A Review of the Events of 1988

The 1989 World Book Year Book

The Annual Supplement to The World Book Encyclopedia

World Book, Inc.
a Scott Fetzer company

Chicago London Sydney Toronto

Printed in the United States of America.
ISBN 0-7166-0489-2
ISSN 0084-1439
Library of Congress Catalog Card Number: 62-4818

Staff

Publisher
William H. Nault

Editor in Chief
Robert O. Zeleny

Editorial
Executive Editor
A. Richard Harmet

Managing Editor
Wayne Wille

Associate Editor
Sara Dreyfuss

Senior Editors
David L. Dreier
Robin Goldman
Jinger Hoop
Mary A. Krier
Barbara A. Mayes
Jay Myers
Rod Such

Contributing Editors
Joan Stephenson
Darlene R. Stille

Research Editor
Irene B. Keller

Senior Indexer
Claire Bolton

Staff Indexer
Beatrice Bertucci

Statistical Editor
Tom Klonoski

Editorial Assistant
Ethel Matthews

Art

Art Director
Alfred de Simone

Senior Artist, Year Book
Nikki Conner

Senior Artists
Melanie J. Lawson
Lucy Smith

Artists
Alice Gardner
Brenda Tropinski
Deirdre Wroblewski

Contributing Artist
Ann Tomasic

Photographs

Photography Director
John S. Marshall

Senior Photographs Editor
Sandra M. Ozanick

Photographs Editors
Elizabeth Greene
Geralyn Swietek

Product Production
Executive Director
Peter Mollman

Director of Manufacturing
Henry Koval

Manufacturing, Manager
Sandra Van den Broucke

Pre-Press Services
Jerry Stack, Director
Lori Frankel
Madelyn Krzak
Barbara Podczerwinski

Proofreaders
Anne Dillon
Marguerite Hoye
Esther Johns
Daniel Marotta

Research Services
Director
Mary Norton

Researcher
Kristina Vaicikonis

Library Services
Mary Kayaian, Head

Cartographic Services
H. George Stoll, Head
Wayne K. Pichler

Contents

See page 108.

See page 140.

A tear-out page of cross-reference tabs for insertion in *The World Book Encyclopedia* appears after page 544.

See page 533.

5

Contributors

Abraham, George (Doc), B.S.; Co-editor and Co-publisher, "The Green Thumb" column. [Gardening]

Abraham, Katherine (Katy), B.S.; Co-editor and Co-publisher, "The Green Thumb" column. [Gardening]

Adachi, Ken, B.A., M.A.; Literary Critic, *The Toronto Star.* [Canadian literature]

Alexander, David T., B.Sc., M.A.; Executive Director, Numismatic Literary Guild. [Coin collecting]

Alexiou, Arthur G., B.S.E.E., M.S.E.E.; Assistant Secretary, Intergovernmental Oceanographic Commission. [Ocean]

Andrews, Peter J., B.A., M.S.; Free-lance writer; biochemist. [Chemistry]

Apseloff, Marilyn Fain, B.A., M.A.; Associate Professor of English, Kent State University. [Literature for children]

Barber, Peggy, B.A., M.L.S.; Associate Executive Director for Communications, American Library Association. [Library]

Bednarski, P. J., B.S.J.; Entertainment-Media Business Reporter, *Chicago Sun-Times.* [Television]

Berman, Howard A., B.A., M.A.H.L., D.Min.; Rabbi, Chicago Sinai Congregation. [Jews and Judaism]

Blackadar, Alfred K., A.B., Ph.D.; Professor Emeritus, The Pennsylvania State University. [Weather; Weather (Close-Up)]

Bourne, Eric, International Affairs Analyst (East Bloc), *The Christian Science Monitor.* [Eastern European country articles; Union of Soviet Socialist Republics (Close-Up)]

Bradsher, Henry S., A.B., B.J.; Foreign affairs analyst. [Asia and Asian country articles]

Brett, Carlton E., M.Sc., Ph.D.; Associate Professor of Geological Sciences, University of Rochester. [Paleontology]

Broad, William J., Science Reporter, *The New York Times.* [Special Report: Back into Space]

Brodsky, Arthur R., B.A., M.S.J.; Senior Editor, *Communications Daily.* [Communications]

Brown, Kenneth, former Editor, *United Kingdom Press Gazette.* [Europe and Western European country articles]

Bruske, Edward H., Reporter, *The Washington Post.* [Courts; Crime]

Campbell, Robert, B.A., M.S., M. Arch.; Architect and architecture critic. [Architecture]

Camper, John, B.A.; Reporter, *Chicago Tribune.* [Special Report: Today's Teens and Drugs]

Campion, Owen, F., A.B.; Associate Publisher, *Our Sunday Visitor* magazine. [Religion; Roman Catholic Church]

Cardinale, Diane P., B.A.; Assistant Communications Director, Toy Manufacturers of America. [Toys and Games]

Cormier, Frank, B.S.J., M.S.J.; former White House Correspondent, Associated Press. [U.S. government articles]

Cormier, Margot, B.A., M.A.; Free-lance writer. [U.S. government articles]

Cromie, William J., B.S., M.S.; Free-lance writer. [Space exploration]

Curry, George E., National Correspondent, *Chicago Tribune.* [Civil rights]

Davidson, Roger M., B.A., Ph.D.; Professor of Government and Politics, University of Maryland, College Park. [World Book Supplement: Congress of the United States]

Dent, Thomas H., B.S.; Executive Director, The Cat Fanciers' Association, Inc. [Cat]

Dugas, Christine, M.A.; Marketing Reporter, *New York Newsday.* [Advertising]

Elsasser, Glen R., B.A., M.S.; Correspondent, *Chicago Tribune.* [Supreme Court of the United States]

Evans, Sandra, B.S.J.; Staff Writer, *The Washington Post.* [Washington, D.C.]

Fanning, Odom, A.B.; Free-lance science writer. [Consumerism; Safety]

Farr, David M. L., M.A., D.Phil.; Professor of History, Carleton University, Ottawa. [Canada; Canadian province articles; Mulroney, Brian; Sauvé, Jeanne M.]

Fisher, Robert W., B.A., M.A.; Senior Economist, U.S. Bureau of Labor Statistics. [Labor]

Fitzgerald, Mark, B.A.; Midwest Editor, *Editor & Publisher* magazine. [Newspaper]

Gatty, Bob, Editor, Periodicals News Service. [Food]

Goldner, Nancy, B.A.; Dance Critic, *The Philadelphia Inquirer.* [Dancing]

Green, Stanley, B.A.; Free-lance writer; author, *The World of Musical Comedy* (1980), *Broadway Musicals Show by Show* (1985). [Popular music (Close-Up)]

Grigadean, Jerry, B.S., M.Mus., Ph.D.; Producer, Grigadean Productions. [Popular music]

Harakas, Stanley Samuel, B.A., B.A.Th., Th.D.; Professor of Christian Ethics, Holy Cross Greek Orthodox School of Theology. [Eastern Orthodox Churches]

Haverstock, Nathan A., A.B.; Affiliate Scholar, Oberlin College. [Latin America and Latin-American country articles]

Herreid, Clyde Freeman, A.B., M.Sc., Ph.D.; Professor of Biological Sciences, State University of New York at Buffalo. [Zoology]

Higgins, James V., B.A.; Auto Industry Reporter, *The Detroit News.* [Automobile]

Hillgren, Sonja, B.J., M.A.; Washington Correspondent, Knight-Ridder Newspapers. [Farm and farming]

Hunzeker, Jeanne M., D.S.W.; Associate Professor of Social Welfare, Southern University at New Orleans. [Child welfare]

Jacobi, Peter P., B.S.J., M.S.J.; Professor of Journalism, Indiana University. [Classical music]

Johanson, Donald C., B.S., M.A., Ph.D.; Director, Institute of Human Origins. [Anthropology]

Kisor, Henry, B.A., M.S.J.; Book Editor, *Chicago Sun-Times.* [Literature]

Knapp, Elaine Stuart, B.A.; Senior Editor, Council of State Governments. [State government]

Knight, Paul G., B.S., M.S.; Instructor, Producer-WPSX/TV, The Pennsylvania State University. [Weather; Weather (Close-Up)]

Kolgraf, Ronald, B.A., M.A.; Publisher, *Adweek* magazine. [Manufacturing]

Langdon, Robert, M.A.; Visiting Fellow, Department of Pacific and SEAsian History, Australian National University. [Pacific Islands]

Larsen, Paul A., P.E., B.S., Ch.E.; Member: American Philatelic Society; Collectors Club of Chicago; Fellow, Royal Philatelic Society, London; past President, British Caribbean Philatelic Study Group. [Stamp collecting]

Lawrence, Al, A.B., M.A., M.Ed.; Associate Director, United States Chess Federation. [Chess]

Lawrence, Richard, B.E.E.; International Economics Correspondent, *The Journal of Commerce.* [International trade]

Lee, Chong-Sik, Ph.D.; Professor of Political Science, University of Pennsylvania. [Special Report: The Two Koreas]

Leff, Donna Rosene, B.S.J., M.S.J., M.P.P., Ph.D.; Associate Professor of Journalism and Urban Affairs, Northwestern University. [City]

Levine, Martin, former Editor, *Consumer Electronics Monthly* magazine; free-lance electronics writer. [Electronics]

Lewis, David C., M.D.; Director, Center for Alcohol and Addiction Studies, Brown University. [Drug abuse]

Liebenow, Beverly B., B.A.; Author and free-lance writer. [Africa and African country articles]

Liebenow, J. Gus, B.A., M.A., Ph.D.; Rudy Professor of Political Science/African Studies, Indiana University. [Africa and African country articles]

Litsky, Frank, B.S.; Sports Writer, *The New York Times.* [Sports articles]

Maki, John M., B.A., M.A., Ph.D.; Professor Emeritus, University of Massachusetts. [Japan]

Maran, Stephen P., B.S., M.A., Ph.D.; Senior Staff Scientist, National Aeronautics and Space Administration-Goddard Space Flight Center. [Astronomy]

Marty, Martin E., Ph.D.; Fairfax M. Cone Distinguished Service Professor, University of Chicago. [Protestantism]

Mather, Ian J., M.A.; Defence Correspondent, *The Observer,* London. [Great Britain; Ireland; Northern Ireland]

Maugh, Thomas H., II, Ph.D.; Science Writer, *Los Angeles Times.* [Biology]

McCarron, John F., B.S.J., M.S.J.; Urban Affairs Writer, *Chicago Tribune.* [Chicago]

McGinley, Laurie, B.S.; Reporter, Transportation and Space, *The Wall Street Journal.* [Aviation; Railroad]

McGraw, Bill, City Hall Bureau Chief, *Detroit Free Press.* [Detroit]

Merina, Victor, A.A., B.A., M.S.; Staff Writer, *Los Angeles Times.* [Los Angeles]

Merkl, Peter H., Ph.D.; Professor of Political Science, University of California at Santa Barbara. [Special Report: The Two Germanys]

Merz, Beverly, A.B.; Associate Editor, *The Journal of the American Medical Association.* [Special Report: Protecting Our Hearing]

Miller, J. D. B., M.Ec., M.A.; Emeritus Professor, Australian National University, Canberra. [Australia; Australia (Close-Up)]

Moores, Eldridge M., B.S., Ph.D.; Professor and Chair, Department of Geology, University of California at Davis. [Geology]

Moritz, Owen, B.A.; Urban Affairs Editor, New York *Daily News.* [New York City]

Morris, Bernadine, B.A., M.A.; Chief Fashion Writer, *The New York Times.* [Fashion]

Newcomb, Eldon H., A.B., A.M., Ph.D.; Folke Skoog Professor of Botany, University of Wisconsin-Madison. [Botany]

Nguyen, J. Tuyet, B.A.; United Nations Correspondent, United Press International. [United Nations]

Ochipinti, Laura A., B.S.; Managing Editor, American Correctional Association. [Prison]

Platiel, Rudy, Reporter, *The Globe and Mail,* Toronto. [Indian, American]

Priestaf, Iris, B.A., M.A.; Ph.D.; Geographer/ Water Resources Specialist, David Keith Todd Consulting Engineers. [Water]

Raeburn, Paul, B.S., Science Editor, Associated Press. [Physics]

Raloff, Janet, B.S.J., M.S.J.; Policy/Technology Editor, *Science News* magazine. [Environmental pollution]

Raven, Peter H., Ph.D.; Director, Missouri Botanical Garden, and Engelmann Professor of Botany, Washington University. [Special Report: Our Vanishing Rain Forests]

Reich, Bernard, B.A., M.A., Ph.D.; Professor of Political Science and International Affairs, George Washington University. [World Book Supplement: Israel]

Reinken, Charles, B.B.A., M.A.; Associate Editor, *The Houston Post.* [Houston]

Robinson, Walter, B.A.; Contributing Editor, *Art in America* magazine. [Art; Special Report: Close Encounters with Public Art]

Sandza, Richard, B.S., M.S.; Correspondent, *Newsweek* magazine. [Armed forces]

Scibilia, Ronald D., A.B., M.A., M.F.A.; West Coast Bureau Chief, International Thomson Retail Press. [Computer]

Shand, David A., B.C.A., B.Com.; First Assistant Secretary, Australian Department of Finance. [New Zealand]

Shapiro, Howard S., B.S.; Editor, *Weekend Magazine, The Philadelphia Inquirer.* [Philadelphia]

Simmons, Mark S., B.A., B.S., D.D.S., M.A.; Director, General Practice Residency Program, University of Minnesota School of Dentistry. [Dentistry]

Spencer, William, A.B., A.M., Ph.D.; Writer; Former Professor of History, Florida State University. [Middle East and Middle Eastern country articles; North Africa country articles]

Stasio, Marilyn, B.A., M.A.; Theater Critic, *The New York Times.* [Theater]

Stein, David Lewis, B.A., M.S.; Author; Urban Affairs Columnist, *The Toronto Star.* [Toronto]

Swanton, Donald W., B.S., M.S., Ph.D., M.B.A.; Chairman, Department of Finance, Roosevelt University. [Bank; Economics; Stocks and bonds]

Thornton, Lee, B.S., M.A., Ph.D.; Professor of Journalism, Howard University. [World Book Supplement: Bush, George Herbert Walker; Quayle, Dan]

Tignor, Robert L., Ph.D.; Professor of History, Princeton University. [World Book Supplement: Egypt]

Toch, Thomas, B.A.; Free-lance journalist. [Education]

Trotter, Robert J., B.S.; Managing Editor/ Executive Editor, *Psychology Today* magazine. [Psychology]

Tuchman, Janice Lyn, B.S., M.S.J.; Managing Editor, *Engineering News-Record.* [Building and construction]

Vesley, Roberta, A.B., M.L.S.; Library Director, American Kennel Club. [Dog]

Voorhies, Barbara, B.S., Ph.D.; Professor of Anthropology, University of California at Santa Barbara. [Archaeology]

Walter, Eugene J., Jr., B.A.; Editor in Chief, *Animal Kingdom* magazine, and Curator of Publications, New York Zoological Society. [Conservation; Zoos]

Weiner, Harte V., B.A., M.F.A., Ph.D.; Lecturer, English Department, Tufts University. [Poetry]

Winchester, Ellen, B.A.; Research Analyst, Gruner + Jahr USA Publishing. [Magazine]

Windeyer, Kendal, President, Windeyer Associates, Montreal, Canada. [Montreal]

Woods, Michael, B.S.; Science Editor, *The Toledo Blade.* [Energy, mining, and health articles; Public health (Close-Up)]

Wuntch, Philip, B.A.; Film Critic, *Dallas Morning News.* [Motion pictures]

1982
1984
1985
1986
1987
1988

The Year in Brief

A short essay captures the spirit of 1988,
and a month-by-month listing highlights
some of the year's significant events.

See page 28 ▶

The modern Olympic Games were organized to encourage world peace and friendship, and in the Olympic year of 1988, it appeared that there had indeed been some progress toward these goals. Although violence—wars or civil strife—still rocked some countries, several conflicts approached resolution.

In May, the Soviet Union began pulling its troops out of war-weary Afghanistan. In June, Vietnam withdrew its top military commanders from Kampuchea (formerly called Cambodia), and peace talks were held between Kampuchean guerrillas and Vietnamese officials. August brought a cease-fire in the long and brutal conflict between Iran and Iraq, when the two nations—at war since 1980—accepted truce terms and later opened talks on a permanent peace. The Middle East saw another important development when the Palestine Liberation Organization (PLO) renounced terrorism and recognized Israel's right to exist, prompting the United States to begin talks with the PLO in December. Angola and Namibia also moved a step closer to peace in December, after Angola, Cuba, and South Africa signed a treaty calling for independence for Namibia and a troop withdrawal from Angola.

The hopes for peace were perhaps fostered by improving relations between the United States and the Soviet Union. In Moscow, on June 1, U.S. President Ronald Reagan and Soviet leader Mikhail S. Gorbachev exchanged documents putting into effect the Intermediate-Range Nuclear Forces (INF) Treaty. In compliance with the treaty, the Soviets began to destroy their land-based intermediate-range nuclear missiles in August, and the United States followed suit in September.

Much of the new spirit of cooperation between the two super-powers stemmed from the more open atmosphere created by Gorbachev's twin policies of domestic reform, called *glasnost* (openness in the flow of information) and *perestroika* (economic restructuring). This loosening of controls, however, allowed discontent to surface within the Soviet Union. Nationalist movements gained momentum in the Soviet Union's three Baltic republics—Estonia, Latvia, and Lithuania—which had been independent countries before World War II. To the southeast, Tartars (also called Tatars) called for the creation of a Tartar homeland, and ethnic Armenians urged that an area in neighboring Azerbaijan be annexed to Armenia.

Violent attempts at change bedeviled other countries in 1988. In Haiti, military coups deposed the president in June and his successor in September. Burma and Israel were beset by turmoil, and ethnic and religious violence rocked Northern Ireland, Burundi, South Africa, India, and Sri Lanka.

In other countries, political struggle took the peaceful form of elections. The United States elected its 41st President, Republican George Bush, two-term Vice President under Ronald Reagan. The campaign struck many as surprisingly ill-tempered, considering that the candidates, Bush and Democrat Michael S.

Dukakis, started the race labeled—respectively—as unassertive and unemotional. The aura of peace and prosperity in the United States—the unemployment rate was fairly low, as was inflation—helped Bush become the first sitting Vice President to win a presidential election since 1836. Bush promised to keep the United States on the course set by President Reagan.

Canadian and French voters also opted to "stay the course" in 1988. In Canada, Prime Minister Brian Mulroney's Progressive Conservative Party won a clear majority in Parliament. His opponent, former Prime Minister John N. Turner of the Liberal Party, had made opposition to a comprehensive U.S.-Canada free-trade agreement a key part of his campaign. Canadian observers saw Mulroney's victory as a mandate for closer economic relations with the United States. In France, François Mitterrand in May became the first president reelected by popular vote in the 30-year history of the Fifth Republic.

Voters in some other countries made changes. Chileans rejected an extension of the term in office of President Augusto Pinochet Ugarte, and Pakistani voters elected their first civilian democratic government since Prime Minister Zulfikar Ali Bhutto was thrown out of office by a coup in 1977. In December 1988, his daughter, Benazir Bhutto, became Pakistan's prime minister.

The worst memories of 1988 for many people may not be linked to affairs of state but to tragedies or natural disasters. On the Fourth of July, Americans woke to news reports that a U.S. Navy warship in the Persian Gulf had mistaken an Iranian airliner filled with civilian passengers for a fighter jet and shot it out of the sky, killing all 290 people on board. The monsoon season brought torrential floods to India and Bangladesh, killing thousands. Sudan was wracked by disasters of near-Biblical proportions, including floods, famine, civil war, and plagues of locusts. Gilbert, the most intense hurricane ever recorded in the Gulf of Mexico, plowed through the West Indies and Mexico in September. In Armenia, a December earthquake caused about 25,000 deaths. Two weeks later, a bomb blew up on a Pan Am World Airways jet over Scotland, killing all 259 people aboard and at least 11 on the ground.

And, like all years, 1988 was a personal triumph for some of us and a disaster for others. It was the best of times for George Bush and Brian Mulroney; for pitcher Orel Hershiser of baseball's Los Angeles Dodgers; for British composer Andrew Lloyd Webber, who had three Broadway hits at the same time; for tennis grand-slammer Steffi Graf; and for most of the more than 11,000 athletes who earned the chance to compete in the Olympic Games. It may have been the worst of times for the athletes who were banned from competition or who lost medals because of using illegal drugs. Most of the rest of us found 1988 to be the usual mixed bag, filled with changes good and bad.   The Editors

January						
					1	2
3	4	5	6	7	8	9
10	11	12	13	14	15	16
17	18	19	20	21	22	23
24	25	26	27	28	29	30
31						

1 The University of Miami defeats the University of Oklahoma 20-14 in the Orange Bowl. The wire services proclaim Miami college football's national champion on January 3.

2 An Ashland Oil Incorporated fuel tank collapses, spilling about 1 million gallons (3.8 million liters) of diesel fuel into the Monongahela River near Pittsburgh, Pa. The spill cuts off water to thousands of homes in Pennsylvania and Ohio.

The United States and Canada sign a free-trade pact that will eliminate tariffs between the two countries by 1999. The pact requires the approval of the Canadian Parliament and U.S. Congress.

8 Governor Evan Mecham of Arizona is indicted on fraud and perjury charges. He denies the charges.

A presidential task force investigating the 1987 stock-market crash proposes major changes, including price limits on stock trading.

13 Japan's Prime Minister Noboru Takeshita meets with U.S. President Ronald Reagan in Washington, D.C., to discuss trade issues. Takeshita also meets with Canada's Prime Minister Brian Mulroney in Toronto, Ont., on January 15.

The Supreme Court of the United States rules that First Amendment rights of free speech and free press do not protect school newspapers, plays, and other school activities from censorship.

President Chiang Ching-kuo of Taiwan dies of a heart attack and is succeeded in the presidency by Vice President Lee Teng-hui.

17 Leslie F. Manigat is elected president of Haiti in a military-run election boycotted by about two-thirds of the eligible voters. He takes office on February 7.

18 Candidates backed by Philippine President Corazon Aquino win a majority of some 16,000 provincial and local posts in Philippine elections.

25 Gunmen in Medellín, Colombia, kidnap and murder Colombia's attorney general after killing his driver and bodyguard.

Ramsewak Shankar is sworn in as the first civilian president of Suriname after nearly eight years of military rule.

26 Australia celebrates its bicentennial with a reenactment in Sydney of the landing in 1788 of the First Fleet, shiploads of convicts who were the first English settlers to arrive there.

The Phantom of the Opera, a musical by British composer Andrew Lloyd Webber, opens on Broadway after a record $18 million in advance ticket sales.

29 The U.S. Department of Health and Human Services issues final rules saying that family-planning programs receiving federal funds may not provide abortion counseling or referrals.

31 The Washington Redskins win Super Bowl XXII, defeating the Denver Broncos 42-10.

Turkish Prime Minister Turgut Ozal and Greek Prime Minister Andreas Papandreou hold the first high-level talks between their two nations since the mid-1970's.

▲
Quarterback Doug Williams leads the Washington Redskins to a 42 to 10 victory over the Denver Broncos in Super Bowl XXII on January 31.

Fireworks light up Sydney Harbour on January
26 during Australia's bicentennial celebration.
▼

▲
U.S. President Ronald Reagan greets Japan's
Prime Minister Noboru Takeshita on January
13, during Takeshita's visit to Washington, D.C.

February						
	1	2	3	4	5	6
7	8	9	10	11	12	13
14	15	16	17	18	19	20
21	22	23	24	25	26	27
28	29					

2 **Canada's Prime Minister Mulroney** dismisses Minister of Supply and Services Michel Côté for violating federal guidelines on conflict of interest.

3 **The Senate** unanimously confirms Judge Anthony M. Kennedy as an associate justice of the Supreme Court of the United States. He takes his seat on February 18.

5 **Federal grand juries** in Miami and Tampa, Fla., indict Panama's military leader, General Manuel Antonio Noriega Morena, on drug trafficking charges.

8 **Australian Immigration Minister** Michael J. Young resigns after charges that he failed to disclose a political donation.

11 **Former White House political director** Lyn Nofziger is convicted of illegal lobbying. He is sentenced on April 8 to 90 days in prison and fined $30,000, but he appeals the conviction.

12 **Two Soviet warships** bump two U.S. Navy vessels in an area of the Black Sea claimed by the Soviet Union but considered international waters by the United States.

13-28 **The Winter Olympic Games** take place in Calgary, Canada. The Soviet Union wins the most medals—29, including 11 gold.

17 **Marine Lieutenant Colonel William R. Higgins** is kidnapped in Lebanon.

21 **Television evangelist Jimmy Swaggart** tells his congregation in Baton Rouge, La., that he has sinned and will not preach for an "indeterminate" time.

George Vassiliou wins election as president of Cyprus, succeeding Spyros Kyprianou.

22 **U.S. Secretary of the Navy** James H. Webb, Jr., resigns, protesting a $12-billion cut in the Navy budget. Reagan appoints William L. Ball III to replace Webb on February 23.

24 **The U.S. Supreme Court** overturns a jury's $200,000 award to evangelist Jerry Falwell for "emotional distress" over a *Hustler* magazine parody, reaffirming that the First Amendment protects satire and criticism of public figures.

South Africa imposes new curbs on antiapartheid activities.

25 **Roh Tae Woo** takes office as president of South Korea in the first peaceful transfer of power since South Korea became an independent nation in 1948.

26 **Panama's National Assembly** ousts President Eric Arturo Delvalle after he announces on February 25 that he is dismissing Noriega. Education Minister Manuel Solís Palma is sworn in as the new president.

28 **Riots**— in which 32 people die—break out in Sumgait in the Soviet republic of Azerbaijan after protests in the neighboring republic of Armenia over Nagorno-Karabakh, an area in Azerbaijan that Armenians want to annex.

Senegal President Abdou Diouf wins reelection, but students riot, claiming vote fraud.

29 **South African police** briefly arrest Archbishop Desmond M. Tutu and other religious leaders as they march to protest the government's February 24 curbs on opposition activities.

▲
The 1988 Winter Olympic Games open on February 13 in Calgary, Canada, and continue until February 28.

15

March						
		1	2	3	4	5
6	7	8	9	10	11	12
13	14	15	16	17	18	19
20	21	22	23	24	25	26
27	28	29	30	31		

2-3   North Atlantic Treaty Organization (NATO) leaders meet in Brussels, Belgium, for the first NATO summit since 1982.

3   Bangladeshi President Hussain Muhammad Ershad's Jatiya Party wins 251 of 299 parliamentary seats in violence-marred elections.

6   British security forces in Gibraltar kill three Irish Republican Army (IRA) guerrillas suspected by British and Spanish authorities of planning a bomb attack.

7   The Writers Guild of America begins a strike against television and motion-picture producers that becomes one of the longest in Hollywood history, lasting until August 8.

8   Sixteen U.S. states hold "Super Tuesday" primaries. Vice President George Bush wins every Republican primary, and Massachusetts Governor Michael S. Dukakis wins the most delegates among the Democratic candidates.

9   Premier Howard Pawley of Manitoba, Canada, announces his resignation.

11   Former National Security Adviser Robert C. McFarlane pleads guilty to four counts of illegally withholding information from Congress about secret White House support of Nicaragua's contra rebels.

13   The world's longest tunnel — the 33.5-mile (53.9-kilometer) Seikan Tunnel—opens in Japan.

15   About 10,000 Hungarians march through Budapest calling for democracy and a free press in one of the largest antigovernment demonstrations since the Soviet-suppressed uprising of 1956.

16   At the funeral of the three IRA guerrillas killed on March 6, an attacker hurls grenades that kill three people.

A federal grand jury in Washington, D.C., indicts former National Security Adviser John M. Poindexter, Lieutenant Colonel Oliver L. North, and two other people on charges of conspiracy, fraud, and theft in connection with the Iran-contra affair. All four plead not guilty.

17-28   Reagan orders more than 3,000 U.S. troops to Honduras on a "training exercise."

20   El Salvador's right wing National Republican Alliance (Arena) wins legislative and municipal elections, capturing 30 seats in the 60-seat National Assembly and the post of mayor of San Salvador.

22   Congress overrides Reagan's veto of the Civil Rights Restoration Act of 1988, which extends federal civil-rights laws to an entire school or other organization if any of its programs receives federal funds.

23   Nicaragua's leftist Sandinista government and the U.S.-supported contra rebels agree to a 60-day cease-fire, beginning on April 1.

29   The United States deputy attorney general, the head of the Justice Department's criminal division, and four top aides resign, reportedly because of their concern over the legal problems of Attorney General Edwin Meese III.

31   Italian and U.S. officials charge 233 suspected members of a Mafia drug ring in the largest drug case ever mounted jointly by the two nations.

▲

Lieutenant Colonel Oliver L. North, shown at 1987 hearings on the Iran-contra affair, is indicted by a federal grand jury on March 16, 1988, for his role in the affair.

◄ U.S. Marines arrive in Honduras for a
"training exercise" on March 17 after reports
that Nicaragua had attacked contra forces
there.

Mourners at a funeral for IRA terrorists in
Belfast, Northern Ireland, duck a grenade
attack that killed three on March 16.
▼

April						
					1	2
3	4	5	6	7	8	9
10	11	12	13	14	15	16
17	18	19	20	21	22	23
24	25	26	27	28	29	30

3 **Postage rates** rise in the United States, with a first-class letter going to 25 cents.

4 **The University of Kansas** wins the National Collegiate Athletic Association men's basketball championship, defeating the University of Oklahoma 83 to 79.

Governor Mecham is removed from office by the Arizona Senate, which convicted him of misconduct charges voted by the state's House of Representatives in February.

5-20 **Shiite Muslim hijackers** seize a Kuwait Airways jetliner; force it to fly to Iran, Cyprus, and Algeria; and kill two passengers before releasing their remaining hostages.

9 **China's National People's Congress** elects Li Peng as the nation's new premier.

11 ***The Last Emperor,*** a historical epic about China, wins nine Academy Awards.

12 **The U.S. Patent and Trademark Office** issues the world's first patent for an animal life form, a mouse with genes altered to make it more useful for cancer research.

13 **Ciriaco De Mita** becomes prime minister of Italy, heading a coalition of the same five parties that governed under Prime Minister Giovanni Goria, who resigned on March 11.

14 **An underwater mine,** which the United States says was planted by Iran, damages the U.S. Navy frigate *Samuel B. Roberts* in the Persian Gulf, injuring 10 crew members. In retaliation, the United States destroys two Iranian oil platforms and damages or sinks six Iranian ships on April 18.

Afghanistan, Pakistan, the Soviet Union, and the United States sign agreements providing for a Soviet withdrawal from Afghanistan.

16 **Khalil al-Wazir,** also known as Abu Jihad, a leader in the Palestine Liberation Organization (PLO), is assassinated in Tunisia.

23 ***Daedalus 88,*** a pedal-powered aircraft, flies 74 miles (119 kilometers) between the Greek islands of Crete and Thira, nearly doubling the distance record for human-powered flight.

25 **An Israeli court** sentences John Demjanjuk, a retired Ukrainian-born U.S. auto worker, to hang after ruling that he was "Ivan the Terrible," a Nazi death-camp guard in Poland.

26 **Manitoba's ruling New Democratic Party** is defeated in provincial elections.

Vice President Bush clinches the Republican presidential nomination by winning the Pennsylvania primary election.

South Korea's ruling Democratic Justice Party fails for the first time to win a majority in elections for the National Assembly.

27 **Reagan and Mulroney** hold a summit meeting in Washington, D.C., to discuss trade and defense issues.

29 **The first California condor** conceived in captivity hatches in San Diego.

Baseball's Baltimore Orioles defeat the Chicago White Sox 9-0 for their first victory of 1988, ending an American League record losing streak of 21 games.

▲
Danny Manning leads the University of Kansas to an 83-79 win over the University of Oklahoma on April 4 to give Kansas the NCAA men's basketball title.

18

◀ An Israeli court on April 25 sentences John (Ivan the Terrible) Demjanjuk to hang for crimes committed as a Nazi death-camp guard in Poland.

◀ *Daedalus 88*, a pedal-powered aircraft, flies 74 miles (119 kilometers) between two Greek islands on April 23, a record distance for such a flight.

A fire is extinguished on one of two Iranian oil platforms destroyed by the United States on April 18. The U.S. attack came four days after a mine reportedly planted by Iran damaged a U.S. frigate in the Persian Gulf.
▼

May						
1	2	3	4	5	6	7
8	9	10	11	12	13	14
15	16	17	18	19	20	21
22	23	24	25	26	27	28
29	30	31				

2-10   Striking Polish workers occupy the Lenin shipyard in Gdańsk, Poland.

5   Polish riot police storm the Lenin steel mill at Nowa Huta, Poland, near Kraków, ending a strike that began on April 26.

Eugene A. Marino becomes archbishop of Atlanta, Ga., the first black Roman Catholic archbishop in the United States.

7-18   Pope John Paul II visits Uruguay, Peru, Bolivia, and Paraguay.

8   François Mitterrand becomes the first French president in history to be reelected by the people.

Rodrigo Borja, a leftist, is elected president of Ecuador, succeeding conservative León Febres-Cordero. Borja takes office on August 10.

9   A book by former White House chief of staff Donald T. Regan claims that "virtually every major move and decision the Reagans made . . . was cleared in advance" with an astrologer.

Gary A. Filmon becomes premier of Manitoba, succeeding Howard Pawley.

9-18   Sikh militants demanding a separate Sikh homeland occupy the Golden Temple in Amritsar, India, the Sikhs' holiest shrine.

10   Mitterrand appoints Michel Rocard, a moderate Socialist, as prime minister of France, succeeding Jacques Chirac.

11   Denmark's Prime Minister Poul Schlüter resigns after an inconclusive parliamentary election on May 10 failed to give him a clear endorsement for his pro-NATO defense policies. Schlüter forms a new three-party coalition government on June 3.

15   Soviet troops begin to leave Afghanistan.

16   Surgeon General of the United States C. Everett Koop issues a report warning that nicotine is "addicting in the same sense as are drugs such as heroin and cocaine."

The U.S. Supreme Court rules that police may search discarded trash without a warrant.

22   Hungary's Communist party replaces János Kádár, its leader since 1956, with Károly Grósz.

24   Reagan vetoes a sweeping overhaul of U.S. trade laws passed by Congress on April 27. The House immediately votes to override the veto, but the Senate attempt to override fails on June 8.

26   The Edmonton Oilers win professional hockey's Stanley Cup, defeating the Boston Bruins in four straight games.

The U.S. government begins mailing a pamphlet about AIDS (acquired immune deficiency syndrome) to more than 106 million households in the first-ever nationwide mailing about a public-health crisis.

27   The U.S. Senate ratifies a treaty with the Soviet Union eliminating intermediate-range nuclear missiles.

29   Reagan arrives in Moscow for his fourth summit meeting with Soviet leader Mikhail S. Gorbachev and his first trip to the Soviet Union.

Pakistan's President M. Zia-ul-Haq fires the nation's prime minister and his Cabinet, and dissolves the National Assembly.

▲
Soviet troops begin to leave Afghanistan on May 15 after the Soviet Union agreed to a gradual troop withdrawal to be completed by February 1989.

◀ Sikh militants surrender on
May 18 after a 10-day siege
by Indian forces on Sikh headquarters at the Golden Temple in Amritsar, India.

▲
The Edmonton Oilers win the Stanley
Cup on May 26, defeating the Boston
Bruins in four straight games.

◀ Eugene A. Marino becomes archbishop of Atlanta, Ga., on May 5.
The appointment made him the first
black archbishop of the Roman Catholic Church in the United States.

June						
			1	2	3	4
5	6	7	8	9	10	11
12	13	14	15	16	17	18
19	20	21	22	23	24	25
26	27	28	29	30		

1   Reagan and Gorbachev exchange documents of ratification putting into force the treaty eliminating intermediate-range nuclear missiles.

5   Religious leaders from some 100 nations gather in Moscow for celebrations marking the 1,000th year of Christianity in Russia.

5, 12   Neither the Socialist Party of French President Mitterrand nor a rival center-right coalition wins a majority in elections for France's National Assembly.

6-8   Up to 2 million South African blacks stay away from work in a strike protesting a labor bill that seeks to curb union powers.

7   Massachusetts Governor Michael S. Dukakis clinches the Democratic presidential nomination by winning California, Montana, New Jersey, and New Mexico primaries.

8   Congress, to provide extra coverage for "catastrophic" illness, approves the largest expansion of Medicare benefits since the program was established in 1965. Reagan signs the bill into law on July 1.

10   Fighting breaks out between South Korean police and students calling for reunification with North Korea after police block a planned meeting with North Korean students at the border village of Panmunjom.

13   A federal jury orders Liggett Group Incorporated to pay a smoker's widower $400,000 in the first ruling holding a tobacco firm partly liable in a smoker's death.

14   Howard H. Baker, Jr., resigns as White House chief of staff, effective July 1, and Reagan names Kenneth M. Duberstein to replace Baker.

19   A military coup ousts Haiti's President Manigat two days after he fires Lieutenant General Henri Namphy. Namphy declares himself president on June 20.

19-21   Leaders of Britain, Canada, France, Italy, Japan, the United States, and West Germany hold an economic summit in Toronto, Canada.

21   The Los Angeles Lakers win the National Basketball Association championship, beating the Detroit Pistons four games to three.

22   Vietnam's National Assembly elects Do Muoi as Council of Ministers chairman (premier).

24   *Who Framed Roger Rabbit,* a film with a unique blend of animation and live action, opens at more than 1,000 theaters throughout the United States.

26   Laos holds elections for district councils in the first nationwide voting since the Communists seized power in 1975. A second round of voting, to elect provincial and municipal committees, takes place on November 20.

28   The first conference of the Soviet Communist Party since 1941 opens in Moscow. It ends on July 1 after endorsing political reforms.

29   The United States Supreme Court upholds the use of special prosecutors to investigate suspected crimes of top federal officials.

30   Vietnam withdraws its high military command from Kampuchea.

France's conservative Archbishop Marcel Lefebvre consecrates four bishops in defiance of the pope. The Vatican excommunicates Lefebvre and the bishops.

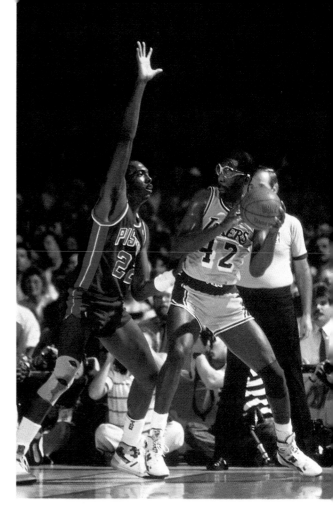

▲
United States President Ronald Reagan and Soviet leader Mikhail S. Gorbachev finalize the Intermediate-Range Nuclear Forces Treaty in Moscow on June 1.

◀ James Worthy of the Los Angeles Lakers stars as the Lakers beat the Detroit Pistons, four games to three, and take the NBA title on June 21.

◀ Bob Hoskins tussles with a cartoon character in *Who Framed Roger Rabbit,* a film acclaimed for its skillful blend of animation and live-action footage, which opened nationwide on June 24.

Religious leaders from 100 nations assemble in Moscow on June 5 to commemorate the 1,000th anniversary of the introduction of Christianity to Russia.
▼

July						
					1	2
3	4	5	6	7	8	9
10	11	12	13	14	15	16
17	18	19	20	21	22	23
24	25	26	27	28	29	30
31						

3   The Navy cruiser U.S.S. *Vincennes* shoots down an Iranian civilian jetliner over the Persian Gulf, killing all 290 people aboard. The *Vincennes* says it mistook the jet for an attacking fighter plane.

5   Attorney General Edwin Meese III, declaring he has been vindicated because a special prosecutor decides not to seek criminal charges against him, announces his resignation. Reagan on July 12 replaces him with former Pennsylvania Governor Richard L. Thornburgh, who takes office on August 12.

6   An explosion on a North Sea oil platform off Scotland kills 167 people in the worst oil-rig accident in the history of North Sea drilling.

Carlos Salinas de Gortari, the candidate of Mexico's long-dominant Institutional Revolutionary Party (PRI), is elected president with 50.4 per cent of the vote, the narrowest margin since the PRI was founded in 1929. He takes office on December 1.

7, 12   The Soviet Union launches two space probes to explore Phobos, a moon of Mars.

11   Masked gunmen fire automatic weapons and hurl hand grenades at tourists aboard a Greek cruise ship in the Aegean Sea, killing nine people.

13   Congress approves a bill that would require companies to give workers 60 days' notice before closing factories or making large layoffs. The bill becomes law without Reagan's signature on August 3.

15   The Teamsters Union elects William J. McCarthy as president, succeeding Jackie Presser, who died on July 9.

16   Florence Griffith Joyner shatters the world record for the women's 100-meter dash, running it in 10.49 seconds at Indianapolis.

20-21   The Democratic National Convention, meeting in Atlanta, Ga., nominates Dukakis for President and Senator Lloyd M. Bentsen, Jr., of Texas for Vice President.

23   Ne Win, Burma's most powerful leader since 1962, resigns as head of the Burma Socialist Programme Party, the nation's only political party. On July 26, the party replaces him with Sein Lwin, who also becomes president of the nation on July 27.

25-28   Kampuchea's four warring factions—the Vietnam-backed government and the three guerrilla factions that oppose it—hold face-to-face peace talks for the first time, in Bogor, Indonesia.

27   Thailand's Prime Minister Prem Tinsulanonda rejects offers by the five parties in his coalition to serve another term following victory in general elections on July 24. Chatichai Choonhavan succeeds him as prime minister on August 9.

Surgeon General Koop issues a landmark report on nutrition calling excess dietary fat a major national health problem.

31   King Hussein I of Jordan says that Jordan is renouncing its claims to the West Bank and Gaza Strip, which Jordan lost to Israel in 1967, and cutting all ties with those areas.

▲

The party's ticket—Michael S. Dukakis, right, and Lloyd M. Bentsen, Jr.—greets supporters at the Democratic National Convention in Atlanta, Ga., on July 21.

◀ Mourners display a drawing of a U.S. warship shooting down an Iranian airliner at a funeral in Teheran, Iran, for victims of the July 3 incident.

Florence Griffith Joyner sets a new world record for the women's 100-meter dash— 10.49 seconds—in Indianapolis on July 16.
▼

◀ Carlos Salinas de Gortari campaigns for the presidency of Mexico, which he won by a narrow margin on July 6.

The Republican National Convention ▶
in New Orleans ends on August 18,
after the party nominated George
Bush and Dan Quayle for President
and Vice President.

August						
	1	2	3	4	5	6
7	8	9	10	11	12	13
14	15	16	17	18	19	20
21	22	23	24	25	26	27
28	29	30	31			

3 **A sweeping overhaul** of U.S. trade laws aimed at reducing the trade deficit is approved by Congress. Reagan signs the bill on August 23.

4 **Congress passes** legislation offering apologies and $20,000 tax-free payments to Japanese Americans put into internment camps during World War II (1939-1945). Reagan signs the bill on August 10.

Representative Mario Biaggi (D., N.Y.) and five other people are convicted of racketeering in a scandal involving Wedtech Corporation, a defense contractor. Biaggi resigns from Congress the next day. He is sentenced on November 18 to five years in prison and fined $242,000.

5 **Secretary of the Treasury** James A. Baker III resigns to head Bush's presidential campaign. Reagan names investment banker Nicholas F. Brady to the Cabinet post, which he takes over on September 16.

8 **The Chicago Cubs** begin their first night game at Wrigley Field, but the game is rained out in the fourth inning.

The Duchess of York gives birth to a daughter, Princess Beatrice of York, who is fifth in line to the British throne.

South Africa, Angola, and Cuba declare a cease-fire in the 13-year-old war in Angola.

9 **Congress approves** a $3.9-billion drought-relief bill, the most generous disaster aid ever given U.S. farmers. Reagan signs it into law on August 11.

Hockey star Wayne Gretzky is traded by the Edmonton Oilers to the Los Angeles Kings in one of the biggest deals in sports history.

12 **The film *The Last Temptation of Christ*,** which depicts Jesus dreaming of life as an ordinary man, opens to scattered protests and sellout crowds in seven U.S. and two Canadian cities.

Sein Lwin resigns as president of Burma and head of its ruling party after a week of violent antigovernment protests in which at least 95 people were killed. He is succeeded on August 19 by Maung Maung.

14 **Violence** in which at least 5,000 people die breaks out between Burundi's Hutu majority and its Tutsi minority.

17 **Pakistan's President Zia** is killed, with the U.S. ambassador and 28 other people, when his plane explodes in midair.

The U.S. Food and Drug Administration approves the drug minoxidil, trade-named Rogaine, the first prescription treatment for baldness available in the United States.

17-18 **The Republican National Convention** in New Orleans nominates Bush for President and Indiana Senator Dan Quayle for Vice President.

20 **Iran and Iraq** begin a cease-fire in their eight-year-old war in the Persian Gulf.

21 **A deadly earthquake** rocks the India-Nepal border, killing at least 1,015 people.

23 **A former U.S. Army sergeant,** Clyde Lee Conrad, and two Hungarian-born Swedish brothers are arrested and charged with passing NATO secrets to Hungarian agents.

▲

Protesters decry the August 12 opening of *The Last Temptation of Christ,* a film that depicts Jesus Christ dreaming of life as an ordinary man.

26

▲ The Duke and Duchess of York pose
with their first child, Princess Beatrice,
after her August 8 birth.

◀ An earthquake on August 21 devas-
tates the Nepal-India border area,
killing at least 1,015 people.

27

September						
				1	2	3
4	5	6	7	8	9	10
11	12	13	14	15	16	17
18	19	20	21	22	23	24
25	26	27	28	29	30	

1-3 Striking Polish workers heed a call by Solidarity leader Lech Walesa to return to work, ending strikes that began on August 16.

7, 9 The U.S. yacht *Stars & Stripes* defeats the challenger *New Zealand* in two straight races off San Diego to retain the America's Cup yachting trophy.

10 Tennis star Steffi Graf of West Germany wins the U.S. Open to take the grand slam, which also includes championships at Wimbledon and the Australian and French opens.

10-19 Pope John Paul II visits Zimbabwe, Botswana, Lesotho, Swaziland, and Mozambique.

11-17 Hurricane Gilbert causes about 300 deaths and more than $10 billion in damage in the West Indies and Mexico.

13 Reagan signs a bill to strengthen the Fair Housing Act of 1968 by extending protection to the disabled and families with children.

17 The 24th Summer Olympic Games begin in Seoul, South Korea, with a record 160 nations taking part.

A military coup in Haiti ousts Namphy. Lieutenant General Prosper Avril declares himself president on September 18.

18 A military coup deposes Burma's civilian President Maung Maung. Armed forces chief Saw Maung forms a ruling military council with himself as the chairman.

19 Poland's Council of Ministers Chairman (premier) Zbigniew Messner and his cabinet resign after criticism of their economic policies, which resulted in two waves of strikes. Mieczyslaw Rakowski succeeds Messner on September 27.

20 The 43rd United Nations (UN) General Assembly elects Dante Caputo of Argentina as its president.

Lauro F. Cavazos takes office as United States secretary of education, the first Hispanic Cabinet member in history.

23 Former presidential aide Michael K. Deaver, convicted in December 1987 of lying under oath to a grand jury, is given a suspended three-year prison sentence and fined $100,000. He says he will appeal the case.

25 Bush and Dukakis meet in a nationally televised debate at Wake Forest University in Winston-Salem, N.C.

27 Canadian sprinter Ben Johnson loses his Olympic gold medal after drug tests show he used illegal muscle-building steroids. Johnson denies using the drugs.

28 Pitcher Orel Hershiser of the Los Angeles Dodgers sets a record for consecutive scoreless innings pitched, with 59.

29 The space shuttle *Discovery* lifts off from Cape Canaveral, Fla., for the first shuttle flight since the *Challenger* exploded in 1986. *Discovery* lands safely on October 3.

30 Congress passes an overhaul of the welfare system designed to move recipients into the work force. Reagan signs the bill October 13.

▲

The space shuttle *Discovery* successfully lifts off on September 29—32 months after the U.S. space program was halted by the explosion of the *Challenger*.

◀ The 24th Summer
Olympic Games open
in Seoul, South Korea,
on September 17.

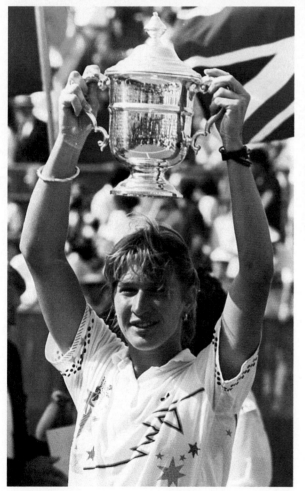

▲
Solidarity leader Lech Walesa meets with striking Polish workers on September 1 and asks
them to return to their jobs.

◀ Steffi Graf of West Germany wins the U.S.
Open, and tennis' grand slam, on September 10.

October						
						1
2	3	4	5	6	7	8
9	10	11	12	13	14	15
16	17	18	19	20	21	22
23	24	25	26	27	28	29
30	31					

1   The Soviet Union replaces Supreme Soviet Presidium Chairman Andrei A. Gromyko with Communist Party General Secretary Gorbachev, giving Gorbachev the nation's two top leadership positions.

2   The 24th Summer Olympic Games end in Seoul, South Korea. The Soviet Union wins the most medals— 132, including 55 gold.

4   Rioting breaks out in Algeria after the government warns that more economic austerity is needed. At least 159 people die in the riots, the worst in Algeria since 1962.

5   Vice presidential candidates Quayle and Bentsen debate in Omaha, Nebr.

Chilean voters reject, 55 to 43 per cent, an extension of the term of President Augusto Pinochet Ugarte, requiring him to hold a presidential election in 1989.

A new democratic Constitution goes into effect in Brazil, replacing the 1969 Constitution of the former military regime.

10   Czechoslovak Prime Minister Lubomir Strougal resigns, reportedly because of differences with Communist Party chief Miloš Jakeš. Ladislav Adamec replaces Strougal on October 12.

13   The Roman Catholic Church announces that new scientific tests prove the Shroud of Turin could not have been the burial cloth of Jesus.

Bush and Dukakis meet at the University of California at Los Angeles for the second debate of the presidential campaign.

18   Congress passes a bill that will make the Veterans Administration a Cabinet department in March 1989. Reagan signs the law on October 25.

19   Two air crashes in India, one in Ahmadabad and one in Gauhati, kill at least 164 people.

20   The Los Angeles Dodgers win the World Series, defeating the Oakland Athletics four games to one.

21   A U.S. grand jury indicts deposed Philippine President Ferdinand E. Marcos and his wife, Imelda, on racketeering charges. The couple deny the charges.

22   Congress approves an antidrug bill that imposes harsh sentences on narcotics users and dealers alike, including the death penalty for drug-related killings. Reagan signs the bill on November 18.

Congress also passes a tax bill including a "taxpayer's bill of rights" restricting Internal Revenue Service agents. Reagan signs it on November 11.

28   Two gray whales who had been trapped in Arctic Ocean ice near Barrow, Alaska, head for open water after U.S. and Soviet rescuers clear a path for them.

Meat packer John Morrell & Company is fined $4.33-million, the most that the Occupational Safety and Health Administration has ever fined an employer, for "willfully" exposing workers to injury. Morrell calls the fine unfair.

30   Kraft Incorporated, the largest U.S. food company, accepts a $13.1-billion take-over bid from food and tobacco giant Philip Morris Companies Incorporated for one of the largest mergers in U.S. history.

▲

Chileans celebrate the result of an October 5 vote rejecting a new eight-year term for President Augusto Pinochet Ugarte and calling for a 1989 election.

◀ Orel Hershiser hurls the Los Angeles Dodgers to a World Series victory on October 20.

Rescuers watch as one of two whales trapped by ice in the Arctic Ocean surfaces. The whales were freed on October 28.
▼

31

November						
		1	2	3	4	5
6	7	8	9	10	11	12
13	14	15	16	17	18	19
20	21	22	23	24	25	26
27	28	29	30			

1   Israeli parliamentary elections fail to give a clear majority to either the conservative Likud bloc or the centrist Labor alignment.

2-4   A computer virus, a program designed to reproduce and transmit itself over electronic networks, disrupts the operation of computers at universities and defense research centers throughout the United States.

3   Algerians, in a national referendum, vote for constitutional changes that may eventually loosen the hold of the National Liberation Front, Algeria's only legal political party.

3-4   A coup attempt led by Sri Lankan mercenaries fails to overthrow the government of the Maldives, an island nation in the Indian Ocean, after Indian troops come to the government's aid.

7-10   A nationwide strike by Sinhalese extremists halts nearly all commerce in Sri Lanka.

8   George Bush wins the U.S. presidency. He says the next day that his campaign manager, former Treasury Secretary Baker, will be secretary of state.

10   The U.S. Department of Energy announces that a $4.4-billion atom smasher, the Superconducting Super Collider (SSC), will be built in Texas.

15   The Soviet Union launches its first reusable spacecraft, the shuttle *Buran* (Snowstorm).

The Palestine National Council, the parliament of the Palestinian people, declares the creation of an independent Palestinian state with Jerusalem as its capital.

President-elect Bush announces that Treasury Secretary Brady will remain in his Cabinet.

16   Benazir Bhutto's Pakistan People's Party wins 92 of 237 seats in the National Assembly, more than twice as many as any other party but not a majority.

The Estonian Supreme Soviet (parliament) declares Estonia "sovereign"—that is, free of the control of any other government. The Soviet government on November 26 holds the declaration invalid.

17   Bush names New Hampshire Governor John H. Sununu as White House chief of staff.

21   Canada's Progressive Conservative Party, led by Prime Minister Mulroney, wins a majority in parliamentary elections.

Bush asks Education Secretary Cavazos and Attorney General Thornburgh to stay on.

22   The U.S. Air Force unveils its long-secret Stealth bomber, designed to evade enemy radar.

Ceremonies mark the 25th anniversary of the assassination of President John F. Kennedy.

26   The United States denies PLO Chairman Yasir' Arafat a visa to visit the UN, charging that he "lends support to acts of terrorism." The UN denounces the U.S. decision on November 30.

29   A cyclone and tidal wave cause at least 3,000 deaths in Bangladesh and India.

Democratic senators elect Senator George J. Mitchell of Maine as majority leader.

30   RJR Nabisco Incorporated, a food and tobacco firm, is bought by Kohlberg Kravis Roberts & Company for $25 billion, the largest corporate buy-out in United States history.

▲
Republican George Bush greets supporters after winning the November 8 U.S. presidential election with 53 per cent of the popular vote.

◀ Students visit the grave-site of U.S. President John F. Kennedy on November 22, 25 years after his assassination.

The U.S. Air Force unveils the B-2 Stealth bomber—designed to evade enemy radar—on November 22.
▼

◀ Canadian Prime Minister Brian Mulroney is applauded by his family after his party wins a clear majority in Canada's November 21 parliamentary elections.

December						
				1	2	3
4	5	6	7	8	9	10
11	12	13	14	15	16	17
18	19	20	21	22	23	24
25	26	27	28	29	30	31

2 **Benazir Bhutto** takes office as prime minister of Pakistan, becoming the first woman elected to head a Muslim nation.

2-6 **The space shuttle *Atlantis*** carries out a secret military mission.

4 **Carlos Andrés Pérez** of the ruling Democratic Action party is elected president of Venezuela.

5 **PTL founder Jim Bakker** is indicted by a federal grand jury in Charlotte, N.C., on fraud and conspiracy charges.

6 **President-elect Bush names** Robert A. Mosbacher secretary of commerce.

Rebel Argentine soldiers surrender, ending a five-day revolt that sought a shakeup in army leadership and an end to prosecution of officers for human-rights abuses.

7 **Soviet leader Gorbachev** announces sweeping military cutbacks in an address to the UN General Assembly in New York City. He also meets with President Reagan and President-elect Bush.

A devastating earthquake causes about 25,000 deaths in the Soviet republic of Armenia.

12 **Pakistan's Acting President** Ghulam Ishaq Khan is elected to the presidency by members of Pakistan's National Assembly and provincial assemblies.

13-15 **The UN General Assembly** convenes a special session in Geneva, Switzerland, so that Arafat, denied a U.S. visa, can address the Assembly.

14 **The United States agrees** to direct talks with the PLO after Arafat renounces terrorism, recognizes Israel's right to exist, and endorses two UN resolutions as a basis for peace negotiations. The talks begin on December 16 in Tunis, Tunisia.

Bush picks U.S. Trade Representative Clayton K. Yeutter as secretary of agriculture. On December 16, he names former Senator John G. Tower of Texas as secretary of defense, and on December 19, Representative Jack F. Kemp of New York as secretary of housing and urban development.

19 **Israel's two major parties,** Likud and Labor, agree to form a coalition with Yitzhak Shamir remaining as prime minister.

Prime Minister Ranasinghe Premadasa is elected president of Sri Lanka.

21 **A Pan Am World Airways jumbo jet crashes** in Lockerbie, Scotland, killing all 259 people aboard and at least 11 people on the ground.

The investment firm of Drexel Burnham Lambert Incorporated pleads guilty to securities fraud charges and agrees to pay $650 million in fines.

22 **Angola, Cuba, and South Africa** sign an agreement providing for the independence of Namibia and the withdrawal of Cuban troops from Angola.

Four more members of Bush's Cabinet are named— Louis W. Sullivan (health and human services), Manuel Lujan, Jr. (interior), Edward J. Derwinski (veterans affairs), and Samuel K. Skinner (transportation). On December 24, Bush picks Elizabeth Hanford Dole as secretary of labor.

30 **Canada's Senate** gives final approval to the U.S.-Canadian free-trade agreement.

▲

Benazir Bhutto—the first woman to head a modern Islamic nation—is sworn in as Pakistan's prime minister in Islamabad on December 2.

34

◀ Soviet leader Mikhail S. Gorbachev, right, poses with U.S. President Ronald Reagan, center, and President-elect George Bush near the Statue of Liberty during Gorbachev's December visit to the United States.

Armenians gather around a fire in the midst of the devastation caused by a December 7 earthquake that killed tens of thousands of people near the Soviet-Turkish border.
▼

1982
1985
1986
1987
1988

Special Reports

Five articles and a two-part feature give special treatment to subjects of current importance and lasting interest.

See page 83 ▶

By William J. Broad

Back into Space

After being grounded for 32 months, the United States space shuttle program was again underway, reviving plans and hopes for the nation's future in space.

The United States space program appeared to be back on track in 1988, after an extraordinary period of turmoil. During that time, the nation's main space-launching vehicles—the space shuttles—were grounded for 32 months, along with their important payloads and hopes for the U.S. future in space. This turmoil was triggered in the cold blue sky over Florida's Cape Canaveral on the morning of Jan. 28, 1986, when the 25th shuttle flight ended about 73 seconds after liftoff with the explosion of the space shuttle *Challenger*. All seven crew members were killed in history's worst space disaster. But on Sept. 29, 1988, the U.S. shuttle fleet once again became spaceborne. The shuttle *Discovery* lifted off at the John F. Kennedy Space Center at Cape Canaveral amid the cheers and applause of about 250,000 spectators and thousands of workers and officials of the National Aeronautics and Space Administration (NASA).

Although the launching of *Discovery* got all the attention, an equally important but little-noticed event occurred less than a month earlier. On September 5, the Department of Defense lofted a Titan 2, the first of a new generation of rockets intended to diminish military reliance on the troubled shuttle program. As the new booster carried a secret payload into space from Vandenberg Air Force Base in California, Secretary of the Air Force Edward C. Aldridge, Jr., proclaimed 1988 "the year of space launch recovery," saying the new rocket fleet would ensure "this nation's access to space for many years to come."

Behind the celebrations, however, lurked a continuing sense of disarray in the U.S. space program. Serious questions remained about how best to use the space shuttle, the world's first reusable spacecraft. Unlike rockets that can be used only once, the space shuttle takes off like a rocket and lands like an airplane, and, except for an external fuel tank, is entirely reusable. When the shuttle was first built in the early 1980's, it was intended to be the principal and, ultimately, the only means of launching U.S. commercial, military, or scientific satellites. Those payloads had previously been launched on expendable rockets. After the shuttle demonstrated its ability to fly into space and return safely, plans were made to do away with the U.S. fleet of expendable rockets.

The *Challenger* disaster of 1986, however, put an end to this policy, which had been characterized by some space experts as "putting all our eggs in one basket." In the aftermath of the explosion, the Administration of President Ronald Reagan decided to remove all commercial cargoes from the shuttle to encourage the growth of a private commercial rocket industry. And the Department of Defense argued successfully for its own launch fleet of expendable rockets, with the aim of launching as many as 20 rockets a year by 1991.

No longer would the U.S. space program have "all its eggs in one basket," but still unanswered was the question: How would the shuttle then be used? A vehicle that was designed to serve

The author:
William J. Broad is a
science reporter for
The New York Times.

three purposes—launching commercial, military, and scientific cargoes—now seemed to serve only one—science—and even the scientific community was divided on the usefulness of the shuttle. A sizable segment of space scientists wanted a separate fleet of expendable rockets to send unmanned spacecraft into the solar system.

NASA proposed that the shuttle be used to build the first permanently occupied U.S. space station. But it was not at all certain in 1988 that Congress would continue to approve funding for the controversial station, which has been described as an orbiting research laboratory. When President Reagan first gave the go-ahead for the station in 1984, NASA estimated its cost at $8-billion. But by 1988, that cost estimate had risen to $25 billion, according to a study by the National Research Council, an agency of the National Academy of Sciences. Thus, the long-term future of the shuttle fleet was far from secure, and another disaster of *Challenger* proportions could destroy the shuttle program.

Complicating the future of the U.S. space program is the number of players that help shape it. NASA and the Department of Defense have the chief responsibility for overseeing space operations. They get pressure in support of favored projects from the aerospace industry and the scientific community. The White House is ultimately responsible for setting policy, and Congress plays a pivotal role with its power to appropriate funds. The result is that the space program sometimes resembles a patchwork quilt, sewn together by a series of compromises among these diverse centers of power. For example, NASA originally won the Defense Department's support for building the shuttle by agreeing to carry military payloads, but the military, in turn, insisted on radical changes in the shuttle's design. The result was a bigger, more cumbersome orbiter that could carry heavy military payloads, rather than the sleek craft NASA first proposed.

By the mid-1980's, there were still more players. In 1986, the Department of Commerce and the Department of Transportation were given the responsibility of helping oversee the development of private commercial industry in space. Almost immediately, NASA and the Commerce Department became embroiled in a dispute over the department's plan for a privately developed, small-scale space station to be visited but not lived in by astronauts. NASA officials saw this plan as a rival to their proposal for a larger, permanently occupied station. The White House approved the private space station over NASA's objections, but Congress failed to fund it in 1988, creating more uncertainty about the future direction of the space program.

Finally, rival spacefaring nations have also played a role in shaping the U.S. space program by virtue of the competition they have created. As a result of the *Challenger* disaster, China, the 13 nations represented in the European Space Agency (ESA),

  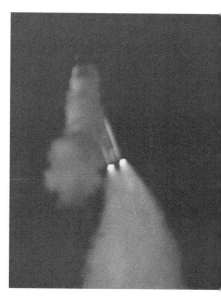

Space setbacks

The U.S. space program experienced its greatest tragedy and worst set-backs in 1986. The space shuttle *Challenger* exploded in January, *above left,* killing all seven crew members. The subsequent failures of two unmanned rockets—a Titan, *above center,* in April, and a Delta, *above right,* in May grounded the U.S. space program.

and the Soviet Union have all made inroads by obtaining commercial payloads previously meant for launch on the shuttle. The Soviet Union, in particular, has gradually taken a considerable lead in many space accomplishments. For example, the Soviets have had a permanently occupied space station—*Mir* (Peace) —since March 1986 while NASA's planned space station— *Freedom*—will not be ready for occupation until 1997, if then. The Soviets have also announced their intention to send a cosmonaut crew to Mars, while the future of U.S. astronauts in space exploration is far from clear. In November, the Soviets launched their first reusable spacecraft, the *Buran* (Snowstorm), which is similar in design to the U.S. shuttles.

At the start of the space age in 1957, things had been clearer. The United States had been motivated to enter space because the Soviet Union had launched the world's first artificial satellite, *Sputnik 1.* Not only was national prestige at stake, but also there was the threat that the Soviets could use space for military purposes, and by seizing the high ground of space, obtain military superiority.

Four years after *Sputnik 1,* on April 12, 1961, the Soviets again upstaged the United States when cosmonaut Yuri A. Gagarin became the first human being in space. The United States responded with the Apollo moon program. Project Apollo led to the dramatic July 20, 1969, moon landing of astronauts Neil A. Armstrong and Edwin E. Aldrin, Jr., a feat of technological prowess that dazzled the world.

In retrospect, the Apollo program of the 1960's represented the golden years of the U.S. space program, though it came with a large price tag. "No single space project," President John F. Kennedy declared on May 25, 1961, "will be more important for the long-range exploration of space. And none will be so difficult or expensive to accomplish." That expense ultimately came to $24 billion. Funding on the scale of the Apollo program for a single project was never to be repeated.

Public interest in the six moon missions that followed the original landing gradually lessened. When the missions ended in December 1972, the space program had lost some of its luster, and critical voices in Congress grew louder in calling for a diversion of funds from the heavens to the war on poverty at home.

In the early 1970's, NASA forged a comprehensive plan to send astronauts to Mars by way of a permanent space station serviced by a reusable space shuttle. But the Administration of President Richard M. Nixon—beset by the war in Vietnam, urban decay, and economic concerns—rejected the plan as too costly, approving only the shuttle. On April 12, 1981, exactly 20 years after Gagarin became the first man to orbit Earth, the

Investigating *Challenger*
Public confidence in the space program was further eroded when a presidential commission investigating the *Challenger* explosion, *left*, learned that the disaster could have been prevented. Prior to the launch, space officials had been warned of the possible failure of O-ring seals in a booster rocket, *below*.

September 1988—Shuttle flights resume with orbiter *Discovery*.

 January 1986—The *Challenger* shuttle explodes, killing all seven crew members.

 January 1986—*Voyager 2* flies past the planet Uranus.

 April 1981—The first reusable spacecraft, the shuttle *Columbia,* is launched into space.

 November 1980—*Voyager 1* flies past the planet Saturn.

 March 1979—*Voyager 1* flies past the planet Jupiter.

 December 1978—*Pioneer-Venus 1* begins orbiting the planet Venus.

 July 1976—*Viking 1* lander becomes first probe to land on the planet Mars.

 May 1973—The first U.S. space station, *Skylab,* is launched into Earth orbit.

 November 1971—*Mariner 9* becomes the first spacecraft to orbit Mars.

 July 1969—Astronaut Neil A. Armstrong becomes the first person to set foot on the moon.

 December 1968—*OAO-2* is the first astronomical observatory in space.

 July 1965—*Mariner 4* returns first close-up photographs of Mars.

 April 1965—*Early Bird* is the first commercial communications satellite.

Milestones in the U.S. space program

The United States has had a continuing presence in space ever since January 1958, with astronaut missions, unmanned interplanetary spacecraft, or various Earth-orbiting satellites.

 July 1962—*Telstar 1* transmits first live transatlantic TV program.

 February 1962—John H. Glenn, Jr., is the first U.S. astronaut to orbit Earth.

 May 1961—Alan B. Shepard, Jr., becomes the first U.S. astronaut in space.

 Astronauts in space

 Interplanetary spacecraft

 U.S. satellite

 April 1960—*Transit 1B* is launched as the first navigation satellite.

 February 1959—*Vanguard 2* becomes first weather satellite.

 January 1958—*Explorer 1* becomes first U.S. satellite.

space shuttle *Columbia* thundered aloft from Cape Canaveral, initiating the era of reusable space vehicles. NASA officials argued that the reusable shuttle would be cheaper in the long run than expendable rockets and could eventually pay for itself by hauling commercial payloads into space.

In 1983, inspired in part by the repeated success of the shuttle flights in the previous two years and the promise of more powerful space technologies to come, President Reagan called on U.S. scientists to design a space-based defense system that would render enemy missiles "impotent and obsolete." Reagan's proposal, called the Strategic Defense Initiative or "Star Wars" project, was envisioned as a five-year, $26-billion effort that would reach its peak in the late 1980's in a dazzling array of space experiments, many carried aloft by the shuttle.

Then, in 1984, in a similar optimistic vein, Reagan called for the creation of America's first permanently occupied space station "within a decade." Describing it as a base from which the moon or Mars might be colonized, he said, "We can follow our dreams to distant stars." The station, too, was to be carried aloft by the shuttle.

These and other plans suffered a dire setback with the *Challenger* explosion. Yet another setback came a few months later, in April 1986, when an Air Force Titan 34D unmanned rocket —the largest U.S. rocket—exploded above its launching pad at Vandenberg, destroying a spy satellite and grounding the Titan fleet for extensive repairs. It was the second failure in a row for the big Titan rocket, another having been lost in August 1985. The nation that had landed men on the moon and, over the course of decades, had pioneered many types of advanced space technology now had no way to loft large payloads into space.

In the shock of failure and its aftermath, various government investigations and probes disclosed information that seriously eroded public confidence in NASA and U.S. competence in space. A 12-member commission appointed by President Reagan to investigate the *Challenger* explosion found that some NASA officials had prior knowledge of the defect that caused the explosion—the failure of rubber seals known as *0 rings* used on the solid-fuel booster rockets that help launch the shuttle. The commission learned that some officials had been aware of problems with the 0 rings—which were vital to seal joints on the boosters and prevent hot gases from leaking—as early as the second shuttle mission in November 1981. In fact, it was later disclosed that the booster rockets had been redesigned to eliminate the 0 ring problem, and these redesigned rockets were on order at the time of the disaster.

On the eve of the *Challenger* launch, engineers for Morton Thiokol, Incorporated, makers of the booster rockets, warned that unusually cold temperatures at the launch site could affect

Among the space goals other nations met during 1986 while the U.S.
shuttles were grounded were the Soviet Union's *Mir* space station, *above
left*, and the European Space Agency's *Giotto* probe of Halley's Comet
(seen in an artist's rendering, *above right*).

the performance of the seals. The engineers recommended
postponing the launch, but they were overruled by Morton
Thiokol management. The commission learned that Morton
Thiokol had come under pressure to approve the launch from
NASA officials at the George C. Marshall Space Flight Center in
Huntsville, Ala. The O rings did fail, and gases as hot as 5000°F.
(2760°C) leaked from a joint in the right solid-fuel booster
rocket, causing a rupture in the external fuel tank and igniting
the explosion. In their haste to launch the *Challenger*, NASA
officials grounded the shuttle fleet for the next 2½ years.

Adding to the damage to NASA's reputation was the commission's discovery of a serious communication failure within
NASA's ranks. Top NASA managers were not informed of the
engineers' warnings on the eve of the launch. And concern about
the safety of the joint design was not communicated to top management until 1985. As a result, the commission recommended
new communication and decision-making procedures.

NASA's recovery from the launching crisis was expensive. Repairs to the shuttle system took nearly three years and cost $2.4-
billion. From 400 to 600 changes were made to key systems and
support gear.

While the shuttle was grounded...

During the 32 months that the United States space shuttle fleet was grounded—from January 1986 to September 1988—the Soviet Union and the European Space Agency made considerable headway in space while the United States achieved little.

Soviet Union

February 1986—*Mir* (Peace) space station begins orbiting Earth.

March 1986—*Vega 1* and *Vega 2* spacecraft fly by Halley's Comet.

May 1987—The Energia—the world's most powerful rocket—is successfully tested.

December 1987—Cosmonauts set record stay of 326 days in space on board *Mir*.

January 1988—Totals show that during 1987, the Soviets launched 95 rockets that carried 116 satellites.

July 1988—The Soviets launch two spacecraft to Phobos, a moon of Mars. (One probe goes out of control en route.)

September 1988—The Soviet Union's first reusable spacecraft, the *Buran* (Snowstorm), is unveiled. It is launched in November.

European Space Agency

February 1986—Ariane rocket launches two research satellites.

March 1986—*Giotto* spacecraft flies past Halley's Comet; two communications satellites are launched.

September 1987—Ariane rocket launches two communications satellites.

March 1988—Ariane rocket launches two communications satellites.

June 1988—New Ariane-4 rocket launches three satellites.

United States

February 1986—Atlas rocket launches Defense Department payload.

September 1986—Atlas rocket launches weather satellite.

February 1987—Titan rocket launches military satellite.

October 1987—Titan-34D rocket launches military satellite.

The most important changes in the three remaining U.S. space shuttles—*Discovery, Columbia*, and *Atlantis*—were made in the design of the flawed solid-fuel booster rocket. Hundreds of other changes were made in the shuttles themselves as well as in their systems and support gear on the ground. These changes would also be incorporated in a fourth orbiter that was being assembled in 1988 at a cost of $2.8 billion and was scheduled to replace *Challenger* in 1991. Additions to the ships included a new hatch that can be blown off in an emergency, an escape pole so astronauts can bail out at high altitudes, and a slide to help them escape the craft while on the ground.

While the shuttle was under repair, the first breath of renewal for the U.S. space program came in October 1987 when a Titan 34D rocket lofted a secret military payload. It was the first large American cargo to be sent into space in more than two years. In

The latest look of the U.S. space fleet includes a new generation of military rockets, *above left,* new private commercial rockets, *above center,* and a fourth orbiter—now under construction—for NASA's shuttle fleet, *above right.*

The United States space fleet

Military rockets

Number	Type	Payload	First launching
11	Atlas 2	7.5 short tons (6.7 metric tons)	1991
20	Delta 2	5.5 short tons (4.9 metric tons)	Fall 1988
14	Titan 2	2.4 short tons (2.2 metric tons)	September 1988
23	Titan 4	20 short tons (18.1 metric tons)	Fall 1988

Private commercial rockets

Company	Number of launches planned from 1989 to 1992, as of June 1988	Type of cargo
Conatec	2 (Black Brant rocket)	Materials-processing experiments.
General Dynamics Corporation	6 (modified Atlas rocket)	U.S. government weather and research satellites; European commercial communications satellite.
Martin Marietta Corporation	4 (modified Titan rocket)	International communications satellites; British military satellite; Japanese communications satellite.
McDonnell Douglas Corporation	8 (modified Delta rocket)	U.S. government research satellites; commercial and government communication satellites for Great Britain, India, and Indonesia.

NASA's space transportation system

Shuttle	Number of missions from 1988 to 1990	Type of mission
Atlantis	6 (1 in 1988; 1 in 1989; 4 in 1990)	Secret Pentagon missions; launch spacecraft to Venus; launch spacecraft to sun.
Columbia	6 (2 in 1989; 4 in 1990)	Secret Pentagon mission; launch communications satellite; astronomy mission; scientific research.
Discovery	7 (1 in 1988; 3 in 1989; 3 in 1990)	Launch tracking satellites; secret Pentagon missions; launch *Hubble Space Telescope;* launch astronomy satellite.

September 1988, a Titan 2 rocket successfully carried another secret military payload into orbit. The Titan 2 was the first of a new generation of at least 68 rockets being built to diminish the military's reliance on the space shuttle. With dozens of military reconnaissance and communications satellites awaiting transport into space, the Air Force estimated that the launching rate for the new rockets would peak in 1991 at about 20 launchings a year. The new rockets will consist of 14 Titan 2's, an 11-story-high rocket made by Martin Marietta Corporation; 20 Delta 2's, a 13-story-high rocket made by McDonnell Douglas Corporation; 11 Atlas 2's, a 15-story-high rocket made by General Dynamics Corporation; and 23 Titan 4 rockets, a 20-story-high launcher also made by Martin Marietta. In addition to these, the Air Force was lobbying Congress for even more rockets, saying it needed a total of $11.7 billion to spend on new boosters.

Some experts have argued that the Pentagon cannot possibly use all of the 68 rockets it has ordered. These experts have charged that the build-up is both an overreaction to previous launch failures and an attempt to diminish NASA's importance.

"This is far more rockets than they know what to do with," according to John E. Pike, head of space policy for the Washington-based Federation of American Scientists. He adds that the space shuttles, if their flight rate became frequent enough, could routinely launch U.S. military satellites in the 1990's.

Air Force officials counter such arguments by saying that in the interest of national security, a reserve of rockets is necessary. Never again, they say, can the United States afford to be in a position in which a string of launching failures cripples its ability to loft military satellites into space.

Where space funds go
The U.S. military space budget has gained ascendancy over NASA's civilian program.

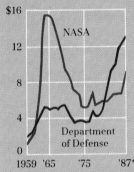

Billions of dollars

*Estimate.
Source: Office of Management and Budget.

Another sign of renewal for the U.S. space program was evident in the time, money, and political support that Congress and the White House gave NASA to rebuild the shuttles. The shuttle had been designed, built, and operated during a period when NASA was under enormous pressure from Congress and the White House to hold down costs. As a result, budget cutbacks forced NASA to redesign the shuttle 50 times before it was launched in 1981. The decision to use the less reliable but cheaper solid-fuel booster rockets—instead of more reliable and more expensive liquid-fuel boosters—was perhaps the most fateful of the early design changes that resulted from congressional budget pressure.

Congress significantly increased NASA's budget during the redesign period that followed the *Challenger* catastrophe. By 1988, the physical elements of the U.S. shuttle fleet appeared to be in the best shape ever, having undergone more testing and fine-tuning than when the shuttles were first built. In theory, the orbiters were capable of meeting a demanding schedule of 10 or more missions a year—a schedule NASA planned for the 1990's.

But the real beneficiary from the launching crisis has clearly been the Pentagon. Not only did the Pentagon manage to assemble a multibillion-dollar rocket fleet from scratch, but also it laid claim to nearly half the space shuttle flights scheduled for 1988 and 1989. Of the nine shuttle missions NASA has scheduled during that period, four are listed as secret Pentagon missions.

Although the White House and Congress cooperated to strengthen NASA and to provide the Pentagon with a separate fleet of rockets, no such benefits befell the U.S. scientific community. In a blow to space scientists, NASA in 1988 decided to delay two key astronomical missions because of postponements in the resumption of shuttle flights. A shortage in rocket fuel arising from the explosion of a solid-rocket fuel plant in Nevada in May 1988 also helped set back the schedule. The most notable postponement was the $1.5-billion *Hubble Space Telescope,* NASA's top scientific project, a telescope 42 feet (13 meters) in length that will orbit Earth. The telescope is expected to enable scientists to see seven times farther than they can with ground-based telescopes, which must peer through distortions caused by Earth's atmosphere. The launching was pushed back five months, from June 1989 to December 1989. Like many NASA payloads awaiting transport into orbit, the space telescope is in storage, costing the space agency $7 million a month to keep it ready for flight. The other delay was that of the $70-million Astro project, a cluster of three advanced telescopes meant to scan the heavens from within the shuttle's payload bay. This project was pushed back from November 1989 to March 1990.

Many space scientists remain skeptical that the shuttle can be relied on to meet a launching schedule. Launch delays have become routine, and if major problems develop, delays can be long. This has caused great concern because some of the shuttle's most important space science missions involve interplanetary expeditions. Launching spacecraft to other planets must be precisely timed to take advantage of the changing alignments in the orbits of the planets. A significant delay in a shuttle launch could mean that the alignments would no longer be advantageous, postponing a planetary mission possibly for years. For this reason, many space scientists would prefer to have more reliable expendable rockets launch planetary probes. NASA has repeatedly asked for money to buy such rockets but has been turned down by Congress and the White House.

In 1988, NASA had only two planetary missions scheduled. The spacecraft *Magellan,* equipped with instruments to map the surface of the planet Venus, was due to be launched in April 1989. *Galileo,* a spacecraft built with West Germany to survey Jupiter and its moons, was to be launched in October 1989.

The *Challenger* disaster heightened the long-standing conflict between proponents of manned and unmanned space flight.

Many prominent scientists had opposed NASA's emphasis on manned flight from the beginning of the space age and shared the view of physicist James A. Van Allen, the discoverer of the Van Allen belts of electrically charged particles that surround Earth. In an influential article in *Scientific American* in January 1986, Van Allen wrote that "the overwhelming majority of scientific and utilitarian achievements in space have come from unmanned . . . spacecraft." So, too, space scientists tended to be skeptical of the proposed space station, believing that robot satellites can do much of what a manned station could, at less cost and with equal or greater efficiency. Theirs has generally been a losing battle, however, given the political support for astronaut missions that has existed since the early days of space flight.

Controversy also surrounded U.S. plans for commercial projects in space. In 1986, President Reagan ordered most commercial payloads to be removed from shuttle missions, calling instead for the creation of a new private rocket industry devoted to the launching of commercial cargoes into space. By 1988, the nation's aerospace corporations were hard at work building huge rockets to loft 20 large commercial payloads—mostly communications satellites—at a total contract cost of more than $1-billion. The first of the launchings was scheduled for early 1989.

But experts were divided on whether the flurry of private rocket-related activity was a flash in the pan or a fundamental shift in the way U.S. aerospace companies operate. Some space experts said it was unlikely that many more payload orders will materialize for the infant industry, adding that foreign rivals—China, the European Space Agency, and the Soviet Union—have already snapped up much of the available business. "We remain optimistic, but it's fair to say the commercial space launch business has gotten a lot more competitive," said Richard E. Brackeen, president of Martin Marietta Commercial Titan Incorporated in Denver, one of the new commercial rocket companies.

Frustrated with the lack of available U.S. launchers, firms with satellites ready for launching have increasingly turned to foreign rivals. In 1988, Payload Systems Incorporated of Wellesley, Mass., became the first American company to contract to have the Soviet Union carry commercial experiments into orbit, marking a major success for the Soviet drive to market its once-secretive space program. The U.S. experiments, to be conducted on the Soviet space station *Mir*, were meant to exploit the near weightlessness of space to grow protein crystals for new drugs.

Less successful in their space commerce endeavors were two major American companies that battled the U.S. government for the right to launch communications satellites on Soviet rockets. Amid the launching crisis, the companies—General Motors Corporation and General Electric Company—urged the govern-

Who shapes the U.S. space program?

The United States space program is pulled in many directions by various and often competing interests. NASA's proposal to build a permanently occupied space station, for example, came under criticism from numerous sources and had to contend with rival proposals. Not only NASA but also the White House; Congress; the departments of Commerce, Defense, and Transportation; the aerospace industry; the scientific community; and public opinion all play a role in shaping America's future in space.

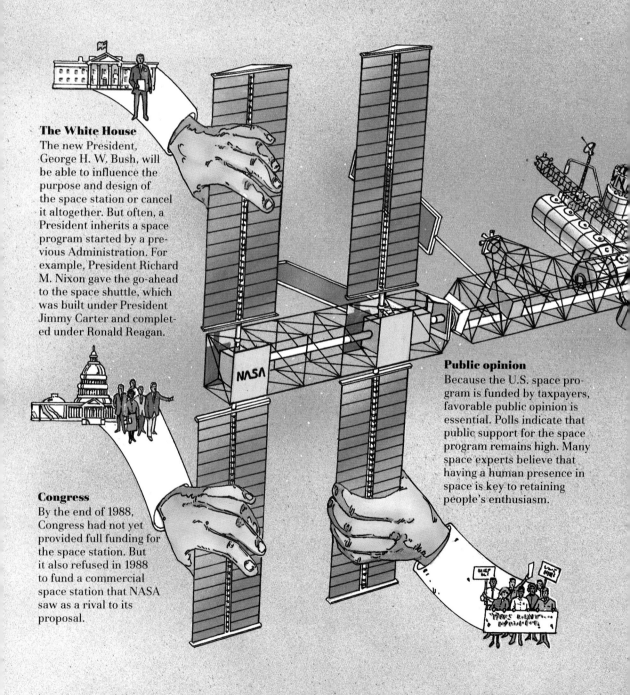

The White House

The new President, George H. W. Bush, will be able to influence the purpose and design of the space station or cancel it altogether. But often, a President inherits a space program started by a previous Administration. For example, President Richard M. Nixon gave the go-ahead to the space shuttle, which was built under President Jimmy Carter and completed under Ronald Reagan.

Congress

By the end of 1988, Congress had not yet provided full funding for the space station. But it also refused in 1988 to fund a commercial space station that NASA saw as a rival to its proposal.

NASA

Public opinion

Because the U.S. space program is funded by taxpayers, favorable public opinion is essential. Polls indicate that public support for the space program remains high. Many space experts believe that having a human presence in space is key to retaining people's enthusiasm.

The Department of Defense

The Defense Department refused to support NASA's proposed space station unless it had access to the station for military research. This position jeopardized an agreement with Europe, Canada, and Japan to build the station jointly for peaceful purposes until a compromise was reached in September 1988.

The aerospace industry

With its considerable lobbying power and political influence—due in part to the thousands of jobs it has created—the aerospace industry plays a major role in shaping U.S. space policy. The industry has been an enthusiastic backer of the proposed space station.

Commerce and Transportation

The departments of Commerce and Transportation have become involved in the space program to help launch a private commercial space industry. The Commerce Department proposed building a small, unoccupied space station that would be serviced by the space shuttle. NASA opposed the plan, arguing that it would duplicate NASA's large-scale manned station.

The scientific community

Much of the scientific community questions the cost and usefulness of a permanently occupied space station. Many scientists have argued instead for an unmanned space platform that would carry out scientific research at less expense.

ment to drop its ban on the launching of U.S.-made satellites by Soviet rockets. The ban was imposed by the White House for national security reasons to prevent Soviet-bloc nations from receiving high-technology equipment that might have military application. Both General Motors and General Electric have subsidiaries that make and market space satellites. In response to their pleas, the Reagan Administration merely stiffened its opposition, saying Western technological secrets might fall into Soviet hands. Some observers, however, said the deeper reason was the fear that freedom to use Soviet rockets would doom the commercial rocket industry in the United States.

Even so, the lobbying by the industrial giants may have ultimately paid off. In September 1988, the Reagan Administration approved export of three satellites for commercial launch on Chinese rockets—the first U.S. satellites to go to a Communist country. The approval by the White House was subject to agreement by China on strict controls to prevent the misuse or diversion of American technology.

In addition to China and the Soviet Union, other foreign rivals posed a challenge to the hopes of the U.S. commercial rocket industry. The most formidable was the European Space Agency, which uses the Ariane rocket to launch satellites from its base at the Kourou Space Center in French Guiana. Although the ESA also experienced launch failures shortly after the *Challenger* disaster, it quickly recovered and by 1988 was dominating the commercial market for satellite launching that had once been monopolized by the United States. Between September 1987 and June 1988, the ESA launched seven satellites, including two U.S. commercial satellites. And the ESA had contracts for nearly 50 commercial satellite launches going into the 1990's, far more than any other space agency. Japan was also expected to enter the satellite-launching business in the 1990's.

These rival spacefaring nations were not only becoming commercial space powers, they were also achieving significant goals in space science. In 1986, two Soviet spacecraft—*Vega 1* and *2*—made the first encounters with Halley's Comet, followed by the ESA's *Giotto* spacecraft and two smaller Japanese probes. The United States did not have a Halley's Comet mission.

In the long run, the *Challenger* disaster and the launching crisis that followed it probably triggered a healthier division of labor in the American space program. And the outlines of the realignment were clearly visible in 1988.

No longer on a commercial footing, NASA's shuttles were freed from the burden of trying to be all things to all users. The shuttle program could now focus instead on building the proposed space station. The space station received an important boost on Sept. 29, 1988—the same day as *Discovery*'s successful launch—when Canada, the ESA, Japan, and the United States signed an agreement to build and operate the space station together, with the United States having the major role in its construction. So long as the shuttles remain reliable and the proposed space station retains the political support of the White House and Congress, the shuttle in the 1990's will probably be used primarily to ferry the components of the space station into orbit. Future shuttle missions will resemble construction projects. Still to be determined, however, is whether the space station will be viewed mainly as a scientific research station or as a transportation center where rockets can be built and launched for missions to the moon and Mars.

Now with its own rocket fleet, the Pentagon will maintain its independence in the lofting of important military satellites. This should help protect the nation's critical outposts of spy satellites.

As for the developing private space industry, its fate will hinge to a large extent on the usual elements of commercial success— the balance of supply and demand. Years will undoubtedly pass before it is clear whether enough payloads will materialize to sustain a thriving industry, or whether foreign rivals are already so well entrenched that they can underprice and outcompete U.S. firms.

What the future holds for the more exotic plans and options for the U.S. space program—such as the "Star Wars" defense system—will be decided by President George H. W. Bush. The cost of exploring and exploiting the heavens, however, will undoubtedly increase. The annual space budgets of the Defense Department and NASA already total more than $30 billion a year—two-thirds of it going to the military. If components of a "Star Wars" defense system are actually put in orbit, the military's space budget will soar. And the Congressional Budget Office has estimated that NASA's budget alone could triple—to $30 billion annually—by the year 2000 if the United States embarked both on building a space station and sending astronauts to Mars. Such estimated expenses, combined with soaring budget deficits, would probably cause the government to lower its sights.

The spendthrift days of the Apollo moon program are probably gone forever. Nevertheless, a renewed space program, tempered by tragedy but encouraged by national resolve, may still push the United States toward new frontiers.

For further reading:

Mark, Hans. *The Space Station: A Personal Journey*. Duke Univ. Press, 1987.

McConnell, Malcolm. *Challenger: A Major Malfunction*. Doubleday, 1987.

McDougall, Walter A. *The Heavens and the Earth: A Political History of the Space Age*. Basic Bks., 1985.

Trento, Joseph J. *Prescription for Disaster: From the Glory of Apollo to the Betrayal of the Shuttle*. Crown, 1987.

By John Camper

Today's Teens and Drugs

More than half of today's high school
seniors have tried drugs—and the drugs
they use are more dangerous than ever.

Chuck's parents were worried. Their 15-year-old son had become increasingly irritable, and his moods sometimes turned violent, leading to wild shouting matches with his father. His high school grades, never the greatest, had grown worse, and there were calls from school saying Chuck hadn't shown up.

Chuck always had an explanation, and his parents were anxious to believe him. They began to wonder if he had a learning disability, but counselors at his suburban Chicago school couldn't seem to figure out what was wrong.

Then his mother found marijuana in his dresser drawer, and things began to fall into place. Chuck's parents learned to their astonishment that he had been taking drugs since he was 11, stealing up to $100 a week from his father's billfold to support his habit. He had started with cigarettes, then used alcohol and marijuana, then progressed to amphetamines, opium, cocaine, LSD, and PCP. "Everything but heroin," Chuck recounted later.

"I still can't believe he took drugs at 11," said his mother.

"There's always denial on the parents' part," said his father.

That is understandable. In the 1950's, when Chuck's parents were growing up, less than 1 per cent of American teen-agers had tried any illicit drug. By 1987, at least 57 per cent had tried an illegal drug, and 36 per cent had tried a drug other than marijuana, according to an annual survey of high school seniors by the University of Michigan's Institute for Social Research.

Recent polls show that Americans of all ages consider drugs the biggest problem facing the nation's schools and, according to some polls, the biggest problem facing the United States. Americans spend an estimated $140 billion a year on illegal drugs, which cost the nation more than $60 billion in lost productivity, crime, and medical bills. The cost in personal suffering and family disruption cannot be measured. The United States has a higher rate of drug abuse than any other industrialized nation, according to the National Institute on Drug Abuse (NIDA).

Although the annual University of Michigan survey is the most thorough source available on teen-agers' drug use, it probably understates the problem because it does not include teens who have dropped out of school. Drug use varies considerably among different geographic areas, socioeconomic groups, and subcultures. Dropouts are more likely to use drugs than are students who remain in school—and the reasons they take drugs, their access to drugs, and even the types of drugs they take are markedly different as well. But because the drug culture outside the schools is intertwined with a multitude of social, economic, and legal tangles that thwart both analysis and control, drug use there is far more difficult to identify and treat.

Among students, however, the Michigan study shows some recent decreases in drug use. Use of marijuana, the most popular illicit drug, has declined since the late 1970's. In 1987, 36.3 per cent of the students reported having used marijuana during the previous year, compared with 50.8 per cent in 1979. And cocaine

The author:
John Camper is a reporter for the *Chicago Tribune*.

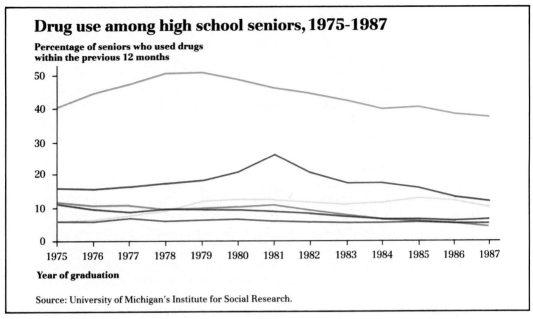

Drug use among high school seniors, 1975-1987

Percentage of seniors who used drugs within the previous 12 months

Year of graduation

Source: University of Michigan's Institute for Social Research.

Marijuana/ hashish

Stimulants

Cocaine

Hallucinogens

Opiates (excluding heroin)

Depressants

use declined substantially for the first time: In 1987, 10.3 per cent of the seniors reported using cocaine within the past year, compared with 12.7 per cent in 1986. (That decline does not necessarily reflect use of a new form of cocaine called *crack*, which was included on the survey for the first time in 1987.) The use of most other illegal drugs tapered off or held steady.

These improvements, while encouraging, are limited. Of particular concern is the finding that teen-age use of alcohol and tobacco has not declined in the past three years. Two-thirds of the seniors had drunk alcohol within the month prior to the survey, and 37.5 per cent had drunk heavily (five or more drinks in one sitting) within the previous two weeks. And, the researchers note, "cigarette smoking—the substance-using behavior that will take the lives of more of these young people than all of the others combined—has not dropped among high school seniors since 1984." Some 18.7 per cent of the seniors smoke daily.

The public is less concerned about alcohol and tobacco than about other drugs, primarily because these are both legal substances—though it's illegal for teen-agers to buy alcohol, and many states restrict the purchase of tobacco. Still, teen-age drinking and smoking have worrisome implications. Researchers have found that teen-agers who drink and smoke are more likely to try illegal drugs. Many experts consider tobacco a "gateway drug" that can lead to marijuana, which in turn can lead to stronger drugs. Of course, smoking does not automatically lead to abuse of other substances. But young people who avoid tobacco are statistically much less likely to take up illicit drugs.

Perhaps more disturbing, the Michigan study also documents the growing popularity of another "gateway" practice: the use of

Use of most drugs by high school seniors has tapered off or held steady in the 1980's. Heroin use (not shown) was 1 per cent or less in all years listed. (The 1981 peak in stimulant use reflects a change in phrasing of the survey question, not an actual change in drug use.)

certain legal—but toxic—substances as *inhalants*. The percentage of students who "sniff" aerosols and solvents such as spray paint, nail-polish remover, glue, and gasoline rose to a high of 6.9 per cent in 1987. A survey by the Texas Commission on Alcohol and Drug Abuse found that inhalant abuse in that state was more common among younger students than older ones, probably because the substances are cheap and readily accessible to children. As inhalant abusers get older, they are more likely to come into contact with—and begin using—illegal drugs.

Hazards of drug use

While health professionals, politicians, and activists have long debated the physical consequences and moral questions of drug use, one risk to drug users has remained constant: Drugs are against the law. Buying or selling even small amounts of drugs can have serious legal consequences. For example, John Zaccaro, Jr., the 24-year-old son of 1984 vice presidential candidate Geraldine A. Ferraro, served three months of house arrest in 1988 for selling one-quarter of a gram of cocaine to an undercover agent in 1986. Zaccaro was also told to pay a $1,500 fine and work 300 hours in community service. Although Zaccaro's family argued that his celebrity status led to an unduly harsh punishment, the mandatory sentence (which was suspended in Zaccaro's case) was one to five years in jail.

In addition to being illegal in itself, drug abuse often leads to theft or other criminal activity as users seek ways to pay for an expensive habit. Also, many users—even those who live in "good" neighborhoods—come into frequent contact with the criminal subculture of drug distribution.

Even if a drug user escapes arrest, the stigma attached to illegal activity can cause serious career problems later in life. Douglas H. Ginsburg, a federal judge, was forced to withdraw his nomination to the Supreme Court of the United States in 1987 after he admitted smoking marijuana as a college student in the 1960's and later as a law school professor.

The illegality of drugs contributes indirectly to their physical hazard. Because drugs are unregulated, a user has no way of assessing their strength or purity. A dose may be strong enough to kill. And legal substances abused as inhalants can kill, too.

The more common physical dangers of most drugs are perhaps less obvious—but no less real—than sudden death from overdose. Drugs can cause severe damage to the heart, lungs, brain, and reproductive organs. Pregnant women who use even small quantities of drugs can cause harm to their unborn children.

Drugs can also contribute to death from other causes. Users of *intravenous drugs* (drugs injected into the body) are at high risk for AIDS (acquired immune deficiency syndrome), a fatal disease spread through sharing contaminated hypodermic needles as well as by sexual contact. And all drug users risk injury or death if they drive under the influence of a drug.

Facing page: One risk of drug use remains constant: Drugs are against the law, and a criminal record lasts a lifetime. Even if a drug user escapes arrest, the association with illegal activity can ruin a career years later.

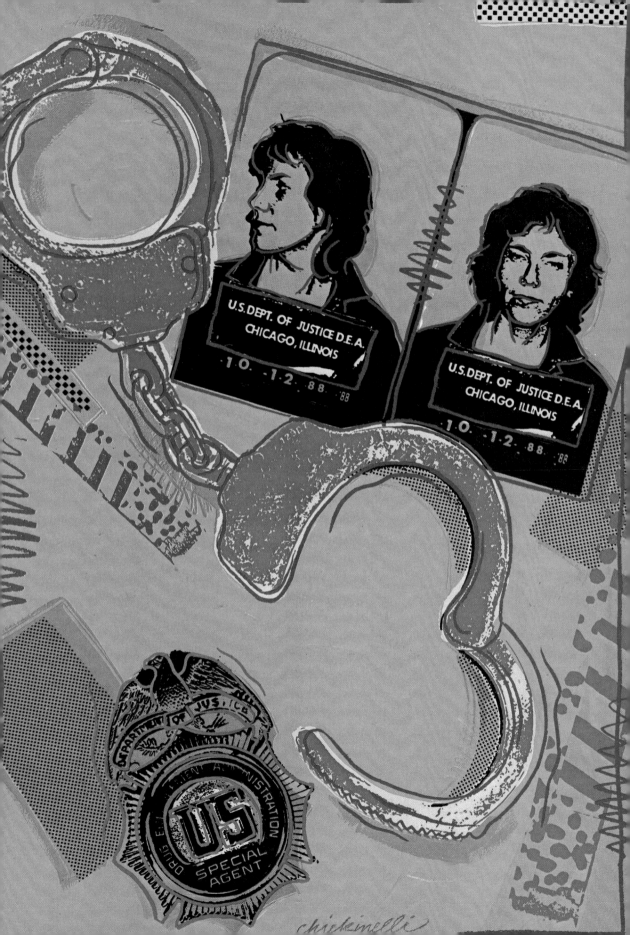

U.S. DEPT. OF JUSTICE D.E.A.
CHICAGO, ILLINOIS
.10. -12. 88. '88

U.S. DEPT. OF JUSTICE D.E.A.
CHICAGO, ILLINOIS
.10. -12. 88. '88

US
SPECIAL
AGENT

chickinelli

The drugs students use

Category of drug	Usual methods of administration	Possible immediate effects	Possible harmful effects
Marijuana (also THC and hashish)	Usually smoked; sometimes taken orally	*Euphoria* (feelings of happiness and well-being), hunger, disorientation, relaxed inhibitions	Over long term, may impair memory and learning, damage lungs, possibly impair fertility
Stimulants (including cocaine and amphetamines)	Cocaine can be sniffed, smoked, or injected; amphetamines are usually taken orally	Alertness, excitement, euphoria, increased heart rate and blood pressure, insomnia, loss of appetite	Agitation, hallucinations, convulsions; overdose may cause heart failure and death
Depressants (including alcohol, barbiturates, and methaqualone)	Taken orally	Slurred speech, disorientation, deep sleep, "drunken" behavior	Breathing difficulty, weak and rapid pulse; overdose may cause coma and death
Hallucinogens (including LSD and PCP)	LSD taken orally; PCP can be eaten, smoked, or injected	Illusions, hallucinations, poor time and distance sense; PCP can cause violent behavior	Flashbacks, psychosis; PCP may cause loss of memory, convulsions, coma, and death
Opiates (including heroin, opium, morphine, and codeine)	Heroin usually injected; other opiates may be eaten, smoked, or injected	Euphoria, drowsiness, weakened breathing, narrowed pupils, nausea	Overdose may cause breathing difficulty, vomiting, convulsions, coma, and death

Source: Adapted from Drug Enforcement Administration, U.S. Department of Justice.

The immediate effects of a drug may be pleasurable, but overdose or long-term use can bring physical damage or death. All these drugs produce psychological or physical dependence — or both.

While drug-related death always remains a possibility, drug use can wreak havoc with living, too. Drug users often have problems in school, and that can cause trouble later in life. "Drug use impairs memory, alertness, and achievement," wrote U.S. Secretary of Education William J. Bennett in a booklet distributed to U.S. schools in 1987. "When a student clouds his mind with drugs, he may become a lifelong casualty."

Social and psychological risks go beyond poor education. Adolescence is the time when most young people learn how to deal with adult problems. Drugs allow youths to avoid those problems—and the learning experiences that accompany them.

A study published in July 1988 by psychologists at the University of California at Los Angeles (UCLA) underscores the psychological and social damage resulting from regular teen-age drug use. The psychologists kept track of 700 Los Angeles youths for eight years. The study showed that those who had used drugs more than once a week as teen-agers were more likely to develop serious personal, social, and economic problems as young adults, even if they had stopped taking drugs by then.

That study confirmed findings by sociologist Denise Kandel of Columbia University in New York City. She tracked 1,600 high school students in New York state from 1971 to 1984. By the time the students were 24, those who had used marijuana daily in high school were five times as likely to have been arrested, two to three times as likely to have consulted a mental health professional, four times as likely to have dropped out of school, and more than twice as likely to have lost or changed jobs.

The drugs students use

Although illegal substances come in and out of fashion, a few types account for most drug abuse among students today.

Marijuana, by far the most widely used illegal drug, consists of the dried leaves and flowers of the hemp plant. When smoked or eaten, the drug produces a dreamlike, intoxicating effect. Responses vary widely, and might include restlessness or relaxation, hunger, and enhancement or distortion of the senses.

The public perception of marijuana has undergone dramatic changes in the last 50 years. In the 1940's and 1950's, authorities claimed the drug invariably led to stronger drugs, degradation, and madness. Those dire warnings were largely ignored by the young people of the late 1960's and early 1970's, who smoked the drug without going mad or turning to stronger substances.

But in recent years, scientists have found that marijuana is not harmless. Today's marijuana is considerably stronger than that of the 1960's, and it can cause short-term memory loss and inhibit learning. When smoked, it is more damaging to the lungs than even tobacco. Some doctors believe it can reduce the sperm count in males and disrupt the menstrual cycle in females.

Heavy users may develop both a physical and psychological dependence on marijuana. And while marijuana does not automatically lead to stronger drugs, people who use stronger drugs almost always used marijuana previously.

Cocaine use rose sharply among young people from 1975, when 5.6 per cent of the seniors said they had used it within the

A young person who uses drugs typically keeps special equipment for particular kinds of drugs. Items associated with cocaine use, *left,* include a grinder for cocaine powder (in red), a mirror and razor blade used to arrange the powder into "lines" that are sniffed through a straw, pipes for smoking crack, and vials and packages for storing the drugs. Supplies used for smoking marijuana and similar drugs, *right,* might include papers and pipes.

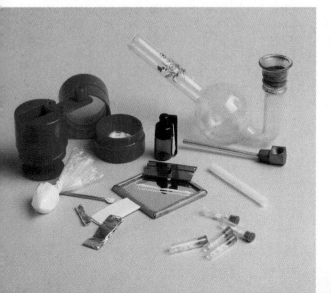

past year, to 1985, when it reached a high of 13.1 per cent. Cocaine, made from the leaves of the coca plant, generally appears as a white powder. Inhaled or injected, cocaine delivers a quick rush of excitement and euphoria that lasts up to an hour.

This "high" is followed by a sense of depression that encourages further use of the drug for relief. Other physical effects are more severe, ranging from burns and sores in the lining of the nose to death—from heart failure, respiratory paralysis, or brain hemorrhage. Users generally become psychologically (and possibly physically) dependent on the drug, requiring more frequent doses to sustain the high. Animals offered an unlimited supply of cocaine will keep using it until it kills them.

In recent years, cocaine has also come in a cheap, smokable form called crack. Crack is the most addictive form of cocaine —and the deadliest. Because crack is a recent entry on the drug scene, and because it is most popular as a "street" drug, few statistics on its use exist. Four per cent of the seniors in the 1987 Michigan survey had used crack in the last year.

Stimulants, chiefly *amphetamines*, were used by 12.2 per cent of the seniors surveyed in 1987; that reflects a steady decline since 1981. Usually taken as pills, stimulants increase alertness and decrease appetite. The drugs speed up the pulse and breathing rate and raise the blood pressure, providing a feeling of energy. They can cause restlessness and anxiety in the short term; over time, they can cause *hallucinations* (imaginary visions) and *paranoia* (irrational fear and distrust). Like cocaine, which is also classed as a stimulant, most "uppers" are strongly habit-forming and encourage repeated use.

Depressants, such as *barbiturates* and *methaqualone* (known by the trade name Quaaludes), were used by 4.1 per cent of the seniors in the 1987 survey, also showing a decline since 1981. Depressants cause many of the same effects as alcohol, including slurred speech, deep sleep, and confusion. They may bring on depression and are a leading cause of drug-related deaths—not only from overdose but also from suicide. They are physically addictive; addicts who quit suddenly may suffer severe withdrawal symptoms, including convulsions and delirium.

Hallucinogens were used by 6.4 per cent of the students in the survey; that figure has held relatively steady for four years. Once called *psychedelic drugs*, hallucinogens distort the user's perceptions and produce a wide range of unpredictable effects, varying from disorientation to delusions or visions. Recurrent hallucinations called *flashbacks* may occur weeks or months after use.

The most common hallucinogens are the manufactured chemicals *LSD* and *PCP*. LSD, which is usually taken orally, can cause wild illusions or panic, but few physical effects. PCP—which usually comes in powder form and is eaten or smoked—is far more dangerous. Users may become violent and experience loss of memory, speech difficulties, and prolonged psychotic reactions. PCP may also cause convulsions, coma, and death.

Opiates, mostly derivatives of the opium plant, have been used for centuries as painkillers. These highly addictive drugs produce a brief feeling of euphoria followed by drowsiness. Larger doses can cause nausea, vomiting, breathing difficulty, coma, and death. Withdrawal is uncomfortable and difficult.

Until the appearance of crack, *heroin*, an injectable opiate, was considered the "hardest"—or most dangerous—drug in common use. Less than 1 per cent of the students in the survey said they used heroin in the last year. Other opiates, such as *codeine, morphine,* and *opium*, were used by 5.3 per cent. Both figures have remained relatively steady for 12 years.

Why students use drugs

Given drugs' potential to end or ruin lives, why do teen-agers use them? According to opinion surveys, the most common answers teens give are "to fit in with others," "to have a good time," and "to feel older." Yet millions of teen-agers manage to fit in, have fun, and grow up without using drugs. There must be other factors that cause some teens to take such a grave risk.

Chuck, who has spent countless hours talking to counselors about his drug problem, explained, "Everybody was partying, and I wanted to be accepted by them. So I did drugs, because that's what they were doing. But I still felt I wasn't the same as them. I didn't fit in. So I decided, 'I can't be as smart as they are or as cool as they are, but I can do more drugs than they can.' "

Psychologists would say Chuck was overly affected by *peer pressure*—the influence of other people his age—and *low self-esteem*, the feeling that he was somehow not up to other people's standards. Substance abuse professional Ken L. Barun described this situation in his 1988 book *How to Keep the Children You Love Off Drugs:* "To join the Jocks Club, you have to be an exceptional athlete. Membership in the Mensa Club requires a high IQ. The Drug Club has the lowest standards of all—you only have to drink, smoke a joint, and so on—and for many kids lacking confidence or an identity, it provides a common denominator for acceptance, without any other requisites."

Researchers point out that students who already have social problems—such as difficulty in school or family troubles—are the ones most likely to use drugs. But well-adjusted teens are not immune. They are surrounded by stimuli that seem to tell them drug use is acceptable. Advertising promotes pills for quick relief of everything from backache to constipation. Parents drink to relax after a tough day, or light up a cigarette to ease tension, or take prescription tranquilizers such as Valium or Librium. The media tell of athletes and performers who use drugs. Song lyrics, movies, and novels portray drug use as common, even normal. Some young people are intrigued by the counterculture of the late 1960's and early 1970's, when drug use skyrocketed in an era of permissiveness and protest.

Certain characteristics of the 1980's may help create a new climate for drug abuse. The high incidence of divorce and the trend to smaller family units have left many young people with only an overworked single parent to keep tabs on them. In more and more families, both parents work outside the home, leaving children unsupervised after school. At the same time, many students have jobs that provide them with money to buy drugs even if they don't have a wealthy parent to rob, as Chuck did.

Facing page: Some young people turn to drugs because they lack confidence in themselves or doubt their ability to "fit in." Doing drugs is, for them, a way to gain acceptance from others.

Prevention—and cure

Practically every school teaches its students about drugs and their dangers, sometimes as early as elementary school. NIDA has been helping parents organize antidrug groups since 1977. In addition, groups such as Youth to Youth, the Just Say No Foundation, and Students Against Driving Drunk help students organize their own antidrug efforts.

Programs place less emphasis on the dangers of drug use than they once did. Researchers point out that teen-agers tend to discount "scare stories"; they think of themselves as immortal and don't consider the long-range consequences of their actions. Instead, many teachers and counselors are attacking the situations that might cause students to turn to drugs. They try to teach students how to solve problems on their own, in order to develop self-confidence so they can resist pressures to try drugs. This is the rationale for former first lady Nancy Reagan's Just Say No campaign, which has spawned more than 10,000 clubs.

Some critics contend that programs such as Just Say No may be naive in advocating abstinence as the definitive solution to teen drug use. They note that many teens will be tempted to try

something illegal at some point, and that an occasional experiment is not the same thing as serious or chronic drug use. In fact, the UCLA study shows that teens who simply dabbled with illegal substances—using drugs less than once a month, for example—did not appear to suffer any long-term ill effects.

Still, attempts to prevent students from starting drugs have some advantages over programs that focus on stopping those who have started. Some studies suggest that a person who does not start drugs by the age of 20 probably never will. In addition, it may be easier to keep people from trying drugs than to cure them once they have become dependent. Treatment may require weeks of hospitalization and months of counseling—and it may be hard to get. Although the United States has some 10,000 drug treatment centers, addicts often must wait months for admission.

Also, few people agree on which treatment programs work best. Some programs for teen drug users rely on group therapy, in which youths share experiences and learn from one another. Others use family therapy, on the theory that the child's drug use may be tied to family problems. In still others, drug users have one-on-one counseling sessions with therapists.

When Chuck's parents discovered his drug problem, Chuck agreed to get counseling. For six months, Chuck succeeded in convincing both his counselor and his parents that he had quit drugs for good. Then on New Year's Eve, he stole $6,000 from his parents and disappeared on a weeklong drug binge. After he was found and arrested at a nearby suburban motel, his parents gave him an ultimatum: Enter a hospital drug-treatment program or face the juvenile courts on his own.

He chose the hospital. "I thought I'd walk in the door and they'd touch me on the head and I'd walk out a completely different person," he said later. "But it was hard work. I had to see how unmanageable my life had become. And they let me know that if I didn't want to help myself, they'd kick me out."

After six weeks in the hospital, Chuck went back to school but continued to spend his afternoons at a drop-in center. At the time of our interview, he had been off drugs for eight months. He considered himself lucky; of the 30 young people who were in the hospital with him, all but 2 were back on drugs.

Long-term solutions

On a broader scale, the U.S. government has expended a great deal of money and effort to try to reduce drug use. The federal budget for enforcing drug laws rose from $800 million in 1981 to $2.5 billion in 1988. Much of that was spent on the difficult task of cutting off drug supplies from Latin America and Asia.

In 1988, some outspoken scholars, law-enforcement officials, and civic leaders became so discouraged by the failure to stem the flow of drugs that they proposed an approach that has been suggested periodically ever since drugs were first prohibited: Make them legal. Proponents of this alternative said legalization would take the profit out of drug dealing and eliminate much drug-related crime. The billions of dollars now spent on law enforcement could then be spent on education and treatment programs. Still, the public did not appear to favor legalization, and political leaders vied to be the toughest on drugs.

Politics aside, many observers were cautiously optimistic that teen-age drug use might continue to decline. David F. Musto, a historian and psychiatrist at Yale University in New Haven, Conn., said the United States may be repeating a pattern that appeared during an epidemic of heroin and cocaine use in the early 1900's. According to Musto, that cycle begins with a sharp increase in drug use, followed by a gradual decline, followed by a period of widespread public intolerance. The United States may now be entering that intolerant phase, he suggests.

The Michigan study seems to bear out that theory. Fully 87 per cent of the seniors in 1987 disapproved of trying cocaine, a jump of seven percentage points over 1986. For a decade, the proportion of students who saw "great risk" in using cocaine even once or twice had hovered around one-third; in 1987 it leaped to nearly one-half. The researchers attributed that change in part to the 1986 cocaine-related deaths of two young sports heroes —University of Maryland basketball star Len Bias and Cleveland Browns football player Don Rogers.

Even marijuana, once thought so benign, is considered dangerous by many of today's high school seniors. From 1978 to 1987, the proportion of seniors who felt regular marijuana use carried great risk jumped from 35 to 74 per cent. The public also is becoming less tolerant of the two major legal drugs, alcohol and tobacco. State after state has raised the drinking age and toughened drunken-driving laws. And more and more local governments are banning smoking in public places. As people's concern with physical fitness grows, unhealthful activities such as smoking and heavy drinking are no longer fashionable.

Officials hope that the decline in students' drug use means illicit drugs are becoming less fashionable, too. Still, even if the numbers are decreasing, the impact of drugs on users and their families is as strong—and as devastating—as ever.

For further information:

These groups can provide additional resources on student drug use:

The Just Say No Foundation
    1777 N. California Boulevard
    Suite 210
    Walnut Creek, CA 94596

National Clearinghouse of Alcohol
    and Drug Information
    P.O. Box 2345
    Rockville, MD 20852

National Institute on Drug Abuse
    5600 Fishers Lane
    Rockville, MD 20857

National Parents' Resource Institute
    for Drug Education (PRIDE)
    100 Edgewood Avenue
    Suite 1002
    Atlanta, GA 30303

Students Against Driving Drunk
    P.O. Box 800
    Marlboro, MA 01752

Youth to Youth
    700 Bryden Road
    Columbus, OH 43215

By Walter Robinson

Close Encounters with Public Art

Art is enlivening our public
spaces and also stirring up
at least its share of conflict.

Y|ou round a corner, and there it is—an assemblage of steel or stone, a vibrant mural, or a strikingly landscaped area. It may be beautiful. It may be bizarre. It may even be humorous. But chances are, it catches your eye and captures your imagination. You have just had an encounter with public art.

In the last 25 years, public art has become an increasingly familiar sight throughout the United States and Canada. The term *public art* usually refers to large sculptures, murals, or artist-designed spaces in public areas. Some of the most cherished national symbols of the United States, such as the Statue of Liberty in New York City and Mount Rushmore National Memorial in the Black Hills of South Dakota, qualify as public art.

Public art encompasses the abstract and realistic works that grace civic squares and lobbies of office buildings. Public art is also found in parks and plazas, at airports, in train stations and subways, on the outside walls of buildings, and even in old mining sites and gravel pits. Artists today design everything from bus-stop shelters to huge city parks and gardens.

Most people agree that public art enlivens urban and rural spaces and gives us a richer, more stimulating environment. Its insistence on being part of everyday life makes it very different from the art displayed in the more sheltered confines of museums and galleries. Art lovers visit these places to seek out art. But public art, in its own way, seeks out people—whether they are art lovers or not. For this reason, public art—just because it *is* public—stirs up controversy.

Many public artworks created since the 1960's have been particularly controversial because they broke from the traditional image of what art "should" look like. Few statues of heroes on horses are commissioned today. Instead, artists are creating richly diverse works from all manner of materials. There are no well-defined categories to describe all the different types of public art being created in the 1980's, but most fall into one of several broad groups.

One of the most common types of public art is sculpture used to accent the public plazas and lobbies of large—and often impersonal—office buildings. These works, usually abstract metal sculptures, are sometimes called "plop art" because many are simply plopped down at some location, with no meaningful relation to the buildings that surround them or to the people who live or work in the area. Still, many of these works do complement their sites and provide the passer-by with both visual relief and a sense of the human spirit of creativity.

Another type of public art is environmental art or *earthworks*. These are large works usually sculpted out of the landscape and composed of earth, water, or other natural elements. Not surprisingly, most environmental art is found in rural areas.

Earthworks have come to the city, however, thanks to earthwork artists and sculptors who have adapted natural elements to urban spaces. Using rocks, plants, and other natural materials,

The author:
Walter Robinson is contributing editor of *Art in America* magazine in New York City.

as well as sculpture, artists transform barren plazas, empty lots, or *traffic islands* (areas in the center of traffic circles or between traffic lanes) into environments that offer a peaceful place to rest in the midst of urban bustle. As these artists seek a greater role in designing urban spaces, they often collaborate with architects and developers in planning urban projects.

There are also outdoor *murals* (designs or pictures that decorate walls). Murals brighten up the bare walls of office or apartment buildings and may be part of a community renewal project to beautify a decaying neighborhood. In many cases, artists work with local residents to create murals that capture the flavor of the neighborhood. Other artists decorate walls with *friezes* (horizontal bands of sculptured designs) or *reliefs* (figures that stand out from the surface in which they are cut or shaped).

Perhaps the most flamboyant type of public artworks are those that appear to be media events rather than works of art. With *spectacle art*, as it is sometimes called, the preparation and creation of the work are an integral part of the art experience. Spectacle artists may work with hot-air balloons or *lasers* (devices that produce very narrow and intense beams of light). They may wrap buildings with brightly colored fabric. But no matter what materials they use, their art is always transitory—it exists for only a few hours, days, or weeks. Although few people may actually see the work firsthand, it can reach a national audience through the news media, photographs, and films.

If the look of public art has changed over the years, so has the way in which these works are funded. In the past, civic groups or private citizens sponsored most public art in the United States. But during the Great Depression of the 1930's, the federal government—for the first time—became a major art patron. The government sponsored art as a way to provide work for painters, writers, and other artists through an agency called the Works Progress Administration (WPA), which Congress created in 1935. From 1935 to 1943, the WPA and other federal agencies paid some 12,000 artists to paint countless murals on the walls of government buildings.

City collections

Many cities boast growing outdoor sculpture collections. Visitors to Houston can enjoy *the vaquero* by Luis Jimenez, a 1982 fiberglass and *epoxy* (synthetic resin) sculpture that enlivens the city's Moody Park, *above,* and Spanish artist Joan Miró's 1982 steel sculpture *Personage and Birds,* which graces the plaza of the Texas Commerce Towers, *below.*

The proliferation of public art since the 1930's is due in large part to an increase in funding from many sources—not just the federal government. Sponsors of public artworks also include state and local governments, corporations, individuals, and private nonprofit institutions, such as museums and universities.

In a 1987 survey, the National Endowment for the Arts (NEA) —a federal agency established in 1965 to promote the arts in the United States—identified 195 ongoing public-art programs run by state or local governments or nonprofit organizations. Many state and local arts councils make grants that partially fund public-art commissions undertaken by civic organizations and other groups. The NEA's own Art in Public Places program annually makes more than 20 public-art grants, ranging from $5,000 to $50,000. In 1986 alone, the NEA contributed a total of $417,625 to 24 public-art projects. Since it was founded, the NEA has helped underwrite more than 500 such projects in 47 states and Washington, D.C. The NEA's 1987 survey listed about 25 state and local art councils with public-art grant programs similar to that of the NEA. Among the states leading the public-art movement are New York, New Jersey, and Minnesota.

Many government agencies also commission public art directly, often through "per cent for art" programs, which earmark a fraction of public construction budgets—usually about 1 per cent—for on-site artwork. One of the most frequent users of the per cent for art program in the federal government is the Art-in-Architecture project of the General Services Administration (GSA), the agency that designs and constructs new federal buildings throughout the United States. Since the federal government adopted the per cent for art policy in 1963, the GSA has sponsored some 250 artworks at federal courthouses and office buildings. At present, 23 states and at least 74 cities and counties have some type of per cent for art program. These programs often involve community leaders, art professionals, and ordinary citizens in the selection and installation of public artworks.

Governments are not the only supporters of public art, however. An increasing number of private businesses are installing

Funding options

Public art is funded in many ways. For example, Robert Graham's bronze sculpture *Monument to Joe Louis, below,* was given to Detroit in 1986 by *Sports Illustrated* magazine. But *La Grande Vitesse* (*The Grand Rapids*), *below right,* a 1969 steel work by Alexander Calder, was funded by the federal government and by many businesses and citizens of Grand Rapids, Mich.

art in the plazas or lobbies of their buildings or in other publicly accessible spaces. Essentially private commissions, such artworks are selected and paid for by the company to create a better environment for their employees or to promote a positive corporate image. Companies are also encouraged by the government to sponsor public art. For example, in Philadelphia, Los Angeles, and other cities, municipal redevelopment agencies and planning boards require or encourage private developers to include public art in their real estate projects. Federal and state environmental protection regulations have also led a number of mining companies to consider earthworks as an inexpensive form of land reclamation. Private commissions, however, are not usually subject to public review.

Many public artworks come about in ways that combine public and private resources. For instance, a *bas-relief* (a wall sculpture in which figures stand out only slightly from the background) called *Back to School*, which depicts eight residents of New York City's South Bronx, was conceived and financed entirely by the two artists who made it. John Ahearn and Rigoberto Torres, seeking to produce a work of art for the block on which they lived, convinced a private landlord in 1987 to let them use a wall of his building. The two then made the sculpture over a two-year period, donating the materials and their own labor.

In contrast, Alexander Calder's *La Grande Vitesse* (1969), located in the VandenBerg Plaza in Grand Rapids, Mich., was part of an urban-renewal effort. It was selected by a panel appointed jointly by the mayor of Grand Rapids and by the NEA. The $127,900 price tag for this project included $45,000 from the NEA—its first public-art grant—with most of the remaining funds raised locally from business and individual contributions.

Thanks to such collaborative funding efforts, more people than ever before have the opportunity to experience public art. But the growth of the public-art movement has not been trouble-free. Art is by its nature provocative and usually calls forth widely diverging opinions as to its suitability and value. Abstract works may draw criticism for being unresponsive to community taste, while figurative or realistic works may cause controversy when they address themes considered by some people to be improper or inappropriate. In most such controversies, artists must defend their works aesthetically—as a challenge to the public's imagination—and also philosophically, as part of the artist's right to free expression.

One of the most celebrated public-art controversies of recent years involves a work called *Tilted Arc* by sculptor Richard Serra. The GSA in 1982 installed the gently curving wall—made of steel and measuring 120 feet (36.6 meters) long and 12 feet (3.6 meters) tall—in the plaza of the Jacob K. Javits Federal Building in New York City. Many government workers in adjacent office buildings, including some judges and GSA administrators, mounted an effort to remove *Tilted Arc*. They said it was an eyesore that blocked public use of the plaza. To forestall removal of *Tilted Arc*, Serra took the GSA to court, arguing that his sculpture should be protected as free speech under the First Amendment to the U.S. Constitution. Although the court in 1987 rejected Serra's argument, the GSA has still not decided whether to remove the work. Whatever the outcome for *Tilted Arc*, the controversy has forced the GSA to revise its art commission process to include more input about any future work from the community and from the architects of surrounding buildings.

Another abstract work has also had its share of well-publicized turmoil. In 1982, the Fine Arts Commission in Washington, D.C., unveiled Maya Ying Lin's memorial honoring the U.S. military personnel who served in the Vietnam War (1957-1975). The memorial, situated on a 2-acre (0.8-hectare) site, is a V-shaped, black granite wall, 500 feet (152 meters) long and inscribed with the names of the more than 50,000 Americans killed in the Vietnam War. When the design was first unveiled, some critics interpreted it as a "black gash of shame." Others said it failed to express the heroism of those who served in Vietnam. After considerable controversy, the commission in 1984 added a more traditional bronze sculpture by artist Frederick Hart, depicting a group of three soldiers.

But the controversy still wasn't over. In 1988, at the insistence of some veterans' groups, another sculpture—a statue of a female Army nurse—was approved for the site. These compromises have quieted most critics—though opponents of the additions say they detract from the simplicity of Lin's work. Even so, most agree today that the Vietnam Veterans Memorial is one of the most dramatic and emotionally charged public artworks in the United States.

Even public art that is not abstract can cause controversy. In 1978, a storm of protest arose over efforts to commemorate the four student protesters killed by National Guardsmen during an anti-Vietnam War demonstration in 1970 at Kent State University in Ohio. A private foundation had commissioned sculptor George Segal to create a bronze monument to the students. His simple sculpture, titled *Abraham and Isaac*, was a modern interpretation of the well-known Bible story. It showed a standing figure holding a knife over a kneeling one. The artist intended the work to symbolize forgiveness. University officials, however, refused to install the work on campus, apparently viewing it as a reminder of an unfortunate tragedy and concerned that its violent theme might provoke campus unrest. The work was eventually installed at Princeton University in New Jersey.

Public artworks are also sometimes destroyed by their owners without notifying the artist or going through any public review process. In 1980, a sculpture designed by Isamu Noguchi in 1975 for the lobby of a New York City bank was destroyed without the artist's knowledge. Employees and customers of the bank said the work, which was suspended from the ceiling, was "threatening." In 1987, a St. Louis, Mo., park designed by environmental artist Alan Sonfist and installed just a year earlier was bulldozed by order of a city parks official, who said it was an "eyesore." According to the city official, the park was so poorly maintained it looked like a "construction site." In this case too, the artist was not informed in advance, nor was the city's public-art review process followed before the park was destroyed.

Such cases have caused many artists and public-art advocates to lobby for what are called "moral rights" laws for artists. In general, moral rights laws prohibit the destruction or alteration of an artist's work by its owner and allow artists to sue for damages if the alteration detracts from their reputation. Such laws have long existed in Europe, but in the United States, artists usually surrender control of their works when the works are sold, unless otherwise specified in a contract. Since 1980, four states—California, New York, Massachusetts, and Maine—have adopted limited moral rights protection for artists. To date, no major moral rights cases have come to light, and it remains to be seen whether these laws provide practical—or just symbolic—protection for artists' works.

Vandalism or neglect can destroy or mutilate public artworks as well. Such problems have led many public-art agencies to allot a portion of their budgets for ongoing maintenance and repair, and have also led artists to include provisions for upkeep in their contracts.

It stands as a testament to the health of the public-art movement in the United States that it is still flourishing despite these problems. And every time someone stops to gaze at an abstract sculpture in a plaza, or walks through a traffic island transformed with plants and rocks by an environmental artist, or smiles at the unexpected pleasure of seeing a mural of many colors where once there was a dull brick wall, the support for public art grows just a bit stronger.

Art in conflict

Public art has been known to stir up conflict. One controversy involves a large steel wall entitled *Tilted Arc, above.* The wall, created by Richard Serra and funded by the General Services Administration (GSA), was installed in the plaza of the Jacob K. Javits Federal Building in New York City in 1982. Public outcry against the work—which was called an "eyesore"—was so strong that the GSA considered moving it, an action that prompted Serra to take GSA to court. Maya Ying Lin's Vietnam Veterans Memorial in Washington, D.C., *below,* one of the most emotionally charged public artworks in the United States, was severely criticized after its 1982 unveiling.

Sculpture in public places

Public sculpture is the most common type of public art. Some of these works are called "plop art" because they have no meaningful relation to their surroundings. But as the examples on these two pages show, public sculpture can be visually exciting, evoking a sense of drama or whimsy.

The slashing diagonals and seemingly precarious balance of Isamu Noguchi's *The Red Cube* (1967), *right,* a steel and aluminum sculpture 28 feet (8.5 meters) high, add energy to the Marine Midland Building Plaza in New York City.

A woman stops to contemplate the last move of *The Winner* (1983), *left,* J. Seward Johnson, Jr.'s cigar-smoking chess player. The life-sized bronze sculpture —complete with chessboard and immovable chess pieces—is located in the Hughes Justice Complex in Trenton, N.J.

Group of Four Trees (1972), *left,* an epoxy and fiberglass sculpture by French artist Jean Dubuffet in the Chase Manhattan Bank Plaza in New York City, has curving lines that soften the vertical pull of surrounding buildings.

Metal wolves stand beside a wall of rolling hills in Canadian artist John McEwen's 1981 steel sculpture *Western Channel, below,* outside the Performing Arts Center of the University of Lethbridge, in Alberta, Canada.

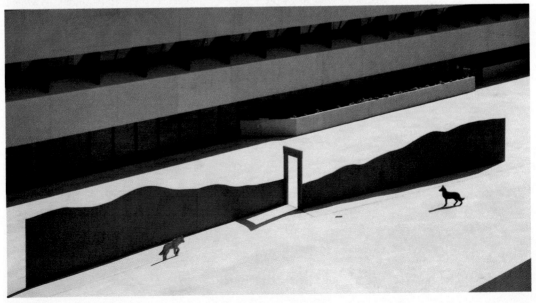

Art from the land

Environmental art—or earthworks—is literally sculpted out of the landscape. The tools of the earthworks artist are rocks, earth, plants, and water. In some cases, earthworks artists are hired to beautify old mining pits and other scarred landscape as part of land-reclamation projects.

Robert Smithson's *Spiral Jetty* (1970), a 1,500-foot (460-meter) coil made of rocks, juts into Great Salt Lake in Utah, *above.* A giant catfish, *right,* is one of five earth forms that make up *Tumuli Effigy,* a 200-acre (80-hectare) earthwork near Ottawa, Ill. The work, designed by Michael Heizer, was a land-reclamation project. It was completed in 1986 on the site of a former coal mine.

Artist Robert Morris transformed an old gravel pit in King County, Washington, into a grassy amphitheater called *Earthwork at Johnson Pit #30.* The 4-acre (1.6-hectare) work, *below,* was completed in 1979.

In Robert Irwin's *Nine Spaces Nine Trees* (1983), *above,*
walls of lavender *scrim* (thin material) divide the plaza of the
Public Safety Building in Seattle into nine "rooms" containing plum trees and seats for passers-by.

Transforming city spaces

Having artists convert empty lots,
barren lots, building interiors,
and other spaces into beautiful—
and many times restful—environments is a recent trend in public
art. Today, many artists work
with building and city developers
to incorporate their ideas into
new urban projects. These artist-
designed spaces often combine
sculpture with plants and other
natural materials.

In 1984, artist Nancy Holt transformed
two traffic islands in Rosslyn, Va., near
Arlington, into *Dark Star Park, right.* With
its five large concrete spheres—or "dark
stars"—steel pipes, and ponds, the park
has become a neighborhood landmark.

82

Colorful, undulating walls and a neon ceiling sculpture convey a sense of flight to travelers walking through the United Airlines terminal in Chicago's O'Hare International Airport, *left.* The sculpture, unveiled in 1987, is the work of artist Michael Hayden.

Visitors stop to contemplate *The Upper Room* (1987), a plaza in New York City's Battery Park City, *below.* Designed by Ned Smyth, the plaza features ornate mosaic columns, benches, tables, and a pyramid-topped *pergola* (arbor).

Children in the South Bronx, a section of New York City, skip rope below artist John Ahearn's plaster frieze *Jumping for Joy* (1986), *far left*. Ahearn created the frieze using neighborhood children as models. Richard Haas's 1985 mural *Arch de Fontainebleau, left,* is so realistic it is called a *trompe-l'oeil* (optical illusion). It appears on a wall of the Fontainebleau Hilton hotel in Miami Beach, Fla.

Outdoor murals: walls with a view

Murals are designs or pictures on walls. Some artists paint murals that reflect the history of local neighborhoods. Other artists decorate walls with *friezes* (horizontal bands of sculptured designs). But whatever the medium, murals can brighten the bare walls of buildings like nothing else.

Los Angeles history is depicted on a mural that runs 1.5 miles (2.4 kilometers) along a concrete flood-control wall in Venice, Calif., *below.* Called *The Great Wall of Los Angeles,* the mural was begun in 1983 under the direction of artist Judith Baca.

In *Public Projection, 1985,* Polish-born artist Krzysztof Wodiczko projected an image of a huge eye onto the Swiss Parliament building in Bern, *right.* For two weeks in 1983, 11 tiny islands in Biscayne Bay off the coast of Miami, Fla., were almost unrecognizable when Bulgarian-born artist Christo surrounded them with skirts of pink plastic 200 feet (60 meters) wide, *far right.* He called the work *Surrounded Islands.*

Making a spectacle of art

Wrapping islands with brightly colored fabric or sending bright balloons up in the air may not sound like art—but it is. These flamboyant works are often called *spectacle art.* Spectacle art is usually short-lived, but, thanks to photographs and films, it can be experienced by a wide audience.

Crowds gathered in Richmond, Va., in June 1981 to experience artist Howard Woody's *Red Wedge Dispersal, below,* an art spectacle in which five large balloons were released at different times.

By Peter H. Raven

Our Vanishing Rain Forests

Tropical rain forests are being cut down at a ferocious pace. Unless this destruction stops, the world will pay a staggering price in climatic change and lost species.

Throughout the tropics, a relentless orgy of destruction is taking place. In western Brazil, fires rage day and night for months on end as vast areas of the world's largest rain forest are burned to make way for cattle ranches and farms. On the islands of Indonesia, in Southeast Asia, the stillness of forests is shattered by the piercing whine of loggers' chain saws, followed by the crash of falling trees. In west Africa, Ivory Coast peasants push their way into rain forests partially cleared by timber cutters, there to fell even more trees in an effort to carve farmland from wilderness.

The world's tropical rain forests are disappearing at an alarming rate. During the approxi-

Many trees in tropical rain forests are supported by growths called *buttresses* that extend from the lower part of the trunk. Where the ground is shaded by a dense canopy of leaves, the forest floor is largely free of vegetation, foreground. In brighter areas, background, plants grow in profusion.

The author:
Peter H. Raven is director of the Missouri Botanical Garden in St. Louis and a professor of botany at Washington University, also in St. Louis.

mately 20 minutes you will spend reading this article, between 1 and 2 square miles (2.6 and 5.2 square kilometers) of rain forest will be destroyed. Conservationists estimated in the late 1970's that some 25,000 square miles (65,000 square kilometers) of tropical forest—an area about the size of West Virginia—were being destroyed annually. Another 25,000 square miles, those experts said, were being severely damaged. In 1987 and 1988, however, scientists obtained evidence that the rate of destruction is now even higher than that.

The causes of this ceaseless onslaught are clear: population pressures and economic necessity in the developing nations of the tropics. The consequences awaiting us if we fail to put a stop to it are also becoming evident: probable changes in the earth's climate and the loss of countless varieties of plants and animals, many of which could be of great value to humanity. Tropical rain forests are not just exotic and beautiful; they are an integral part of our planet, and their disappearance would be a tragedy that would affect everyone. We must act soon to save the forests that remain to us.

Where rain forests flourish

Tropical rain forests grow almost exclusively within the borders of the hot, wet tropics, a geographical band 3,200 miles (5,100 kilometers) wide that circles the globe, with the equator as its centerline. These lush forests cover large areas of Central and South America, Southeast Asia, and central Africa. More than 80 per cent of the world's tropical rain forest area lies in just nine countries—Bolivia, Brazil, Colombia, Peru, and Venezuela in South America; Indonesia and Malaysia in Southeast

Tropical rain forests contain at least half of the world's species of plants and animals. Plants called *epiphytes, top,* grow on tree branches and obtain water and nutrients from the humid forest air. Most of the animal species in rain forests are insects, such as the striped moth, *above,* perching on a leaf in a Costa Rican rain forest. The vast majority of plant and insect species in tropical rain forests are still undiscovered.

Asia; and Gabon and Zaire in Africa. Smaller stands of rain forest are found elsewhere in the tropics, including parts of Australia and India.

As their name suggests, tropical rain forests get an abundance of rain. Thundershowers may pelt a rain forest on 200 or more days of the year, and annual precipitation usually totals 80 to 160 inches (100 to 200 centimeters).

The trees of tropical rain forests, broad-leaved and green throughout the year, typically grow to heights of 100 to 200 feet (30 to 60 meters), and some tower as high as 325 feet (100 meters). These huge trees have shallow roots that grow close to the surface of the soil, where they extract nutrients from leaves and other matter that falls to the forest floor. Many of the trees have large growths called *buttresses* that extend from the base of the trunk and may help keep the tree upright. The tops of the trees crowd together to form a leafy covering, or *canopy,* so dense that even on the brightest afternoon the ground below is as dark as the bottom of a well.

The rich life of the rain forest

Although a rain forest may appear impenetrable from the air or along its margins, the forest interior is usually open and largely free of low-growing vegetation. Most kinds of plants, which need a great deal of light for growth, cannot flourish in the shadow world of the forest floor. Only in the occasional patch of sunshine where a tree has died and fallen, creating a gap in the canopy, does the spacious forest become a tangled jungle.

And yet, tropical rain forests are the richest natural environments on earth. Occupying just 7 per cent of the world's land area, they contain at least 50 per cent—and perhaps a much higher proportion—of all species of plants and animals.

Several hundred species of trees may be found in a single 2½-acre (1-hectare) section of tropical forest. That amounts to more species of trees than occur in the United States and Canada together, and many more than in Europe. Most of the life in a rain forest, however, is confined to the sun-bathed canopy. There, plants grow in amazing abundance. Climbing woody vines, or *lianas,* are rooted in the soil but coil upward around the tree trunks toward the sunlight. Other kinds of plants, called *epiphytes,* grow on

A dwindling band of green

Tropical rain forests grow throughout the warm, wet tropics – a region 3,200 miles (5,100 kilometers) wide circling the globe between the Tropic of Cancer and Tropic of Capricorn. Forest clearing has reduced the world's original rain forest areas by some 50 per cent, with most of the destruction occurring since about 1940. In the 1980's, the remaining rain forests have been cleared or seriously damaged at an estimated rate of at least 50,000 square miles (130,000 square kilometers) a year, an area approximately the size of New York state. The devastation has been caused primarily by loggers, subsistence farmers, and cattle ranchers.

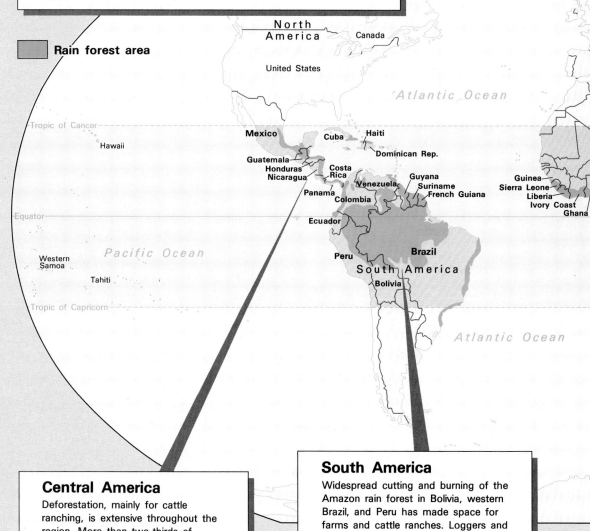

Rain forest area

Central America

Deforestation, mainly for cattle ranching, is extensive throughout the region. More than two-thirds of original rain forest areas are gone.

South America

Widespread cutting and burning of the Amazon rain forest in Bolivia, western Brazil, and Peru has made space for farms and cattle ranches. Loggers and sugar cane growers have cleared much of Brazil's coastal forests. Ecuadorean forests are almost totally destroyed.

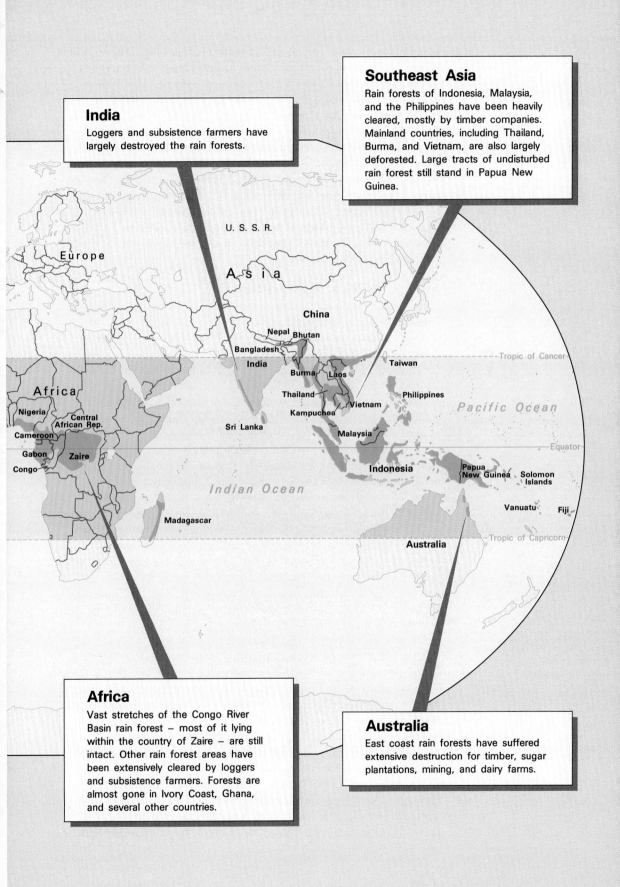

India

Loggers and subsistence farmers have largely destroyed the rain forests.

Southeast Asia

Rain forests of Indonesia, Malaysia, and the Philippines have been heavily cleared, mostly by timber companies. Mainland countries, including Thailand, Burma, and Vietnam, are also largely deforested. Large tracts of undisturbed rain forest still stand in Papua New Guinea.

Africa

Vast stretches of the Congo River Basin rain forest – most of it lying within the country of Zaire – are still intact. Other rain forest areas have been extensively cleared by loggers and subsistence farmers. Forests are almost gone in Ivory Coast, Ghana, and several other countries.

Australia

East coast rain forests have suffered extensive destruction for timber, sugar plantations, mining, and dairy farms.

U. S. S. R.

Europe

Asia

China

Nepal Bhutan

Bangladesh

India

Burma Laos

Taiwan

Thailand

Vietnam

Philippines

Kampuchea

Pacific Ocean

Africa

Sri Lanka

Nigeria

Central African Rep.

Malaysia

Cameroon

Gabon

Zaire

Congo

Indonesia

Papua New Guinea

Solomon Islands

Equator

Indian Ocean

Madagascar

Vanuatu

Fiji

Tropic of Cancer

Tropic of Capricorn

Australia

tree surfaces, obtaining moisture and nutrients from the humid air of the canopy. How many plant species exist in the tropics is unknown, but botanists estimate their number at 165,000.

Animals, too, abound in the treetops: monkeys, birds, snakes, bats, squirrels, lizards—and above all, insects. In a single square mile of tropical rain forest in Peru, scientists recently identified more than 1,600 species of butterflies, more than twice the number recorded for the entire United States and Canada. In an even smaller section of the Peruvian forest—a mere 2½ acres—investigators counted an astounding 12,000 species of beetles. While the number of all insect and other animal species in the tropics can only be approximated, biologists feel certain that the total is at least 3 million, and some have calculated that it may be as high as 10 million.

The furious pace of destruction

Scientists estimate that in the last few centuries tropical forested areas have been reduced by more than 50 per cent. Most of that loss has occurred since about 1940. Today, rain forests cover some 2.2 million square miles (5.7 million square kilometers) of the tropics, an area about three-fourths the size of the United States, excluding Alaska.

At the destruction rate previously estimated by environmentalists—50,000 square miles (130,000 square kilometers) a year—all the remaining tracts of rain forest would be cleared or ruined within another 45 years. But because the pace at which the forests are being laid waste has accelerated, that timetable no longer holds. It is now quite possible that only a few large areas of rain forest where relatively few people live—notably sections of the Amazon region in South America and the interior of the Congo River Basin in Africa—will survive the first few decades of the next century. Most other rain forests will be reduced to small patches and reserves within the next 20 to 30 years. As the forests disappear, the problems of the tropical nations will mount. Malnutrition will spread. Political instability will grow. And the potential of tropical land to feed and support people will be drastically diminished.

Clearly, by ravaging their forests, tropical nations are acting against their own long-term interests—not to mention those of humanity and Planet Earth. Unfortunately, these struggling Third World countries do not have the luxury of worrying about the long term. Desperately trying to cope with mushrooming populations, widespread poverty, and a general lack of resources, the developing nations of the tropics understandably have tended to adopt economic policies aimed at making life better now and to let the future take care of itself.

The governments of all but a few developing nations have, however, recognized population growth as the chief cause of their woes and are trying to bring the problem under control. It is a daunting challenge. The global human population, which will reach 5.2 billion in 1989, is climbing by nearly 90 million each year, and more than 90 per cent of that increase is occurring in developing countries. What makes the situation particularly ominous is the fact that 40 to 45 per cent of the people in those countries, twice the proportion of Western industrialized countries, are under 15 years old. Even if these young people have small families when they reach adulthood, there are so many of them that the populations of their countries will continue to grow for at least another two or three generations. The best we can hope for is that world population will stabilize at a level of approximately 10.5 billion people about the year 2050.

Closely intertwined with the headache of zooming population growth is the problem of poverty. The developing countries have almost 75 per cent of the world's people but only about 15 per cent of the world's goods. As the population of the Third World rises, that 15 per cent must be spread ever thinner. In 1988, the World Bank—an agency of the United Nations (UN)—estimated that more than 1 billion people, nearly 30 per cent of the total population of developing countries, are living in absolute poverty. For those people, obtaining the necessities of life for themselves and their families from day to day is an almost hopeless task. About half of these unfortunates are chronically malnourished. UN officials estimate that the yearly global death toll of 55 million includes some 14 million babies and children in developing nations who die of starvation and related diseases.

People immersed in poverty, as well as cash-strapped Third World governments seeking to elevate their national standard of living and pay foreign debts, have little choice but to exploit whatever resources are available. And in most tropical countries, two of the most obvious resources are the rain forests and the lands they occupy.

Loggers, farmers, ranchers wreak havoc

Tropical rain forests have long been under assault by loggers seeking valuable mahogany, rosewood, and other hardwoods. But the demand for wood has grown so great that loggers no longer take only selected trees but instead remove all the trees in an area, a practice known as *clear-cutting*. The export of timber brings much-needed foreign exchange to tropical nations, and so the plunder goes on. In west Africa, logging is expected to deplete most of the remaining rain forests by the end of the century. Logging is also having a major impact on the forests of Southeast Asia. In the Philippines, only about one-third of the forests that existed 30 years ago still stand. Indonesia's rain forests, the largest in that part of the world, are being cut down at a breakneck pace that could leave the islands of Sumatra and Celebes largely denuded within a few years.

Loggers are not the only ones taking wood from the forests. Some 1.5 billion people in developing countries depend on firewood as their principal source of energy, and in many regions of

The economics of destruction

Tropical Third World nations exploit their forests to obtain scarce foreign currency and to meet the needs of hungry people. A number of Central and South American governments have offered tax incentives for the establishment of cattle ranches, *above*. Logging, *right*, has long been a major factor in tropical forest destruction. In west Africa and Southeast Asia, many once-mighty rain forests are now all but gone.

the tropics the poor are chopping down trees faster than they can be regrown. Although this is still a relatively minor problem, it is likely to become more serious as population pressures mount.

Some of the most extensive devastation is being caused by subsistence farmers and—especially in Latin America—cattle ranchers. The fires in western Brazil have been ignited by ranch developers and hundreds of thousands of land-hungry settlers trying to carve pasturelands and homesteads from the Amazon forest. The newcomers fell trees with ax and saw and leave them to dry in the sun. Then, from June through October, a season of diminished rainfall, they burn them.

Despite alarms raised by some environmentalists in the 1980's, most of the world was only vaguely aware that the western Amazon region was being ravished on a mammoth scale. But in 1987 and 1988, satellite pictures revealed graphically the extent of the damage being done to the Brazilian forestlands. Analysts at a National Aeronautics and Space Administration (NASA) facility in Greenbelt, Md., reported in summer 1988 that the Amazon fires were far worse than anyone had realized.

The NASA researchers said their studies agreed with a finding announced the year before by scientists in Brazil: that some 77,000 square miles (200,000 square kilometers) of Brazilian rain forest were destroyed in 1987. Of that area, according to the Brazilian investigators, about 47,000 square miles (122,000 square kilometers) were previously cleared forest that had partially regrown; the other 30,000 square miles (78,000 square kilometers) were virgin forest. The satellite images also revealed widespread fires in the forests of Bolivia and Peru. The pictures showed beyond a doubt that the amount of forest being lost in

The pressure of population
The mushrooming populations and widespread poverty of many tropical countries have put tremendous pressure on the forests. This family of homesteaders in western Brazil is typical of poor people throughout the tropics who have invaded rain forests by the hundreds of thousands to farm the often-barren soil.

The burning of the Amazon forest

A tower of thick smoke darkens the sky as an expanse of rain forest in Brazil is devoured by flames. The massive cutting and burning of the Amazon forest in the 1980's, mostly for farms and cattle ranches, has denuded vast tracts of land. Smoke from fires is adding hundreds of millions of tons of carbon dioxide (CO_2) to the atmosphere and thus is contributing to global warming by intensifying the *greenhouse effect*—the retention of solar energy in the earth's atmosphere. In addition, the loss of countless trees, which absorb CO_2 from the air, makes matters even worse.

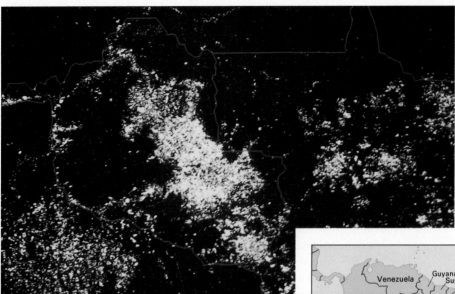

the tropics each year had increased dramatically.

Whereas in Africa and Southeast Asia, deforestation—through the sale of timber —provides some genuine economic benefits, the lands from which the trees have been cleared are virtually worthless. The soil of many rain-forest areas does not lend itself to farming or even to the raising of cattle. A large proportion of the nutrients in a tropical rain forest is held in the tissues of trees and other plants, rather than in the soil. Felling and burning the trees to create farmland—a practice known as *slash-and-burn* agriculture—releases large amounts of nutrients to the soil, which is then able to support a crop. But after a few years of cultivation, the soil returns to its original low fertility, and the farmer must move on to another part of the forest and start anew.

Ranchers, too, will likely be disappointed. In most cases, the thin rain-forest soil quickly gives up most of its fertility to pasture grasses. The nutritional quality of the grasses then declines steadily, and cattle raising ceases to be economical (and in fact, it is usually only government tax subsidies that make it profitable in the first place). The ranch operators depart, leaving behind them a wasteland.

A composite picture, *above left,* made from satellite images beamed to earth from Aug. 1 to Sept. 18, 1987, shows the extent of fires in the western Amazon region during that brief period. Farmers and cattle ranchers set some 170,000 fires in that area in all of 1987, and on the worst day—September 9—the satellite detected 7,603 fires.

Changes in the earth's climate

The world will pay a price for the leveling of the rain forests; how heavy that price will be depends on how long the destruction continues. Already in many deforested areas, soil that had been held in place by tree roots is being eroded by wind and rain—what rain still falls. More often than not, the downpours that once came with almost clockwork regularity now occur infrequently. Well over half of the rainfall that drenches a tropical forest is generated by the forest itself. Water in the forest returns to the air through plant *transpiration* (evaporation from leaves), forms clouds, and descends again as rain. When the forest is cleared, this recycling ends.

Forests also moderate the temperature of the atmosphere in at least two ways. For one thing, they soak up great amounts of sunlight, thereby cooling the overlying air. Cut down the trees, and the air grows warmer. More significantly, forests absorb carbon dioxide (CO_2) from the air. Many scientists think a build-up of carbon dioxide in the atmosphere, primarily from the burning of coal, oil, and natural gas in the industrialized countries, is increasing the *greenhouse effect*—a global warming caused when solar energy striking the earth is prevented from being radiated back into space. If current trends continue, the intensified greenhouse effect could, by the end of the next century, turn many agricultural lands into semideserts and melt the polar icecaps, flooding coastal areas on every continent.

Although the industrialized countries continue to be the main source of excess carbon dioxide, rain-forest cutting over the last few decades has, according to some estimates, been responsible for at least one-fifth of the total CO_2 increase. As the remaining forests dwindle with each passing year, the probability of a future climatic disaster becomes ever higher.

The devastation going on in Brazil is increasing that probability even further. Not only are huge stretches of rain forest no longer there to remove carbon dioxide from the air, but also the burning of the trees is adding hundreds of millions of tons of the greenhouse gas to the atmosphere. Brazilian and American scientists calculated in 1988 that the Amazon fires account for fully one-tenth of the current global production of CO_2 resulting from human activity.

Extinction of species

Deforestation's contribution to the greenhouse effect, however significant, is overshadowed by a potential calamity of even greater magnitude: the extinction of innumerable species of plants and animals. The climatic consequences of forest clearing could perhaps be reversed, though only slowly, by planting new trees to replace those that were cut down. But once a species is gone, it is gone forever.

Although biologists have identified many of the plant and ani-

The price to be paid

A heightened greenhouse effect is just one of the consequences we face if rain-forest destruction is not stopped. Another is severe erosion, which is already occurring in some countries. In Madagascar, for example, rivers run red with soil washed from the tree-stripped land, *top*. The most serious effect, however, will be the loss of untold numbers of plant and animal species. Some endangered species, such as Brazil's golden lion tamarin, *above*, might survive in zoos, but countless others will be driven to extinction before they are even discovered.

mal species of the tropical forests, including most of the trees and larger animals, the great majority of life forms still await discovery. A group of insects collected from the treetops of the Amazon rain forest, for example, will consist almost entirely of species never before seen by any scientist. If forest clearing is not brought under control, untold numbers of species will perish without our ever knowing of their existence. In countries where the forest cover has already been reduced to less than one-tenth its original extent—Madagascar and Sri Lanka, for instance —large-scale extinction has already begun.

How many species would ultimately be wiped out by the near-total deforestation of the tropics is anyone's guess, but the number would be staggering. By even the most conservative estimate, we stand to lose a million species—one-fourth of the world total—during the next 20 to 30 years. That works out to an extinction rate of at least 100 species a day—more than 1,000 times faster than normal. And remember, that is a *conservative* estimate. The actual extinction rate in coming years could be several hundred species a day.

The loss of a million or more species is an extremely serious matter for both science and humanity. Each of those plants and animals is unique, with its own characteristics and collection of genes. There is no telling what benefits could result from the study of just a fraction of

Racing against time, scientists are trying to learn all they can about the plants and animals of the rain forests. In Costa Rica, researchers, *above,* are hoisted into a forest canopy to search for new species, and a botanist, *above right,* examines the roots of a tropical plant. Through such studies, scientists seek not only to catalog as many species as possible but also to understand the relationships between them. Over the years, research in tropical forests has identified many species that are valuable to humanity.

the organisms within the tropical forests. Scientists might gain new insights into plant growth, the recycling of nutrients within ecosystems, and plant-insect interactions. The genes of many animals and plants could prove useful in the rapidly advancing field of genetic engineering. Still other plants might yield food for the hungry or medicines for the treatment of cancer and heart disease.

This is not just idle speculation. Scientists have already acquired a wealth of knowledge from research in the rain forests. The products of the forests, moreover—woods, resins, edible oils, waxes, fruits and vegetables, and a variety of drugs, to name just a few—are among the world's most important natural commodities.

With respect to drugs, tropical forests are a virtual treasure house of incalculable value to medical science. Some 40 per cent of the prescriptions written each year in the United States contain at least one substance originally derived from a living organism—in most cases, a tropical plant. Malaria, for example, has long been treated with quinine, a compound extracted from a tree native to the Peruvian rain forest, and doctors often prescribe reserpine, obtained from a Southeast Asian shrub, for high blood pressure.

Another important drug from the rain forest is curare, a muscle relaxant derived from several South American plants that is employed in abdominal and heart surgery. Curare was first used as an arrow poison by Indians of the Amazon. As a side note, it should be mentioned that these people, helpless against the inroads of civilization, are dying out from disease and homelessness. Some 200,000 of them remain, about one-fifth the number estimated in the Amazon in 1900. The way things are going, the Indians of the South American forests could—like other inhabitants of the rain forest—be consigned to oblivion.

Hope for the rain forests

Fortunately, the news from the tropics is not all grim. We may take some hope from the fact that an increasing number of tropical countries are finally moving to protect at least a portion of their forests. In Bolivia, for example, the government in 1987 set aside about 4,700 square miles (12,200 square kilometers) of forestland and adjoining savanna as a reserve. In Brazil, patches of virgin forest ranging in size from 2.5 to 2,500 acres (1 to 1,000 hectares) have been left standing in some areas that were cleared for cattle ranches. These forest islands—being studied to determine how large a reserve must be to safeguard its species—were a government response to Brazil's growing environmental movement. That concession, though puny compared with the magnitude of the problem, showed that tropical governments are not insensitive to conservationist concerns. As if to underscore that fact, Brazil's President José Sarney went on Brazilian national television in October 1988 to promise an end to the mass burning of the Amazon forests and to the tax subsidies that led to much of it.

International efforts to protect the tropical forests have also been gathering force. In 1986, some 40 major producers and consumers of rain forest timber, including the United States, formed the International Tropical Timber Organization (ITTO) under a charter of the United Nations. ITTO's main responsibility is to further the *sustained management* of tropical forests. In sustained management, a forest is viewed as a permanent resource that provides a variety of profitable products in addition to timber, rather than as a onetime resource that is simply "mined" and abandoned. A key part of this approach is the reforestation of areas that have been logged. In its first major undertaking, ITTO is sponsoring a project in the Brazilian state of Acre aimed at determining whether sustained management will work in the Amazon rain forest.

Balanced forest use is also being promoted under the Tropical Forest Action Plan, developed by the World Resources Institute —a Washington, D.C.-based conservation organization— together with the World Bank and other agencies of the United Nations. The institute is just one of many prominent environmental groups that are striving to save the rain forests.

Quinine, a drug used to treat malaria, is derived from the cinchona tree, *above,* native to Peru. Dozens of medicines in use today were originally obtained from tropical plants, and botanists are certain that many still-unknown rain-forest plants could be of great benefit in treating cancer, heart disease, and other maladies. Likewise, among the countless kinds of insects and other animals in the forests, there may be hundreds or thousands with potentially valuable genetic traits.

Turning forestlands to new uses offers a way for tropical nations to derive long-term benefits from their rainforest areas. Although many projects of this type—such as the planting of pine trees amid the charred remains of a Brazilian rain forest, *right,* to supply wood for a paper-pulp mill—are controversial, they can ease economic pressures and so help save remaining forests.

In fostering a sane approach to the exploitation of forest resources, conservation groups and government agencies must take into account the population pressures existing in many tropical countries. Where overpopulation is a factor, sustained management can succeed only if the landless poor are still given a share of the forest. Many scientists think the best solution to this predicament is to replace slash-and-burn agriculture with *agroforestry,* a form of sustained management in which trees and crops are grown together. The rain-forest soil can be enriched with fertilizers, enabling settlers to grow crops from year to year without having to burn any trees.

Sustained management offers our best hope for the rain forests, but we have only begun to turn the corner in that direction. According to at least one estimate, the acreage devoted to sustained use constitutes no more than 0.1 per cent of the world's total rain-forest area. In most countries, only 1 tree is planted for every 10 that are cut; in Africa, the ratio is more like 1 to 30.

Despite the dawning realization among tropical nations that their economic survival depends on using their forests wisely, the desire—and necessity—for short-term revenue often compels them to continue their destructive ways. Much of the money raised by tropical countries each year goes for payments on foreign debt. Taking note of that fact, many conservationists and world leaders have called for programs to ease the financial obligations of tropical Third World nations that protect their forests.

At least one such plan—sponsored by a private U.S. environmental organization, Conservation International—has already been put into effect. It was Conservation International that persuaded Bolivia to establish its forest-and-savanna reserve in 1987. The organization worked out an arrangement whereby the Bolivian government was forgiven $650,000 in debts to foreign banks in return for creating the reserve. But most debt-ridden tropical nations will need a bigger financial incentive than that. For conservation-credit programs to have a major impact, they will need solid government support from the United States and other industrialized nations, which control a major proportion of the world's wealth.

As the tropical forests continue to fall, and to burn, we must redouble our efforts to save the tracts that remain. It is tempting to condemn the tropical nations for their pillage of the rain forests, but that would be pointless. Rather, we must give those nations every assistance we can to help them manage their forests wisely. If we succeed in that task, all the world will benefit. If we fail, all the world will suffer. The challenge is before us to preserve one of our planet's greatest natural resources, and we must meet that challenge out of respect for future generations.

Tranquil and beautiful, yet vibrant with life, tropical rain forests are a resource of incredible richness and one that we cannot afford to squander. With wise management, a portion of the earth's remaining rain forests can be preserved for future generations while also providing continuing economic benefits for the countries that own them.

For further reading:
Caufield, Catherine. *In the Rainforest: Report from a Strange, Beautiful, Imperial World.* University of Chicago Press, 1986.
Forsyth, Adrian, and Miyata, Kenneth. *Tropical Nature: Life and Death in the Rain Forests of Central and South America.* Scribner, 1984.
Mitchell, Andrew W. *The Enchanted Canopy.* Macmillan, 1986.

The divisions between the two Koreas
and the two Germanys widened during
the late 1940's and early 1950's. North
Korea invaded South Korea in 1950,
forcing refugees to flee the advancing
troops, *above*. The Berlin airlift of 1948
and 1949, *opposite page*, defeated an
attempt by the Soviet Union to force
the Western Allies out of Berlin.

Divided Countries

On the occasion of the 50th anniversary of the beginning of World War II (1939-1945), *The World Book Year Book* presents a special two-part section. A set of companion articles looks at the two divided countries that resulted from that conflict, East and West Germany and North and South Korea, and how they have developed on their separate paths.

By Peter H. Merkl

The Two Germanys

Under different political systems, the
two states have grown into economic
powerhouses that maintain a lively
trade in goods—if not in ideas.

Preceding pages: The Berlin Wall, built by East Germany in 1961 to prevent its citizens from fleeing to the West, stands as a symbol of the profound political differences that keep the two Germanys separated.

One Sunday evening in June 1988, some 50,000 young West Germans attended a rock concert presented by American singer Michael Jackson in West Berlin. A few blocks away, about 5,000 East Germans huddled in a square to catch the music drifting over the Berlin Wall, the fortified structure that separates West Berlin from East Berlin and East Germany. Not all 5,000 East Germans were rock fans, however. As many as 2,000 of them were members of East German security forces. When West German reporters and television crews tried to photograph and interview the East German crowd, these forces smashed broadcasting equipment and chased away the camera crews.

The rock-concert episode was another incident in the history of the confusing relationship between the two Germanys. This history has been marked by recurring confrontations interspersed with gestures of cooperation. In fact, a few days after the violence of the rock concert, representatives of the two Germanys and more than 100 other countries met in East Berlin to discuss the creation of nuclear-weapons-free zones in Europe.

Why is the relationship between the two Germanys so confusing? If East Germany will not allow its young people to attend a musical performance only a few blocks away in the West, can there be much hope that the two Germanys will ever agree on anything as serious as arms limitation? From time to time, politicians in West Germany suggest that the countries might be combined in the foreseeable future. Is this empty rhetoric, or is there really a chance for German reunification?

The division of a nation

Inter-German relations are confusing today because less than 50 years ago, a beaten Germany was divided into two states with opposing political and economic systems. The roots of this division of Germany extend back to the earliest days of the 1800's, when some 200 large and small German states were loosely organized in a union known as the Holy Roman Empire. By that time, other European peoples such as the English, French, and Spaniards had established *nation-states,* and German nationalists wanted to follow suit. (A *nation* is a group of people who share a culture, history, or language and have a feeling of national unity; a *state* is an area of land whose people have an independent government; and a *nation-state* is a nation and a state with the same boundaries.)

German nationalism succeeded in the 1800's, partly by the voluntary unification of German states and partly by the use of force against non-German states such as France that contested the boundaries—and the authority—of the emerging German nation. In 1871, a German Empire was formed.

Success gave way to disaster in the early 1900's, however. The empire's growing ambitions led to World War I (1914-1918), which Germany and its allies lost. The empire was replaced by a republic, in which there arose an ultranationalistic movement

The author:
Peter H. Merkl is a professor of political science at the University of California at Santa Barbara.

The Cold War between the Soviet bloc and the West brought grim times to Germany in 1948, when a Soviet blockade led to the Berlin airlift, *above left.* East-West tensions relaxed in the 1960's, giving rise in 1970 to the meeting, *above,* of West Germany's Chancellor Willy Brandt, left, and East German Prime Minister Willi Stoph in Erfurt, East Germany.

dedicated to renewing Germany's struggle for power—and this time to fighting for an empire based on racial domination. When a severe economic depression hit Germany in the early 1930's, this National Socialist (Nazi) movement promised to improve living and working conditions for Germans. Led by Adolf Hitler, the Nazis came to power in 1933 and started World War II in 1939. After a long series of German victories, the tide of war turned.

When the European phase of World War II ended on May 8, 1945, victorious troops of the Soviet Union occupied a large area in the eastern part of defeated Germany. Most of the remaining territory was in the hands of the Soviets' Western Allies—chiefly the United States, Great Britain, and France.

After the war, the four Allied powers stationed troops in what were intended to be temporary occupation zones that had been agreed upon in 1944 and 1945. Each of the four also occupied a sector of Berlin, the German capital, which lay deep within the Soviet occupation zone. The occupation of Germany began officially on June 5, 1945.

The Soviets had already begun to redraw the map of Germany, chopping off about 25 per cent of the German lands. The Soviets gave most of this territory to Poland and attached the remainder to the Soviet Union.

In July and August 1945, the leaders of the United States, the Soviet Union, and Great Britain met at Potsdam, Germany, to determine the future of Germany. The leaders agreed that final boundaries would be set at a peace conference, and that a four-power Allied Control Council—with France as the fourth power—would govern Germany as a single state.

The Iron Curtain descends

The planned peace conference never took place, however, because the wartime alliance between the Soviet Union and the Western powers broke up. A major reason for the breakup was the spread of Communism in Eastern Europe. Aided by the

111

East and West Germany at a glance

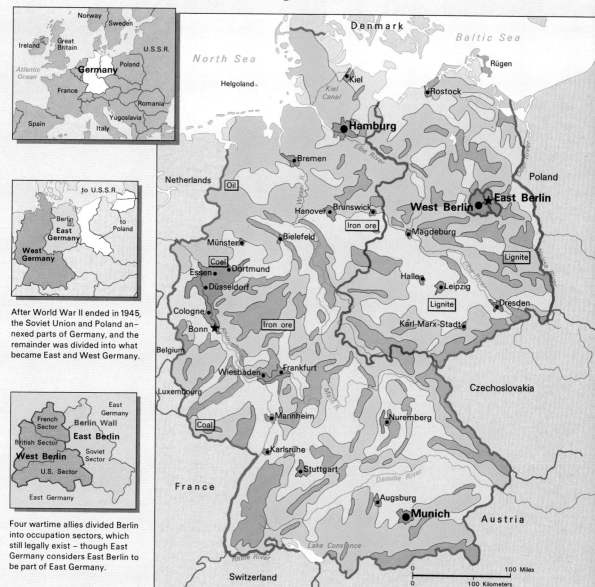

After World War II ended in 1945, the Soviet Union and Poland annexed parts of Germany, and the remainder was divided into what became East and West Germany.

Four wartime allies divided Berlin into occupation sectors, which still legally exist – though East Germany considers East Berlin to be part of East Germany.

Urban-industrial area

Cropland

Mostly grazing land

Forestland

Boundary

★ National capital

● Major city

• Other large city

Coal Major mining resource

West Germany

Area .... 96,005 sq. mi. (248,651 km²)

Population 60,839,000

Work force .. 25,257,000

Data includes West Berlin

East Germany

Area .... 41,768 sq. mi. (108,178 km²)

Population 16,606,000

Work force .. 7,929,000

Data includes East Berlin

Work, money, and purchasing power in the two Germanys

Amounts of work needed to make key purchases

Item	Hours:minutes needed to buy item*	
	West Germany	East Germany
Manufactured goods		
Man's shoes, leather	5:26	24:01
Woman's dress, blended fabrics	4:44	31:10
Color TV, approx. 60 centimeter (24-inch)	81:34	1,008:56
Passenger automobile, 1,500-cubic-centimeter engine	694:33	4,375:00
Washing machine	59:09	491:04
Refrigerator with freezer compartment	29:54	272:19
Sheets, cotton, set	2:43	21:20
Gasoline, 1 liter (0.26 gallon)	0:06	0:18
Foods		
Rye bread, 1 kilogram (2.2 pounds)	0:12	0:07
Sugar, 1 kilogram	0:07	0:17
Butter, 1 kilogram	0:36	1:39
Eggs, 10	0:10	0:36
Milk, 1 liter	0:05	0:07
Coffee, 250 grams	0:21	4:28
Services		
Electricity, 75 kilowatt-hours	2:00	1:20
Railroad ticket, weekly	1:46	0:27
City bus ticket	0:08	0:02
Rent, two-room apartment, 1 month	26:32	13:24

*Based on prices and average hourly wages in mid-1985.
Source: German Institute for Economic Research.

West Germans work fewer hours for the money needed to buy TV sets and other consumer goods, but in East Germany, state subsidies make rent and other necessities less expensive.

Gross national product per capita*

Thousands of dollars

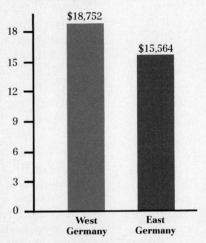

*Amounts are for 1986. Figure for West Germany was supplied by the West German government. East German figure is based on an estimate by the German Institute for Economic Research.

Both Germanys have vigorous economies, but total output per person is higher in West Germany.

Net monthly income per worker's household*

Thousands of dollars

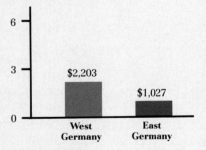

*Figures are for 1987.
Source: Federal Republic of Germany (West Germany).

Workers' households in West Germany are more prosperous, on the average, than their East German counterparts. Figures include welfare benefits and other income apart from wages.

Soviets, Communist parties had quickly taken control of several European nations. Communists ruled Albania, Bulgaria, Poland, Romania, and Yugoslavia by March 5, 1946, when Britain's wartime prime minister, Winston Churchill, cautioned the West against the further spread of Communism. Churchill warned in a speech in Fulton, Mo.: "Beware . . . time may be short. . . . From Stettin in the Baltic to Trieste in the Adriatic, an Iron Curtain has descended across the continent."

The economic situation was grim on both sides of the Iron Curtain—East and West—but not simply because of wartime destruction. One condition that gave rise to the prewar depression still existed—the division of the European economy into individual economies of various states. This division had prevented goods from flowing freely between states and so had retarded the European economy as a whole. On June 5, 1947, United States Secretary of State George C. Marshall proposed the European Recovery Program, a plan to use a massive infusion of U.S. dollars to help start a new, integrated European economy. The United States invited all four occupied zones of Germany to participate in the program, which became known as the Marshall Plan. The Soviets refused U.S. aid for their zone, however, fearing that American influence would follow.

The two Germanys emerge

By this time, it had become apparent that the victorious powers could not agree on an occupation policy. The U.S. military government said in the summer of 1947 that the Allied Control Council had stopped working in matters of major importance.

One such matter was a need to replace the almost worthless German money then in circulation. The Western Allies began working on a plan to introduce a new currency in their zones. This plan triggered Soviet walkouts from meetings of the Allied Control Council, and in March 1948 the Soviets stopped attending the meetings. The next month, the Soviets instituted a partial blockade of West Berlin.

In June, the Western Allies issued a new currency in their zones. That same month, the Soviets completed the blockade, closing off all rail, water, and highway routes through the Soviet zone to West Berlin.

Opposite page: A gleaming mall in Stuttgart symbolizes West Germany's development into a modern, market-oriented state, with a wealth of goods and services available to ordinary consumers.

The Western powers rose to this challenge by supplying food, coal, and other necessities to the West Berliners by air. The airlift was a tremendous operation. At its peak, one aircraft landed in Berlin every 1 to 2 minutes. From July 1948 to May 1949, when the Soviets lifted the blockade, some 213,000 flights carried more than 1.7 million short tons (1.5 million metric tons) of supplies to Berlin.

Meanwhile, the Western zones had united under a German economic council, and by the end of the blockade, German politicians had written a constitution for a republic consisting of these zones. In September 1949, this Federal Republic of Ger-

Mass transit in East Berlin is typical of the consumer services and goods that are heavily subsidized in East Germany's controlled economy. Subsidies make the prices of such necessities much lower than in West Germany.

many (West Germany) was founded, with Bonn, a city on the Rhine River, as its capital. In October 1949, the Soviet zone became the German Democratic Republic (East Germany).

East Germany considered East Berlin to be its capital. Berlin as a whole was still legally separate, however, from both East Germany and West Germany—and it remains so to this day. Thus, East Berlin legally could not be the capital of East Germany. And, although West Berlin was—and still is—closely associated with West Germany, it could not be fully incorporated into West Germany.

West Germany was the larger and more heavily populated of the two states. West Germany and West Berlin had a total area of about 95,000 square miles (246,000 square kilometers) and, in 1950, a population of approximately 52 million. The area of East Germany and East Berlin was about 42,500 square miles (110,000 square kilometers), and the combined population was approximately 18 million.

Rapid recovery in the West

The new Western state rapidly repaired the economic and political damage that the war had wrought. In the 1950's, West Germany's economy grew at an annual rate of 7.9 per cent.

Two major factors responsible for West Germany's rapid recovery were the Marshall Plan and the outward-looking policies of Konrad Adenauer, West Germany's first *chancellor* (prime minister). In 1951, West Germany joined with Belgium, France, Italy, Luxembourg, and the Netherlands in forming an organization to manage their coal and steel industries. It worked so well that in 1957 the six nations formed an organization to develop nuclear power for peaceful purposes such as the production of electricity; and a trading bloc to enable capital, labor, goods, and services to flow freely among them. The countries in these organizations came to be known collectively as the European Community (EC or Common Market).

Another factor responsible for West Germany's rapid growth was a dramatic opening of markets for West German exports. This opening resulted from shortages caused by the Korean War (1950-1953) and from waning British influence in countries such as Egypt and Iran. Yet another factor was the demand of West Germans for all kinds of goods—household appliances, automobiles, and other consumer products—that had been unavailable since World War II. The willingness of West German workers to postpone wage increases also was an immense help.

Furthermore, ethnic German refugees who entered West Germany after the war made up for losses in the labor force caused by wartime deaths of soldiers and civilians. Most of the refugees came from parts of Czechoslovakia and Poland in which Germans had lived for centuries. Other refugees came from the part of Germany that the Soviets chopped off. And many Germans fled the Soviet occupation zone (and later, East Germany).

Adenauer stabilizes West Germany

Adenauer's policies drew praise from West Germany's allies and made West Germans feel safe from the spread of Communism. These results and West Germany's economic prosperity increased the popularity—and thus the size—of Adenauer's party, the conservative Christian Democratic Union (CDU), and its "sister" party in Bavaria, the Christian Social Union (CSU). The growth of the CDU-CSU helped erase a threat to West Germany's stability—a lack of dominant political parties.

West Germany began its political life with as many as eight parties represented in its parliament. The CDU-CSU combination won only about 30 per cent of the votes in West Germany's first parliamentary election, held in August 1949. Adenauer's policies proved to be so popular, however, that in 1957 the CDU-CSU won a parliamentary majority.

Adenauer provided further stability by integrating West Germany militarily with the West. In 1954, he guided his nation into the North Atlantic Treaty Organization (NATO), which had been formed in 1950 to provide for the common defense of its member nations in the event of an armed attack. Thus, as the 1950's drew to a close, West Germany had completed a westward turn. West Germany was a Western-style democracy, a world-class economic power, and a member of the major Western economic community and the principal Western military alliance.

The unintended state

At the end of World War II in 1945, not even the Soviet Union intended to create a separate East German state. At first, the Soviets even permitted relatively free elections in their zone, but the Communists lost. Nevertheless, the Soviets, aided by German Communists they appointed to local offices, carried out Communist economic policies in the Soviet occupation zone. They seized all private landholdings of more than 100 hectares (247 acres) and gave most of this land to about 500,000 small farmers and landless farmworkers. They organized the remainder of the land they had taken into collective farms similar to those in the Soviet Union. The Soviets and their German allies also seized factories and turned them over to local governments, cooperatives, and an economic commission.

In addition, the Soviets communized political life in their zone. They forced the large Social Democratic Party (a socialist party) to merge with the Communist Party to form the Socialist Unity Party (SED) and established new parties—which they controlled. By the time the Communists created the German Democratic Republic in 1949, the Soviet zone had been transformed into a dictatorship. East Germany's borders with the West were fortified with a death strip of barbed wire, land mines, and guard dogs.

Only the Soviet Union and a handful of Soviet satellite nations recognized the East German government diplomatically, and many of its own citizens did not respect it. Large numbers of young and better-educated East Germans began to flee through West Berlin to West Germany.

East Germany builds the wall

In 1950, East Germany formally integrated its economy into that of the Soviet bloc by joining the Council for Mutual Economic Assistance (COMECON), the bloc's common market. East Germany's economy grew rapidly, but could not keep up with economic growth in West Germany. Because of West Germany's rising prosperity and political freedom, the exodus from East Germany grew by leaps and bounds. From 1949 through 1952, a total of almost 500,000 East Germans fled to the West; from 1953 through 1956, more than 1 million followed.

In 1955, East Germany joined with the Soviet Union, Albania, Bulgaria, Czechoslovakia, Hungary, Poland, and Romania to sign the Warsaw Pact, forming a military alliance of Soviet-bloc nations. Thus, the division of Germany was sealed. Left in the midst of East Germany was West Berlin, a democratic island in the middle of a Communist ocean.

In late 1958, Soviet leader Nikita S. Khrushchev threatened to sign a peace treaty with East Germany and implied that such a treaty would end all Allied occupation rights in Berlin. Khrushchev renewed his threat in June 1961, and the flight to the West intensified. In July 1961, 30,000 East Germans fled to West Germany, most of them via West Berlin. And in the first 12 days of August, more than 17,000 East Germans fled to West Berlin.

Alarmed by heavy losses of well-educated, productive citizens, East Germany built the Berlin Wall between the East and West sectors of the city, beginning in the early morning hours of August 13. The construction of the wall was sudden, surprising, and effective, virtually ending flight to the West.

Ulbricht transforms East Germany

Once the last exit to the West was sealed off by the wall and other barriers, East Germany could develop its economy more strictly along Communist lines with little risk that many of its citizens would react by fleeing. The government completed the take-over of most industries. Agriculture had already been totally collectivized in 1959 and 1960. East Germany also expanded trade to many Western and Third World countries.

The Rhine River, Europe's busiest inland waterway, is a major trade artery for West Germany, the world's top exporter.

Young boxers in East Berlin fight in a *Spartakiad,* a sports competition for East German young people. Each year, Spartakiads take place throughout the country, helping East Germany to produce an astonishing number of world-class athletes.

Under Walter Ulbricht, who in 1950 had become the general secretary of the SED—and thus the nation's leader—East Germany became one of the most industrialized countries in the world, and the most prosperous Communist nation. During the Ulbricht years, East Germany improved its system of sports training, which to this day produces an astonishing number of world-class athletes. The Ulbricht regime also took a lively interest in the development of science and technology.

In the mid-1960's, East Germany asked other countries for diplomatic recognition. West Germany responded by restating a threat, first issued in 1955, to withdraw its own recognition from any country—except the Soviet Union—that recognized East Germany. This threat led East Germany to redouble its efforts to assert its existence as a separate state and, in 1967, to proclaim a separate East German citizenship.

Brandt reaches out to the East

By this time, the spirit of *détente* (an easing of strained tensions) was in the air. Détente in relations with the Soviets was a policy of U.S. President John F. Kennedy, who served from 1961 until his assassination in 1963; and of his successor, Lyndon B. Johnson. Richard M. Nixon, who succeeded Johnson in 1969, continued the policy.

In the spirit of détente, Willy Brandt, who became West Germany's first Social Democratic chancellor in 1969, began a campaign called *Ostpolitik* (Eastern policy), aimed at the establishment of normal diplomatic and trade relations with West Germany's Communist neighbors. He entered into treaty negotiations with the Soviet Union, Poland, and Czechoslovakia.

Brandt had no illusion that Ostpolitik might lead to reunification. He did not even intend to extend diplomatic recognition to East Germany, but only to acknowledge that it was a second state within one German nation.

East Germany's reaction to Ostpolitik was frosty, even defensive. For too many years, East Germany's regime had used the mutual hostility of the East and the West as a justification for pursuing its own harsh policies. Nevertheless, East Germany's Prime Minister Willi Stoph agreed—probably because of Soviet pressure—to exchange official visits with Brandt in 1970.

In 1971, Brandt persuaded the four occupying powers to negotiate an agreement among themselves concerning the status of Berlin. The leaders of East Germany were uneasy about the negotiations. Ulbricht feared that the Soviets would negotiate away East Germany's ability to put pressure on West Germany by disrupting ground traffic between West Germany and West Berlin, and that the negotiators might grant West Germany closer ties to West Berlin. He also had a fear regarding East Berlin—that the Soviets would acknowledge its status as part of a city not legally attached to either of the two Germanys.

In addition, Ulbricht strongly resisted an improvement of relations between West Germany and the Soviet Union. As a result, he lost favor with the Soviets and in May 1971 was forced to resign. Ulbricht's successor was Erich Honecker, who had been Ulbricht's deputy in charge of party affairs and the nation's military and security forces.

East-West treaties signed

Ulbricht's fears regarding West Berlin were realized in an agreement signed by the four powers in September 1971. The Soviets guaranteed that Western nations would have access to West Berlin by road, rail, and waterway. The Soviets also acknowledged the right of the West German government to represent West Berlin abroad. And most important, the four-power agreement and later negotiations between the two Germanys committed East Germany to allow larger numbers of West Germans and West Berliners to visit East Germany. For initiating the relaxation of tensions between West Germany and Communist states, Brandt won the 1971 Nobel Peace Prize.

East-West negotiations continued. In a treaty signed in 1972, the two Germanys promised to treat each other as equals. The United Nations admitted the two Germanys in 1973, and Western countries—but not West Germany—began to grant diplomatic recognition to East Germany.

East Germans relax on the Baltic coast, one of the country's top vacation spots. East Germans find it easy and inexpensive to "get away from it all"— especially within their own country. Adult workers receive at least 18 days of paid vacation per year, and labor unions provide subsidized travel and lodging packages.

Cooperation at arm's length

During the past 15 years, the two Germanys have continued to cooperate even during times of East-West crisis, such as the Soviet invasion of Afghanistan in December 1979. Trade has boomed between the two Germanys, and West Germany even allows East Germany to export goods to other EC countries as if the goods were West German. Thus, East Germany does not have to pay the EC tariffs charged to nonmembers. Furthermore, West Germany has extended financial credits to East Germany.

But in spite of their continuing economic cooperation, the two Germanys have grown no closer politically. West Germany's present chancellor, Helmut Kohl of the CDU, continues to pursue Ostpolitik, but Honecker has continued to build his foreign policy around loyalty to the Soviet Union.

No easy comparison

Honecker's domestic policy has stressed the production of consumer goods and the improvement of welfare programs. Although East Germany is still under firm Communist control, life there has become more pleasant.

It is difficult to compare daily life in the two Germanys because of differences in how prices of goods and services are set. In West Germany, market forces—supply and demand —establish most prices. In East Germany, the government establishes prices. Education and medical services are free in East

Germany, and East Germans pay less than West Germans for such necessities as rent and personal transportation. Prices in East Germany are higher, however, for such "luxuries" as automobiles and television sets.

Economists suggest that the average standard of living of East German workers has dropped to a level of little more than one-half that of West German workers since the building of the Berlin Wall. Meanwhile, West Germany's standard of living has grown to rival that of the United States.

Little hope of reunification

There has been no sign that the two Germanys will reunify. Both West and East Germans have long ceased to pay attention to West German politicians' ritual calls for reunification. Moreover, allies of both Germanys have not been willing to go beyond mere lip service to reunification and frequently have hinted that they are uneasy about the power and potential menace of a reunified Germany. Indeed, Germany's division into two politically opposed states, each integrated into one of the two major opposing blocs, has had the unintended effect of keeping the ghost of German expansionism at bay.

Some political observers also speculate that East and West Germans, after four decades of separate living under different systems, may have become estranged. On the one hand, most East Germans are able to watch West German television and listen to radio broadcasts from all over Western Europe. Also, as many as 25 per cent of West German families have relatives in the East. On the other hand, after more than 40 years, East Germans evidently have become more content with the Communist system, and they are proud of their economic achievements.

A recent visit symbolized the two Germanys' attempts to improve their relations, and the political gulf that remains between them. In September 1987, East Germany's Honecker made a historic trip to Bonn, West Germany, for talks with Kohl. No general secretary of the SED had ever visited West Germany. During the visit, Kohl commented that "the whole German people must be free to choose reunification." Honecker replied, "Socialism [Communism] and capitalism cannot be unified any more than fire and water."

East Germany's reaction to Michael Jackson's concert showed how far Honecker's government will go to prevent the "fire and water" from getting too close together. The regime may have had little interest in preventing a relatively small and peaceful crowd of East German youngsters from listening to one of the best-known entertainers of the world's leading capitalist nation—even though his music was "decadent." But the treatment inflicted on the Western news crews revealed a strong interest: preventing the broadcast of what might be interpreted as an indication that East Germans would rather be on the other side of the Berlin Wall—or that they wish there were no wall.

By Chong-Sik Lee

The Two Koreas

The division of Korea produced sharply diverging states—an isolated Communist dictatorship in the North and a tumultuous new democracy in the South.

The streets of Seoul, the capital of South Korea, were empty—an unusual sight in that bustling city of 10 million people. Buses and subway trains carried only a few passengers. Most Koreans had hurried home and were now gathered in front of their television sets to watch the live broadcast of an extraordinary meeting.

Under the auspices of the Red Cross, 100 Koreans had been allowed to travel across the line that separates North Korea from South Korea to meet with relatives living on the other side. After Korea was divided into two sectors in 1945, these Koreans—along with many thousands of other citizens—had become separated from their family members. In four decades, no

125

The author:
Chong-Sik Lee, who was born in Korea, is professor of political science at the University of Pennsylvania in Philadelphia and the author of several books on Korea.

one else had been given permission to visit estranged relatives, a tragic situation for members of a culture that places extreme importance on maintaining strong family ties. Relations between the governments of North and South Korea had been so hostile that even the exchange of letters had been prohibited.

Koreans watching the televised reunions saw a stooped elderly woman wearing a tight-fitting, short jacket and a long full skirt—traditional Korean dress. She, a South Korean, was small and so old that she walked unsteadily.

A man in his 50's approached her. A citizen of North Korea, he wore Western-style clothing—a suit and tie. His eyes widened as he recognized the woman, and he began to weep.

"Mother, Mother," he sobbed. "Forgive this unfilial son. Please forgive me."

The elderly woman looked at him coolly, without expression. Sometime during the decades since the teen-aged boy and his young mother were separated, the mother had become senile. She never recognized the weeping middle-aged man as her son.

Many Koreans—hundreds of thousands of them separated from their own families—also cried that September evening in 1985. The reunion had come too late.

One nation, divisible

Korea had been a unified nation for centuries. Koreans can trace their origins to hundreds of years before the time of Christ, when a nation called Chosun (The Land of the Morning Calm) was founded in the northwest of the small, mountainous Korean Peninsula. In 108 B.C., China conquered this kingdom and ruled it until A.D. 313. After the Chinese were ousted, the Korean Peninsula was ruled by three rival kingdoms—Koguryo, Paekche, and Silla. In 668, Silla vanquished the other two kingdoms, unifying the people and creating a single, distinct culture.

Although Koreans borrowed heavily from some aspects of Chinese civilization, there was no mistake about their own cultural identity. Their language, for example, belongs to the Koreans alone. The people also had their own social customs and distinctive style of clothing. The nation developed a centralized system of government, and most citizens followed the teachings of Confucianism, which encourages people to be kind and faithful, to respect their parents, and to honor their ancestors.

For centuries, the small peninsula surrounded by the powerful nations of Japan, Russia, and China was subject to several invasions. From the 1600's to the late 1800's, however, the Korean people managed to avoid invasion by closing the country to foreigners. This period, during which Korea was known as the Hermit Kingdom, came to an end in 1910, when Japan conquered Korea and ruled it as a colony. Korea remained a Japanese territory for more than 30 years. Freedom from the Japanese—and, unintentionally, Korea's division—came with Japan's defeat by the Allies in World War II (1939-1945).

In December 1950, during the Korean War, Korean refugees cross the icy Taedong River as they flee south from Pyongyang and advancing North Korean and Chinese troops, *above.* In this way, the war led to the disruption of thousands of families. On July 27, 1953, *left,* generals from the United States, left, and North Korea, right, sign the truce that ended the war, leaving Korea divided.

In 1943, the Soviet Union and the United States, sure of their coming victory, had agreed to eventually grant Korea its independence from Japan but had not agreed on other details. About one week before Japan surrendered, the Soviets unexpectedly sent soldiers into Korea. United States officials, having seen the Soviet Union try to impose Communism on Poland and other recently liberated countries in Eastern Europe, feared that the pattern would be repeated in Korea unless the United States stepped in. On Aug. 14, 1945, the U.S. government dispatched a telegram to the Soviet leader, Joseph Stalin, proposing to "divide the task of disarming Japanese forces in Korea." Stalin promptly agreed. Soviet forces occupied the territory north of the 38th

parallel of north latitude, an imaginary line running from east to west that cuts Korea approximately in half. United States troops moved into the southern territory.

Dividing Korea was easy, but unifying it again proved impossible. The United States and the Soviet Union were at odds over matters in the Middle East and Eastern Europe, and as relations between the two major powers became chillier, compromise and reconciliation became virtually impossible on any issue, including the fate of Korea.

After two years of failed negotiations with the Soviets, the United States asked the United Nations (UN) to take over the task of reuniting Korea. The UN decided to hold general elections throughout Korea as a first step toward establishing an independent government. Because this proposal was similar to the position the United States had taken before the deadlock, the Soviet Union refused to go along with the plan. As a result, UN-supervised elections were held in South Korea only, leading to the establishment of a state called the Republic of Korea. The territory occupied by the Soviets held its own elections, creating a Communist state, the Democratic People's Republic of Korea.

The split was now official. Soviet and U.S. troops left Korea in 1948 and 1949, respectively. The United States had indeed prevented the Soviets from placing all of Korea under its control, but the division of a formerly united people was the price paid.

The widening gulf

Left alone, the two Koreas were unable to coexist peacefully. Politicians on both sides of the 38th parallel adopted opposing positions. In the North, the Korean Communists advocated radical changes, calling for land reform, government confiscation of factories and other major enterprises from their owners, and the establishment of rule by the Communist party. Koreans in the South opposed radicalism, though they advocated moderate reforms. Making the situation more emotional was the feeling of people on both sides that their opponents were traitors to Korea, more interested in serving the cause of either the United States or the Soviet Union.

An inequality in the strength of the two new states also led to instability. The economic balance favored the North, where Korea's hydroelectric power stations, mines, and major industries were located. Another North Korean advantage was the country's shared border with its protector nation, the Soviet Union, which actively assisted in building up North Korea's armed forces. The United States, on the other hand, was separated by thousands of miles of ocean from South Korea and did not provide it with heavy equipment.

On June 25, 1950, the North Koreans attempted to gain control of the entire peninsula by launching the Korean War—or, as those in the North termed it, "The Just War for National Liberation and Unification." Airplanes, tanks, and heavy artillery

Opposite page: Soldiers patrol Korea's Demilitarized Zone (DMZ), a strip of land 4 kilometers (2½ miles) wide, wreathed in barbed wire, that marks the border between North and South.

moved south across the 38th parallel. The South Korean Army was no match for the well-equipped North Koreans. Seoul—only 26 miles (42 kilometers) from the 38th parallel—was captured within three days. Less than two months later, the North Korean Army had captured the entire peninsula except for a small enclave in the southeast.

The United States quickly intervened, preventing the North Koreans from making a complete conquest. Eventually, U.S. and South Korean forces drove most of the North Korean Army out of the entire peninsula and into Chinese territory. The UN, seeing North Korea as the aggressor in the conflict, provided support for the U.S. operation. But China, another Communist state, bolstered the North Korean forces by sending in its own troops.

Battles were fierce and prolonged, and the conflict became one of the most destructive wars in history. In three years, 4 million people were killed or maimed. Hundreds of thousands of North Koreans sought haven in the South, tearing families apart.

Finally, in July 1953, the UN and the North Koreans signed an armistice agreement in the town of Panmunjom, near the 38th parallel. South Korea's first president, Syngman Rhee, who wanted the Communists driven off the peninsula at any cost, refused to take part in the truce talks. It no longer mattered that the former combatants were a single people sharing a common ancestry, tradition, and language. The wounds suffered during the war made it impossible for people to shake off their hatred, fear, and suspicion of those on the other side.

Thirty-six years later, little has changed. Technically still at war, both sides maintain powerful armies—two of the largest in the world—ready for combat at a moment's notice. The demilitarized zone (DMZ), which extends 2 kilometers (1¼ miles) on each side of the line of separation between North and South Korea, is as impregnable as the Himalaya. Constantly patrolled, the DMZ is a tangle of barbed wire, land mines, machine guns, rocket launchers, and loudspeakers broadcasting propaganda to the other side.

North Korea: Stability and regimentation

After the war, the two Koreas followed drastically different paths of economic and political development. South Korea followed the Western pattern of development and experienced many political turnovers, fluctuations in policies, and periods of civil unrest. North Korea, on the other hand, followed the Soviet model by building a tightly organized, disciplined, and indoctrinated society.

North Korean politics have been completely dominated by one man—Kim Il-song—who, during the 1930's, had been the leader of a small band of Koreans who waged a guerrilla war against the Japanese. After Japan surrendered to the Allies, Kim ascended to top posts in the Korean Workers' Party—as North Korea's Communist party is called—and the North Korean

North and South Korea at a glance

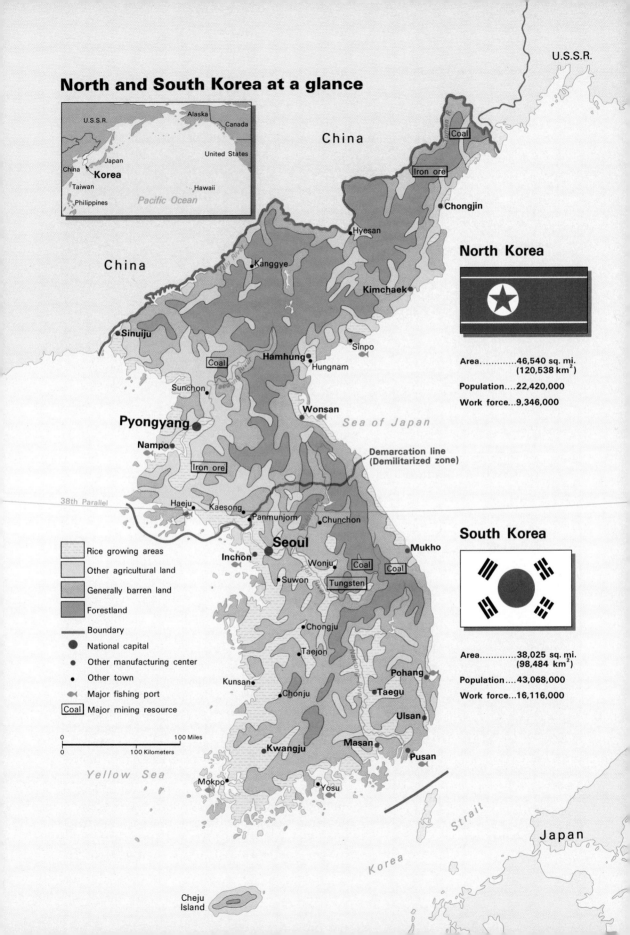

U.S.S.R.

Alaska
Canada
U.S.S.R.
Japan
China United States
Korea
Taiwan Hawaii
Philippines *Pacific Ocean*

China

Coal

Iron ore

● Chongjin

● Hyesan

North Korea

Kanggye

Kimchaek ●

● **Sinuiju**

Sinpo

Hamhung ● Coal

Sunchon ● Hungnam

Area............46,540 sq. mi.
(120,538 km^2)

Population....22,420,000

Work force...9,346,000

● **Wonsan**

Pyongyang ●

Sea of Japan

Nampo ●

Iron ore

Demarcation line
(Demilitarized zone)

38th Parallel

Haeju ● Kaesong ●

Panmunjom ●

● Chunchon

Seoul ●

● Mukho

Inchon ●

Wonju ● Coal

Suwon ● Coal

Tungsten

South Korea

● Chongju

● Taejon

● Pohang

Kunsan ●

● Chonju **Taegu**

Area............38,025 sq. mi.
(98,484 km^2)

Population....43,068,000

Work force...16,116,000

Ulsan

Masan

● **Kwangju** **Pusan**

Mokpo ● Yosu

Legend

	Rice growing areas
	Other agricultural land
	Generally barren land
	Forestland
——	Boundary
●	National capital
●	Other manufacturing center
●	Other town
	Major fishing port
Coal	Major mining resource

0   100 Miles
0   100 Kilometers

Yellow Sea

Korea Strait

Japan

Cheju
Island

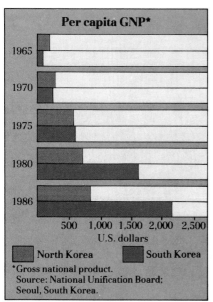

Per capita GNP*					
1965					
1970					
1975					
1980					
1986					
500	1,000	1,500	2,000	2,500	
U.S. dollars					

North Korea   South Korea

*Gross national product.
  Source: National Unification Board;
  Seoul, South Korea.

A comparison of the per capita *gross national product* (GNP)—the value of all goods and services produced—in North and South Korea shows the South's economic boom of the 1970's and 1980's. Foreign-investment and export policies fueled the spectacular growth.

government. Under Kim's leadership, the government conducted a massive indoctrination campaign to remake the party, the army, and the state—indeed the entire North Korean people—into the spiritual heirs of the band of guerrillas Kim had once led. The guerrillas were lauded as self-sacrificing, self-reliant, and disciplined heroes filled with love for Korea and hatred for its enemies. All North Koreans were expected to be similarly dedicated to their nation and loyal to their leader.

When North Korea became independent in 1948, Kim became the new nation's premier, the Communist party's chairman, and the North Korean Army's commanding general. His titles changed during the next four decades—he is now president of the state instead of premier and the party's general secretary instead of chairman—but there has been no change in his status as North Korea's supreme leader.

Although North Korea's political system is in many ways similar to that of the Soviet Union and other Communist nations, the society's true foundation is the personality of Kim. North Korean citizens are taught that their existence is

justified only when they fulfill the tasks assigned to them by their leader. Kim is exalted by the party and the government as the "Sun of the Nation." Statues and busts of him are displayed in most public buildings; his photographs occupy prominent places in homes; a button bearing his likeness is worn by every North Korean adult. Kim's kinglike status was reaffirmed in 1977, when the government designated his son, Kim Chong-il (pronounced *kihm jung ihl*), as his successor.

Not only was the entire society reorganized to follow Kim, but the country's economic structure was also radically altered. Private ownership of businesses was abolished soon after the war. The government now owns and operates all factories, as well as all other businesses such as retail stores and restaurants. All the farmlands have been collectivized to form cooperatives.

North Korea's industries grew rapidly after the war, but the Communist system proved to have limitations. North Korea's technology is behind that of many countries, and its government-operated businesses do not encourage innovation or experimentation. Worker morale has declined. To make matters worse, the perceived military threat from South Korea forces North Korea to spend heavily on its army—as much as 20 per cent of the value of all goods and services produced. This means that less money can be devoted to helping the economy grow.

Today, per capita income in North Korea is estimated to be about half that in South Korea. Because Kim places much em-

Economic contrasts
North Korea's economy is dependent on its heavy industries, such as the iron and steel complex in Chongjin, *opposite page*. South Korea, on the other hand, has developed a diversified and technologically advanced economy. Securities traders in Seoul, *above*, monitor the value of stocks in companies that manufacture textiles, automobiles, electronic products, and other goods.

133

A visitor to Seoul, the capital of South Korea, *right,* finds a teeming, modern city. Automobiles—a rarity in the North—are so numerous in Seoul as to be a nuisance.

In the North, religion is actively discouraged and is replaced with a reverence for President Kim Il-song. Workers at a factory near Pyongyang, *below,* mount a picture of Kim in preparation for an outdoor rally.

phasis on bolstering the army and heavy industries such as steel mills and chemical plants, consumer goods are in short supply. Bad weather during the 1980's also reduced agricultural output and food supplies. As a result, most North Koreans lead austere lives.

South Korea: Political chaos and economic growth

South Korea followed a different path, moving toward a Western type of democracy. But establishing a true democracy in the South proved to be much more difficult than creating a dictatorship in the North. South Korea's Constitution is similar to those of the United States and Western European countries, providing for a separation of powers between branches of the government and guaranteeing liberties to individual citizens. But the Constitution has been more a statement of goals than a reflection of realities.

Unlike the situation in North Korea, the leadership of South Korea has changed several times, typically because of civil unrest or military take-overs. In most cases, once a leader has attained power, he has forcibly amended or revised the Constitution to suit his purposes.

In 1987, widespread demonstrations against President Chun Doo Hwan—whose administration was marred by large-scale corruption and the imprisonment and torture of his political opponents—led to what may prove to be an important turning point in South Korea's history. The voters in South Korea, well-educated and exposed to many electoral campaigns and many dictatorships, are politically sophisticated. No longer willing to tolerate governmental hypocrisy, the citizens caused so much civil unrest that officials were forced to respond. On June 29, 1987, Roh (pronounced *Noh*) Tae Woo, the ruling party's candidate to succeed Chun, announced that a new, more democratic constitution would be proposed and that the upcoming presidential election would be fair and democratic. The new Constitution was put up for vote and ratified by a huge majority, and in February 1988, Roh narrowly won the presidency. It was believed that Roh would need extraordinary skill to maintain South Korea's political stability, but there was no doubt that the nation had weathered an important crisis.

One factor in Roh's favor was South Korea's rapidly growing economy. In the late 1960's, President Park Chung Hee adopted an export-oriented industrial policy that would prove extremely successful. At the time, few business people had enough money to build factories, and the country was not technologically advanced. Park encouraged Korean entrepreneurs to borrow money or enter into joint ventures with foreign investors and to export the goods they produced. South Korea's large pool of industrious workers—a 54-hour workweek is typical—helped many enterprises succeed. This led to increases in the country's level of technological advancement and brought money into

The standard of living for a family in South Korea, *above,* is typically higher than that of a family in the North. The South's economic boom has driven up per capita income and increased the production of consumer goods such as clothing, appliances, and electronic products.

South Korea. South Korean companies then scoured the world for new markets for their goods.

Today, South Korea's economy is one of the most rapidly growing in the world. The state exports light industrial products such as shoes and textiles and heavy industrial products such as oil tankers, automobiles, and steel. It is also a strong competitor in the electronics market.

Although pockets of poverty remain in South Korea, two decades of economic growth have produced a huge jump in most people's standard of living. When surveyed in 1987, more than half of the population said they considered themselves middle class. South Korean streets are crowded with automobiles of all kinds, many of which are privately owned. A good selection of foods is sold in markets and restaurants, and stores are full of merchandise produced in Korea or imported from abroad. Like the middle class in other countries, middle-class South Koreans also enjoy a full range of entertainments, including television, theater, and sporting events.

Widely diverging paths

Thus, North and South Korea have truly become different states, motivated by sharply contrasting ideals. In the North, fulfillment of Kim's wishes is the standard for government and citizens to follow. In the South, on the other hand, democratic principles and the improvement of living standards have served as yardsticks for the nation's success.

A second contrast between the two parts of Korea is the difference in the extent of the government's power. In the North, Kim and the Communist party control every aspect of the society, including the way people behave and think. In the South, the people have generally been free to lead their own lives—except in the case of those suspected of being involved in antigovernment activities, who have been subject to arrest and imprisonment. Also, the government of North Korea has complete control over the nation's economy, while the South Korean economy depends on private enterprise.

A third important difference is the extent of openness toward the outside world. North Korea is an extremely closed society—another Hermit Kingdom. The government maintains diplomatic and trade relations with many Third World and Western countries, but the ruling party has imposed restrictions on the flow of information to and from the nation. Even such basic information as population statistics are difficult for anyone outside North Korea to obtain. North Koreans are forbidden to travel outside their country unless they are on an official mission, and few outsiders are allowed into North Korea.

Inevitably, North Korean perceptions of the rest of the world are highly distorted. Their closed society contrasts with the open

Accustomed to a relative scarcity of consumer products, North Koreans clamor for the chance to buy chewing gum in a Pyongyang department store, *below.*

A North Korean man consoles his weeping South Korean sister at their reunion in Seoul. Separated by the division of Korea 40 years earlier, they were allowed to spend a few hours together in 1985 by agreement of their two states. Since the division, only 100 citizens have been allowed to cross the DMZ to meet with relatives.

society of South Korea. Thousands of business people and tourists fly in and out of Seoul International Airport each day. Newspapers, magazines, and movies from the West are easily accessible.

Repairing the rift

The myriad differences between North and South have made them uneasy, if not openly hostile, neighbors. In 1974, North Korean terrorists tried to assassinate South Korean President Park, killing his wife in the attempt. In 1987, North Korean terrorists apparently set off a bomb aboard a South Korean airliner, causing 115 deaths. North Korea disclaims responsibility for both events, however, and charges that they were South Korea's own doing.

The 1988 Summer Olympics presented an opportunity for cooperation, which did not materialize. North Korea had strenuously objected to the selection of Seoul as the site of the Olympics, arguing that North and South Korea should co-host the events. Although the Seoul Olympics Committee offered to hold some athletic contests in North Korea and invited North Korean athletes to participate in the Olympics as members of a joint Korean team or as a separate North Korean team, these offers were not acceptable to the North Koreans, who unsuccessfully attempted to organize a Communist-bloc boycott of the games. Seoul anticipated terrorist attacks from the North during the games, but fortunately this fear proved to be unfounded. The games went off smoothly, and South Koreans took great pride in how well their country played host.

Despite the recurring conflicts between the two Koreas, there is hope for a reduction in hostilities. One impetus is the improvement of relations among the major powers—the United States, the Soviet Union, China, and Japan. All four powers desire to maintain peace on the Korean Peninsula. In the late 1980's, pressure also began building inside North and South Korea to change each government's confrontational attitude toward the other. During South Korea's 1987 and 1988 electoral campaigns, for example, practically all of the candidates argued for "opening up to the North."

In the North, leaders came to realize that they must reduce the cost of maintaining a huge army in order to boost the civilian economy. A reduction of tension will also be necessary if North Korea is to successfully encourage foreigners to invest in North Korean businesses.

There have even been a few hesitant steps in the direction of reunification. Representatives from the North and South met and issued a joint communiqué on July 4, 1972, pledging to work toward unification. The two sides then engaged in several months of negotiations, which, though unsuccessful, created a feeling of euphoria among Koreans on both sides of the DMZ.

There were other dramatic developments. For example, North Korea in 1984 sent relief goods after South Korea suffered a devastating flood. Although South Korea did not need such assistance—President Chun had offered economic aid to North Korea only 20 days earlier—the North's gesture was accepted. This friendly exchange led to meetings of representatives of the two governments for trade talks. It also initiated the family reunions of September 1985.

These events can be interpreted in various ways. Some Koreans cite the negative results of more than 15 years of negotiations and conclude that a lasting improvement of relations—not to mention unification—will never happen. But others say that the very fact that the two sides are talking to each other marks a vast improvement over the situation before 1970.

Nothing could more graphically show the Korean people's desire for unification than the tears that welled into the eyes of the citizens who watched the dramatic 1985 reunions. Many hope that a reduction of tension will allow others to fulfill their dream of seeing long-lost relatives. And in time, perhaps, the attitude of the people toward each other will evolve from hatred into something approaching brotherhood.

For further reading:
Clough, Ralph N. *Embattled Korea: The Rivalry for International Support.* Westview Press, 1987.
Kihl, Young Whan. *Politics and Policies in Divided Korea: Regimes in Contest. 1845-1983.* Westview Press, 1983.
Koh, Byung Chul. *The Foreign Policy Systems of North and South Korea.* University of Calif. Press, 1984.

By Beverly Merz

Protecting Our Hearing

**Despite assaults on our ears by a
noisy world, there are simple, effective
ways to safeguard our hearing.**

Despite the festive atmosphere at the Hendersons' Christmas
open house, Carl realized that he wasn't enjoying parties the
way he once did. He felt annoyed when he tried to talk to his
fellow partygoers. The room was so noisy he had to struggle to
make out what people were saying. He had felt the same way at
his office party earlier that week. It had been hard to follow the
jokes and stories his co-workers were telling. "What's happen-
ing? I'm barely 45 and I'm turning into an old fogy," he thought.

Over the next few months, Carl became increasingly irritable.
He yelled at his teen-aged sons for mumbling. He found it difficult to concentrate on presentations at sales meetings. He
seemed to miss part of what his companions were saying at
lunch. When Carl began to decline social invitations and cancel
business appointments, his wife became alarmed. She suggested
that Carl talk to his old college roommate, now the family doctor.

After listening to Carl's story, the doctor made a suggestion.
He knew that Carl had spent his college vacations working in a
steel mill and that he had played the drums in a rock band
throughout college and graduate school. He suspected that Carl's
increasing sense of isolation was the result of a hearing loss and

recommended that he see an *otologist*, a doctor specializing in hearing disorders.

The family doctor's suspicions turned out to be right. Carl was suffering from *presbycusis*, a gradual hearing loss due to age. In Carl's case, it was compounded by noise damage. Although neither presbycusis nor noise damage can be reversed, they may be treated. An *audiologist*—a person trained to determine how well a patient hears—fitted Carl with a hearing aid for each ear. Within a few weeks, he had become accustomed to the slightly distorted and amplified sound provided by the devices and was surprised at how easily he could hear conversation again. He began to enjoy being with people once more.

Carl is not alone. He is one of more than 16 million Americans, including former President Ronald Reagan, who have a hearing loss. Two million of these Americans are seriously hearing-impaired or completely deaf. About 25 per cent of those over age 75 have a hearing loss severe enough to interfere with their ability to understand normal conversation. But hearing defects are not unique to older age groups. One in every 1,500 babies born in the United States has a hearing problem. And surveys of U.S. students entering college indicate that up to 60 per cent have a minor hearing defect.

Fortunately, advances in electronics are enabling many people like Carl to cope with hearing loss. The newest hearing aids are more effective, smaller, and less conspicuous than previous aids. Even more revolutionary, some people with severe hearing loss are benefiting from surgically implanted devices that by-pass damaged areas of the ear. And other devices, such as those that enable people with hearing impairments to watch TV or use the telephone, are making everyday life easier.

Hearing: from sound waves to brain waves

Hearing loss may result from damage to any of the ear's three parts: the outer ear, the middle ear, or the inner ear. The outer ear consists of the fleshy curved part on the outside of the head and the *external auditory canal*, the tunnellike opening in the ear. At the end of the external auditory canal is the *eardrum*, a thin membrane stretched tightly over the canal.

The middle ear is a small chamber containing three tiny bones—the hammer, the anvil, and the stirrup. These bones, which are linked, connect the eardrum to the inner ear.

The bottom of the chamber forming the middle ear opens into a narrow passage called the Eustachian tube, which leads to the back of the throat. Usually, the Eustachian tube is collapsed. It opens when you swallow, sneeze, yawn, or blow your nose. It also opens when the air pressure changes rapidly, such as when you take off or land in an airplane. When the tube opens, air passes between the middle ear and the throat, equalizing the pressure on the inner and outer sides of the eardrum and preventing the membrane from rupturing.

The author:
Beverly Merz is an associate editor of *The Journal of the American Medical Association.*

How we hear

Sound enters the ear through the external auditory canal and strikes the *eardrum,* causing it to vibrate. The vibrations—amplified and transmitted by tiny bones called the *hammer, anvil,* and *stirrup*—create waves in the membranes in the *organ of Corti,* a structure in the snail-shaped *cochlea.* The waves cause the movement of tiny hairs on sensory cells known as *hair cells.* This action in turn creates electrical impulses that travel via the *auditory nerve* to the brain. The brain interprets the impulses as sound.

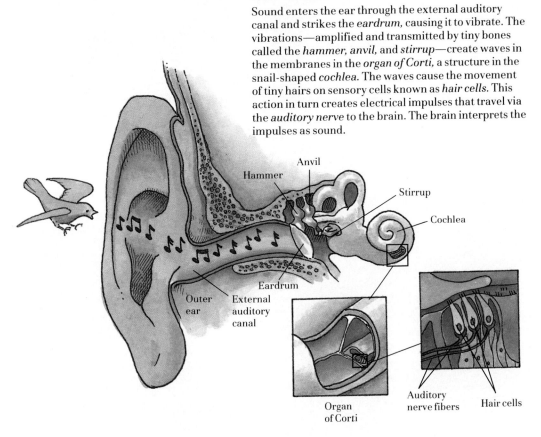

Anvil

Hammer

Stirrup

Cochlea

Eardrum

Outer ear

External auditory canal

Organ of Corti

Auditory nerve fibers

Hair cells

The inner ear has three principal parts, the most important of which is the *cochlea,* a structure shaped like a snail shell. All three sections contain *hair cells,* specialized sensory cells with tiny hairlike projections. These cells are attached to the fibers of the *auditory* (hearing) nerve. More than 15,000 of the 40,000 hair cells that we normally have at birth are found in one of three fluid-filled ducts that wind through the cochlea. These cells, together with supporting cells, make up the *organ of Corti,* the actual organ of hearing.

When a clock ticks, when a musician pulls a bow across the strings of a violin, or when the surf pounds the shore, sound waves are produced. When these waves reach the ear, they travel through the external auditory canal to the eardrum, causing it to vibrate. The vibrations pass from the eardrum to the middle ear, where the stirrup vibrates, causing pressure changes in the inner ear. These pressure changes create waves that travel along the organ of Corti. The waves cause filaments on the hair cells to bend. A loud noise causes the movement of a greater number of filaments and causes them to bend farther than does a soft noise. The bending of the filaments causes the release of a chemical that creates electric impulses that travel

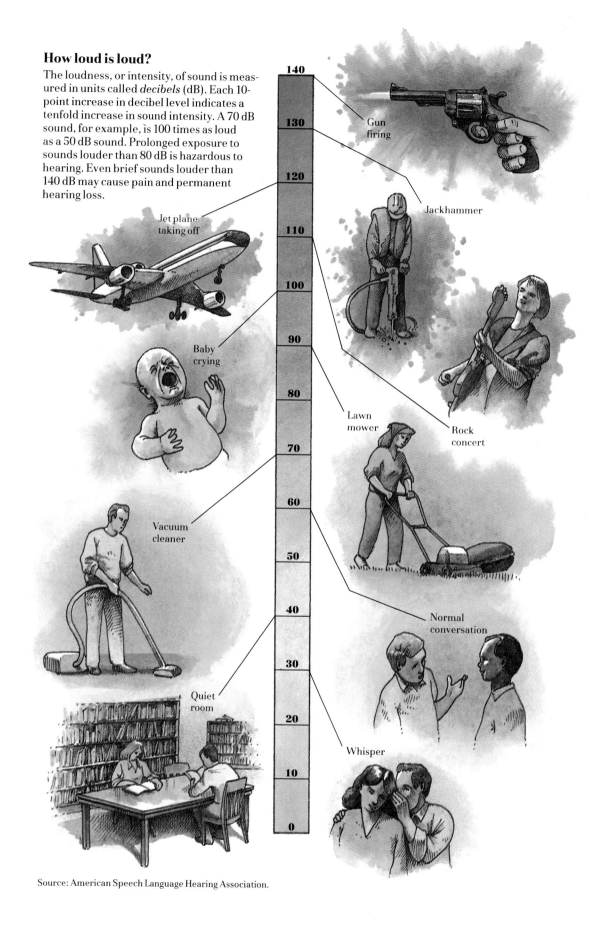

How loud is loud?

The loudness, or intensity, of sound is measured in units called *decibels* (dB). Each 10-point increase in decibel level indicates a tenfold increase in sound intensity. A 70 dB sound, for example, is 100 times as loud as a 50 dB sound. Prolonged exposure to sounds louder than 80 dB is hazardous to hearing. Even brief sounds louder than 140 dB may cause pain and permanent hearing loss.

140

130 — Gun firing

120 — Jackhammer

Jet plane taking off

110

100

90

Baby crying

80

Lawn mower

70 — Rock concert

Vacuum cleaner

60

50

40 — Normal conversation

30

Quiet room

20

Whisper

10

0

Source: American Speech Language Hearing Association.

via the auditory nerve to the brain, where they are interpreted as sound. Some sound is also transmitted to the inner ear by the temporal bone, which encases most of the ear.

What can go wrong

Some people are born with defective hearing because the structures of the ear or the auditory nerve did not develop properly. In addition, because hearing is such a complicated process, there are many points at which something can go wrong, producing hearing loss later in life. For example, sound waves may not be transmitted properly to the inner ear. The hair cells may not respond to the traveling wave, or they may fail to stimulate an electric impulse in the auditory nerve fibers. Or the impulses may not be transmitted properly along the auditory nerve or processed correctly by the brain.

Each type of hearing loss can be caused in several ways—by aging, exposure to loud noises, head injury, infection, and certain drugs. Except for loss due to hereditary defects or aging, however, most hearing loss can be prevented.

Like Carl, many Americans suffer from a gradual hearing loss caused by aging. This condition, called *presbycusis*, occurs as the organ of Corti in the cochlea begins to deteriorate. Some hearing specialists believe presbycusis is simply the result of cells wearing out. With the death of hair cells and auditory-nerve cells, the ability to hear certain sounds is lost. An estimated 60 per cent of all Americans over age 65 have presbycusis. People with presbycusis often have difficulty hearing high-pitched sounds and following conversation in noisy environments. They may also suffer from *tinnitus*, a ringing or buzzing in the ears.

Exposure to loud noise, which is defined as loud unwanted sound, is another of the most common—and hardest to avoid—sources of hearing loss. The intensity of sound—basically, its loudness—is measured in units called *decibels* (dB). Each 10-point increase in decibel level indicates a tenfold increase in intensity. For example, the noise produced by a chain saw, which registers about 90 dB, is 1,000 times louder than that produced by a vacuum cleaner, which registers at 60 dB. (The loudness of a sound also depends on its *frequency*, the rate at which the sound waves are vibrating. Our ears are less sensitive to sounds near the upper and lower limits of the frequencies we can hear. As a result, high-frequency and low-frequency sounds do not seem as loud as sounds from the middle of the frequency range, even if they all register at the same decibel level.)

Studies of factory workers whose hearing was measured before and after several months on a high-noise job have suggested that prolonged exposure to noise above 85 to 90 dB can cause permanent hearing loss. Experiments with animals have indicated that high-decibel noise can destroy large numbers of hair cells.

Protecting your ears

Protecting your ears against noise is simpler than restoring lost hearing.

Wear ear protectors when operating loud machinery.

Keep a safe distance from loudspeakers at concerts and discos.

Cover your ears when confronted by sudden, loud noise.

Other studies have revealed that the type of hearing loss associated with excessive exposure to noise can occur surprisingly early. For example, audiologist David Lipscomb, then at the University of Tennessee in Knoxville, in the late 1960's found measurable high-frequency hearing loss in nearly 4 per cent of the sixth-graders, 11 per cent of the ninth-graders, and nearly 11 per cent of the high school seniors he tested. In another study, of college freshmen, reported in 1969, Lipscomb found that more than 60 per cent had significant hearing loss. About 15 per cent of the male students had what Lipscomb calls "retirement ears"—that is, their hearing was only as good as or was even worse than that of men aged 60 to 69.

When people with normal hearing are exposed to noises above the caution zone of 80 to 90 dB, their hair cells become flattened and incapable of creating electric impulses. Usually, if the noise exposure has been brief, the hair cells—and hearing—return to normal. Repeated exposure, however, can cause hair cells to lose their flexibility and even die. This can result in permanent hearing loss.

Unfortunately, our world offers many opportunities for prolonged noise exposure. The roar of automobile and bus engines,

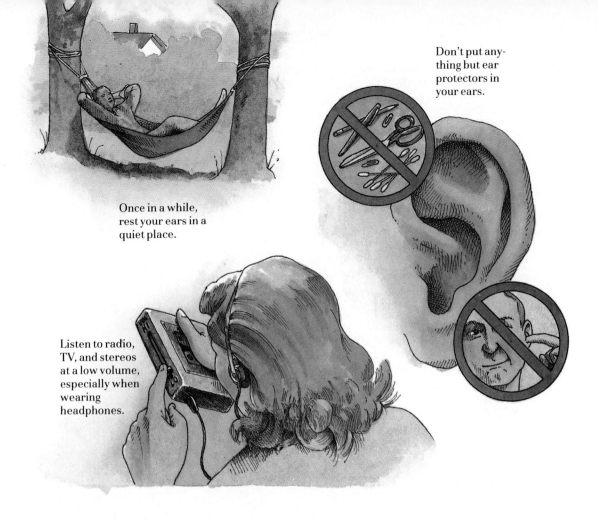

Once in a while,
rest your ears in a
quiet place.

Don't put any-
thing but ear
protectors in
your ears.

Listen to radio,
TV, and stereos
at a low volume,
especially when
wearing
headphones.

the din of building construction, and other common urban noises
have raised the background decibel level in cities to a mildly
unsettling 70 to 80 dB. Because we live in a world filled with
noise, we must learn to protect our ears.

One way is with ear protectors. They range from small foam
plugs worn in the external auditory canal to large muffs that
cover the ear completely. Most ear protectors reduce noise
levels by 20 or 30 dB. A protector will not provide adequate
protection, however, unless it completely seals off the auditory
canal. That is why wearers should carefully follow the manufacturer's directions. Hearing experts recommend wearing ear
protectors when firing guns; when operating power tools, vacuum cleaners, lawn mowers, or snow blowers; and when riding
in snowmobiles, speedboats, or small airplanes.

Of course, no one can be prepared for sudden, unexpected
high-decibel bursts of sound, such as those made by an ambu-
lance siren or a jackhammer. Although it may be impossible to
avoid loud noises, you can usually lower the decibel level of the
sound entering your ears by covering your ears with your hands.

Ironically, an increasingly common cause of hearing loss today
is sounds people want to hear, particularly music. Fans standing

near the loudspeakers at rock concerts and discos may be bombarded by as much as 120 dB. At close range, small radios can deliver 90 dB and large stereo systems a painful 140 dB. And although using headphones may protect other people from excess noise, it may be at the wearer's expense, because the sound is channeled directly into the ear.

Because this cause of hearing loss is self-inflicted, it is relatively easy to avoid. The simplest approach is to stay as far away as possible from the loudspeakers at discos and rock concerts—or to avoid these places altogether—and to learn to listen to radio, television, and recorded music at a lower volume, especially when wearing headphones.

One thing we can do to preserve our hearing is to see that the background noise of the home is as low as possible. We can do this by choosing carpeting and draperies that muffle sound, by buying appliances that have relatively quiet motors, and by establishing "maximum volume" limits for radios, stereo equipment, and television sets. Parents can also help their children avoid noise damage by buying them a set of earplugs and teaching them how and when to use them.

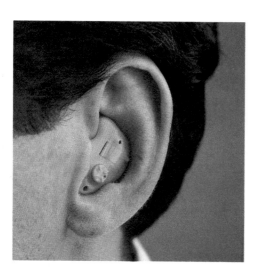
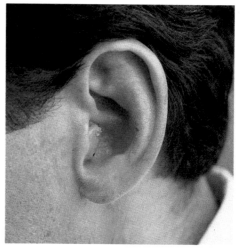
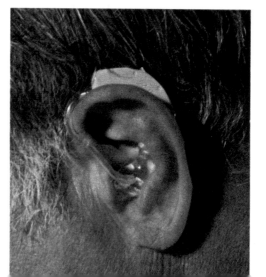

Types of hearing aids
Hearing aids enable people with hearing loss to regain at least some of their hearing. Hearing aids come in several styles. In-the-ear aids, *above,* the most popular type of hearing aid, fit into the bowl-shaped opening of the outer ear. Canal aids, *above right,* fit inconspicuously into the external auditory canal. They are less powerful than in-the-ear devices. Behind-the-ear hearing aids, *right,* are more powerful and less expensive than in-the-ear aids.

148

Injury is another common source of hearing loss. The eardrum is one of the ear's most vulnerable structures. Because it is stretched so tightly, it can be torn by a relatively weak force—such as that delivered by a gentle slap—traveling through the auditory canal. It can also be damaged by inserting objects, such as cotton swabs, into the external auditory canal. For this reason, otologists advise patients not to try to clean the canal or remove wax from it.

Sudden changes in pressure, such as those experienced when flying or scuba diving, can also cause the membrane to rupture. This usually occurs when the Eustachian tube is blocked or cannot open to equalize pressure in the middle and outer ear. Because colds, hay fever, and other sinus conditions can cause swelling in the nose and throat that may block the Eustachian tube, people suffering from these conditions should avoid flying and scuba diving. If flying is absolutely necessary, taking antihistamines or decongestants before and during the flight may reduce the swelling enough to allow the Eustachian tube to open.

A ruptured eardrum, though painful, does not necessarily result in permanent hearing loss. Unless the ear becomes infected, the membrane usually heals on its own, and any temporary hearing loss is restored.

Blows to the head can also displace or fracture the tiny bones of the middle ear so that they are no longer able to transmit vibrations to the cochlea. Such injuries can produce severe hearing losses if they are not surgically corrected. Displaced bones can be repositioned. Fractured bones can be replaced by transplanted bones from people who have died or by stainless steel substitutes.

Head injuries may also cause vibrations of the skull that are violent enough to result in permanent damage to the hair cells of the inner ear. People with such injuries may experience the same type of high-frequency hearing loss caused by excessive noise. A skull fracture through the cochlea usually produces total hearing loss in the affected ear.

Infections

Infections, another common source of hearing loss, are more likely to affect children than adults. "Swimmer's ear," for example, one of the most common childhood infections, occurs when water harboring bacteria or fungi gets trapped in the auditory canal. As the microorganisms multiply and infect the ear, the tissues of the middle ear swell and press against the eardrum. Antibiotics usually can destroy the infection.

Middle ear infections strike more than 50 per cent of all children. These infections are usually caused by an infection of the nose or throat that has spread through the Eustachian tube to the middle ear. If fluid has accumulated in the middle ear, a doctor may have to make a small hole in the eardrum and insert a tiny drainage tube. In most cases, however, antibiotics alone

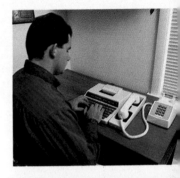

Getting the message
Electronic devices can make life easier for people with severe hearing loss. A special telecommunications device, *top,* enables deaf people to make and receive telephone calls. The user types the message on a keyboard. The words are then transmitted over the telephone and appear on the screen of the recipient's device or are printed on paper. In close-captioned TV, *above,* the gist of a program's conversation appears on the screen.

149

Electronic ears

Electronic devices that are surgically implanted in the ear have provided new options for some people whose hearing is too severely impaired to benefit from conventional hearing aids. These devices, which by-pass damaged areas of the ear, do not provide their wearers with normal hearing, however.

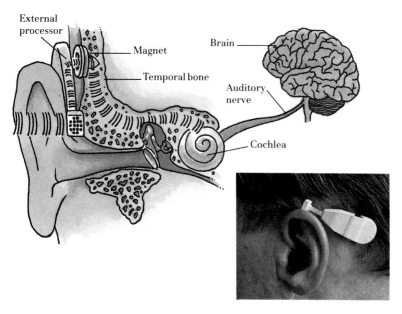

External processor

Magnet

Temporal bone

Brain

Auditory nerve

Cochlea

The bone conductor implant

The bone conductor implant is designed for people with a damaged middle ear but functional nerve cells in the inner ear. The device uses the temporal bone to by-pass the middle ear. An external processor, held against the head by a magnet screwed into the temporal bone, converts sound waves to vibrations. The vibrations are then transmitted to the magnet and conducted through the temporal bone to the sensory cells in the cochlea. The sensory cells create electrical impulses, which travel via the auditory nerve to the brain.

The cochlear implant

The cochlear implant is designed for people with severely damaged hair cells but some surviving auditory nerve cells. A microphone picks up and magnifies sounds, which are converted into electrical signals by a processor and passed along to an external transmitter. An internal receiver implanted behind the ear picks up the signals and transmits them to electrodes implanted in the cochlea. The electrodes provide direct electrical stimulation of the auditory nerve, which carries the signals to the brain for interpretation.

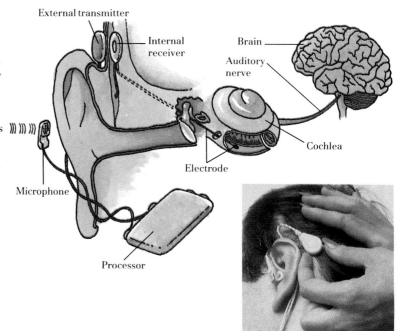

External transmitter

Internal receiver

Brain

Auditory nerve

Cochlea

Electrode

Microphone

Processor

can clear up the infection in a few days. In fact, the use of antibiotics has transformed the disease from the major cause of hearing loss in children to little more than a nuisance.

Drugs: cure and cause

Although some drugs can clear up diseases or relieve conditions that cause hearing loss, other drugs can cause hearing loss by damaging hair cells or the auditory nerve. Among them are such antibiotics as streptomycin and neomycin, and *diuretics*—drugs taken to eliminate excess fluid by people who have high blood pressure or kidney disease. It is a good idea for patients taking these drugs to be alert for any change in their hearing so that their doctor can change their prescription.

Aspirin is the most commonly used drug associated with hearing loss. People who take aspirin in large doses or for a long time may experience tinnitus and minor hearing loss. Both conditions can be reversed by lowering the dose of aspirin taken or switching to another drug.

Hearing aids: opening a window on sound

Most people with a hearing loss can regain at least part of their hearing with a hearing aid. Because most hearing losses affect both ears, hearing specialists recommend that patients wear two hearing aids. But less than 40 per cent of the 2 million people who wear hearing aids in the United States do so.

All hearing aids consist of the same basic parts: a microphone, which picks up sound and converts it to an electric signal; an amplifier, which magnifies the signal; a receiver, which converts the signal back into sound; and a device that directs the sound into the ear. A battery provides the power for the hearing aid, and a volume control adjusts the loudness.

Hearing aids come in several styles. One of the most popular, used by about 50 per cent of the Americans who wear hearing aids, fits into the bowl-shaped opening of the outer ear. Because this type of aid can be adjusted to amplify certain frequencies, it can be used by people with a wide range of hearing loss.

About 25 per cent of hearing-aid wearers use canal aids, which resemble earplugs and fit snugly in the external auditory canal. They have become increasingly popular since President Reagan began to use one in 1983. Less conspicuous than in-the-ear aids, they are also less powerful and are recommended only for people with mild to moderate hearing loss. These aids can also be adjusted to amplify wanted sounds, such as conversation, and tune out unwanted sounds, such as traffic noises.

Another 25 per cent of hearing-aid wearers use an aid that fits behind the ear. It consists of a crescent-shaped plastic case that is hooked over the ear and houses a battery, microphone, amplifier, and receiver. A small plastic tube connects the aid to an earpiece that fits in the external auditory canal. These devices are more powerful than in-the-ear aids, and less expensive.

A tiny percentage of hearing-aid wearers use miniaturized devices housed in the temples of wide-rimmed glasses and connected to earpieces by tubes. An equally small percentage use body aids, boxlike devices usually carried in a shirt pocket and connected to a buttonlike earpiece by an electric cord. These aids are usually worn by people with severe hearing loss.

All hearing aids amplify sound. They make soft sounds louder and improve their wearers' ability to hear bird calls and other sounds at higher frequencies than they normally would hear.

But hearing aids cannot restore hearing completely. If they could make faint sounds audible, louder sounds would blast intolerably. Nor can hearing aids restore the ability to hear the full range of frequencies, especially the high-frequency sounds often inaudible to people with hearing loss. That is why the sound they produce is often described as "tinny."

Finally, most available models do not amplify sounds selectively. For example, people wearing hearing aids in a restaurant may hear the talk at several other tables besides their own. In contrast, most people with normal hearing have an amazing ability to focus on the sounds they want to hear.

Making everyday life easier

Although hearing aids improve face-to-face communications, they cannot be used when talking on most telephones. This is because the telephone converts sound into electromagnetic waves, which most hearing aids cannot pick up. Many people who wear hearing aids use either special phones that allow the listener to increase the volume or removable couplers that fit on the earpiece. These couplers also amplify sound but can be moved from phone to phone. Unless users wear less powerful canal aids, however, they must remove their hearing aids before using phones with amplification devices. Otherwise, the sound volume may be too great.

People whose hearing loss is so severe that amplified telephones are not helpful may use a telecommunications device for the deaf (TDD). These devices transfer typed messages over telephone lines. The sender types a message on a small keyboard, and the words appear on a small display screen on the recipient's device. People with a TDD who want to communicate with hearing people who don't have one may do so through a message center. The people at the center receive the message, print it out, and read it over the telephone to the hearing recipient. Hearing people may also use the center to send messages to a person with a TDD.

Other electronic devices are allowing people with a hearing loss to enjoy television. Since the introduction of closed-captioned television in the 1970's, the major TV networks, as well as some cable systems, have made a wide variety of programs accessible by running subtitles that deliver the gist of the conversation at the bottom of the screen. The captions appear only when an adapter is added to the television set or on special TV sets with built-in adapters, however. People with a moderate hearing loss can use special earphones that amplify a television's audio signal and screen out surrounding noise.

Electronic "ears"

Engineering advances have also produced new options in the form of surgically implanted electronic hearing devices for some people with severe hearing loss. The cochlear implant, for example, is designed for people with profound hearing loss who would not benefit from a hearing aid. Such people must have some surviving auditory nerve fibers, however. First developed in the 1960's, cochlear implants were not approved for use in the United States by the Food and Drug Administration (FDA) until 1984, after years of debate about their effectiveness. By late 1988, about 3,000 of the devices had been implanted in patients worldwide, most of them in the United States. But experts agree that the implants have limited use. A panel of experts convened by the FDA in 1988 concluded that fewer than 150,000 hearing-impaired Americans would be candidates for a cochlear implant.

Cochlear implants do not enable deaf people to distinguish words. In fact, people with these implants may hear only static or clicks, buzzes or beeps. The devices do, however, help the wearers connect certain sounds with lip movements and so make lip reading easier. Newer models, which contain several electrodes, have considerably improved the clarity of the sound transmitted. Engineers predict that further refinements, such as filters that pick up only those sounds made by voices, may eventually enable people with cochlear implants to understand speech without lip reading.

In 1987, the FDA approved the use of another implant, this one for people with damaged middle ears who are subject to the recurring ear infections that affect some wearers of hearing aids. The middle ear implant, called the Xomed Audiant bone conductor, was developed by researchers at the Oregon Hearing Research Center in Portland and the Central Ear Research Institute in Oklahoma City, Okla. By late 1988, about 500 patients had been fitted with the device.

The middle ear implant uses the bones of the skull to transmit sound vibrations to the cochlea and so by-passes the middle ear altogether. Like the cochlear implant, the middle ear implant is expected to be useful for a limited number of deaf people. It works only for those people whose nerve cells in the inner ear are functional.

Despite the promise of increasingly sophisticated hearing devices, it will be a long time—if ever—before people with severe hearing loss will be able to completely regain their hearing. Prevention—protecting against head injuries, treating infections that can spread to the inner ear, and above all, keeping the noise level down—is still the best medicine.

1982
1983
1984
1985
1986
1987
1988

The Year on File

Contributors to *The World Book Year Book* report on the major developments of 1988. The contributors' names appear at the end of the articles they have written, and a complete roster of contributors, listing their professional affiliations and the articles they have written, is on pages 6 and 7.

Articles in this section are arranged alphabetically by subject matter. In most cases, the article titles are the same as those of the articles in *The World Book Encyclopedia* that they update. The numerous cross-references guide the reader to a subject or information that may be in some other article or that may appear under an alternative title. "See" and "See also" cross-references appear within and at the end of articles to direct the reader to related information elsewhere in *The Year Book*. "In *World Book,* see" references point the reader to articles in the encyclopedia that provide background information to the year's events reported in *The Year Book.*

See page 427 ▶

Advertising

Advertising. Current events such as the Olympic Games, the United States presidential election, and *glasnost*, the new Soviet policy of openness in the flow of information, created opportunities for the U.S. advertising industry in 1988. In May, Soviet television viewers saw Michael Jackson perform in commercials for Pepsi-Cola—the first U.S. advertiser to buy time on Soviet television. Two advertising agencies based in New York City, Young & Rubicam and Ogilvy & Mather, arranged to form joint ventures with Soviet advertising agencies. And the Soviet Union's advertising association became the first Soviet member of the International Advertising Association.

Political ads. Every four years, the U.S. advertising industry receives a windfall of revenues from the presidential election and the Olympics. In 1988, ads costing $250 million promoted Vice President George Bush, the Republican Party candidate who was elected President, and Massachusetts Governor Michael S. Dukakis, the Democratic Party hopeful.

The Olympic Games turned out to be less of an advertising bonanza than expected. The American Broadcasting Companies (ABC) paid $309 million for the TV rights to the Winter Games in Calgary, Canada. ABC's revenue from commercials aired during its Olympic telecasts did not make up for this payment and the cost of producing the telecasts.

The National Broadcasting Company (NBC), which televised the Summer Games in Seoul, South Korea,

had to give advertisers extra commercial time to make up for the fact that an unexpectedly low number of viewers tuned into the games. Television broadcasters sell commercial time on the basis of a guaranteed number of viewers. When the actual number of viewers falls short of the guaranteed viewership, the broadcaster must give the advertiser extra time. Advertisers paid $330,000 for each 30-second prime-time commercial aired during the Summer Games.

As usual, advertisers used the Olympic Games to introduce ad campaigns and to air commercials created especially for the event. For the Winter Games, for example, the Coca-Cola Company paid for the writing of a song that a chorus of young people from 30 countries sang at the opening ceremonies. The song later appeared in Coca-Cola commercials.

During the Summer Games, the Metropolitan Life Insurance Company ran a commercial featuring Charlie Brown and some of his "Peanuts" comic-strip pals running a 400-meter race. And Eastman Kodak Company introduced a campaign for its batteries that starred Stevie Wonder singing a theme he wrote for the commercials.

An antismoking commercial cost the agency that produced it millions of dollars worth of business. In April, Saatchi & Saatchi DFS Compton created a commercial for Northwest Airlines showing passengers cheering an announcement that the airline would ban smoking on all flights. Tobacco giant RJR Nabisco

Bill Whitehead; reprinted with permission from
Advertising Age. © 1988 Crain Communications, Inc.

"I never could've done it without corporate sponsorship."

Incorporated—which manufactures such cigarettes as Winstons and Camels—then took its $80-million cookie and candy account away from Saatchi.

The tobacco industry came under heavy attack in Canada, which in 1988 banned all tobacco advertising on radio and television, and in newspapers and magazines, except for foreign magazines. The ban also prohibited tobacco advertising in stores.

Aspirin ads. Results of a study published in January 1988 indicated that aspirin can help reduce the risk of heart attack. Soon after the publication of the results, Rorer Pharmaceutical Corporation of Fort Washington, Pa., touted the study's conclusions in ads for its product Ascriptin, a combination of aspirin and an antacid. But the attorneys general of New York and Texas complained that the company went too far in using the study to promote Ascriptin. Later in the year, Rorer agreed to halt the ads.

Seashore shell sell. In the summer of 1988, one advertiser saw an opportunity in the pollution of East Coast beaches by medical waste and other debris. The Bahamas, an island nation off the Florida coast and a major tourist attraction, ran print ads showing a huge conch shell on a pristine beach. The headline read, "The only things that wash up on our beaches."

The advertising industry continued to feel the effects of the hostile take-over of JWT Group, Incorporated, of New York City by London-based WPP Group PLC in 1987. In March 1988, a group of executives at Lord, Geller, Federico, Einstein—a unit of JWT—decided to leave JWT to start their own agency. WPP filed suit to prevent the defectors from soliciting business from JWT clients and trying to hire JWT employees. WPP later accused the former executives of sabotaging Lord, Geller's business.

WPP was concerned about preventing a $125-million client, International Business Machines Corporation (IBM), from moving to the new agency. But IBM snubbed both of the feuding agencies and took its business to Wells, Rich, Greene, and Litas: U.S.A. in New York City.

In July, Robert J. Coen, senior vice president and director of forecasting for McCann-Erickson Incorporated, an advertising agency based in New York City, predicted that the Olympic Games and the presidential election would help boost spending on advertising in the United States by 8.4 per cent in 1988. Coen noted that since 1985, spending on advertising has grown more rapidly in certain other countries than in the United States. He predicted that the biggest gainers in 1988 would be Spain and Italy.

After 24 years as the largest advertiser in the United States, Procter & Gamble Company (P & G) lost out to Philip Morris Companies, Incorporated, according to an annual study of ad spending published by *Advertising Age* magazine. Philip Morris' 1987 advertising budget was $1.5 billion, compared with $1.4 billion for P & G. Christine Dugas

In *World Book*, see **Advertising.**

Afghanistan. The Soviet Union began on May 15, 1988, the first stage of a planned withdrawal of its troops from Afghanistan, which it had invaded in 1979. The withdrawal, scheduled to be completed by Feb. 15, 1989, did not end the war between the Communist regime in Kabul and Islamic guerrillas seeking to topple the government.

The withdrawal agreement, negotiated under the auspices of the United Nations (UN), was signed by Afghanistan, Pakistan, the Soviet Union, and the United States in Geneva, Switzerland, on April 14. The planned withdrawal was part of a larger agreement calling for the restoration of a nonaligned Afghan state. The agreement was made possible by an offer, announced on February 8 by Soviet leader Mikhail S. Gorbachev, to withdraw Soviet troops supporting the Kabul regime even if it meant the Afghan regime would fall to the Islamic resistance.

The Soviets, who reported suffering 49,099 casualties in Afghanistan as of May 1, said they would continue supplying arms to Kabul. The United States said it would go on helping resistance guerrillas, who reported in 1987 that more than 1 million Afghans had died in the war.

By Aug. 15, 1988, half the estimated 115,000 Soviet troops had left, according to UN observers, and Soviet forces remained in only 6 of the country's 31 provinces. The Afghan Army also pulled back from some provinces, yielding them to the resistance, but the Communists fought to hold such larger towns as Qandahar and Jalalabad despite the Soviet withdrawal. On December 2, the Soviet Union and Afghan rebels began their first direct talks to reach a political settlement for the country after Soviet withdrawal.

Coalition attempt. Although Afghan leader Najibullah—who uses only one name—was the dominant political leader in the country, he attempted during the year to bring the resistance into a coalition government. In May, Sultan Ali Keshtmand, a Communist, was replaced as prime minister by Mohammad Hassan Sharq, who said he belonged to no party. Resistance leaders based in Peshawar, Pakistan, scorned cooperation with Sharq, however, labeling him a secret agent of the Soviet police.

Resistance politics. The Peshawar leaders, who spoke for only some of the guerrillas operating inside Afghanistan, maneuvered among themselves throughout 1988 to try to organize an Islamic government that might take over from the Communists. The most dynamic leader, Gulbuddin Hekmatyar, advocated rule by strict Muslim traditions but was opposed by others.

Economic pacts. During 1988, the Soviet Union signed numerous agreements providing economic aid from Soviet provinces to local governments in Afghanistan. Plans for continued economic ties indicated that Moscow expected to keep some influence in that country even after the withdrawal. Henry S. Bradsher

See also **Asia** (Facts in brief table). In *World Book,* see **Afghanistan.**

157

Africa

The Organization of African Unity (OAU)—an association of 49 African nations—in 1988 celebrated the 25th anniversary of its founding. Ironically, the OAU era has been marked less by unity than by civil wars, prolonged armed struggles between nations, border clashes, and other forms of conflict. There were signs in 1988, however, that hopes for peace had improved.

Angola and South Africa reach accord. The most promising development was an easing of hostilities in southwestern Africa after more than two decades of armed struggle. With the United States acting as mediator, diplomats from South Africa, Angola, and Cuba—which has some 50,000 soldiers in Angola to support the government—began a series of peace talks in May. By September, the discussions had secured the withdrawal of all South African troops from Angola. South African forces had occupied southern Angola off and on since 1975, allegedly to track down guerrillas who were fighting for the independence of Namibia, which has been controlled by South Africa since 1920.

On Dec. 22, 1988, South Africa, Angola, and Cuba signed a peace agreement at the United Nations (UN). The pact grants Namibia its independence in April 1989. A second agreement, signed by Cuba and Angola, calls for the withdrawal of all Cuban troops from Angola over a 27-month period ending on July 1, 1991. South Africa had made Namibian independence contingent on the Cubans being sent home.

The major issue not negotiated was an end to Angola's civil war—regarded by Angola as a "domestic question." The main rebel force, the National Union for the Total Independence of Angola (UNITA), is supported by South Africa and the United States and occupies roughly one-third of the country. Several African leaders in 1988 were pressing for the inclusion of UNITA in the government of Angola.

Several factors led to the Angolan/Namibian negotiations. Most important, perhaps, was South Africa's desire to disengage itself from the conflict. South African troops suffered heavy losses in February and were decisively defeated in fighting at the Angolan town of Cuito Cuanavale. Another major factor was the influence of the United States and the Soviet Union. At the Moscow summit meeting between President Ronald Reagan and Soviet leader Mikhail S. Gorbachev in May and June, officials of the two nations agreed to cooperate in trying to ease regional conflicts in Africa and other parts of the world.

Other hopeful developments. The conflicting claims of Somalia and Ethiopia to ownership of the Ogaden region in eastern Ethiopia—a cause of war in the late 1970's and of strained relations since then —were apparently laid to rest in 1988. In April, the two nations agreed to a restoration of diplomatic ties, an exchange of prisoners, and the withdrawal of troops from their common border.

The reestablishment of diplomatic ties in May between Morocco and Algeria after a 12-year lapse paved the way for a UN *referendum* (direct vote of the people) on the fate of Western Sahara. On the basis of historic claims, Morocco occupied the territory in 1976 as Spanish forces withdrew. Algeria has given military aid to the Polisario Front, a rebel movement that has struggled for Western Sahara's independence. Morocco and the Polisario Front agreed to the referendum in the disputed territory in August, but rebel attacks on Moroccan positions in September left the fate of the plan in doubt.

The long hostility between Chad and Libya also appeared to be nearing an end in 1988. Libya's head of state, Muammar Muhammad al-Qadhafi, who supported the losing side in a 25-year Chadian civil war that ended in 1987, claims Libyan ownership of the Aozou Strip, a piece of territory in northern Chad. Under UN prodding, Qadhafi tried in 1988 to resolve that issue peacefully with Chad's President Hissein Habré. In October, Chad and Libya renewed diplomatic ties, though Habré would not agree to release Libyan prisoners of war or remove French support troops.

Other settlements in 1988 included the resolution of long-standing border disputes between Nigeria and Benin, Mali and Burkina Faso, and Mali and Mauritania. The leaders of Ghana and Nigeria met in April to put aside more than two decades of bitterness stemming from the periodic deportations they have imposed on workers from each other's nation. And in September, President Samuel K. Doe of Liberia, who has often accused Sierra Leone of taking part in coup attempts against him, agreed to a reconciliation with that country's government.

Malawi's relations with Mozambique, long strained by Malawi's formal diplomatic links with South Africa, also improved in 1988. Malawi sent several hundred troops to Mozambique to help guard a vital rail line against attacks by the rebel Mozambique National Resistance (Renamo).

Where violence still reigned. Renamo's continued destruction of bridges, railroads, and other installations in Mozambique was one of the major unresolved armed conflicts in Africa in 1988. A U.S. Department of State report issued in April documented atrocities carried out by Renamo against civilians, including women and children. The violence in Mozambique has caused some 1 million people to flee to Malawi and other neighboring countries.

New outbreaks of civil war in Burundi and Somalia also swelled the ranks of the continent's refugees. In

South African troops cross the Okavango River into Namibia in August during their withdrawal from Angola as part of a regional peace plan.

Africa

Burundi, violence erupted in August between members of the privileged Tutsi clan, who make up roughly 14 per cent of the population, and the Hutu majority. Estimates of the dead ranged from 5,000 to 25,000; many more people were left homeless or forced to seek refuge in Tanzania and other nearby countries. In Somalia, the leading clan in the north—long resentful of the unequal distribution of government jobs and resources—rebelled in May against the clans that dominate national politics. Battles raged in the north throughout late spring and much of the summer, but government forces maintained the upper hand.

In Sudan, a civil war that has continued with only a brief interruption since the nation gained independence in 1956 reached a new intensity during 1988. The people of southern Sudan, the great majority of whom are Christians or followers of traditional African religions, demand the right to govern themselves. They have resisted efforts of the Muslim-dominated government in the north to apply Islamic law throughout the nation.

Despite a reported build-up of Cuban forces in Ethiopia, rebel groups seeking the secession of the Eritrea and Tigre areas of Ethiopia won major battles from March through June. Conflict there as well as in the Oromo region has frustrated the efforts of international relief agencies to get food to refugees.

In Uganda, President Yoweri Museveni's National Resistance Army continued to fight rebel groups in the north and east. In June, however, one of the two major antigovernment factions, the Uganda People's Democratic Army, signed a peace agreement.

Aborted coups, alleged coup plots, and treason trials were reported from a number of African countries during the year, including Benin, Congo, Equatorial Guinea, Gambia, Kenya, Liberia, Mauritania, Niger, São Tomé and Príncipe, Senegal, Somalia, and Swaziland. In addition, many dictatorial regimes continued to crack down on people who criticized government policies or used strikes or boycotts as a form of protest.

Popular government. In three nations under military rule, however, there was hope for the restoration of popular government. In Nigeria in April, the regime of President Ibrahim Babangida set in motion a process expected to lead to civilian rule under a two-party system by 1992. In June 1988, Uganda's President Museveni promised a return to civilian government by 1990, with a national referendum to determine whether multiparty competition should be permitted. The military rulers of Ghana maintained their strong control of the central government in 1988 but said that democracy would be encouraged in local elections. In December, Ghana held elections for members of 110 district assemblies.

Senegal, one of just six nations in black Africa with a multiparty system—the others are Botswana, Gambia, Madagascar, Mauritius, and Sudan—held presi-

Coffee workers marching in a May Day parade in Goma, Zaire, carry a sign praising the nation's head of state, President Mobutu Sese Seko.

dential and legislative elections in February. But violence erupted when supporters of the main opposition candidate charged that the Socialist Party of President Abdou Diouf—the declared winner in the election—had engaged in electoral fraud and had limited other candidates' access to the media.

Under the single-party systems of most African countries, presidents normally run unopposed. Thus, President Daniel T. arap Moi of Kenya and President Paul Biya of Cameroon faced no challengers in their reelection bids in 1988. In parliamentary and local elections, however, an increasing number of single-party states give voters a choice—provided that all candidates are members in good standing of the dominant party. Such competitive elections were held during the year in Kenya, Cameroon, and Mali, and voters rejected a number of incumbents.

Food and famine. Nine of the 42 sub-Saharan African nations—Angola, Benin, Botswana, Chad, Ethiopia, Madagascar, Malawi, Mozambique, and Niger—needed large amounts of emergency food aid in 1988. During the year, those and 26 other African countries received more than 4.6 million short tons (4.4 million metric tons) of donated food.

Drought, which had been the major natural threat to Africa's food supply for two decades—and which again afflicted Ethiopia—was replaced in 1988 by another of nature's scourges: insects. In the spring, swarms of crop-devouring desert locusts—the worst locust plague in 30 years—spread across northern Africa and the Sahel, the region just south of the Sahara.

Another natural pest, a South American mealy bug that has spread to 31 African countries, was increasing as a problem in 1988. The bug attacks the cassava plant, a root crop that provides almost half the dietary calories of some 200 million Africans. Instead of using pesticides, agricultural officials released wasps that feed on mealy bugs into fields of cassava.

In Ethiopia, Mozambique, and Sudan, civil war outpaced natural forces in disrupting the food supply. Those conflicts prevented the cultivation of crops, turned farmers into refugees, and interfered with the distribution of emergency food to famine areas. Both guerrilla forces and government troops tried to starve the opposing side's civilian base of support. In April, the Ethiopian government prevented all except a few relief agents from distributing food in rebel areas.

Crushing debts. The foreign debt for all of sub-Saharan Africa—other than Nigeria and South Africa—passed the $110-billion mark in 1988. Just paying the interest on that mountain of debt consumed an estimated one-third of all export earnings, leaving little for education, health, and economic development. Three-fourths of Africa's creditors are Western governments—rather than private banks, which hold most other Third World debt. At a June meeting in Toronto, Canada, representatives of the major industrialized nations discussed debt relief for Africa. At the urging of France's President François

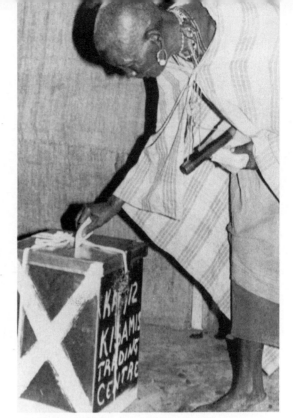

An elderly woman in Kisamis, Kenya, casts her vote in March as the nation holds one-party—but competitive—elections for the National Assembly.

Mitterrand, the creditor nations agreed to stretch out loan repayment, renegotiate interest rates, and consider canceling some debts.

Wildlife. Alarmed at the dwindling numbers of many animal species unique to the continent, African governments continued to step up their conservation efforts in 1988. Wildlife experts noted a few success stories. The population of addax—large antelope that live in the deserts of northern Africa—has increased. Strong government measures in Rwanda are protecting the mountain gorilla from poachers. And Zimbabwe has hired 500 armed scouts to guard the black rhinoceros, which was nearing extinction.

The greatest danger, according to the African Wildlife Foundation, is the killing of elephants by ivory poachers. Largely because of poaching, the elephant population has dropped from an estimated 1.3 million in 1977 to about 700,000. The escalating price for ivory—from $2 per pound (0.45 kilogram) in 1960 to $68 today—has intensified the problem. Wildlife officials warned that only strict conservation efforts by African governments, better marking of legally obtained ivory, and consumer boycotts of contraband ivory will curb the wanton destruction of elephant herds.   J. Gus Liebenow and Beverly B. Liebenow

See also the various African country articles. In the Special Reports section, see **Our Vanishing Rain Forests.** In *World Book*, see **Africa.**

Agriculture. See **Farm and farming.**

Facts in brief on African political units

Country	Population	Government	Monetary unit*	Exports†	Foreign trade (million U.S.$) Imports†
Algeria	24,700,000	President Chadli Bendjedid; Prime Minister Kasdi Merbah	dinar (26.3 = $1)	8,500	7,200
Angola	9,733,000	President José Eduardo dos Santos	kwanza (29.9 = $1)	1,100	1,400
Benin	4,585,000	President Mathieu Kerekou	CFA franc (297 = $1)	131	329
Botswana	1,284,000	President Quett K. J. Masire	pula (1.9 = $1)	653	535
Burkina Faso (Upper Volta)	8,894,000	Popular Front President, Head of State, & Head of Government Blaise Compaoré	CFA franc (297 = $1)	82	324
Burundi	5,290,000	President Pierre Buyoya; Prime Minister Adrien Sibomana	franc (114 = $1)	169	207
Cameroon	10,874,000	President Paul Biya	CFA franc (297 = $1)	2,200	1,700
Cape Verde	358,000	President Aristides Pereira; Prime Minister Pedro Pires	escudo (71.6 = $1)	3	59
Central African Republic	2,836,000	President & Prime Minister André-Dieudonné Kolingba	CFA franc (297 = $1)	145	140
Chad	5,529,000	President Hissein Habré	CFA franc (297 = $1)	99	206
Comoros	502,000	President Ahmed Abdallah Abderemane	CFA franc (297 = $1)	23	42
Congo	2,117,000	President Denis Sassou-Nguesso; Prime Minister Ange Edouard Poungui	CFA franc (297 = $1)	1,300	618
Djibouti	327,000	President Hassan Gouled Aptidon; Prime Minister Barkat Gourad Hamadou	franc (170 = $1)	96	205
Egypt	51,205,000	President Mohammad Hosni Mubarak; Prime Minister Atef Sedky	pound (2.2 = $1)	2,900	11,500
Equatorial Guinea	389,000	President Obiang Nguema Mbasogo; Prime Minister Cristino Seriche Bioko	ekuele (297 = $1)	17	41
Ethiopia	47,709,000	President Mengistu Haile-Mariam; Prime Minister Fikre-Selassie Wogderess	birr (2 = $1)	390	900
Gabon	1,245,000	President Omar Bongo; Prime Minister Léon Mébiame	CFA franc (297 = $1)	1,500	800
Gambia	798,000	President Sir Dawda Kairaba Jawara	dalasi (6.8 = $1)	59	73
Ghana	14,786,000	Provisional National Defense Council Chairman Jerry John Rawlings	cedi (231 = $1)	863	783
Guinea	6,706,000	President and Prime Minister Lansana Conté	syli (440 = $1)	538	511
Guinea-Bissau	929,000	President João Bernardo Vieira	peso (650 = $1)	9	57
Ivory Coast	11,277,000	President Félix Houphouët-Boigny	CFA franc (297 = $1)	3,400	1,600
Kenya	23,727,000	President Daniel T. arap Moi	shilling (19.2 = $1)	1,171	1,462
Lesotho	1,686,000	King Moshoeshoe II; Military Council Chairman Justinus M. Lekhanya	loti (2.3 = $1)	25	343
Liberia	2,494,000	President Samuel K. Doe	dollar (1 = $1)	408	259
Libya	4,271,000	Leader of the Revolution Muammar Muhammad al-Qadhafi; General People's Committee Secretary (Prime Minister) 'Umar Ibrahim al-Muntasir	dinar (0.28 = $1)	5,000	4,500

*Exchange rates as of Dec. 1, 1988, or latest available data (source: Deak International).   †Latest available data.

Country	Population	Government	Monetary unit*	Exports†	Foreign trade (million U.S.$) Imports†
Madagascar	11,240,000	President Didier Ratsiraka; Prime Minister Victor C. Ramahatra	franc (1,327 = $1)	350	453
Malawi	7,928,000	President H. Kamuzu Banda	kwacha (2.85 = $1)	240	260
Mali	9,088,000	President Moussa Traoré	CFA franc (297 = $1)	175	295
Mauritania	1,973,000	President Maaouiya Ould Sidi Ahmed Taya	ouguiya (79 = $1)	400	494
Mauritius	1,123,000	Governor General Sir Veerasamy Ringadoo; Prime Minister Sir Aneerood Jugnauth	rupee (1.33 = $1)	676	685
Morocco	24,086,000	King Hassan II; Prime Minister Azzedine Laraki	dirham (9.1 = $1)	2,450	3,800
Mozambique	15,542,000	President Joaquím Alberto Chissano; Prime Minister Mario da Graca Machungo	metical (626 = $1)	80	480
Namibia (South West Africa)	1,319,000	Administrator-General Louis Pienaar	rand (2.3 = $1)	878	652
Niger	6,894,000	Supreme Military Council President Ali Saibou; Prime Minister Oumerou Mamane	CFA franc (297 = $1)	251	309
Nigeria	109,408,000	President Ibrahim Babangida	naira (3.55 = $1)	6,970	5,500
Rwanda	6,939,000	President Juvénal Habyarimana	franc (75.3 = $1)	162	379
São Tomé and Principe	114,000	President Manuel Pinto de Costa	dobra (73.3 = $1)	10	3
Senegal	7,177,000	President Abdou Diouf	CFA franc (297 = $1)	525	805
Seychelles	70,000	President France Albert René	rupee (5.3 = $1)	5	90
Sierra Leone	4,021,000	President Joseph S. Momoh	leone (37 = $1)	137	155
Somalia	6,535,000	President Mohamed Siad Barre; Prime Minister Mohamed Ali Samantar	shilling (244 = $1)	99	363
South Africa	35,839,000	State President Pieter Willem Botha	rand (2.3 = $1)	21,000	14,000
Sudan	24,188,000	Supreme Council President Ahmed al-Mirghani; Prime Minister Al-Sadiq Al-Mahdi	pound (4.5 = $1)	369	760
Swaziland	736,000	King Mswati III; Prime Minister Sotja Dlamini	lilangeni (2.3 = $1)	311	353
Tanzania	25,079,000	President Ali Hassan Mwinyi; Prime Minister Joseph Warioba	shilling (122 = $1)	411	1,150
Togo	3,345,000	President Gnassingbé Eyadema	CFA franc (297 = $1)	191	233
Tunisia	7,729,000	President Zine El-Abidine Ben Ali; Prime Minister Hedi Baccouche	dinar (0.88 = $1)	2,900	3,500
Uganda	16,811,000	President Yoweri Museveni; Prime Minister Samson Kisekka	shilling (164 = $1)	352	325
Zaire	33,797,000	President Mobutu Sese Seko; Prime Minister Sambwa Pida N'Bagui	zaire (260 = $1)	1,824	1,411
Zambia	7,643,000	President Kenneth David Kaunda; Prime Minister Kebby Musokotwane	kwacha (9.8 = $1)	689	517
Zimbabwe	10,137,000	President Robert Gabriel Mugabe	dollar (2.15 = $1)	1,300	1,000

AIDS

AIDS. The United States Department of Health and Human Services on May 26, 1988, began an unprecedented effort to inform the American public about AIDS (acquired immune deficiency syndrome). AIDS is a disorder that affects the body's disease-fighting immune system. It is caused by the human immunodeficiency virus (HIV), which infects and destroys cells essential to the immune system.

The government effort involved the mailing of more than 106 million copies of a frank, explicit booklet on AIDS to every American household. According to officials, it was the most ambitious attempt ever made to inform the American public about a disease. The eight-page pamphlet, *Understanding AIDS*, described how AIDS is spread and outlined steps the public can take to reduce the risk of infection. Surgeon General of the United States C. Everett Koop urged families to read and discuss the pamphlet.

AIDS cases rise. On September 23, the World Health Organization (WHO) estimated that at least 250,000 cases of AIDS had occurred worldwide. Epidemiologist Jonathan M. Mann, director of WHO's AIDS program, said that 5 million to 10 million people in about 138 countries had already been infected with HIV. During an AIDS conference held in June in Stockholm, Sweden, he predicted that about 1 million new AIDS cases would occur by 1993.

By Dec. 31, 1988, a total of 82,764 cases of AIDS and 46,344 AIDS deaths had been reported in the United States since the AIDS epidemic was first identified in 1981, according to the U.S. Centers for Disease Control (CDC) in Atlanta, Ga. Since Jan. 1, 1988, alone, 20,540 cases and 5,155 deaths had occurred.

Babies tested. The CDC announced on August 23 that more than 1 million newborn babies would be tested for AIDS during 1989 to study transmission of HIV. The test will use blood that is routinely taken from babies by pinprick to test for diseases.

Deadlier than believed. Scientists at the CDC on June 3, 1988, reported evidence showing that infection with HIV is far more serious than was previously believed. Medical authorities had hoped that only a fraction of people infected with the virus would develop AIDS. But a study involving 6,000 homosexual and bisexual men found that almost every person infected with HIV will develop AIDS and die unless a cure is discovered.

Vaccines. The National Institute of Allergy and Infectious Diseases announced on August 25 that a second potential AIDS vaccine would be tested on volunteers at six university medical centers in the United States. Human trials of the first potential AIDS vaccine began in 1987.   Michael Woods

In *World Book*, see **AIDS.**

Air force. See Armed forces.

Air pollution. See Environmental pollution.

Alabama. See State government.

Alaska. See State government.

United States Surgeon General C. Everett Koop explains *Understanding AIDS*, a pamphlet mailed to millions of U.S. households in May and June.

Albania, a long-time isolationist Communist state, in 1988 sharply attacked Soviet leader Mikhail S. Gorbachev's policies of *glasnost* (openness in the flow of information) and *perestroika* (economic and social restructuring). Yet Albania continued to pursue its own brands of glasnost and perestroika. One major result of Albania's new openness in foreign relations—and a measure of its previous policy of isolation—was its participation in the first conference of the Balkan nations since the end of World War II in 1945.

At the Balkan conference, held in Belgrade, Yugoslavia, in February 1988, political observers gave high marks to Albania's Foreign Minister Reis Malile for his readiness to cooperate with the other nations—Bulgaria, Greece, Romania, Turkey, and even Yugoslavia, whose relations with Albania are complicated by ethnic conflict. This conflict involves the status of Kosovo, a province in Yugoslavia. Most residents of Kosovo are ethnic Albanians, many of whom want to upgrade Kosovo to a republic within Yugoslavia. The Yugoslav government has often alleged that Albania wants to absorb Kosovo. While in Belgrade, however, Malile said that he saw Kosovo as a potential bridge to good relations between Albania and Yugoslavia, and that Albania had no territorial claims on Kosovo.

Soviet policies attacked. The June 1988 conference of the Communist Party of the Soviet Union drew the sharpest anti-Soviet comment from Albania in several years. The major newspaper of Albania's Communist party charged on July 9 that the conference "opened doors to all the anti-Communist and counterrevolutionary elements to slander and attack everything sound, socialist, and revolutionary in the life of the Soviet Union."

International agreements. Albania did not allow its ideology to stand in the way of an expansion of economic and technological contacts with Western countries. In 1988, Albania signed economic agreements with France, Greece, Italy, Switzerland, Turkey, and West Germany.

The most significant of these accords was the pact signed with West Germany because it dealt with four areas in which Albania performed poorly in 1987—agriculture, energy, transportation, and construction. Low productivity in these areas dragged down the two segments of the economy that Albania considers top priorities—exports and consumer goods.

Domestic perestroika. Albania continued to cut the number of people involved in the administration of the economy, to hire younger, professionally trained people to manage business enterprises, and to relax the central control of business management. The changes in control are giving added responsibility to local managers of individual business units such as factories and farms.   Eric Bourne

See also **Europe** (Facts in brief table). In *World Book*, see **Albania.**

Alberta. The Winter Olympic Games were held at Calgary, Alberta, for 16 days in February 1988. More than 1,750 athletes from a record 57 countries took part. Some events were delayed because of high winds and warm chinook air currents, but the games were the most profitable in the history of the Winter Olympics. See **Olympic Games.**

The Lubicon Lake Indians, a small band whose land claims had been frustrated by years of court battles, declared themselves a sovereign nation—that is, free of the control of any other government—on Oct. 6, 1988. On October 15, the Indians erected roadblocks around a 3,900-square-mile (10,000-square-kilometer) area they claimed as their traditional hunting grounds. The disputed area, in northwestern Alberta, is used for logging and oil and gas drilling. Police removed the blockade on October 20. Two days later, the band and the province reached a preliminary settlement that would give the Indians control over 95 square miles (250 square kilometers) of wilderness.

On Sept. 24, 1988, six oil companies and the federal and provincial governments announced an agreement to work toward producing synthetic crude oil from the oil sands around Fort McMurray in northern Alberta. They agreed to cooperate in a $4-billion plan (Canadian dollars; $1 = U.S. 84 cents as of Dec. 31, 1988) to produce 75,000 barrels of oil per day by the mid-1990's.   David M. L. Farr

See also **Canada.** In *World Book*, see **Alberta.**

Algeria. Riots broke out in Algiers—Algeria's capital—and nearby areas on Oct. 4, 1988, leading the government to declare a state of emergency. The rioters, mostly young people, protested high prices, unemployment averaging 40 per cent, corruption, and the monopoly of power held by the ruling National Liberation Front (FLN), Algeria's only legal political party. The rioters burned government buildings and shops and destroyed luxury cars belonging to FLN leaders. Although the rioting was spontaneous, Islamic fundamentalists took an active part, leading demonstrations from Algiers' mosques. The official death toll was 159, but independent sources said more than 500 people were killed.

President Chadli Bendjedid, who had earlier introduced reforms to shore up the economy, announced changes in the political system. The changes were approved in a referendum on November 3. Under the new system, the National Popular Assembly, Algeria's parliament, will appoint the prime minister. The cabinet will report to parliament instead of to the FLN. The changes were to take effect in 1989. Independents and representatives of professional groups will also be allowed to run for the Assembly.

On Dec. 22, 1988, Chadli was elected to a third five-year term, getting 81 per cent of the votes in an uncontested election. The government said his reelection was another endorsement of the political changes begun in the fall.

Western Sahara. Algeria restored diplomatic relations with Morocco in May. The move ended a 12-year break caused by Algerian support for Polisario Front guerrillas fighting for the independence of Western Sahara, controlled by Morocco. With the opening of the Moroccan-Algerian border, telephone and electricity links between the two countries were restored. Rail service resumed in September.

Algeria and the Polisario Front took a major step toward resolving the conflict in Western Sahara in August when they accepted in principle a United Nations (UN) peace settlement. The plan included a UN-supervised cease-fire and a referendum allowing residents of the region to choose between independence and integration with Morocco.

Regional relations. Algeria's relations with Tunisia and Libya also improved in 1988. In June, Chadli convened the first North African summit meeting, which included the leaders of Tunisia, Morocco, Libya, and Mauritania. The five leaders agreed to abolish passports and visas for travel within the region.

Also in 1988, two Algerian-funded projects in Tunisia—a cement factory and diesel engine assembly plant—went into production. Closer ties with other North African states stood to benefit Algeria's deteriorating economy, which was hit by declining oil revenues and competition from Greece, Spain, and Portugal for its citrus and wine exports.   William Spencer

See also **Africa** (Facts in brief table). In *World Book*, see **Algeria.**

Rebel UNITA troops in Jamba, Angola, form ranks in June before a picture of their leader, Jonas Savimbi, meeting with U.S. President Ronald Reagan.

Angola. The withdrawal of South African troops from Angola on Sept. 1, 1988, and the promise of independence for South African-controlled Namibia (Angola's neighbor to the south) increased hopes for an end to Angola's 13-year civil war. During the year, a number of African leaders urged Angola's President José Eduardo dos Santos to form a coalition government with all the factions that helped end Portugal's colonial rule in 1975. Dos Santos' Popular Movement for the Liberation of Angola (MPLA) had offered amnesty to individual rebels but refused to deal with the main opposition group, the National Union for the Total Independence of Angola (UNITA).

A major factor in South Africa's exit from Angola was the reinforced strength of Cuban forces assisting the MPLA. From late 1987 to mid-1988, the number of Cuban troops in Angola increased from about 37,000 to an estimated 50,000.

South African forces found themselves on the run both on the ground and in the air. At the town of Cuíto Cuanavale in March 1988, Cuban and Angolan troops ended a long siege and compelled the South African and UNITA forces to retreat into Namibia. And during much of the year, Cuban-piloted Soviet MIG fighters outmaneuvered older South African planes. Increasing casualties and the cost of the war led to growing peace demands within South Africa.

A further pressure toward peace came from Soviet and United States leaders. At a Moscow summit meeting in May and June, the two superpowers agreed to cooperate to end regional conflicts in Asia, Latin America, and Africa. Even before that, the United States had initiated talks between South Africa, Angola, and Cuba.

In a series of meetings in the summer and fall, diplomats and military advisers from the United States and the warring nations hammered out a comprehensive peace plan, including a 27-month timetable for the withdrawal of Cuban troops from Angola. South Africa had indicated that unless the Cubans were sent home, it would not fulfill a pledge to grant Namibia its independence in June 1989. Angola, Cuba, and South Africa signed the peace argeement on Dec. 22, 1988. The pact did not include a formula for ending the internal fighting between the Angolan government and UNITA, but observers felt it was a step in that direction.

Economy. Until the civil war ends, the battered Angolan economy is unlikely to recover. The departure of the Cubans, however, would mean that Angola need no longer use earnings from its exports to finance foreign troops. Optimism regarding the economy was spurred during the year by new oil discoveries and an increase in oil production. The government's trade policies also boosted corn production.

J. Gus Liebenow and Beverly B. Liebenow

See also **Africa** (Facts in brief table). In *World Book,* see **Angola.**

Anthropology. The origin of modern-looking human beings, *Homo sapiens sapiens*, continued to be the focus of much discussion in 1988. In an article published in March, anthropologists Christopher B. Stringer and Peter Andrews of the British Museum (Natural History) in London contended that fossil and genetic evidence strongly supports the theory that modern-looking human beings evolved comparatively recently in Africa. This single-origin theory is one of two main theories proposed by anthropologists to explain the development of *H. sapiens sapiens*.

The single-origin theory suggests that modern-looking human beings evolved in one place—probably Africa—between 100,000 and 200,000 years ago from *archaic* (early) *Homo sapiens*. At that time, groups of archaic *H. sapiens* also lived in Asia and Europe. All members of this group had evolved from *Homo erectus*, an early form of human beings who spread out of Africa, where they had originated, from 1 million to 1.5 million years ago. About 100,000 years ago, groups of *H. sapiens sapiens* migrated from Africa, replacing existing populations of archaic *H. sapiens* in Asia and Europe.

Scientists supporting the single-origin theory believe that modern-looking human beings may have replaced *H. sapiens* because their more advanced anatomy, including a larger brain, or cultural superiority—such as more sophisticated hunting skills—enabled them to compete more successfully for food and other natural resources. Some have suggested that a fully developed language was the critical factor.

The second theory of the origins of *H. sapiens sapiens* suggests that modern-looking human beings evolved independently in a number of places from ancestral populations of *H. erectus* over a period that lasted hundreds of thousands of years. According to this theory, there was enough contact between different groups of *H. erectus* or of archaic *H. sapiens* to prevent the development of different species of modern-looking human beings. These groups were the ancestors of modern racial groups, however.

Stringer and Andrews argued that the fossil evidence supports the single-origin theory. They pointed out that the oldest known *H. sapiens sapiens* fossils have been found at sites in eastern and southern Africa dated to about 100,000 years ago. The oldest known *H. sapiens sapiens* fossils from eastern Asia, Australia, and Europe are considerably younger. In fact, the oldest modern-looking human fossils from western Europe are only 35,000 years old.

Genetic studies. Stringer and Andrews also used evidence from genetic studies to bolster their argument for the single-origin theory. A 1987 study by scientists at the University of Hawaii in Honolulu and the University of California at Berkeley concluded that every person living today can trace his or her maternal ancestry to a woman who lived in Africa about 200,000 years ago. This conclusion was based on studies of a substance called *mitochondrial deoxyribonu-cleic acid* (mtDNA) found outside the nucleus of cells.

MtDNA, which is involved in producing energy for cells, is passed from generation to generation only through the female line. When the scientists compared samples of mtDNA from people whose ancestors came from various parts of the world, they found a greater number of *mutations* (genetic changes) in the mtDNA of people with exclusively African ancestors. This suggested that modern human beings have existed in Africa longer than anywhere else. Calculations of the mtDNA mutation rate led the scientists to conclude that the ancestral woman lived in Africa sometime between 140,000 and 290,000 years ago.

Qafzeh fossils. New evidence supporting the single-origin theory was reported in February 1988 by a team of scientists headed by physicist Bernard Vandermeersch of the Laboratory of Anthropology at the University of Bordeaux in France. The scientists theorized that *H. sapiens sapiens* fossils found in Israel may represent one of the first groups of modern-looking human beings to have migrated from Africa. The fossils, found in a cave called Qafzeh, near Nazareth, in 1973, were recently dated to 92,000 years ago. That date is only slightly later than the date for the oldest known *H. sapiens sapiens* fossils found in Africa.

Neanderthal side branch. The Qafzeh fossils also suggest that Neanderthals were not direct ancestors of modern human beings. Fossil evidence indicates that Neanderthals lived in southwestern Europe as long as 200,000 years ago but did not arrive in the Middle East until about 60,000 years ago. Because this date is 30,000 years after the earliest known date for *H. sapiens sapiens* fossils in this area, it is unlikely that *H. sapiens sapiens* descended from Neanderthals.

Toolmaking. Contrary to a commonly accepted belief, early human beings may not have been the only *hominids* capable of making and using tools, according to research reported in May 1988 by anatomist Randall L. Susman of the State University of New York at Stony Brook. (Hominids include modern human beings and our closest human and prehuman ancestors.) A ruggedly built hominid called *Australopithecus robustus* may also have been a toolmaker.

Susman based his theory on an analysis of 1.8-million-year-old fossil hand bones of *A. robustus* found in a cave in South Africa. *A. robustus*, which became extinct about 1 million years ago, existed at the same time as several species of early human beings. Anthropologists have long believed that *A. robustus* was not advanced enough to make or use tools.

Susman reported that the fingertips of *A. robustus* were broad, like human fingertips. Ape fingertips, in contrast, are narrow. According to Susman, *A. robustus'* thumbs were also remarkably human. The fossil thumbs showed signs of a muscle, used for precision grasping, previously found only in modern human beings and human ancestors.   Donald C. Johanson

See also **Archaeology.** In *World Book*, see **Anthropology; Prehistoric people.**

Archaeologists examine a clay jar found with the skeleton of a Moche warrior-priest in a 1,500-year-old tomb filled with treasure in Peru.

Archaeology. The discovery in Peru of one of the richest unlooted tombs ever found in the Western Hemisphere was reported in September 1988. The tomb, which is about 1,500 years old, is that of a high-ranking Moche warrior-priest. The Moche Indians, a warlike people who were also sophisticated farmers and artisans, dominated the northwestern coast of what is now Peru from A.D. 100 to 700. The tomb was found by archaeologist Walter Alva of the Brüning Archaeological Museum in Lambayeque, Peru. It is near the village of Sipán, about 420 miles (680 kilometers) northwest of Lima.

The tomb lay in a huge pyramid that had been looted often. Alva was drawn to the pyramid in February 1987, after local police arrested grave robbers who had in their possession spectacular gold and silver artifacts plundered from the pyramid. Following the looters' lead, Alva launched an excavation of the pyramid.

The tomb he discovered is the first burial place of a high-ranking Moche individual excavated by scientists that had not been looted by grave robbers. In the tomb were the skeletal remains of a Moche lord who was in his 30's at his death, and more than 100 precious ornaments and pieces of clothing and decorated ceramics. The bones of two women (probably wives of the lord), three male attendants, and a dog surrounded the remains.

The Moche lord was covered in beautifully crafted jewelry, much of it made of gold, silver, and turquoise, and wrapped in three shrouds of finely worked textiles. The body had been put in a wooden coffin, which was then placed in a room within a burial platform made of adobe bricks near the base of the pyramid.

Found with the remains were a large solid gold headdress and strands of gold and silver beads in the shape of peanuts. In his right hand, the Moche lord held a ceremonial rattle decorated with the picture of a warrior beating a prisoner. On his chest was a shield of pure gold weighing about 2 pounds (1 kilogram).

According to anthropologist Christopher B. Donnan of the University of California at Los Angeles—an expert on ancient Peru—the tomb was probably that of a high-ranking warrior-priest. Images of warrior-priests on pieces of Moche art show that the same trappings found in the tomb are associated with that office. The warrior-priest, who is always shown with a spotted dog at his feet, is frequently pictured sacrificing war prisoners.

Origins of farming. An analysis of plant and animal remains from one of the oldest known villages in the world, Tell Abu Hureyra in northern Syria, has revealed new evidence that the origins of farming and settled village life in southwestern Asia were more complicated than archaeologists had believed. The findings at Tell Abu Hureyra, which was occupied nearly continuously from 9500 B.C. to 5000 B.C., were reported in April 1988 by a team of scientists headed by archaeologist Andrew Moore of Yale University in

Forty years after its discovery in Israel, a 2,000-year-old Dead Sea Scroll is unrolled for infrared filming that might reveal indistinct or unseen letters.

New Haven, Conn. The site was excavated in 1974 before being submerged by a lake that was created by the construction of a dam across the nearby Euphrates River.

The scientists found that the first settlement at the site, which lasted from 9500 B.C. until 8100 B.C., was inhabited year-round by people who ate wild plants and animals. This discovery was a surprise because most archaeologists have long accepted the theory that farming led to the development of permanent villages. Moore and his colleagues speculated that the inhabitants maintained their hunting and gathering life style—and settled permanently in the area—because of the region's exceptionally abundant and diverse species of plants and animals. The village was abandoned about 8100 B.C., probably because the climate changed and food became less plentiful.

Farmers resettled the site in 7600 B.C. Although they grew a variety of crops, including grains, beans, and peas, they continued to hunt wild animals, especially the gazelles that passed near the village on annual migrations. This mixed farming and hunting economy lasted nearly 1,000 years, until the people at the site suddenly began domesticating sheep and goats. This may have occurred because of the overkilling of the gazelles. Thus, the record at Tell Abu Hureyra indicates that people lived permanently at the site for nearly 4,000 years before depending fully upon domesticated plants and animals for their food.

Clovis cache. The largest collection of Clovis spearpoints and other stone and bone tools ever found in North America was discovered in an apple orchard in central Washington, according to a report published in April 1988. Clovis spearpoints, which are named for Clovis, N. Mex., where they were first discovered in the 1920's, were used by Ice Age hunters from 11,000 to 11,500 years ago. They are the oldest artifacts discovered in the New World whose age is undisputed. They have been found throughout North America among the skeletal remains of bison, mammoth, and other Ice Age animals. Traces of bovine blood were found on three of the tools, suggesting that the tools were used for killing or butchering bison.

Shroud of Turin. The leader of the Roman Catholic Church in Turin, Italy, reported in October 1988 that the Shroud of Turin, a burial cloth apparently bearing the image of a crucified man and venerated for centuries by many Christians as the burial cloth of Jesus Christ, could not have been His shroud. The finding was made by scientists from three research centers who dated small pieces of the linen cloth, using an advanced form of radiocarbon dating, and found that the linen probably was woven between A.D. 1260 and 1380—that is, much later than Christ's death in A.D. 30.　Barbara Voorhies

In *World Book*, see **Agriculture** (History of agriculture); **Archaeology; Egypt, Ancient; Shroud of Turin.**

Glass towers dominate the new National Gallery of Canada, designed by Israeli-born Canadian architect Moshe Safdie, which opened in Ottawa, Ont., in May.

Architecture. Much of the architectural world's attention turned in 1988 toward Paris, where a vast series of civic buildings moved toward completion. The new buildings, called the *Grands Projets* (Major Projects), had been undertaken by the government of French President François Mitterrand.

Most controversial among the Grands Projets was a remodeling of the national art museum, the Louvre, by Chinese-born American architect I. M. Pei. The remodeling featured a glass pyramid 65 feet (19.8 meters) tall as the main entrance to the museum. Unveiled in March and nearly complete at year's end, Pei's pyramid drew praise from many Parisians. Others thought, however, that the stark modernity of the pyramid clashed with the architecture of the Louvre, the oldest section of which dates from about 1200.

Other Mitterrand projects nearing completion included a new Paris Opéra and the Parc de la Villette, a park in La Villette on the outskirts of Paris. The park's competition-winning design came from French-Swiss architect Bernard Tschumi, who was named during 1988 as dean of Columbia University School of Architecture in New York City. Tschumi's design features 30 bright-red steel structures called "follies" housing snack bars and other park facilities.

Noteworthy buildings. Perhaps the most widely noted single building of 1988 was the new National Gallery of Canada in Ottawa, Ont., which opened in May. Israeli-born Canadian architect Moshe Safdie

(who lives in Cambridge, Mass.) designed the gallery, which stands high on a promontory commanding a view of the Ottawa River. The building is made of pink Canadian granite, with tall octagonal glass towers. It features an ingenious system of interior skylights that reflect sunlight two stories down into some of the gallery spaces.

Other notable buildings of 1988 included:
● Parliament House, the national capitol of Australia, which was opened in Canberra on May 9 by Queen Elizabeth II. The design by American architect Romaldo Giurgola gained widespread praise, though some Australians thought the building too grand for their nation's informal way of life.
● Olympic Village in Seoul, South Korea—a vast, 5,600-apartment complex designed by Korean-born American architect Kyu Sung Woo to house Olympic athletes and visitors. After the Olympics, the complex became a residential neighborhood and shopping center.
● Rowes Wharf by Skidmore, Owings & Merrill of Chicago, a combination of a hotel, offices, and condominium apartments on the Boston waterfront. The complex includes a waterfront plaza where ferryboats can dock.

Competitions—events in which many architects submit designs for the same building and a jury picks the best—continued to make news in 1988. The most notable competition of the year was the one for a new central library in Chicago. The city had hoped to attract hundreds of entrants but—because of a requirement that the architect, contractor, and developer could charge the city no more than $140 million for building the library—only five actually entered. Thomas H. Beeby, a partner in the Chicago firm of Hammond Beeby & Babka Incorporated and dean of the Yale School of Architecture in New Haven, Conn., won with a well-planned neoclassic building.

In Hartford, Conn., local architect Tai Soo Kim, known for his National Museum of Modern Art in South Korea, won a competition for a new city office tower. A design by New York City architect Robert A. M. Stern was chosen for the Norman Rockwell Museum in Stockbridge, Mass. And Moshe Safdie was selected to design a ballet and opera house in Toronto, Canada.

Prominent exhibitions of 1988 included a much-publicized show called "Deconstructivist Architecture" that ran from June to August at the Museum of Modern Art in New York City. Organized by noted architect Philip Johnson, the exhibition proposed that a new style of architecture is emerging. It displayed work by Frank O. Gehry, Bernard Tschumi, and five other architects from around the world, dubbed *deconstructivists*. They all design buildings in a jagged style with many precarious-looking angles and distorted interiors.

In Chicago, a major exhibit, "Chicago Architecture 1872-1922: Birth of a Metropolis," appeared from July to September at the Art Institute of Chicago.

The preservation movement scored a victory when the congregation of Unity Temple in Oak Park, Ill., voted unanimously to conclude an agreement with the Landmarks Preservation Council of Illinois. The agreement will protect the Unity Temple building, designed by the great American architect Frank Lloyd Wright and completed in 1908.

Controversies of various kinds continued in architecture. In New York City, St. Bartholomew's Church challenged the constitutionality of the New York City landmarks law in federal court. The city has repeatedly refused to give St. Bartholomew's, a landmark Episcopal church, permission to replace its chapter house on Park Avenue with a new office tower. The church says it needs the income from the proposed tower to continue its services to the poor. The case is widely regarded as critical for the future of architectural preservation.

In Washington, D.C., there was debate over a proposal to add a statue of a U.S. Army nurse to the Vietnam Veterans Memorial, as well as an American flag at the juncture of the memorial's two black-granite walls bearing the names of the war dead. The American Institute of Architects opposed any further change to the memorial, designed by Maya Ying Lin and regarded as a masterpiece.   Robert Campbell

In the Special Reports section, see **Close Encounters with Public Art**. In *World Book*, see **Architecture**.

Argentina. Approaching the final year of his six-year term and ineligible to succeed himself, Argentine President Raúl Alfonsín seized upon a minor rebellion in January 1988 to purge Argentina's armed forces of officers disloyal to democracy. But even so, Alfonsín had to cut short a visit to the United States on December 2 to fly home and put down a second military coup attempt. The military rebellion ended on December 6, but there were reports that Alfonsín agreed to a key demand put forward by the rebels as a condition for ending the revolt.

Argentines were slated to go to the polls on May 14, 1989, to elect a new president. The opposition Justicialist Party—identified with the late dictator Juan Perón—picked Carlos Saúl Menem, governor of La Rioja province, as its presidential candidate in the party's first-ever primary on July 9, 1988. Menem became the early favorite by promising increased spending on social programs, higher wages, and a five-year moratorium on foreign debt payments—all popular stands with workers.

The ruling Radical Civic Union party chose Eduardo Angeloz, the governor of Córdoba province and a moderate who faces an uphill struggle to win. A third, minor party—the right wing Democratic Center—selected Álvaro Alsogaray, an economist who held high government posts under recent military regimes.

Austerity measures. Although Alfonsín retained the personal popularity he enjoyed because of his

An Argentine soldier loyal to the government of President Raúl Alfonsín stands guard during an unsuccessful military rebellion in January.

Arizona

confrontations with the military, the Argentine president during 1988 was forced to impose unpopular belt-tightening measures that placed a heavy burden on blue-collar workers. For example, on August 2, the government imposed a 30 per cent price increase on most public services and utilities and ordered cuts in government spending.

Alfonsín pointed to these austerity measures as he tried to persuade foreign governments and commercial banks to keep on lending to Argentina. During a visit to the United States from May 30 to June 2, he asked bankers and U.S. officials to help put in place a system that would reduce payments on Argentina's $55-billion foreign debt, while providing for a net inflow of new credit to the country. In October, Argentina paid about $100 million in overdue interest to foreign banks out of a total of $1.2 billion in arrears.

Missile deal. Great Britain—still technically at war with Argentina since the 1982 Falkland Islands conflict—voiced alarm over a newspaper report that Alfonsín had struck a deal with China to jointly manufacture missiles capable of reaching the Falklands from Argentina. Alfonsín visited China from May 13 to 16, 1988. Argentina lost the 1982 war but still claims sovereignty over the Falklands.   Nathan A. Haverstock

See also **Latin America** (Facts in brief table). In *World Book*, see **Argentina.**

Arizona. See **State government.**

Arkansas. See **State government.**

Armed forces. The United States armed forces started 1988 heavily committed in the Persian Gulf, where the eight-year-old war between Iran and Iraq still raged. The U.S. Navy devoted vast resources—more than 30 ships at times—to escorting Kuwaiti tankers through the gulf to ensure oil deliveries to Europe and Japan.

The heaviest fighting came after the Navy frigate U.S.S. *Samuel B. Roberts* hit a mine in international waters of the gulf on April 14. Ten sailors were seriously injured, and the explosion tore a gaping hole in the warship's hull.

Four days later, after the Navy confirmed that the mines had been laid by Iran, U.S. forces struck back with a vengeance. Navy warships assisted by U.S. marines destroyed the Sassan and Sirri oil platforms. The United States said that the Iranian military used both platforms as radar stations. The Iranians retaliated by firing on a U.S. helicopter and attacking the cruiser U.S.S. *Wainwright* and the frigate U.S.S. *Simpson.* The Navy then received White House approval to strike again. A-6 attack aircraft from the aircraft carrier U.S.S. *Enterprise* outside the gulf attacked two Iranian frigates, causing serious damage. No U.S. ships were damaged, though one U.S. helicopter was lost.

Iranian airliner tragedy. On July 3, the crew of the cruiser U.S.S. *Vincennes*, the Navy's most sophisticated Persian Gulf ship, accidentally shot down an Iranian civilian airliner, killing all 290 people aboard.

At the time, the *Vincennes* was engaged in surface combat with a group of Iranian speedboats. Inside the ship's combat-information center, the crew mistook the airliner for an attacking Iranian F-14 fighter. Intelligence had predicted that Iran would try to sink a U.S. warship on the Fourth of July weekend. When the airliner flew toward the *Vincennes* and failed to turn away, despite repeated radio warnings, the Navy said, the ship fired two missiles, at least one of which hit the plane, destroying it. On August 19, the Navy released the results of its investigation into the incident. It said that human errors induced by combat stress had led the ship's crew into thinking the approaching airliner was a hostile fighter.

On July 18, Iran announced that it would accept United Nations (UN) Security Council Resolution 598 calling for a cease-fire in the Iran-Iraq war. Iran cited the downing of the airliner as a decisive factor in its acceptance of the truce. On August 20, the cease-fire took effect under the watchful eyes of UN observers. With hostilities seemingly ended, the U.S. Navy on September 27 abandoned ship-by-ship escort operations, changing to a "zone defense" of gulf ships.

Arms control. In December 1987, the United States and the Soviet Union had signed the Intermediate-Range Nuclear Forces (INF) Treaty agreeing to eliminate their medium-range nuclear missiles. The treaty required ratification by both the U.S. Senate and the Supreme Soviet, the parliament of the Soviet Union.

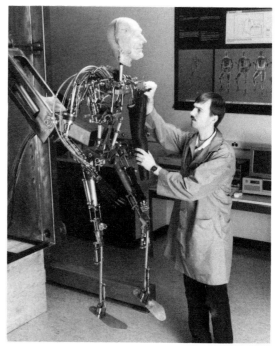

A technician adjusts "Manny," a robot under development for the United States Army to test the durability of protective clothing.

Vice President George Bush and a Soviet official watch as a Pershing II missile engine is destroyed in September in compliance with the INF Treaty.

Senate ratification hinged on lawmakers' concerns over how Soviet fulfillment of the treaty could be verified. After the Administration of President Ronald Reagan agreed to build a new generation of spy satellites, the Senate ratified the treaty by a 93-5 vote on May 27— the eve of President Reagan's meeting with Soviet leader Mikhail S. Gorbachev in Moscow. The Supreme Soviet had already ratified the pact on May 23, and on June 1 the two leaders exchanged documents putting the INF Treaty into force.

On August 1, the Soviets dynamited four SS-12 missiles, the first missiles destroyed under the INF Treaty. On September 8, the United States destroyed two Pershing missile engines, the first American weapons components destroyed under the pact.

Strategic Arms Reduction Talks (START) continued throughout 1988 in Geneva, Switzerland. The talks often bogged down, however, over Soviet insistence on limiting American plans to develop the space-based missile defense system known as the Strategic Defense Initiative (SDI), or "Star Wars."

New weapons. With the passage of the National Defense Authorization Act for the 1989 fiscal year (which began on Oct. 1, 1988), Congress authorized the construction of the Navy's first new class of submarine in 20 years—the SSN-21 Seawolf attack submarine. Planned for launch in 1994, the SSN-21 will be the biggest and most expensive attack submarine ever built. The first five boats will cost nearly $10 billion,

and several harbors will have to be dredged to accommodate the submarine's 34-foot (10.4-meter) draft.

On October 14, the Navy contracted to replace its aging fleet of antisubmarine aircraft, Lockheed P-3 Orions. Lockheed Corporation won the contract to build the new generation of aircraft, named the LRAACA, for Long-Range Air Anti-Submarine Capability Aircraft. The first of as many as 125 of the planes will be delivered in 1994. The total cost of the new aircraft was estimated at $4.9 billion.

On Nov. 22, 1988, the Air Force pulled back the veil of secrecy surrounding the B-2, nicknamed the Stealth bomber, rolling out the aircraft at the Northrop Corporation's Palmdale, Calif., plant. The plane's winglike shape and other features reportedly help it avoid detection by enemy radar. The Air Force also acknowledged that the aircraft had exceeded its budget, with 130 planes costing as much as $42 billion (in 1981 dollars) rather than the $36 billion planned.

Bribery and espionage. A Pentagon bribery scandal was revealed on June 14, 1988, when the Federal Bureau of Investigation (FBI) and the Naval Investigative Service unveiled a two-year joint investigation capped by a search of 31 homes and offices. Former Assistant Secretary of the Navy Melvyn R. Paisley is the central figure in what the FBI called a kickback scheme. Since 1987, Paisley had worked as a consultant to major defense contractors, including McDonnell Douglas Corporation.

173

Armed forces

Paisley is suspected of providing McDonnell Douglas with confidential Pentagon plans and specifications to help the firm win defense contracts. McDonnell Douglas denied the charges, as did Paisley's attorney.

On Aug. 23, 1988, West German police arrested Clyde Lee Conrad, a retired U.S. Army sergeant. Conrad, who spent most of his 20 years in the Army in West Germany, was charged with selling North Atlantic Treaty Organization (NATO) secrets to Hungarian intelligence agents. He was accused of working with seven other people in West Germany and Sweden.

Personnel policies. The findings of a special panel studying the role of women in the military prompted Secretary of Defense Frank C. Carlucci III to order on February 2 a sweeping expansion of that role. By year-end, women were eligible for about 24,000 Army, Navy, Air Force, and Marine jobs previously designated for men.

Defense budget. On February 18, the Reagan Administration submitted its proposed budget for the 1989 fiscal year. In seeking just $299.5 billion for defense—only a 2.8 per cent increase over the $291.4-billion appropriated for defense in fiscal 1988—Reagan signaled the end of the massive weapons build-up that began in 1981. The budget proposed reducing the size of the armed forces by some 36,000, canceling several weapons programs, and retiring older ships and aircraft. The largest single item in the request was $4.9 billion for SDI research and development.

Congress responded by cutting key weapons systems, including the SDI. Reagan then vetoed the budget, setting off two months of intense negotiations. Finally, on Sept. 30, 1988, hours before it was to take effect, Congress passed a compromise budget appropriating $282.4 billion for defense, and Reagan signed it into law on October 1. The measure retained an $800-million cut in SDI funding.

In protest against a cut in the Navy budget that would require abandoning the Administration's goal of a 600-ship Navy, Secretary of the Navy James H. Webb, Jr., resigned on February 22. He was replaced by former White House lobbyist William L. Ball III.

Other developments. On October 25, President Reagan signed a law elevating the Veterans Administration to Cabinet-level status. The President also approved the creation of a politically independent commission to decide which military bases should be closed. On December 29, the panel recommended abolishing 86 bases in the United States. Defense Secretary Carlucci endorsed the recommendations on Jan. 4, 1989. The base closings also required the approval of Congress, which had to either accept or reject the panel's list in its entirety. The base closings would save the government an estimated $693 million annually.   Richard Sandza

In *World Book*, see the articles on the branches of the armed forces.

Army. See **Armed forces.**

The Stealth bomber, designed to evade radar detection, is unveiled by the U.S. Air Force at a Northrop Corporation plant in Palmdale, Calif., in November.

The Art Institute of Chicago's new wing, which features a skylit central court, opened on September 17 with a retrospective of Paul Gauguin's works.

Art. Major museum exhibitions of 1988 included important shows of work by French artists from several periods. Museums in France, Canada, and the United States teamed up to organize a major retrospective of the work of impressionist master Edgar Degas. The exhibition, which included Degas's bathers, ballet dancers, race-track scenes, portraits, and historical subjects—about 300 works in all—premiered at the Grand Palais in Paris from Feb. 9 to May 16, 1988. The show then appeared at the National Gallery of Canada in Ottawa, Ont., from June 16 to August 28 and at the Metropolitan Museum of Art in New York City from Sept. 27, 1988, to Jan. 8, 1989.

"The Art of Paul Gauguin" featured more than 230 paintings, prints, sculptures, and other works by the postimpressionist artist, who traveled to Tahiti and other exotic locales in search of uncorrupted, simple people. The exhibition appeared at the National Gallery of Art in Washington, D.C., from May 1 to July 31, 1988, and at the Art Institute of Chicago from September 17 to December 11. It was to hang at the Grand Palais in early 1989.

United States museums gave elaborate treatment to three French masters from other periods. "Poussin: The Early Years in Rome," the first major North American exhibition of work by the baroque artist Nicolas Poussin, was on view at the Kimbell Art Museum in Fort Worth, Tex., from Sept. 24 to Nov. 27, 1988. The show included 36 paintings and 58 drawings on mythi-cal and Biblical themes. The first full-scale U.S. survey of the work of rococo court painter Jean-Honoré Fragonard appeared at the Metropolitan Museum from Feb. 6 to May 8, 1988. The exhibition, which included some 95 paintings and 130 drawings, had premiered in 1987 at the Grand Palais. "Courbet Reconsidered" offered a fresh perspective on the French realist Gustave Courbet. The exhibition of almost 100 paintings and drawings premiered at the Brooklyn Museum in New York City from Nov. 4, 1988, to Jan. 16, 1989, and was to travel to Minneapolis, Minn., in early 1989.

European moderns. Several shows featured artists who worked in the experimental art community of Paris in the early 1900's. To commemorate the 25th anniversary of the death of Georges Braque, the collage artist who helped found the cubism movement, the Solomon R. Guggenheim Museum in New York City displayed 100 of Braque's works from June 10 to Sept. 11, 1988. "Perpetual Motif: The Art of Man Ray," which featured 268 photographs, paintings, and other works by American-born dadaist and surrealist Man Ray, premiered at the National Museum of American Art in Washington, D.C., from Dec. 2, 1988, to Feb. 20, 1989, and was scheduled for Los Angeles, Houston, and Philadelphia in 1989. A show of 105 works by Swiss-born surrealist sculptor Alberto Giacometti appeared at the Hirshhorn Museum in Washington, D.C., from Sept. 15 to Nov. 13, 1988, and then traveled to the San Francisco Museum of Modern Art to run from Dec. 15, 1988, to Feb. 5, 1989.

From Oct. 28, 1988, to Feb. 26, 1989, the Montreal Museum of Fine Arts in Canada presented more than 150 works by the Russian-born artist Marc Chagall. The pieces, once part of Chagall's estate, were given to French museums under a policy that allows an artist's heirs to donate artwork to the French government instead of paying estate taxes.

Italian art from Venice, Siena, and Florence also highlighted the 1988 museum season. "The Art of Paolo Veronese: 1528-1588," which commemorated the 400th anniversary of the Venetian painter's death, opened Nov. 13, 1988, at the National Gallery of Art, to run to Feb. 20, 1989. "Painting in Renaissance Siena: 1420-1500," which presented about 140 altarpiece panels and manuscript illuminations, opened Dec. 20, 1988, at the Metropolitan Museum, to run to March 19, 1989. "Michelangelo: Draftsman/Architect," which appeared at the National Gallery of Art from Oct. 9 to Dec. 11, 1988, included some 81 works in the largest U.S. show ever devoted to the Florentine master's drawings.

Ancient cultures of Egypt, Greece, and Japan were also featured in 1988 exhibitions. "Cleopatra's Egypt: Age of the Ptolemies"—nearly 150 examples of Egyptian statuary, jewelry, vessels, figurines, and other objects dating from the years 305 to 30 B.C.—appeared at the Brooklyn Museum from Oct. 7, 1988, to Jan. 2, 1989, and was to travel to Detroit and to Munich, West Germany, in 1989.

"The Human Figure in Early Greek Art," a collection of 67 bronzes, marbles, and pottery figures dating from 900 to 400 B.C., appeared at the National Gallery of Art from Jan. 31 to June 12, 1988; at the Nelson-Atkins Museum of Art in Kansas City, Mo., from July 16 to Oct. 2, 1988; and at the Los Angeles County Museum of Art from Nov. 13, 1988, to Jan. 15, 1989. The show was also scheduled to tour to Chicago and Boston in 1989. "Japan: The Shaping of Daimyo Culture 1185-1868," the most comprehensive exhibition ever of art and artifacts from Japan's feudal age, was on view at the National Gallery of Art from Oct. 30, 1988, to Jan. 23, 1989.

German expressionism, new and old, continued to be popular in 1988 exhibitions. The first U.S. museum retrospective of Anselm Kiefer, a 43-year-old West German neoexpressionist painter, appeared at the Art Institute of Chicago from Dec. 5, 1987, to Jan. 31, 1988; the Philadelphia Museum of Art from March 6 to May 1; the Los Angeles Museum of Contemporary Art from June 12 to September 11; and the Museum of Modern Art in New York City from Oct. 17, 1988, to Jan. 3, 1989. "German Expressionism 1915-1925: The Second Generation," which featured some 200 paintings, sculptures, and graphics by such artists as Max Beckmann, Otto Dix, Käthe Kollwitz, and George Grosz, premiered at the Los Angeles County Museum of Art from Oct. 9 to Dec. 31, 1988, and was due to

travel in 1989 to Fort Worth, Tex., and two West German cities.

Still-life painting formed the focus for two major exhibitions. "A Prosperous Past: The Sumptuous Still Life in the Netherlands 1600-1700" appeared at Harvard University's Fogg Art Museum in Cambridge, Mass., from Oct. 1 to Nov. 27, 1988, and at the Kimbell Art Museum from Dec. 10, 1988, to Jan. 29, 1989. Thirty-two paintings by Raphaelle Peale, the first great American still-life painter, appeared at the National Gallery of Art from Oct. 16, 1988, to Jan. 29, 1989, and were scheduled to travel to Philadelphia.

The Venice Biennale, a huge international show of contemporary art that has been hosted by the city of Venice, Italy, every other year since 1895, ran from June 26 to Sept. 25, 1988. Artists from 40 countries participated. The show's grand prize went to American artist Jasper Johns, whose pop paintings were shown in the newly renovated U.S. pavilion in Venice's public gardens. The Johns show later appeared at the Philadelphia Museum of Art from Oct. 23, 1988, to Jan. 8, 1989.

The museum building boom continued in 1988. The National Gallery of Canada opened its new $130-million building—designed by Israeli-born Canadian architect Moshe Safdie and constructed of glass, rose granite, and concrete—on May 21. The Art Institute of Chicago unveiled its new $23-million annex on September 17. The three-story addition, designed by Chicago architect Thomas H. Beeby, has 66,640 square feet (6,000 square meters) of gallery space. On December 11, the Princeton University Art Museum opened its $8.25-million new wing, designed by Philadelphia architects Mitchell/Giurgola. And the St. Louis Art Museum completed its $31-million renovation of its west wing, originally built in 1904 by Cass Gilbert.

Auctions continued to make front-page news in 1988—not only for record-breaking prices, but also for unusual collections and causes. The New York City-based auction house of Sotheby's conducted historic sales in Beijing (Peking in the traditional Wade-Giles spelling) and in Moscow. In Beijing, on June 5, 73 contemporary Chinese artworks and other items brought a total of nearly $500,000. Auction proceeds were earmarked to help pay for restoration of China's Great Wall and the Italian city of Venice. On July 7, in Moscow, Sotheby's auctioned 101 works by 29 contemporary Soviet artists and 18 works by avant-garde artists of the early 1900's. The event—the first international art auction in Soviet history—brought a total of $3.6 million, more than three times the expected revenue. The top sale price among the contemporary works went to Grisha Bruskin's 1986 painting *Fundamental Lexicon*, which sold for $416,000.

In a 10-day event beginning on April 23, Sotheby's in New York City sold off the collection of pop artist Andy Warhol, who died in 1987. Warhol's eclectic collection of nearly 10,000 objects, ranging from flea-market trinkets to rare antiques and contemporary paintings, brought a total of $25.3 million. By the terms of the artist's will, the proceeds were to help establish the Andy Warhol Foundation for the Visual Arts. The foundation, which is scheduled to begin operation in 1989, will make grants to support visual-arts organizations in the United States and in other countries, arts publications, performing-arts projects with visual-arts components, and preservation of parks and landmarks.

Auctions in New York City and London in 1988 set new price records, most of them occurring within a three-week span in November. On November 10, Sotheby's in New York City sold *False Start*, a 1959 painting by Jasper Johns, for $17 million—the highest recorded price for a work by a living artist. That topped the record of $7 million that another Johns piece had set only the day before. *False Start* had first been sold in 1960 for $3,150, and only half of that sum had gone to the artist.

On November 14, Pablo Picasso's 1901 painting *Maternity* sold at Christie's auction house in New York City for $24.7 million, the highest price ever paid for a painting created in the 1900's. That record stood for only two weeks; on November 28, Picasso's 1905 painting *Acrobat and Young Harlequin* brought $38.5-million at Christie's in London.   Walter Robinson

In the Special Reports section, see **Close Encounters with Public Art**. In *World Book*, see **Art and the arts; Painting; Sculpture.**

Asia led the world in economic growth in 1988, and most Asian countries prospered. Farmers saw less prosperity than city dwellers did, but generally good weather and rising commodity prices helped them. A few countries were hit by flooding or severe earthquakes, however. Diplomatic activity gave hopes of ending the region's largest wars, but millions of Asians continued to live as refugees.

From Japan and South Korea to Thailand and India came reports of booming economies. Although some countries, particularly Vietnam and China, experienced economic problems, Asia's overall rate of economic growth was about 6 per cent, compared with about 3.5 per cent for the world's industrial nations.

For the Asian struggling to grow enough food on a small piece of land, the main factor in relieving hardship was better weather than 1987's droughts and floods. After four years of subnormal rainfall, monsoon rains gave India bumper crops in 1988. Across Southeast Asia, weather was fairly normal, except for a drought in Laos that reduced crops there by about 20 per cent. Most parts of East Asia were also able to grow adequate amounts of food.

Floods. Bad weather forced China to import food to feed its population of more than 1 billion people, however, and two areas of South Asia just below the Himalaya experienced severe flooding during the monsoon. According to experts, the monsoon rainfall was so destructive primarily because deforestation of

Bangladesh was swamped by catastrophic floods for the second consecutive year in 1988. About 25 million Bangladeshis were left homeless.

Great Britain's Prime Minister Margaret Thatcher is greeted by children at a refugee camp for Kampucheans during her August trip to Thailand.

the mountains allowed rain water to cascade down the slopes rather than soak into the soil. As a result, for the second year in a row, Bangladesh had the worst floods ever recorded. About three-quarters of the country was affected, and 25 million people were left temporarily homeless. The Punjab region in India and Pakistan also suffered damaging floods.

Earthquakes. Nature also beset Asia with earthquakes in the geologically active region north of India. On August 21, an earthquake hit central and eastern Nepal and adjacent parts of India. Nepal officials said the quake killed at least 721 people, caused more than $200 million in damage, and dealt a major blow to economic development in the impoverished, technology-lacking area. The earthquake also killed at least 294 people in India. On November 6, an even stronger earthquake hit 800 miles (1,300 kilometers) to the east in China's Yunnan Province along the Burmese border. About 730 people died in this remote region.

Hopes for peace. Insurgencies continued in several Asian countries, including a Communist attempt to take power and a Muslim regional separatist movement in the Philippines, Tamil separatism in Sri Lanka, various separatist efforts in Burma, and a Sikh demand for independence from India. But negotiations brought some hope of peace in the two largest wars —in Afghanistan and Kampuchea (formerly called Cambodia).

Under the auspices of the United Nations (UN), Afghanistan, Pakistan, the Soviet Union, and the United States agreed in Geneva, Switzerland, on April 14, that Soviet troops would be withdrawn from Afghanistan by Feb. 15, 1989. By Aug. 15, 1988, as agreed, half of the troops had left. The Soviets had entered Afghanistan in 1979 to keep that country's Communist regime from falling to Islamic guerrillas.

Vietnam, which had invaded Kampuchea in 1978 to set up a friendly Communist regime, announced in 1988 the withdrawal of half of the Vietnamese troops that had been fighting the resistance there. Vietnam promised to withdraw the remaining troops sometime in 1990. But several international meetings during 1988 failed to resolve whether power in Kampuchea would shift to a popularly accepted coalition or to the largest resistance group—the Khmer Rouge—whose atrocities had been responsible for more than 1 million deaths in the late 1970's.

Three months of localized border fighting between Thailand and Laos ended in a cease-fire on February 19. By late February, Vietnam had withdrawn half of the 40,000 troops it had stationed in Laos.

A confrontation that stopped short of war occurred in the Spratly Islands in the South China Sea. China, Taiwan, Vietnam, the Philippines, and Malaysia all claim some of these tiny coral atolls. Each nation has some outposts on the islands, which are believed to contain oil reserves. Vietnam accused China of sending

Facts in brief on Asian countries

Country	Population	Government	Monetary unit*	Exports†	Foreign trade (million U.S.$) Imports†
Afghanistan	18,136,000	President & People's Democratic General Secretary Najibullah; Prime Minister Mohammad Hassan Sharq	afghani (50.6 = $1)	565	848
Australia	16,315,000	Governor General Sir Ninian Stephen; Prime Minister Robert Hawke	dollar (1.15 = $1)	22,600	26,100
Bangladesh	112,335,000	President Hussain Muhammad Ershad; Prime Minister Moudud Ahmed	taka (32.2 = $1)	820	2,300
Bhutan	1,538,000	King Jigme Singye Wangchuck	Indian rupee (15.0 = $1) & ngultrum (15.0 = $1)	15	69
Brunei	267,000	Sultan Sir Hassanal Bolkiah	dollar (1.9 = $1)	2,200	625
Burma	40,090,000	Military Council Chairman and Prime Minister Saw Maung	kyat (4.8 = $1)	407	627
China	1,097,432,000	Communist Party General Secretary Zhao Ziyang; Premier Li Peng; President Yang Shangkun; Central Military Commission Chairman Deng Xiaoping	yuan (3.72 = $1)	31,100	43,200
India	813,445,000	President R. Venkataraman; Prime Minister Rajiv Gandhi	rupee (15.0 = $1)	11,700	17,100
Indonesia	178,505,000	President Suharto; Vice President Sudharmono	rupiah (1,716 = $1)	15,000	11,100
Iran	53,141,000	President Ali Khamenei; Prime Minister Mir Hosein Musavi-Khamenei	rial (67.7 = $1)	12,300	10,000
Japan	123,980,000	Emperor Hirohito; Prime Minister Noboru Takeshita	yen (122 = $1)	210,800	127,500
Kampuchea (Cambodia)	6,855,000	People's Revolutionary Party Secretary General & Council of State President Heng Samrin (Coalition government: President Prince Norodom Sihanouk; Vice President Khieu Samphan; Prime Minister Son Sann)	riel (100 = $1)	3	28
Korea, North	22,420,000	President Kim Il-song; Premier Yon Hyong Muk	won (0.97 = $1)	1,700	2,000
Korea, South	43,068,000	President Roh Tae Woo; Prime Minister Kang Young Hoon	won (688 = $1)	46,900	40,500
Laos	3,923,000	Acting President Phoumi Vongvichit; Prime Minister Kaysone Phomvihan	kip (430 = $1)	59	205
Malaysia	16,954,000	Paramount Ruler Sultan Iskandar Yang di-Pertuan Agong; Prime Minister Mahathir bin Mohamed	ringgit (2.68 = $1)	13,900	10,800
Maldives	207,000	President Maumoon Abdul Gayoom	rufiyaa (8.8 = $1)	23	52
Mongolia	2,093,000	People's Great Khural Presidium Chairman Jambyn Batmonh; Council of Ministers Chairman Dumaagiyn Sodnom	tughrik (3.36 = $1)	no statistics available	
Nepal	18,054,000	King Birendra Bir Bikram Shah Dev; Prime Minister Marich Man Singh Shrestha	rupee (24 = $1)	130	365
New Zealand	3,389,000	Governor General Sir Paul Reeves; Prime Minister David R. Lange	dollar (1.55 = $1)	5,880	6,100
Pakistan	109,741,000	President Ghulam Ishaq Khan; Prime Minister Benazir Bhutto	rupee (18.6 = $1)	3,700	5,400
Papua New Guinea	3,738,000	Governor General Sir Kingsford Dibela; Prime Minister Rabbie Namaliu	kina (0.82 = $1)	1,033	978
Philippines	59,660,000	President Corazon Aquino	peso (20.7 = $1)	5,200	6,200
Singapore	2,673,000	President Wee Kim Wee; Prime Minister Lee Kuan Yew	dollar (1.95 = $1)	22,500	25,500
Sri Lanka	17,215,000	President J. R. Jayewardene; Prime Minister Ranasinghe Premadasa	rupee (33 = $1)	1,200	1,950
Taiwan	20,289,000	President Lee Teng-hui; Prime Minister Yu Kuo-hwa	dollar (28.1 = $1)	39,800	24,200
Thailand	54,835,000	King Bhumibol Adulyadej; Prime Minister Chatichai Choonhavan	baht (25.1 = $1)	8,800	9,200
Union of Soviet Socialist Republics	289,280,000	Communist Party General Secretary & Supreme Soviet Presidium Chairman Mikhail S. Gorbachev; Council of Ministers Chairman Nikolai I. Ryzhkov	ruble (0.67 = $1)	97,053	88,874
Vietnam	64,807,000	Communist Party General Secretary Nguyen Van Linh; Council of State Chairman Vo Chi Cong; Council of Ministers Chairman Do Muoi	dong (2,600 = $1)	785	1,590

*Exchange rates as of Dec. 1, 1988, or latest available data (source: Deak International).   †Latest available data.

warships into the area in January. On March 14, Chinese and Vietnamese ships fought briefly there, and each country built up garrisons on its atolls, but the tension subsided.

Refugees. Wars kept millions of Asians in miserable refugee camps. The UN launched an effort to rehabilitate the 3 million Afghan refugees living in Pakistan and another 2.5 million now in Iran when the war in Afghanistan ends. Removing the millions of land mines planted by the Soviets in Afghanistan was a major problem.

And refugees continued to pour out of Indochina. Since the Vietnam War ended in 1975, 1.6 million refugees have left Vietnam, Kampuchea, and Laos. Most have been resettled outside the region—the United States has taken 860,000, for example—but some 150,000 refugees remain in camps in Thailand, Malaysia, and other Southeast Asian countries. Another 300,000 Kampucheans, considered "displaced" rather than refugees, live in Thai camps.

Most Indochinese refugees in 1988 were fleeing the economic hardships caused by the Communist regimes in their homelands, especially Vietnam. But nearby countries were unwilling to accept the refugees, saying that the people were not victims of political persecution but economic migrants who might become stuck in those already overpopulated countries.

An international conference on the refugee problem was held in Bangkok, Thailand, in October to prepare for a greater effort to relieve the plight of refugees in 1989. Vietnam attended and asked other countries to fund the return of Vietnamese refugees to Vietnam.

Under an "orderly departure program" sponsored by the UN, the number of people leaving Vietnam with visas reached a monthly record of 3,233 in September 1988. The emigrants included several hundred of the estimated 25,000 Amerasian children fathered by U.S. servicemen during the Vietnam War, who were beginning to be resettled in the United States.

Maldives coup attempt. Mercenaries made an unsuccessful attempt to seize control of the Maldives, a country of some 207,000 people, mainly Muslims, living on about 210 coral islands off the southwestern tip of India. Before dawn on November 3, more than 100 gunmen came ashore at Male, the capital, and attacked the residence of President Maumoon Abdul Gayoom, who had won reelection to a third five-year term on September 23 with 96 per cent of the vote. The mercenaries reportedly had been hired from a small group of Tamil separatist militants in nearby Sri Lanka. The soldiers were led by Abdullah Luthufi, a onetime aide to former Maldivian President Ibrahim Nasir, whose followers had tried to overthrow Gayoom in 1980 and 1983. Nasir, now a businessman in Singapore, denied any involvement.

Gayoom escaped from his residence and appealed to India for help. By early evening, while the gunmen

Tibetan refugees living in New Delhi, India, burn a Chinese flag on March 12 to commemorate a 1959 Tibetan uprising against Chinese rule.

were still trying to capture the government security headquarters in Male, 1,600 Indian paratroopers arrived. They quickly restored order, with the day's fighting killing 14 and wounding 40. Many of the gunmen fled in three ships, taking 24 hostages, 4 of whom were killed before the Indian Navy captured the gunmen early on November 6. Five days later, Gayoom was inaugurated for his third term.

Singapore held parliamentary elections on September 3. Prime Minister Lee Kuan Yew called the elections on only 17 days' notice as a referendum on his rule, which had been increasingly criticized for being dictatorial.

After 29 years as the leader of the small island nation, Lee was quick to move against his opponents. Eight alleged Marxists who had been arrested in 1987 and released were detained again on April 19, 1988, for publicly complaining that they had been tortured while in custody. Lee also accused outsiders of interfering in Singapore's affairs. The circulation of several international publications was restricted on the charge that their reporting interfered in local affairs.

On May 7, a U.S. diplomat was asked to leave the country because, according to local authorities, he was becoming too involved in Singapore's politics. The diplomat had met with Francis T. Seow, a former solicitor general who had been jailed after representing the eight alleged Marxists in court. The United States insisted, however, that the diplomat was merely following the normal diplomatic practice of talking with members of all political sides.

In the September elections, Lee's People's Action Party won 63 per cent of the vote—down slightly from the previous election—and 80 of the 81 seats in Parliament. In the most hotly contested race, Seow lost narrowly. Lee was sworn in on September 13, three days before his 65th birthday, for his eighth term as prime minister.

Brunei, an oil-rich country of 267,000 people in Southeast Asia, remained under the absolute rule of Sultan Sir Hassanal Bolkiah. On January 27, the government dissolved the main political party, the Brunei National Democratic Party, and officials later arrested two party leaders. The party had in late 1987 called publicly for the sultan to end a 25-year-old state of emergency, give up the prime minister's post, and call elections.

Hong Kong continued to boom economically, with many new buildings going up. But worries grew about what will happen politically after China takes control of Hong Kong in 1997 under an agreement made with Britain in 1984. In April 1988, a committee named by China released the draft of a constitution for Hong Kong that many citizens felt failed to live up to the guarantees of freedom promised by China. Skilled professionals began to emigrate.   Henry S. Bradsher

See also the various Asian country articles. In the Special Reports section, see **Our Vanishing Rain Forests** and **The Two Koreas**. In *World Book*, see **Asia**.

Astronomy. Several exciting discoveries, including a remarkable pulsar and an Einstein ring, marked the year 1988 in astronomy. Astronomers also found rare light echoes from a supernova and learned that the planet Pluto has an atmosphere.

A deadly pulsar. Using the 305-meter (1,000-foot) radio telescope at Arecibo, Puerto Rico, astronomers on March 3 discovered a *pulsar* that showers Earth with pulses of radio energy hundreds of times per second. A pulsar is a highly magnetized, rapidly rotating, and extremely compact star. Beams of radio waves from the pulsar sweep across the sky as it spins on its axis, like radar scanning the sky. When a beam crosses Earth, astronomers observe it as a pulse of radio energy from the direction of the pulsar. The new-found pulsar is spinning so rapidly that its pulses are received at an average rate of 625 times per second.

Astronomers Andrew S. Fruchter, Daniel R. Stinebring, and Joseph H. Taylor of Princeton University in New Jersey also discovered that this pulsar has a remarkable feature. They noticed that the rate of the pulses increases or decreases once every 9 hours and 10 minutes. They identified this interval as the orbital period of the pulsar as it orbits a companion star. When the pulsar is on that part of its orbit in which it is moving toward Earth, the pulses arrive more frequently than their average rate. When the pulsar is orbiting away from Earth, the pulses arrive less frequently than average.

Further, the Princeton astronomers found that once in each orbital period, the pulses disappear for about 50 minutes. Their disappearance indicates that the pulsar is being eclipsed as it orbits behind its companion star.

Calculations revealed the startling information that the pulsar's companion is at least 50 per cent larger than our sun, yet has a mass only about 20 times greater than Jupiter, the largest planet in our solar system. The researchers concluded that the companion star was once much more massive, but that a wind of high-energy atomic particles from the pulsar is blasting into the star, heating it and driving its matter off into space.

Confirmation came on May 9. Pulsar specialist Shrinivas R. Kulkarni of the Palomar Observatory in southern California, working with Fruchter and astronomer Stanislaus Djorgovski of Palomar, used the 60-inch (152-centimeter) telescope there to detect the companion star.

The astronomers found that as the companion star follows its orbit, it gets alternately brighter and fainter. When the companion star is behind the pulsar, the hemisphere that faces the pulsar also faces Earth. At this point, the star appears at least 16 times brighter than when the companion star is in front of the pulsar and the hemisphere that faces Earth no longer faces the pulsar. The greater brightness of the hemisphere that faces the pulsar is due to the heating of the star by the pulsar's wind.

One of the world's largest radio telescopes—300 feet (90 meters) in diameter—at Green Bank, W. Va., collapsed in November in a major setback for astronomy.

A celestial ring. In June, radio astronomers led by Jacqueline N. Hewitt of the Haystack Observatory in Westford, Mass., reported finding an object that gives off radio waves in the shape of an elliptical ring. The astronomers used the world's most powerful radio telescope—the Very Large Array Telescope near Socorro, N. Mex.

Hewitt concluded that the object may be the first known *Einstein ring*—the image of a distant celestial object, distorted to a ring shape by the bending of its visible light or radio waves by the gravitational field of another object. Physicist Albert Einstein speculated in 1936 that the light from a distant star might be bent so that as seen from Earth it would appear as a ring. This bending would occur if another star was at the right distance and position between the more distant star and Earth.

Einstein concluded that such a phenomenon was highly unlikely, but he overlooked the more likely possibility that a similar effect will occur if an intervening object is located in front of an extremely distant galaxy. If Hewitt's interpretation is correct, the object she discovered is a powerful radio galaxy, its appearance altered by the gravity of a huge mass located on a line of sight between the galaxy and Earth.

An atmosphere on Pluto. On June 9, planetary scientist James L. Elliott of the Massachusetts Institute of Technology in Cambridge and his colleagues studied a rare *occultation* of a star by the planet Pluto. (An occultation is the passage of a planet, moon, or asteroid in front of another object in space.)

Elliott and his colleagues made their observations on the Kuiper Airborne Observatory, a C-141 jet aircraft operated by the National Aeronautics and Space Administration (NASA) and equipped with a 36-inch (90-centimeter) telescope. Other investigators watched with telescopes at Mount John and other locations in New Zealand as well as in Tasmania and Queensland, Australia. The astronomers found that the star began to fade before Pluto passed in front of it, and that it brightened gradually after Pluto had gone by. If Pluto had no atmosphere, the star would have faded abruptly, then brightened abruptly again. The investigators concluded that Pluto has an atmosphere of methane gas. The atmosphere caused the gradual fading of the star and the slow brightening observed when the star reappeared.

Interstellar echoes. On March 3, astronomer Arlin Crotts of the University of Texas in Austin discovered two faint, concentric arcs of light around Supernova 1987A, a massive star that was observed exploding in February 1987. Crotts identified the arcs, which he photographed with a 40-inch (100-centimeter) telescope at the Las Campanas Observatory in northern Chile, as *light echoes*—reflections of the supernova explosion from clouds of interstellar dust.

The inner and outer arcs were located on clouds situated about 440 and 950 *light-years*, respectively, in

182

front of the supernova as seen from Earth. A light-year is the distance light travels in a year—about 5.9 trillion miles (9.5 trillion kilometers). The light echoes took about a year longer to reach Earth than the direct rays of the supernova, which took about 160,000 years to arrive. Through the remainder of 1988, the two concentric arcs of light grew larger and became visible as complete circles around the supernova.

Meanwhile, astronomers using infrared telescopes aboard the Kuiper Airborne Observatory and others using NASA's unmanned *Solar Maximum Mission* satellite monitored radiation from the supernova that revealed the presence of heavy chemical elements, including iron and cobalt, which were created in its explosion. This finding confirmed a theory first proposed in the 1940's that supernovae explosions create iron and other heavy elements.

Faraway galaxies. In August 1988, astronomers led by Kenneth Chambers, a graduate student at Johns Hopkins University in Baltimore, said they had identified the most distant known galaxy. Using the 84-inch (213-centimeter) telescope on Kitt Peak in Arizona, they found that the galaxy designated 4C41.17 is so far away that it took 15 billion years for its light to reach Earth. The galaxy is enveloped by a cloud of hydrogen gas more than 300,000 light-years in diameter.   Stephen P. Maran

In *World Book*, see **Astronomy.**

Australia. In 1988, Australia celebrated the 200th anniversary of the arrival of the British in what is now the city of Sydney. Australians took the Australian Bicentennial Authority's slogan—"Let's Make It Great in 88"—to heart, planning hundreds of events to commemorate the historic occasion. See **Close-Up.**

Government. The Australian Labor Party government led by Prime Minister Robert Hawke enjoyed considerable public support in 1988. The Labor Party's favorable standing with the public was helped by dissension within the opposing National and Liberal parties. The National Party appeared to exert more influence on the National-Liberal coalition, even though it had fewer members in Parliament and its position on the economy and other issues was more extreme. The National Party's image, however, suffered from conflicts between its members of Parliament from Queensland and New South Wales.

Political upset. Control of the government of New South Wales changed for the first time in 12 years after state elections on March 19. The National-Liberal coalition defeated the Labor Party and won a majority in the state parliament.

On March 25, Liberal leader Nick Greiner became premier of New South Wales, succeeding Labor leader Barrie Unsworth. Greiner focused on changes in education, health, and other state services. In a state election in Victoria on October 1, the Labor government under John Cain was reelected.

Fireworks fill the sky over Sydney Harbour on January 26 as Australians celebrate the bicentennial of the arrival of the first European settlers.

Visitors take in the sights of World Expo 88—with the theme "Leisure in the Age of Technology"—which opened a six-month run in Brisbane in April.

Race relations. A series of discussions about Asian immigration and the rights of Aborigines, the descendants of Australia's original inhabitants, marked 1988. Several conservative groups, especially National Party members, demanded a reduction in the number of Asian immigrants allowed to enter Australia. They felt a reduction was necessary to encourage "national cohesion" among Australians. Liberal Party leader John Howard appeared to want a similar reduction.

Discussions about the plight of the Aborigines, one of Australia's most pressing social problems, heated up during the year. To call attention to their problems, many Aborigines staged peaceful demonstrations during some bicentennial events, and Gerry Hand, minister for Aboriginal affairs, boycotted the opening bicentennial ceremony on January 26 in Sydney in a gesture of support.

On January 27, a government commission led by former Supreme Court Justice James Muirhead launched an investigation into a highly emotional question—why a large number of Aborigines die while in police custody. Since 1980, there have been more than 100 such deaths.

Hayden resigns. Foreign Minister William Hayden resigned from his post and from Parliament in August to succeed Sir Ninian Stephen as governor general in 1989. (The governor general is Australia's local head of state and is the representative of Queen Elizabeth II, who is also the Australian monarch.)

Economy. Improved commodity prices and continued economic growth helped spur the Australian dollar in 1988 to its highest level against most major foreign currencies since January 1985. The Australian dollar rose from a low of $A 1 = U.S. 65 cents in January 1987 to about U.S. 87 cents in December 1988. The economy grew at a rate of about 3.5 per cent. Inflation and unemployment both fell during 1988 from 8 per cent to 7 per cent.

These positive conditions were offset by a substantial foreign debt and trade deficit caused by a high demand for imported goods and services. Treasurer Paul Keating attempted to deal with these problems in his "minibudget" released on May 25 and in his formal budget, which was announced on August 24. The main feature of both was an estimated budget surplus for the 1988-1989 fiscal year of $5.5 billion, the largest surplus in Australian history. A smaller surplus in the 1987-1988 fiscal year was used to repay some of Australia's $3.7-billion federal debt. Keating proposed repaying an even larger percentage of the federal debt in the 1988-1989 fiscal year.

To minimize inflation and reduce imports, Keating announced plans to delay cuts in personal income tax until the 1989-1990 fiscal year. The company tax rate, however, was slashed from 49 to 39 per cent on July 1, 1988.

Foreign trade. Australia's agricultural exports enjoyed a good year in 1988. Wheat and grain exports

Australia's Birthday Bash

On Jan. 26, 1988, Australians celebrated the 200th anniversary of the first British settlement on the continent of Australia. On that day in 1788, Captain Arthur Phillip landed at Sydney Cove with a fleet of ships carrying convicts and guards from England. For the convicts, Australia was to be their prison. As it turned out, that prison settlement was actually the beginning of a new nation.

The 1988 bicentennial celebration naturally centered on the state of New South Wales, the colony Phillip founded. But grants from the federal government's Australian Bicentennial Authority—and the efforts of many local communities—ensured that there were events to mark the bicentennial in all of Australia's six states and two territories.

The opening ceremony in Sydney on January 26 was a fitting start to Australia's yearlong party. The weather was perfect as thousands of small boats joined an international contingent of tall sailing ships in Sydney Harbour to greet a replica of the First Fleet—the first shiploads of convicts and guards that landed at Sydney Cove. The 11 ships that made up the fleet had set sail for Australia from Portsmouth, England, in May. Almost 2 million people lined the harbor to witness the sailing spectacular. The day was capped by a keynote address by Charles, Prince of Wales, on the steps of the famous Sydney Opera House, and by a colorful fireworks display over the Sydney Harbour Bridge.

Protesters supporting Aboriginal rights hold a demonstration as Australia's bicentennial celebration gets underway in January 1988.

From that point on, an immense variety of events—musical, dramatic, educational, commemorative, ethnic, and sporting—took place throughout the year. Among the highlights were visits from New York City's Twyla Tharp Dance Company and the Chicago Symphony Orchestra; the loan of two giant pandas from China for the Taronga Zoological Park in Sydney and the Royal Melbourne Zoological Gardens; a naval review of ships from many countries; airplane and yacht races around Australia; an international soccer competition; an international Scout Jamboree; and a special touring bicentennial exhibition.

Some of the events were a bit unusual. Tasmania hosted the World Penny Farthing Championship, where cyclists raced old-fashioned penny-farthing bicycles with huge front wheels, and the World Kiting Festival. The Great Gumnut Underarm Throwing Competition took place on Bribie Island off the coast of Queensland. (A gumnut is a nut produced by a gum tree, a type of eucalyptus tree.) Left-handed golfers held a festival in Coolangatta; and the Federation of Australian Astrologers held their international conference in Perth. Beltana in South Australia saw its population of seven swell to thousands on September 3 when New Zealand-born soprano Dame Kiri Te Kanawa appeared in a concert billed as "Opera in the Outback."

On April 30, World Expo 88 opened its doors in Brisbane for a six-month run. Pavilions from more than 40 countries, including the United States and Japan, addressed the theme "Leisure in the Age of Technology." The Australian pavilion highlighted the country's cultural heritage, featuring plays by Aboriginal playwrights. Expo 88 also had an amusement-park atmosphere, offering visitors dancing and comedy revues, water shows, circus events, and two parades every day.

Although these events were enjoyed by many people, some Australians questioned whether they should be celebrating the anniversary of the British settlement at all because of the wrongs done by white people to the Aborigines, the dark-skinned people who were Australia's earliest inhabitants, over the past 200 years. Aborigine activists said the bicentennial was the celebration of an invasion by whites, who robbed the Aborigines of their land and culture. During many bicentennial events, Aborigines and their supporters conducted nonviolent demonstrations in protest. When Queen Elizabeth II dedicated the new Parliament House in Canberra on May 9, the ceremony was interrupted by protesters demanding land rights for Aborigines.

Despite the protests by some, the celebrations left most Australians with good memories of bicentennial fun as well as with a feeling of unity as a nation.   J. D. B. Miller

Australia

benefited from a decline in grain exports from the United States—due to drought. Beef and sugar exports also did well, partly because of a decline in world supplies, and partly because of a more liberal Japanese import policy. On June 23, Japan agreed to gradually increase its imports of Australian beef over the next three years.

Foreign affairs. Australia's connections with the Association of Southeast Asian Nations and with South Pacific states continued to be strong, though there was some concern about political instability on the islands of Fiji and Vanuatu.

In spite of New Zealand's withdrawal from the ANZUS mutual defense treaty in 1987, Australia's relations with its neighbor continued to be good. On Oct. 12, 1988, Australia and New Zealand extended their 1983 Closer Economic Relations agreement, which called for the gradual removal of all trade restrictions between the countries. The agreement provided for eliminating tariffs by 1990.

Constitutional referendum. Australians voted in a national referendum on September 3 proposing changes in the country's Constitution. The federal government sponsored the referendum, which was opposed by the National and Liberal parties.

One proposed change called for members of both houses of the federal Parliament to serve four-year terms. At present, senators serve six-year terms, and representatives serve three-year terms. The referendum also included changes to satisfy the demand from some groups for an Australian bill of rights. These proposals called for "fair and democratic elections" throughout the country and provided guarantees of freedom of religion and trial by jury. All the proposals were heavily defeated, confirming the view of some Australians that constitutional amendment is impossible unless it is supported by all political parties.

Education. The federal government on June 16 announced plans to eliminate the country's program of free higher education. The government proposed that students pay for their own university education through a tax levied on their income after they graduate or by paying for courses at the beginning or end of their education. In spite of protests from students, the proposal was included in the federal budget.

3-D money. Australia became one of the first countries to put a *hologram* (three-dimensional image) on its currency when it introduced new plastic $10 bills in January. A hologram of Captain James Cook, the British explorer who claimed part of Australia for Great Britain in 1770, appears in one corner of the bill. Although it feels like traditional paper money, the plastic currency is expected to last longer. Bank officials also hope the hologram will make it impossible for counterfeiters to duplicate the money. Australia plans to replace all its currency with plastic bills over the next three years.   J. D. B. Miller

See also **Asia** (Facts in brief table). In *World Book*, see **Australia**.

Austria. Controversy over Kurt Waldheim, Austria's president and former secretary-general of the United Nations, continued through 1988. In 1987, Waldheim was barred from entering the United States because of his activities as an officer in the German Army during World War II (1939-1945). An international commission of historians established by the Austrian government to investigate Waldheim's wartime activities reported on Feb. 9, 1988, that it had found no evidence that he was a war criminal. The Israeli member of the commission, Yehuda L. Wallach, claimed, however, that Austria had put pressure on the commission to soften its conclusions.

The commission ruled that Waldheim was not personally responsible for any war crimes committed by his army unit during his service in Greece and Yugoslavia, but was aware that atrocities were being committed. The commission said also that he "must have been aware of war crimes against Jews and civilians during 1942 and 1943."

Foreign reactions. After the report was issued, Great Britain's Prime Minister Margaret Thatcher announced that her country's Ministry of Defence would reopen the files of six British commandos who were executed after being interrogated at the German army headquarters where Waldheim was an officer. The United States government announced that it was pursuing an independent investigation of Yugoslavia's records that give details of the wartime deportation and execution of Yugoslav men, women, and children.

Resignation threat. Austria's Chancellor Franz Vranitzky threatened to resign on Feb. 14, 1988, unless the Waldheim controversy calmed down "in the foreseeable future." On February 23, the Socialist Party, to which Vranitzky belongs, called on Waldheim to resign because he had not kept an election promise to increase national prestige. Waldheim, a member of the conservative People's Party, said he had a duty to stay in office.

Libel action dropped. Waldheim dropped a libel action on July 1 against Edgar M. Bronfman, president of the World Jewish Congress, concerning remarks about Waldheim's wartime activities. Waldheim accused the United States of refusing to help the Austrian courts prepare his case.

Annexation anniversary. On March 11, Austria marked the 50th anniversary of the country's annexation by Nazi Germany. At ceremonies in the former Imperial Palace in Vienna, Vranitzky called for unity to build up a society that had been destroyed by internal divisions 50 years earlier.

The economy expanded by only 1.8 per cent in 1988—the third consecutive year in which Austria failed to keep pace with other Western industrialized countries. The unemployment rate was 5.6 per cent and rising.   Kenneth Brown

See also **Europe** (Facts in brief table). In *World Book*, see **Austria**.

Automobile. United States automakers entered 1988 with dread, fearing that the stock-market crash of Oct. 19, 1987, had signaled the start of a general decline in automotive sales. Instead, car and truck sales quickly regained strength in 1988, helping the industry to record the third best sales year in its history. Unabated consumer interest in new cars and trucks pushed total 1988 sales to an estimated 15.65 million, the fourth consecutive year that combined car and truck sales broke through the 15-million mark. Before the mid-1980's boom, the last time overall sales had exceeded 15 million was in 1978. As 1988 drew to a close, the auto industry and independent economists saw no immediate end to what had become the longest period of sales strength in U.S. automotive history.

Production. Automakers believed that the stock-market crash would depress sales throughout 1988. Even before the year opened, U.S. automakers began to make production cuts. But by February 1988 it was clear that consumers had retained their buying mood. After strong January sales, U.S. automakers revised their plans, beefing up production instead. In February, General Motors Corporation (GM) increased production by 175,000 vehicles and restored the jobs of 8,600 laid-off workers, setting a pattern of production strength that lasted throughout the year.

A changed market? So impressive was the industry's 1988 performance that experts began to speculate that the fundamental nature of the U.S. car market had changed. In the past, the market had been known for boom-and-bust cycles in which sales rose for about three years and then declined for a similar period. But by 1988, after four years of strong sales, it appeared that stability was the key word—at least for the immediate future. Experts predicted that annual car sales would average around 10 million, while truck sales would stabilize at about 5 million.

Competition and the economy. Lloyd E. Reuss, executive vice president of North American automotive operations for GM, attributed the new stability to the increasing competition in the North American automotive market. Each of the world's major automakers fought for a share of the profitable U.S. market in the 1980's, and additional competition arrived regularly—such as South Korea's Hyundai Motor Company, which made its debut in 1987. Reuss and other industry experts said that the intense competition in the market place kept prices low and forced automakers to offer a steady stream of new products to encourage sales. Reuss calculated that new cars and trucks were introduced in the United States in 1988 at the rate of approximately one per week.

Other industry observers, including Louis R. Ross, executive vice president in charge of North American car and truck operations at Ford Motor Company, said the industry's new stability can also be explained by the rise of double-income households in the 1980's. Such households—where both husbands and wives hold full-time jobs—typically need two cars.

Other economic factors also continued to favor car and truck purchases. Gasoline prices and interest rates in the United States remained stable, and consumer confidence in the economy's health remained high.

Auto prices. The strength of the U.S. market was not the only good news for GM, Chrysler Corporation, and Ford. By the end of 1988, they had clearly halted the sales growth of Japanese and European imports. Part of this victory was due to manufacturing improvements that substantially increased the quality of domestic cars. But pricing also gave the Detroit automakers an edge. The sharp decline in the value of the U.S. dollar against foreign currencies since 1985 forced Japanese and European automakers to raise their prices at a faster rate than U.S. manufacturers.

Import figures reflected the weakening position of Japanese and European automakers in the U.S. market. In the first 10 months of 1988, imports held a 28.9 per cent share of the U.S. auto market. This was down from 30.5 per cent for the same period in 1987. On January 29, Japan's Ministry of International Trade and Industry announced that Japan would continue its annual export quota of 2.3 million cars but might consider lifting the quota if U.S. sales of Japanese-built cars continue to decline.

The distinction between imported and domestic vehicles continued to fade in 1988. During the year, Japanese automakers emerged as major producers of cars and trucks in the United States, while at the same

The first Ford Probes, sporty compacts built by Japan's Mazda Motor Corporation for Ford in Michigan, arrive in Japan for a September introduction.

Automobile

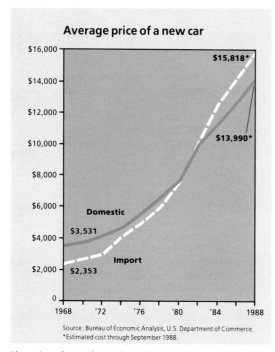

Average price of a new car

- $16,000
- $14,000
- $12,000
- $10,000
- $8,000
- $6,000
- $4,000
- $2,000
- 0

$15,818*

$13,990*

Domestic

$3,531

Import

$2,353

1968 '72 '76 '80 '84 1988

Source: Bureau of Economic Analysis, U.S. Department of Commerce.
*Estimated cost through September 1988.

The price of new domestic and imported automobiles continued to rise sharply in 1988, with import prices nearly triple those of 1978 models.

time U.S. companies were steadily increasing the number of foreign-produced parts in their cars and trucks.

Transplant plants. The number of transplant assembly plants—auto plants in the United States wholly or partly owned and managed by foreign firms—underwent significant expansion in 1988. In March, the Honda Motor Company, the first Japanese company to assemble cars in the United States, broke ground in East Liberty, Ohio, for its second American car-assembly plant. In May, Toyota Motor Company started production at its car-assembly plant in Georgetown, Ky. Toyota officials said the plant would probably be expanded beyond its current production capacity of 200,000 cars per year.

Nissan Motor Company announced in October that it would expand production capacity at its Smyrna, Tenn., plant from 265,000 cars and trucks per year to about 400,000. Diamond-Star Motors, a joint venture between Chrysler and Mitsubishi Motors Corporation, began producing cars in September at its Normal, Ill., assembly plant.

By the end of 1988, six transplant plants, capable of producing 1 million vehicles by 1989, were in operation in the United States. A study by the Japan Development Bank in Tokyo found that production at transplant plants could reach 2.13 million vehicles by 1990 if the output of Canadian-based assembly plants owned by Japanese firms were included.

New deal. One new joint venture between a Japanese and an American firm was finalized during 1988. In September, Ford signed an agreement with Nissan to jointly produce and assemble small vans in Avon Lake, Ohio, beginning in 1991.

Production downside. But events in 1988 also showed that there is no guarantee the transplant plants would be successful. Production declined at New United Motors in Fremont, Calif., a joint venture between GM and Toyota managed by Toyota. There was also one complete plant failure—Volkswagen of America closed its New Stanton, Pa., assembly plant in July, after 10 years of production there.

New cars. Dozens of new car and truck models were introduced in 1988. GM unveiled restyled Cadillac Fleetwood and DeVille models, while Ford rolled out the highly successful Ford Probe and the anxiously awaited Ford Thunderbird Super Coupe. The Super Coupe features the U.S. auto industry's first *supercharged engine* since the mid-1950's. (A supercharged engine has a special pump that increases the power of the engine by forcing extra air into the cylinders.) Diamond-Star marketed a new Plymouth Laser sports coupe. Toyota introduced a restyled Cressida luxury car. Nissan rolled out the all-new Nissan 240SX and the Maxima sedan. GM also introduced a new family of Japanese-made Chevrolet cars and trucks under the Geo name.   James V. Higgins

In *World Book*, see **Automobile**.

Automobile racing. The cars were similar—sleek open-wheel, open-cockpit roadsters with aerodynamic wings to keep them from sailing off the ground at high speed—but they differed in weight. The lighter ones competed in 16 Formula One Grand Prix international races for the World Drivers Championship, and the best of those in 1988 were the McLaren-Hondas. The heavier versions ran 15 races in the Championship Auto Racing Teams (CART) series, and the best of those in 1988 were the Penske-Chevrolets.

Formula One. In 1988, there were 10 Formula One races in Europe and 1 each in the United States, Canada, Brazil, Mexico, Japan, and Australia. The McLaren team, using Honda engines for the first time, won 15 of the 16 races, including the first 11. Of the two McLaren drivers, 28-year-old Ayrton Senna of Brazil won 8 races, and teammate Alain Prost of France won 7. Senna's victories included the Detroit Grand Prix on June 19, the only Formula One race held in the United States.

The only non-McLaren winner was Gerhard Berger of Austria, who won the Grand Prix of Italy on September 11 in a Ferrari. The final leaders were Senna with 91 points, Prost with 87, and Berger with 41.

Most of the leading cars, including the McLarens, used 1.5-liter turbocharged engines. Starting in 1989, all Formula One cars will be restricted to less-expensive 3.5-liter engines without turbochargers to pump extra air into their cylinders.

Bill Elliott of Dawsonville, Ga., in a Ford Thunderbird, beat Rusty Wallace of Charlotte, N.C., in a Pontiac Grand Prix, for the series title, 4,488 points to 4,464. Each won six races. Elliott earned $1,554,639, and Wallace got $1,411,567.

The first and richest race of the series was the $1,548,455 Daytona 500 on February 14 in Daytona Beach. Fifty-year-old Bobby Allison of Hueytown, Ala., won in a Buick, 2½ car lengths ahead of his 26-year-old son, Davey, in a Ford. On June 19 in Long Pond, Pa., Bobby Allison was critically injured in a race accident and later started a long rehabilitation.

Other races. In drag racing, 52-year-old Eddie Hill of Wichita Falls, Tex., broke two records for cars in the Top Fuel Class. From a standing start, he reached 288.83 mph (464.83 kph) on March 20 in Gainesville, Fla., and covered a quarter-mile in 4.936 seconds on October 9 in Baytown, Tex.

In endurance racing, Porsches had won for seven straight years in the 24 Hours of Le Mans in France and for 11 straight years in the 24 Hours of Daytona. In 1988, Jaguars ended both winning streaks with XJR-9 prototypes. The winning drivers were Jan Lammers of the Netherlands and Johnny Dumfries and Andy Wallace of Great Britain on June 11 to 12 at Le Mans and John Nielsen of Denmark, Raul Boesel of Brazil, and Martin Brundle of Great Britain on January 30 to 31 in Daytona Beach.   Frank Litsky

In *World Book*, see **Automobile racing.**

Race car driver Rick Mears holds up three fingers in a salute symbolizing his third victory in the Indianapolis 500 automobile race in May.

CART. The best-known race in this series was the May 29 Indianapolis 500. Penske's team became the first to take all three front-row positions in the field of 33, with Rick Mears of Bakersfield, Calif., on the pole; Danny Sullivan of Louisville, Ky., starting second; and Al Unser, Sr., of Albuquerque, N. Mex., third. Each drove a Penske PC-17 chassis with a Chevrolet V8 engine.

Mears won his third Indy 500 by seven seconds, about 700 yards (640 meters). He earned a record winner's share of $804,853 from a purse of $5.02-million, the largest in auto-racing history. Two hours after the finish, stewards rescinded a two-lap penalty against Emerson Fittipaldi of Brazil, saying he had made up time legally during a yellow flag, and restored him to second place. Unser dropped to third.

Sullivan won the CART series title with 171 points to 136 for Bobby Rahal of Dublin, Ohio, in a Lola-Judd. In the 15 races, Sullivan won 4.

NASCAR. Safety became a major concern in the National Association for Stock Car Auto Racing's (NASCAR) 29-race, $16.7-million series for late-model sedans. To limit high speeds on the fastest tracks—in Daytona Beach, Fla., and Talladega, Ala.—restrictor plates were bolted onto the carburetor to limit the amounts of fuel and air entering the engine. That change reduced horsepower in the four races on those tracks from 650 in 1987 to about 420 in 1988 and made races safer and more competitive.

Aviation. Turmoil between labor and management at Eastern Airlines and a special federal investigation into the airline and its parent company, Texas Air Corporation, dominated aviation news in the United States in 1988. At the heart of the dispute between Eastern's labor unions and management were issues of wages and flight safety. Eastern's unions repeatedly accused the airline of skimping on safety to save money. Eastern executives charged that the unions exaggerated safety problems to avoid taking needed pay cuts.

On February 5, Texas Air, which also owns Continental Airlines, reported a record loss of $466.2 million for 1987. The company also announced plans to sell Eastern's profitable shuttle service, which flies between Washington, D.C., New York City, and Boston, to a newly created Texas Air company. The plan infuriated Eastern's unions. They claimed that Texas Air was trying to ruin Eastern by selling a money-maker.

Prodded by Congress, the U.S. Department of Transportation (DOT) on April 13 opened an investigation into Texas Air's finances and Eastern's safety practices. A few days later, it began investigating the safety of Continental Airlines as well. On June 2, the DOT found Texas Air fit to run airlines and concluded that Continental and Eastern were safe, but said Eastern's labor-management hostility could threaten safety. To avoid that, Eastern's management and unions on July 5 signed an agreement pledging to preserve safety.

Aviation

But Eastern's troubles continued. On July 22, the airline said it would eliminate 4,000 jobs and cut service to 14 U.S. cities. On August 30, it defeated union efforts to block the layoffs in court.

On October 12, real estate developer Donald J. Trump announced plans to buy Eastern's shuttle service, which he would rename the "Trump Shuttle." The purchase would require government approval, and Eastern's unions vowed to fight the take-over in court.

Accidents. A Delta Air Lines Boeing 727 jetliner on August 31 crashed on take-off at Dallas-Fort Worth International Airport, killing 13 of the 107 people aboard. It was the worst U.S. airline accident in 1988. On September 15, federal investigators ruled out engine failure, but said it would be months before the cause of the accident was determined.

A bizarre accident involving an Aloha Airlines Boeing 737 jet on April 28 raised safety concerns about older airliners. The 19-year-old jet, one of the oldest 737's in use, lost part of the top of its *fuselage* (body) while flying over Hawaii. A flight attendant was swept to her death, but the pilots landed the plane safely. The exact cause of the accident was not known, but investigators suspected structural problems due to metal fatigue. The Federal Aviation Administration (FAA) ordered more frequent inspections of older aircraft and directed airlines to take steps to prevent metal fatigue in older planes.

On August 28, an air-show disaster at Ramstein U.S. Air Force Base near Frankfurt, West Germany, killed at least 70 people, most of them spectators, and injured hundreds of others. During an exhibition flight, three Italian Air Force jets collided and one crashed into a crowd of onlookers.

On October 19, at least 164 people died in two air crashes in India, one in Ahmadabad and the other in Gauhati. And on March 17, an Avianca Airlines Boeing 727 slammed into a mountain in northern Colombia, killing all 137 persons aboard.

Service and fares. Flight delays and consumer complaints against U.S. airlines, which rose sharply in 1987, fell in 1988 as the FAA improved its air-traffic-control procedures and as airlines worked to provide better service. In many cases, flight delays decreased because airlines stretched out their schedules, not because passengers reached their destinations quicker.

During the year, a growing number of aviation experts warned that the United States faced a severe, long-term shortage of airport space. To try to reduce crowding at one airport, voters in Denver on May 17 approved construction of a new, $3-billion airport to replace Denver's Stapleton International Airport. The new airport would be the first major U.S. airport opened since 1974. But Continental Airlines and United Airlines, which provide most flights to Denver, objected to the plan, saying the airport would be too expensive. Because the airlines had been expected to

Rescue workers aid passengers of an Aloha Airlines jet that lost part of the top of its fuselage during a flight over Hawaii on April 28.

Three Italian Air Force jets collide during an August 28 air show in West Germany before one crashed into a crowd of onlookers. At least 70 people died.

help pay for the airport, their objections raised doubts about when—and if—it would be built.

Meanwhile, U.S. airlines in 1988 increased fares to bolster revenues. In the first seven months of 1988, fares rose an average of 10 per cent over the same period in 1987. The fare increases sparked concerns that the wave of airline mergers in the 1980's had hurt competition. By late 1988, eight airlines controlled more than 90 per cent of U.S. air traffic.

Safety. The FAA in March 1988 launched an investigation into the safety of commuter airlines after a string of fatal commuter crashes in late 1987 and early 1988 killed more than 50 people. The investigation focused on maintenance and pilot training.

In an effort to reduce the risk of midair collisions, the FAA, on June 16, ordered private pilots flying near most large and medium-sized airports to use equipment that enables their altitude to be read on radar screens by air-traffic controllers. Commercial airliners already have the equipment.

Transportation Secretary James H. Burnley IV ignited a controversy on November 14 when he ordered that all airline pilots, railroad engineers, and interstate truckdrivers undergo random testing for drug use, beginning in late 1989. The unions representing railroad workers and pilots objected strongly, saying they would sue the Transportation Department.

On Dec. 29, 1988, the FAA ordered increased security measures for U.S. airlines in the Middle East and Europe. The tightened security was prompted by the December 21 bombing of a Pan American World Airways jet in Scotland, in which 270 people died.

No smoking. Another aviation issue that made headlines in 1988 was smoking on airliners. Under federal law, smoking on U.S. airline flights of two hours or less was banned beginning April 23.

FAA problems. The FAA has long been criticized as being slow to act on safety problems, and in 1988 several plans to improve the agency emerged, including a proposal by some members of Congress to take the FAA out of the DOT. These ideas were highly controversial, and none were implemented in 1988.

In a major step toward modernizing its aging air-traffic-control system, the FAA awarded a $3.6-billion contract on July 26 to International Business Machines Corporation (IBM) to develop the Advanced Automation System. The system will replace existing radar with sophisticated equipment to make controllers more efficient and air travel safer. The contract was challenged by Hughes Aircraft Company, the losing bidder, but was upheld by a federal review board.

Aircraft sales. On September 22, Delta Air Lines announced plans to buy as many as 215 jetliners, valued at $10.5 billion, from McDonnell Douglas Corporation and the Boeing Company. If the entire purchase is made, it would be the biggest aircraft acquisition ever made.   Laurie McGinley

In *World Book*, see **Aviation.**

Awards and prizes

Awards and prizes presented in 1988 included the following:

Arts awards

Academy of Motion Picture Arts and Sciences. "Oscar" Awards: **Best Picture,** *The Last Emperor.* **Best Actor,** Michael Douglas, *Wall Street.* **Best Actress,** Cher, *Moonstruck.* **Best Supporting Actor,** Sean Connery, *The Untouchables.* **Best Supporting Actress,** Olympia Dukakis, *Moonstruck.* **Best Director,** Bernardo Bertolucci, *The Last Emperor.* **Best Original Screenplay,** John Patrick Shanley, *Moonstruck.* **Best Screenplay Adaptation,** Mark Peploe and Bernardo Bertolucci, *The Last Emperor.* **Best Cinematography,** Vittorio Storaro, *The Last Emperor.* **Best Film Editing,** Gabriella Cristiani, *The Last Emperor.* **Best Original Score,** Ryuichi Sakamoto, David Byrne, and Cong Su, *The Last Emperor.* **Best Original Song,** Franke Previte, John DeNicola, and Donald Markowitz, "(I've Had) The Time of My Life." **Best Foreign-Language Film,** *Babette's Feast* (Denmark). See **Cher; Douglas, Michael.**

American Academy and Institute of Arts and Letters. **Gold Medal for Biography,** author James Thomas Flexner. **Gold Medal for Music,** composer Milton Babbitt. **Arnold W. Brunner Memorial Prize in Architecture,** Arata Isozaki.

American Dance Festival. **Samuel H. Scripps-American Dance Festival Award,** Erick Hawkins, American dancer and choreographer.

American Film Institute. Life Achievement Award, actor Gregory Peck.

American Institute of Architects. Honor Awards, Eisenman Robertson Architects, New York City, for IBA Social Housing in West Berlin, West Germany; Esherick Homsey Dodge and Davis, San Francisco, for Monterey Bay Aquarium in Monterey, Calif.; Frank O. Gehry and Associates Incorporated, Venice, Calif., for a guest house near Minneapolis, Minn.; Gwathmey Siegel & Associates Architects, New York City, for the Library and Science Building at Westover School, Middlebury, Conn.; Hugh Newell Jacobsen, Washington, D.C., for a residence in La Romana, Dominican Republic; Moore Ruble Yudell, Santa Monica, Calif., for Tegel Harbor Housing in West Berlin; Morphosis, Santa Monica, for the Kate Mantilini Restaurant in Beverly Hills, Calif.; Eric Owen Moss, Culver City, Calif., for 8522 National Boulevard, a warehouse turned into an office building in Culver City; Murphy/Jahn, Chicago, for the United Airlines Terminal 1 Complex at O'Hare International Airport in that city; I. M. Pei & Partners, New York City, for the Jacob K. Javits Convention Center in that city; Piano + Fitzgerald, Architects, Houston, for the Menil Collection, an art museum in that city; James Stewart Polshek and Partners, New York City, for the Carnegie Hall restoration in that city; Scogin Elam and Bray Architects, Incorporated, Atlanta, Ga., for the High Museum at Georgia-Pacific Center in that city; Skidmore, Owings & Merrill, Chicago, for the United Gulf Bank in Manama, Bahrain; Tod Williams Billie Tsien and Associates, New York City, for Feinberg Hall at Princeton University in New Jersey.

American Music Awards. Pop/Rock Awards: **Female Vocalist,** Whitney Houston. **Male Vocalist,** Paul Simon. **Duo or Group,** Bon Jovi. **Single,** "I Wanna Dance with Somebody (Who Loves Me)," Whitney Houston. **Album,** *Graceland,* Paul Simon.

Soul Music/Rhythm and Blues Awards: **Female Vocalist,** Anita Baker. **Male Vocalist,** Smokey Robinson. **Duo or Group,** Cameo. **Single,** "Bad," Michael Jackson. **Album,** *Rapture,* Anita Baker.

Country Music Awards: Female Vocalist, Reba McEntire. **Male Vocalist,** Randy Travis. **Duo or Group,** Alabama. **Single,** "Forever and Ever, Amen," Randy Travis. **Album,** *Always & Forever,* Randy Travis.

Video Awards: Pop/Rock and Soul Music/Rhythm and Blues, "When I Think of You," Janet Jackson. **Country,** "Forever and Ever, Amen," Randy Travis.

Avery Fisher Prize. American pianist André Watts.

Cannes International Film Festival. Golden Palm Grand Prize, *Pelle the Conqueror* (Denmark). **Special Jury Prize,** *A World Apart* (Great Britain). **Jury Prize,** *Thou Shalt Not Kill* (Poland). **Best Actor,** Forest Whitaker, *Bird* (United States). **Best Actress,** Barbara Hershey, Jodhi May, and Linda Mvusi, *A World Apart.* **Best Director,** Fernando Solanas, *The South* (Argentina).

Capezio Dance Award. American tap dancer Charles (Honi) Coles.

Hyatt Foundation. Pritzker Architecture Prize, Gordon Bunshaft (United States) and Oscar Niemeyer (Brazil).

John F. Kennedy Center for the Performing Arts. Honors, choreographer Alvin Ailey; comedian George Burns; actress Myrna Loy; violinist Alexander Schneider; theatrical producer Roger L. Stevens, founding chairman of the Kennedy Center.

MacDowell Colony. Edward MacDowell Medal, writer William Styron.

National Academy of Recording Arts and Sciences. Grammy Awards: **Record of the Year,** "Graceland," Paul Simon. **Album of the Year,** *The Joshua Tree,* U2. **Song of the Year,** "Somewhere Out There," James Horner, Barry Mann, and Cynthia Weil, songwriters. **Best New Artist,** Jody Watley.

Pop Awards: **Pop Vocal Performance, Female,** "I Wanna Dance with Somebody (Who Loves Me)," Whitney Houston. **Pop Vocal Performance, Male,** *Bring on the Night,* Sting. **Pop Vocal Performance by a Duo or Group,** "(I've Had) The Time of My Life," Bill Medley and Jennifer Warnes. **Pop Instrumental Performance,** *Minute by Minute,* Larry Carlton.

Rock Awards: **Rock Vocal Performance, Female or Male,** *Tunnel of Love,* Bruce Springsteen. **Rock Vocal Performance by a Duo or Group,** *The Joshua Tree,* U2. **Rock Instrumental Performance,** *Jazz from Hell,* Frank Zappa.

Rhythm and Blues Awards: **Rhythm and Blues Vocal Performance, Female,** *Aretha,* Aretha Franklin. **Rhythm and Blues Vocal Performance, Male,** "Just to See Her," Smokey Robinson. **Rhythm and Blues Vocal Performance by a Duo or Group,** "I Knew You Were Waiting (for Me)," Aretha Franklin and George Michael. **Rhythm and Blues Instrumental Performance,** *Chicago Song,* David Sanborn. **Rhythm and Blues Song,** "Lean on Me," Reggie Calloway and Bill Withers, songwriters.

Video Awards: **Performance Music Video,** *The Prince's Trust All-Star Rock Concert,* Elton John, Tina Turner, Sting, and others. **Concept Music Video,** *Land of Confusion,* Genesis.

Country Awards: **Country Vocal Performance, Female,** *80's Ladies,* K. T. Oslin. **Country Vocal Performance, Male,** *Always & Forever,* Randy Travis. **Country Vocal Performance, Duet,** "Make No Mistake, She's Mine," Ronnie Milsap and Kenny Rogers. **Country Vocal Performance, Group,** *Trio,* Dolly Parton, Linda Ronstadt, and Emmylou Harris. **Country Instrumental Performance,** "String of Pars," Asleep at the Wheel. **Country Song,** "Forever and Ever, Amen," Paul Overstreet and Don Schlitz, songwriters.

Jazz Awards: **Jazz Fusion Performance, Vocal or Instrumental,** *Still Life,* Pat Metheny Group. **Jazz Vocal Performance, Female,** *Diane Schuur and the Count Basie Orchestra,* Diane Schuur. **Jazz Vocal Performance, Male,** "What Is This Thing Called Love?" Bobby McFerrin. **Jazz Instrumental Performance, Solo,** *The Other Side of 'Round Midnight,* Dexter Gordon. **Jazz Instrumental Performance, Group,** *Marsalis Standard Time Volume I,* Wynton Marsalis. **Jazz Instrumental Performance, Big Band,** *Digital Duke,* The Duke Ellington Orchestra conducted by Mercer Ellington.

Classical Awards: **Performance by a Soloist with Orchestra,** *Mozart: Violin Concertos Nos. 2 and 4 in D,* Itzhak Perlman with James Levine conducting the Vienna Philharmonic. **Performance by a Soloist Without Orchestra,** *Horowitz in Moscow,* Vladimir Horowitz. **Orchestra Recording,** *Beethoven: Symphony No. 9 in D Minor,* Sir Georg Solti conducting the Chicago Symphony Orchestra. **Opera Recording,** *Strauss: Ariadne auf Naxos,* James Levine conducting the

Vienna Philharmonic. **Choral Performance,** *Hindemith: When Lilacs Last in the Dooryard Bloom'd,* Robert Shaw conducting the Atlanta Symphony Chorus and Orchestra.

National Academy of Television Arts and Sciences. Emmy Awards, Comedy: Best Series, "The Wonder Years." **Lead Actor,** Michael J. Fox, "Family Ties." **Lead Actress,** Beatrice Arthur, "The Golden Girls." **Supporting Actor,** John Larroquette, "Night Court." **Supporting Actress,** Estelle Getty, "The Golden Girls."

Drama Awards: Best Series, "thirtysomething." **Lead Actor,** Richard Kiley, "A Year in the Life." **Lead Actress,** Tyne Daley, "Cagney & Lacey." **Supporting Actor,** Larry Drake, "L.A. Law." **Supporting Actress,** Patricia Wettig, "thirtysomething."

Other Awards: Drama or Comedy Special, *Inherit the Wind.* **Miniseries,** "The Murder of Mary Phagan." **Variety, Music, or Comedy Program,** *Irving Berlin's 100th Birthday Celebration.* **Lead Actor in a Miniseries or Special,** Jason Robards, *Inherit the Wind.* **Lead Actress in a Miniseries or Special,** Jessica Tandy, *Foxfire.* **Supporting Actor in a Miniseries or Special,** John Shea, *Baby M.* **Supporting Actress in a Miniseries or Special,** Jane Seymour, *Onassis: The Richest Man in the World.*

National Society of Film Critics Awards. Best Film, *The Unbearable Lightness of Being.* **Best Actor,** Michael Keaton, *Beetlejuice* and *Clean and Sober.* **Best Actress,** Judy Davis, *High Tide.* **Best Supporting Actor,** Dean Stockwell, *Tucker* and *Married to the Mob.* **Best Supporting Actress,** Mercedes Ruehl, *Married to the Mob.* **Best Director,** Philip Kaufman, *The Unbearable Lightness of Being.* **Best Screenplay,** Ron Shelton, *Bull Durham.* **Best Cinematography,** Henri Alekan, *Wings of Desire.* **Best Documentary,** *The Thin Blue Line.* **Special Award for Originality,** Pedro Almodovar, *Women on the Verge of a Nervous Breakdown.*

New York Drama Critics Circle Awards. Best New Play, *Joe Turner's Come and Gone,* August Wilson. **Best New Foreign Play,** *The Road to Mecca,* Athol Fugard. **Best Musical,** *Into the Woods,* Stephen Sondheim and James Lapine.

New York Film Critics Circle Awards. Best Film, *The Accidental Tourist.* **Best Actor,** Jeremy Irons, *Dead Ringers.* **Best Actress,** Meryl Streep, *A Cry in the Dark.* **Best Supporting Actor,** Dean Stockwell, *Married to the Mob* and *Tucker.* **Best Supporting Actress,** Diane Venora, *Bird.* **Best Director,** Chris Menges, *A World Apart.* **Best Screenplay,** Ron Shelton, *Bull Durham.* **Best Cinematography,** Henri Alekan, *Wings of Desire.* **Best Foreign Film,** *Women on the Verge of a Nervous Breakdown* (Spain). **Best Documentary,** *The Thin Blue Line.*

Antoinette Perry (Tony) Awards. Drama Awards: Best Play, *M. Butterfly.* **Leading Actor,** Ron Silver, *Speed-the-Plow.* **Leading Actress,** Joan Allen, *Burn This.* **Featured Actor,** B. D. Wong, *M. Butterfly.* **Featured Actress,** L. Scott Caldwell, *Joe Turner's Come and Gone.* **Direction,** John Dexter, *M. Butterfly.*

Musical Awards: Best Musical, *The Phantom of the Opera.* **Leading Actor,** Michael Crawford, *The Phantom of the Opera.* **Leading Actress,** Joanna Gleason, *Into the Woods.* **Featured Actor,** Bill McCutcheon, *Anything Goes.* **Featured Actress,** Judy Kaye, *The Phantom of the Opera.* **Direction,** Harold Prince, *The Phantom of the Opera.* **Book for a Musical,** James Lapine, *Into the Woods.* **Score for a Musical,** Stephen Sondheim, *Into the Woods.* **Choreography,** Michael Smuin, *Anything Goes.*

Best Reproduction of a Play or Musical, *Anything Goes.*

United States government. National Medal of Arts, art patron Brooke Astor; novelist Saul Bellow; art historian Sydney J. Freedberg, chief curator at the National Gallery of Art; music patron Francis Goelet; actress Helen Hayes; photographer and film director Gordon Parks; architect I. M. Pei; choreographer Jerome Robbins; pianist Rudolf Serkin; theatrical producer Roger L. Stevens, founding chairman of the Kennedy Center for the Performing Arts; art patron Obert C. Tanner; composer Virgil Thomson.

Theater legend Helen Hayes receives the National Medal of Arts from President Ronald Reagan at a White House ceremony in August.

Journalism awards

American Society of Magazine Editors. National Magazine Awards: General Excellence, Circulation over 1 Million, *Parents Magazine;* **Circulation of 400,000 to 1 million,** *Fortune;* **Circulation of 100,000 to 400,000,** *Hippocrates;* **Circulation Under 100,000,** *The Sciences.* **Personal Service,** *Money.* **Special Interests,** *Condé Nast Traveler.* **News Reporting,** *The Washingtonian* and *Baltimore Magazine.* **Public Interest,** *The Atlantic.* **Design,** *Life.* **Photography,** *Rolling Stone.* **Essays and Criticism,** *Harper's.* **Fiction,** *The Atlantic.* **Feature Writing,** *The Atlantic.* **Single-Topic Issue,** *Life.*

Long Island University. George Polk Memorial Awards: National Reporting, Mike Masterson, Chuck Cook, and Mark N. Trahant, *The* (Phoenix) *Arizona Republic,* for their exposé of mismanagement and corruption in the U.S. Bureau of Indian Affairs. **Local Reporting,** Ron Ridenhour, *CityBusiness*—a biweekly newspaper in New Orleans, La.—for uncovering a city tax scandal. **Metropolitan Reporting,** *The Charlotte* (N.C.) *Observer* for its more than 500 articles on evangelist Jim Bakker and the PTL ministry. **Foreign Reporting,** Nora Boustany, *The Washington* (D.C.) *Post,* for her coverage of the plight of Palestinian refugees and hardship in Lebanon. **Political Reporting,** the Washington, D.C., bureau of Knight-Ridder Incorporated for general excellence. **Financial Reporting,** James B. Stewart and Daniel Hertzberg, *The Wall Street Journal,* for their articles on the Oct. 19, 1987, stock-market collapse and its aftermath. **Sports Reporting,** Chris Mortensen, *The Atlanta* (Ga.) *Journal/Constitution,* for a series of articles on commercialization of amateur sports by sports agents and college athletes. **Science Reporting,** *Science News.* **Magazine Reporting,** Roger Rosenblatt, *Time,* for his examination of the Soviet Union. **Local Television Reporting,** Margie Nichols, WSMV-TV, Nashville, Tenn., for her series on insurance frauds that prey on senior citizens. **Foreign Television Reporting,** Gordon Manning, National Broadcasting Company (NBC), for

Awards and prizes

Cher, playing a widow who finds romance, shares a toast with her father in *Moonstruck*. Her performance won her the 1988 Academy Award as best actress.

two major projects, "Changing China" and "A Conversation with Mikhail Gorbachev." **Network Television Reporting,** Cable News Network (CNN) for its national and international news. **Radio Reporting,** Larry Bensky, Pacifica Radio, for coverage of the Iran-contra hearings.

Career Award, Murray Kempton, columnist for *Newsday,* Long Island, New York.

The Society of Professional Journalists, Sigma Delta Chi. Sigma Delta Chi Distinguished Service Awards, Newspaper Awards: General Reporting, Circulation More than 100,000, Jacqui Banaszynski, *St. Paul* (Minn.) *Pioneer Press Dispatch,* for her series on the life and death of a victim of AIDS (acquired immune deficiency syndrome). **General Reporting, Circulation Less than 100,000,** Paul Nyden, *The Charleston* (W. Va.) *Gazette,* for a series on medical malpractice claims and insurance settlements. **Editorial Writing,** Jane E. Healy, *The Orlando* (Fla.) *Sentinel,* for editorials protesting overdevelopment in Florida's Orange County. **Washington Correspondence,** Tom Fiedler, Jim McGee, and James Savage, *The Miami* (Fla.) *Herald,* for stories on how presidential candidate Gary Hart met with Miami model Donna Rice in a Washington, D.C., townhouse. **Foreign Correspondence,** Guy Gugliotta, Jeff Leen, and Jim Savage, *The Miami Herald,* for a series about the Colombian cocaine trafficking ring known as the Medellín Cartel. **News Photography,** Michel duCille, *The Miami Herald,* for photographs showing how crack, a form of cocaine, dominated the lives of people in a public housing project. **Editorial Cartooning,** Paul Conrad, *Los Angeles Times.* **Public Service in Newspaper Journalism, Circulation More than 100,000,** *Dallas Times Herald,* for a series that explained the effects of the Immigration Reform and Control Act of 1987. **Public Service in Newspaper Journalism, Circulation Less than 100,000,** *The* (Montgomery) *Alabama Journal,* for its series on infant mortality in that state.

Magazine Awards: Magazine Reporting, Stephen Fried, *Philadelphia* magazine, for a story on how a suburban police

officer had been sexually molesting boys for 25 years. **Public Service in Magazine Journalism,** *The Washington Post Magazine,* for a story about a father's struggle to cope with the kidnapping of his infant son from a hospital.

Radio Awards: Radio Spot-News Reporting, KNX-AM, Los Angeles, for its coverage of an October 1987 earthquake. **Public Service in Radio Journalism,** "MonitoRadio," the weekend radio news program of *The Christian Science Monitor,* for a series on children in Third World nations. **Editorializing on Radio,** Catherine Cahan, WBBM-AM, Chicago, for editorials calling for flexible hours in Chicago health clinics.

Television Awards: Television Spot-News Reporting, Allen Pizzey, Paul Vittoroulis, and Georges Ioannides, CBS News, for a report on efforts to rescue sailors from a burning Cypriot tanker in the Persian Gulf. **Public Service in Television Journalism, Stations in the Top 50 Markets,** KING-TV, Seattle, for a documentary about sex education. **Public Service in Television Journalism, Small-Market Stations,** WBRZ-TV, Baton Rouge, La., for a documentary that examined how state and city officials failed to appeal court judgments costing taxpayers millions yearly. **Editorializing on Television,** Phil Johnson, WWL-TV, New Orleans, for a series uncovering problems at a state prison for young offenders.

Research About Journalism: Randall P. Bezanson, Gilbert Cranberg, and John Soloski, for *Libel Law and the Press.*

University of Georgia. George Foster Peabody Broadcasting Awards, American Broadcasting Companies (ABC) Radio News for its firsthand account of action in the Persian Gulf; Blackside, Incorporated, Boston, for "Eyes on the Prize: America's Civil Rights Years"; Kevin Brownlow and David Gill for their film archive research and restoration; CNN for its live coverage of the October 1987 stock-market crash; The Center for New America Media Incorporated, New York City, for *American Tongues,* a documentary about regional speech in the United States; CKVU-TV, Vancouver, Canada, for *AIDS and You;* Karl Haas for "Adventures in Good Music," his classical music series on radio; "Hallmark Hall of Fame" and CBS-TV for the dramas *Foxfire* and *Pack of Lies;* KNBC-TV, Los Angeles, for *Some Place Like Home,* about hospices for AIDS patients; K-PAL Radio, North Little Rock, Ark., for its full-time children's programming; KQED, San Francisco, in association with El Teatro Campesino, for a series on Mexican American culture; Long Bow Group, Incorporated, in association with the Public Broadcasting Service (PBS) for *Small Happiness* on the series "One Village in China"; "MacNeil/Lehrer NewsHour" for its series on Japan; Mutual Broadcasting System, Arlington, Va., for its documentary examining superstar fund-raising events; National Public Radio, Washington, D.C., for the story on "Weekend Edition" of a boy paralyzed in a shooting incident; Niemack Productions Incorporated in association with Home Box Office for its documentary on alcohol-related highway deaths; Paramount Pictures Corporation for *The Big Good-Bye* on "Star Trek: The Next Generation"; Louis Rudolph Films and Brice Productions in association with Fries Entertainment and NBC-TV for *LBJ: The Early Years;* Titus Productions in association with Polymuse, Incorporated, and Home Box Office for *Mandela,* about South African leader Nelson Mandela; 20th Century Fox Television in association with NBC-TV for "L.A. Law"; WCPO-TV, Cincinnati, for *Drake Hospital Investigation,* tracking a serial killer at the hospital; WCVB-TV, Boston, for *Inside Bridgewater,* documenting conditions at a Massachusetts facility for the criminally insane; WGBH-TV, Boston, and KCET, Los Angeles, for *Spy Machines,* about spy satellites and other technology, on "Nova"; WNET/Thirteen, New York City, for *A Season in the Sun,* about East African wildlife, on "Nature"; WNET/Thirteen, in association with PBS, for presenting *Shoah,* a Claude Lanzmann film about the Holocaust; WRC-TV, Washington, D.C., for *Deadly Mistakes,* about laboratory errors in cancer testing; WSM Radio, Nashville, for an inquiry into the impact of increasing crime in that city; WSMV-TV, Nashville, for "4 the Family," a series dedicated to enhancing family life; WXXI-TV, Rochester, N.Y., for *Safe Haven,* a documentary about European refugees imprisoned in New York state during World War II.

Literature awards

Academy of American Poets. Lamont Poetry Selection, *Unfinished Painting,* Mary Jo Salter. **Walt Whitman Award,** *Blackbird Bye Bye,* April Bernard.

American Library Association. Newbery Medal, *Lincoln: A Photobiography,* Russell Freedman. **Caldecott Medal,** *Owl Moon,* C. John Schoenherr, illustrator.

Association of American Publishers. National Book Awards: Fiction, *Paris Trout,* Pete Dexter. **Nonfiction,** *A Bright Shining Lie: John Paul Vann and America in Vietnam,* Neil Sheehan. **Medal for Distinguished Contribution to American Letters,** Jason Epstein, editorial director, Random House.

Booker Prize. *Oscar and Lucinda,* Peter Carey.

Canada Council. Governor General's Literary Awards, English-Language: Fiction, *A Dream Like Mine,* M. T. Kelly. **Poetry,** *Afterworlds,* Gwendolyn MacEwen. **Drama,** *Prague,* John Krizanc. **Nonfiction,** *The Russian Album,* Michael Ignatieff. **Translation,** *Enchantment and Sorrow: The Autobiography of Gabrielle Roy,* translated by Patricia Claxton. **Children's Literature (Text),** *Galahad Schwartz and the Cockroach Army,* Morgan Nyberg. **Children's Literature (Illustration),** *Rainy Day Magic,* Marie-Louise Gay.

French-Language: Fiction, *L'Obsédante Obèse et autres agressions,* Gilles Archambault. **Poetry,** *Les Heures,* Fernand Ouelette. **Drama,** *Un oiseau vivant dans la gueule,* Jeanne-Mance Delisle. **Nonfiction,** *La Petite Noirceur,* Jean Larose. **Translation,** *L'homme qui se croyait aimé, ou La vie secrète d'un premier ministre,* translated by Ivan Steenhout. **Children's Literature (Text),** *Le Don,* David Schinkel and Yves Beauchesne. **Children's Literature (Illustration),** *Venir au monde,* Darcia Labrosse.

Canadian Library Association. Book of the Year for Children Award, *A Handful of Time,* Kit Pearson. **Amelia Frances Howard-Gibbon Illustrator's Award,** *Rainy Day Magic,* Marie-Louise Gay.

Columbia University. Bancroft Prizes in American History, *Unfree Labor: American Slavery and Russian Serfdom,* Peter R. Kolchin; *The Rise of American Air Power: The Creation of Armageddon,* Michael S. Sherry.

Ingersoll Foundation. Ingersoll Prizes: T. S. Eliot Award for Creative Writing, novelist Walker Percy. **Richard M. Weaver Award for Scholarly Letters,** University of Chicago sociologist Edward Shils.

National Book Critics Circle. National Book Critics Circle Awards, Fiction, *The Counterlife,* Philip Roth. **General Nonfiction,** *The Making of the Atomic Bomb,* Richard Rhodes. **Biography/Autobiography,** *Chaucer: His Life, His Works, His World,* Donald R. Howard. **Poetry,** *Flesh and Blood,* C. K. Williams. **Criticism,** *Dance Writings,* Edwin Denby. **Citation for Excellence in Reviewing,** Josh Rubins, free-lance critic.

PEN American Center. Faulkner Award, *World's End,* T. Coraghessan Boyle.

Nobel Prizes. See Nobel Prizes.

Public service awards

American Institute for Public Service. Thomas Jefferson Awards, James Chappell and Joanna Chappell, founders of the Banyan House, a shelter for drug addicts and alcoholics in West Palm Beach, Fla.; Peter Frazza, a disabled former police officer who heads the National Disabled Law Officers Association in Nutley, N.J.; Surgeon General of the United States C. Everett Koop for his efforts to educate the public about AIDS; Lola T. Martin, head of a literacy program in Hempstead, N.Y.; deaf actress Marlee Matlin; J. T. Pace of Mauldin, S.C., a national spokesman for literacy; Bruce Ritter, founder of Covenant House, which helps homeless and abused children in New York City; James W. Rouse, head of a foundation in Columbia, Md., that provides affordable housing; and Amy Marie Windom, a high school student in Richmond, Va., who tutors other students and helps run a local chapter of Students Against Driving Drunk.

Carnegie Hero Fund Commission. Carnegie Medals, Michael Allen, Conroe, Tex.; George A. Andrews, Fairfield, Calif.; Donna Marie Bell, Ingleside, Ill.; Todd Allen Brill, Elkhart, Ind.; Thomas J. Cathcart, Ellenville, N.Y.; Hsien-li Chang, San Francisco; Jeffrey G. Chipley, Estevan, Canada (posthumous); John E. Conner, Trenton, N.J.; Berman P. Detty, Frankfort, Ohio; Bruce Dobbs, Fairfax Station, Va.; Vernon W. Gist, England, Ark.; Connie Sue Gries, Evansville, Ind.; Arthur H. C. Ham, Arnprior, Canada; Guy A. Keally, Johnson City, Tenn.; Thomas William Luzak, Walton, Ky.; Thomas C. Morris, Jr., Sugar Hill, Ga.; James Michael Paradis, Lynn, Mass. (posthumous); Richard C. Pool, England, Ark.; Larry B. Pulai, Saskatoon, Canada; Fred A. Thomas, Jr., Wilkes-Barre, Pa.

National Association for the Advancement of Colored People. Spingarn Medal, Frederick Douglass Patterson, founder of the United Negro College Fund (posthumous).

Templeton Foundation. Templeton Prize for Progress in Religion, Inamullah Khan, secretary-general of the Pakistan-based World Muslim Congress, for bringing together world religious leaders to discuss disarmament, human rights, and economic development.

United States government. Presidential Medal of Freedom, entertainer Pearl Bailey; Secretary of Commerce Malcolm Baldrige (posthumous); labor leader Irving J. Brown; former Chief Justice of the United States Warren E. Burger; economist Milton Friedman; Jean F. MacArthur, widow of General Douglas MacArthur; hotel and restaurant executive J. Willard Marriott, Jr. (posthumous); former Deputy Secretary of Defense David Packard.

Awards and prizes

Michael J. Fox smiles at winning his third straight Emmy Award as best lead actor in a comedy series for his role in "Family Ties."

Pulitzer Prizes

Journalism. Public Service, *The Charlotte Observer* for revealing the misuse of funds by the PTL ministry headed by evangelist Jim Bakker. **General News Reporting,** *The Alabama Journal,* for its series on infant mortality in that state; *Lawrence* (Mass.) *Eagle-Tribune,* for its series uncovering flaws in the state prison-furlough system. **Investigative Reporting,** Dean Baquet, William C. Gaines, and Ann Marie Lipinski, *Chicago Tribune,* for their series about waste and conflicts of interest in the Chicago City Council. **Explanatory Journalism,** Daniel Hertzberg and James B. Stewart, *The Wall Street Journal,* for their articles about an investment banker charged with insider trading and about the aftermath of the October 1987 stock-market collapse. **Specialized Reporting,** Walt Bogdanovich, *The Wall Street Journal,* for a series on faulty testing by medical laboratories. **National Reporting,** Tim Weiner, *The Philadelphia Inquirer,* for a three-part series on secret federal spending for defense and intelligence. **International Reporting,** Thomas L. Friedman, *The New York Times,* for coverage of Israel. **Feature Writing,** Jacqui Banaszynski, *St. Paul Pioneer Press Dispatch,* for a series on the life and death of an AIDS victim. **Commentary,** Dave Barry, *The Miami Herald,* for his humor columns. **Criticism,** Tom Shales, *The Washington Post,* for his television criticism. **Editorial Writing,** Jane E. Healy, *The Orlando Sentinel,* for editorials protesting overdevelopment in Florida's Orange County. **Editorial Cartooning,** Doug Marlette, *The Atlanta Constitution* and *The Charlotte Observer.* **Spot News Photography,** Scott Shaw, *The Odessa* (Tex.) *American,* for photographs of the October 1987 rescue of 18-month-old Jessica McClure from an abandoned well in Midland, Tex. **Feature Photography,** Michel duCille, *The Miami Herald,* for photographs showing how crack, a form of cocaine, dominated the lives of people in a public housing project.

Letters. Biography, *Look Homeward: A Life of Thomas Wolfe,* David Herbert Donald. **Fiction,** *Beloved,* Toni Morrison. **General Nonfiction,** *The Making of the Atomic Bomb,* Richard Rhodes. **History,** *The Launching of Modern American Science 1846-1876,* Robert V. Bruce. **Drama,** *Driving Miss Daisy,* Alfred Uhry. **Poetry,** *Partial Accounts: New and Selected Poems,* William Meredith.

Music. Music Award, *12 New Études for Piano,* William Bolcom.

Science and technology awards

Columbia University. Louisa Gross Horwitz Prize, Thomas R. Cech, University of Colorado, Boulder; Phillip A. Sharp, Massachusetts Institute of Technology (M.I.T.).

Gairdner Foundation. Gairdner Foundation International Awards, Albert Aguayo, McGill University, Montreal, Canada; Michael J. Berridge, Cambridge University, England; Thomas R. Cech, University of Colorado; Michael A. Epstein, Oxford University, England; Robert J. Lefkowitz, Duke University Medical Center, Durham, N.C.; Yasutomi Nishizuka, Kobe University, Japan.

Albert and Mary Lasker Foundation. Albert Lasker Basic Medical Research Award, Thomas R. Cech, University of Colorado; Phillip A. Sharp, M.I.T. **Albert Lasker Clinical Medical Research Award,** Vincent P. Dole, Rockefeller University.

Royal Society of Canada. Thomas W. Eadie Medal, Arthur A. Axelrad, Mount Sinai Hospital, Toronto. **Flavelle Medal,** Robert H. Haynes, York University, Toronto. **McLaughlin Medal,** Adolfo J. de Bold, Ottawa Heart Institute. **Rutherford Medal in Chemistry,** Raymond J. Andersen, University of British Columbia, Vancouver. **Rutherford Medal in Physics,** Claude Leroy, McGill University, Montreal.

Royal Swedish Academy of Sciences. Crafoord Prize, Pierre Deligne, Institute of Advanced Study, Princeton, N.J.; Alexandre Grothendieck, Université des Sciences et Techniques du Languedoc, Montpellier, France (award declined).

United States government. National Medal of Science, William O. Baker, Bell Telephone Laboratories, Murray Hill, N.J.; Konrad E. Bloch, Harvard University; D. Allan Bromley, Yale University; Michael S. Brown, University of Texas; Paul C. W. Chu, University of Houston; Stanley N. Cohen, Stanford University; Elias J. Corey, Harvard University; Daniel C. Drucker, University of Florida; Milton Friedman, Stanford University; Joseph L. Goldstein, University of Texas Southwestern Medical Center; Ralph E. Gomory, International Business Machines Corporation (IBM); Willis M. Hawkins, Lockheed Corporation; Maurice R. Hilleman, Merck and Company; George W. Housner, California Institute of Technology; Eric R. Kandel, Columbia University and New York State Psychiatric Institute; Joseph B. Keller, Stanford University; Walter Kohn, University of California at Santa Barbara; Norman F. Ramsey, Harvard University; Jack Steinberger, European Laboratory for Particle Physics, Geneva, Switzerland; Rosalyn S. Yalow, Mount Sinai School of Medicine.

National Medal of Technology, John L. Atwood, Rockwell International Corporation; Arnold O. Beckman, Beckman Instruments; Paul M. Cook, Raychem Corporation; Raymond Damadian, Fonar Corporation; Robert H. Dennard, IBM; Harold E. Edgerton, M.I.T.; Clarence L. Johnson, Lockheed Corporation; Edwin H. Land, founder of the Polaroid Corporation; Paul C. Lauterbur, University of Illinois; David Packard, Hewlett-Packard Company.

University of Southern California. John and Alice Tyler Prize for Environmental Achievement, Bert R. J. Bolin, International Meteorological Institute, Stockholm, Sweden.
Sara Dreyfuss

Bahamas. See **Latin America.**

Bahrain. See **Middle East.**

Ballet. See **Dancing.**

Bangladesh in 1988 suffered its second consecutive year of devastating summertime floods. Three-fourths of the country was affected, with high-water records broken in most areas. Parts of Dhaka, the capital, were flooded for the first time in memory.

In September, President Hussain Muhammad Ershad said that his nation had never before faced a natural disaster of such proportions. An estimated 25 million of Bangladesh's 112 million people were left temporarily homeless. People huddled on roofs and lived in trees. Relief camps provided some people with a place to stay, but most camps lacked adequate drinking water, food, and medical care. Consumption of tainted water led to widespread outbreaks of diarrhea, which contributed to the flood's death toll, estimated at 1,600. Property damage was estimated at up to $2 billion, and about one-third of the year's food crop was destroyed.

Although some flooding is normal in Bangladesh, which lies in the delta of the Ganges and Brahmaputra rivers, environmental experts agreed that the catastrophic floods of 1987 and 1988 were primarily caused by deforestation of the Himalaya in India, Nepal, and Bhutan—all of which are upstream of Bangladesh. Once denuded, the Himalaya does not have enough vegetation to soak up the monsoon rains and release them gradually. Instead, silt-laden water cascades down to the delta. In September, Ershad tried to organize a regional plan to reduce flooding, but India obstructed it. None of the upstream countries were eager to have their valleys flooded to hold back water, and reforestation projects would take many years.

Nature dealt Bangladesh another savage blow when a hurricane hit the Bay of Bengal coastline on November 29. The hurricane's towering tidal wave killed at least 3,000 people.

Economic conditions were hurt by nature and by labor strikes in late 1987 and early 1988. Already one of the world's poorest countries, Bangladesh saw its living standards decline further in 1988. The garment industry showed growth in 1988, however, replacing jute as the nation's main export.

Elections to choose 44,000 mayors and members of local councils were held on February 10. On March 3, the fourth parliamentary election since Bangladesh's independence in 1971 filled all 300 seats of the legislature. Because the two main opposition parties boycotted the election, Ershad's Jatiya Dal (National Party) obtained 256 seats. On March 27, Ershad swore in Moudud Ahmed, a former deputy prime minister, as prime minister.

A constitutional amendment enacted on June 7 made Islam the state religion of Bangladesh. Opposition politicians called the amendment illegal and unnecessary, and said it would complicate relations with non-Muslims.   Henry S. Bradsher

See also **Asia** (Facts in brief table). In *World Book*, see **Bangladesh.**

Bank. The year 1988 was essentially a good one for the United States economy, but the banking system still suffered from years of bad loans and difficult changes. The U.S. economy expanded for a sixth straight year, a peacetime record. The gross national product (GNP)—the total of goods and services produced by the nation—grew at a 3.9 per cent annual rate in 1988. Unemployment also fell, from 6.1 per cent in 1987 to 5.3 per cent in 1988, the lowest level of joblessness since 1973.

Economies throughout the world expanded as well in 1988. Canada's grew at 2.2 per cent with unemployment of 7.8 per cent (down from 8.6 per cent), Great Britain's at 4 per cent with 8 per cent unemployment (down from 9.8 per cent), and Japan's at 5.6 per cent with 2.8 per cent unemployment.

When a nation's economy is good, people worry about inflation more than unemployment. The U.S. inflation rate had been just under 4 per cent per year since 1982, but it edged up to 4.4 per cent in 1987 and stayed there in 1988. Canada's inflation had also risen from 4.2 per cent in 1987 and early 1988 to 5 per cent in the last half of 1988. Great Britain's inflation rate rose from 5.9 per cent to 6.4 per cent in the same period. In Japan, the price level remained relatively flat in 1988 with an inflation rate of less than 1 per cent.

When inflation fears begin, people look to the nation's *central bank*—a government agency that

A Chicago police captain holds the remains of a chemically coated check that disintegrated hours after being deposited by a con artist in March.

Bank

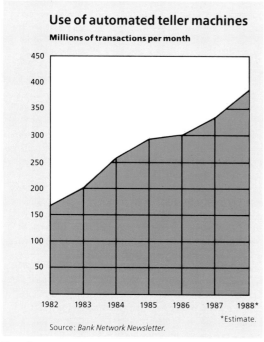

Use of automated teller machines
Millions of transactions per month

Source: *Bank Network Newsletter.*

*Estimate.

Use of automated teller machines, with which people can make deposits and withdraw limited sums of cash 24 hours a day, has more than doubled since 1982.

regulates banking and performs other financial services—to slow the rate of growth of the money supply. The U.S. central bank is the Federal Reserve System—often called simply the Fed. In 1988, the Fed permitted the *monetary base* (the total quantity of bank reserves and currency in the hands of the public) to rise by a steady 6 per cent for the year, with a slight slowing in the second half.

The money supply slowed more dramatically. *M1*, the money supply consisting of currency in the hands of the public and checking account balances, began the year at $752 billion. M1 rose to $780 billion in July and remained in that range through the end of October. The year-end total of $786 billion represented about 4.5 per cent growth for the year.

M1 consists mostly of "money to spend," only part of which pays interest. *M2*, the more broadly defined money supply, consists of M1 plus "money to hold," including savings accounts, certificates of deposit, and money-market funds and money-market deposit accounts at banks. M2 began the year at $2,905 billion and rose smoothly at about a 7.3 per cent annual rate to $3,030 billion in the first week of August. It ranged between $3,025 billion and $3,040 billion during the fall, then rose to about $3,066 billion by year's end.

Money supplies grew considerably more quickly in most other nations in 1988. The broadly defined money supply grew in Canada by 8.8 per cent, in

Britain by 20.1 per cent, in Japan by 10.9 per cent, and in Australia by 13.5 per cent over the year.

Interest rates. Short-term interest rates in the United States rose generally through 1988. The three-month Treasury-bill (T-bill) rate opened the year at 5.9 per cent, passed 7 per cent in mid-August, and ended the year at 8.1 per cent. The prime rate, the rate banks announce as the rate they charge their best corporate customers, was 8.75 per cent in January, dropped to 8.5 per cent in February, rose to 10 per cent in August, and ended December at 10.5 per cent.

As short-term rates rose, the Fed increased the discount rate, the rate of interest it charges banks to borrow its reserves. The discount rate rose from 6 per cent, where it had been since August 1987, to 6.5 per cent.

Long-term rates showed less obvious increases in 1988, and the spread between long-term and short-term rates narrowed in the second half of the year. Corporate AAA bonds, the bonds issued by corporations with the highest credit rating, began the year at 10.0 per cent and fell to 9.4 per cent at the end of February before returning to 10.0 per cent by the end of June. They hovered at about 10 per cent until the beginning of September and then began to fall, finishing December at 9.8 per cent. Five-year Treasury bonds began January at 8.4 per cent, fell to 7.7 per cent in early March, surpassed 9 per cent in August, and fell below 8.5 per cent by the end of October. Treasury bonds ended the year at 9.1 per cent. The spread between AAA bond rates and T-bill rates shrank to 2.1 per cent in October, indicating that short-term rates would probably drop in 1989.

The deposit insurance crisis. United States banks and savings and loan institutions (S&L's) continued to fail in large numbers in 1988 with 200 bank failures and 205 S&L's closed or merged with other institutions. The failures were especially prevalent in the West and Southwest. In those regions, poor harvests and depressed oil and mineral prices, coupled with risky lending on the part of some bank managers, caused many borrowers to fail to pay bank loans when due, eroding bank assets.

When a bank or S&L fails, depositors do not necessarily lose money because most deposits are insured by government agencies—the Federal Deposit Insurance Corporation (FDIC) in the case of banks and the Federal Savings and Loan Insurance Corporation (FSLIC) for S&L's. These agencies charge the institutions premiums of one-twelfth of 1 per cent of all deposits to insure accounts of up to $100,000 each.

Normally, failed banks are merged with healthy ones—minus the failed management. The insurance agency uses part of its reserves from previously collected premiums to cover the bad loans that caused the bank to fail. It is rare for the insurance agency to actually close a bank and pay off the depositors.

When there are many sick banks and few healthy ones, however, it is harder to find a merger partner and the agency's monetary contribution must be greater. More failed banks have to be closed and the depositors reimbursed. If the insurance agency is especially short of cash, it cannot afford to close all the ailing banks and may try to keep some of them going. The agency takes over the job of collecting anything possible on the banks' loans.

The FDIC's reserves had fallen by the end of 1988 from $20 billion to $18.3 billion. The big problem, however, was the FSLIC, which was technically out of money by July. It has, however, the authority to borrow up to $3 billion from the U.S. Treasury.

M. Danny Wall, the chairman of the Federal Home Loan Bank Board, which oversees federally chartered S&L's, estimated in October that it would cost $50-billion to close down all the failing S&L's and pay off their depositors. Other estimates ranged up to $100-billion. FDIC Chairman L. William Seidman on November 30 called for closing the 100 shakiest S&L's in 1989 at an estimated cost of $30 billion. The FSLIC had begun 1988 with reserves of less than $12 billion and was widely expected to require an appropriation from Congress. Congress responded in May 1988 with the Southwest Plan, a federal program to assist the many insolvent S&L's in the economically depressed Southwestern States. Under the plan, such S&L's will operate for up to 10 years backed by bonds with an FSLIC guarantee.   Donald W. Swanton

In *World Book*, see **Bank.**

Baseball. In 1986, the Los Angeles Dodgers finished 15 games under .500, and in 1987, they finished 16 games under. Then the team was rebuilt so well that it won the world championship in 1988.

The New York Mets were favored in the National League championship play-off, but the Dodgers beat them in an exciting struggle, 4 games to 3. The Oakland Athletics were favored in the World Series, but the Dodgers beat them, 4 games to 1.

Orel Hershiser of the Dodgers ended the season by pitching 59 consecutive scoreless innings, breaking the major league record of 58 set by Don Drysdale of the Dodgers 20 years earlier. Hershiser was also a star in the postseason competition. He unanimously won the Cy Young Award as the National League's outstanding pitcher in the regular season and was voted the Most Valuable Player in the National League play-off and again in the World Series.

The Dodgers' most important acquisition in 1988 was Kirk Gibson, a fast, hard-hitting outfielder who played for the Detroit Tigers until an arbitrator made him a free agent in January. Gibson was voted the National League's Most Valuable Player. The American League's Most Valuable Player was Oakland outfielder José Canseco, who became the first major league player ever to hit 40 home runs and steal 40 bases in one season.

Highlights. Major league attendance set a record for the fourth straight year, reaching 52,957,752. The

club owners said the average major league salary was $419,629, also a record. In August, night baseball came to Wrigley Field in Chicago, where the Cubs had been the last major league team to play all home games in sunlight.

Throughout the season, there were fewer runs and home runs, more shutouts, and lower earned-run averages. Tom Browning of the Cincinnati Reds pitched a perfect game, and pitchers in eight other games carried no-hitters into the ninth inning.

Baseball Commissioner Peter V. Ueberroth declined a second five-year term, and the major-league club owners elected National League President A. Bartlett Giamatti as his successor on September 8. Giamatti was formerly the president of Yale University in New Haven, Conn., and a professor of Renaissance literature there.

The New York Yankees fired Billy Martin in June as manager for the fifth time in 10 years. In the Yankees' revolving-door system, he was succeeded by Lou Piniella, the general manager, who preceded Martin as manager.

League races. In the National League, the Dodgers won the Western Division by 7 games over Cincinnati. The Mets beat the Pittsburgh Pirates by 15 games in the Eastern Division.

During the regular season, the Mets won 10 of their 11 games against the Dodgers. After the Mets took a lead of two games to one in the play-off, Gibson—in great pain from a damaged right knee and a strained left hamstring muscle—won the fourth game for the Dodgers, 5-4, with a two-run home run in the 12th inning. The Dodgers won the seventh and deciding game, 6-0, behind Hershiser's five-hit pitching.

In the American League, the Oakland A's finished with a 104-58 record, the best in the major leagues. They won the Western Division by 13 games over the Minnesota Twins. The Boston Red Sox were struggling with a 43-42 record before they replaced manager John McNamara with third-base coach Joe Morgan, and they won the Eastern Division by 1 game over Detroit.

The play-off matched Boston's pitching against Oakland's power. The A's won in four straight games, 2-1, 4-3, 10-6, and 4-1. Canseco hit three home runs. Dennis Eckersley of the A's pitched well in relief in all four games and was voted the play-off's Most Valuable Player.

World Series. Oakland was favored, and Dodger manager Tommy Lasorda said of his team, "We shouldn't even be on the same field as the A's." Then the Dodgers demolished them.

On October 15, in the first game, Gibson received painkilling injections in both legs. Then, as a pinch hitter in the bottom of the ninth inning, he hit a two-out, two-strike home run and limped around the bases to give the Dodgers a dramatic 5-4 victory.

The Dodgers won the second game, 6-0, behind Hershiser's three-hit pitching. The A's won the third

Final standings in major league baseball

American League

Eastern Division

	W.	L.	Pct.	G.B.
Boston Red Sox	89	73	.549	
Detroit Tigers	88	74	.543	1
Milwaukee Brewers	87	75	.537	2
Toronto Blue Jays	87	75	.537	2
New York Yankees	85	76	.528	3½
Cleveland Indians	78	84	.481	11
Baltimore Orioles	54	107	.335	34½

Western Division

	W.	L.	Pct.	G.B.
Oakland Athletics	104	58	.642	
Minnesota Twins	91	71	.562	13
Kansas City Royals	84	77	.522	19½
California Angels	75	87	.463	29
Chicago White Sox	71	90	.441	32½
Texas Rangers	70	91	.435	33½
Seattle Mariners	68	93	.422	35½

American League champions—Oakland Athletics (defeated Boston Red Sox, 4 games to 0)

Offensive leaders

Batting average—Wade Boggs, Boston	.366
Runs scored—Wade Boggs, Boston	128
Home runs—José Canseco, Oakland	42
Runs batted in—José Canseco, Oakland	124
Hits—Kirby Puckett, Minnesota	234
Stolen bases—Rickey Henderson, New York	93
Slugging percentage—José Canseco, Oakland	.569

Leading pitchers

Games won—Frank Viola, Minnesota	24
Win average (15 decisions or more)—Frank Viola, Minnesota (24-7)	.774
Earned run average (162 or more innings)—Allan Anderson, Minnesota	2.446
Strikeouts—Roger Clemens, Boston	291
Saves—Dennis Eckersley, Oakland	45
Shutouts—Roger Clemens, Boston	8

Awards*

Most Valuable Player—José Canseco, Oakland
Cy Young—Frank Viola, Minnesota
Rookie of the Year—Walt Weiss, Oakland
Manager of the Year—Tony LaRussa, Oakland

National League

Eastern Division

	W.	L.	Pct.	G.B.
New York Mets	100	60	.625	
Pittsburgh Pirates	85	75	.531	15
Montreal Expos	81	81	.500	20
Chicago Cubs	77	85	.475	24
St. Louis Cardinals	76	86	.469	25
Philadelphia Phillies	65	96	.404	35½

Western Division

	W.	L.	Pct.	G.B.
Los Angeles Dodgers	94	67	.584	
Cincinnati Reds	87	74	.540	7
San Diego Padres	83	78	.516	11
San Francisco Giants	83	79	.512	11½
Houston Astros	82	80	.506	12½
Atlanta Braves	54	106	.338	39½

National League champions—Los Angeles Dodgers (defeated New York Mets, 4 games to 3)
World Series champions—Los Angeles Dodgers (4 games to 1)

Offensive leaders

Batting average—Tony Gwynn, San Diego	.313
Runs scored—Brett Butler, San Francisco	109
Home runs—Darryl Strawberry, New York	39
Runs batted in—Will Clark, San Francisco	109
Hits—Andres Galarraga, Montreal	184
Stolen bases—Vince Coleman, St. Louis	81
Slugging percentage—Darryl Strawberry, New York	.545

Leading pitchers

Games won—Orel Hershiser, Los Angeles, and Danny Jackson, Cincinnati (tie)	23
Win average (15 decisions or more)—David Cone, New York (20-3)	.870
Earned run average (162 or more innings)—Joe Magrane, St. Louis	2.18
Strikeouts—Nolan Ryan, Houston	228
Saves—John Franco, Cincinnati	39
Shutouts—Orel Hershiser, Los Angeles	8

Awards*

Most Valuable Player—Kirk Gibson, Los Angeles
Cy Young—Orel Hershiser, Los Angeles
Rookie of the Year—Chris Sabo, Cincinnati
Manager of the Year—Tommy Lasorda, Los Angeles

*Selected by Baseball Writers Association of America.

game, 2-1, on first baseman Mark McGwire's ninth-inning home run. The Dodgers won the fourth game, 4-3, and closed out the series by winning the fifth game, 5-2, on October 21 on Hershiser's four-hit pitching. In his last seven weeks, including the play-off and the World Series, Hershiser had a 9-0 record in 11 starts. For postseason play, each Dodger earned an additional $108,664, and each player on the A's received $86,220.

Stars. Frank Viola of Minnesota won the Cy Young Award in the American League. Third baseman Chris Sabo of Cincinnati and shortstop Walt Weiss of Oakland were the rookies of the year. Lasorda and Oakland's Tony LaRussa were the managers of the year. Third baseman Wade Boggs of Boston led the Ameri-

can League in batting for the fourth straight year with a .366 average.

The Associated Press all-star team had Hershiser as the right-handed pitcher; Viola as the left-handed pitcher; Eckersley as the relief pitcher; Benito Santiago of the San Diego Padres catching; Will Clark of the San Francisco Giants at first base; Ryne Sandberg of the Cubs at second base; Alan Trammell of Detroit at shortstop; Boggs at third base; Paul Molitor of the Milwaukee Brewers as the designated hitter; and Canseco, Kirby Puckett of Minnesota, and Mike Greenwell of Boston in the outfield.

Hall of Fame. Willie Stargell, a Pittsburgh outfielder for 21 years, was voted into the National Baseball Hall of Fame in Cooperstown, N.Y., in his first year

Los Angeles Dodger pitcher Orel Hershiser tossed a record 59 consecutive shutout innings, reaching the mark in a game against San Diego in September.

of eligibility. Stargell retired after the 1982 season with 475 home runs and a career .282 batting average. Pitcher Jim Bunning just missed being elected, getting 317 votes when he needed 321. For the first time since it was formed in 1956, the veterans committee failed to elect anyone to the Hall of Fame.

Arbitration. For years, the major league players contended that the club owners had violated the collective-bargaining agreement by conspiring to restrict movement of free agents. The players were upheld by arbitrators in 1987 and 1988.

In September 1987, arbitrator Thomas T. Roberts ruled that the owners had acted in collusion after the 1985 season. On Jan. 22, 1988, Roberts made seven of the affected players free agents again. The only one of the seven who then signed with another team was Gibson, who joined the Dodgers for $4.5 million over three years.

On August 31, arbitrator George Nicolau found similar collusion after the 1986 season. On October 24, he declared 14 of the players involved to be free agents again.

There were few free-agent moves after the end of the 1987 season. In one major move, the Yankees signed Jack Clark, the St. Louis Cardinals' power-hitting first baseman, for $3 million over two years. After the 1988 season, however, the Yankees traded him to San Diego.   Frank Litsky

In *World Book*, see **Baseball.**

Basketball. The University of Kansas unexpectedly won the National Collegiate Athletic Association's (NCAA) 1988 championship tournament for men. Louisiana Tech won the NCAA women's championship. In professional basketball, the Los Angeles Lakers became the first team to win two consecutive National Basketball Association (NBA) championships since the Boston Celtics did it in 1968 and 1969.

Men's college season. No single team dominated the regular college season. The best record among the major colleges was Temple's 29-1. Temple's only loss came by 1 point to Nevada-Las Vegas. Arizona finished the regular season at 31-2; North Carolina A & T at 26-2; Oklahoma at 30-3; Purdue and Loyola Marymount at 27-3; Xavier (Ohio) at 26-3; and Bradley at 26-4. Kansas had an unremarkable 21-11 record.

After the regular season, the Associated Press (AP) and United Press International (UPI) polls named the same leaders. Temple was ranked first, Arizona second, Purdue third, Oklahoma fourth, Duke fifth, and Kentucky sixth. Kansas was ranked 33rd in the AP poll and received no votes in the UPI poll. After being eliminated early in the Big Eight Conference tournament, Kansas received an at-large invitation to the NCAA tournament and was given odds of 50-1 to win.

The 50th annual NCAA tournament started with 64 teams in four regional competitions. The East regional produced three major upsets that eliminated Indiana, the defending national champion; Syracuse, which

Basketball

had gone to the Final Four in 1987; and Temple, the first-ranked team.

Final Four. The regional winners advanced to the Final Four in Kansas City, Mo. They were Duke and Kansas, each in the Final Four for the second time in three years; Oklahoma, the highest-scoring team with a 104-point average per game; and Arizona.

In the national semifinals on April 2, Kansas defeated Duke, 66-59, and Oklahoma eliminated Arizona, 86-78. That brought two teams from the Big Eight to the final on April 4. Oklahoma was favored to beat Kansas for the third time in the season. But Kansas shot with 71 per cent field-goal accuracy in the first half, Kansas forward Danny Manning sank four free throws in the last 14 seconds of the game, and Kansas won, 83-79. Manning finished with 31 points, 18 rebounds, five steals, and two blocked shots and was voted the tournament's Most Valuable Player.

On June 13, Larry Brown resigned as Kansas coach to coach the San Antonio Spurs of the NBA for $3.5-million over five years, the highest-paying coaching contract ever in professional or college basketball. On November 1, the NCAA put Kansas on three-year probation and banned it from its 1989 tournament for recruiting violations during Brown's tenure.

Manning and Bradley guard Hersey Hawkins were frequently cited as the year's best players. Hawkins was the regular-season scoring leader, averaging 36.3 points per game. The popular choices for the All-

University of Kansas forward Danny Manning leads his team to the NCAA title with an 83 to 79 victory over Oklahoma in the final on April 4 in Kansas City, Mo.

National Basketball Association standings

Eastern Conference

Atlantic Division

	W.	L.	Pct.	G.B.
Boston Celtics	57	25	.695	
New York Knicks	38	44	.463	19
Washington Bullets	38	44	.463	19
Philadelphia 76ers	36	46	.439	21
New Jersey Nets	19	63	.232	38

Central Division

	W.	L.	Pct.	G.B.
Detroit Pistons	54	28	.659	
Atlanta Hawks	50	32	.610	4
Chicago Bulls	50	32	.610	4
Cleveland Cavaliers	42	40	.512	12
Milwaukee Bucks	42	40	.512	12
Indiana Pacers	38	44	.463	16

Western Conference

Midwest Division

	W.	L.	Pct.	G.B.
Denver Nuggets	54	28	.659	
Dallas Mavericks	53	29	.646	1
Utah Jazz	47	35	.573	7
Houston Rockets	46	36	.561	8
San Antonio Spurs	31	51	.378	23
Sacramento Kings	24	58	.293	30

Pacific Division

	W.	L.	Pct.	G.B.
Los Angeles Lakers	62	20	.756	
Portland Trail Blazers	53	29	.646	9
Seattle SuperSonics	44	38	.537	18
Phoenix Suns	28	54	.341	34
Golden State Warriors	20	62	.244	42
Los Angeles Clippers	17	65	.207	45

NBA champions—Los Angeles Lakers (defeated Detroit Pistons, 4 games to 3)

Individual leaders

Scoring

	G.	F.G.	F.T.	Pts.	Avg.
Michael Jordan, Chicago	82	1,069	723	2,868	35.0
Dominique Wilkins, Atlanta	78	909	541	2,397	30.7
Larry Bird, Boston	76	881	415	2,275	29.9
Charles Barkley, Philadelphia	80	753	714	2,264	28.3
Karl Malone, Utah	82	858	552	2,268	27.7
Clyde Drexler, Portland	81	849	476	2,185	27.0
Dale Ellis, Seattle	75	764	303	1,938	25.8

Rebounding

	G.	Tot.	Avg.
Michael Cage, L.A. Clippers	72	938	13.03
Charles Oakley, Chicago	82	1,066	13.00
Akeem Olajuwon, Houston	79	959	12.1
Karl Malone, Utah	82	986	12.0

America team were Hawkins, Manning, forward Sean Elliott of Arizona, center J. R. Reid of North Carolina, and guard Gary Grant of Michigan.

College women. After the regular season, the AP poll listed Tennessee (28-2), the defending national champion, first; Iowa (27-1), second; Auburn (28-2), third; Texas (24-2), fourth; and Louisiana Tech (27-2), fifth. They were among the 48 teams chosen for the NCAA women's tournament. In separate voting for Player of the Year, the Naismith Trophy went to Rutgers forward Sue Wicks and the Wade Trophy to Louisiana Tech guard Teresa Witherspoon.

In the Final Four semifinals held on April 1 in Tacoma, Wash., Louisiana Tech upset Tennessee, 68-59, and Auburn defeated Long Beach State, 68-55.

In the April 3 final, Louisiana Tech—trailing by 14 points at half-time—turned to a smaller, faster line-up and won, 56-54. Erica Westbrooks, a Louisiana Tech forward, contributed 25 points, seven rebounds, and six steals and was voted the tournament's Most Valuable Player.

NBA season. The NBA's regular season went much as expected. From October 1987 to April 1988, the 23 teams played 82 games each. The division winners were the Lakers (62-20) by 9 games over the Portland Trail Blazers; Boston (57-25) by 19 games over the Washington Bullets and the New York Knicks; the Detroit Pistons (54-28) by 4 games over the Chicago Bulls and the Atlanta Hawks; and the Denver Nuggets (54-28) by 1 game over the Dallas Mavericks.

Of the 16 teams that qualified for the play-offs, the Lakers and the aging Celtics seemed likely to gain the finals, as they had so often in the past. But the Celtics did not make it.

The Lakers eliminated San Antonio (3 games to 0), the Utah Jazz (4-3), and Dallas (4-3). The Celtics got by the Knicks (3-1) and Atlanta (4-3), then lost to Detroit (4-2) in the conference final.

The championship series matched the Lakers' speed against the Pistons' power. The Pistons took a 3-2 lead in games and were one victory short of the championship when the Lakers rallied on their home court in Inglewood, Calif.

On June 19, the Lakers won, 103-102, on two free throws in the last 14 seconds by 41-year-old center Kareem Abdul-Jabbar. Isiah Thomas, the Pistons' playmaker, finished that game with 43 points, eight assists, six steals, and a sprained right ankle.

Thomas needed crutches to walk, but he played much of the seventh and deciding game on June 21. Thomas scored 10 points, but the Lakers won, 108-105. Lakers forward James Worthy had 36 points, 16 rebounds, and 10 assists and was voted Most Valuable Player of the finals.

Other stars. At age 25, Michael Jordan of Chicago was the league's most spectacular player with his gravity-defying moves. He was the Most Valuable Player in the regular season and the all-star game, the defensive Player of the Year, and the scoring champion with an average of 35.0 points per game. The all-star team comprised Jordan and Earvin (Magic) Johnson of the Lakers at guard, Akeem Olajuwon of the Houston Rockets at center, and Larry Bird of the Celtics and Charles Barkley of the Philadelphia 76ers at forward.

Other developments. On April 26, the owners and the players reached a six-year collective-bargaining agreement that was expected eventually to raise the players' average salary of $533,000 to almost $1 million. Attendance rose for the fifth consecutive season to 12,654,374. Expansion teams started playing in the 1988-1989 season in Charlotte, N.C., and Miami, Fla.   Frank Litsky

In *World Book*, see **Basketball.**

The 1987-1988 college basketball season

College tournament champions

NCAA (Men) Division I: Kansas
      Division II: Lowell (Mass.)
      Division III: Ohio Wesleyan
NCAA (Women) Division I: Louisiana Tech
      Division II: Hampton (Virginia)
      Division III: Concordia-Moorhead (Minn.)
NAIA (Men): Grand Canyon (Ariz.)
      (Women): Oklahoma City
NIT (Men): Connecticut
      (Women): De Paul
Junior College (Men): Hutchinson (Kansas)
      (Women): Kilgore (Texas)

College champions

Conference	School
American South	Louisiana Tech—New Orleans (tie; regular season)
	Louisiana Tech (tournament)
Atlantic Coast	North Carolina (regular season)
	Duke (tournament)
Atlantic Ten	Temple*
Big East	Pittsburgh (regular season)
	Syracuse (tournament)
Big Eight	Oklahoma*
Big Sky	Boise State*
Big South	Coastal Carolina (regular season)
	Winthrop (tournament)
Big Ten	Purdue
Colonial Athletic	Richmond*
East Coast	Lafayette (regular season)
	Lehigh (tournament)
Eastern College Athletic-Metro	Fairleigh Dickinson*
Eastern College Athletic-North	Siena (regular season)
	Boston U. (tournament)
Ivy League	Cornell
Metro	Louisville*
Metro Atlantic	La Salle*
Mid-American	Eastern Michigan*
Mid-Continent	Southwest Missouri State
Mid-Eastern	North Carolina A & T*
Midwestern City	Xavier*
Missouri Valley	Bradley*
Ohio Valley	Murray State*
Pacific Coast Athletic	Nevada-Las Vegas (regular season)
	Utah State (tournament)
Pacific Ten	Arizona*
Southeastern	Kentucky*
Southern	Marshall (regular season)
	Tennessee-Chattanooga (tournament)
Southland	North Texas State*
Southwest	Southern Methodist*
Southwestern Athletic	Southern-Baton Rouge*
Sun Belt	North Carolina-Charlotte*
Trans America Athletic	Arkansas-Little Rock—Georgia Southern (tie; regular season)
	Texas-San Antonio (tournament)
West Coast Athletic	Loyola Marymount*
Western Athletic	Brigham Young (regular season)
	Wyoming (tournament)

*Regular season and conference tournament champions.

Belgium

Belgium ended a period of political chaos on May 6, 1988, when King Baudouin I asked Wilfried A. E. Martens to form a new coalition government. Martens had resigned as prime minister on Oct. 15, 1987, after a long-running dispute involving Belgium's two major ethnic groups split his moderate Christian Social Party along ethnic lines.

The split in Martens' party prompted the collapse of his government, a coalition with the right wing Liberals. After resigning, Martens stayed on as caretaker prime minister.

Ethnic conflict. Most Belgians belong to one of the two major ethnic groups—the Flemings, who speak Dutch, and the Walloons, whose language is French. Most Flemings live in northern Belgium, which is called Flanders; most Walloons live in southern Belgium, known as Wallonia. The metropolitan area that includes Brussels, the capital of Belgium, is officially bilingual.

Friction between the two groups has hindered economic development in Belgium. The event that triggered Martens' 1987 resignation was a compromise arranged by Martens to give French-speaking minorities who live in Dutch-speaking regions more power in regional affairs. Officials elected by such minorities, however, would have to take a test to show that they can speak Dutch.

Socialists join government. Martens surprised political observers by forming a new government in coalition with the Socialists, rather than the Liberals. The Socialists had not participated in a governing coalition since 1944. Martens' 1988 coalition also included a small party representing Flemish interests. The new government was sworn in on May 9.

The governing parties held 150 of the 212 seats in the House of Representatives, the more powerful of the two houses of Parliament. Martens said that, with this majority, he intended to press on with a federalization plan and an austerity program.

Regional control. On August 5, the Senate approved the first phase of Martens' federalization plan, under which control of almost 50 per cent of the national government's funds will be handed over to Wallonia, Flanders, and the Brussels metropolitan area. The three regions will control their own schools, economic policies, public works programs, and research and development efforts in an attempt to minimize their historic friction.

Martens' austerity program, designed to curb inflation, would cut Belgium's budget deficit from its current level of 8 per cent of *gross national product* (the total output of goods and services) to 7 per cent in 1989. In a budget announced on August 15, the coalition promised to cut spending on health care and defense in 1989.   Kenneth Brown

See also **Europe** (Facts in brief table). In *World Book*, see **Belgium**.

Belize. See **Latin America.**

Benin. See **Africa.**

Bentsen, Lloyd Millard, Jr. (1921-   ), a Democratic senator from Texas, waged two political campaigns during 1988: one as a senator seeking reelection and the other as the running mate of Democratic presidential candidate Michael S. Dukakis. Although Bentsen won reelection to the Senate on November 8, he and Dukakis lost to Republicans Vice President George Bush and Indiana Senator Dan Quayle. See **Elections; Dukakis, Michael S.**

Some political experts questioned Dukakis' selection of Bentsen as a running mate. A conservative Democrat, Bentsen supports some things that Dukakis opposes, such as mandatory school prayer and aid to *contra* rebels fighting the Marxist government in Nicaragua. But Democratic leaders hoped that Bentsen's more conservative stance on some issues would offset Dukakis' liberal image. They also expected the Texan to enhance Dukakis' popularity in the South.

Bentsen was born on Feb. 11, 1921, in Mission, Tex. He received a law degree in 1942 from the University of Texas at Austin. In 1948, he was elected to the U.S. House of Representatives, a position he held for three terms. He left politics to become president and chief executive officer of an insurance company in Houston in 1955.

Bentsen returned to politics in 1970, defeating Bush in a Senate race. In 1987, he was named chairman of the Senate Finance Committee.   Mary A. Krier

Bhutan. See **Asia.**

Bhutto, Benazir (1953-   ), became prime minister of Pakistan on Dec. 2, 1988, the first woman to hold the highest office in a modern Muslim nation. Bhutto was named prime minister after her Pakistan People's Party on November 16 was elected to more seats in parliament than any other party. She had been a visible leader of the movement opposing Pakistan's President M. Zia-ul-Haq, who died in an airplane crash on August 17. Upon taking office, she announced that "11 years of tyranny are over." See **Pakistan.**

Bhutto was born on June 21, 1953, in Sind Province, the daughter of Zulfikar Ali Bhutto, who was Pakistan's prime minister from 1971 until 1977. She attended convent schools in Pakistan and then Radcliffe College in Cambridge, Mass. Bhutto graduated in 1973 with a bachelor of arts degree and then enrolled in Oxford University in England, where she received a bachelor's degree in 1977.

Bhutto returned to Pakistan in 1977, a few weeks before a coup led by Zia overthrew her father's government. After the elder Bhutto was executed in 1979 by Zia's regime, Benazir Bhutto became an outspoken opponent of Zia. She was jailed several times and spent nearly nine years in self-imposed exile, finally returning to Pakistan in 1986.

In late 1987, Bhutto married Asif Ali Zardari. In September 1988, less than two months before the November election, Bhutto gave birth to the couple's first child, a son named Bilawal.   Jinger Hoop

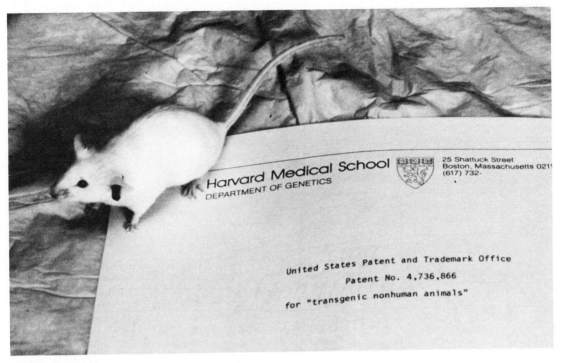

A cancer-prone laboratory mouse, genetically engineered by Harvard Medical School scientists, in 1988 became the first patented animal.

Biology. Scientists in 1988 found several ways to turn mice into effective models for research on AIDS (acquired immune deficiency syndrome) and other human diseases. In September 1988, researchers at Stanford University School of Medicine in California reported that they had developed working human immune systems in mice by implanting human fetal tissue into mice whose own immune systems did not work. That same month, researchers at the Medical Biology Institute in La Jolla, Calif., reported similar results from injecting human blood cells into mice. In December, researchers at the Hospital for Sick Children in Toronto, Canada, altered mice by transplanting human bone marrow cells into them.

By the end of the year, both of the California groups were able to infect their altered mice with the virus that causes AIDS, creating a promising new tool for studying the disease. Until now, AIDS research has relied on chimpanzees—which are expensive and in danger of extinction—because they are the only animals besides human beings that can be naturally infected with the virus.

Genome map. Scientists worldwide continued in 1988 to discuss plans for a coordinated effort to map all human genes. Genes, which determine all inherited traits, are made up of a chemical substance called *deoxyribonucleic acid* (DNA) and are arranged in a particular order on the chromosomes in a human cell. A map of the human *genome*—the approximately

100,000 human genes and the 3 billion units of DNA they comprise—could help researchers identify the causes of inherited diseases and develop ways to prevent or treat them.

Such a project, which would involve geneticists working independently as well as in central laboratories, might cost $3 billion and take at least 15 years. In the United States, both the National Institutes of Health (NIH) and the Department of Energy have taken early steps in leading gene-mapping efforts. Japan and several European countries also committed resources to genome projects in 1988. And geneticists from around the world formed a group called the Human Genome Organization to coordinate gene-mapping work internationally.

Missing genes. A major exception to a fundamental rule of biology was reported in June by researchers from the University of California at Los Angeles and the University of Washington in Seattle. A basic principle of biology is that all genetic information is contained in DNA. Cells use this information to produce proteins and other cellular components.

The researchers found, however, that in a family of disease-causing parasites called *kinetoplastids*, the DNA of some genes is garbled and unusable. An unknown mechanism in the cell apparently provides additional information so that the garbled genes can be used to produce functional proteins. The researchers added that human beings and other mammals have

Biology

segments of DNA that appear to be genes but are missing crucial parts. Such "pseudogenes" might also use genetic information carried elsewhere in the cell.

Intentional evolution. Bacteria may be able to partly direct their own evolution by choosing or even stimulating genetic changes that will benefit them, biologists reported in September. Scientists had previously thought that *mutations*—changes in DNA typically caused by chemicals or radiation—occur completely at random, and that long-term, evolutionary change in a given species results from the accumulation of mutations that help the organism survive and reproduce.

In separate studies, researchers at the Harvard School of Public Health in Boston and the University of Connecticut in Storrs placed bacteria in a culture containing food that the bacteria were unable to process. In both studies, some of the bacteria responded with the specific series of mutations that enabled them to use the food. They then passed the mutated genes on to their descendants. The scientists concluded that microorganisms can produce or choose mutations in direct response to particular needs as well as by chance. These results may alter scientists' views of how microorganisms evolved into more complicated life forms.

A new category of genetic diseases—caused by defects in *mitochondria*, the energy-producing parts of cells—has been discovered by researchers at the Emory University School of Medicine in Atlanta, Ga. Although nearly all of a cell's genes are located in its nucleus, each mitochondrion contains a few genes that give instructions for making the proteins involved in energy production.

The researchers reported in July that a disease called Leber's hereditary optic neuropathy, which leads to blindness, is caused by a defect in a mitochondrial gene. Because mitochondrial genes come only from the mother, the disease is passed down maternally. The researchers are looking at other maternally inherited diseases to see if they are caused by similar mitochondrial defects.

Gene transplant. NIH researchers received permission from an NIH advisory panel in October to perform the first authorized attempt at genetic engineering in human beings. The experiment was approved by the Food and Drug Administration in December but still required approval from the head of the NIH.

The researchers want to implant a gene for antibiotic resistance into white blood cells that have been treated with *interleukin-2*, a protein that enhances the cells' ability to fight tumors. Such cells are used in an experimental cancer therapy. The gene would not affect the cells' tumor-fighting activity, but would act as a marker to enable the researchers to trace the cells in the patients' bodies. The attempt may help scientists both in developing better cancer therapies and in learning how to make genetically engineered cells work in human beings.   Thomas H. Maugh II

In **World Book**, see **Biology.**

Boating. In the 137-year history of America's Cup yachting, no series involved more controversy or bitterness than the 1988 defense won by the United States over New Zealand. Since the 1940's, America's Cup races had been sailed in sloops of the 12-Meter class, actually 65-foot (20-meter) boats of similar design. The 1988 races, however, were sailed in vastly different boats—the U.S. defenders in a sleek twin-hulled catamaran and the New Zealand challengers in a huge monohull sloop twice the size of boats in the 12-Meter class.

The United States had regained the cup from Australia in 1987 and then had received challenges from 21 clubs in 10 nations for a traditional defense in 1991. It also received a surprise challenge from Michael Fay, a New Zealand banker whose 12-Meter boat lost in 1987.

Fay challenged for a 1988 series to be sailed in a large, high-technology boat. He said his challenge was legal under the 100-year-old Deed of Gift, which established the rules for America's Cup racing. The deed specifies that the rules be interpreted by the New York State Supreme Court. The defending San Diego Yacht Club refused Fay's challenge, but the court upheld Fay.

Sail America, the defending syndicate, then yielded and accepted Fay's challenge. Later, the syndicate said it would defend in a boat of its choice and, in a surprise move, chose a catamaran.

The challenging yacht *New Zealand* was 132 feet (40 meters) long and 90 feet (27 meters) on the water line, with a mast about as high as a 16-story building. The defending *Stars & Stripes* was only 60 feet (18 meters) long and weighed 6,000 pounds (2,700 kilograms), compared with *New Zealand*'s 70,000 pounds (32,000 kilograms).

The best-two-of-three-race series began on September 7, off San Diego. Fay said it would be a mismatch because catamarans usually go much faster than monohulls, and he said that if he lost, he would go to court on the grounds that he was denied a fair match.

Dennis Conner, the defending syndicate's manager, sailed *Stars & Stripes* to runaway victories by margins of 18 minutes 15 seconds in the first race on September 7 and 21 minutes 10 seconds in the second race on September 9. Pending a reversal by the court, the cup remained in the United States, and the next challenge was scheduled for 1991 in a boat class to be determined later.

Powerboats. In the races for unlimited hydroplanes—big boats powered by old airplane engines—*Miss Budweiser* won four of the nine races and the series title. The driver was Tom D'Eath of Fair Haven, Mich. In the U.S. series for offshore boats, Al Copeland of New Orleans drove his *Popeyes/diet Coke* to four victories in the eight races and the overall championship. Television star Don Johnson won the world offshore title.   Frank Litsky

In **World Book**, see **Boating; Sailing.**

Boitano, Brian (1963-   ), of the United States narrowly defeated Canadian favorite Brian Orser to win the men's figure-skating event on Feb. 20, 1988, at the Winter Olympics in Calgary, Canada. Then, at the world championships in March in Budapest, Hungary, Boitano regained the world title in men's figure skating, which he had held in 1986 and lost to Orser in 1987. See **Ice skating; Olympic Games.**

Boitano was born on Oct. 22, 1963, in Sunnyvale, Calif., where he still resides. An avid roller skater as a child, he began ice skating at age 8. When he was 14, while attending Peterson High School in Sunnyvale, he became the 1978 U.S. Junior Men's champion. He drew early notice for his technical feats: In 1982, he became the first skater to perform a triple axel in the U.S. national competition, and in 1983 he was the first to complete all six different triple jumps in a world championship competition.

Boitano placed fifth in the 1984 Winter Olympics and held the U.S. men's title from 1985 through 1988. In all, he has won 12 gold medals in international competition, earned more than 50 titles, and skated in exhibitions throughout the world.

Known for his precision and his powerful jumps, Boitano pioneered such challenging maneuvers as the 'Tano Triple, which consists of three revolutions in the air with one arm extended overhead. The world champion skater plans to continue his skating career as a professional.   Robin Goldman

Bolivia. About half of Bolivia's foreign creditors sold back $334 million in debt at 11 per cent of its face value, it was reported on Aug. 11, 1988. The transaction cut Bolivia's total foreign debts by nearly half.

The Bolivian government also followed through in 1988 on another agreement to reduce its debt. In 1987, Bolivia had made an unusual agreement with Conservation International whereby the Washington-based nonprofit group bought up $650,000 of deeply discounted debt for about $100,000. In 1988, the Bolivian legislature honored its part of the bargain by creating a nearly 4-million-acre (1.6-million-hectare) conservation area in the north-central part of Bolivia. The area, which adjoins an established reserve of 334,000 acres (135,200 hectares), is rich in endangered species, including the jaguar, giant armadillo, maned wolf, and four-eyed opossum. United States Secretary of the Treasury James A. Baker III had endorsed such exchanges of debt for conservation rights as a way of relieving the debt problems of developing nations.

On a visit to Oruro, a depressed tin-mining center, on May 11, Pope John Paul II delivered a sharp attack on free-market capitalism, blaming it for Bolivia's economic woes. At Santa Cruz—a major focus of cocaine trafficking—the pope warned 200,000 Bolivians against the illicit drug trade.   Nathan A. Haverstock

In *World Book*, see **Bolivia.**

Books. See **Canadian literature; Literature; Literature for children.**

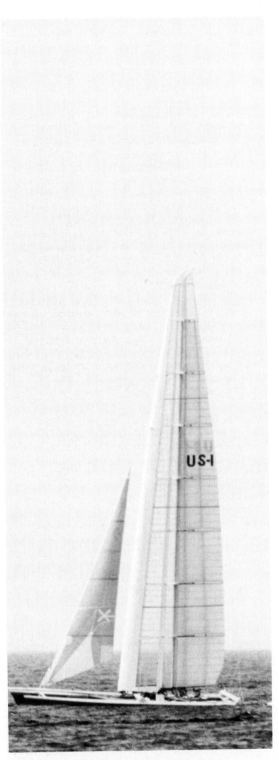

The twin-hulled catamaran *Stars & Stripes,* the United States defender, won the America's Cup yacht races off San Diego in September.

Botany. Scientists made further breakthroughs in the genetic engineering of grain crops in 1988. Geneticists at Sandoz Crop Protection Corporation in Palo Alto, Calif., reported in April that they had successfully transferred a foreign gene into *maize* (corn) cells. The cells developed into mature plants, all of whose cells contained the inserted gene. The experiment represented the first time a foreign gene had been introduced into a grain crop plant. Researchers hope eventually to use gene transfer to give grain plants such useful traits as resistance to insects and diseases.

Plant hemoglobin, a pigment related to the oxygen-carrying molecule in blood, may be more widespread than once thought. Before 1988, hemoglobin had been detected only in the root nodules of a few plants. Bacteria in the root nodules take nitrogen gas from the soil and turn it into a form the plants can use. The hemoglobin brings oxygen to the nodules and the bacteria. In January, scientists at the Commonwealth Scientific and Industrial Research Organization (CSIRO) laboratory in Canberra, Australia, reported that they had found the hemoglobin gene and a small amount of hemoglobin in a plant whose roots have no nodules. The scientists speculated that the gene might be in all plants and that hemoglobin might help roots use oxygen. 　　Eldon H. Newcomb

In *World Book*, see **Botany**. In the Special Reports section, see **Our Vanishing Rain Forests**.

Botswana. See **Africa**.

Bowling. In April 1988, Pete Weber, the son of Hall of Famer Dick Weber, won the richest tournament and the richest winner's purse on the Professional Bowlers Association of America (PBA) tour. In August, PBA Commissioner Joseph R. Antenora suspended the younger Weber for six months for failing to honor commitments for a tournament and a television interview. Weber was already on probation for similar incidents and for violating the PBA code of conduct.

Weber's big victory came in the $500,000 United States Open, held from April 10 to 16 in Atlantic City, N.J. In the championship game of the five-man stepladder final, he defeated Marshall Holman of Medford, Ore., 203 to 171. The victory was worth $100,000. After the 31 tournaments of the winter and the spring-summer tour, Weber's $154,203 ranked him third in earnings. At the age of 26, he already had more than $900,000 in earnings, making him the fourth leading earner in the history of the tour.

Men's tour. The yearlong tour consisted of 37 tournaments worth $6 million in prize money. The leading money-winner was Brian Voss of Tacoma, Wash., with $225,485, a record. Joe Berardi of Wellington, Fla., was the only bowler to win three tournaments during the year.

The three most important tournaments, including the U.S. Open, were played in an eight-week span in winter. In the first of those tournaments, the $270,000 PBA national championship, held from March 6 to 12

in Toledo, Ohio, Voss won by beating Todd Thompson of Reno, Nev., in the final game, 246 to 185. In the $250,000 Firestone Tournament of Champions, held from April 25 to 30 in Akron, Ohio, Mark Williams of Beaumont, Tex., won for the second time in four years, beating Tony Westlake of Edmond, Okla., in the final game, 237 to 214.

On January 23 in Grand Prairie, Tex., Bob Benoit of Topeka, Kans., played in a five-man final for the first time. He rolled a perfect 300—the first time anyone had done that—and won a $100,000 bonus.

Sam Maccarone of Glassboro, N.J., and Pete Mc-Cordic of Houston became winners, too. Maccarone, who had never won in 6 years on the tour, won twice in five weeks. McCordic, who had never won in 15 years on the tour, won twice in six weeks.

Women. After one year of rival tours by the Ladies Pro Bowlers Tour (LPBT) and the Ladies Touring Players Association (LTPA), the women were back to one tour. The LTPA became dormant, and the LPBT staged 17 tournaments with almost $1 million in purses.

The most successful woman was 27-year-old Lisa Wagner of Palmetto, Fla. She won the richest tournament, the $200,000 U.S. Open, held from March 27 to April 2 in Winston-Salem, N.C., and six overall. She became the first woman to earn $100,000 in one year, her $105,500 breaking the record of $81,452 by Aleta Sill of Detroit in 1984. 　　Frank Litsky

In *World Book*, see **Bowling**.

Boxing. The seemingly unending saga of Mike Tyson—in and out of the ring—provided headlines during much of 1988. At age 22, Tyson was recognized as the world heavyweight champion by the three major governing bodies—the World Boxing Council (WBC), the World Boxing Association (WBA), and the International Boxing Federation.

Tyson won his three title defenses in 1988, earning $33.5 million for less than seven rounds of boxing. He knocked out 38-year-old Larry Holmes of Easton, Pa., in four rounds on January 22 in Atlantic City, N.J. Then on March 21 in Tokyo, he knocked out Tony Tubbs of Cincinnati, Ohio, in two rounds. Finally, he knocked out Michael Spinks of St. Louis, Mo., in one round on June 27 in Atlantic City. The previously undefeated Spinks lasted only 91 seconds.

In February, Tyson married Robin Givens, a 24-year-old television actress. After the death of Jimmy Jacobs, Tyson's co-manager, on March 23, Givens and her mother, Ruth Roper, encouraged Tyson to break his contract with the surviving manager, Bill Cayton. Cayton and Tyson seemingly settled their differences in July when Cayton reduced his standard one-third share of Tyson's earnings. Later, Tyson sued Cayton to break the revised contract.

Tyson had many problems. He drove his $180,000 Bentley into a parked car and then tried to give it away. On August 23, during an early-morning brawl with Mitch Green—a heavyweight Tyson had once

Heavyweight champion Mike Tyson towers over challenger Michael Spinks, knocked out in the first round of a bout in June in Atlantic City, N.J.

beaten in the ring—Tyson broke his right hand. Tyson drove another car into a tree on September 4 in what was reported as a suicide attempt, though he denied that. His wife said he was being treated for manic-depression. Tyson's mood swings were well known, but he alternated between acknowledging and denying that he had emotional problems.

Cayton and others who had known Tyson for years said Tyson's wife and mother-in-law were manipulating him. On October 7, his wife filed for divorce, and her lawyer said Givens did not want any of Tyson's money. But Givens later filed a $125-million libel suit against Tyson. See **Tyson, Mike.**

Other. Sugar Ray Leonard ended his latest retirement to fight Donny Lalonde of Canada on November 7 in Las Vegas, Nev. Leonard knocked out Lalonde in the ninth round to win the WBC light-heavyweight title and the WBC's newly created super middleweight title. But on November 15, Leonard retired again and relinquished both titles.

Thomas Hearns, who in 1987 became the first fighter to win four world championships, became the first to win five titles, beating Leonard to that goal by only a few days and only because a new governing body—the World Boxing Organization (WBO)—was created just days before the fight. Hearns defeated James Kinchen in a split decision at Las Vegas to win the WBO super middleweight title.   Frank Litsky

See also **Olympic Games.** In *World Book*, see **Boxing.**

World champion boxers

World Boxing Association

Division	Champion	Country	Date won
Heavyweight	Mike Tyson	U.S.A.	1987
Cruiserweight	Evander Holyfield	U.S.A.	1986
Light heavyweight	Virgil Hill	U.S.A.	1987
Super middleweight	Park Chong-pal	South Korea	1987
	Fulgencio Obelmejias	Venezuela	May '88
Middleweight	Sumbu Kalambay	Italy	1987
Super welterweight	Julian Jackson	U.S. Virgin Islands	1987
Welterweight	Marlon Starling	U.S.A.	1987
	Tomas Molinares	Colombia	July '88
	vacant		Dec. '88
Super lightweight	Juan Martin Coggi	Argentina	1987
Lightweight	Julio César Chávez	Mexico	1987
Super featherweight	Brian Mitchell	South Africa	1986
Featherweight	Antonio Esparragoza	Venezuela	1987
Super bantamweight	Julio Gervacio	Dominican Republic	1987
	Bernardo Pinango	Venezuela	March '88
	Juan José Estrada	Mexico	June '88
Bantamweight	Wilfredo Vasquez	Puerto Rico	1987
	Kaokor Galaxy	Thailand	May '88
	Moon Sung-kil	South Korea	Aug. '88
Super flyweight	Khaosai Galaxy	Thailand	1984
Flyweight	Fidel Bassa	Colombia	1987
Junior flyweight	Myung-Woo Yuh	South Korea	1985
Strawweight	Leo Gâmez	Venezuela	Jan. '88

World Boxing Council

Division	Champion	Country	Date won
Heavyweight	Mike Tyson	U.S.A.	1986
Cruiserweight	Carlos DeLeón	Puerto Rico	1986
	Evander Holyfield	U.S.A.	April '88
Light heavyweight	Donny Lalonde	Canada	1987
	Sugar Ray Leonard	U.S.A.	Nov. '88
	vacant		Nov. '88
Super middleweight	Sugar Ray Leonard	U.S.A.	Nov. '88
	vacant		Nov. '88
Middleweight	Thomas Hearns	U.S.A.	1987
	Iran Barkley	U.S.A.	June '88
Super welterweight	Gianfranco Rosi	Italy	1987
	Donald Curry	U.S.A.	July '88
Welterweight	Jorge Vaca	Mexico	1987
	Lloyd Honeyghan	Great Britain	March '88
Super lightweight	Roger Mayweather	U.S.A.	1987
Lightweight	José-Luis Ramirez	Mexico	1987
	Julio César Chávez	Mexico	Nov. '88
Super featherweight	Azumah Nelson	Ghana	Feb. '88
Featherweight	Azumah Nelson	Ghana	1984
	vacant		
	Jeff Fenech	Australia	March '88
Super bantamweight	Jeff Fenech	Australia	1987
	vacant		
	Daniel Zaragoza	Mexico	Feb. '88
Bantamweight	Miguel Lora	Colombia	1985
	Raul Perez	Mexico	Nov. '88
Super flyweight	Jesus Rojas	Colombia	1987
	Gilberto Roman	Mexico	April '88
Flyweight	Sot Chitalada	Thailand	1984
	Kim Yong-gang	South Korea	July '88
Junior flyweight	Jung-Koo Chang	South Korea	1983
	Jerman Torres	Mexico	Dec. '88
Strawweight	Hiroki Ioka	Japan	1987
	Napa Kaitwanchai	Thailand	Dec. '88

Brady, Nicholas Frederick

Brady, Nicholas Frederick (1930-   ), became United States secretary of the treasury on Sept. 16, 1988. In November, President-elect George Bush said Brady would keep his post in the new Cabinet.

Brady, formerly chairman of the New York City investment banking firm of Dillon, Read & Company, Incorporated, was largely unknown outside financial circles before the stock-market collapse of 1987. Named by President Ronald Reagan to head a probe of the crash, Brady organized a group of experts who concluded that massive selling by large institutional investors was the main cause of the crash.

Brady was born on April 11, 1930, in New York City and grew up on a family estate in Far Hills, N.J. He attended Yale University in New Haven, Conn., graduating in 1952, and earned a master's degree in business administration from Harvard University in Cambridge, Mass., in 1954. He then joined Dillon, Read, which in the 1920's his father had helped build into one of the most prominent investment banking firms in the United States. Brady was instrumental in reviving the company's by-then declining fortunes.

Brady, a Republican, served in the U.S. Senate from April to December 1982, filling the unexpired term of Senator Harrison A. Williams, Jr. (D., N.J.). Williams had been expelled from the Senate after being convicted of bribery and conspiracy.

Brady is married to the former Katherine Douglas. They have four children.   David L. Dreier

Brazil. A new Constitution for Brazil went into effect on Oct. 5, 1988, replacing the 1969 charter of Brazil's former military regime. The new Constitution provides for the direct election of Brazil's president for the first time since 1960 and sets the minimum voting age at 16, the youngest voting age in South America.

During the political compromising that preceded approval of the Constitution, incumbent President José Sarney's term was extended by one year to March 1990 so that he will complete a five-year term in office. Sarney was originally elected to a four-year term, but the new Constitution calls for the president to serve five years.

The 1988 Constitution abolishes the president's powers to make laws by decree. Brazil's new legal framework also transfers substantial powers from the president to the legislative branch.

Ethnic diversity. Two ethnic celebrations in 1988 underscored Brazil's diverse population of 147 million. On May 13, Brazilians marked the 100th anniversary of the abolition of slavery. Brazil has the largest black population of any nation outside Africa. Half of all Brazilians are descended from slaves.

The anniversary was an occasion to protest lingering racism. "We have gone from the hold of the ship to the basement of society," declared Zézé Motta, Brazil's leading black actress and campaigner for black advancement. The rate of illiteracy is 37 per cent among blacks, compared with 15 per cent among whites. Of 559 members of Congress, only 7 consider themselves blacks.

A second ethnic celebration marked the 80th anniversary of the arrival of the first group of Japanese immigrants to Brazil. In 1988, Brazil had 1 million citizens of Japanese descent—the largest such concentration anywhere in the world outside of Japan.

About half of these citizens of Japanese origin have settled in the industrial state of São Paulo, where they have prospered in many industries, including banking and the manufacture of paper, plastics, fertilizers, and electronics. Farmers of Japanese descent produce an estimated 70 per cent of all the vegetables and fruit consumed in the São Paulo metropolitan area—home to more than 12.5 million people.

Farm output. Brazilian farmers took advantage of the drought that struck many parts of the United States in 1988 to add an extra $1.5 billion to their earnings from exports of soybeans. Hardly cultivated in Brazil 15 years ago, soybeans in 1988 surpassed coffee in dollar earnings as Brazil became the world's second-leading soybean exporter.

In nationwide municipal elections on November 15, parties to the right and left of Sarney's centrist Brazilian Democratic Movement Party captured many posts. The results showed widespread dissatisfaction with Brazil's 1,000 per cent annual inflation and other economic problems.   Nathan A. Haverstock

In *World Book*, see **Brazil.**

British Columbia. Premier William N. Vander Zalm, conservative and controversial leader of the Social Credit government, announced in February 1988 that his government would not provide public medical insurance for abortions unless the woman's life was in danger. The Supreme Court of the province overturned that decision on March 7, ruling that the province could not withhold funds for medical services from women. The premier responded in April by announcing a $20-million (Canadian dollars; $1 = U.S. 84 cents as of Dec. 31, 1988) public program to discourage abortion and promote family life.

Two leading members of the Social Credit cabinet resigned in the space of a week in June and July 1988, claiming that they could not carry out their duties because of interference from the premier's office. Both Brian Smith, attorney general, and Grace McCarthy, economic development minister and onetime deputy premier, had been rivals of Vander Zalm for party leadership in 1986. Smith and McCarthy criticized what they saw as Vander Zalm's arbitrary decision-making and attempts to centralize power in the premier's office. Dissatisfaction with Vander Zalm's leadership was also demonstrated at a by-election—a special election to fill a vacancy in the provincial legislature—on June 8, when the Social Credit Party lost a seat it had held for 22 years.   David M. L. Farr

In *World Book*, see **British Columbia.**
Brunei. See Asia.

Building and construction. Work started early in 1988 on what will be the highest all-reinforced-concrete building in the world. The 946-foot (288-meter) office building at 311 S. Wacker Drive in Chicago will rise 87 feet (27 meters) above the previous recordholder, a Chicago building named Water Tower Place. The designers said they were not shooting for a record, but they believed the all-concrete system was best economically and structurally for their building.

The Bank of China's Hong Kong branch, the fifth tallest building in the world and the tallest outside the United States, was topped out at a height of 1,209 feet (369 meters) on Aug. 8, 1988. The quadruple eights of the date—8/8/88—made it a day of good fortune, according to Chinese tradition. A team of Americans designed the composite steel-and-concrete structure.

The last segment of the record-setting span of the Dame Point Bridge in Jacksonville, Fla., was installed in July 1988, and the bridge neared completion at year-end. It has the longest cable-stayed concrete box-girder span in the United States, with a 1,300-foot (400-meter) main span and two 650-foot (200-meter) back spans. The bridge provides 175 feet (53 meters) of clearance over the shipping channel of the St. Johns River.

Channel tunnel. The first year of work on the English Channel Tunnel ran behind schedule and over budget in 1988, and projected construction costs rose from $8.3 billion to $8.8 billion. Still, Eurotunnel—an association of 5 banks and 10 construction companies that owns and operates the privately financed venture—forecast a 6 per cent increase in traffic revenues and believed lost time could be made up to open the tunnel in 1993 as scheduled.

The tunnel—the first to be constructed under the English Channel—will allow electric trains to run between Dover, England, and Calais, France. Of the tunnel's 31 miles (50 kilometers), 23.5 miles (37.5 kilometers) will lie underwater. That will top the record set by the Seikan Tunnel, a 33.5-mile (53.9-kilometer) railway tunnel linking the islands of Honshu and Hokkaido in Japan. The Seikan Tunnel, which was completed in March 1988 after 24 years of work, includes a 14.6-mile (23.3-kilometer) section beneath the Tsugaru Strait.

Bank building fire. On May 4, flames broke out in the 62-story First Interstate Bank Building in Los Angeles. It took nearly 300 fire fighters four hours to control the fire, which killed 1 person and injured more than 30, gutted floors 12 through 16, and caused $450 million in damage. The cause remained unknown, though officials ruled out arson.

The fire broke out even as workers were installing a sprinkler system that, once in place, might have limited the fire to part of one floor. The installation was voluntary; Los Angeles did not require sprinklers in buildings built before the City Council passed a sprin-

Egyptian workers begin restoration of the Sphinx's neck and shoulders. A stone slab fell off the 5,000-year-old monument in February 1988.

Starting from the bottom of a huge vertical shaft, Channel tunnel workers in France begin boring under the English Channel toward England.

New contracts down. The U.S. construction industry experienced a dip in new contracts for the second consecutive year in 1988. Contracts awarded for new construction in the first eight months of the year (excluding residential work) totaled $107.3 billion, down 5 per cent from the first eight months of 1987, according to construction economists at McGraw-Hill Incorporated, a leading source of construction-industry data. The private sector accounted for $62-billion of the contracts awarded, the federal government accounted for $4.3 billion, and other public sources accounted for $41 billion of the total.

Contracts awarded for manufacturing plants, waste-water-treatment plants, highways, hospitals, office buildings, warehouses, multifamily housing, and hotels all declined. The McGraw-Hill economists cited financial jitters after the 1987 stock-market crash, congressional budget-cutting efforts, and the impact of reality on the bloated commercial and apartment markets as factors in the downswing.

In the public sector, postal-service contracts took a nose dive in the first eight months of 1988, with contract awards plummeting 76 per cent compared with the same period in 1987. The drop came after Congress slashed a major postal-service construction program in January. But prospects for postal-service construction began looking up in October when the U.S. Postal Service Board of Governors signed a $12.9-billion, five-year capital-investment program that included $6.7 billion for new construction and repairs.

Private-sector growth areas. Contracts for airport runways, parking, and service roads were up 20 per cent in the first eight months of 1988. That rise constituted the logical second phase to the contracts for new terminals, hangars, and cargo buildings that were awarded at a rate averaging $100 million per month in 1987.

Competition among universities to replace obsolete research laboratories with larger and more sophisticated facilities led to $1.6 billion in laboratory construction contracts as of September 1988. McGraw-Hill figures indicated that laboratory construction accounted for 60 per cent of all work on university campuses in 1988.

In hospitals, contracts awarded were down nationally by 26 per cent in the first eight months of 1988. But the volume of new plans for projects being announced was on the rise with a movement toward more clinics and smaller projects.

Family housing. With mortgage rates in 1988 averaging 1 to 2 percentage points above those of 1987, the U.S. Department of Commerce projected that single-family and multifamily housing starts would drop to 1.5 million units in 1988—down about 6 per cent from the 1.6 million units started in 1987. Single-family housing starts alone were expected to drop to 970,000 units, down from the 1.02 million units started in 1987. Janice Lyn Tuchman

In *World Book*, see **Building; Construction; Tunnel.**

kler ordinance in 1974. The bank building was completed in 1973. In a swift response to the fire, the council passed a law in July requiring all buildings higher than 75 feet (23 meters) to have sprinkler systems. Only New York City and Massachusetts have similar rules.

The Williamsburg Bridge, which links Brooklyn and Manhattan across the East River in New York City, was closed from mid-April to late July for emergency repairs. City officials questioned whether the 1,600-foot (490-meter) suspension span, whose structural members were deeply corroded, should be repaired or replaced.

The city held an international competition for new bridge designs and received 25 proposals. In the end, however, city officials compromised with a plan to repair the suspension spans and build new elevated approach roads. The project will cost an estimated $359 million and take up to 7 years. A new bridge would cost an estimated $875 million and take up to 12 years to build.

Quality guidelines. In 1988, the American Society of Civil Engineers produced guidelines for building-in quality. A preliminary edition of *The Manual of Professional Practice for Quality in the Constructed Project* appeared in early May for trial use and comment. Forty authors produced its 24 chapters, and more than 4,000 people reviewed it. A final version is scheduled for January 1990.

Bulgaria. Mystery surrounded the sudden political downfall of Chudomir Aleksandrov on July 20, 1988. Aleksandrov, 53, was a leading member of a new generation of economic planners and a strong advocate of accelerating the pace of an economic restructuring program begun in the late 1970's. In 1984, he had become first deputy prime minister in charge of coordination of economic policy and a full member of the Politburo, the executive board of Bulgaria's Communist Party. In 1985, he was put in charge of a special commission on energy.

Political observers had seen Aleksandrov as a leading candidate to succeed Bulgaria's leader, 77-year-old Todor Zhivkov. On July 20, 1988, however, the Communist Party Central Committee removed Aleksandrov from the Politburo. Some observers said that he fell because of his strong support of restructuring—known as *perestroika* in the Soviet Union—and because Zhivkov believed that the Soviets regarded Aleksandrov more favorably than Zhivkov.

More perestroika, less glasnost. At a Communist Party conference held on January 28 and 29, Zhivkov urged that party officials be limited to two five-year terms. He also called for the legalization of non-Communist organizations—but not anti-Communist groups.

In a document published on April 26, Zhivkov severely criticized violations of restrictions on the discussion of government policies. In the Soviet Union, such discussions have become more common, thanks to a new policy of *glasnost* (openness in the flow of information). In fact, Soviet leader Mikhail S. Gorbachev has urged officials in his country to be more open in the discussion of past and present errors in Soviet domestic policy. Zhivkov, however, is extremely sensitive about open discussion of Bulgaria's policies because he has been responsible for them since becoming the head of the Communist Party in 1954.

Trade activities. Bulgaria continued in 1988 to increase its economic contacts with the West. In March, Bulgaria signed a 10-year joint marketing agreement with the West German firm Volkswagen AG to sell a Volkswagen automobile called HM Bulgaria. In April, Bulgaria's minister for foreign economic relations, Andrei Lukanov, made a 10-day visit to the United States for trade talks.

Ties with the Soviet Union remained paramount, however. Bulgaria rapidly increased its technological exports to the Soviet Union during 1988. Leading the wave of exports were data-processing and telecommunications equipment. Soviet leader Gorbachev's move to modernize the Soviet economy calls for large shipments of such products, and the Soviet space program continually requires technological updating. Soviet space missions reportedly rely on Bulgarian supercomputers. Eric Bourne

See also **Europe** (Facts in brief table). In *World Book*, see **Bulgaria.**

Burkina Faso. See Africa.

Burma was wracked by violence during 1988 in an indecisive effort to end the military dictatorship of General Ne Win. Ne Win, who seized power in 1962, had created a system of government devoted to the "Burmese way to socialism," a mixture of Buddhism, isolationism, and state control of all political and economic activity. But the result of Ne Win's rule was the impoverishment of a once-rich nation. Ne Win conceded in 1987 that his policies might have been wrong—but then instituted an economic program that further worsened conditions.

Months of rioting. Mounting public frustration over the government's unwillingness or inability to do anything about Burma's deteriorating standard of living triggered a week of rioting led by students and other members of the opposition in Rangoon, the capital, in March 1988. At least 100 people were killed, and officials eventually admitted that 41 rioters had suffocated in a police van after being arrested. In June, protests spread to other cities, and the death toll rose to more than 200.

Ne Win resigned on July 23 from his only official position, chairman of the ruling Socialist Programme Party. General Sein Lwin—who was widely hated and feared for having brutally suppressed student demonstrations—was named party chairman on July 26 and became president of Burma the next day. This touched off more rioting in several cities. Students and other rioters fought security personnel—in some cases

Protesters in Rangoon in August decry the regime of General Sein Lwin, who became president of Burma on July 27 and stepped down on August 12.

Burundi

beheading members of Burma's detested police force—and were themselves shot down by government troops. On August 12, as the number of deaths climbed into the hundreds, Sein Lwin resigned all his posts.

Maung Maung, a former civilian adviser to Ne Win, took over the presidency on August 19. The public's demands for democratic rule grew stronger, however, and massive, often violent, antigovernment demonstrations continued throughout the country.

Military take-over. On September 18, General Saw Maung, the army chief of staff, was summoned to the home of Ne Win. A short time later, officials announced that Maung Maung had resigned and a 19-member State Law-and-Order Restoration Council had taken power, with Saw Maung in charge. This military coup and the widespread suspicion that Ne Win was actually running the country from behind the scenes sparked labor strikes and more rioting. The council announced on September 27 that security forces had killed 342 rioters and wounded 219.

Saw Maung promised "free and fair" elections, but many Burmese feared that the ruling party, renamed the National Unity Party, would control the voting. By December, more than 150 parties had registered, but no election date had been set. Economic conditions remained poor.   Henry S. Bradsher

See also **Asia** (Facts in brief table). In **World Book**, see **Burma**.

Burundi. The long-suppressed hostility between Burundi's ruling Tutsi (also spelled *Tusi*) caste group, which constitutes roughly 14 per cent of the population, and the subordinate Hutu majority erupted into violence on Aug. 14, 1988. The strife broke a peace that had been imposed by the Tutsi-dominated army since 1972, when an estimated 100,000 people, mainly Hutu, were killed after a failed coup attempt.

Observers estimated that more than 5,000 people—both Tutsi and Hutu—were killed in the latest clash and that another 100,000 were made homeless or forced to seek refuge in neighboring countries. The violence was attributed to Hutu frustration at being denied political power and access to educational and economic opportunities. The government charged that Hutu agitators, backed by the leaders of neighboring Rwanda, initiated the bloodshed.

President Pierre Buyoya had tried earlier in the year to placate the Hutu by releasing political prisoners and relaxing government control over Hutu farmers and business people. He also stopped harassing the Roman Catholic Church, a champion of Hutu rights.

Buyoya met with the presidents of Zaire and Rwanda on August 30 about the crisis. The flood of refugees from Burundi strained ties with its neighbors.   J. Gus Liebenow and Beverly B. Liebenow

See also **Africa** (Facts in brief table). In **World Book**, see **Burundi**.

Bus. See Transit.

Hutu people from Burundi, refugees from violence that erupted in August between Hutus and the rival Tutsis, receive food at a relief camp in Rwanda.

Bush, George H. W. (1924-   ), 43rd Vice President of the United States, was elected President on Nov. 8, 1988. Bush and his running mate, Senator Dan Quayle of Indiana, won a solid victory over the Democratic presidential ticket, headed by Governor Michael S. Dukakis of Massachusetts. See **Elections**.

Throughout the year, Bush's activities, even the performance of his official duties, were weighted with heavy overtones of electoral politics. On July 14, for example, the Vice President represented the United States at a United Nations (UN) Security Council meeting on the U.S. Navy's accidental downing of an Iranian airliner on July 3, with a loss of 290 lives. The assignment, which customarily would have gone to the secretary of state or the ambassador to the UN, enabled Bush to spotlight his diplomatic experience.

In August, Bush's White House physician, Rodney W. Savage, said the Vice President was "an unusually active and healthy man" with no history of serious medical problems. His "most bothersome clinical problem," the doctor said, was mild osteoarthritis of the hips and knees. Bush and his wife, Barbara, reported on April 21 that they paid $86,396 in federal income tax in 1987 on an adjusted gross income of $308,396.   Frank Cormier and Margot Cormier

In the World Book Supplement section, see **Bush, George Herbert Walker**.

Business. See Bank; Economics; International trade; Labor; Manufacturing.

214

Cabinet, United States. The year 1988 was one of change for the United States Cabinet. By year-end, President Ronald Reagan had named three new members to his Cabinet, President-elect George Bush had made appointments to his Administration's Cabinet, and a new Cabinet department was created.

On July 5, U.S. Attorney General Edwin Meese III announced his resignation after an independent prosecutor recommended that criminal charges not be brought against him. Meese, who had been the subject of a 14-month criminal investigation, said that the recommendation of prosecutor James C. McKay "vindicated" him. President Reagan on July 12 named Richard L. Thornburgh, former governor of Pennsylvania, as Meese's successor.

On August 5, James A. Baker III said he would step down as treasury secretary to manage Bush's presidential campaign. Reagan named Nicholas F. Brady, an investment banker and former New Jersey senator, as Baker's replacement.

On August 9, Secretary of Education William J. Bennett said he would retire in September. To succeed him, Reagan appointed Lauro F. Cavazos, president of Texas Tech University in Lubbock. When he was sworn in on September 20, Cavazos became the first Hispanic Cabinet member in U.S. history.

Bush's Cabinet. After Bush's victory in the November presidential election, one of his first moves was to appoint Baker as secretary of state. By the end of December, Bush had chosen the rest of his Cabinet, except for the secretary of energy. Those appointments were: Robert A. Mosbacher, chairman of a Houston oil firm, as secretary of commerce; U.S. Trade Representative Clayton K. Yeutter as secretary of agriculture; Jack F. Kemp, representative from New York, as secretary of housing and urban development; Elizabeth Hanford Dole, former transportation secretary, as secretary of labor; John G. Tower, former senator from Texas, as secretary of defense; Manuel Lujan, Jr., representative from New Mexico, as secretary of the interior; Louis W. Sullivan, a black Atlanta physician and educator, as secretary of health and human services; and Samuel K. Skinner, Chicago mass-transit official, as secretary of transportation.

Bush named Edward J. Derwinski, former representative from Illinois, to serve as the country's first secretary of veterans affairs. On October 25, Reagan had signed legislation making the Veterans Administration the 14th Cabinet department. The measure was to go into effect in March 1989.

Bush also said he would retain Treasury Secretary Brady, Attorney General Thornburgh, and Education Secretary Cavazos in his Cabinet.   Mary A. Krier

See also **Brady, Nicholas F.; Cavazos, Lauro F.; Thornburgh, Richard L.** In *World Book*, see **Cabinet.**
California. See Los Angeles; State government.
Cambodia. See Kampuchea.
Cameroon. See Africa.

Canada. In a historic national election on Nov. 21, 1988, Prime Minister Brian Mulroney's Progressive Conservative (PC) Party won a decisive victory, taking 169 of the 295 seats in the House of Commons. The victory confirmed Canada's participation in the broad free-trade agreement signed by Mulroney and United States President Ronald Reagan in January 1988.

The agreement, which will eliminate tariffs on virtually all trade between the two countries, was ratified by the U.S. House of Representatives in August and by the U.S. Senate in September. Canada's opposition parties and the Canadian Senate, which had stalled approval of the agreement, had indicated that they would no longer block it if a national election resulted in a PC victory. After the election, the Commons approved the agreement on December 24, and the Senate added final approval on December 30. The pact went into effect on Jan. 1, 1989.

The free-trade issue was confusing to many Canadians, especially because the agreement was set forth in a 2,500-page document full of technical language. The Mulroney government argued that the agreement continued the trend toward freer trade between the two countries (more than 70 per cent of Canada-U.S. trade was already free of duties); that it offered Canada more secure access to the U.S. market; that it provided improved procedures for settling trade disputes; and that it would help Canada enhance its competitiveness in the harsher international trading environment of the 1990's. Canada's long-term prosperity, the PC's claimed, depended upon a more liberal atmosphere for trade in North America.

The Liberal Party, led by John N. Turner, and the New Democratic Party (NDP), led by Edward Broadbent, opposed the agreement. Both parties argued that Canada should not depend too heavily on trade with the United States but should actively promote better trade links with Asia and Europe.

In addition, opponents claimed that the free-trade agreement was flawed in not defining exactly what sorts of government assistance would be considered unacceptable subsidies of private business. This omission might put at risk some social and economic programs partly funded by the federal government, such as unemployment insurance, public health-care support, and assistance to disadvantaged regions. Free trade, the opponents argued, would also make it more difficult for Canada to control its economy and would lead, over time, to a weakening of Canada's independence.

The opposition arguments often took an emotional tone, touching on the nervousness that many Canadians felt at the thought of closer economic ties with the United States. The opposition drew backing from organized labor, church organizations, and many writers and artists. Supporters of the agreement included the business community, manufacturers, producers of raw materials, and economists. Eight of the 10 provincial premiers backed free trade.

Calgary

Bienvenue

The Olympic Winter Games open on February 13 in Calgary, Alberta, *left*. More than 1,750 athletes from a record 57 countries took part.

217

Canada

Federal spending in Canada

Estimated budget for fiscal 1988-1989*

Ministry (includes the department and all agencies for which a minister reports to Parliament):	Millions of dollars†
Agriculture	2,188
Atlantic Canada Opportunities Agency	306
Communications	
Canadian Broadcasting Corporation	907
Canadian Film Development Corporation	102
Other	704
Consumer and corporate affairs	
Canada Post Corporation	196
Other	144
Employment and immigration	4,547
Energy, mines and resources	
Atomic Energy of Canada Limited	142
Other	1,038
Environment	796
External affairs	3,361
Finance	38,887
Fisheries and oceans	679
Governor General	8
Indian affairs and northern development	3,309
Justice	528
Labour	211
National defence	11,200
National health and welfare	30,857
National revenue	1,371
Parliament	237
Privy Council	84
Public works	
Canada Mortgage and Housing Corporation	1,704
Other	1,293
Regional industrial expansion	1,435
Science and technology	825
Secretary of state	3,541
Solicitor general	
Royal Canadian Mounted Police	1,033
Other	1,009
Supply and services	800
Transport	3,333
Treasury Board	942
Veterans affairs	1,649
Total	**119,366**

*April 1, 1988, to March 31, 1989.
†Canadian dollars; $1 = U.S. 81 cents as of May 1988.

Spending since 1983

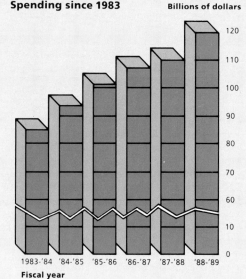

Billions of dollars

1983-'84 '84-'85 '85-'86 '86-'87 '87-'88 '88-'89

Fiscal year

Source: Treasury Board of Canada.

ing free trade than for the PC's, under Canada's parliamentary system the party holding the largest number of seats in the Commons forms the government. Mulroney's victory thus meant that the free-trade agreement could go ahead.

The 1988 election was important for other reasons as well. The PC's, in opposition for much of the 1900's, showed for the second time that they possessed strong support. They also captured the allegiance of Quebec, once a Liberal stronghold. In addition, some observers suggested that the results promised a more effective House of Commons than had been produced by the PC landslide in 1984, because the stronger and broader-based opposition would provide a healthier setting for legislative action.

Legislation. The Mulroney government found much of its 1988 legislative program in addition to the free-trade measure blocked by the Senate. New legislation requires the consent of both the House of Commons, whose members are elected, and the Senate, whose members are appointed.

In April, the Senate attached to the Meech Lake Accord several amendments that proved unacceptable to the PC government. The Meech Lake Accord, signed by Mulroney and the 10 provincial premiers in June 1987, was designed to bring Quebec under the provisions of Canada's 1982 constitution, which Quebec had originally rejected. The resolution supporting the accord required the endorsement of the 10 provincial legislatures—all except Manitoba and New Brunswick have approved it—and both houses of Parliament. The Commons ratified the resolution in October 1987 and reaffirmed its approval in June 1988, overriding the Senate's changes.

The Senate also blocked legislation to provide federal funding for child-care facilities. The Senate was still studying the bill when Mulroney's election call dissolved Parliament. Because of the election, the measure required reintroduction in both houses under the new Parliament.

After almost a year's delay, the Senate approved statutes to improve procedures for determining refugee status and to curb the activities of people responsible for the entry of bogus refugees. The bills were intended to help the government deal with the 80,000 refugee claimants in Canada awaiting hearings.

The Senate acted more swiftly to pass a new Environment Act, which laid down tough standards for the production and disposal of toxic chemicals. Two other statutes banned tobacco advertising and guaranteed federal employees a smoke-free workplace.

Japanese-Canadian compensation. The government met a long-standing grievance of Japanese Canadians regarding their forced relocation and confinement in the early 1940's during World War II. On Sept. 22, 1988, Mulroney declared that the government would award about $21,100 to each of the 12,000 surviving Japanese Canadians who were relocated during the war. (Unless otherwise noted, monetary amounts in this article are in Canadian dollars; $1 = U.S. 84 cents as of Dec. 31, 1988.)

Abortion. Members of the Commons could not agree on how to handle the regulation of abortions after the Supreme Court of Canada struck down Canada's abortion laws in January. To discover Parliament's sentiments on the subject, the Mulroney government introduced for discussion a resolution that would have allowed abortions in the early stages of a pregnancy but denied them in later stages. In a July debate, the Commons soundly defeated the resolution along with five amendments from members of the legislature that suggested other options for regulating abortion. The debate offered the government no clear path for future legislation, and Mulroney deferred the issue.

Language. The relative precedence of Canada's two official languages—English and French—continued to be a volatile issue in 1988. In July, Parliament passed legislation to protect linguistic minorities (French speakers in most of Canada and English speakers in Quebec). Nine members of Mulroney's PC majority voted against the bill, which guaranteed that government services would be available in both languages. Mulroney immediately fired one of the dissidents from a parliamentary post.

On December 15, the Canadian Supreme Court struck down a controversial Quebec law that prohibited the use of English on public signs. Three days later, Quebec's Prime Minister Bourassa announced a new law that would allow bilingual signs indoors but restrict exterior signs to French. In doing so, he invoked a seldom-used provision of the Canadian and Quebec constitutions to exempt the law from court challenges. Both French- and English-speaking groups declared the compromise unsatisfactory.

Canada's economy boomed in 1988. With a 4 per cent growth rate estimated, the gross national product (GNP)—the total value of all goods and services produced—was expected to be $590.9 billion for the year. Strong trends in business investment, housing construction, and exports fueled the growth, making 1988 the sixth consecutive year of expansion. Unemployment fell in June to 7.6 per cent, its lowest rate in seven years, but climbed to 7.8 per cent by November. Much of the economic expansion was concentrated in Ontario, where the jobless rate was well below the national average.

The Bank of Canada followed a high interest rate policy to restrain spending and inflation. The bank's rate, which determines commercial lending terms, topped 11 per cent in December. The increase in the cost of living hovered around 4 per cent for the year. Backed by a strong economy, the Canadian dollar strengthened against U.S. currency. Its year-end figure of U.S. 84 cents was a six-year high.

Budget. The PC government presented its fourth budget on Feb. 10, 1988. Finance Minister Michael H. Wilson announced no new taxes aside from an increase in levies on gasoline and aviation fuel. Using

The Ministry of Canada*

Brian Mulroney—prime minister
Charles Joseph Clark—secretary of state for external affairs; acting minister of justice and attorney general of Canada
John Carnell Crosbie—minister for international trade
Donald Frank Mazankowski—deputy prime minister; president of the Queen's Privy Council for Canada; government House leader; minister of agriculture; minister responsible for privatization and regulatory affairs
Elmer MacIntosh MacKay—minister of national revenue
Arthur Jacob Epp—minister of national health and welfare
Robert R. de Cotret—minister of regional industrial expansion; minister of state (science and technology)
Henry Perrin Beatty—minister of national defence; acting solicitor general of Canada
Michael Holcombe Wilson—minister of finance
Harvie Andre—minister of consumer and corporate affairs; minister responsible for Canada Post Corporation
Otto John Jelinek—minister of supply and services; acting minister of public works
Thomas Edward Siddon—minister of fisheries and oceans
Charles James Mayer—minister of state (grains and oilseeds)
William Hunter McKnight—minister of Indian affairs and northern development; minister of Western economic diversification
Benoît Bouchard—minister of transport
Marcel Masse—minister of energy, mines, and resources
Barbara Jean McDougall—minister of employment and immigration; minister responsible for the status of women
Gerald Stairs Merrithew—minister of veterans affairs; minister for the purposes of the Atlantic Canada Opportunities Agency Act
Monique Vézina—minister of state (employment and immigration); minister of state (seniors)
Frank Oberle—minister of state (science and technology); acting minister of state (forestry)
Lowell Murray—leader of the government in the Senate; minister of state (federal-provincial relations); acting minister of communications
Paul Wyatt Dick—associate minister of national defence
Pierre H. Cadieux—minister of labour
Jean J. Charest—minister of state (youth); minister of state (fitness and amateur sport)
Thomas Hockin—minister of state (finance)
Monique Landry—minister for external relations and international development
Bernard Valcourt—minister of state (small businesses and tourism); minister of state (Indian affairs and northern development)
Gerry Weiner—minister of state (multiculturalism and citizenship)
Douglas Grinslade Lewis—minister of state; minister of state (Treasury Board); acting president of the Treasury Board
Pierre Blais—minister of state (agriculture)
Lucien Bouchard—secretary of state of Canada; acting minister of the environment
John Horton McDermid—minister of state (international trade); minister of state (housing)
Shirley Martin—minister of state (transport)

*As of Dec. 31, 1988. Seven cabinet members lost or ceded their seats in the House of Commons in the November 1988 general election. Prime Minister Mulroney was expected to name new cabinet members and reassign responsibilities early in 1989.

Premiers of Canadian provinces

Province	Premier
Alberta	Donald R. Getty
British Columbia	William N. Vander Zalm
Manitoba	Gary A. Filmon
New Brunswick	Frank J. McKenna
Newfoundland	Brian Peckford
Nova Scotia	John Buchanan
Ontario	David Peterson
Prince Edward Island	Joseph A. Ghiz
Quebec	Robert Bourassa
Saskatchewan	Grant Devine

Commissioners of territories

Northwest Territories	Nick Sibbeston
Yukon Territory	Tony Penikett

Canada, provinces, and territories population estimates

	1987	1988
Alberta	2,380,400	2,401,100
British Columbia	2,925,700	2,984,000
Manitoba	1,079,000	1,084,700
New Brunswick	712,300	714,400
Newfoundland	568,200	568,100
Northwest Territories	51,700	51,800
Nova Scotia	878,900	883,900
Ontario	9,270,700	9,430,800
Prince Edward Island	127,300	128,700
Quebec	6,592,600	6,639,200
Saskatchewan	1,014,000	1,011,200
Yukon Territory	24,400	25,300
Canada	**25,625,200**	**25,923,200**

City and metropolitan population estimates

	Metropolitan area 1987 estimate	City 1986 census
Toronto, Ont.	3,501,600	612,289
Montreal, Que.	2,942,700	1,015,420
Vancouver, B.C.	1,412,700	431,147
Ottawa-Hull	833,100	
Ottawa, Ont.		300,763
Hull, Ont.		58,722
Edmonton, Alta.	788,400	573,982
Calgary, Alta.	677,400	636,104
Winnipeg, Man.	631,100	594,551
Quebec, Que.	607,400	164,580
Hamilton, Ont.	566,900	306,728
London, Ont.	347,500	269,140
St. Catharines-Niagara	346,900	
St. Catharines, Ont.		123,455
Niagara Falls, Ont.		72,107
Kitchener, Ont.	316,900	150,604
Halifax, N.S.	300,000	113,577
Victoria, B.C.	260,400	66,303
Windsor, Ont.	256,700	193,111
Oshawa, Ont.	210,400	123,651
Saskatoon, Sask.	204,000	177,641
Regina, Sask.	189,400	175,064
St. John's, Nfld.	162,200	96,216
Chicoutimi-Jonquière	159,800	
Chicoutimi, Que.		61,083
Jonquière, Que.		58,467
Sudbury, Ont.	147,500	88,717
Sherbrooke, Ont.	132,200	74,438
Trois-Rivières, Que.	130,600	50,122
Thunder Bay, Ont.	123,100	112,272
Saint John, N.B.	122,000	76,381

larger revenues from economic growth, Wilson reduced the federal deficit for the third year in a row. The deficit had been $38.3 billion when the PC's took office in 1984. Wilson projected a deficit of $29.3-billion for 1987-1988, and in June he reduced that estimate to $28.3 billion. According to a September report, the 1987-1988 deficit stood even lower, at $28.08 billion.

Total spending for 1988-1989 was estimated at $132.3 billion, an increase of 5.5 per cent over the previous year. Government revenues for 1988-1989 were predicted at $103.3 billion.

A new personal and corporate income-tax structure, announced by Wilson in 1987, went into effect in January 1988. The second phase of Wilson's tax-re-form program, which called for a more broad-based national sales tax incorporating provincial sales taxes, was under discussion with the provinces.

Peacekeeping honors. Canadians took pride in the international recognition given to United Nations (UN) peacekeeping forces, which won the 1988 Nobel Peace Prize for helping resolve conflicts by providing truce supervision. Since the first such unit was established in 1949, Canadian troops have been involved in more peacekeeping operations in more places than troops of any other country. About 80,000 Canadians have served with the UN forces, and 78 have been killed. In 1988, Canada provided two UN peacekeeping detachments: In May, a small force of officers observed the Soviet withdrawal from Afghanistan, and in August, 500 Canadian soldiers helped monitor the border between Iran and Iraq.

On Oct. 26, 1988, Canada was elected to one of the nonpermanent two-year seats on the UN Security Council. Canada has served on the Security Council once every 10 years since the UN was formed in 1945.

France and fish. Canada and France continued to argue about maritime boundaries around France's tiny colonies St.-Pierre and Miquelon, which lie close to the southern coast of Newfoundland. Canada maintained that France is entitled only to a 12-nautical-mile (22-kilometer) territorial sea around the islands. France claimed a 200-nautical-mile (370-kilometer) boundary around the islands.

The dispute escalated in 1988 with two ship seizures. On April 14, Canadian patrol vessels impounded a St.-Pierre trawler and charged the 21 people on board—17 crew members and 4 local politicians—with illegally fishing in Canadian waters. The men were released April 18 on bail. On May 5, France seized a Canadian fishing vessel off St.-Pierre and charged its five-member crew with illegal fishing. The boat and crew were released on May 6 after the Canadian government posted bail.

Negotiations were suspended for most of the summer. On September 21, Canada called for nonbinding mediation to reach a settlement. The dispute drew attention to Canada's fear that European fishing was depleting fish stocks.

Canadian-Soviet relations exhibited both cooperation and tension during 1988. The cooperation occurred on a joint Canadian-Soviet venture to ski across the frozen Arctic from the Soviet Union to the North Pole and on to one of Canada's Arctic Islands. Four Canadians and nine Soviets took part in the grueling 1,730-kilometer (1,075-mile) journey, which took 91 days. It was the first long Arctic crossing made without vehicles or sled dogs.

Friction came in June in a series of expulsions of Canadian and Soviet diplomats for allegedly attempting to collect military and industrial information. Canada began the exchange by expelling eight Soviet diplomats. Moscow responded by expelling two Canadian representatives and, after other expulsions from

Prime Minister Brian Mulroney and his wife, Mila, vote in Canada's general election in November 1988. Mulroney was elected to a second term.

both sides, by forbidding 25 Soviets to continue working at the Canadian Embassy in Moscow. After negotiations in June, both countries drew back from further actions, and diplomatic relations returned to normal.

South Africa. Canada kept up its pressure against *apartheid* (racial segregation) in South Africa. In late January, C. Joseph Clark, secretary of state for external affairs, visited the nations bordering South Africa. He announced that Canada would provide those countries with development assistance but stopped short of committing Canada to military aid in Mozambique. In August, representatives of eight Commonwealth countries met in Toronto, Ont., to discuss further steps against apartheid. (The Commonwealth is an association that includes Great Britain, Canada, and about 50 other nations that were once British colonies.) They called for heavier penalties for sanctions violators and announced plans for a program to counter South African propaganda and censorship.

Facts in brief. Population: 25,890,000. Government: Governor General Jeanne M. Sauvé; Prime Minister Brian Mulroney. Monetary unit: dollar. Value of foreign trade: exports, $120,631,000,000; imports, $110,498,000,000.   David M. L. Farr

See also the Canadian provinces articles; **Canadian literature; Filmon, Gary A.; Montreal; Mulroney, Brian; Sauvé, Jeanne M.; Toronto.** In *World Book*, see **Canada.**

Canadian literature. The largest Canadian publishing venture of 1988 was the second edition of *The Canadian Encyclopedia*, which was revised and expanded from three to four volumes. The 2,736-page revision included 1,700 new entries and 1,000 new charts, maps, chronologies, and illustrations.

Fiction. Major novels included Margaret Atwood's *Cat's Eye*, which explored women's issues, and Robertson Davies' *The Lyre of Orpheus*, the last book of a trilogy about a group of characters and their varied links with Canadian culture. Also of great interest was Morley Callaghan's *A Wild Old Man on the Road*, a deeply felt chronicle of a writer's search for meaning. Hugh Hood produced *Tony's Book*, the seventh in a projected 12-novel series about the lives of several generations of a middle-class Canadian family.

Other notable novels included David Helwig's *A Postcard from Rome;* Daphne Marlatt's *Ana Historic;* W. O. Mitchell's *Ladybug, Ladybug;* and David Adams Richards' *Nights Below Station Street.*

Major first novels of 1988 included Neil Bissoondath's *A Casual Brutality*, a study of racism, politics, and exile set in Toronto, Ont., and the Caribbean. Other excellent debuts were Janice Kulyk Keefer's *Constellations*, Rick Salutin's *A Man of Little Faith*, and Linda Spalding's *Daughters of Captain Cook.*

Among the many fine short-story collections were David Carpenter's *God's Bedfellows*, Shirley Faessler's *A Basket of Apples*, Timothy Findley's *Stones*, Mavis Gallant's *In Transit*, and Bharati Mukherjee's *The Middleman and Other Stories*. W. P. Kinsella's *The Further Adventures of Slugger McBatt* featured baseball stories written with verve and expertise.

Notable mystery and thriller novels included Howard Engel's *A Victim Must Be Found*, Peter Robinson's *A Dedicated Man*, John Ralston Saul's *The Paradise Eater*, Eric Wright's *A Question of Murder*, and Scott Young's *Murder in a Cold Climate*. Josef Skvorecky produced *Sins for Father Knox*, a collection of mystery stories.

Biographies and memoirs. Biographies of well-known political figures included Judy Steed's *Ed Broadbent: The Pursuit of Power*, a portrait of the leader of Canada's New Democratic Party, and James Swift's *Odd Man Out*, which described the life and times of Liberal Party politician Eric Keirans.

Several biographies and autobiographies focused on European themes. In *So Many Miracles*, actor Saul Rubinek told the story of his parents' experience during the Holocaust. In *A Journey to Yalta*, Sarah Klassen recounted her Mennonite family's struggle for survival during the Russian Revolution. And in *A Soviet Odyssey*, Suzanne Rosenberg described her childhood in Montreal, Que., her incarceration in a Soviet labor camp, and her return to Canada.

Two daughters explored the lives of their celebrated actor fathers: Martha Harron in *Don Harron: A Parent Contradiction*, and Bronwyn Drainie in *Living the Part: John Drainie and the Dilemma of Canadian Stardom.*

Canadian literature

Robertson Davies signs a copy of his novel, *The Lyre of Orpheus*, published in 1988 to complete a trilogy about Canadian characters and culture.

Other arts figures who were the subjects of biographies in 1988 included actor William Hutt in Keith Garebian's *William Hutt: A Theatre Portrait*, singer Gordon Lightfoot in Maynard Collins' *If You Could Read My Mind*, jazz pianist Oscar Peterson in Gene Lees's *Oscar Peterson: The Will to Swing*, and opera singer Teresa Stratas in Harry Rasky's *Stratas*.

Literary biographies included Paul Stuewe's *The Storms Below*, a study of the life and work of popular Toronto writer Hugh Garner, and Mary McAlpine's *The Other Side of Silence*, a critical examination of Vancouver, B.C., novelist Ethel Wilson. In *The Memoirs of a Literary Blockhead*, Robin Skelton offered a lighthearted recollection of his life as poet, editor, critic, and teacher, and in *Best Seat in the House: Memoirs of a Lucky Man*, Robert Fulford told the story of his influential career as journalist and cultural critic.

Essays and criticism. Josef Skvorecky, a Czechoslovak-born novelist and critic, offered his often-biting thoughts on politics, movies, jazz, and literature in *Talkin' Moscow Blues*. *Crossing the River*, edited by Kristjana Gunnars, brought together essays by scholars commemorating the work of the late novelist Margaret Laurence. *Carry on Bumping*, a collection of essays by authors, poets, and booksellers, took its inspiration from editor John Metcalf's controversial views on Canadian writing and publishing.

History. Popular historian Pierre Berton's *The Arctic Grail* shed new light on the quest to conquer the frozen North. George Woodcock, author and editor of more than 80 books, produced *A Social History of Canada*. Barry Broadfoot continued his series of oral histories with *Next-Year Country*, which gave a voice to the people of the Canadian prairies.

Among books on war were Daniel Dancocks' *Welcome to Flanders Fields*, a description of Canada's entry into World War I at the Battle of Ypres in 1915; Brian Nolan's *King's War*, an analysis of Prime Minister W. L. Mackenzie King's actions during World War II (1939-1945); and Denis Smith's *Diplomacy of Fear*, a look at Canada's Cold War with the Soviet Union.

Alison Griffiths and David Cruise mapped out the building of the Canadian Pacific Railway in *Lords of the Line*, and Anne Collins' *In the Sleep Room* described experiments in brainwashing conducted by the United States Central Intelligence Agency in Montreal in the 1960's. Ian Mulgrew's *Unholy Terror* examined the history of Canada's Sikh community, while Harold Troper and Morton Weinfeld analyzed the tensions between Canadian Ukrainians and Jews in *Old Wounds*. In *No Time to Wave Goodbye*, British-born Canadian Ben Wicks tells how London children—including himself—were sent to the British countryside during World War II, and Geoffrey Bilson's *The Guest Children* looks at those sent to Canada.

Politics. The most controversial political book of 1988 was Greg Weston's *Reign of Error*, a study of John N. Turner and his leadership of the Liberal Party. Jeffrey Simpson's *Spoils of Power* dealt with the issue of political patronage, and Peter Newman collected his journalistic essays on people and power politics in *Sometimes a Great Nation*.

Business and finance. Patricia Best and Ann Shortell examined Canada's most controversial financial empire in *The Brass Ring: Power, Influence, and the Brascan Empire*. Diane Francis' *Contrepreneurs* looked at white-collar swindlers operating in Canada.

Awards. The Governor General's Literary Awards for books published in 1987 went to M. T. Kelly for *A Dream Like Mine* (English fiction); Gwendolyn MacEwen for *Afterworlds* (English poetry); Michael Ignatieff for *The Russian Album* (English nonfiction); John Krizanc for *Prague* (English drama); Gilles Archambault for *L'Obsédante Obèse et autres agressions* (French fiction); Fernand Ouellette for *Les Heures* (French poetry); Jean Larose for *La Petite Noirceur* (French nonfiction); and Jeanne-Mance Delisle for *Un oiseau vivant dans la gueule* (French drama).

Patricia Claxton won the Canada Council translation prize for her English translation of *Enchantment and Sorrow: The Autobiography of Gabrielle Roy*, and Ivan Steenhout and Christiane Teasdale won for their French translation of Heather Robertson's novel *Willie: A Romance*. Paul Quarrington received the Stephen Leacock Memorial Award for humor for his novel *King Leary*.   Ken Adachi

In *World Book*, see **Canadian literature**.
Cape Verde. See **Africa**.

Cat. The United States Postal Service honored the domestic cat with its release on Feb. 5, 1988, of a special four-stamp block. The stamps pictured the Siamese, exotic shorthair, Abyssinian, Himalayan, Maine coon, Burmese, American shorthair, and Persian cats, with two breeds appearing on each stamp.

Figures released by Market Research Corporation of America in 1988 indicated that, although the estimated number of pet cats in the United States had dropped slightly since 1987, the cat was still the most popular pet in the United States. According to The Cat Fanciers' Association (CFA), the Persian remained the most popular breed.

CFA's National Best Cat for 1988 was Grand Champion South Paw Wish Upon A Star, a white Persian male bred and owned by Judy and Greg Brocato of Rome, Ga. For the third consecutive year, the award for National Best Kitten went to Vicki Dickerson, Barbara Farrell, and Clifford Farrell, all of Salinas, Calif. The award-winning kitten for 1988 was Grand Champion Windborne California Dreamin, a white Persian female bred by Dickerson.

Grand Champion and Grand Premier Briarson Babette of Midinite, a brown-patched tabby American shorthair, was 1988 Best Altered Cat. Babette, owned by Lucia A. Pozzi of New Brighton, Minn., was bred by Sheree Dachman of Denver and Brian Pearson of Kansas City, Mo.   Thomas H. Dent

In *World Book*, see **Cat.**

Cavazos, Lauro Fred (1927-   ), was sworn in as United States secretary of education on Sept. 20, 1988. Cavazos, formerly the president of Texas Tech University in Lubbock, became the first Hispanic ever to hold a Cabinet post. Some critics charged that Cavazos' appointment was a ploy to win Hispanic support for Vice President George Bush in his campaign for the presidency. Many educators, however, praised the choice of Cavazos. After the election, President-elect Bush asked him to remain in the Cabinet.

Cavazos was born on Jan. 4, 1927, on the famous King Ranch near Kingsville, Tex., where his father spent 43 years as a foreman. He attended Texas Tech, graduating in 1949, and earned a doctorate in *cytology* (the study of cells) in 1954 at Iowa State University of Science and Technology in Ames.

From 1954 to 1964, Cavazos taught at the Medical College of Virginia in Richmond. He was named chairman of the Anatomy Department at Tufts University School of Medicine in Boston in 1964 and dean in 1975.

In 1980, Cavazos became president of Texas Tech. In that post, he increased black and Hispanic enrollment and instituted a policy requiring periodic performance reviews of tenured professors.

Cavazos is married to the former Peggy Ann Murdock. They have 10 children.   David L. Dreier

Central African Republic. See **Africa.**
Chad. See **Africa.**

Chemistry. Chemist Keith N. Slessor and his colleagues at Simon Fraser University in Burnaby, Canada, reported in March 1988 that they had synthesized *retinue pheromone*, a group of five chemicals that control honey bee colonies. The queen bee transfers these chemicals to other bees by licking and touching them. The pheromone is responsible for a variety of bee activities, including gathering together as a swarm.

The researchers identified the five chemicals from more than 100 compounds present in the queen's *mandibular* (jaw) gland. Two of the five chemicals have been known for several years. In 1985, however, Slessor's group found that one of those two is actually a pair of compounds that are mirror images of each other. The researchers identified the remaining two chemicals in the pheromone in 1988. The Canadian researchers then synthesized the five chemicals, mixed them, put them into glass tubes, and placed the tubes—now synthetic queens—in hives. The bees in these hives stopped building special cells that they ordinarily construct for new queens, licked the synthetic queens, and touched them with their antennae. Pheromone samples deposited in other places caused bees to gather at those places.

The most important potential use of the pheromone may be to encourage the pollination of crops, especially fruits, by luring bees to crops they otherwise would ignore. Each year, bees pollinate some $20-billion worth of crops in North America.

Honey producers also may benefit from the substance because it can keep queenless colonies calm during shipment. In addition, the pheromone may stimulate worker bees to raise young bees more rapidly and to bring more nectar and pollen to the hive, thus providing more honey per colony.

Researchers are already testing the pheromone to restrict the spread of aggressive South American "killer bees." These bees developed in Brazil in the late 1950's and the 1960's, and by late 1987 had reached as far north as the Isthmus of Tehuantepec in southern Mexico. Experts predicted that swarms of killer bees would reach Texas by late 1989 or early 1990. If that happens, eradication efforts will begin in the United States. Researchers are trying to develop a chemical mixture to attract killer bees into boxes where they could be destroyed.

Bright bite. Biting into a piece of wintergreen candy creates a bluish flash due to the phenomenon of *triboluminescence*, the emission of light by some materials when they are rubbed, crushed, or broken. People have known about this phenomenon for nearly 400 years. In June 1988, Linda M. Sweeting, a chemist at Towson State University in Baltimore, explained it.

She said that, as materials such as wintergreen candy begin to crack, patches of positive and negative electric charge form on opposite sides of the cracks. Electrons then jump across the cracks to neutralize the

An engineer tests a paint powder that is charged electrically and blown onto metals. The charge holds the powder in place as it is baked on.

ria. These chemicals, unlike glucans, are easily washed away with water, so they should help reduce the number of cavity-causing bacteria in the mouth. Taylor hopes that the chemicals will someday be used in toothpaste and mouthwash.

Tiny rulers. To measure something very small requires a ruler with extremely small distances between the measuring lines. There is no ruler, however, able to measure distances on the next generation of microcircuits, which are expected to have parts measuring in the range of a few billionths of a meter. But in January 1988, researchers at the University of Minnesota in Minneapolis and Brookhaven National Laboratory on Long Island, N.Y., reported that they had come close to making such a ruler.

Minnesota chemist Larry L. Miller and his colleagues attached iridium metal atoms, which served as ruler markings, to rodlike molecules. The scientists then looked at the molecules with a scanning transmission electron microscope, which uses a moving beam of electrons to scan a specimen. The atoms showed up as spots a few billionths of a meter apart.

Unfortunately, the distances between the spots were not uniform enough to enable the molecules to be used as rulers, and the molecules were too flexible. The researchers are working to find a way to attach the iridium at more precise intervals and to make the molecules stiffer.   Peter J. Andrews

In *World Book*, see **Bee; Chemistry.**

differences in charge. Many of the jumping electrons hit nitrogen molecules in the air. These molecules emit light that has the same blue-white hue as lightning.

Sweeting and her co-workers made this discovery using extremely sensitive light detectors to measure the intensity of colors given off as wintergreen candy was crushed. There is no immediate application for Sweeting's work, but her findings expanded knowledge of how energy flows into and out of molecules.

Plaque blockers. In September 1988, chemist K. Grant Taylor of the University of Louisville in Kentucky announced a new weapon in the fight against tooth decay—plaque blockers. Plaque is a sticky film on the teeth made up of saliva, food particles, and bacteria. When sugar, starches, and certain bacteria become trapped in plaque, acids are formed. The acids can dissolve tooth enamel and cause cavities, a $16-billion-a-year problem in the United States.

Researchers have already developed substances aimed at removing plaque, but Taylor is trying to prevent plaque from forming. He and his colleagues have manufactured chemicals that are similar to glucan molecules, which are major constituents of plaque. These chemicals can block the action of certain bacterial *enzymes* (proteins that influence chemical reactions without themselves changing), preventing these enzymes from helping to build plaque.

The chemicals developed by the Louisville researchers can also attach themselves to troublesome bacte-

Cher (1946-   ) won the Academy of Motion Picture Arts and Sciences Award for best actress on April 11, 1988. She received the Oscar for her role in the romantic comedy *Moonstruck* as a tough widow who falls in love with the younger brother of the man she has agreed to marry. Cher had been nominated for an Oscar in 1984 for her role in *Silkwood* (1983).

Cher was born Cherilyn Sarkisian in El Centro, Calif., on May 20, 1946. She dropped out of school at age 16 to study acting but soon began singing backup at a recording studio in Hollywood, Calif. There she met Salvatore (Sonny) Bono, with whom she formed a musical duo. They were married in 1964.

In 1965, Sonny and Cher released "I Got You, Babe," which established the duo as recording stars. From 1971 to 1974, the two also hosted their own television comedy show. After her divorce from Bono in 1975, Cher continued to work as a musical performer, mainly in lavish shows in Las Vegas, Nev.

In 1981, Cher moved to New York City to pursue an acting career. She made her serious acting debut in 1982 in the Broadway production of *Come Back to the 5 & Dime, Jimmy Dean, Jimmy Dean*. She repeated her role in the 1982 film version of the play. Cher's other film credits include *Mask* (1985), *The Witches of Eastwick* (1987), and *Suspect* (1987).

Cher has a daughter from her marriage to Bono and a son from a brief marriage to rock musician Gregg Allman.   Barbara A. Mayes

Chess. Women's world chess champion Maya Chiburdanidze of the Soviet Union successfully defended her title in a close match against Nana Ioseliani, also of the Soviet Union. The match took place in September and November in Telavi, a city in the Soviet republic of Georgia.

Olympiad. A Soviet team won the gold medal for men at the biennial Chess Olympiad held in Salonika, Greece, from November 12 to 30. England won the silver medal, and the Netherlands won the bronze medal. Hungary won the gold medal for women.

U.S. championship. Michael Wilder, 26, of Princeton, N.J., surprised a powerful and more experienced field of players by winning the 1988 United States championship. The tournament was held from October 1 to 17 in Cambridge Springs, Pa.

Other tournaments. A long series of candidates' elimination matches began in January to select a player to challenge world champion Gary Kasparov of the Soviet Union in 1990. The first seven of these matches took place at the World Chess Festival, held from Jan. 23 to Feb. 20, 1988, in Saint John, Canada. Joel Benjamin of New York City and Yasser Seirawan of Seattle won the two major tournaments held at the festival, attended by nearly 1,000 players.

Max Dlugy of New York City topped a field of more than 1,200 to win the World Open on July 4 in Philadelphia. On August 20, Dmitry Gurevich of New York City won the U.S. Open in Boston.

Younger players. Competing in Timişoara, Romania, in August, 10-year-old John Viloria of Yonkers, N.Y., captured the world under-10 chess title for an unprecedented second consecutive year. Viloria, born on May 29, 1978, qualified by being under 10 on Jan. 1, 1988. Stuart Rachels, 18, of Birmingham, Ala., won the 1988 U.S. Junior Invitational Championship in Amherst, Mass. In St. Louis, Mo., Andrew Serotta, 18, of Lansdale, Pa., won the U.S. Junior Open for the second time in a row.

In April, the Royal Knights Chess Team, 12 students from Junior High School 99 from the East Harlem area of New York City, toured the Soviet Union as official guests. Their visit inaugurated the U.S.-Soviet Chess Friendship Games.

A record-breaking 2,144 U.S. school players competed in national team chess championships in 1988. Dalton School of New York City won its second consecutive elementary school team championship, in a tournament held in Detroit from April 22 to 24. On May 6 and 7 in Memphis, Horace Mann School of New York City became champion for the eighth grade and below, while Dalton School and Metcalf School of Minneapolis, Minn., tied for the championship for the ninth grade and below. The team from University High School of Tucson, Ariz., won the high school championship, held from April 15 to 17 in Albuquerque, N. Mex.   Al Lawrence

In *World Book*, see **Chess.**

World chess champion Gary Kasparov of the Soviet Union takes on 59 young opponents simultaneously in New York City in February.

Wrigley Field, home of the Chicago Cubs, is all aglow on the evening of August 8 as the Cubs play their first-ever home game under the lights.

Chicago.

The city's political leaders spent much of 1988 jockeying for position following the sudden death of Mayor Harold Washington on Nov. 25, 1987. The stage for that contest was set a week later, on December 2, when a biracial coalition of regular Democratic City Council members elected Eugene Sawyer, an alderman from a black middle-class ward on the South Side, as acting mayor. Sawyer was opposed then, and throughout 1988, by a minority faction led by Alderman Timothy C. Evans. See **Sawyer, Eugene.**

On April 25, the Chicago Board of Election Commissioners ordered a special mayoral election to be held in April 1989, and on November 21 the Illinois Supreme Court upheld that order. By year-end, numerous mayoral hopefuls had declared their candidacy, including Sawyer, Evans, Cook County State's Attorney Richard M. Daley, and Aldermen Juan Soliz and Lawrence Bloom.

Budget and taxes. In December, the City Council approved a $2.9-billion municipal budget for 1989 that avoided higher property taxes by raising fees on business licenses, building permits, and landing privileges at Chicago-O'Hare International Airport. Property taxes were raised earlier in the year, on July 29, when the council reluctantly approved a $50-million increase to fund city labor contracts.

Race relations. The political turmoil that followed the death of Mayor Washington was played out against a backdrop of heightened racial tensions,

typified by two widely publicized incidents. On May 5, Mayor Sawyer was forced by adverse public opinion to fire a top black assistant, Steve Cokely, for making numerous anti-Semitic statements, including an accusation that Jewish doctors were inoculating black children with the virus that causes AIDS (acquired immune deficiency syndrome).

Less than a week later, on May 11, a group of black aldermen accompanied by police stormed into the School of the Art Institute of Chicago and removed a painting—part of a student art exhibit—that depicted Harold Washington clothed in frilly women's lingerie. The two incidents stirred heated debate over black-Jewish relations, racial sensitivities, and First Amendment rights.

Library design. On June 20, an 11-member jury of experts chose a neoclassic design by Chicago architect Thomas H. Beeby for the city's new central library. On October 13, ground was broken in the downtown area for the $140-million structure, which will be the largest municipal library ever built in the United States. The library is scheduled to open in mid-1991.

Airport safety. On Oct. 3, 1988, the Federal Aviation Administration (FAA) ordered cutbacks in the number of airplane landings at O'Hare Airport following a sharp increase in the number of errors made by air-traffic controllers there. The FAA pledged to improve equipment and staffing levels at the O'Hare control tower, but the cutbacks convinced many that

Chicago would need an additional airport by early in the next century.

Corruption. During the year, prosecutors obtained more indictments and convictions of judges and other officials involved in bribery schemes. On October 18, Associate Judge Martin Hogan became the most recent of more than 70 defendants, including 14 judges, to be sentenced in the four-year-old Operation Greylord probe of corruption within the Cook County court system. And on April 8, former Alderman Wallace Davis was sentenced to eight years in prison for accepting bribes from a federal informant in the Operation Incubator probe of corruption at City Hall.

School reform. Public dissatisfaction with the Chicago public schools reached new heights during a four-week teachers' strike in the fall of 1987, making school reform a major political issue in 1988. A blue-ribbon panel established by Mayor Washington made several proposals, including a recommendation that school principals and parents' councils be given more authority in the management of their schools.

After some sparring with Illinois Governor James R. Thompson, the state legislature on December 1 overwhelmingly passed a bill ordering cuts in the Chicago educational bureaucracy and giving parents an unprecedented degree of authority in operating the city's schools. Thompson signed the bill on December 12.   John F. McCarron

See also **City.** In *World Book*, see **Chicago.**

Child welfare. The Congress of the United States in 1988 passed important legislation supporting education programs for children and teen-agers. On April 20, the lawmakers approved a bill that will continue virtually all federal funding for elementary and high schools through 1993. The bill also authorized a total of $275 million for various projects, including counseling for potential high school dropouts and tutoring programs for students lacking basic academic skills. President Ronald Reagan signed the bill into law on April 28, 1988.

Day care. Recognizing the need of many working parents for affordable child-care services, Congress spent much of the year debating whether to increase federal support for day care. In September, the Senate Labor Committee approved a major bill, the Act for Better Child Care Services—nicknamed ABC—aimed at helping low- and moderate-income families.

The $2.5-billion measure would have provided funds through state agencies to help pay families' child-care costs, to expand existing day-care centers, and to establish more such facilities. The bill also called for the development of federal health and safety standards for child care.

The bill died in the Senate when its supporters could not muster enough votes to end debate and bring it to a vote. The bill's sponsor, Senator Christopher J. Dodd (D., Conn.), said he would reintroduce the bill in the 101st Congress in January 1989.

Social policy analysts in the United States expect the demand for child care to continue growing as ever greater numbers of mothers enter the work force. By 1995, according to most estimates, two-thirds of preschoolers in the United States and three-fourths of school-age children will have mothers working outside the home.

Homeless children. Child welfare experts estimated in 1988 that families with children now make up more than one-third of the homeless population in the United States. In some areas, the proportion was found to be much higher. Figures compiled on U.S. cities in 1987 showed, for example, that in Trenton, N.J., and Providence, R.I., at least half of the homeless were families with children.

Estimates of the number of homeless Americans vary widely—from a low of 250,000 to a high of 3 million. People take to the streets for a variety of reasons. Many of the homeless are apparently renters who have been forced out of their apartments and have been unable to find another place to live.

In 1988, the Children's Defense Fund—a private child welfare organization in Washington, D.C.—reported that each year some 2.5 million Americans lose their apartments because of condominium conversions, redevelopment projects, or building abandonment by landlords.   Jeanne M. Hunzeker

In *World Book*, see **Child welfare.**

Children's books. See Literature for children.

Chile. On Oct. 5, 1988, Chile's voters rejected another eight-year term for President Augusto Pinochet Ugarte, the 72-year-old military dictator who has ruled the country since 1973. In a yes-or-no plebiscite, 54.7 per cent of the more than 7 million Chilean voters said no to another term for Pinochet, while 43 per cent voted yes. Chilean youths celebrated the outcome with caravans of automobiles and demonstrations along the streets of Santiago, the capital.

Under the terms of a new Constitution approved by the Chilean people in 1980, Pinochet must now set a date for new presidential and congressional elections in December 1989. The new president would take office on March 11, 1990. The Constitution allows Pinochet to retain his title as commander in chief of the army for at least four more years, regardless of the outcome of the elections.

Opposition unites. Some 16 parties made up the coalition that opposed Pinochet in the plebiscite, and many observers doubted that they would be able to unite behind a single candidate in the 1989 elections. On Oct. 14, 1988, however, the coalition announced that it would back a single candidate in 1989. The announcement indicated an unexpected degree of unity between the two major parties in the coalition—the Christian Democrats and the Socialists.

It was a bitter feud between these two parties that some experts contend opened the way for the military coup in 1973 that deposed President Salvador Allende

Chileans celebrate a vote in October forcing President Pinochet, the military dictator who has ruled since 1973, to hold an election in 1989.

Gossens, the leader of the Socialist Party. The coup was led by Pinochet and ended in Allende's death.

Exile's end. On Sept. 1, 1988, prior to the plebiscite, Pinochet ended 15 years of forced exile imposed on members of Allende's family and other political opponents of the military regime. A total of 339 people were allowed to return to Chile. The first to end her exile was novelist Isabel Allende Bussi, the daughter of Salvador Allende, who told reporters on her arrival in Santiago, "I am here to demonstrate my right to live in my country." Also free to return was Luis Corvalán, secretary general of the Chilean Communist Party, who was in exile in Moscow.

The economy. Chile's gross national product—the value of all goods and services produced—has grown at an annual rate of 2.6 per cent during the 15 years of military rule. Following the nationalization of many industries under Allende, Pinochet returned more than 500 state-run enterprises to the private sector and reduced government jobs by 200,000.

Chile's workers, however, have failed to benefit from the growth rate, with minimum wages hovering at the equivalent of $48 per month. Estimates of the number of Chileans living in extreme poverty range from 15 per cent of the population, according to the government, to 40 per cent, according to the opposition.　　Nathan A. Haverstock

See also **Latin America** (Facts in brief table). In *World Book*, see **Chile**.

China

China struggled with economic problems during 1988. Plagued by inflation and government corruption, China's leaders curtailed an economic reform program that had permitted more free enterprise but led to shortages. Grain production remained inadequate, and officials acknowledged that their efforts to control population growth had been unsuccessful.

Mixed results came from the 10-year effort to change China's Communist economic system, a system in which the government controlled all aspects of the economy and emphasized political ideology rather than motivating workers with financial incentives to be more productive. By 1988, the loosening of economic control had brought greater prosperity to many farmers and some city dwellers. It made China the world's largest producer of agricultural products and, according to official statistics, the fifth-largest industrial power. But, because the country's population is now a staggering 1.097 billion, the average reported income was only about $280 a year, though many people earned additional income they did not report.

Income was unevenly distributed, however. After decades of limits on the amount of money people could earn and the type and quantity of goods they could buy, the reforms brought to some the appearance of wealth. Relatively rich Chinese were able to purchase a limited amount of consumer goods, particularly the "four new essentials"—television sets, refrigerators, washing machines, and tape recorders. Chinese banks also began issuing credit cards.

Officials amended the Constitution in April 1988 to modify the prohibition on land sales, making it legal to transfer the long-term use of land. The Constitution was also changed to legalize private businesses that employ eight or more people. On June 29, the government relaxed controls on these businesses, which, along with smaller firms, employed about 25 million people and accounted for 2 per cent of China's industrial output and 12 per cent of its retail trade.

Inflation. By mid-1988, however, the economy was in danger of running out of control. Domestic production could not keep up with demand, and China was not making enough money on exports to pay for all the imported goods that consumers wanted. Too much money was chasing too few goods—a classic cause of inflation. In June, retail prices were at least 19 per cent higher than they had been one year earlier. The inflation rate was later estimated at 50 per cent in some cities. Runs on banks and panic buying

Japanese Prime Minister Noboru Takeshita, third from right, visits the Museum of the Toreador Warriors in Xi'an (Sian), China, in August.

China's Acting Premier Li Peng addresses the National People's Congress on March 25, a few days before he was named premier.

resulted as people tried to spend their money before it decreased further in value and before prices rose.

China's leaders reacted with alarm. They remembered that rampant inflation in the 1940's had undermined public support for China's previous regime and helped bring about its downfall in 1949.

The situation provoked debates within the leadership. Zhao Ziyang, general secretary of the Chinese Communist Party, led a group that believed the solution was to move more rapidly through the awkward transition from totally controlling the economy to unleashing the energies of private enterprise. The key to this change was reforming the government's price-control policy so that the price of an item reflected its true cost. Zhao thought that the current policy of only partially decontrolling prices—so that some prices were set by the market place in order to stimulate production while others were set by the government—had distorted the economy and encouraged inflation. In addition, many state-owned businesses whose prices were set by the government were losing money and requiring massive government subsidies.

Another group, led by Li Peng, China's Soviet-educated premier, wanted slower, more cautious changes that would ensure continued state control of the economy. Li's group worried about the unemployment that would result if businesses that could not break even or make a profit were closed. Already, 30 million of China's 130 million urban workers were employed by the government in essentially useless jobs, according to a June 13 report in *People's Daily*, the Communist Party newspaper. Li and his supporters also worried about the social problems that might be caused by a widening gap between those who prospered in a free-enterprise system and those who could not compete as well. And Li feared that eliminating price subsidies would cause prices to rise faster than wages.

Zhao's reforms slowed. The two groups discussed the problem at the annual summer meeting of the Politburo, the Communist Party's top policymaking body, from August 15 to 17. A report produced at the conference promised continued reforms through 1993, though they were to be implemented more slowly and carefully than those of the previous decade. After the meeting, Li's State Council, or cabinet, announced that there would be no more price increases in 1988 and no major pricing reforms in 1989.

Zhao's prestige seemed to have suffered from the failure of his reforms to live up to expectations. Zhao's urge to move quickly was discounted even by the man who had selected him for his high office, Deng Xiaoping (Teng Hsiao-p'ing in the traditional Wade-Giles spelling). Deng, who remained China's most powerful figure though he headed neither the party nor the government, remarked that economic reform efforts had "been bold enough," and that China now should proceed "in a more cautious way."

The party's main forum, the Central Committee, met in Beijing (Peking) from September 26 to 30. The committee announced that for the next two years it would focus on "improving the economic environment and rectifying the economic order."

On September 26, Zhao announced that China would cut its level of investment in construction projects. This policy was an effort to avoid contributing to inflation by paying wages for work that did not directly produce goods that workers could spend those wages on. More than 100 projects were canceled or postponed.

The government in October reimposed price controls on many commodities such as staple foods and some items basic to industry, and imposed a 20 per cent cut in spending on most government and party agencies. These steps were widely interpreted as a victory of Li's views over Zhao's.

Increasing corruption. During the year, the government intensified its efforts to stamp out corruption. Because shortages enabled officials to profit from their positions, corruption had reached its worst level in four decades of Communist rule.

A survey reported in June found that 83 per cent of China's city residents believed the bureaucracy was corrupt, and 63 per cent of officials admitted to corrupt practices. A party official disclosed that from 1983 to 1987, about 150,000 people were expelled from the party on charges of corruption.

New officials. When the Communist Party Central Committee met on March 15, Zhao produced a major report that included a list of names for top government jobs—the first time the party had openly shown that it assigned people to government jobs. The National People's Congress, China's party-controlled parliament, went into session on March 25 and voted for Zhao's list on April 8. Li Peng, who had filled the post of acting premier since Zhao gave up the job in 1987, became premier on April 9. The Congress then approved Li's 41-member State Council, which included officials who were younger and better educated than members of the previous council.

Yang Shangkun, an 81-year-old veteran of the civil war that brought the Communists to power in 1949, was elected China's president—a figurehead position—succeeding Li Xiannian. Another revolutionary soldier, 80-year-old Wang Zhen, became vice president. Deng was reelected chairman of the government's Central Military Commission, which gave him command of China's army.

Population statistics. The head of the state Family Planning Commission, Peng Peiyun, reported on November 1 that China was failing to meet its goal of restraining population growth. Authorities had hoped that the population would be only 1.2 billion by the year 2000, but Peng said that the population might reach 1.27 billion by then. Some foreign experts made even higher projections. With about 20 per cent of the world's people living on just 7 per cent of its land

area—and with only a small portion of that land suitable for farming—China would be hard-pressed to feed an even larger population.

A scientific survey of the body size of Chinese citizens was reported on November 4. Chinese men averaged 167 centimeters (5 feet 5¾ inches) in height and 59 kilograms (130 pounds) in weight. Women averaged 157 centimeters (5 feet 1¾ inches) and 52 kilograms (114½ pounds).

Natural disasters. Drought and floods in 1987 had made feeding China's people difficult and necessitated importing grain in 1988. Heat waves, floods, and typhoons in 1988 caused another grain shortage. More than 20 per cent of China's crops were damaged by drought along the middle and lower Yangtze River, while flooding in northeast China and along the central coast caused thousands of deaths and damaged crops on 10 per cent of the nation's farmland.

On November 6, an earthquake rocked a mountainous area of Yunnan Province. About 730 people died, and 300,000 were left homeless.

Unrest in Tibet. Despite police suppression, Tibetans continued the riots against Chinese rule begun in 1987. In an anti-Chinese demonstration on March 5, 1988, three Chinese policemen reportedly were killed, and the police then shot and killed a 15-year-old Buddhist monk and at least four other Tibetans. On December 10, some 35 monks and nuns demonstrated for Tibetan rights. Foreign witnesses said Chinese police fired on the demonstrators without provocation, killing at least 2 monks.

The Dalai Lama, the long-exiled Buddhist spiritual leader to whom most Tibetans profess loyalty, proposed on June 15 that Tibet become a "self-governing democratic political entity" while China would retain authority for its defense and foreign affairs. This apparent abandonment of the goal of complete independence for Tibet angered some of the Dalai Lama's followers. Chinese officials, though not interested in giving up total control, offered to talk with the Dalai Lama, and he proposed a meeting in 1989.

Military ranks were restored and soldiers began wearing emblems indicating their status on Oct. 1, 1988, 23 years after all official signs of military rank were abolished. The armed forces were put on stricter rations, however, and Zhao warned them not to expect major funding increases until the national economy improved. The government also scrapped extensive plans for navy research.

The armed forces intensified their efforts to make money by manufacturing exports. In 1988, China became the world's fifth-largest arms exporter, primarily through sales of missiles and other weaponry to Middle Eastern nations.   Henry S. Bradsher

See also **Asia** (Facts in brief table); **Li Peng; Taiwan.** In *World Book,* see **China.**

Churches. See Eastern Orthodox Churches; Jews and Judaism; Protestantism; Religion; Roman Catholic Church.

City

City. As federal and state funding for housing, education, health care, and commercial development continued to decline in 1988, cities in the United States faced the challenge of standing on their own. The decline in funding was particularly disheartening to mayors of large and middle-sized cities, who found themselves trying to cope with the problem of poverty and all its related social ills, including illiteracy, homelessness, teen-age pregnancy, and infant mortality.

A report released by the U.S. Conference of Mayors in October 1988 said that if just a small percentage of the $291.4 billion spent by the federal government for defense in 1988 had been shifted to urban needs, billions of dollars would have been available to invest in education, housing and community development, social services, mass transit, employment programs, and public health. Instead, in the fiscal year beginning Oct. 1, 1988, the federal government eliminated funding for the Urban Development Action Grants program, which provides money for a variety of city projects.

The mayors' report also contained the results of a survey of 52 large cities in the United States. The survey found that although 38 per cent of these cities had special agencies to help children, child-care programs in the cities were insufficient. The majority of the cities surveyed also reported that the problems of inadequate education and school dropouts had worsened over the past five years.

John O. Norquist waves to supporters after being elected mayor of Milwaukee on April 5. Norquist is the city's first new mayor in 28 years.

City children. Of the 18.5 million children who live in U.S. urban areas, 29 per cent live in poverty, according to 1987 figures released in 1988 by the U.S. Bureau of the Census, an agency of the U.S. Department of Commerce. Nowhere was the tragedy of childhood poverty more evident in 1988 than among babies born in urban areas. Infant mortality rates—the number of deaths per 1,000 live births—in U.S. cities continued to exceed those of cities in nearly all other industrialized nations. Although the 1987 infant mortality rate (the latest available figure) for the United States was 10.6, the rate in Detroit was 19.7, the highest among U.S. cities. Chicago, with a rate of 16.6, had the country's second-worst record. And in Harlem, a section of New York City, the rate stood at a staggering 27.6.

Race relations. The economic gap between blacks and whites continued to widen in 1988, creating tension in some cities. In October 1988, the Census Bureau reported that in 1987 the average income of black families in the United States was only a little more than half the average income of white families. Census Bureau data released in August 1988 found that the 1987 poverty rate—the proportion of the population with income below the government's official poverty level of $11,611 for a family of four—was 10.5 per cent for white Americans, but 33.1 per cent for blacks and 28.2 per cent for Hispanics.

The gap between poor and wealthy black families also widened during the year. According to the Census Bureau, the average income of the poorest 20 per cent of black families fell 23.6 per cent between 1978 and 1987, from $5,022 to $3,837 after adjusting for inflation. During the same period, however, the average income for the top 20 per cent of black families rose from $51,858 to $55,107.

Census dilemma. The U.S. Bureau of the Census faced two lawsuits in 1988, both dealing with the upcoming 1990 census. One suit challenged the bureau's undercounting of residents in inner-city neighborhoods, but the other questioned the bureau's plan to count illegal aliens. The outcome of both cases could have an impact on larger U.S. cities because undercounting reduces the number of congressional representatives from inner cities, and because some federal aid programs are based on population.

In April 1988, the Federation for American Immigration Reform and 40 members of Congress filed suit in a Pennsylvania federal court to prevent the Census Bureau from counting illegal aliens in the 1990 census. But in June 1988, Chicago, New York City, the state of New York, and the Mexican American Legal Defense and Educational Fund filed a petition to intervene in the lawsuit, demanding that illegal aliens be counted. Those parties, plus California and other groups, filed a second lawsuit in New York state in November to force the Census Bureau to adjust the results of the 1990 census to include people not counted.

The homeless. United States cities from coast to coast struggled in 1988 to deal with the problem of

50 largest cities in the United States

Rank	City	Population*	Per cent change in population since 1980	Unemployment rate†	Mayor‡
1.	New York City	7,262,700	+2.5	3.6%	Edward I. Koch (D, 1/90)
2.	Los Angeles	3,259,300	+9.8	5.1	Thomas Bradley (NP, 6/89)
3.	Chicago	3,009,530	+0.1	6.5	Eugene Sawyer (D, 5/89)
4.	Houston	1,728,910	+7.3	7.7	Kathryn J. Whitmire (NP, 1/90)
5.	Philadelphia	1,642,900	−2.7	4.7	W. Wilson Goode (D, 1/92)
6.	Detroit	1,086,220	−9.7	7.3	Coleman A. Young (D, 1/90)
7.	San Diego	1,015,190	+16.0	4.5	Maureen F. O'Connor (D, 6/92)
8.	Dallas	1,003,520	+10.9	6.5	Annette G. Strauss (NP, 5/89)
9.	Phoenix	914,350	+12.8	4.8	Terry Goddard (D, 12/89)
10.	San Antonio	894,070	+13.1	8.7	Henry G. Cisneros (D, 4/89)
11.	Baltimore	752,800	−4.3	5.0	Kurt L. Schmoke (D, 12/91)
12.	San Francisco	749,000	+10.3	3.8	Art Agnos (NP, 1/92)
13.	Indianapolis	719,820	+2.7	4.1	William H. Hudnut III (R, 12/91)
14.	San Jose	712,080	+13.1	4.2	Thomas McEnery (D, 12/90)
15.	Memphis	652,640	+1.0	4.8	Richard C. Hackett (I, 12/91)
16.	Washington, D.C.	626,000	−1.9	2.9	Marion S. Barry, Jr. (D, 1/91)
17.	Jacksonville	610,030	+12.8	5.1	Thomas L. Hazouri (D, 7/91)
18.	Milwaukee	605,090	−4.9	3.8	John O. Norquist (D, 4/92)
19.	Boston	573,600	+1.9	3.0	Raymond L. Flynn (D,1/92)
20.	Columbus, Ohio	566,030	+0.1	4.9	Dana G. Rinehart (R, 1/92)
21.	New Orleans	554,500	−0.6	9.3	Sidney J. Barthelemy (D, 5/90)
22.	Cleveland	535,830	−6.6	5.7	George V. Voinovich (R, 11/89)
23.	Denver	505,000	+2.5	5.8	Federico Peña (D, 6/91)
24.	El Paso	491,800	+15.6	11.9	Jonathan W. Rogers (NP, 4/89)
25.	Seattle	486,200	−1.5	4.8	Charles Royer (NP, 1/90)
26.	Nashville, Tenn.	473,670	+4.0	4.4	William H. Boner (D, 9/91)
27.	Austin, Tex.	466,550	+25.2	6.9	Lee Cooke (NP, 5/91)
28.	Oklahoma City	446,120	+10.4	4.9	Ronald J. Norik (D, 4/91)
29.	Kansas City, Mo.	441,170	−1.5	4.7	Richard L. Berkley (NP, 4/91)
30.	Fort Worth, Tex.	429,550	+11.5	7.0	Bob Bolen (NP, 4/89)
31.	St. Louis, Mo.	426,300	−5.9	6.2	Vincent L. Schoemehl, Jr. (D, 4/89)
32.	Atlanta, Ga.	421,910	−0.7	5.6	Andrew J. Young, Jr. (D, 1/90)
33.	Long Beach, Calif.	396,280	+9.6	5.1	Ernie Kell (D, 7/90)
34.	Portland, Ore.	387,870	−2.2	4.9	J. E. (Bud) Clark (NP, 12/92)
35.	Pittsburgh, Pa.	387,490	−8.6	6.1	Sophie Masloff (D, 11/89)
36.	Miami, Fla.	373,940	+7.8	5.0	Xavier L. Suarez (NP, 11/89)
37.	Tulsa, Okla.	373,750	+3.6	6.9	Rodger A. Randle (D, 5/90)
38.	Honolulu, Hawaii	372,330	+1.2	2.7	Frank F. Fasi (R, 1/93)
39.	Cincinnati, Ohio	369,750	−4.1	5.6	Charles J. Luken (D, 11/89)
40.	Albuquerque, N. Mex.	366,750	+10.4	6.6	Ken Schultz (NP, 12/89)
41.	Tucson, Ariz.	358,850	+6.0	4.8	Thomas J. Volgi (D, 12/91)
42.	Oakland, Calif.	356,960	+5.2	4.9	Lionel J. Wilson (D, 7/89)
43.	Minneapolis, Minn.	356,840	−3.8	3.0	Donald M. Fraser (D, 1/90)
44.	Charlotte, N.C.	352,070	+7.9	3.2	Sue Myrick (D, 11/89)
45.	Omaha, Nebr.	349,270	+1.9	3.9	Walter M. Calinger (NP, 5/89)
46.	Toledo, Ohio	340,680	−3.9	5.7	Donna Owens (R, 12/89)
47.	Virginia Beach, Va.	333,400	+27.2	4.4	Meyera E. Oberndorf (NP, 7/92)
48.	Buffalo, N.Y.	324,820	−9.2	3.9	James D. Griffin (D, 12/89)
49.	Sacramento, Calif.	323,550	+17.3	5.4	Anne Rudin (NP, 12/89)
50.	Newark, N.J.	316,300	−3.9	3.8	Sharpe James (D, 7/90)

*1986 estimates (source: U.S. Bureau of the Census).
†June 1988 figures for metropolitan areas (source: U.S. Bureau of Labor Statistics).
‡The letters in parentheses represent the mayor's party, with *D* meaning Democrat, *R* Republican, *I* Independent, and *NP* nonpartisan. The date is when the term of office ends (source: mayors' offices).

50 largest cities in the world

Rank	City	Population
1.	Mexico City	10,061,000
2.	Seoul, South Korea	9,645,932
3.	Tokyo	8,353,674
4.	Moscow	8,275,000
5.	Bombay, India	8,227,332
6.	New York City	7,262,700
7.	São Paulo, Brazil	7,033,529
8.	Shanghai	6,880,000
9.	London	6,767,500
10.	Jakarta, Indonesia	6,503,449
11.	Cairo, Egypt	5,875,000
12.	Beijing (Peking)	5,760,000
13.	Teheran, Iran	5,734,199
14.	Hong Kong	5,659,000
15.	Tianjin (Tientsin), China	5,300,000
16.	Karachi, Pakistan	5,208,170
17.	Bangkok, Thailand	5,153,902
18.	Rio de Janeiro, Brazil	5,093,232
19.	Delhi, India	4,884,234
20.	Leningrad, Soviet Union	4,295,000
21.	Santiago, Chile	4,225,299
22.	Lima, Peru	4,164,597
23.	Shenyang (Shen-yang), China	4,130,000
24.	Bogotá, Colombia	3,982,941
25.	Pusan, South Korea	3,516,807
26.	Ho Chi Minh City, Vietnam	3,419,978
27.	Sydney, Australia	3,364,858
28.	Wuhan (Wu-han), China	3,340,000
29.	Calcutta, India	3,305,006
30.	Madras, India	3,276,622
31.	Los Angeles	3,259,300
32.	Guangzhou (Canton), China	3,220,000
33.	Madrid, Spain	3,188,297
34.	Berlin (East and West), East and West Germany	3,062,979
35.	Chicago	3,009,530
36.	Yokohama, Japan	2,992,644
37.	Baghdad, Iraq	2,969,000
38.	Lahore, Pakistan	2,952,689
39.	Buenos Aires, Argentina	2,908,001
40.	Melbourne, Australia	2,832,893
41.	Rome	2,830,569
42.	Istanbul, Turkey	2,772,708
43.	Chongqing (Ch'ung-ch'ing), China	2,730,000
44.	Pyongyang, North Korea	2,639,448
45.	Osaka, Japan	2,636,260
46.	Harbin, China	2,590,000
47.	Hanoi, Vietnam	2,570,905
48.	Chengdu (Ch'eng-tu), China	2,540,000
49.	Bangalore, India	2,476,355
50.	Kiev, Soviet Union	2,409,000

Sources: 1986 Bureau of the Census estimates for cities of the United States; censuses or government estimates for cities of other countries.

the homeless. The National Academy of Sciences (NAS) in Washington, D.C., in a dramatic and emotional supplement to its September 1988 report on the health needs of the poor, expressed "anger and dismay" over the "national scandal" of homelessness. The NAS estimated that as many as 2 million Americans are homeless for one or more nights a year.

In August, Dorothy King, a Denver woman who runs a shelter for abused women, broke into a vacant house owned by the U.S. Department of Housing and Urban Development (HUD). Such houses are left vacant when their owners default on federally subsidized mortgages. King intended to force HUD and city officials to lease some of Denver's vacant houses as shelters for the homeless. King was jailed for three days on trespassing charges, but she succeeded in persuading federal and city officials to permit the homeless to occupy some of Denver's empty houses. In December, King was found guilty of the August charges and given a 10-day suspended sentence.

Housing. The National Housing Preservation Task Force, an organization representing owners of private, federally subsidized housing projects, issued a report in February 1988 that added to the concerns of housing experts. The task force estimated that federal subsidies on more than 1.4 million privately owned housing developments would expire in 1990, and another 750,000 would expire by 1995. The end of the federally subsidized programs would mean the displacement of low-income families, who, as tenants in such housing developments, pay a maximum of 30 per cent of their income for rent.

San Diego had success with a program to increase available low-cost housing for the homeless. In 1987, the city relaxed building codes and granted low-interest loans to developers who built single-room-occupancy hotels, a traditional source of low-cost urban housing. In August 1988—one year after the program began—more than 500 units were occupied and another 1,500 were planned.

President Ronald Reagan on September 13 signed into law a bill that extends the open housing provisions of the 1968 Civil Rights Act. The new law protects families with children under age 18, the elderly, and the disabled against housing discrimination. The bill also allows the government to levy fines of $10,000 to $50,000 against those who discriminate in housing sales or rentals on the basis of race, color, sex, religion, or national origin.

Air quality. On Aug. 31, 1988, more than 60 United States cities found themselves in violation of federal ozone and carbon monoxide air pollution standards. In 1987, Congress had extended deadlines under the Federal Clean Air Act to give cities more time to reduce pollution. For cities that did not comply, such as Los Angeles and Chicago, the Environmental Protection Agency ordered a halt on the construction of factories or other projects that could lead to increased air pollution.

To curb Los Angeles' air-pollution problem without relying on federal help, Mayor Thomas Bradley imposed one of the strictest truck bans in the United States on Sept. 28, 1988. The measure bans 70 per cent of heavy-duty trucks from the city's streets and roads during morning and evening rush hours. Mayor Bradley also ordered supermarkets and other receivers of trucked goods to stay open at least four hours at night to allow off-peak deliveries.

Garbage. During the year, many U.S. cities turned to incinerators to solve garbage-disposal problems caused by landfill shortages and groundwater pollution from buried garbage. In the spring of 1988, the city of Bridgeport, Conn., started operating a new— and controversial— type of incinerator that does not cause significant pollution. The plant burns waste at extremely high temperatures to destroy dioxin and other pollutants. The superheated steam that is produced is used to heat downtown buildings and to generate electricity for a local power plant. In August, officials reported that the burning garbage produced only trace amounts of dioxin.

Crime. Although violent crime continued its steady decline in the United States in 1988, drug-related murders and gang violence increased in urban areas. A study by the U.S. Department of Justice released in January found that as many as three-fourths of all men arrested for serious crimes in the largest U.S. cities had used drugs shortly before their arrest. Of the 12 cities studied, New York City, Washington, D.C., and San Diego had the highest percentages of arrested suspects who tested positive for illegal drug use.

Washington, D.C.'s murder total for 1988 was a record 372. Crime experts attributed the rise in murders to fights among drug dealers and crimes committed by drug users.

Elections. Milwaukee elected its first new mayor in more than two decades when voters on April 5 chose State Senator John O. Norquist, a Democrat, to succeed 70-year-old Mayor Henry W. Maier. Maier, also a Democrat, had retired after a 28-year term. In another April election, voters in Tulsa, Okla., unseated Republican Mayor Dick Crawford by electing Democrat Rodger A. Randle.

In elections held on November 8, voters in Honolulu, Hawaii, reelected Mayor Frank F. Fasi, a Republican, while voters in Wilmington, Del., reelected Democrat Daniel Frawley. In Wichita, Kans., voters chose to change their system of government, replacing a part-time mayor appointed by the City Council with a full-time elected mayor.

On November 21, the Illinois Supreme Court upheld a ruling ordering a mayoral election in Chicago in April 1989 to fill the two years then remaining in the term of Mayor Harold Washington, who died in November 1987. Eugene Sawyer, an alderman, became acting mayor.   Donna Rosene Leff

See also **Elections** and articles on individual cities. In *World Book*, see **City.**

Civil rights. On Sept. 13, 1988, United States President Ronald Reagan signed into law a bill hailed as the most important U.S. civil rights law in the last 20 years. The law, the Fair Housing Amendments Act of 1988, greatly strengthened federal laws banning housing discrimination based on race, color, sex, religion, or national origin. The new law, for the first time, established a procedure by which the federal government can impose heavy fines on those found guilty of housing discrimination. The law also expanded protection against housing bias directed at the elderly, people with disabilities, and families with children under 18.

Protection restored. Another important development in civil rights was the passage by Congress of the Civil Rights Restoration Act of 1988. It reversed a 1984 decision by the Supreme Court of the United States that had narrowed the scope of federal antidiscrimination laws. Although President Reagan vetoed the act, Congress easily overrode the veto on March 22, 1988— the Senate by a vote of 74-23 and the House by a vote of 292-133.

In *Grove City College v. Bell*, the high court had ruled that under a 1972 law barring sex discrimination in schools and colleges that receive federal funds, only the specific department found guilty of discrimination—not the entire institution—could lose its federal funds. Because the 1972 law was similar to three other federal antibias laws, the Reagan Administration decided that the ruling could be applied to discrimination based on race, disability, and age as well. In passing the Civil Rights Restoration Act, however, Congress said the Supreme Court had misread its original intention, which was to provide systemwide protection against all types of discrimination covered by federal law.

Japanese American reparations. An estimated 60,000 surviving Japanese Americans who were forcibly sent to internment camps during World War II will receive $20,000 each under legislation signed on Aug. 10, 1988, by President Reagan. About 77,000 American citizens and 43,000 legal and illegal alien residents of Japanese ancestry were interned because the government believed—with little evidence—that they posed a threat to U.S. security. About 450 surviving Aleut Indians evacuated from the Aleutian and Pribilof islands in Alaska for their own safety will receive $12,000 each. Many of the Indians removed from the islands died because of poor living conditions in the camps where they were housed.

International report. In its annual report released in October 1988, Amnesty International, a human rights group based in London, reported human rights abuses in 135 countries in 1987. It was the largest number of countries cited since the group was founded in 1961.

According to the report, thousands of people were kidnapped, tortured, or killed by secret death squads linked to government forces, especially in Latin Amer-

President Reagan congratulates Rep. Norman Mineta (D., Calif.) at the signing of a bill compensating Japanese Americans interned during World War II.

ica. The report also cited the massacres of unarmed members of the Dinka people in Sudan and the mass killings of Kurdish civilians in Iraq. In addition, Amnesty International criticized the Soviet Union for sending political prisoners to jail, exile, or psychiatric hospitals. The organization, which opposes capital punishment, also condemned the use of the death penalty in the United States as "arbitrary, racially biased, and unfair."

FBI spying. In January, lawyers for the Center for Constitutional Rights, a civil rights group based in New York City, reported that they had obtained documents showing that from 1983 to 1985 the Federal Bureau of Investigation (FBI) had spied on U.S. peace groups opposed to the Reagan Administration's policies in Central America. The documents, obtained under the Freedom of Information Act, disclosed that the FBI had investigated members of about 100 peace groups. Most of the surveillance had focused on members of the Committee in Solidarity with the People of El Salvador (CISPES).

The FBI initially defended its actions, saying that it had received information linking CISPES to a terrorist group in El Salvador. Agents, however, failed to establish any such link. On Sept. 14, 1988, FBI Director William S. Sessions, citing "mistakes in judgment," announced that he had disciplined six FBI agents, including the former head of the agency's terrorism section, for their part in the affair.

On September 30, a U.S. district judge in Texas found the FBI guilty of discriminating against Hispanic agents in both promotions and working conditions.

Congressional antibias action. The House of Representatives voted on October 4 to extend protection against job discrimination based on race, color, national origin, religion, sex, disability, or age to its own employees for the first time. In the past, Congress had exempted itself from federal job discrimination statutes. The Senate did not pass similar legislation.

Yonkers settlement. Brought to the verge of bankruptcy by heavy fines, the city of Yonkers, N.Y., on September 10 finally abandoned a three-year legal battle against a court-ordered housing desegregation plan. In 1985, a federal court found that the city had intentionally and unlawfully promoted racial segregation in housing and education. The case, initiated in 1980, was the first in which the U.S. government had linked the two types of segregation in one lawsuit. By the time the Yonkers City Council voted to accept the plan, the city had paid $1.6 million in fines and faced severe cutbacks in services.

The fines were imposed in August 1988 after the City Council, under intense pressure from residents who opposed the order, voted against implementing the plan, which Yonkers city officials had agreed to in January. Under the desegregation order, the city was to construct 200 units of low-income housing in mostly white neighborhoods by March 1, 1989, and to build 800 units of moderate-income housing within four years. In June 1988, the Supreme Court refused to hear the city's last appeal of the ruling. Residents of the neighborhoods in which the housing was to be built had argued that the new housing would lower property values and that Yonkers already had more low-income housing than most neighboring towns.

Free speech. In a major ruling on freedom of speech, the Supreme Court unanimously held on February 24 that television evangelist Jerry Falwell was not entitled to damages from *Hustler* magazine, which had satirically depicted him as an incestuous drunkard. At the bottom of the parody, *Hustler's* editors had included a disclaimer reading, "Ad parody—not to be taken seriously." The justices overturned a judgment of $200,000 for emotional distress awarded to Falwell by a federal jury in Virginia in 1984. Writing for the majority, Chief Justice William H. Rehnquist said that the parody was "doubtless gross and repugnant in the eyes of most." But he noted that the First Amendment protects satire and criticism of public figures from being found libelous to allow "breathing space" to freedom of expression.

AIDS. President Reagan on Aug. 2, 1988, ordered federal agencies to adopt rules that would prevent discrimination against employees infected with the virus that causes AIDS (acquired immune deficiency syndrome). In doing so, Reagan rejected a recommendation made by a presidential commission on AIDS that he endorse federal legislation prohibiting discrimination against AIDS victims. Reagan said the legislation was unnecessary because 36 states, including the 2 states with the highest number of reported cases of AIDS—New York and California—already had statutes protecting AIDS victims.

Klan judgment. On October 6, a federal jury in Atlanta, Ga., ordered two white supremacist groups and 11 individuals to pay a total of $1 million in damages to protesters attacked during a civil rights march in Georgia in 1987. During the interracial "brotherhood walk" in all-white Forsyth County, several hundred members of the Ku Klux Klan and the Southern White Knights and their sympathizers threw stones and bottles and shouted epithets at participants.

Howard Beach sentences. Three white teenagers convicted of manslaughter and assault for attacking three black men in the Howard Beach section of New York City in 1986 were sentenced in early 1988. One of the black men was killed by a passing car after the youths, who were among a group of up to 12 white men, chased him onto a highway.

The three men were given prison sentences ranging from the maximum of 10 to 30 years to 5 to 15 years. Three other defendants in the case convicted of misdemeanor riot charges were sentenced in September to 16 weekends in prison and ordered to perform 200 hours of community service work. A seventh defendant was acquitted.   George E. Curry

In *World Book*, see **Civil rights.**

Classical music. More than 200 performers proved once again in June 1988 that music is an international language. Members of the New York Philharmonic and the Soviet State Symphony Orchestra gathered on the stage of an outdoor theater in Moscow's Gorki Park to make music together. The performance was the farewell concert of the Philharmonic's tour of the Soviet Union.

Gennadi Rozhdestvensky, the conductor of the Soviet Symphony, led the combined orchestras in Dimitri Shostakovich's Symphony No. 5. The Philharmonic's conductor, Zubin Mehta, was in charge during a performance of Hector Berlioz' *Symphonie Fantastique.* For an encore, Mehta led the orchestras in a rousing rendition of John Philip Sousa's "The Stars and Stripes Forever" as fireworks burst overhead.

Earlier in 1988, Soviet and United States musicians collaborated on a three-week festival in Boston in March and April. It was the brainchild of Sarah Caldwell, artistic director of the Opera Company of Boston, and Soviet composer Rodion Shchedrin. Dozens of contemporary Soviet works received their first U.S. hearing, including a Requiem by Alfred Schnittke.

New York City also attempted to make music on a grand scale during the First New York International Festival of the Arts, a monthlong display of 20th-century creativity held in June and early July. The festival's 350 performances included several United States premieres.

Birthdays and anniversaries. As part of its 50th-anniversary celebration, Tanglewood, the Boston Symphony's summer festival in Lenox, Mass., presented a four-day festival in August honoring composer-conductor Leonard Bernstein, who turned 70 in 1988. Bernstein had already been feted in March at "A Leonard Bernstein Song Celebration"—a gala tribute at New York City's Alice Tully Hall.

In 1988, another premier conductor, Herbert von Karajan, turned 80. One of the most honored American composers, Elliott Carter, also celebrated his 80th birthday during the year. The San Francisco Symphony Orchestra devoted several concerts to Carter's music during October and November, including the U.S. premiere of his Oboe Concerto. French composer Olivier Messiaen had his 80th birthday in 1988. Other notable anniversaries included the Pittsburgh (Pa.) Opera's 50th and the centenary of the Concertgebouw, the renowned concert hall in Amsterdam, the Netherlands, which was renovated for the occasion.

Bartók's homecoming. In July, Hungarian composer Béla Bartók, who died in 1945, went home. Bartók had left his native Hungary in 1940, despairing of events in Europe. He spent the last five years of his life in the United States and was buried in the New York City area. In recent years, however, the Hungarian government had made overtures to Bartók's sons, suggesting that the composer's remains be reburied in his homeland, and Bartók's family consented. The composer's remains were interred in Budapest.

A world devastated by nuclear war was the setting for a new production of
Richard Wagner's *The Twilight of the Gods* in Bayreuth, West Germany, in 1988.

Beethoven's 10th. A reconstruction of the first movement of Ludwig van Beethoven's planned 10th symphony in October met with mixed reviews. Barry Cooper, a professor of music at the University of Scotland at Aberdeen, pieced together the reconstruction from sketches Beethoven had made for the symphony. The results were performed first by the Royal Liverpool Orchestra in London, then by the American Symphony Orchestra in New York City.

Unusual works. The U.S. premieres of two intriguing operatic works won favorable reactions. Krzysztof Penderecki's *The Black Mask*, a horror tale, had a successful summer run at the Santa Fe (N. Mex.) Opera. Audiences also liked John Cage's first opera, *Europeras 1 & 2*, which was presented at the adventurous PepsiCo Summerfare festival in Purchase, N.Y. The Cage work is a collage of fragments from 70 different operas, mostly repeated as parody.

Glass plus. Three stage works by minimalist composer Philip Glass were introduced during 1988. The American Repertory Theater in Cambridge, Mass., and the Kentucky Opera in Louisville joined to present *The Fall of the House of Usher*, based on a tale by American writer Edgar Allan Poe. One critic found the work "curiously detached from the terrifying events implied by the story." More happily received was *The Making of the Representative for Planet 8*, based on a 1982 novel by British writer Doris Lessing, which the Houston Grand Opera premiered in July 1988. The compos-

er's ethereal musical style seemed well suited to Lessing's science-fiction story.

Glass's *1000 Airplanes on the Roof* had a summer debut in Vienna, Austria. It tells the story of a quiet man who is transported to an alien spaceship, subjected to medical experiments, and made to forget what was done to him. The opera explores his struggle to remember.

Operatic premieres. In October, West Berlin's Deutsche Oper premiered *Los Alamos* by American composer Marc Neikrug. The antinuclear opera centers on the place in New Mexico where the atomic bomb was developed.

Other operatic premieres in 1988 included *Monday*, the third part of Karlheinz Stockhausen's seven-opera cycle called *Light*. It was introduced in June at La Scala in Milan, Italy. The Paris Opéra presented Maurice Ohana's *La Celestine* in June. The New York City Opera debuted Jay Reise's *Rasputin* in September. The work, based on the story of the Russian monk's life, brought both boos and cheers from the opening-night audience. Peter Maxwell Davies' opera *Resurrection* also premiered in September, in Darmstadt, West Germany. And in November the Dallas Opera presented its first commissioned work, Dominick Argento's *The Aspern Papers*, based on an 1888 novella by American writer Henry James.

New looks. Operatic directors continued to play games with old plots. Peter Sellars updated Richard

Wagner's *Tannhäuser* for Chicago's Lyric Opera, setting the action in a Miami, Fla., motel room and a crystal cathedral and making the hero a television evangelist. He set Wolfgang Amadeus Mozart's *The Marriage of Figaro* in New York City's Trump Tower for a production at the Summerfare festival.

Orchestras in 1988 seemed intent on expanding the repertory for instruments not well served by concertos. The Chicago Symphony commissioned a Trumpet Concerto from Karel Husa and a Flute Concerto from Gunther Schuller. The St. Louis (Mo.) Symphony Orchestra presented a Guitar Concerto by Joseph Schwantner.

Less prominent orchestras also sought out new works. The Charlotte (N.C.) Symphony, for instance, introduced Dan Locklair's *Creation's Seeing Order*, and the New Jersey Symphony Orchestra presented the world premiere of Steven Jaffe's *Four Images for Orchestra*. The Buffalo (N.Y.) Philharmonic and that city's Schola Cantorum—marking its 50th anniversary—commissioned a *Te Deum* by Argento, which the two ensembles presented in March.

Other orchestral premieres included: Alvin Singleton's *After Fallen Crumbs* (Atlanta, Ga.); Christopher Rouse's Symphony No. 1 (Baltimore); Ezra Laderman's Symphony No. 6 (Houston); Anthony Davis' Violin Concerto (Kansas City, Mo.); and *Morning Litany* by Nancy Galbraith (Pittsburgh).

Director changes. The Atlanta Symphony Orchestra's Robert Shaw retired after 21 years as music director. Yoel Levi replaced him. Lorin Maazel took over as music director of the Pittsburgh Symphony, and Christoph Eschenbach became director of the Houston Symphony Orchestra. Lofti Mansouri became the new general director of the San Francisco Opera. Zubin Mehta announced in November that he will leave his post with the New York Philharmonic in 1991.

Budget woes. Financial problems were never far from the minds of musical companies in 1988. The Baltimore Symphony endured a lengthy strike, and the New Orleans Symphony Orchestra canceled the second half of its 1987-1988 season because of a budget shortfall. The Vancouver (Canada) Symphony Orchestra suspended operations in January while civic leaders sought new funds, and the Nashville Symphony filed for bankruptcy. On the other hand, the New World Symphony gave its first performance in Miami in February. Artistic director Michael Tilson Thomas selected 86 young musicians from nearly 1,000 applicants during auditions held in 17 cities.

Special events of 1988 included the Bavarian State Opera's staging of all 15 operas by Richard Strauss at West Germany's Munich Festival in July. In October, the Israel Philharmonic performed Gustav Mahler's Symphony No. 2 in C minor, known as "The Resurrection," at the foot of the mountain fortress of Masada to mark Israel's 40th birthday.   Peter P. Jacobi

In *World Book*, see **Classical music; Opera.**

Clothing. See **Fashion.**

Coal production in the United States soared toward record levels in 1988 due to improved economic conditions and increased use of coal by electric power plants.

Production up, exports down. The United States Department of Energy (DOE) reported on September 26 that 465.8 million short tons (422.6 million metric tons) of coal was produced during the first half of 1988, about 5.7 per cent more than during the first half of 1987. Coal exports during the period increased by almost 12 per cent, to about 41 million short tons (37 million metric tons).

The National Coal Association (NCA) predicted on July 19, 1988, that coal production would reach record levels for the second straight year. The NCA, an industry organization located in Washington, D.C., said that 926 million short tons (840 million metric tons) of coal would be produced during 1988. Production would be about 9 million short tons (8 million metric tons), or 1 per cent, greater than the record 917 million short tons (832 million metric tons) produced in 1987, according to the NCA.

Increased industrial and manufacturing activity and the 1988 summer drought were largely responsible for the increases, according to the NCA. The drought produced poor conditions for hydroelectric generating stations, decreasing the flow of rivers and the amount of water stored in reservoirs. As a result, coal-fired power plants had to produce more electricity to meet the demand.

The NCA predicted that United States coal exports for all of 1988 would decline, due to increased competition from Venezuela, Colombia, and China, but said the rate of decline would not be as steep as in previous years. The NCA expected exports to total 79 million short tons (72 million metric tons), compared with 79.6 million short tons (72.2 million metric tons) in 1987.

British coal. Great Britain's Undersecretary of State for Energy W. Michael H. Spicer on May 11, 1988, said the British government planned to sell the nationally owned coal industry to private investors. But he said the sale probably would not occur until after the next general election in 1992.

An explosion on June 1, 1988, killed 51 coal miners working underground in a mine near Borken, West Germany, northeast of Frankfurt.

New mines. Mining officials in Tanzania in eastern Africa said in August that a new $110-million coal mine would make the country self-sufficient in coal. The mine, located 570 miles (920 kilometers) southwest of Dar es Salaam, would produce 160,000 short tons (150,000 metric tons) per year, ending the need to import coal from Zimbabwe and Zambia.

China in August announced discovery of a huge new coal deposit in Shanxi (Shansi) province. The deposit covers an area of 125 square miles (324 square kilometers) and contains an estimated 3.7 billion short tons (3.4 billion metric tons) of coal.

Coin collecting

Labor woes. About 10,000 coal-mine supervisors in Great Britain staged a one-day strike on February 1 that closed 100 of Britain's 102 pit mines. The strikers sought better pay and production bonuses. Thousands of coal miners in Poland went out on strike from August 16 until September 3 demanding higher pay, safer working conditions, and government recognition of Solidarity, the outlawed labor union. Miners in the Australian states of New South Wales and Queensland went out on strike in June and again in July to protest against changes in work schedules and low pay.

New uses for coal. The DOE on September 28 announced that it would spend $537 million on a group of clean-coal technology projects in 12 states. The projects will demonstrate improved techniques that could reduce air pollution in the 1990's from coal-burning electric power plants and industrial facilities. Electric utilities and other private firms sponsoring the projects agreed to contribute more than $800 million.

The DOE on August 24, 1988, announced a three-year research program to develop a locomotive engine powered by synthetic gas made from coal. The DOE awarded $4 million to Caterpillar, Incorporated, of Peoria, Ill., to develop an experimental version of the new engine.   Michael Woods

See also **Energy supply; Environmental pollution; Mining.** In *World Book*, see **Coal.**

A silver dollar is sealed in a plastic holder after being quality-graded by a company launched in 1988 in response to consumer doubts about coin values.

Coin collecting. The United States Mint in May 1988 issued coins commemorating the Summer Olympic Games in Seoul, South Korea. Two coins were issued—a $1 silver coin and a $5 gold coin. Those face values were considerably lower than the prices of the coins. The silver dollar was priced at $27 for the uncirculated coin and $29 for the proof coin; the gold piece sold for $225 uncirculated and $235 proof.

On the *obverse* (front) of the $1 coin, the Statue of Liberty's torch is shown receiving the flame of the Olympic torch. The reverse depicts the five interlinked Olympic rings. The obverse of the gold coin features the head of Nike, the Greek goddess of victory. The reverse portrays a stylized Olympic flame beneath the five-ring symbol.

The U.S. Olympic Committee receives $7 from the sale of each silver coin and $35 from each gold coin. Sales of the coins were expected to raise about $105-million for the committee.

New coin designs? The U.S. Senate on September 16 approved legislation to redesign the reverse side of the penny, nickel, dime, and quarter. The bill called for designs pertaining to American constitutional ideas, such as freedom of speech and assembly and the separation of powers in government. The House of Representatives, however, failed to act on the bill before the end of the 100th Congress.

Cracking down on fraud. To protect consumers from unscrupulous rare-coin dealers, the coin industry stepped up a self-policing effort that began in 1987. In March 1988, a program to accredit coin dealers was launched by the Industry Council for Tangible Assets (ICTA), an organization of individuals and companies dealing in coins, art objects, and other valuable commodities.

To obtain ICTA certification, dealers must submit to a rigorous background check and an investigation of their business procedures. By year-end, about 50 dealers had been accredited.

In another move to help coin buyers, the American Numismatic Association, jointly with the Federal Trade Commission, issued a *Consumer Alert on Investing in Rare Coins.* It warned that coin purchases can be a "financial disaster" for unwary investors.

Auction prices. In April, a buyer at a Toronto, Canada, auction submitted a winning bid of $353,430 for a 1911 Canadian *pattern* (new design) silver dollar—the highest price paid for a coin at a North American auction in 1988. At a March auction in New York City, a 1911-D Indian head $10 gold piece brought $120,000, and in June the finest known 1792 U.S. half *disme* (dime) sold for $100,000 at a sale in Long Beach, Calif.

Gold and silver prices remained relatively stable throughout 1988. At year-end, gold was $411 per troy ounce (31 grams), and silver sold for $6 per troy ounce.   David T. Alexander

In *World Book*, see **Coin collecting.**

Colombia. Colombia's Attorney General Carlos Mauro Hoyos Jimenez was kidnapped and later found murdered on Jan. 25, 1988, outside the city of Medellín. Hoyos was the latest victim of Colombian drug traffickers who have also killed a minister of justice and several supreme court judges since 1986.

Drug traffickers have declared "total war" on anyone who seeks their extradition to the United States to face drug charges. Hoyos was in Medellín to investigate the December 1987 release of a suspected drug trafficker who was facing extradition.

In August, Colombian officials said that the country's two largest drug rings—one in Medellín and another in the city of Cali—had gone to war with each other. Police attributed 80 slayings to the warfare.

The reported cause of the violence was territorial. The Medellín gang, which has long controlled drug distribution in the Miami, Fla., area, was reportedly attempting to force its way into the New York City market.

Oil. With help from foreign oil companies, Colombia has tripled its oil output in the last 10 years. Exports of more than 250,000 barrels per day in 1988 meant that oil was becoming almost as valuable to the economy as coffee.   Nathan A. Haverstock

See also **Latin America** (Facts in brief table). In *World Book*, see **Colombia.**

Colorado. See **State government.**

Common Market. See **Europe.**

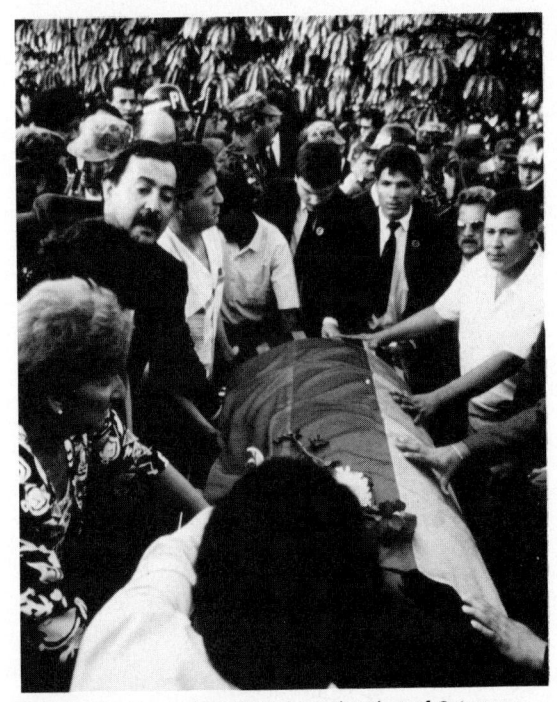

Mourners surround the flag-draped casket of Colombian Attorney General Carlos Mauro Hoyos Jimenez, assassinated in January by drug traffickers.

Communications. The most controversial issues of 1988 in the United States telecommunications industry concerned two variations on regular telephone service. One was the so-called *976 services*, such as "gab" lines on which many people can talk with one another at the same time. The other involved alternative operator service (AOS) companies, which provide operators for users in such locations as hotel rooms and pay telephones in airports. (The term *976 services* stems from the use of the prefix *976* in the telephone numbers of some of these services.)

One problem with 976 services was that many young callers ran up hundreds of dollars in gab line charges of which parents were unaware until they received their telephone bills. After being swamped with complaints from parents, several telephone companies canceled gab lines.

Another problem with 976 services was the nature of one particular type of service—telephone pornography. Parents and other individuals who opposed such services on moral grounds complained to telephone companies and the federal government. By the end of 1988, most telephone companies offered to block individual consumers' access to some or all 976 services at no cost to the consumer.

AOS restrictions. Many consumers complained that AOS companies charged much more than the consumers had expected. Regulatory agencies in Florida and other states warned consumers to beware of AOS providers. Other regulators, such as those in Kentucky, ordered AOS firms to stop doing business in their states. The Federal Communications Commission also investigated AOS charges but took no action because AOS services were not federally regulated.

Gateways. All seven regional holding companies (RHC's) moved closer to making *gateways* (connections) to new, interactive information services available to consumers. RHC's are telephone companies that were formed on Jan. 1, 1984, when the American Telephone and Telegraph Company (AT&T) broke up. The new services include *audiotex*, which provides voice messages such as weather reports and flight schedules; and *videotex*, which supplies information displayed on a computer screen.

United States District Judge Harold H. Greene, who is overseeing RHC activities, ruled on March 7, 1988, that the RHC's may provide information and data storage necessary to enable them to offer gateways to services that would be used with personal computers or computer terminals in the home, as well as electronic mail. The RHC's, however, must not provide the content of the information services.

By the end of September 1988, all the RHC's except American Information Technologies Corporation (Ameritech) had announced that they at least would conduct trials of videotex gateways, and BellSouth Corporation had started a limited commercial service in Atlanta, Ga. Ameritech, BellSouth, and Southwestern Bell Corporation of St. Louis, Mo., also announced

Earl Engleman, *The Wall Street Journal*;
permission, Cartoon Features Syndicate

"If elected I promise the return
of single-page phone bills . . . !"

trials of audiotex gateway services. On September 20,
Prodigy, a videotex business sponsored by Sears, Roe-
buck and Company and International Business Machines Corporation (IBM), began regular service in
Atlanta; Hartford, Conn.;. and the California cities of
Los Angeles, Sacramento, San Diego, San Francisco,
and Santa Barbara.

Transatlantic laser hook-up. The first fiberoptic
cable laid under the Atlantic Ocean went into service
on December 14. The cable contains hair-thin strands
of glass called optical fibers. Messages flash through
these fibers encoded as pulses of laser light. The cable
can carry 40,000 telephone calls simultaneously, twice
the capacity of all the transatlantic copper cables
combined. AT&T operates the cable.

AT&T chief dies. James E. Olson, chairman of
AT&T, died on April 18, shortly before the company
announced its best financial results since the 1984
breakup. Olson, 62, had spent just 20 months on the
job—the shortest chairmanship in AT&T's history.

Industry observers credited Olson for his role in the
reshaping of AT&T after the breakup, his cost-cutting
strategies, and his emphasis on AT&T's core businesses
such as long-distance service. Through the first half of
1988, AT&T held about 70 per cent of the long-distance market. AT&T President Robert E. Allen, 53,
succeeded Olson.   Arthur R. Brodsky

In *World Book*, see **Communication.**

Comoros. See **Africa.**

Computer. The year 1988 saw strong growth in the
computer industry. Dataquest, Incorporated, a mar-
ket-analysis firm located in San Jose, estimated that in
1988 more than 10 million personal computers, with a
total value of $22.4 billion, were sold in the United
States—a jump of 16.5 per cent in individual computers and 21 per cent in dollars. The global sales figures
were no less impressive: The number of computers
sold rose 13 per cent to 19 million and the dollar value
increased 17 per cent to $38.6 billion. The year also
saw plenty of drama, including a "virus" epidemic,
battles between various market factions fighting over
hardware and software standards, and a legal action.

The virus epidemic began on November 2, when
a renegade program attacked computers in United
States Department of Defense networks. A *computer
virus* is a small program designed to do mischief,
sometimes by deleting data or altering information
and sometimes by merely inserting a message. A virus
is inserted by a computer user into a floppy disc or
transmitted to a data network, and eventually embeds
itself in computer operating systems.

A virus spreads from these operating systems to
other computers—sometimes extremely rapidly. The
November virus flashed through Internet, a group of
networks used mainly by government-funded researchers at universities. Within hours, the virus had
infected thousands of computer systems. By November
4, programming experts had "cured" many of these
systems and put them back into the network. The
virus was planted by Robert T. Morris, Jr., a 23-year-
old computer science graduate student who apparently intended it only as a harmless stunt.

Hardware competition. Among the big gainers in
sales were the two market leaders, International
Business Machines Corporation (IBM) and Apple Computer, Incorporated, of Cupertino, Calif. IBM shipped
its 3-millionth PS/2 model in late 1988, and Apple
announced that the 2-millionth Macintosh had
reached the market. But while IBM's PS/2 line struggled to become a dominant standard, the Macintosh
gained favor in the business community. There was
evidence, however, that both were being overshadowed by a third line of products—machines whose
design conforms to the so-called Industry Standard
Architecture, established by the original IBM PC and
its later enhanced version, the IBM PC/AT.

Software struggle. UNIX, an operating system
created by American Telephone and Telegraph Company (AT&T) in the 1970's and popular in academic
and engineering circles, began to attract wider interest in 1988. Two groups—the Archer Group, led by
AT&T, and the Open Software Foundation, led by
IBM—fought for what industry observers called a
$5-billion slice of the personal computer (PC) pie.

On October 31, IBM and Microsoft Corporation of
Redmond, Wash., finally introduced Presentation
Manager, graphical interface software that enables
the user to manipulate what appears on the computer

The NEC UltraLite laptop computer has a 78-key keyboard and 640 kilobytes of main memory, yet weighs only 4.4 pounds (2 kilograms) with batteries.

screen by using a mouse to point at commands and pictorial representations of commands. Presentation Manager is designed to give IBM-compatible machines much of Macintosh's ease of use and flexibility. Presentation Manager is the first major software designed specifically for OS/2, an operating system developed by IBM and Microsoft.

Lawsuit. Apple Computer dropped a bombshell in March 1988, when it sued Microsoft and Hewlett-Packard Company of Palo Alto, Calif., for copyright infringement. Apple alleged that the two companies misappropriated the Macintosh's graphical interface in Microsoft's *Windows* and Hewlett-Packard's *New Wave* software.

Jobs unveils NeXT. The most eagerly awaited hardware introduction of 1988 occurred on October 12, when Steven P. Jobs, president and chief executive officer of NeXT, Incorporated, of Palo Alto, demonstrated a computer called the NeXT Computer System. Jobs has targeted the machine for use in university education and said sales would be directed to that market. The $6,500 machine includes an erasable optical disc that holds 256 million characters of information, equivalent to 128,000 double-spaced typewritten pages; digital-quality sound; a high-resolution, 17-inch (43-centimeter) monochrome monitor; and a software package designed for educators and students. A laser printer, available for an additional $2,000, runs on software built into the computer.

Powering up. Computers designed around the powerful 80386 microprocessor, a 32-bit chip made by Intel Corporation of Santa Clara, Calif., were the machines of choice in 1988. A bit is a 0 or 1, the basic "letters" of the computer "alphabet." A 32-bit chip handles 32 bits of data at a time, twice as many as previous processors. The more bits a chip can handle at once, the faster the computer operates.

Compaq Computer Corporation of Houston in June introduced the first personal computer that operates at a speed of 25 million electronic pulses per second, making it the fastest on the market. (A computer operates by sending pulses of electricity through electric circuits.) Other companies, including IBM and Advanced Logic Research, Incorporated, of Irvine, Calif., soon introduced equally fast-operating computers.

Portables and laptops. One of the year's strongest trends in personal computers was the growth of sales of portable and laptop machines. Some 1 million such computers were sold in 1988. Portables became faster, offered more memory storage, and incorporated much better displays. NEC Information Systems of Boxborough, Mass., made the lightest MS-DOS portable on the market, the 4.4-pound (2-kilogram) UltraLite, which sold for $2,999.   Ronald D. Scibilia

See also **Electronics.** In *World Book*, see **Computer; Microprocessor.**
Congo. See Africa.

Congress of the United States

Congress of the United States. The Democratic-controlled 100th Congress of the United States
adjourned on Oct. 22, 1988, after achieving an impressive election-year legislative record. The lawmakers
got their work done in spite of partisan frictions between Democrats and Republicans and sharp bickering with the "lame duck" Administration of President
Ronald Reagan. The final action of the session was
passage of a $2.8-billion bill to combat the thriving
traffic in illegal drugs—a measure spurred by campaign-season zeal to do something about a seemingly
unsolvable problem.

Also enacted during the year were a catastrophic
illness insurance plan for Medicare participants, a
major overhaul of the federal welfare system, the
most extensive revision of trade laws since World War
II (1939-1945), an inflation-adjusted freeze on defense
spending, and two major bills to strengthen civil rights
enforcement. Other legislation included a $1.2-billion
program to fight AIDS (acquired immune deficiency
syndrome), a measure requiring 60 days' notice of
plant closings and large-scale layoffs, a program making reparations to Japanese Americans interned during World War II, Senate ratification of the Intermediate-Range Nuclear Forces (INF) Treaty with the Soviets,
and an ending of military aid to the Nicaraguan *contra* rebels. An election- year drought in the nation's
heartland brought swift action in August on a $3.9-
billion aid package for farmers and ranchers.

But Congress also ducked its share of controversy. It
deferred until 1989 the task of making hard choices in
dealing with massive federal budget deficits. A bill to
limit congressional campaign spending died on February 26 as Democrats failed to overcome a Republican
filibuster against it. On September 26, Senate Democrats again threw in the towel as a Republican filibuster foiled their preelection drive to raise the minimum wage. A campaign-season package of "pro-
family" initiatives also died in the Senate on October
7, as yet another Republican talkathon tied up legislation to provide child-care assistance and parental
leaves for workers. Efforts to fashion a compromise
bill to combat acid rain and urban smog were abandoned on October 4.

The drug bill passed the Senate by voice vote after
clearing the House of Representatives 346 to 11. It
permits the death penalty for those convicted in federal courts of drug-related killings and establishes
fines of up to $10,000 for those convicted of possess-
ing even small amounts of such illicit drugs as marijuana and cocaine. The legislation also allows courts,
starting in September 1989, to deny certain federal
benefits, such as welfare payments and disability
compensation, to drug offenders. The measure provides $484.8 million for antidrug programs in the 1989
fiscal year in addition to $3.5 billion appropriated
earlier in the year, and it allows for added spending of
$2.8 billion over several years.

Surrounded by colleagues on May 27, Senators Bob Dole, left, and Robert C. Byrd
tell President Reagan, in Finland, that the Senate has ratified the INF Treaty.

244

Members of the United States Senate

The Senate of the first session of the 101st Congress consisted of 55 Democrats and 45 Republicans when it convened in January 1989. Senators shown starting their term in 1989 were elected for the first time in the Nov. 8, 1988, elections. Others shown ending their current terms in 1995 were reelected to the Senate in the 1988 balloting. The second date in each listing shows when the term of a previously elected senator expires.

State	Term	State	Term	State	Term
Alabama		**Louisiana**		**Ohio**	
Howell T. Heflin, D.	1979-1991	J. Bennett Johnston, Jr., D.	1972-1991	John H. Glenn, Jr., D.	1974-1993
Richard C. Shelby, D.	1987-1993	John B. Breaux, D.	1987-1993	Howard M. Metzenbaum, D.	1976-1995
Alaska		**Maine**		**Oklahoma**	
Theodore F. Stevens, R.	1968-1991	William S. Cohen, R.	1979-1991	David L. Boren, D.	1979-1991
Frank H. Murkowski, R.	1981-1993	George J. Mitchell, D.	1980-1995	Don Nickles, R.	1981-1993
Arizona		**Maryland**		**Oregon**	
Dennis DeConcini, D.	1977-1995	Paul S. Sarbanes, D.	1977-1995	Mark O. Hatfield, R.	1967-1991
John McCain III, R.	1987-1993	Barbara A. Mikulski, D.	1987-1993	Bob Packwood, R.	1969-1993
Arkansas		**Massachusetts**		**Pennsylvania**	
Dale Bumpers, D.	1975-1993	Edward M. Kennedy, D.	1962-1995	John Heinz, R.	1977-1995
David H. Pryor, D.	1979-1991	John F. Kerry, D.	1985-1991	Arlen Specter, R.	1981-1993
California		**Michigan**		**Rhode Island**	
Alan Cranston, D.	1969-1993	Donald W. Riegle, Jr., D.	1976-1995	Claiborne Pell, D.	1961-1991
Pete Wilson, R.	1983-1995	Carl Levin, D.	1979-1991	John H. Chafee, R.	1976-1995
Colorado		**Minnesota**		**South Carolina**	
William L. Armstrong, R.	1979-1991	David F. Durenberger, R.	1978-1995	Strom Thurmond, R.	1956-1991
Timothy E. Wirth, D.	1987-1993	Rudy Boschwitz, R.	1978-1991	Ernest F. Hollings, D.	1966-1993
Connecticut		**Mississippi**		**South Dakota**	
Christopher J. Dodd, D.	1981-1993	Thad Cochran, R.	1978-1991	Larry Pressler, R.	1979-1991
Joseph Lieberman, D.	1989-1995	Trent Lott, R.	1989-1995	Thomas A. Daschle, D.	1987-1993
Delaware		**Missouri**		**Tennessee**	
William V. Roth, Jr., R.	1971-1995	John C. Danforth, R.	1976-1995	James Sasser, D.	1977-1995
Joseph R. Biden, Jr., D.	1973-1991	Christopher S. (Kit) Bond, R.	1987-1993	Albert A. Gore, Jr., D.	1985-1991
Florida		**Montana**		**Texas**	
Bob Graham, D.	1987-1993	Max Baucus, D.	1978-1991	Lloyd M. Bentsen, Jr., D.	1971-1995
Connie Mack III, R.	1989-1995	Conrad Burns, R.	1989-1995	Phil Gramm, R.	1985-1991
Georgia		**Nebraska**		**Utah**	
Sam Nunn, D.	1972-1991	J. James Exon, D.	1979-1991	Edwin Jacob Garn, R.	1974-1993
Wyche Fowler, Jr., D.	1987-1993	Robert Kerrey, D.	1989-1995	Orrin G. Hatch, R.	1977-1995
Hawaii		**Nevada**		**Vermont**	
Daniel K. Inouye, D.	1963-1993	Harry M. Reid, D.	1987-1993	Patrick J. Leahy, D.	1975-1993
Spark M. Matsunaga, D.	1977-1995	Richard H. Bryan, D.	1989-1995	James M. Jeffords, R.	1989-1995
Idaho		**New Hampshire**		**Virginia**	
James A. McClure, R.	1973-1991	Gordon J. Humphrey, R.	1979-1991	John W. Warner, R.	1979-1991
Steven D. Symms, R.	1981-1993	Warren B. Rudman, R.	1980-1993	Charles S. Robb, D.	1989-1995
Illinois		**New Jersey**		**Washington**	
Alan J. Dixon, D.	1981-1993	Bill Bradley, D.	1979-1991	Brock Adams, D.	1987-1993
Paul Simon, D.	1985-1991	Frank R. Lautenberg, D.	1982-1995	Slade Gorton, R.	1989-1995
Indiana		**New Mexico**		**West Virginia**	
Richard G. Lugar, R.	1977-1995	Pete V. Domenici, R.	1973-1991	Robert C. Byrd, D.	1959-1995
Dan R. Coats, R.*	1989-1991	Jeff Bingaman, D.	1983-1995	John D. Rockefeller IV, D.	1985-1991
Iowa		**New York**		**Wisconsin**	
Charles E. Grassley, R.	1981-1993	Daniel P. Moynihan, D.	1977-1995	Robert W. Kasten, Jr., R.	1981-1993
Tom Harkin, D.	1985-1991	Alfonse M. D'Amato, R.	1981-1993	Herbert Kohl, D.	1989-1995
Kansas		**North Carolina**		**Wyoming**	
Robert J. Dole, R.	1969-1993	Jesse A. Helms, R.	1973-1991	Malcolm Wallop, R.	1977-1995
Nancy Landon Kassebaum, R.	1978-1991	Terry Sanford, D.	1986-1993	Alan K. Simpson, R.	1979-1991
Kentucky		**North Dakota**			
Wendell H. Ford, D.	1974-1993	Quentin N. Burdick, D.	1960-1995		
Mitch McConnell, R.	1985-1991	Kent Conrad, D.	1987-1993		

*Coats was appointed by Indiana Governor Robert D. Orr to fill the Senate seat vacated by Dan Quayle, elected Vice President.

Members of the United States House of Representatives

The House of Representatives of the first session of the 101st Congress consisted of 259 Democrats and 174 Republicans, with 2 vacancies (not including representatives from American Samoa, the District of Columbia, Guam, Puerto Rico, and the Virgin Islands), when it convened in January 1989, compared with 258 Democrats and 177 Republicans when the second session of the 100th Congress convened. This table shows congressional district, legislator, and party affiliation. Asterisk (*) denotes those who served in the 100th Congress; dagger (†) denotes "at large."

Alabama
1. H. L. Callahan, R.*
2. William L. Dickinson, R.*
3. vacant
4. Tom Bevill, D.*
5. Ronnie G. Flippo, D.*
6. Ben Erdreich, D.*
7. Claude Harris, D.*

Alaska
†Donald E. Young, R.*

Arizona
1. John J. Rhodes III, R.*
2. Morris K. Udall, D.*
3. Bob Stump, R.*
4. Jon L. Kyl, R.*
5. Jim Kolbe, R.*

Arkansas
1. Bill Alexander, D.*
2. Tommy F. Robinson, D.*
3. John P. Hammerschmidt, R.*
4. Beryl F. Anthony, Jr., D.*

California
1. Douglas H. Bosco, D.*
2. Wally Herger, R.*
3. Robert T. Matsui, D.*
4. Vic Fazio, D.*
5. Nancy Pelosi, D.*
6. Barbara Boxer, D.*
7. George E. Miller, D.*
8. Ronald V. Dellums, D.*
9. Fortney H. (Pete) Stark, D.*
10. Don Edwards, D.*
11. Tom Lantos, D.*
12. Tom J. Campbell, R.
13. Norman Y. Mineta, D.*
14. Norman D. Shumway, R.*
15. Tony Coelho, D.*
16. Leon E. Panetta, D.*
17. Charles Pashayan, Jr., R.*
18. Richard H. Lehman, D.*
19. Robert J. Lagomarsino, R.*
20. William M. Thomas, R.*
21. Elton Gallegly, R.*
22. Carlos J. Moorhead, R.*
23. Anthony C. Beilenson, D.*
24. Henry A. Waxman, D.*
25. Edward R. Roybal, D.*
26. Howard L. Berman, D.*
27. Mel Levine, D.*
28. Julian C. Dixon, D.*
29. Augustus F. (Gus) Hawkins, D.*
30. Matthew G. Martinez, D.*
31. Mervyn M. Dymally, D.*
32. Glenn M. Anderson, D.*
33. David Dreier, R.*
34. Esteban E. Torres, D.*
35. Jerry Lewis, R.*
36. George E. Brown, Jr., D.*
37. Alfred A. McCandless, R.*
38. Robert K. Dornan, R.*
39. William E. Dannemeyer, R.*
40. Christopher Cox, R.
41. William D. Lowery, R.*
42. Dana Rohrabacher, R.
43. Ronald C. Packard, R.*
44. Jim Bates, D.*
45. Duncan L. Hunter, R.*

Colorado
1. Patricia Schroeder, D.*
2. David E. Skaggs, D.*
3. Ben Nighthorse Campbell, D.*
4. Hank Brown, R.*
5. Joel Hefley, R.*
6. Daniel Schaefer, R.*

Connecticut
1. Barbara B. Kennelly, D.*
2. Samuel Gejdenson, D.*
3. Bruce A. Morrison, D.*
4. Christopher Shays, R.*
5. John G. Rowland, R.*
6. Nancy L. Johnson, R.*

Delaware
†Thomas R. Carper, D.*

Florida
1. Earl Hutto, D.*
2. Bill Grant, D.*
3. Charles E. Bennett, D.*
4. Craig T. James, R.
5. Bill McCollum, R.*
6. Clifford B. Stearns, R.
7. Sam M. Gibbons, D.*
8. C. W. Bill Young, R.*
9. Michael Bilirakis, R.*
10. Andy Ireland, R.*
11. Bill Nelson, D.*
12. Thomas F. Lewis, R.*
13. Porter J. Goss, R.
14. Harry A. Johnston II, D.
15. E. Clay Shaw, Jr., R.*
16. Lawrence J. Smith, D.*
17. William Lehman, D.*
18. Claude D. Pepper, D.*
19. Dante B. Fascell, D.*

Georgia
1. Lindsay Thomas, D.*
2. Charles F. Hatcher, D.*
3. Richard B. Ray, D.*
4. Ben Jones, D.
5. John Lewis, D.*
6. Newt Gingrich, R.*
7. George Darden, D.*
8. J. Roy Rowland, D.*
9. Edgar L. Jenkins, D.*
10. Doug Barnard, Jr., D.*

Hawaii
1. Patricia F. Saiki, R.*
2. Daniel K. Akaka, D.*

Idaho
1. Larry E. Craig, R.*
2. Richard H. Stallings, D.*

Illinois
1. Charles A. Hayes, D.*
2. Gus Savage, D.*
3. Marty Russo, D.*
4. George Sangmeister, D.
5. William O. Lipinski, D.*
6. Henry J. Hyde, R.*
7. Cardiss Collins, D.*
8. Dan Rostenkowski, D.*
9. Sidney R. Yates, D.*
10. John Edward Porter, R.*
11. Frank Annunzio, D.*
12. Philip M. Crane, R.*
13. Harris W. Fawell, R.*
14. J. Dennis Hastert, R.*
15. Edward R. Madigan, R.*
16. Lynn M. Martin, R.*
17. Lane A. Evans, D.*
18. Robert H. Michel, R.*
19. Terry L. Bruce, D.*
20. Richard J. Durbin, D.*
21. Jerry F. Costello, D.*
22. Glenn Poshard, D.

Indiana
1. Peter J. Visclosky, D.*
2. Philip R. Sharp, D.*
3. John Patrick Hiler, R.*
4. vacant
5. James Jontz, D.*
6. Danny L. Burton, R.*
7. John T. Myers, R.*
8. Frank McCloskey, D.*
9. Lee H. Hamilton, D.*
10. Andrew Jacobs, Jr., D.*

Iowa
1. Jim Leach, R.*
2. Thomas J. Tauke, R.*
3. David R. Nagle, D.*
4. Neal Smith, D.*
5. Jim Ross Lightfoot, R.*
6. Fred Grandy, R.*

Kansas
1. Pat Roberts, R.*
2. James C. Slattery, D.*
3. Jan Meyers, R.*
4. Dan Glickman, D.*
5. Bob Whittaker, R.*

Kentucky
1. Carrol Hubbard, Jr., D.*
2. William H. Natcher, D.*
3. Romano L. Mazzoli, D.*
4. Jim Bunning, R.*
5. Harold (Hal) Rogers, R.*
6. Larry J. Hopkins, R.*
7. Carl C. (Chris) Perkins, D.*

Louisiana
1. Robert L. Livingston, Jr., R.*
2. Corrinne C. (Lindy) Boggs, D.*
3. W. J. (Billy) Tauzin, D.*
4. Jim McCrery, R.*
5. Thomas J. (Jerry) Huckaby, D.*
6. Richard Hugh Baker, R.*
7. James A. (Jimmy) Hayes, D.*
8. Clyde C. Holloway, R.*

Maine
1. Joseph E. Brennan, D.*
2. Olympia J. Snowe, R.*

Maryland
1. Roy P. Dyson, D.*
2. Helen Delich Bentley, R.*
3. Benjamin L. Cardin, D.*
4. Thomas McMillen, D.*
5. Steny H. Hoyer, D.*
6. Beverly B. Byron, D.*
7. Kweisi Mfume, D.*
8. Constance A. Morella, R.*

Massachusetts
1. Silvio O. Conte, R.*
2. Richard E. Neal, D.
3. Joseph D. Early, D.*
4. Barney Frank, D.*
5. Chester G. Atkins, D.*
6. Nicholas Mavroules, D.*
7. Edward J. Markey, D.*
8. Joseph P. Kennedy II, D.*
9. John Joseph Moakley, D.*
10. Gerry E. Studds, D.*
11. Brian J. Donnelly, D.*

Michigan
1. John Conyers, Jr., D.*
2. Carl D. Pursell, R.*
3. Howard E. Wolpe, D.*
4. Frederick S. Upton, R.*
5. Paul B. Henry, R.*
6. Bob Carr, D.*
7. Dale E. Kildee, D.*
8. Bob Traxler, D.*
9. Guy Vander Jagt, R.*
10. Bill Schuette, R.*
11. Robert W. Davis, R.*
12. David E. Bonior, D.*
13. George W. Crockett, Jr., D.*
14. Dennis M. Hertel, D.*
15. William D. Ford, D.*
16. John D. Dingell, D.*
17. Sander M. Levin, D.*
18. William S. Broomfield, R.*

Minnesota
1. Timothy J. Penny, D.*
2. Vin Weber, R.*
3. Bill Frenzel, R.*
4. Bruce F. Vento, D.*
5. Martin O. Sabo, D.*
6. Gerry Sikorski, D.*
7. Arlan Stangeland, R.*
8. James L. Oberstar, D.*

Mississippi
1. Jamie L. Whitten, D.*
2. Mike Espy, D.*
3. G. V. (Sonny) Montgomery, D.*
4. Mike Parker, D.
5. Larkin Smith, R.

Missouri
1. William L. (Bill) Clay, D.*
2. Jack Buechner, R.
3. Richard A. Gephardt, D.*
4. Ike Skelton, D.*
5. Alan D. Wheat, D.*
6. E. Thomas Coleman, R.*
7. Mel Hancock, R.
8. Bill Emerson, R.*
9. Harold L. Volkmer, D.*

Montana
1. Pat Williams, D.*
2. Ron Marlenee, R.*

Nebraska
1. Doug Bereuter, R.*
2. Peter Hoagland, D.
3. Virginia Smith, R.*

Nevada
1. James H. Bilbray, D.*
2. Barbara F. Vucanovich, R.*

New Hampshire
1. Robert C. Smith, R.*
2. Charles C. Douglass III, R.

New Jersey
1. James J. Florio, D.*
2. William J. Hughes, D.*
3. Frank Pallone, Jr., D.
4. Christopher H. Smith, R.*
5. Marge Roukema, R.*
6. Bernard J. Dwyer, D.*
7. Matthew J. Rinaldo, R.*
8. Robert A. Roe, D.*
9. Robert G. Torricelli, D.*
10. Donald M. Payne, D.
11. Dean A. Gallo, R.*
12. Jim Courter, R.*
13. H. James Saxton, R.*
14. Frank J. Guarini, D.*

New Mexico
1. Steven H. Schiff, R.
2. Joe Skeen, R.*
3. William B. Richardson, D.*

New York
1. George J. Hochbrueckner, D.*
2. Thomas J. Downey, D.*
3. Robert J. Mrazek, D.*
4. Norman F. Lent, R.*
5. Raymond J. McGrath, R.*
6. Floyd H. Flake, D.*
7. Gary L. Ackerman, D.*
8. James H. Scheuer, D.*
9. Thomas J. Manton, D.*
10. Charles E. Schumer, D.*
11. Edolphus Towns, D.*
12. Major R. Owens, D.*
13. Stephen J. Solarz, D.*
14. Guy V. Molinari, R.*
15. Bill Green, R.*
16. Charles B. Rangel, D.*
17. Ted Weiss, D.*
18. Robert Garcia, D.*
19. Eliot L. Engel, D.
20. Nita M. Lowey, D.
21. Hamilton Fish, Jr., R.*
22. Benjamin A. Gilman, R.*
23. Michael R. McNulty, D.
24. Gerald B. Solomon, R.*
25. Sherwood L. Boehlert, R.*
26. David O'B. Martin, R.*
27. James T. Walsh, R.
28. Matthew F. McHugh, D.*
29. Frank Horton, R.*
30. Louise M. Slaughter, D.
31. William Paxon, R.
32. John J. LaFalce, D.*
33. Henry J. Nowak, D.*
34. Amory Houghton, Jr., R.*

North Carolina
1. Walter B. Jones, D.*
2. Tim Valentine, D.*
3. Martin Lancaster, D.*
4. David E. Price, D.*
5. Stephen L. Neal, D.*
6. Howard Coble, R.*
7. Charlie Rose, D.*
8. W. G. (Bill) Hefner, D.*
9. J. Alex McMillan III, R.*
10. Cass Ballenger, R.*
11. James McClure Clark, D.*

North Dakota
†Byron L. Dorgan, D.*

Ohio
1. Thomas A. Luken, D.*
2. Willis D. Gradison, Jr., R.*
3. Tony P. Hall, D.*
4. Michael G. Oxley, R.*
5. Paul E. Gillmor, R.
6. Bob McEwen, R.*
7. Michael DeWine, R.*
8. Donald E. Lukens, R.*
9. Marcy Kaptur, D.*
10. Clarence E. Miller, R.*
11. Dennis E. Eckart, D.*
12. John R. Kasich, R.*
13. Donald J. Pease, D.*
14. Thomas C. Sawyer, D.*
15. Chalmers P. Wylie, R.*
16. Ralph Regula, R.*
17. James A. Traficant, Jr., D.*
18. Douglas Applegate, D.*
19. Edward F. Feighan, D.*
20. Mary Rose Oakar, D.*
21. Louis Stokes, D.*

Oklahoma
1. James M. Inhofe, R.*
2. Mike Synar, D.*
3. Wesley W. Watkins, D.*
4. Dave McCurdy, D.*
5. Mickey Edwards, R.*
6. Glenn English, D.*

Oregon
1. Les AuCoin, D.*
2. Robert F. Smith, R.*
3. Ron Wyden, D.*
4. Peter A. DeFazio, D.*
5. Denny Smith, R.*

Pennsylvania
1. Thomas M. Foglietta, D.*
2. William H. (Bill) Gray III, D.*
3. Robert A. Borski, Jr., D.*
4. Joseph P. Kolter, D.*
5. Richard T. Schulze, R.*
6. Gus Yatron, D.*
7. W. Curtis Weldon, R.*
8. Peter H. Kostmayer, D.*
9. E. G. (Bud) Shuster, R.*
10. Joseph M. McDade, R.*
11. Paul E. Kanjorski, D.*
12. John P. Murtha, D.*
13. Lawrence Coughlin, R.*
14. William J. Coyne, D.*
15. Don Ritter, R.*
16. Robert S. Walker, R.*
17. George W. Gekas, R.*
18. Doug Walgren, D.*
19. William F. Goodling, R.*
20. Joseph M. Gaydos, D.*
21. Thomas J. Ridge, R.*
22. Austin J. Murphy, D.*
23. William F. Clinger, Jr., R.*

Rhode Island
1. Ronald K. Machtley, R.
2. Claudine Schneider, R.*

South Carolina
1. Arthur Ravenel, Jr., R.*
2. Floyd Spence, R.*
3. Butler Derrick, D.*
4. Liz J. Patterson, D.*
5. John McK. Spratt, D.*
6. Robert M. (Robin) Tallon, D.*

South Dakota
†Tim Johnson, D.*

Tennessee
1. James H. Quillen, R.*
2. John J. Duncan, Jr., R.*
3. Marilyn Lloyd, D.*
4. James H. Cooper, D.*
5. Bob Clement, D.*
6. Bart Gordon, D.*
7. Donald K. Sundquist, R.*
8. John S. Tanner, D.
9. Harold E. Ford, D.*

Texas
1. Jim Chapman, D.*
2. Charles Wilson, D.*
3. Steve Bartlett, R.*
4. Ralph M. Hall, D.*
5. John W. Bryant, D.*
6. Joe Barton, R.*
7. Bill Archer, R.*
8. Jack Fields, R.*
9. Jack Brooks, D.*
10. J. J. (Jake) Pickle, D.*
11. J. Marvin Leath, D.*
12. James C. Wright, Jr., D.*
13. Bill Sarpalius, D.*
14. Greg Laughlin, D.
15. Eligio (Kika) de la Garza, D.*
16. Ronald D. Coleman, D.*
17. Charles W. Stenholm, D.*
18. Mickey Leland, D.*
19. Larry Combest, R.*
20. Henry B. Gonzalez, D.*
21. Lamar S. Smith, R.*
22. Tom DeLay, R.*
23. Albert G. Bustamante, D.*
24. Martin Frost, D.*
25. Michael A. Andrews, D.*
26. Richard K. Armey, R.*
27. Solomon P. Ortiz, D.*

Utah
1. James V. Hansen, R.*
2. Wayne Owens, D.*
3. Howard C. Nielson, R.*

Vermont
†Peter P. Smith, R.

Virginia
1. Herbert H. Bateman, R.*
2. Owen B. Pickett, D.*
3. Thomas J. (Tom) Bliley, Jr., R.*
4. Norman Sisisky, D.*
5. Lewis F. Payne, Jr., D.*
6. James R. Olin, D.*
7. D. French Slaughter, R.*
8. Stanford E. (Stan) Parris, R.*
9. Frederick C. Boucher, D.*
10. Frank R. Wolf, R.*

Washington
1. John R. Miller, R.*
2. Al Swift, D.*
3. Jolene Unsoeld, D.
4. Sid Morrison, R.*
5. Thomas S. Foley, D.*
6. Norman D. Dicks, D.*
7. Jim McDermott, D.
8. Rod Chandler, R.*

West Virginia
1. Alan B. Mollohan, D.*
2. Harley O. Staggers, Jr., D.*
3. Robert E. Wise, Jr., D.*
4. Nick J. Rahall II, D.*

Wisconsin
1. Les Aspin, D.*
2. Robert W. Kastenmeier, D.*
3. Steven Gunderson, R.*
4. Gerald D. Kleczka, D.*
5. Jim Moody, D.*
6. Thomas E. Petri, R.*
7. David R. Obey, D.*
8. Toby Roth, R.*
9. F. James Sensenbrenner, Jr., R.*

Wyoming
†Dick Cheney, R.*

Nonvoting representatives
American Samoa
Faleomavaega Eni Hunkin, D.

District of Columbia
Walter E. Fauntroy, D.*

Guam
Ben Blaz, R.*

Puerto Rico
Jaime B. Fuster, D.*

Virgin Islands
Ron de Lugo, D.*

Congress of the United States

Other legislation passed in the final days of the session included bills creating an independent commission to determine which military bases are unneeded and should be closed, and toughening penalties against illegal insider trading in the stock market. The lawmakers also approved a bill to make "technical" corrections in the 1986 tax overhaul law; and a $1.3-billion, two-year program to provide food, shelter, job training, and counseling for the homeless.

Medicare expanded. On July 1, 1988, Reagan signed a landmark bill designed to protect 33 million elderly and disabled Medicare participants from "catastrophic" hospital, doctor, and outpatient drug bills. The most sweeping Medicare overhaul since the program was created in 1965, the measure gives Medicare participants unlimited free hospitalization effective Jan. 1, 1989, after payment of an annual deductible of $560 in 1989, which will rise with inflation thereafter. In 1988, patients paid a $540 deductible for each "spell of illness," and Medicare payments ended after the 60th day. The new law also phases in assistance in paying for prescription drugs starting in 1990, and places a $1,370 ceiling on annual patient outlays under Part B of Medicare, which covers doctor bills, laboratory fees, and outpatient services.

Welfare reform. A years-long effort to overhaul the U.S. welfare system ended in 1988 with passage of the Family Support Act, a law designed to help poor people get off the welfare rolls by providing education, job training, and work programs. The Senate passed the measure 96 to 1 on September 29, and passage by the House followed a day later, 347 to 53. Reagan signed the legislation on October 13.

The revised program was estimated to cost an extra $3.3 billion over five years. A key provision requires welfare parents with children over age 3 to enroll in state-operated basic-education, job training, job search, or work programs. By 1995, 20 per cent of those eligible for welfare would be required to enter such programs. The compromise measure also requires employers to withhold child-support payments from the paychecks of parents absent from the home.

At White House insistence, Democrats agreed that in two-parent welfare families, at least one parent would have to work 16 hours a week in unpaid community programs starting in 1994. The White House agreed to a provision requiring states to continue child-care subsidies and Medicaid benefits for one extra year to families that work their way off welfare.

Trade-law revisions. After four years of effort to enact a trade bill, the House voted 312 to 107 for trade legislation on April 21, 1988, and Senate approval followed, 63 to 36, on April 27. Reagan vetoed the bill on May 24, largely due to a provision requiring businesses to give 60 days' notice of plant closings or massive layoffs. After the Senate was unable to override the veto, the advance-notice requirement was dropped, and the bill won final passage on August 3. Reagan signed the bill on August 23.

The measure requires the federal government to fight more aggressively against unfair trade practices by other countries and to try harder to open foreign markets to American exports. The plant-closing notification requirement was adopted by Congress as separate legislation, and Reagan, mindful of the political popularity of the measure, let it become law on August 13 without his signature.

Another controversial trade measure, calling for stiff curbs against imports of textiles, clothing, and shoes, cleared Congress on September 9. But on September 28, Reagan vetoed the bill as "protectionist," and neither chamber could muster enough votes to override his action. On the same day as the veto, the President signed legislation to implement a major free-trade agreement with Canada. The President and Canadian Prime Minister Brian Mulroney had agreed in January to the pact, which would create the world's largest free-trade zone. Congress easily approved the accord, and approval by the Canadian Parliament followed in late December.

Civil rights. Reagan also used his veto pen on March 16, rejecting a civil rights bill designed to restore broad antidiscrimination protections scaled back by the Supreme Court of the United States in 1984. In a 6 to 3 ruling, the court had placed limits on federal laws that prohibited institutions receiving U.S. government funds from discriminating on the basis of sex. Reagan said he supported overturning the court's 1984 decision but felt the new bill would "vastly and unjustifiably expand the power of the federal government over the decisions and affairs of private organizations. . . ." Congress overrode the veto on March 22. The vote in the Senate was 73 to 24, in the House 191 to 133. Congress later passed, and Reagan signed, a bill to strengthen civil rights protections under the Fair Housing Act of 1968.

Protecting "whistle-blowers." Congressional efforts to protect federal workers who expose fraud and abuse came to naught in October. Although the "whistle-blower" bill was passed by both houses without a single dissenting vote, Reagan announced on October 26 that he was refusing to sign the legislation because it might help "employees who are not genuine whistle-blowers" to avoid disciplinary action. Because Congress had already adjourned, it had no opportunity to override Reagan's decision.

Defense. On July 14, Congress sent Reagan a $300-billion defense authorization bill for the 1989 fiscal year that trimmed 20 per cent from his request for the Strategic Defense Initiative (SDI). SDI, known popularly as "Star Wars," is a proposed space-based line of defense against enemy ballistic missiles. The bill also shifted funds from the multiple-warhead MX missile, favored by the Administration, to the single-warhead Midgetman, which is preferred by Congress.

Reagan vetoed the measure on August 3, accusing Congress of playing "partisan politics." Unable to override the veto, Congress passed a compromise

House Speaker James C. Wright, Jr. (D., Tex.), denies in June that his new book was published under improper circumstances—one of several ethics charges against him.

authorization bill on September 28 by lopsided margins. SDI money cuts were not restored, but Congress agreed to drop some proposed curbs on SDI and other weapons programs and allowed an extra $100 million for the MX. Reagan signed the bill on September 29.

Federal budget. A remarkable aspect of the congressional session was an absence of partisan bickering over the annual budget resolution and the appropriations bills that followed. Relative harmony was possible because, in the wake of the October 1987 stock-market crash, congressional leaders and Reagan agreed on the broad outlines of a budget that would hold the federal deficit in check in the 1989 fiscal year, which began on Oct. 1, 1988. Reagan submitted a $1.09-trillion budget on February 18, and Congress essentially stuck to his blueprint while making shifts in spending priorities.

The House amazed even itself by passing 13 annual appropriations bills by June 29, the earliest that had happened in 28 years. The Senate, which like the House had repeatedly failed in the past to make timely appropriations, completed its budget work at 11:57 p.m. on September 30—just three minutes before the new fiscal year began.

As part of the defense appropriation bill, Congress refused to provide any military aid to the contra rebels fighting the Marxist Sandinista government of Nicaragua, but it gave the contras an extra $27 million in humanitarian assistance. The House rejected, by a 219-211 vote on February 3, Reagan's request for $36.3 million in contra aid that included $3.6 million in military assistance.

Ethics bill. In its rush toward adjournment, Congress on October 21 passed an ethics bill to tighten curbs on lobbying by former federal officials and to include for the first time members of Congress and their top staff aides. Under the bill, former executive-branch employees would have been banned for life from lobbying on matters in which they were "personally and substantially involved" while in government. The measure would also have forbidden members of Congress to lobby any congressional colleague or staff member for a year after leaving office and imposed a similar restriction on former staff aides. Reagan vetoed the bill, saying it went too far.

Congress had its own ethical problems. On August 5, Representative Mario Biaggi (D., N.Y.) resigned after being convicted on federal corruption charges for the second time in less than a year. Biaggi was found guilty of using his influence illegally to obtain federal contracts for the Wedtech Corporation of New York City. He had been a House member for 20 years.

On November 21, another congressional figure in the Wedtech affair was indicted. Representative Robert Garcia (D., N.Y.) and his wife were charged in federal court with receiving more than $150,000 in bribes from Wedtech officials. They denied any wrongdoing.

Connecticut

On October 17, Representative Pat Swindall (R., Ga.) was indicted on federal perjury charges stemming from a grand jury investigation of "laundered" drug profits—that is, drug profits whose illegal origin had been disguised. The House Committee on Standards of Official Conduct had voted on June 23 to investigate allegations that Swindall sought to negotiate an $850,000 house loan from two men even though he was warned that the men might be trying to launder drug money. Swindall was defeated for reelection.

On June 10, the House Committee on Standards announced that it would look into allegations that Speaker James C. Wright, Jr. (D., Tex.), had committed several breaches of ethics, including intervening improperly with federal banking regulators in Texas and receiving unusually high royalties for his book *Reflections of a Public Man.* Wright said he welcomed the probe, predicting it would clear him.

New majority leader. Senate Democrats of the incoming 101st Congress met on November 29 and elected Senator George J. Mitchell of Maine as the new majority leader. He succeeded Senator Robert C. Byrd of West Virginia, who gave up the post after 11 years to become chairman of the Appropriations Committee.   Frank Cormier and Margot Cormier

See also **United States, Government of the.** In the World Book Supplement section, see **Congress of the United States.**

Connecticut. See State government.

Conservation. In January 1988, a group of environmental organizations charged that oil drilling near Alaska's Prudhoe Bay had polluted the North Slope tundra, a fragile ecosystem, and destroyed large areas of wildlife habitat. Claiming that the oil industry had committed more than 1,500 violations of antipollution laws, the conservationists said that the same destruction could occur in northeastern Alaska's Arctic National Wildlife Refuge if oil drilling were allowed there. The refuge is a calving ground for the largest herd of migratory caribou in the world, a nesting site for thousands of migrating waterfowl, and home to polar bears, wolves, and large numbers of other Arctic mammals.

In 1987, the United States Department of the Interior had recommended that exploratory drilling be permitted along the coastal section of the refuge, where prospectors estimated that there was a 20 per cent chance of finding a major petroleum pool. Despite the conservationists' warning, in February 1988 the Senate Committee on Energy and Natural Resources granted the oil industry permission to proceed with exploratory drilling.

On May 10, environmentalists made public a preliminary report on the impact of petroleum development on the Prudhoe Bay area. The document—which had been prepared by the U.S. Fish and Wildlife Service (FWS) but had not been released—revealed that the bay sustained far greater environmental damage than

had been expected when full-scale oil exploration began in 1972. For instance, about 11,000 acres (4,450 hectares) of wildlife-supporting vegetation had been destroyed—almost double the amount predicted—and the populations of wolves, bears, and most bird species had declined.

The document appeared to confirm the conservationists' charges. They expressed hope that the FWS report would strengthen the prospects of protecting the Arctic National Wildlife Refuge.

Wildlife recoveries. In 1988, the black-footed ferret appeared to be recovering from its brush with extinction. After disease nearly exterminated the only known colony of the ferret in 1985, the Wyoming Game and Fish Department captured the 18 survivors and took them to a breeding station. In 1987, 7 kits were born and raised, and in May and June 1988, 38 young were born. If reproduction continues at this rate, officials plan to begin reintroducing the black-footed ferret to the wild in 1991.

Two of four pairs of red wolves released into the Alligator River National Wildlife Refuge on the coast of North Carolina in 1987 produced cubs in 1988. Once fairly common in the Southeastern United States, the species became extinct in the wild in 1978, when the few remaining red wolves were taken to captive-breeding centers.

In September 1988, the FWS announced that the whooping crane population in the United States was expected to exceed 200 by year-end—the largest crane population since the early 1900's. In 1941, only 15 whooping cranes were in existence but, beginning in the late 1970's, biologists boosted the population through captive breeding. They then created a second flock to protect the species from extinction should some disaster strike the main population. The biologists accomplished this by transferring whooping crane eggs to the nests of sandhill cranes, who became "foster parents" for the whooper chicks that were born.

Protecting endangered species. On September 28, Congress passed legislation to reinstate the Endangered Species Act. The original law expired in September 1985 but was extended by special appropriations while conservation-minded members of Congress worked to strengthen the law's protection of threatened species.

The new legislation included provisions for more closely monitoring plants and animals that are not yet listed as protected species and for improving safeguards for endangered plants on public or private land.

Another special provision of the bill was aimed at curbing the slaughter of African elephants. Ivory poaching caused the species' population to drop from some 1.3 million in 1979 to about 730,000 in 1988. The revised act would bar ivory imports from countries not making adequate efforts to halt poaching and from nations that do not have native elephant populations.

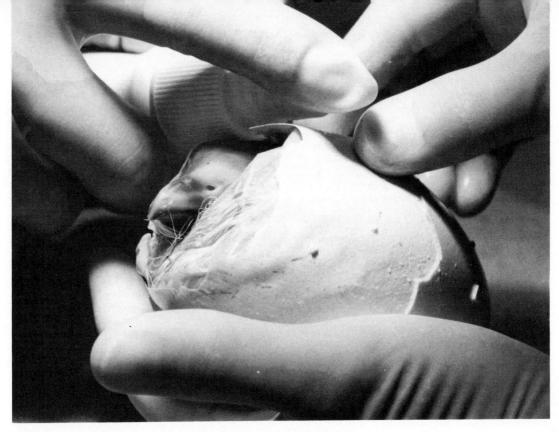

A worker at San Diego Wild Animal Park helps the first California condor ever conceived and hatched in captivity emerge from its shell on April 29.

President Ronald Reagan signed the bill into law in October.

Wildfires raged through national parks and forests in six Western states from July through September 1988. Fire swept through 2 million acres (810,000 hectares) of wilderness—1 million acres (405,000 hectares) in Yellowstone National Park alone. Glacier National Park was severely damaged, and 2 million acres of Alaskan forest were also ravaged by wildfires. See **Forest fires.**

Ocean dumping. Beginning in early summer, the waters and beaches of the Northeastern coast of the United States and some of the Great Lakes were contaminated by sewage and medical wastes washing ashore. The unsanitary conditions in some areas curtailed tourism, causing losses of millions of dollars.

Legislators moved to combat rising pollution levels in October, when Congress passed a bill banning ocean dumping of sewage sludge, and imposing heavy fines on violators. The bill was signed into law in November. Other new legislation outlawed unauthorized dumping of hospital waste into offshore waters.

Acid rain. Evidence of the environmental damage caused by acid rain mounted during 1988. On April 24, the Environmental Defense Fund, a public-interest organization based in New York City, stated that acid rain, as well as sewage and agricultural chemical runoff, was responsible for massive—and increasingly

frequent—kills of marine plants and animals in Atlantic coastal waters.

Acid rain contains nitrogen oxides, which are emitted by electric power plants and automobiles. When acid rain falls on a body of water, these chemicals cause an excessive growth of algae, which shuts off the oxygen supply to other aquatic creatures.

A survey of 500 freshwater streams in the Eastern United States released on May 21 by the U.S. Environmental Protection Agency demonstrated that acidification was far more widespread than previously known. Other researchers reported in July that thousands of trees in forests along the Eastern Seaboard had died since the early 1980's because of air pollutants such as airborne acids. Scientists studying lakes in the Sierra Nevada mountains in California stated in August that some bodies of water showed heavy acidity while others, though not yet permanently damaged, might become poisoned because of acid build-up in snow.

On August 5, Reagan reversed his previous policy on acid rain by agreeing to freeze emission levels of nitrogen oxides at the 1987 level for seven years. His action made it possible for the United States to join in a major international treaty designed to reduce acid rain.   Eugene J. Walter, Jr.

See also **Environmental pollution; Ocean.** In the Special Reports section, see **Our Vanishing Rain Forests.** In *World Book*, see **Conservation.**

Consumerism

Consumerism. Consumer prices climbed during 1988 at about the same rate as in 1987. As determined by the Consumer Price Index (CPI), the federal government's measurement of changes in the cost of goods and services, consumer prices in the United States rose 4.4 per cent in 1988, the same rate of inflation as in 1987, compared with only 1.1 per cent in 1986. The CPI is compiled by the Bureau of Labor Statistics (BLS), an agency of the Department of Labor.

Food prices were affected by the summer's severe drought, which helped push the food CPI up 5.2 per cent in 1988. The drought not only decreased grain harvests but also forced many farmers to reduce their livestock herds, suggesting that meat prices would continue to rise in 1989. The average food-price rise since 1982 has been about 3.5 per cent.

The prices of fuel oil provided some good news for consumers. For the first 11 months of 1988, gasoline prices dropped 0.5 per cent, and the price of home heating oil fell a precipitous 9.6 per cent, because of weakness in worldwide petroleum markets. Health-care costs, on the other hand, continued to climb more rapidly than other prices, rising 6.5 per cent for the first 11 months.

The monthly rise of 0.3 per cent in the CPI for urban wage earners in September, which ends the federal government's fiscal year, triggered an automatic 4 per cent cost-of-living increase in 1989 benefits for at least 47.8 million U.S. citizens. Those expected to receive the increase included 38.5 million social security beneficiaries; civil service, military, and railroad retirees; and some military veterans. The average benefit for a retired worker was to rise to $537 per month from $516. The maximum social security check for a worker retiring at 65 in 1989 would be $899 monthly, up $28 from 1988.

Getting money quicker. Banks traditionally have put a "hold" on a check deposit. This practice allows the bank to use the money, sometimes for two weeks or more, while the bank, not the depositor, draws the interest during this *float* period. (Money that is unavailable to either the check's payer or its receiver, but only to the bank, is called a float.)

A federal law that took effect on September 1 shortens the float period. For example, deposits made at teller windows in the form of cash, government checks, and cashier's checks may be held for no more than one banking day. Other regulations made by the Board of Governors of the Federal Reserve System vary the float period, however, generally from one to seven days.

Air travel. According to the Federal Trade Commission, airline deregulation has saved consumers $100-billion in fares since 1977. The June 1988 issue of *Consumer Reports* magazine agreed that deregulation has spurred competition, "bringing the benefits of air travel to millions of consumers who previously could not afford to fly." The number of airline passengers

New York City Mayor Edward I. Koch joins demonstrators protesting a rise in ticket prices at two of the city's movie-theater chains in January.

increased 63 per cent between 1978 and 1987, and total revenues soared 140 per cent to $45 billion. Critics say, however, that the competitive benefits of deregulation are limited; one or two airlines may dominate in many areas, effectively acting as a local monopoly and charging whatever consumers will pay.

Drugs. For the first time since 1976, a ban was placed in 1988 on color additives that are used in cosmetics and drugs and which may cause cancer. As required by a court order, the Food and Drug Administration (FDA) banned, effective July 17, Red Dyes numbers 8, 9, and 19 and Orange Dye number 17.

In May, the FDA ordered Roche Laboratories (a division of Hoffmann-La Roche Incorporated of Nutley, N.J.), manufacturer of Accutane, a drug used in the treatment of severe acne, to take additional measures to prevent the use of Accutane by pregnant women. The drug had been linked to serious birth defects. Prior to the FDA order, Accutane prescriptions carried a label warning of the drug's dangers. The new measures include asking physicians and their patients to sign a consent form that states the risks of the drug and warns patients taking Accutane to avoid pregnancy. Also, package inserts must include a picture of a baby deformed by Accutane.

Accutane is prescribed for up to 200,000 people in the United States each year. The FDA estimated birth defects due to Accutane at 600 to 1,300 each year. Roche said only 62 cases of such defects had been officially reported.

Aspirin warning. An FDA regulation, which became effective on December 9, requires a stronger, permanent label on nonprescription aspirin products. It warns that aspirin-containing drugs should not be given to children or teen-agers for chicken pox or flu. Numerous public health studies have confirmed a significant association between aspirin, when given to young people for those two viral infections, and the development of Reye's syndrome, a disease of the liver and central nervous system.

Radon in household air. Federal agencies in 1988 warned consumers about the hazards of radon, an invisible, odorless radioactive gas produced by the decay of uranium in rock and soil. Scientists have long known that radon is a threat to the health of people who live in houses built on radioactive soil or in dwellings that incorporate such radioactive material in walls or foundations. The National Academy of Sciences' National Research Council estimated that radon is responsible for 5,000 to 20,000 lung cancer deaths per year in the United States.

On September 12, the Environmental Protection Agency and the Public Health Service released a survey of 11,000 houses in seven states. They found that nearly 1 house in 3 exceeded the level considered acceptable—4 picocuries of radon per liter (110 picocuries per cubic foot) of air. (A picocurie is one-trillionth of a *curie*, a unit for measuring radioactivity.) The two agencies advised that every single-family

house and every apartment below the third floor be tested for radon. Testing involves placing an inexpensive collector in the house for about a week, then having a laboratory measure the radon build-up. On September 28, President Ronald Reagan signed a bill calling for a 3-year, $15.5-million program to deal with radon in schools and federal buildings.

Restitutions. On Jan. 25, 1988, the U.S. Department of Justice accused the Hertz Corporation—a car-rental company—of overcharging customers and their insurance carriers for repairs to accident-damaged vehicles. The Hertz Corporation, estimating that it had collected more than $13 million in overcharges over seven years through such practices, had already begun a refund program.

On February 23, Texaco Incorporated agreed to pay the U.S. Department of Energy $1.25 billion to settle a complaint that Texaco had overcharged customers for crude oil and refined products between 1973 and 1981, when federal price controls were in effect. The settlement brought the government's total recovery from settlements and judgments against oil companies that allegedly overcharged customers to more than $7.3 billion. State governments and consumers have shared in the recovery.   Odom Fanning

See also **Aviation; Bank; Drugs; Environmental pollution; Food; Public health; Safety.** In *World Book*, see **Consumerism.**

Costa Rica. See **Latin America.**

Courts. There were controversies and arguments about judges and judicial nominations to federal courts in the United States during 1988. Democrats led by Senator Edward M. Kennedy (D., Mass.) criticized the Administration of President Ronald Reagan for appointing too few women and members of minority groups to the federal bench. Through the end of 1987, the Reagan Administration had selected 6 blacks and 31 women for federal court jobs. Administration officials responded that they had tried to find more women and minorities but that the pool of qualified applicants was too small.

After sometimes emotional proceedings, the U.S. House of Representatives on August 3 voted 413 to 3 to impeach Judge Alcee L. Hastings of Florida on charges of conspiracy to obtain a bribe in a criminal case in 1981. Hastings, who had been acquitted of the charges in a 1983 jury trial, claimed the continuing investigation of his conduct was inspired by racism because he is black.

Congressman John Conyers, Jr. (D., Mich.), also a black, voted to recommend impeachment and rejected the charge of racism. In addition, an appeals court concluded that Hastings' earlier acquittal had been based on perjury.

Tobacco ruling. In a landmark decision on June 13, 1988, a federal jury in Newark, N.J., found a tobacco company liable in a smoker's lung-cancer death. After a four-month trial, the jury awarded $400,000 in

John Demjanjuk, accused of Nazi crimes in World War II, listens to translated testimony at his trial in Jerusalem. In April, he was sentenced to death.

damages to Antonio Cipollone on behalf of his wife, Rose, who died in 1984. The jury ruled that Liggett Group Incorporated's advertising prior to 1966—when warning labels became required by law—wrongly implied that its cigarettes were safe. The decision was the first of its kind in more than 300 tobacco-liability lawsuits filed since 1954.

LaRouche convicted. A federal jury in Alexandria, Va., on Dec. 16, 1988, convicted independent presidential candidate Lyndon H. LaRouche, Jr., of tax and mail fraud and conspiracy. The jury also convicted six LaRouche associates of mail fraud and conspiracy to cheat supporters whose $30 million in loans were never repaid. Sentencing was set for January 1989. Defense attorneys said they planned to appeal.

U.S. versus the PLO. The International Court of Justice, also known as the World Court, in The Hague, the Netherlands, ruled on April 26 that the U.S. government must submit to arbitration to resolve a dispute over an attempt to force the Palestine Liberation Organization (PLO) to close its mission to the United Nations (UN) in New York City. The United States had ordered the PLO mission vacated under a 1987 federal law aimed at curbing terrorism. Officials in the Reagan Administration ceased their efforts to close the PLO mission after a federal judge in New York City ruled on June 29 that the U.S. Congress, in approving the antiterrorist act in question, had not intended it to supersede UN provisions for arbitration.

Nazi conviction. John Demjanjuk was convicted in an Israeli court and sentenced on April 25 to death for war crimes committed in a Nazi extermination center during World War II (1939-1945). Demjanjuk was identified as the executioner called "Ivan the Terrible" because of his role in helping kill more than 850,000 men, women, and children at the Nazi death camp of Treblinka in German-occupied Poland. He continued to maintain that he was not "Ivan the Terrible" but the innocent victim of mistaken identity.

Racism ruling. Faced with millions of dollars in fines levied by a federal judge, the divided City Council of Yonkers, N.Y., on September 10 voted to build 1,000 units of low- and moderate-income housing. United States District Court Judge Leonard B. Sand, on August 2, acting on a lawsuit filed by the Department of Justice, had levied fines of up to $1 million a day against the city after finding that officials of the predominantly white community outside New York City had discriminated for years against blacks by refusing to build public housing units in white neighborhoods.

Rail wreck verdict. The engineer of a Conrail freight locomotive was sentenced on March 29 by a judge in Baltimore to five years in prison after pleading guilty to a single count of manslaughter stemming from a fatal collision between his train and an Amtrak passenger train in January 1987. The engineer, Ricky L. Gates, admitted that he had smoked marijuana shortly before the freight train he was driving ran through a switch and plowed into the Amtrak train. The Amtrak train carried 600 passengers, 16 of whom were killed and 176 injured. On July 15, 1988, Gates was sentenced to an additional three years in prison for obstructing a federal investigation of the crash.

Sensational cases. A highly publicized trial in New York City of what had come to be called the "preppie murder," because both the accused murderer and the victim had wealthy parents and belonged to a circle of preparatory school graduates, ended on March 25. The accused, Robert E. Chambers, Jr., now 21 years old, pleaded guilty to first-degree manslaughter in the death of 18-year-old Jennifer Levin. The woman had been strangled in August 1986 during a sexual encounter in New York City's Central Park.

A New York state grand jury, after a seven-month investigation, concluded on Oct. 6, 1988, that a young black woman's story about being abducted and molested by a gang of white men was a fabrication. The grand jury concluded that the black teen-ager, Tawana Brawley, had hidden in a vacant apartment for four days during November 1987, written racial slurs on her body, and made up the abduction story. Brawley had refused to testify before the grand jury.

New York State Attorney General Robert Abrams called for an investigation into the conduct of Brawley's attorneys, who had advised their client not to cooperate with investigators. Abrams also said he was beginning a civil and criminal investigation of Al Sharpton, a New York City clergyman who had acted as a spokesman for Brawley and conducted rallies to publicize the case.

The Baby M case. The New Jersey Supreme Court, in a decision that was expected to have national ramifications on the question of surrogate parenting, on February 3 struck down a parenting contract in the so-called Baby M case. The court found that the agreement made by Mary Beth Whitehead to bear a child for William Stern and his wife, Elizabeth, through artificial insemination for a $10,000 fee was invalid because it constituted "the sale of a child or, at the very least, the sale of a mother's right to her child." The court ruled, however, that Baby M (for Melissa) should remain with the Sterns because it was in the child's best interests to do so. A state Superior Court judge in April granted Whitehead, who has remarried and is now known as Whitehead-Gould, unsupervised visitation rights.

Product tampering conviction. In what was believed to be the first conviction for murder by product tampering, a Seattle woman, Stella Nickell, on June 17 was sentenced to 90 years in prison. Nickell was convicted of killing her husband, Bruce, and a stranger in 1986 with Excedrin capsules poisoned with cyanide.   Edward H. Bruske

See also **Civil rights; Crime; Supreme Court of the United States.** In *World Book*, see **Court.**

Crime. Efforts to stem the flow of illegal drugs into the United States took on global proportions in 1988. In February, federal grand juries in Tampa and Miami, Fla., indicted Panamanian leader General Manuel Antonio Noriega Morena on charges that he participated in drug trafficking. Further indictments in October revealed the results of a huge federal probe of international *laundering* (transferring to obscure the illegal source) of drug money allegedly carried out by the Luxembourg-based Bank of Credit and Commerce International, the world's seventh-largest privately owned bank. Indictments in Tampa and five other U.S. cities named 85 alleged conspirators in the laundering of $34 million in drug proceeds. Those charged included nine bank officials and top associates of the Medellín cocaine cartel based in Colombia.

Colombian drug kingpin Carlos Enrique Lehder Rivas, meanwhile, was convicted on May 19 on charges of smuggling 3.3 short tons (3 metric tons) of cocaine into the United States. A federal judge in Jacksonville, Fla., sentenced Lehder Rivas, a key figure in the Medellín drug cartel, to life plus 150 years in prison.

In an election-year effort against escalating drug problems, the Congress of the United States in October passed a $2.6-billion bill that included funds for stepped-up drug enforcement and increases in drug-abuse prevention efforts and in rehabilitation programs. See **Drug abuse.**

Iran-contra affair. The investigation of a scheme to sell arms to Iran and divert proceeds to the *contra* rebels fighting against Nicaragua's government resulted in criminal charges in 1988 against the affair's most prominent figures—several current and former high-ranking members of President Ronald Reagan's Administration. See **Iran-contra affair.**

Meese investigation. Another former member of the Reagan Administration faced charges of impropriety in 1988. On July 5, U.S. Attorney General Edwin Meese III, a long-time friend and political ally of the President, announced his resignation following a lengthy investigation by independent prosecutor James C. McKay that had undercut Meese's support on Capitol Hill. Meese said at his resignation that McKay's findings "completely vindicated" him. But McKay, while declining to seek an indictment against Meese, stated in a report made public on July 18 that Meese "probably" had violated the law four times while in office by permitting a false income tax return to be filed, failing to pay capital gains taxes when they were due, and twice violating federal conflict-of-interest laws.

Pentagon corruption. On June 14, after a two-year probe, federal investigators revealed allegations indicating widespread corruption in the awarding of U.S. defense contracts. See **United States, Government of the.**

In other defense-related matters, the U.S. Army announced on March 10 that Bell Helicopter Textron

A detective gathers up $147,000 found during a drug bust—reportedly the largest seizure of brown heroin in United States history—in Chicago in May.

Incorporated had agreed to pay about $88 million to the federal government to settle fraud charges resulting from a Department of Justice investigation into allegations that the company had overcharged the U.S. Army for helicopter spare parts. Officials called it the biggest settlement ever of a defense-contract fraud case. And on March 24, Motorola Incorporated agreed to plead guilty to charges that it defrauded the Pentagon of about $5 million on Navy weapons contracts and consented to pay $16.7 million in civil and criminal fines.

Apple juice scam. Prosecution of white-collar crime netted two former officials of the Beech-Nut Nutrition Corporation, who on February 17 were found guilty in a U.S. district court of intentionally selling apple-flavored sugar water labeled as pure apple juice for babies. Former Beech-Nut President Neils L. Hoyvald and former Vice President John F. Lavery both were convicted on 448 counts of violating food and drug, conspiracy, and mail-fraud laws.

Crime on Wall Street. Wall Street investor Ivan F. Boesky, who had pleaded guilty in 1987 to improperly dealing in insider information to make millions on the stock market, began to serve a three-year prison sentence on March 24, 1988. Boesky cooperated with investigators in a widening probe of illegal stock dealings.

On September 7, the U.S. Securities and Exchange Commission (SEC) charged investment brokers Drexel

Burnham Lambert Incorporated, and the company's chief junk-bond specialist, Michael Milken, with multi-billion-dollar insider trading fraud. SEC officials called the case—which included the rigging of corporate take-overs and the manipulation of stock prices—one of the most sweeping ever filed against a Wall Street firm. On December 21, Drexel agreed to plead guilty to fraud charges and pay $650 million in fines.

In other action, the SEC on January 12 charged a 23-year-old New Yorker, David P. Bloom, an unregistered investment adviser, with buying millions of dollars worth of artwork and other luxury items with $10 million that investors had given him to buy stocks. Bloom turned over assets worth more than $8 million.

Gun control. Several events in 1988 focused renewed attention on the issue of handgun ownership in the United States. On September 29, a judge in the District of Columbia declared a mistrial in the case of nationally known newspaper columnist Carl T. Rowan, who had been charged with unlawful possession of a handgun. Rowan was charged after he shot and wounded one of two teen-agers trespassing in his backyard pool in Washington, D.C. Rowan—a vocal advocate of gun control—claimed that the gun belonged to his son, a former Federal Bureau of Investigation (FBI) agent, who testified that district police had told him he was not required to register the weapon. District prosecutors said they would not press the case against Rowan after the mistrial was declared.

Congress on September 15 voted down proposed legislation that would have required at least a seven-day waiting period for would-be handgun purchasers. In Maryland, however, after a bitterly contested election battle, voters on November 8 approved a unique statute aimed at eliminating sales of cheap handguns known as Saturday night specials. The law, which overcame an unprecedented $4-million campaign by the National Rifle Association and other opponents, established a state commission to decide which handguns may be sold in Maryland.

Siege at computer firm. On February 16, a former employee of ESL, Incorporated, a computer-manufacturing company in Sunnyvale, Calif., allegedly conducted an armed assault on the firm, shooting to death seven workers. Authorities said the assailant, Richard W. Farley, a 39-year-old software engineer, had been spurned by a female employee of the firm and dismissed in 1986 for sexual harassment.

School shooting spree. A baby sitter armed with three guns on May 20 invaded an elementary school in Winnetka, an affluent suburb of Chicago, opening fire in a second-grade classroom and killing an 8-year-old boy and wounding five other children. Laurie Wasserman Dann, 30, who was said to have suffered emotional problems, later barricaded herself at a nearby home, wounding one of the occupants. Police stormed the house and found Dann dead of a self-inflicted gunshot wound.

Landlady arrested. Los Angeles police on November 16 arrested a Sacramento landlady after seven bodies had been found in shallow graves in the yard of her unlicensed boarding house. Police theorized that the victims were poisoned and secretly buried so that the landlady, Dorothea Montalvo Puente, could continue to cash their social security and welfare checks. By year-end, Montalvo Puente had been charged with one count of murder.

"I cashed the checks, yes," Montalvo Puente admitted, but she denied killing anyone. In 1982, she was convicted and served 2½ years in prison for forgery, grand theft, and "administering a stupefying drug" to elderly men she met in bars and then robbed. Although Sacramento police knew of the woman's record, she was questioned and released on Nov. 11, 1988, following discovery of the first corpse. She disappeared the next day and eluded police until a citizen tipoff led to her arrest in Los Angeles.

Slight rise in crime rate. The United States crime rate rose 1.8 per cent in 1987, the Justice Department reported on Oct. 9, 1988, marking an end to a five-year decline. The Reagan Administration had attributed that decline, in part, to tougher law enforcement. Some academic experts, however, emphasized that the age group most likely to commit crimes—those in their mid- to late teens—had decreased in the 1980's.   Edward H. Bruske

In *World Book*, see **Crime.**

Cuba. The signing of a pact at the United Nations Headquarters in New York City on Dec. 22, 1988, marked the success of negotiations designed to help end the civil war in Angola and to withdraw the Cuban and South African troops that have backed the opposing sides. Cuba has had troops in Angola since 1975, when Angola's civil war began. The number of Cuban troops has increased over the years and in 1988 totaled about 50,000. The Cuban forces were defending the Angolan government from attack by rebels supported by the United States and South Africa.

In London in May, for the first time since the civil war began, representatives from Cuba, Angola, the United States, and South Africa met at the same conference table to discuss peace prospects. On August 8, following a round of talks held in Geneva, Switzerland, the four powers declared a truce agreement, though a number of key issues, including a timetable for Cuba's withdrawal, were left unresolved.

The December pact calls for withdrawal of the Cuban troops by July 1, 1991. A second pact signed by Cuba, Angola, and South Africa is to bring independence to Namibia, which has been ruled by South Africa since World War I. Cuban withdrawal from Angola had been a South African condition for Namibian independence.   Nathan A. Haverstock

See also **Latin America** (Facts in brief table). In *World Book*, see **Cuba.**

Cyprus. See **Middle East.**

Czechoslovakia continued in 1988 to drag its feet in carrying out Soviet leader Mikhail S. Gorbachev's policy of *perestroika* (restructuring) and made no political concessions to Gorbachev's policy of *glasnost* (openness in the flow of information). The Czechoslovak government also continued to justify the 1968 invasion of Czechoslovakia by its Communist neighbors. But Soviet journalists who had reported from Prague during the invasion said at an anniversary seminar on Aug. 25, 1988, that no situation justified such interference with one Communist state by others.

Business as usual. As expected, Czechoslovakia's change of leadership in December 1987 brought about essentially no change in policy in 1988. Miloš Jakeš, who replaced Gustáv Husák as the nation's leader in December 1987, visited Moscow on Jan. 11, 1988, to discuss reform with Gorbachev. Commenting on the discussion, Jakeš emphasized his intent to maintain "effective ideological reins" on Czechoslovakia's political and economic structures—despite a July 1987 decree curbing the centralized control of business enterprises.

Jakeš' insistence on a slow pace of reform prompted a less patient top official to resign. Prime Minister Lubomir Strougal quit on Oct. 10, 1988, and was succeeded on October 12 by Ladislav Adamec, an economist and the prime minister of the Czech Socialist Republic, one of the two republics that make up Czechoslovakia.

Invasion reexamined. After his January meeting with Gorbachev, Jakeš said that neither his government nor the Soviets saw any reason to revise their views of the 1968 invasion—despite the fact that the invasion was caused by Czechoslovak policies strongly resembling perestroika and glasnost. In 1968, the Czechoslovak government under Alexander Dubček tried to implement sweeping reforms. The Soviet bloc crushed the reform movement in August 1968, as troops from the Soviet Union, Bulgaria, East Germany, Hungary, and Poland invaded Czechoslovakia. In 1969, Czechoslovakia's Communist Party dismissed Dubček and installed Husák.

Church and state conflict turned violent on March 25, 1988, when police broke up a crowd of 2,000 people at a candlelight rally in Bratislava, the capital of the Slovak Socialist Republic, the nation's other republic. The rally may have been the largest demonstration for religious freedom ever held in Czechoslovakia.

The government was already under pressure to grant its citizens more freedom to practice their religion. In the summer of 1987, Augustin Navratil, a Roman Catholic lay activist, began to circulate a petition for religious freedom. On Jan. 4, 1988, the archbishop of Prague, František Cardinal Tomášek, publicly supported it. By early March, more than 400,000 people had signed the petition.   Eric Bourne

See also **Europe** (Facts in brief table). In *World Book*, see **Czechoslovakia.**

Dancing

The death of American choreographer Robert Joffrey on March 25, 1988, was a serious loss to the dance world. As founder and director of the Joffrey Ballet, he had given young experimental choreographers such as Twyla Tharp and Laura Dean their first access to a wide audience. Joffrey was also the driving force behind revivals of a number of ground-breaking ballets of the early 1900's.

Joffrey presentations. The Joffrey Ballet's major production in 1988 indicated that, under the leadership of Gerald Arpino—named as artistic director in April—the company was continuing in the tradition of its founder. On October 26, at the opening of the monthlong Robert Joffrey Memorial Season at the City Center Theater in New York City, the company revived *Cotillon*, the "lost" masterpiece of Russian-born choreographer George Balanchine, who died in 1983. Created in 1932 for the Ballets Russes de Monte Carlo, the ballet was dropped from the dance repertory in the mid-1940's.

The story of a young girl who is touched by the hand of fate at a ball, *Cotillon* is considered the first—and some critics say the best—of Balanchine's many ballets dealing with the mysteriousness of life, represented in this case by a haunted ballroom. *Cotillon* was reconstructed by American dance historian Millicent Hodson and her husband, art historian Kenneth Archer. The two had reconstructed the Joffrey Ballet's production of Vaslav Nijinsky's *The Rite of Spring* (1913) in 1987.

Another 1988 Joffrey Ballet production was *Concerto Grosso*, which premiered in February at the Olympic Arts Festival in Calgary, Canada. The work featured choreography by James Kudelka, music by Jean Papineau-Couture, and scenery by Sylvain Labelle, all of whom are Canadian.

City Ballet. To celebrate its 40th anniversary, the New York City Ballet produced the American Music Festival at the New York State Theater in New York City. Held from April 26 to May 15, the festival presented 35 ballets set to music by American composers, including 19 world premieres. Organized by Peter Martins, artistic codirector of the City Ballet, the festival broke the company's long-standing tradition of performing only classical ballet and presented works by such modern dance choreographers as Paul Taylor, Laura Dean, Lar Lubovitch, and William Forsythe.

Even before the festival began, observers wondered if Martins was breaking a tradition worth keeping. By the time it was over, many critics felt the doubts had

Amy Rose and John Gardner flirt in the American Ballet Theatre's revival of Leonide Massine's 1938 ballet *Gaîté Parisienne* in June.

Dancing

Dancers of the Joffrey Ballet perform in a reconstructed version of *Cotillon* (1932), George Balanchine's "lost" masterpiece, in October.

been justified. It was generally conceded that none of the new works brought out the best in the dancers. Some critics also maintained that in surveying all types of American music, the festival was too diverse in nature to make an artistic statement. Previous dance festivals, produced under the guidance of Balanchine, had concentrated on just one composer. Finally, some critics felt that the festival confirmed suspicions that the company has been suffering an identity crisis since Balanchine's death.

American Ballet Theatre. In June 1988, at the Metropolitan Opera House in New York City, American Ballet Theatre (ABT) premiered *Drink to Me Only with Thine Eyes* by choreographer Mark Morris. It was set to a score by American composer Virgil Thomson. Notable for its clear, classical style and musicality, the work was considered a breakthrough for Morris, one of the most promising choreographers in the United States. Many observers felt that the Morris piece did more for American music and ballet than the entire American Music Festival.

The ABT had a banner year in other ways as well. Artistic director Mikhail Baryshnikov's policy of developing young dancers from within the ranks bore fruit in 1988. The company never looked stronger or more unified in style. The ABT also had the honor of presenting the world premiere of *The Informer* by Agnes De Mille on March 13 in Los Angeles. Set to Celtic dance tunes, *The Informer* was De Mille's first dance

since 1978. In October, the ABT made a two-week appearance in Paris in the company's first European season in 11 years.

The ABT closed its season at the Opera House with two new productions. One was the company premiere of *Fandango*, a 1964 ballet by Antony Tudor. The other was a new work by Clark Tippet, an ABT dancer, set to barbershop quartet music. It was titled *S.P.E.B.S.Q.S.A. (Society for the Preservation and Encouragement of Barber Shop Quartet Singing in America)*.

The ABT's artistic leadership was strengthened when Twyla Tharp announced on July 1, 1988, that she was disbanding her own dance company and joining the ABT as artistic associate. She said that the administrative duties of running her own troupe gave her too little creative time. Taking a group of her own dancers with her to the American Ballet Theatre, Tharp planned to choreograph a new dance for the ABT's 1988-1989 season.

U.S.-Soviet dance thaw. The era of *glasnost* (openness in the flow of information) in the Soviet Union was felt in dance. On Sept. 27, 1988, Baryshnikov announced that Andris Liepa, a star of the Bolshoi Theater Ballet, would be a guest artist with the ABT for the 1988-1989 season. It was the first time that a Soviet dancer had been granted an extended leave of absence to perform in the West. Earlier in 1988, Liepa and his frequent Bolshoi partner Nina Ananiashvili gave several guest performances with the City Ballet. In August, Natalia Makarova danced in Paris with the Kirov, the company from which she had defected in 1970.

Entire companies also profited from the cultural thaw between the United States and the Soviet Union. The Dance Theatre of Harlem became the first dance group to travel to Russia since the United States and the Soviet Union signed a cultural exchange agreement in 1985. The group performed there for five weeks in May and June 1988.

A group of 50 dancers from the Bolshoi, led by Maya Plisetskaya, participated in Making Music Together, a Soviet-American cultural exchange festival held in Boston in March and April. The highlights of the program were Plisetskaya's versions of *Anna Karenina* and *The Sea Gull*. Plisetskaya also danced in the October 4 opening for the three-week season of the Martha Graham Dance Company at the City Center.

The Paris Opéra Ballet revealed its avant-garde side when it toured Costa Mesa, Calif.; New York City; and Washington, D.C., from June 14 to July 31. Artistic director Rudolf Nureyev included in the program works by leading European experimentalists William Forsythe and Maguy Marin and a highly controversial production by choreographer Robert Wilson of Gabriele D'Annunzio's 1911 ballet, *The Martyrdom of Saint Sebastian*. In a more traditional vein, the Royal Danish Ballet presented two ballets, including *Napoli* (1842),

The Paul Taylor Dance Company performs in Taylor's *Counterswarm,*
a new work inspired by insects, which premiered in April in New York City.

by Danish choreographer August Bournonville in Washington, D.C., and New York City in June.

Premieres. Paul Taylor was prolific in 1988. In addition to a work for the American Music Festival, he created three pieces for his own troupe. Two of them —*Brandenburgs* and *Counterswarm*—debuted during his troupe's annual April engagement at the City Center. The third premiered in Philadelphia on November 10. Choreographer Martha Graham's 178th work, *Night Chant,* premiered on October 13 at the City Center. It was set to traditional Navajo music.

Other news. In September, the Mark Morris Dance Company took up residence at the Théâtre de la Monnaie, the opera house of Brussels, Belgium. It was the first time that an entire U.S. dance company had moved to Europe. Brussels gave Morris' young troupe, formerly based in Seattle, a budget of $1.5 million. A budget deficit equal to that amount led the Dallas Ballet to temporarily close down in January. The company reorganized, however, and presented a reduced season in the fall.

The National Ballet of Canada, based in Toronto, Ont., announced in August that Canadian-born dancer and choreographer Reid Anderson would become the company's artistic director in 1990. The company, which appeared in California and New York City during the summer of 1988, is currently led by Valerie Wilder and Lynn Wallis.   Nancy Goldner

In *World Book,* see **Ballet; Dancing.**

De Mita, Ciriaco (1928-   ), became prime minister of Italy on April 13, 1988, succeeding Giovanni Goria, who had resigned after serving for only 7½ months. Both Goria and De Mita are members of the Christian Democrat Party, and both their governments were a coalition of the same five parties that had governed the country since 1981. See **Italy.**

Goria resigned on March 11, 1988, after two of the coalition partners—the Socialists and the Social Democrats—opposed his proposal to resume the construction of a nuclear power plant north of Rome. In negotiations leading to the formation of De Mita's government, the Socialists obtained De Mita's promise to convert the plant to nonnuclear fuel. De Mita also pledged to work with Socialist leader Bettino Craxi to limit a major source of government instability—secret voting in Parliament.

Luigi Ciriaco De Mita was born on Feb. 2, 1928, in Nusco, a town east of Naples. He obtained a law degree at Catholic University in Milan, then served as a law professor at that university. He joined the Christian Democrat Party in the early 1950's and was first elected to Parliament in 1963.

De Mita served in various governments as minister for the development of the southern part of Italy, minister of industry, and trade minister. In 1982, he became the leader of the Christian Democrat Party.

The new prime minister is married and is the father of four children.   Jay Myers

Deaths

Deaths in 1988 included those listed below, who were Americans unless otherwise indicated. An asterisk (*) indicates that the person has a biography in *The World Book Encyclopedia.*

Addams, Charles (1912-Sept. 29), cartoonist whose delightfully ghoulish creations appeared in *The New Yorker* magazine.

Adler, Kurt Herbert (1905-Feb. 9), Austrian-born conductor who directed the San Francisco Opera from 1953 to 1981.

Albery, Sir Donald (1914-Sept. 14), British theater manager knighted in 1977.

Allegro, John Marco (1923-Feb. 17), British linguist, archaeologist, and author of the best seller *The Dead Sea Scrolls* (1956).

Alpert, George (1898-Sept. 11), president of the New York, New Haven & Hartford Railroad Company from 1956 to 1968; helped found Brandeis University in 1947.

*Alvarez, Luis W.** (1911-Sept. 1), physicist who won the Nobel Prize for physics in 1968 for his use of bubble chambers to detect new subatomic particles.

Ameche, Alan (1933?-Aug. 8), Heisman Trophy winner as the best college football player of 1954; Baltimore Colts running back from 1955 to 1960.

Andrewes, Sir Christopher (1896-Dec. 31), British virologist who helped discover the influenza virus.

Arias Madrid, Arnulfo (1901-Aug. 10), three-time president of Panama—in 1940 and 1941, from 1949 to 1951, and in 1968.

Armstrong, Henry (Henry Jackson) (1912-Oct. 22), boxer who held the featherweight, lightweight, and welterweight championships in 1938, the first man to hold three world titles simultaneously.

Artukovic, Andrija (1899-Jan. 16), Yugoslav official known as the Butcher of the Balkans because he supervised a network of Nazi concentration camps during World War II (1939-1945).

Ashby, Hal (1930-Dec. 27), motion-picture director whose films included *Harold and Maude* (1971) and *Coming Home* (1978).

Ashmole, Bernard (1894-Feb. 25), British archaeologist, art historian, and expert on ancient Greek sculpture.

*Ashton, Sir Frederick** (1904-Aug. 18), British choreographer who helped establish the modern classical style of ballet.

Baker, Chet (Chesney H. Baker) (1929-May 13), jazz trumpeter.

Barragán, Luis (1902-Nov. 22), leading Mexican architect; winner of the 1980 Pritzker Architecture Prize.

Barry, Robert R. (1915-June 14), Republican representative from New York from 1959 to 1965.

Bauduc, Ray (1909-Jan. 8), jazz drummer and composer who, with bassist Bob Haggart, wrote the 1930's hits "South Rampart Street Parade" and "Big Noise from Winnetka."

Bauer, David (1924-Nov. 9), Canadian Roman Catholic priest who helped found Canada's national hockey team.

Bearden, Romare H. (1914-March 12), abstract painter and collage artist whose works depicted black American life.

Bell, Richard A. (1913-March 20), Canadian minister of citizenship and immigration in 1962 and 1963.

Benton, Brook (Benjamin Peay) (1931-April 9), pop singer whose hits included "Just a Matter of Time" (1958) and "Rainy Night in Georgia" (1970).

Besser, Joe (1907?-March 1), actor who replaced Curly Howard in The Three Stooges comedy team from 1955 to 1959.

Bible, Alan H. (1909-Sept. 12), Democratic senator from Nevada from 1954 to 1975.

Bingham, Barry, Sr. (1906-Aug. 15), former owner and publisher of *The Louisville* (Ky.) *Times* and *The Courier-Journal* newspapers.

Bishop, Isabel (1902-Feb. 19), artist who painted everyday activities of women in a representational style.

Boswell, Vet (Helvetia Boswell) (1911?-Nov. 12), last surviving member of the popular 1930's singing trio the Boswell Sisters.

Bourne, Geoffrey H. (1909-July 19), Australian-born nutritionist and anatomist.

Boxer, Mark (1931-July 20), British cartoonist and editor who used the pen name Marc.

Boyington, Pappy (Gregory Boyington) (1912-Jan. 11), Marine aviator who commanded the famous Black Sheep squadron during World War II.

Brewster, Kingman (1919-Nov. 8), president of Yale University from 1963 to 1977 and U.S. ambassador to Great Britain from 1977 to 1981.

Brockway, Lord (A. Fenner Brockway) (1888-April 28), British Labour Party leader.

Brown, Lawrence (1905-Sept. 5), trombonist with the Duke Ellington orchestra for decades.

Brownson, Charles B. (1914-Aug. 4), Republican representative from Indiana from 1951 to 1959.

Butler, Daws (Charles Dawson Butler) (1916-May 18), the voice of Yogi Bear, Huckleberry Hound, and many other cartoon characters.

Butterfield, Billy (Charles William Butterfield) (1917-March 18), jazz trumpeter.

Caliguiri, Richard S. (1931-May 6), mayor of Pittsburgh, Pa., since 1977.

Caniff, Milton A. (1907-April 3), comic-strip artist who created "Terry and the Pirates" and "Steve Canyon."

Cardin, L. J. Lucien (1919-June 13), judge on the Tax Court of Canada since 1983 and minister of public works and minister of justice in the 1960's.

Milton A. Caniff,
"Steve Canyon" artist

Robert A. Heinlein,
science-fiction writer

Luis W. Alvarez,
Nobel physicist

Robert Joffrey,
founder of Joffrey Ballet

Deps

Carradine, John (Richmond Reed Carradine) (1906-Nov. 27), lanky character actor; father of actors David, Robert, Keith, and Bruce Carradine.

Carter, Billy (William A. Carter III) (1937-Sept. 25), brother of former President Jimmy Carter.

Carver, Raymond (1938-Aug. 2), short-story writer and poet who chronicled blue-collar life.

Castellano, Richard (1933-Dec. 10), actor who played the Mafia lieutenant Clemenza in *The Godfather* (1972).

*Caswell, Hollis L. (1901-Nov. 22), educator; president of Teachers College, Columbia University, from 1954 to 1962. He became a member of the World Book Editorial Advisory Board in 1936 and was its chairman from 1948 until his retirement in 1966.

*Chiang Ching-kuo (1910-Jan. 13), prime minister of Taiwan from 1972 to 1978 and president since 1978.

Clements, Sir John (1910-April 6), British actor and director who appeared in many plays with his wife, Kay Hammond.

Cohen, Nat (1905-Feb. 10), British film producer.

Cohn, Al (Alvin G. Cohn) (1925-Feb. 15), jazz tenor saxophonist and composer.

Coleman, Sheldon (1901-Sept. 21), chairman of the Coleman Company, Incorporated, makers of Coleman lanterns and other camping gear.

Connelly, Christopher (1941?-Dec. 7), actor who starred in the TV series "Peyton Place" and "Paper Moon."

Cook, Bun (Frederick J. Cook) (1903-March 19), Canadian hockey star who played left wing for the New York Rangers from 1926 to 1936; member of the International Hockey Hall of Fame.

Cooper of Stockton Heath, Lord (John Cooper) (1908-Sept. 2), general secretary of Great Britain's National Union of General and Municipal Workers from 1962 to 1973.

Cournand, André F. (1895-Feb. 19), French-born physician who shared the Nobel Prize for physiology or medicine in 1956 for developing a method of exploring the interior of the heart with a catheter.

Cousins, William E. (1902-Sept. 14), Roman Catholic archbishop of Milwaukee from 1959 to 1977.

Croudip, David (1959?-Oct. 10), special teams captain for the Atlanta Falcons football team.

Cunningham, Glenn (1910-March 10), former world recordholder in the mile run.

Daley, John F. (1887-Aug. 31), oldest former major league baseball player; shortstop for the St. Louis Browns in 1912.

Daniel, Dan (Wilbur C. Daniel) (1914-Jan. 23), Democratic representative from Virginia from 1969 until his death.

Daniel, Price M. (1910-Aug. 25), Democratic senator from Texas from 1953 to 1957 and governor of that state from 1957 to 1963.

Daniels, Billy (1915?-Oct. 7), big-band singer whose theme song was "That Old Black Magic."

Dart, Raymond A. (1893-Nov. 22), Australian anthropologist who in 1924 discovered the first fossil remains of an apelike, prehuman creature called *Australopithecus*.

Davis, Glenn R. (1914-Sept. 21), Republican representative from Wisconsin from 1947 to 1957 and from 1965 to 1975.

Dawn, Hazel (Hazel Tout) (1894-Aug. 28), singer and actress known as "The Pink Lady" who starred in the original Ziegfeld Follies and in silent films.

Day, Dennis (Owen Patrick Eugene Denis McNulty) (1917-June 22), singer who starred with comedian Jack Benny.

Dearden, John F. Cardinal (1907-Aug. 1), Roman Catholic archbishop of Detroit from 1959 to 1981.

Debo, Angie (1890-Feb. 21), historian and author of many books about American Indian and Oklahoma history.

Dell, Gabe (Gabriel del Vecchio) (1920?-July 3), actor who was one of the original Dead End Kids in films.

Dent, John H. (1908-April 9), Democratic representative from Pennsylvania from 1958 to 1979.

Devereux, James P. S. (1903-Aug. 5), Republican congressman from Maryland from 1951 to 1959.

Frederick Douglass
Patterson, educator

Sheilah Graham,
Hollywood columnist

Joshua Logan,
Broadway director

Pappy Boyington,
"Black Sheep" leader

Divine (Harris Glenn Milstead) (1945-March 7), female impersonator who starred in the films *Pink Flamingos* (1972) and *Hairspray* (1988).

Dodd, Bobby (Robert Lee Dodd) (1908?-June 21), football coach at Georgia Institute of Technology from 1945 to 1966.

Domengeaux, James (1907-April 11), Democratic representative from Louisiana from 1941 to April 1944 and from November 1944 to 1949.

Doráti, Antal (1906-Nov. 13), Hungarian-born symphony conductor.

Downie, Allan W. (1901-Jan. 26), British bacteriologist who played a leading role in ridding the world of smallpox.

Drees, Jack (1917?-July 27), long-time television sports announcer.

Drees, Willem (1886-May 14), prime minister of the Netherlands from 1948 to 1958.

Duggan, Andrew (1923-May 15), versatile, craggy-faced character actor.

Dulski, Thaddeus J. (1915-Oct. 11), Democratic representative from New York from 1959 to 1975.

Duncan, John J. (1919-June 21), Republican congressman from Tennessee since 1965.

*Duncan, Robert (1919-Feb. 3), poet.

Du Pont, Pierre S., III (1910?-April 9), chemical industry executive and father of former Governor Pierre S. du Pont IV of Delaware.

Eames, Ray (1916-Aug. 21), designer who, with her husband, Charles, created some of the most imaginative furniture of the 1900's.

263

Deaths

Edwards, Jimmy (1920-July 7), British radio and TV comedian whose trademark was a handlebar mustache.
Eldridge, Florence (1901-Aug. 1), actress who appeared with her husband, Fredric March, on stage and screen.
*****Estes, Eleanor** (1906-July 15), author of children's books who received the Newbery Medal in 1952 for *Ginger Pye*.
Estes, Elliott M. (1916-March 24), president of General Motors Corporation from 1974 to 1981.
Evans, Gil (Ian Ernest Gilmore Green) (1912-March 20), jazz composer and arranger born in Canada of Australian parents.
Eyskens, Gaston (1905-Jan. 3), prime minister of Belgium in 1949, from 1958 to 1961, and from 1968 to 1972.
Faure, Edgar J. (1908-March 30), twice prime minister of France, first in 1952 and again in 1955 and 1956.
Fennelly, Parker W. (1891?-Jan. 22), actor known for his portrayal of old Yankee characters.
Ferrari, Enzo (1898-Aug. 14), Italian sports car builder.
*****Feynman, Richard P.** (1918-Feb. 15), physicist who shared the 1965 Nobel Prize in physics for devising a theory by which scientists could predict the effects of electrically charged particles on each other in a radiation field.
Freeman, Cynthia (Beatrice Cynthia Freeman Feinberg) (1915?-Oct. 22), author of best-selling romance novels, including *Come Pour the Wine* (1980).
Frey, Leonard (1939?-Aug. 24), actor best-known for his roles in *The Boys in the Band* (1970) and *Fiddler on the Roof* (1971).
Fröbe, Gert (1912-Sept. 5), German actor who played the title role in the 1964 James Bond film *Goldfinger*.

Fuchs, Klaus (1911-Jan. 28), German-born physicist convicted of giving U.S. and British atomic bomb secrets to the Soviet Union in the 1940's.
Galbreath, John W. (1897-July 20), real estate developer, horse breeder, and former co-owner of baseball's Pittsburgh Pirates.
Gascon, Jean (1920-April 20), Canadian actor and director; artistic director of the Stratford Festival in Ontario from 1969 to 1974.
Gibb, Andy (1958-March 10), British pop singer, born in Australia; younger brother of the Bee Gees rock group.
Gildea, James H. (1890-June 5), Democratic congressman from Pennsylvania from 1935 to 1939.
Gillars, Mildred E. (Axis Sally) (1900-June 25), actress who broadcast Nazi radio propaganda to Allied troops during World War II.
Gittins, Chriss (1902?-Aug. 21), British actor who had played Walter Gabriel on the British Broadcasting Corporation (BBC) radio serial "The Archers" since 1953.
Gollan, Frank (1901-Oct. 5), Czechoslovak-born pediatrician who isolated the polio virus in 1948 and invented the heart-lung machine in the 1950's.
Goossens, Leon J. (1897-Feb. 12), British oboist.
Graham, Sheilah (Lily Sheil) (1908?-Nov. 17), British-born Hollywood columnist who chronicled her relationship with novelist F. Scott Fitzgerald in her autobiography *Beloved Infidel* (1958).
Guinness, Jonathan B. (1930-Feb. 27), British financier and member of the wealthy Guinness brewing family.
Guinness, Loel (Thomas Loel Evelyn Bulkeley Guinness) (1906-Dec. 31), heir of the banking branch of Britain's Guinness family and member of Parliament from 1931 to 1945.
Hall, Al (1915-Jan. 18), jazz bassist.
Hamilton, Sir Denis (1918-April 7), British journalist; chairman of Reuters news agency from 1979 to 1985.
Hamilton, Hamish (1900-May 25), leading British publisher, born in the United States.
Hargreaves, Roger (1935-Sept. 12), British children's author who created the Mr. Men and Little Miss characters.
Harty, Russell (1934-June 8), one of Great Britain's top TV talk-show hosts.
Hawtrey, Charles (George F. J. Hartree) (1914-Oct. 27), British actor who starred in the long-running series of *Carry On* films.
Hayter, Stanley W. (1901-May 4), British-born artist who founded the influential printmaking workshop Atelier 17 in Paris in 1927.
*****Heinlein, Robert A.** (1907-May 8), science-fiction writer whose most popular novel was *Stranger in a Strange Land* (1961).
Higgins, Colin (1941-Aug. 5), screenwriter and director, born in New Caledonia and raised in Australia, who wrote the cult classic *Harold and Maude* (1971).
Hildreth, Horace A. (1902-June 2), Republican governor of Maine from 1945 to 1949.
Hinkle, Clarke (1912-Nov. 9), fullback for the Green Bay Packers from 1932 to 1941; member of the Pro Football Hall of Fame.
Hoest, Bill (1926-Nov. 7), cartoonist who created "The Lockhorns" comic strip.
Holbert, Al (1947?-Sept 30), racing driver who won five Grand Touring season titles and three 24 Hours of Le Mans championships.
Holman, M. Carl (Moses Carl Holman) (1919-Aug. 9), civil rights leader and president of the National Urban Coalition.
Horton, Vaughn (George Vaughn Horton) (1911?-Feb. 29), country music composer who wrote "Mockin' Bird Hill" (1949); member of the Songwriters Hall of Fame.
Household, Geoffrey (1900-Oct. 4), British adventure novelist best known for *Rogue Male* (1939).
Houseman, John (Jacques Haussmann) (1902-Oct. 31), actor, director, and producer who won the 1973 Academy Award for best supporting actor for his role in *The Paper*

John Carradine,
versatile actor

Roy Orbison,
rock music pioneer

Christina Onassis,
shipping heiress

Carl O. Hubbell,
Hall of Fame pitcher

Chase; born in Romania, raised in Great Britain, and since 1943 a U.S. citizen.

Howard, James J. (1927-March 25), Democratic representative from New Jersey since 1965.

Howard, Trevor (1916-Jan. 7), rugged British motion-picture actor known for playing military officers and gentlemen.

Hubbell, Carl O. (1903-Nov. 21), pitcher for the New York Giants from 1928 to 1943; member of the National Baseball Hall of Fame.

Huffman, Gregory (1952-May 20), leading dancer with the Joffrey Ballet from 1972 to 1983.

Hulton, Sir Edward (1906-Oct. 8), British founder of the magazine *Picture Post.*

Hurd, Clement G. (1908-Feb. 5), illustrator of the children's classic *Goodnight Moon* (1947).

Hurkos, Peter (Pieter Van Der Hurk) (1910?-June 1), Dutch-born psychic.

Hurley, Lucille S. (1922-July 28), Latvian-born nutritionist who linked dietary deficiencies with birth defects.

Issigonis, Sir Alec (1906-Oct. 2), British automobile designer, born in Turkey, who created the popular Morris Minor and Mini.

Jacobson, Lord (Sydney Jacobson) (1908-Aug. 13), former editor of Britain's *Daily Herald* and *The Sun* newspapers.

Jenner, Albert E., Jr. (1907-Sept. 18), lawyer who participated in the investigation into the assassination of President John F. Kennedy and in the impeachment proceedings against President Richard M. Nixon.

*****Joffrey, Robert** (Abdullah Jaffa Bey Khan) (1930-March 25), founder and artistic director of the Joffrey Ballet.

Johnson, Harold T. (1907-March 16), Democratic representative from California from 1959 to 1981.

Johnson, Thomas F. (1909-Feb. 1), Democratic congressman from Maryland from 1959 to 1963.

Johnson, Wallace E. (1902?-April 27), cofounder of the Holiday Inn hotel chain.

Jonas, Charles R. (1904-Sept. 28), Republican representative from North Carolina from 1953 to 1973.

Jordan, James E. (1896-April 1), actor who played Fibber on the radio series "Fibber McGee and Molly" from 1935 to 1957.

Jung, J. W. (1888?-March 11), founder of the Jung Seed Company in Randolph, Wis., one of the largest mail-order garden companies.

Kennon, Robert F. (1902-Jan. 11), Democratic governor of Louisiana from 1952 to 1956.

Kid Chocolate (Eligio Sardinias) (1910-Aug. 8), Cuban boxer who held the world junior lightweight title from 1931 to 1933; member of the Boxing Hall of Fame.

Kiesinger, Kurt Georg (1904-March 9), chancellor of West Germany from 1966 to 1969.

Killian, James R., Jr. (1904-Jan. 29), engineer who was the first presidential assistant for science and technology, from 1957 to 1959.

Kinnear, Roy (1934-Sept. 20), British comic actor.

Kluszewski, Ted (Theodore B. Kluszewski) (1924-March 29), power-hitting first baseman with the Cincinnati Reds from 1947 to 1957 and with three other major league clubs until 1961.

Knapp, Florence (1873-Jan. 11), retired teacher thought to be the world's oldest person.

Kolodin, Irving (1908-April 29), music critic and long-time music editor of *Saturday Review* magazine.

Kuenn, Harvey E. (1930-Feb. 28), baseball player who had a lifetime batting average of .303 in 15 seasons, most of them with the Detroit Tigers and San Francisco Giants.

Laing, Hugh (Hugh Skinner) (1911-May 10), ballet dancer, born in the British West Indies, who specialized in the ballets of British choreographer Antony Tudor.

*****L'Amour, Louis** (Louis D. LaMoore) (1908-June 10), author of best-selling novels about the American West.

Laski, Marghanita (1915-Feb. 6), British novelist who wrote *The Victorian Chaise-Longue* (1953).

Louis L'Amour, author of Westerns

John Houseman, distinguished actor

John N. Mitchell, Watergate attorney general

M. Carl Holman, civil rights leader

Lassiter, Luther (Wimpy Lassiter) (1919?-Oct. 25), six-time world billiards champion.

Leach, Wilford (1932-June 18), New York Shakespeare Festival director from 1978 to 1987.

Lee of Asheridge, Baroness (Jennie Lee) (1904-Nov. 16), Great Britain's minister of state for the arts from 1967 to 1970.

Lemnitzer, Lyman L. (1899-Nov. 12), U.S. Army general who served as chairman of the Joint Chiefs of Staff from 1960 to 1962.

Levchenko, Anatoly (1941?-Aug. 6), Soviet cosmonaut.

Lexcen, Ben (Robert Miller) (1936-May 1), Australian yacht designer whose *Australia II* won the America's Cup yacht race in 1983.

Lizio, Celeste (1908?-Dec. 16), Italian-born restaurant owner and pizza maker known as "Mama Celeste."

Loewe, Frederick (1901-Feb. 14), Austrian-born composer who collaborated with lyricist Alan J. Lerner on such musicals as *My Fair Lady* (1956) and *Camelot* (1960).

*****Logan, Joshua** (1908-July 12), dramatist and director whose best-known hit was the musical *South Pacific* (1949).

Looney, Joe Don (1943?-Sept. 24), football star at the University of Oklahoma, later with five professional teams.

Lower, Arthur R. M. (1889-Jan. 7), one of Canada's most widely read historians.

Ma Haide (George Hatem) (1908?-Oct. 3), Chinese physician, born in the United States, who led the effort to wipe out leprosy and venereal disease in China.

MacBride, Sean (1904-Jan. 15), Irish human rights activist who was co-winner of the 1974 Nobel Peace Prize.

Deaths

*Malenkov, Georgi M.** (1902-Jan. 14), premier of the Soviet Union from 1953 to 1955.

Mansfield, Irving (1908?-Aug. 25), TV producer and publicist who promoted the novels of his wife, Jacqueline Susann.

Maravich, Pete (1948-Jan. 5), basketball star who spent most of his career with the Atlanta Hawks and the New Orleans Jazz; member of the Basketball Hall of Fame.

Marchand, Jean (1918-Aug. 28), Canadian labor leader and politician who held six cabinet posts between 1965 and 1975.

Marshall, Sir John Ross (1912-Aug. 31), prime minister of New Zealand in 1972.

Matlovich, Leonard P. (1944?-June 22), Air Force sergeant whose 1975 discharge for homosexuality became a rallying point for gay-rights activists.

McClory, Robert N. (1908-July 24), Republican congressman from Illinois from 1963 to 1983.

McCracken, James (1926-April 30), operatic tenor.

McCree, Floyd J., Sr. (1923-June 16), mayor of Flint, Mich., from 1966 to 1968; one of the first black mayors of a U.S. city.

McMahon, Sir William (1908-March 31), prime minister of Australia in 1971 and 1972.

Meeker, Ralph (Ralph Rathgeber) (1920-Aug. 5), actor who starred on Broadway in *Picnic* (1953).

Melen, Ferit (1906-Sept. 3), prime minister of Turkey in 1972 and 1973.

Memphis Slim (Peter Chatman) (1915-Feb. 24), blues pianist.

Méndez, Aparicio (1904-June 26), president of Uruguay from 1976 to 1981.

*Miki, Takeo** (1907-Nov. 14), prime minister of Japan from 1974 to 1976.

*Mitchell, John N.** (1913-Nov. 9), attorney general of the United States from 1969 to 1972 who became a central figure in the Watergate political scandal and the only attorney general ever convicted of a felony.

Moore, Colleen (Kathleen Morrison) (1900-Jan. 25), silent-film star whose famous doll house, the Fairy Castle, is displayed at the Museum of Science and Industry in Chicago.

Moore, Davey (1960?-June 3), World Boxing Association junior middleweight champion in 1982 and 1983.

Moses, Sir Charles (1900-Feb. 9), British-born general manager of the Australian Broadcasting Commission from 1935 to 1965.

Napier, Alan (Alan Napier-Clovering) (1903-Aug. 8), British character actor best known as the butler on the 1960's TV series "Batman."

Neddermeyer, Seth H. (1907-Jan. 29), physicist whose research led to the discovery of subatomic particles called *muons.*

*Nevelson, Louise** (1900-April 17), Russian-born American sculptor best known for her large wall sculptures made of wood scraps.

Newhouse, Norman N. (1906?-Nov. 6), publishing executive.

Nicholls, Sir Douglas R. (1906-June 4), governor of South Australia in 1976 and 1977; first Aborigine governor of an Australian state.

Nichols, Bill (William F. Nichols) (1918-Dec. 13), Democratic representative from Alabama from 1967 until his death.

Nissen, Greta (Grethe Ruzt-Nissen) (1906-May 15), Norwegian-born silent-film star.

*Noguchi, Isamu** (1904-Dec. 30), sculptor known for creating abstract works in highly polished stone.

Norstad, Lauris (1907-Sept. 12), U.S. Air Force general who commanded North Atlantic Treaty Organization forces in Europe from 1956 to 1963.

Northumberland, Duke of (Hugh A. Percy) (1914-Oct. 11), British nobleman.

Nusbaum, Orpha (1875-March 30), woman recognized as the world's oldest person after the January death of Florence Knapp.

O'Donnell, Madeline Foy (1908?-July 5), next-to-last living member of the Seven Little Foys vaudeville troupe. Only Irving Foy survives.

O'Farrell, Robert A. (1896-Feb. 20), baseball catcher whose major league career lasted from 1915 to 1935, most of it with the Chicago Cubs and St. Louis Cardinals.

Ogilvie, Richard B. (1923-May 10), Republican governor of Illinois from 1969 to 1973.

Oliver, Sy (Melvin James Oliver) (1910-May 27), jazz trumpeter and composer who wrote such 1940's hits as "Opus One" and "Easy Does It."

Olson, James E. (1925-April 18), chairman and chief executive officer of the American Telephone & Telegraph Company from 1986 to 1988.

Onassis, Christina (1950-Nov. 19), daughter of Greek shipping tycoon Aristotle S. Onassis.

O'Neill, Sir Con (1912-Jan. 11), British diplomat who led the negotiations that brought Great Britain into the European Community (EC or Common Market) in 1973.

Orbison, Roy (1936-Dec. 6), rock-music pioneer whose hits included "Crying" (1961) and "Pretty Woman" (1964).

O'Rourke, Heather (1975-Feb. 1), child actress who exclaimed "They're heeeere!" and "They're baaaack!" in the *Poltergeist* movies.

Osborn, Paul (1901-May 12), playwright who created *Morning's at Seven* (1939) and *The World of Suzie Wong* (1958).

Ouimet, J. Alphonse (1908-Dec. 20), Canadian TV executive; president of the Canadian Broadcasting Corporation from 1958 to 1967.

Raymond A. Dart,
Australian scientist

Max C. Robinson,
TV news anchorman

Kim Philby,
British double agent

Ted Kluszewski,
baseball slugger

Pagels, Heinz R. (1939-July 24), physicist and author of popular books about science, including *The Cosmic Code* (1982) and *Perfect Symmetry* (1985).

Palmieri, Charlie (1928?-Sept. 12), salsa pianist whose style blended Latin music and jazz.

Parish, Peggy (Margaret C. Parish) (1927-Nov. 18), author of the *Amelia Bedelia* series of children's books.

Passman, Otto E. (1900-Aug. 13), Democratic representative from Louisiana from 1947 to 1977.

Paton, Alan (1903-April 12), South African author whose acclaimed novel *Cry, the Beloved Country* (1948) focused on the plight of blacks in white-dominated South Africa.

Patterson, Frederick Douglass (1901-April 26), founder of the United Negro College Fund.

Peart, Lord (T. Frederick Peart) (1914-Aug. 26), leader of the British House of Commons from 1968 to 1970, leader of the House of Lords from 1976 to 1979, and then leader of the opposition in the Lords from 1979 to 1982.

Pendleton, Clarence M., Jr. (1930-June 5), first black chairman of the U.S. Commission on Civil Rights.

Pham Hung (1912-March 10), Vietnam's Council of Ministers chairman (prime minister) since June 1987.

Philby, Kim (Harold A. R. Philby) (1912-May 11), British double agent who defected to the Soviet Union in 1963.

Piñero, Miguel (1946-June 16), Puerto Rican-born dramatist and former prison inmate who wrote the play *Short Eyes* (1974).

Prater, Dave, Sr. (1938?-April 9), singer who, with his partner, Sam Moore, made up the soul-music duo Sam and Dave.

Pratt, Babe (Walter Pratt) (1916-Dec. 16), Canadian hockey player who was one of the sport's highest-scoring defensemen; member of the Hockey Hall of Fame.

Pratte, Yves (1925-June 26), justice of the Supreme Court of Canada from 1977 to 1979.

Pressburger, Emeric (1902-Feb. 5), Hungarian-born British screenwriter and producer who cowrote and codirected *The Red Shoes* (1948).

Presser, Jackie (1926-July 9), president of the Teamsters Union since 1983.

Price, C. Melvin (1905-April 22), Democratic representative from Illinois since 1945.

Provenzano, Anthony (1917-Dec. 12), reputed organized-crime leader, nicknamed Tony Pro.

Rabi, Isidor Isaac (1898-Jan. 11), physicist, born in Austria-Hungary, who won the 1944 Nobel Prize in physics for his work on measuring the magnetic properties of atoms.

Raby, Albert A. (1933?-Nov. 23), civil rights leader.

Raines, Ella (Ella W. Raubes) (1921-May 30), actress whose best-known role was in the suspense film *Phantom Lady* (1944).

Ramsey, Anne (1929?-Aug. 11), veteran character actress who played the domineering mother in *Throw Momma from the Train* (1987).

Ramsey of Canterbury, Lord (Arthur M. Ramsey) (1904-April 23), archbishop of Canterbury from 1961 to 1974.

Rankin, Sir Hugh (1899-April 25), British aristocrat famous for his eccentricity.

Raschi, Vic (1919-Oct. 14), pitcher for the New York Yankees baseball team from 1946 to 1953.

Rees, Lloyd (1895-Dec. 2), Australian artist known for his landscape paintings.

Rhys Williams, Sir Brandon (1927-May 18), Conservative member of the British Parliament since 1968.

Ricci, Robert (1905-Aug. 8), cofounder and head of the French fashion house of Nina Ricci.

Rich, Irene (Irene Luther) (1891-April 22), silent-film and radio star.

Richter, Curt Paul (1894-Dec. 21), psychobiologist credited with the discovery of biorhythms.

Righter, Carroll (1900-April 30), astrologer who wrote a syndicated daily column.

Jackie Presser,
Teamsters president

Pete Maravich,
basketball star

Louise Nevelson,
Russian-born sculptor

Mohammed Zia-ul-Haq,
Pakistani president

Ritchie, Roland A. (1910-June 5), justice of the Supreme Court of Canada from 1959 to 1984.

Robinson, Max C. (1939-Dec. 20), first black news anchorman on U.S. network television.

Rooney, Art (1901-Aug. 25), founder of the Pittsburgh Steelers football team.

Roosevelt, Franklin D., Jr. (1914-Aug. 17), Democratic representative from New York from 1949 to 1955; son of President Franklin D. Roosevelt and Eleanor Roosevelt.

Rose, George (1920-May 4), British-born actor who won Tony Awards for his roles in *My Fair Lady* in 1976 and *The Mystery of Edwin Drood* in 1986.

Ross, Lanny (Lancelot P. Ross) (1906-April 25), radio actor and singer whose theme song was "Moonlight and Roses."

Rothschild, Baron Philippe de (1902-Jan. 20), French winemaker.

Rouse, Charles (1924-Nov. 30), jazz saxophonist best known for his collaboration with pianist Thelonious Monk.

Roush, Edd J. (1893-March 21), outfielder with the Cincinnati Reds and the New York Giants from 1917 to 1931; member of the National Baseball Hall of Fame.

Rukeyser, Merryle S. (1897-Dec. 21), financial columnist syndicated in some 200 newspapers. Two of his four sons, Louis and William, also became financial writers.

Ruska, Ernst (1906-May 27), West German electrical engineer who shared the 1986 Nobel Prize for physics for his invention of the electron microscope.

St. Johns, Adela Rogers (1894-Aug. 10), pioneering woman journalist.

Deaths

Jean Marchand,
Canadian statesman

Barbara Woodhouse,
British dog trainer

Andy Gibb, British
pop singer

Edd J. Roush, baseball
Hall of Famer

Saragat, Giuseppe (1898-June 11), president of Italy from 1964 to 1971.

Satterfield, David E., III (1920-Sept. 30), Democratic representative from Virginia from 1965 to 1981.

Saxon, Charles D. (1920-Dec. 6), cartoonist who lampooned the prosperous and the sophisticated for *The New Yorker* magazine.

Scherer, Gordon H. (1906-Aug. 13), Republican congressman from Ohio from 1953 to 1963.

Schoenbrun, David F. (1915-May 23), veteran journalist for CBS News.

Schonfield, Hugh J. (1901-Jan. 24), British Biblical scholar who wrote the best seller *The Passover Plot* (1965).

Schwinn, Frank V. (1920?-Jan. 12), chairman and chief executive officer of Schwinn Bicycle Company.

Scott, Sheila (1927-Oct. 20), British actress and aviator who in 1971 became the first solo flier to cross the North Pole.

Shulman, Max (1919-Aug. 28), writer and humorist who created the TV series "The Many Loves of Dobie Gillis."

Silkin, Lord (Samuel C. Silkin) (1918-Aug. 17), British attorney general from 1974 to 1979.

Silva, Trinidad, Jr. (1950?-July 31), actor who portrayed a gang leader on TV's "Hill Street Blues" and in the movie *Colors* (1988).

Simak, Clifford D. (1904-April 25), science-fiction writer.

Simon, Bernie (1928?-April 14), Democratic mayor of Omaha since February 1987.

Sitwell, Sir Sacheverell (1897-Oct. 1), British author and art critic; younger brother of poet Dame Edith Sitwell.

Solomon (Solomon Cutner) (1902-Feb. 2), British pianist.

Spellman, Gladys Noon (1918-June 19), Democratic representative from Maryland from 1975 to 1981.

Staley, Oren Lee (1923-Sept. 19), first president of the National Farmers Organization, established in 1955 to help its members get better prices for their products.

Steele, Bob (Robert N. Bradbury, Jr.) (1906-Dec. 22), actor who played Trooper Duffy on TV's "F Troop" in the 1960's.

Steptoe, Patrick C. (1913-March 21), British gynecologist who pioneered the technique of *in vitro fertilization* that resulted in 1978 of the world's first "test-tube baby."

Stevens, Siaka P. (1905-May 29), president of the African nation of Sierra Leone from 1971 to 1985.

Stewart, Bennett M. (1912?-April 26), Democratic congressman from Illinois from 1979 to 1981.

Stonehouse, John T. (1925-April 14), former British Cabinet minister who faked his own drowning in Florida in 1974 to evade bankruptcy.

Strauss, Franz Josef (1915-Oct. 3), premier of the West German state of Bavaria since 1978.

Sullivan, Leonor K. (1903-Sept. 1), the only woman ever elected to Congress from Missouri; a Democrat who served from 1953 to 1977.

Symington, Stuart (1901-Dec. 14), Democratic senator from Missouri from 1953 to 1977.

Szeryng, Henryk (1918-March 3), Polish-born violinist.

Thompson, Mickey (1928?-March 16), automobile racer who set nearly 500 speed and endurance records in the 1950's.

Thomson, Vernon W. (1905-April 2), Republican governor of Wisconsin from 1957 to 1959 and U.S. representative from that state from 1961 to 1975.

*****Tinbergen, Nikolaas** (1907-Dec. 21), Dutch-born British biologist who won the 1973 Nobel Prize in physiology or medicine for his studies of animal behavior.

Trench, Sir David (1915-Dec. 4), governor of the British colony of Hong Kong from 1964 to 1971.

Truong Chinh (1908-Sept. 30), general secretary of Vietnam's Communist party from 1941 to 1956 and in 1986.

Utley, T. E. (Thomas E. Utley) (1921-June 21), leading British journalist, blind since childhood.

Vinson, Eddie (1917-July 2), blues singer and saxophone player nicknamed Cleanhead because of his shaven head.

Wankel, Felix (1902-Oct. 9), West German engineer who invented the Wankel rotary engine.

Wickersham, Victor E. (1906-March 15), Democratic representative from Oklahoma from 1941 to 1947 and from 1949 to 1965.

Williams, Edward Bennett (1920-Aug. 13), criminal lawyer and owner of the Baltimore Orioles baseball team.

Williams, G. Mennen (1911-Feb. 2), Democratic governor of Michigan from 1949 to 1960.

Williams, John J. (1904-Jan. 11), Republican senator from Delaware from 1947 to 1971.

Williams, Kenneth (1926-April 15), British actor who starred in 22 of the *Carry On* movie comedies.

Willman, Noel (1918-Dec. 24), actor and director, born in Northern Ireland, who won a Tony Award in 1961 for directing *A Man for All Seasons.*

Wood, Louise A. (1910-May 16), national executive director of the Girl Scouts of the U.S.A. from 1961 to 1972.

Woodhouse, Barbara (1910-July 9), British animal trainer who starred in the BBC TV series "Training Dogs the Woodhouse Way."

Wrather, Bonita Granville (1923-Oct. 11), child film star of the 1930's; later a motion-picture producer.

Zia-ul-Haq, Mohammed (1924-Aug. 17), leader of Pakistan who seized power in 1977 and declared himself president in 1978.

Zumwalt, Elmo R., III (1946?-Aug. 13), Vietnam War veteran who attributed his cancer to the herbicide Agent Orange sprayed in Vietnam on orders of his father, Admiral Elmo Zumwalt, Jr.   Sara Dreyfuss

Delaware. See **State government.**

Democratic Party. The United States general election of Nov. 8, 1988, resulted in the third straight defeat of a Democratic presidential ticket. But the loss, coming after midsummer polls had indicated a likely Democratic victory, was made less painful by Democratic gains of one seat in the Senate and five in the House of Representatives.

The Democratic presidential nominee, Governor Michael S. Dukakis of Massachusetts, picked Senator Lloyd M. Bentsen, Jr., of Texas—a man more conservative than himself—as his vice presidential running mate. Dukakis hoped Bentsen would help put Texas in the Democratic column, but that was not to be. The Republican tide rolled through Texas and 39 other states as the winning candidate, Vice President George Bush, received about 53 per cent of the nationwide vote to 46 per cent for Dukakis.

The electoral vote count was far more lopsided—426 to 111. Dukakis carried only the District of Columbia and 10 states: Hawaii, Iowa, Massachusetts, Minnesota, New York, Oregon, Rhode Island, Washington, West Virginia, and Wisconsin.

Polls taken by ABC News as voters left polling places showed that Dukakis scored best among voters under age 25 and over 59 and among those earning less than $20,000 a year. The polls also found that 52 per cent of women voters preferred Dukakis, as did 90 per cent of blacks, 71 per cent of Jews, and 53 per cent of Roman Catholics.

The primaries. The long campaign for the Democratic presidential nomination generated little enthusiasm among the voting public. The seven aspirants, most of whom were relatively unknown nationally, were sometimes referred to as the "seven dwarfs." In the February 8 Iowa caucuses, the candidates' first big test, Representative Richard A. Gephardt of Missouri, campaigning on the theme of protecting American industry from foreign competition, won narrowly over Senator Paul Simon of Illinois. Dukakis placed third, and civil rights leader Jesse L. Jackson was fourth. Bringing up the rear were former Governor Bruce E. Babbitt of Arizona, former Senator Gary Hart of Colorado, and Senator Albert A. Gore, Jr., of Tennessee.

One of the biggest tests came on March 8, called "Super Tuesday" because 20 states, including 14 Southern or border states, held Democratic primaries or caucuses. Gore carried 6 states and placed second in another 5. Jackson won 5 states and placed second in 11. Dukakis won in 7 states, including the 2 offering the most delegates—Florida and Texas.

Jackson's strong showing on Super Tuesday surprised many political observers. But the biggest surprise came on March 26, when Jackson won 53 per cent of the vote in Michigan to 29 per cent for Dukakis.

Although Jackson continued to do well, Dukakis did better.On April 5, he outpolled Jackson 48 to 28 per cent in the Wisconsin primary, and two

At the Democratic convention in Atlanta, Ga., in July, Jesse Jackson, left, joins ranks with party standardbearers Michael Dukakis, center, and Lloyd Bentsen.

Democratic Party

weeks later in the New York primary, Dukakis prevailed by a margin of 51 to 37 per cent. On June 7, Dukakis clinched the nomination by winning primaries in California, Montana, New Jersey, and New Mexico.

In Senate races, a mixture of Democratic gains and losses netted one extra seat, resulting in a 55 to 45 Democratic edge. In Connecticut, Democratic Attorney General Joseph Lieberman narrowly upset Republican Senator Lowell P. Weicker, Jr., while in Nebraska former Democratic Governor Robert Kerrey defeated Republican Senator David K. Karnes. Democratic Governor Richard H. Bryan of Nevada defeated Republican Senator Chic Hecht, and former Democratic Governor Charles S. Robb of Virginia easily defeated Republican Maurice Dawkins to take over the seat of retiring Republican Senator Paul S. Trible, Jr. Only one Democratic senator, John Melcher of Montana, was defeated. But Republicans took over seats held by two retiring Democratic senators—John C. Stennis of Mississippi and Lawton Chiles of Florida. On November 29, Democratic senators elected Senator George J. Mitchell of Maine as the new majority leader, succeeding Robert C. Byrd of West Virginia, who stepped down from the leadership post.

House of Representatives. Democrats took heart from the fact that, for the first time since 1960, the party capturing the presidency failed to increase its strength in the House of Representatives. Quite the contrary, Democrats netted 7 extra seats to expand their lopsided margin to 260 to 175. Among the newly elected House Democrats were two women, Jolene Unsoeld of Washington state and Nita M. Lowey of New York. Their victories increased the number of women representatives to a record-tying 14.

Democratic casualties in the House included 14-term Congressman Fernand J. St Germain of Rhode Island, chairman of the House Committee on Banking, Housing, and Urban Affairs. St Germain, who was being investigated by the House Ethics Committee because of discrepancies in his official financial-disclosure statements, was the first standing committee chairman to be defeated since 1980. Another Democrat going down to defeat was Representative Bill Chappell, Jr., of Florida, whose name had figured prominently in an ongoing scandal involving military weapons purchases.

In state contests, Democrats picked up one governorship, giving them a 28 to 22 margin over the Republicans. Democrats may have found a new rising star in Indiana, where Evan Bayh, the 32-year-old secretary of state, defeated Republican Lieutenant Governor John M. Mutz to become the first Democratic governor in 20 years. Bayh is the son of former Senator Birch Bayh, who was defeated in 1980 by Republican Dan Quayle—Bush's running mate in 1988.   Frank Cormier and Margot Cormier

See also **Bentsen, Lloyd M., Jr.; Dukakis, Michael S.; Elections; Republican Party.** In *World Book*, see Democratic Party.

Denmark. A general election on May 10, 1988, failed to resolve a political crisis involving Denmark's nuclear-arms policy and the country's membership in the North Atlantic Treaty Organization (NATO). Denmark had prohibited the presence of nuclear weapons in its territory in peacetime. On April 14, 1988, Denmark's Folketing (parliament) voted to require the government to draw this prohibition to the attention of visiting naval vessels entering Denmark's waters. Conservative Prime Minister Poul Schlüter said that this vote would force his administration to look again at continuing Denmark's membership in NATO, because NATO allies Great Britain and the United States refuse to disclose whether their vessels carry nuclear weapons.

To gather political backing for his opposition to the vote, Schlüter decided to call a general election. On April 19, he announced the May 10 election.

Visits canceled. On April 23, NATO Secretary-General Lord Carrington canceled a visit to Denmark and warned that Denmark's antinuclear policy had "grave implications." Great Britain and the United States canceled visits by six of their warships to four Danish ports.

The election failed to break the deadlock over the nuclear issue. Schlüter's center-right minority coalition of Conservatives, Liberals, Center Democrats, and the Christian People's Party held its 70 seats in the 179-member Folketing. The Progress Party, which often voted with the coalition, won 16 seats. So, even with the help of the Progress Party, Schlüter was still four votes short of the majority (90 seats) he needed to overturn the nuclear vote. Schlüter therefore resigned on May 11, enabling Denmark's eight political parties to negotiate the formation of a new government.

Three weeks of political stalemate neared an end on May 31 when Queen Margrethe II asked Schlüter to form another minority government. Schlüter then forged a three-party coalition of Conservatives, Liberals, and Radical Liberals. This coalition held 67 seats in the Folketing.

The crisis ended on June 7 when Schlüter announced a compromise. The Radical Liberals, who on April 14 voted for the measure requiring notification of NATO warships, had agreed to allow the ships to visit Danish waters without divulging whether they carry nuclear weapons. In return, Schlüter had admitted the Radical Liberals to his coalition.

Container law overturned. The European Court of Justice, the judicial branch of the European Community (EC or Common Market), ruled on May 24 that Denmark's ban on nonreturnable beer and soft-drink containers violated EC regulations. The court said that the ban was "an artificial barrier to trade." Denmark banned such containers in 1981.Danish brewers export 75 million cans of beer each year. Bottles are used in Denmark, however.   Kenneth Brown

See also **Europe** (Facts in brief table). In *World Book*, see **Denmark.**

Dentistry. The National Institute of Dental Research (NIDR) in Bethesda, Md., reported in May 1988 that preliminary studies strongly indicate that AIDS (acquired immune deficiency syndrome) is not spread by saliva or other oral fluids. According to NIDR researcher Phillip Fox, human saliva contains a substance that appears to prevent the human immunodeficiency virus (HIV), which causes AIDS, from infecting cells in the mouth.

These studies support the theory that oral contact is not a route through which the disease spreads. Fox said that the NIDR will continue to work to isolate the substance in saliva that is responsible for blocking HIV. Once identified, such a substance could be used to develop a drug to control AIDS.

Look, Ma, no cavities. About half of the school-children in the United States have no signs of tooth decay or cavities, according to a report issued by the NIDR in June 1988. In a survey of nearly 40,000 children under the age of 17, conducted during the 1986-1987 school year, the NIDR found that 50 per cent of the children had no cavities or other tooth decay.

The NIDR said the survey showed that the 15-year decline in tooth decay in the United States is continuing, thanks to better dental care and to widespread *fluoridation* (the addition of *fluorides*, chemicals that prevent tooth decay, to water supplies). A similar survey conducted in 1979-1980 found that 36.6 per cent of schoolchildren had no tooth decay. Only an estimated 28 per cent of children were cavity-free in the early 1970's.

Detecting heart problems. Researchers at the University of Minnesota School of Dentistry in Minneapolis reported in September 1988 that patients undergoing dental surgery or other complex dental treatment that may aggravate hidden heart abnormalities can now be tested for heart problems in the dentist's office. The researchers monitored the heart rhythms of more than 5,000 patients using a simple electrocardiograph, a device that produces an *electrocardiogram* (EKG or ECG), a record of the electrical signals produced by the heart, in just 60 seconds. The patients were hooked up to the device by *electrodes* (small metal plates that conduct electricity) placed on their wrists and ankles. After transmitting the signals over the telephone to a *cardiology technician* (a nurse trained to interpret EKG's), the researchers received immediate information on the patients' heart rate and heart rhythm. They found evidence of abnormal heart rhythm in 17 per cent of the patients.

By performing an EKG in their office, dentists can quickly determine the best course of treatment for their patients, according to the Minnesota researchers. This may include referring a patient to a *cardiologist* (a doctor specializing in treating heart diseases) before proceeding with dental treatment, the dental researchers said.   Mark S. Simmons

In *World Book,* see **Dentistry.**

Detroit. Redevelopment projects continued to put a new face on Detroit in 1988, though not without generating some major controversies. Meanwhile, crime—especially among young people—remained one of the city's most troublesome problems.

Redevelopment. City officials hoped the various renewal projects would breathe life into Detroit. City Airport, on Detroit's east side, opened to major commercial flights on July 8, ending a 40-year period in which the facility was used mainly for freight, commuter, and corporate flights. The city spent $20 million to modernize the airport terminal and parking facilities. Citizen protests, however, stopped a planned expansion of the airport into a neighboring city-owned cemetery.

In November, Michael Ilitch, founder of the Little Caesars pizza chain and owner of the Detroit Red Wings professional hockey team, opened the restored Fox Theatre. The 5,000-seat theater, built in 1928, is one of the largest and grandest movie houses in the United States. Renovated at a cost of $35 million, the Fox and its adjacent office tower will serve as the centerpiece of a $300-million rehabilitation of a deteriorated neighborhood just north of downtown.

In February, Detroit Mayor Coleman A. Young and the Chrysler Corporation signed an agreement to redevelop a neighborhood on the city's east side. A 637-acre (258-hectare) industrial park is to be established on the cleared tract.

U.S. children without cavities or tooth decay

Source: National Institute of Dental Research.

A National Institute of Dental Research study released in 1988 found that more U.S. children were cavity-free in 1986-1987 than in 1979-1980.

Detroit

The city's purchase of property in the east side neighborhood prior to the bulldozing came under the scrutiny of the Federal Bureau of Investigation (FBI). The FBI probe was launched after four businessmen received $40 million more than the city's original offer for three buildings that were housing used industrial machinery.

Crime. Detroit continued in 1988 to be one of the most crime-ridden cities in the United States. Much of the violent crime was committed by youths, and drugs were often a factor.

A computer study of FBI crime reports from 1979 through 1986, released in 1988, showed that Detroit's juvenile homicide rate was the highest of the 10 largest U.S. cities. Between January and mid-October 1988, 222 youngsters aged 16 and under had been shot in Detroit, 39 fatally. Many of the accused or suspected assailants in those shootings were also in their teens or younger.

Detroit's biggest drug problem in 1988, like that of many other U.S. cities, had become *crack,* a smokable and highly addictive form of cocaine. During the year, police conducted a "CrackDown" on the drug, and drug-related arrests increased.

Many Detroit residents complained about drug dealers running rampant in their neighborhoods, and some people—frustrated with what they viewed as police inaction—took the law into their own hands. In October, two men were acquitted of arson in the burning of a suspected "crack house" even though they admitted setting the fire.

Voters reject gambling. In early 1988, Mayor Young appointed a committee to study the possibility of allowing casino gambling in Detroit as a way of spurring the city's economic growth. Although the committee later recommended that the city open its doors to gambling, Detroit residents were unconvinced. In August, voters overwhelmingly approved an ordinance that would ban casinos in Detroit if the state legislature ever decides to allow casino gambling in Michigan. It was the third antigambling vote in Detroit since 1976.

Catholic churches face closure. In September, Detroit's Edmund Cardinal Szoka recommended the closing of 42 Roman Catholic churches in the city —most of them in inner-city neighborhoods—because of declining memberships. A coalition of priests and parishioners vowed to fight the closings, and at year-end most of the churches were appealing the cardinal's recommendation.

Automobile industry riding high. Despite the October 1987 stock-market crash, the 1988 model year, which ended on September 30, was a banner year for the automobile industry, the anchor of Detroit's economy. Americans bought a surprising 15.65 million cars and trucks, including imports, making 1988 the third best sales year in history for the automobile industry.   Bill McGraw

See also **City.** In *World Book,* see **Detroit.**

Disasters. The worst natural disaster of 1988 was a devastating earthquake that rocked the Caucasus Mountains in the Soviet Union on December 7. The quake rumbled across the Soviet republics of Armenia, Azerbaijan, and Georgia, killing about 25,000 people and leaving another 500,000 homeless. It did the worst damage in northwestern Armenia near the Turkish border, causing large-scale destruction in the cities of Leninakan and Kirovakan and all but wiping out the town of Spitak.

Disaster followed disaster on December 11, when a military transport plane carrying troops to join the earthquake rescue effort crashed on its approach to Leninakan airport. All 78 people aboard—9 crew members and 69 Soviet soldiers—died in the crash. Then on December 12, a Yugoslav Air Force transport plane carrying medical supplies for quake victims crashed near Yerevan, the Armenian capital, killing another 7 crew members.

The year's worst disasters also included two other killer earthquakes and a combination cyclone and tidal wave, all of which struck in Asia. An earthquake that rocked the mountains of the Himalaya on the border between India and Nepal killed at least 721 people in Nepal and 294 in India, making it the deadliest to strike the Himalaya since 1934. The quake struck shortly before daybreak on Aug. 21, 1988, when most people in the area were asleep. Many of the victims died in their houses, which collapsed around them. A second earthquake shook a remote area of southern China near the Burmese border on November 6, causing about 730 deaths.

On November 29, a cyclone generated a 15-foot (4.5-meter) tidal wave in the Bay of Bengal that hammered the southern coast of Bangladesh and eastern India. The storm and tidal wave took at least 3,000 lives in Bangladesh and India. Officials feared that the death toll might rise as high as 15,000.

Disasters that resulted in 30 or more deaths in 1988 included the following:

Aircraft crashes

Jan. 18—Near Chongqing (Ch'ung-ch'ing), China. A Southwest China Airline plane crashed minutes before landing, killing all 108 passengers and crew.

Feb. 27—Surgut, Soviet Union. An Aeroflot airliner crashed on a runway in Siberia and burst into flames, causing about 50 deaths.

March 17—Near Cúcuta, Colombia. An Avianca jetliner crashed in the mountains during a storm, killing all 137 passengers and crew aboard.

May 6—Brønnøysund, Norway, near Namsos. All 36 people aboard a Norwegian airliner died after it slammed into a mountain.

Aug. 28—Ramstein, West Germany. Three Italian fighter jets collided at an air show, sending one of the jets hurtling in flames into a crowd of spectators and killing at least 70 people.

Sept. 9—Near Bangkok, Thailand. A bolt of lightning caused an Air Vietnam jetliner to crash, killing 76 people.

Sept. 15—Near Bahir Dar, Ethiopia. An Ethiopian Airlines jetliner ran into a flock of birds shortly after take-off and crashed in flames, causing at least 31 deaths.

Survivors view the wreckage left behind by a December 7 earthquake that killed about 25,000 people in the Soviet republic of Armenia.

Oct. 7—Linfen, Shanxi (Shansi) province, China. A sightseeing plane crashed into a hotel and exploded, killing 42 of the 46 people aboard.

Oct. 17—Rome. A Uganda Airlines jetliner approaching the Rome airport in thick fog hit the tops of several buildings and crashed, causing 32 deaths.

Oct. 19—Ahmadabad, India. An Indian Airlines jetliner trying to land in heavy fog crashed and exploded, killing at least 130 people.

Oct. 19—Gauhati, India. A propeller plane slammed into a hill, killing all of the plane's 34 passengers.

Dec. 11—Near Leninakan, Soviet Union. A Soviet military transport plane crashed, killing all 78 people aboard—69 soldiers who were going to join earthquake rescue efforts and the plane's 9 crew members.

Bus and truck crashes

March 7—Henan (Honan) province, China. A bus plunged off a mountain road into a gorge, killing 39 passengers.

March 16—Madhya Pradesh state, India. At least 90 members of a wedding party died after their bus overturned and caught fire.

March 20—Cachoeira, Brazil. A truck carrying pilgrims to a Roman Catholic shrine crashed through a guard rail and tumbled over a cliff, causing 65 deaths.

July 21—Kahuta, Pakistan, near Islamabad. As many as 71 people died after their bus was swept away by floodwaters while crossing a bridge.

Aug. 12—Northern Iran. Two buses collided on the Teheran-Tabriz highway, killing 30 people.

Aug. 31—Near Sarajevo, Yugoslavia. A bus ran into a load of bricks dropped on the road and plunged into a reservoir, causing 30 deaths.

Sept. 25—Punjab state, India. A bus crashed into a canal, leaving 69 people dead.

Oct. 9—Assam state, India. A bus skidded off a mountain road and plunged into a river, taking at least 38 lives.

Oct. 12—Shaanxi (Shensi) province, China. A bus traveling in the rain without windshield wipers fell into a ditch and caught fire, killing 43 people.

Dec. 23—Liaoning province, China. An express passenger train slammed into a bus crossing the railroad tracks, causing at least 46 deaths.

Earthquakes

Aug. 21—India and Nepal border. An earthquake struck the Himalaya, triggering landslides and floods and killing at least 1,015 people.

Nov. 6—Yunnan province, China. An earthquake destroyed several mountain villages and killed about 730 people.

Dec. 7—Armenia, Soviet Union. A powerful earthquake near the Soviet-Turkish border caused about 25,000 deaths.

Explosions and fires

Jan. 7—Hunan province, China. Paint thinner caught fire on a train, killing 34 people.

March 20—Lashio, Burma. A fire that started in a kitchen swept through more than 2,000 buildings, killing at least 113 people in the largest death toll ever reported in a fire in Burma.

April 10—Near Islamabad and Rawalpindi, Pakistan. A leaky artillery shell at an army weapons depot set off explosions of rockets, grenades, and mortars that killed about 100 people.

June 4—Arzamas, Soviet Union. A freight train hauling explosives blew up, causing at least 83 deaths.

June 22—Al Qusiyah, Egypt. Forty-seven pilgrims, including 27 children, were burned or trampled to death in a blaze at a monastery.

July 6—Off eastern Scotland. An explosion and fire on a North Sea oil rig killed 167 people.

Disasters

Dec. 11—Mexico City. Illegal fireworks exploded in a crowded street market, starting a fire that spread to five buildings and killing at least 62 people.
Dec. 31—Chittagong, Bangladesh. A fire swept through two barges in dry dock in the port of Chittagong, causing at least 33 deaths.

Landslides and avalanches

Feb. 2—Huánuco department, Peru. A mud slide caused by torrential rains left 30 people dead and more than 70 missing and feared dead.
Feb. 17—Cusco department, Peru. A mud slide buried up to 50 people alive.
March 26—Arandgul, Pakistan. An avalanche that hit a village at night killed at least 50 people.
June 23—Catak, Turkey, near Trabzon. A landslide buried much of the village of Catak and caused up to 300 deaths.
Sept. 6—Morobe province, Papua New Guinea. A mud slide swept over five mountain villages and killed at least 76 people.
Oct. 2—Fredonia, Colombia, near Medellín. A landslide caused by heavy rains buried several farms, killing as many as 40 people.

Mine disasters

Jan. 25—Near Nueva Rosita, Mexico. An explosion and fire caused by a short circuit in a coal mine killed 41 miners.
May 29—Shanxi (Shansi) province, China. At least 49 miners died in a gas explosion at a coal mine.
June 1—Borken, West Germany, near Frankfurt. A coal-mine explosion killed 51 miners.
Mid-June—Taiyuan (Tai-yuan), China. A gas explosion in a coal mine killed and buried all 40 miners working there.

Shipwrecks

Jan. 4—Bangladesh. A ferry collided with a barge and capsized in the Jamuna River, leaving more than 160 people missing and feared dead.
May 28—Off Indonesia. At least 200 people drowned after an overloaded ferry sank in the Java Sea.
July 15—Amazon River, Brazil. A ferry struck the underwater hulk of another boat and sank, causing 59 confirmed deaths and leaving another 30 people missing and presumed drowned.
July 21—Min River, China. At least 133 people were feared drowned after their ferry sank while sailing from Yibin (I-pin) to Leshan (Le-shan).
July 23—Tokyo Bay, Japan. A Japanese navy submarine collided with a fishing boat, killing 30 people.
Aug. 6—Near Katihar, Bihar state, India. A ferry capsized in the Ganges River, causing an estimated 400 deaths.
Aug. 17—Lake Tanganyika, Africa. A ferry sinking caused more than 50 deaths.
Aug. 24—Near Manikganj, Bangladesh. A boat carrying Muslim pilgrims to a holy site sank after it was swamped by high waves on the Padma River, drowning about 60 passengers.
Oct. 14—Off Leyte island, Philippines. At least 55 people drowned after a ferry sank in rough seas.
Dec. 14—Southern China. An overloaded ferry taking schoolchildren on a field trip capsized and sank, drowning at least 55 youngsters.
Dec. 27—Near Munshiganj, Bangladesh. A river ferry sank after being rammed by a cargo ship, leaving 200 passengers missing and feared dead.
Dec. 31—Rio de Janeiro, Brazil. A pleasure boat on a New Year's Eve cruise sank in Rio de Janeiro harbor, leaving at least 53 passengers drowned and about 30 missing.

Storms and floods

February—Rio de Janeiro state, Brazil. Floods and mud slides killed nearly 300 people.

Late May—Southeast China. Heavy rains triggered widespread flooding that killed at least 149 people.
Late May—Philippines. Typhoon Susan caused flooding that left as many as 36 people dead.
Mid-June to mid-September—Bangladesh. Floods that began with the June monsoon rains killed an estimated 1,600 people.
Mid-July—Pilar, Brazil. Flooding killed at least 64 people.
Late July-early August—Zhejiang (Chekiang) province, China. A torrential rainstorm on July 29 and 30 caused floods that left at least 264 people dead and more than 50 missing.
Aug. 8—Zhejiang province. A typhoon killed 100 people and left 81 missing.
Mid-August—Khartoum, Sudan. Floods caused by torrential rains on August 4 and 5 killed at least 91 people.
Mid-August—Northern Nigeria. Torrential rains left up to 50 people dead in Kano state and 26 in Borno state, many due to collapsed buildings.
Sept. 11-17—West Indies and Mexico. Hurricane Gilbert caused about 300 deaths.
Mid-September—Hunan and Hubei (Hupeh) provinces, China. Torrential rains and widespread flooding left about 170 people dead.
Late September-early October—northern India. Devastating floods in the four states of Haryana, Himachal Pradesh, Jammu and Kashmir, and Punjab left at least 1,000 people dead.
Early October—Punjab province, Pakistan. Floods killed 104 people.
Oct. 17-23—South and Central America. Hurricane Joan killed at least 385 people in Colombia, Venezuela, Panama, Costa Rica, and Nicaragua. Nearly 200 others were missing.
Oct. 19—Southern Bangladesh. A storm lashed the Bangladesh coast along the Bay of Bengal, killing at least 35 people and leaving up to 1,500 missing.
Oct. 24-25—Philippines. Typhoon Ruby took at least 114 lives on land and sank the ship *Dona Marilyn* in the Visayan Sea, drowning about 300 other people.
Nov. 7—Philippines. Typhoon Skip claimed at least 90 lives.
Late November—Malaysia and southern Thailand. Heavy rains that began on November 19 caused floods and mud slides that killed at least 450 people and perhaps 1,000.
Nov. 29—Southern Bangladesh and eastern India. A cyclone and tidal wave caused at least 3,000 deaths in Bangladesh and India.

Train wrecks

Jan. 24—Yunnan province, China. A passenger train derailed and overturned, killing 88 people.
June 27—Paris. Brake failure caused a commuter train to ram another commuter train at the Gare de Lyon, causing 56 deaths.
July 8—Near Quilon, India. Six cars of a passenger train derailed and plunged into a lake, killing at least 105 people.
Oct. 9—Lapovo, Yugoslavia, near Belgrade. Two cars of a passenger train derailed and slammed into a parked freight train, causing at least 33 deaths.
Dec. 12—London. Two commuter trains crashed during morning rush hour, and a third train slammed into the wreckage, killing 33 people.

Other disasters

March 12—Kathmandu, Nepal. At least 70 people died at a soccer game when they were trampled in a stampede to escape a sudden hailstorm.
May 12—Aguascalientes, Mexico. Four floors of a building under construction collapsed, killing as many as 58 workers.
July 31—Butterworth, Malaysia. A crowded pier collapsed, causing at least 31 deaths.
Dec. 5—Yaoundé, Cameroon. A false alarm that a high school was about to collapse triggered a stampede that left about 60 students dead.   Sara Dreyfuss
Djibouti. See Africa.

274

Dog. The Westminster Kennel Club held its 112th annual show on Feb. 8 and 9, 1988, in New York City's Madison Square Garden. A male Pomeranian, Champion Great Elms Prince Charming II, owned by Skip Piazza of Avondale, Pa., and Olga Baker of Seabrook, Tex., was chosen best-in-show by Judge Michelle Billings of Fort Lauderdale, Fla. The dog, called Prince, was the first Pomeranian to win the top award.

In 1987, the American Kennel Club (AKC) registered 1,187,400 dogs. The three most popular breeds were the cocker spaniel, the poodle, and the Labrador retriever. Golden retrievers, German shepherd dogs, chow chows, beagles, miniature schnauzers, dachshunds, and Shetland sheepdogs made up the balance of the top 10 breeds in 1987.

The Canadian Kennel Club celebrated its centennial in 1988 by holding four days of all-breed shows, specialty shows, and obedience trials from August 30 through September 2 at the Metro Toronto Convention Center in Toronto, Ont. Judge R. William Taylor of Franklin Centre, Que., selected a Shih Tzu, Canadian and American Champion Shente's Brandy Alexander, for best-in-show. The champion was owned by Margaret Brown of St. Catharines, Ont., and Luke Ehrict of Kleinberg, Ont. High-in-trial was won by a golden retriever, Meadowpond Rumpelstiltskin, owned by Madeline Stuck of Vestal, N.Y.   Roberta Vesley

In *World Book*, see **Dog.**

Dominican Republic. See **West Indies.**

Lucky Dog, the unlucky winner of the Ugliest Dog in Connecticut contest, is cuddled by its owner, Nathan Williams of Noank, in July.

Douglas, Michael (1944-   ), won the Academy of Motion Picture Arts and Sciences Award for best actor on April 11, 1988. Douglas won the Oscar for his performance as Gordon Gekko, a ruthless corporate raider, in *Wall Street.*

Michael Kirk Douglas, the oldest son of actor Kirk Douglas, was born on Sept. 25, 1944, in New Brunswick, N.J. He attended the University of California at Santa Barbara, receiving a B.A. degree in drama in 1968. After college, Douglas continued his study of drama at the Neighborhood Playhouse and the American Place Theatre, both in New York City.

His first major acting role was in a 1969 television drama, *The Experiment.* After a few years of appearances in television and feature films, Douglas starred in the popular television series "The Streets of San Francisco" from 1972 to 1974.

Douglas also began to work as an independent film producer in the early 1970's. The first feature he produced, *One Flew over the Cuckoo's Nest* (1975), was a huge popular success and received five Academy Awards. He then produced and starred in *The China Syndrome* (1979), *Romancing the Stone* (1984), and *The Jewel of the Nile* (1985). Douglas' acting credits also include starring roles in *A Chorus Line* (1985) and in the 1987 blockbuster *Fatal Attraction.*

Douglas married Diandra Luker in 1977. The couple have one son.   Jinger Hoop

Drought. See **Water; Weather.**

Drug abuse. On Nov. 18, 1988, President Ronald Reagan signed into law one of the most far-reaching antidrug bills in United States history. Among other provisions, the legislation allows up to a $10,000 fine for possession of even small amounts of illicit drugs and permits the death penalty for people who kill or order killings while committing drug-related felonies. The law also creates a Cabinet-level "drug czar" to coordinate government antidrug efforts; establishes a one-year pilot program to test new driver's license applicants for drug use; requires health warning labels on alcoholic beverages; allows the President to impose sanctions against countries involved in laundering drug money; and expands drug prevention, treatment, and research programs.

Drugs and disease. AIDS (acquired immune deficiency syndrome) continued to spread in 1988 among users of *intravenous drugs* (drugs injected into the body). Intravenous drug users were the second-largest group—following homosexuals—at high risk for contracting the fatal disease, chiefly by sharing contaminated needles but also by having sex with infected users. As of 1988, 26 per cent of all AIDS patients were intravenous drug users.

A report released in June 1988 by the President's AIDS commission cited the control of intravenous drug use as a crucial factor in limiting the spread of AIDS among drug users, their sex partners, and their unborn babies. In November, New York City began giv-

275

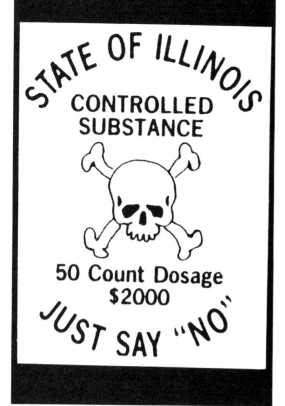

Illinois began in January to require a tax stamp on illegal drugs, not to raise money but to provide an additional legal weapon against drug dealers.

ing free clean needles to drug abusers in a controversial experiment to slow the spread of AIDS.

In May, the U.S. Centers for Disease Control in Atlanta, Ga., reported a link between drug abuse and hepatitis A, a liver disease. Intravenous drug use was already known to be a risk factor for hepatitis B, a blood-borne form of the disease that, like AIDS, can be transmitted through contaminated needles.

Drug testing by employers increased in 1988. By 1988, half of the 500 largest U.S. companies regularly tested at least some workers or job applicants. In November, the Supreme Court of the United States heard arguments from a railroad-workers' union on the constitutionality of a federal requirement to screen railroad employees for drug use.

In June, the White House announced that it would begin random drug testing of employees of the Executive Office of the President. The decree came within hours after disclosures that three White House guards had been suspended for suspected off-duty use of cocaine and that two National Security Council secretaries had been fired some months earlier for drug use. The departments of Justice and Agriculture also announced employee drug-testing programs. The Department of Transportation and the Veterans Administration, as well as the military, already had testing programs in place.   David C. Lewis

In the Special Reports section, see **Today's Teens and Drugs.** In *World Book*, see **Drug abuse.**

Drugs. Two unlikely prescription drugs—the first effective antiwrinkle cream and the first prescription treatment for baldness—caused excitement among appearance-conscious people in the United States during 1988.

On January 22, *dermatologists* (doctors who specialize in treating skin disorders) at the University of Michigan in Ann Arbor reported that the drug tretinoin—sold under the brand name Retin-A—can reduce facial wrinkles and age spots caused by exposure to the sun. Retin-A, which contains a derivative of vitamin A, had long been used to treat severe acne. The study, which included only 30 patients, found that regular application of Retin-A cream could make the skin appear smoother, clearer, and more youthful. The study was published in *The Journal of the American Medical Association* (*JAMA*) and accompanied by an editorial that hailed the findings but noted uncertainty about Retin-A's long-term effects.

Within days of the *JAMA* report, patients deluged physicians with requests for Retin-A prescriptions. Shortages of the drug, which is manufactured by Ortho Pharmaceutical Corporation of Raritan, N.J., developed in some parts of the United States. Retin-A's popularity led the U.S. Food and Drug Administration (FDA) to warn consumers about indiscriminate use of the medication. FDA Commissioner Frank E. Young on July 5 called the use of Retin-A as an antiwrinkle cream "an expensive therapeutic gamble." He emphasized the limited scientific evidence of Retin-A's effectiveness.

Young also announced a crackdown on health fraud that had emerged as a result of publicity about Retin-A. He said that unlicensed manufacturers had started to sell other drugs under the Retin-A name.

Baldness treatment. On August 17, the FDA approved Rogaine, the first prescription drug to treat hair loss. Rogaine is manufactured by the Upjohn Company of Kalamazoo, Mich. Its active ingredient—minoxidil—previously had been approved for treatment of high blood pressure. Physicians recognized its hair-restoring effect when patients taking minoxidil reported unexpected hair growth. Experts noted, however, that Rogaine is not a cure-all for baldness. Studies showed that it stimulates hair growth in only a small number of balding men, and does not help men who are totally bald. Also, the drug must be used regularly for several years, or newly grown hair will fall out.

Cosmetic warning. The FDA on April 4 warned 22 cosmetics manufacturers to change claims made on the labels of skin-care products being promoted for an alleged "antiaging" effect. The FDA said that cosmetics can claim only to cleanse or superficially beautify the skin. Cosmetics sold on the grounds that they retard aging or rejuvenate the skin are illegally claiming to act like drugs.

Acne drug. Concern also arose in 1988 over the side effects of Accutane, a prescription drug used in

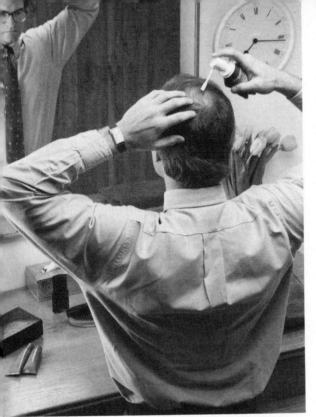

A man applies Rogaine, the first prescription drug to treat baldness, to his scalp. The U.S. Food and Drug Administration approved the drug on August 17.

cause stomach upsets and ulcers, but also the researchers found a small increase in the incidence of strokes among the men who took aspirin in the study. On February 24, the FDA, concerned about possible side effects, cautioned aspirin manufacturers against running advertisements that promote the use of aspirin for preventing heart attacks.

Arthritis relief. The world's most widely prescribed arthritis drug became available in the United States on August 4 following approval by the FDA. The drug—diclofenac sodium—is marketed under the trade name Voltaren by CIBA-Geigy Pharmaceuticals of Summit, N.J. Authorities estimated that 64 million prescriptions for Voltaren were written worldwide in 1987.

Drug approval. The FDA on October 19 outlined new procedures to speed up the approval of drugs for AIDS (acquired immune deficiency syndrome), cancer, and other serious illnesses. The procedures will allow the FDA to work with drug developers to produce more data in less time. According to the FDA, this should significantly reduce the number of years it takes for a drug to be approved. The regulation change was sparked by complaints that the drug approval process, which can take anywhere from three to seven years, was delaying potential treatments for critically ill AIDS patients.   Michael Woods

See also **Drug abuse; Medicine.** In *World Book*, see **Drug.**

the treatment of severe acne. On May 26, the FDA said it would require Accutane's manufacturer, Hoffmann-La Roche Incorporated of Nutley, N.J., to issue strong new warnings to prevent pregnant women from using the drug. Accutane can cause birth defects, including severe mental retardation, and facial malformations, such as missing or misplaced ears.

The FDA estimated that since Accutane was introduced in 1982, it has caused birth defects in 600 to 1,300 cases. The agency emphasized that pregnant women—or women who might become pregnant—should not use the drug. Hoffmann-La Roche agreed to include a photograph of a baby deformed by Accutane in the brochure packaged with the drug. The company also took other steps to make doctors and patients more aware of Accutane's hazards.

Aspirin and the heart. Medical researchers at Boston's Harvard Medical School and Brigham and Women's Hospital on January 26 reported on a study indicating that healthy men who take a single aspirin tablet every other day can reduce their risk of a heart attack by almost 50 per cent. The five-year study monitored the health of 22,071 men. Half of the men took one aspirin tablet every other day, while the rest took a *placebo* (inactive substance). The researchers said that aspirin showed an "extreme beneficial effect" in reducing fatal and nonfatal heart attacks.

They warned, however, that not everyone should start taking aspirin regularly. Not only can aspirin

Dukakis, Michael Stanley (1933-   ), won the Democratic Party's nomination for President of the United States on July 20, 1988, but lost the election on November 8 to his Republican opponent, Vice President George Bush. See **Elections.**

Dukakis began 1988 as one of seven Democratic candidates. But he won nomination on the first ballot at the party's convention in Atlanta, Ga., in July by a better than 2 to 1 margin over his lone remaining opponent, Jesse L. Jackson.

In his acceptance speech, Dukakis attacked the huge federal deficit, called for "an economic future that will provide good jobs at good wages for every citizen of this land," and challenged the country to "end the shame of homelessness." He decried "the avalanche of drugs that is pouring into this country" and declared that "this election is not about ideology. It's about competence."

Dukakis stressed these themes in his campaign against Bush. Only in the last days before the election did he respond forcefully to Bush's attacks on his record and political philosophy. Election analysts said that the main reasons for Dukakis' loss may have been his failure to respond to Bush earlier, as well as the difficulty of defeating an incumbent Vice President during relatively peaceful and prosperous times. After the election, Dukakis resumed full-time duties as governor of Massachusetts, the office he has held since 1983.   Jay Myers

277

Eastern Orthodox Churches

Eastern Orthodox Churches. During 1988, the Russian Orthodox Church observed the 1,000th anniversary of the introduction of Christianity to Russia. According to historians, Grand Prince Vladimir I, pagan ruler of the city of Kiev in what is now the Soviet Union, converted to Christianity in about the year 988. Observances of the anniversary were given unusual support by the Soviet government.

The celebration began on June 5, 1988, with a Russian Orthodox Divine Liturgy held at Epiphany Cathedral in Moscow. A number of religious leaders attended the liturgy. Disputes between the Russian and Greek Orthodox churches, however, prevented Patriarch Demetrios of Constantinople, Turkey, from participating in it.

The 700-year-old Danilov Monastery in Moscow was restored for the anniversary, and the Soviet government returned control of the monastery to the church. On May 30, United States President Ronald Reagan visited the Danilov Monastery while in the Soviet Union for a summit meeting. Reagan called for more religious freedom in the Soviet Union.

Celebration at Patmos. In September, the Greek Orthodox Church commemorated the 900th anniversary of the establishment of the monastery of Saint John the Theologian—the author of the Book of Revelation in the Bible—by Saint Christodoulos on the Greek island of Patmos. Patriarch Demetrios proclaimed Patmos a "holy island."

Dukakis candidacy. The candidacy of Massachusetts Governor Michael S. Dukakis for the office of U.S. President was of great interest to the Orthodox Church in the United States. Dukakis was the first person with an Eastern Orthodox background to be nominated by a major political party for the office. His status as a member of the Orthodox Church was widely debated, however, because his wife, Katharine (known as Kitty), is Jewish and their marriage did not take place in the Orthodox Church, and because he supports women's right to abortion. The Orthodox Church has consistently opposed abortion.

Film protest. The film *The Last Temptation of Christ* provoked a strong reaction in the Eastern Orthodox community when it opened in U.S. and Canadian theaters in August. Several Orthodox churches strongly condemned the film, which portrays Jesus as dreaming of life as an ordinary human being. Nikos Kazantzakis, the author of the novel on which the film is based, was born in Greece and baptized in the Greek Orthodox Church but rejected membership in it.

Archbishop Iakovos, primate of the Greek Orthodox Archdiocese of North and South America, played an instrumental role in arranging the January 31 meeting between Prime Ministers Andreas Papandreou of Greece and Turgut Ozal of Turkey. The meeting, in Davos, Switzerland, reduced tensions between the two countries.   Stanley Samuel Harakas

In *World Book,* see **Eastern Orthodox Churches.**

Bishops gather for a council in Zagorsk, Soviet Union, in June as part of celebrations marking the 1,000th anniversary of Christianity in Russia.

278

Economics. The United States economy had its sixth consecutive year of growth in 1988, setting a record for the longest period of peacetime economic expansion in U.S. history. Overall, the year's economic news continued to be good, though many Americans worried about the country's tremendous trade and budget deficits and about possible aftershocks of the October 1987 stock-market crash. Although the deficits did provide cause for concern, the financial collapse that some experts had predicted would follow the 1987 crash never came in 1988.

By the end of 1988, it appeared that the gross national product (GNP) for all of the year—the total value of all goods and services produced—would total about $3.996 trillion in 1982 dollars. (To make year-to-year comparisons easier, economists often measure GNP in the dollars of an earlier year. In the mid- and late 1980's, they used 1982 dollars.) The $3.996 trillion for 1988 would represent a growth of about 3.9 per cent over the 1987 GNP. Economic growth slowed in the second half of 1988, but there were no signs that the economy was slipping into a recession. In fact, many economists viewed this slowdown as a healthy trend, because a slower growth rate after years of expansion tends to put less upward pressure on prices.

Inflation. The inflation rate for 1988 as measured by the Gross National Product Deflator—also called the Implicit Price Index or Implicit Price Deflator—was 3.4 per cent at the end of the year. The Consumer Price Index (CPI)—the most commonly used measurement of changes in the cost of goods and services—rose at an annual rate of 4.4 per cent, the same rate of inflation as in 1987. The drought that hit the United States in the summer of 1988 boosted food prices, which increased 5.2 per cent. The dry weather shriveled grain harvests, and shortages of livestock feed forced farmers to reduce their herds.

Employment and production. The unemployment rate averaged 5.3 per cent in 1988, its fifth straight year of decline. The number of jobs available to Americans grew 2.3 per cent during the year to reach a new high of 115 million jobs. This meant that there were 26 million more jobs available in 1988 than at the end of 1982, when the current cycle of economic expansion began. The rate of job expansion in the United States during this period was twice that of any other country. But even though more jobs were available, about 6.7 million Americans were still unemployed at the end of 1988.

The 5.3 per cent unemployment rate meant that only about 5 out of every 100 Americans who were looking for work in 1988 were unable to find a job. A different way to measure employment is the *employment rate*. This is the number of employed people divided by the total number of working-age people. In December 1988, the employment rate in the United States stood at a record 62.6 per cent. In 1983, the employment rate was 56.2 per cent.

Economists attribute the long-term rise in the employment rate to a number of factors. One is that "baby boomers"—people born during the post-World War II period of rapid population growth in the United States that lasted from 1946 to 1964—have passed from entry-level jobs to more stable employment, with fewer people entering the labor market. Whether this long-term rise in the rate is a benefit to the economy or a detriment is a matter of debate among economists.

What is not debatable is the changing face of the U.S. labor market in 1988. After six years of economic expansion, there were jobs looking for workers. An index of the volume of help-wanted advertising rose from 155 at the end of 1987 to 160 at the end of 1988.

Workers in the United States were more productive in 1988. The index of output per hour worked rose from 109.9 in the fourth quarter of 1987 to 110.4 by October 1988. Approximately 84 per cent of the United States industrial capacity was in use by the end of 1988, up from 80 per cent at the end of 1986.

Interest rates began to rise in 1988. This is a typical occurrence in the late stages of an expansion cycle. The Board of Governors of the Federal Reserve System (the Fed) announced on August 9 that it was raising its *discount rate*—the interest rate on loans to banks and other financial institutions—from 6.0 per cent to 6.5 per cent. The board said it ordered the hike, the first increase in the discount rate since September 1987, to help reduce inflationary pressures on the economy.

The Fed's action had an immediate effect, raising rates on certificates of deposit (CD's) and Treasury bills to their highest levels since before the October 1987 stock-market crash. The three-month Treasury bill rate, which began 1988 at 5.7 per cent, rose past 7 per cent by the end of August and reached 8 per cent in early December. It ended 1988 at 8.1 per cent.

For long-term rates, however, the picture was different during 1988. At the start of the year, the interest rates on corporate AAA bonds, the bonds issued by corporations with the highest credit rating, stood at 10.0 per cent. They dipped to 9.4 per cent at the end of February, then rose back to about 10 per cent by the end of June. They hovered at about 10 per cent until the first week of September, when they started to drop. They bottomed out at 9.4 per cent in early November and ended 1988 at 9.8 per cent.

Investment. Although the growth rate of the U.S. economy was slowing down, there were signs that the expansion would continue over the next few years. In 1988, U.S. businesses spent $431 billion on new plants and equipment, an increase of 10.6 per cent from 1987. According to most economists, such increased capital expenditure usually points toward future economic growth. Manufacturing expenditures rose 12.1 per cent during the year. New orders for manufactured goods during the first 10 months of 1988 were up a surprising 72 per cent.

Economics

Leaders of the world's major industrialized nations gather for an economic summit meeting in Toronto, Canada, in June.

Government spending. Despite an expanding economy, the United States government continued to spend more than it received in taxes in 1988. The deficit for the fiscal year 1988 (which ended on Sept. 30, 1988) was an estimated $155.1 billion. In comparison, the deficit for fiscal 1987 was about $148 billion. The total net federal debt passed the $2-trillion mark for the first time in mid-1988 and was still rising at year-end. Interest on this debt reached $150 billion per year. This deficit increase occurred despite a 12 per cent increase in federal income taxes collected in 1987 and a similar increase in 1988. In contrast, state and local governments had a collective surplus of about $59 billion in 1988.

International scene. In general, the economic climate of other countries was also good in 1988. The real GNP—adjusted for inflation—for most industrialized nations rose during the year. Japan's GNP increased by 5.6 per cent; Great Britain's by 4.0 per cent; and Australia's by 3.5 per cent. Countries such as Peru and Mexico, with faltering economies, continued to experience a declining GNP.

As in the United States, the unemployment rates in other industrialized countries generally fell during 1988. Japan's rate of joblessness hovered around 2.8 per cent; but Great Britain's plunged from 9.4 per cent to 8; West Germany's fell from 9.0 per cent to 8.6; and Canada's dropped from 8.4 per cent to 7.9.

Inflation was moderate in most industrialized coun-

tries. In Japan, the inflation rate stabilized at about 2.8 per cent after reaching a record 3.2 per cent in 1987. In Great Britain, it hovered around 6 per cent, and in Australia, it fell from 8 per cent to 7 per cent.

The economic situations of developing countries did not improve in 1988. High interest rates and continuing debt problems plagued many countries. In Brazil, the inflation rate—which stood at a staggering 480 per cent at the beginning of 1988—passed the 1,000 per cent mark by year-end. This meant that prices in Brazil increased nearly 30 per cent each month. In the past, such runaway inflation usually signaled economic—and even political—collapse. But Brazil's government prevented this calamity by tying almost all prices and wages to the inflation rate.

In Latin America, overall GNP growth continued at a rate of less than 1.5 per cent in 1988, as it had for the previous five years. Because the GNP has not been growing at the same pace as the area's population, more people in Latin America are growing poorer.

Soviet Union and China. The economic changes going on in the Soviet Union and China slowed in 1988. In the Soviet Union, the changes are part of what its leaders call *perestroika*, or restructuring. In China, they are called *socialism with Chinese characteristics*. But in both countries, hopes dwindled that their large, government-run economies could be easily revitalized. Reforms became bogged down in bureaucracy and economic difficulties.

Selected key U.S. economic indicators

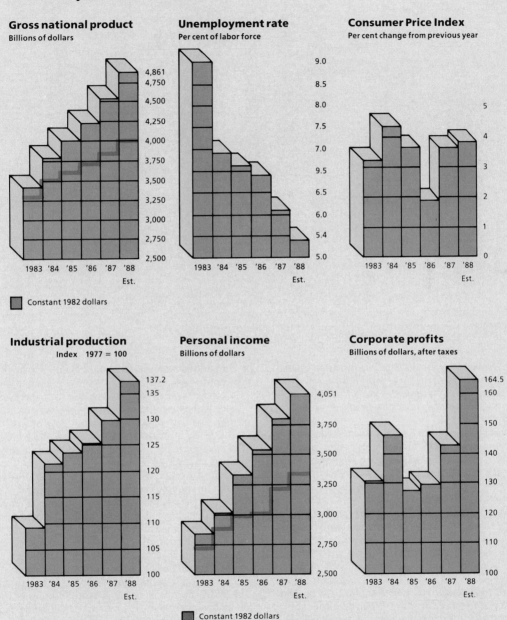

Gross national product
Billions of dollars

4,861
4,750
4,500
4,250
4,000
3,750
3,500
3,250
3,000
2,750
2,500

1983 '84 '85 '86 '87 '88 Est.

■ Constant 1982 dollars

Unemployment rate
Per cent of labor force

9.0
8.5
8.0
7.5
7.0
9.5
6.5
6.0
5.4
5.0

1983 '84 '85 '86 '87 '88 Est.

Consumer Price Index
Per cent change from previous year

5
4
3
2
1
0

1983 '84 '85 '86 '87 '88 Est.

Industrial production
Index 1977 = 100

137.2
135
130
125
120
115
110
105
100

1983 '84 '85 '86 '87 '88 Est.

Personal income
Billions of dollars

4,051
3,750
3,500
3,250
3,000
2,750
2,500

1983 '84 '85 '86 '87 '88 Est.

■ Constant 1982 dollars

Corporate profits
Billions of dollars, after taxes

164.5
160
150
140
130
120
110
100

1983 '84 '85 '86 '87 '88 Est.

The most frequently used measure of the nation's total economic performance is the gross national product (GNP). The GNP measures the value in current prices of all goods and services produced by a country in a year. Constant dollars show the amounts adjusted for inflation. The unemployment rate is the percentage of the total labor force that is unemployed and actively seeking work. The Consumer Price Index (CPI) measures inflation by showing the change in prices of selected goods and services consumed by urban families and individuals. Industrial production is a monthly measure of the physical output of manufacturing, mining, and utility industries. Personal income is current income received by individuals, nonprofit institutions, and private trust funds before taxes. Corporate profits are quarterly profit samplings from major industries.

All 1988 figures are estimates from The Conference Board. Figures for other years are from the U.S. Council of Economic Advisers.

Economics

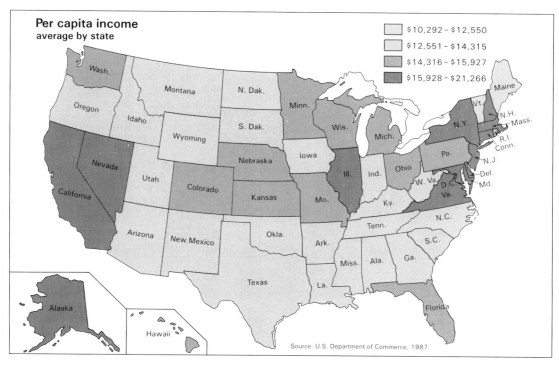

Per capita income
average by state

☐	$10,292 – $12,550
☐	$12,551 – $14,315
■	$14,316 – $15,927
■	$15,928 – $21,266

Source: U.S. Department of Commerce, 1987.

New England had the highest per capita income in the United States in 1987, according to figures released in 1988 by the U.S. Department of Commerce.

In the Soviet Union, lines to buy food and other consumer items were longer, not shorter. An attempt to give farmers 50-year leases on farmland had attracted fewer than 1.5 per cent of all Soviet farmers by the end of 1988.

China was forced to halt investment spending for "nonproductive investments" such as hotels. In July, statistics released by the Chinese government showed that the country's inflation rate had reached its highest level in almost 40 years and that retail prices had jumped 19 per cent in 1988.

World trade, which has been expanding since 1983 at an annual rate of 5.5 per cent, continued to grow at the same pace in 1988. During much of the year, the trade atmosphere continued to warm as economies of more countries grew and as more trade barriers were lowered. One of the most significant agreements to lower such barriers was that between the United States and Canada. The two countries approved a free-trade agreement that will eliminate duties on virtually all trade between them by 1999 (see **Canada**).

One of the few disturbances in the trade atmosphere was a dispute that erupted in late December between the United States and the European Community (EC or Common Market). The EC banned imports of U.S. meat from livestock that have been given growth hormones, and the United States responded with 100 per cent tariffs on many European foods.

The United States has had a trade deficit—an excess of imports over exports—since the end of 1982. The 1987 deficit was a record $154 billion, and the 1988 deficit was expected to be only slightly smaller. This deficit is financed largely by the purchase of U.S. securities by investors in other countries. And, indeed, the private net purchase of U.S. securities by foreigners was about $125 billion in 1988.

A country that runs a trade deficit year after year sooner or later sees the value of its currency fall against other nations' currencies. For example, Japan exports more manufactured goods to the United States than it imports from the United States. In 1983, it took 250 Japanese yen to buy one U.S. dollar, but by the end of 1988, it took only 125 yen.

Thus, the U.S. dollar—though still a strong currency—is less expensive for foreigners to buy than it was in the past. And investors in other countries continue to want dollars, so perhaps the U.S. trade deficit is caused not so much by Americans' appetite for imported goods as by foreign investors' appetite for American securities—which must be paid for by selling goods to Americans.

Acquisition fever hit the U.S. food industry in 1988. One of the largest take-overs in U.S. history took place on October 30 when Philip Morris Companies Incorporated, a food and tobacco firm, purchased food giant Kraft Incorporated for $13.1 billion. A month later, on November 30, Kohlberg Kravis Roberts & Company, an investment firm, bought RJR Nabisco Incorporated, another food and tobacco firm, for $25 billion—the largest corporate buy-out in U.S. history. Then, on December 18, the Pillsbury Company, a U.S. food and restaurant firm, agreed to be acquired by Grand Metropolitan PLC, a British food and liquor company, for $5.75 billion.

Economic illiteracy. The majority of high school students in the United States are unable to define basic economic terms such as *inflation* or *profits*, according to a report issued December 28 by the Joint Council on Economic Education, an independent, nonprofit educational organization in New York City. The report was based on the results of a multiple-choice test that was given to more than 8,000 students nationwide in 1987. Only 34 per cent of the students correctly identified profits as "revenues minus costs," while only 25 per cent rightly defined inflation as "a sustained rise in prices."

William B. Walstad, an economics professor at the University of Nebraska in Lincoln and one of the authors of the study, called the results "shocking" and said that the country's schools are "producing a nation of economic illiterates." The report recommended that all high school students be required to take a course in economics.   Donald W. Swanton

See also **Bank; International trade; Labor; Manufacturing; Stocks and bonds;** and individual country articles. In *World Book*, see **Economics.**

Ecuador. In his inaugural speech on Aug. 10, 1988, President Rodrigo Borja of the Democratic Left Party sought to reassure Ecuadorean business interests and the international financial community about his program for social change. "No one needs to be nervous about the presence of our government," Borja said.

The 53-year-old career politician and law professor denied that he had plans to nationalize Ecuador's private sector. But he said that he will introduce greater government regulation of an economy hit hard by decreased oil revenues and mismanagement.

Borja's inauguration provided an opportunity for a minisummit of Latin-American leaders who converged on Quito, the capital, to witness his swearing in. Nicaragua's President Daniel Ortega, who was denied entry to Ecuador for the inaugural by Borja's conservative predecessor, met with Borja in Quito on August 11. Ortega congratulated the left-leaning Borja on his victory, and Borja announced the restoration of diplomatic relations with Nicaragua.

United States Secretary of State George P. Shultz, who also attended the inauguration, met privately with several heads of state. In public, he expressed his displeasure with a new mural in Ecuador's National Congress building. The mural depicts a skull wearing a Nazi helmet painted with the letters *CIA*, for the U.S. Central Intelligence Agency.   Nathan A. Haverstock

See also **Latin America** (Facts in brief table). In *World Book*, see **Ecuador.**

Education. Five years of educational reform and a $56-billion increase in spending only marginally improved public schools in the United States, leaving student achievement "unacceptably low," U.S. Secretary of Education William J. Bennett concluded in a report published in April 1988. Written at President Ronald Reagan's request, the 61-page study, *American Education: Making It Work*, said that "undeniable progress" had taken place in the wake of school-reform efforts, and that, in general, school performance had improved "a little bit." But Secretary Bennett charged that improvement was taking place at a "disappointingly slow" pace and that American students still performed at "excessively low levels of achievement."

The report was issued on the fifth anniversary of the publication of *A Nation at Risk*, a federally sponsored study of American education that concluded that the educational foundations of the United States were "being eroded by a rising tide of mediocrity." *A Nation at Risk*'s alarming findings and powerful prose helped spark a nationwide effort to improve public education.

In addition to measuring the progress of this effort, the Bennett report proposed a new agenda for school reform that included toughening the content of courses in the lower grades, establishing a core academic curriculum for all students, making textbooks more difficult, and providing more intellectually challenging instruction for minority and disadvantaged students. The report also called for changing state regulations so that people without degrees in education could become teachers and principals, and increasing the number of *magnet schools*, specialized programs that draw students from beyond the boundaries of regular attendance zones.

The discouraging message of the Bennett report was reinforced by two major assessments of student achievement released later in the year. The National Assessment of Educational Progress (NAEP) reported in June that, despite gains in mathematics achievement made during the 1980's—especially by minority students—U.S. high school students still possessed a "dismal" level of math proficiency. The NAEP, which is mandated by Congress to regularly assess student achievement, based its conclusions on a nationwide test of nearly 12,000 eleventh-graders. In September, a similar NAEP assessment of science achievement concluded that American students' understanding of science is distressingly poor, despite some recent improvements.

Model curriculums. In August, Bennett released a sequel to his 1987 report, *James Madison High School: A Curriculum for American Students*. In the earlier work, Bennett had proposed a rigorous academic core curriculum for U.S. high schools. He urged that all students be taught a common body of knowledge through a demanding course of study that would include four years of English; three years each of

President Reagan announces the nomination of Lauro F. Cavazos, right, as secretary of education. He became the first-ever Hispanic Cabinet member .

mathematics, social studies, and science; two years of foreign language; and one year of art and music.

Bennett's 1988 report provided a model curriculum for elementary schools. He proposed that students be exposed to good literature in the early grades and be given intensive instruction in academic subjects, with foreign-language study beginning by fourth grade.

Blackboard jungle. United States urban schools were the focus of considerable attention in 1988. Arguing that the education reform movement of the 1980's had largely by-passed the "most deeply troubled schools," the trustees of the Carnegie Foundation for the Advancement of Teaching in Princeton, N.J., in March called for a comprehensive initiative to rescue urban education.

In the 38-page report—*An Imperiled Generation: Saving Urban Schools*—they painted a bleak picture of inner-city schools as institutions burdened by bureaucracy, decaying facilities, uncompromising unions, and low expectations for students. The Carnegie trustees called for reforms that included holding schools accountable for the performance of their students, intervening in ineffective schools, reducing enrollments at crowded schools, and giving more authority to teachers and principals.

The difficult conditions that prevail in some inner-city schools received widespread publicity in 1988. A dispute in Paterson, N.J., over the 1987 decision of high school principal Joe Clark to expel 66 of his stu-

dents without due process and to lock fire doors to keep out drug dealers evolved into a national news story in January 1988. The publicity landed the colorful principal—who was said to patrol the halls of his school wielding a baseball bat—on the cover of *Time* magazine and earned him praise from President Ronald Reagan. More important, the story prompted a national debate on how educators should combat crime and drug use in urban schools.

Attempting to reform one of the most troubled urban school systems, the Illinois legislature in July passed legislation that made sweeping changes in the organization of Chicago public schools. In what some education experts called a radical move, the lawmakers dissolved the current Chicago Board of Education and mandated the creation of parent-led councils to oversee the direction of individual schools. The legislation also gave local schools greater decision-making authority and greater control over their budgets, and it denied school principals lifetime tenure.

In September, Illinois Governor James R. Thompson returned the legislation, unsigned, to the lawmakers. He proposed two controversial amendments that spurred the legislators to draft a compromise bill that nonetheless retained most features of the original. In December, the Illinois legislature approved the bill, and Thompson signed it on December 12.

Questions about achievement tests. The use and abuse of standardized testing was another significant issue in 1988. After Friends of Education, a West Virginia advocacy group, challenged the accuracy of achievement tests taken by many U.S. elementary school students, the Department of Education in February announced that it would prepare a "consumer guide" on standardized testing.

Friends of Education had published a study in 1987 that revealed that the overwhelming majority of elementary school pupils in the United States scored above the levels that were accepted as the national average on major commercially written standardized tests. The advocacy group claimed that the skewed results were caused by "average" scores being out of date and set artificially low. The organization also charged that the publishers of the achievement tests did little to inform the public of how the results could be misinterpreted.

State school reform. In May, Minnesota lawmakers made their state the first to permit students to attend any school system in the state. The Minnesota law, which is to take full effect in 1991, calls for the state's per-pupil educational funds to follow students to their new school systems and provides transportation for underprivileged students. In the 1980's, many reformers have advocated giving parents and students greater freedom of choice in choosing schools, on the grounds that such a policy would force each school to improve its programs or lose students and funding to more effective schools.

New Jersey education officials also attracted publicity when they initiated proceedings in May to take over the operation of the Jersey City school system. Acting under the jurisdiction of a New Jersey "academic bankruptcy" law—one of several such state laws enacted in the 1980's—Education Commissioner Saul Cooperman issued an order requiring the Jersey City public schools to show cause why the district should not be taken over and operated by the state. Cooperman called the district's schools "bleak" and its bureaucracy rife with political patronage, cronyism, and fiscal misdealings. In accordance with the New Jersey law, hearings before an administrative law judge were begun in July 1988 and scheduled to continue until January 1989, when the judge is to recommend whether or not the state should assume the operation of the Jersey City schools.

Skyrocketing costs. The rapidly rising cost of a college education became another major issue in 1988. In the summer, various educational associations estimated the total cost of tuition, fees, and room and board at prestigious private U.S. universities at nearly $20,000 per year. The figure prompted Secretary Bennett and other critics to charge that colleges and universities were enriching themselves at their students' expense.

The average annual expenditure per college student reached $14,565 during the 1988-1989 school year, according to the U.S. Department of Education. This figure was nearly $900 higher than that of one year

earlier, and, after adjusting for inflation, up 31 per cent since the 1980-1981 school year.

Despite evidence—including results of a survey of 11 colleges released in March 1988 by Brandeis University in Waltham, Mass.—that more blacks were applying for college admission, civil rights advocates and others voiced concern in 1988 over the impact of rising college costs on minorities, the poor, and even the middle class. The problem became an issue in the 1988 presidential campaign. Both Michael S. Dukakis, the Democratic nominee, and George Bush, the Republican who won the election, spoke repeatedly during the campaign about the importance of education to the economic future of the United States. Bush pledged that, if elected, he would strive to become "the education President," and Dukakis announced a plan that would permit students to pay back college loans over a lifetime through payroll withholding.

The total U.S. education bill was estimated at $328-billion for 1988-1989, a one-year increase of $20 billion. Spending at the elementary and secondary levels was estimated at $196 billion, a 6 per cent increase from the previous year. Expenditures for higher education were estimated at $132 billion, up 6.6 per cent.

Enrollments. Total enrollment in U.S. schools and colleges reached 58.5 million in fall 1988, nearly 100,000 higher than the previous year. About 46 million students were enrolled in public and private elementary and secondary schools, an increase of 80,000 from the 1987-1988 school year. College enrollment increased only marginally during the same period. A total of 12.6 million students were enrolled in institutions of higher education at the beginning of the 1988-1989 school year. In all, more than 25 per cent of the U.S. population participated in the educational process either as students or educators.

According to a September announcement by the U.S. Bureau of the Census, a greater percentage of the U.S. population has completed high school or college than ever before. More than 75 per cent of Americans over 24 have earned high school diplomas, and almost 20 per cent have college degrees. The education level has been increasing for many years. In 1940, only about 25 per cent had completed high school and less than 5 per cent had completed college.

New education secretary. Bennett resigned as secretary of education in September. He had said in May that he would resign in mid-September because the November presidential election would make it impossible for there to be any serious accomplishments in the last months of the Reagan Administration. Bennett was replaced by Lauro F. Cavazos, formerly president of Texas Tech University in Lubbock. Cavazos became the first Hispanic member of the U.S. Cabinet in history. On November 21, President-elect Bush said Cavazos would be asked to remain in the Cabinet post.   Thomas Toch

See also **Cavazos, Lauro F.** In *World Book*, see **Education.**

Egypt

Egypt. A nine-year territorial dispute with Israel was resolved on Sept. 29, 1988, when an international arbitration panel awarded Taba, a small Israeli-occupied oceanfront resort in the Sinai Peninsula, to Egypt. Taba was the only part of the Sinai that was not returned to Egypt by Israel under the 1979 peace treaty between the two countries.

The return of Taba strengthened President Mohammad Hosni Mubarak's position in his own country and with other Arab leaders, but it had little effect on Egyptian-Israeli relations. In January, rioters swept through Cairo protesting Israeli actions to suppress the Palestinian uprising in the occupied West Bank and Gaza Strip. The Egyptian government also criticized Israel's actions and in November joined other Arab states in recognizing the independent Palestinian state declared by the Palestine National Council that month. At the same time, however, Egypt continued to call for a negotiated solution to the Palestinian problem and was the first Arab country to announce its support for a United States peace plan proposed in February.

In February, Mubarak reestablished diplomatic ties with Tunisia and Yemen (Aden). That left Algeria, Libya, and Syria as the only Arab states still refusing to restore relations broken off when Egypt signed the 1979 peace treaty with Israel. In March 1988, Egypt and Libya withdrew troops from their common border. In July, Egypt was reinstated in the Arab League Educational, Cultural and Scientific Organization, from which it had been suspended in 1979.

Relations with the United States remained close despite Egypt's sympathy for the Palestinian cause and continued criticism of Israel. In March, the United States and Egypt signed an agreement that allows the Egyptian arms industry the same rights to bid on American military contracts as members of the North Atlantic Treaty Organization and several other U.S. allies, such as Israel. In November, the United States and Egypt signed an agreement to jointly manufacture the M1-A1 tank, the most sophisticated U.S. tank.

Fundamentalism. The trial of members of a secret group called Egypt's Revolution, dedicated to undermining Egypt's peace with Israel, began in November. The defendants were charged with killing or wounding three Israeli diplomats between 1984 and 1986. The group's alleged leader, Khaled Abdel Nasser, is the son of Gamal Abdel Nasser, Egypt's president from 1956 to 1970. The younger Nasser, living in exile in Yugoslavia, was tried in absentia.

The economy. Heavy foreign debts and chronic budget deficits continued to hamper economic development. By July, Egypt's foreign debt had reached $45 billion, most of it owed to the United States. On the positive side, revenues from the Suez Canal rose to $1.3 billion, aided by discounts that increased supertanker traffic. William Spencer

See also **Middle East** (Facts in brief table). In the World Book Supplement section, see **Egypt.**

Elections. Republican George Bush, Vice President of the United States for eight years under President Ronald Reagan, was elected 41st President of the United States on Nov. 8, 1988. Bush scored a convincing victory over Democrat Michael S. Dukakis, the governor of Massachusetts, but shied away from claiming a mandate. Bush carried 40 states and received about 48.9 million votes, or 53 per cent of the total, as he piled up an impressive 426 electoral votes. Dukakis carried 10 states and the District of Columbia as he gathered about 41.8 million votes, or 46 per cent of the total, and 111 electoral votes. (One West Virginia elector cast her presidential vote in the Electoral College for Dukakis' running mate, Senator Lloyd M. Bentsen, Jr., of Texas, instead of for Dukakis.)

Bush's vice presidential running mate was Senator Dan Quayle of Indiana, a controversial figure throughout the campaign. The youthful Quayle posed a sharp contrast with the older, more experienced Bentsen. In the end, however, Quayle's presence on the ticket was not as important a factor as some political analysts had thought it would be.

Turned-off voters. Polling in the fall indicated widespread voter dissatisfaction with both presidential candidates and their often negative campaigns. A record number of Americans stayed away from the polls, breaking a 40-year-old mark for low turnout. Just over 50 per cent of eligible voters cast ballots, down from 53.1 per cent in the 1984 presidential election. The previous low turnout of 51.1 per cent was recorded in 1948 when Democratic President Harry S. Truman upset Republican Thomas E. Dewey.

Polls taken by ABC News as voters left polling places indicated that 49 per cent of Bush's supporters were interested mainly in stopping Dukakis, while 50 per cent of Dukakis voters were most intent on stopping Bush—further evidence of a marked lack of enthusiasm for the candidates. Bush had majority support among all age groups except those under 25 years of age or over 59. Bush was backed by 3 out of 5 voters earning more than $40,000 a year, and Dukakis had a similar margin of support from those earning less than $20,000. Fifty-four per cent of men favored Bush, while 52 per cent of women voted for Dukakis. The governor also received 90 per cent of the black vote and 71 per cent of the Jewish vote.

The voters' preferences in the fall had changed considerably since midsummer, when polls indicated that Dukakis had a commanding 17-point lead over Bush. The Vice President began his ascendancy in August after suggesting that Dukakis was a far-out liberal, soft on crime and national defense, a supporter of gun control and the American Civil Liberties Union (ACLU), and an opponent of capital punishment. Bush made much of a Dukakis veto, based on an advisory opinion by the Massachusetts Supreme Court, of a bill to require elementary-school teachers to lead classes in reciting the Pledge of Allegiance. The Republican campaign also trumpeted the case of

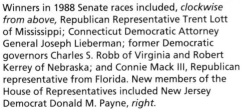

Winners in 1988 Senate races included, *clockwise from above,* Republican Representative Trent Lott of Mississippi; Connecticut Democratic Attorney General Joseph Lieberman; former Democratic governors Charles S. Robb of Virginia and Robert Kerrey of Nebraska; and Connie Mack III, Republican representative from Florida. New members of the House of Representatives included New Jersey Democrat Donald M. Payne, *right.*

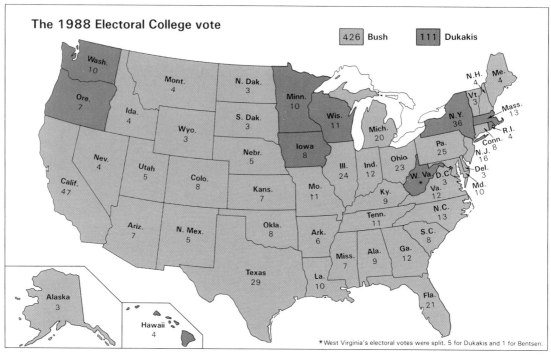

The 1988 Electoral College vote

| 426 | Bush | 111 | Dukakis |

Wash. 10
Mont. 4
N. Dak. 3
Minn. 10
N.H. 4
Me. 4
Vt. 3
Ore. 7
Ida. 4
S. Dak. 3
Wis. 11
Mich. 20
N.Y. 36
Mass. 13
R.I. 4
Conn. 8
Wyo. 3
Nebr. 5
Iowa 8
Pa. 25
N.J. 16
Nev. 4
Utah 5
Colo. 8
Ill. 24
Ind. 12
Ohio 23
Del. 3
Calif. 47
Kans. 7
Mo. 11
W. Va. 5
D.C. 3
Va. 12
Md. 10
Ky. 9
Ariz. 7
N. Mex. 5
Okla. 8
Ark. 6
Tenn. 11
N.C. 13
S.C. 8
Miss. 7
Ala. 9
Ga. 12
Texas 29
La. 10
Fla. 21
Alaska 3
Hawaii 4

*West Virginia's electoral votes were split. 5 for Dukakis and 1 for Bentsen.

George Bush won 426 of the 538 electoral votes in the 1988 election. Michael S. Dukakis got 111 votes, and 1 Democratic elector voted for Lloyd M. Bentsen, Jr.

William Horton, Jr., known as Willie Horton, a convicted murderer who tortured a Maryland man and raped the man's fiancée while on furlough from a Massachusetts prison.

A number of weeks passed before Dukakis hit back, accusing Bush of spreading "garbage" and "lies" about his record and "dragging truth into the gutter." Republicans had their own complaints about Democratic tactics, accusing Dukakis of distorting Bush's position on social security and other issues and unfairly linking him to Panama's strongman, General Manuel Antonio Noriega Morena, who has been accused of drug dealing. Many voters were repelled by both campaigns. A *Newsweek* magazine poll in October found that 64 per cent of the public believed the campaign was more negative than past races.

Congress. Democratic gains in the Senate and House of Representatives had some party leaders claiming that if voters had bestowed any mandate, it was to Democrats to pursue their congressional priorities. In the election, Democrats scored a net gain of one seat in the Senate and five seats in the House. Although voters were kind to House incumbents—more than 98 per cent were reelected—three Republican senators and one Democratic senator lost.

In the Senate races, Connecticut's Democratic Attorney General Joseph Lieberman narrowly upset three-term Republican Senator Lowell P. Weicker, Jr. Former Democratic Governor Robert Kerrey of Nebraska

defeated Republican Senator David K. Karnes, who made the mistake of declaring, "We need fewer farmers." In Nevada, Democratic Governor Richard H. Bryan defeated one-term Republican Senator Chic Hecht. Democrats also picked up a Senate seat in Virginia, where former Democratic Governor Charles S. Robb overwhelmed a little-known Republican, Maurice Dawkins, to win the seat vacated by retiring Republican Senator Paul S. Trible, Jr.

Republicans took control of a Senate seat in Montana as Republican Conrad Burns, a Yellowstone County commissioner, upset Democratic Senator John Melcher. In Mississippi, Republican Representative Trent Lott defeated Democratic Representative Wayne Dowdy to win the Senate seat of retiring Democrat John C. Stennis. The seat of another retiring Democrat, Senator Lawton Chiles of Florida, was claimed by Republican Representative Connie Mack III, who edged out Democratic Representative Kenneth H. (Buddy) MacKay.

Two others newly elected to the Senate were Republicans Slade Gorton of Washington and James M. Jeffords of Vermont. Gorton, a former senator, narrowly defeated five-term Representative Mike Lowry to take over the seat of retiring Republican Daniel J. Evans. Jeffords, a seven-term House member, won the seat of retiring Republican Robert T. Stafford, easily defeating Democrat William B. Gray.

The net result of these changes was a 55 to 45 Democratic edge in the 1989 Senate. The previous margin had been 54 to 46.

Democrats also increased their already lopsided control of the House, marking the first time since 1960 that the party winning the presidency failed to increase its strength in the House. In the 100th Congress, Democrats had an edge of 255 to 177, with 3 vacancies. In the 101st Congress, their margin was to be 259 to 174, with 2 vacancies, for a net gain of 7. The margin had been 260 to 175, but Democratic Representative Bill Nichols of Alabama died after winning reelection, and in Indiana, Republican Representative Dan R. Coats was appointed to fill the Senate seat vacated by Quayle.

Ethics problems cost some House members their seats. Representative Fernand J. St Germain (D., R.I.), chairman of the House Committee on Banking, Housing, and Urban Affairs, was upset by a political newcomer, Republican lawyer Ronald K. Machtley, after the House Committee on Standards of Official Conduct began looking into suspected ethical lapses by St Germain. Democratic Representative Bill Chappell, Jr., of Florida, whose name figured in a Pentagon weapons-purchasing scandal in 1988, was edged out by Republican Craig T. James.

On the Republican side, Representative Pat Swindall of Georgia lost his bid for a third term after being indicted on federal perjury charges involving a home loan that may have come from illegal drug profits. And in New York, Republican Representative Joseph J. DioGuardi lost a close contest to Democrat Nita M. Lowey, a former assistant New York secretary of state, after being accused of improper campaign financing.

Lowey was one of two newly elected women representatives; the other was Democrat Jolene Unsoeld of Washington state. The election of Lowey and Unsoeld raised the House's female membership to 14, equaling a previous high mark.

In state races, Democrats picked up one governorship, thereby padding their margin over the Republicans to 28-22. In Indiana, Democrat Evan Bayh, the 32-year-old secretary of state, defeated Republican Lieutenant Governor John M. Mutz to become the state's first Democratic governor in 20 years. Bayh is the son of former Senator Birch Bayh, who was defeated in 1980 by Quayle. In West Virginia, Republican Governor Arch A. Moore, Jr., was decisively beaten in his bid for a fourth term by Democratic businessman Gaston Caperton. The Republicans picked up a governorship in Montana, where state Senator Stan Stephens defeated former Democratic Governor Thomas L. Judge.

Nationwide, Democrats lost about 50 seats in state legislatures. That outcome contrasted sharply with Democratic losses of 302 state seats in 1980 and 330 seats in 1984. In another striking contrast to recent presidential election years, only two state legislative chambers changed hands. Democrats gained control of the New Mexico Senate, while Republicans took

charge of the Vermont Senate. Republicans gained control of 10 chambers in 1980 and 7 in 1984.

State issues. Voters in 41 states acted on more than 230 ballot initiatives. In California, voters approved a measure to roll back property and casualty insurance rates by 20 per cent from 1987 levels and establish an elected insurance commissioner to review proposed rate increases. The insurance industry vowed to challenge the outcome in the courts, and at least 47 insurance companies stopped writing policies in California. See **State government.**

Californians also approved a measure requiring that certain sex offenders be screened for AIDS (acquired immune deficiency syndrome), but they defeated a proposal that would have required doctors to report the names and addresses of known or suspected carriers of the AIDS virus. The tobacco industry spent $18-million in a futile attempt to beat back a California proposal to increase the state cigarette tax by 25 cents a pack, with proceeds from the tax to be used for health programs.

Another large special-interest group—the National Rifle Association (NRA)—received a setback in Maryland. Although the NRA spent $4 million to persuade voters to overturn a state law controlling handgun sales, Marylanders gave solid approval to the law. The vote marked the first time that the NRA position did not prevail in a statewide referendum.

Gay rights suffered a reverse in Oregon, where voters repealed Democratic Governor Neil Goldschmidt's order banning state government discrimination against homosexuals. Oregonians also voted overwhelmingly to deny parole, probation, or sentence reduction for repeat felony offenders. California, Oklahoma, and New Mexico approved other anticrime measures.

Three states—Arizona, Colorado, and Florida—voted to make English their only official language. And bans on state-financed abortions were adopted in Arkansas, Colorado, and Michigan.

Voters in South Dakota, Utah, and Colorado defeated measures to limit government spending or roll back property taxes and other assessments. Arkansas voters, on the other hand, rejected a proposal that would have made it easier to hike property and income taxes.

State lotteries were approved in Idaho, Kentucky, Indiana, and Minnesota. Virginians approved betting on horse races for the first time. And the nuclear power industry position won in Massachusetts and Nebraska. Massachusetts voters declined to shut down the state's two nuclear plants, and Nebraskans rejected a proposal to withdraw from a multistate plan that would locate a low-level radioactive-waste site in the state.   Frank Cormier and Margot Cormier

See also **Congress of the United States; Democratic Party; Republican Party; State government.** In *World Book,* see **Election; Election campaign.**
Electric power. See Energy supply.

Electronics

Electronics. The remnants of the United States consumer electronics industry made a last stand in 1988. At midnight on January 1, Thomson S.A., one of France's largest manufacturers, took possession of the General Electric (GE) and RCA Consumer Electronics business from General Electric Company. The transfer left Zenith Electronics Corporation as the sole remaining U.S. company making television sets.

Throughout the first half of 1988, however, Zenith's management considered offers to sell the company. But the company appeared to remove itself from the auction block in June.

In 1988, U.S. consumers for the first time bought fewer videocassette recorders (VCR's) than they had the year before. Manufacturers and retailers struggled to make a profit on VCR's, color TV sets, and other electronic products.

Sharper video coming. The industry found some hope in new technologies that surfaced during 1988. Chief among them was high-definition television (HDTV) technology, which promises to deliver higher-quality wide-screen images to U.S. households. A TV set builds up a television image by a scanning technique that puts several hundred lines of picture information on the TV screen. The scanning is so rapid that we see a single image, and we usually are not aware of the lines. But the number of lines determines the sharpness of the picture—the more lines, the sharper the picture. The current standard for the United States calls for the transmission of 525 lines to the TV set, which, for certain technical reasons, puts fewer than 500 lines on the screen. Most HDTV systems under development in the United States start with 1,050, rather than 525, lines—providing a much more detailed picture than available on a standard TV set.

In September, the Federal Communications Commission (FCC)—which regulates broadcasting in the United States—made sure that a changeover to HDTV will not make older TV sets and VCR's obsolete overnight. The FCC ruled that whatever HDTV system it eventually approves will have to be compatible with previously purchased equipment. Thus, the HDTV broadcast signal will have to provide the information that an older TV set needs to produce its approximately 500-line picture.

Playback technology. In October, Intel Corporation, a major U.S. semiconductor manufacturer, unveiled Digital Video Interactive technology, which stores up to 72 minutes of picture and sound data on a compact disc and plays it back when instructed to do so by a computer. Intel bought the technology from GE and plans to license it to manufacturers of such products as educational tools and video games.

Video games enjoyed a resurgence in 1988. Sales of video game players and game cartridges were estimated at $2.4 billion in 1988.   Martin Levine

See also **Computer.** In *World Book*, see **Electronics; Television.**

© Mischa Richter; reproduced with
permission of Cartoonists and Writers Syndicate

El Salvador. As El Salvador headed toward presidential elections in March 1989, gunfire and explosions punctuated the nights in San Salvador, the capital. Elsewhere, leftist rebels mounted scattered attacks throughout the small country.

President José Napoleón Duarte, in the last year of his five-year term, was dying of cancer. Following exploratory surgery on June 7, 1988, at Walter Reed Army Medical Center in Washington, D.C., Duarte's doctors said he had only months to live.

Duarte's Christian Democratic Party seemed seriously ailing, too. Unable to unite behind a single candidate and amid charges of meddling on behalf of one candidate by the United States ambassador, the party split. Fidel Chávez Mena, who was foreign minister at the time of El Salvador's 1969 war with Honduras, became the candidate of one faction. Julio Adolfo Rey Prendes, a wealthy businessman and the former mayor of San Salvador, became the candidate of another, which called itself the Authentic Christian Democratic Party.

The right wing National Republican Alliance on May 28 named Alfredo Cristiani, a wealthy coffee grower, as its presidential candidate. Leftist rebels vowed to disrupt the elections.   Nathan A. Haverstock

See also **Latin America** (Facts in brief table). In *World Book*, see **El Salvador.**

Employment. See Economics; Labor.

Endangered species. See Conservation.

Energy supply. A long heat wave and drought during the summer of 1988 strained the generating capacity of electric utilities in many parts of the United States. The extreme heat increased demand for electricity for air conditioning, and the drought decreased the flow of rivers used by hydroelectric power plants. Some nuclear power stations, which need large quantities of water to cool plant components, also had to cut output because of low river levels. At the same time, favorable economic conditions increased the consumption of electricity by factories and other industries. Overall, consumption of electricity increased by 5 per cent during the first half of the year.

In August, utilities in the Midwest reported record demands for electricity, and they partially disconnected service to some large industrial consumers and thousands of residential customers. Utilities in the Northeast were forced to conserve electricity by reducing the voltage of electricity supplied to customers. Utility companies repeatedly urged customers to conserve energy.

U.S. energy consumption. The U.S. Department of Energy (DOE) on September 26 reported that the consumption of all forms of energy in the United States totaled 41 quadrillion British thermal units (B.T.U.'s) of energy in the first half of 1988, 6 per cent more than was used during the same period in 1987. Domestic energy production, however, increased by only 2 per cent, making the United States more reliant on imported sources of energy.

Synthetic fuels plant sold. The DOE on October 31 sold the Great Plains Coal Gasification Plant to the Basin Electric Power Cooperative of Bismarck, N. Dak. The $2.1-billion plant, the only U.S. commercial synthetic-fuels facility, was built in the 1970's.

Basin Electric was selected from nine prospective buyers competing to purchase the plant, which produces about 142 million cubic feet (4 million cubic meters) of synthetic natural gas daily from coal. The DOE took over the plant, located in Beulah, N. Dak., in 1985 after private sponsors defaulted on more than $1.5 billion in federal loans. Basin Electric said that under its purchase proposal, which is spread over 21 years, the government could eventually recover the full $1.5 billion.

Nuclear accident liability. President Ronald Reagan on August 20 signed legislation increasing the nuclear power industry's liability for nuclear accidents. The law is an extension of the 1954 Price-Anderson Act (legislation that set up a no-fault insurance pool for the nuclear industry, with a limit on liability). It makes the owners of nuclear power plants liable for up to $7.1 billion in damages resulting from a single nuclear accident—10 times more than the current level. The amount of the liability would increase with the licensing of new reactors and inflation.

Nuclear plant purchase stalled. New York state and the Long Island Lighting Company on May 27 reached an agreement to close the controversial Shoreham nuclear power plant. The $5.3-billion plant, located on Long Island about 55 miles (90 kilometers) east of New York City, was completed in 1984. But it never went into commercial operation because state and local officials refused to participate in emergency evacuation planning. The officials contended that the residents of Long Island could not be safely evacuated if a serious accident occurred. The agreement called for New York state to purchase Shoreham for $1 and dismantle the plant. But the agreement expired on December 2, when the New York state legislature adjourned without acting on the matter.

Nuclear waste. The DOE on September 13 announced a delay in the opening of the Waste Isolation Pilot Plant (WIPP), the first permanent repository for storing nuclear wastes in the United States. The $700-million facility, located 26 miles (40 kilometers) east of Carlsbad, N. Mex., originally was scheduled to open in October. WIPP consists of huge rooms, corridors, and ventilation shafts mined from salt deposits about 2,150 feet (655 meters) below the desert. It was designed to store millions of cubic feet of radioactive wastes resulting from the production of nuclear weapons. The DOE said that safety-related questions about the facility's design and construction must be resolved before the repository can be opened.

Safety concerns at nuclear sites. Controversy occurred during 1988 over the safety of government plants involved in the production of fuel for nuclear weapons. On October 4, the DOE acknowledged that the department and its predecessor, the U.S. Atomic Energy Commission, had kept secret a number of serious reactor accidents at the Savannah River Plant near Aiken, S.C. The accidents, which occurred between 1957 and 1985, included melting of nuclear fuel, leaks of reactor coolant water, and extensive radioactive contamination inside the plant. Safety concerns forced the DOE to shut the last active reactor at the plant in August 1988 because of an unexplained power surge.

On October 8, the DOE halted the processing of nuclear material at the Rocky Flats Plant near Boulder, Colo., after three employees were contaminated with plutonium. And state officials in Ohio on October 18 urged the DOE to close the Feed Materials Production Center in Fernald, near Cincinnati, after revelations that the facility had been discharging potentially dangerous radioactive wastes into the environment.

Plant fined. The U.S. Nuclear Regulatory Commission on August 11 announced the largest fine ever imposed on the owner of a nuclear power plant. The NRC said it would fine the Philadelphia Electric Company $1.25 million for safety violations at the Peach Bottom nuclear power station in Delta, Pa., near the Maryland border. The NRC also fined 33 workers at the plant from $500 to $1,000 each for sleeping on the job or showing other inattention to duty.

New nuclear plants. The International Atomic Energy Agency—a component of the United Nations

Israeli researchers display their version of a magnetohydrodynamic generator—a highly efficient means of producing electricity—in July.

based in Vienna, Austria—reported in February that 23 new nuclear power plants went into commercial operation in 1987, bringing the world total of nuclear plants to 417. The agency said that nuclear energy produced about 16 per cent of the world's electricity supply during 1987.

The Mexican government on October 14 ordered the start-up of the country's first nuclear power plant, located on the Gulf of Mexico at Laguna Verde in the state of Veracruz. Environmentalists expressed concern about the safety of the $3.5-billion plant and protested the government's decision.

Solar energy. Chronar Incorporated of Trenton, N.J., on September 8 announced plans to build the world's largest photovoltaic station for converting sunlight directly into electricity. The $125-million facility, to be located in the California desert about 60 miles (100 kilometers) east of Los Angeles, would use solar cells to produce 50 megawatts of electricity, enough to supply about 25,000 homes. Chronar officials said the plant would be seven times larger than any similar existing facility.

Compressed air. Construction began on October 28 on the first full-scale compressed-air energy-storage plant in the United States. When completed in 1991, the $65-million plant will use electricity generated at night, when demand is low, to compress air into underground caverns about 1,500 feet (460 meters) deep. During the day, when demand for

electricity increases, the air will be heated and released, spinning a turbine and generating electricity.

The Alabama Electric Cooperative is building the plant in McIntosh, about 40 miles (64 kilometers) north of Mobile, Ala., with help from the Electric Power Research Institute (EPRI) of Palo Alto, Calif. EPRI, the research and development arm of the electric utility industry, said that compressed-air energy-storage plants could have wide application throughout the United States.

Wind energy farms. Great Britain on March 23 announced plans to build its first *wind energy farms*, complexes of wind turbines that will supply electricity for about 15,000 people. W. Michael H. Spicer, Great Britain's undersecretary of state for energy, said three wind energy farms would be built by 1992. Each farm will have 25 *wind turbines*, or high-technology windmills. Spicer said wind energy eventually could contribute up to 20 per cent of Great Britain's electricity supply.

Blackout in Quebec. A severe ice storm on April 18 damaged an electrical substation of Hydro-Québec, the provincially owned utility. The damage cut off electricity to about 85 per cent of the Canadian province. The utility was unable to begin restoring power until the following day.   Michael Woods

In *World Book*, see **Energy supply.**
Engineering. See **Building and construction.**
England. See **Great Britain.**

Environmental pollution. Scientists found increasing evidence in 1988 that the pollutants unleashed by human activities may be seriously altering the earth's environment.

Greenhouse effect. The devastating droughts that afflicted the United States and China in the summer of 1988 may be among the first signs that pollution levels in the atmosphere are becoming high enough to initiate a global climatic warming, according to James E. Hansen, a climate expert with the National Aeronautics and Space Administration (NASA). Hansen testified before the U.S. Senate in June. Although many other scientists dispute the idea that the summer's record high temperatures were linked to present pollution levels, most agree that such a climate change is likely if atmospheric pollution continues to increase at the current rate.

Because of their ability to trap infrared radiation, certain gases—such as the carbon dioxide (CO_2) emitted by burning coal, oil, and natural gas—are known as "greenhouse" gases. Like the glass windows in a greenhouse, these gases let sunlight through to warm the earth but absorb much of the heat that is radiated from the earth's surface, thus warming the atmosphere. When atmospheric levels of these pollutants are high, the greenhouse gases trap even more heat and can raise the temperature of the entire planet. This "greenhouse effect" could dramatically alter the world's climate—possibly melting the polar icecaps, which could raise the sea level enough to flood coastal cities around the world.

On October 31, an international treaty was signed that would limit nations' future emissions of another greenhouse gas, nitrogen oxides, to their 1987 emission levels. Nitrogen oxides, formed by the combustion of fuels, can also cause acid rain and smog. By year-end, the treaty had been ratified by only 1 of the 16 nations required—the United States.

The ozone hole. The annual thinning of the stratospheric ozone layer above Antarctica appeared as expected in August 1988. But for the first time since this "ozone hole" was first reported in 1985, the thinning was far less severe than scientists had expected. The greatest loss was a 15 per cent depletion—far less than the 50 per cent thinning in 1987.

The NASA scientists in Greenbelt, Md., who first reported the 1988 ozone levels suspected that unusual weather patterns may have been responsible for the change. Typically, rotating polar winds confine ozone-destroying pollutants to an area above Antarctica. The pollutants and the ozone then undergo complex chemical reactions that result in a loss of ozone. Atypical weather patterns in 1988 may have prevented the rotating winds from confining the pollutants long enough to cause much breakdown of ozone. Scientists predict that in 1989 the wind pattern will return to normal and the ozone layer will again thin greatly.

The breakdown of atmospheric ozone is not limited to the skies above Antarctica, however. In May 1988, scientists with the National Oceanic and Atmospheric Administration reported the first clear evidence that similar ozone-destroying reactions were occurring over the North Pole, though to a far lesser degree than in the Antarctic. Between January and March, three groups of scientists, including an international panel of more than 100 experts, also reported finding a thinning of the ozone layer throughout the Northern Hemisphere's middle-latitude skies.

Because thinning of stratospheric ozone can subject plants and animals to potentially harmful levels of solar ultraviolet radiation, in September 1987 24 nations signed a treaty, known as the Montreal Protocol, agreeing to cut in half the production of the chemicals posing the greatest threat to the ozone layer. By the end of 1988, 30 nations (including the United States) had ratified the treaty—enough to permit its enactment on Jan.1, 1989.

But in September, the U.S. Environmental Protection Agency (EPA) announced that the results of a new analysis indicated that the ozone-damaging effects of chlorofluorocarbons (CFC's)—used as refrigerants and spray propellants—and related chemicals are worse than scientists envisioned when the treaty was written. As a result, on September 26, EPA Administrator Lee M. Thomas proposed revising the treaty to call for a ban on the production of CFC's and other chemicals that destroy ozone.

Radon levels worrisome. On September 12, the EPA announced that a seven-state survey of indoor radon levels had found worrisome amounts of this naturally occurring radioactive gas in at least 1 out of every 3 homes tested. Radon—which can enter a building by seeping out of soils, building materials, or water—has been linked to increased risk of lung cancer. The EPA survey found especially high levels in North Dakota, where geologic conditions created a radon "hot spot" that is potentially as serious as that of Pennsylvania's Reading Prong area, where 60 per cent of the 22,000 houses tested in 1986 were found to have radon levels above the EPA's recommended maximum.

The EPA recommended that individuals consider taking corrective action to limit the seepage of radon into their homes if tests show indoor radon concentrations at or above 4 picocuries per liter (110 picocuries per cubic foot) of air. (A picocurie is one-trillionth of a curie, a unit used to measure radioactivity.) According to Richard J. Guimond, director of the EPA's radiation programs, this level of exposure to radon poses about the same risk of lung cancer as smoking half a pack of cigarettes daily or receiving 100 to 200 chest X rays annually.

In a 1987 survey of 10 other states, the EPA found potentially hazardous levels of radon in 1 out of every 5 homes surveyed. Taken together, the two surveys indicate that radon constitutes a major national health risk, according to Assistant Surgeon General of the United States Vernon N. Houk. On Sept. 12, 1988,

Environmental pollution

Workers try to contain a diesel-fuel spill on the Monongahela River near Pittsburgh, Pa., after the collapse of a fuel tank in January.

Houk issued a "national radon health advisory," recommending that all U.S. homes be tested for radon and that action be taken if potentially dangerous levels are found.

Acid rain effects. An April 1988 study by the Environmental Defense Fund (EDF), a public-interest group based in New York City, found that nitrates—a little-studied component of acid rain—could have deadly effects on East Coast waters such as Chesapeake Bay. Nitrates contain nitrogen, which in large amounts can cause an overgrowth of algae and other small aquatic plants. These "algal blooms" quickly consume much of the available oxygen in the water, suffocating other aquatic life.

Using government data, EDF scientists showed that acid rain causes at least one-fourth of the nitrogen pollution in Chesapeake Bay and other East Coast waters. Algal blooms are a serious problem that will become more widespread as long as acid rain continues to dump large quantities of nitrogen into these waters, according to the EDF scientists.

Medical waste became a concern in 1988 when paraphernalia such as hypodermic syringes and vials of blood washed ashore on U.S. beaches. More than 2 million short tons (1.8 million metric tons) of infectious medical wastes are generated in the United States each year. "Yet there are no federal regulations governing the disposal of this dangerous refuse," noted Representative Thomas A. Luken (D., Ohio) at an August 31 hearing held in Cleveland to investigate illegal waste dumping.

Because disposal of toxic substances can be expensive, many waste handlers illegally dump the garbage, often in open waters. A bill signed into law by President Ronald Reagan on November 2 set up an experimental program in New York, New Jersey, Connecticut, and states along the Great Lakes requiring medical-waste generators to certify that waste is disposed of properly. If any waste fails to arrive at its approved destination, Environmental Protection Agency headquarters must be notified and a criminal investigation begun.

Asbestos hazard. The EPA reported on February 29 that an estimated 20 per cent of the offices, industrial facilities, and apartment buildings in the United States contain asbestos, a group of fiberlike minerals once used as insulation. In 43 per cent of the buildings in which asbestos insulation was found, it was damaged and likely to shed fibers into the air. Those fibers could be inhaled, causing lung problems, including cancer. Because the asbestos was typically found in insulating wraps around boilers or pipes, the EPA said that few people—with the exception of maintenance workers—would be exposed to dangerous levels of the substance.   Janet Raloff

See also **Conservation; Ocean.** In the Special Reports section, see **Our Vanishing Rain Forests.** In *World Book,* see **Environmental pollution.**
Equatorial Guinea. See **Africa.**

Ethiopia. The government of President Mengistu Haile-Mariam, while remaining committed to military rule and a socialist economy, adopted new agricultural policies in February 1988. The regime removed some of the controls on farmers, began paying higher crop prices, distributed improved seeds and fertilizers, and introduced new programs for soil and water conservation.

Famine relief. The United Nations (UN) estimated in June that approximately 7 million of Ethiopia's more than 47 million people were dependent on foreign food aid in 1988. From October 1987 to March 1988, Western donors gave or pledged 1.2 million short tons (1 million metric tons) of food to Ethiopia.

Among those donors was the Soviet Union, which pledged 250,000 short tons (227,000 metric tons) of wheat. Although the Soviet Union is Ethiopia's ally and has supplied the Mengistu regime with $4 billion worth of arms since 1978, the promised wheat shipments were the first Soviet emergency food assistance.

Civil war. The Ethiopian regions of Eritrea and Tigre, which for more than two decades have been fighting for their independence, continued to be torn by conflict in 1988. Early in the year, the Eritrean People's Liberation Front and the Tigrean People's Liberation Front won dramatic victories against government troops. But a midyear counteroffensive by Mengistu's troops—with massive support from the Soviet Union—reversed most of the rebel gains.

A peace pact Ethiopia signed in April with neighboring Somalia, a long-time foe, helped turn the tide in the civil war. Because the treaty called for both countries to withdraw troops from their common border, the Ethiopian government had thousands of additional soldiers to throw against the rebels.

Waging war was a higher priority for the government during the year than famine relief. On April 6, the government ordered the foreign staffs of more than 45 international relief agencies to leave Eritrea and Tigre, despite the fact that those were the areas of greatest famine. The United States Department of State, UN agencies, and others charged that the Mengistu regime wanted a free hand—that is, no witnesses—to crush the rebellions and that it was using starvation as a weapon. Mengistu argued that Ethiopia had enough trucks, food, and trained relief workers, so foreigners were no longer needed.

As a result of the government's decree, an estimated 2 million famine victims in the rebel areas were cut off from food supplies. After negotiations, a few UN relief workers were allowed to remain.

Some food aid was smuggled into rebel areas from Sudan, Ethiopia's neighbor to the west. Relations between the two nations were strained. Each accused the other of backing rebels to undermine its government. J. Gus Liebenow and Beverly B. Liebenow

See also **Africa** (Facts in brief table). In *World Book*, see **Ethiopia.**

Starving Ethiopians wait for food at an aid-distribution center in Wik'ro in March as the African country is once again hit by drought and famine.

Europe. The European Community (EC or Common Market) cleared the way in 1988 for the elimination of all tariffs and other trade barriers between its 12 member nations by 1992. At summit meetings in February and June, EC leaders resolved long-standing crises that had threatened the open-market plan—a disagreement over the EC budget and a dispute concerning EC agricultural policies.

With these crises resolved, the three strongest EC powers—Great Britain, West Germany, and France—argued about such matters as tax adjustments and the establishment of a single currency for the EC. Strong opposition built up in Great Britain to the concept of the federalization of the EC to transform the community into a "United States of Europe." (The other EC nations are Belgium, Denmark, Greece, Ireland, Italy, Luxembourg, the Netherlands, Portugal, and Spain.)

Prediction of prosperity. The European Commission, the EC's executive branch, claimed that the opening of the EC market would save the EC almost $300-billion by sweeping away restrictions that keep prices high and economic growth low. The commission predicted that, over five to six years, consumer prices would fall by 6 per cent while *gross domestic product* would rise by 4.5 per cent. (Gross domestic product is the total value of the goods produced and services performed within the borders of a nation or a group of nations.) The commission said also that unemploy-

ment in the EC nations would drop by 2 million over the same period.

Toward 1992. The European Commission in 1988 introduced 90 per cent of the proposals required to meet the 1992 target date. In 1988, the EC abolished haulage quotas that a member country could impose on trucks registered in other member countries, ended restrictions on the free flow of capital across frontiers, and changed immigration laws to permit highly skilled individuals to move around the EC at will.

First summit. The leaders of the EC nations, meeting from February 11 to 13 in Brussels, Belgium, had a stormy discussion but finally compromised on the budget and the Common Agricultural Policy, which fixes production targets and price supports. They scheduled the budget to rise from $51.7 billion in 1988 to $62.7 billion in 1992. The extra money is to come from each country's *value-added tax* (VAT, a kind of sales tax) and from payments based on each country's *gross national product* (total output of goods and services by facilities owned by a country's citizens, even if the facilities are in another country).

The EC leaders established limits on the quantities of cereal grains—such as wheat and oats—and oil-seeds—such as peanuts and soybeans—that the EC plans to subsidize fully during the next four years. The EC expected these limits to reduce substantially the meat and butter "mountains" and wine "lakes" that resulted from previous overproduction. The EC leaders

Greece's Prime Minister Andreas Papandreou, right, welcomes Turgut Ozal —the first Turkish premier to visit Greece in 16 years—to Athens in June.

Facts in brief on European countries

Country	Population	Government	Monetary unit*	Exports†	Foreign trade (million U.S.$) Imports†
Albania	3,317,000	Communist Party First Secretary and People's Assembly Presidium Chairman Ramiz Alia; Prime Minister Adil Çarçani	lek (5.5 = $1)	428	363
Andorra	51,000	The bishop of Urgel, Spain, and the president of France	French franc & Spanish peseta	no statistics available	
Austria	7,555,000	President Kurt Waldheim; Chancellor Franz Vranitzky	schilling (12.2 = $1)	22,500	26,800
Belgium	9,897,000	King Baudouin I; Prime Minister Wilfried A. E. Martens	franc (36.2 = $1)	68,600 (includes Luxembourg)	68,000
Bulgaria	8,977,000	Communist Party General Secretary & State Council Chairman Todor Zhivkov; Prime Minister Georgi Atanasov	lev (5.1 = $1)	14,500	15,300
Czechoslovakia	15,774,000	Communist Party General Secretary Miloš Jakeš; President Gustáv Husák; Prime Minister Ladislav Adamec	koruna (40 = $1)	21,900	21,970
Denmark	5,121,000	Queen Margrethe II; Prime Minister Poul Schlüter	krone (6.6 = $1)	21,300	22,900
Finland	4,953,000	President Mauno Koivisto; Prime Minister Harri Holkeri	markka (4.0 = $1)	16,360	15,330
France	55,813,000	President François Mitterrand; Prime Minister Michel Rocard	franc (5.9 = $1)	124,900	129,400
Germany, East	16,736,000	Communist Party Secretary-General & State Council Chairman Erich Honecker; Prime Minister Willi Stoph	mark (1.7 = $1)	27,900	27,600
Germany, West	60,421,000	President Richard von Weizsäcker; Chancellor Helmut Kohl	mark (1.7 = $1)	243,000	191,000
Great Britain	56,658,000	Queen Elizabeth II; Prime Minister Margaret Thatcher	pound (0.54 = $1)	107,000	126,000
Greece	10,044,000	President Christos Sartzetakis; Prime Minister Andreas Papandreou	drachma (144 = $1)	5,600	10,100
Hungary	10,664,000	Hungarian Socialist Workers' Party General Secretary Károly Grósz; Prime Minister Miklós Németh; President János Kádár	forint (62.5 = $1)	15,400	15,800
Iceland	252,000	President Vigdís Finnbogadóttir; Prime Minister Steingrimur Hermannsson	krona (47.6 = $1)	1,096	1,115
Ireland	3,601,000	President Patrick J. Hillery; Prime Minister Charles Haughey	pound (punt) (0.64 = $1)	12,600	11,600
Italy	57,489,000	President Francesco Cossiga; Prime Minister Ciriaco De Mita	lira (1,278 = $1)	97,800	99,400
Liechtenstein	29,000	Prince Franz Josef II; Prime Minister Hans Brunhart	Swiss franc	no statistics available	
Luxembourg	369,000	Grand Duke Jean; Prime Minister Jacques Santer	franc (40 = $1)	68,600 (includes Belgium)	68,000
Malta	354,000	Acting President Paul Xuereb; Prime Minister Edward Fenech Adami	lira (0.32 = $1)	527	943
Monaco	29,000	Prince Rainier III	French franc	no statistics available	
Netherlands	14,703,000	Queen Beatrix; Prime Minister Ruud Lubbers	guilder (1.95 = $1)	80,500	75,600
Norway	4,171,000	King Olav V; Prime Minister Gro Harlem Brundtland	krone (6.48 = $1)	18,200	20,300
Poland	38,269,000	Communist Party First Secretary & President Wojciech Jaruzelski; Council of Ministers Chairman Mieczyslaw Rakowski	zloty (1,000 = $1)	21,700	21,200
Portugal	10,474,000	President Mário Soares; Prime Minister Aníbal Cavaço Silva	escudo (143 = $1)	7,200	9,600
Romania	23,155,000	Communist Party General Secretary & President Nicolae Ceaușescu; Prime Minister Constantin Dăscălescu	leu (8.6 = $1)	12,500	10,600
San Marino	23,000	2 captains regent appointed by Grand Council every 6 months	Italian lira	no statistics available	
Spain	39,499,000	King Juan Carlos I; President Felipe González Márquez	peseta (113 = $1)	27,200	35,100
Sweden	8,371,000	King Carl XVI Gustaf; Prime Minister Ingvar Carlsson	krona (6.0 = $1)	37,300	32,700
Switzerland	6,485,000	President Otto Stich‡	franc (1.45 = $1)	37,500	41,000
Turkey	55,377,000	President Kenan Evren; Prime Minister Turgut Ozal	lira (1,762 = $1)	8,000	11,000
Union of Soviet Socialist Republics	289,280,000	Communist Party General Secretary & Supreme Soviet Presidium Chairman Mikhail S. Gorbachev; Council of Ministers Chairman Nikolai I. Ryzhkov	ruble (0.59 = $1)	97,053	88,874
Yugoslavia	23,752,000	President of the Presidency Raif Dizdarević; Federal Executive Council President Branko Mikulić	dinar (4,095 = $1)	10,400	11,800

*Exchange rates as of Dec. 1, 1988, or latest available data (source: Deak International). †Latest available data.
‡Stich will be succeeded on Jan. 1, 1989, by Jean-Pascal Delamuraz.

also agreed to increase funding for regional development, urban renewal, and job-creation programs in the EC's poorest areas.

At the second summit, held on June 27 and 28 in Hannover, West Germany, Great Britain's Prime Minister Margaret Thatcher said that the EC was moving too quickly. Thatcher declared that Britain would not accept two major changes—a standardization of VAT's in the 12 EC countries, and a dismantling of border controls. She had already told the British Parliament that a VAT on fuel, children's clothing, and shoes would be imposed only "over my dead body."

A lifting of border controls would end the system of checking individuals and their belongings at points of entry from one member nation to another. Border checks make it more difficult for terrorists to travel and often turn up illegal items such as drugs and diseased animals.

Another point of disagreement was a plan to replace the 12 nations' currencies with a single EC currency. Thatcher declared after the summit meeting, "I do not share the dream of a United States of Europe with a single currency."

Britain has always refused to join the European Monetary System (EMS), founded in 1979 to stabilize currency exchange rates. President François Mitterrand of France said, however, that the countries favoring the establishment of a Central European Bank to handle the single currency were in a position to "pull the others along." (All the EC nations except Britain, Greece, Portugal, and Spain are in the EMS.)

Tax proposals. Great Britain was not the only EC nation that had doubts about some of the open-market plans. Denmark, Ireland, and Italy would have to cut individual and corporate income taxes sharply to bring them into line with the rest of the EC. By contrast, Portugal, Spain, and Luxembourg would have to increase direct taxes.

A standardization of *excise taxes* (charges levied on the manufacture, sale, or use of various items) would force certain nations to make drastic adjustments. Britain, for example, would have to reduce taxes on cigarettes and alcohol by 50 per cent. But Italy, France, Spain, and Greece would face huge increases in these excise taxes.

Shocking prediction. Jacques Delors, who was reelected president of the EC Commission on June 28, shocked many members of the European Parliament—the EC's legislative branch—on July 6 with his predictions on that Parliament's future role. The European Parliament currently has a largely advisory role. Delors told that body, however, that the present system of national parliaments would have to give way to the "embryo" of a European government within seven years. The European Parliament would gain powers, he said, almost equivalent to those now exercised by national parliaments. And within 10 years, 80 per cent of social, economic, and financial legislation would be of European rather than national origin.

Pact with COMECON. The EC on June 25 signed a declaration of "mutual recognition" with the Council for Mutual Economic Assistance (COMECON), the Soviet-led trading bloc. The signing ended almost 30 years of hostility between the two organizations. Diplomats said that the declaration would accelerate talks between EC and COMECON nations concerning the establishment of diplomatic relations and the initiation or extension of trade and economic pacts.

COMECON's future to the year 2005 was the focus of that organization's 44th summit meeting, held in Prague, Czechoslovakia, on July 5, 1988. East Germany and Romania, which have rigid economies and hard-line internal policies, were lukewarm to any changes in COMECON policies. The two countries represent economic extremes. Romania's economy is the poorest in all Europe, while East Germany is the most prosperous nation in the Eastern bloc.

Ethnic conflict plagued Eastern Europe. In Yugoslavia, Serbs and Montenegrins protested against what they termed the mistreatment of ethnic Serbs and ethnic Montenegrins living in the province of Kosovo. Most residents of Kosovo are ethnic Albanians.

Hungary condemned Romania for launching a massive resettlement program in which some 7,000 Romanian villages would be demolished, with their residents moved to urban agricultural-industrial centers. About 2,000 of the villages are populated by ethnic Hungarians or ethnic Germans.

Ethnic conflict reached even the Soviet Union. Ethnic Armenians living in a region within the Azerbaijan Soviet Socialist Republic (S.S.R.), 1 of the 15 union republics that make up the Soviet Union, demanded that their region become a part of the neighboring Armenian S.S.R. And in the three formerly independent Baltic republics—the Estonian, Latvian, and Lithuanian S.S.R.'s—long-suppressed nationalist feelings surfaced at demonstrations and rallies.

A tremendous earthquake struck the Armenian S.S.R. on December 7, killing about 25,000 people. The quake destroyed at least two-thirds of the buildings in Leninakan, a city with a population of 220,000, and half the buildings in Kirovakan, a city of 162,000. Soviet leader Mikhail S. Gorbachev on December 8 cut short a visit to the United States, returning to the Soviet Union to deal with the disaster.

NATO challenge. The North Atlantic Treaty Organization (NATO), meeting in Brussels on March 2 and 3, established guidelines for "credible nuclear and conventional deterrence." Since 1987, when the United States and the Soviet Union agreed to eliminate intermediate-range nuclear missiles, NATO had been considering ways to strengthen its deterrent forces.

During the meeting—NATO's first summit since 1982—United States President Ronald Reagan said that NATO was now "ready to get down to business." The NATO leaders challenged Soviet leader Gorbachev to cut conventional forces in Europe and called for the modernization of nuclear weapons.

Soviet troops in February 1988 prepare to remove a nuclear missile from East Germany under the terms of a 1987 arms pact with the United States.

Lord Carrington of Great Britain ended his term as NATO's secretary-general. He was succeeded on July 1, 1988, by Manfred Wörner, formerly the defense minister of West Germany. (The members of NATO are Canada, Iceland, Norway, Turkey, and the United States, plus all the EC nations except Ireland.)

Country politics. France's President Mitterrand was reelected on May 8, defeating conservative Prime Minister Jacques Chirac. Mitterrand appointed Michel Rocard, a Socialist, as prime minister. A general election on June 5 and 12 failed, however, to establish a Socialist majority in Parliament. See **Rocard, Michel.**

Denmark faced a government crisis over its policy of forbidding ships armed with nuclear weapons to enter Danish waters. An election held on May 10 failed to resolve the crisis. Prime Minister Poul Schlüter finally built a new minority government around a compromise deal allowing Western warships into Danish waters without their having to divulge whether they are carrying nuclear arms.

Prime Minister Wilfried A. E. Martens of Belgium ended five months of political chaos by forming a coalition that took office on May 9. The coalition depended upon a shaky compromise between Belgium's two major ethnic groups—the Dutch-speaking Flemings, who live in the north, and the French-speaking Walloons, who live in the south.

Italy's 47th government since the end of World War II in 1945 resigned on March 11, 1988, because the two major partners in the ruling coalition disagreed about how to finish a partially built nuclear power plant. The Christian Democrats wanted to complete it as a nuclear facility, while the Socialists favored installing coal-burning equipment. Ciriaco De Mita, a Christian Democrat, yielded to the Socialists and put together a new coalition. De Mita was sworn in as prime minister on April 13. See **De Mita, Ciriaco.**

Terrorist attacks. Britain's struggle against the Provisional Irish Republican Army (IRA), the military arm of the Sinn Féin party in Northern Ireland, spilled over to West Germany on August 5 when IRA bombers blasted part of a British Army barracks in Düsseldorf. The blast injured three servicemen and a German civilian. The IRA struck again on August 13, when it murdered a furloughed British soldier in his car in Ostend, Belgium.

Masked gunmen attacked a tourist ferryboat off Greece on July 11. Nine people died, and another 80 were injured. Authorities in Greece linked the attack to attempts to gain the release of a suspected Palestinian terrorist held by Greece.

On December 21, a Pan Am World Airways jumbo jet exploded in midair over Lockerbie, Scotland, killing all 259 people aboard and at least 11 on the ground. British investigators determined that a terrorist bomb caused the explosion

Disasters. The worst disaster in the history of drilling for oil beneath the North Sea occurred on July 6,

Explosion

when explosions rocked the Piper Alpha rig, owned by Occidental Petroleum Corporation, a United States firm. The accident killed 167 people.

The explosions, triggered by a build-up of gas, produced flames that were visible almost 60 miles (100 kilometers) away. The shutdown of the rig cut North Sea oil production by about 15 per cent. Lost production of oil and gas cost Occidental $5 million a day.

Three Italian air force jets collided and fell flaming to earth on August 28, during an air show at the U.S. air base at Ramstein, West Germany. Thirty-four people died on the spot, and more than 350 others were injured. By year-end, the death toll had risen to 70.

The worst railway accident in the history of Paris occurred on June 27, when two commuter trains collided. Fifty-six people died as a result of the collision.

Favorable report. The Organization for Economic Cooperation and Development (OECD), an association of 24 nations, reported on May 19 that economic expansion in all OECD countries was entering its sixth year. The average inflation rate among OECD members had declined, and international cooperation had been strengthened largely through greater coordination of economic policies and efforts to stabilize currency exchange rates.   Kenneth Brown

See also the various European country articles. In the Special Reports section, see **The Two Germanys.** In *World Book*, see **Europe.**

Explosion. See **Disasters.**

Farm and farming. The worst drought in recorded weather history in the United States scorched crops in most key farming regions during the early part of the 1988 growing season. For the entire season, the drought was the fourth worst in history. Barges moving grain backed up for miles as the Mississippi River fell to the lowest levels ever recorded. Congress and the Administration of President Ronald Reagan responded with a $3.9-billion drought-relief measure to compensate farmers for lost and damaged crops. This compensation, along with higher crop prices as a consequence of the drought, eased the financial impact on farmers. Despite the drought, the recovery that began in 1987 from the farm economic crisis of the early 1980's continued in 1988. Net farm income was a relatively strong $38 billion to $40 billion, down about 15 per cent from a 1987 record of $46 billion.

Drought slashed the 1988 U.S. harvest of corn—the nation's major crop used for livestock feed, industrial products, and human food. The harvest was 4.67 billion bushels, down 34 per cent from 1987.

Winter wheat harvested in early summer escaped much damage. But other crops worsened each week as rain fell infrequently or not at all.

The entire wheat harvest was down 14 per cent, but the spring wheat crop fell 54 per cent, and spring-planted durum wheat, used to make pasta, fell 50 per cent. Oat production declined 44 per cent to become the smallest harvest in history. Soybean production

fell 21 per cent, and the grain sorghum harvest declined 26 per cent.

By contrast, cotton production rose 3 per cent; peanuts, 14 per cent; and rice, 24 per cent. Beef production dropped less than 1 per cent, pork production jumped 9 per cent, and poultry output rose 4 per cent.

Farmers with crops that escaped serious drought damage and those who had built up inventories from past years benefited from higher crop prices later in the year. Subsidies, drought relief, and federally subsidized crop insurance (optional for farmers) helped cushion the impact of the drought. The Department of Agriculture estimated that about 15,000 commercial farms were hard-hit financially by the lack of rain.

Drought relief. As the drought parched pastures in late spring and early summer of 1988, the federal government allowed livestock producers to use acreage that had been idled under the annual farm program for grazing animals and harvesting hay. To keep animals alive, producers were permitted to cut hay from land idled under the 10-year conservation reserve. The Agriculture Department also subsidized feed purchases for some livestock producers.

By early July, Secretary of Agriculture Richard E. Lyng, along with Democratic and Republican congressional leaders, agreed to work jointly on a drought-relief package. To avoid making the drought an issue in the November 8 presidential election, the two political parties cooperated with unusual speed to complete action on the legislation by August 9.

With more than 100 farmers assembled in the Rose Garden of the White House, President Reagan signed the $3.9-billion bill into law on August 11. After the Agriculture Department established regulations to carry out the law, the department's county offices began accepting applications for relief on October 1.

The law permitted grain and cotton farmers to keep advance subsidies to cover losses of up to 35 per cent. Unlike most past drought relief, which was limited to grain and cotton, the 1988 law offered compensation for all crops. For losses between 35 and 75 per cent, farmers received 65 per cent of their expected predrought income. They received 90 per cent of predrought income for losses greater than 75 per cent.

Congress also streamlined existing livestock assistance. This enabled farmers who grow crops for livestock to more readily receive federal reimbursement for feed purchases or to buy government-owned feed at a discount.

World supplies. The drought produced the steepest one-year decline in the world's grain stocks ever recorded. Due to drought in the United States, world corn production fell 14 per cent and world soybean production fell 9 per cent. Drought also trimmed crops in Canada, contributing to a 1 per cent decline in world wheat production. Rice production rose 4 per cent, and cotton climbed 5 per cent.

Global beef production fell 1 per cent, pork rose 4 per cent, and poultry increased 3 per cent.

A farmer near Amsterdam, N.Y., stirs up a cloud of dust in a field parched
by the drought that plagued much of the United States during the summer.

Climate speculation. The 1988 drought was the
worst on record for the early months of the growing
season since modern weather records were first kept
in the late 1800's. For the entire summer, only three
previous droughts—in 1934, 1936, and 1954—were
worse than that of 1988. Serious drought also hit at
least part of the nation's crops in 1980, 1983, and
1986.

The drought of 1988 highlighted concerns about
the *greenhouse effect*, a global warming caused by a
build-up in the atmosphere of certain gases, particularly carbon dioxide produced by the burning of oil
and coal. The gases prevent solar energy from being
radiated back away from the earth, thus raising the
temperature of the atmosphere. Some scientists,
however, said the 1988 drought was due to cyclical
weather patterns and not directly attributable to the
greenhouse effect.

As examples of these cyclical patterns, Norton
Strommen, the Agriculture Department's chief mete-
orologist, cited a warming trend that began in the
late 1800's, a cooling period in the early 1970's, and
the current warming that began in the late 1970's.

Farm Credit System. On January 6, President
Reagan signed into law a bill passed by Congress in
December 1987 that committed the federal government to back the sale of bonds designed to infuse up
to $4 billion into the Farm Credit System. This feder-
ally regulated, farmer-owned network of banks had

lost billions of dollars due to declining land values in
the mid-1980's and to farm failures.

An agency established by the law, the Federal Agricultural Mortgage Corporation, distributed funds to
Farm Credit System banks in 1988. But on May 20, it
also forced the liquidation of the Federal Land Bank
of Jackson, Miss., one of the system's 12 regional
banks that lend money to farmers for the purchase of
real estate. Farm credit officials determined that a
cash infusion could not save the bank.

The farm credit law also provided for the restructuring of farmers' loans made by Farm Credit System
banks and by the Farmers Home Administration, an
agency of the Agriculture Department that lends
money to farmers who cannot get credit elsewhere.

In November, the lending agency mailed out about
80,000 notices to farmers who were behind on repaying their loans. The letters gave farmers options for
renegotiating past-due debt and interest. Officials
predicted, however, that more than one-third of the
farmers who had suffered losses in the farm crisis of
the early 1980's had no option left but foreclosure.

Although grain and cotton farmers remained dependent on government subsidies to supplement their
income in 1988, federal expenditures for farm programs declined to $13.1 billion in fiscal 1988. This was
half of a $25.8-billion record set in 1986.

Farmland prices. The national average price of
1 acre (0.4 hectare) of farmland rose to $564 in 1988,

Agricultural statistics, 1988

World crop production
(million units)

Crop	Units	1987-1988*	1988-1989*†	% U.S. 1988-1989
Coarse grains‡	Metric tons	790	713	20
Corn	Metric tons	445	386	31
Wheat	Metric tons	504	503	10
Rice (rough)	Metric tons	453	471	2
Barley	Metric tons	181	166	4
Soybeans	Metric tons	103	94	44
Cotton	Bales§	80	84	18
Coffee	Bags#	103	93	0.2
Sugar (centrifugal)	Metric tons	104	107	6

*Crop year.   †Preliminary.
‡Corn, barley, sorghum, rye, oats, millet, and mixed grains.
§480 pounds (217.7 kilograms) net.
#132.3 pounds (60 kilograms).

Output of major U.S. crops
(millions of bushels)

Crop	1987-1988*	1988-1989*†
Corn	7,064	4,671
Sorghum	741	546
Wheat	2,107	1,812
Soybeans	1,923	1,512
Rice (rough)‡	128	158
Potatoes‡	385	352
Cotton§	14.8	15.3
Tobacco#	1,191	1,333

*Crop year.   †Preliminary.
‡1 million hundredweight (45.4 million kilograms).
§1 million bales (480 million pounds) (217.4 million kilograms).
#1 million pounds (454,000 kilograms).

U.S. production of animal products
(millions of pounds)

	1987-1988*	1988-1989*†
Beef	21,825	23,336
Pork	15,700	15,611
Total red meat‡	38,250	39,695
Eggs§	5,625	5,734
Turkey	4,050	3,933
Total milk#	1,458	1,453
Broilers	16,850	16,149

*Crop year.   †Preliminary.
‡Beef, pork, veal, lamb, and mutton.
§ 1 million dozens.
#100 millions of pounds (45.4 million kilograms).

up $16 an acre from 1987. It was the first increase in average land values since the average price rose to $832 in 1982 before tumbling for the next five years. Drought held down land prices for a few months in 1988, but upward momentum was renewed in the third quarter of the year.

The volume of exports of U.S. farm products rose for the second consecutive year in 1988. An increase in 1987 had been the first since 1980. The value of farm exports rose in 1988 by more than $7 billion to $35.2-billion.

Some agricultural exports, particularly wheat to the Soviet Union and China, were subsidized under a program established in 1985 to compete against subsidies offered by the European Community (EC or Com-

mon Market). The U.S. exporters also sold large quantities of unsubsidized corn and soybeans to the Soviet Union.

Soviet and U.S. negotiators, after eight months of talks, agreed on November 28 to extend a five-year grain trade agreement between the two countries until the end of 1990. The agreement required the Soviets to buy 9 million metric tons (10 million short tons) of U.S. grain a year.

Idled land. American farmers took more than 78 million acres (31.6 million hectares) of cropland out of production in 1988, surpassing a record set in 1983. The total area of idled land was almost as great as the total acreage of grain harvested in the 12 EC nations. More than two-thirds of the affected U.S. acreage was idled under the annual farm program that requires farmers to set aside land to qualify for federal subsidies. The remainder was highly erosion-prone land taken out of production for 10 years to reduce wind erosion or the runoff of soil into streams, lakes, and rivers.

Before drought struck, the Agriculture Department required wheat farmers to idle 27.5 per cent of their acreage to qualify for farm subsidies in 1988. Corn, grain sorghum, and barley farmers were required to set aside 20 per cent of their acreage to qualify for subsidies and were offered optional payments to idle another 10 per cent.

To replenish grain stocks reduced by drought, Agriculture Secretary Lyng asked farmers to bring millions of acres back into production in 1989. He asked them to idle only 10 per cent of wheat, corn, sorghum, and barley acreage to qualify for subsidies.

New secretary. On Dec. 14, 1988, President-elect George Bush designated U.S. Trade Representative Clayton K. Yeutter as his secretary of agriculture.

Genetic engineering. The world's first patent for a genetically engineered animal, a mouse, was issued on April 12 by the U.S. Patent and Trademark Office to Harvard Medical School in Boston. To make cancer research more efficient, scientists developed a strain of mice that were engineered to contract cancer more easily than the mice often used in research.

The patent decision opened a debate over whether scientists should be able to patent genetically engineered farm animals and thus collect money from sales of those animals. Bills were introduced in Congress to ban or restrict livestock patenting, but Congress took no final action.

The transfer of a foreign gene into a corn plant was announced in April by researchers at the Sandoz Crop Protection Corporation in Palo Alto, Calif. This marked the first time a gene had been successfully transplanted into a cereal crop plant. The technique developed may one day be used to insert genes that could provide corn plants with insect resistance or other desirable traits.   Sonja Hillgren

See also **Food; Weather.** In *World Book*, see **Agriculture; Farm and farming.**

Fashion. The short skirts, the poufs and ruffles, and the sense of exaggerated femininity that took the fashion industry by storm in 1987 gave way to a more sober look in 1988. By fall, clothes were slimmer, slicker, and less exaggerated. Colors took on classic hues, sparked with clear, sharp accents of red, blue, or violet. But although the look may have changed, the energy generated by 1987's wild excesses and youthful abandon remained.

The fall of the miniskirt. Choice became the byword of the fashion industry during 1988. More than ever before, women demanded a variety of clothes from which to choose. Although the world's top designers—including Christian Lacroix, Emanuel Ungaro, and Hubert de Givenchy—seemed to agree in 1987 that the new look was short, many women declined to bare their thighs. Exactly how many inches above the knee the hemline rose was determined by what a woman saw in her mirror, the shapeliness of her legs, and her attitude toward clothes. Many women chose conservative hemlines on the grounds that short skirts were inappropriate for the workplace.

Not surprisingly, the resistance to the miniskirt among working women caused a reaction in the fashion industry in 1988. Karl Lagerfeld was the first to respond. In his spring and summer Chanel couture collection, shown in Paris in January, he introduced a handful of suits with long, narrow skirts, which brought a note of stark elegance to the fashion free-for-all. Dramatically different in tone from the flamboyant styles that everyone—including Lagerfeld —had shown previously, the suits pointed to a new, calmer fashion direction. The following month, American designer Donna Karan showed a few summer dresses in black or navy cotton with hemlines ranging from just below the knee to midcalf.

By March, when the 1988 fall and winter collections were introduced, the change in hemline length appeared complete. Designers unveiled skirts and dresses with hemlines just above or just below the knee. Some designers took the downward direction started by Lagerfeld and Karan even farther by showing calf-length skirts, but the longer length did not dominate the fashion scene.

Sales stupor. During the 1988 spring selling season, fashion retailers in the United States and Europe complained about lagging sales. Some attributed the problem to the stock-market crash in October 1987, but others insisted business was slow because of the miniskirt. They said that many women, believing short skirts were just a fad, opted to buy nothing rather than invest in skirts and dresses that would quickly go out of style.

The return of trousers. The important new fashion event during 1988 was the reemergence of loose, flowing trousers, which had not been an important part of high fashion since the 1970's. Trousers received endorsements from such diverse designers as Calvin Klein and Giorgio Armani.

Long skirts with a fluid, elegant look replaced thigh-baring miniskirts in the 1988 fall collection of Italian designer Giorgio Armani.

Filmon, Gary Albert

Fashion leaders. Some reputations were enhanced by the upheaval of 1988. In Paris, Yves Saint Laurent regained his reputation as a fashion front-runner after what many observers considered to be a slump. His 1988 fall collection, unveiled in the spring, was hailed as one of his best.

Lacroix, the new star of French couture, made his mark on evening clothes. Short bubble-shaped skirts, which he inspired, were the rage, and their success focused new attention on custom-made evening styles, the most expensive branch of the fashion industry.

In Milan, Italy, Armani set the style for women's soft tailored suits. New York sportswear designers Donna Karan, Calvin Klein, Ralph Lauren, and Louis Dell'Olio for Anne Klein softened the look of their clothes. They also offered a larger variety of dressy fashions and evening wear.

Beene honored. During September and October, American designer Geoffrey Beene, who in 1988 celebrated his 25th anniversary in the business, was honored as a leading creator of fashion with a retrospective at the National Academy of Design in New York City. Beene's designs reflect influences from Japan; Vienna, Austria; and the 1920's. During the six-week retrospective, which opened on September 20, his clothes were displayed on mannequins as if they were works of art.   Bernadine Morris

In *World Book*, see **Clothing; Fashion.**

Filmon, Gary Albert (1942-   ), was sworn in as premier of the province of Manitoba, Canada, on May 9, 1988. As leader of Manitoba's Progressive Conservative (PC) Party, Filmon became head of a minority government; the conservatives held only 25 of the legislature's 57 seats. See **Manitoba.**

Filmon was born on Aug. 24, 1942, in Winnipeg, Man. He married Janice Wainwright in 1963 while studying engineering at the University of Manitoba, where he earned a bachelor's degree in 1964 and a master's degree in 1967. He worked as a consulting engineer before joining his father-in-law's Winnipeg business school, Success/Angus Business College, as an administrator in 1969. Filmon bought the college and became its president in 1971.

Filmon served on the Winnipeg City Council from 1975 through 1979. In October 1979, he was elected to the Manitoba Legislative Assembly from the district of Tuxedo. In January 1981, he was appointed to the Executive Council (cabinet) of Manitoba's Premier Sterling R. Lyon as minister of consumer and corporate affairs and environment. He was reelected to the provincial legislature in 1981 and 1986. In December 1983, Filmon, a moderate, was chosen to replace the right wing Lyon as leader of Manitoba's PC's.

In addition to serving as premier, Filmon is chairman of the Treasury Board and minister of federal-provincial relations. The Filmons live in Winnipeg and have four children.   Robin Goldman

Finland. Mauno Koivisto won a second six-year term as president in a national election on Jan. 31 and Feb. 1, 1988. He ran as the candidate of the Social Democratic Party and some smaller parties. Koivisto polled 47.9 per cent of the votes. Koivisto's good showing in the polls reflected the public's high regard for him as the "father" of Finland's present economic boom.

Paavo Väyrynen, leader of the opposition Center Party, surprised political observers by edging out Prime Minister Harri Holkeri, a member of the conservative National Coalition Party, for second place. Väyrynen won 20 per cent of the votes to Holkeri's 18 per cent.

Because Koivisto won less than 50 per cent of the votes, Finland's 301-member electoral college automatically received the authority to decide who would become president. This body, which is elected by the Finnish people, selected Koivisto on February 15.

Presidential powers questioned. After the election, Finnish politicians increased their support for removing some powers of the presidency. Koivisto has been reluctant to use certain of these powers and has indicated support for ending them. These powers include the authority to dissolve the Eduskunta (parliament), call elections, and form a new government. The president also has special responsibility for foreign policy.

Koivisto strongly prefers that the prime minister run the country, and he was deeply critical of how his predecessor, Urho Kekkonen, dissolved the Eduskunta in the 1970's. Furthermore, Koivisto believes that the president should serve no more than two terms. Kekkonen was president for 25 years.

Koivisto also wishes to preserve the broad-based coalition government that has become popular with the Finns. The Cabinet includes members of both the National Coalition and Social Democratic Parties.

Exports rise. Finland's exports grew in 1988, led by a 5 per cent hike in deliveries to Western countries. Exports to Communist countries continued to decline.

Deliveries to the Soviet Union dropped by 7 per cent because of Finland's need to balance its trade with the Soviets. Finland and the Soviet Union trade by barter, and the value of the bartered goods is supposed to balance. The value of Finland's shipments had exceeded that of the goods received from the Soviets, forcing the Finns to export less to the Soviet Union.

Production in Finland ran at 100 per cent of capacity throughout the year. Finland's output of goods increased by 4.5 per cent, reaching its highest level in the 1980's. Imports continued to grow in volume, but not in cost, largely because the price of crude oil dropped.   Kenneth Brown

See also **Europe** (Facts in brief table). In *World Book*, see **Finland.**

Fire. See **Disasters; Forest fires.**
Flood. See **Disasters.**
Florida. See **State government.**
Flower. See **Gardening.**

Food. The United States food industry fell on harder times in 1988 as a result of one of the most severe droughts in U.S. history. Grain production dropped sharply and pushed food prices up, though large stockpiles from past harvests blunted the drought's impact. By the end of the year, food prices were up 5.2 per cent, helping drive up the overall Consumer Price Index—the most widely used measure of inflation—by 4.4 per cent over 1987 levels.

Thanks to an expanding economy, however, the proportion of disposable income (spending money left over after taxes) that went for food continued to decline. Americans spent 14.3 per cent of their disposable income on food in 1988, compared with 16.7 per cent in 1987.

U.S. agriculture. The severe summer drought cut U.S. grain production to about 31 per cent below 1987 levels. Hard hit were corn (off 34 per cent) and soybeans (off 21 per cent). Wheat production fell 14 per cent overall; the winter wheat crop, harvested before the drought, remained at 1987 levels, but spring wheat declined 54 per cent. Large stockpiles of most crops, however, ensured adequate supplies for domestic and export needs. Analysts saw the reduction in stockpiles as potentially leading to a change in farm policy, allowing more acres to be planted in 1989.

World grain production fell for the second year in a row. The 4 per cent drop chiefly reflected poor North American harvests. Europe, the Soviet Union, and most of Asia had good harvests that led to a 2 per cent rise in foreign grain production.

World consumption of grains exceeded production, and grain stockpiles were the lowest in 40 years. Low production, high consumption, and inadequate distribution systems led to food shortages in parts of Africa. The number of seriously malnourished people worldwide grew as high as 600 million.

Grocery store sales rose 5.5 per cent over 1987, but in *real terms* (after allowing for inflation), the growth rate was only 1.2 per cent. Reversing a trend, more grocery stores opened than closed in 1988.

Remodeling of stores was common as retailers added new departments to satisfy consumer demands for one-stop shopping and specialty items. The size of a typical new store grew to 47,000 square feet (4,370 square meters). The European-style "hypermarket," a 200,000-square-foot (19,000-square-meter) combination department store and food store, gained a toehold in the market place.

Convenience and variety remained important to two-paycheck families and working singles. The line between grocery stores and take-out restaurants blurred, as grocery stores expanded their selections of ready-to-eat and prepared heat-and-serve foods. In response to consumer interest in nutrition information, many stores improved shelf labeling or offered informational publications.

Consumers continued to translate awareness of nutrition into food choices that were lower in fat,

Brian Duffy, © 1988, Des Moines Register and Tribune Company. Reprinted with permission.

sodium, and cholesterol. They chose leaner meats, more fish and poultry, low-fat dairy products, and a wider variety of fresh fruits and vegetables. At the same time, expensive gourmet foods—many loaded with calories and fat—remained popular.

Eating out accounted for nearly 41 per cent of money spent on food. Sales for all eating and drinking establishments soared to $213.5 billion—a 2.9 per cent increase in real terms. Menu prices crept up 4.2 per cent, slightly higher than 1987's 4.0 per cent. Diners opted for more nutritious foods and less alcohol. Ethnic foods, particularly Asian and Latin cuisines, remained popular.

Fast-food establishments continued to outpace other segments of the industry with sales of $60.4-billion, showing a 4.3 per cent increase in real terms. Pizza, spurred by home-delivery services, gained on hamburgers as the most-consumed fast food. Take-out services expanded beyond fast food into more traditional sectors, as restaurants competed with take-out services at grocery stores.

Food safety. In October, the U.S. Environmental Protection Agency announced changes in its rules on pesticide residues in food. Earlier regulations prohibited any contamination of processed foods by cancer-causing pesticides registered since 1972. The new rules use a weaker safety standard, but they apply to older pesticides as well as new ones and to raw products as well as processed foods.

Football

Fat as foe. In July, U.S. Surgeon General C. Everett Koop issued a report stating that dietary changes could improve the health of many Americans. Koop particularly disapproved of saturated fats, which have been linked to such leading causes of death as cancer, heart disease, and diabetes.

In August, Public Voice for Food and Health Policy, a consumer group based in Washington, D.C., criticized high levels of saturated fats in school lunches. The group recommended that the U.S. Department of Agriculture set limits on fat, sodium, and sugar in lunches served under its school-lunch program.

Amid general consumer concern over fat, two food companies raced to produce fat substitutes. In January, the NutraSweet Company unveiled plans to market Simplesse—a protein-based fat substitute—by mid-1989. Meanwhile, Procter & Gamble waited for its fat substitute, an artificial substance called Olestra, to wend its way through the Food and Drug Administration's approval system.

In May, however, researchers in Texas reported that one type of saturated fat, found in beef and chocolate, may not be as harmful as once thought. Scientists at the University of Texas Southwestern Medical Center in Dallas reported that the fat, called stearic acid, may actually help lower cholesterol levels in the blood.   Bob Gatty

See also **Farm and farming.** In *World Book*, see **Food; Food supply.**

Football. The major titles in 1988 football were won by the San Francisco 49ers of the National Football League (NFL), the Winnipeg Blue Bombers of the Canadian Football League (CFL), and the University of Notre Dame among colleges. Continued crackdowns on illegal recruiting and payments to college players marred the college season.

Pro. Through the player draft, schedule formats, and rules changes, the NFL had been trying for years to achieve parity among its 28 teams. In 1988, it succeeded to a large degree. There were no clearly dominant teams. There was, however, one relocated team: The St. Louis Cardinals moved to Phoenix.

In the National Football Conference, the division champions were the Chicago Bears (12-4), the San Francisco 49ers (10-6), and the Philadelphia Eagles (10-6). The teams that qualified for wild-card berths in the play-offs were the Minnesota Vikings (11-5) and the Los Angeles Rams (10-6).

The American Football Conference division champions were the Cincinnati Bengals (12-4), the Buffalo Bills (12-4), and the Seattle Seahawks (9-7). The wild-card teams were the Houston Oilers (10-6) and the Cleveland Browns (10-6).

As the regular season neared its end, many teams stayed in contention for play-off berths. On the last Sunday of the season, when the tie-breaking system was invoked, the New Orleans Saints and New York Giants were eliminated despite 10-6 records.

For the first time ever, the two teams that played in the previous Super Bowl failed to qualify for the play-offs. The Washington Redskins, who won Super Bowl XXII, finished the 1988 season at 7-9. The Denver Broncos, the Super Bowl losers, were 8-8.

The season was disastrous for several former power-houses. The Dallas Cowboys finished with a 3-13 record, last in their division. Also last were the Pittsburgh Steelers (5-11) and the Miami Dolphins (6-10).

Play-offs. The 1988-1989 play-offs began with the wild-card games on December 24 and 26. Houston upset Cleveland, 24-23, after a quick whistle had wiped out a Cleveland touchdown. Minnesota eliminated the Rams, 28-17.

The following weekend, in the National Conference play-offs, Chicago defeated Philadelphia, 20-12, in a game played in thick fog for the last 32 minutes. San Francisco routed Minnesota, 34-9, as quarterback Joe Montana threw three touchdown passes to wide receiver Jerry Rice in the first 16 minutes. In the American Conference play-offs, Cincinnati rushed for 254 yards (232 meters) in beating Seattle, 21-13, and Buffalo beat Houston, 17-10, and qualified for its first championship game in 22 years.

In the conference championship games on Jan. 8, 1989, San Francisco won the National Conference title, defeating Chicago, 28-3. Montana passed for three of the 49ers' four touchdowns, two of them to Rice. Montana completed 17 of 27 passes for 288 yards (263 meters). Bear quarterback Jim McMahon, in his first start since October 30, was 14 of 29 for 121 yards (111 meters) and threw one interception.

Cincinnati came back from a last-place finish in the 1987 season to win the American Conference championship, beating Buffalo 21-10. The Bengals rushed for 175 yards (160 meters), most of them by Elbert (Ickey) Woods, who scored two touchdowns.

That sent San Francisco and Cincinnati into Super Bowl XXIII on Jan. 22, 1989, in the new Joe Robbie Stadium in Miami, Fla. San Francisco won, 20-16, in a contest that NFL Commissioner Pete Rozelle called "the finest" of the 23 Super Bowls played. Although both teams were NFL leaders in offense, the game became a defensive struggle with the score tied on three occasions—3-3 at the half, 6-6, and 13-13. In the final minutes, Jim Breech kicked a 40-yard (37-meter) field goal to put the Bengals ahead, 16-13.

With only 3 minutes and 10 seconds remaining, Montana led the 49ers on a 92-yard (84-meter) drive. The winning touchdown came on a pass from Montana to John Taylor with 34 seconds remaining. Rice made 11 receptions for 215 yards (197 meters) and one touchdown, and was named Most Valuable Player. It was San Francisco coach Bill Walsh's third Super Bowl victory. On January 26, Walsh resigned and was succeeded by defensive coordinator George Seifert.

Other stars. It was a memorable year for coach Mike Ditka of Chicago. First, the former tight end was

National Football League final standings

American Conference

Eastern Division	W.	L.	T.	Pct.
Buffalo Bills	12	4	0	.750
Indianapolis Colts	9	7	0	.563
New England Patriots	9	7	0	.563
New York Jets	8	7	1	.531
Miami Dolphins	6	10	0	.375

Central Division				
Cincinnati Bengals	12	4	0	.750
Cleveland Browns	10	6	0	.625
Houston Oilers	10	6	0	.625
Pittsburgh Steelers	5	11	0	.313

Western Division				
Seattle Seahawks	9	7	0	.563
Denver Broncos	8	8	0	.500
Los Angeles Raiders	7	9	0	.438
San Diego Chargers	6	10	0	.375
Kansas City Chiefs	4	11	1	.281

National Conference

Eastern Division	W.	L.	T.	Pct.
Philadelphia Eagles	10	6	0	.625
New York Giants	10	6	0	.625
Washington Redskins	7	9	0	.438
Phoenix Cardinals	7	9	0	.438
Dallas Cowboys	3	13	0	.188

Central Division				
Chicago Bears	12	4	0	.750
Minnesota Vikings	11	5	0	.688
Tampa Bay Buccaneers	5	11	0	.313
Detroit Lions	4	12	0	.250
Green Bay Packers	4	12	0	.250

Western Division				
San Francisco 49ers	10	6	0	.625
Los Angeles Rams	10	6	0	.625
New Orleans Saints	10	6	0	.625
Atlanta Falcons	5	11	0	.313

Super Bowl champions—San Francisco 49ers (defeated Cincinnati Bengals, 20-16)

Individual statistics

Leading scorers, touchdowns	TD's	Rush	Rec.	Ret.	Pts.
Eric Dickerson, Indianapolis	15	14	1	0	90
Ickey Woods, Cincinnati	15	15	0	0	90
James Brooks, Cincinnati	14	8	6	0	84
Mark Clayton, Miami	14	0	14	0	84
Robb Riddick, Buffalo	14	12	1	1	84
Lorenzo Hampton, Miami	12	9	3	0	72
Curt Warner, Seattle	12	10	2	0	72
Mike Rozier, Houston	11	10	1	0	66

Leading scorers, kicking	PAT	FG	Longest	Pts.
Scott Norwood, Buffalo	33-33	32-37	49	129
Gary Anderson, Pittsburgh	34-35	28-36	52	118
Dean Biasucci, Indianapolis	39-40	25-32	53	114
Tony Zendejas, Houston	48-50	22-34	52	114
Pat Leahy, New York Jets	43-43	23-28	48	112
Norm Johnson, Seattle	39-39	22-28	47	105
Rich Karlis, Denver	36-37	23-36	51	105
Matt Bahr, Cleveland	32-33	24-29	47	104
Nick Lowery, Kansas City	23-23	27-32	51	104
Chris Bahr, L.A. Raiders	37-39	18-29	50	91

Leading quarterbacks	Att.	Comp.	Yards	TD's	Int.
Boomer Esiason, Cincinnati	388	223	3,572	28	14
Dave Krieg, Seattle	228	134	1,741	18	8
Warren Moon, Houston	294	160	2,327	17	8
Bernie Kosar, Cleveland	259	156	1,890	10	7
Dan Marino, Miami	606	354	4,434	28	23
Ken O'Brien, New York Jets	424	236	2,567	15	7
Jim Kelly, Buffalo	452	269	3,380	15	17
Steve DeBerg, Kansas City	414	224	2,935	16	16
John Elway, Denver	496	274	3,309	17	19

Leading receivers	Number caught	Total yards	Avg. gain	TD's
Al Toon, New York Jets	93	1,067	11.5	5
Mark Clayton, Miami	86	1,129	13.1	14
Drew Hill, Houston	72	1,141	15.8	10
Andre Reed, Buffalo	71	968	13.6	6
Mickey Shuler, New York Jets	70	805	11.5	5
Vance Johnson, Denver	68	896	13.2	5
Stephone Paige, Kansas City	61	902	14.8	7
Ernest Givins, Houston	60	976	16.3	5
Earnest Byner, Cleveland	59	576	9.8	2
Jim Jensen, Miami	58	652	11.2	5
John L. Williams, Seattle	58	651	11.2	3

Leading rushers	No.	Yards	Avg.	TD's
Eric Dickerson, Indianapolis	388	1,659	4.3	14
John Stephens, New England	297	1,168	3.9	4
Gary Anderson, San Diego	225	1,119	5.0	3
Ickey Woods, Cincinnati	203	1,066	5.3	15
Curt Warner, Seattle	266	1,025	3.9	10
Mike Rozier, Houston	251	1,002	4.0	10
Freeman McNeil, N.Y. Jets	219	944	4.3	6
James Brooks, Cincinnati	182	931	5.1	8
Thurman Thomas, Buffalo	207	881	4.3	2
John L. Williams, Seattle	189	877	4.6	4

Leading punters	No.	Yards	Avg.	Longest
Harry Newsome, Pittsburgh	65	2,950	45.4	62
Ralf Mojsiejenko, San Diego	85	3,745	44.1	62
Mike Horan, Denver	65	2,861	44.0	70
Rohn Stark, Indianapolis	64	2,784	43.5	65
Reggie Roby, Miami	64	2,754	43.0	64

Individual statistics

Leading scorers, touchdowns	TD's	Rush	Rec.	Ret.	Pts.
Greg Bell, L.A. Rams	18	16	2	0	108
Neal Anderson, Chicago	12	12	0	0	72
Ricky Sanders, Washington	12	0	12	0	72
Keith Byars, Philadelphia	10	6	4	0	60
Roger Craig, San Francisco	10	9	1	0	60
Henry Ellard, L. A. Rams	10	0	10	0	60
Jerry Rice, San Francisco	10	1	9	0	60

Leading scorers, kicking	PAT	FG	Longest	Pts.
Mike Cofer, San Francisco	40-41	27-38	52	121
Mike Lansford, L.A. Rams	45-48	24-32	49	117
Morten Andersen, New Orleans	32-33	26-36	51	110
Chuck Nelson, Minnesota	48-49	20-25	49	108
Chip Lohmiller, Washington	40-41	19-26	46	97
Luis Zendejas, Philadelphia	35-36	20-27	50	95
Kevin Butler, Chicago	37-38	15-19	45	82
Greg Davis, Atlanta	25-27	19-30	52	82
Eddie Murray, Detroit	22-23	20-21	48	82

Leading quarterbacks	Att.	Comp.	Yards	TD's	Int.
Wade Wilson, Minnesota	332	204	2,746	15	9
Jim Everett, L.A. Rams	517	308	3,964	31	18
Joe Montana, San Francisco	397	238	2,981	18	10
Neil Lomax, Phoenix	443	255	3,395	20	11
Phil Simms, N.Y. Giants	479	263	3,359	21	11
Bobby Hebert, New Orleans	478	280	3,156	20	15
Randall Cunningham, Philadelphia	560	301	3,808	24	16
Doug Williams, Washington	380	213	2,609	15	12
Steve Pelluer, Dallas	435	245	3,139	17	19

Leading receivers	Number caught	Total yards	Avg. gain	TD's
Henry Ellard, L.A. Rams	86	1,414	16.4	10
Eric Martin, New Orleans	85	1,083	12.7	7
J. T. Smith, Phoenix	83	986	11.9	5
Keith Jackson, Philadelphia	81	869	10.7	6
Roger Craig, San Francisco	76	534	7.0	1
Ricky Sanders, Washington	73	1,148	15.7	12
Anthony Carter, Minnesota	72	1,225	17.0	6
Art Monk, Washington	72	946	13.1	5
Keith Byars, Philadelphia	72	705	9.8	4

Leading rushers	No.	Yards	Avg.	TD's
Herschel Walker, Dallas	361	1,514	4.2	5
Roger Craig, San Francisco	310	1,502	4.8	9
Greg Bell, L.A. Rams	288	1,212	4.2	16
Neal Anderson, Chicago	249	1,106	4.4	12
Joe Morris, N.Y. Giants	307	1,083	3.5	5
John Settle, Atlanta	232	1,024	4.4	7
Earl Ferrell, Phoenix	202	924	4.6	7
Dalton Hilliard, New Orleans	204	823	4.0	5
Stump Mitchell, Phoenix	164	726	4.4	4
Rueben Mayes, New Orleans	170	628	3.7	3

Leading punters	No.	Yards	Avg.	Longest
Jim Arnold, Detroit	97	4,110	42.4	69
Bryan Wagner, Chicago	79	3,282	41.5	70
Maury Buford, N.Y. Giants	73	3,012	41.3	66
Mike Saxon, Dallas	80	3,271	40.9	55
Greg Horne, Phoenix	79	3,228	40.9	66

The 1988 college football season

1988 college conference champions

Conference	School
Atlantic Coast	Clemson
Big Eight	Nebraska
Big Sky	Idaho
Big Ten	Michigan
Big West	Fresno State
Ivy League	Cornell—Pennsylvania (tie)
Mid-American	Western Michigan
Ohio Valley	Eastern Kentucky
Pacific Ten	Southern California
Southeastern	Auburn—Louisiana State (tie)
Southland	Northwest Louisiana
Southwest	Arkansas
Southwestern	Jackson State
Western Athletic	Wyoming
Yankee	Delaware

Major bowl games

Bowl	Winner	Loser
All-American	Florida 14	Illinois 10
Aloha	Washington State 24	Houston 22
Amos Alonzo Stagg (Div. III)	Ithaca (N.Y.) 39	Central (Iowa) 24
Blue-Gray	Blue 22	Gray 21
California	Fresno State 35	Western Michigan 30
Cotton	UCLA 17	Arkansas 3
Fiesta	Notre Dame 34	West Virginia 21
Florida Citrus	Clemson 13	Oklahoma 6
Freedom	Brigham Young 20	Colorado 17
Gator	Georgia 34	Michigan State 27
Hall of Fame	Syracuse 23	Louisiana State 10
Holiday	Oklahoma State 62	Wyoming 14
Independence	Southern Mississippi 38	Texas-El Paso 18
Japan Bowl	East 30	West 7
Liberty	Indiana 34	South Carolina 10
Orange	Miami 23	Nebraska 3
Palm (Div. II)	North Dakota State 35	Portland State (Ore.) 21
Peach	North Carolina State 28	Iowa 23
Rose	Michigan 22	Southern California 14
Senior	South 13	North 12
Sugar	Florida State 13	Auburn 7
Sun	Alabama 29	Army 28
NCAA Div. I-AA	Furman (S.C.) 17	Georgia Southern 13
NAIA Div. I	Carson-Newman (Tenn.) 56	Adams State (Colo.) 21
NAIA Div. II	Westminster (Pa.) 21	Wisconsin-LaCrosse 14

All-American team (as picked by AP)

Offense

Tight end—Wesley Walls, Mississippi
Wide receivers—Hart Lee Dykes, Oklahoma State; Jason Phillips, Houston
Tackles—Andy Heck, Notre Dame; Tony Mandarich, Michigan State
Guards—Anthony Phillips, Oklahoma; Mike Utley, Washington State
Center—Jake Young, Nebraska
Quarterback—Steve Walsh, Miami
Running backs—Darren Lewis, Texas A & M; Barry Sanders, Oklahoma State
Place kicker—Kendall Trainor, Arkansas
Return specialist—Tyrone Thurman, Texas Tech

Defense

Ends—Frank Stams, Notre Dame; Broderick Thomas, Nebraska
Down linemen—Wayne Martin, Arkansas; Mark Messner, Michigan; Tracy Rocker, Auburn
Linebackers—Keith DeLong, Tennessee; Mike Stonebreaker, Notre Dame; Derrick Thomas, Alabama
Defensive backs—Louis Oliver, Florida; Markus Paul, Syracuse; Deion Sanders, Florida State
Punter—Keith English, Colorado

Player awards

Heisman Trophy (best player)—Barry Sanders, Oklahoma State
Lombardi Award (best lineman)—Tracy Rocker, Auburn
Outland Award (best interior lineman)—Tracy Rocker, Auburn

voted into the Pro Football Hall of Fame in Canton, Ohio, with wide receiver Fred Biletnikoff, defensive tackle Alan Page, and linebacker Jack Ham. In midseason, Ditka suffered a mild heart attack but missed only one game. An Associated Press poll voted Ditka the NFL Coach of the Year, quarterback Norman (Boomer) Esiason of Cincinnati the Player of the Year, tailback Roger Craig of San Francisco the Offensive Player of the Year, and linebacker Mike Singletary of Chicago the Defensive Player of the Year.

Problems. The five-year collective-bargaining agreement between the NFL club owners and their players expired on Aug. 31, 1987. Despite a 24-day strike early in the 1987 season, no agreement had been reached by the end of the 1988 season.

In November 1988, the owners offered the players a choice of two new collective-bargaining agreements. One—plan A—would have increased many benefits. Plan B would have created free agency for a limited number of players but would also have limited key benefits. The owners said that if no agreement was reached on the offer by Feb. 1, 1989, they would unilaterally impose plan B.

The players' union criticized both plans and said it wanted unrestricted free agency for all players with six or more years in the league. The union also awaited a trial on its federal antitrust suit against the league.

The NFL's other problems included drug suspensions and quarterback injuries. In 1988, its second year of leaguewide drug testing, the NFL suspended 23 players as second-time offenders and 1 as a third-time offender. The 23 were suspended for 30 days, and the third-time offender, running back Tony Collins of the Indianapolis Colts, was suspended for at least a year.

The 23 included such Pro Bowl players as linebacker Lawrence Taylor of the Giants, defensive end Bruce Smith of Buffalo, defensive end Dexter Manley of Washington, and 1987 rushing champion Charles White of the Rams. In addition, defensive back David Croudip of the Atlanta Falcons died in October of a cocaine overdose.

Game injuries sidelined such outstanding quarterbacks as Bernie Kosar of Cleveland, Warren Moon of Houston, John Elway of Denver, McMahon of Chicago, and Dave Krieg of Seattle. Of the 28 starting quarterbacks in the league, only 6 started every game.

On the positive side, the Seattle team was sold for $99 million and the New England Patriots for $85-million, the highest prices ever for professional sports franchises. Television ratings were relatively steady in 1988, though previous years had marked a decline.

The financially troubled Canadian Football League survived after the players on the eight teams had agreed to salary cuts. The Winnipeg Blue Bombers upset the British Columbia Lions, 22-21, in the Grey Cup championship game on November 27 in Ottawa, Ont. The Blue Bombers were the first team in CFL history to win the Grey Cup after failing to post a

Oklahoma State running back Barry Sanders eludes a tackler during a season in which he set several rushing records. In December, he won the Heisman Trophy.

Barry Sanders, Oklahoma State tailback, set major-college single-season records for touchdowns (39), rushing yards (2,628 [2,403 meters]), and 300-yard rushing games (4). He won the Heisman Trophy as college football's outstanding player with 1,878 points to 912 for quarterback Rodney Peete of Southern California and 582 for quarterback Troy Aikman of UCLA.

Sanders was the first junior to win the award since Herschel Walker in 1982. Sanders' win was even more remarkable because he is unusually short for a football player at a major college. Sanders stands only 5 feet 8 inches (173 centimeters) tall.

The National Collegiate Athletic Association (NCAA), the major governing body for college sports, enforced its strict and complex code barring coaches and boosters from giving more benefits to players than the rules allowed. It penalized the football programs at Oklahoma, Oklahoma State, Texas A & M, Houston, and Illinois. Penalties also were leveled against the University of Cincinnati in football and basketball. The penalties included probation up to three years, bans on bowl appearances and television revenue, and loss of athletic scholarships.

The longest losing streak in major-college history ended on October 8 when Columbia beat Princeton, 16-13, after Princeton missed a 48-yard (44-meter) field goal on the last play. Columbia, which had lost 44 straight games, finished at 2-8.　　Frank Litsky

In *World Book*, see **Football.**

winning record during the regular season. Winnipeg was 9-9 going into the championship game.

In the United States, the Arena Football League played its second season of a scaled-down indoor game. After the season, the owners of four of the six clubs tried, without success, to buy out Jim Foster, the league's founder and commissioner.

College. Notre Dame and West Virginia, each with 11 victories in 11 games, were the only major teams to finish the regular season undefeated and untied. Nebraska and Wyoming were 11-1, and Miami of Florida, Southern California, Auburn, Florida State, and Arkansas were 10-1.

During the season, teams that ranked first in the Associated Press and United Press International weekly polls were Miami, then the University of California at Los Angeles (UCLA), then Notre Dame. After the regular season, both polls ranked Notre Dame first, Miami second, West Virginia third, Florida State fourth, and Southern California fifth.

Because the major colleges had rejected a proposed one-game play-off for the national championship, the unofficial championship was decided in the postseason bowl games. Notre Dame beat West Virginia, 34-21, in the Fiesta Bowl on Jan. 2, 1989, in Tempe, Ariz., as quarterback Tony Rice passed for two touchdowns. The next day, in the final wire-service polls, Notre Dame was ranked first, Miami second, Florida State third, Michigan fourth, and West Virginia fifth.

Forest fires. Fires raged out of control in Yellowstone National Park in the summer of 1988, peaking in September as 13 separate blazes roamed over half of the park's 2,219,785 acres (898,315 hectares). The fires, which cost an estimated $120 million to control, also sparked a political fire storm over the "natural burn" policy of the United States National Park Service. Since 1972, officials have considered natural fires essential to the forest's life cycle. Such fires are allowed to burn out unless they threaten lives or property.

The 1988 fires were started in June by lightning, and unusually dry conditions encouraged the fires to spread as the flames fed on large quantities of dead wood and other litter on Yellowstone's forest floor. High winds, which carried embers for distances of more than 1 mile (1.6 kilometers), fanned the fires to unexpected proportions. On July 21, Secretary of the Interior Donald P. Hodel ordered all fires battled aggressively. The effort eventually involved more than 9,000 fire fighters.

In early September, flames threatened the tourist complex at Old Faithful geyser, and officials closed the park for the first time in its 116-year history. The blaze skirted the historic Old Faithful Inn, but scorched nearby pines and destroyed several outbuildings. By the time the fires were controlled in late September, they had gutted about 15 buildings in the park.

The fires' effects. Critics of the "let-it-burn" policy, including congressmen from Wyoming, Montana,

Fires burn out of control in Yellowstone National Park. The fires ranged over half of the park's area in the summer and fall of 1988.

and Idaho—the states in which Yellowstone is located —contended that the Park Service had encouraged a disaster. But conservationists maintained that the fires had actually helped the forest by clearing an over-abundance of old trees and promoting the growth of new ground vegetation that will feed the park's wild-life.

In October, park officials reported that the damage was less severe than had been feared. The fires killed only 9 of the park's 2,500 bison and 250 of its 32,000 elk. At least one-third of the land within the fire zones escaped the flames entirely; only 20,000 acres (8,100 hectares) were burned severely enough to wipe out all life. Grass and flowers had already begun to spring up in the ash-enriched soil, and experts pre-dicted more diversity of plant and bird species. To maintain tourism, officials planned to promote the park as a demonstration of natural rebirth.

Other fires, however, created more damage. The same dry conditions that fueled the Yellowstone fires fed major blazes in California, Colorado, Idaho, Mon-tana, Utah, Washington, and Wyoming. Those fires seared more than 1 million acres (405,000 hectares), not including Yellowstone. More than twice that area burned in Alaska. All told, flames swept over 6 million acres (2.4 million hectares) nationwide, making 1988 the worst year for forest fires since 1924. Ten people died fighting the fires.   Robin Goldman

In **World Book**, see **Yellowstone National Park.**

France. President François Mitterrand won a second term of office in general elections in April and May 1988. His leading opponent was Prime Minister Jacques Chirac, with whom Mitterrand had estab-lished an unprecedented power-sharing arrangement in 1986. Mitterrand, a Socialist, and Chirac, a member of the conservative Rally for the Republic (RPR) party, were opposed politically but had agreed to work together.

First vote. Mitterrand faced eight other candidates in the first round of voting on April 24, 1988. Among them were Jean-Marie Le Pen, leader of the far-right National Front, and former Prime Minister Raymond Barre, an independent who was supported by the centrist French Democratic Union.

Mitterrand won 34 per cent of the vote to Chirac's 20 per cent, 17 per cent for Barre, and 14 per cent for Le Pen. The two leaders, Mitterrand and Chirac, ad-vanced to the second round of voting, scheduled for May 8.

Prisoner, hostages freed. On May 6, Chirac made a popular move by arranging for the return to France of Captain Dominique Prieur, a French secret service agent. In 1985, she had helped to blow up the Green-peace ship *Rainbow Warrior* in Auckland Harbour, New Zealand. The explosion resulted in the death of a photographer working for Greenpeace, an environ-mentalist organization opposed to France's nuclear-weapons tests in the Pacific Ocean.

310

A New Zealand court convicted Prieur and another agent, Alain Mafart. New Zealand and France then reached an agreement allowing the two agents to live in exile on Hao, a small French island in the Pacific. The agents were to remain under house arrest in Hao for three years. Mafart returned to France in December 1987, however, after the French government said that he had a stomach ailment.

Mitterrand wins. In the second round of balloting, Mitterrand won 54.5 per cent of the votes. After the election, Mitterrand pledged himself to a "program of national unity" to prepare France for a profound change in the 12-nation European Community (EC or Common Market). The EC plans to transform itself in 1992 into a single market with no tariffs or other barriers to trade.

Rocard succeeds Chirac. On May 10, 1988, Mitterrand appointed Michel Rocard prime minister. Rocard, a moderate Socialist, had fought hard for many years to swing his party toward the political center. He supported Mitterrand's idea that the Socialist Party had to broaden its appeal to centrists to gain enough political power to govern the country. Rocard's support of this concept had made him a popular politician. See **Rocard, Michel.**

France votes again. Rocard immediately scheduled a general election to break the right wing's grip on the National Assembly, the more powerful of the two houses of Parliament. In the first round of voting on June 5, the RPR polled 40.5 per cent of the votes to 37.5 per cent for the Socialists. Only about 66 per cent of the eligible voters cast ballots. This was a record low turnout for the years since World War II, which ended in 1945.

In the second round of voting on June 12, 1988, Mitterrand did not get the majority he had sought for his Socialist government. The Socialists won 276 of the 577 seats in the National Assembly, leaving them 13 short of the 289 needed for a majority. The RPR and other conservatives won 271 seats. The Communists dropped from 35 seats to 27. The election was a blow for the National Front, which lost 34 of its 35 seats. A June 26 vote in French Polynesia gave 1 seat to an independent and another to a Socialist.

Rail disaster. Fifty-six people died and another 40 were injured when two commuter trains collided in Paris on June 27. A suburban express apparently lost its braking power and hurtled into a packed train that was stopped at an underground platform.

Strikes hit Paris and other cities from October 19 to 22. Nearly 5 million employees of state-owned businesses took to the streets to demonstrate for higher wages. Rocard refused to yield to the strikers' demands.   Kenneth Brown

See also **Europe** (Facts in brief table). In *World Book*, see **France.**

Gabon. See Africa.

Gambia. See Africa.

Games. See Toys and games.

Gardening. People who choose gardening as a hobby today are younger and more affluent than ever before, according to a study released in 1988 by the National Gardening Association, a nonprofit organization based in Burlington, Vt. In 1987, 70 million United States households spent a total of $17.5 billion on lawns and gardens. That represents an increase of 23 per cent over the $14.2 billion spent in 1986. Of those households, 25 per cent had an annual income of more than $40,000, up from 18 per cent in 1985. And 49 per cent represented consumers between the ages of 30 and 49, up from 39 per cent in 1985.

Year of the Dahlia. The National Garden Bureau, a Chicago-based educational arm of the seed industry, proclaimed 1988 the Year of the Dahlia. The dahlia, a tuberous flowering plant that originated in Central America, became popular in Europe in the 1700's and returned to the Americas as a garden plant. Compact varieties that grow readily from seeds have helped make the dahlia a popular annual and one of the most commonly grown bedding flowers.

New pesticides. In March 1988, the Environmental Protection Agency (EPA) approved a new biological pesticide that kills microscopic *nematodes* (worms) that attack plants. The pesticide's active ingredient is a substance called *chitin* that occurs naturally in the shells of clams and similar shellfish. The pesticide was designed as a substitute for chemical pesticides and is marketed under the name ClandoSan. In June, the EPA approved a microbial pesticide—a pesticide that works by infecting insects or other pests with a disease. The active microbe in the new pesticide kills the larvae of the Colorado potato beetle. The beetle, which has become resistant to conventional chemical insecticides, attacks potatoes, tomatoes, and eggplant. The pesticide, called M-One, contains a variety of the bacterium *Bacillus thuringiensis.* Another species of this bacterium is used to fight gypsy moths, cabbage butterflies, and related pests. The pesticide is harmless to human beings and domestic animals.

Supercarrot. The USDA's Vegetable Crops Research Unit in Madison, Wis., has produced a "supercarrot" that has three to five times the usual amount of *carotene*, a chemical that gives carrots their color and nutritional value. The human body converts carotene into vitamin A. Two supercarrots weekly allow a person to produce enough vitamin A to prevent the type of blindness caused by a vitamin A deficiency. The sweet, dark-orange carrot, called Beta 3, was first released for trial production in developing countries where many people suffer from vitamin A deficiency. The supercarrot's creators began releasing the carrot to U.S. seed companies in 1988. The new carrot was expected to be available to the public in 1989 or 1990.   George (Doc) Abraham and Katherine (Katy) Abraham

In *World Book*, see **Gardening.**

Gas and gasoline. See Energy supply; Petroleum and gas.

Genetic engineering. See Biology.

Geology

Geology. One of the most exciting geologic events of 1988 was a conference held in Snowbird, Utah, in October. More than 100 scientists gathered to discuss evidence for theories linking meteorite impacts with mass extinctions and geologic change.

The most prominent of these theories is one proposed in 1979 by a team of scientists headed by physicist Luis W. Alvarez of the University of California at Berkeley (who died in September 1988). The scientists proposed that the mass extinctions at the end of the Cretaceous Period 65 million years ago, which included the disappearance of the dinosaurs, was the result of a meteorite impact. According to the theory, the impact created huge clouds of dust that blocked the sun, cooling the earth's climate.

At the Snowbird conference, a team led by geochemist Stanley V. Margolis of the University of California at Davis reported finding the first concrete evidence of debris from the meteorite. In mineral grains found in deep-sea sediments from Spain, the scientists discovered small particles of iron, nickel oxides, and sulfides identical to those found around known meteorite impact sites. This was the first identification of the minerals that carry rare elements such as iridium in rocks that were formed 65 million years ago. Iridium is rare on the earth but more plentiful in asteroids.

The scientists did not contend that the impact caused the extinction of the dinosaurs, however. They reported finding evidence in the sediments that many species of marine plants and animals were already becoming extinct 65 million years ago.

Meteorite impacts may also be connected with volcanic eruptions and the breakup of continents, according to a theory presented at the conference by geophysicist W. Jason Morgan of Princeton University in New Jersey. He suggested that meteorite impacts might trigger massive outpourings of lava. Morgan noted that several huge volcanic deposits, particularly those in southwestern India, also date from about 65 million years ago. The Indian lavas were deposited just before India separated from Africa and Madagascar.

Deep-sea vent. A mysterious glowing vent of extremely hot water on the floor of the Pacific Ocean was discovered in August by a team of scientists led by marine geologist John R. Delaney of the University of Washington in Seattle. The scientists found the faintly lighted vent while working 7,200 feet (2,200 meters) below the ocean surface in the submersible *Alvin* 180 miles (290 kilometers) west of Vancouver, Canada.

The vent is one of hundreds scientists have found at the midoceanic ridges where new ocean crust is formed by an upwelling of molten rock. The water spurting from the vent is seawater that seeped down to the chamber of molten rock underlying the ridge, where it was rapidly heated.

The scientists are puzzled about the cause of the glow. The molten rock below the ridge glows, but it lies at least ½ mile (0.8 kilometer) beneath the ocean

floor, too far down to be seen at the vent. In addition, the water at the vent is too hot to provide a home for any *bioluminescent animals* (animals that give off their own glow). The scientists speculated that chemical reactions in the hot water produce the light.

Puzzling earthquake. A moderately severe earthquake that struck the foothills of the Himalaya in Nepal in south-central Asia on August 21 apparently originated deeper in the earth than scientists had expected for earthquakes in this region. The quake killed at least 1,015 people.

The Himalaya began to form about 55 million years ago when a large section of the earth's crust called a *tectonic plate*, containing what is now India, collided with Asia. India is still drifting northward into Asia at the rate of 2 inches (5 centimeters) per year. As a result, many large earthquakes occur in northern India, Pakistan, Nepal, Bhutan, and Tibet.

Up to now, geologists believed these earthquakes originated in the crust of the earth, along a huge, nearly horizontal *fault* (break in the crust) 3 to 6 miles (5 to 10 kilometers) below the surface. This fault extends from beneath the southern Himalaya to central India. The Nepal earthquake, however, occurred about 42 miles (70 kilometers) below the surface in the *mantle* (the region of hot solid rock between the crust and core). Eldridge M. Moores

In *World Book*, see **Geology**.

Georgia. See **State government**.

Germany, East. East Germany's leader, Erich Honecker, made a historic visit to Paris from Jan. 7 to 9, 1988. No other East German head of state had ever visited France before. During his visit, Honecker met President François Mitterrand and Prime Minister Jacques Chirac. This was Honecker's first official meeting with any leader of the Western powers—France, the United States, and Great Britain—who in 1971 joined the Soviet Union in signing an agreement that still defines the status of Berlin.

Demonstrators punished. Tens of thousands of East Germans have been demanding to be allowed to move to the West. In the spring of 1988, hundreds demonstrated in East Berlin, Leipzig, Jena, Dresden, and Wismar, and many subsequently received heavy fines and jail sentences.

Protestant church leaders accused Honecker of failing to keep his promises. In early March, Honecker had held a church-and-state "summit meeting" with Bishop Werner Leich, chairman of the East German Protestant church council. During the meeting, Honecker declared that the government would never interfere with the right of individuals to practice their religion. Three days later, however, police surrounded the Sophien Church in East Berlin and refused entry to many people.

Youth confrontation. In East Berlin on January 17, police detained more than 100 young political activists who tried to conduct an unauthorized demonstration during an official rally. The authorities later released all but 22 of them, and put the 22 on trial for unlawful assembly and other crimes. The trials triggered protests in both East and West Germany.

By February 1, the 22 had been convicted and sentenced to prison terms ranging from six months to one year. Three days later, however, East Germany released four of the prisoners, with the understanding that they would go to West Germany. By February 9, the authorities had released the remaining 18, some of whom were told that they would have to leave East Germany for certain periods of time.

Compensation for Jews. Heinz Gallinski, chairman of the Central Council of the Jews in Germany, announced on June 8 that East Germany was considering paying $100 million in compensation to Jewish survivors of the Holocaust—the murder of about 6 million Jews by Germany's Nazi regime during World War II (1939-1945). Gallinski made his announcement after meeting Honecker.

Gallinski said that the money would come from East Germany's profits on trade deals with the United States. East Germany had previously opposed compensating Holocaust survivors on the grounds that East Germany bore neither moral nor historical responsibility for Nazi crimes.   Kenneth Brown

See also **Europe** (Facts in brief table). In the Special Reports section, see **The Two Germanys**. In *World Book*, see **Germany**.

Germany, West. Chancellor Helmut Kohl's center-right coalition government lost ground in two state elections in early 1988. State elections have a special national significance in West Germany because the Bundesrat, one of the two houses of the national Parliament, represents the states. Each state appoints three to five members of the state government to the Bundesrat. The Bundesrat is not as powerful as the other house, the Bundestag, but has the power to review most legislation.

Voters went to the polls in the state of Baden-Württemberg on March 20 and in Schleswig-Holstein on May 8. In Baden-Württemberg, Kohl's party, the Christian Democratic Union (CDU), lost 3 per cent of the votes it had won in the last election in 1984, and lost 2 of its 68 seats. Nevertheless, the CDU kept its majority in the state parliament. Only two small parties, the right wing Republican Party and the radical right National Democratic Party, won more votes than in 1984.

Heavy loss. In Schleswig-Holstein, the CDU suffered a crushing defeat after ruling there for 38 years. The Social Democrat Party won by a landslide, with more than 55 per cent of the votes to about 33 per cent for the CDU. This result left Kohl with an advantage of only two seats in the Bundesrat.

Kohl blamed the loss in Schleswig-Holstein on the "Barschel affair" of October 1987. The affair involved the state's prime minister, Uwe Barschel, a member of

Soviet leader Mikhail S. Gorbachev, left, toasts West Germany's Chancellor Helmut Kohl in October in Moscow, marking their first formal talks.

the CDU. Barschel had committed suicide after it was disclosed that he had directed a "dirty tricks" campaign against a political opponent.

Tax cut. The 1988 election setbacks jeopardized Kohl's plans for reforms in West Germany's tax laws. The government said that it needed to cut taxes to stimulate the economy. After decades of expansion, West Germany's rate of economic growth fell below 2 per cent in 1988, the lowest among the major industrialized countries of the West.

Amid some calls for deep cuts in tax rates, Kohl hoped that his modest program of tax reform would halt the economic slide. Although he had to make some compromises, Kohl pushed a tax cut through the Bundestag in July.

Strauss dies. Franz Josef Strauss, chairman of the Christian Social Union (CSU) party and prime minister of the state of Bavaria, died on October 3. Theo Waigel succeeded him as chairman, and Max Streibl—also a member of the CSU—became the state's new prime minister. The CSU functions as a branch of the CDU in Bavaria.

Bundestag chief quits. Philipp Jenninger resigned as president of the Bundestag on November 11, one day after making a controversial speech to that body to mark the 50th anniversary of a Nazi atrocity known as *Kristallnacht* (Night of Glass). On that night in 1938, Nazis smashed windows of stores owned by Jews—giving rise to the term Kristallnacht—destroyed homes owned by Jews, demolished synagogues, and rounded up some 30,000 Jews for shipment to concentration camps.

In his speech, Jenninger tried to remind Germans of how the Nazis had "blinded and seduced" their ancestors. Jenninger condemned the Nazis, but in his explanation recited anti-Semitic and other pro-Nazi statements typical of those used in the 1930's by Nazi supporters. During long passages of such statements, Jenninger did not provide point-by-point counterarguments, so he sounded somewhat as if he were presenting a case for Nazism—though he intended to do exactly the opposite.

As he spoke, about 50 members of the Bundestag walked out of the parliament chamber. After the speech, critics said that Jenninger's recitation had been extremely offensive, and that the Kristallnacht anniversary was not the time to mention past support and enthusiasm for the Nazis—even in condemnation. Rita Süssmuth succeeded Jenninger in the Bundestag presidency.

Soccer riots. West German police in Stuttgart, Düsseldorf, Frankfurt, and Munich used tear gas and flares to quell battles between West German, British, Dutch, and Irish soccer fans during the European football championships in June. The police arrested hundreds of fans during the riots.   Kenneth Brown

See also **Europe** (Facts in brief table). In the Special Reports section, see **The Two Germanys.** In *World Book,* see **Germany.**

Ghana. The economy of Ghana improved significantly in 1988 after almost two decades of decline. The upturn was due largely to an economic recovery program instituted in 1982 by Ghana's leader, Jerry John Rawlings. Rawlings introduced a program of agricultural diversification to reduce Ghana's historic dependence upon cacao, which had accounted for 60 to 65 per cent of its export earnings.

During 1988, a total of 53 new exports—including pineapples, papayas, avocados, lobsters, and shrimp—helped improve Ghana's trade balance. At the same time, an emphasis on the production of corn, sorghum, yams, and cassava reduced the chronic shortages of basic foods in local markets.

Rawlings has also promoted the development of light industry, such as furniture making, and has encouraged foreign companies to prospect in Ghana for oil and minerals. The production of gold increased by 13 per cent in 1987 and 1988 as a result of new discoveries and the refurbishing of abandoned mines.

Rawlings' plan for greater grass-roots democracy was launched at year-end with the election of members to 110 newly created district assemblies. The assemblies, which will carry out legislative and administrative functions at the local level, are designed to increase citizen involvement in local development projects.   J. Gus Liebenow and Beverly B. Liebenow

See also **Africa** (Facts in brief table). In *World Book,* see **Ghana.**

Golf. Curtis Strange won the United States Open in 1988, and Alexander (Sandy) Lyle of Scotland won the Masters. Gary Player of South Africa captured three major titles for seniors. They were among the year's most successful male golfers.

The Professional Golfers' Association (PGA) year-round tour for men encompassed 52 tournaments for $39 million in prize money. Some players from other countries who competed on that tour also took part in a European tour of 38 tournaments paying more than $18 million. The PGA tour for senior men and the Ladies Professional Golf Association (LPGA) tour for women each comprised 38 tournaments worth almost $13 million.

PGA. Strange won four tournaments and Lyle three on the PGA tour, and Strange won the points competition for PGA Player of the Year. Severiano (Seve) Ballesteros of Spain, Chip Beck, Joey Sindelar, Ken Green, David Frost, Lanny Wadkins, Bill Glasson, and Steve Pate won two tournaments each.

When Lyle also won the World Match Play Championship on October 10 in Wentworth, England, he became the first golfer to earn $1 million in worldwide purses in one year. Five weeks later, Strange became the first player to earn $1 million on just the PGA tour in one year, ending 1988 as the tour's leading money-winner with $1,147,644.

Grand slam. The first of the four grand-slam tournaments was the $1-million Masters, held from April 7

Alexander (Sandy) Lyle celebrates his birdie putt on the 18th green as he becomes the first British golfer to win the Masters, in Augusta, Ga., in April.

to 10 in Augusta, Ga. Lyle, with a 72-hole score of 281, beat Mark Calcavecchia by one stroke. In the final round, Lyle lost the lead when he went three over par on the 11th to the 13th holes, the famous Amen Corner. But on the 18th hole, he hit an almost-perfect 145-yard (133-meter) bunker shot and then sank a 10-foot (3-meter) birdie putt.

In the United States Open from June 16 to 20 in Brookline, Mass., Nick Faldo of England and Strange tied at 278, 2 strokes ahead of Pate, Mark O'Meara, and D. A. Weibring. The next day, in an 18-hole play-off, Strange shot 71 and beat Faldo by 4 strokes.

In the British Open, held from July 14 to 18 at the Royal Lytham and St. Anne's Golf Club, St. Anne's-on-the-Sea, England, Ballesteros finished at 273 and won by 2 strokes under Nick Price, a South African who lives in Orlando, Fla. Ballesteros rallied with a final-round 65 that included a 135-yard (123-meter) 9-iron approach shot on the 16th hole that stopped 3 inches (7.6 centimeters) from the cup.

In the $1-million PGA championship, held from August 11 to 14 in Edmond, Okla., Paul Azinger led by 4 strokes during the third round. Jeff Sluman rallied with a closing 65 for 272 and beat Azinger by 3 strokes. On the fifth hole the last day, Sluman sank a 115-yard (105-meter) sand-wedge shot for an eagle 3 and never trailed after that.

Seniors. Before Player became 50 years old, he was a dominant player on the PGA tour. He became even more dominant in 1988 on the senior tour. He beat Chi Chi Rodriguez by 3 strokes in the PGA Seniors championship; Billy Casper, Jr., by 1 stroke in the British Seniors Open; and Bob Charles of New Zealand by 2 strokes in an 18-hole play-off in the U.S. Senior Open. In the only major tournament that Player failed to win, Casper beat Al Geiberger by 2 strokes in the Senior Tournament Players Championship.

For the year, Player won five tour tournaments plus the British Seniors Open. Charles won five tournaments; Orville Moody won four; and Bruce Crampton of Australia, Rodriguez, and Dave Hill won three each.

LPGA. At least three women's tournaments were in financial trouble, and many of the female pros felt their tour was stagnating. The women players decided they wanted new direction, and John D. Laupheimer, commissioner for more than six years, resigned. He was replaced by William True, a marketing executive.

In the LPGA's major tournaments, Amy Alcott defeated Colleen Walker by 2 strokes in the Nabisco Dinah Shore; Sherri Turner's two closing birdies beat Alcott by 1 stroke in the LPGA championship; Sally Little's closing 20-foot (6-meter) birdie putt beat Laura Davies by 1 stroke in the Du Maurier Classic; and Liselotte Neumann of Sweden won by 3 strokes from Patty Sheehan in the U.S. Open. Nancy Lopez, Ayako Okamoto, Betsy King, Julie Inkster, and Rosie Jones won three tournaments each. Turner led in earnings with $350,851.   Frank Litsky

In *World Book*, see **Golf**.

Great Britain

Great Britain. Prime Minister Margaret Thatcher's political agenda dominated 1988. With a comfortable majority in the House of Commons, her Conservative Party government pressed ahead with major reforms. But as the year progressed, economic troubles grew.

On February 25, Energy Secretary Cecil Parkinson announced plans to privatize the government-owned Central Electricity Generating Board (CEGB), which supplies electricity to local utilities in England and Wales. Parkinson said the sale, the largest one attempted by Thatcher's government, would create a modern, competitive electrical industry. But John L. Prescott, a spokesman for the opposing Labour Party, denounced the measure as a "triumph of ideology over common sense." Legislation approving the public sale of the CEGB was introduced into Parliament on November 22.

Health and taxes. Two vulnerable areas for Prime Minister Thatcher during the year were the National Health Service—the country's state-funded medical care system—and the local taxation system. The government was accused by the Labour opposition of starving the National Health Service of its resources. The media played up the charges, highlighting cases of children unable to have heart operations because of a shortage of specially trained nurses.

But the year's most controversial issue was a bill replacing the local property tax with a "community charge," a tax levied equally on all adults. The bill became law on July 29, 1988, and will go into effect in Scotland in May 1989 and in England and Wales in 1990. The opposition in Parliament labeled the measure a "poll tax," and said it would hurt the poor.

Fears that the new law would lead to large increases in local taxes for most families almost defeated the measure in Parliament. The government barely avoided a humiliating loss on April 18 by promising an extra 130 million pounds (about $247 million) in rebates to reduce the impact of the tax on the poor.

The budget. In the annual 1988-1989 budget announced on March 15, Chancellor of the Exchequer Nigel Lawson cut the income-tax rate from 27 to 25 per cent, and replaced higher tax rates, which ranged from 40 to 60 per cent, with a single-tax rate of 40 per cent. Many hailed Lawson's tax reductions, which created a total personal income tax savings of 4 billion pounds (about $7.4 billion). Labour Party members, however, complained that the tax break would benefit only the middle class. They interrupted Lawson's budget speech to the House of Commons with chants of "Shame, shame."

The benefits of the tax reductions were short-lived. Large trade deficits forced Lawson to raise the Bank of England's base lending rates a number of times during the year in an attempt to dampen domestic demand for imports. This pushed up interest rates for home loans, effectively wiping out the tax concessions and causing inflation to rise to 6.4 per cent by October.

Britain's tiny Princess of York, Beatrice Elizabeth Mary, born August 8, sleeps in the arms of her mother, Sarah Ferguson, the Duchess of York.

Internal battles. The Labour Party failed to exploit the Conservative government's economic difficulties during the year. Instead, its leaders plunged the party into a six-month internal struggle. The battle began on March 23, when Tony Benn, a senior member of the Labour Party's left wing, challenged Labour leader Neil G. Kinnock for control of the party, and Eric Heffer, another senior left wing member, challenged Roy Hattersley, the party's right wing deputy leader. Both Benn and Heffer opposed the party's shift toward the center under Kinnock.

Labour members decided the party's direction during an election at its annual conference in Blackpool in October. Kinnock was announced the winner on October 2 with 89 per cent of the vote. Hattersley also won by a comfortable margin. The left wing's crushing defeat strengthened Kinnock's position.

New party name. On March 3, the Liberal Party and the Social Democratic Party (SDP) finalized their merger and adopted a new name—the Social and Liberal Democratic Party. At its inaugural conference in Blackpool on September 26, the party voted to be known as "the Democrats" for short. David Owen, SDP leader and one of its founding members, strongly opposed the merger and refused to join the new party, causing a split among SDP members. On July 28, the Democrats overwhelmingly elected Jeremy J. (Paddy) Ashdown, a member of Parliament and former Royal Marine, as their new leader.

Education. On July 29, the Education Reform Act became law, introducing major changes in Britain's education system. One change gave state schools the right to transfer from the local education system to a centrally administered system if a majority of parents approved the move. By the end of the year, about 400 schools had inquired about the new measure.

In 1988, secondary school students in England, Northern Ireland, and Wales took a new examination—the General Certificate of Secondary Education (GCSE)—to qualify for entry into college. The GCSE exam replaced the General Certificate of Education exam, which had been given to pupils with abilities well above average, and the Certificate of Secondary Education exam, given to average or above-average students. The GCSE was designed to provide a single exam for students of all abilities.

Close call for prince. Tragedy struck close to Britain's royal family on March 10 when an avalanche swept away two members of Prince Charles's skiing party in Klosters, Switzerland. Major Hugh Lindsay, 34, a close friend of the prince's, was killed, and another friend broke both legs. Prince Charles and the rest of the party managed to scramble to safety. Princess Diana and Sarah Ferguson, the Duchess of York, who would have been with the party if the duchess had not fallen earlier in the day, were resting in their chalet at the time of the disaster. A report issued by Swiss authorities on June 27 found that Prince Charles

and his party chose to ignore an avalanche warning and had "set off the fatal avalanche," but said that there were no grounds for prosecution.

New princess. On August 8, the Duchess of York gave birth to a daughter, the first child for her and her husband, Prince Andrew, the Duke of York. The child, named Beatrice Elizabeth Mary, became the fifth in line of succession to the British throne.

Union disputes. Rivalry between 12 unions on March 17 put an end to the Ford Motor Company's plan to build a 40-million-pound (about $73-million) automobile electronic parts plant in Dundee, Scotland. In 1987, Ford and the Amalgamated Engineering Union negotiated a deal in which the union would represent all hourly workers at the new plant. Eleven other unions, which also represent workers at Ford's existing British plants, strongly opposed the deal. When the unions refused to promise not to cause disruptions, Ford opted not to build the plant.

The most serious split in the 120-year history of the Trades Union Congress (TUC) occurred on September 5, when the TUC's General Council voted to expel the Electrical, Electronic, Telecommunications and Plumbing Union (EETPU). The EETPU was accused of breaking a TUC rule that bars unions, in contracts with employers, from agreeing never to strike in return for being recognized as the only union representing employees. The 330,000-member EETPU had signed such contracts with two companies.

The bodies of two British soldiers killed during an Irish Republican Army funeral in Belfast, Northern Ireland, are returned to England on March 23.

Great Britain

Although the TUC said the action was necessary because the EETPU did not abide by TUC rules, others speculated that the real reason was the EETPU's action during a printing strike in 1986 and 1987. The union had replaced striking members of three printing unions after newspaper owner Rupert K. Murdoch moved his printing operations to a computerized plant.

Spycatcher resolution. A three-year battle waged by the British government to prevent publication of the memoirs of a former MI5 agent (British counterintelligence officer) ended on October 13. The House of Lords, Britain's court of appeal, ruled that extracts from Peter Wright's book, *Spycatcher: The Candid Autobiography of a Senior Intelligence Officer*, could be printed by British newspapers. *Spycatcher*, which had already been published in the United States, Australia, and many other countries, was banned in Britain pending the outcome of the hearing.

Although the court removed the ban, it agreed with the government that former intelligence agents had a lifelong obligation to remain silent. The court refused to permit Heinemann (William) Limited of London, the book's publisher, to print *Spycatcher* in Britain but said that imported copies could be sold.

Soccer violence. English soccer fans maintained their reputation for violence during 1988. From June 12 to 18, more than 300 English supporters were arrested after riots broke out during the European Nations Cup soccer finals held in West Germany. On June 15, Prime Minister Thatcher apologized to West German Chancellor Helmut Kohl and promised tough measures against soccer "hooligans." On June 16, the British government proposed a number of such measures, including a compulsory membership program. Fans wanting to gain admission to games played by any of the 92 soccer clubs in England would have to carry identification cards. If approved by Parliament, the membership plan would begin in August 1989.

Pub hours. A restriction on Britain's public houses —or pubs—was lifted on August 22 when a law went into effect permitting them to stay open 12 hours a day between 11 a.m. and 11 p.m., Monday through Saturday. Pubs, which sell alcoholic drinks, had been forced to close between 3 p.m. and 5:30 p.m. under a law introduced during World War I (1914-1918).

Accidents. The worst disaster in the history of North Sea oil drilling occurred on July 6, 1988, when an oil rig called Piper Alpha exploded in flames, killing 167 people. The rig, located 120 miles (200 kilometers) northeast of Aberdeen, Scotland, belonged to the Occidental Petroleum Corporation of Los Angeles. The fires were extinguished on July 29.

On December 12, the worst train crash in Great Britain in more than 10 years occurred when two commuter trains, packed with passengers, collided outside London and the wreckage was hit by an empty freight train. Thirty-three people died.   Ian J. Mather

See also **Ireland; Northern Ireland.** In *World Book*, see **Great Britain.**

Greece and Turkey agreed in 1988 on a plan to cool their dispute over the ownership of the oil-rich floor of the Aegean Sea. In March 1987, this dispute had brought them to the brink of war. Greece's Prime Minister Andreas Papandreou and his Turkish counterpart, Turgut Ozal, met in Davos, Switzerland, on Jan. 31, 1988, to work out an agreement.

The two countries' foreign ministers, meeting in Athens, Greece, on May 27, agreed that Greece and Turkey would respect each other's sovereignty and each other's right to use the waters and international airspace of the Aegean Sea. The two countries also lifted their three-year-old vetoes on the construction of North Atlantic Treaty Organization (NATO) military installations in their territories.

Papandreou welcomed Ozal to Athens on June 13 in the first official visit by a Turkish prime minister to Greece in 36 years. After three days of talks with Ozal, Papandreou said the two countries might sign a nonaggression pact.

Personal and political problems hounded Papandreou in late 1988. On August 25, he flew to London for open heart surgery. His wife did not accompany him on the trip. Instead, he traveled with his mistress, Dimitra Liani. On September 15, he said that he would obtain a divorce.

George Koskotas, a political ally of Papandreou, mysteriously vanished after being arrested in connection with the disappearance of millions of dollars from the Bank of Crete, which he owned. By the end of 1988, two ministers of the Greek government had resigned in the wave of the investigation of the Koskotas affair, and Koskotas himself was in a Boston jail fighting extradition to Greece.

Cyprus talks. Leaders of the ethnic Greek and ethnic Turkish communities in Cyprus agreed in 1988 to try to settle their differences. That island has been divided between the two groups since 1974. In 1983, the Turkish Cypriots declared their part of the island an independent nation, the Turkish Republic of Northern Cyprus. Only Turkey recognizes this republic.

United Nations Secretary-General Javier Pérez de Cuéllar arranged for President George Vassiliou of Cyprus and Rauf R. Denktaş, acting president of the Republic of Northern Cyprus, to meet on Aug. 23 and 24, 1988, in Geneva, Switzerland. At the meeting, the leaders agreed to begin talks on September 15 on the reunification of the two communities.

Terrorism. Nine people died and more than 80 were injured on July 11, when Arab gunmen hurled grenades and fired machine guns aboard a Greek ferry packed with tourists off the island of Aiyina (Aegina). Greek officials suggested that the attack's purpose was to induce Greece to release from prison Mohammed Rashid, a suspected Palestinian terrorist wanted by the United States.   Kenneth Brown

See also **Europe** (Facts in brief table). In *World Book*, see **Cyprus; Greece.**

Grenada. See **Latin America.**

Grósz, Károly (1930-   ), became Hungary's leader on May 22, 1988, when delegates to a national convention of the Hungarian Socialist Workers' Party (HSWP)—Hungary's Communist party—elected him general secretary. He succeeded János Kádár, 75, who had led Hungary since 1956. Grósz continued as prime minister, a post he had held from June 1987 until November 1988. Then he stepped down to focus on his role as general secretary of the party, and Miklós Németh succeeded him in the post of prime minister. See **Hungary.**

Grósz was born in Miskolc, in northeastern Hungary, and graduated from the HSWP academy and from Loránd Eötvös University in Budapest. He went to work for the HSWP in 1950. From 1958 to 1961, he was editor of the party's newspaper in the Miskolc region. In 1962, he became secretary of the committee for radio and television.

From 1968 to 1973, Grósz was deputy head of the Propaganda Department, which controls publishing and broadcasting in Hungary. After a stint as chief of a regional party organization, he returned to Budapest in 1974 to lead the Propaganda Department. Grósz became HSWP chief in the Miskolc region in 1979 and leader of the party organization in Budapest in 1984, and was named to the Politburo, the party's policymaking body, in 1985.

Grósz is married. He and his wife are reported to have two sons.   Jay Myers

Guatemala. Vinicio Cerezo, Guatemala's first elected civilian president in more than 30 years, survived an attempted coup on May 11, 1988. But in its aftermath, Cerezo was reportedly more dependent than ever on military support to stay in power. The mutiny was led by three army colonels with help from several influential and wealthy civilians. Guatemala's defense minister announced the arrest of six army officers and the forced retirement of three others on May 13. On May 17, eight civilians were charged with inciting rebellion.

The mutiny was prompted by Cerezo's efforts to negotiate with left wing Guatemalan rebels. Conservative army officers and wealthy landowners and business leaders were also furious that Cerezo sought to increase Guatemalan contacts with Communist Cuba. Finally, there was resentment that Cerezo had failed to attract increased aid from the United States. The U.S. government later sought to dampen such feelings by boosting economic and military assistance to the country to a total of $150 million in 1988.

During 1988, the stagnant Guatemalan economy was battered by strikes in both the private and public sectors, as President Cerezo imposed unpopular austerity measures.   Nathan A. Haverstock

See also **Latin America** (Facts in brief table). In *World Book*, see **Guatemala.**

Guinea. See **Africa.**

Guyana. See **Latin America.**

Haiti. Political turmoil held Haiti firmly in its grip during 1988. Military coups—one in June and a second in September—rocked the nation. Violent attacks on dissidents were followed by reprisals against those who carried out the attacks, and a breakdown in the chain of command split the nation's armed forces.

It was not until October 21 that Lieutenant General Prosper Avril, installed as Haiti's president after the September coup, told the Haitian people of his plans for their future. Avril—who broke with past military precedents on September 19 by naming a Cabinet composed almost entirely of civilians—said in October that he would reinstate an independent electoral council to oversee new presidential elections at an undetermined future date.

Avril came to power after a September 17 coup led mainly by noncommissioned officers (noncoms) angered over the corruption of their officers. The noncoms were also said to have been outraged by a September 11 attack on a Roman Catholic Church in Port-au-Prince in which at least 13 people were killed and more than 70 wounded by former members of the *Tontons Macoutes*, the secret police of deposed dictator Jean-Claude Duvalier.

Although Avril was associated with the Duvalier dictatorship, the dissident noncoms reportedly chose him because he had distanced himself from the repressive acts carried out by the former Tontons Macoutes with the apparent support of other military

Lieutenant General Prosper Avril declares himself president of Haiti in September, following a coup that ousted military ruler Henri Namphy.

Americans John Brewer, left, and Jeff Worthington were winners in the 800-meter wheelchair race at the 1988 Paralympic Games in Seoul, South Korea.

leaders. Among his first acts as president, Avril retired Colonel Jean-Claude Paul, the commander of Haiti's largest, best-trained, and most brutal military unit. Paul had been indicted by a federal grand jury in Miami, Fla., on March 9 on drug trafficking charges. Paul died on November 6, reportedly after eating a bowl of soup that may have been poisoned.

Paul's indictment had played a role in an earlier military coup, on June 19, when disgruntled officers led by Lieutenant General Henri Namphy overthrew civilian President Leslie F. Manigat. Manigat had been considered the military's hand-picked candidate in a January 17 election that was boycotted by the four most popular presidential candidates due to election irregularities. During his brief term, however, Manigat was credited with having made a beginning in rooting out corruption within Haiti's tax bureau and the state-owned telephone and cement companies. Two days prior to Manigat's overthrow, he had fired Namphy and announced a major military reorganization, including the reassignment of more than 30 officers.

Following the second coup, Haitians hoped for a return to democracy. Many expressed cautious optimism that the noncommissioned officers who engineered the coup and who seemed closer to the democratic aspirations of Haitians would carry out the pledge for new elections.   Nathan A. Haverstock

See also **Latin America** (Facts in brief table). In *World Book*, see **Haiti.**

Handicapped. The Fair Housing Amendments Act of 1988, passed by the United States Congress in August and signed into law in September, extended federal protection for the first time to cover housing discrimination against people with mental or physical disabilities. The law, which strengthened the 1968 Fair Housing Act, also bars discrimination on the basis of race, age, sex, religion, or national origin, and discrimination against families with children under 18.

Under the law, disabled renters are entitled to modify their dwelling to accommodate their disability as long as they return the dwelling to its original condition when they move. In addition, the law requires that multiunit housing built for occupancy after early 1991 must be "reasonably accessible and adaptable" for people with disabilities.

The Civil Rights Restoration Act, enacted in March, reversed the effects of a 1984 decision by the Supreme Court of the United States that had narrowed the scope of federal antidiscrimination laws.

The court had ruled that a 1972 federal law barring sex discrimination in schools and colleges that receive federal funds applied only to the specific department or program receiving the money and not to the entire school. Although the 1984 ruling focused only on sex discrimination, the Administration of President Ronald Reagan interpreted the decision as also applying to laws prohibiting discrimination based on race, age, or disability. Under the new law, all parts of an institution receiving federal funds are forbidden to discriminate on the basis of sex, race, age, or disability, even if only one part of the institution receives money from the government.

Gallaudet protest. A weeklong class boycott by students at Gallaudet University in Washington, D.C., the only liberal arts college for the deaf in the United States, in March 1988 led to the appointment of the school's first deaf president. The students, who viewed their protest as a demonstration for the rights of the deaf, shut down the school on March 7, the day after Gallaudet's board of trustees chose Elisabeth A. Zinser, vice president of academic affairs at the University of North Carolina at Greensboro, as president. Zinser, who is not hearing impaired, was chosen over two deaf candidates. The boycott won support from the school's faculty and alumni as well as consumer groups, labor unions, and politicians.

Zinser resigned on March 11 and was replaced by I. King Jordan, Jr., dean of Gallaudet's College of Arts and Sciences and one of the two deaf candidates for president. In addition, the students won the appointment of a deaf person as the new chairman of the university's board of trustees and the restructuring of the board to include a majority of hearing-impaired trustees.   Barbara A. Mayes

In *World Book*, see **Handicapped.**
Harness racing. See **Horse racing.**
Hawaii. See **State government.**

Health and disease. Scientists on May 10, 1988, reported the discovery of a virus that causes serious liver disease in thousands of people who receive blood transfusions each year.

The scientists, who are members of a research team at Chiron Corporation, a genetic engineering firm in Emeryville, Calif., hope the discovery will lead to more accurate methods of screening donated blood for the virus. Medical authorities hailed the discovery as a major advance toward increasing the safety of blood transfusions.

Scientists have been trying since the 1970's to isolate the virus, which causes non-A, non-B hepatitis—a potentially serious inflammation of the liver. Non-A, non-B hepatitis is the most common complication caused by blood transfusions, which are given to 4 million people each year in the United States. Blood banks have used tests to detect non-A, non-B virus contamination since 1986, but these tests are so inaccurate that an estimated 200,000 Americans are infected with the virus each year. About 100,000 of these patients develop chronic hepatitis, which causes nausea, vomiting, weakness, abdominal pain, and other symptoms. About 10,000 hepatitis victims eventually develop liver damage.

Of mice and men. Two groups of scientists in September 1988 reported the first successful transplant of the major elements of the human immune system—the system that helps the body fight off disease—into laboratory mice. Authorities said the altered mice would provide a powerful new tool for understanding the causes of AIDS (acquired immune deficiency syndrome) and other diseases and for testing new drugs and vaccines. One group of researchers—working at Stanford University in California—injected mice with fetal tissues responsible for the development of the human immune system. The other group—at the Medical Biology Institute, an independent research center in La Jolla, Calif.—injected mice with human immune cells taken from healthy adults. In December 1988, another research team—at the Hospital for Sick Children in Toronto, Canada—reported similar results from transplanting human bone marrow cells into mice.

VDT hazard. Debate over the possible health effects of *video display terminals* (VDT's)—the TV-like screens of computers on which data are displayed—continued in 1988. Researchers at the University of California at Berkeley on August 10 reported evidence that working long periods at a VDT may damage the eye's ability to focus. The study identified an unusual incidence of focusing problems among people who worked at VDT's for an average of six hours daily for more than four years. Previous studies found that VDT's cause temporary eye strain but no permanent eye damage. By 1990, an estimated 70 million VDT's will be in use in offices and homes.

Genetic breakthrough. Scientists at Massachusetts Institute of Technology in Cambridge reported on May 5, 1988, the discovery of a second genetic code that could help explain the causes of some human diseases. The code—different from the genetic code long recognized by biologists—explains how a molecule called *transfer ribonucleic acid* (transfer RNA) assembles protein molecules from building blocks called amino acids. Twenty amino acids are used in the manufacture of proteins, and each of the 20 connects with a transfer RNA molecule that "fits" only that particular amino acid. The researchers discovered that just one tiny segment of a transfer RNA molecule determines which amino acid the molecule attaches to.

Transplant device. On June 15, medical researchers at the University of California at Irvine announced the development of an experimental device that substantially extends the life of hearts and other organs donated for transplantation. The computerized apparatus mimics the environment inside the human body. The device pumps a blood substitute through the heart, enabling the heart to continue beating slowly. With existing techniques, it is often difficult and sometimes impossible to transplant donated organs to recipients in distant cities because organs begin to deteriorate within a few hours after removal from a donor. The new apparatus could keep donated human hearts alive for three days, and kidneys and livers for up to seven days, according to the researchers.

Hobbies

Alzheimer's clue. New evidence linking Alzheimer's disease to a virus infection was reported on July 1 by Yale University scientists in New Haven, Conn. Alzheimer's disease is a disorder that has caused memory loss and intellectual deterioration in about 2.5 million people in the United States. When the Yale scientists injected blood from relatives of Alzheimer's patients into laboratory animals, the animals developed brain changes closely resembling those known to result from infection with a slow-acting virus, which causes symptoms long after the initial infection.

Inherited cancer. Scientists at the University of Utah in Salt Lake City on August 31 reported that 1 out of every 3 people may inherit genes that increase their risk of developing cancer of the colon and rectum. The genes make people susceptible to intestinal *polyps* (growths that sometimes become cancerous).

Alcoholism and genes. In September, medical researchers at the University of California at San Francisco reported evidence of a genetic component in the development of alcoholism. They found that the white blood cells of alcoholics show an abnormal response to alcohol that may explain why some people become addicted to alcohol.   Michael Woods

See also **AIDS; Drugs; Medicine; Public health.** In the Special Reports section, see **Protecting Our Hearing.** In *World Book*, see **Health; Disease.**

Hobbies. See **Coin collecting; Stamp collecting; Toys and games.**

Hockey. The Edmonton Oilers, the National Hockey League's (NHL) best team in the 1980's, won the Stanley Cup play-offs in 1988. Edmonton center Wayne Gretzky, the best player in the 1980's, failed to win the Most Valuable Player award, however, for the first time since 1980. And in a blockbuster trade in August 1988 that left Canada weeping, Edmonton traded "The Great" Gretzky to the Los Angeles Kings.

During the 1987-1988 regular season, the Oilers finished with 99 points in 80 games and placed second to the Calgary Flames (105 points) in their division. The other division winners were the Montreal Canadiens (103), the Detroit Red Wings (93), and the New York Islanders (88).

The New Jersey Devils, qualifying for the play-offs for the first time, took the Boston Bruins to the full seven games in their conference finals. When the fourth game ended with a Boston victory, Devils coach Jim Schoenfeld yelled at referee Don Koharski and, Koharski said, shoved him. The league suspended Schoenfeld for the next game, but the Devils obtained a temporary restraining order from a New Jersey court. When Schoenfeld appeared for the game, the three game officials left, and amateur officials were recruited to replace them. The league then gave Schoenfeld a hearing and suspended him for the next game. It also fined him $1,000 and the Devils $10,000.

Stanley Cup. Edmonton easily advanced to the finals by eliminating the Winnipeg Jets (4 games to 1),

National Hockey League standings

Prince of Wales Conference

Charles F. Adams Division

	W.	L.	T.	Pts.
Montreal Canadiens	45	22	13	103
Boston Bruins	44	30	6	94
Buffalo Sabres	37	32	11	85
Hartford Whalers	35	38	7	77
Quebec Nordiques	32	43	5	69

Lester Patrick Division

	W.	L.	T.	Pts.
New York Islanders	39	31	10	88
Washington Capitals	38	33	9	85
Philadelphia Flyers	38	33	9	85
New Jersey Devils	38	36	6	82
New York Rangers	36	34	10	82
Pittsburgh Penguins	36	35	9	81

Clarence Campbell Conference

James Norris Division

Detroit Red Wings	41	28	11	93
St. Louis Blues	34	38	8	76
Chicago Black Hawks	30	41	9	69
Toronto Maple Leafs	21	49	10	52
Minnesota North Stars	19	48	13	51

Conn Smythe Division

Calgary Flames	48	23	9	105
Edmonton Oilers	44	25	11	99
Winnipeg Jets	33	36	11	77
Los Angeles Kings	30	42	8	68
Vancouver Canucks	25	46	9	59

Stanley Cup winner—
Edmonton Oilers (defeated Boston Bruins, 4 games to 0)

Scoring leaders	Games	Goals	Assists	Pts.
Mario Lemieux, Pittsburgh	77	70	98	168
Wayne Gretzky, Edmonton	64	40	109	149
Denis Savard, Chicago	80	44	87	131
Dale Hawerchuk, Winnipeg	80	44	77	121
Luc Robitaille, Los Angeles	80	53	58	111
Peter Stastny, Quebec	76	46	65	111
Mark Messier, Edmonton	77	37	74	111
Jimmy Carson, Los Angeles	80	55	52	107
Hakan Loob, Calgary	80	50	56	106
Michel Goulet, Quebec	80	48	58	106
Mike Bullard, Calgary	79	48	55	103
Steve Yzerman, Detroit	64	50	52	102

Leading goalies (25 or more games)	Games	Goals against	Avg.
Pete Peeters, Washington	35	88	2.78
Brian Hayward, Montreal	39	107	2.86
Patrick Roy, Montreal	45	125	2.90
Reggie Lemelin, Boston	49	138	2.93

Awards

Calder Trophy (best rookie)—Joe Nieuwendyk, Calgary
Hart Trophy (most valuable player)—Mario Lemieux, Pittsburgh
Lady Byng Trophy (sportsmanship)—Mats Naslund, Montreal
Masterton Trophy (perseverance, dedication to hockey)—Bob Bourne, Los Angeles
Norris Trophy (best defenseman)—Ray Bourque, Boston
Ross Trophy (leading scorer)—Mario Lemieux, Pittsburgh
Selke Trophy (best defensive forward)—Guy Carbonneau, Montreal
Smythe Trophy (most valuable player in Stanley Cup)—Wayne Gretzky, Edmonton
Vezina Trophy (most valuable goalie)—Grant Fuhr, Edmonton

Calgary (4-0), and Detroit (4-1). Edmonton swept the finals from Boston, 4 games to 0. It was the Oilers' fourth Stanley Cup in five years.

Gretzky had won the Hart Trophy as the NHL's Most Valuable Player for eight straight seasons and the Ross Trophy as the scoring champion for seven straight seasons. This time, he finished third in the voting for Most Valuable Player after Pittsburgh Penguins center Mario Lemieux and Edmonton goalie Grant Fuhr. Gretzky won the Smythe Trophy as the Stanley Cup play-offs' Most Valuable Player, however, and on March 1 his 1,050th career assist sent him past the retired Gordie Howe as the NHL's all-time assist leader.

The stars. On Dec. 30, 1987, Gretzky badly strained a knee ligament and missed 13 games. That helped Lemieux win the scoring title with 168 points, while Gretzky finished second with 149.

Lemieux was voted the all-star center, with Gretzky on the second team. Also on the first team were Luc Robitaille of the Kings and Hakan Loob of Calgary at wing, Ray Bourque of Boston and Scott Stevens of Washington on defense, and Fuhr in goal.

On Aug. 9, 1988, Edmonton unexpectedly traded Gretzky and two other players to the Kings for center Jimmy Carson, number-one draft pick Martin Gelinas, three future number-one draft choices, and $15 million.   Frank Litsky

In *World Book*, see **Hockey.**

Hogan, Paul (1940-   ), brought his brand of low-key Australian humor back to motion-picture theaters in 1988 with the release of *"Crocodile" Dundee II.* The movie, a sequel to the 1986 box-office hit *"Crocodile" Dundee,* once again featured Hogan as the tough man from Australia's outback. It became one of the top-grossing movies of the year.

Hogan was born on April 23, 1940, in Sydney. After dropping out of high school at age 15, he tried a variety of jobs, including chauffeur and salesman. In 1963, he took a job building scaffolds on the Sydney Harbour Bridge.

On a dare from co-workers, Hogan appeared on a television talent show in 1972. His performance as a blindfolded, tap-dancing knife thrower was such a hit that he was offered a comedy spot on another TV show. Less than a year later, Hogan had his own TV show—"The Paul Hogan Show"—which ran for nine years and has been syndicated in 30 countries. Hogan also appeared on U.S. television in commercials for the Australian Tourist Commission.

Hogan developed the idea of *"Crocodile" Dundee* in 1984 and helped write the screenplay. He made his movie debut in the film, which became the highest-grossing film in Australian history.

Hogan and his wife, Noelene, were married in 1958. They divorced in 1981 but remarried less than a year later. The couple separated again in 1988. They have five children.   Mary A. Krier

Honduras. Violent anti-American demonstrations that left five people dead erupted in Tegucigalpa, the capital, on April 7, 1988. The protests followed the seizure two days earlier of Juan Ramón Matta Ballesteros. He was conveyed out of the country to face drug-trafficking charges in the United States, though the Honduran Constitution forbids the extradition of a Honduran citizen for crimes committed in another country. The seizure of Matta Ballesteros was reportedly carried out in cooperation with U.S. agents.

The protest riots mainly involved students from the National Autonomous University of Honduras and the National Teachers' School, both in Tegucigalpa. Protesters inflicted extensive damage on a U.S. Embassy compound and set fire to some 25 automobiles belonging to U.S. diplomats. The riots were symptomatic of deepening anti-U.S. sentiment and Honduran frustration over the continuing presence of U.S.-backed Nicaraguan *contra* rebels in their country.

On October 4, Honduran Foreign Minister Carlos López Contreras proposed a solution to the Central American conflict in a speech before the United Nations (UN) General Assembly. He asked for a UN peacekeeping force to patrol Honduran borders and keep out rebels seeking to topple the governments of El Salvador and Nicaragua.   Nathan A. Haverstock

See also **Latin America** (Facts in brief table). In *World Book,* see **Honduras.**

Horse racing. In 1988, Alysheba and Personal Ensign won major thoroughbred honors, and Mack Lobell was the outstanding harness-racing horse, just as he was in 1987. After the season, all three 4-year-olds were retired for breeding.

Thoroughbred. In 1987, Alysheba was the champion 3-year-old. In 1988, competing in five states, he won seven of his nine races. Six victories came in Grade I stakes, the most important races.

Alysheba's last race was his most significant. On November 5, in the $3-million Breeders' Cup Classic at Churchill Downs in Louisville, Ky., he beat Seeking the Gold by half a length. The victory made Alysheba the leading money-winner in horse-racing history, his $6,679,242 breaking the record of $6,597,947 by the retired John Henry.

The Breeders' Cup program, the highlight of the thoroughbred year, consisted of seven races with purses ranging from $1 million to $3 million. Personal Ensign rallied to beat Winning Colors, the Kentucky Derby winner, by a nose in the $1-million Breeders' Cup Distaff. That lifted her record to 13 victories in 13 races, and she became the first major thoroughbred to retire undefeated since Colin in 1908.

Horses trained by D. Wayne Lukas won three Breeders' Cup races and finished second in three others. In the $1-million race for juvenile (2-year-old) fillies, his horses finished 1-2-3. His Breeders' Cup winners were Open Mind in the Juvenile Fillies, Is It True in the

Winning Colors, ridden by jockey Gary Stevens, holds off Forty Niner to win the Kentucky Derby by a neck at Churchill Downs in Louisville in May.

Major horse races of 1988

Race	Winner	Value to winner
Arlington Million	Mill Native	$600,000
Belmont Stakes	Risen Star	1,303,720*
Breeders' Cup Classic	Alysheba	1,350,000
Breeders' Cup Distaff	Personal Ensign	450,000
Breeders' Cup Juvenile	Is It True	450,000
Breeders' Cup Juvenile Fillies	Open Mind	450,000
Breeders' Cup Mile	Miesque	450,000
Breeders' Cup Sprint	Gulch	450,000
Breeders' Cup Turf	Great Communicator	900,000
Budweiser Irish Derby	Kahyasi	487,553
Cartier Million (Ireland)	Corwyn Bay	716,461
Epsom Derby (England)	Kahyasi	537,554
Hollywood Futurity	King Glorious	495,000
Japan Cup (Japan)	Pay the Butler	1,016,078
Jockey Club Gold Cup Stakes	Waquoit	637,800
Kentucky Derby	Winning Colors	611,200
Molson Export Challenge Stakes	Ballindaggin	600,000
Pimlico Special	Bet Twice	425,000
Preakness Stakes	Risen Star	413,700
Prix de l'Arc de Triomphe (France)	Tony Bin	787,500
Rothmans International Stakes (Canada)	Infamy	508,680
Melbourne Cup (Australia)	Empire Rose	737,604
Santa Anita Handicap	Alysheba	550,000
Super Derby	Seeking the Gold	600,000
Travers Stakes	Forty Niner	653,100
Woodward Handicap	Alysheba	498,600

Major U.S. harness races of 1988

Race	Winner	Value to winner
Cane Pace	Runnymede Lobell	$175,137
Hambletonian	Armbro Goal	578,400
Little Brown Jug	B J Scoot	147,029
Meadowlands Pace	Matt's Scooter	519,500
Woodrow Wilson	Kassa Branca	520,500

*Includes $1 million bonus.
Sources: *The Blood-Horse* magazine and United States Trotting Association.

$1-million Juvenile, and Gulch in the $1-million Sprint.

Triple Crown races. In the $786,200 Kentucky Derby on May 7 at Churchill Downs, Winning Colors beat Forty Niner by a neck, with Risen Star third. In the Preakness on May 21 at Pimlico in Baltimore, Winning Colors and Forty Niner faded, and Risen Star won by 1¼ lengths. In the Belmont Stakes on June 11 at Elmont, N.Y., Risen Star won by 14¾ lengths. His time of 2 minutes 26⅖ seconds for the 1½ miles was the second-fastest ever for the Belmont, behind the 2 minutes 24 seconds set in 1973 by his sire, Secretariat.

Harness racing. Mack Lobell won 18 of 20 races. In 1987, he set world trotting records for the mile over a 1-mile track (1 minute 52⅕ seconds) and a five-eighths-of-a-mile track (1 minute 54⅕ seconds). On Aug. 5, 1988, at Saratoga Raceway in Saratoga Springs, N.Y., he broke the remaining record by winning over a half-mile track in 1 minute 56 seconds.

Matt's Scooter, a Canadian-bred 3-year-old, paced the fastest mile in history, 1 minute 48⅖ seconds, on September 23 in a time trial over the Red Mile in Lexington, Ky. From August to October, Matt's Scooter also won the Messenger Stake, the Meadowlands Pace, the Confederation Cup, and the Prix d'Été.

Horse of the Year. In January, Ferdinand was voted the 1987 Horse of the Year. Alysheba and Personal Ensign were contenders for the 1988 title, thoroughbred racing's highest honor.   Frank Litsky

In *World Book*, see **Harness racing; Horse racing.**

Hospital. A major expansion of the United States Medicare program, approved by Congress in June 1988, provided unlimited hospital care for the 33 million elderly and disabled people covered by the program. On July 1, President Ronald Reagan signed the legislation, intended to protect the elderly and disabled from the high costs of catastrophic illness. Catastrophic illnesses—such as cancer—can require lengthy medical care that depletes a family's savings.

Under the new legislation, Medicare patients will be entitled to unlimited free hospital care after paying a single annual charge of $560 for 1989. Previously, patients were eligible for only 60 days of free hospital care annually. The legislation also provided improved Medicare coverage of doctors' bills and other health-care expenses. The cost of the new benefits would be borne by Medicare beneficiaries through higher monthly premiums and an income-tax surcharge on the more-affluent beneficiaries.

Shorter stays. The average length of a patient's stay in a U.S. hospital dropped 22 per cent between 1980 and 1985, according to a May 24 study by the U.S. Department of Health and Human Services (HHS). The study found that the average hospital stay in 1985 lasted 5.7 days, compared with 7.4 days in 1980. Authorities attributed the decrease to medical advances that permit faster diagnosis and treatment, and economy measures that encourage patients to be discharged from the hospital early.

Charity care. Hospitals that operate for profit provide substantially less free care to needy patients than nonprofit hospitals, concluded a study published in the May 5, 1988, issue of *The New England Journal of Medicine*. The study, commissioned by Volunteer Trustees of Not-for-Profit Hospitals in Washington, D.C., examined hospital spending on charity—or uncompensated care—in five states. It found that nonprofit hospitals spend 50 to 90 per cent more money on charity care than do for-profit hospitals.

Nursing shortage. An HHS panel concluded in July that the shortage of nurses in the United States has left unfilled 117,000 hospital jobs for registered nurses. The study blamed the shortage on undesirable working conditions, poor salaries and benefits, and other factors. The American Hospital Association (AHA) on May 16 reported that the nursing shortage had worsened during 1987, forcing some hospitals to temporarily shut down emergency departments and other facilities. The AHA, an industry group based in Chicago, said that 78 per cent of U.S. hospitals reported difficulty in hiring enough nurses, compared with 76 per cent in 1986.

On strike. A 19-day strike of more than 9,000 nurses in Alberta, Canada, ended on Feb. 11, 1988. Their union—United Nurses of Alberta—reached an agreement with the province's hospitals on pay and benefit increases.   Michael Woods

In *World Book*, see **Hospital.**

Housing. See Building and construction.

Houston. The economy of Houston, which had faltered for four years, showed a moderate upturn in 1988. By August, unemployment was 6.3 per cent, down from a record high of 10.7 per cent in May 1986. Retail sales and home sales increased, while foreclosures declined. Sales-tax collections in July 1988 were 24 per cent above those of July 1987.

Troubles continued, however, for businesses and individuals that had invested heavily in Houston real estate. By year-end, more than 15 local banks had failed, and a number of Houstonians had filed for bankruptcy.

Budget troubles. In April, Mayor Kathryn J. Whitmire told the City Council that the city faced a budget shortfall of $55 million. The council took action during the summer, raising property tax rates 18.9 per cent and hiking water and sewer rates 8 per cent.

County government. On October 4, Harris County, of which Houston is the county seat, raised property taxes an average of 18 per cent.

Scandals cost two county officials their jobs in 1988. On January 5, Commissioner Bob Eckels resigned from the county commission and paid a $2,000 fine after investigators concluded that he had acted unethically in accepting free work—the construction of a 1-mile (1.6-kilometer) road at his ranch—from a contractor.

On September 13, the board of the county Mental Health/Mental Retardation Authority fired Executive Director Eugene Williams after learning that Williams was drawing more than twice his official salary, and that during his tenure the authority had purchased a building for $3.3 million from a company that bought it only hours earlier for $2.1 million. No indictment was filed, but at year-end county officials were looking into Williams' activities as the authority's executive director.

Law enforcement. In January, a probe began into allegations that some Houston police officers had conducted illegal narcotics searches, planted drugs on suspects, and lied in court to obtain convictions against accused drug dealers. In February, 106 narcotics cases were dismissed on those grounds, and the following month two officers were indicted for perjury. Their cases were pending at year-end.

Violent crime in Houston dropped 7.8 per cent in 1987, with homicides down 20.8 per cent and sexual assaults down 23.1 per cent. Police Chief Lee P. Brown attributed the improvement to better law enforcement and improved public education programs on crime prevention.

Education. On July 8, trustees of the Houston Independent School District voted to raise property taxes by 8 cents per $100 valuation and to give the district's teachers raises of 5 to 10 per cent. On September 6, the district unveiled a $629-million construction plan that included the building of 14 new schools and the renovation of all 232 existing schools in the district.

Houston

Health and science. City health officials announced in January that 770 new cases of AIDS (acquired immune deficiency syndrome) were reported in Houston in 1987, bringing the city's total to 1,764. On Aug. 23, 1988, the University of Houston (UH) signed a long-term contract with E. I. du Pont de Nemours & Company for the development of advances made by UH physicist Paul C. W. Chu in the field of *superconductivity*. (Superconductivity is the ability of some materials, when chilled, to conduct electric current without resistance, thus wasting almost no energy.)

Transit. On January 16, 60 per cent of the voters participating in a local *referendum* (direct vote) approved a $2.57-billion program for rail-transit construction and street improvements. In midsummer, Houston opened its first major tollways, the Hardy Toll Road and the Sam Houston Tollway. On November 15, Amtrak resumed rail service between Houston and Dallas, which had been halted since 1981.

Professional sports. On Jan. 10, 1988, the Houston Oilers lost 34-10 to the Denver Broncos in an American Football Conference semifinal play-off game, ending their Super Bowl chances. The Houston Astros stayed in contention most of the season to lead baseball's National League Western Division, but lost 13 of their last 17 games and finished 12½ games out of first place. *Charles Reinken*

See also **City.** In *World Book*, see **Houston.**

Hungary. The Hungarian Socialist Workers' Party, Hungary's Communist party, changed leaders and approved a package of Western-style political reforms at a national conference of the party on May 20 to 22, 1988. The changes apparently had the full approval of the Soviet Union.

Hungary's leader, János Kádár, was retired as general secretary of the party, a post he had held since 1956. The 75-year-old Kádár was succeeded by Prime Minister Károly Grósz, 57. In November, Grósz resigned as prime minister to focus on his duties as party chief, and Miklós Németh, 40, became the new prime minister. Both Grósz and Németh favor economic reforms that would increase the role of private initiative in Hungary's socialist system. See **Grósz, Károly.**

The delegates at the convention also removed Kádár and 7 of his closest allies from the Politburo, the party's policymaking body, and added 6 reform-minded individuals to that group. The changes reduced the number of Politburo members from 13 to 11. In addition, the delegates replaced more than 40 members of the party's 106-member Central Committee, which handles party affairs between national conferences.

A new generation. The Kádár era had been identified with Hungary's 1968 New Economic Mechanism (NEM), a program that introduced features of a free-market system into Hungary's economy. At first, the NEM helped the economy grow. Then, a global reces-

Hungary's leader Károly Grósz, visiting the United States in July, takes time out from affairs of state to meet Mickey Mouse in Disneyland.

sion in the early 1980's and a restraining hand by Soviet leader Leonid I. Brezhnev—a firmly orthodox Communist—led to an economic standstill. Impatient with this standstill, reform-minded officials—and, increasingly, young workers in the rank and file of the Communist party—looked forward to the replacement of the party's aging leadership.

The May conference surpassed their most optimistic hopes. The sweeping personnel changes reduced the average age of the Politburo from the mid-60's to 52, giving Hungary the youngest leadership in the Communist bloc.

Political reforms. A position paper approved at the conference called for numerous political reforms, including expanding the number of elections in which voters may choose between two candidates, limiting the number of terms served by certain party officials, and granting more power to local branches of the party. One of the new members of the Politburo, 55-year-old Imre Pozsgay, said that the party should make room for non-Communist opinions.

Non-Communist organizations flourished throughout 1988. Journalists ignored censorship regulations and campaigned for a law that would grant more independence to news media. On September 3, writers and reform economists launched a group called the Democratic Forum. Other organizations founded in 1988 were the Federation of Young Democrats and Hungary's first independent labor union, the Democratic Trade Union of Scientific Employees.

'Twixt East and West. Hungary's changing position in Europe was evident in a 30 per cent jump in exports to the West. On June 30, Hungary became the first Communist state to sign a comprehensive trade agreement with the European Community (EC or Common Market), the West European trading bloc.

Grósz made a successful visit to the United States from July 20 to 27. He met with both major candidates for President, talked to U.S. and international bankers, and then ended his trip with a two-hour discussion with President Ronald Reagan. Grósz spent July 27 to 29 in Canada. Earlier in 1988, as prime minister, Grósz had visited Great Britain and West Germany.

A quarrel with Romania, a neighboring Communist country, worsened in March 1988, when Romania said that it intended to tear down some 7,000 villages in Romania and replace them with 500 agricultural-industrial settlements. Many of the villages are peopled by ethnic Hungarians.

On June 27, about 40,000 Hungarians demonstrated against the plan in Budapest, the capital of Hungary. Reports reached London in August that Romania had already demolished 16 villages. On August 28, Grósz discussed the resettlement issue and a number of other matters with Romania's President Nicolae Ceauşescu. Ceauşescu refused to reconsider the resettlement plan.   Eric Bourne

See also **Europe** (Facts in brief table). In *World Book*, see **Hungary**.

Ice skating. Brian Boitano of Sunnyvale, Calif., and Katarina Witt of East Germany swept the major figure-skating championships in 1988. Among the successful speed skaters were Bonnie Blair of Champaign, Ill.; Yvonne van Gennip of the Netherlands; and Karin Enke Kania of East Germany.

Figure skating. Experts regarded the 24-year-old Boitano as probably the best technical skater ever. In the United States championships, held from January 4 to 9 in Denver, he won his fourth consecutive men's title. In the Winter Olympic Games, held from February 13 to 28 in Calgary, Canada, he beat his long-time rival, Brian Orser of Penetanguishene, Canada, for the gold medal. Then, in the world championships, held from March 22 to 26 in Budapest, Hungary, Boitano won by beating Orser again.

Witt won her sixth straight European women's title on January 14 in Prague, Czechoslovakia. She won her second straight Olympic gold medal on February 27, and her fourth world championship in five years on March 26 in Budapest. At the Olympics, Witt was challenged by Debi Thomas of San Jose, but Thomas' hopes collapsed when she landed badly on a difficult combination jump 15 seconds into her free-skating program. Thomas finished third behind Witt and Elizabeth Manley of Ottawa, Canada, in the Olympics. The three skaters finished in the same order in the world championships.

Soviet couples dominated international competition. In pairs, the favored Ekaterina Gordeeva and Sergei Grinkov won the Olympic gold medals, though Elena Valova and Oleg Vasiliev upset them for the world championship on March 23. In ice dancing, Natalya Bestemianova and Andrei Bukin won the Olympic gold medal and their fourth world title.

Speed skating. Blair was the most successful U.S. speed skater in the Olympics, winning a gold medal in the women's 500 meters in 39.10 seconds, a world record. She also won a bronze in the 1,000 meters and finished fourth in the 1,500 meters. On February 14, hours after learning of his sister's death from leukemia, Dan Jansen of West Allis, Wis., tried to win a gold medal in the men's 500 meters but fell on the first turn. Jansen fell again in the 1,000 meters, ending U.S. hopes for a gold medal in men's speed skating. Eric Flaim of Pembroke, Mass., won a silver medal.

The Olympic races produced seven world records in 10 events. East German women won 10 of 15 medals. Of the 5 they lost, Blair won 2 in the shortest races, and van Gennip won 3 golds in the longest races.

American men won both world championships—Flaim (overall) and Jansen (sprints). The women's world champions were Kania (overall) and Christa Rothenburger of East Germany (sprint).   Frank Litsky

See also **Boitano, Brian; Olympic Games; Witt, Katarina.** In *World Book*, see **Ice skating.**

Iceland. See Europe.

Idaho. See State government.

Illinois. See Chicago; State government.

Immigration

Immigration. A one-year amnesty program for many illegal aliens, established by a sweeping 1986 United States immigration law, expired on May 4, 1988, despite efforts in Congress to extend it. Although the Immigration and Naturalization Service (INS) had estimated that about 3.9 million illegal aliens met the requirements of the program and that 2 million would actually apply, the final count was about 1.4 million. Under the program, illegal aliens who had resided continuously in the United States since before Jan. 1, 1982, could seek temporary legal-resident status. Temporary legal aliens would be eligible after 18 months to apply for permanent resident status, which in turn would let them seek U.S. citizenship after five years.

In March 1988, in a move to encourage applications, the INS approved a 60-day extension for aliens who began but did not complete the application process by the May 4 deadline. On April 20, the U.S. House of Representatives voted 213 to 201 to extend the deadline to November 30, the expiration date for a related, smaller amnesty program for agricultural workers. The measure died in the Senate on April 28, when supporters fell 4 votes short of the 60 needed to cut off debate by opponents.

INS Commissioner Alan C. Nelson said 55 per cent of the 1.4 million applicants lived in California. More than 17 per cent lived in Texas and almost 7 per cent in Illinois. The median age of the applicants was 30, and more than 70 per cent had entered the United States from Mexico.

Totals and trends. The Center for Immigration Studies, a private research group, predicted in July that between 1981 and 1990 the number of legal immigrants would equal or exceed the record 8.7 million registered between 1901 and 1910. The center noted that the new arrivals are primarily of Asian and Hispanic descent, whereas those who came in the early 1900's were mostly from Europe.

The National Bureau of Economic Research reported in January 1988 on a study showing that the immigration influx of the 1980's has had little impact on U.S. job markets outside of California, Florida, New York, and Texas. The greatest job impact was felt by other immigrants, according to Richard B. Freeman, a Harvard University economist who coordinated the two-year study.

The sanctuary movement, aimed at helping Central American refugees, won a major legal victory on August 2, when a federal district court jury in Albuquerque, N. Mex., acquitted a Lutheran minister and a free-lance writer of illegally smuggling two Salvadoran women into the country. The defendants were the first members of the sanctuary movement to be prosecuted since eight activists were convicted in May 1986 of smuggling or harboring illegal immigrants.   Frank Cormier and Margot Cormier

In *World Book*, see **Immigration.**

Income tax. See Taxation.

India. The monsoon winds that sweep over India from the Arabian Sea brought plentiful rain in 1988, reviving agriculture in the rural areas where most of India's 813 million people live and spurring economic growth in the cities. But Prime Minister Rajiv Gandhi's government was buffeted by regional problems and faced increasing political opposition.

The return of normal amounts of rainfall after four years of drought was the biggest event in the lives of most Indians during 1988. Food reserves, which had been partially depleted during the drought, were expected to be replenished by 1988's 22 per cent increase in grain yields.

Tragically, the rain also was responsible for about 1,000 deaths caused by flooding in Punjab and other states in northwest India during September and October. Experts blamed the partial deforestation of the Himalaya for the rapid runoff of rainfall, which otherwise would have soaked into the soil of the mountain woodlands and flowed gradually onto the plains.

Violence in Punjab took at least 2,000 lives during 1988 as the state degenerated into widespread lawlessness. The bloodshed originated with a militant minority of the Sikh religious community that used terrorism to advance its demands for the creation of a separate Sikh nation.

An estimated 2,000 Sikh terrorists killed more than 750 people during the first four months of 1988. In May, Indian paramilitary forces staged a 10-day siege of the Sikh Golden Temple in Amritsar, the terrorists' headquarters, clearing the temple. In the next few days, terrorists killed 245 people in retaliation, including many migrant Hindu laborers.

Gandhi attempted to work with moderate Sikhs for a solution to the strife in Punjab, but the terrorists continued murdering Sikh and Hindu leaders. Under heavy police protection, Gandhi visited Punjab on September 21 and made political and economic concessions intended to reconcile the warring factions, but violence continued. Amnesty International, a human-rights organization based in London, said Indian police had killed scores of Sikh militants in staged encounters. The government called Amnesty's interpretation of events "one-sided."

During the year, the government signed agreements to end two other regional insurgencies. In July and August, more than 7,000 members of the Gurkha National Liberation Front, a separatist group, laid down their weapons and agreed to end their two-year battle for the creation of a state for Nepali-speaking residents of northern West Bengal. On August 12, guerrillas in Tripura in eastern India agreed to end their eight-year fight for a separate homeland. In Mizoram and Nagaland, two other eastern states, however, settlements with former separatist rebels went sour. In response, Gandhi ousted officials of the state governments.

Continuing opposition to Gandhi. Candidates of Gandhi's Congress Party were defeated in special elec-

Sikh terrorists, their hands raised in surrender, leave the Sikh Golden
Temple in Amritsar after a 10-day siege by Indian police in May.

tions on June 16 for four seats in Parliament and six
state assembly seats. The most important contest—for
the Parliament seat once held by Gandhi's grandfather, Jawaharlal Nehru, and later by Gandhi's mother,
Indira Gandhi, each of whom later became prime
minister—was won by Vishwanath Pratap Singh. In
1987, Singh had been fired from Gandhi's cabinet, reportedly for threatening to expose government corruption, and had then formed the opposition People's Front. Singh's parliamentary campaign attacked
Gandhi and accused his government of corruption.

Seven small regional political parties created an
opposition alliance called the National Front on Sept.
17, 1988. On October 11, several important opposition
leaders and their parties joined together to create the
People's Party, with Singh as president, and this party
became the nucleus of the National Front. Singh's
main challenger for leadership was Ramakrishna
Hegde, a former head of the Karnataka state government. Hegde had resigned his government post on
August 10 because of charges that he tapped the telephones of his political foes, but the resulting furor over
phone tapping by Gandhi's government hurt it also.

Polls showed that many Indians believed Gandhi
tolerated corruption and nepotism and acted auto-
cratically. Singh and others focused their criticism of
the government on charges of corruption, including
allegations that large kickbacks had been made to
politicians for a $1.3-billion defense contract. But

rivalries among the opposition politicians raised questions about their ability to stay united throughout the
1989 parliamentary election campaigns.

Plagued by charges of corruption that appeared in
India's newspapers, the government introduced a
parliamentary bill to tighten the legal definition of
defamation (slander or libel) and prescribe a mandatory jail sentence for it. But after the public protested
this apparent attempt to muzzle the press, the government postponed action on the bill.

Other developments. An attempt to launch a
space satellite on July 13 failed when the five-stage
rocket intended to propel the satellite into orbit
plunged into the Bay of Bengal. It was India's second
such attempt. The first—in 1987—also failed.

Gandhi visited China from Dec. 19 to 23, 1988, the
first such trip by an Indian prime minister since 1954.
Soviet leader Mikhail S. Gorbachev visited India in
November.

The economy was expected to grow by about 10
per cent in 1988—four times the growth rate in 1987,
when the drought severely hampered the economy.
Because the expected growth rate would be well
ahead of the population growth rate of more than 2
per cent, per-capita income was also expected to
increase. Nonetheless, more than one-third of India's
people live in poverty.   Henry S. Bradsher

See also **Asia** (Facts in brief table). In *World Book*,
see **India**.

329

Indian, American

Indian, American. Indians from the United States and Canada campaigned for independence for native populations on an international scale in 1988. At a press conference in Moscow in May during the summit meeting between President Ronald Reagan and Soviet leader Mikhail S. Gorbachev, activists with the American Indian Movement complained to the international news media that although Reagan criticized the human-rights record of the Soviet Union, Native Americans continued to suffer in hunger and poverty.

And at the headquarters of two United Nations (UN) agencies in Geneva, Switzerland, North American Indians and other peoples who had become minorities in countries where they were the original inhabitants lobbied unsuccessfully against amendments proposed by the Canadian delegation on two separate issues. One amendment—before the UN subcommittee on human rights in February—involved changes to a proposed study of treaties. The other amendment—before the International Labor Organization in June—concerned the wording of a declaration of the rights of indigenous peoples.

Land-claims settlements. On Oct. 22, 1988, the province of Alberta, Canada, settled a long-running dispute with the Lubicon Lake Indians by agreeing to give them control over 95 square miles (250 square kilometers) of government-owned wilderness they had long claimed as their homeland. Earlier in October, the 477-member Indian band, frustrated over years of fruitless land-rights negotiations, had declared itself an independent nation. On October 15, the band blocked off access to the disputed area, which includes hundreds of U.S. and Canadian oil wells. Canadian police dismantled the blockade after five days, and the agreement between the Indians and Alberta's Premier Donald R. Getty followed two days later. At year-end, the Indians were still negotiating with the federal government.

The Lubicon Lake agreement capped off a series of Canadian land-claims settlements made during 1988. In July, the Council of Yukon Indians, which represents 5,500 members of 13 bands, voted to approve most provisions of an agreement-in-principle that gave them control over about 16,000 square miles (41,500 square kilometers) of land and more than $170 million. (All dollar amounts in this article are in U.S. dollars.)

Then, on September 5, Canadian Prime Minister Brian Mulroney signed a tentative agreement to make 13,000 Native Americans in the Northwest Territories the largest private landholders in North America. The deal would award $405 million and full title to about 3,800 square miles (10,000 square kilometers) of land, and surface rights to an additional 65,600 square miles (170,000 square kilometers), to the Dene Indians and *métis* (people of mixed Indian and white ancestry).

In one of the largest land-claim settlements ever in the United States, the Puyallup Indians agreed in August to drop claims to 300 acres (120 hectares) in

A poster highlights an American Indian group's 1988 campaign to persuade sports organizations to abandon Indian-related team names.

Tacoma, Wash., in exchange for cash, land, and job training worth a total of $162 million.

Protests. Mohawk Indians of the Kahnawake reserve blocked off a highway in suburban Montreal, Canada, for two days in June to protest a police raid. The police had seized $365,000 worth of duty-free cigarettes and arrested 17 Mohawks for illegally selling cigarettes to non-Indians.

In the United States, the National Congress of American Indians (NCAI), which represents 150 tribal governments, passed a resolution in March asking for the removal of Ross O. Swimmer, assistant secretary of the U.S. Bureau of Indian Affairs (BIA). The NCAI was angered by a number of Swimmer's initiatives, including a 1987 plan to turn control of BIA-run schools over to states or tribal councils. The NCAI said most tribal councils are not ready to operate schools and that control would therefore revert to the states.

Supreme Court decisions. In April 1988, the Supreme Court of the United States rejected an appeal by Alaskan Indians who wanted to hunt migratory birds in the spring and summer. The court also decided in April to allow the U.S. government to cut timber and build a road in a national forest in California that is sacred to three tribes. A lower court had halted the project, saying it infringed on the Indians' constitutional rights.   Rudy Platiel

In *World Book*, see **Indian, American.**
Indiana. See **State government.**

Indonesia. On March 10, 1988, the People's Consultative Assembly unanimously elected President Suharto to a fifth five-year term. Suharto, who turned 67 in 1988, has held the presidency since 1967.

Although his election was unchallenged, Suharto stirred opposition by selecting Sudharmono, a 60-year-old military lawyer, as vice president. Sudharmono was a former general, but his appointment was opposed by Indonesia's politically powerful armed forces, who regarded him as a bureaucrat with leftist tendencies.

Uneasy military. Since 1983, Sudharmono had been chairman of the Golkar political organization, a ruling coalition of top generals and government and business leaders. The generals feared that Sudharmono's appointment and his possible succession to the presidency could mean their loss of influence in Golkar. But on October 25, Wahono, a Golkar member favored by the generals, was elected party chairman.

Army leaders and some newspapers also campaigned against a revival of the Communist Party, which had been crushed in 1965, as a way of warning the public to beware of leftist influences.

The second most powerful person in Indonesia, General Benny Murdani, was retired from his post as commander of the armed forces by Suharto on February 27. General Try Sutrisno was appointed his successor. Murdani, Suharto's long-time intelligence chief, had become critical of some aspects of the regime. When Suharto reorganized his Cabinet on March 21, he made Murdani defense minister, a post with little real power.

The new Cabinet included a career diplomat, Ali Alatas, as foreign minister. Alatas sought to increase Indonesia's international role by promoting Indonesia as the leader of the Nonaligned Movement, an organization of developing countries and other political groups. The movement chose Yugoslavia for the leadership position, however.

Economy. In June, monthly exports of items other than oil and gas—including timber, rubber, and manufactured goods—surpassed $1 billion for the first time. This was a milestone in Indonesia's efforts to diversify its economy, which had been dangerously dependent on oil and gas when world prices for petroleum products dropped in the mid-1980's. Economists said that an improvement in the government's policies had increased trade opportunities.

International organizations including the World Bank, which provides loans to countries for development projects, predicted that Indonesia's new policies would mean five years of economic growth, averaging 5 per cent per year. But unemployment and the more widespread underemployment—when people cannot find full-time jobs that pay a sufficient wage—remained a major problem as Indonesia's work force grew by about 3 per cent per year.   Henry S. Bradsher

See also **Asia** (Facts in brief table). In *World Book*, see **Indonesia.**

International trade volume in 1988 rose by about 7 per cent, the highest rate since 1984. United States export volume soared by 25 per cent, and Japan's imports increased by 15 per cent. These increases reflected both Japan's extraordinary economic growth and the U.S. dollar's depreciation since 1985, which made U.S. goods cheaper in other countries.

Huge trade imbalances continued to trouble the world economy, especially among the United States, Japan, and West Germany. Some progress, however, was made in reducing these imbalances. The U.S. balance-of-payments deficit—which reflects transactions in merchandise and services, and government and corporate money transfers—declined moderately from a record $154 billion in 1987. Japan's payments surplus, meanwhile, receded somewhat. Nevertheless, by the end of 1988, the U.S. foreign debt approached $500 billion. This rising debt, some economists warned, could destroy the stability of world markets and cause a global recession.

At the economic summit held from June 19 to 21, 1988, in Toronto, Canada, the leaders of Canada, France, Great Britain, Italy, Japan, the United States, and West Germany vowed to reinforce the dollar by reaffirming their support for stable exchange rates. The seven leaders also approved proposals to improve economic policy coordination among their governments. For the first time, they invited the "newly industrialized economies" of the Far East—Hong Kong, Singapore, South Korea, and Taiwan—to enter into broad economic policy discussions.

The debt burden of developing nations continued to rise in 1988, though at the slowest rate since the onset of the debt crisis in 1982. By the end of 1988, the debt was estimated at $1.25 trillion. There were some signs that the debt problem might be easing. Compared with the developing countries' exports, both the debt and payments on the debt declined during the year.

Promises of increased financing by both the World Bank and the International Monetary Fund (IMF), two United Nations agencies, improved the developing countries' prospects. The World Bank's lending resources expanded by $74.8 billion. The bank also opened a new agency called the Multilateral Investment Guaranty Agency to help developing nations attract foreign investment. The IMF announced programs to help developing countries offset higher international interest rates and to provide longer and cheaper loans to nations undertaking economic reforms. The governments of major industrial countries, meanwhile, said they would reduce the debt burdens of the world's poorest nations through loan write-offs, lower interest rates, or longer repayment terms.

The three most heavily indebted developing countries—Argentina, Brazil, and Mexico—received special assistance. Brazil won a major agreement from its creditor banks, including $5.2 billion in new loans, and lower interest and longer repayment terms on $63-

The president of McDonald's Restaurants of Canada, left, and the Soviet ambassador to Canada celebrate a May decision to open 20 restaurants in Moscow.

billion of outstanding debt. The U.S. Department of the Treasury offered Mexico a $3.5-billion line of credit, and the World Bank announced a $1.25-billion aid package for Argentina.

New U.S. trade bill. President Ronald Reagan on August 23 signed a landmark U.S. trade bill intended to promote exports while protecting domestic industries from unfairly priced imports. The new law authorizes the United States to negotiate lower tariffs and otherwise liberalize trade with nations subscribing to the General Agreement on Tariffs and Trade (GATT).

In December, the United States and about 100 other nations, under the auspices of the GATT, announced in Montreal, Canada, tentative procedures for negotiating by 1990 a series of trade-liberalizing accords. A dispute between the United States and the European Community (EC or Common Market) blocked any conclusive agreements in Montreal, however.

Trade frictions. On September 28, Reagan signed legislation passed by Congress on September 19 to put into effect the U.S. part of the U.S.-Canadian free-trade agreement. The pact provides for duty-free trade between the two countries by 1999.

The free-trade agreement also required the approval of the Canadian Parliament and became a major issue in Canada's parliamentary election on November 21. The Progressive Conservatives (PC's) of Prime Minister Brian Mulroney supported the agreement. Both major opposition parties—the Liberal

Party of former Prime Minister John N. Turner and the New Democratic Party led by Edward Broadbent—opposed the pact. They said it would destroy Canadian businesses and force Canada to integrate its economy completely with that of the United States. In the election, the PC's won a majority in the House of Commons, and the free-trade agreement received final approval on December 30.

The U.S. government expressed growing concern during 1988 over the large trade and payments surpluses of South Korea and Taiwan. The United States terminated, effective Jan. 1, 1989, tariff-free treatment on hundreds of South Korean and Taiwanese products as well as on goods from Hong Kong and Singapore.

United States trade frictions with Japan eased somewhat after Japan agreed to relax import quotas on beef, oranges, and other food items. In a rare trade reprisal, the United States raised tariffs on Brazilian paper, chemical, and electronic products after Brazil denied patent protection for U.S. pharmaceutical manufacturers. The United States also retaliated against an EC ban on hormone-treated U.S. meat by imposing 100 per cent tariffs on certain European foods. Both the EC ban and the U.S. tariffs went into effect on Jan. 1, 1989.   Richard Lawrence

See also **Economics.** In *World Book*, see **International trade.**

Iowa. See **State government.**

Iran. After a year's delay, Iran on July 18, 1988, accepted United Nations (UN) Security Council Resolution 598, which called for a cease-fire and peace negotiations to end Iran's eight-year war with Iraq. The UN had passed the resolution in July 1987.

In addition to halting hostilities, Iran's decision ended a long and often bitter dispute between rival factions within the country over the conduct of the war. The dispute had divided the Iranian leadership and had begun to undermine public confidence in the regime of Iran's leader, Ayatollah Ruhollah Khomeini.

Battlefield defeats were a key factor in Iran's decision to suspend hostilities. The reverses began in April 1988, when Iraq's forces recaptured the Fao Peninsula near the head of the Persian Gulf. In June, an Iraqi attack recovered the marshy Majnoon Islands northeast of Al Basrah, Iraq's second-largest city. Further defeats followed, and by early July, Iranian forces had been driven from Iraqi territory.

Another key factor in Iran's decision to accept the resolution was the resumption of Iraq's air war against Iranian industrial plants. In late February, Iraq began firing Soviet-designed Scud B surface-to-surface missiles at Iranian cities—including Teheran, Iran's capital—previously believed to be out of range. The missiles, 140 of which fell on the Iranian capital alone, caused few casualties and relatively little damage. But the attacks had a devastating effect on public morale as schools closed and residents fled to nearby mountain areas or resorts along the Caspian Sea for refuge.

The Iranian war effort suffered another setback in April when United States naval vessels in the Persian Gulf put one-fourth of the Iranian Navy out of action. In a daylong battle, U.S. ships sank or damaged four patrol boats and two frigates.

Jetliner disaster. On July 3, the U.S. Navy cruiser *Vincennes* shot down an Iranian commercial jetliner by mistake, killing all 290 people aboard (see **Armed forces**). Hard-line supporters of the war, notably Khomeini's designated successor, Ayatollah Hossein Ali Montazeri, called for retaliation against U.S. installations and personnel. But Khomeini overruled them.

Opposition attacks. The Mujaheddin-e-Khalq (People's Crusaders), the only organized Iranian opposition group to the Khomeini regime still in existence, took advantage of Iraqi battle successes to launch several raids into Iran from bases in Iraq. In June, Mujaheddin units took part in the capture of the Iranian border town of Mehran.

Internal debate. Rival factions within the Iranian government waged their own battles over the conduct of the war. In May, Mehdi Bazargan, a former prime minister and the head of the token opposition Liberation Movement of Iran, wrote an open letter to Khomeini accusing him of trafficking in the blood of martyrs by continuing to insist on a victory in the war. Antiwar rallies were held in several cities, and delegations of *mullahs* (religious leaders) warned Khomeini that the war was sapping morale. In the end, it was

Khomeini's own decision—which he said "was more deadly than poison"—to accept the cease-fire.

Executions. At least 300 people were executed in Iran in 1988 in the most violent political crackdown in the country since the 1980 revolution, according to a report issued in December 1988 by Amnesty International, a human rights group based in London. The group said thousands may have died in the wave of executions, which began in June. Those killed included Kurds, supporters of the Mujaheddin-e-Khalq, and members of left wing groups.

Elections for a new Majlis (parliament) were held in April and May. Because political parties are banned in Iran, candidates represented professional or business groups, workers, or special interest groups such as the clergy. The reformists, who advocate state intervention in the economy, including land reform and the nationalization of industry, won 146 of the 244 seats up for election. Traditionalists, who support a free-market economy, strict adherence to Islam, and efforts to export the Iranian revolution, won 80 seats.

Foreign relations. Iran improved its image abroad in 1988 by restoring links with a number of countries. Iran and France reestablished diplomatic relations in June. France had broken off relations in July 1987 over accusations that an Iranian diplomat in Paris had been involved in terrorist activities. Iran restored relations with Canada in July 1988. In December, Great Britain reopened its embassy in Teheran, which had been closed in 1979.

But Saudi Arabia broke off relations in April 1988 after Khomeini rejected Saudi demands that only 50,000 Iranian pilgrims attend the annual Islamic pilgrimage to Mecca, Saudi Arabia, Islam's most sacred city. The Saudis feared a repeat of the bloody riots that occurred during the 1987 pilgrimage.

Social policy. Khomeini played a pivotal role in 1988 in resolving political deadlocks between reformists and traditionalists that had blocked bills on land reform, education, and other social programs. In January, he announced that the government could legitimately enact measures for the good of society even if these measures were considered anti-Islamic by conservative mullahs. He also appointed a special committee to mediate between the Majlis and the Council of Guardians, the conservative religious body that has final approval over legislation.

The economy. The war with Iraq left 123,000 Iranians dead and 500,000 wounded by official count and was estimated to have cost Iran $24 billion in military expenditures and $23 billion in lost oil revenues. Before the cease-fire, industry was operating at only 42 per cent of capacity because of Iraqi raids. With inflation at 75 per cent, a 25 per cent unemployment rate, and shortages of such basic commodities as meat and sugar, the war's end came none too soon for the Iranian people. William Spencer

See also **Iran-contra affair; Iraq; Middle East** (Facts in brief table). In *World Book*, see **Iran**.

Iran-contra affair. Prosecution of key figures in the Iran-contra affair—the White House scandal involving the sale of arms to Iran and the diversion of profits from those sales to *contra* rebels in Nicaragua—was put off in 1988 until at least January 1989. The delay came as judges, prosecutors, and defense attorneys argued about prospects for fair trials. President Ronald Reagan announced on Dec. 1, 1988, that he would pardon none of the defendants and would block use in the trial of classified documents that would threaten national security.

The investigation proceeds. On January 19, the Supreme Court of the United States rejected an attempt by Marine Lieutenant Colonel Oliver L. North to block an investigation of his role in the scandal. North, a former National Security Council (NSC) staff member, was the person most closely involved with the day-to-day management of the undercover operation, which was carried out in 1985 and 1986. The high court let stand a federal appeals court ruling that upheld the authority of the U.S. attorney general to assign the case to a special prosecutor.

On March 11, 1988, Robert C. McFarlane, former national security adviser to President Reagan, pleaded guilty to four misdemeanor counts of purposely misleading Congress by withholding information about White House efforts to support the contras. Sentencing of McFarlane was deferred.

Four key figures indicted. A federal grand jury on March 16 indicted North; Rear Admiral John M. Poindexter, President Reagan's former national security adviser; and two other central figures in the Iran-contra affair on charges of conspiring to defraud the U.S. government. In addition, North and Poindexter were charged with trying to cover up their activities. Poindexter, who succeeded McFarlane as Reagan's national security assistant, had been North's NSC boss.

The two others indicted were retired Air Force Major General Richard V. Secord and Albert A. Hakim, an Iranian-born businessman. Working together, Secord and Hakim negotiated many phases of the arms sales and arranged most related financial transactions. The defendants all pleaded not guilty.

Separate trials. On June 8, U.S. District Judge Gerhard A. Gesell ordered separate trials for all four defendants. Gesell said that was the only way they could get fair treatment because all but Secord had been granted limited immunity for testifying before congressional investigators in 1987. In a joint trial, the judge said, none of the accused could use, in his own defense, information that fellow defendants had presented in their congressional testimony.

Prosecutor Lawrence E. Walsh said a day later he would bring North to trial first. North had retired from the Marine Corps on May 1 because, he said, continued service would be "inconsistent" with his plans to mount a "vigorous defense." In December, Gesell scheduled North's trial to begin on Jan. 31, 1989.   Frank Cormier and Margot Cormier

Iraq. Victory celebrations throughout Iraq marked the Aug. 20, 1988, cease-fire that halted hostilities in the country's eight-year war with Iran. On August 8, both countries had formally accepted United Nations (UN) Security Council Resolution 598, which called for the cease-fire and negotiations for a permanent peace settlement.

Iraq had originally accepted the resolution after its passage in July 1987, but Iran had refused to take similar action, insisting that Iraq must be declared the aggressor in the conflict and forced to pay war reparations. After Iran agreed to the resolution on July 18, 1988, however, Iraq hedged for several weeks before finally accepting.

Military success. The Iraqis were somewhat justified in claiming victory in the war, as the fighting had tilted sharply in their favor earlier in 1988. Iraqi forces recaptured the Fao Peninsula near the head of the Persian Gulf in April in a lightning offensive that marked their first advance into Iranian-held territory since 1982.

A second Iraqi attack in May recaptured the area around Shalamcheh, an Iraqi port on the Shatt al Arab River. Its capture in January 1987 had brought Iranian forces within artillery range of Al Basrah, Iraq's second-largest city and its major port.

On June 25, 1988, a third major Iraqi offensive recovered the Majnoon Islands, a marshy area northeast of Al Basrah believed to contain a 30-billion-barrel oil field, Iraq's largest reserve. The area had been held by Iran since 1984.

In June 1988, Iraqi troops and the allied Mujaheddin-e-Khalq (People's Crusaders)—an Iranian group opposed to the government of Iranian leader Ayatollah Ruhollah Khomeini—captured the Iranian border town of Mehran. In July, Iraqi units captured the important border towns of Halabjah and Al Amarah in northeast Iraq, driving the Iranian Army and its Kurdish allies across the border.

Air war. Earlier in 1988, Iraqi aircraft bombed Iranian cities with devastating psychological effect. Beginning in February, some 140 Soviet-designed Scud B surface-to-surface long-range missiles hit Teheran, Iran's capital, which had been thought to be beyond the range of those missiles.

Kurdish attacks. In August and September, following the cease-fire, the regime of President Saddam Hussein turned on Iraq's Kurds, many of whom had supported the Iranians in an attempt to win independence from Iraq. Several battalions of Kurdish rebels had fought with Iranian forces on the mountainous central front.

In the offensive into Kurdish areas, the Iraqi Army destroyed villages suspected of sheltering the rebels. At least 60,000 Kurdish refugees fled into Turkey. After the operation, the Kurds repeated previous accusations that the Iraqis were using chemical weapons, specifically mustard gas, to kill civilians. In March, Kurds had charged Iraqi forces with using chemical

Iraqi soldiers pose before a bullet-riddled portrait of Iran's leader Ayatollah Khomeini to cheer the April recapture of the Fao Peninsula.

weapons to attack the Kurdish border town of Halabjah after its capture by the Iranians. Thousands of Kurdish civilians were reportedly killed or injured. In September, the United States, Great Britain, West Germany, and Japan asked the UN to investigate the charges.

The economy stood to gain enormously from an end to eight years of debilitating war. Aside from 350,000 to 400,000 Iraqi casualties and thousands of refugees displaced by the fighting, the war had cost Iraq an estimated $65.5 billion, including $33 billion in military costs and billions in lost oil revenues due to damaged installations.

To speed the reconstruction process, Hussein formed a new ministry of civilian and military industries in July. It would supervise the transition from a wartime to peacetime economy. One goal within reach would be a 75 per cent increase in non-oil exports. In March, Iraq reported the discovery of a new sulfur field, which increased reserves to 567 million short tons (515 million metric tons), and of an aluminum silicon reserve estimated at 330 million short tons (300 million metric tons). Both would add significantly to the country's export potential.

Killing. Hussein's oldest son, Odai, was jailed on October 21 for allegedly killing a drunken bodyguard. Hussein ordered an investigation.   William Spencer

See also **Iran; Middle East** (Facts in brief table). In *World Book*, see **Iraq.**

Iron and steel

Ireland enjoyed a period of political stability in 1988. Prime Minister Charles Haughey was popular despite the painful economic measures he backed to help strengthen the country's weak economy. Opinion polls showed that his Fianna Fáil (Soldiers of Destiny) party had the support of more than half of Ireland's voters for what he described as the "new reality"—the urgent need to tackle the country's huge national debt.

Economy. Finance Minister Ray MacSharry on Jan. 27, 1988, announced a tough budget to deal with the national debt of 24 billion Irish pounds (about $38-billion). It called for cuts in public spending and hikes in the prices of gasoline and cigarettes.

Ireland's unemployment rate remained high. By year-end, 20 per cent of the work force was unemployed. High unemployment, coupled with a sluggish economy, caused an estimated 30,000 people to leave Ireland to seek better employment opportunities in other countries.

There was some good economic news in 1988, however. The government gained a surprise windfall from a tax amnesty program it announced in January. The program produced 500 million Irish pounds (about $716 million)—17 times the predicted amount—by the time it ended in September.

Relations with Britain became strained in 1988. In January, the British Court of Appeal in a retrial upheld the convictions of six Irish people found guilty of bomb attacks in Birmingham, England, in 1974. The retrial had resulted from new evidence showing that a scientist may have faked evidence at the first trial and that the defendants had confessed to the crime after being beaten. This decision was followed by an announcement that Great Britain would not prosecute the Royal Ulster Constabulary officers who in 1982 killed six unarmed people suspected of belonging to the outlawed Irish Republican Army (IRA).

The Irish government protested both decisions, but Prime Minister Haughey decided not to retaliate by halting border-security cooperation with British troops in Northern Ireland. This cooperation had been established under the Anglo-Irish Agreement signed in 1985 by the governments of Great Britain and Ireland. On Nov. 11, 1988, the Irish government issued a full review of the agreement.

On December 13, Ireland's attorney general refused to extradite an Irish Roman Catholic priest to Britain on terrorism charges, saying the priest could not get a fair trial there. (Under extradition, a prisoner is turned over to the jurisdiction of another country or state.) Controversy over the decision further strained relations between the two countries.

Prisoner policy. On January 19, the Irish Supreme Court ruled that because their offenses were political, IRA members could not be protected from extradition to Northern Ireland.   Ian J. Mather

See also **Northern Ireland.** In *World Book*, see **Ireland.**

Iron and steel. See Steel industry.

Israel

Israel. After seven weeks of feverish, often rancorous negotiations following an inconclusive national election, Israel's two major political parties agreed on Dec. 19, 1988, to form another coalition government. The Likud bloc and the Labor Party had formed a similar government after the 1984 election, which had also failed to produce a clear winner.

Under the agreement, Yitzhak Shamir, the leader of the Likud bloc, was to remain as prime minister. Shimon Peres, the leader of the Labor Party, was named as finance minister. The new government was sworn in on Dec. 22, 1988. Given Likud and Labor's deep policy differences, however, it was uncertain whether the new government would be able to deal effectively with the Palestinian uprising in the occupied territories or to negotiate with the Palestine Liberation Organization (PLO), which recognized Israel's right to exist in December.

Stalemate. The results of the parliamentary election, held on November 1, underscored the deep divisions among Israelis over future dealings with their Arab neighbors and the Palestinian *intifada* (uprising) in the Israeli-occupied West Bank and Gaza Strip. During the election campaign, Shamir had strongly defended the government's harsh measures to suppress Palestinian unrest and ruled out any peace settlement that required Israel to give up the occupied territories. In contrast, Peres advocated an Israeli withdrawal from the Gaza Strip and parts of the West Bank in return for a peace treaty safeguarding Israel's existence.

Neither Likud nor Labor won the 61 seats needed to form a majority in the 120-seat Knesset (parliament). The election, which drew a record 80 per cent of Israel's eligible voters, ended in a virtual draw with Likud winning 40 seats and Labor taking 39. Smaller parties—some to the right of Likud, others to the left of Labor—won the balance of the seats. The surprise winners in the election were four ultrareligious parties—Shas, Degel HaTorah, Agudat Israel, and the National Religious Party—which gained 15 per cent of the popular vote and 18 Knesset seats.

On November 14, Israel's President Chaim Herzog officially invited Shamir to form a government. With Likud and Labor separated by serious policy differences, the four religious parties seemed to hold the balance of power and were courted by both parties.

Religious demands. In return for their support, the four parties demanded concessions opposed by many Israelis and American Jews. For example, they wanted the government to prohibit sports events and close theaters on the Jewish sabbath.

The most controversial demand, however, involved changes in the Law of Return. This law allows anyone born of a Jewish mother or anyone who converts to Judaism to immigrate to Israel and immediately receive citizenship. (Under Jewish law, the religion of the child is determined by the mother.)

Palestinians throw rocks at Israeli security forces on the West Bank in March, the third month of violent protests against the Israeli occupation.

Under the proposed amendments, immigrants to Israel born to mothers converted to Judaism by Conservative or Reform rabbis or immigrants themselves converted by Reform or Conservative rabbis would not be legally regarded as Jews by the Israeli government. Only conversions performed by Orthodox rabbis would be recognized.

The proposed changes caused a storm of protest among American Jews, most of whom are Conservative or Reform. Also faced with mounting opposition from the Israeli public to a government that included the ultrareligious parties, Likud and Labor agreed to form another coalition. Several prominent members of both the Labor Party and the Likud bloc, however, opposed the coalition, and Shamir and Peres were criticized for compromising with the opposition.

The Palestinian question. Two of the most pressing problems facing the new government were Israel's isolation in refusing to deal with the PLO and the Palestinian uprising in the occupied territories. In a dramatic diplomatic development, Yasir Arafat, chairman of the PLO, announced on December 14 that the PLO recognized Israel's right to exist in peace and security, and renounced terrorism. The United States then announced that the PLO had satisfied U.S. conditions for direct talks and opened discussions the next day. Israeli leaders rejected Arafat's statement as "meaningless," and reacted with shock and anger to the U.S. decision to talk directly with the PLO (see **Middle East**).

Unrest. The intifada in the occupied territories continued without letup throughout 1988. By mid-December, at least 330 Palestinians and 13 Jews had been killed and 7,000 people injured in the violence.

The Israeli Army and police tried various methods to suppress the uprising. They deported Palestinian activists, jailed thousands of Palestinians without charges, and destroyed the homes of people accused of participating in demonstrations or throwing stones at Israeli troops. The army also imposed strict curfews and periodically sealed off refugee camps in the Gaza Strip and parts of the West Bank. In January, the Israeli government instituted a policy of beating protesters in the occupied territories. Israeli officials said the change from using live ammunition to beatings would save lives. Soldiers also, however, beat Palestinians in house-to-house searches.

The Israeli actions prompted widespread international criticism. In January, members of the United Nations Security Council, including the United States, condemned the deportations of Palestinian activists. Amnesty International, a human rights organization based in London, deplored the conditions in Israeli detention camps.

The intifada also drove a wedge into Israeli society. Although many Israelis supported the government's actions in the occupied territories, others criticized them and demonstrated in protest. The harsh measures served only to heighten Palestinian resistance.

Israeli Arabs. Israel's own Arab population, previously quiet on the Palestinian unrest, began not only to actively support the uprising but also to display a new-found political activism seeking to end discrimination in jobs, education, civil service posts, and housing. The first Arab political party in Israel's history was formed in June. The platform of the Democratic Arab Party called for equal rights for Israeli Arabs, an international Middle East peace conference, and a binational state in what is now Israel and the occupied territories. The party won one seat in the November election.

Other developments. On September 19, Israel launched an experimental earth-orbiting satellite, thus becoming one of only eight nations with rockets capable of putting a satellite in space. The craft, which was code-named *Ofek* (Horizon), was designed to collect data on solar energy and the earth's magnetic field. Expected to remain in space for only about one month, the satellite was seen as a step toward the development of a reconnaissance satellite that would make Israel less dependent on the United States for military intelligence.

On March 24, Israeli nuclear technician Mordechai Vanunu was convicted of treason and espionage for selling information on Israel's Dimona nuclear center to a London newspaper. He was sentenced to 18 years in prison.　　William Spencer

In the World Book Supplement section, see **Israel**.

Italy. Prime Minister Giovanni Goria resigned on March 11, 1988, because of a dispute over a partially built nuclear power plant. This was Goria's third resignation since taking office on July 29, 1987. The most recent had occurred on Feb. 10, 1988, but President Francesco Cossiga had persuaded Goria to stay on until Parliament passed the national budget—which it did on March 10.

The nuclear issue had prevented Goria from forming a stable government, a coalition of Christian Democrats, Socialists, Republicans, Social Democrats, and Liberals—the same five parties that had governed the country since 1981. The issue concerned the Montalto di Castro nuclear power station north of Rome. The country was split over whether to complete the construction of the station as a nuclear plant or as a coal-burning facility. The Socialists and the Social Democrats opposed nuclear power. In addition, a national *referendum* (direct vote of the people) in 1987 had canceled the development of nuclear power, and closed the two reactors already built in Italy.

New leader. At Cossiga's request, Ciriaco De Mita, chairman of the Christian Democratic Party, struggled to develop a program on which a new coalition could be based. On April 12, 1988, De Mita forged a coalition of the five governing parties. He was sworn in as prime minister the next day. See **De Mita, Ciriaco**.

De Mita compromised with the Socialists to build his coalition. He needed support from Italy's left wing to remain in power, and in order to exclude Italy's powerful Communist Party from the government, he had to turn to the Socialists. In return for the backing of the Socialists, De Mita made two major concessions —a promise that the Montalto di Castro power station would be completed as a coal-burning plant, and a pledge to initiate a public employment program in Italy's economically deprived south.

Of Italy's 57 million people, 20 million live in the south, which is primarily an agricultural region. The unemployment rate in the south is 20 per cent, compared with 7.6 per cent in the industrial north.

Since the 1950's, the Italian government has poured $100 billion into the south to foster the development of industry. In addition, the government has offered financial incentives to companies to build factories there.

Adviser shot. De Mita received a severe setback on April 16, when the terrorist Red Brigades organization murdered Roberto Ruffilli, his close adviser. Ruffilli was a member of Parliament, a professor of history at the University of Bologna, and a leading strategist in the Christian Democratic Party. He had advised De Mita on constitutional reform and on ways to prevent the collapse of coalition governments—a problem that has dogged Italy. The Red Brigades announced their crime with this message: "We have carried out an attack on the heart of the state."

Communist support. De Mita received a boost from an unexpected source—the Communist Party, which had not supported an Italian government since 1978. That party's chairman, Alessandro Natta, said he would support the coalition government in a proposed radical reform of the operating procedures of Italy's Parliament.

Reform measures included a decrease in the duplication of functions between the two houses of Parliament and a reduction in the use of secret ballots in Parliament. Currently, members of political parties participating in a coalition government may vote in secret against the government. Such balloting has tended to destabilize Italy's governments. Parliament voted on October 13 to abolish the secret ballot, except on issues involving civil rights, linguistic minorities, electoral and parliamentary rules, and certain appointments.

Natta resigned on June 13, a month after suffering a heart attack. On June 21, Achille Occhetto succeeded him. But Occhetto, a moderate, gave only qualified support to the reform measures.

U.S. jets. On June 30, Parliament accepted a proposal to base 72 United States F-16 fighter planes at a cruise missile site at Cosimo, Sicily. The F-16's are to be moved from Torrejón, near Madrid, Spain, within three years.   Kenneth Brown

See also **Europe** (Facts in brief table). In *World Book*, see **Italy**.

Ivory Coast. See **Africa**.
Jamaica. See **West Indies**.

Japan. Emperor Hirohito—Japan's emperor since 1926—became critically ill on Sept. 19, 1988, when he suffered an attack of intestinal bleeding. The news media reported that he had cancer, though there was no official confirmation. One year earlier, Hirohito had undergone surgery for a pancreatic ailment and related intestinal blockage. Hirohito's advanced age—he turned 87 in 1988—was a complicating factor in his illness. The Imperial Household Agency, which is in charge of the emperor's affairs, was criticized for not releasing full details of his illness, particularly regarding the possibility of cancer.

The state of the emperor's health created widespread concern. Tens of thousands of Japanese citizens, both young and old, signed special books that expressed wishes for his speedy recovery. Schools canceled their customary autumn festivals, and a Cabinet minister canceled an official visit abroad. Individuals in the public eye called off parties and other private celebrations to avoid appearing disrespectful.

In late September, the English-language edition of a leading Japanese newspaper erroneously published an editorial lamenting the emperor's death. As a result, the editor in chief of the parent paper and the editor of the English edition lost their positions. Hirohito died on Jan. 7, 1989.

Expanding role in world affairs. Japan began in 1988 to be a more active participant in international politics, in keeping with its position as one of the wealthiest industrialized democracies. During the year, Prime Minister Noboru Takeshita visited the United States, Canada, Western Europe, South Korea, and China.

Speaking in London on May 4 at the conclusion of his tour of Western Europe, Takeshita announced a major new foreign-policy initiative. It had three principal elements: pursuing a new approach to working toward international peace; strengthening programs for international cultural exchange; and increasing Japan's assistance to Third World nations.

In pursuit of its goal to aid developing nations, Japan on June 14 announced a five-year plan for providing $50 billion in foreign assistance. The new plan would make Japan the biggest supplier of foreign aid, supplanting the United States. The 1988 Japanese budget allocated $10 billion for such aid.

Japan's attempts to promote peace included a $20-million contribution to the United Nations in April. The funds were targeted for peacekeeping efforts in Afghanistan and the Middle East. In July, Foreign Minister Sosuke Uno announced that Japan was considering financing an international military force to ensure peace and security in Kampuchea (formerly called Cambodia), as well as sending personnel to monitor that country's upcoming elections.

Japan attempted to influence the chaotic political situation in Burma, which was rocked by violent antigovernment protests in August, by urging the Burmese government to create economic stability in order to develop political stability. Japan was Burma's largest foreign-aid donor.

Relations with the United States. Takeshita made his first official visit to Washington, D.C., in January. He and U.S. President Ronald Reagan talked on a first-name basis, continuing the practice of Reagan and former Prime Minister Yasuhiro Nakasone. In a communiqué issued after their meeting, President Reagan pledged to continue his efforts to reduce the U.S. federal budget deficit and to veto protectionist trade bills, and Takeshita promised to stimulate Japan's demand for U.S.-made goods in order to reduce Japan's trade surplus with the United States. He also pledged to speed up the liberalization of Japan's interest-rate policy.

Some progress was made in correcting the trade imbalance, according to Japan's Ministry of Finance, which announced in January that Japan's trade surplus with the United States in 1987 was $52.1 billion, up only $700 million from 1986. This represented a significantly lower rate of increase than that of previous years. Japan's overall trade surplus for 1987 was $79.8 billion, a decrease of about 3.5 per cent from 1986.

On March 29, 1988, Japanese and U.S. officials announced that U.S. contractors would be allowed to bid on large Japanese public-works projects, including an airport near Osaka. Although the United States had long pressed for such an agreement, U.S. contractors were slow in responding to the new opportunity, according to a U.S. trade official.

The Japanese government announced on June 20 that it would remove all quotas on imported beef and oranges by 1991 and remove quotas on imported orange juice by 1992, thus ending another serious trade dispute between the United States and Japan. Under the plan, the quotas will be gradually liberalized until they are phased out. Japan will then establish gradually decreasing tariffs on these imports.

Investment in the United States. Throughout the year, Japanese companies continued to acquire U.S. firms. On February 16, Bridgestone Corporation, Japan's leading tire manufacturer, purchased three-fourths of the tire operations of Firestone Tire & Rubber Company. On September 30, the Saison Group, a huge retail and service organization, paid $2.27 billion in cash for the U.S. Intercontinental hotel chain.

The Japanese also continued to amass large holdings of U.S. real estate. An estimated $16 billion in such property was purchased by the Japanese in 1988, raising the total value of Japanese-owned U.S. real estate to $40 billion. This is about 1.5 per cent of the value of all real estate in the United States.

Economy. According to a survey by *American Banker* magazine in July, the world's 10 largest banks—as measured by deposits—were all Japanese. The Dai-Ichi Kangyo Bank led with deposits of $275.3-billion in 1987. The small number of banks in Japan

A Japanese woman prays for the health of Emperor Hirohito, whose serious illness in late 1988 distressed the Japanese people.

Japan

In February, Japanese protesters call for the return of four islands near Hokkaido held by the Soviet Union since the end of World War II in 1945.

—only 200, compared with some 14,000 in the United States—was one reason for Japan's prominence in this area.

After Japan's monthly unemployment rate hit a record high of 3.2 per cent in May 1987, it stabilized at about 2.8 per cent in early 1988. The improvement resulted from an increase in jobs in the sales and service sectors, reflecting the rising domestic demand for goods and services.

The government tried to bring an end to Tokyo's wild three-year-long real estate boom by limiting the prices paid in large transactions and instructing banks to cut back drastically on loans for real estate. Real estate in some areas had been priced at $250,000 per square yard ($209,000 per square meter)—and prices three times as high were not unheard of.

Takeshita called a special session of Japan's Diet (parliament) on July 29 to consider a new bill for tax reform, a hot political issue in Japan. The bill called for, among other things, a 3 per cent sales tax, which was particularly unpopular, and a cut in income taxes. Takeshita's objectives were to reduce Japan's budget deficit, finance care for the nation's rapidly growing aged population, and make the tax burden more fair. The bill was finally passed on December 24.

For the fiscal year ending in March 1988, Japan's budget deficit was $86 billion, about one-fifth of the *gross national product*, the value of all goods and services produced by the nation. The total amount of public debt had grown to about $1 trillion. Salaried workers paid a disproportionately high share of their income in taxes because tax was automatically deducted from their wages while self-employed people were allowed to calculate their own taxes.

Other developments. On March 13, the Seikan Tunnel, the world's longest undersea tunnel, opened to rail traffic. The 33.5-mile (53.9-kilometer) tunnel links the main Japanese island of Honshu with the island of Hokkaido. The Seto Ohashi Bridge Complex, the first bridge to connect Honshu with Shikoku, Japan's fourth-largest island, opened on April 10. The two-deck span, which cost $8.8 billion, is 6 miles (9.7 kilometers) long, making it the longest bridge of its type in the world.

In September, the Soviet Union informally suggested that Japan could lease four disputed islands just northeast of Hokkaido. The Japanese and the Soviets both claim ownership of the islands, which were occupied by the Soviets at the end of World War II in 1945. The informal proposal was the first relaxation of the Soviet position in the dispute.

On December 27, Takeshita reshuffled his Cabinet, replacing ministers tainted by a stock-trading scandal. Three days later, however, the newly appointed minister of justice resigned after admitting that he had accepted political contributions from the corporation involved in the scandal.   John M. Maki

See also **Asia** (Facts in brief table). In *World Book*, see **Japan**.

340

Jews and Judaism.
Jews throughout the world commemorated two significant historical events in 1988—the 40th anniversary of the creation of the state of Israel and the 50th anniversary of *Kristallnacht* (Night of Glass), an event in November 1938 when Nazis destroyed synagogues and Jewish property in Germany.

Israel's milestone. From April 21 to 23, Israel celebrated its 40th anniversary. The actual anniversary of independence was on May 14, 1988, but Israel celebrated according to the Hebrew calendar. The world's Jewish community used the occasion to express solidarity for the country. Many communities around the world marked the day with worship services, cultural events, and celebrations highlighting Israel's major accomplishments during its brief history.

Some of these celebrations, however, reflected the concern many Jews have over the continuing turmoil between Jews and Arabs in Israel, the Gaza Strip, and the West Bank. Many Jews—in Israel and around the world—oppose Israel's occupation of these areas and other Arab territories. During the year, they strongly urged the Israeli government to return "land for peace." An escalation in the number of Palestinian demonstrations and riots in 1988 intensified the moral conflict over the issue among many Jews.

Law of Return. A further source of tension among Jews in 1988 arose after Israel's November 1 elections. Neither the conservative Likud bloc nor the more moderate Labor Party won a majority in the country's Knesset (parliament). Following the election, Likud began working to set up a coalition government with four smaller Orthodox-religious political parties that would give it a majority in the Knesset. To win the support of these parties, Likud began pressuring the Knesset to amend Israel's Law of Return. This law grants citizenship to any Jew who chooses to settle in Israel. Because this law also applies to converts, Orthodox leaders want to restrict this right to Jews converted by Orthodox rabbis.

Reform and Conservative Jews in Israel and the United States vehemently oppose this proposed restriction. They believe it will destroy the unity of Jews around the world and compromise support for Israel from Jews in other countries. The issue seemingly was resolved when Likud and Labor agreed on December 19 to form another coalition government. See **Israel.**

Kristallnacht. November 9 marked the 50th anniversary of a Nazi attack on Jewish communities in Germany in 1938. Kristallnacht—so named for the broken glass that littered the streets of towns where Jews were attacked—is regarded as the beginning of the *Holocaust*, the murder of 6 million European Jews by the Nazis during World War II (1939-1945). In November 1938, the German government sponsored "demonstrations" that led to the destruction of thousands of synagogues and Jewish homes and businesses. More than 30,000 Jews were arrested, and an estimated 100 Jews were killed.

Around the world, Christians and civic officials joined Jews in memorial services in November to commemorate the event. Thousands of synagogues were lit up throughout the night in remembrance of the burning of the synagogues in Germany. Many church leaders recalled the silence of Christians in 1938. In a memorial service in Chicago, Joseph Cardinal Bernardin spoke of the "moral blindness" of the world at that time and observed that the Holocaust "is a deep wound that is still bleeding." He added that the Roman Catholic Church is working on a "dialogue of reconciliation between Jews and Christians."

Holocaust museum. In a ceremony in Washington, D.C., on Oct. 5, 1988, U.S. President Ronald Reagan dedicated the cornerstone of a new museum that will be a national center for the study of the Holocaust. When completed in 1990, the Holocaust Memorial Museum will offer exhibitions, lectures, and public education programs on the Holocaust and its meaning today.

The October dedication was attended by Holocaust survivors, religious leaders, members of Congress, and foreign ambassadors. During the ceremony, Reagan paid tribute to the Holocaust victims and said that the world must ensure that "from now until the end of days, all humankind stares this evil [the Holocaust] in the face" so that it "knows what this evil looks like and how it came to be."   Howard A. Berman

In *World Book*, see **Jews; Judaism.**

Jordan.
King Hussein I abruptly announced on July 31, 1988, that he was severing financial and administrative ties between Jordan and the Israeli-occupied West Bank. The West Bank was a part of Jordan until 1967, when Israel occupied the territory during the Six-Day War. Hussein said the action was in accordance with the decision made at the 1974 Arab League summit to designate the Palestine Liberation Organization (PLO) as the sole representative of the Palestinian people.

Breaking the links. The day before the announcement, Hussein had dissolved Jordan's 60-member House of Representatives, the lower house of the country's legislature. About half the members of the House were Palestinian.

On Aug. 4, 1988, the Jordanian government stopped paying the salaries of some 21,000 West Bank civil servants, teachers, and health workers. Long-time employees were pensioned off. The Jordanian ministry responsible for West Bank affairs was closed. The government also set a two-year time limit on Jordanian passports issued to Palestinians. On July 28, Hussein had canceled a five-year development program for the West Bank launched in 1986. The project had been plagued by political difficulties and had failed to attract outside funding.

Effects of the decision. Hussein's decision to cut ties with the West Bank pleased Jordanian nationalists, who felt that the country should concentrate on enhancing its own identity as a nation instead of wrestling with the problems of the Palestinians on the West Bank. The move was also expected to save the government about $20 million per month in wages and salaries.

One factor in Hussein's decision was Jordan's belief that the United States had failed to exert enough pressure on Israel to accept a political settlement for the occupied territories proposed by the United States in February. In May, Hussein criticized the United States for continuing to support Israel despite the refusal by Israel's Prime Minister Yitzhak Shamir to go along with the plan.

The economy. Increased imports and a drop in value of the Jordanian dinar, the country's unit of currency, slowed economic growth below the record rise achieved in 1987. Export revenues covered only one-fourth of the import bill, creating Jordan's first trade deficit since 1983.

An encouraging sign was increased world demand for phosphates and potash, Jordan's principal mineral resources. In September 1988, the Arab Potash Company, headquartered in Amman, recorded its first profit since it was established in 1984. The company benefited from a rise in potash prices from $60 to $81 per metric ton (1.1 short tons).   William Spencer

See also **Middle East** (Facts in brief table). In *World Book*, see **Jordan**.

Judaism. See **Jews and Judaism**.

Kampuchea. During 1988, a number of international meetings sought a way to end Vietnam's military occupation of Kampuchea (formerly called Cambodia) and transfer power from the Vietnamese-backed government to an opposition coalition led by Kampuchea's former leader, Prince Norodom Sihanouk. A major difficulty was the need to prevent the Khmer Rouge—a Communist group that killed more than 1 million people when it ruled Kampuchea from 1975 to 1979—from returning to power.

On May 25, Vietnamese officials announced the withdrawal of 50,000 troops from Kampuchea—saying that this was half its force there, though other estimates of the total ran to 140,000. Vietnam had pledged in February that its troops would be completely withdrawn by 1990.

All parties to the conflict met for the first time under the auspices of the Association of Southeast Asian Nations at Bogor, Indonesia, from July 25 to 28. Because Vietnam sought to link its withdrawal to some kind of guarantee that the Khmer Rouge would be kept from power, the meeting was inconclusive.

The Khmer Rouge in August offered to reduce the size of its guerrilla force and agreed to let an international peacekeeping force ensure that it did not seize power after the Vietnamese troops left. Despite these assurances, Sihanouk and other non-Communist Kampucheans feared that the Khmer Rouge would again try to dominate the country.

The United Nations (UN) in October reported "outrageous violations of human rights" in refugee camps run by the Khmer Rouge along the border of Thailand. A UN resolution passed on November 3 called for Vietnam to leave Kampuchea and demanded that the nation never return to the "universally condemned policies and practices" of the Khmer Rouge regime.

Sihanouk, his non-Communist coalition partner, and the prime minister of the Vietnamese-backed government met near Paris on November 7 and 8, but the Khmer Rouge boycotted the meeting. Those in attendance set up a group to work on a settlement but agreed that they would not meet again until September 1989.

On an October visit to Washington, D.C., Sihanouk hinted that his coalition's guerrilla supporters were receiving U.S. military aid—counter to a U.S. policy against supplying arms to the guerrillas. Later press reports said that in 1982 the United States had begun secretly funneling "nonlethal" aid to the guerrillas through Thailand (see **Thailand**). Meanwhile, China also worked through Thailand—but to supply the Khmer Rouge guerrillas.   Henry S. Bradsher

See also **Asia** (Facts in brief table). In *World Book*, see **Kampuchea**.

Kansas. See **State government**.

Kentucky. See **State government**.

Kenya. See **Africa**.

Korea, North. A woman arrested for the 1987 terrorist bombing of a South Korean airliner that killed 115 people confessed on Jan. 15, 1988, that she was a North Korean agent and that she helped plant the bomb. The woman, Kim Hyon Hui, said that the bombing was directed by Kim Jong-il, the son and designated successor of North Korea's President Kim Il-song. North Korea vehemently denied her statement.

Despite having agreed in 1987 to repay foreign debts that, including interest, amounted to $900-million, North Korea failed during 1988 to meet its obligations to international banks. Nonetheless, President Kim announced during the September 9 celebrations of North Korea's 40th anniversary that he wanted to "develop economic and technical cooperation and cultural exchange" with countries that did not have formal relations with North Korea. Observers speculated that Kim was worried that because South Korea was increasing its contacts with North Korea's major allies—China and the Soviet Union—the North might be left relatively isolated. In October, North Korea repeated a long-standing proposal that North and South Korea unite to form a single nation that combines Communist and capitalist systems of government.   Henry S. Bradsher

See also **Asia** (Facts in brief table); **Korea, South**. In the Special Reports section, see **The Two Koreas**. In *World Book*, see **Korea**.

Korea, South

Korea, South. Roh Tae Woo took office on Feb. 25, 1988, as South Korea's first popularly elected president. The former general, who assumed power in the first peaceful and legal presidential transition in the country's 40-year history, emphasized his concern for ordinary people by inviting taxi drivers and street sweepers to his inauguration.

Roh (pronounced *Noh*) named Lee Hyun Jae, a former president of Seoul National University, as prime minister on February 11. A recently retired chairman of the joint chiefs of staff, Oh Ja Bok, was named defense minister on February 19. At first, Roh retained seven members of the cabinet of his predecessor, Chun Doo Hwan, whom he had helped bring to power in 1980 after a military coup, but in December, Roh reorganized his cabinet. He replaced Lee with Kang Young Hoon and replaced Oh with General Lee Sang Hoon.

Election results. Roh had won election on Dec. 16, 1987, because his two main challengers, Kim Young Sam and Kim Dae Jung, split the opposition vote. The two Kims tried to put together a unified opposition slate for the April 26, 1988, elections for the National Assembly, South Korea's parliament. Their long rivalry could not be overcome, however, and they again led separate parties that divided the opposition vote.

Roh's Democratic Justice Party nonetheless won only 125 parliamentary seats with 34 per cent of the vote, thus failing to get a majority of the 299 seats. Kim Young Sam's Reunification Democratic Party won 59 seats with 24 per cent of the ballots cast, and Kim Dae Jung's Party for Peace and Democracy won 70 seats with 19 per cent of the vote. Kim Jong Pil, a former prime minister who also ran for the presidency in 1987, led his New Democratic Republican Party to win 35 seats with 15 per cent of the vote.

The two elections showed that South Korea was sharply divided along regional lines. Each of the opposition parties had a strong base in one part of the country, and Seoul, the capital, was hotly contested by all. The opposition parties were unable to put together a coherent program, and Roh's party maneuvered in the Assembly to win votes on various issues.

Roh sets new tone. Chun's younger brother, Chun Kyung Hwan, was arrested on March 31 on charges of influence-peddling and embezzling millions of dollars while Chun Doo Hwan was president. The former president apologized publicly on April 13 for his brother's misdeeds and resigned as chairman of the Council of Elder Statesmen, a role through which he had hoped to retain some influence. Chun Kyung Hwan was convicted of bribery, tax evasion, and other charges and was sentenced on September 5 to seven years in jail. Roh used the case to emphasize his personal and political break with his former patron.

In a nationally televised address on November 23, Chun apologized for human-rights violations and corruption during his administration. He promised to

Costumed performers, balloons, and fanfares mark the September 17 opening ceremonies of the 1988 Summer Olympic Games in Seoul, South Korea.

Opposition leader Kim Dae Jung posts results in South Korea's April election. The ruling party failed, for the first time, to win a parliamentary majority.

surrender millions of dollars to the government. In hopes of further defusing the public anger over Chun's legacy, Roh on December 20 released or reduced the jail sentences of almost 400 political prisoners and restored the civil rights of about 1,600 others who had opposed the government.

A change in the government's attitude toward the press and the military was demonstrated after a journalist who had criticized the military was stabbed and beaten on August 6. Before Roh took office, it would not have been unusual for such an assault to go unpunished. But an investigation of the August case spurred by the public's anger led to the arrest of two brigadier generals of the powerful Army Intelligence Command and the dismissal of the command's head.

Student demonstrations also lost some of their power under Roh's administration. The students' often-violent rallies for democracy had helped persuade Chun to allow the 1987 election, but under Roh, the demonstrations' focus shifted to calls for unification with North Korea and expressions of anti-American and nationalist sentiments. Unlike the student demonstrations of earlier years, the 1988 protests won little popular support.

Successful Olympics. The buoyant mood in South Korea reached a peak as the nation hosted the largest Summer Olympic Games ever staged. Despite fears of terrorist attacks by North Korea, extensive security measures and good planning made the Summer Games, which were held in Seoul from September 17 to October 2, a success. See **Olympic Games.**

Roh sought to capitalize on the resulting feeling of national pride in a speech to the National Assembly on October 4. Promising "clean and trustworthy government," he said that South Koreans had "now acquired the confidence that we can do anything to which we put our minds."

Unification efforts. Roh made a number of proposals during 1988 to improve relations with Communist North Korea. On July 7, he called for trade between the two countries, which have been divided since 1945, and he also authorized family visits and student exchanges. On July 18, the South Korean National Assembly proposed a joint meeting with parliamentarians in the North, but talks on the proposal broke off on August 26.

Roh proposed on August 15 a summit meeting with North Korean leader Kim Il-song "to work out practical ways to bring about national integration." Kim responded on September 8 with an invitation for Roh to visit Pyongyang, North Korea's capital, under certain conditions. On October 4, Roh said that he was willing to go, but the conditions were left unclear. Roh called for an international conference on Korean unification in an October 18 speech to the United Nations in New York City. It was the first such appearance by a leader of South or North Korea.

While North Korea remained isolated from most

major Western countries, the South's growing economic strength attracted trade initiatives from the North's Communist allies. China expanded its trade with South Korea to some $3 billion in 1988 despite the lack of diplomatic ties between the two countries. The Soviet Union explored opportunities for trade and for South Korean investment in developing the Soviet Far East. On September 13, South Korea said it and Hungary had agreed to exchange permanent missions. This was the first step toward establishing diplomatic relations with any Communist nation.

Economic growth. South Korea continued in 1988 the strong economic growth that had increased the average income sixfold in 30 years and made South Korea one of the world's most notable economic success stories. The nation's phenomenal growth was built on a policy of manufacturing goods for export using imported raw materials paid for with huge foreign loans. Although workers' wages were rising faster than productivity, thus increasing production costs, South Korea remained a competitive exporter, producing steel more cheaply than Japan or the United States, for example. By 1988, South Korea earned $10 billion per year more than it spent on imports and loan repayment.   Henry S. Bradsher

See also **Asia** (Facts in brief table); **Korea, North.** In the Special Reports section, see **The Two Koreas.** In *World Book*, see **Korea.**

Kuwait. See **Middle East.**

Labor. The unemployment rate in the United States fell to one of its lowest levels in 14 years in 1988, hitting 5.3 per cent. This meant that only 53 out of every 1,000 people in the U.S. labor force were unable to find a job. Wage increases continued to inch upward, but at a moderate rate. The U.S. Bureau of Labor Statistics Employment Cost Index—the broadest measure of wage change—showed an increase of 4.7 per cent from September 1987 to September 1988.

Collective bargaining. Despite the U.S. economy's sixth consecutive year of economic growth, wage and benefit increases won by employees in collective-bargaining agreements during 1988 remained moderate. Collective-bargaining agreements are negotiated by employees as a group, usually with a union representing them in negotiations. During the first nine months of the year, workers received an annual wage increase of 2.7 per cent, compared with a 2.1 per cent increase during the same period in 1987.

Approximately 1.4 million workers in 1988 were covered by major collective-bargaining agreements—those applying to 1,000 workers or more. During the first nine months of the year, these agreements provided average annual wage increases of 2.4 per cent over the life of contracts. The last time these contracts were negotiated, they yielded wage increases averaging 2.6 per cent.

The wave of wage and benefit concessions agreed to by employees during the 1980's as a way to help

their employers compete in the market place subsided somewhat in 1988, but was still evident. During the year, employers continued to provide bonuses, profit-sharing, and other one-time payments tied to productivity and profitability instead of permanent wage increases. Workers continued to seek agreements that would protect their jobs, a concern that usually arises during periods of recession, not in years of economic expansion, such as 1988.

Coal contract. The United Mine Workers of America (UMW) on Jan. 31, 1988, agreed to a five-year contract with the Bituminous Coal Operators' Association, just one day before a strike deadline. The contract increased wages by 25 cents an hour on Feb. 1, 1988, and called for two other wage hikes—a 35-cent increase on Feb. 1, 1989, and a 45-cent increase on Feb. 1, 1990.

The contract's job-security provisions permit miners who are laid off to bid on jobs at nonunion operations specified by the agreement. An estimated $20-million in employer contributions will be used to fund education and training provisions. The UMW ratified the contract on February 9.

Oil deals. Competition from cheaper imported oil and from coal mined by nonunion operations in the Western United States buffeted the U.S. oil industry in 1988 and weakened the bargaining position of oil workers. An agreement reached by the Oil, Chemical and Atomic Workers International Union and the

Changes in the United States labor force

	1987	1988
Total labor force	**121,421,000**	**123,370,000**
Armed forces	1,736,000	1,709,000
Civilian labor force	119,685,000	121,660,000
Total employment	112,233,000	116,676,000
Unemployment	7,452,000	6,693,000
Unemployment rate	6.0%	5.3%
Change in real earnings of production and nonsupervisory workers (private nonfarm sector)*	−0.9%	+3.9%
Change in output per employee hour (private nonfarm sector)†	+1.2%	+0.8%

*Constant (1977) dollars. 1987 change from December 1986 to December 1987; 1988 change from October 1987 to October 1988 (preliminary data).

†Annual rate for 1987; for 1988, change is from third quarter 1987 to third quarter 1988 (preliminary data).

Source: Bureau of Labor Statistics.

William J. McCarthy greets employees of the Teamsters Union after being elected on July 15 to succeed Jackie Presser as the union's president.

Amoco Chemical Company at the beginning of the year turned into a "pattern" settlement—a settlement that is adopted by a number of companies within a particular industry with little or no change.

The settlement, which was approved by the union on January 31, called for Amoco to pay a one-time lump-sum payment of $900 and provide wage increases of 30 cents an hour starting on Feb. 1, 1988, with a 3 per cent increase in February 1989. The agreement also provided improvements in health-care coverage. During the year, similar settlements were adopted by the Atlantic Richfield Company, Shell Oil Company, and other oil refineries. Still, petroleum workers at some U.S. companies, such as the Mobil Oil Corporation, struck over local issues while accepting the pattern settlement.

Kenosha woes. Autoworkers in Kenosha, Wis., were dealt a blow on Jan. 27, 1988, when Chrysler Corporation announced that it would close two of the town's plants. One of the plants was the 86-year-old assembly plant Chrysler acquired when it purchased the American Motors Corporation in 1987.

The United Automobile Workers (UAW) union and Wisconsin officials vehemently protested the closings, which put almost 5,500 employees out of work. Chrysler responded to the protests by providing more than $30 million to help laid-off workers. In May, the company agreed to give laid-off workers 24 weeks of sup-

plemental unemployment benefits. Both plants closed their doors in December.

Chrysler contract. On May 5, the UAW reached an agreement with Chrysler on a 28-month contract intended to give Chrysler employees the same benefits as UAW workers at Ford Motor Company and General Motors Corporation (GM). The pact provided workers with a $1,000 "early settlement" bonus in cash or stock; a profit-sharing provision; performance bonuses equaling 3 per cent of qualified earnings in October 1988 and October 1989; and cost-of-living adjustments. The settlement also provided a job-security program similar to the employment-guarantee programs at Ford and GM. Chrysler workers ratified the contract on May 11.

Rubber match. The United Rubber, Cork, Linoleum and Plastic Workers of America reached an agreement with Uniroyal-Goodrich Tire Company in February. Although the contract provided no wage increases until April 1991, workers received cost-of-living adjustments based on changes in the Consumer Price Index, and "equity units" in the company that could be redeemed for cash under certain circumstances. The union said that the agreement was not a pattern settlement and would not apply to contract negotiations with the Firestone Tire & Rubber Company and Goodyear Tire & Rubber Company.

During the spring, union workers at Goodyear threatened to strike despite the company's weakened financial position, which resulted from fighting off a British take-over bid. Workers rejected an April 21 pact that called for no general wage increase but provided a 25-cents-an-hour increase as an advance against future cost-of-living increases. The pact also improved pensions, raising the pension rate from $20 per year of service to $23.50. It also included a clause to ensure the continued unionization of any Goodyear plant that may be sold.

On May 17, however, workers agreed to a contract that essentially encompassed the terms outlined in the April 21 pact. The agreement was ratified on June 5.

Roadblock. In an effort to bring stability to what some labor leaders called the economic "chaos" of the trucking industry in the United States, the Teamsters Union executive board on March 31 accepted an agreement with trucking industry employers, even though 63.5 per cent of the union's members voted against it. The board's unusual action was based on a 1961 provision in the union's Constitution that permits the executive board to approve a contract if less than two-thirds of the membership oppose it.

The new trucking pact provided a 35-cents-per-hour increase in April 1988 and possible similar increases in April 1989 and April 1990. The bargainers revised the two-tier pay plan, which permits employers to use lower wage scales for workers hired after a certain date. The revisions give higher starting pay to new employees and help workers employed for a minimum of 18 months progress more quickly to the standard wage rates paid older employees.

The Times. After an agonizingly long bargaining round that lasted more than a year, the New York Times Company in 1988 reached agreement with no less than 14 unions in staggered procession. The contracts had expired on March 30, 1987, but were extended by the company and the unions as both parties worked to solve the problem of job security in an industry beset by burgeoning technological change.

The security issue dwarfed concerns over pay and benefit changes. In the new six-year agreement between the International Mailers Union and the New York Times Company, for example, workers won pay increases totaling more than $215 per week. But more important was the lifetime guarantee of employment for workers hired before 1990.

Writers strike. The 9,000 members of the Writers Guild of America on August 8 returned to work, ending a 22-week strike against the Alliance of Motion Picture and Television Producers that had affected motion picture and TV production and programming. The strike, which began on March 7, occurred over the amount and types of *residuals*—payments writers receive when programs they scripted are rerun. The new contract gives them the chance to secure higher residuals, especially in foreign markets.

Electric coalition. The General Electric Company and a coalition of 12 unions on June 26 agreed to a contract calling for an immediate 2.5 per cent wage

Members of the Writers Guild of America picket MGM Studios in New York City in March. The strike lasted 22 weeks, disrupting fall TV schedules.

hike and an additional 1.5 per cent increase in June 1989 and June 1990. Workers also received an immediate payment of $165, with an additional $900 to be paid in 1989. Retirement and pension benefits also were improved.

A number of unions involved in the settlement, however, condemned the pact for not providing workers with adequate wage gains and job-security provisions. Even so, on July 7, the International Union of Electronic, Electrical, Technical, Salaried, and Machine Workers, the largest union in the coalition, ratified the contract by a vote of 5 to 1.

Government labor policies. On August 2, President Ronald Reagan ordered federal agencies to set up guidelines that will prevent discrimination against employees afflicted with AIDS (acquired immune deficiency syndrome). President Reagan did not, however, issue an executive order or express support for federal legislation prohibiting discrimination on the basis of AIDS, two actions recommended in June by the President's AIDS commission.

On June 27, President Reagan signed into law the Employee Polygraph Protection Act of 1988. The law protects most new employees from having to submit to a lie detector test as a condition for being hired. It also prevents current employees from having to undergo such a test unless they are suspected of committing a theft or some other crime that results in an economic loss for the employer.

Teamsters changes. On July 9, Teamsters Union President Jackie Presser died, just months after taking a leave of absence due to ill health. Presser had been president since 1983.

The Teamsters Union quickly moved to select a successor to complete the remaining three years of Presser's term. On July 15, the union selected William J. McCarthy as its new president. McCarthy, international vice president of the union for New England, defeated Weldon L. Mathis, the union's secretary-treasurer, who had been serving as acting president and had been favored to win the post.

Crime connection. The U.S. government in 1988 continued to take action to free the Teamsters Union from what it called "organized-crime control." On June 28, the U.S. Department of Justice filed a suit under federal racketeering laws to force out Teamster leaders and hold new elections. Other unions and the American Federation of Labor and Congress of Industrial Organizations rallied to the Teamsters' defense, condemning the government's move as union busting.

New leader. At the 31st convention of the American Federation of Government Employees, held in August in Miami, Fla., John N. Sturdivant was elected president, becoming one of the highest-ranking black labor leaders in the United States. Sturdivant defeated incumbent Kenneth T. Blaylock.   Robert W. Fisher

See also **Economics.** In *World Book*, see **Labor force.**
Laos. See Asia.

Latin America quietly whittled away at its foreign debts during 1988. Creative and competent finance ministers tested new approaches to the debt problem. On December 19, United States President-elect George Bush pledged his Administration to helping them fashion "a whole new look" at a debt problem that he called "enormous" in "our own hemisphere."

During 1988, Latin-American governments were able to persuade their foreign creditors that political stability involves more than a good international credit rating. To maintain stability, they argued, people's needs must be met and cannot be put off until the debt problem is solved. The governments also sought to convince foreign creditors that Latin America, with its enormous human and material resources, is a prime target for future investment.

Brazil—Latin America's largest debtor—showed considerable ingenuity in coping with its debt problem, while simultaneously, in coming to terms with its creditors, lifting a moratorium it had declared in 1987 on interest payments. During a six-month period beginning in April 1988, Brazilian authorities converted some $1.1 billion in overdue debt into needed investments in industries ranging from paper manufacturing and farming to tourism. The method used was "debt-for-equity" auctions, whereby banks trade debts owed them for new investments in assets, not unlike home owners who take out a line of credit on the value of the equity in their home. During the

same period, informal conversions—a similar process carried out without government assistance—wiped out another $4 billion in Brazilian debt.

Privatization was the watchword in some countries. Argentina and Chile, for example, trimmed their budgets by continuing to sell inefficient publicly owned companies to private firms. Foreign banks proved helpful in several cases. Foreign commercial banks sold back to Bolivia nearly half of its foreign debt at 11 per cent of its paper value. Chase Manhattan Bank, headquartered in New York City, accepted commodities in payment on debt owed by Peru.

To encourage what are called *debt for nature* swaps, the United States Department of the Treasury allowed U.S. banks to take tax deductions for the full value of debts sold at discount to nonprofit conservation groups. The groups bought the discounted debts in exchange for agreements with Latin-American governments to set aside land to preserve the environment and protect endangered species. Such agreements have trimmed the foreign debts of Bolivia, Costa Rica, and Ecuador.

During 1988, many foreign banks—plus the World Bank, an agency of the United Nations (UN)—increased the funds they set aside as reserves to absorb possible losses on their Latin-American loans. For example, in May, Citicorp announced that it was setting $3 billion aside as reserves, largely due to Brazil's moratorium on interest payments.

Mexico's newly elected President Carlos Salinas de Gortari waves during his inaugural parade in December, which was marked by protests charging vote fraud.

Pope John Paul II greets Indians in Bolivia in May during a four-nation tour of Latin America that also included Paraguay, Peru, and Uruguay.

In October, the U.S. government rescued Mexico, Latin America's second-largest debtor, with a loan of up to $3.5 billion. The loan was intended to tide the nation over during a difficult period of political transition and hard times.

Action to help resolve the debt crisis was not limited to non-Communist nations. Cuba pardoned a $50-million debt owed by Nicaragua. The Soviet Union rescheduled nearly $1 billion in debt owed by Peru, an obligation incurred in the 1970's when a left-leaning military government bought Soviet-made arms.

Japan's plan. During 1988, Japan struck out on its own in trying to help resolve the problems of debt-ridden Latin-American nations. Japan also sought to lay a basis for future trade and investment in Latin America. Under the Japanese plan, the debts of Brazil and Mexico would be divided into two parts. Commercial banks would be able to swap one part for guaranteed bonds, backed by reserves on deposit at the International Monetary Fund, an agency of the UN. Borrowers would be obliged to set aside a percentage of their export earnings to pay off the debts—an arrangement that some Latin-American governments have long favored.

The Japanese have earmarked a total of $30 billion to help alleviate Third World debt problems. Nearly two-thirds of this assistance will be funneled through such agencies as the World Bank and the Inter-American Development Bank (IDB).

An IDB study issued on September 18 reported that since the debt crisis began in 1982, the net flow of foreign capital to Latin America has decreased by 80 per cent. The development bank sought to play a larger role in resolving the debt problem, following the February 1988 election of Uruguayan Foreign Minister Enrique Iglesias as its president.

Drug war. Shocking revelations concerning the extent of drug trafficking in Latin America emerged at congressional hearings in April chaired by U.S. Senator John F. Kerry (D., Mass.). Also during 1988, several high-ranking Latin-American officials were indicted by United States grand juries probing drug-smuggling operations.

On March 1, the U.S. Department of State reported that despite all efforts, the United States was losing the war on drugs. The production of coca, marijuana, and opium-poppy crops seemed beyond the control of any single government, according to the State Department. The report cited a 10 per cent increase in the production of coca—used to make cocaine—in Bolivia, Colombia, and Peru in 1987. These countries, together with Ecuador, are the major sources of the drug. Although U.S. troops were used in 1986 to shut down cocaine-processing laboratories in Bolivia, the State Department said that Bolivian drugmakers were back in business by 1988.

The U.S. Department of Justice indicted, in absentia, a number of Latin-American officials, diplomats, and

349

Facts in brief on Latin-American political units

Country	Population	Government	Monetary unit*	Exports†	Foreign trade (million U.S.$) Imports†
Antigua and Barbuda	85,000	Governor General Sir Wilfred Jacobs; Prime Minister Vere C. Bird	dollar (2.7 = $1)	25	181
Argentina	32,425,000	President Raúl Alfonsín	austral (15.5 = $1)	6,800	4,700
Bahamas	247,000	Governor General Sir Henry Taylor; Prime Minister Lynden O. Pindling	dollar (1 = $1)	825	1,600
Barbados	259,000	Governor General Sir Hugh Springer; Prime Minister Lloyd Erskine Sandiford	dollar (2.3 = $1)	300	559
Belize	179,000	Governor General Minita Gordon; Prime Minister Manuel Esquivel	dollar (2.2 = $1)	75	110
Bolivia	7,014,000	President Víctor Paz Estenssoro	boliviano (2.6 = $1)	495	750
Brazil	147,399,000	President José Sarney	cruzado (570 = $1)	22,400	15,600
Chile	12,796,000	President Augusto Pinochet Ugarte	peso (245 = $1)	2,900	3,000
Colombia	30,164,000	President Virgilio Barco Vargas	peso (328 = $1)	5,400	3,900
Costa Rica	2,721,000	President Oscar Arias Sánchez	colón (81.3 = $1)	1,077	1,163
Cuba	10,426,000	President Fidel Castro	peso (0.76 = $1)	6,400	9,200
Dominica	76,000	President Clarence Seignoret; Prime Minister Eugenia Charles	dollar (2.7 = $1)	28	57
Dominican Republic	6,824,000	President Joaquín Balaguer	peso (8.3 = $1)	718	1,400
Ecuador	10,490,000	President Rodrigo Borja	sucre (483 = $1)	2,000	2,100
El Salvador	5,900,000	President José Napoleón Duarte	colón (5.3 = $1)	755	884
Grenada	87,000	Governor General Sir Paul Godwin Scoon; Prime Minister Herbert Blaize	dollar (2.7 = $1)	28	83
Guatemala	8,935,000	President Vinicio Cerezo	quetzal (3.1 = $1)	650	610
Guyana	846,000	President Hugh Desmond Hoyte; Prime Minister Hamilton Green	dollar (10.0 = $1)	214	209
Haiti	6,216,000	President Prosper Avril	gourde (5 = $1)	191	326
Honduras	4,952,000	President José Azcona del Hoyo	lempira (3.8 = $1)	875	957
Jamaica	2,484,000	Governor General Sir Florizel Glasspole; Prime Minister Edward Seaga	dollar (6.1 = $1)	596	964
Mexico	86,988,000	President Carlos Salinas de Gortari	peso (2,310 = $1)	16,200	12,000
Nicaragua	3,745,000	President Daniel Ortega	córdoba (920 = $1)	251	775
Panama	2,370,000	President Manuel Solís Palma; Panamanian Defense Forces Commander Manuel Antonio Noriega Morena	balboa (1 = $1)	327	1,250
Paraguay	4,118,000	President Alfredo Stroessner	guaraní (1,000 = $1)	316	578
Peru	21,790,000	President Alan García Pérez; Prime Minister Armando Villanueva Del Campo	inti (617 = $1)	2,500	2,800
Puerto Rico	3,282,000	Governor Rafael Hernández Colón	U.S. dollar	11,600	10,100
St. Christopher and Nevis	48,000	Governor General Clement Arrindell; Prime Minister Kennedy Alphonse Simmonds	dollar (2.7 = $1)	34	63
St. Lucia	151,000	Acting Governor General Stanislaus Anthony James; Prime Minister John Compton	dollar (2.7 = $1)	24	141
St. Vincent and the Grenadines	142,000	Acting Governor General Henry Harvey Williams; Prime Minister James Mitchell	dollar (2.7 = $1)	68	87
Suriname	397,000	Commander of the National Army Désiré D. Bouterse; President Ramsewak Shankar	guilder (1.8 = $1)	332	320
Trinidad and Tobago	1,263,000	President Noor Mohamed Hassanali; Prime Minister A. N. R. Robinson	dollar (5.4 = $1)	1,400	1,200
Uruguay	2,983,000	President Julio María Sanguinetti	peso (432 = $1)	1,140	910
Venezuela	19,244,000	President Jaime Lusinchi	bolívar (7.5 = $1)	10,400	8,100

*Exchange rates as of Dec. 1, 1988, or latest available data (source: Deak International).   †Latest available data.

military and police officers on drug charges in 1988. On February 5, General Manuel Antonio Noriega Morena, chief of Panama's Defense Forces and a long-time collaborator with the U.S. Central Intelligence Agency, was indicted by federal grand juries in Miami and Tampa, Fla., on charges of international cocaine smuggling. On March 9, Colonel Jean-Claude Paul, commander of Haiti's best-trained army unit, was indicted by a Miami grand jury on charges of conspiring to ship cocaine to the United States from an airstrip on his farm. Paul was later ousted from his position and died mysteriously—possibly a victim of poisoning—in November.

As 1988 progressed, U.S. drug-enforcement officials repeated charges that drug-generated corruption was widespread within the Mexican government. In February, newspaper reports indicated that such corruption was also becoming rooted within the military of Honduras, a key U.S. ally in Central America. On April 5, however, responding to U.S. pressures, Honduran military officials seized reputed drug kingpin Juan Ramon Matta Ballesteros at his home in Tegucigalpa, the capital of Honduras. Ballesteros, who escaped from a U.S. federal prison in 1971 and who was wanted in the United States on drug charges, was flown to the Dominican Republic, where he was denied entry and placed in the custody of U.S. marshals.

There was mounting evidence during 1988 that Brazil was becoming a crossroads for drug shipments to the United States and Western Europe. In June, U.S. officials found a sizable shipment of cocaine concealed within cedar boards shipped from Brazil's Amazon Basin to Tampa.

On August 3, U.S. President Ronald Reagan vetoed an amendment tacked onto a defense bill that would have involved U.S. military forces in the war against drugs. Reagan vetoed the bill on grounds that it would unconstitutionally involve the military in civilian law enforcement. But the federal government funded the stationing of about 100 National Guardsmen along the Mexican border in early August to determine the effectiveness of military forces in this role.

Amazon conservation. Brazil's President José Sarney announced on October 12 the suspension of tax breaks and other incentives for Amazon land developers. The incentives were blamed for the hasty destruction of vast regions of tropical forest. Sarney said he was moved to action after a survey by Brazilian scientists counted more than 7,600 fires in the Amazon Basin in a single day. The fires are usually started to clear land for farming.

Earlier in the year, the Brazilian government announced plans to use a 250,000-acre (100,000-hectare) tract in the western part of the Amazon Basin as a model for tropical forest development. Under the plan, an undisturbed jungle will be protected and preserved, though its inhabitants may continue to profit from harvesting precious hardwoods, rubber,

U.S. troops parachute into Honduras in a March training exercise after Nicaraguan troops reportedly crossed the border in pursuit of *contra* rebels.

nuts, spices, and other useful plants. In the Special Reports section, see **Our Vanishing Rain Forests.**

Elections. The most surprising election in 1988 occurred in July in Mexico, where the long-dominant Institutional Revolutionary Party narrowly escaped defeat amid charges of vote fraud. In a plebiscite in Chile in October, voters rejected another term for President Augusto Pinochet Ugarte, a military dictator who has ruled the country for 15 years. In Paraguay in February, 75-year-old President Alfredo Stroessner easily won reelection to his eighth five-year term, to become one of the longest-ruling leaders of this century. In Suriname, a civilian president—Ramsewak Shankar—was elected in January, ending nearly eight years of military rule.

Hispanics in the United States. "Suddenly, Both Parties Are Speaking Spanish," *The New York Times* headlined an article on August 14. The article noted that "for the first time in American history both the Presidential and Vice Presidential candidates of a major party, the Democrats, are fluent in Spanish." The Democratic and Republican parties spent heavily on campaign advertising to influence Hispanics in such key states as California, Florida, New York, and Texas.

President Reagan in August named Lauro F. Cavazos, president of Texas Tech University in Lubbock, to the post of secretary of education. Cavazos became the first Hispanic ever to hold Cabinet rank. See **Cabinet, United States.**

Law

Archaeological finds. Peruvian archaeologist Walter Alva was the leader of a National Geographic Society-backed expedition that unearthed a treasure-trove of artifacts made by the Moche Indians, who flourished along Peru's north coast from A.D. 100 to 700. Following the trail of grave robbers, the expedition excavated the unlooted tomb of a Moche warrior-priest near the village of Sipán. The scientists found gold and silver artwork rivaling the treasures discovered in the tomb of Egyptian King Tutankhamen in 1922, according to anthropologist Christopher B. Donnan of the University of California at Los Angeles. See **Archaeology.**

In another development, physicists, archaeologists, ethnomusicologists, and craftworkers in the United States discovered clay whistles, ocarinas, and flutes produced by ancient South Americans before the 1400's to be skillfully engineered to emit a wide range of sounds. X-ray examinations showed that the instruments had many hidden chambers. Once dismissed by museum keepers as mere toys, the instruments were actually more advanced than the wooden recorders and metal flutes produced in Europe during the same period.   Nathan A. Haverstock

See also articles on the various Latin-American countries. In *World Book*, see **Latin America** and articles on the individual countries.

Law. See **Civil rights; Courts; Crime; Supreme Court of the United States.**

Lebanon. Lebanon's strife-torn government was brought to a near standstill in 1988 after parliament failed to elect a new president to succeed Amine Gemayel, whose six-year term expired on September 23. The failure dimmed already faint hopes that the various Lebanese sects and power blocs would end their violent civil conflict. Under the Lebanese political system, the president, traditionally a member of the Christian Maronite community, is elected by the National Assembly, Lebanon's parliament.

Franjieh rejected. A number of Maronite leaders, including Suleiman Franjieh, who served as president from 1970 to 1976, presented themselves as candidates. Franjieh was the choice of Syria's President Hafiz al-Assad, who maintains 25,000 troops in Lebanon. But Muslim members of the Assembly opposed Franjieh because they associated him with the 1975-1976 civil war and because his government had failed to introduce power-sharing reforms into the Lebanese political system.

Franjieh was also opposed by Gemayel's Christian supporters and by the Lebanese Forces, an anti-Syrian Christian militia, because of his ties to Syria. In August, the Lebanese Forces blocked Franjieh's election by preventing members of the Assembly from attending a scheduled parliamentary election, thereby leaving the Assembly without a quorum.

Two governments. The election process was still deadlocked on September 23, when Gemayel's term

Shiite militiamen—backed by Syrian troops—continue to battle against their pro-Iranian Shiite rivals in the southern suburbs of Beirut, Lebanon, in May.

352

officially ended. The outgoing president, who by law could not succeed himself, then named General Michel Aoun, the Maronite Christian commander of the Lebanese Army, as the head of an interim military government. The existing civilian government headed by Muslim Prime Minister Salim al-Huss, who had never resigned, declared itself the legitimate authority in the country. Al-Huss was also supported by the Lebanese Forces. As a result, Lebanon was left with two governments—a Muslim-Christian government based in West Beirut and an all-Christian government in East Beirut.

The hostage problem. Lebanon continued to be a dangerous place for foreigners in 1988. In February, two Scandinavians working for the United Nations (UN) Relief and Works Agency for Palestine Refugees in the Near East were kidnapped near Sidon. The agency suspended its Lebanese services as a result. That same month, unknown gunmen seized Marine Lieutenant Colonel William R. Higgins, the American commander of the UN Truce Supervision Organization, which monitors the border between Israel and Lebanon.

In May, however, three French hostages held since 1985 were freed by the pro-Iranian group Islamic Jihad (Holy War) for the Liberation of Palestine. Two West German hostages were also released—one in March, the other in September. An Indian professor with resident-alien status in the United States was freed in October, and a Swiss hostage was released in December. But there was no word on the whereabouts of Anglican Church envoy Terry Waite, or of nine American hostages held in Lebanon.

Civil conflict lessened somewhat during 1988 as Syrian troops extended their security zone to cover about 70 per cent of Lebanon. In January, they broke a siege of Palestinian refugee camps by Amal (Hope), the largest Shiite Muslim militia, that had lasted nearly three years and caused 2,500 casualties. But efforts to end the ongoing struggle between Amal and the Hezbollah (Party of God) militia, Amal's principal rival for control of the Shiite community, were largely ineffective. Cease-fires arranged by negotiators from Iran—Hezbollah's main backer—or by diplomats from Syria broke down almost before they could be implemented.

The economy. A draft budget issued by the al-Huss government in October set revenues at $26-billion and expenditures at $41 billion. But in practical terms, the effort was meaningless, because of wild fluctuations in the value of the Lebanese currency. Also, the government's power to collect taxes was undercut by the militias' control of the ports, which enabled them to siphon off export revenues for their own use. Almost the only resource standing between Lebanon and bankruptcy was its gold reserves, held by the Central Bank.   William Spencer

See also **Middle East** (Facts in brief table). In *World Book*, see **Lebanon.**

Lee Teng-hui (1923-   ), vice president of Taiwan, succeeded to the presidency upon the death of President Chiang Ching-kuo on Jan. 13, 1988. Under Taiwan's Constitution, Lee will serve the remainder of Chiang's term, which ends in 1990. Lee—the first president born in Taiwan rather than mainland China—pledged to continue his predecessor's policies, including working toward reunification with the mainland. See **Taiwan.**

Lee was born in a rural area in northern Taiwan on Jan. 15, 1923, during the Japanese occupation of the island. He attended Kyoto Imperial University in Japan and National Taiwan University in Taipei; graduating in 1948 with a degree in agricultural economics. Lee completed his education in the United States, receiving a master's degree in agricultural economics from Iowa State University of Science and Technology in Ames in 1953, and in 1968 earning a doctorate in the same field from Cornell University in Ithaca, N.Y.

Lee taught economics at National Taiwan University periodically from 1948 to 1978. In 1957, he also began working as an administrator for Taiwan's Joint Commission on Rural Reconstruction.

Lee was appointed mayor of Taipei, the capital, in 1978, and three years later, he became governor of Taiwan province. He was designated vice president of the country in 1984.

Lee and his wife, the former Tseng Wen-hui, have two daughters.   Jinger Hoop

Lefebvre, Marcel (1905-   ), a French archbishop and leader of a movement supporting traditional Roman Catholic rites, initiated the first *schism* (split) in the church in more than 100 years on June 30, 1988. The schism occurred when Lefebvre consecrated four bishops in defiance of orders from Pope John Paul II in a Mass in Ecône, Switzerland. The pope excommunicated Lefebvre and the bishops. Lefebvre's movement reportedly has as many as 100,000 followers. See **Roman Catholic Church.**

Marcel Lefebvre was born on Nov. 29, 1905, in Tourcoing, France. He was educated at Sacred Heart College in Tourcoing and the French Seminary in Rome and was ordained a priest in 1929. In 1932, he entered the congregation of the Holy Ghost Fathers and was sent to Africa. He became archbishop of Dakar, Senegal, in 1948.

The archbishop's dispute with the Vatican began in 1960, when he served as a member of the preparatory commission for Vatican Council II, a council held from 1962 to 1965 to update Roman Catholic doctrine. Lefebvre opposed most of the Vatican II reforms, such as using the *vernacular* (local language) instead of Latin in the Mass and promoting better relations with other religions.

Lefebvre founded the fraternity of St. Pius X in 1969. The Vatican withdrew its approval of the seminary in 1975. In 1976, it banned Lefebvre from performing all priestly functions.   Mary A. Krier

Leonard, Elmore

Leonard, Elmore (1925-   ), saw his 26th novel, *Freaky Deaky*, become a best seller within weeks of its publication in May 1988. Although Leonard has been published since the 1950's and has been recognized as a top writer of crime novels, mysteries, and Westerns, only three of his books have made the best-seller lists. The other two were *Glitz* (1985) and *Bandits* (1987).

Elmore John Leonard, Jr., was born on Oct. 11, 1925, in New Orleans. From 1943 to 1946, he served with the United States Navy, fighting in the South Pacific during World War II. He later attended the University of Detroit, graduating in 1950. He began his career as a novelist by writing Westerns in his spare time while working as an advertising copywriter. His first novel, *The Bounty Hunters*, appeared in 1953.

After his fifth novel, *Hombre* (1961), was made into a motion picture in 1967, Leonard started writing full-time and began producing crime novels. His urban thrillers earned critical praise for their realistic dialogue, deadpan humor, and street-smart characters ranging from cops and ex-convicts to drug dealers and terrorists. Leonard also writes short stories and screenplays.

Leonard has five children by his first wife, Beverly Cline, whom he married in 1949 and divorced in 1977. He married Joan Shepard in 1979; they live in Birmingham, Mich.   Robin Goldman

Lesotho. See Africa.

Li Peng (1928-   ), China's acting premier, was confirmed as premier on April 9, 1988. Li had taken over the post in November 1987, when Premier Zhao Ziyang resigned to become general secretary of the Chinese Communist Party. As premier, Li holds one of the highest leadership positions in the Chinese government.

Li was born in Chengdu (Ch'eng-tu in the traditional Wade-Giles spelling) in October 1928, the son of parents active in the Communist Party. In 1931, Li's father was killed by political opponents. Today, the elder Li is considered a martyr to the cause of Chinese Communism. Young Li was adopted by Zhou Enlai (Chou En-lai), who later became China's first premier.

In 1945, when Li was 17, he joined the Communist Party. Three years later, he traveled to the Soviet Union to study engineering at the Moscow Power Institute. In 1955, Li returned to China, where he worked as an engineer at power plants in the northeast, eventually becoming director of the Beijing (Peking) Electric Power Administration, a position he held from 1966 to 1979. In 1979, Li was appointed to China's Ministry of Power Industry. In 1985, Li was elected to China's ruling Politburo, and in 1987, he was named to the standing committee of the Politburo—China's most powerful policymaking body.

Li and his wife, Zhu Lin, an electrical engineer, have a daughter and two sons.   Jinger Hoop

Liberia. See Africa.

Library. Public libraries in the United States are busier than ever, according to an annual survey conducted by the Library Research Center at the University of Illinois at Urbana-Champaign and reported in August 1988. In 1987, total public library circulation of books and other materials increased 6.3 per cent, the largest increase in the past 10 years, the Library Research Center said. Americans borrowed an average of 5.7 library items per capita in 1987.

Library improvements. Several public libraries gained increased funding in 1988. In Phoenix, 58 per cent of the city's voters approved a record $55-million bond proposal for a new central library and branch improvements. On March 8, voters in Dade County, Florida, approved a tax that will generate $47 million solely for the purchase of books for the Miami-Dade Public Library System.

After an international design competition, the Chicago Public Library selected a neoclassic design by local architect Thomas H. Beeby for a new central library scheduled for completion by 1991. The building will cost $140 million and will have an area of 757,031 square feet (70,330 square meters), making it the largest city library in the United States.

ALA versus FBI. Librarians confronted the Federal Bureau of Investigation (FBI) in 1988 over the FBI's Library Awareness Program, a program to monitor the use of United States libraries by suspected spies. Although the program has been in effect for more than 10 years, the library community first learned of it in June 1987, when two FBI agents approached Paula T. Kaufman, a librarian at Columbia University in New York City, and asked her for circulation records of scientific journals. Kaufman refused the request because New York state law prohibits revealing library checkout records, as do laws in 37 other states. The FBI agents also asked her to report any "suspicious" activities of foreigners, people with accents, or "foreign-sounding names." Other librarians reported that the FBI had asked them to watch library patrons who might be doing research for foreign intelligence services.

The American Library Association (ALA) filed requests under the Freedom of Information Act seeking release of "full documentation regarding the FBI's Library Awareness Program." The ALA also passed a resolution opposing the program and demanding that it cease. The FBI defended the activity as a necessary part of its counterintelligence effort. In November 1988, however, the agency said the program is limited to libraries in the New York City area and declared that cooperation would be strictly voluntary.

Leningrad library fire. On February 14 and 15, fire destroyed much of the Library of the Academy of Sciences of the U.S.S.R. in Leningrad. The library's 13 million volumes made up a vast research treasure built around a collection donated by Russia's Czar Peter the Great in 1714. Library officials said that 400,000 books were destroyed, 3.6 million were damaged by water, 10,000 became infected with mold, and 7.5 million

The design for Chicago's new central library, chosen in June by a jury of librarians and architects, is a neoclassic building by Thomas H. Beeby.

needed preventive care. A library conservation team from the United States went to Leningrad from March 28 to April 1 to advise the restoration efforts.

ALA changes. Margaret E. Chisholm, director of the Graduate School of Library and Information Science at the University of Washington in Seattle, served as president of the 47,000-member ALA and presided over the ALA's 107th annual conference attended by 16,550 participants in New Orleans from July 9 to 14, 1988. At the conclusion of the conference, F. William Summers, dean of the School of Library and Information Studies at Florida State University in Tallahassee, took over as ALA president.

Children's reading. The ALA continued a national campaign begun in 1987 to put a library card into the hands of every child in the United States. Congress designated September 1988 as "National Library Card Sign-Up Month." Television, radio, and print advertisements featured the message, "The Best Gift You'll Ever Give Your Child . . . A Library Card." The campaign produced impressive results as thousands of librarians organized statewide and local efforts. The West Virginia Library Commission, for example, reported that more than 105,000 students applied for library cards. The New York Public Library signed up more than 60,000 young patrons in six weeks. Louisville, Ky., gained more than 50,000 new "card-carrying readers."   Peggy Barber

In *World Book*, see **Library.**

Libya. Leader of the Revolution Muammar Muhammad al-Qadhafi reversed direction in both foreign and domestic policy in 1988. He improved Libya's ties with its neighbors in an attempt to enhance Libya's image abroad. In August, Qadhafi called for greater involvement by the private sector in production to shore up the deteriorating economy.

Regional fence-mending. On a visit to Tunisia in February, Qadhafi agreed to compensate the Tunisian government for the 21,000 Tunisian workers abruptly expelled from Libya in 1985. In May 1988, the two countries signed an agreement permitting the free movement of citizens across their common border. Tunisians and Libyans were to carry a common identification card but would retain separate citizenship. Qadhafi also agreed to submit the dispute between Libya and Tunisia over the ownership of offshore oil resources in the Gulf of Gabes to binding arbitration by the International Court of Justice.

Also in May, Qadhafi declared that Libya's war with Chad over the Aozou Strip, which ended in a cease-fire in 1987, had been a mistake, and he offered financial aid toward Chad's reconstruction. In October 1988, Libya and Chad announced a restoration of diplomatic ties and agreed to seek a peaceful solution to the 15-year conflict over the strip, a uranium-rich border area claimed by both countries. In March, Qadhafi announced that Libyan Army units stationed along the Egyptian border would be withdrawn. A "sister provinces" plan was established between al-Khufra, in southern Libya, and Sudan's Darfur province, with funds for roadbuilding and agriculture earmarked for the impoverished Sudanese province.

Terrorism. There was some evidence of a revival of Libyan-backed terrorism abroad. In February, three Libyans were arrested in Senegal for attempting to smuggle weapons and explosives into that far-western African country. In addition, an individual who carried a Libyan passport led a terrorist attack on the Greek tourist ship *City of Poros* on July 11. Nine people were killed and more than 80 were injured by grenades and machine-gun fire in that attack.

Internal changes. In March, Qadhafi ordered the release of all political prisoners in Libya. He started off the process by personally driving a bulldozer through the gate of Tripoli's prison. In addition, March 12 was declared "Freedom Day," and political opponents of the regime in exile were invited to return, with guarantees of their safety. Several did so.

In June, the General People's Congress, Libya's legislative body, approved a 12-point Human Rights Charter developed by Qadhafi. Its provisions include abolition of the death penalty, an end to revolutionary courts, guarantees of a fair and honest trial for all citizens, the right to education and suitable employment, a ban on the employment of house servants, and the outlawing of Libyan production and use of nuclear and chemical weapons. The charter also permits the formation of labor unions and professional leagues, though political parties are still forbidden. Officials of Amnesty International, an international human rights organization based in London, visited Libya in August and expressed satisfaction with the country's progress in human rights.

The economy. Libya continued to wrestle with the effects of an economic recession caused by a decline in oil revenues, which supply nearly all of the government's income, and the economy's limited capacity to produce consumer goods. Per capita income in 1988 continued to drop. Oil revenues of $7 billion in 1988 represented a 60 per cent decline from 1980, the last year of the oil boom.

Two promising developments were the start-up in September 1988 of the Tobruk oil refinery and a new offshore oil field, with a production capacity of 50,000 barrels per day (bpd). The refinery has a capacity of 220,000 bpd.

Qadhafi's pet economic project, the Great Man-Made River, begun in 1987, continued on schedule. The project is a pipeline for carrying water from underground reservoirs in the Sahara northward to farmland along the Mediterranean coast. By August 1988, approximately 250 miles (400 kilometers) of the projected 2,500-mile (4,000-kilometer) pipeline had been laid.　　William Spencer

See also **Africa** (Facts in brief table); **Chad.** In *World Book*, see **Libya.**

Liechtenstein. See **Europe.**

Literature. The year 1988 saw the return of the traditional novel in the United States. The most successful American fiction of the year championed traditional techniques—such as character development, complex plots, and large themes—rather than minimalism, a style fashionable in the early 1980's that looked inward and focused on small details.

Thomas Flanagan's *The Tenants of Time*, a novel about revolutionary politics in Ireland in the 1800's, made dazzling use of multiple narrators. Equally impressive was *Libra*, in which Don DeLillo not only constructed a vivid mirror of the American spirit of the 1960's but also created a fascinating fictional character based on Lee Harvey Oswald, accused of assassinating President John F. Kennedy.

Larry McMurtry's *Anything for Billy*, an epic of the American West, built on the mythology surrounding the life of Billy the Kid. Another epic historical novel, Jane Smiley's *The Greenlanders*, told of the Scandinavian settlers of Greenland in the 900's.

Edward Abbey's *The Fool's Progress*, a hefty comic novel, described the awakening of an environmentalist. Anne Tyler added to her reputation with *Breathing Lessons*, an affectionate novel about a woman addicted to meddling in the lives of others. Pete Dexter won the 1988 National Book Award for fiction with *Paris Trout*, a novel about the murderer of a teen-aged black girl in rural Georgia.

Two respected writers produced highly ironic novels. Alison Lurie's *The Truth About Lorin Jones* satirized the excesses of feminism. John Updike returned to the old convention of the *epistolary novel*—a novel written in the form of letters—in *S.*, a comedy about a Boston doctor's wife who leaves her unfaithful husband to join a Hindu religious community.

Other important American novels were Alice Adams' *Second Chances*, Louis Auchincloss' *The Golden Calves*, Thomas Berger's *The Houseguest*, Jay Cantor's *Krazy Kat*, Gretel Ehrlich's *Heart Mountain*, Louise Erdrich's *Tracks*, Joanne Greenberg's *Of Such Small Differences*, Judith Grossman's *Her Own Terms*, Alice Hoffman's *At Risk*, Susan Isaacs' *Shining Through*, William Kennedy's *Quinn's Book*, Susan Kenney's *Sailing*, Eric Kraft's *Herb 'n' Lorna*, Beverly Lowry's *Breaking Gentle*, Gloria Naylor's *Mama Day*, J. F. Powers' *Wheat That Springeth Green*, Paul West's *The Place in Flowers Where Pollen Rests*, William Wiser's *The Circle Tour*, and Larry Woiwode's *Born Brothers*.

Among the notable first novels were Michael Chabon's *The Mysteries of Pittsburgh*, Kathryn Davis' *Labrador*, Abby Frucht's *Snap*, and Mary McGarry Morris' *Vanished*.

Leading the short-story collections was Harold Brodkey's *Stories in an Almost Classical Mode*, a long book of sharply observed tales that were both exhilarating and exhausting. Minimalism endured in the work of Raymond Carver, whose *Where I'm Calling From* brought together 37 stories on marriage and other domestic issues. Carver died on August 2.

Other first-rate collections were Ethan Canin's *Emperor of the Air*, Andre Dubus's *Selected Stories*, Mary Gaitskill's *Bad Behavior*, Michael Martone's *Safety Patrol*, Kermit Moyer's *Tumbling*, James Salter's *Dusk and Other Stories*, Isaac Bashevis Singer's *The Death of Methuselah and Other Stories*, Elizabeth Spencer's *Jack of Diamonds and Other Stories*, and Pamela Zoline's *The Heat Death of the Universe and Other Stories*.

Fiction from outside North America. Novels from England included Peter Ackroyd's *Chatterton*, a novel based on the short, suicidal life of the poet Thomas Chatterton; Doris Lessing's *The Fifth Child*, a frightening tale of the collapse of family values; Iris Murdoch's *The Book and the Brotherhood*, a novel of academic revolutionaries in contemporary England; and Fay Weldon's *The Hearts and Lives of Men*, a satirical novel of marriage and divorce.

Other important novels from abroad were Australian writer Peter Carey's *Oscar and Lucinda*, a love story involving a priest and a young heiress; Nigerian writer Chinua Achebe's *Anthills of the Savannah*, a political novel set in a mythical West African country; and Italian writer Primo Levi's *The Drowned and the Saved*, a novel about the Holocaust, published after the author's death. (Levi died in April 1987.)

Two other fine novels were Colombian Nobel laureate Gabriel García Márquez' *Love in the Time of Cholera*, a powerful love story; and Palestinian Anton Shammas' *Arabesques*, about a young Arab's search for his family origins in the Holy Land.

Biography. The year 1988 was exceptionally rich in the study of literary lives. The late Richard Ellmann's *Oscar Wilde* reexamined the scandalous yet generous life of the British playwright and poet. Michael Holroyd began a projected three-volume study of a great Irish playwright with *Bernard Shaw, Volume 1, 1856-1898: The Search for Love*. Brenda Maddox' *Nora: The Real Life of Molly Bloom* convincingly argued that Nora Barnacle, the wife of Irish novelist James Joyce, was a far stronger individual than the obedient wallflower described in most Joyce biographies. Garry O'Connor's *Sean O'Casey* entertainingly revealed how the great Irish playwright had invented much of his official life story.

Four biographies centered on American writers. Gerald Clarke's *Capote* scrutinized, in an almost novelistic manner, the tormented life of Truman Capote. Scott Donaldson's *John Cheever* honored Cheever's genius and reserve while being frank about his faults. Judy Oppenheimer's *Private Demons* presented short-story writer Shirley Jackson as a tragic but gifted personality whose inner life both helped and hindered her writing. And Arnold Rampersad's *The Life of Langston Hughes* shed considerable light on an extremely private poet.

Two biographies, both titled *Tolstoy*, reexamined the life of Russian author Leo Tolstoy. Martine de Courcel's book focused on the unity of Tolstoy's reli-

Author Louise Erdrich, whose mother was a Chippewa Indian, continued her series of novels about American Indians with *Tracks* in 1988.

gious and artistic lives, and A. N. Wilson's work emphasized his creative imagination.

Peter Gay's *Freud: A Life for Our Time* offered a massive and even-handed look at Sigmund Freud, the founder of psychoanalysis. Elisabeth Young-Bruehl's *Anna Freud* examined the considerable contributions Freud's daughter made to her father's field.

Roy M. Cohn, the lawyer who aided in Senator Joseph R. McCarthy's anti-Communist "witch hunt" in the 1950's, was the subject of two biographies: the sympathetic *Autobiography of Roy Cohn*, rewritten by Sidney Zion from Cohn's manuscript, and the critical *Citizen Cohn* by Nicholas von Hoffman.

Martin Gilbert completed his official biography of Britain's legendary prime minister with an eighth volume, *Winston S. Churchill: Never Despair, 1945-1965*. William Manchester looked at the same figure in *The Last Lion; Winston Spencer Churchill: Alone, 1932-1940*.

Autobiography. Many of 1988's autobiographies focused on the literary world. Novelist Philip Roth examined his life in *The Facts*. In *Lovesong: Becoming a Jew*, black author Julius Lester told how he converted to Judaism. In *Flights of Passage*, Princeton University Professor Samuel Hynes provided an amusing yet shrewdly observant memoir about coming of age as a Marine aviator during World War II.

Three leading figures of the arts world offered candid memoirs. In *Elia Kazan: A Life*, the noted the-

Literature

Author John Updike, right, presents the Edward MacDowell Medal for excellence in the arts to novelist William Styron in August 1988.

ater and film director freely discussed the often startling details of his long career. Swedish film director Ingmar Bergman did the same in *The Magic Lantern*. And in *Perfect Pitch*, Nicolas Slonimsky, one of the world's foremost musical lexicographers, provided a fascinating memoir.

Political autobiographies included *Fear No Evil*, in which Soviet dissident Natan Sharansky—formerly known as Anatoly Shcharansky and now an Israeli citizen—told of his long imprisonment in the Soviet Union, and *Reunion*, in which American activist Tom Hayden recalled his part in the student antiwar movement of the 1960's and 1970's.

Letters. Among the year's important collections of correspondence were *The Letters of T. S. Eliot: Vol. 1, 1898-1922*, encompassing the poet's life up to age 34, including the publication of *The Waste Land*; *A Literate Passion*, the letters of writers and lovers Henry Miller and Anaïs Nin; *We Dream of Honour*, poet John Berryman's revealing letters to his mother, who was often blamed for the insanity that led to his suicide; *Selected Letters of Richard Wagner*, which showed, among other things, how the great composer dealt with his paranoia; and *Bernard Shaw: Collected Letters, 1926-1950*—the last of four volumes of his correspondence—which vividly recalled the Irish playwright's wide-ranging mind and biting wit.

History. One of the year's most impressive works of nonfiction was Neil Sheehan's *A Bright Shining Lie*,

which, in the guise of a biography of controversial U.S. Army officer John Paul Vann, retold in stunning detail the entire American involvement in the Vietnam War. The book won the 1988 National Book Award for nonfiction. James M. McPherson's skillful *Battle Cry of Freedom* won praise as perhaps the best one-volume study of the Civil War to date. Also widely honored was Eric Foner's *Reconstruction: America's Unfinished Revolution, 1863-1877*.

Especially intriguing was *The Rise and Fall of the Great Powers*, Paul Kennedy's exploration of how a combination of foreign commitments and gigantic military budgets have caused the decline of the great powers of the last 500 years. The book contained sharp lessons for both U.S. and Soviet readers. McGeorge Bundy's *Danger and Survival* traced the history of the "tradition of nonuse" of nuclear weapons.

Taylor Branch's *Parting the Waters* reexamined the achievements of civil rights leader Martin Luther King, Jr. The 20th anniversary of the tempestuous, violence-ridden 1968 Democratic National Convention in Chicago was marked by several engrossing books, among them *The Year of the Barricades* by David Caute and *Chicago '68* by David Farber.

New history books continued to focus on the history of Germany's Third Reich. Claudia Koonz's *Mothers in the Fatherland* provocatively examined how women embraced Hitler's ideology during the early years of the Nazi movement. *Born Guilty* by Peter Sichrovsky ably explored the lasting feelings of complicity among 14 children of Nazi war criminals in Germany. *Racial Hygiene* by Robert Proctor investigated the evident willingness of German medical professionals to participate in Nazi programs of genocide.

The distinguished journalist I. F. Stone drew lessons for modern times from an event of the 400's B.C. in *The Trial of Socrates*. Religious historian Elaine Pagels' *Adam, Eve and the Serpent* proposed that as early Christianity changed from a dissident sect to an imperial religion, its focus changed from human freedom to sin and depravity.

Contemporary affairs. William Greider's *Secrets of the Temple* investigated the powerful, often secret role the Board of Governors of the Federal Reserve System plays in the life of the United States. *Buying into America* by Martin and Susan Tolchin examined the perils of increased foreign investment in the United States.

Domestic affairs occupied several writers. Jonathan Kozol's *Rachel and Her Children* took an impassioned look at the plight of the homeless in the United States, especially in New York City's welfare hotels. John Crewdson's *By Silence Betrayed* examined the widespread sexual abuse of children. Howard Kohn's *The Last Farmer* offered a moving personal chronicle about the decline of the American family farm.

David Wise's *The Spy Who Got Away* analyzed the case of Edward Lee Howard, an intelligence agent who deeply embarrassed the U.S. government when he defected to the Soviet Union in 1985. From Israel came David Grossman's *The Yellow Wind*, which attempted to give Israeli Jews a look into Palestinian hearts.

The growth of AIDS (acquired immune deficiency syndrome) inspired several books on the fatal illness. Two books were deeply affecting memoirs of living with the disease: Paul Monette's *Borrowed Time* and French author Emmanuel Dreuilhe's *Mortal Embrace*.

Science. In *Elephant Memories*, Cynthia Moss told the 13-year history of 25 elephants in Kenya, revealing their close-knit bonds as well as their peril in the face of the African country's exploding human population. Timothy Ferris' *Coming of Age in the Milky Way* richly chronicled the awakening of humankind to the immensity of the universe.

Best sellers included Tom Wolfe's *The Bonfire of the Vanities*, a 1987 book on the best-seller list for more than a year; Tom Clancy's *Cardinal of the Kremlin*; James A. Michener's *Alaska*; Rosamunde Pilcher's *The Shell Seekers*; Judith Krantz's *Till We Meet Again*; Stephen W. Hawking's *A Brief History of Time*; Lee Iacocca's *Talking Straight*; Charles Higham's *The Duchess of Windsor*; Robert Kowalski's *The 8-Week Cholesterol Cure*; and Harvey Mackay's *Swim with the Sharks Without Being Eaten Alive*.   Henry Kisor

See also **Awards and prizes** (Literature awards); **Canadian literature; Literature for children; Poetry; Publishing.** In *World Book*, see **Literature.**

Literature for children. Children's books published in 1988 included more books for the very young. For older readers, informational books explored a wide range of topics, and much fiction involved current issues.

In what some critics called his finest work ever, Maurice Sendak illustrated the 1988 publication by Farrar, Straus & Giroux of *Dear Mili*, a story by Wilhelm Grimm discovered in 1983. Grimm's tale, found in a letter he wrote to a child friend in 1816, stirred controversy over its strong religious overtones and an ending in which the young heroine and her mother die.

Other outstanding books of 1988 included the following:

Picture books
Annabelle Swift, Kindergartener by Amy Schwartz (Orchard Bks.). Lucy tells her younger sister Annabelle how to behave in kindergarten, with amusing results. Ages 4 to 7.

The Boy of the Three-Year Nap by Dianne Snyder, illustrated by Allen Say (Houghton Mifflin). Taro, the laziest boy in the village, comes up with a plan to gain wealth and a rich bride. His mother has a plan, too. Ages 5 to 9.

The Boy Who Ate the Moon by Christopher King, illustrated by John Wallner (Philomel Bks.). Beautiful paintings capture a boy's imaginative adventure when he eats the moon. Ages 3 to 7.

The Chinese Mirror adapted by Mirra Ginsburg, illustrated by Margot Zemach (Harcourt Brace Jovanovich). When a villager brings home a small mirror, the first ever seen in his village, the reactions cause havoc. Ages 5 to 8.

Company's Coming by Arthur Yorinks, illustrated by David Small (Crown). Aliens land in Shirley and Moe's yard, but Shirley takes charge. Comical illustrations. Ages 4 to 8.

Farmer Schulz's Ducks by Colin Thiele, illustrated by Mary Milton (Harper & Row). When cars begin hitting the farmer's ducks, he and his family have to come up with solutions. Lovely water colors. Ages 3 to 7.

The Green Lion of Zion Street by Julia Fields, illustrated by Jerry Pinkney (Macmillan). In lilting verse, imagery, and Black English, the story tells of a group of children who meet a green lion as they go to school. Ages 5 to 8.

I Want to Be an Astronaut by Byron Barton (Crowell). Illustrations with bold, outlined colors show what a boy wants to see in space. Ages 4 to 6.

Kirsty Knows Best by Annalena McAfee, illustrated by Anthony Browne (Knopf). Paintings show the sharp contrast between Kirsty's daydreaming and her everyday life. Ages 5 to 9.

The Legend of the Indian Paintbrush retold by Tomie dePaola (Putnam). Little Gopher tries to become a great painter in a tale of the origin of a wild flower. Ages 3 to 7.

Literature for children

Lincoln: A Photobiography by Russell Freedman won the 1988 Newbery Medal from the American Library Association as the best children's book.

Picnic with Piggins by Jane Yolen, illustrated by Jane Dyer (Harcourt Brace Jovanovich). Piggins solves a mystery on a picnic. Bright paintings include rich detail. Ages 4 to 8.

The Rumor of Pavel and Paali adapted by Carole Kismaric, illustrated by Charles Mikolaycak (Harper & Row). Twin brothers wager over good and evil. Paali gives up his eyes for food but learns powerful secrets and is suitably rewarded. Gorgeous paintings. Ages 6 to 9.

The Secret in the Matchbox by Val Willis, illustrated by John Shelley (Farrar, Straus & Giroux). Bobby Bell's secret causes turmoil in his classroom. Droll color paintings. Ages 5 to 9.

Storm in the Night by Mary Stolz, illustrated by Pat Cummings (Harper & Row). Grandfather tells Thomas how he felt as a boy during a bad storm. Lovely, dark paintings. Ages 4 to 8.

The Tea Squall by Ariane Dewey (Greenwillow Bks.). Short, delightful tall tales from six female relatives of famous American tall-tale heroes, told over tea and an incredible assortment of food. Ages 7 to 10.

Two Bad Ants by Chris Van Allsburg (Houghton Mifflin). Frightening adventures and an ant's-eye-view of ordinary objects combine to make a fascinating book. Ages 4 to 8.

Upside-Downers by Mitsumasa Anno (Putnam). Pictures that can be viewed right side up and upside down, accompanied by rhymed text. Ages 4 to 9.

Where's the Baby? by Pat Hutchins (Greenwillow Bks.). In rhymed text, a monster family follows a messy trail to find the baby. Funny characters and situations. Ages 4 to 7.

Zekmet the Stone Carver; A Tale of Ancient Egypt by Mary Stolz, illustrated by Deborah Nourse Lattimore (Harcourt Brace Jovanovich). The pharaoh demands that his minister of state design overnight a monument that will last forever. Ages 8 to 12.

Poetry

Birches by Robert Frost, illustrated by Ed Young (Holt & Co.). Frost's fine poem accompanies luminous impressionistic paintings. The entire poem is reprinted alone at the end. Ages 5 and up.

Greens by Arnold Adoff, illustrated by Betsy Lewin (Lothrop, Lee & Shepard Bks.). Adoff celebrates the spring and green objects in this small collection of poems. Ages 4 to 8.

The Music of What Happens: Poems That Tell Stories selected by Paul Janeczko (Orchard Bks.). Fascinating narrative poems on various subjects should grip every reader. Ages 12 and up.

Sing a Song of Popcorn: Every Child's Book of Poems selected by Beatrice de Regniers and others (Scholastic). Excellent poems are illustrated by nine Caldecott Medal winners, including Maurice Sendak, Arnold Lobel, Diane and Leo Dillon, and others. All ages.

Space Songs by Myra Cohn Livingston, illustrated by Leonard Everett Fisher (Holiday House). Often-haunting poems and paintings about satellites, the moon, meteors, and more. Ages 8 and up.

Tail Feathers from Mother Goose: The Opie Rhyme Book by Iona and Peter Opie (Little, Brown). Each double-page spread has illustrations by a different artist for one or more nursery rhymes. All ages.

Fantasy

Born into Light by Paul Samuel Jacobs (Scholastic). Children mysteriously appear one night. But who are they? Ages 11 and up.

The Clothes Horse and Other Stories by Allan Ahlberg, illustrated by Janet Ahlberg (Viking Kestrel). Figurative expressions form the basis for funny tales, such as a story of a horse really made out of clothes. All ages.

The Hawk's Tale by John Balaban, illustrated by David Delamare (Harcourt Brace Jovanovich). The adventures of three friends on a quest, richly told and illustrated. Ages 8 to 11.

In the Beginning: Creation Stories from Around the World by Virginia Hamilton, illustrated by Barry Moser (Harcourt Brace Jovanovich). Fascinating tales, with explanations for each, have haunting paintings. All ages.

The Last Slice of Rainbow and Other Stories by Joan Aiken, illustrated by Alix Berenzy (Harper & Row). Nine remarkable tales of magic, fairies, and wonder. Ages 9 to 12.

For one minute,
three minutes,
maybe even a hundred minutes,
we stared at one another.

John Schoenherr's illustrations for *Owl Moon,* by Jane Yolen, won the 1988 Caldecott Medal for "the most distinguished American picture book for children."

The Mermaid Summer by Mollie Hunter (Harper & Row). Eric Anderson defies a mermaid and is banished from home, but Anna and Jon are determined to bring him back. Ages 8 to 12.

Tales from the Enchanted World by Amabel Williams-Ellis, illustrated by Moira Kemp (Little, Brown). Fascinating illustrations accompany a fine mixture of tales from several countries. Ages 8 and up.

Urn Burial by Robert Westall (Greenwillow Bks.). When Ralph discovers an alien creature, frightening events occur. Ages 12 and up.

Fiction

Black Star, Bright Dawn by Scott O'Dell (Houghton Mifflin). Bright Dawn takes the place of her injured father in a dog-sled race across Alaska. Ages 8 to 14.

Borrowed Children by George Ella Lyon (Orchard Bks.). Amanda, 12, must leave school to care for her family when her mother becomes ill. She is rewarded with a trip to Memphis, where she learns about family and values. Ages 10 to 12.

The Boy from Over There by Tamar Bergman, translated by Hillel Halkin (Houghton Mifflin). A European war orphan learns to adapt in Israel, thanks to Rina, who befriends him. Ages 12 and up.

The Burning Questions of Bingo Brown by Betsy Byars (Viking Kestrel). Bingo is full of questions about life and love. His teacher, who is losing his grip on reality, adds to those questions.

The Facts and Fictions of Minna Pratt by Patricia MacLachlan (Harper & Row). When Minna falls in love with Lucas, even her attitude toward playing her cello changes. Ages 9 to 12.

Fallen Angels by Walter Dean Myers (Scholastic). Richie Perry joins the army and discovers the vivid horrors of the Vietnam War. Ages 12 and up.

Granny Was a Buffer Girl by Berlie Doherty (Orchard Bks.). Jess gathers family stories and discovers that pain and disappointment are part of life. Ages 12 and up.

The Hideout by Sigrid Heuck, translated by Rika Lesser (Dutton). Rebecca, her memory lost after an air raid, forms a bond with a boy living on his own near her orphanage. A stark, moving tale. Ages 10 to 14.

The Last Silk Dress by Ann Rinaldi (Holiday House). Susan, a 14-year-old growing up in the South during the Civil War, must cope with a mentally unbalanced mother and her own changing beliefs about the war. Ages 12 and up.

Maudie in the Middle by Phyllis Reynolds Naylor and Lura Schield Reynolds, illustrated by Judith Gwyn Brown (Atheneum Pubs.). Maudie is either too young or too old and feels put-upon and unloved. Her attempts to gain attention often backfire. Ages 7 to 11.

Maybe I'll Move to the Lost & Found by Susan Haven (Putnam). Friends have a falling-out when a new girl moves in. Ages 10 and up.

Memory by Margaret Mahy (Macmillan). Jonny

befriends elderly Sophie West and finds that she cannot care for herself. Ages 12 and up.

The Village by the Sea by Paula Fox (Orchard Bks.). Emma, visiting her bitter aunt and kind uncle while her father undergoes surgery, meets Bertie, and their toy village becomes absorbing, easing her problems. Ages 9 to 11.

Animals, people, places, and projects

Anthony Burns: The Defeat and Triumph of a Fugitive Slave by Virginia Hamilton (Knopf). Burns, captured in Boston, recalls his earlier slave days. Includes excerpts from the Fugitive Slave Act of 1850 and a bibliography. Ages 12 and up.

Henry by Nina Bawden (Lothrop, Lee & Shepard Bks.). A true story of a red squirrel named Henry and his effect on the family that adopts him. Ages 8 to 12.

Micromysteries: Stories of Scientific Detection by Gail Kay Haines (Dodd, Mead). Fascinating accounts of scientists' searches for the secrets of rubber, the cause of a mysterious disease, a treatment for diabetes, and more, with the frustrations and failures as well as the successes. Ages 12 and up.

Moonseed and Mistletoe: A Book of Poisonous Wild Plants by Carol Lerner (Morrow). A fascinating account, with clear drawings and paintings, of how dangerous these plants can be. Ages 10 and up.

Rain of Troubles by Laurence Pringle (Macmillan). The book shows the effects of industrial pollutants and reveals attempts to delay or forgo corrections. Ages 12 and up.

Rescue: The Story of How Gentiles Saved Jews in the Holocaust by Milton Meltzer (Harper & Row). Meltzer vividly shows where and how Jews were saved from the Nazis in Europe during World War II (1939-1945). Ages 12 and up.

Smoke and Ashes: The Story of the Holocaust by Barbara Rogasky (Holiday House). The horrors of the Nazi extermination program are told in stark prose and often shocking photographs. Ages 13 and up.

The Way Things Work by David Macaulay (Houghton Mifflin). Using the adventures of woolly mammoths as a theme, Macaulay explains the elements, movement, electricity, and much more in almost 400 pages of lively and witty drawings and information. Ages 12 and up.

Awards in 1988

The Newbery Medal for the best American children's book was awarded to Russell Freedman for *Lincoln: A Photobiography*. The Caldecott Medal for "the most distinguished American picture book for children" went to John Schoenherr, the illustrator of *Owl Moon*. The Mildred L. Batchelder Award cited Margaret K. McElderry Books, a branch of Macmillan Publishing Company, for its publication of *If You Didn't Have Me* by Ulf Nilsson.   Marilyn Fain Apseloff

In *World Book*, see **Caldecott Medal; Literature for children; Newbery Medal.**

Lloyd Webber, Andrew (1948-   ), a British composer and theater producer, added to his string of box-office successes with the 1988 Broadway opening of his blockbuster musical *The Phantom of the Opera*. The play, which premiered in London in 1986, brought to three the number of Lloyd Webber hits playing simultaneously on Broadway in 1988. The other two were *Cats* (1981) and *Starlight Express* (1984).

Lloyd Webber was born in London on March 22, 1948, to musician parents. He began to study the violin at age 3 and composed his first song at age 9. Lloyd Webber briefly attended Magdalen College at Oxford University and the Royal College of Music in London. While at Oxford, he met lyric writer Tim Rice, who became his collaborator on a number of musicals.

Their first success was *Joseph and the Amazing Technicolor Dreamcoat*, originally a short piece written in 1967 for a boys' choir at a London school. Later expanded to two acts, the musical was first staged in 1973. Lloyd Webber and Rice, whose partnership dissolved in the late 1970's, also wrote the rock opera *Jesus Christ Superstar* (1971), released as a film in 1973, and *Evita* (1978).

Lloyd Webber's other works include *Jeeves* (1975), *Song and Dance* (1982), and *Requiem* (1985), a memorial Mass for his father.

Lloyd Webber is married to British actress Sarah Brightman. He has two children from a previous marriage.   Barbara A. Mayes

Los Angeles residents in 1988 witnessed a year of escalating street violence caused by youth gangs. Reacting to public anger and fear, the Los Angeles City Council on April 12 approved $4.5 million in additional police overtime pay to put more officers on the streets. On June 21, the City Council approved an ordinance imposing a 10 p.m. curfew on teen-agers to enable police to stop suspicious youngsters and possible gang members from loitering on the streets at night. The Los Angeles County Board of Supervisors passed an identical measure on November 8.

Despite the crackdown, however, the violence continued. The Los Angeles Police Department reported a total of 257 gang-related homicides in 1988, exceeding the 1987 total of 205.

High-rise fire. On May 4, a fire at the 62-story First Interstate Bank Building in downtown Los Angeles, the city's tallest skyscraper, left 1 person dead and more than 30 injured. The fire prompted the City Council to pass an ordinance on July 15 requiring some 350 older high-rises to be equipped with automatic sprinklers and fire-resistant elevator lobbies on every floor.

Discrimination suits. The United States Department of Justice filed suit against Los Angeles County on September 8, alleging that the county had discriminated against Hispanic voters. The civil action contended that the County Board of Supervisors violated the Voting Rights Act of 1965 when it redrew the five

A fire causing one death and more than 30 injuries sweeps five floors of the 62-story First Interstate Bank Building in Los Angeles on May 4.

erty owners are required to fix leaky faucets and toilets and are forbidden to use water to hose off paved areas such as patios, sidewalks, and driveways. The law also bars restaurants from serving water to diners except on demand and prohibits the operation of decorative fountains that do not recycle water. In addition, the council passed a new ordinance requiring property owners to install water-saving devices.

Culture. The local arts community won a major victory on November 22 when the City Council agreed to create a new program to shape the city's cultural policy and generate up to $20 million annually for the arts. The council established the Los Angeles Endowment for the Arts, a program within the Cultural Affairs Department that will be funded through fees imposed on municipal and private development projects. The program will also receive a share of revenues from the city's hotel bed tax.

Sports. It was a year of downtown parades for local sports teams as the city celebrated a pair of world championships. In the spring, throngs of sports fans honored the Los Angeles Lakers, champions of the National Basketball Association, and in the fall the Los Angeles Dodgers baseball team was cheered after its victory in the World Series.   Victor Merina

See also **City**. In *World Book*, see **Los Angeles**.

Louisiana. See **State government**.

Luxembourg. See **Europe**.

Madagascar. See **Africa**.

county districts established in 1981 for the election of supervisors. That remapping, the Justice Department said, diluted the voting power of the county's Hispanics, thereby denying them fair political representation. The Mexican American Legal Defense and Educational Fund and the American Civil Liberties Union Foundation of Southern California had filed a similar, class-action lawsuit against the county on August 24. In replying to both lawsuits, county officials denied that they had discriminated against Hispanics.

Voters nix oil drilling. On November 8, Los Angeles voters rejected Occidental Petroleum Corporation's quest to drill for oil beneath Pacific Palisades, a coastal community near Will Rogers State Beach. A majority of voters—52.3 per cent—approved a ballot proposition that repealed three city ordinances granting Occidental the right to drill in that area. A rival measure, supported by the oil company, won the support of only 34.3 per cent of the voters. Occidental and its environmentalist opponents had relied on intensive television advertising and direct-mail appeals to push their positions during the hotly contested race.

Mandatory water conservation was ordered by the City Council on April 26 in response to months of drought. The conservation plan was also prompted by concerns that urban growth may be overburdening the city's sewer system.

Under the law, which was last invoked in Los Angeles during a major drought in 1977 and 1978, all prop-

Magazine advertising revenues in the United States increased in 1988 by about 10 per cent over 1987, reaching a total of $5.9 billion. The number of advertising pages also rose in 1988, totaling nearly 167,000, an increase of 7 per cent.

The combined circulation per issue of all consumer magazines surveyed by the Audit Bureau of Circulations (ABC) in the United States was 349.9 million during the first six months of 1988, a 4 per cent increase over the same period in 1987. (The ABC is an independent organization that issues circulation figures, verified by auditors, for magazines and other periodicals.)

An annual survey conducted by the Magazine Publishers of America (MPA) and the accounting firm of Price Waterhouse & Company indicated that U.S. magazines were more profitable in 1987 than in 1986. The surveyed magazines showed a pretax operating profit of 13.6 per cent, compared with 11.0 per cent in 1986.

According to a survey conducted in late 1987 by Mediamark Research, Incorporated, 94 per cent of all U.S. adults read magazines, and they read almost 10 different issues per month. The average magazine reader is 38 years old, has at least a high school education, is married, is employed full-time, and has household income 11 per cent above the U.S. average.

Awards. The MPA named Jack D. Rehm, president and chief executive officer of Meredith Corporation in

Leading magazines in the United States

The following were the magazines with the highest average paid circulation—including sub-scriptions and single-copy sales—for the first six months of 1988, as determined by the Audit Bureau of Circulations, an independent company that issues circulation figures verified by auditors.

Magazine	Circulation
1. *Modern Maturity*	17,924,783
2. *Reader's Digest*	16,964,226
3. *TV Guide*	16,917,545
4. *National Geographic Magazine*	10,516,837
5. *Better Homes and Gardens*	8,152,478
6. *Family Circle*	5,900,794
7. *McCall's*	5,146,554
8. *Woman's Day*	5,138,280
9. *Good Housekeeping*	5,027,865
10. *Ladies' Home Journal*	5,013,761
11. *Time*	4,737,912
12. *Guideposts*	4,371,861
13. *National Enquirer*	4,303,631
14. *Redbook*	4,007,564
15. *Star*	3,623,058
16. *Sports Illustrated*	3,438,999
17. *Playboy*	3,405,786
18. *Newsweek*	3,315,369
19. *People Weekly*	3,277,839
20. *Cosmopolitan*	3,013,759

Source: Audit Bureau of Circulations, *FAS-FAX Report*, June 30, 1988.

Des Moines, Iowa, to receive the 1988 Henry Johnson Fisher Award as publisher of the year, the magazine publishing industry's most prestigious honor. The Stephen E. Kelly Award and the accompanying prize of $100,000, granted for outstanding advertising in magazines, went to Ogilvy & Mather, Incorporated, for that agency's campaign for the American Express Green Card.

The American Society of Magazine Editors presented its National Magazine Awards for editorial excellence in April. Winners were *Money* for personal service; *Condé Nast Traveler* for special interests; *The Washingtonian* and *Baltimore Magazine* for news reporting; *The Atlantic* for feature writing, public interest, and fiction; *Life* for design and single-topic issue; *Rolling Stone* for photography; and *Harper's* for essays and criticism. In the category of general excellence, which is presented in four groups according to circulation size, the winners were *The Sciences* (less than 100,000); *Hippocrates* (100,000 to 400,000); *Fortune* (400,000 to 1 million); and *Parents Magazine* (more than 1 million).

New magazines appearing in 1988 included *Lear's*, for women over 40, and *Sassy* and *Model*, for teen-aged girls. Diamandis Communications, Incorporated, launched *Memories*, a collection of nostalgic stories and photographs. A number of magazines aimed at college students failed, including *Newsweek on Campus* and *Campus Voice*.

Changes. In what was reported to be the largest magazine acquisition in history, News America Publishing, owned by Australian-born media magnate Rupert K. Murdoch, purchased Triangle Publications in August for $3 billion. Triangle publishes *TV Guide*, whose circulation of nearly 17 million makes it the top-selling weekly magazine in the United States. Other Triangle magazines are *Seventeen*, *Good Food*, and the *Daily Racing Form*.

In June, Peter G. Diamandis sold Diamandis Communications to Hachette S.A., the Paris-based publishing giant, for $712 million. The sale included some of the best-known consumer magazines in the United States, such as *Woman's Day*, *Car and Driver*, *Road & Track*, and *Popular Photography*.

American Express Publishing Corporation spent well over $1 million in August to acquire its fourth magazine, *L.A. Style*, from the newspaper *L.A. Weekly*. *L.A. Style* is a three-year-old monthly with a circulation of 500,000. In March, Sandra Yates and Anne Summers, executives at Fairfax Publications (U.S.) Limited, bought *Ms.* and *Sassy* from Fairfax for an undisclosed sum. John J. Beni resigned as president of Gruner + Jahr USA, publisher of *Parents Magazine*, in May and was replaced by Elizabeth Crow, formerly editor in chief.   Ellen Winchester

In *World Book*, see **Magazine**.

Maine. See **State government**.

Malawi. See **Africa**.

Malaysia experienced political turmoil in 1988 even as it became more prosperous due to industrial growth and a rise in world prices for its rubber and palm oil exports. Prime Minister Mahathir bin Mohamed's narrow 1987 reelection as president of the United Malays National Organization (UMNO), the dominant political party, was challenged in the Kuala Lumpur High Court in early 1988. The case was brought to court by Tunku (Prince) Razaleigh Hamzah and other members of UMNO who had opposed Mahathir's reelection on the grounds that his regime was corrupt. On February 4, the court dismissed the challenge but ruled that UMNO was unlawful because its branches had not been legally registered.

New UMNO. Mahathir competed with his opponents to form a new party that would inherit the assets of UMNO. On February 8, Tengku Abdul Rahman, UMNO's founder and Malaysia's first prime minister, denounced Mahathir for jailing 106 political activists and other dissidents and for shutting down three newspapers in October 1987. Calling for Mahathir's resignation as prime minister, Rahman, Razaleigh, and their supporters sought to form a new party. But on February 13, Mahathir and his supporters created UMNO Baru (New UMNO), which became Malaysia's largest party. .

Shakeup of the judiciary. Parliament amended the Constitution on March 18 to reduce the power of Malaysia's courts. Mahathir had introduced the amendments after judges ruled against the government on several occasions.

On June 12, the king, Paramount Ruler Sultan Iskandar Yang di-Pertuan Agong, acting on Mahathir's advice, suspended the head of the judicial system, Tun Mohammed Salleh Abas, accusing him of being biased against the government. A tribunal of five Malaysian and Commonwealth judges was named to consider the charges against Salleh, but on July 2, five Supreme Court judges ordered these proceedings halted. Four days later, the king suspended the Supreme Court judges and lifted their order to halt the tribunal's proceedings. The tribunal removed Salleh from office on August 8 and recommended the dismissal of two of the Supreme Court judges but exonerated the other three. The situation left critics of the government fearful that the independence of the judicial branch had been seriously weakened.

Economic growth. According to official calculations, the nation's economy grew at a 4.7 per cent rate in 1987, and the projected growth rate for 1988 was even higher. Part of the rise could be credited to new policies that cut government spending and encouraged foreign investment.   Henry S. Bradsher

See also **Asia** (Facts in brief table). In **World Book**, see **Malaysia**.

Maldives. See Asia.

Mali. See Africa.

Malta. See Europe.

Manitoba. The governing New Democratic Party (NDP) suffered a dramatic defeat in the legislature on March 8, 1988, when it lost a vote of confidence on its budget. Premier Howard Pawley, Canada's only NDP provincial head, resigned the next day, saying that he would let someone else lead the party into the election, called for April 26. At an NDP convention on March 30, Gary Doer, minister for urban affairs under Pawley, was chosen as party leader. He asked Pawley to carry on as caretaker premier until the election.

Doer's NDP ran a poor third in the April voting, winning only 12 of the 57 seats in the legislature. The Progressive Conservatives won the largest number of seats—25—allowing the party to form a minority government. The Liberals, whose leader, Sharon Carstairs, had held the party's only seat in the legislature, took a surprising 20 seats. Observers attributed the defeat of the NDP to the party's record of careless management of provincial corporations, high premium increases in public automobile insurance, and unpopular taxes.

Conservative leader Gary A. Filmon, an engineer and businessman, became premier of Manitoba on May 9. His government announced it would give priority to cutting the provincial deficit, reducing the number of senior public-service positions, and eliminating a tax on business payrolls.   David M. L. Farr

See also **Canada; Filmon, Gary Albert**. In **World Book**, see **Manitoba**.

Manufacturing. "The health of manufacturing improved significantly in 1988" in the United States, according to Alexander B. Trowbridge, president of the National Association of Manufacturers (NAM). The manufacturing renaissance that began in 1987 was partly the result of action by U.S. manufacturers to streamline and modernize their operations. Another contributing factor was the decline of the U.S. dollar. The combination worked to make U.S.-made goods more competitive both at home and abroad. As one manufacturing executive observed in Industry Week magazine, "The 'Made in the U.S.A.' label can now be taken off the endangered species list."

The drop in the value of the dollar, which started in 1986, continued in 1988. As a result, from 1985 to 1987, U.S. products became 22.2 per cent cheaper in France; 21.3 per cent cheaper in Italy; 27.9 per cent in West Germany; and 28.4 per cent in Japan, according to the Department of Labor.

The ability to compete in price opened up overseas markets, which had been closed to U.S. manufacturers for years due to the dollar's inflated value. When exports began to increase in mid-1987, the factory sector began to rebound. Manufacturing accounted for about 66 per cent of total exports in 1988.

Productivity. United States manufacturers also became more competitive in world markets due to increased productivity. From 1982 to 1987, productivity in the manufacturing sector rose at the highest rate in three decades. The rise is a direct reaction to foreign competition, which was taking markets away from U.S. companies by selling higher-quality products at lower prices. Other countries were able to capture markets because their costs were significantly lower than those of U.S. companies.

American manufacturers had to be able to produce goods faster, more efficiently, and at higher quality in order to remain competitive. They did so by closing aging factories, cutting payrolls, and employing factory automation and computer technology. Measured in output per worker hour, U.S. productivity grew at an annual rate of 4.8 per cent from 1983 to 1987, compared with an annual rate of 2.4 per cent over the years between 1960 and 1982. Manufacturers improved productivity at an annual rate of 5.2 per cent in the third quarter of 1988.

In effect, the United States became a low-cost producer nation, and busy factories have reflected this change. In November 1988, factories ran at 84.5 per cent of capacity, the highest level since July 1979. In some industries—such as paper, chemicals, metals, and aerospace—factories were producing at 95 per cent of capacity.

Not all industries prospered, however. In 1988, U.S. manufacturers were no longer producing videocassette recorders or compact disc players, and only Zenith Electronics Corporation still made television sets. Japan was the only producer of facsimile machines and small office copiers.

Executives study computer-integrated manufacturing at the Systems Integration Center of the Basic Industry Research Laboratory in Evanston, Ill.

Employment. More than 300,000 new manufacturing jobs were created in 1987, and the manufacturing boom continued to create jobs in 1988. In November 1988 alone, manufacturing created 71,000 new jobs. That was in addition to 99,000 new manufacturing jobs in October. It was the largest two-month gain in factory jobs since 1983.

Manufacturing jobs have been found traditionally in the so-called *rust-belt* states of the Midwest. But in 1988, employment gains in the manufacturing sector spread more widely than ever across the United States, according to economist Steven R. Malin of the Conference Board, a business research group. States in the Southeast and West, for example, added more manufacturing jobs than traditional manufacturing states in the North and East. Growth occurred in California, North Carolina, and Florida, while Ohio, Michigan, and Pennsylvania lost manufacturing jobs.

Factory wages in the United States in 1988 remained extremely competitive in relation to international averages. The average U.S. factory wage in October rose at an annual rate of 3.8 per cent to $9.49 per hour. Following a dramatic slowdown in the rise of U.S. factory wages since 1983, U.S. labor costs in 1988 were 30 per cent lower than West Germany's and 10 per cent lower than Japan's. In 1985, U.S. costs were slightly higher than West Germany's and 59 per cent higher than Japan's.

A growing number of foreign companies opened

plants in the United States to take advantage of less expensive labor and lower transportation and construction costs. Four Japanese automakers—Honda Motor Company, Toyota Motor Company, Nissan Motor Company, and Mazda Motor Corporation—began producing cars in the United States. In 1988, Mitsubishi Motors Corporation began constructing a plant in Houston to make fork-lift trucks.

Some U.S. companies that had shifted manufacturing operations overseas in recent years returned some operations to the United States in 1988 as a result of declining production costs. The Tandy Corporation transferred production of its Color Computer 3 from South Korea to Fort Worth, Tex., for example.

Downsizing. To become more competitive in the global market place, U.S. manufacturers have taken a number of dramatic cost-cutting steps, while using technology and increased worker productivity to make strides in production. For example, Ford Motor Company has slashed $5 billion in operating costs since 1979 and has cut its work force by 30 per cent. These moves have enabled the company to lower its *break-even point*—the point at which costs and income are equal—by 40 per cent.

General Motors Corporation (GM) invested large sums—more than $11 billion in 1986—in technology to reduce costs by $13 billion over four years. In 1988 alone, GM obtained cost savings of $4 billion. *Industry Week* noted that GM can now assemble a Grand Prix automobile at its $1.1-billion plant in Fairfax, Kans., in 28.3 hours, compared with the 45.5 hours required at an older plant—a productivity improvement of 25 to 30 per cent.

Factory automation. The USX Corporation (formerly United States Steel Corporation) produces a ton of steel in less than 4 work hours today, compared with 10 work hours just a few years ago. Its production costs are now comparable with those in Japan.

Rockwell International Corporation spent more than $1.5 billion from 1986 to 1988—most of it for high-technology production techniques such as computer-integrated manufacturing (CIM)—to improve quality and productivity in the aerospace field. Similarly, Caterpillar Incorporated, whose construction equipment was taking a pounding from overseas competitors, improved product quality through extensive use of computers in production and quality control. The company regained its former share of the market and became a profitable operation again.

American manufacturers borrowed tactics from Japanese and other companies, involving—from the conception of a product through its sale—teams of production, engineering, marketing, and design people. Extensive use of CAD/CAM (computer-aided design and computer-aided manufacturing) systems and corresponding software led to an 18.5 per cent rise in sales of these systems in 1988 to $5.3 billion.

More than 81 per cent of the electronic components assembled in the United States in 1988 were assembled automatically, compared with less than 50 per cent in 1983. A Motorola Incorporated plant in Florida, for example, assembled a line of the company's pagers using total robot automation in one-hundredth of the normal time. The robots assemble, adjust, and check for accuracy. Only 12 workers are needed to monitor the operation and load parts.

Industrial production in 1988 reflected the growth in manufacturing. According to the Department of Commerce, orders for *durable goods* (goods expected to last at least three years) rose 2.9 per cent in November to $122.9 billion. Much of this increase was due to continued strong defense spending for tanks and military aircraft.

The backlog of unfilled durable-goods orders continued to be strong. Total unfilled orders rose 0.8 per cent in October to $436 billion. Through October 1988, new orders for durable and *nondurable goods* (goods expected to last less than three years) totaled $222.2 billion, compared with $206.7 billion for the same period in 1987.

Capital spending —that is, spending on new equipment and factory construction—stagnated between 1985 and 1987. In 1987, manufacturers spent $388.7 billion on modernization and improvements, up only 1.7 per cent from 1986. But the tide turned in 1988, when manufacturers appeared to realize that they had to replace older, less efficient equipment if they were to remain competitive in world markets.

Capital spending became one of the strongest sectors in the 1988 economy, increasing more than 8 per cent to $419.9 billion. This was the largest increase since 1985. In some industries, 1988 spending was expected to rise by 11 per cent over 1987.

Machine tool orders are one indicator of future investment in manufacturing plants and equipment. These power-driven devices are used to cut and shape metal parts. After two dismal years in 1986 and 1987, the machine tool industry was back on its feet in 1988, fueled by orders from the automotive, construction machinery, defense, and aerospace industries.

Orders were strong in November, up 6.4 per cent over October, to $279 million. Sales through the first 11 months of 1988 were $3.3 billion, 74 per cent higher than the same period in 1987. Eleven-month 1988 orders for U.S. machine tools from foreign customers surged by 80 per cent from the same period in 1987, to $461 million.

Productivity improvements helped domestic steel producers increase their share of steel used to make machine tools from 50 per cent in 1986 to 70 per cent in 1988.   Ronald Kolgraf

In *World Book*, see **Manufacturing.**
Marine Corps, U.S. See Armed forces.
Maryland. See State government.
Massachusetts. See State government.
Mauritania. See Africa.
Mauritius. See Africa.

Medicine. The lack of progress in successfully developing an artificial human heart sparked a controversy in the United States in 1988. On May 12, the National Institutes of Health (NIH) in Bethesda, Md., announced a halt in funding for research to develop an artificial heart. The NIH said it had provided about $240 million for artificial heart research since 1964, yet no artificial heart capable of permanently replacing the human heart had been developed.

But objections from Congress forced the NIH to reverse its action and confirm on July 2, 1988, that funding for the program would continue. The agency maintained, however, that success for the artificial heart program still appeared unlikely.

Claude J. M. Lenfant, director of the National Heart, Lung, and Blood Institute, which is part of the NIH, argued that research funds allocated for artificial hearts should instead be spent on left ventricular assist pumps, devices threaded into the heart's *ventricles* (lower chambers) to partially replace an ailing heart. Assist pumps work with a beating heart and are often used to help patients awaiting a heart transplant or experiencing complications after heart surgery.

Small heart pump. Doctors at the Texas Heart Institute in Houston on April 26 performed the first implant of a small assist pump designed to treat patients suffering from heart failure. The pump, called the Nimbus Hemopump, is about the size of a pencil eraser. It is threaded into the heart through an artery in the leg, and can remain inside the left ventricle for up to seven days.

Treating breast cancer. In May, the National Cancer Institute (NCI) issued a special alert recommending a major change in the treatment of breast cancer. Vincent T. DeVita, Jr., NCI director, said that all women who undergo surgery for breast cancer should receive follow-up drug or hormone treatment.

The NCI, which is part of the National Institutes of Health, previously recommended such postsurgical therapy only for women whose cancer had spread to the underarm *lymph nodes*, glandlike bodies that return fluids from body tissues to the blood. The new recommendation was based on three studies which established that follow-up treatment of women who had breast cancer but no evidence of cancer in the lymph nodes greatly reduced the risk that the cancer would spread to other parts of the body. DeVita estimated that if all patients who had breast cancer surgery received postsurgical drug or hormone therapy, about 5,000 lives could be saved each year in the United States.

Mammogram benefits. NCI scientists on September 20 reported the first convincing evidence that early detection of breast cancer by *mammograms* (low-dose X rays of the breast) helps reduce deaths from breast cancer among women under age 50. Authorities have long agreed on the benefits of routine mammograms for women over 50, but experts

disagreed about the benefits of mammograms for women in their 40's. The NCI researchers found that periodic mammograms reduced the rate of death due to breast cancer by about 24 per cent among women between 40 and 49 years of age.

Stroke surgery. Only about one-third of surgical operations to prevent strokes are clearly justified, medical researchers at the University of California at Los Angeles and at several private organizations reported in the March 24 issue of *The New England Journal of Medicine*. The operation—carotid endarterectomy—involves the removal of fatty deposits that block blood flowing to the brain through arteries in the neck. The researchers said that about one-third of such operations are unjustified and another one-third are questionable.

Saving newborns' sight. The results of a study conducted at 23 medical centers throughout the United States and reported on March 29 show that surgically freezing part of the eye can save thousands of premature infants from blindness or permanent visual damage. In the procedure, called *cryotherapy*, a thin probe filled with a refrigerant is applied to specific points of the eye to stop the growth of abnormal blood vessels.

Cryotherapy was designed to treat premature infants born with *retinopathy of prematurity*, a previously untreatable condition. The disease causes excessive growth of blood vessels, bleeding, and scarring

Doctors in Bethesda, Md., discuss cancer treatments with Soviet physicians in Moscow via satellite TV hookup during a cancer summit on March 29.

inside the eye. The National Eye Institute, which funded the study, said that cryotherapy can reduce by 50 per cent the risk of blindness or visual impairment in infants with the disease.

Fetal tissue controversy. A debate over the use of tissue from aborted fetuses in medical research arose in 1988. It began in January when a team of doctors led by Ignacio Madrazo of Mexico City reported that they successfully used tissue from a spontaneously aborted fetus to treat patients with Parkinson's disease, a brain disorder that causes tremors, muscle rigidity, and other symptoms. The doctors transplanted tissue from the brain and adrenal glands of a fetus into the brains of two Parkinson's patients. They reported that the transplants helped to relieve symptoms of the disease.

Groups in the United States opposed to abortion objected to the procedure, saying that it might encourage more abortions. In April, the U.S. Department of Health and Human Services banned the use of fetal-tissue transplants in research funded by the U.S. government until completion of a study on the procedure's ethical and legal aspects. On September 16, the study panel concluded that research involving tissue from aborted fetuses is acceptable and that it should continue.

Contraceptive cap. On May 23, the U.S. Food and Drug Administration approved prescription sale of the cervical cap, a birth control device that is widely used in Europe. The cap, manufactured by Lamberts (Dalston) Limited, a British firm, is a cuplike rubber device that blocks entry of sperm into the uterus. Studies found that the cap is more comfortable and convenient than the diaphragm, a similar device.

Liver transplants. Surgeons in Europe and the United States performed the world's first "split-liver" transplants in 1988, raising hopes that more people awaiting transplants can benefit from a limited supply of donor livers. On February 2, a surgical team at the University of Hannover in West Germany performed the first such procedure, cutting a donated liver in half and transplanting the halves into two different recipients. A second split-liver transplant took place on May 1 in Paris. On July 12, surgeons at the University of Chicago hospitals performed the first transplant in which two infants received portions of a liver from a single donor. One of the infants died, however, 36 hours later.

Delivering babies. The American College of Obstetricians and Gynecologists (ACOG) on October 26 issued new guidelines intended to reduce the number of babies delivered by Caesarean section, an operation in which a baby is removed from the uterus by cutting through the abdominal and uterine wall. The ACOG, a medical organization in Washington, D.C., said that women who have had one baby by Caesarean section should be encouraged to attempt normal labor and delivery in subsequent pregnancies. Repeat Caesarean sections, the ACOG said, should be performed only

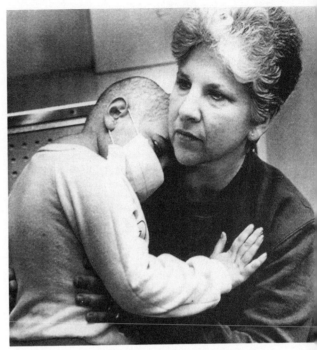

Brooke Ward of Raleigh, N.C., is held by her mother after becoming the first bone-marrow recipient matched through a national donor program in March.

when there are specific medical reasons for the surgery. Caesarean sections should no longer be performed routinely.

Help from fish. A study published in the September 22 issue of *The New England Journal of Medicine* reported that taking fish oil capsules can dramatically improve the success of coronary angioplasty. Angioplasty, an alternative to coronary by-pass surgery, involves guiding a tiny balloon into coronary arteries that are clogged with fatty deposits. When inflated, the balloon compresses the deposits, restoring the flow of blood to the heart.

The study, which was conducted at the Veterans Administration Medical Center in Dallas, found that fish oil capsules helped prevent the arteries of angioplasty patients from becoming clogged again. This problem, which is a major drawback of the procedure, occurs in about one-third of all angioplasty patients.

Twins go home. Benjamin and Patrick Binder, Siamese twins who were born joined at the back of the head and were separated in 22 hours of surgery in September 1987, were discharged from Baltimore's Johns Hopkins Hospital in April 1988. The boys, 14 months old, returned to Ulm, West Germany, with their parents.   Michael Woods

See also **AIDS; Drug abuse; Drugs; Health and disease; Public health.** In the Special Reports section, see **Protecting Our Hearing.** In *World Book*, see **Heart; Medicine.**

Mental illness

Mental illness. The National Institute of Mental Health (NIMH) in Rockville, Md., on May 4, 1988, began an intensive nationwide campaign to inform the public about the symptoms and treatment of clinical depression. Psychiatrist Lewis L. Judd, director of the institute, said that clinical depression strikes about 10 million people in the United States each year but that only one-third of them receive adequate treatment.

Clinical depression is not just "the blues," or the brief periods of sadness or disappointment that are a normal part of life. Rather, it involves a profound sense of despair that may last for months. It can virtually incapacitate its victims, leaving them unable to work, care for their families, or perform other tasks. Approximately 15 per cent of severely depressed people commit suicide. The NIMH reported that untreated depression costs the United States $14.2 billion annually in lost wages and productivity.

The national campaign—entitled "Depression/Awareness, Recognition, and Treatment" or D/ART—is designed to correct the widespread misconception that depression is not a legitimate illness but is just a passing mood or a sign of personal weakness. Judd estimated that 80 to 90 per cent of all cases of depression can be treated effectively with antidepressant medication, psychotherapy, or both.

Suit settled. Psychologists in the United States in October claimed a major victory in their long struggle with psychiatrists to gain equal professional recognition. It came when psychiatrists, in settling a lawsuit brought by the American Psychological Association (APA) in 1985, gave psychologists greater access to training programs that prepare professionals to perform psychotherapy. In the past, these programs refused to admit psychologists.

Although trained to care for the mentally ill, psychologists—unlike psychiatrists—are not physicians and therefore cannot prescribe medicine or admit patients to hospitals. The APA, a professional organization of psychologists based in Washington, D.C., said the October settlement could permit Medicare and other health insurance programs to reimburse nonphysician psychotherapists for their services.

Inadequate care. Two studies in 1988 criticized the lack of adequate services for the mentally ill in the United States. One study, conducted by Congress and released on April 3, estimated that about 29 million Americans suffer from some type of mental illness that requires professional treatment. Yet the study found that many mental health services are fragmented, inappropriate, or ineffective.

Despite the trend to treat patients in community outpatient programs rather than in mental hospitals, "a desperate lack of community services" still exists for the most severely mentally ill. The report said 75 per cent of mental health services are provided by the community, but only 30 per cent of government funding goes to community or outpatient services.

The other study, issued on September 13 by the Health Research Group in Washington, D.C., and the National Alliance for the Mentally Ill in Arlington, Va.—both consumer health groups—concluded that inadequate care for people with serious mental illness is the greatest single failure of American medicine. The study cited low-quality hospital care and a lack of rehabilitation services and housing for the seriously mentally ill. It also included a state-by-state ranking of the quality of mental health services available for the seriously mentally ill.

Ruling on alcoholism. The Supreme Court of the United States on April 20 ruled that the Veterans Administration can define alcoholism as "willful misconduct," rather than a disease, in determining eligibility for benefits. The court said that Congress had "reasonably determined" that the government could classify veterans whose alcoholism is not rooted in physical or mental illness as "at least to some extent responsible for their disabilities."

Mental health groups and medical authorities criticized the court's decision, citing evidence that alcoholism is a disease. In November, President Ronald Reagan signed into law a bill overriding the court's ruling. Under the new law, the Veterans Administration must, in the granting of benefits, consider chronic alcoholism a disease.   Michael Woods

See also **Psychology.** In *World Book*, see **Mental illness.**

Mexico. On Dec. 1, 1988, Carlos Salinas de Gortari was sworn in for a six-year term as Mexico's president, but the inaugural ceremony was marked by a walkout by more than 100 opposition lawmakers and by street demonstrations protesting vote fraud.

The inauguration came at a particularly troubled time in Mexico's history. The 40-year-old Salinas won his office by the narrowest of margins—receiving just 50.4 per cent of the popular vote. The July 6 elections were marred by charges of widespread vote fraud—charges that appeared to many critics to be bolstered by a weeklong delay in announcing the official election results.

Salinas was the first presidential candidate from the long-dominant Institutional Revolutionary Party (PRI) to face significant opposition. Since the party was founded in 1929, the PRI has won every presidential election in Mexico.

Salinas' leading opponent was the charismatic Cuauhtémoc Cárdenas, former governor of Michoacán state, who left the PRI to run as the candidate of the populist National Democratic Front. Cárdenas won 31.1 per cent of the vote, according to the official results, though Cárdenas contended that vote fraud had denied him victory.

The son of Lázaro Cárdenas, Mexico's president from 1934 to 1940 and one of the most popular political figures in Mexico's modern history, Cárdenas won 3 out of every 4 votes cast in Mexico City. Most observ-

Mexico's Carlos Salinas de Gortari, left, shakes hands with voters as he campaigns for the presidency, which he won by a slim majority in July.

ers interpreted the PRI's poor showing in the capital city as an indication of deep concern about government corruption and mismanagement of the economy. Voters in Mexico City have traditionally been the PRI's base of support and have, in turn, benefited most from government subsidies that support low food prices and modest subway fares.

In the months between the election and the inauguration, Cárdenas stumped the country to protest electoral fraud. On occasion, he appeared jointly with Manuel Clouthier of the conservative National Action Party, who won 17.1 per cent of the vote.

U.S. loan. Widespread discontent with the election results and a weakening economy threatened to undermine the Salinas administration even before he took office. To forestall such an event, the United States government announced on October 17 its largest loan ever to a debt-stricken nation—up to $3.5 billion. The loan will help Mexico cope with disastrous shortfalls in its oil earnings, which are projected at only $5 billion in 1989, compared with $15.6-billion in the peak year of 1982.

The loan was also seen as a political effort to aid Salinas. During the campaign, Cárdenas called for a moratorium on interest payments on Mexico's swelling foreign debt of more than $100 billion.

Cárdenas' proposal was as bold as his father's action in nationalizing foreign-owned oil companies in 1938. Most of Mexico's foreign debts are held by United

States banks. The United States grant was expected to offset pressure from Cárdenas until Salinas could consolidate his hold on power and obtain long-term financial help from the World Bank and the International Monetary Fund, both of them agencies of the United Nations.

Challenges facing Salinas. As budget and planning minister in Mexico's previous administration, Salinas was known for his insistence on trimming government subsidies. The subsidies were popular with the poor, who make up a majority of Mexico's population. He was also an advocate of selling unprofitable state-owned enterprises to the private sector—an unpopular position because of the increased unemployment it has caused.

As president, Salinas must tread a narrow path. He must confront continuing economic hard times and resentment from workers who feel that they have unfairly borne the brunt of austerity measures. He must also maintain the support of organized labor, including Joaquín Hernández Galicia, head of the powerful oil workers' union. Observers expected that this 210,000-member union would continue to look for favorable treatment from the government in return for political support.   Nathan A. Haverstock

See also **Latin America** (Facts in brief table); **Salinas de Gortari, Carlos.** In *World Book*, see **Cárdenas, Lázaro; Mexico.**

Michigan. See **Detroit; State government.**

Middle East

The various conflicts that have kept tensions in the Middle East at a high level in recent years proved to be more susceptible to arbitration in 1988 than at any time since 1979, when Egypt became the first Arab state to recognize the existence of Israel as a nation. There was even some movement toward resolving the seemingly unresolvable conflict between Israel and the Palestinians.

The strife among ethnic groups and a number of wars between neighboring states that had plagued regional stability began to wind slowly down in 1988, partly because of war-weariness and the high cost of military conflict. But effective intervention by the United Nations (UN) and international pressure also played important roles.

Concerns about population increases and living standards increasingly forced Middle Eastern countries to look inward and concentrate their efforts on economic development. At the same time, regional conflicts continued to affect the development process, with most Middle Eastern countries still devoting a large percentage of their revenues to arms purchases.

Iran-Iraq War. In July 1988, Iran formally accepted UN Security Council Resolution 598, which called for a cease-fire and peace negotiations in Iran's eight-year war with Iraq. Iraq had accepted the resolution in 1987. The conflict had resulted in nearly 1 million casualties and cost more than $100 billion in economic damage and lost oil revenues. When the cease-fire went into effect on Aug. 20, 1988, the two countries' armies were approximately where they had been when the war began in September 1980.

But peace talks held under UN auspices made little progress. The hatred generated by years of conflict hardened the two countries' terms for peace.

Iran and Iraq also argued over the establishment of borders, the exchange of prisoners, and the assignment of blame for starting the war. By year-end, the only thing the two countries had agreed on was an exchange of sick and wounded prisoners.

Gulf action. The cease-fire also helped restore a measure of stability to the Persian Gulf. Shortly after hostilities ended, the multinational naval force stationed in the gulf to protect oil-tanker traffic from Iranian attacks began to withdraw. A battle between United States and Iranian naval forces in the gulf in April, which cost Iran one-fourth of its navy, had helped push Iran toward the peace table. Another key factor was the accidental downing of an Iranian commercial airliner on July 3 by the U.S. Navy cruiser *Vincennes*. All 290 people aboard the plane died.

Chemical weapons. A particularly ominous aspect of the Iran-Iraq war was Iraq's alleged use of chemical weapons. Mustard gas and other chemical agents reportedly played a large part in successful Iraqi spring

offensives. In March, Kurdish rebels fighting for independence from Iraq accused Iraqi forces of using chemical weapons to attack the Kurdish border town of Halabjah, Iraq. Thousands of Kurdish civilians were reportedly killed then and in similar attacks in August and September. The U.S. Senate in September passed bills to suspend economic credits to Iraq and ban further sales of chemical materials and technology to protest Iraq's use of chemical weapons.

Western Sahara. In August, the government of Morocco and leaders of the Polisario Front guerrillas agreed in principle to a UN-sponsored peace plan. The Polisario Front has been fighting for independence for Western Sahara, which Morocco claims, since 1976. The UN plan called for an immediate cease-fire, with a

An Iranian fireboat sprays a burning oil rig in the Persian Gulf, one of two Iranian rigs and six vessels damaged by U.S. forces on April 18.

2,000-member UN peacekeeping force to monitor the truce. On Sept. 20, 1988, the UN Security Council approved plans for a *referendum* (direct vote) for the territory, which is recognized as the Sahrawi Arab Democratic Republic by 71 nations despite Morocco's occupation. The people of the territory would choose between integration with Morocco or independence.

Sudan. Attempts to end the bloody civil war in Sudan failed. The government and the rebel Sudanese People's Liberation Army (SPLA), which controls most of southern Sudan, agreed in late November to cease hostilities and hold a constitutional convention in December. But the agreement broke down in late December. The latest upsurge in the long conflict had been triggered in 1983 by attempts by the North's Muslim majority to impose Islamic law over the South's largely non-Muslim population.

Palestinian uprising. The Palestinian uprising on the Israeli-occupied West Bank and Gaza Strip, which began in December 1987, continued without letup during 1988. The Palestinians kept up the pressure on Israeli forces by throwing stones and firebombs and holding demonstrations.

To crush the uprising, the Israeli Army beat protesters, destroyed the houses of people suspected of

Facts in brief on Middle Eastern countries

Country	Population	Government	Monetary unit*	Exports†	Foreign trade (million U.S.$) Imports†
Bahrain	503,000	Amir Isa bin Sulman Al-Khalifa; Prime Minister Khalifa bin Sulman Al-Khalifa	dinar (0.38 = $1)	2,600	2,400
Cyprus	697,000	President George Vassiliou (Turkish Republic of Northern Cyprus: Acting President Rauf R. Denktaş)	pound (0.5 = $1)	561	1,470
Egypt	51,205,000	President Mohammad Hosni Mubarak; Prime Minister Atef Sedky	pound (2.3 = $1)	2,900	11,500
Iran	53,141,000	President Ali Khamenei; Prime Minister Mir Hosein Musavi-Khamenei	rial (67.7 = $1)	12,300	10,000
Iraq	17,610,000	President Saddam Hussein	dinar (0.32 = $1)	12,100	10,500
Israel	4,447,000	President Chaim Herzog; Prime Minister Yitzhak Shamir	shekel (1.6 = $1)	7,100	10,400
Jordan	3,967,000	King Hussein I; Prime Minister Zaid Rifa'i	dinar (0.46 = $1)	733	2,400
Kuwait	1,998,000	Amir Jabir al Ahmad al Sabah; Prime Minister & Crown Prince Saad Al Abdullah Al Sabah	dinar (0.28 = $1)	7,400	5,800
Lebanon	2,898,000	Acting Prime Minister Michel Aoun‡	pound (484 = $1)	500	2,200
Oman	1,413,000	Sultan Qaboos bin Said	rial (0.38 = $1)	2,800	2,600
Qatar	342,000	Amir & Prime Minister Khalifa bin Hamad Al Thani	riyal (3.45 = $1)	1,900	890
Saudi Arabia	13,474,000	King & Prime Minister Fahd ibn Abd al-Aziz Al Saud	riyal (3.75 = $1)	25,000	19,000
Sudan	24,188,000	Supreme Council President Ahmed Ali al Mirghani; Prime Minister Al-Sadiq Al-Mahdi	pound (4.5 = $1)	369	760
Syria	12,177,000	President Hafiz al-Assad; Prime Minister Mahmud al-Zu'bi	pound (33.5 = $1)	1,300	2,700
Turkey	55,377,000	President Kenan Evren; Prime Minister Turgut Ozal	lira (1,761 = $1)	8,000	11,000
United Arab Emirates	1,534,000	President Zayid bin Sultan Al Nahayyan; Prime Minister Rashid ibn Said al Maktum	dirham (3.67 = $1)	8,300	6,500
Yemen (Aden)	2,408,000	Supreme People's Council Presidium Chairman Haydar Abu Bakr al-Attas; Council of Ministers Chairman Yasir Sa'id Nu'man	dinar (.34 = $1)	316	762
Yemen (Sana)	7,691,000	President Ali Abdallah Salih; Prime Minister Abdel Aziz Abdel Ghani	rial (9.75 = $1)	11	1,300

*Exchange rates as of Dec. 1, 1988, or latest available data (source: Deak International). †Latest available data.
‡Acting Prime Minister Salim al-Huss still has the support of many Muslim leaders.

throwing stones or demonstrating, jailed Palestinians without trial, sealed off the occupied territories, and imposed strict curfews. By mid-December, at least 330 Palestinians and 13 Israelis had died in the violence.

Israel's standing abroad was seriously damaged by extensive television coverage of the army's treatment of Palestinian protesters. The uprising not only focused global attention on the issue of Palestinians' civil and political rights but also drove a wedge into Israeli society. Although many Israelis supported the army's harsh measures, many other Israelis criticized the government's policy in the occupied territories as brutal.

Israel was also criticized for deporting Palestinian activists. In January, the United States voted with other UN Security Council members for a resolution calling on Israel to halt the deportations.

Economic costs. Although Israeli forces maintained physical control of the occupied territories, the unrest increasingly affected Israel's economy. In March, the European Community (EC or Common Market) refused to ratify a preferential trade agreement for Israeli exports. Israel stood to lose $8 million from flower exports alone to EC markets. In addition, tax revenues lost because of the mass resignation of Palestinian tax collectors cost the Israeli government some $180 million a year. Work stoppages by Palestinian laborers employed in Israel brought Israel's construction industry to a halt. With once-profitable West Bank markets closed to Israeli manufacturers by Palestinian boycotts, and military costs of the occupation reaching $2 million to $3 million per month, the occupied territories increasingly became an economic drain as well as a political liability.

Hussein bows out. The Palestinian uprising generated a significant realignment of players in regional politics. In July, Jordan's King Hussein I formally cut that country's financial and legal links with the West Bank. He explained his action as a response to the Palestinians' desire for a separate state represented by the Palestine Liberation Organization (PLO). Although the cutoff in Jordanian funds initially strained the resistance, other Arab states took up the slack. In September, they pledged $126 million in immediate aid and a $43-million monthly subsidy.

A Palestinian state. Although the leadership of the uprising remained in local hands, the growing solidarity of the resistance movement led the PLO to take action to preserve its position as the representative of the Palestinian people. In November, the Palestine National Council, the governing body of the PLO, meeting in Algeria, approved by a 5 to 1 margin a declaration proclaiming the establishment of an independent Palestinian state. According to the PLO declaration, the state would include the West Bank, the Gaza Strip, and the Arab sector of Jerusalem. The council also endorsed UN Resolutions 242 and 338 as the basis for an international peace conference. Resolution 242, adopted in 1967, indirectly recognizes Israel's right to exist. Resolution 338, adopted in 1973, calls for the implementation of Resolution 242. But the council did not recognize Israel by name.

The PLO announcement brought wild rejoicing on the West Bank and the Gaza Strip, even though Israeli forces placed both areas under curfew to prevent violence and cut down on the celebrations. At least 27 countries recognized the proposed Palestinian state, including Cuba, India, Turkey, and Yugoslavia in addition to the Arab states. East Germany, Greece, and the Soviet Union did not extend formal recognition but welcomed the action as a step toward peace.

U.S. reactions. Initially, the United States and Israel refused to modify their opposition to the PLO. In March 1988, the United States had tried to close down the PLO's observer mission to the United Nations in New York City, calling it a "nest of terrorism." But the United States dropped the matter after the International Court of Justice, a UN agency, ruled that the United States is prohibited by treaty from interfering in UN matters.

In December, the Administration of President Ronald Reagan refused to permit PLO Chairman Yasir Arafat to enter the United States to address the UN General Assembly, citing his past association with terrorism. Most countries denounced the move, and the Assembly held a special session in Geneva, Switzerland, on December 13 to hear Arafat.

Recognition of Israel. In his UN speech and at a meeting on December 7 with four American Jews in

Passengers from a Kuwaiti airliner hijacked by Muslim terrorists in April are released in Algeria. The hijackers killed two of their hostages.

Stockholm, Sweden, Arafat, in a historic turnabout, announced PLO support for UN Resolutions 242 and 338 and accepted the existence of Israel as a state in the Middle East. The United States and Israel, however, said Arafat's statements did not go far enough in recognizing Israel's existence and renouncing terrorism. So on December 14, Arafat read a declaration in English recognizing Israel's right to exist in peace and security and renouncing terrorism in all its forms. Reagan immediately authorized direct talks between the PLO and the United States, lifting a ban on such contact that the United States had imposed in 1975. The talks began on Dec. 16, 1988, in Tunis, Tunisia.

Israeli political turmoil. The PLO declaration and U.S. announcement not only left Israel isolated in its refusal to deal with the PLO but also complicated the already difficult attempts to form a new Israeli government. In parliamentary elections held on November 1, the hard-line Likud bloc edged out the Labor Party. The Likud leader, Prime Minister Yitzhak Shamir, had said he would never allow anything more than limited local self-government for the occupied territories.

The Likud bloc's narrow victory led Shamir to negotiate with Israel's small ultrareligious parties in order to gain a majority in the Knesset (parliament). Widespread opposition by the Israeli public and American Jews to the religious parties' participation in the Cabinet led Likud to begin negotiations on November

375

Mining

20 with the Labor Party to form a government of national unity. Such a government had been formed after the last Israeli elections in 1984. On Dec. 19, 1988, the two parties announced the formation of a new coalition government to be headed again by Shamir.

Lebanese elections. Attempts to elect a new president of Lebanon to succeed Amine Gemayel, whose term expired in September, failed because of divisions between Christians and Muslims as well as conflict within the Christian community. At year-end, Lebanon had no president but two competing governments, a Muslim-Christian government in West Beirut and an all-Christian government in East Beirut.

Hostages freed. Seven hostages—five French, one German, and one Swiss—held in Lebanon were released during 1988. An Indian professor with resident-alien status in the United States was freed in October. But the kidnapping of several Red Cross and refugee-aid officials—later released—and of an American officer assigned to the UN Truce Supervision Organization in southern Lebanon underlined the vulnerability of foreigners, regardless of background or status, in Lebanon's civil conflict.   William Spencer

See also **Iran-contra affair** and articles on the various Middle Eastern countries. In the World Book Supplement section, see **Egypt; Israel.** In *World Book,* see **Middle East** and individual Middle Eastern country articles.

Mining. After six years of negotiations, 33 nations agreed on June 2, 1988, to open all of Antarctica to strictly controlled prospecting, mining, and oil drilling. The agreement would become binding when ratified by 16 of the 20 nations that signed the Antarctic Treaty in 1959 to regulate activities in the southernmost continent and its offshore waters. The 1988 agreement replaced an informal, voluntary halt on Antarctic minerals development that had been in effect since 1980.

Under the new agreement, prospecting would be allowed in Antarctica for the first time, using seismic and other techniques with little environmental impact. In seismic prospecting, geologists set off small explosions and study how the resulting shock waves travel through the rock layers, revealing what lies underground. Large-scale exploration and development, involving blasting or drilling, would require approval from a special commission. The commission would consider the environmental impact in reaching a decision. Geologists believe that Antarctica has large deposits of gold, copper, uranium, and coal in addition to extensive offshore fields of crude oil and natural gas.

Discoveries. Pennzoil Company, an oil firm based in Houston, announced on September 29 that its mining division had discovered major deposits of gold and silver on the island of Borneo in Indonesia. The deposits contained an estimated 15 million troy ounces (467 billion grams) of gold and 800,000 troy ounces (25 million grams) of silver.

Geologists on Aug. 29, 1988, reported the discovery of a major deposit of beryllium near the town of Mo, also called Mo i Rana, in northern Norway. Beryllium is a valuable strategic metal used to control the rate of nuclear reactions in atomic power plants and other nuclear reactors. Geologists estimated the deposit was sufficient to meet all of Western Europe's needs for beryllium for 10 years.

A take-over battle involved two of the world's biggest gold-mining firms during the year. Minerals and Resources Corporation of Luxembourg on September 21 said it would attempt to buy Consolidated Gold Fields PLC of London for $4.9 billion. Gold Fields resisted the attempt, and on October 11 filed an antitrust suit in federal district court in New York City to prevent the take-over. The suit alleged that the take-over would create a monopoly in the world gold market and illegally restrain trade in the United States.

China announced plans on July 29 to expand gold-mining operations. Bai Meiqing, deputy secretary of China's State Council (cabinet), said gold production would double by 1993 but would require increased foreign investment to help pay for prospecting and mining operations. China already ranks as the world's sixth-largest gold producer, after South Africa, the Soviet Union, Australia, the United States, and Canada.

International ventures. Comalco Limited, a big Australian aluminum company, agreed in August to supply 1 million metric tons (1.1 million short tons) of bauxite or aluminum ore each year to the Soviet Union. The bauxite would be shipped from a Comalco mine on the Cape York Peninsula in northern Queensland to the Soviet Union for conversion into aluminum. Comalco would be a joint owner of the refining and smelting facilities.

Brazil's Constituent Assembly in April voted to prohibit foreign-controlled mining companies from operating in the country. The measure—part of Brazil's new Constitution that took effect in October—requires 55 foreign mining companies to find Brazilian partners or leave the country. The foreign companies account for about 20 per cent of the $3 billion in minerals produced by Brazil each year.

Mexican mine sold. In an effort to transfer government-owned resources to private industry, Mexico on April 21 announced the sale of a big copper mine in Sonora. Grupo Protexa of Monterrey assumed $910-million of Mexico's foreign debt in return for the mine.   Michael Woods

In *World Book,* see **Mining.**

Minnesota. See **State government.**
Mississippi. See **State government.**
Missouri. See **State government.**
Mongolia. See **Asia.**
Montana. See **State government.**

376

Montreal. Contrary to widespread predictions of economic problems made when Mayor Jean Doré took office in November 1986, Montreal's economy continued to boom in 1988, the city's second year under a socialist municipal government. Twenty-one major development projects were announced for the downtown office sector. Residences—mostly condominiums—were built at such a pace that supply outran demand, and the vacancy rate in the Montreal area was one of the highest in Canada, with nearly 5 per cent of all apartments empty at any given time.

Unemployment dropped to about 9 per cent—close to the Canadian average and about twice that of the United States. Inflation hovered around 5 per cent, compared with 4.4 per cent in the United States.

Tax rates for property owners in Montreal, among the highest in Canada, were capped in 1988 with maximum increases of 15 per cent for most taxpayers. Taxes increased at or near that maximum, however, for 56 per cent of the property owners, while taxes decreased for only a few. In most cases, tax bills for homeowners have doubled in the past five years.

In March, there was a public outcry when tax bills for developers of major office projects were cut by as much as 18 per cent, and the boom in construction of condominiums caused the destruction of more than 20,000 low-cost housing units.

The battle over language became increasingly bitter in 1988. As the province struggled with constitutional challenges to laws mandating the use of French, Montreal merchants who displayed signs in English suffered from broken windows and other vandalism. The city government added to the dispute by forbidding the use of English in crime-prevention signs displayed in public places. See **Quebec.**

The language dispute took an ugly turn when the largest French-language newspaper, *La Presse,* used the issue as a forum for anti-Semitic opinion. The paper expressed support of a movement in Outremont—an affluent French-language suburb—to prevent Hasidic Jews from erecting a synagogue, on the grounds that they spoke English and had not integrated with the Quebec community.

Racial confrontations. Montreal saw the first major conflict between blacks and whites in the city's history in the wake of a November 1987 shooting of an unarmed black teen-ager by a white police officer. The police officer, Allan Gosset, claimed the death was an accident and was acquitted of criminal charges in February 1988, though the police force later disciplined and discharged him. The event, however, caused a wave of protest among the members of Montreal's small black community—mainly first-generation immigrants from the Caribbean—who marched, demonstrated, and prepared petitions. Throughout the year, court cases demonstrated that the city police force had a record of treating blacks harshly. The city responded by increasing sensitivity training for police officers.

The question of free trade between the United States and Canada divided the city deeply. Some Montreal-area industries, such as clothing and light manufacturing, depend heavily on tariff barriers. Others—such as the pulp and paper industry, technology, and mining—would like greater access to U.S. markets. The consensus among Montreal's government and its population favored free trade. Canada's Senate gave final approval to the free-trade agreement on December 30.

Media. A new English-language daily newspaper, *The Montreal Daily News,* started publishing in March 1988. The *News,* a tabloid featuring sports and crime news, competes with the 200-year-old *Gazette.* Despite some predictions of failure, the *News* was still appearing six days a week at year-end.

Politics. In late 1988, the coalition built by Mayor Doré showed signs of breaking apart. Doré came under increasing criticism from members of his own party, the Montreal Citizen's Movement (MCM). One member, Pierre-Yves Melançon, resigned from party ranks on October 28 to sit as an independent member of the City Council. Melançon charged that the MCM was undemocratic. Three other council members resigned from Doré's caucus in December, citing similar reasons. The defections, however, were no threat to Doré, who at year-end controlled 52 of the 58 council seats.   Kendal Windeyer

See also **Canada.** In *World Book,* see **Montreal.**

Morocco. The 12-year conflict in Western Sahara, which has drained Morocco's resources, tied down its army, and affected Morocco's relations with other African states, seemed to be approaching a solution in 1988. The first sign of a breakthrough was the resumption of diplomatic ties between Morocco and Algeria, which has supported the Polisario Front guerrillas in their effort to win Western Sahara's independence from Morocco. Morocco's King Hassan II met with Algeria's President Chadli Bendjedid during a historic summit meeting of North African heads of state in June. The two leaders agreed to reopen their common border and restore rail and communication links.

In August, Hassan and the Polisario Front agreed in principle to a peace plan for Western Sahara sponsored by the United Nations (UN) and the Organization of African Unity. The plan included a cease-fire and a *referendum* (direct vote), which would allow the people of the territory to choose between independence and integration with Morocco. The cease-fire was violated almost immediately, however, when 2,000 Polisario Front guerrillas invaded the Oum Dreiga region and fought several battles with Moroccan troops. Both sides suffered heavy casualties.

Spanish settlement. Another issue involving Moroccan territorial claims was resolved in 1988. In August, the Cortes, Spain's parliament, passed a law formally making the Spanish enclaves of Ceuta and Melilla on Morocco's Mediterranean coast a part of

Spain, with locally elected legislatures. Both Spain and Morocco have claimed the two enclaves since Morocco became independent in 1956. In compensation, Spain gave Morocco $1.1 billion in loans and backed Morocco's attempts to obtain preferential treatment for its exports to the European Community (EC or Common Market). In May 1988, the EC agreed to allow Morocco to ship 17,500 metric tons (19,000 short tons) of fish per year duty-free to European markets.

The economy. One compelling reason for a solution to the conflict in Western Sahara was the war's effect on the Moroccan economy. With the war costing up to $2 million a day, Morocco could ill afford to continue the struggle. The restoration of rail links with Algeria allowed for expanded trade, particularly exports of Moroccan farm products.

An agricultural surplus due to plentiful rains lifted hopes of overcoming Morocco's perennial deficit crisis. Exports in 1988 increased 15.3 per cent to $2.8 billion, while strict controls held imports at $4.2 billion. The 1988-1992 Five Year Plan, approved in February by the Chamber of Representatives, Morocco's legislature, forecast economic growth at 4 per cent annually. In August 1988, the World Bank, a UN agency, which had been insisting on economic reforms as a condition for additional loans, made a stand-by loan of $225 million for agricultural development.   William Spencer

See also **Middle East** (Facts in brief table). In *World Book*, see **Morocco.**

Morrison, Toni (1931-   ), won the Pulitzer Prize for fiction in March 1988 for *Beloved* (1987), the haunting story of an escaped slave in the pre-Civil War South who kills her baby daughter rather than allow the child to be taken by slave catchers. Like Morrison's other novels, *Beloved* was praised for its lyrical but precise language, its powerful characters, and its depiction of black culture as a world filled with magic and poetry.

Toni Morrison was born Chloe Anthony Wofford on Feb. 18, 1931, in Lorain, Ohio, near Cleveland. She earned a bachelor of arts degree in 1953 from Howard University in Washington, D.C., and a master of arts degree in 1955 from Cornell University in Ithaca, N.Y. After teaching at Texas Southern University in Houston for two years, she joined the faculty of Howard University, a position she held until 1964.

Morrison wrote her first four novels while working as an editor at Random House, a publishing company in New York City, where she specialized in books by black writers. Her first novel, *The Bluest Eye*, was published in 1970. Her second novel, *Sula* (1973), brought her national recognition. *Song of Solomon* (1977), which won the National Book Critics Circle Award for fiction in 1978, and *Tar Baby* (1981) became best sellers. Morrison left Random House in 1983 to write full-time.

Morrison has two sons from a marriage that ended in divorce in the mid-1960's.   Barbara A. Mayes

Motion pictures. The most publicized film of 1988 was never shown in much of the United States, Canada, and Europe. *The Last Temptation of Christ*, directed by Martin Scorsese of *Taxi Driver* (1976) and *The Color of Money* (1986) acclaim, had lengthy engagements in metropolitan areas and good runs in smaller cities. It received largely favorable reviews. But in many small towns, the film was not shown at all.

For a while, it looked as if *The Last Temptation* might never be shown anywhere. Some Christians were offended by a brief segment in which the film's Jesus, played by Willem Dafoe, hallucinates during the Crucifixion. He dreams of marriage and family life, and the hallucination scenes include fleeting footage of sex between Jesus and Mary Magdalene, played by Barbara Hershey. Religious groups threatened to boycott theater chains that showed *The Last Temptation* or to sabotage the theaters. Fundamentalist preachers called for a boycott against all products of MCA, Incorporated, the parent company of Universal Pictures, which released the film in the United States. Universal moved up the film's release from late September to August 12, a move viewed by some as a ploy to cash in on the publicity.

The controversy over *The Last Temptation of Christ* reached worldwide proportions. The film, based on a 1955 novel by the Greek author Nikos Kazantzakis, was banned in Greece, as was the novel more than 30 years earlier. The Roman Catholic archbishop of Dublin and primate of Ireland, Desmond Connell, objected to the showing of the Scorsese film. Some of the most violent demonstrations occurred in France, where the movie received largely hostile reviews. Demonstrations in Paris continued for more than three days and resulted in injuries to 13 police officers. In Besançon, arsonists burned down a movie theater showing *The Last Temptation*. In Marseille, stink bombs forced viewers out of auditoriums.

Other controversies. *The Last Temptation of Christ* was not the only film to stir controversy during 1988. In *Colors*, Robert Duvall gave a riveting performance as a tired policeman coping with gang warfare in Los Angeles. The Guardian Angels, a volunteer crime-fighting group, as well as various official law-enforcement agencies, objected to the film, claiming that it glorified gang membership. Three theaters in Los Angeles pulled *Colors* off their screens after minor violence broke out among audiences. In April, a young man wearing gang *colors* (membership insignia) was shot to death as he waited in line to see the movie at a Stockton, Calif., theater. *Colors* played without incident, however, in the rest of the United States.

The Accused, in which Jodie Foster played the victim of a barroom gang rape, also caused debate, presumably because of the character played by Foster. Some viewers thought the film excused the crime of rape by portraying a victim who was "asking for it."

Hot box office. Summer continued to be prime movie playtime in the United States. The U.S. motion-

Bob Hoskins plays Eddie Valiant, the human star of *Who Framed Roger Rabbit*, a blend of animation and live action never before achieved in motion pictures.

picture industry tallied record-breaking grosses in the summer of 1988. Four films topped the $100-million figure. *Who Framed Roger Rabbit* led, followed by *Coming to America*, which proved the star power of Eddie Murphy. *Big*, with Tom Hanks, and *"Crocodile" Dundee II*, with Paul Hogan, also grossed in excess of $100 million. For the year, the U.S. box-office total was almost $4.4 billion, a record.

Sylvester Stallone's *Rambo III* was a disappointment in the United States, grossing $50 million, less than one-third the amount earned by its 1985 predecessor, *Rambo: First Blood, Part II*. The film became a target of jokes by comedians and even other filmmakers. In the comedy *Twins*, for example, Arnold Schwarzenegger compares his muscles with Stallone's on a *Rambo III* poster and sneers. The Stallone film was a giant success overseas, however, and was expected to earn in excess of $150 million in foreign receipts by the end of 1988.

Strong women's roles reemerged in many 1988 films. Jodie Foster won praise for her gutsy role in *The Accused*, as did many other actresses, including Barbara Hershey as an antiapartheid activist mother in *A World Apart* and Melanie Griffith as a secretary on the rise in *Working Girl*. Critics also lauded Sigourney Weaver as the dedicated anthropologist Dian Fossey in *Gorillas in the Mist*, Shirley MacLaine as an eccentric piano teacher in *Madame Sousatzka*, Meryl Streep as an innocent mother on trial for the murder of her

baby in *A Cry in the Dark*, and Amy Irving as an upscale New Yorker courted by a pickle merchant in *Crossing Delancey*. Still other notable roles were those of Diane Keaton as a divorced woman fighting for custody of her daughter in *The Good Mother*, Michelle Pfeiffer as a Mafia widow in *Married to the Mob*, Christine Lahti as a former antiwar activist fleeing the Federal Bureau of Investigation (FBI) in *Running on Empty*, Debra Winger as an FBI agent in *Betrayed*, and Jessica Lange as a Southern belle with hidden resources in *Everybody's All-American*. Newcomers Annabeth Gish, Lili Taylor, and Julia Roberts gave fine performances as waitresses with their eyes on the future in *Mystic Pizza*.

Strong male roles were also plentiful. Gene Hackman won praise for his performance as a world-weary FBI agent investigating the disappearance of three civil rights workers in 1964 in *Mississippi Burning*. Eric Bogosian was acclaimed for his role as a radio talk-show host who carries his hostility to dangerous extremes in *Talk Radio*. Edward James Olmos received commendation for playing an inspiring ghetto schoolteacher in *Stand and Deliver*, and Ben Kingsley won critical honors as a lonely spy in *Pascali's Island*. William Hurt's performance as a grieving father in *The Accidental Tourist* earned favorable comment, as did the wildly comic portrayals of John Cleese and Kevin Kline in *A Fish Called Wanda*.

Tom Hanks won considerable praise for two widely

Martin Scorsese's *The Last Temptation of Christ*, which depicts Jesus dreaming
of life as an ordinary man, attracts protesters at its August opening.

differing roles. *Big* featured a brilliant comic performance by Hanks as a lovable boy in a man's body.
Other films with similar themes included *Like Father,
Like Son*; *Vice Versa*; and *18 Again*. Hanks rose to
superstardom with his strong, bitter portrayal of a
stand-up comic in the uneven *Punchline*.

Kevin Costner's performance as a veteran minor-
league baseball player in *Bull Durham* was endorsed
by both critics and public. Don Ameche got the best
reviews of his long and possibly underrated career in
Things Change, in which he played a shoeshine man
whose resemblance to a Mafia don temporarily
changes his life. Dustin Hoffman and Tom Cruise won
widespread praise for their performances as an autis-
tic man and his streetwise brother in *Rain Man*.

The return of successful animation was an
endearing aspect of 1988. *Who Framed Roger Rabbit*,
a product of the Walt Disney Company, co-produced
by Steven Spielberg and with special effects by George
Lucas, was 1988's biggest box-office hit in the United
States as well as a major success in Europe. Kathleen
Turner, who provided the voice of the vamp Jessica
Rabbit, had the year's most quoted line when she
drawled, "I'm not bad. I'm just drawn that way."

The Land Before Time, a comedy featuring dinosaurs, was created by former Disney animators Don
Bluth, Gary Goldman, and John Pomeroy and became
a major attraction. The Disney studio's *Oliver & Company*, based loosely on British novelist Charles Dickens'

Oliver Twist (1837-1839), also drew large audiences
and appreciative comments.

Horror films made a flurry at the box office. *Hal-
loween 4*, *Nightmare on Elm Street 4*, and *Friday the
13th, Part VII* drew the expected crowds. The inventive
Child's Play, in which a working mother combats her
child's demonic doll, was noteworthy for its special
effects and its emotional manipulations.

Reruns. The 1962 thriller *The Manchurian Candidate*, featuring splendid work by Frank Sinatra, Janet
Leigh, Laurence Harvey, and Angela Lansbury, was
reissued to theaters prior to its release on videocassette. Its critical reception was even more favorable
the second time around. The videocassette release in
October of Universal's 1982 blockbuster *E.T.: The
Extra-Terrestrial* achieved record-breaking success,
with advance sales of nearly 12 million cassettes.

Documentaries and imports. Errol Morris' *The
Thin Blue Line* proved the power of film. The documentary drama, which showed at film festivals
throughout the United States, maintained that Randall Dale Adams, a drifter convicted of killing a Dallas
policeman in 1976, was actually innocent. The film led
to a barrage of news stories, and a Dallas judge recommended a new trial for Adams.

The West German *Wings of Desire*, the Spanish
Women on the Verge of a Nervous Breakdown, and
the Indian *Salaam Bombay!* achieved success on American shores, while the Italian film *The Legend of the*

Holy Drinker seemed certain to join their company. British directors examined the sins of the idle rich in *White Mischief* and *A Handful of Dust*.

On the international scene, Swiss filmmaking continued its strong growth in 1988. Switzerland, a country of 6.5 million people, turns out more than 20 full-length features annually. Two lavish Swiss films, *Gemini, the Twin Stars* and *Quicker than the Eye*, seemed destined for U.S. distribution.

French filmmakers also benefited from government aid. Cultural Minister Jack Lang pledged nearly $12-million in aid for motion-picture exhibition and the creation of a special fund to promote French cinema.

American motion pictures flourished throughout the world. Comedies rarely transfer well to other cultures, but *Big* was a worldwide hit. *Who Framed Roger Rabbit* proved the cross-cultural appeal of animation. *"Crocodile" Dundee II* broke attendance records in Great Britain, Japan, and several South American countries. *Fatal Attraction*, a 1987 blockbuster in the United States, was a 1988 phenomenon worldwide. In Japan, the movie played with its original ending, in which Glenn Close commits suicide after framing Michael Douglas for her murder. United States audiences saw a different version. The gangster film *The Untouchables*, a 1987 success in the United States, was an even bigger hit overseas.

The antiapartheid film *Cry Freedom*, which had won critical endorsement but small audiences in its 1987

release in the United States, continued to have problems. In July 1988, South African police seized all prints of the film within seven hours of its release in Johannesburg, saying it threatened public safety. South Africa's board of censors banned another antiapartheid film, *A World Apart*.

Ironically, considering the South African government's tight censorship of motion pictures, South Africa's tax laws make it both easy and profitable to invest in filmmaking. As a result, independent filmmaking boomed in South Africa, though most of the films made there were low-budget action pictures such as *American Ninja* and *Mercenary Fighters*.

Other news. Two new museums devoted to motion-picture and television history opened in 1988—the Museum of the Moving Image in London and the similarly named American Museum of the Moving Image in New York City.

In November, humor columnist Art Buchwald and producer Alain Bernheim filed a $5-million lawsuit against Paramount Pictures. The suit claimed that the Eddie Murphy film *Coming to America*, about an African prince who comes to New York City, was based on a Buchwald story that he and Bernheim sold to the studio in 1983. Paramount said the idea for the film came from Murphy.   Philip Wuntch

See also **Awards and prizes** (Arts awards); **Cher; Douglas, Michael; Hogan, Paul.** In *World Book*, see **Motion picture.**

Meryl Streep stars as an Australian mother accused of murdering her baby in *A Cry in the Dark*, based on the real-life story of Lindy Chamberlain.

Mozambique

Mozambique. The civil war in Mozambique, which began when the country obtained its independence from Portugal in 1975, continued in 1988. During the year, the ruling Front for the Liberation of Mozambique (Frelimo) offered amnesty to guerrillas of the Mozambique National Resistance (Renamo), a rebel group trying to destabilize the government. Some 1,600 of Renamo's estimated 20,000 troops accepted the offer and defected to the government's side.

President Joaquím Alberto Chissano spent much of 1988 forging peaceful ties with other countries. In July, Chissano visited neighboring Malawi as a gesture of appreciation to Malawi's President H. Kamuzu Banda for his generous treatment of Mozambican refugees. Of the estimated 1 million Mozambicans who have fled the civil war, some 700,000 are in Malawi. In September, Chissano received a visit from South Africa's State President Pieter Willem Botha.

As a result of Chissano's diplomatic efforts, economic and military support for Frelimo poured into Mozambique from nations in Western Europe, Africa, and the Soviet bloc. That assistance included nearly 40,000 troops from Tanzania, Zambia, and Zimbabwe. Even South Africa—alleged to be Renamo's primary backer—promised to train and equip Frelimo troops. South Africa and Mozambique agreed on May 26 to revive a 1984 nonaggression pact that pledged South Africa to cease its support for Renamo.

A report issued in April 1988 by the United States Department of State asserted that Renamo troops had murdered an estimated 100,000 civilians over the previous two years and committed numerous atrocities, many against women and children. According to the report, rebel forces destroyed whole villages, including health clinics and schools.

Meeting at midyear, Mozambique, Portugal, and South Africa agreed to work together to restore electric power service from the Cabora Bassa Dam. Power lines from the dam, which has the capacity to meet all of Mozambique's electrical needs as well as 8 per cent of South Africa's, have been kept out of commission by Renamo sabotage since 1983.

The economy. Putting aside many failed socialist programs, Frelimo encouraged the development of private farms and businesses in 1988. The government also abolished a number of price controls and devalued the nation's currency by 22.4 per cent to dampen the 160 per cent inflation rate and reduce a severe trade deficit.

Religious tolerance. In an effort to promote good will among the citizenry, Chissano's Marxist government showed a new tolerance toward religion in 1988, a trend that began the year before. Christians and Muslims, whose activities had been severely restricted since 1975, were allowed to reopen their boarded-up places of worship and operate their own schools.   J. Gus Liebenow and Beverly B. Liebenow

See also **Africa** (Facts in brief table). In *World Book*, see **Mozambique.**

Mulroney, Brian (1939-   ), prime minister of Canada, led his Progressive Conservative (PC) Party to a decisive victory in a national election on Nov. 21, 1988. The victory, in which the PC's won 169 seats for a majority in the 295-seat House of Commons, marked the first time in 35 years that a Canadian prime minister had won two consecutive majority terms and the first time in the 1900's the PC's had done so. The win also cleared the way for a much-debated free-trade agreement between Canada and the United States, making Mulroney the first Canadian prime minister to gain countrywide support for a program to establish closer economic relations between the two countries.

Mulroney's popularity among Canadians fluctuated widely during his four-year tenure as prime minister, according to surveys of public opinion. By 1986, the middle of his term, only 16 per cent of Canadians considered Mulroney the best leader for the country. By the eve of the 1988 election, however, 40 per cent of Canadians preferred Mulroney, citing his competence, ideas and policies, likability, and trustworthiness.   David M. L. Farr

See also **Canada.** In *World Book,* see **Mulroney, Brian.**

Music. See **Classical music; Popular music.**

Namibia. See **Africa.**

Navy. See **Armed forces.**

Nebraska. See **State government.**

Netherlands welcomed Queen Elizabeth II of Great Britain and Prince Philip, Duke of Edinburgh, who arrived on July 2, 1988, for a two-day visit to mark the 300th anniversary of the accession of the Dutch Prince William of Orange to the English throne. William was invited to assume the throne by English politicians who were dismayed by King James II's promotion of Roman Catholicism in largely Protestant England. After William arrived in England, James gave up his throne. William's accession became known as the Glorious Revolution because it established Parliament's right to control succession to the throne and to limit the power of the monarch.

Homosexual rights protest. Queen Beatrix and Prince Claus of the Netherlands accompanied Elizabeth and Philip to the anniversary celebrations. During a celebration in Amsterdam, demonstrators protested against Clause 28, a new British law that makes it unlawful for public authorities to "promote" homosexuality. Protesters waved banners proclaiming homosexual rights, but the monarchs ignored them as they walked to historic Nieuwe Kerk (New Church), where the Netherlands' kings and queens are crowned.

Terrorist murders. At 1:30 a.m. on May 1, a spray of bullets killed an off-duty British Royal Air Force (RAF) serviceman who had returned to his car after spending the evening at a pub in Roermond. About 30 minutes later, a car bomb exploded in Nieuw Bergen,

A squatter stands guard in Amsterdam, the Netherlands, in July as police officers try to evict squatters from an abandoned warehouse.

killing two RAF men and wounding another. The outlawed Provisional Irish Republican Army claimed responsibility for the killings.

Oil find. The Netherlands in January reported striking oil near a suburb of Rotterdam. The oil happens to be located under one of Western Europe's largest oil refineries. The owner of the refinery, Royal Dutch/Shell, said that the deposit also contains a substantial amount of natural gas.

Soccer win. Dutch sports fans rejoiced on June 25, when the Netherlands won its first major international championship in soccer. The Dutch defeated the Soviet Union to capture the European Nations Cup in Munich, West Germany.

Slower growth. The Organization for Economic Cooperation and Development (OECD), an association of 24 industrialized nations, said that the economy of the Netherlands would grow by only about 1.5 per cent in 1988. The OECD also forecast a weakening in growth of private consumption, along with smaller gains in the number of people employed and higher prices for consumer goods.

By mid-1988, exports were heading for a 3 per cent rise. Inflation remained low, at just over 1 per cent, and the government cut spending to offset a rising national debt.   Kenneth Brown

See also **Europe** (Facts in brief table). In *World Book*, see **Netherlands**.

Nevada. See State government.

New Brunswick. Following the overwhelming election victory of the Liberal Party in October 1987, New Brunswick entered 1988 as the only Canadian province to have a legislature consisting of only one party. The Liberals, under Premier Frank J. McKenna, held all 58 seats. In February 1988, McKenna rejected requests by the Progressive Conservative (PC) and New Democratic opposition parties for direct financial assistance. Instead, he gave both parties government-owned office space, allowed their representatives access to legislative committees, and funded a research staff to assist them in the legislative library.

Countering 17 years of PC government, the Liberals made proposals for change in almost every aspect of New Brunswick life. The first legislative session, however, was concerned mainly with housekeeping measures. The Liberals' first budget, announced on April 6, raised taxes and cut back on social programs. The provincial income tax rate was raised two percentage points to 60 per cent of federal tax, one of the highest rates in Canada. The province's debt increased 22 per cent during fiscal year 1987-1988 to $2.92 billion (Canadian dollars; $1 = U.S. 84 cents as of Dec. 31, 1988).   David M. L. Farr

In *World Book*, see **New Brunswick**.

New Hampshire. See State government.

New Jersey. See State government.

New Mexico. See State government.

New York. See New York City; State government.

New York City. The crack epidemic left its mark on New York City in 1988. In the borough of Queens in February, a war among rival gangs selling this smokable and highly addictive form of cocaine led to the assassination of a police officer, Edward Byrne, as he sat in a patrol car guarding the home of a witness in a drug case. In October, two police officers were slain within hours of one another in crack-related shootouts. And the principal of a Bronx elementary school was arrested in November for allegedly buying two vials of crack on a Harlem street.

Despite an austere municipal budget, the administration of Mayor Edward I. Koch implemented a $118-million police initiative called Tactical Narcotics Teams in March to combat the growing trafficking in narcotics. The program, which involved some 600 police officers, was expected to increase the annual number of drug arrests in the city by at least 21,000.

City charter. In November, New York City voters approved five changes to the city's charter, including provisions providing $28 million in public financing for the 1989 mayoral race; curbs on conflicts of interest among city officials; and new maintenance requirements for roads and bridges. The maintenance issue arose after the 85-year-old Williamsburg Bridge, which links Brooklyn with Manhattan, was closed early in 1988 for badly needed repairs.

Trials. Bess Myerson, Mayor Koch's cultural affairs commissioner and a former Miss America (1945), on

New York City

Richard R. Green, newly named chancellor of the New York City school system and the first black to hold that post, walks to City Hall in January.

December 22 was found innocent of bribery and conspiracy after a nearly three-month trial. Also cleared were her codefendants, retired New York Supreme Court Judge Hortense W. Gabel and Myerson's companion, contractor Carl A. Capasso. Myerson had been accused of hiring Sukhreet Gabel, the judge's daughter, as a $19,000-per-year administrative aide in return for the judge's lowering divorce payments for Capasso.

On August 4, Democratic U.S. Representative Mario Biaggi, former Bronx Borough President Stanley Simon, and three other defendants were convicted in a federal court of extortion and racketeering. The five had been charged with promoting government contracts for the Wedtech Corporation, a military supply firm in the Bronx. Biaggi's son, lawyer Richard Biaggi, was acquitted of racketeering charges but convicted of five other felonies, including helping his father obtain a bribe from Wedtech. On August 5, Congressman Biaggi announced his resignation.

A tale of rape doubted. Another crime failed to come to trial in 1988—because investigators concluded that it never happened. After examining evidence for seven months, a state grand jury concluded on October 6 that Tawana Brawley, a black teen-ager, lied about being abducted, raped, and subjected to racial humiliations by six white men in suburban Wappingers Falls in November 1987. The jury said that the girl, 15 years old at the time of the reported attack,

most likely concocted the story to escape punishment for staying away from home for several days.

The sensational and racially charged case attracted national attention throughout most of the year. Black activists rallied to the girl's cause, and she was promised financial assistance by actor Bill Cosby and heavyweight boxing champion Mike Tyson. After the grand jury released its report, a number of people—including Brawley's lawyers and family adviser—continued to insist that the girl's story was true and that state officials were guilty of a cover-up.

New officials. Minneapolis School Superintendent Richard R. Green was named chancellor of the New York City school system in January. Green became the first black ever to hold that post.

In November, the city got its first-ever black district attorney with the appointment of Robert Johnson, a criminal court judge, as district attorney for the Bronx. Johnson will complete the term of Bronx District Attorney Mario Merola, who died in 1987.

Chase Manhattan Bank announced in November 1988 that it would move 5,000 workers from its Manhattan headquarters to downtown Brooklyn, rather than to a new waterfront development across the Hudson River in Jersey City, N.J. New York state and city agencies provided a record $235 million in tax, property, and electricity subsidies to Chase as an inducement to stay in the city.   Owen Moritz

See also **City.** In *World Book,* see **New York City.**

New Zealand experienced continuing economic problems during 1988. The year saw a dramatic decline in public support for the Labour Party government headed by Prime Minister David R. Lange. Although the government's economic policies of tight monetary controls and high interest rates significantly reduced inflation, they caused a record rise in unemployment. By year-end, about 10 per cent of the work force was unemployed.

The government continued plans to sell government-owned businesses to repay a portion of New Zealand's massive debt of $39 billion (New Zealand dollars; $NZ 1 = U.S. 63 cents as of Dec. 31, 1988). During the year, the government sold a number of businesses, including the Petroleum Corporation, New Zealand Steel, and Air New Zealand. The 1988-1989 budget presented on July 28 provided for a surplus of $NZ 2.2 billion based on the sale of such enterprises.

Tax changes. On February 10, Prime Minister Lange and Finance Minister Roger Douglas announced a new two-tier tax system to substantially cut tax rates for businesses and individuals. The system replaced a previously proposed single tax rate plan. As a result of the new system, the corporate tax rate was cut on April 1 from 48 per cent to 28 per cent. This was followed by an October 1 reduction in the maximum personal income tax rate from 48 per cent to 33 per cent and 24 per cent on annual incomes of $NZ 30,875 or less.

A major political crisis occurred in Prime Minister Lange's government near the end of 1988. In mid-December, Finance Minister Douglas, the architect of the government's economic policies, was dismissed because of policy differences with Lange. Lange appointed David F. Caygill to succeed Douglas.

Public services. In April, New Zealand's Parliament passed a controversial bill that brought about radical changes in the country's public services. The bill removed guaranteed job security for almost 200,000 government employees.

Free trade. In an important move, New Zealand and Australia extended their 1983 Closer Economic Relations Agreement on Oct. 12, 1988. The agreement provided for the removal of all *tariffs* (taxes on imports) between the two countries by July 1, 1990.

Racial tensions between New Zealanders of European (primarily British) descent and Maoris (New Zealanders of Polynesian descent) escalated during 1988. Maoris comprise about 10 per cent of the population. Maori groups were concerned about high unemployment and poverty, problems that are more severe among Maoris than among New Zealanders of European descent. European New Zealanders were concerned about a Court of Appeal decision that recognized certain Maori claims to land and fishing and forestry rights.   David A. Shand

See also **Asia** (Facts in brief table). In *World Book*, see **New Zealand.**

Newfoundland, Canada's federal government, and a consortium of five oil companies announced a tentative agreement on July 18, 1988, to develop the Hibernia oil field, located in the North Atlantic Ocean about 200 miles (320 kilometers) southeast of St. John's. The field is estimated to contain 525 million barrels of oil, which would be brought ashore over an 18-year period starting in the mid-1990's. The project was expected to cost $8.5 billion (Canadian dollars; $1 = U.S. 84 cents as of Dec. 31, 1988), $5.2 billion of that for start-up costs. It would be the largest and most expensive energy development in Canada and the largest economic undertaking ever for the Atlantic Provinces. The development was intended to help the economy of Newfoundland, which has Canada's highest unemployment rate and lowest per capita income.

Newfoundland became the only province in Canada without a railway when the line across the island was closed in September 1988. Running 547 miles (880 kilometers) from Channel-Port aux Basques on the southwest tip of Newfoundland to St. John's on the east coast, the freight railway had been a lifeline since it was built in 1881. But revenues had fallen as trucking took over transportation needs on the island. The federal government agreed to provide $813 million to improve the highway across the island and to assist communities hurt by the railway's closing, which eliminated about 640 jobs.   David M. L. Farr

See also **Canada.** In *World Book*, see **Newfoundland.**

Newsmakers of 1988 included the following:

Whale of a rescue. After being trapped by an unseasonal ice pack near Barrow, Alaska, for three weeks, two California gray whales headed for open water on October 28, thanks to the efforts of an international group of rescuers. There were originally three trapped whales, but one is believed to have died. The predicament of the two remaining whales, nicknamed Crossbeak and Bonnet, gained worldwide attention. They finally escaped after Soviet icebreakers cut a path to the open sea. Eskimos, scientists, and environmentalists from the United States monitored the whales' health and helped cut 200 holes in the ice so that the whales could come up for air during their 5-mile (8-kilometer) swim to freedom.

Orel history. "As long as we all live, none of us will ever see any pitcher accomplish what Orel has done; he'll go down in history." The speaker was no slouch himself—the National League's 1988 Most Valuable Player, Kirk Gibson—and the person he was earmarking for the history books was Los Angeles Dodger teammate Orel Hershiser. What Hershiser accomplished was a record 59 consecutive shutout innings (breaking former Dodger Don Drysdale's 20-year record) to end the season, followed by an unparalleled pitching performance in the league championship series and the World Series. Named the Most Valuable Player in both series, Hershiser ended the year as the Cy Young Award winner. But perhaps his

Pop singer Cyndi Lauper, 35, gives her mom a hug and shows off her diploma after graduating from Richmond Hill High School in New York City in July.

most incredible number was an earned run average of 0.44 in his last 14 outings of the year.

British eagle. Michael (Eddie the Eagle) Edwards was the only ski jumper from Great Britain to compete in the Winter Olympics in Calgary, Canada, in February 1988. He finished last in the competition, but he placed first in the hearts of his countrymen—and the rest of the world. The 24-year-old plasterer from Cheltenham, England, entered the games with neither a sponsor nor a coach—nor any great skill. During his jumps in the 70- and 90-meter events, his arms flailed and his landings were rocky. But what he lacked in control, he made up for in spirit. To those who tried to stop him from jumping, he said, "I know I'm not a world-class jumper, but at the moment I'm the best jumper Great Britain has. I'm going for the gold as much as anybody." Maybe in four years, Eddie.

What they did for love. The disappearance in Chicago on April 2, 1988, of newlyweds Scott Swanson, 23, and Carolyn MacLean, 22, which captured national attention, ended on July 26. That day, the parents of both college students received word from the couple that they were living in San Diego.

MacLean said she and Swanson ran away because pressures from the material world, their family, and from military authorities—Swanson was to begin serving in the U.S. Army in May—threatened to keep them apart.

Friends of the couple—as well as the police—were baffled as to why Swanson and MacLean waited four months to let their families know they were alive, especially since the couple knew of the extensive search being conducted by state and federal authorities. In apologizing to their family and friends, the couple said they had no idea their disappearance would generate so much publicity, and they were afraid to return. The couple, who were secretly married just before they disappeared, had a second wedding ceremony in a Haddonfield, N.J., church on November 26.

Papa panda Pe-Pe dies. A panda who fathered seven cubs—the largest number born in captivity outside China—died on July 20 in Mexico City of cancer. The 13-year-old panda, called Pe-Pe, was taken to Mexico from China in 1975 with his mate, Ying-Ying. Four of Pe-Pe's offspring still survive, and so will Pe-Pe—in a way. The Mexico City Zoo planned to preserve the panda's body for a special display.

Hockey hubbub. When Wayne Gretzky, superstar of Canada's Edmonton Oilers hockey team, got married on July 16 to Hollywood actress and model Janet Jones, the elaborate nuptials were dubbed "Canada's royal wedding." About 700 guests attended the ceremony, and 5,000 loyal Gretzky fans stood outside St. Joseph's Roman Catholic Basilica in Edmonton to get a glimpse of the couple and wish them well.

But the well-wishing turned sour when the Oilers announced on August 9 that Gretzky had been traded to the Los Angeles Kings—apparently at Gretzky's request. Canadians, stunned and angered by the

Michael (Eddie the Eagle) Edwards, Britain's only Olympic ski jumper, shows off his less-than-polished form in February at the Winter Olympics.

news, blamed Gretzky's bride for his defection to the United States. In September, however, the press reported that Gretzky had verbally agreed to sign a contract with the Oilers in June but that the team's management had decided to trade him to the Kings in a deal involving other players, draft picks, and U.S. $15 million.

Flying high. On May 11, Bridgette Ellis, 9, became the youngest pilot to fly solo. She took to the air in a small, homemade aircraft for a three-minute flight over the Fox Valley Flying Club near Montgomery, Ill.

In another record-breaking feat, Christopher Lee Marshall, an 11-year-old boy from Oceana, Calif., became the youngest pilot to cross the Atlantic Ocean. Marshall, accompanied by a retired Navy pilot, began his flight in San Diego on July 7 and made stops in Canada, Greenland, Iceland, and Scotland. He landed his plane at Le Bourget Airport in Paris on July 14.

She's in the money. On September 7, Sheelah Ryan, a real estate broker from Winter Springs, Fla., turned in the winning Florida lottery ticket to claim $55.16 million, the largest lottery prize ever won by one person in North America. Ryan came up with the lucky number by picking the first six numbers she came across on the front page of her local newspaper. "I've had three firsts today," she said in a press conference in Tallahassee. "It has been my first plane ride . . . my first press conference . . . [and] this is the first time I've ever won $55 million." The largest lottery prize in North America—$60.8 million—was shared by three people in California on October 30.

Lady of the lakes. Swimmer Vicki Keith of Kingston, Canada, became the first person to swim across all five Great Lakes when she completed her crossing of Lake Ontario on August 30. Keith began on July 1, when she swam across Lake Erie. In all, she swam about 190 miles (300 kilometers) and helped raise more than $200,000 for handicapped children.

Sailing solo. Braving savage storms, Kay Cottee of Australia became the first woman to complete a nonstop solo boat trip around the world on June 5. During her 189-day voyage, the 34-year-old boatbuilder had no physical contact with another boat or person. Cottee sailed a 36-foot (11-meter) sloop.

So long, Wilberforce. A long-time resident of 10 Downing Street in London, the official home of Great Britain's prime minister, died in his sleep on May 19. The resident, called Wilberforce, had lived there rent-free since 1973. He spent his days lying on the front doorstep or walking through the building looking for mice. A companion to four prime ministers, including Margaret Thatcher, he held the title of "the best mouser in Britain." Wilberforce, a black-and-white cat, died at his retirement home in Essex, England.

Going, going, gone. What was billed as one of the largest auctions in history got underway on April 23 in New York City. It took 10 days for the auction house of Sotheby's to sell off the 10,000 objects amassed by American pop artist Andy Warhol, who died in 1987. Warhol's unusual collection included 175 pottery cookie jars; jewelry; paintings; and plastic wrist watches featuring cartoon characters Judy Jetson and Fred Flintstone. Sotheby's estimated that the collection would go for $10 million to $15 million, but competitive bidding pushed up prices, resulting in a total of $25.3 million. All the proceeds went to the Andy Warhol Foundation for the Visual Arts.

The password is "fraud." People wanted by the police should take a lesson from Kerry Ketchem: Don't appear on a nationally broadcast television show. Ketchem was arrested on January 14 in Los Angeles on charges of fraud when he tried to pick up the prize he won as a contestant on the TV game show "Super Password." Using the name Patrick Quinn, Ketchem won $58,600 to become the biggest winner in the show's history. Unfortunately for Ketchem, who was wanted by police in Alaska and Indiana, a "Password" viewer recognized him and tipped off authorities.

New war chief. On February 4, Sioux Indians in the United States named Phillip Stevens, the great-grandson of Chief Standing Bear—who fought resettlement of his people in the 1800's—as their war chief, and gave him the task of leading the fight to recover unoccupied government-owned land in South Dakota. The Sioux say the land was taken from them illegally 110 years ago. Stevens, who heads his own engineering firm, is the first Sioux to be named war chief in more than 100 years.

Protester sued. S. Brian Willson, a protester who lost both his legs when he was struck by a Navy train during a demonstration, found himself the defendant in a lawsuit filed by the train's crewmen on January 8. The injury occurred in September 1987, when Willson and two other protesters sat down on railroad tracks leading from the Concord Naval Weapons Station in California to protest the train's shipment of arms to Central America.

Ralph Dawson, David Humiston, and Robert Mayfield—the train's civilian crew—said that they suffered humiliation, mental anguish, and loss of earnings as a result of the incident. They charged Willson with intentional neglect and infliction of emotional distress. Willson's lawyer called the lawsuit the "most cruel and insensitive legal maneuver I have seen." On Jan. 29, 1988, Willson filed a civil rights lawsuit against the men and the Navy.

Second *Wind*? Fans of Margaret Mitchell's *Gone with the Wind* (1936)—one of the most popular novels of all time—may eventually find out if Scarlett O'Hara and Rhett Butler get back together. In a literary auction in New York City on April 25, Warner Books won the right to publish the novel's sequel. The new tale will be written by Alexandra Ripley, a writer from Virginia. Warner plans to publish the book in 1990.

Keep on pedaling. Greek bicyclist Kanellos Kanellopoulos broke three records for human-powered

The May 13 TV marriage of "Sesame Street" characters Maria and Luis, played by Sonia Manzano and Emilio Delgado, has Big Bird as a happy onlooker.

Hockey star Wayne Gretzky gives well-wishers the "thumbs up" sign after marrying actress Janet Jones on July 16 in Edmonton, Canada.

flight on April 23 when he flew 74 miles (119 kilometers) over the Aegean Sea in a plane powered only by his own legs. Kanellopoulos flew an ultralight plane called the *Daedalus 88*, named after the legendary Daedalus of ancient Greece, who tried to fly with wings made of leather and wax.

Kanellopoulos' trip from Crete to the island of Thira (also called Santorini) took 3 hours 54 minutes. He traveled at a speed of approximately 18 miles (29 kilometers) per hour and flew about 15 feet (4.6 meters) above the water. When he crash-landed on Thira, he had broken the 1979 records for human-powered straight-line flight and duration aloft, and the 1987 distance record.

No more bunnies. The era of the Playboy bunny ended in the United States on July 31 when the last U.S. club—in Lansing, Mich.—closed its doors. Since Playboy Enterprises in Chicago opened the first Playboy Club in 1960, the main attraction had been its Playboy bunnies—waitresses clad in scanty costumes complete with bunny ears and cotton-puff tails. During its heyday, Playboy had 22 clubs throughout the world. In 1988, there were 5 clubs left, 4 in Japan and 1 in the Philippines.

An era also may be ending for Hugh M. Hefner, Playboy's 62-year-old founder. On July 23, he became engaged to Kimberley Conrad, a 24-year-old Canadian model. The two planned to wed in 1989. Hefner has been single since a 1959 divorce.

But did he read them all? On August 17, writer Gustav Hasford was charged with stealing 10,000 books from 70 libraries around the world. Hasford, who along with director Stanley Kubrick and Michael Herr adapted Hasford's Vietnam War novel into the 1987 movie *Full Metal Jacket*, insisted he was innocent. Police discovered the stash of books in a rented storage locker on the campus of California Polytechnic State University in San Luis Obispo, Calif. On December 3, Hasford pleaded no contest to charges of possessing stolen property. He faced a possible six-month jail term.

Arctic error? Admiral Robert E. Peary, the American explorer who claimed to have been the first man to reach the North Pole, may have actually been miles away from his destination, according to astronomer Dennis Rawlins of Baltimore on October 12. Rawlins said a copy of Peary's original navigational notes, which he found at Johns Hopkins University in Baltimore, showed that Peary knew he was about 120 miles (190 kilometers) away from the North Pole on April 6, 1909, the day he claimed to have reached it. The National Geographic Society, which sponsored Peary's expedition, said that it would examine the notes, but added it was possible the readings were made on April 5, the day before Peary claimed to have reached the pole.

It's still a mouthful. The Welsh town that sported the longest name in Great Britain shaved off a few letters in 1988 to make it a bit more "tidy," according to a city official on November 11. The town—Llanfairpwllgwyngyllgogerychwyrndrobwllllantysiliogogogoch—will now be known on maps and signs as just Llanfair Pwllgwyngyll. In English, the original tongue-twisting, 58-letter name meant "St. Mary's Church in the hollow of the white hazels near to the rapid whirlpool of Llantysilio by the red cave."

Poignant letters. Two pen pal letters, a post card, and two small photographs sent in 1940 by 11-year-old Anne Frank and her 14-year-old sister Margot from Amsterdam, the Netherlands, to two girls in Iowa were sold at auction on Oct. 25, 1988. The correspondence was sent to Betty Ann Wagner and her sister Juanita before the Nazi occupation of the Netherlands during World War II (1939-1945). In 1942, the German-Jewish Frank family was forced to hide from the Nazis in the attic of an Amsterdam building. The letters, written in English, describe the Frank girls' life at home and at school.

The Wagner girls, who lived on a farm in Danville, never got any more mail from Anne or Margot. After the war, they received a letter from Otto Frank saying that his daughters died in a Nazi concentration camp. A friend convinced the Wagners that the letters they had kept for almost 50 years would be of interest to the world. An unidentified buyer purchased the correspondence at an auction in New York City for $165,000.   Mary A. Krier

Newspaper reporting in the United States came under increasing fire in 1988. Much of the criticism focused on the use of anonymous sources, a practice that has become much more widespread over the past two decades. On July 22, a Minneapolis, Minn., jury ruled that a newspaper's promise of confidentiality is, in effect, a contract. The jury ordered the Minneapolis *Star Tribune* and the *St. Paul Pioneer Press Dispatch* to pay $700,000 to a man named in a story after he had been promised anonymity. The *Star Tribune* later banned use of anonymous sources.

Reporting on the private lives of public individuals remained controversial in 1988. Such reporting led to the suicide of a judge in Seattle on August 18. The judge killed himself after learning that the *Seattle Post-Intelligencer* planned to report allegations that he had coerced teen-agers to have sex with him.

Editorials muted. At least once, newspaper reporting and newspaper economics became hard to separate. That case involved two Detroit newspapers that had sought the permission of the United States government to merge in a *joint operating agreement* (JOA). Under a JOA, two newspapers share production facilities and cooperate in the advertising and circulation areas. The two newsrooms, however, must continue to compete with each other.

Both Detroit newspapers were losing money, with the red ink absorbed by the huge chains that owned them—Knight-Ridder Newspapers, Incorporated,

owner of the *Detroit Free Press*; and the Gannett Company, owner of *The Detroit News*. While the *Free Press* was waiting for U.S. Attorney General Edwin Meese III to make a decision on the proposed JOA, that normally liberal newspaper took what it conceded was a "cautious" stance in editorials about Meese. And the *Free Press* did not publish several anti-Meese editorial cartoons drawn by its own cartoonist, though they were syndicated in other newspapers.

On August 8, Meese approved the JOA, but a group of opponents temporarily blocked the arrangement in a federal appeals court. Knight-Ridder said it will shut down the 156-year-old *Free Press* if the JOA is rejected. At year-end, the court had not lifted the stay.

Other news. The Supreme Court of the United States ruled on January 13 that high school officials may censor school-sponsored student publications if the censorship has a "valid educational purpose." The ruling brought an outcry from many First Amendment advocates. A survey by *Editor & Publisher* magazine indicated that most newspaper editorialists supported the decision. They maintained that a school acts as a publisher and that the "censorship" is merely the kind of editing done at any paper.

On December 31, Cox Enterprises Incorporated ceased publication of its 92-year-old daily, *The Miami (Fla.) News.*   Mark Fitzgerald

See also **Awards and prizes** (Journalism awards). In *World Book*, see **Newspaper.**

Nicaragua. The Sandinista government and rebel forces known as *contras* reached a cease-fire agreement on March 23, 1988, ending full-scale fighting that had claimed some 25,000 lives since 1981. For the remainder of 1988, talks between the two sides continued, and the cease-fire was extended several times, though occasional skirmishes were reported.

Under the terms of the accord, which went into effect on April 1, the contras agreed to end military actions and to enter special cease-fire zones within Nicaragua but without surrendering their weapons. The Sandinistas, in turn, agreed to grant amnesty to some 3,300 contra prisoners and to "guarantee unrestricted freedom of expression" within Nicaragua.

The cease-fire, however, did not mean an end to conflict. On July 11, the Sandinistas ordered U.S. Ambassador Richard H. Melton and seven other U.S. diplomats to leave the country on grounds of interference in Nicaragua's internal political affairs. On September 20, support for the Sandinista charges came from Speaker of the House James C. Wright, Jr. (D., Tex.). Wright confirmed that the U.S. Central Intelligence Agency, with presidential approval, was secretly supporting opponents of the Sandinista regime in the hope of provoking an overreaction by the Sandinistas. The Administration of President Ronald Reagan rebuked Wright, saying he had disclosed classified information, but Wright said his information was already a matter of public record.

Adolfo Calero, leader of the *contra* rebels fighting the Sandinista government in Nicaragua, signs a cease-fire accord with the government in March.

Rivalries among contra leaders reached a breaking point when, in mid-July, senior contra field commander Colonel Enrique Bermúdez denounced Pedro Joaquín Chamorro, the rebels' chief political operative, on grounds of corruption. Chamorro then failed to win reelection to the contra leadership. Bermúdez, a former member of the National Guard under dictator Anastasio Somoza Debayle, took personal command of political as well as military affairs. Seven contra field commanders resigned in protest. On July 26, the contras announced another reshuffle, and Bermúdez resigned as military commander.

Congressional funding. The U.S. Congress approved $27 million in aid to the contras before taking a break in August for the national election campaign. The money was to be spent to provide food, clothing, shelter, and medical aid, but not military supplies.

Economy. The Nicaraguan economy continued to reel under the impact of the civil war. In February, the Sandinistas introduced a new currency—the new córdoba—in an effort to counteract inflation. The new córdoba was declared the equivalent of 1,000 old córdobas. Nicaraguan authorities waged an uphill battle during the year to confiscate contraband goods and products sold at prices above those decreed by the government.   Nathan A. Haverstock

See also **Latin America** (Facts in brief table). In *World Book*, see **Nicaragua**.

Niger. See **Africa**.

Nigeria. Oil earnings, which account for 95 per cent of Nigeria's foreign exchange, dropped to about $6-billion in 1988—down from a high of about $25-billion in 1980. In July, the government of President Ibrahim Babangida took steps to attract new industries and foreign investment to Nigeria. Among other measures, the government offered incentives to foreign investors and authorized the sale of many government-owned businesses to private buyers.

Belt-tightening provokes riots. Public discontent with austerity measures aimed at strengthening the economy erupted in violence in the city of Jos on April 13 when a student demonstration escalated into rioting. When workers in other cities joined a strike to support the students, the government closed several universities. Many students, together with a number of their labor-unionist supporters, were arrested and jailed.

Civilian rule. In October, Babangida, who assumed the office of president in a 1985 military coup, repeated his pledge to return Nigeria to civilian rule in 1992. The 536 members of the Constituent Assembly—450 elected in April 1988, the rest appointed by the military—held their first working meeting on June 14 to begin reviewing the draft of a new national constitution.

The constitution provides for a two-party political system, a two-house legislature, and a popularly elected president. It also contains provisions guaranteeing the protection of religious and ethnic minorities. If all goes according to plan, the two parties will be designated in 1990, and elections for local, state, and federal officials will be held in 1991 and 1992.

Nigerians received mixed signals during 1988 regarding the military regime's commitment to democracy. On the one hand, they were reassured by the government's relative toleration of media criticism and its announcement in January of amnesty for former civilian President Shehu Shagari, who was deposed in 1983. On the other hand, the government, in addition to cracking down on the student rioters and their supporters, disbanded several labor unions and detained individual journalists it considered too outspoken in their opposition.

Foreign relations. The Babangida government moved in 1988 to end long-standing bad feelings with Ghana. The ill will stemmed from periodic mass deportations that the two countries have imposed on each other's citizens during periods of economic stress.

Nigeria took a stronger stance against white-dominated South Africa during the year. The Babangida regime pressured Equatorial Guinea into breaking diplomatic ties with South Africa, and the army said it would create a force in 1989 to protect African countries from attack—particularly attack by South Africa.   J. Gus Liebenow and Beverly B. Liebenow

See also **Africa** (Facts in brief table). In *World Book*, see **Nigeria.**

Nobel Prizes in peace, literature, economics, and the sciences were awarded in 1988 by the Norwegian Storting (parliament) in Oslo and by the Royal Academy of Science, the Caroline Institute, and the Swedish Academy of Literature in Stockholm, Sweden.

The peace prize was awarded to the peacekeeping forces of the United Nations (UN). In its citation, the Nobel committee noted that "the UN forces represent the manifest will of the community of nations to achieve peace through negotiations."

Since the UN's founding in 1945, about 500,000 UN soldiers—drawn from regular and reserve armed forces units from 58 member nations—have taken part in 14 peacekeeping operations. In 1988, about 10,000 UN troops were on duty in the Middle East and South Asia. See **United Nations.**

The literature prize went to Egyptian novelist Naguib Mahfouz, 77, the first Arabic-language writer to win the award. Mahfouz was praised as a writer "who, through works rich in nuance—now clear-sightedly realistic, now evocatively ambiguous—has formed an Arabian narrative art that applies to all mankind."

Mahfouz was born in 1911 in Cairo, Egypt's capital, and has lived there his entire life. He first became widely known for his writing about the city in a major work, *The Cairo Trilogy*. Mahfouz has written 40 novels and short-story collections, several plays, and more than 30 screenplays.

The economics prize was given to economist Maurice Allais, 77, of France "for his pioneering contributions to the theory of markets and efficient utilization of resources." Known as the "founding father of the French school of modern economics," Allais is the first French citizen to win the economics prize.

Two of Allais's principal works were studies on state-owned monopolies, such as utilities. Both studies were published in the 1940's. After World War II, Allais taught at the École Nationale Supérieure des Mines de Paris until his retirement in 1979.

The physics prize was shared by three United States physicists—Leon M. Lederman, 66, director of the Fermi National Accelerator Laboratory in Batavia, Ill.; Melvin Schwartz, 55, a former Stanford University professor who now heads a computer firm in California; and Jack Steinberger, 67, a researcher at the European Laboratory for Particle Physics (CERN) in Geneva, Switzerland. The three physicists were awarded the prize for their discovery of a subatomic particle called the *muon neutrino*. The discovery was made in 1961 and 1962.

The muon neutrino later proved to be a useful tool for understanding the properties of subatomic particles. Lederman once called the muon neutrino "barely a fact" because it had no measurable mass and could pass through dense matter undisturbed.

The chemistry prize went to three West German scientists for determining the structure of certain

Leon M. Lederman diagrams an experiment of the type that won him and two other physicists the 1988 Nobel Prize for physics in October.

proteins necessary for *photosynthesis*—the process by which plants and certain bacteria use energy from sunlight to make food. The winners were Johann Deisenhofer, 45, of the Howard Hughes Medical Institute in Dallas; Robert Huber, 51, of the Max Planck Institute for Biochemistry in Martinsried, West Germany; and Hartmut Michel, 42, of the Max Planck Institute for Biophysics in Frankfurt.

In 1982, Michel found a technique to put the proteins in a crystalline form so that their structure could be studied. The structure was determined in 1985 in collaboration with Deisenhofer and Huber. The Nobel committee noted that their work led to greater understanding of photosynthesis and represented a step toward the goal of artificial photosynthesis.

The physiology or medicine prize was shared by two U.S. biochemists and a British pharmacologist for discoveries leading to pathbreaking drug treatments that have saved millions of lives. The winners were Gertrude B. Elion, 70, and George H. Hitchings, 83, both researchers at Wellcome Research Laboratories in Research Triangle Park, N.C., and Sir James W. Black, 64, of King's College Hospital Medical School of the University of London.

The three researchers were cited for discovering "important principles" that led to new drug treatments for such health problems as heart disease, herpes infections, leukemia, malaria, stomach ulcers, and transplant rejection. By discovering how genetic material is processed differently by normal cells, cancer cells, and viruses, for example, Elion and Hitchings provided the key to the development of certain new drugs. These drugs interfere with the formation of genetic material in cancer cells and viruses without harming normal cells.

The two biochemists also developed an antimalaria drug and azidothymidine (AZT), the only drug approved by the United States Food and Drug Administration that has proved effective in prolonging the lives of people suffering from AIDS (acquired immune deficiency syndrome).

Black discovered two important new groups of drugs—*beta-blockers*, which block the stimulating effect of adrenalin on the heart, and *H-2 receptor-antagonists*, used in the treatment of stomach ulcers. Beta-blockers are used to treat high blood pressure, heart attacks, and *angina pectoris* (chest pains caused by an inadequate flow of blood to the heart).

1987 winners. The winners of Nobel Prizes in 1987 were Costa Rica's President Oscar Arias Sánchez for peace, exiled Soviet poet Joseph Brodsky for literature, Robert M. Solow of the United States for economics, K. Alex Müller of Switzerland and J. Georg Bednorz of West Germany for physics, Donald J. Cram and Charles J. Pedersen of the United States and Jean-Marie Lehn of France for chemistry, and Japanese-born Susumu Tonegawa for physiology or medicine.   Rod Such

In *World Book*, see **Nobel Prizes.**

Noriega Morena, Manuel Antonio (1934-   ), the military ruler of Panama, was indicted on charges of drug trafficking by federal grand juries in Miami and Tampa, Fla., on Feb. 5, 1988. During 1988, however, Noriega successfully resisted demands for his resignation. See **Panama.**

Born in Panama in 1934, Noriega was educated at a military school in Lima, Peru. Returning to Panama, he was commissioned a sublieutenant in the National Guard, Panama's army. Noriega took part in an October 1968 coup led by Brigadier General Omar Torrijos Herrera. During an unsuccessful countercoup attempt in December 1969, Noriega remained loyal to Torrijos and was promoted to lieutenant colonel and chief of military intelligence.

On Torrijos' death in 1981, Noriega became the National Guard's chief of staff under General Rubén Darío Paredes, but in 1983, Noriega succeeded Paredes and promoted himself to general. He also combined the navy and air force with the National Guard, which was renamed the Panamanian Defense Forces. In 1985, Noriega forced the resignation of civilian President Nicolás Ardito Barletta Vallarina, reportedly because Barletta regarded Noriega as a suspect in a murder. In January 1988, Panama's former consul general Jóse I. Blandón testified that Noriega was heavily involved in illicit drug traffic.   Rod Such

North Carolina. See **State government.**
North Dakota. See **State government.**

Northern Ireland. An escalation of violence between the outlawed Irish Republican Army (IRA) and British troops overshadowed all other events in Northern Ireland in 1988. On January 25, controversy erupted when the British government announced that eight Royal Ulster Constabulary (RUC) officers who killed six unarmed IRA suspects in three separate incidents in 1982 would not be prosecuted. Although the government said that the officers had tried "to pervert justice," it added that their actions were in the interest of national security. The decision raised new debate over whether the RUC had a "shoot to kill" policy against suspected IRA terrorists in 1982.

Gibraltar incident. British Special Air Service (SAS) officers shot to death three IRA terrorist suspects in Gibraltar, a British dependency on the southern coast of Spain, on March 6. Although the IRA admitted that the three were preparing to plant a car bomb, they were all unarmed. At an inquest, the SAS officers said they had shot the three—two men and a woman—because they thought their lives and the lives of others were threatened. On September 30, a jury found that the three had been lawfully killed.

More terrorism. On March 16, Michael Stone, a man who called himself a "free-lance loyalist paramilitary," killed three mourners in a Belfast cemetery who were attending the funeral of the IRA members slain in Gibraltar. Three days later—on March 19—two British soldiers, armed but in civilian dress, apparently

Mourners at an IRA funeral in Belfast on March 16 take cover to escape
gunfire and grenades from a terrorist. Three were killed, some 60 injured.

blundered into the path of an IRA funeral procession
in Belfast and were pulled from their car and killed by
the crowd.

The IRA in May began a campaign of violence
against off-duty British troops. On May 1, three British
servicemen were killed in two attacks in the Netherlands. On June 15, six British soldiers, who had taken
part in a charity race near Belfast, were killed by an
IRA bomb that exploded in their van.

The first successful IRA attack in England since 1984
occurred on Aug. 1, 1988, when an IRA bomb exploded in a British Army barracks in London, killing one
soldier and wounding nine others. Three other attacks
quickly followed. On August 5, three British soldiers
were injured when a bomb went off at a British Army
base in West Germany. On August 13, a British soldier
was shot to death in his car in Ostend, Belgium. Eight
British soldiers were killed on August 20 after their
bus was hit by a bomb in Omagh, Northern Ireland.

British action. Although the British government rejected demands during the year to imprison IRA suspects without trial, it announced on October 19 that
suspects accused of terrorist crimes could no longer
remain silent without it being held against them at
their trial. Britain also banned television and radio
interviews with members of the IRA and Sinn Féin
(Ourselves Alone), its political wing.   Ian J. Mather

See also **Ireland**. In *World Book*, see **Northern Ireland**.

Northwest Territories. On Sept. 5, 1988, in a tiny
Indian village on the shores of the Great Slave Lake,
Canada's Prime Minister Brian Mulroney signed an
agreement-in-principle that would make 13,000 Dene
Indians and *Métis* (people of mixed Indian and white
ancestry) the largest nongovernment landowners in
North America. The native peoples—inhabitants of
the Mackenzie River Valley—would gain full ownership of about 3,800 square miles (10,000 square kilometers) of land and surface rights to another 65,600
square miles (170,000 square kilometers).

Other provisions gave the Dene and Métis a share in
oil, gas, and mineral royalties. Indian hunting rights
were confirmed over a much larger territory. In addition, $500 million (Canadian dollars; $1=U.S. 84 cents
as of Dec. 31, 1988) would be paid to the native peoples in cash over 20 years beginning in 1990. Self-
government was not included in the pact and would
need to be negotiated separately. Mulroney said the
pact marked a "day of justice" for northern peoples.

Mulroney signed an agreement on September 6
with the Northwest Territories government. The pact
transferred federal management powers for onshore
oil drilling to the territory, along with a share of oil
and gas royalties. In addition, the territorial government will participate in drawing up regulations for
offshore drilling in the Beaufort Sea.   David M. L. Farr

See also **Canada**. In *World Book*, see **Northwest
Territories**.

Norway. Prime Minister Gro Harlem Brundtland shuffled her cabinet on June 13, 1988, appointing ministers who strongly favored Norway's joining the European Community (EC or Common Market). Norway had decided in a *referendum* (vote of the people) in 1972 not to join the EC. Political observers predicted that, if Brundtland's government wins a general election scheduled for September 1989, she will hold another referendum on EC membership.

NATO deal. The government agreed on Jan. 24, 1988, to allow German combat troops to enter Norway for the first time since 1940, when Nazi Germany conquered Norway during World War II. The soldiers who entered Norway in 1988 were West Germans, part of a North Atlantic Treaty Organization (NATO) force.

Heavy-water inquiry. On May 19, 1988, Norway began an investigation into the sale to Romania of *heavy water*, a chemical that can be used in making nuclear weapons. This was the third such inquiry in two years. The government said that 12.5 metric tons (13.8 short tons) of heavy water produced in Norway and sold to Romania were intended for use in two nuclear reactors due to be completed in 1988, and denied allegations that the heavy water had been resold to Israel to make atomic weapons.

Seals hit fishing. Seals, which eat fish, migrated into Norway's northern fishing waters in numbers not seen since the 1800's, heavily damaging the country's multimillion-dollar fishing industry. Directorate of Fisheries spokesman Sigbjorn Lomelde said on June 22, 1988, that the inshore waters between the North Cape and the Soviet border were almost barren of fishing boats. Normally, hundreds of boats would have been working there.

Minister of Fisheries Bjarne Mork Eidam tried to persuade the Soviets to double the total quota of fish that may be taken from the White Sea, which is south of the Kola Peninsula—where the Soviet Union borders Norway. The present annual quota is 70,000 short tons (63,500 metric tons), of which Norway's share is 16,600 short tons (15,000 metric tons). The Norwegians wanted the quota to be increased to 150,000 short tons (136,100 metric tons), but the Soviets said that the present quota was fair.

Economy better. The Organization for Economic Cooperation and Development (OECD), made up of 24 industrialized nations, reported that Norway's economic outlook improved in 1988. The main causes of the improvement included a rebound in oil prices after a slump in 1986, and increases in planned spending on energy and industry. The OECD noted that Norway had made progress toward stabilizing—and even reducing—its people's demand for consumer goods following what the OECD termed excessive growth in 1986 and 1987. But Norway continued to have labor shortages in 1988. Kenneth Brown

See also **Europe** (Facts in brief table). In *World Book*, see **Norway.**

Nova Scotia. Scandals plagued the Progressive Conservative (PC) administration of Premier John Buchanan in 1988. Cabinet member Edmund Morris resigned his post in January after he was convicted of violating the province's Freedom of Information Act. Gregory MacIsaac, a PC member of the legislature, was sentenced in March to a year in jail for falsifying his expense account. Deputy Premier Roland Thornhill resigned in April over irregularities concerning a bank loan but was reinstated to the cabinet in December. Despite the scandals, Buchanan won his fourth consecutive term in a narrow victory in a September 6 election. Buchanan's 10 years in the post made him, at age 57, Canada's longest-serving provincial premier in office.

The PC's entered the election holding 40 seats in the 52-seat legislature but emerged with only 28 seats. They lost 7 seats on Cape Breton Island, where coal miners and steelworkers demonstrated their frustration at high unemployment. The Liberals, under a new leader, Vincent MacLean, increased their standing from 6 to 21 seats. The New Democratic Party kept 2 of its 3 seats, and an independent held the remaining seat. The popular vote was close—43 per cent for the PC's, 39 per cent for the Liberals, and 16 per cent for the New Democratic Party. David M. L. Farr

See also **Canada.** In *World Book*, see **Nova Scotia.**
Nuclear energy. See **Energy supply.**
Nutrition. See **Food.**

Ocean. Scientists aboard the Ocean Drilling Program's research drill ship, the *JOIDES Resolution*, targeted the Kerguelen Plateau, one of the world's largest underwater geologic features, for several months of exploration in early 1988.

The Kerguelen Plateau lies more than 1,000 meters (3,300 feet) below the ocean surface in the remote subantarctic region of the Indian Ocean. Sample cores of the sea floor taken during the expedition provided a geologic record of the origin and evolution of the giant plateau, revealing its fascinating 97-million-year history. The cores indicated that the region was once a barren land mass that evolved into a lush forest and then slowly subsided.

The oldest material recovered was basement rock that resembled neither the basalts generated at mid-ocean ridges nor those that form such islands as Hawaii. The oceanographers also found evidence that the Kerguelen rock had formed either above or very near sea level, indicating that the plateau was a land mass during its early history.

The first sediment accumulation occurred when the plateau was a marsh or flood plain. The oceanographers found fingernail-sized fragments of fossilized wood in the sediment, indicating that the land mass once had a climate that was warm and moist enough to support a lush forest.

The next layers of sediment were deposited after the plateau began to subside—about 66 million to 97

394

million years ago. These layers contained fossilized marine invertebrates, such as clams, sponges, and sea urchins, and fossils of other sea creatures. The researchers also found the tooth of a large marine vertebrate, possibly a giant swimming lizard.

Subsidence continued until 1.6 million years ago. Since then, blooms of microscopic algae and layers of rocks carried by icebergs from Antarctica have left a record in sample cores of the climate changes that occurred during the ice ages.

Ocean dumping. A number of unusual events in 1988 fueled growing international concern that the oceans are increasingly at risk from pollution. But the alarming appearance of at least 400 dolphin carcasses on the east coast of the United States in 1987 was probably not linked to ocean pollution, according to an official at the National Oceanic and Atmospheric Administration. An April 1988 report suggested that the dolphins died of natural causes, and that changing currents in the Atlantic Ocean simply washed an unusually large number of dolphins to shore.

In June 1988, however, scientists and environmental experts from West Germany, the Netherlands, and the Scandinavian countries met in Kiel, West Germany, to discuss ways of dealing with a disastrous slimy algae bloom in the North Sea. The bloom caused the deaths of thousands of fish, which washed ashore in southern Scandinavia and northern Germany. In Bonn, West Germany, environmentalists demanded an immediate halt to the dumping of untreated wastes into the North Sea. These nutrient-rich wastes were believed to have contributed to the sudden flourishing of the gluey, yellow-green algal slime.

By September, 7,000 dead seals had also washed ashore in Denmark, Sweden, and the island of Sylt in the North Sea. Biologists said that the seals had died of a viral infection related to canine distemper, however, and preliminary reports indicated that the deaths were not connected with the algal slime.

During the 1980's, the closing of U.S. beaches because of bacterial contamination has become commonplace. But in 1988, a different kind of ocean pollution concerned public health officials. For several weeks during the summer, New York beaches from Staten Island to Long Island were periodically closed because potentially hazardous medical waste—sutures, hypodermic needles, catheter bags, and vials of blood—had washed ashore. New York's problem was by no means unique. Hospital waste, along with a distasteful array of other garbage, floated ashore on beaches from Maine to Texas. In October, the Congress of the United States approved a bill making the disposal of medical waste into the ocean a federal crime.   Arthur G. Alexiou

In *World Book*, see Ocean.

Ohio. See State government.

Oklahoma. See State government.

Old age. See Social security.

Secretary of the Interior Hodel, right, and Florida Governor Martinez explore a coral reef threatened by offshore drilling near Key Largo.

Olympic Games

The Olympic year of 1988 started with the Winter Olympics in February in Calgary, Canada, best remembered for high winds and unseasonably warm weather. The year ended with the games of the XXIV Olympiad, held from September 17 to October 2 in Seoul, South Korea. There were fears of security threats from North Korea and international terrorists, but there were no such incidents. Instead, this highly successful competition may be remembered mostly for drugs.

The most-awaited event in Seoul was the showdown in the men's 100-meter dash between Ben Johnson of Canada and Carl Lewis of the United States. Johnson won in 9.79 seconds, breaking his 1987 world record. But three days later, the gold medal and the record were stripped from Johnson when a drug test showed he had ingested *stanozolol*, a performance-enhancing anabolic steroid banned by the International Olympic Committee (IOC).

Winter Games. As a concession to television, the Winter Olympics were extended for the first time to 16 days, from February 13 to 28. They were held in Calgary, Alberta, a city of 636,104 and the oil and natural-gas capital of Canada.

Calgary built excellent facilities for the Olympic competitions—the $98-million Olympic Saddledome for hockey and figure skating; the $45-million Canada Olympic Park for bobsledding, luge, and ski jumping; the $30-million enclosed speed-skating oval; the $19-million Nakiska complex for Alpine skiing; and the $10-million Canmore Nordic Centre for cross-country skiing. Even with all those expenses, the organizers managed to turn a $46-million profit to benefit Canadian amateur sports. (These amounts are Canadian dollars, with $1 = U.S. 84 cents as of Dec. 31, 1988.)

The speed-skating oval was enclosed for protection—not so much from the fierce winter as from the warm February winds known as *chinooks* that blow in from the Rocky Mountains, about 55 miles (89 kilometers) to the west. Twice in a three-day period, the temperature soared to 70°F. (21°C). Snow melted, and the icy bobsled and luge courses became soft.

The competition attracted more than 1,750 athletes from a record 57 nations. There were such unexpected cold-weather athletes as a luge racer from the Philippines and a bobsled team from Jamaica. There was also Michael (Eddie the Eagle) Edwards, a British ski jumper who attracted many fans. Edwards finished 58th and last in the 70-meter ski jump and called it "the greatest day of my life."

Of the 46 gold medals, 11 went to the Soviet Union, 9 to East Germany, and 5 to Switzerland. In total medals, the leaders were the Soviet Union with 29, East Germany with 25, and Switzerland with 15. The United States was far down in the standings with 6 medals—2 gold, 1 silver, and 3 bronze. Canada won 5 medals—2 silver and 3 bronze.

Olympic gold medalists in action, *clockwise from right:* Turkey's Naim Suleymanoglu, known as the Pocket Hercules, lifts three times his body weight; U.S. diver Greg Louganis repeats his 1984 Olympic performance, capturing both diving golds; swimmer Kristin Otto of East Germany wins one of her six golds—the 1988 record; Matti Nykänen of Finland soars to one of his three gold medals in ski jumping; Jackie Joyner-Kersee of the United States leaps a hurdle on her way to a world-record 7,291 points in the heptathlon; and East Germany's Katarina Witt displays the form that won her the figure-skating medal.

The U.S. showing disappointed the American Broadcasting Companies, Incorporated (ABC), which had paid $309 million for U.S. television rights. ABC showed 94½ hours of the Olympics, but its ratings suffered when the U.S. hockey team failed to qualify for the medal round.

Medalists. The only gold medals for the United States came from Brian Boitano of Sunnyvale, Calif., in men's figure skating and Bonnie Blair of Champaign, Ill., in women's 500-meter speed skating. Those two sports produced all six U.S. medals.

In figure skating, Debi Thomas of San Jose won a bronze medal in women's singles, and the team of Jill Watson of Bloomington, Ind., and Peter Oppegard of Knoxville, Tenn., won the bronze in pairs. In speed skating, Eric Flaim of Pembroke, Mass., won a silver in the men's 1,500 meters, and Blair won a bronze in the women's 1,000 meters. Dan Jansen of West Allis, Wis., a world champion speed skater, competed only hours after his sister's death and fell in his two races.

There were heroes from other nations. Yvonne van Gennip of the Netherlands won three gold medals in speed skating in beating the once-dominant East German women. The figure-skating champions included Katarina Witt of East Germany, and pairs and dance teams from the Soviet Union. Canada's Elizabeth Manley won a silver medal in figure skating. Alberto Tomba of Italy and Vreni Schneider of Switzerland took two gold medals each in slalom and giant slalom skiing. The Soviets won in hockey and

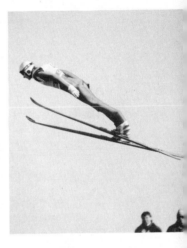

Official results of the 1988 Olympic Games

Winners of the Winter Olympics in Calgary, Canada, February 13-28

Event	Winner	Country	Mark
Men's skiing			
Downhill	Pirmin Zurbriggen	Switzerland	1:59.63
Combined	Hubert Strolz	Austria	36.55 pts.
Super giant slalom	Franck Piccard	France	1:39.66
Giant slalom	Alberto Tomba	Italy	2:06.37
Slalom	Alberto Tomba	Italy	1:39.47
Cross-country:			
15-kilometer	Mikhail Deviatiarov	U.S.S.R.	41:18.9
30-kilometer	Alexei Prokurorov	U.S.S.R.	1:24:26.3
50-kilometer	Gunde Svan	Sweden	2:04:30.9
40-kilometer relay	Ottosson, Wassberg Svan, Mogren	Sweden	1:43:58.6
70-meter jump	Matti Nykänen	Finland	229.1 pts.
90-meter jump	Matti Nykänen	Finland	224.0 pts.
Team	Nikkola, Nykänen, Ylipulli, Puikkonen	Finland	634.4 pts.
Nordic combined (individual)	Hippolyt Kempf	Switzerland	
Nordic combined (team)	Müller, Pohl, Schwarz	W. Germany	
Women's skiing			
Downhill	Marina Kiehl	W. Germany	1:25.86
Combined	Anita Wachter	Austria	29.25 pts.
Super giant slalom	Sigrid Wolf	Austria	1:19.03
Giant slalom	Vreni Schneider	Switzerland	2:06.49
Slalom	Vreni Schneider	Switzerland	1:36.69
Cross-country:			
5-kilometer	Marjo Matikänen	Finland	15:04.0
10-kilometer	Vida Ventsene	U.S.S.R.	30:08.03
20-kilometer	Tamara Tikhonova	U.S.S.R.	55:53.6
20-kilometer relay	Nagueikina, Gavriliuk, Tikhonova, Reztsova	U.S.S.R.	59:51.1
Ice hockey	U.S.S.R.	U.S.S.R.	7 wins, 1 loss
Men's speed skating			
500 meters	Uwe-Jens Mey	E. Germany	:36.45†

Event	Winner	Country	Mark
1,000 meters	Nikolai Guliaev	U.S.S.R.	1:13.03*
1,500 meters	Andre Hoffmann	E. Germany	1:52.06†
5,000 meters	Tomas Gustafson	Sweden	6:44.63†
10,000 meters	Tomas Gustafson	Sweden	13:48.20†
Women's speed skating			
500 meters	Bonnie Blair	U.S.A.	:39.10†
1,000 meters	Christa Rothenburger	E. Germany	1:17.65†
1,500 meters	Yvonne van Gennip	Netherlands	2:00.68*
3,000 meters	Yvonne van Gennip	Netherlands	4:11.94†
5,000 meters	Yvonne van Gennip	Netherlands	7:14.13†
Biathlon			
10-kilometer event	Frank-Peter Rötsch	E. Germany	25:08.1
20-kilometer event	Frank-Peter Rötsch	E. Germany	56:33.33
30-kilometer relay	Vassiliev, Chepikov, Popov, Medvedtsev	U.S.S.R.	1:22:30.0
Bobsledding			
Two-man	Ianis Kipours, Vladimir Kozlov	U.S.S.R.	3:53.48
Four-man	Fasser, Meier, Fässler, Stocker	Switzerland	3:47.51
Figure skating			
Men's singles	Brian Boitano	U.S.A.	3.0
Women's singles	Katarina Witt	E. Germany	4.2
Pairs	Ekaterina Gordeeva, Sergei Grinkov	U.S.S.R.	1.4
Ice dancing	Natalya Bestemianova, Andrei Bukin	U.S.S.R.	2.0
Men's luge			
Singles	Jens Müller	E. Germany	3:05.548
Doubles	Joerg Hoffmann, Jochen Pietzsch	E. Germany	1:31.940
Women's luge			
Singles	Steffi Walter	E. Germany	3:03.973

Winners of the Summer Olympics in Seoul, South Korea, September 17-October 2

Event	Winner	Country	Mark
Archery			
Men	Jay Barrs	U.S.A.	338 pts.
Women	Kim Soo-Nyung	S. Korea	344 pts.
Team (men)	S. Korea	S. Korea	986 pts.
Team (women)	S. Korea	S. Korea	982 pts.
Boxing			
Light flyweight	Ivailo Hristov	Bulgaria	
Flyweight	Kim Kwang-Sun	S. Korea	
Bantamweight	Kennedy McKinney	U.S.A.	
Featherweight	Giovanni Parisi	Italy	
Lightweight	Andreas Zuelow	E. Germany	
Light welterweight	Viatcheslav Janovski	U.S.S.R.	
Welterweight	Robert Wangila	Kenya	
Light middleweight	Park Si-Hun	S. Korea	
Middleweight	Henry Maske	E. Germany	
Light heavyweight	Andrew Maynard	U.S.A.	
Heavyweight	Ray Mercer	U.S.A.	
Super heavyweight	Lennox Lewis	Canada	
Canoeing, men			
500-meter kayak singles	Zsolt Gyulay	Hungary	1:44.82
500-meter kayak tandems	Ferguson, MacDonald	New Zealand	1:33.98
500-meter Canadian singles	Olaf Heukrodt	E. Germany	1:56.42
500-meter Canadian tandems	Reneiski, Jouravski	U.S.S.R.	1:41.77
1,000-meter kayak singles	Greg Barton	U.S.A.	3:55.27
1,000-meter kayak tandems	Barton, Bellingham	U.S.A.	3:32.42
1,000-meter kayak fours	Gyulay, Csipes, Hodosi, Abraham	Hungary	3:00.20
1,000-meter Canadian singles	Ivan Klementiev	U.S.S.R.	4:12.78
1,000-meter Canadian tandems	Reneiski, Jouravski	U.S.S.R.	3:48.36

Event	Winner	Country	Mark
Canoeing, women			
500-meter kayak singles	Vania Guecheva	Bulgaria	1:55.19
500-meter kayak tandems	Schmidt, Nothnagel	E. Germany	1:43.46
500-meter kayak fours	Schmidt, Nothnagel, Portwich, Singer	E. Germany	1:40.78
Cycling, men			
Individual road race	Olaf Ludwig	E. Germany	4:32:22
Sprint	Lutz Hesslich	E. Germany	
1,000-meter time trial	Aleksandr Kirichenko	U.S.S.R.	1:04.499
4,000-meter individual pursuit	Gintautas Umaras	U.S.S.R.	4:32.00
4,000-meter team pursuit	Ekimov, Kaspoutis, Nelubine, Umaras	U.S.S.R.	4:13.31
100-kilometer team time trial	Ampler, Kummer, Landsmann, Schur	E. Germany	1:57:47.7
50-kilometer points race	Dan Frost	Denmark	38 pts.
Cycling, women			
Sprint	Erika Salumiae	U.S.S.R.	
82-kilometer road race	Monique Knol	Netherlands	2:00:52
Equestrian			
Three-day event, individual	Mark Todd	New Zealand	42.6 pts.
Three-day event, team	Erhorn, Baumann, Kaspareit, Ehrenbrink	W. Germany	225.95 pts.
Dressage, individual	Nicole Uphoff	W. Germany	1,521 pts.
Dressage, team	Klimke, Uphoff, Linsenhoff, Theodorescu	W. Germany	4,302 pts.
Show-jumping, individual	Pierre Durand	France	1.25 pts.

*New Olympic record.   †New world record.   **Tied Olympic record.   ‡Tied Olympic and world record.

Event	Winner	Country	Mark
Show-jumping, team	Beerbaum, Brinkman, Hafemeister, Sloothaak	W. Germany	17.25 pts.

Fencing, men

Event	Winner	Country	Mark
Individual foil	Stefano Cerioni	Italy	
Team foil	Romankov, Mamedov, Aptsiaouri, Ibraguimov, Koretskii	U.S.S.R.	
Individual epee	Arnd Schmitt	W. Germany	
Team epee	Lenglet, Srecki, Riboud, Henry, Delpla	France	
Individual sabre	Jean-François Lamour	France	
Team sabre	Nébald, Szabo, Bujdoso, Gedoevari, Csongradi	Hungary	

Fencing, women

Event	Winner	Country	Mark
Individual foil	Anja Fichtel	W. Germany	
Team foil	Fichtel, Funkenhauser, Weber, Bau, Klug	W. Germany	

Gymnastics, men

Event	Winner	Country	Mark
All-around	Vladimir Artemov	U.S.S.R.	119.125 pts.
Vault	Lou Yun	China	19.875 pts.
Pommel horse	Lyubomir Gueraskov; Zsolt Borkai; Dmitri Bilozerchev (tie)	Bulgaria Hungary U.S.S.R.	19.950 pts.
Horizontal bar	Vladimir Artemov; Valeri Lyukin (tie)	U.S.S.R. U.S.S.R.	19.900 pts.
Parallel bars	Vladimir Artemov	U.S.S.R.	19.925 pts.
Rings	Holger Behrendt; Dmitri Bilozerchev (tie)	E. Germany U.S.S.R.	19.925 pts.
Floor exercise	Sergei Kharlkov	U.S.S.R.	19.925 pts.
Team	Gogoladze, Nouvikov, Kharkov, Bilozerchev, Artemov, Lyukin	U.S.S.R.	593.35 pts.

Gymnastics, women

Event	Winner	Country	Mark
All-around	Elena Shushunova	U.S.S.R.	79.662 pts.
Balance beam	Daniela Silivaş	Romania	19.924 pts.
Uneven parallel bars	Daniela Silivaş	Romania	20.000 pts.
Vault	Svetlana Boguinskaya	U.S.S.R.	19.905 pts.
Floor exercise	Daniela Silivaş	Romania	19.937 pts.
Rhythmic	Marina Lobatch	U.S.S.R.	60 pts.
Team	Baitova, Chevtchenko, Strajeva, Boguinskaya, Lachtchenova, Shushunova	U.S.S.R.	395.475 pts.

Judo

Event	Winner	Country	Mark
132 pounds (60 kg)	Kim Jae-Yup	S. Korea	
143 pounds (65 kg)	Lee Kyung-Keun	S. Korea	
157 pounds (71 kg)	Marc Alexandre	France	
172 pounds (78 kg)	Waldemar Legien	Poland	
190 pounds (86 kg)	Peter Seisenbacher	Austria	
209 pounds (95 kg)	Aurelio Miguel	Brazil	
Over 209 pounds	Hitoshi Saito	Japan	

Modern pentathlon

Event	Winner	Country	Mark
Individual	Janos Martinek	Hungary	5,404 pts.
Team	Martinek, Mizser, Fabian	Hungary	15,886 pts.

Rowing, men (all distances 2,000 meters)

Event	Winner	Country	Mark
Single sculls	Thomas Lange	E. Germany	6:49.86
Double sculls	Florun, Rienks	Netherlands	6:21.13
Four sculls	Poli, Farina, Tizzano, A. Abbagnale	Italy	5:53.37
Pairs without coxswain	Holmes, Redgrave	Great Britain	6:36.84
Pairs with coxswain	C. Abbagnale, G. Abbagnale, Di Capua	Italy	6:58.79
Fours without coxswain	Schröder, Greiner, Brudel, Förster	E. Germany	6:03.11
Fours with coxswain	Klawonn, Eichwurzel, Niesecke, Schmeling, Reiher	E. Germany	6:10.74

Event	Winner	Country	Mark
Eights with coxswain	Domian, Eichholz, Klein, Männig, Mellinghaus, Möllenkamp, Rabe, Schultz, Wessling	W. Germany	5:46.05

Rowing, women (all races 2,000 meters)

Event	Winner	Country	Mark
Single sculls	Jutta Behrendt	E. Germany	7:47.19
Double sculls	Peter, Schröter	E. Germany	7:00.48
Four sculls	Förster, Mundt, Schramm, Sorgers	E. Germany	6:21.06
Pairs without coxswain	Arba, Homeghi	Romania	7:28.13
Fours with coxswain	Walther, Doberschütz, Hornig, Siech, Rose	E. Germany	6:56.00
Eights with coxswain	Balthasar, Haacker, Kluge, Neunast, Schrör, Stange, Strauch, Wild, Zeidler	E. Germany	6:15.17

Shooting, open

Event	Winner	Country	Mark
Skeet	Axel Wegner	E. Germany	222 pts.**
Trapshooting	Dmitri Monakov	U.S.S.R.	222 pts.*

Shooting, men

Event	Winner	Country	Mark
Air pistol	Taniou Kiriakov	Bulgaria	687.9 pts.*
Free pistol	Sorin Babii	Romania	660 pts.*
Rapid-fire pistol	Afanasi Kouzmine	U.S.S.R.	698 pts.†
Small-bore rifle, prone	Miroslav Varga	Czechoslovakia	703.9 pts.*
Free rifle, three positions	Malcolm Cooper	Great Britain	1,279.3 pts.*
Rifle, running game target	Tor Heiestad	Norway	689 pts.**
Air rifle	Goran Maksimovic	Yugoslavia	695.6 pts.*

Shooting, women

Event	Winner	Country	Mark
Air pistol	Jasna Sekaric	Yugoslavia	489.5 pts.†
Sport pistol	Nino Saloukvadze	U.S.S.R.	690 pts.*
Air rifle	Irina Chilova	U.S.S.R.	498.5 pts.*
Standard rifle, three positions	Silvia Sperber	W. Germany	685.6 pts.*

Swimming and diving, men

Event	Winner	Country	Mark
50-meter freestyle	Matt Biondi	U.S.A.	:22.14†
100-meter freestyle	Matt Biondi	U.S.A.	:48.63*
200-meter freestyle	Duncan Armstrong	Australia	1:47.25†
400-meter freestyle	Uwe Dassler	E. Germany	3:46.95†
1,500-meter freestyle	Vladimir Salnikov	U.S.S.R.	15:00.4
100-meter backstroke	Daichi Suzuki	Japan	:55.05
200-meter backstroke	Igor Polianski	U.S.S.R.	1:59.37
100-meter breaststroke	Adrian Moorhouse	Great Britain	1:02.04
200-meter breaststroke	József Szabo	Hungary	2:13.52
100-meter butterfly	Anthony Nesty	Suriname	:53.00*
200-meter butterfly	Michael Gross	W. Germany	1:56.94*
200-meter medley	Tamas Darnyi	Hungary	2:00.17†
400-meter medley	Tamas Darnyi	Hungary	4:14.75†
400-meter medley relay	Berkoff, Schroeder, Biondi, Jacobs	U.S.A.	3:36.93†
400-meter freestyle relay	Jacobs, Dalbey, Jager, Biondi	U.S.A.	3:16.53†
800-meter freestyle relay	Dalbey, Cetlinski, Gjertsen, Biondi	U.S.A.	7:12.51†
Platform diving	Greg Louganis	U.S.A.	638.61 pts.
Springboard diving	Greg Louganis	U.S.A.	730.80 pts.

Swimming and diving, women

Event	Winner	Country	Mark
50-meter freestyle	Kristin Otto	E. Germany	:25.49*
100-meter freestyle	Kristin Otto	E. Germany	:54.93
200-meter freestyle	Heike Freidrich	E. Germany	1:57.65*
400-meter freestyle	Janet Evans	U.S.A.	4:03.85†
800-meter freestyle	Janet Evans	U.S.A.	8:20.20*
100-meter backstroke	Kristin Otto	E. Germany	1:00.89
200-meter backstroke	Krisztina Egerszegi	Hungary	2:09.29*
100-meter breaststroke	Tania Dangalakova	Bulgaria	1:07.95*

Event	Winner	Country	Mark
200-meter breaststroke	Silke Hörner	E. Germany	2:26.71†
100-meter butterfly	Kristin Otto	E. Germany	:59.00*
200-meter butterfly	Kathleen Nord	E. Germany	2:09.51
200-meter medley	Daniela Hunger	E. Germany	2:12.59*
400-meter medley	Janet Evans	U.S.A.	4:37.76
400-meter freestyle relay	Otto, Meissner, Hunger, Stellmach	E. Germany	3:40.63*
400-meter medley relay	Otto, Hörner, Weigang, Meissner	E. Germany	4:03.74*
Synchronized swimming (solo)	Carolyn Waldo	Canada	200.15 pts.
Synchronized swimming (duet)	Waldo, Cameron	Canada	197.717 pts.
Platform diving	Xu Yanmei	China	445.2 pts.
Springboard diving	Gao Min	China	580.23 pts.

Table tennis, men

Singles	Yoo Nam Kyu	S. Korea	
Doubles	Longcan, Qingquang	China	

Table tennis, women

Singles	Chen Jing	China	
Doubles	Jung-Hwa, Young Ja	S. Korea	

Tennis, men

Singles	Miloslav Mecir	Czechoslovakia	
Doubles	Flach, Seguso	U.S.A.	

Tennis, women

Singles	Steffi Graf	W. Germany	
Doubles	Shriver, Garrison	U.S.A.	

Track and field, men

100 meters	Carl Lewis	U.S.A.	:9.92*
200 meters	Joe DeLoach	U.S.A.	:19.75*
400 meters	Steve Lewis	U.S.A.	:43.87
800 meters	Paul Ereng	Kenya	1:43.45
1,500 meters	Peter Rono	Kenya	3:35.96
5,000 meters	John Ngugi	Kenya	13:11.70
10,000 meters	Brahim Boutaib	Morocco	27:21.46*
110-meter hurdles	Roger Kingdom	U.S.A.	:12.98*
400-meter hurdles	Andre Phillips	U.S.A.	:47.19*
3,000-meter steeplechase	Julius Kariuki	Kenya	8:05.51*
Marathon	Gelindo Bordin	Italy	2:10.32
400-meter relay	Bryzgine, Krylov, Mouraviev, Savine	U.S.S.R.	:38.19
1,600-meter relay	Everett, S. Lewis, Robinzine, Reynolds	U.S.A.	2:56.16‡
20-kilometer walk	Jozef Pribilinec	Czechoslovakia	1:19.57
50-kilometer walk	Viacheslav Ivanenko	U.S.S.R.	3:38.29
High jump	Gennadi Avdeenko	U.S.S.R.	7 ft. 9½ in. (2.38 m)
Long jump	Carl Lewis	U.S.A.	28 ft. 7¼ in. (8.72 m)
Triple jump	Hristo Markov	Bulgaria	57 ft. 9¼ in.* (17.61 m)
Pole vault	Sergei Bubka	U.S.S.R.	19 ft. 4¼ in.* (5.90 m)
Discus throw	Jürgen Schult	E. Germany	219 ft. 5 in.* (66.82 m)
Javelin throw	Tapio Korjus	Finland	276 ft. 6 in. (84.28 m)
Shot-put	Ulf Timmermann	E. Germany	73 ft. 8¾ in.* (22.47 m)
Hammer throw	Sergei Litvinov	U.S.S.R.	278 ft. 2½ in.* (84.80 m)
Decathlon	Christian Schenk	E. Germany	8,488 pts.

Track and field, women

100 meters	Florence Griffith Joyner	U.S.A.	:10.54
200 meters	Florence Griffith Joyner	U.S.A.	:21.34†
400 meters	Olga Bryzgina	U.S.S.R.	:48.65*
800 meters	Sigrun Wodars	E. Germany	1:56.10
1,500 meters	Paula Ivan	Romania	3:53.96*
3,000 meters	Tatiana Samolenko	U.S.S.R.	8:26.53*
10,000 meters	Olga Bondarenko	U.S.S.R.	31:05.21*
100-meter hurdles	Jordanka Donkova	Bulgaria	:12.38*
400-meter hurdles	Debra Flintoff-King	Australia	:53.17*
400-meter relay	Brown, Echols, Griffith Joyner, Ashford	U.S.A.	:41.98

Event	Winner	Country	Mark
1,600-meter relay	Ledovskaia, Nazarova, Piniguina, Bryzgina	U.S.S.R.	3:15.18†
High jump	Louise Ritter	U.S.A.	6 ft. 8 in.* (2.03 m)
Long jump	Jackie Joyner-Kersee	U.S.A.	24 ft. 3½ in.* (7.40 m)
Discus throw	Martina Hellmann	E. Germany	237 ft. 2 in.* (72.30 m)
Javelin throw	Petra Felke	E. Germany	245 ft. 0 in.* (74.68 m)
Shot-put	Natalya Lisovskaya	U.S.S.R.	72 ft. 11½ in. (22.24 m)
Marathon	Rosa Mota	Portugal	2:25.40
Heptathlon	Jackie Joyner-Kersee	U.S.A.	7,291 pts.†

Weight lifting

115 pounds or less	Sevdalin Marinov	Bulgaria	595 lbs.† (270 kg)
123 pounds or less	Oxen Mirzoin	U.S.S.R.	645 lbs.* (292.5 kg)
132 pounds or less	Naim Suleymanoglu	Turkey	755 lbs.† (342.5 kg)
149 pounds or less	Joachim Kunz	E. Germany	749½ lbs. (340 kg)
165 pounds or less	Borislav Guidikov	Bulgaria	826½ lbs.* (375 kg)
182 pounds or less	Israil Arsamakov	U.S.S.R.	832 lbs. (377.5 kg)
198 pounds or less	Anatoli Khrapatyi	U.S.S.R.	909¼ lbs.* (412.5 kg)
220 pounds or less	Pavel Kouznetsov	U.S.S.R.	936¾ lbs.* (425 kg)
242 pounds or less	Yuri Zakharevitch	U.S.S.R.	1,003 lbs.† (455 kg)
over 242 pounds	Alexandre Kurlovich	U.S.S.R.	1,019½ lbs.* (462.5 kg)

Wrestling (freestyle)

106 pounds or less	Takashi Kobayashi	Japan	
115 pounds or less	Mitsuru Sato	Japan	
126 pounds or less	Sergei Beloglazov	U.S.S.R.	
137 pounds or less	John Smith	U.S.A.	
149 pounds or less	Arsen Fadzaev	U.S.S.R.	
163 pounds or less	Kenneth Monday	U.S.A.	
181 pounds or less	Han Myang-Woo	S. Korea	
198 pounds or less	Makharbek Khadartsev	U.S.S.R.	
220 pounds or less	Vasile Puscasu	Romania	
Over 220 pounds	David Gobedjichvili	U.S.S.R.	

Wrestling (Greco-Roman)

106 pounds or less	Vincenzo Maenza	Italy	
114 pounds or less	Jon Ronningen	Norway	
125 pounds or less	Andras Sike	Hungary	
136 pounds or less	Kamandar Madjidov	U.S.S.R.	
150 pounds or less	Levon Djoulfalakian	U.S.S.R.	
163 pounds or less	Kim Young-Nam	S. Korea	
180 pounds or less	Mikhail Mamiachvili	U.S.S.R	
198 pounds or less	Atanas Komchev	Bulgaria	
220 pounds or less	Andrzej Wronski	Poland	
Over 220 pounds	Alexandre Kareline	U.S.S.R.	

Yachting

Finn class	José Luis Doreste	Spain	38.1 pts.
Tornado class	Le Deroff, Henard	France	16 pts.
470 class (men)	Peponnet, Pillot	France	34.7 pts.
470 class (women)	Jolly, Jewell	U.S.A.	26.7 pts.
Soling class	Schümann, Flach, Jäkel	E. Germany	11.7 pts.
Flying Dutchman	Bojsen-Möller, Grönberg	Denmark	31.4 pts.
Star class	McIntyre, Bryn Vaile	Great Britain	45.7 pts.
Board sailing	Bruce Kendall	New Zealand	35.4 pts.

Team sports

Basketball (men)		U.S.S.R.	
Basketball (women)		U.S.A.	
Field hockey (men)		Great Britain	
Field hockey (women)		Australia	
Handball (men)		U.S.S.R.	
Handball (women)		S. Korea	
Soccer (men)		U.S.S.R.	
Volleyball (men)		U.S.A.	
Volleyball (women)		U.S.S.R.	
Water polo (men)		Yugoslavia	

dominated cross-country skiing. The East Germans swept the three luge titles and the two individual biathlon events.

Summer Games. There was apprehension in 1981 when the IOC awarded the 1988 Summer Olympics to Seoul. The city is only 30 miles (48 kilometers) south of the demilitarized zone separating South Korea from its hostile neighbor, North Korea, and military action or terrorism seemed possible. In addition, South Korea has no diplomatic relations with Soviet-bloc nations.

Most of the Soviet-bloc nations boycotted the 1984 Summer Olympics in Los Angeles, and another boycott was feared. The possibility of a boycott seemed to increase when North Korea demanded to co-host the games. The IOC and South Korea rejected that demand, though they offered to allow North Korea to stage all or part of five Olympic sports. North Korea rejected that proposal and did not take part in the games.

Cuba, Ethiopia, and the Seychelles sympathized with North Korea and did not enter the Olympics. Madagascar entered, but then stayed home. Nicaragua, torn by civil war, declined to compete, and Albania did not respond to its invitation.

Otherwise, for the first time since the 1972 Olympic Games in Munich, West Germany, virtually all nations took part in the Olympics. In all, a record 160 nations sent 9,627 athletes, also a record.

For months before the Olympics, radical student groups demanding reunification with North Korea staged violent demonstrations in Seoul. During the Olympics, South Korea stationed 100,000 security personnel in Seoul to prevent disruptions.

Many of the Olympic facilities were built for the 1986 Asian Games. The major competition sites were clustered in Olympic Park, across the street from the Olympic Village, and in the nearby Seoul Sports Complex. South Korea spent $1.4 billion in permanent improvements, and together with private sources spent another $1.7 billion on sports facilities and operating expenses.

Drugs. Serious drug testing came to the Olympics in 1976, but in the years that followed, some methods of cheating evaded the testers. The drugs that most concerned Olympic officials were *anabolic steroids*—artificial forms of the male sex hormone testosterone. These steroids, used in conjunction with weight lifting and a high-protein diet, build muscles, making the athletes stronger and able to train harder. Some female athletes also use them.

The IOC and various international sports federations ban steroids because of possible dangerous side effects. The side effects include cancer, circulatory problems, liver damage, and impotence.

The glow of Johnson's Olympic victory over Lewis was still alive on September 27 when the IOC announced Johnson's disqualification. Johnson denied taking steroids and suggested that someone had put a banned substance in a drink handed to him after the

Figure skater Brian Boitano earns a gold medal—one of only two won by U.S. athletes at the Winter Olympics in Calgary, Canada, in February.

race. IOC physicians discounted that possibility, saying the drug had been in Johnson's system for a much longer time.

Johnson left Korea for his home in Scarborough, Canada, the next day, still protesting his innocence. George M. (Jamie) Astaphan, a physician who had treated Johnson for years, said he gave Johnson steroids in May to combat bursitis, but not the steroids disclosed in the test. Astaphan said he knew nothing about those steroids.

The Canadian government banned Johnson for life from representing Canada in track and field. Johnson's commercial contracts, worth millions of dollars, were canceled. Anita DeFrantz of Los Angeles, a member of the IOC, said of Johnson's situation: "It's cowardly. It's cheating. It's disgusting. It's vile."

It was also not uncommon. Before the Olympics, national Olympic committees disqualified four Canadian weight lifters, three Belgian cyclists, and a U.S. swimmer—Angel Myers—after drug tests.

During the Olympics, the IOC disqualified 10 athletes—5 weight lifters, 2 modern pentathletes, a judo player, a wrestler, and Johnson. The drugs involved were amphetamines; anabolic steroids; diuretics (which help athletes lose weight and also disguise the use of other drugs, including steroids); beta-blockers (which help steady the hands); and caffeine (in amounts taken by tablet or injection as opposed to the normal amounts of caffeine in coffee or tea).

Canada's Ben Johnson leads the 100-meter dash at the Summer Olympics in September, but he later was stripped of his gold medal when a drug test showed steroid use.

When two Bulgarian weight lifters who had won gold medals were found to have used *furosemide*—a diuretic—the entire Bulgarian weight-lifting team went home. When two Hungarian weight lifters were found to have used anabolic steroids, their team left, too.

Richard Pound of Canada, a vice president of the IOC, proposed that weight lifting be eliminated from the Olympics until it is free of its drug problem. And on October 2, the day the Olympics ended, the United States and the Soviet Union signed an agreement for a joint crackdown on drug use among athletes.

Competition. The Olympics ran for 16 days—from September 17 to October 2. There were 237 medal events in 26 sports. In addition, there were three demonstration sports—baseball, tae kwon do, and women's judo—and two exhibition sports—bowling and badminton.

The major medal winners were the Soviet Union with 132, East Germany with 102, and the United States with 94. In gold medals, it was the same three—the Soviet Union with 55, East Germany with 37, and the United States with 36. Canada won 10 medals, including 3 gold.

The biggest individual gold-medal winner was Kristin Otto, an East German swimmer who won six golds in six tries. She showed her versatility by taking the 100-meter freestyle, the 100-meter backstroke, and the 100-meter butterfly.

Matt Biondi of Moraga, Calif., swam seven events and won seven medals—five gold, one silver, and one bronze. Janet Evans of Placentia, Calif., won three gold medals in her three swimming events. Canada's Carolyn Waldo won two gold medals in synchronized swimming. In gymnastics, Vladimir Artemov of the Soviet Union won four gold medals and a silver; his teammate, Dmitri Bilozerchev, won three gold and a bronze; and Daniela Silivaş of Romania won three gold, two silver, and a bronze.

During the U.S. Olympic trials in July, Florence Griffith Joyner of Los Angeles, known for her flamboyant running clothes and long fingernails, became the world's ranking female sprinter, setting a world record in the 100-meter dash at a trial in Indianapolis. In the Olympics, she won the 100-meter dash and set a world record in the 200-meter dash with a time of 21.34 seconds. She ran on one gold-medal relay team and another that finished second. She won three gold medals and one silver.

Her sister-in-law, Jackie Joyner-Kersee of Newport Beach, Calif., won gold medals in the long jump and the heptathlon, in which she broke her previous world record with 7,291 points. Carl Lewis, who won four gold medals in the 1984 Olympics, won two gold and one silver.

Greg Louganis of Boca Raton, Fla., won the two gold medals in men's diving, as he did in 1984. This time, in the springboard qualifying, his head hit the board and he sustained a wound that required four stitches. Greg Barton of Homer, Mich., a world champion, won two gold medals in kayaking, the first ever by an American. The U.S. teams won in men's volleyball and women's basketball, but the favored men's basketball team took only the bronze, while the Soviets won the gold.

Tennis returned to the Olympics for the first time since 1924. Steffi Graf of West Germany, who had just completed a grand slam of the world's four major tennis tournaments, won the gold in women's singles.

No achievement was greeted with more awe than the weight lifting of Naim Suleymanoglu of Turkey. Standing only 5 feet (150 centimeters) tall and weighing 132 pounds (60 kilograms), he raised 419 pounds (190 kilograms)—more than three times his body weight—over his head. He became known as the Pocket Hercules.

Controversy. Controversial decisions are the norm in amateur boxing. In Seoul, they were also frequent.

When Byun Jong-il of South Korea lost a decision to Ivailo Hristov of Bulgaria, five Koreans—a coach, a trainer, and three security officers—rushed into the ring and punched and kicked the referee, Keith Walker of New Zealand. The International Amateur Boxing Association (AIBA) suspended five officials of the South Korean Boxing Federation indefinitely. It also suspended Byun because he sat in the ring for 67 minutes and refused to leave. The Korean public and the press were outraged by the conduct of their countrymen. They were also outraged that the National Broadcasting Company (NBC)—which televised the Summer Olympics to the United States—embarrassed them by showing news film of the incident more often than they thought necessary.

On the last day of boxing, Park Si-Hun of South Korea won a gold medal with a controversial 3 to 2 decision over Roy Jones of Pensacola, Fla. Koreans apologized for the decision. AIBA officials voted Jones the best boxer in the Olympics, and later they suspended the three judges who had voted for Park.

The U.S. women's gymnastics team would have won a bronze medal except for a technicality. Because an alternate U.S. gymnast inadvertently stayed on the podium while a teammate was competing, the Americans were penalized a half-point. The violation was reported by an international official from East Germany. The East Germans finished third with 390.875 points, edging out the Americans with 390.575 points.

New schedule. The IOC voted on September 15 to hold the 1994 Winter Olympics in Lillehammer, Norway. Under a recently adopted system to stagger the games, the Summer and Winter Olympics will be held at two-year intervals, instead of both occurring every four years. The 1992 Winter Olympics were scheduled to be held in Albertville, France.   Frank Litsky

See also **Boitano, Brian; Witt, Katarina.** In *World Book*, see **Olympic Games.**

Oman. See Middle East.

Ontario. Canada's 1988 economic boom was felt strongly in Ontario, the country's manufacturing and financial center. Economic growth outpaced Canada's national average, and the jobless rate of 5.1 per cent remained the lowest among Canada's provinces.

The Liberal government of Premier David Peterson continued to enjoy popularity. The Progressive Conservative Party captured 1 legislative seat in an April 1988 by-election (a special election to fill a vacancy) in London, Ont., giving that party 17 assembly members, but the Liberals still held 94 of the 130 seats. The New Democratic Party held 19 seats.

Economy. In a controversial move, the Peterson government announced in April that it would increase the sales tax by 1 percentage point, to 8 per cent, and raise the provincial personal income tax by the same proportion. A similar increase in income tax was promised for 1989. The new taxes were expected to yield an additional $1.3 billion in 1988. (All monetary amounts in this article are in Canadian dollars, with $1 = U.S. 84 cents as of Dec. 31, 1988.)

The need for added revenue arose from the escalating costs of social and medical programs and from a determination to curb the growth in the province's deficit. In presenting the budget on April 20, Treasurer Robert Nixon estimated that total spending in 1988 would grow to $37.9 billion with a deficit of $473 million—the lowest deficit in 19 years. Additional funds were allotted for housing.

Sunday shopping. An emotional issue was a government proposal to allow each of Ontario's approximately 800 municipalities to draw up its own rules governing shopping hours on Sunday. Existing rules restricted Sunday shopping while permitting municipalities to designate tourist areas where certain shops might remain open.

The two opposition parties strongly opposed the Sunday-shopping legislation, and opposition members of the legislature staged a filibuster when the measure was introduced in April. They claimed that once Sunday shopping was permitted across the province, no municipality would be able to reject it because of the competition from stores in adjoining towns. After tying up legislative business for 10 days, the opposition agreed to a truce when the government promised to hold public hearings on the issue before proceeding with the legislation. At hearings during the summer, church and labor groups mounted a strong campaign against Sunday shopping.

Free trade. The government continued to oppose free trade with the United States by sponsoring a bill, passed in July, controlling transfer of water. The measure arose from fears that the U.S.-Canada free-trade agreement might put Canada's fresh water at risk by treating it as a commodity.   David M. L. Farr

See also **Canada; Toronto.** In *World Book*, see Ontario.

Opera. See Classical music.

Oregon. See State government.

Pacific Islands. Agreement on a 10-year peace plan between New Caledonia's ethnic French citizens and *Kanaks*—descendants of the original Melanesian inhabitants—was the major achievement in the Pacific Islands in 1988. The agreement, reached on June 26, came after several years of heated confrontation between the French, who want the territory to remain a part of France, and the Kanaks, who favor independence for New Caledonia. In a referendum in France on November 6, 80 per cent of the voters approved the agreement, but voter turnout was only 37 per cent.

Under the agreement, France will rule New Caledonia until June 1989. Then, three federal provinces, governed by elected executive councils, will be created. These councils will make up a territorial congress for the entire territory. In 1998, a referendum will determine the future government system.

The agreement came two months after the independence issue appeared to bring New Caledonia to the brink of civil war. Events culminated on April 22, when a group of Kanaks killed four French policemen and took 27 French hostages on Ouvéa, one of the territory's Loyalty Islands. Although 11 hostages were released on April 24, a French *magistrate* (law officer) and seven policemen who tried to initiate talks with the captors were taken hostage on April 27. All the hostages were freed on May 5 in a controversial military-style operation, mounted by French commandos, that left 15 Kanaks and 2 commandos dead.

Palau setback. The future of Palau's relationship with the United States continued to be uncertain in 1988. On August 29, the Palau Supreme Court ruled that a 1987 referendum on the issue was invalid. In the referendum, 73 per cent of Palau's voters agreed to drop a provision in their Constitution closing their islands to nuclear-powered ships and weapons of the United States. The provision has long prevented the implementation of a Compact of Free Association between Palau and the United States, which would grant Palau limited self-government in "free association" with the United States.

On August 20, Palau President Lazarus Salii was found shot to death in his home in Koror, the capital. Police investigators believed it was a case of suicide. On November 2, voters elected businessman Ngiratkel Etpison president.

Papua New Guinea got a new government on July 4 when Prime Minister Paias Wingti lost a vote of confidence in Parliament. Rabbie Namaliu, who had become opposition leader only six days earlier, became the new prime minister. Namaliu was elected opposition leader when Michael Somare gave up the post. As the new prime minister, Namaliu promised to stop the "moral rot and ethical corruption" that he said had marked the country's political leadership over the previous three years.

The defeat of the Wingti government ended several months of political chaos. Wingti had forestalled

Facts in brief on Pacific Island countries

Country	Population	Government	Monetary unit*	Exports†	Foreign trade (million U.S.$) Imports†
Australia	16,315,000	Governor General Sir Ninian Stephen; Prime Minister Robert Hawke	dollar (1.15 = $1)	22,600	26,100
Fiji	758,000	President Ratu Sir Penaia Ganilau; Prime Minister Ratu Sir Kamisese Mara	dollar (1.42 = $1)	246	368
Kiribati	69,000	President Ieremia Tabai	Australian dollar	1	12
Nauru	9,000	President Hammer DeRoburt	Australian dollar	93	73
New Zealand	3,389,000	Governor General Sir Paul Reeves; Prime Minister David R. Lange	dollar (1.55 = $1)	5,880	6,100
Papua New Guinea	3,738,000	Governor General Sir Kingsford Dibela; Prime Minister Rabbie Namaliu	kina (0.82 = $1.01)	1,033	978
Solomon Islands	314,000	Governor General Sir Baddeley Devesi; Prime Minister Ezekiel Alebua	dollar (2.08 = $1)	65	59
Tonga	108,000	King Taufa'ahau Tupou IV; Prime Minister Prince Fatafehi Tu'ipelehake	pa'anga (1.28 = $1)	5	41
Tuvalu	9,000	Governor General Tupua Leupena; Prime Minister Tomasi Puapua	Australian dollar	1	3
Vanuatu	150,000	President Ati George Sokomanu‡; Prime Minister Walter H. Lini	vatu (104 = $1)	14	58
Western Samoa	169,000	Head of State Malietoa Tanumafili II; Prime Minister Tofilau Eti	tala (2.16 = $1)	11	43

*Exchange rates as of Dec. 1, 1988, or latest available data (source: Deak International). †Latest available data. ‡Sokomanu was arrested on Dec. 21, 1988, charged with inciting mutiny.

defeat earlier in the year. In April, he reinstated Ted
Diro as defense minister even though Diro was facing
perjury charges. Diro's support allowed Wingti on
April 23 to pass a motion adjourning Parliament until
June 27. When Parliament resumed, however, Diro
deserted him.

Vanuatu president jailed. Ati George Sokomanu,
Vanuatu's president, and five of the country's leading
politicians were jailed in December following a failed
attempt to replace the government of Prime Minister
Walter H. Lini. On December 21, Sokomanu was
charged with inciting mutiny in the country's police
and paramilitary forces as well as with unlawfully
swearing in the five politicians as an interim government. Earlier, the five had been charged with *sedition*
(causing rebellion) and taking unlawful oaths. Among
them was Barak Sope, secretary-general of Lini's Van-
ua'aku Party, who had been named prime minister of
the interim government.

Sope and Lini had been on a collision course since
December 1987. At that time, Sope tried to topple Lini
on the grounds that a stroke had undermined his
health. On May 23, Lini dismissed Sope from his cabinet after he allegedly organized a riotous march on
Lini's office. Several months of political turmoil followed, marked by the expulsions and resignations of
members of Parliament. By November 8, only 23 seats
in Vanuatu's 46-seat Parliament were filled.

Special elections took place on December 12 to fill
the 18 seats formerly occupied by members of the
opposition party. The by-elections, which were partially boycotted, gave Lini's party an overwhelming
majority in Parliament. But when Parliament recon-
vened on December 16, Sokomanu announced he was
dissolving it pending new elections. Lini claimed that
Sokomanu had no constitutional authority for this
action, and Parliament ignored Sokomanu's order.
When Sokomanu swore in his five ministers two days
later, Lini quickly had them arrested.

Fiji's new Constitution. On November 21, Fiji's
traditional chiefs approved a draft of a new Constitution, which had been announced by the government
on September 15. The Constitution provides for a
single-chamber parliament of 71 members—59
elected and 12 appointed. Ethnic Fijians will have 28
elective seats, Indians (people whose ancestors were
brought to Fiji from India as plantation laborers) and
other groups will have 30 seats, and Rotumans (inhabitants of the island of Rotuma, a Fiji dependency) will
have 1 seat.

Of the 12 appointed members, 8 will be nominated
by the president and 4 by the prime minister. The
president's nominees must include the armed forces
commander. The present commander is Sitiveni Ra-
buka, who led two coups in 1987. The first elections
under the new Constitution are expected to be held in
December 1989.   Robert Langdon

In *World Book*, see **Pacific Islands.**
Painting. See Art.

Pakistan. President M. Zia-ul-Haq was killed on Aug.
17, 1988, when the air force transport plane he was
riding in crashed near Bahawalpur. The crash killed all
of the 30 people aboard, including 10 senior Pakistani
army officers and the United States Ambassador to
Pakistan, Arnold L. Raphel. In October, a Pakistani
investigation team said that the crash was probably
caused by "a criminal act or sabotage."

Upon Zia's death, Ghulam Ishaq Khan, a 73-year-old
career civil servant who was chairman of the Senate,
became acting president under the Constitution. He
was supported by Lieutenant General Mirza Aslam
Beq, who became the head of Pakistan's politically
powerful armed forces.

Ishaq Khan and Beq supported Zia's plan to hold
national and provincial assembly elections on November 16. Zia had on May 29 dismissed Prime Minister
Mohammed Khan Junejo and his Cabinet and dissolved the assemblies, accusing Junejo of being ineffective and the National Assembly of being incompetent and corrupt.

Election results. The Islamic Democratic Alliance, a
coalition of nine political parties including Junejo's
Pakistan Muslim League, in November won only 55 of
the 207 contested seats in the 237-member National
Assembly. Junejo and most other elderly leaders of his
once-powerful party lost their seats. The Pakistan
People's Party (PPP) won the largest number of
seats—92. After a vote to fill 20 seats reserved for
women, the PPP gained 12 more seats. The PPP had
been founded by Zulfikar Ali Bhutto, who headed
Pakistan's government from 1971 until 1977, when he
was ousted in a military coup led by Zia. Bhutto was
executed by Zia's government in 1979 for conspiracy
to murder a political opponent while serving as prime
minister. In the 1988 election, the PPP was led by
Bhutto's 35-year-old daughter, Benazir.

New prime minister and president. Benazir
Bhutto won support from a majority of Assembly
members and was named prime minister. She took
office on December 2, becoming the first woman to
govern a Muslim country in modern times. Bhutto
advocated reconciliation with Zia's supporters rather
than revenge for her father's death; continuation of
Pakistani support for guerrillas fighting Afghanistan's
Communist regime; and respect for the importance of
Pakistan's armed forces (see **Bhutto, Benazir**). An
electoral college of the National Assembly, Senate,
and provincial assemblies on December 12 elected
Ishaq Khan to a five-year term as president.

Ethnic violence. More than 120 Indian immigrants
were killed by unidentified gunmen in Hyderabad on
September 30. Survivors of the attack believed that
their assailants were ethnic Pakistanis. In an act of
revenge the next day in nearby Karachi, Indian immigrants attacked Pakistani residents. As many as 100
people died.   Henry S. Bradsher

See also **Asia** (Facts in brief table). In *World Book*,
see **Pakistan.**

405

Paleontology

Paleontology. A discovery in Montana in 1988 provided new details of the early life cycle of ancient reptiles. The unearthing of dinosaur eggs containing the fossilized skeletons of dinosaur embryos was reported in March 1988 by paleontologist John R. Horner of the Museum of the Rockies in Bozeman, Mont., and anatomist David B. Weishampel of Johns Hopkins University in Baltimore. The dinosaur eggs and their embryos, which are about 75 million years old, were discovered in the remains of regularly spaced mounds lined with vegetation that the scientists concluded were dinosaur nests.

Horner and Weishampel examined the dinosaur eggs using a computerized tomography (CT) scanner, an X-ray device. They found that the embryos represented two types of dinosaurs. The first is a previously unknown kind of *hypsilophodont*, a small, agile dinosaur that walked upright on two legs. A study of the limb joints of the hypsilophodont, named *orodromeus* (mountain runner), suggested that the dinosaur matured rapidly and was able to scamper about in search of food shortly after hatching.

The other embryos are of a type of dinosaur called *maiasaura*, which Horner and another colleague discovered in 1978. Studies of its limb joints, which are less well developed than those of orodromeus, support a theory proposed earlier by Horner that maiasaura was a late developer that spent its early life in the nest, where it was fed by its parents.

Coral in Hawaii. New information about the development of coral reefs in the Hawaiian Islands and ancient ocean currents in the Pacific Ocean was reported in June 1988 by marine biologist Richard W. Grigg of the University of Hawaii in Honolulu.

The Hawaiian Islands and the nearby Emperor Seamounts—sunken former islands—form a chain of volcanic islands. They were created when the *tectonic plate* (a section of the earth's crust and the upper part of the underlying layer, called the mantle) on which the Pacific Ocean sits passed over a *hot spot*, a fixed area of molten rock welling up from the earth's mantle. Because the Pacific Plate was—and still is—moving in a northwesterly direction, the islands and seamounts are older the farther they are from the island of Hawaii, which currently sits over the hot spot. The northwesternmost seamount is about 68 million to 70 million years old. The islands and seamounts, therefore, provide a natural laboratory for studying the evolutionary and ecological changes that have taken place in the island chain during that time.

For his research, Grigg examined the fossil record of reef corals and other organisms along the Hawaiian chain. He found that seamounts farthest to the northwest, which are therefore oldest, lack fossil reef corals even though these former islands originally were created in a subtropical environment favorable to the existence of corals. In fact, fossilized reef corals first appear on the Koko and Yuryaku seamounts in sedi-

A paleontologist holds dinosaur eggs containing embryo skeletons found in Montana. A model of an embryo (inset) is based on X-ray studies of the eggs.

ments dating from about 34 million years ago. Fossil reef corals are found on all the younger seamounts and the Hawaiian Islands.

Grigg theorized that the older seamounts lack fossil coral reefs because the currents in the Pacific Ocean were relatively weak from about 70 million to 34 million years ago. As a result, free-floating coral larvae from reefs in the Indian and Western Pacific oceans that later colonized the younger islands in the Hawaiian chain were not then being carried to the newly formed volcanic islands. Later, the movement of the Pacific Plate carried the islands into water too far north and too cold to support the growth of coral reefs. Grigg's findings support previous research suggesting that a major change in the pattern of currents in the Pacific occurred about 30 million years ago.

Mistaken identity. A previously unknown type of dinosaur was identified in 1988 from fossils that were mislabeled after they were found more than 60 years ago. Paleontologist Robert T. Bakker of the University of Colorado in Boulder reported in April that a fossil dinosaur skull discovered in Montana in the early 1940's was really that of a pygmy tyrannosaur named *nanotyrannus*. A smaller version of tyrannosaurus rex, nanotyrannus was 17 feet (5 meters) long and weighed 1,000 pounds (450 kilograms). The skull was previously believed to be that of a flesh-eating dinosaur called a *gorgosaur*.   Carlton E. Brett

In *World Book*, see Coral; Dinosaur; Paleontology.

Panama. General Manuel Antonio Noriega Morena, commander of the Panamanian Defense Forces, was indicted on Feb. 5, 1988, by grand juries in Miami and Tampa, Fla., on charges of drug trafficking. The indictments led to a bizarre stand-off in United States-Panama relations.

On February 25, Panama's titular president, Eric Arturo Delvalle, sought to remove Noriega, but Delvalle was himself deposed, forced into exile, and replaced by Manuel Solís Palma, who was backed by Noriega. In reaction, the Administration of U.S. President Ronald Reagan on March 2 froze $50 million in Panamanian funds held by U.S. banks in an effort to oust Noriega.

For several weeks, Panama reeled under the impact of U.S. government efforts to shut down the country's economy. With currency in short supply, paydays for Panamanian workers and soldiers were delayed. Panamanians took to the streets to protest Noriega's continued rule, but a general strike had limited success. Panamanian affiliates of U.S. companies were finally forced to ignore U.S. government injunctions against bringing in more money to meet their payrolls and continue operations.

Resourceful. Noriega proved more resourceful and resilient than U.S. policymakers had expected. He retained the loyalty of the army even in the face of mounting accusations concerning his past involvement in drug trafficking. These included the testimony at

hearings before the U.S. Congress that Noriega had a personal bank account ranging from $20 million to $25 million. Deposits were reportedly made via an extensive money-laundering network that used banks in Tampa, New York City, Luxembourg, England, and Uruguay and phony corporations in the Bahamas.

By the end of 1988, even Panamanians who ardently hoped for Noriega's departure were convinced that the United States would be unable to force his resignation. Some Panamanians even rallied to Noriega's support.

Members of the U.S. Congress called for the renegotiation of the Panama Canal treaties, under which Panama will become the sole authority over the waterway in 1999. The congressional representatives argued that the Panamanian government could not be trusted to administer the canal. Americans remaining in the Canal Zone were reportedly subjected to increased harassment by Panamanian officials during the stand-off between the two governments.

Arias. On August 10, Arnulfo Arias Madrid died in Miami at 87 years of age. Arias was elected president of Panama three times and was ousted from power by Panama's military three times.   Nathan A. Haverstock

See also **Latin America** (Facts in brief table); **Noriega Morena, Manuel Antonio.** In *World Book*, see Panama.

Papua New Guinea. See Asia; Pacific Islands.
Paraguay. See Latin America.
Pennsylvania. See Philadelphia; State government.

Peru. Peruvian President Alan García Pérez imposed new austerity measures on Sept. 6, 1988—and still more belt-tightening on November 23—after a bitter debate within his own party, the American Popular Revolutionary Alliance. Citing a lack of cooperation with his policies, García Pérez reportedly offered to resign but was persuaded to remain in office until the end of his term in 1990.

The Peruvian economy was battered by inflation, which reached a record 1,700 per cent in 1988. And García Pérez's popularity plummeted in a September poll that showed only 16 per cent of Peruvians approved of his performance in office, compared with 96 per cent approval in August 1985.

When rumors spread of a possible military coup, both the defense minister and the head of the joint chiefs of staff denied such a possibility. But the military was reportedly concerned about the lack of progress in putting down an eight-year rebellion by the left wing guerrilla group Sendero Luminoso (Shining Path). In January 1988, the rebels called for an alliance of workers, peasants, and owners of small businesses, and reportedly began trying to organize urban workers. The group's leader, Abimael Guzmán Reynoso, emerged from hiding to give an interview to a left wing newspaper in July.   Nathan A. Haverstock

See also **Latin America** (Facts in brief table). In *World Book*, see **Peru.**
Pet. See Cat; Dog.

Petroleum and gas

Petroleum and gas. A last-minute compromise by Iran enabled the Organization of Petroleum Exporting Countries (OPEC) in November 1988 to reach a new oil production accord designed to halt the plunge in world oil prices and help the organization regain control over output. The pact was the first signed by all 13 members of the oil cartel since 1986.

The accord came only after Iran, under intense pressure from other OPEC members, agreed to allow Iraq an equal production quota. Iraq had refused to sign previous production agreements because its quota was lower than that of Iran, its opponent in a bitter war.

Most oil industry observers had believed prospects for a new accord were dim. OPEC members on June 14, 1988, had agreed to maintain the 1987 limit on their output of crude oil—a total of 16.6 million barrels per day (bpd)—and sell it for no less than $18 per barrel. But Iraq and the United Arab Emirates announced that they would exclude themselves from the agreement, and other OPEC members quickly disregarded their quotas. After a truce in the long war between Iran and Iraq went into effect on Aug. 20, 1988, Iraq began pumping even more oil to obtain the funds needed to rebuild its economy.

By October, OPEC members were producing more than 20 million bpd, and the price of some Persian Gulf oil had tumbled to less than $10 per barrel—the lowest level since 1986. Also by October 1988, Saudi Arabia was producing 6.5 million bpd, its highest level since 1982, in an attempt to push prices lower and force other OPEC members to honor their quotas.

Under the November agreement, Iran and Iraq may pump 2.6 million bpd each. As part of the compromise, however, that total was higher than Iran's previous quota of 2.4 million bpd. In addition, Iran retained its percentage share of OPEC's total output, set at 18.5 million bpd for the first half of 1989. The percentage shares of other OPEC members were reduced to compensate for the increase for Iran and Iraq. The agreement was expected to raise oil prices by $4 per barrel and cost consumers an additional $60 billion per year.

Texaco payouts. Texaco Incorporated on April 7 paid the Pennzoil Company $3 billion, settling a four-year dispute between the two oil firms. In 1985, a state court in Houston ordered Texaco to pay Pennzoil $10.53 billion for interfering with a merger between Pennzoil and the Getty Oil Company. But Texaco and Pennzoil agreed on the smaller settlement.

Texaco on Aug. 29, 1988, agreed to pay the Department of Energy (DOE) $1.25 billion to settle a complaint that it had overcharged customers for crude oil sold between 1973 and 1981, when government price controls were in effect.

Corporate news. Tenneco Incorporated on Oct. 10, 1988, announced that it had sold the assets of the Tenneco Oil Company, its oil and natural gas subsidiary, for $7.3 billion. Tenneco, the 10th largest United States oil firm, owned about 10 per cent of all U.S. crude oil and natural gas reserves. The two largest purchasers were the Chevron Corporation, which paid $2.57 billion for Tenneco's natural gas reserves in the Gulf of Mexico, and the Amoco Corporation, which paid $900 million for natural gas fields in the Rocky Mountain region. Tenneco, a large, diversified firm, said it would use the money from the sale to reduce its debt and concentrate on other business activities.

Sun Company Incorporated, a major petroleum refiner, said on July 5 that it would buy the smaller Atlantic Petroleum Corporation for $513 million. Atlantic owns or supplies about 1,000 gasoline service stations in the United States.

Oil reserve debate. A 1988 government reassessment of the amount of undiscovered crude oil and natural gas in the United States came under fire by the oil industry. The U.S. Geological Survey (USGS) in March issued preliminary estimates suggesting that domestic petroleum and gas reserves may be 40 per cent smaller than previously believed. The new estimates, based on actual drilling results, suggested that the United States has 33.4 billion barrels of undiscovered crude oil that could be recovered with conventional technology. In 1981, the USGS had estimated that the United States had 54.6 billion barrels of undiscovered crude oil. The latest USGS estimate of natural gas resources also fell by about 40 per cent, from 427 trillion cubic feet (12 trillion cubic meters) to 254 trillion cubic feet (7 trillion cubic meters).

An oil derrick rises above the surrounding buildings in Ivry, France, a few miles from the heart of Paris. Oil was discovered there in August.

Black smoke pours from the Piper Alpha oil platform in the North Sea off Scotland after an explosion and fire on July 6 that killed 167 people.

The American Gas Association, an industry group based in Arlington, Va., criticized the new estimates as unrealistically low. The association maintained that about 400 trillion cubic feet (11 trillion cubic meters) of natural gas remain to be discovered.

U.S. usage. The DOE on Aug. 8, 1988, estimated that the United States would use 17 million barrels of oil per day in 1988, the most since 1980. The DOE said the increase, representing about 310,000 bpd, was due to low world oil prices and strong economic conditions. Domestic oil production during the first eight months of 1988 averaged 9.9 million bpd. The United States imported an average of 6.9 million bpd of crude oil and petroleum products during that period. The DOE also predicted a continuing decline in domestic oil production during 1989 and increasing dependence on imported oil.

Oil & Gas Journal, a respected industry publication, reported on Feb. 29, 1988, that Alaska had overtaken Texas as the number-one oil-producing state. By that date, Alaskan oil production had reached 2.1 million bpd, compared with 2.06 million bpd in Texas.

Offshore drilling. The U.S. Department of the Interior on June 6 postponed a controversial plan to lease 1.1 million acres (445,000 hectares) of land off the northern California coast for offshore oil and gas drilling. Area residents had objected to the plan because they feared environmental damage resulting from oil spills. In support of the plan, oil industry groups cited a national need for the estimated 790 million barrels of oil and 1.5 trillion cubic feet (42 billion cubic meters) of natural gas in the region.

President Ronald Reagan on August 23 signed legislation that repealed the windfall profits tax on domestic oil. The tax, which went into effect in 1980, was intended to recover some of the profits oil companies made after the government eliminated price controls on domestic oil. The tax raised about $77.3 billion. Government officials predicted the repeal would encourage additional production of domestic oil.

Canadian energy projects. The Canadian government on July 18, 1988, announced that it would provide up to $2.23 billion in grants and loan guarantees to develop the Hibernia oil field, about 200 miles (320 kilometers) off the eastern coast of Newfoundland. The field, believed to contain up to 650 million barrels of oil, will be developed by a group of five oil companies headed by Mobil Oil Canada Limited. It will be Canada's largest and most expensive energy project.

Canada on September 25 agreed to help another group of oil companies finance a $3.27-billion project to extract crude oil from oil sands in northern Alberta, about 300 miles (480 kilometers) northeast of Edmonton. The project, headed by Imperial Oil Limited of Toronto, Ont., was expected to produce about 77,000 bpd by the mid-1990's.

Platform disaster. An explosion and fire on July 6, 1988, destroyed Occidental Petroleum Corporation's

409

Philadelphia

Piper Alpha oil platform in the North Sea, 120 miles (190 kilometers) northeast of Aberdeen, Scotland, killing 167 people. It was the worst oil rig accident in the North Sea since drilling began there in 1968. The accident forced the closing of six other oil rigs that were connected to Piper Alpha by transmission lines, and it reduced Great Britain's oil production by 300,000 bpd.

Tallest platform. Contractors on June 1, 1988, lowered the world's tallest offshore oil drilling platform onto the floor of the Gulf of Mexico, about 150 miles (240 kilometers) south of New Orleans. The platform, named Bullwinkle, stands 1,615 feet (492 meters) high. Shell Offshore, Incorporated, a part of the Royal Dutch/Shell Group, will use the platform in a $500-million project to develop new offshore oil and natural gas wells.

Soviet records. The Soviet Union established world records for both crude oil and natural gas production in 1987, *Oil & Gas Journal* reported on Feb. 15, 1988. Soviet oil production averaged 12.48 million bpd, and gas production totaled 25.7 trillion cubic feet (728 billion cubic meters).

Parisian oil strike. Société Nationale Elf Aquitaine, the French oil company, on August 29 announced an oil strike in a suburb of Paris. Elf, the world's 11th largest oil company, discovered oil while drilling in Ivry.   Michael Woods

In *World Book*, see **Gas; Petroleum**.

Philadelphia. Using a city regulation that empowers officials to seal houses they declare "public nuisances," Philadelphia Mayor W. Wilson Goode on July 25, 1988, began a campaign against *crack*, a concentrated, smokable form of cocaine. Goode moved to close down the city's "crack houses"—buildings and single-family dwellings, most of them abandoned, where drug dealers were selling crack and other narcotics. City authorities had pinpointed some 500 addresses that were being used as crack houses. Ten Pennsylvania State Police officers were dispatched to Philadelphia to work with city police in rooting out the drug operations. In some houses, police seized hundreds of vials of crack.

The mayor took the action after two children—innocent bystanders in clashes between suspected members of drug rings—were struck down by bullets. On July 12, 6-year-old Ralph Brooks, Jr., was partially paralyzed by a stray bullet; six days later, Marcus Yates, 5, was killed in a drug-related shoot-out at a candy store.

On June 10, a new police commissioner, Willie L. Williams, was sworn in. Williams, 44, who is the first black police commissioner in Philadelphia's history, said that tackling the city's drug business and ending drug-related violence would be his highest priority.

Union transition. Earl Stout, president of Philadelphia's District Council 33 of the American Federation of State, County and Municipal Employees (AFSCME) since 1974, was defeated in a bid for reelection on May 10, 1988. After a bitter campaign, the members of the city workers' union voted 7,428 to 5,756 to elect James Sutton, head of the sanitation workers' local, as their new president.

Stout, one of the city's most influential labor leaders, had won large wage increases and strong benefits packages for union members over the years. But he had been formally reprimanded three times by national officials of AFSCME for violations of the union's bylaws. Sutton campaigned on the issue of restoring accountability to the union.

Human rights concert. About 75,000 people converged on John F. Kennedy Stadium on September 19 for a seven-hour rock concert sponsored by Amnesty International, the London-based human-rights organization.

The concert was part of a tour to promote Amnesty International's work on behalf of torture victims and political prisoners and to commemorate the 40th anniversary of the United Nations Universal Declaration of Human Rights. Philadelphia was the only East Coast stop on the six-week, 35,000-mile (56,000-kilometer) tour, which featured rock stars Bruce Springsteen and Peter Gabriel, among others.

Convention center. Land was cleared during the year for a proposed convention center to be constructed in the heart of Center City, Philadelphia's downtown area, even though several government bodies had not yet agreed to fund the project. The Philadelphia City Council, in particular, was studying different aspects of the proposal before considering a bond issue of more than $215 million to pay for the center's construction.

From hearings and reports, it was clear that most City Council members supported the project. Some of them, however, said they would insist that a maximum be placed on construction costs and that the project not endanger the Reading Terminal Market, a huge, nearly century-old collection of food stalls and restaurants in the middle of the proposed construction area.

Corrupt judges. Twelve Philadelphia judges resigned or were removed from office in 1988 by the Pennsylvania Supreme Court. The purge resulted from Federal Bureau of Investigation charges in 1987 that the judges had accepted cash gifts from the city's roofers union.

Nicodemo (Little Nicky) Scarfo, the reputed leader of organized crime in Philadelphia, had also been in league with the roofers union. Sentenced in 1987 to 14 years in prison and fined $150,000 for an extortion attempt, Scarfo was convicted of murder and conspiracy on Nov. 19, 1988, in Philadelphia along with 16 associates. They were found guilty of plotting 13 murders and carrying out 9, extorting money from drug dealers, and running gambling and loan-sharking rackets.   Howard S. Shapiro

See also **City**. In *World Book*, see **Philadelphia**.

Philippines. President Corazon Aquino voiced hopes for an end to the 20-year-old Communist guerrilla movement in her state-of-the-nation address on July 25, 1988, saying that 1988 "may be remembered as the year the insurgency was broken." Her claim was partly based on the February and March captures of eight leaders of the Communists' New People's Army (NPA), though on November 12 one of them, the NPA commander, escaped from army custody. The government also seized computer disks belonging to the Communists that listed the names of guerrillas and described procedures for raising money abroad, buying foreign weapons, and training recruits.

The military did not share Aquino's optimism, however. A report prepared by the armed forces in May said that, overall, the guerrillas had taken the initiative in major engagements. Soldiers also complained that their equipment was inadequate.

On January 14, Defense Minister Rafael Ileto resigned. Ileto said that he had taken the appointment 14 months earlier after the Communist insurgency had become alarmingly powerful because the Aquino government had not addressed the needs of the people. He said that he resigned because he had been unable to reorganize the armed forces due to "divisive elements and controversial issues." General Fidel V. Ramos, the armed forces chief of staff, replaced Ileto as defense minister on January 21.

Elections. Candidates supported by Aquino won a majority of some 16,000 provincial and municipal posts filled in elections on January 18. The elections, the first free local elections held since 1971, were considered another step toward restoring democracy. They were marred by campaign violence, however, with about 100 people killed.

Continuing charges of corruption. Vice President Salvador Laurel, who broke politically with Aquino in 1987 though he retained his government post, criticized Aquino in an open letter published on August 13. He charged that the Philippines had gone "from bad to worse" during her presidency, citing such problems as government corruption, difficulty maintaining law and order, and the Communist insurgency. Laurel and former Defense Minister Juan Ponce Enrile on August 27 launched a new political party, the Union for National Action.

Although their party won little support, the public increasingly criticized Aquino for failing to reduce the corruption that seemed firmly rooted in the Philippine government. The Chamber of Commerce and Industry estimated that about one-third of the nation's revenue for the year had been lost due to corruption and inefficiency. Even the chairman of the Presidential Commission on Good Government was forced to resign on July 19 after being accused of "ineptness, incompetence, and corruption."

Marcos indictment. Former President Ferdinand E. Marcos and his wife, Imelda, were indicted in New York City on October 21 on charges of stealing more

Former Philippine first lady Imelda Marcos arrives at a federal court in New York City on October 31 to answer charges of embezzlement and racketeering.

Physics

than $100 million in Philippine government funds to invest in the United States, hiding their U.S. assets, and obstructing U.S. justice. Marcos claimed that the allegations could not be proved. His associates had earlier denied well-publicized reports that Marcos offered in July to return $5 billion to the Philippines if allowed to return there from exile in Hawaii.

Other developments. On October 17, the Philippines and the United States signed an agreement allowing the United States to continue using its military bases in the Philippines until 1991. In return, the United States will give the Philippines $962 million in military and economic aid. The agreement was controversial in the Philippines, which had requested $2.4-billion in aid.

The economy grew by more than 6 per cent in 1988 as business people expressed their confidence in the nation's stability by increasing the level of investment. The World Bank, an international lending organization affiliated with the United Nations, found that about 30 million of the country's 60 million people lived in "absolute poverty," however, and said that the situation of the poor was worsening. The bank emphasized the importance of reducing the growth of the population, which could reach 100 million in 30 years. Family planning is controversial in the predominantly Roman Catholic nation.   Henry S. Bradsher

See also **Asia** (Facts in brief table). In *World Book*, see **Philippines.**

Physics made big news in 1988 with the announcement of the site for the proposed Superconducting Super Collider (SSC), a particle accelerator that will be the largest scientific instrument ever built; and with increases in the temperature at which materials *superconduct* (conduct electricity without resistance). Also in 1988, a modified particle accelerator failed to operate as planned.

SSC site. United States Secretary of Energy John S. Herrington announced on November 10 that the SSC will be built in Texas. Plans call for the machine to be housed in an oval tunnel 53 miles (85 kilometers) in circumference, at a cost of about $4.4 billion. The SSC is to accelerate two beams of protons to nearly the speed of light (186,282 miles [299,792 kilometers] per second) and to a combined energy of 40 trillion electron volts. (One electron volt is the amount of energy an electron gains when it moves across an electric field of 1 volt.)

Some 10,000 superconducting electromagnets will steer the proton beams around the tunnel and direct the beams into head-on collisions. Physicists expect the collisions to create subatomic particles never before observed, enabling researchers to probe more deeply into the interior of the atom. Texas was chosen in a competition among 25 states, which proposed 43 sites for the SSC.

Superconductivity gain. Only certain materials superconduct, and they do so only when cooled to

Pouring nitrogen on an experimental motor chills certain parts so that they become superconducting, causing a magnetic action that rotates the motor.

extremely low temperatures. The temperature at which a given material becomes capable of superconducting is that material's *critical temperature.*

Superconductivity has been of limited commercial value because, for most potential applications, the cost of cooling superconductors to their critical temperature exceeds the savings resulting from the loss of electrical resistance.

A material discovered in 1986 led to research that may soon sharply increase the value of superconductivity. The discovery of this material raised the record high critical temperature from −418°F. (−250°C), where it had remained since 1973, to −406°F. (−243°C). Physicists suspected that similar materials might have even higher critical temperatures, so a worldwide frenzy of research began. By the end of 1987, the record high critical temperature had reached −283°F. (−175°C).

In February 1988, physicists Allen M. Hermann and Zhengzhi Z. Sheng of the University of Arkansas in Fayetteville reported that a compound of calcium, barium, thallium, copper, and oxygen became superconducting at a temperature above −279°F. (−173°C). In March, physicist Paul M. Grant, chemist Edward M. Engler, and their colleagues at International Business Machines Corporation (IBM) Almaden Research Center in San Jose announced that they had varied the Arkansas researchers' formula slightly and pushed the critical temperature up to −234°F. (−148°C). The advances achieved in 1988 moved superconductivity closer to such applications as generating, transmitting, and storing electric power; and even magnetically levitating trains.

The accelerator that failed to operate as expected was the Stanford Linear Collider (SLC) in California. The SLC was the first accelerator to produce head-on collisions between two beams that pass through each other only once.

United States physicists had spent $115 million in a crash program to modify the SLC to produce beams of this type. The previous version produced only one beam.

The researchers' goal was to collide the two beams to make large numbers of *Z particles*—subatomic objects that were numerous for an instant after the *big bang*, the explosion in which the universe was born some 10 billion to 20 billion years ago. The SLC scientists proved that the new accelerator created beams of Z particles, but these beams did not last long enough to enable the scientists to do the experiments they had planned.

The researchers had hoped to beat a European team that is spending $1 billion to build a completely new accelerator to produce Z particles. The delays at the Stanford collider considerably diminished hopes of a U.S. victory.   Paul Raeburn

In *World Book*, see **Particle accelerator; Physics; Superconductivity.**

Poetry. Major poets both within and outside the United States published collections of previous work in 1988. The leading American collection was *New and Collected Poems* by Richard Wilbur, U.S. poet laureate in 1987 and 1988. The book includes the full text of Wilbur's six previous collections, 27 new poems, and the text of the cantata "On Freedom's Ground," written in collaboration with composer William Schuman to honor the Statue of Liberty. James Schuyler's *Selected Poems* includes poems of short lines as well as longer pieces in a more conversational style; most document the poet's experiences of urban life in New York City. And in *Poems, 1963-1983*, C. K. Williams compiled poems he wrote before his award-winning *Flesh and Blood*.

British poet Philip Larkin's *Collected Poems* brings together the works of that acclaimed poet, who died in 1985. Expatriate Polish poet and 1980 Nobel laureate Czeslaw Milosz, whose stark, emblematic poems cover both personal and political themes, brought out *The Collected Poems, 1931-1987*.

New works. Major poets with new books in 1988 included W. S. Merwin, whose *The Rain in the Trees* underscores the irony that civilization is often at odds with art. For James Merrill, the irony lies with the contradictions in civilization itself; his new book, *The Inner Room*, highlights the shortcomings of modern life in precise, witty rhyme. John Hollander, another poet known for technical mastery, brought out *Harp*

Lake, a collection of poems on topics ranging from the meaning of Jerusalem to a "painting" in words. New volumes by other established poets included *In Other Words: New Poems* by May Swenson, *The West Door* by Alfred Corn, *Shades* by Heather McHugh, and *Streamers* by Sandra McPherson.

Single volumes by two Nobel laureates appeared in 1988. Joseph Brodsky, a Soviet-born dissident who is now a U.S. citizen, presented new poems as well as his translations of his earlier work in *To Urania*. Nigerian poet Wole Soyinka used images from both African and Western myth, history, and literature to express political themes in *Mandela's Earth and Other Poems*.

Books by emerging poets included the five winners of the National Poetry Series open competition: *The Good Thief* by Marie Howe, *The Singing Underneath* by Jeffrey Harrison, *The Hand of God and a Few Bright Flowers* by William Olsen, *A Guide to Forgetting* by Jeffrey Skinner, and *New Math* by Cole Swenson. Another noteworthy first book was *Torque* by David Rivard, winner of the Agnes Lynch Starrett poetry prize.

Nemerov named. In May 1988, the Library of Congress appointed Howard Nemerov the third poet laureate of the United States. Nemerov—a poet, essayist, novelist, and critic as well as a professor of English at Washington University in St. Louis, Mo.—replaced Wilbur in September.   Harte V. Weiner

In *World Book*, see **Poetry.**

Poland suffered in 1988 from internal disorders that had been common since December 1981, when the government suppressed the independent labor union Solidarity. Strikes, government threats, the use of troops, arrests, and a state of near-total emergency in major industrial cities racked Poland from April to September 1988.

During the year's first major wave of labor unrest, strikers occupied the Lenin steel mill in Nowa Huta from April 26 to May 5 and the Lenin shipyard in Gdańsk, the birthplace of Solidarity, from May 2 to 10. A second wave of strikes began on August 16 at Poland's largest coal mine. The strike spread to other miners, to dockworkers in Szczecin, to Lenin shipyard workers, and to other groups. Those strikes ended between September 1 and 3 when the strikers heeded a call by Solidarity leader Lech Walesa to return to work. Despite all the turmoil, the Communist regime managed to avoid a confrontation with Solidarity—which had been declared illegal in 1982—and other opposition groups.

New prime minister. To relieve the tremendous political and social stresses that had built up throughout the country, the regime in mid-September 1988 dismissed Council of Ministers Chairman (prime minister) Zbigniew Messner and his entire Cabinet, and promised to hold talks with opposition groups.

Mieczyslaw Rakowski succeeded Messner as prime minister. Rakowski had been the government's chief

Lech Walesa, leader of the outlawed Polish labor union Solidarity, addresses strikers in May at the Lenin shipyard in Gdańsk, Poland.

negotiator with Solidarity in 1981, when the union was legal, but strongly supported the union's suppression in December of that year.

Rakowski had wanted to bring non-Communists into his government and offered portfolios to four prominent independents. They declined, however.

On December 23, the head of the Polish regime, Communist Party First Secretary and President Wojciech Jaruzelski, made sweeping changes in the party's ruling Politburo. The changes replaced a number of veterans and hard-liners with younger moderates.

Walesa broadcasts views. On November 30, Walesa took part in an unprecedented, 42-minute debate broadcast live on Poland's state-run television network. During the debate, Walesa demanded that the Polish government legalize Solidarity. "I am going to fight for Solidarity because Poland needs Solidarity," he said. "Solidarity in misery. Solidarity in work. Solidarity in uplifting the country."

Gorbachev praises, prods. During a visit to Warsaw in July 1988, Soviet leader Mikhail S. Gorbachev praised Jaruzelski's leadership. Gorbachev's references to Poland's reform efforts, however, were somewhat restrained, perhaps because of remarks made by Jaruzelski in an interview in the Soviet magazine *New Times* just before Gorbachev's visit. In the interview, Jaruzelski expressed what Gorbachev may have interpreted as an excessive reliance on the Soviet Union to support the Polish government.

With the Solidarity experience still uppermost in mind, Poland's leaders were concerned with the unpredictability of reform. Twice during his visit to Poland, however, Gorbachev told the Poles not to "miss the train." He clearly perceived the force of the mood for change in Poland.

Church and state. The government sought the aid of the Roman Catholic Church increasingly throughout 1988 to help ease tensions. Jaruzelski met with Poland's primate, Jozef Cardinal Glemp, on April 12, and after that there were continuing contacts between government officials and bishops and lay Catholic intellectuals.

The economy. The government promised on August 31 to develop a program that would pump $1-billion worth of consumer goods into the market to boost supplies through the winter, while reducing inflation from 70 to 50 per cent by the end of 1988. On September 14, however, a parliamentary commission on reform reported that there could be no economic improvement "without deep restructuring" of the political system to bring "other forces" into government. The sequel to this report was the resignation of Messner and his Cabinet. On December 21, Poland's parliament approved bills to encourage private ownership and foreign investment.   Eric Bourne

See also **Europe** (Facts in brief table). In *World Book*, see **Poland**.

Pollution. See Environmental pollution.

Popular music. Sales rose for both compact discs (CD's) and CD players in 1988, and record companies began to phase out traditional vinyl albums after sales figures showed that most buyers preferred CD's or cassettes. Technological innovations included 3-inch (7.5-centimeter) CD's, which feature a shorter format suitable for single-song releases and mini-albums, and a pocket-sized player for the 3-inch discs. Meanwhile, the industry continued its legal battle to keep consumers from using digital audio tape to duplicate copyrighted music.

Humanitarian efforts. Musicians turned their attention to a broad range of causes in 1988. To promote human rights, Bruce Springsteen headlined the all-star international Human Rights Now! tour, organized by Amnesty International, in the fall. Dire Straits and Stevie Wonder were among 70 performers who raised $4 million for the antiapartheid movement and South African charities at a 10-hour June concert in London marking the 70th birthday of South African political prisoner Nelson Mandela.

Working to aid the homeless were Amy Grant, who toured for Habitat for Humanity International, and jazz artists Herbie Hancock and Chick Corea, who toured for the National Coalition for the Homeless. Yoko Ono, Country Joe McDonald, Richie Havens, and other artists took part in a video documentary, *The Peace Tape*, which was sent free to schools and colleges as an educational tool. And on September 24,

Bruce Springsteen, Tracy Chapman, Senegal's Youssou N'Dour, Sting, an unidentified backup singer, and Peter Gabriel sing in London for Amnesty International.

the Grateful Dead played in New York City to benefit efforts to preserve rain forests.

The Soviet Union's policy of open cultural exchange continued to involve popular musicians in 1988 as Western artists performed in the Soviet Union. In March, Great Britain's David Bowie and Ireland's U2 joined other artists for three concerts in Moscow to benefit the United Nations antidrug campaign. Country musician Roy Clark toured the Soviet Union in November; to help defray the $200,000 cost, Clark collected donations from fans via a network of country-music radio stations in the United States.

The Soviet state record label Melodia issued a double album, *Greenpeace-Breakthrough*, recorded by Western musicians to benefit Greenpeace and other environmental organizations. Saxophonist Paul Winter released *Earthbeat*, billed as the first album of original music created in a Soviet-American collaboration, and toured in the United States with the Dimitri Pokrovsky Singers, a Soviet vocal group.

Surprises and firsts. The year 1988 saw unexpected successes in several styles of music. Jazz vocalist Bobby McFerrin's "Don't Worry, Be Happy" became the first *a cappella* (voice only) song ever to reach the top of *Billboard* magazine's chart of Hot 100 singles. (The *Billboard* charts, an industry standard, rank records according to sales and radio airplay.)

George Michael's dance-oriented *Faith* became the first album by a white solo artist to top the black

albums chart. *Dirty Dancing*, a soundtrack album of oldies and new songs by relatively obscure artists, held the number-one spot on the pop albums chart for 18 weeks. A debut album of sharp social comment by black folk singer Tracy Chapman also topped the pop albums chart. The mainstream rock group Huey Lewis and the News issued an album of diverse styles from around the world.

A debut album by the Traveling Wilburys—an impromptu group formed by top stars Bob Dylan, George Harrison, Jeff Lynne, Roy Orbison, and Tom Petty—jumped to the number-23 spot on the pop albums chart in its second week of release in November. The album was at the number-8 spot when Orbison died of an apparent heart attack on December 6.

Two teen-agers made chart history. Tiffany, age 16, was the first teen-aged girl to have a number-one hit album—*Tiffany*. And with "Foolish Beat," 17-year-old Debbie Gibson was the youngest artist ever to write, produce, and perform a number-one single.

Mainstream rock. U2 received 10 awards, including Artist of the Year, in *Rolling Stone* magazine's readers' poll in March. Among the many veteran artists with comeback albums were Daryl Hall and John Oates, Elton John, Joni Mitchell, Boz Scaggs, Patti Smith, sometime Beach Boy Brian Wilson, and the group Crosby, Stills, Nash, and Young. Heavy-metal music remained strong; in July, for the first time, the top three spots on the pop albums chart

There's No Composer Like This Composer

Irving Berlin, who celebrated his 100th birthday on May 11, 1988, once said, "I don't deserve credit for attaining old age just because I've been lucky enough not to get knocked off by a car or a disease." The credit Americans give Berlin for being one of their favorite popular composers, however, is definitely well deserved, and the songwriter's birthday was marked by worldwide tributes. The most elaborate was a celebration in New York City's Carnegie Hall, where Frank Sinatra sang Berlin's "Always," Tommy Tune tap-danced to the composer's "Puttin' on the Ritz," and Willie Nelson sang his version of Berlin's "Blue Skies."

Other performers at the tribute included Ray Charles, Leonard Bernstein, Shirley MacLaine, and the U.S. Army chorus—an eclectic mix that was itself a testament to the diversity of Berlin's music. Indeed, his songs are so varied that many people fail to realize that they are the work of one person. The composer of sophisticated dance numbers like "Cheek to Cheek" and "Let's Face the Music and Dance" somehow managed to pen such love songs as "All Alone" and "How Deep Is the Ocean?" and the classics "White Christmas" and "God Bless America."

A master composer despite his lack of a formal musical education, Irving Berlin plays his favorite piano keys—the black ones—in the 1930's.

What Berlin's songs have in common is their ability, to an unrivaled degree, to express what Americans feel and believe. Berlin's feelings about love, country, holidays, music, dancing, or show business may be his alone, yet through Berlin's songwriting skill, they are transformed to reflect the feelings of an entire generation. His songs have been a part of our lives for many years. Composer Jerome Kern described Berlin's knack for touching generations of Americans by saying that Berlin "absorbs the vibrations emanating from the people, manners, and life of his time and, in return, gives these impressions back to the world—simplified, clarified, glorified. In short, Irving Berlin has no *place* in American music. He *is* American music."

Yet Berlin's success was unlikely. Born Israel Baline in Temun, Russia, Berlin immigrated to the United States with his family when he was 4 years old and settled on New York City's Lower East Side. After his father died four years later, Berlin quit school to help support his family.

With only two years of schooling and no formal musical training, he began his songwriting career as a lyricist and then taught himself how to play the piano. He never learned to compose in any key except F sharp, but he eventually had a piano made with a clutchlike device that allowed him to change from key to key.

Berlin's first sale, "Marie from Sunny Italy" —written when he was a singing waiter—netted all of 37 cents. When he was 23, Berlin wrote "Alexander's Ragtime Band," which started the ragtime craze and made Berlin a celebrity. A few years later he wrote another hit destined for pop-music immortality, "A Pretty Girl Is Like a Melody."

During the 1920's, Berlin divided his time between writing songs for musical revues and for Tin Pan Alley, as the music-publishing industry was called. His first major film score was for *Top Hat* in 1935, and he went on to write scores for 13 other films, including *Holiday Inn* (1942) and *Easter Parade* (1948). Berlin also created scores for 21 Broadway shows. *Annie Get Your Gun* (1946)—which produced the classics "Anything You Can Do," "I Got the Sun in the Morning," "Doin' What Comes Naturally," and "There's No Business Like Show Business"—was his most successful Broadway show, and *Mr. President* (1962) was his last.

In all, Berlin wrote almost 1,000 songs, some 650 of which were published. He certainly was never one to take his success for granted. "It's harder for me to write songs now than it is for others," he once told a magazine interviewer. "It's difficult to top my previous efforts." Irving Berlin made that statement in 1913, when he was only 25.   Stanley Green

"Teenypoppers" Tiffany, *left,* 16, and Debbie Gibson, *right,* 17, set records in 1988 as the youngest females to top the pop charts.

were held by metal bands—Def Leppard, Guns N' Roses, and Van Halen. Heavy-metal groups AC/DC, Bon Jovi, and Metallica also released new albums.

Music video. MTV, the music-oriented cable-television network, began experimenting in 1988 with more varied programming to retain viewers who had grown bored with its original nonstop-music-video format. At the same time, home videos grew in popularity. Among the music-oriented movies, concerts, and documentaries released on video in 1988 were *Elvis '56; The Real Buddy Holly Story; Buried Alive* (a movie about the Sex Pistols); *Monterey Pop* (1967); and *Ready Steady Go! The Sounds of Motown* (1965). Music videos by Def Leppard, Peter Gabriel, the Grateful Dead, Madonna, Metallica, George Michael, and Sting topped the charts for music video sales. An Australian group, INXS, was the big winner at the MTV Music Video Awards in September, earning five awards.

Black music. For two weeks in April, 7 of the top 10 slots on the pop-singles chart were held by black acts: Terence Trent D'Arby, Whitney Houston, Michael Jackson, the Jets, Billy Ocean, Pebbles, and Jody Watley or Keith Sweat. With "Where Do Broken Hearts Go," Houston set a record of seven consecutive number-one singles. Jackson's 1987 album *Bad* became the first pop album to generate five number-one singles. Among the other black artists with top albums were Bobby Brown, EPMD, Gladys Knight and the Pips, Al B. Sure!, and Stevie Wonder.

Dance and rap. Major record labels began paying more attention to dance music following the 1987 pop-chart success of several acts—such as Exposé, Debbie Gibson, Taylor Dayne, and Stacey Q—that were first popular in dance clubs. A&M records introduced a new dance-oriented label, Vendetta. Hot dance artists of 1988 included Rick Astley, Blue Mercedes, and Information Society. Rap music, boosted by 1987 multiplatinum sales by the Beastie Boys and L. L. Cool J, moved further into the mainstream. Successful rap artists of 1988 included D. J. Jazzy Jeff and the Fresh Prince, Kool Moe Dee, Run-D.M.C., and Salt-N-Pepa.

Jazz. Several events brought attention to classic jazz artists in 1988. The Smithsonian Institution in Washington, D.C., acquired a massive collection of jazz great Duke Ellington's papers and recordings; MusicMasters label began releasing recordings from Yale University's Benny Goodman archive; and Clint Eastwood produced and directed *Bird,* a movie about legendary saxophonist Charlie Parker. Two record companies—A&M and EMI—introduced new jazz labels. Artists with top albums included Betty Carter, Ella Fitzgerald, Bobby McFerrin, Dianne Reeves, David Sanborn, Diane Schuur, and Kirk Whalum.

Country music. In June, Randy Travis' *Always & Forever* ended its record-setting 43 weeks in the number-one spot on the country album chart, and in August his new album, *Old 8 × 10,* began a run of 8

417

With his best-selling debut solo album, *Faith,* British rocker George Michael became the first white singer to top the black albums chart.

weeks in the number-one position. Hank Williams, Jr., won his second consecutive Entertainer of the Year award from the Country Music Association in October, and his album *Wild Streak* reached number one. Veteran performers Alabama, Reba McEntire, George Strait, Dwight Yoakum, and newcomers K. T. Oslin and Ricky Van Shelton also had top albums. In August, Willie Nelson's *Stardust* hit a record 10-year mark on the country albums chart.

Oldies. In April, The Nashville Network, a cable TV network, began a weekly oldies show called "Rock 'N' Roll Palace," hosted by legendary disc jockey Wolfman Jack. Multirecord anthologies featured the works of English guitarist Eric Clapton and music producer Phil Spector. At the Third Annual Rock and Roll Hall of Fame show, held on January 20 in New York City, inductees included the Beach Boys, the Beatles, Bob Dylan, the Drifters, and the Supremes.

Biographies. Albert Goldman's 1988 book *The Lives of John Lennon* sparked protests from Lennon's family and friends, who disputed the book's claims about Lennon's personal life. Audiences and critics were more receptive to a new movie, *Imagine: John Lennon.* Michael Jackson's autobiography, *Moonwalk,* and David Crosby's autobiography, *Long Time Gone,* also appeared in 1988.   Jerry M. Grigadean

See also **Awards and prizes** (Arts awards). In *World Book,* see **Country music; Jazz; Popular music; Rock music.**

Population. The world's population has grown more rapidly in the late 1980's than was projected, the Population Reference Bureau in Washington, D.C., announced in 1988. The United Nations had projected earlier in the decade that the world's population would increase each year by 1.6 per cent, but actual growth rates for the late 1980's have averaged 1.7 per cent. With world population at more than 5 billion in 1988, the seemingly small difference in growth rate represents more than 5 million additional people per year. If growth continues at this rate, the world's population will double by 2028, several years earlier than had been projected.

Regional growth rates. The discrepancy between projected and actual growth rates may be due to higher than expected growth rates in the developing world. The overall growth rate for these nations was 2.1 per cent annually, indicating that their populations would double in 33 years. Two of the highest growth rates were reported in Kenya and the Gaza Strip (an area on the Mediterranean coast where Egypt and Israel meet). Populations in these areas were expected to double in only 17 years.

In industrialized nations, the overall growth rate was 0.6 per cent, a rate at which population doubles in 120 years. In several industrialized countries—including Austria, Denmark, East Germany, Hungary, and West Germany—the population did not increase at all, or even showed a decrease.

United States statistics. On Jan. 1, 1989, the U.S. population totaled approximately 247 million, but the growth rate for the country continued to be fairly low—0.9 per cent annually. For five consecutive years, the U.S. population growth rate was less than 1 per cent, the slowest growth rate for the nation since the 1930's. Since the early 1980's, an average of 3.8 million children have been born in the United States each year, and about 600,000 immigrants have arrived annually.

The low growth rate combined with the aging of the baby boom generation has produced the oldest citizenry in U.S. history. On July 1, 1987, the *median age* of U.S. citizens was 32.1 years, up 0.3 year from the year before, the U.S. Bureau of the Census announced in 1988. (There are as many people older than the median age as there are younger.) People aged 35 to 44 made up the most rapidly growing age group in the United States, followed by those aged 85 and older and then by those aged 75 to 84.

Life expectancy at birth throughout the world showed little change. Children born in the United States, Canada, and Australia were expected to live an average of 74, 76, and 75 years, respectively. Infants born in developing nations, however, had a much shorter expected life span. For example, life expectancy in Gambia was 35 years and in Sierra Leone, 34 years.   Jinger Hoop

See also *Census.* In *World Book,* see **Life expectancy; Population.**

Portugal. A 24-hour general strike called by Portugal's two main labor unions paralyzed much of the country on March 28, 1988. The unions were protesting labor legislation that Prime Minister Aníbal Cavaço Silva's center-right government presented to Parliament on March 3.

The legislation was one of two parts of a package of major reforms by which Cavaço Silva intended to end what he called the excesses of the Armed Forces Movement of 1974—a revolution in which left wing military officers overthrew a dictatorship that had ruled Portugal since 1926. Political confusion following the Armed Forces Movement led to labor and farm policies unlike those of any other Western nation, as well as a commitment to install a Western-style democracy in Portugal.

Labor reform. Portugal's workers have more protection against job loss than do employees in any other Western nation. An employer has little chance of dismissing a worker for reasons other than refusal to carry out orders; and even in cases of such refusal, the employer must do a large amount of complex legal paperwork.

Cavaço Silva's proposal would make it easier to dismiss workers and would permit employers to lay off workers for economic reasons. Parliament passed Cavaço Silva's labor legislation on April 15, but the Supreme Court of Portugal declared that key parts of the employment-reform measure were unconstitutional.

Farm reform. The other part of Cavaço Silva's reform package would end a system of agriculture established shortly after the 1974 revolution. At that time, workers seized land south of Lisbon and set up collective farms. Cavaço Silva's government said that these farms have failed because many of their managers were inexperienced in agriculture, and because of government neglect.

Portugal is scheduled to integrate its economy fully into the European Community (EC or Common Market) in 1992. Arlindo Marques Cunha, Portugal's state secretary for agriculture, maintained that the government must promote efficiency in agriculture to enable individual farmers and farm cooperatives in Portugal to compete effectively with their counterparts in other EC nations. Portugal's agricultural production has declined since the late 1970's.

United States cuts aid. Cavaço Silva told U.S. President Ronald Reagan in Washington, D.C., on February 24 that he was disappointed by cuts in United States military and economic aid. The United States exchanges aid for the right to use Lajes Air Base in the Azores, a group of islands about 800 miles (1,300 kilometers) west of Portugal. United States aid dropped from $208 million in 1985 to $117 million in 1988. Reagan asked the U.S. Congress for $163 million in aid to Portugal for 1989.   Kenneth Brown

See also **Europe** (Facts in brief table). In *World Book*, see **Portugal**.

Fire fighters battle an August 25 blaze that destroyed more than 40 businesses in the historic Chiado district of Lisbon, Portugal.

Postal Service, United States. Anthony M. Frank, 56, a savings and loan official from California, was sworn in as United States postmaster general on March 1, 1988. Frank, formerly the chief executive of San Francisco's First Nationwide Financial Corporation, became the fifth postmaster general in four years. He succeeded multimillionaire Preston R. Tisch, who returned to the family-owned Loews Corporation in New York City after directing the Postal Service since August 1986.

On April 3, 1988, barely a month after Frank took over, the Postal Service adopted long-planned rate increases averaging 16.4 per cent. The cost of a first-class stamp went up 13.6 per cent, from 22 cents to 25 cents. Rates for second-class mail—newspapers and magazines—were hiked by 18 per cent, and rates for third-class mail—for example, catalogs and advertising circulars—were boosted 25 per cent.

Mailers look for alternatives. *The Wall Street Journal* reported on June 27 that, for the first time, second-class and third-class mailers were exploring delivery systems that would by-pass the Postal Service. Among those seeking alternatives were two groups—the Direct Marketing Association and the National Association of Selective Distributors—whose members have long relied on third-class mailing privileges. Officials of those organizations acknowledged, however, that private delivery would not be practical for reaching homes in all parts of the United States.

Nonetheless, critics of the Postal Service contend that it has become an inefficient bureaucracy. One of those critics, James C. Miller III, director of the Office of Management and Budget, called the Postal Service a "monstrosity" and urged repeatedly in 1988 that it be *privatized*—transformed into a private corporation. Postmaster General Frank suggested that *privatization* might be a code word for busting the postal unions.

Service cutbacks. In March, window service at most post offices was reduced by half a day per week as a cost-cutting measure aimed at helping reduce the federal budget deficit. Normal window-service hours were restored on September 10.

Indictments. On October 6, two executives of Recognition Equipment, Incorporated, of Irving, Tex., were indicted on federal charges of conspiring to rig bidding on $400 million in contracts for automated mail-sorting equipment. Peter E. Voss, a vice chairman of the Postal Service's Board of Governors, pleaded guilty to related charges of steering postal contracts in 1986 and was sentenced to four years in prison.

Frank Cormier and Margot Cormier

In *World Book*, see **Post office; Postal Service, United States.**

President of the United States. See **Reagan, Ronald W.; United States, Government of the.** In the World Book Supplement section, see **Bush, George Herbert Walker.**

Prince Edward Island. In a nonbinding popular vote on Jan. 18, 1988, the residents of Canada's smallest province voted in favor of the construction of an 8.7-mile (14-kilometer) link to mainland Canada by a bridge or a tunnel. Historically, only boats and aircraft provided contact with the mainland. About 60 per cent of those voting supported the permanent link, arguing that it would bring more tourists to the largely agricultural province. Opponents claimed that a permanent crossing would destroy the island's pastoral character and eliminate the jobs of about 600 people who operate the ferry service with New Brunswick, Canada.

Premier Joseph A. Ghiz, head of the province's Liberal government, said that environmental assessments would be conducted before the province committed itself to the project, which is expected to take five years and cost up to $1 billion (Canadian dollars; $1 = U.S. 84 cents as of Dec. 31, 1988). In September, the federal government narrowed a field of seven proposals to three, all for bridges.

A ban on Prince Edward Island's mussels and clams, imposed in December 1987 after an outbreak of food poisoning, was gradually lifted in January and February 1988. On March 18, the federal government announced it would provide a $2-million loan to help shellfish producers and distributors recover from the disruption caused by the ban.   David M. L. Farr

In *World Book*, see **Prince Edward Island.**

Prison. Crowding remained the number-one problem plaguing United States prisons and jails in 1988 as inmate populations grew to record numbers. From January through June, the number of inmates in state and federal correctional institutions grew 4 per cent to 604,824, according to the Department of Justice's Bureau of Justice Statistics. The number of women in prison continued to grow faster than the number of men—6.7 and 3.9 per cent respectively. Since 1980, the female inmate population has increased 130 per cent to 30,834, while the number of male inmates has increased 81 per cent to 573,990.

As of Jan. 1, 1988, 32 correctional agencies were operating under court order because federal courts had found crowding or other conditions in violation of the Eighth Amendment to the U.S. Constitution, which forbids "cruel and unusual punishments." Of these, 27 agencies had population limits set by the courts.

To combat crowding, officials explored sentencing alternatives such as early release and house arrest. One house-arrest program came under scrutiny, however, when John Zaccaro, Jr., son of 1984 Democratic vice presidential candidate Geraldine A. Ferraro, served a house-arrest sentence in 1988 in Burlington, Vt., in a $1,500-a-month apartment paid for by his parents. Zaccaro was convicted in June of selling $25 worth of cocaine to an undercover police officer.

Furor over furloughs. Prisons became an issue in the 1988 presidential campaign when Republican

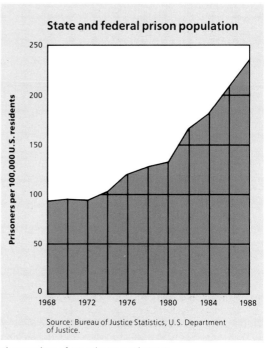

State and federal prison population

Prisoners per 100,000 U.S. residents

1968 1972 1976 1980 1984 1988

Source: Bureau of Justice Statistics, U.S. Department of Justice.

The number of Americans serving sentences of more than one year in state or federal prisons has skyrocketed since 1968.

nominee George Bush criticized Democratic candidate Michael S. Dukakis, governor of Massachusetts, about that state's furlough program. Bush cited the case of William Horton, Jr. (usually called Willie Horton), a convicted murderer who escaped while on weekend release from a Massachusetts prison in 1986 and later stabbed a man and raped a woman in Maryland. As of 1987, all 50 states, as well as the District of Columbia and the federal prison system, offered some sort of temporary release program; 36 of these allowed furloughs for prisoners serving life sentences. Massachusetts tightened its restrictions on furloughs in April 1988 following uproar over the Horton case.

Death penalty. An estimated 2,200 people were on death row in state prisons as of Dec. 31, 1988. Eleven inmates were executed during the year, bringing the total number of executions to 104 since the Supreme Court of the United States reinstated the death penalty in 1976.

AIDS. By October 1987, a total of 1,964 confirmed cases of AIDS (acquired immune deficiency syndrome) had been reported in U.S. prisons and in the largest jails. In August 1988, Philadelphia's correctional system became the fourth to distribute condoms to inmates as part of an AIDS prevention program. New York City, Mississippi, and Vermont also provide condoms to inmates.   Laura A. Ochipinti

In *World Book*, see **Prison.**

Prizes. See **Awards and prizes; Nobel Prizes.**

Protestantism. Protestant *evangelists*—people who seek to convert others—had a difficult year during 1988. One well-known evangelist in the news who had a good year, however, was Billy Graham. On April 17, Graham began a five-city preaching tour in China, where he received favorable notice. In June, Graham traveled to Moscow, where he preached in a Russian Orthodox cathedral as part of the celebrations surrounding the 1,000th anniversary of the introduction of Christianity to Russia. Graham attended along with leaders of the World Council of Churches—an organization of about 300 Protestant, Anglican, Old Catholic (Christians who have split away from the Roman Catholic Church), and Orthodox churches.

More scandals. Headlines on some other evangelists were less benign. Jim Bakker failed to regain control of the evangelistic and entertainment organization called PTL (Praise the Lord or People That Love) based in Fort Mill, S.C., a year after a series of scandals led to his resignation as head of the organization. He faced continuing court battles. On December 5, a federal grand jury indicted Bakker and Richard Dortch, a former top aide, on 24 counts of fraud. If convicted, both men face five years in prison and $250,000 fines on each count. On December 13, a U.S. bankruptcy judge ordered the sale of the PTL's assets—including the Heritage USA amusement park in Fort Mill and its television operation—to Canadian businessman Stephen R. Mernick for $65 million.

Another scandal rocked television evangelism on February 21 when Assemblies of God minister Jimmy Swaggart admitted to his congregation in Baton Rouge, La., that he had committed an unspecified "sin." Later news reports said it had involved sexual misconduct. On March 29, Assemblies of God leaders banned Swaggart from preaching for a year. He was stripped of his ministry on April 8 when he refused to comply with the ban. Later in the year, he began preaching as an independent minister.

In December, the Internal Revenue Service (IRS) confirmed that it was investigating 26 television evangelists. Although the IRS would not reveal the names of those being investigated, *The Washington Post* reported that they included Jerry Falwell, Pat Robertson, and Oral Roberts. The IRS said the investigations are to ensure that the ministries are following the rules for tax-exempt organizations. Those rules prevent excessive salaries and benefits for employees, donations for political activities, and the diversion of contributions for personal use.

Robertson bows out. On May 16, Robertson—who in 1987 told reporters not to call him a TV evangelist and who had been running for President in Republican primaries—withdrew from the race. Although he won some state caucuses, Robertson failed to produce the large number of votes he expected from his "invisible army" of supporters. He endorsed Republican candidate George Bush, who held on to the support of most conservative evangelical voters during the campaign. Robertson, who resigned as chairman of the Christian Broadcasting Network to run as a candidate, returned to the TV enterprise.

Jackson runs well. Jesse L. Jackson, a Baptist minister, lost his bid for the Democratic presidential nomination in 1988. Conservative black evangelicals did not agree with the Democratic Party's support of a woman's right to abortion, but most were strongly behind Jackson, who came in second to the eventual Democratic nominee, Michael S. Dukakis.

Stargazing. Some conservative evangelicals, who generally supported Ronald Reagan during his eight years as President of the United States, expressed disappointment when it was revealed in May 1988 that his wife, Nancy, was extremely interested in astrology. The first lady admitted using the advice of an astrologer to help arrange her husband's schedule. Many Protestants view astrology, which is the study of the alignment of stars and planets and their supposed influence on human affairs, as an unchristian practice.

Ed McAteer, a businessman who heads the Religious Roundtable in Memphis, Tenn., a group concerned about moral issues in the United States, spoke for many Protestants when he said he was "very, very disappointed" over the news and said that the President did not seem to have "a good grasp of Biblical truth." Still, most conservative Protestants continued to regard President Reagan with favor during his last year in office.

C. Kenneth Hall, of Butler, Pa., holds a press conference after being elected head of the Presbyterian Church (U.S.A.) in June in St. Louis, Mo.

Protests. Many conservative Protestants objected to the showing of the film *The Last Temptation of Christ*. The film, which opened in U.S. and Canadian theaters in August, portrays Jesus as dreaming of life as an ordinary human being. Many people found the movie blasphemous, and they organized boycotts against it.

Other militant Protestants stepped up efforts against legalized abortion. The most visible protests occurred in Atlanta, Ga., during and after the Democratic National Convention in July.

Fundamentalist control. In 1988, the fundamentalist faction of the Southern Baptist Convention (SBC), the largest Protestant group in the United States, continued—and, according to some, completed—its 10-year drive to seize control of the SBC. On June 14, at its annual meeting in San Antonio, the SBC elected by the narrow margin of 50.5 per cent to 48.2 per cent fundamentalist Jerry Vines of Jacksonville, Fla., as president.

The close vote indicated the extent of the conflict between the group's conservative fundamentalists, who insist on a strict literal interpretation of the Bible, and more moderate members. During the convention, fundamentalists gained control of all important SBC boards and bureaus.

Hot issues. The questions of abortion and sexuality fired evangelical groups into action in 1988. On May 2, at the general conference of the United Methodist

Church (UMC) in St. Louis, Mo., delegates moved to temper the church's liberal policies. Although their resolution criticizing abortion was milder than those of other Protestant groups, the UMC delegates stepped back from efforts to legitimize homosexual activities and declared that people who admit to being homosexual should not be ordained ministers.

More important, however, was the approval of a theological statement against *pluralism*—a policy that encourages a wide variety of interpretations of doctrines and practices. Opponents say pluralism goes against tradition and encourages ambiguity.

Liberal delegates also resolved to join their conservative colleagues in continuing efforts to stop the drop in membership. Since 1968, the UMC, the second largest Protestant group in the United States, has lost more than 1 million members.

Abortion was a bellwether issue at the 200th general assembly of the Presbyterian Church (U.S.A.), which met in June in St. Louis. Presbyterians Pro-Life, an antiabortion group, brought Mother Teresa, a Roman Catholic nun renowned for her work with the poor, to encourage delegates to take a stronger stand against abortion. The church, in general, supports a woman's right to abortion. The delegates ended up voting to reconsider the abortion policy.

Sexuality was the topic of heated debate in July at the general convention of the Episcopal Church in Detroit. In general, Episcopalians have a more lenient attitude toward homosexuals and abortion than other Protestant groups. But efforts to give official assent to more liberal attitudes toward sexual practices, such as by blessing homosexual marriages or endorsing premarital sexual relations, were voted down.

The United Church of Canada, meeting in Ottawa, Ont., in August, saw its conservative and liberal factions in conflict over the issue of homosexuality. On August 24, delegates passed a resolution to permit the ordination of practicing homosexuals as ministers. Conservatives who opposed the measure talked of breaking away from the church, but delegates worked to avoid a possible schism.

Role of women. Some 500 bishops, representing 70 million Anglicans and Episcopalians around the world, met at the Lambeth Conference in Canterbury, England, in August. The Lambeth Conference takes place every 10 years to set the tone for Anglican and Episcopal church life. Among the issues debated by the bishops was the question of what the ordination of women has done—and will do—to the church. On August 1, they agreed to accept the possible appointment of women bishops. On September 24, Barbara C. Harris, an Episcopal priest, was elected *suffragan* (assistant bishop) of Massachusetts. By Jan. 3, 1989, the required 60 dioceses had approved her election, ensuring her installation as the first woman Episcopal bishop.   Martin E. Marty

See also **Religion**. In *World Book*, see **Protestantism**.

Psychology. A simple psychological test may predict whether a person is more likely to develop cancer or heart disease or remain unaffected by these conditions, according to research described by Hans J. Eysenck, a psychologist at the University of London's Maudsley Hospital, at the August 1988 meeting of the American Psychological Association (APA) in Atlanta, Ga. According to Eysenck, if the test indicates that a person has a disease-prone personality, behavioral therapies designed to change the personality may help protect the person against cancer or heart disease. It may also lengthen the lives of people who already have these diseases.

Eysenck's report was based on research conducted by Ronald Grossarth-Maticek, a Yugoslav psychologist working in West Germany. In the early 1960's, Grossarth-Maticek began measuring the personality traits, smoking and drinking habits, and physical health of a large random sample of volunteers. As a result of these measurements, he divided the volunteers into four groups: Type 1 was classified as cancer-prone; type 2 was classified as heart-disease prone; and type 3 and type 4 as relatively healthy.

According to Grossarth-Maticek, the type 1 cancer-prone person is generally unassertive, overly patient, and tends to avoid conflict. The type 1 person also has feelings of hopelessness and is unable to express negative emotions. The type 2 heart-disease-prone person tends to be easily angered, hostile, and aggressive.

Grossarth-Maticek monitored the volunteers over a 20-year period to learn which people eventually died of cancer or heart disease and which lived a long and healthy life. Based on his description of type 1 personalities, he was able to predict—with a 50 per cent accuracy rate—which of the volunteers would die of cancer. His predictions of who would die of heart disease were nearly as good.

Some epidemiologists who studied Grossarth-Maticek's research found it seriously flawed. According to Eysenck, however, the results raised the question of whether some deaths due to disease can be prevented by changing people's personalities. In Grossarth-Maticek's latest research, which he conducted with Eysenck, he wanted to see if simple behavioral therapy methods, such as relaxation and hypnosis, could help teach type 1 and type 2 people to change the unhealthy aspects of their personality and avoid disease. The researchers took 100 volunteers with cancer-prone personalities and gave 50 of them behavior therapy. The therapy was designed to help them express their emotions more readily, cope with stress, and become more emotionally independent and self-reliant.

The other 50 volunteers received no therapy. When the researchers followed up on the 100 people 13 years later, 45 of the 50 volunteers who received therapy were still alive while only 19 of the 50 volunteers who received no therapy were alive. Similar results were achieved with heart-disease-prone people.

In another study reported by Eysenck, Grossarth-Maticek found that behavioral therapy appears to help people who have cancer live longer. Cancer patients who received such therapy survived an average of five years. Those who did not get therapy survived an average of only three years. According to Eysenck, this research may signal a new era in health care and disease prevention.

Attitude and the immune system. Psychological factors may also play a role in depressing the body's disease-fighting immune system. At the August APA meeting, psychologist Nancy T. Blaney of the University of Miami School of Medicine reported on a continuing five-year study of 100 men who tested positive for HIV (human immunodeficiency virus), which causes AIDS (acquired immune deficiency syndrome).

When a person is infected with HIV, the virus destroys cells essential to the immune system. If the activity of the immune system is lowered for some reason, it leaves the person even more vulnerable to disease. Blaney found that in HIV patients who reported being depressed and anxious, the activity of the immune system was lower than in HIV patients who vigorously and openly vented their emotions and engaged in denial of their condition. According to Blaney, denial—in this case—means "getting on with life" in spite of severe problems.   Robert J. Trotter

See also **Mental illness**. In *World Book*, see **Psychology**.

Increasingly Today, the Word Is "No Smoking!"

What might be called an antismoking revolution gathered strength in the United States and Canada during 1988. Attitudes toward smoking had come full circle from the time, nearly 400 years ago, when tobacco use first spread across Europe after being introduced from the New World. In 1604, England's King James I called smoking —which in those days usually meant puffing on a pipe— "a custome lothsome to the Eye, hateful to the Nose, harmful to the Braine." But nobody was listening, and this novel habit soon became increasingly popular.

Americans in great numbers took up cigarette smoking in the late 1800's. First, most smokers rolled their own, but with the introduction of the first practical cigarette-making machine in the 1880's, mass production became possible. A new industry was born.

In later decades, cigarette smoking became "sophisticated." The movie stars of the 1930's and 1940's, oozing sex appeal and glamor and rarely on screen without a lighted cigarette, probably did more than anyone to give smoking an aura of worldliness. Moviegoers thrilled when Paul Henreid put two cigarettes in his mouth, lit both, and coolly handed one to Bette Davis, his co-star in *Now, Voyager* (1942). Reinforced by advertising, smoking's oh-so-cool image persisted into the 1960's.

The opening shot in the antismoking revolution came in 1964, when Surgeon General Luther L. Terry issued a report implicating cigarette smoking in lung cancer, heart disease, and other serious illnesses. Evidence against cigarettes had

A waitress at a New York City restaurant labels smoking and nonsmoking areas in April as the city puts new limits on lighting up in public.

been building for at least 10 years, but this was the first time the U.S. government had issued a formal warning on the dangers of smoking.

By 1988, the 26 per cent of American adults who still smoked—down from about 42 per cent in 1964—were feeling increasingly beleaguered as that revolution continued to gather force. In a nation preoccupied with health and fitness, many Americans saw smoking as an embarrassing and unhealthy habit. When traveling or eating out, smokers found themselves directed to special sections of airplanes and restaurants where they could light up in company with others similarly hooked.

And it could no longer be denied that *hooked* was the proper word. In May 1988, Surgeon General C. Everett Koop told the world what every three-pack-a-day smoker had long suspected: Cigarette smoking is an addiction—an addiction to nicotine.

In addition to Koop's report, other blows in the antismoking revolution fell during 1988. For example:

● A new federal law prohibited smoking on airline flights of two hours or less within the United States, and one carrier—Northwest Airlines—banned smoking on all domestic and some international flights.

● New York City and Chicago joined hundreds of other cities that have banned or restricted smoking in public places.

● A federal jury in Newark, N.J., found the Liggett Group Incorporated, a major cigarette manufacturer, partially responsible for the cancer death of a smoker. The verdict was the first such ruling in more than 300 liability cases filed against tobacco companies since 1954.

● California banned smoking on commercial flights between California cities and on all buses and trains traveling through the state.

● Without admitting that regular cigarettes are harmful to health, the R. J. Reynolds Tobacco Company introduced Premier, a reduced-smoke cigarette that heats tobacco without burning it. But the product ran into immediate opposition from health groups, and the American Medical Association filed petitions with the states of Arizona and Missouri—where the Reynolds company was test-marketing Premier—asking them to stop distribution of the controversial product.

● Canada passed a law forbidding all tobacco advertising and restricting smoking in federally regulated workplaces.

Surgeon General Koop believes the trend is clear: Smoking is becoming a vanishing habit and one that will eventually be as socially unacceptable as tobacco chewing is today. By the end of the century, he predicts, ashtrays will be as rare as spittoons.   Michael Woods

Public health. Surgeon General of the United States C. Everett Koop in 1988 warned that improper diet is a major health problem in the United States. In a 712-page report on nutrition and health released on July 27, he said that diseases associated with improper diet, such as heart disease, cancer, stroke, and diabetes, account for more than two-thirds of all deaths in the United States. Koop added that for nonsmokers and people who do not drink alcohol excessively, the type of diet they choose can influence their long-term health more than any other action.

The report said that overeating—and eating the wrong kinds of food—is the major nutritional disorder in the United States and most other industrialized countries. It urged Americans to consume less salt, sugar, and foods high in animal fats, such as red meat, eggs, and dairy products. Instead, Americans should eat more low-fat, high-fiber foods, including fruits, vegetables, whole grains, and beans.

Leaner meats. A study conducted by the National Academy of Sciences (NAS) on April 5 recommended new efforts to reduce the amount of fat and *cholesterol* (a fatty substance) in beef, pork, and other meat. The NAS, based in Washington, D.C., advises the federal government on scientific matters.

The study said that traditional techniques used by the U.S. Department of Agriculture (USDA) to grade meat encourage the production of fatty cuts of meat. The study also called for more scientific research on ways to produce milk, meat, and eggs that are low in cholesterol.

Public health woes. On September 7, another NAS report said that the public health system in the United States has fallen into "disarray." The report found that political pressures, poor organization, and complacency had fragmented the public health system, making it difficult for officials to take decisive action on key health problems. The study urged individual states to assess local health problems and determine what services community public health agencies should offer.

Smokeless cigarette. The R. J. Reynolds Tobacco Company on August 29 began selling in test markets a controversial "smokeless" cigarette in an effort to offset the growing social and medical assault on smoking. The new cigarettes, called Premiers, burn without odor or smoke that might annoy nearby nonsmokers. A Premier looks much like a conventional cigarette, but it consists of a burning carbon element that heats a flavor capsule containing tobacco extract and other substances.

A number of medical organizations claimed that advertising for Premiers falsely implied that the cigarettes are safer than other brands. They charged that the new cigarette does not significantly reduce a person's exposure to harmful nicotine and carbon monoxide, and urged the U.S. Food and Drug Administration to take regulatory action against Premiers. Reynolds admitted that Premiers contain nicotine and give off carbon monoxide but insisted that the cigarettes are safer because they produce lesser amounts of tar and other hazardous compounds than conventional brands.

***Salmonella* alert.** In September, the USDA sent state health and agriculture officials a plan for testing poultry flocks for *salmonella*—the bacteria that cause *salmonellosis*, a form of food poisoning. The plan called for testing chickens for the bacteria and restricting the sale of eggs from infected flocks. It was developed after scientists from the U.S. Centers for Disease Control (CDC) in Atlanta, Ga., traced a number of salmonellosis outbreaks in the United States to raw or undercooked eggs.

On April 8, CDC researchers reported that *salmonella* bacteria can enter eggs developing inside the hen, prior to shell formation. This means that the bacteria can be present in clean, unbroken eggs. Previously, health experts believed that *salmonella* bacteria were transmitted primarily in eggs that were dirty or cracked.

Chinese outbreak. An epidemic of *hepatitis A*, an inflammation of the liver caused by a virus, struck China early in 1988. Dai Zhicheng, China's public health minister, on March 21 reported that about 393,000 cases of the disease had occurred since January.   Michael Woods

See also **AIDS; Health and disease; Medicine.** In *World Book*, see **Public health.**

Puerto Rico. Puerto Ricans reaffirmed their desire to maintain their unique commonwealth status in voting for a new chairman of the dominant Democratic Party on March 20, 1988. (As a commonwealth, Puerto Rico receives assistance and protection from the United States government but governs itself in many local matters. In addition, Puerto Ricans—though U.S. citizens—do not pay federal income tax when living on the island.) Puerto Rico's Senate President Miguel Hernández Agosto won with 56 per cent of the vote, defeating former Governor Carlos Romero Barceló, who advocated statehood for Puerto Rico.

The U.S. government was angered when Mexican authorities freed Puerto Rican terrorist William Morales on June 24 and deported him to Cuba. Morales, the leader of a militant faction seeking Puerto Rican independence, had escaped from custody in New York City in 1979. In absentia, he was sentenced to 89 years in prison on weapons and explosives charges. Mexico had refused United States requests for his extradition on grounds that his actions were politically motivated. Morales had served five years in a Mexican prison for his part in the murder of a policeman.

Nathan A. Haverstock

See also **Latin America** (Facts in brief table). In *World Book*, see **Puerto Rico.**

Pulitzer Prizes. See Awards and prizes.

Quayle, Dan. In the World Book Supplement section, see **Quayle, Dan.**

Quebec

Quebec. Prime Minister Robert Bourassa, leading a solid Liberal government, announced plans in March 1988 to build three more hydroelectric dams in the James Bay region of northern Quebec. The James Bay project, which Bourassa began in 1973 during his first term, is now Canada's largest producer of hydroelectric power. Bourassa declared that the new phase would provide $40 billion worth of electricity to Vermont, Maine, and New York state, as well as to neighboring provinces, beginning in 1995. The plan was estimated to cost $7.5 billion. (All monetary amounts in this article are Canadian dollars with $1 = U.S. 84 cents as of Dec. 31, 1988.)

Language. On Dec. 15, 1988, the Supreme Court of Canada struck down a Quebec law that prohibited English on public signs. Three days later, as 15,000 Quebec nationalists rallied in Montreal, Bourassa announced a new law that would allow English signs indoors but limit exterior signs to French. He also invoked a rarely used provision of the Canadian and Quebec constitutions to exempt the new law from court challenges. The compromise angered both French and English factions, and three English-speaking provincial cabinet ministers resigned in protest.

Birth incentives. In response to concern over Quebec's low birth rate, the government's new budget, presented on May 12, included incentives for family growth. Quebec's fertility rate—1.4 children per woman of childbearing age—is one of the lowest in the industrialized world. Under the new provisions, the province will pay a cash bonus of $500 for each of a family's first two children, plus $3,000, paid over two years, for each subsequent child.

The Parti Québécois (PQ), the secessionist political party opposing the governing Liberals, chose Jacques Parizeau as its leader in March. Parizeau, a hard-line separatist, was acclaimed party head without a contest, replacing Pierre Marc Johnson, who resigned as leader in November 1987. An economics professor who served as Quebec's finance minister before the PQ lost power to the Liberals in 1985, Parizeau rejected Johnson's policy of working within the Canadian federation to win power for the province. In September 1988, Parizeau unveiled a revised party platform based on a goal of independence.

Environment. More than 3,000 residents of St.-Basile-le-Grand, near Montreal, fled their homes on August 23 to avoid toxic smoke from a warehouse fire. Stored in the warehouse were some 30,900 gallons (117,000 liters) of oil containing polychlorinated biphenyls (PCB's), deadly chemicals that release cancer-causing fumes when burned. Officials allowed the residents to return on September 10. The episode intensified nationwide concerns over environmental safety. Within a week, the Quebec cabinet tightened regulations on PCB storage. Two weeks after the fire, the federal government announced that Canada would phase out use of PCB's.   David M. L. Farr

See also **Montreal.** In *World Book*, see **Quebec.**

Railroad. On Aug. 9, 1988, the Interstate Commerce Commission (ICC) approved the $1.02-billion sale of Santa Fe Industries' Southern Pacific Railroad to Rio Grande Industries Incorporated. The ICC rejected a competing bid from Kansas City Southern Industries Incorporated.

The 4-0 vote in favor of the sale appeared to end the long-running saga over the future of Southern Pacific. In late 1983, Santa Fe Industries, which owns the Atchison, Topeka & Santa Fe Railway, bought the Southern Pacific Company, owner of Southern Pacific Railroad. The ICC, however, refused to approve the merger of the companies' two railroads, saying that it would hurt competition. In 1987, the commission ordered Santa Fe to sell one of the railroads.

Rio Grande Industries owns the Denver & Rio Grande Western Railroad. Company officials said the Denver & Rio Grande would be merged with Southern Pacific and operated under the Southern Pacific name. The resulting railroad will have about 15,000 miles (24,000 kilometers) of track.

Safety legislation. In June, Congress approved—and President Ronald Reagan signed—legislation that increased fines for violations of rail-safety rules. Under the new law, the Federal Railroad Administration may impose a $10,000 fine for each safety violation, as well as an additional fine of up to $20,000 for a "grossly negligent violation." Under the old law, fines ranged up to $2,500. The law also gives the administration the authority to punish workers who break safety rules. It permits the agency to fine workers and, in some cases, to bar them from jobs that affect safety. In the past, the agency could penalize only railroad companies, not individuals.

Drug tests. Transportation Secretary James H. Burnley IV on November 14 ordered that railroad engineers and other workers involved in train safety undergo random drug tests beginning in late 1989. The order reflected concern about drug use among railroad workers in the wake of the 1987 collision between three Consolidated Rail Corporation (Conrail) locomotives and a National Railroad Passenger Corporation (Amtrak) passenger train. Sixteen people were killed in the accident, which occurred in Chase, Md., after the Conrail locomotives rolled through a stop signal. In January 1988, the National Transportation Safety Board said the Conrail engineer's use of marijuana was a prime cause of the accident. Rail unions denounced the drug-testing order.

Monopoly concerns. On September 20, the Senate Committee on Commerce, Science, and Transportation rejected a proposed bill that would protect shippers from overpricing by railroads that have a monopoly in certain areas of the country. The bill's supporters argued that the ICC should compel monopoly railroads to lower their shipping rates. The railroads, however, said the regulation would hurt the industry.   Laurie McGinley

In *World Book*, see **Railroad.**

Reagan, Ronald Wilson (1911-   ), 40th President of the United States, neared the end of his second term in 1988 still enjoying extraordinary popularity among the American people. Reagan's high public standing was all the more remarkable because, just a year earlier, his Administration had been rocked by the Iran-contra affair, the biggest one-day stock-market drop in history, and months of conflict with the Democratic-controlled Congress.

As if those problems were not enough for the President, 1988 produced its own share of defeats and setbacks. Israel rejected a Reagan Administration peace plan for the Middle East, Congress defeated strenuous White House efforts to win new military aid for *contra* rebels fighting the government of Nicaragua, and Panama's controversial military leader, General Manuel Antonio Noriega Morena, defeated Administration efforts to force his ouster.

But those and other setbacks—including the tragic destruction of an Iranian airliner by a U.S. Navy vessel—were more than balanced by factors and developments that played well with the public. As always, Reagan's amiable personality served him well. The President also benefited from the continued expansion of the U.S. economy and—most important—a springtime summit meeting in Moscow and ratification of an arms control treaty with the Soviet Union.

Destroying nuclear missiles. The treaty with the Soviets called for eliminating all intermediate-range nuclear forces (INF), most of them in Europe, over a three-year period. The pact was the first superpower agreement to dismantle an entire class of missiles—those with a range of 300 to 3,400 miles (480 to 5,600 kilometers). Under the treaty, the Soviets were to destroy about 1,750 warheads on SS-4, SS-20, SS-12, and SS-23 missiles, while the United States would scrap some 400 warheads on Pershing II and ground-launched cruise missiles. The agreement called for elaborate and unprecedented on-site inspection procedures to ensure compliance. The U.S. Senate ratified the treaty, 93 to 5, on May 27.

The INF Treaty had been signed by Reagan and Soviet leader Mikhail S. Gorbachev at a Washington summit in December 1987. The two agreed at that time to press for completion of a follow-up Strategic Arms Reduction Treaty (START), to limit each superpower to 4,900 nuclear missile warheads, in time for a 1988 Moscow summit. But when Reagan announced on March 3, 1988, that he would be visiting Moscow and Leningrad from May 29 to June 2, little progress had been made on START.

The Moscow meeting. The lack of headway in START negotiations left the Moscow summit bereft of specific accomplishments. Nonetheless, the meeting was considered a good-will success by both sides, with Reagan combining the roles of sightseer, preacher of freedom and democracy, and supporter of Gorbachev's efforts to carry out economic and political reforms in the Soviet Union. While complaining that

Reagan and Soviet leader Mikhail S. Gorbachev greet a toddler in Moscow's Red Square on May 31 during a five-day summit meeting.

more could have been achieved at the summit, Gorbachev observed, "We moved one rung, two rungs up the ladder [of friendship and cooperation between the two nations], and this itself is a momentous fact." That feeling of good will was renewed in December, when Gorbachev visited the United States to address the United Nations (UN) General Assembly.

On other fronts, however, developments were not so favorable. On March 16, Reagan failed to persuade Israel's Prime Minister Yitzhak Shamir to go along with a U.S. plan aimed at resolving the violence sweeping the West Bank and Gaza Strip. Shamir rejected Reagan's call for talks between Israel and a joint Jordanian-Palestinian delegation. The talks were to have been held under the umbrella of an international conference including the five permanent members of the UN Security Council.

Also disappointing to Reagan was his failure to force the ouster of Panama's Noriega following the general's U.S. indictment on drug and racketeering charges. Those charges were brought on February 5 by two federal grand juries in Florida. Reagan ordered economic *sanctions* (penalties) against Panama and dispatched 1,300 additional military personnel to American bases there, then tried to negotiate with Noriega. There was talk of Noriega giving up power if charges against him were dropped, but Secretary of State George P. Shultz announced on May 25 that the negotiations had collapsed.

427

Reagan's chief of staff, Howard H. Baker, Jr., left, resigned on July 1 for personal reasons and was succeeded by his deputy, Kenneth M. Duberstein, right.

Reagan also failed in efforts to win congressional approval for fresh military aid to the contras in Nicaragua. He did order a show of force in the region on March 16 after receiving reports that Nicaraguan troops had crossed into neighboring Honduras in an effort to destroy a contra supply base. The President ordered 3,200 U.S. combat troops to Honduras in what was called an "emergency deployment readiness exercise." The "crisis" quickly evaporated, and the troops returned home.

Navy destroys Iranian airliner. The event causing greatest regret to the White House in 1988 occurred on July 3, when the U.S. Navy cruiser *Vincennes* shot down an Iranian airliner over the Persian Gulf, killing all 290 people aboard. Although the *Vincennes* was equipped with the Navy's most sophisticated radar and electronic battle gear, the ship's crew mistook the Iranian A300 Airbus for an F-14 fighter. Acting on that incorrect assessment, the *Vincennes*' commander, Captain Will C. Rogers III, ordered the firing of two missiles at the plane.

Reagan almost immediately sent Iran a diplomatic note expressing "deep regret," and on July 11 he offered compensation to families of the victims. On August 19, the Pentagon blamed the tragedy on a series of human errors but said none of the cruiser's officers or crew would be disciplined.

Earlier in the year, on April 14, the Navy guided-missile frigate *Samuel B. Roberts*, which like the *Vin-*

cennes was protecting sea lanes in the Persian Gulf, was severely damaged by an Iranian mine. Four days later, at Reagan's order, the Navy retaliated by destroying two Iranian oil platforms and sinking or crippling six Iranian vessels. On April 29, the President directed the Navy to extend its protection of gulf shipping to any neutral, non-Communist ships that might seek help during an attack.

Astrology at the White House. President Reagan and his wife, Nancy, became targets of ridicule following the publication in May of the memoirs of former White House chief of staff Donald T. Regan, who reported that Nancy Reagan regularly consulted an astrologer to determine her husband's travel plans and scheduling. The White House did not flatly deny the assertion, but Reagan said his decisions as President had never been influenced "in my mind" by astrology.

On June 9, Mrs. Reagan felt compelled to respond to criticism that she had been overly protective of her husband. She told an audience of business people that she had no apology for shielding Reagan from the pressures of the presidency. "And if that interferes with affairs of state, then so be it," she said. "No first lady need make apologies for looking out for her husband's personal welfare."

Mrs. Reagan again became a figure of controversy in October when *Time* magazine reported that she had borrowed up to $1 million worth of designer clothing and jewels despite her 1982 promise to discontinue the practice. A dispute ensued over whether the Reagans should have reported the loans on the President's financial disclosure forms.

The Reagans' federal income tax return, released by the White House on April 8, showed that the couple paid $86,638 in tax on a 1987 income of $345,359. Charitable contributions totaled $25,407.

Reagan's health holds. White House physician John Hutton reported on January 15 and again on December 10 that Reagan showed no signs of any recurrence of the colon cancer for which he had major surgery in 1985. The President's only reported illness during the year occurred on the night of January 12-13, when he experienced a mild episode of gastro-enteritis.

Staff changes. Reagan's chief of staff, Howard H. Baker, Jr., resigned on July 1 and was replaced by his deputy, Kenneth M. Duberstein. White House Communications Director Thomas C. Griscom, a long-time Baker associate, also left and was succeeded by Mari Maseng, former press secretary to Senate Republican leader Robert J. Dole. Gary L. Bauer resigned as Reagan's domestic policy adviser on October 31 and was succeeded by Franmarie Kennedy-Keel.

Frank Cormier and Margot Cormier

See also **Cabinet; Congress of the United States; United States, Government of the.** In *World Book*, see **Reagan, Ronald Wilson.**

Religion. The role of women in Christianity was a major concern of religious leaders in 1988. The issue was best dramatized on September 24 when delegates at a convention of the Episcopal *diocese* (church district) of Massachusetts elected 58-year-old Barbara C. Harris, rector of an Episcopal church in Philadelphia, as *suffragan* (assistant bishop). Her election needed the approval of 60 other dioceses, and she had the required votes by Jan. 3, 1989.

Harris was the first woman to be elected a bishop in the Episcopal Church in the United States since the church voted to ordain women priests in 1976, though some women priests have been nominated for the office of bishop.

At the Episcopal Church's general convention held in July 1988 in Detroit, bishops and delegates decided—after much debate—that if a local congregation objected to a woman bishop performing church ceremonies, such as ordinations and confirmations, that congregation could petition her to allow them to invite a male bishop to perform those ceremonies. The female bishop, however, would hold full jurisdiction over the congregation.

After Harris' election, the joint Anglican-Roman Catholic theological commission, which is studying a possible reunion between the two churches, pledged "to carry forward the search for greater unity" but admitted that the Anglican Communion's acceptance of women as bishops presents a "major problem" in

U.S. membership reported for religious groups with 150,000 or more members*

African Methodist Episcopal Church	2,210,000
African Methodist Episcopal Zion Church	1,220,260
American Baptist Association	250,000
American Baptist Churches in the U.S.A.	1,568,778
Antiochian Orthodox Christian Archdiocese of North America	280,000
Armenian Church of America, Diocese of the	450,000
Assemblies of God	2,160,667
Baptist Bible Fellowship, International	1,405,900
Baptist Missionary Association of America	227,638
Christian and Missionary Alliance	244,296
Christian Church (Disciples of Christ)	1,086,668
Christian Churches and Churches of Christ	1,071,995
Christian Methodist Episcopal Church	718,992
Christian Reformed Church in North America	225,951
Church of God (Anderson, Ind.)	198,552
Church of God (Cleveland, Tenn.)	505,775
Church of God in Christ	3,709,661
Church of God in Christ, International	200,000
Church of Jesus Christ of Latter-day Saints	3,860,000
Church of the Brethren	154,067
Church of the Nazarene	543,762
Churches of Christ	1,623,754
Conservative Baptist Association of America	225,000
Episcopal Church	2,462,300
Evangelical Lutheran Church in America	5,288,230
Free Will Baptists	200,387
General Association of Regular Baptist Churches	300,839
Greek Orthodox Archdiocese of North and South America	1,950,000
International Church of the Foursquare Gospel	192,327
International Council of Community Churches	200,000
Jehovah's Witnesses	773,219
Jews	5,943,700
Liberty Baptist Fellowship	200,000
Lutheran Church—Missouri Synod	2,614,375
National Baptist Convention of America	2,668,799
National Baptist Convention, U.S.A., Inc.	5,500,000
National Primitive Baptist Convention	250,000
Orthodox Church in America	1,000,000
Polish National Catholic Church	282,411
Presbyterian Church in America	190,960
Presbyterian Church (U.S.A.)	2,967,781
Progressive National Baptist Convention, Inc.	521,692
Reformed Church in America	338,348
Reorganized Church of Jesus Christ of Latter Day Saints	191,618
Roman Catholic Church	53,496,862
Salvation Army	434,002
Seventh-day Adventist Church	675,702
Southern Baptist Convention	14,722,617
Unitarian Universalist Association	173,167
United Church of Christ	1,662,568
United Methodist Church	9,124,575
United Pentecostal Church, International	500,000
Wisconsin Evangelical Lutheran Synod	418,791

*A majority of the figures are for the years 1987 and 1988.
Source: National Council of the Churches of Christ in the U.S.A., *Yearbook of American and Canadian Churches* for 1989.

Religion

achieving that end. (The Anglican Communion includes the Church of England, the Anglican Church of Canada, and the Episcopal Church in the United States.) Pope John Paul II firmly opposes the ordination of women as priests. That position was reaffirmed on September 30, when the pope, in a statement on the role of women in the church and in society, said that women should affirm their feminine qualities, the greatest of which is motherhood.

Russian anniversary. Christian leaders from throughout the world visited the Soviet Union during 1988 to celebrate the 1,000th anniversary of the introduction of Christianity to Russia. Historians believe that Grand Prince Vladimir I, pagan ruler of the city of Kiev in what is now the Soviet Union, converted to Christianity in about A.D. 988.

Anniversary events began on June 5 with a Russian Orthodox Mass celebrated at Epiphany Cathedral in Moscow. Among the religious leaders in attendance were Robert A. K. Runcie, archbishop of Canterbury; American evangelist Billy Graham; and a delegation of Roman Catholic cardinals and bishops.

The celebration highlighted the calming of tensions between the Soviet government and organized religion. On April 29, Soviet leader Mikhail S. Gorbachev met with Russian Orthodox leaders and promised "a new law on freedom of conscience" in the Soviet Union. But Ukrainian and Lithuanian Christian groups in the United States complained that religious groups in the Soviet Union were still being suppressed, and Jewish groups noted that Soviet Jews continued to be frustrated in their efforts to emigrate to Israel.

Shroud of Turin. The Roman Catholic Church on October 13 ended centuries of debate about the authenticity of the Shroud of Turin when it announced that scientific tests proved that the linen cloth could not have been used to wrap the body of Jesus Christ after His death. The shroud is a 14-foot (4.2-meter) strip of cloth bearing the image of a man who had apparently been crucified.

Using *radiocarbon dating*—a process that determines the age of an ancient object by measuring its radiocarbon content—scientists at the University of Arizona in Tucson, the Federal Technical Institute in Zurich, Switzerland, and the University of Oxford in England tested small samples of the cloth. They found that the shroud was actually woven sometime between 1260 and 1380.

Muslim honored. For promoting Islamic unity, Inamullah Khan, secretary-general of the World Muslim Congress in Karachi, Pakistan, was awarded the 1988 Templeton Prize for Progress in Religion. Khan also is a leader of the World Conference on Religion and Peace, which organizes conferences of religious leaders to discuss world problems. He was the first Muslim to win the award.　　Owen F. Campion

See also **Eastern Orthodox Churches; Jews and Judaism; Protestantism; Roman Catholic Church.** In *World Book*, see **Religion.**

Republican Party. Winning the presidency for the fifth time in the last six elections, the Republican Party (GOP) nevertheless faced a mixed outcome in the general election of Nov. 8, 1988. The GOP lost one seat in the Senate and surrendered one governorship. The GOP also lost two of its seats in the House of Representatives and failed to win three vacant seats previously held by Republicans.

The GOP's presidential nominee, Vice President George Bush, scored an impressive victory over Michael S. Dukakis, the Democratic governor of Massachusetts. Although Bush had trailed Dukakis by up to 17 points in midsummer polls, he carried 40 states, received 53 per cent of the nationwide vote, and collected 426 electoral votes. Dukakis carried 10 states and the District of Columbia and received 46 per cent of the vote and 111 electoral votes.

The battle for the nomination. With popular Republican President Ronald Reagan retiring after eight years in office, Bush faced stiff competition for the GOP nomination. In his first big test, at the Iowa caucuses on February 8, Bush was dealt a major blow. Receiving just 19 per cent of the vote, Bush placed third behind Senate Republican leader Robert J. Dole of Kansas, who received 37 per cent, and former television evangelist Marion G. (Pat) Robertson with 25 per cent. The fourth- and fifth-place finishers were Representative Jack F. Kemp of New York and former Governor Pierre S. du Pont IV of Delaware. Ending up in last place was former Secretary of State Alexander M. Haig, Jr., who soon afterward abandoned his candidacy and endorsed Dole.

But Bush was soon riding high. On February 16, he defied most pollsters and topped Dole by 38 to 29 per cent in the New Hampshire primary. Kemp placed third, and Robertson finished last. Du Pont came in fourth and withdrew from the race.

On March 8, called "Super Tuesday" because 17 states held Republican primaries or caucuses that day, Bush won all 16 primaries, and Robertson won the 17th contest—caucuses in Washington state. Dole collected only about 100 Super Tuesday delegates to Bush's 577. Kemp did far worse, gaining just 4 delegates, and he dropped out of the race two days later.

Dole suffered another defeat on March 15 as Bush won the Illinois primary, 55 to 36 per cent. The senator gave up on March 29, making Bush the obvious nominee even before such big states as Pennsylvania, Ohio, New York, and California had been heard from.

Bush versus Dukakis. Determined to overcome Dukakis' lead in the polls, Bush emerged from the Republican National Convention in New Orleans in August as a slashing attacker who kept his opponent on the defensive throughout most of the fall campaign. Bush sought to depict Dukakis as an extreme liberal who was soft on crime and defense.

Little was heard during the campaign from Bush's surprise choice as running mate, Senator Dan Quayle of Indiana. The 41-year-old senator's youth, service in

Flanked by their wives, Vice President George Bush, second from right, and his newly announced running mate, Senator Dan Quayle, greet each other on August 16.

the National Guard during the Vietnam War, lackluster college record, and relative inexperience became hot issues, but in the end the "Quayle factor" had little apparent effect on the outcome of the election.

Senate races. Three Republican senators lost on November 8, compared with one Democrat. On the plus side, the GOP picked up two seats vacated by Democratic retirees while losing one of their own. The net result was a loss of one seat, giving the 1989 Senate a line-up of 55 Democrats to 45 Republicans.

The defeated Republicans were Senators Lowell P. Weicker, Jr., of Connecticut, David K. Karnes of Nebraska, and Chic Hecht of Nevada. Democratic Senator John Melcher of Montana was upset by Republican Conrad Burns, a Yellowstone County commissioner. Former Democratic Governor Charles S. Robb of Virginia won the Senate seat vacated by Republican Paul S. Trible, Jr. But Republican Representative Trent Lott took over the Mississippi seat of retiring Democrat John C. Stennis, and GOP Representative Connie Mack III succeeded retiring Democrat Lawton Chiles in Florida. Two other Republican candidates won seats that had been held by retiring Republicans. Former Senator Slade Gorton of Washington replaced the retiring Daniel J. Evans, and James M. Jeffords, a seven-term House member from Vermont, succeeded retiring Senator Robert T. Stafford.

House of Representatives. For the first time since 1960, the party winning the presidency failed to add to its numbers in the House. The Democratic margin of control was padded by 7 seats, to 260 to 175. The most notable upset in House races was scored by Republican newcomer Ronald K. Machtley of Rhode Island, who defeated 14-term Democrat Fernand J. St Germain, chairman of the House Committee on Banking, Housing, and Urban Affairs. Machtley benefited from accusations that St Germain had violated House ethics rules.

Governorships. Republicans picked up one governorship while losing two. In Montana, Republican state Senator Stan Stephens derailed a comeback attempt by former Democratic Governor Thomas L. Judge. But Republican Governor Arch A. Moore, Jr., of West Virginia lost his bid for a fourth term, and in Indiana, GOP Lieutenant Governor John M. Mutz lost to Democrat Evan Bayh, son of former Senator Birch Bayh. Republican Governor James G. Martin of North Carolina became the first member of his party to win a second term as chief executive of that state.

In state legislatures, Republicans picked up about 50 seats. In only two state legislative chambers did the majority party change. Republicans gained control of the Vermont Senate but lost their majority in the New Mexico Senate.   Frank Cormier and Margot Cormier

See also **Democratic Party; Elections.** In the World Book Supplement section, see **Bush, George H. W.; Quayle, Dan.** In *World Book*, see **Republican Party. Rhode Island.** See **State government.**

Rocard, Michel (1930-   ), was appointed prime minister of France by President François Mitterrand on May 10, 1988. Both Rocard and Mitterrand are Socialists. Rocard succeeded Jacques Chirac, a member of the conservative Rally for the Republic party. Chirac had fallen from power on May 8, when he lost a national election in a bid to topple Mitterrand from the presidency. Political observers saw Mitterrand's appointment of Rocard, a moderate, as an attempt to gain the support of France's political center. See **France.**

Rocard was born on Aug. 23, 1930, in Courbevoie, a suburb of Paris. He attended the National School of Administration, known as the "training ground" for French politicians. After graduating, he worked for the government as a financial auditor.

Rocard led the small United Socialist Party from 1967 to 1973. In 1974, he and most of his followers joined the Socialist Party.

In 1977, Rocard was elected mayor of Conflans-Ste.-Honorine, a position he kept when he became prime minister. Mitterrand named him minister of planning in 1981 and minister of agriculture in 1983. Rocard resigned in 1985 to protest Mitterrand's support of a proposed change in election laws.

Rocard is married to Michèle Legendre, a professor of sociology. They have two children, and the prime minister also has two children from a previous marriage.   Jay Myers

Roman Catholic Church. The National Conference of Catholic Bishops in the United States, meeting at St. John's Benedictine Abbey in Collegeville, Minn., voted on June 27, 1988, to draft a new statement outlining the Roman Catholic Church's position on the moral issues surrounding AIDS (acquired immune deficiency syndrome). The new statement will clarify the controversial *Many Faces of AIDS: A Gospel Response*, a statement on AIDS that was issued by the bishops' administrative committee in December 1987.

The controversy surrounded—in part—the bishops' stand on AIDS education programs in Catholic schools. Although the bishops' 1987 statement reaffirmed the Catholic Church's criticism of condoms as a way to stop the spread of AIDS, it said the bishops would not oppose public information on AIDS prevention that discussed condoms if the information was couched in a moral framework. The document, however, did not clarify whether information on condoms would be permitted in Catholic schools.

A number of bishops also questioned whether Catholic agencies could join the effort to prevent AIDS if the effort urged the use of condoms during sexual intercourse. John Cardinal O'Connor of New York City, Bernard Cardinal Law of Boston, and Archbishop J. Francis Stafford of Denver had said that use of condoms was immoral and could not be tolerated.

Joseph Cardinal Bernardin of Chicago called for the new AIDS statement to be built upon the 1987 state-

ment and upon the recommendations outlined in a letter sent to the bishops from Joseph Cardinal Ratzinger, head of the Vatican's Sacred Congregation for the Doctrine of the Faith. In the letter, Cardinal Ratzinger expressed the Vatican's concern about the reference to condoms and urged them to consult with the Vatican.

At the world AIDS summit in London on January 27, Archbishop Fiorenzo Angelini of the Vatican's Pontifical Commission for Health Care Workers told health experts and government leaders that efforts to prevent or treat the disease must be based upon "the safeguarding of ethical principles which cannot be renounced." He said that the Catholic Church recognizes the need for a united and rapid effort to combat AIDS, but he added that short-term remedies should not be used if they would create "greater damage" in the future.

Third World problems. On February 29, Pope John Paul II issued an *encyclical*, or papal message, on the needs of small, developing countries and on the responsibilities of prosperous countries to further peace and human advancement throughout the world. The encyclical commemorated the anniversary of Pope Paul VI's 1967 encyclical called *On the Development of Peoples,* which dealt with the problems of newly independent nations.

Pope John Paul II's encyclical, entitled *The Social Concerns of the Church,* denounced the world's major powers—both capitalist and Marxist—for imposing their political and ideological views upon people in developing countries and in newly independent nations. It said that the great differences between rich and poor nations and the tensions rising from the exploitation of weaker countries by stronger nations imperiled world peace. The pope denounced foreign aid that requires or promotes population control through artificial methods, such as birth control devices.

Pope John Paul II also warned that the arms race, the enormous debt owed by many developing nations to richer governments, and the political corruption and tyranny found in some countries were serious threats to peace. The encyclical demanded self-determination for developing countries, but with the cooperation and support of wealthier nations.

The role of women. On September 30, Pope John Paul II released a major statement on the role of women in the Catholic Church and in society. Called *The Dignity of Women,* it was a theological response to the movement for equality for women. The pope based his views upon the Bible, and he said that the document was written in "the style and character of a meditation."

In the document, the pope called the historic subordination of women to men an "evil inheritance" and stated that overcoming this subordination is "the task of every human being, whether woman or man." The pope stressed, however, that a woman's identity emerges from her relationship with men. He said the

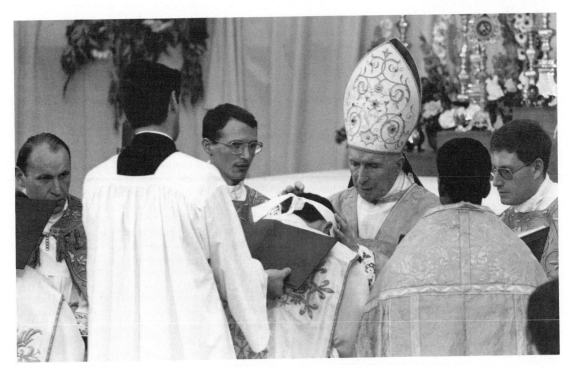

Defying Vatican orders, French Archbishop Marcel Lefebvre ordains a new bishop in Ecône, Switzerland, on June 30. Lefebvre was promptly excommunicated.

Biblical verse—"Husbands, love your wives"—fundamentally affirms a woman as a person, and that it is this love that makes it possible for a woman to lead a fully developed and enriched life.

He extolled what he called women's two vocations —the two roles women are called to fill: being mothers, which affects every aspect of a woman's being, and becoming nuns or other "spiritual" mothers. The pope declared that both vocations were perfectly exhibited by Mary, the mother of Jesus.

According to the pope, the women's liberation movement actually works against women's dignity. He said that women should not appropriate male characteristics at the expense of their femininity, but he did not define those male characteristics. The pope stated that the search for equality between the sexes should not obscure or deny the differences between them.

Archbishop breaks with Vatican. The first *schism* (split) in the Roman Catholic Church in more than 100 years occurred on June 30 when French Archbishop Marcel Lefebvre ordained four bishops in a Mass in Ecône, Switzerland, in defiance of orders from Pope John Paul II. The Vatican responded to the action by excommunicating Archbishop Lefebvre and the four bishops. (Excommunication is the severest penalty that the church can impose on a member.) Bishop Antonio de Castro Mayer, a retired bishop from Brazil who assisted Lefebvre in the ordination, also was excommunicated.

The excommunication culminated a 20-year dispute between Archbishop Lefebvre and the Vatican. The archbishop, who leads a movement supporting traditional Roman Catholic rites, strongly condemns the reforms initiated by the Second Vatican Council, a council held from 1962 to 1965 to update Roman Catholic doctrine. He reportedly has as many as 100,000 followers in Europe and the United States. Although the Vatican banned him from performing priestly functions in 1976, Archbishop Lefebvre has ignored the ban and has continued to offer Mass and ordain priests. See **Lefebvre, Marcel.**

Russian celebration. Vatican Secretary of State Agostino Cardinal Casaroli led a group of nine Roman Catholic officials to the Soviet Union in June to attend the celebration of the 1,000th anniversary of the introduction of Christianity to Russia. The group included Cardinal O'Connor of New York City.

On June 13, Cardinal Casaroli met with Soviet leader Mikhail S. Gorbachev and gave him a letter from Pope John Paul II that reportedly expressed the pope's concern about religious freedom in the Soviet Union. Ukrainian and Lithuanian groups in the United States said that despite the Soviet government's acceptance of the celebrations and Gorbachev's hospitality, Catholics are still repressed in the Soviet Union.

New cardinals. On June 28, Pope John Paul II installed 24 cardinals. Among them was Lithuanian Bishop Vincentas Sladkevicius, who became the second cardinal in the Soviet Union. Archbishops Edmund C. Szoka of Detroit and James A. Hickey of Washington, D.C., also received the honor.

First black archbishop. Pope John Paul II on March 15 named Eugene A. Marino, auxiliary bishop of Washington, D.C., as the archbishop of Atlanta, Ga. With his installation in May, Bishop Marino became the first black Catholic archbishop in the United States.

Other news. During 1988, two new Roman Catholic *dioceses* (church districts) were created in the United States—one in Knoxville, Tenn., and the other in Lexington, Ky.

Pope John Paul II on July 3 declared Rose Philippine Duchesne a saint. Duchesne was a French nun who devoted her life to serving the American Indians living in the Mississippi and Missouri valleys. She died in 1852.

On September 25, Pope John Paul II *beatified* (declared blessed) Junípero Serra, a Franciscan missionary who in 1769 founded the first mission in what is now California. The action is the last step needed before a person can be declared a saint. Some people opposed Serra's beatification because of reports that he abused the Indians who worked for him. On November 20, the pope beatified Katharine Drexel, a Philadelphia heiress who became a nun to educate poor blacks and Native Americans. She died in 1955.   Owen F. Campion

In *World Book*, see **Roman Catholic Church.**

Romania suffered in 1988 from a continuing economic lag and consumer hardship, and became increasingly the odd-man-out in international relations—even within the Soviet bloc. Romania's international relations declined because of what many other nations considered unremitting disregard of human rights by its government.

Both Eastern and Western nations focused their criticism on Romania's rural resettlement project, involving the demolition of some 7,000 Romanian villages—many populated by ethnic Hungarians or Germans—and the moving of their residents to about 500 urban agricultural-industrial settlements. The resettlement plan brought Romania into open conflict with neighboring Hungary, a partner in the Warsaw Pact, the Soviet-led Communist military alliance.

"Worst" repression. United States Secretary of State George P. Shultz on June 16 described Romania's repression of its citizens as "the worst" in Eastern Europe and said the United States had no wish to continue Romania's most-favored-nation (MFN) trading status, which commits the United States to use its lowest tariff rates on all Romanian products. Shultz's condemnation was the bluntest of many expressed by Western governments, including those of Great Britain and West Germany.

In February, Washington had revealed that Romania had renounced continuation of its MFN status because of U.S. "interference" in Romania's internal affairs—

meaning U.S. condemnation of Romania's human rights policy. Romania's MFN status expired in July.

Rationality claimed. Romania's President Nicolae Ceauşescu said that the resettlement program would bring all Romanian agriculture into a rational system. Some Western agricultural experts had once agreed, seeing merit in what seemed to be a plan to reform a backward agriculture increasingly dependent on the labor of women and old men. The appeal of the rationality argument has given way to general distaste for the program, however, because of Romania's disregard for the culture of the villagers—especially the villagers who are not ethnic Romanians.

On August 28, Hungary's leader Károly Grósz discussed the resettlement program with Ceauşescu. But Ceauşescu was as unmoved by the Hungarian leader's arguments as he had been by Western criticism.

Economic gloom. Romania's ambitious industrialization program and Ceauşescu's insistence on making massive payments on the country's foreign debt continued to prevent economic growth. Ceauşescu admitted at the beginning of 1988 that almost all Romania's economic units failed to meet their production quotas in 1987.   Eric Bourne

See also **Europe** (Facts in brief table). In *World Book*, see **Romania.**

Rowing. See **Olympic Games; Sports.**

Russia. See **Union of Soviet Socialist Republics.**

Rwanda. See **Africa.**

Safety. An eruption of problems in several nuclear-weapons plants created a major safety issue in the United States in 1988. Precautionary actions were taken at three facilities. In August, the U.S. Department of Energy shut down three weapons-production reactors at the Savannah River Plant near Aiken, S.C. In September, the Energy Department announced that it would indefinitely postpone opening New Mexico's Waste Isolation Pilot Plant, the first permanent nuclear waste repository in the United States. And one month later, three workers were exposed to unsafe levels of radiation in a plutonium-processing building at the Rocky Flats Plant near Boulder, Colo. That section of the plant was closed. The Savannah River and Rocky Flats plants were scheduled to reopen in 1989.

In early October, the Energy Department acknowledged a long-standing safety problem at the Feed Materials Production Center in Fernald, Ohio, near Cincinnati. The government, but not the public, reportedly had long known that the center had been releasing thousands of tons of radioactive waste into the environment for decades. After years of neglect and haphazard management, many of the 17 facilities in the weapons-production system were falling apart, Secretary of Energy John S. Herrington admitted.

Motor-vehicle safety. Approximately 142,500 people lost their lives in alcohol-related traffic accidents in the United States from 1982 to 1987. This statistic translates into an average of 1 death every 22

Accidental deaths in the United States

	1986-1987*		1987-1988*	
	Number	**Rate†**	**Number**	**Rate†‡**
Motor vehicle	47,600	19.5	49,020	20.3
Home	20,200	8.2	21,300	8.8
Public	18,900	7.7	17,300	7.2
Work	10,700	4.4	10,900	4.6
Total§	**93,500**	**38.2**	**94,100**	**39.3**

*For 12-month period ending June 30.

†Deaths per 100,000 U.S. population.

‡12-month projection based on 1988 data only.

§The total does not equal the sum of the four classes because *Motor vehicle* includes some deaths listed under *Work* and *Home*.

Source: National Safety Council estimates.

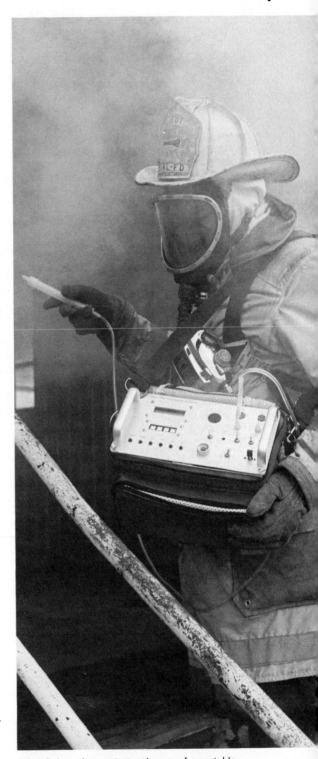

A fire fighter demonstrates the use of a portable toxic-gas detector created at Argonne National Laboratory in Illinois and licensed for sale in 1988.

minutes, the National Highway Traffic Safety Administration (NHTSA) reported in August. The U.S. highway death toll for 1987 was 46,121—identical to the adjusted 1986 toll—according to the NHTSA. But because of an increase in the total number of miles traveled during 1987, the traffic fatality rate for the year was the lowest recorded—2.4 deaths per 100 million miles (160 million kilometers), down from 3.3 in 1980. Secretary of Transportation James H. Burnley IV attributed the decline to increased use of safety belts and campaigns against drunken driving.

A record 45.6 per cent of drivers now use safety belts, according to a Department of Transportation study released in November 1988. This represents a steady increase from 11 per cent reported in 1982. Studies show that using lap or shoulder belts cuts the risk of death or injury by 40 to 55 per cent.

Aircraft safety. Relatively few accidents involving scheduled airliners occurred in the United States in 1988. One of the most dramatic happened when the fuselage of a 19-year-old Aloha Airlines Boeing 737 jet in flight to Honolulu, Hawaii, ripped open on April 28, apparently because of a structural failure. Thirteen of 107 passengers on a Delta Air Lines Boeing 727 jetliner bound for Salt Lake City, Utah, died when the jet crashed and burned shortly after take-off from Dallas-Fort Worth International Airport on August 31. Early reports indicated that engine malfunctioning caused the crash.

Questions arose about the adequacy of airport security measures when a plastic explosive destroyed a Pan American World Airways jumbo jet over Lockerbie, Scotland, on December 21. All 259 people aboard the jet died, as did 11 people on the ground. On December 29, the Federal Aviation Administration tightened security for U.S. airlines overseas.

Occupational safety. On October 28, the Occupational Safety and Health Administration (OSHA) fined John Morrell & Company, a meat-packing company, $4.33 million for "willful" violations at its Sioux Falls, S. Dak., plant. This was the largest fine levied against a single employer in OSHA's 17-year history.

Meat packing has one of the highest injury rates in industry. In 1986, an average of 33.4 injuries were reported per 100 full-time meat-packing workers— three times the overall injury rate for manufacturing workers. The injury rate at the Morrell plant was several times higher than the meat-packing industry average.

Milton J. Schloss, Morrell's chairman of the board, said that the injury rates at the Sioux Falls plant dropped dramatically between April and October 1988. Calling the OSHA action "grossly unfair and totally unjustified," Morrell sought a court order canceling the fine.   Odom Fanning

See also **Aviation; Consumerism; Environmental pollution.** In *World Book*, see **Safety.**
Sailing. See Boating.

Salinas de Gortari, Carlos (1948-   ), took

office as president of Mexico on Dec. 1, 1988. He had been declared the winner of Mexico's July 6 presidential election with 50.4 per cent of the vote. Salinas' victory as the candidate of the Institutional Revolutionary Party (PRI), Mexico's dominant political party, was marred by charges of fraud from his opponents in the election. See **Mexico.**

Born on April 3, 1948, in Mexico City, Salinas spent much of his childhood in the northern state of Nuevo León. His father served as a minister of industry and commerce, as ambassador to the Soviet Union, and as a senator representing Nuevo León.

Salinas graduated from the National Autonomous University of Mexico in Mexico City in 1969. He later did graduate work at Harvard University in Cambridge, Mass., earning master's degrees in public administration in 1973 and in political economy in 1976 and a doctorate in political economy and government in 1978.

After 1978, Salinas returned to Mexico, where he held a series of government jobs, specializing in economic affairs. In 1982, he was appointed to a Cabinet position as minister of budget and planning.

Dubbed the "Atomic Ant" for his small stature and relentless energy, Salinas won a silver medal in horsemanship in the 1971 Pan American Games. He is married to the former Yolanda Cecilia Occelli González. The couple have two sons and a daughter.   Rod Such

Saskatchewan. On Feb. 25, 1988, the Supreme Court of Canada ruled that Saskatchewan must either translate its laws into French or enact a new statute to confirm English as the only language of legislation. A largely ignored 1886 act, which predated the creation of the province in 1905, gave equal status to French and English in the courts and legislature. Only 25,000 of Saskatchewan's 1 million residents speak French as their primary language.

The Progressive Conservative government of Premier Grant Devine, fearing that immediate bilingualism would anger the English-speaking majority, introduced a bill on April 4 to repeal the 1886 act. The new bill authorized the cabinet to order the translation of "key statutes" into French, but other legislation would be valid written in English only. Both languages could be used in the courts and legislature. The federal government, after failing to persuade Devine to move more quickly on French-language protection, offered $60 million (Canadian dollars; $1 = U.S. 84 cents as of Dec. 31, 1988) over 10 years to help the province translate more laws into French.

A dispute over exports of potash, a fertilizer, to the United States was settled on January 7 when Saskatchewan producers agreed not to sell below prices established by U.S. officials as fair value. The agreement removed the threat of U.S. import duties on Canadian potash.   David M. L. Farr

See also **Canada.** In *World Book*, see **Saskatchewan.**

Saudi Arabia broke off diplomatic relations with Iran in April 1988, following a dispute over Saudi attempts to restrict the number of Iranians entering Saudi Arabia in 1988 for the annual *hajj* (pilgrimage) to Mecca, Islam's most sacred city. In March, the Saudis limited the number of Iranians to about 50,000 after failing to obtain assurances from Iran that its pilgrims would not hold political demonstrations. Clashes between Iranian pilgrims and Saudi police in Mecca in 1987 left more than 400 people dead. But Iran's leader, Ayatollah Ruhollah Khomeini, rejected the quota. As a result, no Iranians took part in the July 1988 hajj, held under tight security.

Arms contracts. The government of King and Prime Minister Fahd ibn Abd al-Aziz Al Saud signed a contract with Great Britain on July 3 for the purchase of at least $12 billion in military hardware. The weapons order was the largest ever for the British arms industry.

Saudi Arabia placed the order with Great Britain after the United States Congress delayed approving a request by the Administration of President Ronald Reagan to sell the Saudis $825 million in U.S. weapons. Saudi officials said the delay was caused by a pro-Israel lobby, and the Reagan Administration criticized Congress for preventing the United States from aiding an ally.

Congressional objections to the sale stemmed in part from Saudi purchases in March of medium-range

Sauvé, Jeanne Mathilde (1922-   ), who as governor general of Canada represents head of state Queen Elizabeth II, visited France from Jan. 25 to 29, 1988. The trip was the first official visit to France by a governor general of Canada; France's President Fran-çois Mitterrand had visited Canada in 1987.

The governor general received two royal visitors to Canada in 1988: King Carl XVI Gustaf of Sweden, who spent one week in Canada in March, and Queen Be-atrix of the Netherlands, who started a nine-day visit on May 9. Queen Beatrix had lived in Canada as a child for five years during the Nazi occupation of the Netherlands in World War II (1939-1945).

Sauvé opened two new museums in Ottawa, Ont., in 1988: the National Gallery of Canada on May 21 and the National Aviation Museum on June 17. On February 13, she attended the opening of the Winter Olympic Games in Calgary, Alta. She presented the Order of Canada to Rick Hansen at a ceremony at Rideau Hall, her Ottawa residence, on March 29, 1988. From 1985 to 1987, Hansen pushed himself around the world in a wheelchair to build awareness of the po-tential of disabled persons and to raise money for spinal cord research.

Sauvé confirmed her nonpolitical constitutional role by canceling all of her public engagements during the campaign leading to the federal election on Novem-ber 21.   David M. L. Farr

In *World Book*, see **Sauvé, Jeanne Mathilde.**

Crown Prince Abdallah ibn Abd al-Aziz Al Saud, Saudi Arabia's deputy prime minister, reviews the Welsh Guards on a June visit to Great Britain.

ballistic missiles from China. The Saudis insisted that the missiles were strictly for defense, to help protect Saudi Arabia against attack by Iran. As evidence that it did not intend to acquire nuclear warheads for the missiles, the Saudi government announced in April that it would sign the 1968 Nuclear Nonproliferation Treaty, which limited the spread of nuclear weapons.

The economy. Saudi Arabia in 1988 marked the 50th anniversary of the first Saudi oil strike, which occurred on March 3, 1938. The output from that first well, near Ad Dammam on the Persian Gulf, was 1,600 barrels per day (bpd). In 1988, Saudi oil production was 6.5 million bpd.

But lower oil revenues cast a shadow over economic growth. In January, King Fahd issued a royal decree authorizing the government to borrow money from within the country for the first time in 25 years. With the 1988 budget expected to be in the red, the gov-ernment also announced in January that for the first time it would impose an income tax on foreign com-panies and workers. But the tax was withdrawn only a few days later after foreign firms threatened to re-move their workers.

In June, Saudi Arabia announced it would purchase 50 per cent ownership of three U.S. oil refineries and marketing access to 11,450 gasoline stations from Texaco Incorporated for $1.2 billion.   William Spencer

See also **Middle East** (Facts in brief table); **Petro-leum and gas.** In *World Book*, see **Saudi Arabia.**

Sawyer, Eugene (1934-   ), served as acting mayor of Chicago during 1988. He was elected to that post by the City Council on Dec. 2, 1987, a week after the sudden death of Mayor Harold Washington, who just eight months earlier had won a second four-year term in office. Sawyer's supporters had hoped he would be able to serve the remainder of Washington's term—until 1991—but in November 1988 the Illinois Supreme Court said the city must hold a special may-oral election in 1989. See **Chicago.**

Sawyer was born on Sept. 3, 1934, in Greensboro, Ala. He graduated from Alabama State University in Montgomery in 1956. While at college, he became deeply involved in the civil rights movement.

In 1957, after teaching chemistry for a year at a Mississippi high school, Sawyer moved to Chicago. He was soon a diligent worker for the city's Democratic organization, and in 1971 he was elected to the City Council.

By the time of Mayor Washington's death, Sawyer had served on the City Council longer than any other black and had made many allies among white council members. The backing of the council's white member-ship enabled Sawyer to defeat his rival for the acting mayorship, Alderman Timothy C. Evans, also black.

Sawyer is legally separated from his wife, Eleanor, whom he married in 1975. He has three children from a previous marriage.   David L. Dreier

School. See Education.

Senegal. The multiparty political system of Senegal suffered a severe crisis in the country's February 1988 presidential election. A coalition of parties supporting incumbent President Abdou Diouf of the Socialist Party of Senegal (PS) claimed 73 per cent of the vote, nearly three times the total received by an alliance of opposition parties that supported Abdoulay Wade of the Senegalese Democratic Party (PDS).

Alleging electoral fraud and intimidation, supporters of Wade rioted in Dakar—Senegal's capital—and other cities. Opponents of the Diouf government carried out acts of sabotage against Dakar's water supply and other key targets. On February 29, Diouf declared a state of emergency, and Wade and other PDS leaders were arrested.

The protest led Diouf to make concessions, however, including relaxing an economic austerity program that had been instituted to lower Senegal's foreign debt. On May 12, Wade was released from jail with a one-year suspended sentence, and a week later the state of emergency was lifted.

In July, 9 of Senegal's 17 political parties joined in discussions aimed at reforming the nation's electoral system.   J. Gus Liebenow and Beverly B. Liebenow

See also **Africa** (Facts in brief table). In *World Book*, see **Senegal.**

Sierra Leone. See Africa.

Singapore. See Asia.

Skating. See Hockey; Ice skating; Olympic Games.

Skiing. Alberto Tomba, the brash 21-year-old Italian known as *La Bomba* (the Bomb), joined Swiss veterans in dominating Alpine skiing in the 1987-1988 season. The decline of the United States in skiing continued, partly because of injuries.

During the 1986-1987 season, Swiss men and women won 8 of the 10 titles in the world championships and 9 of 10 in the World Cup competition. In the 1988 Winter Olympics, held from February 13 to 28 in Calgary, Canada, the Swiss did not do quite as well, though they won more medals in Alpine skiing than any other nation—11 of 30. The Swiss gained only 3 of the 10 Alpine gold medals, with Austria also taking 3 golds and Italy 2. In the World Cup series —held from November 1987 through March 1988 in Europe, the United States, and Canada—the Swiss won 6 of the 10 titles.

Men. Tomba started the World Cup season by winning seven of his first nine races, including four straight. He did not take part in downhill races because his mother thought they were too dangerous.

Pirmin Zurbriggen of Switzerland won only two World Cup races, both downhills, but placed consistently well in all types of races. When Tomba fell in his last two races of the season, Zurbriggen retained the World Cup overall title with 310 points to 281 for the second-place Tomba. Zurbriggen won the World Cup titles in downhill and super giant slalom, while Tomba won in slalom and giant slalom. In the Olympics,

Tomba won the slalom and the giant slalom. Zurbriggen took the gold medal in the downhill and the bronze medal in the giant slalom.

Women. The World Cup overall title went to Michela Figini of Switzerland with 244 points to 226 for her teammate, Brigitte Oertli. Figini was the champion in downhill and super giant slalom, Mateja Svet of Yugoslavia in giant slalom, and Roswitha Steiner of Austria in slalom. In the Olympics, another Swiss, Vreni Schneider, won the slalom and giant slalom.

U.S. skiers. On March 19 in Åre, Sweden, Felix McGrath of Norwich, Vt., finished second in a World Cup slalom, the best race by a U.S. man in four years. The best U.S. finish in the Olympics was ninth.

Tamara McKinney of Olympic Valley, Calif., a former World Cup overall champion, suffered a hairline fracture of the left ankle in November 1987 and was not at full strength in the Olympics. Pam Fletcher of Acton, Mass., broke her right leg two hours before the Olympic women's downhill. Injuries sidelined or weakened such leading U.S. women skiers as Debbie Armstrong, Diann Roffe, and Eva Twardokens.

Nordic. The Soviet Union won 5 of the 8 Olympic gold medals and 13 of the 24 total medals. World Cup champions included Gunde Svan of Sweden in men's cross-country, Marjo Matikänen of Finland in women's cross-country, and Klaus Sulzenbacher of Austria in Nordic combined.   Frank Litsky

See also **Olympic Games.** In *World Book,* see **Skiing.**

Soccer. United States soccer experienced an unprecedented high and a perilous low in 1988. Appropriately, the high came on July 4 when the United States was selected to host the quadrennial World Cup competition—the world championship of soccer—in 1994. The low came when the Major Indoor Soccer League (MISL) almost went out of business.

World Cup. Every previous World Cup has been played in Europe, South America, or Mexico. The executive committee of the Fédération Internationale de Football Association—soccer's international governing body—hopes that holding the competition in the United States will stimulate the growth of the sport there.

The 1994 World Cup competition will involve 24 national teams, including the United States, which automatically qualifies for the competition as the host country. The teams will play 52 games in 12 stadiums over a four-week period in June and July 1994.

The United States had qualified for only 3 of the 14 previous World Cups, most recently in 1950. In 1988, the U.S. national team, made up of professionals and amateurs, played in the Summer Olympics and in regional eliminations for the 1990 World Cup, which will be played in Italy. The United States team qualified for a round-robin competition in 1989 with Costa Rica, El Salvador, Guatemala, and Trinidad and Tobago. Two of those five teams will advance to the 1990 World Cup.

A West German player lunges in front of Dutch soccer star Ruud Gullit to keep the ball, but the Netherlands went on to win the European title in June.

MISL. This 10-year-old league played a fast-paced version of soccer in arenas built for basketball and hockey. Of the 11 teams that started the 1987-1988 season, 3 were kept alive by new owners and 2 by fund-raising drives.

In the final week of the regular season, the owners told the players that salaries would have to be cut or the league would collapse. Agreement was reached just before the play-offs. After the play-offs, the players agreed to another pay cut.

The San Diego Sockers filed for bankruptcy. Then in June 1988, they won their fourth league championship in five years, sweeping the Cleveland Force in four games. After the play-offs, 5 of the 11 teams withdrew from the league. Only 7 teams—Baltimore, Dallas, Kansas City, Los Angeles, San Diego, Wichita, and a new franchise in Tacoma, Wash.—agreed to play in the 1988-1989 season.

Europe. On June 25, 1988, the Netherlands defeated the Soviet Union, 2-0, in Munich, West Germany, for the European championship. Mechelen of Belgium beat Ajax Amsterdam of the Netherlands, 1-0, for the European Cup Winners Cup. Liverpool won its first 29 games of the season to tie the English League record, and captured the league title for the ninth time in 13 years. But Liverpool was upset by Wimbledon, 1-0, on May 14 in the English Football Association Cup final.   Frank Litsky

In *World Book,* see **Soccer.**

Social security. The trustees of the United States social security system reported on May 6, 1988, that the system is likely to remain in good shape for the next 60 years. In the most probable scenario of economic and demographic changes, the combined old-age and disability trust funds would remain solvent until the year 2048. But under a more pessimistic scenario, they could run out of funds in 2026.

For the second straight year, the trustees—three Cabinet members and two private citizens—reported an improved outlook for the troubled Hospital Insurance Trust Fund, which finances Medicare. Because of continuing prosperity and efforts to curb outlays, they foresaw the Medicare program remaining solvent until 2005—three years longer than the forecast in 1987. As recently as 1986, the trustees had predicted a bankrupt Medicare fund by 1996.

To keep that fund solvent beyond the next 25 years, the trustees said, benefits would have to be reduced 14 per cent or Medicare contributions increased 16 per cent. The program is financed by a 1.45 per cent payroll tax on most workers.

New health insurance law. On July 1, 1988, President Ronald Reagan signed a "catastrophic" health insurance law that provides the largest increase in Medicare benefits since the program began in 1965. Effective on Jan. 1, 1989, the law gives Medicare participants unlimited hospital benefits for the year once a patient makes an initial payment—$560 in 1989 and more in future years to reflect inflation. In 1988, patients paid a $540 deductible for each hospital stay, and Medicare payments ended after 60 days. The new law also phases in assistance in paying for prescription drugs starting in 1990 and places a $1,370 ceiling on annual outlays by participants in Part B of the Medicare program. Part B covers doctor bills, laboratory fees, and outpatient hospital services.

Payroll deductions. Effective on Jan. 1, 1989, earnings subject to social security payroll taxes were to increase to $48,000, up from $45,000 in 1988, in line with an increase in average wages paid during 1988. The maximum per-worker tax was to rise as a result to $3,604.80 from $3,379.50 in 1987.

Increase in benefits. Also to take effect on Jan. 1, 1989, was a 4 per cent increase in social security benefits under the cost-of-living adjustment (COLA) program. The Social Security Administration estimates that benefit payments rise by $2 billion for each percentage point of inflation.

Higher premiums. Older and disabled Americans participating in Part B were to pay higher premiums starting Jan. 1, 1989. To cover new benefits and increasing health-care costs, monthly premiums were to rise to $31.90 from $24.80. In addition, Medicare beneficiaries with enough income to owe federal income tax will pay a tax surcharge of up to $800 per beneficiary in 1989, rising to a limit of $1,050 per person in 1993.   Frank Cormier and Margot Cormier

In *World Book,* see **Social security.**

Somalia. The prospects for peace between Somalia and Ethiopia in 1988 were the brightest since 1977-1978, when the two countries fought a war over ownership of Ethiopia's Ogaden region. In March 1988, the two nations agreed to resume diplomatic relations, withdraw all of their troops from their common border, exchange prisoners of war, and cease carrying out subversive acts against each other.

The Ethiopian accord was offset by the outbreak of civil war in northern Somalia on May 26 as rebels of the Somali National Movement (SNM) launched an attack on the city of Hargeysa. The SNM—most of whose members are from the Isaaq clan, or ethnic group—seeks regional autonomy. In retaliation for the attack, government forces carried out massive bombing raids against the rebels.

The uprising may have been sparked by a trial in February involving a score of defendants charged with treason. Many of those who were sentenced to death or long prison terms—sentences that were soon commuted—were members of the Isaaq clan.

Escalating prices and shortages of many basic commodities were aggravated by the government's decision in February to control prices for sugar, rice, and pasta. Merchants either hoarded their supplies of those commodities or sold the foods on the black market.   J. Gus Liebenow and Beverly B. Liebenow

See also **Africa** (Facts in brief table). In **World Book**, see **Somalia**.

South Africa. International efforts to isolate South Africa because of its policy of *apartheid* (racial segregation) lost momentum in 1988. The slowdown was due to several factors, including the difficulty of monitoring violations of economic *sanctions* (penalties) imposed against South Africa and the willingness of Japan, Israel, and other nations to fill the gap left by United States and European cuts in trade and investment. The stalled sanctions movement was also attributed to South Africa's efforts to seek a negotiated peace in Angola and Namibia, which led to the signing of a peace pact on December 22.

Challenges to apartheid by South Africa's black majority escalated in 1988. State President Pieter Willem Botha continued his efforts to create a multiracial national council, with a bare majority of black members, to discuss political rights for blacks. But because the council would have only an advisory function, most black leaders rejected the idea.

During the year, the government attempted to neutralize all black opposition by banning 32 major antiapartheid groups from political action and curtailing the activities of a number of black leaders. The government also imposed further restrictions on journalists and widened the scope of censorship.

On June 9, Botha renewed for another year the state of emergency declared in 1986. The emergency decree gives the government the power to hold people in jail without formally charging them with crimes.

In addition, a South African court in November 1988 accepted the government's argument that "treasonable activity" could include speeches and demonstrations as well as acts of violence.

In the absence of peaceful channels for protest, blacks in 1988 increasingly resorted to strikes, boycotts, street demonstrations, and random acts of violence. During a nationwide strike in June, an estimated 2 million black workers stayed away from their jobs for three days. From January through October, about 125 car bombings and other explosions were reported.

Government criticized. In May, the International Commission of Jurists—an organization based in Geneva, Switzerland, that promotes adherence to law throughout the world—criticized South African security forces for their alleged widespread use of torture and violence, even against children.

Mandela out of prison. In August, Botha authorized transferring black antiapartheid leader Nelson Mandela, who had been in jail since 1962, from Pollsmoor Prison near Cape Town to a nearby hospital when Mandela was diagnosed as having tuberculosis. At year's end, Mandela was recuperating at a house on a prison farm.

In November, after granting several stays of execution, the government commuted the death sentences of the "Sharpeville Six" to 18 to 25 years in prison. The five men and a woman, all black, had been convicted of participating in the 1984 killing of a black official, even though the government had failed to prove that they had been directly involved.

Afrikaner disunity. The unity of South Africa's *Afrikaners*—chiefly people of Dutch, German, or French descent, who make up about three-fifths of the white population—was eroded in 1988. Growing numbers of Afrikaners abandoned the ruling National Party (NP), and gave a majority of their votes to the more right wing Conservative Party in October municipal elections.

Also threatening to the NP was the growth of the Afrikaner Resistance Movement, a paramilitary organization of white extremists that seeks the creation of an all-white "homeland." The government has so far dealt gingerly with the organization.

The economy. The government on March 15 announced a budget that included deep cuts in many domestic programs. During the year, the finance ministry acknowledged that economic sanctions have taken a toll; the nation's economic growth has slowed, and, since 1985, foreign investment has fallen by some $10 billion. Inflation in 1988 was about 17 per cent.   J. Gus Liebenow and Beverly B. Liebenow

See also **Africa** (Facts in brief table); **Angola**. In **World Book**, see **South Africa**.

South America. See **Latin America** and articles on Latin-American countries.

South Carolina. See **State government**.

South Dakota. See **State government**.

The *Discovery* blasts off on Sept. 29, 1988, in the first United States space shuttle flight since the *Challenger* exploded in January 1986.

Space exploration.

United States astronauts returned to space on Sept. 29, 1988, after a 32-month absence. The *Discovery* space shuttle blasted off from Cape Canaveral, Fla., following a series of test firings to evaluate redesigned booster rockets and seals. Seals of a previous design had failed on Jan. 28, 1986, causing an explosion that killed the seven crew members of the *Challenger* shuttle.

Officials of the National Aeronautics and Space Administration (NASA) heaved a collective sigh of relief when *Discovery* performed almost flawlessly on a four-day mission. The crew of five astronauts, commanded by Frederick H. Hauck, deployed a tracking data and relay system satellite, one of a network of three satellites that will replace expensive ground-based stations built to track spacecraft in low orbit. The mission ended on October 3 with a perfect landing at Edwards Air Force Base in California.

On December 2, the shuttle *Atlantis* blasted off from Cape Canaveral, carrying a five-member crew commanded by Robert L. Gibson, and a secret military payload. In spite of the secrecy, it was generally known that the crew's main mission was to deploy a spy satellite. The shuttle landed at Edwards Air Force Base on December 6.

Soviet shuttle. The Soviet Union on November 15 launched its first shuttle, the *Buran* (Snowstorm), on an unmanned, computer-controlled flight. The craft orbited Earth twice, then landed successfully.

The *Buran* orbiter looks much like a U.S. orbiter, but the designs differ in two major respects. A U.S. orbiter has on-board launch rockets, while the *Buran* does not; and the *Buran* has jet engines for maneuvering during landing, while U.S. shuttles glide to a landing.

Soviet mishap. Soviet cosmonauts continued to make round trips to the *Mir* space station, which has been in orbit since February 1986. On June 7, 1988, a *Soyuz TM-5* spacecraft blasted off carrying Soviet cosmonauts Viktor Savinykh and Anatoly Solovyov and a Bulgarian pilot, Alexander Alexandrov. The craft docked with *Mir*, and its crew visited with Soviet cosmonauts Vladimir Titov and Musa Manarov, who had been aboard the space station since December 1987. On June 17, 1988, the *TM-5* crew returned to Earth in the *Soyuz TM-4* spacecraft that Titov and Manarov had used.

On August 29, Soviet physician Valery Polyakov, Soviet cosmonaut Vladimir Lyakhov, and Afghan air force pilot Abdul Ahad Mohmand blasted off from Earth in a *Soyuz TM-6* spacecraft. Two days later, they docked with *Mir*. On September 6, Mohmand and Lyakhov left *Mir* in the *TM-5*. Polyakov remained aboard to examine Titov and Manarov.

When a computer fired retrorockets to start the *TM-5*'s descent to Earth, a malfunction shut them down prematurely. Lyakhov terminated a second automatic firing of the retrorockets to prevent the *TM-5* from landing in China. Three hours later, a

United States researchers prepare to test an experimental aluminum space suit in a tank of water that simulates conditions in space.

faulty computer aborted yet another attempt to fire the rockets.

Newspapers throughout the world reported that the cosmonauts were marooned in space. There was little cause for alarm, however. The spacecraft had enough food and water for 48 hours of flight, and its manual control system was functioning.

Flight controllers postponed the landing for 24 hours to study the computer problem and to enable the *TM-5* to orbit to a location from which it could land at the planned site in Soviet central Asia. On September 7, the retrorockets fired properly and the cosmonauts landed safely.

On November 26, a *Soyuz TM-7* spacecraft blasted off, carrying two Soviets and a French astronaut, Jean-Loup Chrétien, to *Mir*. The *TM-7* docked with the space station. On December 21, Chrétien, Titov, and Manarov returned to Earth aboard the *TM-6*. Titov and Manarov had spent a record 366 days in space.

Mars probe fails. On July 7, the Soviets launched the probe *Phobos 1* toward the Martian moon Phobos, followed by the launch of *Phobos 2* on July 12. Plans called for the probes to make close-up measurements of Phobos in 1989. The probes also were scheduled to deploy robot landers.

On the night of Aug. 29-30, 1988, however, a flight controller sent an erroneous message to the computer aboard *Phobos 1*. This message caused the probe to begin tumbling. As a result, its batteries, which depend on sunlight for recharging, went dead. On September 9, Soviet officials said there was almost no chance to regain control of *Phobos 1*.

Unmanned U.S. launches. During the same week, the United States had problems with its most powerful military rocket, the Air Force's Titan 34D. After a normal liftoff on September 2, the upper stage failed, preventing the rocket from boosting a spy satellite into orbit. Three days later, however, the Air Force successfully launched what were reported to be four satellites aboard a Titan 2 missile. This marked the first time that a converted missile, designed to carry a nuclear warhead, orbited satellites.

The United States in 1988 also launched fake Soviet warheads, navigation satellites, and a weather satellite. The mock warheads went aloft to test the ability of Strategic Defense Initiative ("Star Wars") equipment to identify and track them.

A *Geostar* satellite, placed in orbit in March, transmits and receives signals that enable commercial users to determine the positions of trucks and other mobile units. Four navigation satellites that serve both military and civilian users rode Scout rockets into orbit in March, April, May, and June. On September 4, *NOAA-11* joined a network of three weather satellites used in global and local forecasting.

Ariane. United States satellites also went into orbit aboard rockets owned by the 13-nation European Space Agency (ESA). On March 11, an Ariane-3 booster

The first Soviet shuttle entered the space race in 1988. Flying unmanned on November 15, *Buran* (Snowstorm) orbited Earth twice and landed smoothly.

roared away from the ESA's launching base in Kourou, French Guiana, and orbited a U.S. communications satellite and one belonging to France. On July 21, another Ariane-3 orbited a European and an Indian communications satellite. A power failure shortly afterward disabled the Indian satellite.

The first launch of the more powerful Ariane-4 booster took place on June 15. This rocket orbited a privately owned U.S. communications satellite, a European weather satellite, and a West German-built communications satellite for amateur radio operators. On September 8, another Ariane-3 blasted off carrying two privately owned U.S. communications satellites. One reached its designated orbit, but the other veered out of control and could not be saved.

The ESA has established itself as the world leader in launching commercial satellites. President Ronald Reagan took NASA out of this business in August. He ordered NASA to launch only military and scientific payloads, leaving commercial satellite launches to private industry and to other nations.

Israel and China. Israel became a spacefaring nation on September 19 when it orbited a satellite. On August 5, China used a Long March-2 booster to launch a payload that included a West German materials-processing module.   William J. Cromie

In the Special Reports section, see **Back into Space**. In *World Book*, see **Communications satellite; Space travel**.

Spain

Spain. The United States agreed on Jan. 15, 1988, to withdraw 72 F-16 fighter-bombers and some 3,500 troops from Spanish soil within three years. These planes and troops are stationed at Torrejón air base near Madrid, one of four United States bases in Spain.

Socialist President Felipe González Márquez had pledged to reduce the U.S. presence in Spain to encourage Spanish voters to agree to Spain's continuing support of the North Atlantic Treaty Organization (NATO). Under the agreement, the United States will have access to Torrejón in emergencies and will continue to use the other three bases.

During two years of discussions, United States negotiators had maintained that the aircraft and troops were vital to the defense of NATO's southern flank. After reaching agreement with Spain, the United States quickly arranged with Italy to move the fighter unit to Comiso, Sicily.

High unemployment. González faced heavy criticism in January, when the Bank of Spain reported that unemployment in December 1987 had topped 3 million, up 1 million since 1983, when the Socialists came to power. Spain's unemployment rate of 21 per cent was the highest in the European Community (EC or Common Market). Nicolás Redondo, head of the pro-Socialist General Workers Union, called on the government to reverse its economic policies to end "a profound sense of frustration." He complained that only 27 per cent of the workers listed as unemployed received government aid. The Socialist Party responded by promising to create 500,000 positions in which workers would receive on-the-job training. On Dec. 14, 1988, Redondo's union and a Communist-affiliated union led a 24-hour nationwide work stoppage, Spain's first general strike since 1934.

Cabinet reshuffle. González reshuffled his cabinet extensively on July 8, 1988, dismissing four members and adding six. The new members included two union officials and two women—the first women in a Spanish cabinet since the 1930's.

ETA discussions. The Basque separatist group Basque Homeland and Liberty (ETA) on January 28 made an offer aimed at ending its violent campaign for a self-governing homeland. ETA offered the government a 60-day truce in return for an end to "police harassment" and a resumption of talks in Algeria that were broken off late in 1987. On Feb. 19, 1988, the government announced that it had accepted the offer. Informal talks began, but renewed violence in March dimmed hopes for formal negotiations.

Gibraltar shooting. Three members of the Provisional Irish Republican Army (IRA) were shot dead on March 6 by British soldiers in Gibraltar, a British dependency at the southern tip of Spain. According to British authorities, the three were terrorists who had planned to plant a car bomb near the home of the governor of Gibraltar.   Kenneth Brown

See also **Europe** (Facts in brief table). In *World Book*, see **Spain**.

443

Sports

Sports. Amateur sports in the United States were shaken in 1988 by power struggles and charges of mismanagement. The problems attracted special attention in women's gymnastics, bobsledding, boxing, and track and field.

In January 1988, Don Peters succeeded Greg Marsden of the University of Utah in Salt Lake City as coach of the U.S. Olympic women's gymnastics team. Marsden had resigned in 1987 after attacking United States Gymnastics Federation (USGF) officials for their style of work. Mike Jacki, the USGF's executive director, defended the federation and criticized Marsden for insisting on "doing things his way."

Among the assistant coaches picked by Peters was Martha Karolyi, an expert coach of the balance beam. Her husband, the celebrated gymnastics coach Bela Karolyi, was not chosen, but Jacki appointed him to head the U.S. Olympic gymnastics delegation, a ceremonial post.

Peters did not want Bela Karolyi coaching on the floor during the Olympics. Karolyi said he did not care what Peters wanted because, he said, he was Peters' boss. Peters retorted that Karolyi was not his boss. When Karolyi learned he could not coach on the floor, he resigned as head of the delegation.

At the U.S. Olympic trials, four gymnasts personally coached by Karolyi qualified for the Olympic team. None of the gymnasts who were personally coached by Peters won places on the team. Peters then resigned as coach on August 8. Instead of naming a new coach, the USGF decided that the personal coaches of all the Olympian gymnasts could coach their athletes on the floor during the Olympic competition.

Bobsledding controversy. In bobsledding, controversy erupted and team morale fell when Willie Gault qualified for the U.S. Olympic team. Gault, a professional football player for the Chicago Bears, tried out for the bobsledding team only a month before the Winter Olympics in Calgary, Canada. When he made the team, Don LaVigne, who had been with the team all winter, was dropped. LaVigne later was named as an alternate, but he did not compete in the Olympics. Neither did Gault, partly because some of the drivers objected to him.

Boxing. In boxing, the U.S.A. Amateur Boxing Federation on June 11 suspended U.S. Olympic coach Ken Adams for six months for punching a federation official. Over strong objections from fighters and some officials, Tom Coulter, the first assistant coach, was named head coach. Adams went to arbitration and regained his job.

Track and field. Carl Lewis, the best American sprinter, feuded all summer with Russ Rogers, the sprint coach of the U.S. Olympic team, over who would run in the Olympic 400-meter relay. Rogers threatened several times to keep Lewis off the relay team. As it turned out, Lewis was supposed to run in the semifinals and final, but he never got the chance because the U.S. team was disqualified in the first round for passing the baton out of the exchange zone.

Awards. Jim Abbott, a baseball pitcher born without a right hand, won the Sullivan Award as the outstanding amateur athlete in the United States. Abbott, from the University of Michigan in Ann Arbor, helped pitch the United States to a silver medal in the 1987 Pan American Games in Indianapolis and to a gold medal in the 1988 Summer Olympics in Seoul, South Korea.

Among the winners in 1988 were the following:

Cycling. In the major stage races for men, Pedro Delgado of Spain won the Tour de France; Andy Hampsten of Boulder, Colo., the tour of Italy; and Davis Phinney of Boulder, the Coors Classic. Jeannie Longo of France won the women's Tour de France and the women's world pursuit championship. John Tomac of Chatsworth, Calif., won the United States criterium and mountain-bike championships.

Diving. Before the Olympics, where he won two gold medals, Greg Louganis of Boca Raton, Fla., lost two international competitions off the 3-meter springboard to Tan Liangde of China. Louganis won all three U.S. championships outdoors and the platform competition indoors, giving him a record total of 47 national titles. Wendy Lian Williams of Bridgeton, Mo., won the women's platform titles indoors and outdoors.

Fencing. Peter Westbrook of New York City won his 11th United States championship in sabre. The other national champions were Michael Marx of Portland, Ore., in men's foil; Sharon Monplaisir of New York City in women's foil; Jon Normile of Berea, Ohio, in men's epee; and Xandy Brown Robinson of Redondo Beach, Calif., in women's epee.

Marathon. On April 17 in Rotterdam, the Netherlands, Belayneh Densimo of Ethiopia (2 hours 6 minutes 50 seconds) and Ahmed Salah of Djibouti (2:07:07) ran the fastest marathons in history. On November 6, less than three months after arthroscopic knee surgery, Grete Waitz of Norway won the New York City Marathon for the ninth time in 11 years.

Rowing. In a battle of eight-oared crews headed for the Olympics, Great Britain defeated Australia by 12 inches (30 centimeters) on July 3 for the Grand Challenge Cup in the Henley Royal Regatta in England. Hamish McGlashan of Australia upset Andrew Sudduth, the best American, for the Diamond Challenge Cup for single sculls.

Wrestling. The Soviet Union beat the United States, 6-4, on March 27 in Toledo, Ohio, in the decisive match of the two-day, six-nation World Cup freestyle competition. Arizona State University on March 19 won the National Collegiate Athletic Association championship, the first time since 1974 that the University of Iowa or Iowa State University had not won.

Other champions

Archery, U.S. indoor champions: men, Jay Barrs, Mesa, Ariz.; women, Denise Parker, South Jordan, Utah.

Billiards, world champions: pocket, Mike Sigel, Towson, Md.; three-cushion, Torbjorn Blomdahl, Sweden.

Bobsledding, U.S. champions: two-man, Don Hass, Martville, N.Y.; four-man, Bob Horvath, Youngstown, Ohio.

Canoeing, preworld canoe slalom champion: Jon Lugbill, Bethesda, Md.

Casting, U.S. all-around: Steve Rajeff, Poulsbo, Wash.

Court tennis, world: Wayne Davies, New York City.

Croquet, U.S. champion: Reid Fleming, Vancouver, Canada.

Cross-country, world champions: men, John Ngugi, Kenya; women, Ingrid Kristiansen, Norway.

Curling, world champions: men, Eigil Ramssjell, Norway; women, Andrea Schopp, West Germany.

Darts, world champion: Mike Gregory, Great Britain.

Equestrian, world cup champions: jumping, Ian Millar, Perth, Canada; dressage, Christine Stuckelberger, Switzerland.

Susan Butcher embraces a member of her team after winning her third straight Iditarod Trail Sled Dog Race from Anchorage to Nome, Alaska, in March.

Field hockey, Champions Trophy (men): West Germany.

Frisbee, U.S. overall champions: men, Jim Herrick, San Diego; women, Wende Coates, San Diego.

Gymnastics, American Cup all-around champions: men, Marius Toba, Romania: women, Phoebe Mills, Northfield, Ill.

Handball, U.S. four-wall champions: men, Naty Alvarado, Hesperia, Calif.; women, Rosemary Bellini, New York City.

Horseshoe pitching, world champions: men, James Knisley, Bremen, Ohio; women, Diane Lopez, San Francisco.

Iceboating: International DN Class World Cup champion: Mike O'Brien, Hopatcong, N.J.

Judo, U.S. open champions: men, Leo White, Fort Carson, Colo.; women, Margaret Castro Gomez, Groton, Conn.

Lacrosse, U.S. college: Syracuse University, Syracuse, N.Y.

Luge, World Cup champions: men, Markus Prock, Austria; women, Yulia Antipova, Soviet Union.

Motorcycle racing, world 500-cc champion: Eddie Lawson, Upland, Calif.

Paddle tennis, U.S. champions: men, Scott Freedman, Santa Monica, Calif.; women, Denise Yogi, San Gabriel, Calif.

Parachute jump, U.S. combined champions: men, Jim Hayhurst, San Francisco; women, Cheryl Stearns, Fayetteville, N.C.

Platform tennis, U.S. doubles champions: Rich Maier, Upper Nyack, N.Y., and Steve Baird, Harrison, N.Y.

Polo, World Cup: White Birch Farm, Greenwich, Conn.

Racquetball, U.S. champions: men, Ruben Gonzalez, New York City; women, Lynn Adams, San Diego.

Racquets, world champions: James Male, Great Britain.

Rhythmic gymnastics, U.S. all-around champion: Diane Simpson, Evanston, Ill.

Rodeo, U.S. all-around champion: Dave Appleton, Arlington, Tex.

Roller skating, world champions: men's freestyle, Gregg Smith, Seven Hills, Ohio; women's freestyle, Rafaella Del Vinaccio, Italy; men's speed, Tony Muse, West Des Moines, Iowa; women's speed, Marisa Canafoglia, Italy.

Shooting, small-bore rifle three-position champions: U.S., Lones Wigger, Colorado Springs, Colo.; U.S. International, Glenn Dubis, Fort Benning, Ga.

Snowmobile racing, world champion: Bobby Donahue, Wisconsin Rapids, Wis.

Softball, U.S. fast-pitch champions: men, Pay 'n Pak, Bellevue, Wash.; women, Hi-Ho Brakettes, Stratford, Conn.

Squash racquets, world champion: Jahangir Khan, Pakistan. U.S. champions: men, Scott Dulmage, Toronto, Canada; women, Alicia McConnell, New York City.

Squash tennis, U.S. champion: Gary Squires, Darien, Conn.

Surfing, world champions: men, Damien Hardman, Australia; women, Pauline Menczer, Australia.

Synchronized swimming, U.S. champion: Tracie Ruiz-Conforto, Bothell, Wash.

Table tennis, U.S. open champions: men, Jean Philippe Gatien, France; women, Jun Xu, China.

Tae kwon do, U.S. heavyweight champions: men, Jimmy Kim, Cerritos, Calif.; women, Kathy Wagner, Colorado Springs.

Team handball, international champions: World Cup (men), West Germany; USA Cup (women), United States.

Triathlon, Ironman champions: men, Scott Molina, Boulder, Colo.; women, Paula Newby-Fraser, Encinitas, Calif.

Volleyball, U.S. champions: men, Molten, Torrance, Calif.; women, Chrysler Californians, Pleasanton, Calif.

Water polo, U.S. champions: men, Bruin, Los Angeles; women, Hawaii.

Water skiing, U.S. overall champions: men, Carl Roberge, Orlando, Calif.; women, Deena Brush Mapple, Windermere, Fla.

Weight lifting, super-heavyweight champions: European, Leonid Taranenko, Soviet Union; U.S., Mario Martinez, San Francisco.   Frank Litsky

See also **Olympic Games** and articles on the various sports. In *World Book,* see articles on the sports.

445

Sri Lanka

Sri Lanka. Prime Minister Ranasinghe Premadasa of Sri Lanka's United National Party (UNP) was elected president of the strife-torn island nation on Dec. 19, 1988, succeeding J. R. Jayewardene. The new president defeated Sirimavo Bandaranaike of the Sri Lanka Freedom Party (SLFP)—a former prime minister.

Jayewardene ended on September 14 a long period of speculation about whether he would seek reelection, deciding to retire at age 82 after more than 40 years of political prominence. Jayewardene led the UNP to victory in Sri Lanka's most recent parliamentary election, in 1977, becoming prime minister. In 1978, when the Constitution was changed to shift power from the prime minister's office to the presidency, he became president, and he was reelected in 1982.

Parliamentary elections were scheduled for Feb. 15, 1989. In 1982, the UNP extended Parliament's term instead of holding elections, thereby retaining control of Parliament. Ronnie de Mel, Jayewardene's finance minister since 1977, had criticized the term-extension as undemocratic, and he resigned on Jan. 18, 1988. De Mel, who was credited with increasing the level of prosperity in the late 1970's and keeping the economy stable during the guerrilla warfare of the 1980's, joined Bandaranaike's SLFP.

Unrelenting violence. Two terrorist groups, one based in the Sinhalese ethnic majority and the other in the Tamil minority, fought the government throughout 1988.

In the predominantly Sinhalese central and southern part of Sri Lanka, the Marxist People's Liberation Front assassinated some 300 people, including UNP officials. In an effort to overthrow Jayewardene's rule, the Front used mass intimidation and fear to temporarily halt all activity in Colombo, the capital. The threat of terrorism also kept voter turnout low in several local elections.

An even more bloody conflict continued in the north and east, where the Liberation Tigers of Tamil Eelam, a Tamil group, fought for political separation from the Sinhalese, killing many Sinhalese and Muslim villagers. About 45,000 troops from India, who had come to Sri Lanka under a 1987 agreement, failed to defeat the Tamil terrorists. The very presence of Indian troops was controversial, however. Premadasa and Bandaranaike wanted the soldiers to leave, even though the Sri Lankan Army was small and weak.

Jayewardene ordered the merger of the Northern and Eastern provinces on September 9. The Tamil terrorists had sought the merger, but they boycotted elections November 19 for a provincial council.

Economy. Despite the turmoil, rice production rose 21 per cent in the first half of 1988, and industrial production and foreign investment increased. The economic growth rate was only about 2 per cent, however.　　Henry S. Bradsher

See also **Asia** (Facts in brief table). In *World Book*, see **Sri Lanka**.

Stamp collecting. On April 3, 1988, the United States Postal Service raised the cost of a first-class stamp from 22 to 25 cents. A new E-denominated stamp, issued to ensure adequate supplies of first-class postage until sufficient stocks of 25-cent stamps became available, depicted a multicolored view of the earth from outer space.

Eight states that celebrated their 200th anniversary of statehood in 1988—Connecticut, Georgia, Maryland, Massachusetts, New Hampshire, New York, South Carolina, and Virginia—were honored during the year with 22- or 25-cent commemorative stamps. Among other commemorative issues in 1988 were stamps honoring Knute Rockne, Notre Dame University's football coach from 1918 to 1931; the bicentennial of Australia; and the 350th anniversary of the first Finnish settlers in North America. Antarctic explorers Nathaniel B. Palmer, Charles Wilkes, Richard E. Byrd, and Lincoln Ellsworth were honored on a block of four 25-cent stamps, and classic automobiles were featured in a colorful booklet of five 25-cent stamps. The five stamps, which show the autos in color against a black-and-white background, depict a 1928 Locomobile, a 1929 Pierce-Arrow, a 1931 Cord, a 1932 Packard, and a 1935 Duesenberg.

Polls conducted during the year by *Linn's Stamp News* and *Stamp Collector* identified the 50-stamp American wildlife pane as the most popular stamp issue of 1987. Runner-up was a booklet of five stamps picturing early locomotives.

Foreign stamps. Sweden in 1988 released a booklet of six 3.60-kronor stamps honoring the 350th anniversary of New Sweden, a Swedish colony in what is now Delaware and New Jersey. One of the stamps bears a map of New Sweden; the others depict famous Americans of Swedish descent, including poet Carl Sandburg and aviator Charles Lindbergh. Canada issued a block of four 37-cent stamps depicting Canadian butterflies; those pictured are the Canadian tiger swallowtail, the short-tailed swallowtail, Macoun's Arctic, and the northern blue. New Zealand and Australia honored Australia's bicentennial with a joint stamp featuring their respective symbols—the kiwi bird and the koala. And Great Britain issued a new series of stamps depicting famous castles.

New stamp outlets. The Postal Service in 1988 began selling booklets and rolls of stamps at face value in grocery and convenience stores throughout the United States. Some stores even sold limited numbers of stamps at a discount to attract customers. Postal Service officials said they were pleased with the results and would most likely look into other possibilities for making stamps and mail services more widely available.

Auction sales. A number of popular U.S. stamps with inverted designs were sold at auction in 1988. At several auctions in the first half of the year, four 1918 24-cent airmail stamps printed with an upside-down Jenny airplane fetched prices ranging from $99,000 to

$143,000. In April, a buyer at the annual Robert A. Siegel Auction Galleries rarities sale in New York City paid $55,000—$10,000 more than the catalog value—for a fine-quality used 1869 30-cent stamp with a flag-and-shield design on which the flags are inverted.

At a February sale, also at the Siegel galleries, a 2-cent 1902 Pan-American Exposition stamp with an inverted picture of a train and a 4-cent stamp printed with an inverted electric automobile sold, respectively, for $49,500 and $22,000. And in April, an inverted $1 candle-and-candleholder stamp—one of a sheet of such stamps discovered in 1986 by employees of the Central Intelligence Agency—sold for $16,500 at the Greg Manning sale in New York City.

In foreign sales, the Harmers gallery of London sold the finest of three known 1854 4-anna stamps with an inverted head of Queen Victoria for 52,800 pounds—about $99,500—at a May auction. (The anna was a unit of currency in India.) An extremely fine *cover*—an envelope that has gone through the mail—bearing a pair and two singles of the scarce orange-yellow shade of the 1864 ¼-silbergroschen issue of the old German state of Mecklenburg-Strelitz was the star item of Heinrich Köhler's seventh Boker German states sale in March in Wiesbaden, West Germany. This unique postal cover sold for 580,000 marks (about $348,000).   Paul A. Larsen

In *World Book*, see **Stamp collecting.**

State government. The impeachment of a governor, state elections, new lotteries, and radical new approaches to health and automobile insurance were among the major developments in state government in 1988. No state hiked taxes sharply, but a movement to establish state trust funds to finance college tuition and fees gained ground.

Impeachment. Arizona Republican Evan Mecham on April 4 became the first governor to be impeached, convicted, and removed from office since the 1929 conviction of Henry S. Johnston of Oklahoma. The Arizona Senate—which had a Republican majority—convicted Mecham on two charges of misconduct. The Senate held that the governor had tried to stop an investigation of whether one of his aides threatened the life of a member of a grand jury, and that Mecham had made an illegal loan of $80,000 in state funds to his automobile dealership. Acting Governor Rose Mofford, a Democrat who had been secretary of state, became governor to finish Mecham's term.

Elections. Of the 12 governorships contested in the November 8 elections, the Republicans won 7 and the Democrats 5. The results left Democrats in control of 28 statehouses. In legislative races, offsetting gains left the Democrats in control of both chambers in 28 states and the Republicans in 8. See **Elections.**

Lotteries. Idaho, Indiana, Kentucky, and Minnesota voted on November 8 to launch lotteries, joining 28 other states and the District of Columbia. Florida sold a record $95 million worth of instant tickets in the first week of its lottery, which began on January 12.

In August, voters in Missouri approved an increase in the prize money awarded in that state's lottery and the removal of restrictions on advertising the lottery. After the changes took effect, ticket sales picked up.

Insurance. Massachusetts in April enacted the first universal health-insurance program in the United States, designed to make health insurance available to all people in the state by 1992. A major part of the plan focuses on the two-thirds of the uninsured individuals in Massachusetts who are workers or members of workers' families. The program offers incentives to employers to help pay for their employees' insurance. The state will aid small employers with a group-purchasing arrangement and tax credits. Eventually, all Massachusetts businesses will have to offer insurance to all but temporary or seasonal workers. New York, Wisconsin, and other states were testing smaller programs to expand health coverage.

To help pay for medical care for the poor, California voters on Nov. 8, 1988, approved a hike in the cigarette tax. Voters in Georgia approved an Indigent Care Trust Fund. In Missouri, however, voters defeated a measure that would have increased taxes to pay for health care for the uninsured working poor.

Also on November 8, California voters approved a proposal requiring that all premiums for automobile, home, and business insurance be slashed to 80 per

Participants in Florida's first state lottery scratch tickets shortly after the lottery opened at one minute past midnight on January 12.

Selected statistics on state governments

State	Resident population*	Governor†	Legislature† House (D)	(R)	Senate (D)	(R)	State tax revenue‡	Tax revenue per capita‡	Public school expenditures per pupil§
Alabama	4,083,000	Guy Hunt (R)	89	16	30	5	$3,222,000,000	$790	$2,700
Alaska	525,000	Steve Cowper (D)	24	16	8	12	1,062,000,000	2,020	7,240
Arizona	3,386,000	Rose Mofford (D)	24	34	13	17	3,469,000,000	1,020	3,080
Arkansas	2,388,000	Bill Clinton (D)	88	11#	31	4	1,889,000,000	790	2,200
California	27,663,000	George Deukmejian (R)	46	34	24	15#	35,791,000,000	1,290	3,840
Colorado	3,296,000	Roy Romer (D)	26	39	10	25	2,561,000,000	780	4,110
Connecticut	3,211,000	William A. O'Neill (D)	88	63	23	13	4,359,000,000	1,360	5,480
Delaware	644,000	Michael N. Castle (R)	18	23	13	8	989,000,000	1,540	4,820
Florida	12,023,000	Bob Martinez (R)	73	47	25	15	9,846,000,000	820	4,060
Georgia	6,222,000	Joe Frank Harris (D)	144	36	45	11	5,324,000,000	860	3,170
Hawaii	1,083,000	John D. Waihee III (D)	45	6	20	5	1,697,000,000	1,570	3,870
Idaho	998,000	Cecil D. Andrus (D)	20	64	16	23	830,000,000	830	2,650
Illinois	11,582,000	James R. Thompson (R)	67	51	31	28	10,430,000,000	900	4,010
Indiana	5,531,000	Evan Bayh (D)	50	50	20	30	4,774,000,000	860	3,310
Iowa	2,834,000	Terry E. Branstad (R)	61	39	30	20	2,662,000,000	940	3,710
Kansas	2,476,000	Mike Hayden (R)	58	67	16	24	2,085,000,000	840	4,070
Kentucky	3,727,000	Wallace G. Wilkinson (D)	72	28	29	9	3,520,000,000	940	3,110
Louisiana	4,461,000	Charles E. (Buddy) Roemer III (D)	84	21	34	5	3,449,000,000	770	3,010
Maine	1,172,000	John R. McKernan, Jr. (R)	96	55	20	15	1,288,000,000	1,090	3,870
Maryland	4,535,000	William Donald Schaefer (D)	124	17	43	4	5,204,000,000	1,150	4,680
Massachusetts	5,855,000	Michael S. Dukakis (D)	128	32	32	8	8,464,000,000	1,450	4,900
Michigan	9,200,000	James J. Blanchard (D)	61	49	18	20	9,857,000,000	1,070	3,970
Minnesota	4,246,000	Rudy Perpich (D)	81	53	47	20	5,546,000,000	1,310	4,270
Mississippi	2,625,000	Ray Mabus (D)	113	9	45	7	1,943,000,000	740	2,530
Missouri	5,103,000	John Ashcroft (R)	105	58	21	13	3,942,000,000	770	3,340
Montana	809,000	Stan Stephens (R)	52	48	25	25	591,000,000	730	4,060
Nebraska	1,594,000	Kay A. Orr (R)	(unicameral) 49 nonpartisan				1,203,000,000	750	3,420
Nevada	1,007,000	Richard H. Bryan (D)	30	12	8	13	1,118,000,000	1,110	3,570
New Hampshire	1,057,000	Judd Gregg (R)	119	281	8	16	563,000,000	530	3,680
New Jersey	7,627,000	Thomas H. Kean (R)	30	49	23	17	9,491,000,000	1,240	6,170
New Mexico	1,500,000	Garrey E. Carruthers (R)	45	25	26	16	1,575,000,000	1,050	3,470
New York	17,825,000	Mario M. Cuomo (D)	92	58	27	33#	24,676,000,000	1,380	6,380
North Carolina	6,413,000	James G. Martin (R)	72	48	37	13	6,235,000,000	970	3,470
North Dakota	672,000	George A. Sinner (D)	44	62	32	21	573,000,000	850	3,360
Ohio	10,784,000	Richard F. Celeste (D)	59	40	15	18	9,717,000,000	900	3,760
Oklahoma	3,272,000	Henry Bellmon (R)	69	32	31	17	2,669,000,000	820	2,980
Oregon	2,724,000	Neil Goldschmidt (D)	32	28	19	11	2,235,000,000	820	4,380
Pennsylvania	11,936,000	Robert P. Casey (D)	104	99	24	26	11,379,000,000	950	4,750
Rhode Island	986,000	Edward D. DiPrete (R)	83	17	41	9	1,050,000,000	1,070	5,080
South Carolina	3,425,000	Carroll A. Campbell, Jr. (R)	87	37	37	9	3,340,000,000	980	3,040
South Dakota	709,000	George S. Mickelson (R)	24	46	15	20	416,000,000	590	3,050
Tennessee	4,855,000	Ned Ray McWherter (D)	59	40	23	10	3,603,000,000	740	2,870
Texas	16,789,000	William P. Clements, Jr. (R)	93	57	24	7	11,228,000,000	670	3,450
Utah	1,680,000	Norman H. Bangerter (R)	28	47	8	21	1,438,000,000	860	2,490
Vermont	548,000	Madeleine M. Kunin (D)	74	76	16	14	538,000,000	980	4,570
Virginia	5,904,000	Gerald L. Baliles (D)	65	33**	31	9	5,527,000,000	940	3,810
Washington	4,538,000	Booth Gardner (D)	63	35	24	25	5,639,000,000	1,240	3,850
West Virginia	1,897,000	Gaston Caperton (D)	80	20	27	7	1,830,000,000	940	3,660
Wisconsin	4,807,000	Tommy G. Thompson (R)	56	43	20	13	5,674,000,000	1,180	4,640
Wyoming	490,000	Michael Sullivan (D)	23	41	11	19	632,000,000	1,290	6,250

*1987 estimates (source: U.S. Bureau of the Census).
†As of January 1989 (source: state government officials).
‡1987 figures (source: U.S. Bureau of the Census).

§1986-1987 figures per pupil in average daily attendance
 (source: National Education Association).
#One independent.
**Two independents.

cent of their November 1987 levels. The measure, boosted by consumer advocate Ralph Nader, was suspended immediately by the California Supreme Court, pending a challenge by insurance companies. On Dec. 7, 1988, however, the court ruled that other provisions of the measure, including a ban on insurance-company price fixing, could go into effect.

Few tax hikes. No state enacted a major increase in personal income taxes in 1988. Only Louisiana and West Virginia raised sales taxes. The total tax hikes in the 50 states amounted to only $600 million—half of it in higher gasoline taxes in nine states.

Tax revenues in California, Massachusetts, and New York were lower than anticipated, and 18 other states had to deal with projected shortfalls in 1988. Only Louisiana and Texas, however, reported deficits on June 30, the last day of the states' fiscal year 1988. The states as a whole reported revenues of $236.2 billion and expenditures of $231 billion.

Tuition plans. State programs to encourage parents to plan for the cost of their children's higher education mushroomed in 1988. At least 14 states offered either prepayment or savings plans.

The U.S. Internal Revenue Service on March 15 approved Michigan's plan to allow parents to prepay college tuition and fees without paying taxes on the money earned by the payments. The state deposits the payments in a trust, which invests the money. The Michigan plan covers tuition and fees at any college or university supported by the state. Most tuition plans in other states are modeled after the Michigan program.

Illinois and North Carolina in 1988 sold their first college education bonds. The states sell these bonds at a price below face value and will redeem them at face value when they mature.

Education. New Jersey sought to take over the administration of the state's second-largest school district after charging the administrators of the Jersey City School District with gross mismanagement. As 1988 drew to a close, the decision on whether to give control to the state was in the hands of an administrative law judge. State funding of elementary and secondary schools rose 7.4 per cent in fiscal year 1988, and funding for higher education increased 5.2 per cent.

Highway safety. In May, 27 members of a church group died as a result of a collision between the second-hand school bus they were riding near Carrollton, Ky., and a pickup truck driven by a drunken driver. The accident prompted calls for laws to make school buses safer and to increase penalties for driving while drunk. Kentucky's Governor Wallace G. Wilkinson ordered safety inspections of all second-hand school buses, and many school districts in Kentucky began installing emergency pop-out window exits and making other safety improvements.

On July 1, Wyoming became the last state in the nation to raise its legal drinking age to 21. A 1984 federal mandate called for withholding a portion of federal highway funds from states that allowed individuals under 21 to drink. South Dakota, which lost a court challenge to the federal mandate in June 1987, raised its legal drinking age effective April 1, 1988.

Ohio in 1988 became the 10th state to permit judges to order that people convicted of driving while drunk have ignition interlocks installed on their cars. Ignition interlocks measure the amount of alcohol in the driver's breath and will not release a lock on the ignition if that level is too high.

The drive for state laws requiring the use of seat belts had a rocky year in 1988. Montana, Georgia, and Virginia made seat-belt use mandatory. Voters in Oregon, however, rejected a proposal requiring belts. West Virginia's Governor Arch A. Moore, Jr., vetoed a bill to require drivers to buckle up. Wisconsin legislators barely beat back an effort to repeal the state's new seat-belt requirement.

Economic development. The Illinois legislature acted on July 1 to keep the White Sox professional baseball team in Chicago. The state would provide the team with up to $60 million in incentives to move into a new stadium that would be financed by the state. Illinois would raise money for the sports package by imposing a 2 per cent tax on hotels and motels. The state acted to ward off a raid by St. Petersburg, Fla., which is looking for a major league team to play in a new stadium.

Texas won a highly competitive battle to become the home of the proposed Superconducting Super Collider (SSC), a gigantic particle accelerator to be built by the U.S. Department of Energy. Energy Secretary John S. Herrington announced on November 10 that Texas was the preferred site. The SSC would be built inside a ring-shaped tunnel, 53 miles (85 kilometers) in circumference, that would be bored near Waxahachie, Tex. Texas had offered to provide land at no cost to the federal government, and Texas voters had approved a $1-billion bond to support state efforts to obtain the massive project. The U.S. Congress had not yet appropriated the $4.4 billion necessary to build the SSC.

Recycling laws were enacted in several states to deal with growing problems of waste disposal. New York required communities to separate and recycle waste by 1992. Pennsylvania ordered recycling of leaf waste, glass, aluminum, paper, and plastic; communities of 10,000 or more population must begin by 1990, and those of 5,000 to 10,000 population by 1991. Illinois levied a fee for dumping in landfills. Florida began on Jan. 1, 1989, to levy a tax of $1 on each tire sold in the state and set a date after which landfills no longer may accept tires, lead-acid batteries, used oil, or household appliances. Florida also required that localities recycle newspapers, glass, plastic bottles, and aluminum cans.   Elaine Stuart Knapp

In *World Book*, see **State government** and articles on the individual states.

Steel industry

Steel industry prosperity returned to the United States in 1988, after years of heavy financial losses. The industry recorded sharp increases in production, domestic sales, and exports.

During the first half of 1988, production of raw steel totaled 50.4 million short tons (45.7 million metric tons), an increase of 20.1 per cent from the same period in 1987. Sales totaled $16.4 billion, compared with $12.7 billion during the first half of 1987. In addition, U.S. steel mills ran at more than 90 per cent capacity, compared with 75 per cent capacity during the first six months of 1987.

The American Iron and Steel Institute (AISI), the chief association of U.S. steel producers, reported on June 1, 1988, that the recovery actually began in 1987, when the industry earned a profit of $1 billion. That year was the industry's first profitable year since 1981. United States steelmakers lost almost $12 billion from 1982 to 1986, a period when many steel mills closed and steel producers in other countries captured a large share of the U.S. market. The AISI predicted that U.S. steel companies would have to invest $3 billion to $4 billion each year in modernizing their plants to continue competing with foreign steel producers.

Import restrictions. A steel industry study published in September 1988 concluded that voluntary restraint agreements had been a major factor in ending the financial crisis. The agreements, negotiated in 1984 between the United States and 29 steel-producing countries, limited steel imports to the United States to about 20 per cent of all steel used in the country. The lower value of the U.S. dollar also contributed to the recovery by making imported steel more costly.

Despite the boom, U.S. steel firms continued to express concern about the amount of cheap imported steel entering the United States. On Aug. 26, 1988, the AISI said that 11 million short tons (10 million metric tons) of steel were imported during the first half of 1988, an increase of nearly 10 per cent over the same period in 1987. The AISI urged government action to further limit steel imports.

Exports of U.S. steel also surged during 1988. The AISI said that 670,000 short tons (607,000 metric tons) of steel were exported during the first half of 1988, an increase of 25 per cent from the same period in 1987. The USX Corporation, the largest U.S. steel company, in September 1988 estimated that it would export more than 1 million short tons (0.9 million metric tons) of steel in 1988, its largest export total since the mid-1970's. On Aug. 30, 1988, USX announced its first sale of steel to the Soviet Union since the early 1970's. USX agreed to sell 88,000 short tons (80,000 metric tons) of steel tube products for use in oil and natural-gas drilling in the Soviet Union. The sale was the company's largest ever to that country.

Labor losses. The news for steelworkers was not so positive. The AISI reported in May 1988 that employment in the steel industry fell to 163,300 in 1987, the lowest level since the association began keeping records in 1933.

Company news. The LTV Steel Company on May 11, 1988, said it would sell a large steel mill in Warren, Ohio, and a related operation in Canton, China, to the Renco Group Incorporated of New York City. The sale price of the Warren plant, which has about 2,200 employees, was not disclosed, though the United Steelworkers of America estimated it at $140 million.

On July 6, the British Steel Corporation reported a record profit of $738 million for the first quarter of 1988. Krupp Stahl AG, a West German steel company, said in May that it would permit a huge steel mill in Rheinhausen, near Essen, to remain in operation until 1991. Krupp originally planned to close the mill, which has been a landmark in the heavily industrialized Ruhr Valley since the 1890's. But the company decided on a gradual phase-out after protests from workers and government officials. Krupp said the closing was necessary because the plant, which employs more than 5,000 workers, is obsolete and uneconomical.

Mexican loan. The World Bank, an agency of the United Nations, in March 1988 approved a $400-million loan to help modernize and restructure Mexico's steel industry. The United States opposed the loan on the grounds that the move would aggravate the world steel glut and give the Mexican steel industry an advantage in competition.   Michael Woods

In *World Book*, see **Iron and steel.**

Stocks and bonds. Compared with the wild stock-market fluctuations of the previous year—highlighted by the stock-market crash on Oct. 19, 1987—the year 1988 was relatively quiet. But the feeling of calm that pervaded the market was touched with nervousness. Many people remembered that the stock market appeared to recover after the 1929 stock-market crash only to collapse in 1930, setting off the Great Depression. Fortunately, no such collapse occurred in 1988, and none appeared likely.

The Standard & Poor's 500 Index, usually called the S&P 500, which tracks the prices of 500 stocks traded on the New York Stock Exchange (NYSE), closed 1987 at 247.08, but rose to 255.94 on Jan. 4, 1988. By February 8, however, it dropped to 242.63, the year's lowest point. It then bounced up and down between 250 and 275 until October. On October 21, it reached 283.66, a high for the year and a new high since the October 1987 stock-market crash. The index closed 1988 at 277.72.

The Dow Jones Industrial Average (the Dow)—the best-known index of stock prices, which tracks the stocks of 30 well-established industrial corporations—behaved much like the S&P 500 during 1988. After closing 1987 at 1,938.83, the Dow sank to 1,879.14 on January 20, its lowest point in 1988. But by late 1988, it had risen substantially, hitting 2,183.50 on October 21, its highest point since the 1987 crash. The Dow ended the year at 2,168.57.

The Dow calms down

Dow Jones Industrial Average

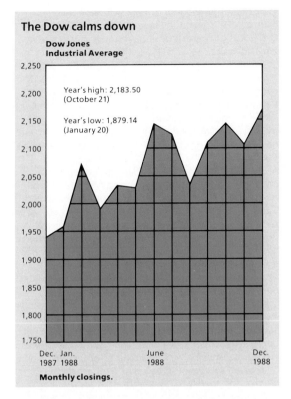

Year's high: 2,183.50 (October 21)

Year's low: 1,879.14 (January 20)

Dec. 1987 — Jan. 1988 — June 1988 — Dec. 1988

Monthly closings.

Other long-term interest rates followed the fluctuations of the corporate bonds. Home-mortgage rates, which began the year at 10.7 per cent, fell to a low of just under 10 per cent at the end of March, rose to 10.9 per cent at the end of August, and fell again to end the year at 10.7 per cent. State and local bonds remained steady during 1988, moving between 7 per cent and 7.5 per cent.

The fall in the bond market at the end of 1988 was in direct contrast to the movement of short-term interest rates, which generally rose during the last quarter of the year. At the beginning of 1988, the spread between rates on *long-term* (10-year or longer) Treasury bonds and three-month Treasury bills was 3.2 percentage points, but by the end of November, the gap had narrowed to 1.3 percentage points.

Insider trading. On September 7, the U.S. Securities and Exchange Commission (SEC) charged Drexel Burnham Lambert Incorporated, a New York City investment firm, and six of its employees with *insider stock trading*—the buying and selling of stocks based on confidential information—and other violations of securities law. The lawsuit, largest brought against a Wall Street firm by the SEC, involved 18 deals made between 1984 and 1986. On December 21, the firm said it would plead guilty to six felony charges and pay $650 million in fines.   Donald W. Swanton

In *World Book*, see **Bond; Investment; Stock, Capital.**

Stock activity elsewhere. Most other stock exchanges throughout the world paralleled the level of activity on the NYSE and the Dow in 1988, remaining quiet and well below the peaks they hit in August 1987. During 1988, stocks on the Australian Stock Exchange hit a low of 1,171 and a high of 1,658, with an increase for the year of 12 per cent. The Toronto Stock Exchange in Canada saw stocks swing between 2,978 and 3,465 for an annual increase of 7.3 per cent. The United Kingdom's Financial Times Ordinary Index, which tracks the prices of stocks sold on the London Stock Exchange, recorded a low of 1,695 and a high of 1,879. The index recorded an annual increase of 3.3 per cent for 1988.

Only Japanese stocks stood out from the pattern. Tokyo's Nikkei Index hit a record high of 30,159 on Dec. 28, 1988. This was 39 per cent more than the index's level at the close of 1987.

The bond market in the United States in 1988 was almost as quiet as the stock market. Corporate AAA bonds, the bonds issued by corporations with the highest credit rating, opened the year at 10.0 per cent, dipped to a low of 9.5 per cent by the end of February, but then rose back to 10 per cent by the end of May. At the end of August, they hit their peak for the year, reaching 10.2 per cent. Over the next few months, they started to fall again, dropping to 9.5 per cent by the end of October. They ended the year at 9.8 per cent.

Sudan, once expected to become the breadbasket of the Middle East, was wracked by famine, civil war, and ruinous economic problems in 1988.

Al-Mahdi reelected. On April 16, Prime Minister Al-Sadiq Al-Mahdi, who had been serving on a caretaker basis since his coalition government fell in August 1987, resigned to form a new government. The National Assembly, Sudan's parliament, overwhelmingly reelected him on April 27, 1988.

Continuing civil war. Despite the formation of a new government in May, Al-Mahdi made little headway in dealing with Sudan's economic problems and civil war. Sudanese in the South, most of whom are Christian or practice local religions, continued to resist the application of Islamic law to the entire country. The imposition of Islamic law in 1983 had led to an upsurge in the long-standing conflict between the North and the South. The rebel Sudanese People's Liberation Army (SPLA) insisted on repeal as the price for peace. In November, the Democratic Unionist Party, the second-largest party in Al-Mahdi's coalition government, signed a peace agreement with the SPLA. The National Assembly rejected the agreement in December, however.

The war also weakened government control over areas of the Muslim North. In May, a separatist movement seized power in Darfur province. The rebels organized a 40,000-soldier army, mostly from the Fur tribe, traditional rivals of Al-Mahdi's Ansar sect.

Supreme Court of the United States

Starving Southerners. The civil war deepened the misery of the people of the South, where most of the fighting was taking place. Their suffering was compounded by a second year of drought, plus swarms of locusts that destroyed essential crops.

Western relief workers accused the government of using starvation and massacres to destroy civilian support for the rebels. The rebels, however, also prevented food supplies from reaching starving people in areas controlled by the government.

Floods. In August, torrential rains devastated Khartoum, Sudan's capital, and left more than 1 million people homeless. Relief agencies charged that some of the food donated for the victims of the flood was commandeered by the army and sold on the black market. In response, the government imposed heavy fines and prison sentences on black marketeers.

Protests. On December 28, the Democratic Unionist Party quit Al-Mahdi's coalition in protest over government increases in food prices. The December 26 price hikes, which included a 500 per cent increase in the cost of sugar, had set off widespread demonstrations and strikes as well as calls for Al-Mahdi's resignation. On December 29, the government rescinded the increases. But at year's end, protests continued and it remained unclear whether the Democratic Unionists would rejoin the government.   William Spencer

See also **Africa** (Facts in brief table). In **World Book**, see **Sudan.**

Supreme Court of the United States. In one of the last public sessions of its 1987-1988 term, the Supreme Court of the United States on June 29, 1988, upheld the authority of an independent counsel to investigate suspected criminal wrongdoing by top government officials. The 7 to 1 ruling, written by Chief Justice William H. Rehnquist, ended a yearlong dispute over whether the 1978 Ethics in Government Act unconstitutionally gives an independent counsel —also called a special prosecutor—too much unchecked power.

The Administration of President Ronald Reagan had argued that the 1978 law improperly stripped the President and the executive branch of the government of their traditional authority to appoint and dismiss prosecutors. The law provides that a special panel of judges select an independent counsel, who can be dismissed by the attorney general only for "good cause."

The high court ruling stemmed from an investigation being conducted by independent counsel Alexia Morrison. Morrison had been looking into charges that former Assistant Attorney General Theodore B. Olson and two other Justice Department officials committed perjury in 1983 when they refused to provide congressional committees with documents concerning the Superfund toxic-waste cleanup program. The three officials challenged the independent-counsel law after Morrison subpoenaed them to tes-

tify before a grand jury in 1987. A United States district court upheld the law, but on Jan. 22, 1988, the U.S. Court of Appeals declared it unconstitutional in a 2 to 1 decision.

The sole dissenter in the Supreme Court's reversal of that decision was Associate Justice Antonin Scalia. The court's newest member, Associate Justice Anthony M. Kennedy, did not participate in the ruling. A former judge on the Ninth Circuit Court of Appeals in Sacramento, Calif., Kennedy took his seat on the high court on February 18 after being unanimously confirmed by the Senate.

Freedom of expression. The 1987-1988 term produced two significant rulings on free speech and freedom of the press. On January 13, the court ruled, 5 to 3, that public school officials have broad authority to censor school newspapers, student theatrical productions, and other "school-sponsored expressive activities." Justice Byron R. White said in the majority opinion that students do not enjoy the same First Amendment rights of free speech as adults when they participate in school-sponsored activities.

The decision came in a case brought by three former students of Hazelwood East High School in suburban St. Louis, Mo. The students, who had been staff members of the school newspaper, charged that the Hazelwood East principal violated their rights in 1983 when he refused to allow the paper to print articles on divorce and teen-age pregnancy.

The court delivered another landmark First Amendment ruling on February 24 when it held, 8 to 0, that evangelist Jerry Falwell could not recover damages solely on the basis of emotional distress caused him by a 1983 *Hustler* magazine parody. Chief Justice Rehnquist said that although the *Hustler* piece was "doubtless gross and repugnant in the eyes of most," it was obviously satirical and thus could not be considered libelous.

Opening private clubs. Striking a blow against discrimination, the court on June 20 unanimously (9 to 0) upheld a New York City ordinance that prohibits large private clubs from denying membership to women and minorities. The ordinance, similar to laws enacted in recent years in other cities, applies to any club with more than 400 members that provides regular meal service and routinely receives payment from nonmembers using the facilities for business purposes.

In his written opinion, Justice White rejected claims that the law violates the constitutionally protected right of association. "If women and minorities are to have equal access to the market place," he declared, "some so-called private clubs that are commonplace for business discussions and other activities related to the market place must be subject to antidiscrimination law."

Taking another·unanimous stand against discrimination, the court on June 29 ruled, 8 to 0, that Clara Watson, a black former employee of the Fort Worth Bank and Trust, could use statistics to challenge the

Anthony M. Kennedy signs his oath as the high court's newest member on February 18 as Chief Justice William Rehnquist, right, and Justice Antonin Scalia look on.

bank's decision not to promote her and need not prove she had been the victim of intentional discrimination. For the first time, the court said that a company's use of "subjective" assessments of employee performance—that is, evaluations of employees' originality, judgment, ambition, and the like— violates the 1964 Civil Rights Act if that policy adversely affects members of minority groups and women more than other employees. The 1964 law prohibits job discrimination on the basis of color, race, sex, religion, and national origin.

Teen-age counseling. In an opinion relating to the separation of church and state, the court on June 29 upheld, 5 to 4, a federal law funding sex counseling by religious groups. The law, the 1981 Adolescent Family Life Act, aims at persuading teen-aged girls to avoid sex and—in the case of girls who are pregnant —to choose adoption over abortion.

Although the majority of the justices agreed with the dissenters that the law had in some cases been financing the teaching of religious doctrine, they said the act was constitutional as it was written by Congress. The court sent the case back to a federal district court in Washington, D.C., with instructions to look into violations of the law's secular intent and to suggest remedies.

In another decision concerning religion, the court ruled on April 19 that building a federal road through a national forest area sacred to American Indians

would not violate the First Amendment's guarantee of religious freedom. The area in question, in the Six Rivers National Forest in California, has been used by Indians for religious rituals for at least 200 years.

Other important rulings by the Supreme Court in 1988 included the following decisions:
● A 6 to 2 ruling on May 16 that police, without a search warrant, may look for evidence in garbage that people leave outside their homes.
● A 5 to 3 decision on March 23 upholding a federal law denying or restricting the right of families of striking workers to receive food stamps.
● A 5 to 4 ruling on June 24 that a North Dakota law allowing school districts to charge students a fee for transporting them to and from school does not violate the equal-protection rights of poor families.
● A 5 to 4 decision on June 27 that severely limits a defense contractor's liability for deaths or injuries caused by the faulty design of aircraft, land vehicles, and other kinds of equipment. Liability cannot be imposed, the court said, if the equipment conforms to "reasonably precise specifications" approved by the U.S. government and the contractor has warned the government of potential dangers.   Glen R. Elsasser

See also **Courts.** In *World Book*, see **Supreme Court of the United States.**
Surgery. See **Medicine.**
Suriname. See **Latin America.**
Swaziland. See **Africa.**

Sweden

Sweden. Prime Minister Ingvar Carlsson's Social Democrats lost three seats in the Riksdag (parliament) in a general election held on Sept. 18, 1988. The loss cut the Social Democrats' representation to 156 seats in the 349-seat Riksdag. The Communists, who support Carlsson, won 21 seats, giving the left wing parties a majority.

Enter the Greens. The environmentalist Green Party won 20 seats, becoming the first new party to enter the Riksdag in 70 years. The Greens had pledged "to launch an all-out attack on the ongoing devastation of the environment" if elected to the Riksdag. Political observers said, however, that the success of the Greens was due to voters' wish to return to an "age of innocence" before Sweden was rocked by assassination and scandal.

Minister resigns. Minister of Justice Anna-Greta Leijon resigned on June 7 because of a scandal involving an unofficial investigation into the assassination of Prime Minister Olof Palme in 1986. Although Swedish authorities have arrested several suspects, the assassins have never been found.

Leijon allowed a publisher, Ebbe Carlsson (no relation to the prime minister), to conduct an investigation financed by a $370,000 contribution from Tomas Fischer, a businessman. Private investigators smuggled illegal telephone-tapping equipment into Sweden to use against Kurdish refugees living in Sweden. Critics charged that Leijon gave Ebbe Carlsson letters of introduction to the British Secret Service and to other authorities said to have possessed information that Palme's life had been threatened.

Warning ignored? On June 11, critics said that the Swedish secret police had ignored a warning from the British intelligence service that Palme was in danger. The British reportedly had learned of a plot involving Iran's secret police and the Kurdish Workers' Party. The Iranians were said to be angered over Palme's attempts to help negotiate a settlement of Iran's war with Iraq and to block the sale of Swedish arms to Iran. The Kurdish Workers' Party is committed to establishing an independent Kurdish state on the borders of Iran, Iraq, and Turkey. Sweden ruled in 1984 that the party was a terrorist group.

Carlsson questioned. Prime Minister Carlsson faced tough questioning on Aug. 4, 1988, at a public inquiry into his government's role in setting up the private investigation. The prime minister denied that the government had sanctioned the investigation and said he found the suggestion "deeply insulting."

Industrialist charged. Prosecutors in December charged Refaat el-Sayed, former president of the biotechnology firm Fermenta AB, with 14 counts of fraud, insider trading, perjury, and breach of *fiduciary duty* (executive responsibility). He allegedly defrauded the firm of $50 million.   Kenneth Brown

See also **Europe** (Facts in brief table). In *World Book*, see **Sweden.**

Sweden's King Carl XVI Gustaf and Queen Silvia cross a river in Delaware in April as they mark 350 years of Swedish settlement in America.

Swimming. Kristin Otto of East Germany and Matt Biondi of Moraga, Calif., won the most honors in swimming in 1988. Janet Evans of Placentia, Calif., broke the most individual world records. David Berkoff of Huntington Valley, Pa., with his unusual underwater start in the backstroke, and Greg Louganis of Boca Raton, Fla., with a come-from-behind victory in Olympic diving, stirred the most attention.

The Summer Olympic Games in Seoul, South Korea, were the highlight of the year. In the swimming events, from September 18 to 25, the 22-year-old Otto won six gold medals in her six races, including a rare triple in the 100-meter freestyle, the 100-meter backstroke, and the 100-meter butterfly.

The 22-year-old Biondi won five gold medals, one silver, and one bronze in his seven Olympic races. He broke world records in the 50-meter freestyle, the 400-meter freestyle relay, the 800-meter freestyle relay, and the 400-meter medley relay. Biondi finished second in the 100-meter butterfly, losing to Anthony Nesty of Suriname by one-hundredth of a second.

In the United States indoor championships, held from March 22 to 26 in Orlando, Fla., Evans won four events and set women's world records of 8 minutes 17.12 seconds for the 800-meter freestyle and 15 minutes 52.10 seconds for the 1,500-meter freestyle. In the Olympics, just after she became 17 years old, she lowered her 1987 world record in the 400-meter freestyle to 4 minutes 3.85 seconds. She also won Olympic

454

U.S. swimmer Matt Biondi races to a silver medal in the 100-meter butterfly final at the Summer Olympics, where he also won five gold medals and one bronze.

gold medals in the 800-meter freestyle and the 400-meter individual medley. See **Olympic Games.**

World records fell during 1988 in 10 of the 17 swimming events for men and 5 of the 17 for women. In the Olympics, the men broke 9 world records, the women 2.

In the United States Olympic trials, held from August 8 to 13 in Austin, Tex., Angel Myers of Americus, Ga., bettered the U.S. records for the women's 50-meter freestyle (25.40 seconds) and the 100-meter freestyle (54.95 seconds). Three weeks later, she was disqualified from the Olympic team and stripped of the records because she failed a routine drug test.

Berkoff bettered the world record for the 100-meter backstroke twice (54.95 and 54.91 seconds) in the Olympic trials and in his preliminary heat of the Olympics (54.51 seconds). He finished second in the Olympic final to Daichi Suzuki of Japan after a sluggish start. In all his races, Berkoff swam his first 30 to 35 meters underwater using extended arms and a dolphin kick. After the Olympics, the sport's world governing body banned the underwater style.

Louganis won the gold medal in springboard diving despite hitting his head on the board during preliminaries. He won the platform title on his final dive, overtaking China's Xiong Ni to win his second gold medal and become the first man to win two diving golds in consecutive Olympics.   Frank Litsky

In *World Book*, see **Swimming.**

Switzerland was rocked in late 1988 by a scandal involving *money laundering* (the transfer of money to conceal its illegal source). The scandal caused the political downfall of Elisabeth Kopp, Switzerland's minister of justice and police, the nation's vice president-elect, and the first woman to serve in a Swiss cabinet.

Kopp's husband, Hans, had been on the board of a company that was under investigation in connection with the laundering of drug money. Elisabeth Kopp admitted that, on October 27, she had tipped off her husband about the investigation. Hans Kopp had then resigned.

Elisabeth Kopp resigned on December 12. Both Kopps denied doing anything wrong.

Royal mishap. Switzerland was the scene of a skiing accident on March 10 involving Prince Charles, heir to the throne of Great Britain. The prince and his companions were skiing on a steep, unmarked slope near Klosters. They had ignored warnings by Swiss authorities of possible avalanches.

Moments after the prince skied down the slope, an avalanche swept down the mountainside. The prince was not hurt, but a friend, Major Hugh Lindsay, was killed, and another friend, Patricia Palmer-Tomkinson, broke both legs. Swiss authorities reported on June 27 that the group had caused the avalanche, but held no individual responsible.   Kenneth Brown

See also **Europe** (Facts in brief table). In *World Book*, see **Switzerland.**

Syria. During 1988, the government of Syrian President Hafiz al-Assad found itself increasingly mired in the internal politics of neighboring Lebanon. Although the 25,000-member Syrian peacekeeping force stationed in Lebanon extended its security zone over about 70 per cent of the country, President Assad was unable—or possibly unwilling—to impose order throughout Lebanon.

Intervention. Syrian forces intervened in southern Lebanon in January to end a three-year siege of Palestinian refugee camps by Amal (Hope), the largest Shiite Muslim militia. The conflict had resulted in more than 2,500 deaths. The Syrians took action again in late May to halt weeks of bloody fighting between Amal and the Iran-backed Hezbollah (Party of God) militia, Amal's chief rival for the leadership of Lebanon's Shiite Muslims.

Power broker. Assad's chief concern was not so much ending Lebanon's civil struggle as preserving Syria's role as power broker between Lebanese factions without engaging in massive military intervention. To this end, he made a major effort in August and September to stage-manage Lebanon's presidential election to secure the selection of a pro-Syrian candidate. Assad's first choice was Suleiman Franjieh, an elder statesman in the Christian Maronite community who had served as Lebanon's president from 1970 to 1976. Franjieh had also spent time in exile in Syria. But Franjieh's election was blocked by the Lebanese Forces, a Christian militia, because of his ties to Syria. Assad then threw his support to Mikhail Daher, a Christian politician and friend of Franjieh's. But Daher also failed to win endorsement by the National Assembly, Lebanon's parliament.

Arafat meeting. In April, Assad met with Yasir Arafat, chairman of the Palestine Liberation Organization (PLO), for the first time since 1983, when Assad expelled Arafat from Syria. The reconciliation coincided with the funeral of Arafat's military chief, Khalil al-Wazir, also called Abu Jihad. Wazir was assassinated in Tunis, Tunisia, on April 16, 1988, allegedly by Israeli agents. But Arafat's insistence on an independent Palestinian presence in Lebanon ran counter to Assad's interest in preserving Syria's dominant position there.

The economy. Significant increases in oil production and a fivefold rise in wheat and cotton harvests resulted in a strong economic performance in 1988. Exports reached $101 million, while imports totaled $75 million, resulting in a trade surplus after at least a decade of trade deficits. Oil output of 1.1 million barrels per day from the newly developed Thayyem oil field in southwestern Syria was sufficient to meet all domestic fuel needs. The budget, passed by the People's Council, Syria's legislature, in July, was balanced at $4.6 billion, a 20 per cent increase over 1987's budget.   William Spencer

See also **Lebanon; Middle East** (Facts in brief table). In *World Book*, see **Syria.**

Taiwan. President Chiang Ching-kuo died of a heart attack on Jan. 13, 1988. His death, which came after years of declining health, ended a dynasty established in China more than 60 years earlier by his father, President Chiang Kai-shek. The elder Chiang had moved his government to Taiwan in 1949 when the Communists won control of China, and he remained Taiwan's most powerful leader until his death in 1975.

Vice President Lee Teng-hui succeeded Chiang Ching-kuo, despite the reported opposition of Chiang Kai-shek's widow and other elderly leaders of the ruling political party, the Kuomintang. Lee, the first president born in Taiwan rather than China, was popular with the island's native Taiwanese—80 per cent of Taiwan's population of 20 million.

Lee was named acting chairman of the Kuomintang by the party's Central Standing Committee on Jan. 27, 1988. At the committee's next meeting in February, the membership agreed to encourage aged, conservative party members to retire from their posts in the legislative *yuan* (council) and other government jobs, hoping to clear the way to continue the reforms started by Chiang Ching-kuo. On July 8, the Kuomintang's 13th Congress elected Lee party chairman. On July 12, in the first free elections ever held for seats on the Kuomintang's Central Standing Committee, the 1,209 delegates at the Congress gave Lee's supporters 147 of a total of 180 seats. Some conservatives, including Prime Minister Yu Kuo-hwa, won by embarrassingly slim margins.

Cabinet changes. Lee retained Yu when he reshuffled his cabinet on July 20, however. But, in general, younger, reform-minded technical experts were named to the cabinet, and for the first time, native Taiwanese outnumbered those born in China. In addition, 10 of the new members had been educated in the United States.

Relations with the United States were troubled by the disappearance in January of Chang Hsien-yi, a deputy director of Taiwan's Nuclear Energy Research Institute. The press reported that Chang had given state secrets about nuclear-weapons development to the United States. Taiwan denied that it was developing nuclear weaponry but in March agreed to stop the construction of a reactor capable of producing plutonium, a key component of nuclear arms.

Economy. Taiwan's trade with China reached $2.5-billion in 1988, and Taiwanese businesses began to invest in China as well. Taiwan, which is strongly anti-Communist, also began establishing trade relations with the Soviet Union and Eastern Europe. Despite the opposition of conservatives, a trade delegation was sent to Moscow. Taiwan's economy continued to grow rapidly, but its stock market collapsed in October after rising 276 per cent in 10 months.   Henry S. Bradsher

See also **Asia** (Facts in brief table); **China; Lee Teng-hui.** In *World Book*, see **Taiwan.**

Tanzania. See Africa.

Taxation. The Congress of the United States passed a major tax bill on Oct. 22, 1988, minutes before adjourning for the year. The bill, which was designed to extend some popular tax breaks and make "technical" corrections in the massive 1986 tax overhaul law, will not increase federal revenues. Some groups' taxes will rise by $4.1 billion over three years, while other taxpayers' assessments will be reduced by the same amount.

The House of Representatives passed the compromise measure 358 to 1, and the Senate added its approval by voice vote. President Ronald Reagan signed the legislation on November 11.

The bill will raise some taxes by speeding up corporate tax payments, restricting the use of life insurance policies as tax shelters, and reducing the amount of taxes that businesses working under federal contracts can defer until a contract is completed. The bill will also raise the taxes of some individuals who use their homes as offices and impose a new tax of 45 cents per pound (0.4 kilogram) on pipe tobacco. Another provision, aimed at discouraging companies from using assets in their employees' pension funds to help finance take-overs of other companies, imposes a 15 per cent excise tax on the withdrawal of such pension fund assets.

Tax benefits in the bill include the continuation through 1989 of a provision for mutual-fund shareholders, exempting them from having to deduct their proportionate share of the fund's expenses. Among other benefits are an extension through 1989 of a 20 per cent research and development tax credit; a "taxpayer bill of rights" to strengthen the position of individuals in disputes with the tax-collecting Internal Revenue Service; an extension through 1989 of a credit given to employers who hire economically disadvantaged workers; a provision exempting from taxation the interest earned on U.S. savings bonds redeemed to pay for college or vocational education; the liberalization of a tax credit for low-income housing; and an exemption from the diesel-fuel tax for farmers using that fuel for off-road vehicles.

Higher taxes for Medicare. In a separate bill, Congress imposed an income tax surcharge on Medicare participants with enough income to pay federal taxes. The purpose of the surcharge, which takes effect in 1989, is to help finance Medicare coverage for "catastrophic" illnesses. Under the law, signed by President Reagan in July 1988, participants will pay a "supplemental premium" based on their federal income tax liability. The 1989 rate would be $22.50 per $150 of tax liability, rising to $42 per $150 by 1993. For 1989, the maximum supplemental premium would be $800 per individual, or $1,600 for a husband and wife. By 1993, the maximum surcharge will increase to $1,050 per individual or $2,100 for a married couple.   Frank Cormier and Margot Cormier

In *World Book*, see **Taxation.**

"Oh, drat! I put a 'love' stamp on the IRS envelope."

Television. Although the United States television audience might not have been fully aware of it, a strike by television writers greatly affected what they saw in 1988. For 22 weeks beginning on March 7, about 2,500 TV scriptwriters—members of the Writers Guild of America—were out on strike. The writers struck the Alliance of Motion Picture and Television Producers, whose members make virtually all of television's dramatic programming, over royalties and creative rights.

The strike ended on August 8, far too late for the three dominant U.S. networks—the National Broadcasting Company (NBC), Capital Cities/ABC Inc. (ABC), and CBS Inc.—to prepare for their fall premiere season, which usually begins in September. A fledgling fourth network, Fox Broadcasting Company, which scheduled fewer programs and was affiliated with fewer stations, was also affected.

Instead of their customary line-up of new shows, the networks showed a combination of specials, documentaries, and rebroadcasts of programs. Many new programs and fresh episodes of returning series were not seen until November or later.

Special programming events marked the television year. ABC paid $309 million for the rights to telecast nearly 100 hours of the Winter Olympics in February from Calgary, Canada, and later said it lost more than $65 million. NBC paid $300 million to air a staggering 179½ hours of the Summer Olympics from

Top-rated U.S. television series

The following were the most-watched television series for the 31-week regular season—Sept. 20, 1987, through April 17, 1988—as determined by the A. C. Nielsen Company.

1. "The Cosby Show" (NBC)
2. "A Different World" (NBC)
3. "Cheers" (NBC)
4. "The Golden Girls" (NBC)
5. "Growing Pains" (ABC)
6. "Who's the Boss?" (ABC)
7. "Night Court" (NBC)
8. "60 Minutes" (CBS)
9. "Murder, She Wrote" (CBS)
10. "The Wonder Years" (ABC)
11. "ALF" (NBC)
12. (tie) "Moonlighting" (ABC)
    "L.A. Law" (NBC)
14. "NFL Monday Night Football" (ABC)
15. "Matlock" (NBC)
16. "Amen" (NBC)
17. "Family Ties" (NBC)
18. "CBS Sunday Movie" (CBS)
19. (tie) "In the Heat of the Night" (NBC)
    "My Two Dads" (NBC)
21. "Valerie's Family" (NBC)
22. "Dallas" (CBS)
23. (tie) "Head of the Class" (ABC)
    "NBC Sunday Night Movie" (NBC)
25. "Newhart" (CBS)

Seoul, South Korea, in September and October. Although NBC made a profit, it was criticized by some South Koreans for what they thought was negative coverage of their country and its athletes.

In December, after losing a bid to broadcast the 1992 Summer Olympics, CBS rebounded with a stunning upset. The network, which had not covered major league baseball for more than 20 years, announced that it would pay $1 billion for exclusive broadcasting rights for the World Series, League Championship Series, All-Star Game, and 12 regular-season games for four years starting in 1990. The agreement meant that NBC's Saturday "Game of the Week," a staple on television since the mid-1960's, would go off the air in 1990.

Presidential race. Television was a principal player in the 1988 presidential election. The winner—the Republican candidate, Vice President George Bush—and to a lesser extent, his Democratic opponent, Massachusetts Governor Michael S. Dukakis, were criticized for airing negative campaign commercials. Most of the commercials attacked and sometimes distorted the opponent's political stands. But some political experts observed that those kinds of commercials were successful and predicted that they would become more common in future campaigns.

In January, Dan Rather, anchorman for "The CBS Evening News," was embroiled in controversy when he got into a heated 9½-minute on-air discussion with Bush regarding the Iran-contra affair. Some public-opinion polls of viewers concluded that Rather had badgered Bush.

Dukakis and Bush took part in two televised debates during the campaign. Senator Lloyd M. Bentsen, Jr. (D., Tex.), Dukakis' running mate, debated Senator Dan Quayle (R., Ind.), Bush's running mate. Their one debate may have provided the most-remembered remark of the entire campaign. Quayle, 41, relatively unknown, at one point in the debate compared his experience with that of John F. Kennedy, who was only 43 when he was elected President in 1960. Bentsen retorted, "Senator, you're no Jack Kennedy."

Trash TV. Two television talk programs raised eyebrows. "The Morton Downey Jr. Show," shown nightly on hundreds of stations, featured Downey, an often abusive talk-show host. Downey regularly berated guests, particularly those who seemed to defend liberal positions. "Geraldo," a weekday talk show hosted by former ABC newsman Geraldo Rivera, also caused controversy. In November, when a program featuring civil rights activist Roy Innis and several white supremacists degenerated into a fistfight and chair-throwing melee, Rivera was hit by a flying chair and suffered a broken nose. Mainly because of Downey's and Rivera's shows and a few other programs that seemed especially exploitative, broadcasting critics decried what they called "trash TV" or "tabloid television."

Prime time. As usual, the focus of television's energy and effort was in prime time—between 8 and 11 p.m., Eastern Standard Time. But the established networks, with programming aired by more than 630 affiliated stations, continued to see viewership erode, as it has for the last several years. An increasing number of viewers were attracted to the more than 340 independent stations. Those stations had no network affiliation and typically aired network reruns and old movies. More than half the homes in the United States were also wired to receive cable television, which offered dozens of programming alternatives. In addition, more than half of the 90 million U.S. television households had videocassette recorders, enabling them to play prerecorded movies or other programs that they had rented or bought.

By late October, the three major networks had only a 69 per cent share of the prime-time audience, the first time that percentage had slipped below 70 per cent. In the late 1970's, when less competition existed, the networks maintained a 91 per cent share.

In November, ABC aired the first 18 hours of a 30-hour miniseries, "War and Remembrance," the longest miniseries ever. A World War II drama starring Robert Mitchum and based on Herman Wouk's best-selling 1978 novel of the same title, it cost $110 million to make. But it lost at least $23 million, partly because ABC could no longer attract an audience large enough to draw the necessary advertising. Ratings were lower than anticipated. Following a huge

Actors John Goodman and Roseanne Barr star in "Roseanne." The hit comedy about a razor-tongued mom and her family premiered on ABC in October.

success airing Wouk's "Winds of War" in 1983, ABC had intended to show "War and Remembrance" in 1989 but pushed up part of the telecast because of the writers' strike. The remaining 12 hours of the drama were scheduled to air in February 1989.

For the fourth consecutive season in 1988, NBC was the top-rated network in prime time. NBC's "The Cosby Show," which entered its fifth season in the fall, was still television's top program.

New programs. Many new comedies began in the fall, but perhaps the best was ABC's "Roseanne," starring comedian Roseanne Barr as a sharp-tongued mother. One of the most unusual of the successful programs was ABC's midseason replacement "The Wonder Years," a soft-hearted comedy that served as a retrospective on suburban adolescence in the late 1960's. Fred Savage, a teen-ager, starred, and though only a few episodes aired in 1988, it received television's Emmy Award as the best comedy series.

Other noteworthy new programs included "TV 101" on CBS, about a high-school teacher who turns the school newspaper into a television show; NBC's "Midnight Caller," about a former police officer who becomes a radio talk-show host; and "Almost Grown," on CBS, which traced the hurried and confusing lives of affluent adults who grew up in the 1960's. An NBC miniseries, "Favorite Son," starring Harry Hamlin, was the story of a handsome young senator catapulted by events into the presidential spotlight.

Television revivals. ABC briefly brought back "Mission: Impossible," the adventure drama that had been a hit in the 1960's on CBS. And CBS tried two new comedies with two well-established stars. Unfortunately, neither Dick Van Dyke in "The Van Dyke Show" nor Mary Tyler Moore in "Annie McGuire" made it. The programs were canceled in December.

Cable television in October saw the beginning of a new channel, Turner Network Television (TNT), started by Ted Turner, the cable entrepreneur who also began Cable News Network, Headline News channel, and the so-called SuperStation WTBS.

Public television. The noncommercial Public Broadcasting Service (PBS) began "The American Experience," a weekly documentary series that retraced important events in American history. In its 18th season, "Masterpiece Theatre" presented a seven-part drama, *A Perfect Spy*, based on spy novelist John le Carré's best seller. And in November, near the 25th anniversary of President Kennedy's assassination in Dallas on Nov. 22, 1963, "Nova," the PBS science series, reinvestigated the killing using new scientific methods that were not available 25 years ago. The program was one of several Kennedy documentaries that aired on television near the anniversary of his death.   P. J. Bednarski

See also **Awards and prizes.** In *World Book*, see **Television.**

Tennessee. See **State government.**

Tennis

Tennis. Steffi Graf, a 19-year-old West German, recorded tennis' first grand slam in 18 years in 1988 by sweeping the women's singles titles in the four grand-slam championships in the same year. The championships were the Australian, French, and United States opens, and the All-England Lawn Tennis Championship (Wimbledon). Mats Wilander of Sweden won three of those four men's titles.

Graf, with her powerful ground strokes, became the first single-year grand-slam winner since Margaret Smith Court of Australia in 1970. The only others to win those four titles in one year were Don Budge in 1938, Maureen Connolly in 1953, and Rod Laver of Australia in 1962 and 1969. In 1984, the International Tennis Federation (ITF) recognized Martina Navratilova as a grand-slam winner and awarded her a $1-million bonus because she won the four titles in succession, though not in the same year.

Graf actually went one better. Tennis returned to the Olympic Games for the first time since 1924, and professionals were allowed to play. Graf won the women's gold medal for what became known as a ''golden grand slam.''

In the grand-slam tournaments, Graf won the Australian Open on a hard court in Melbourne on January 23, the French Open on clay in Paris on June 4, Wimbledon on grass on July 2, and the U.S. Open on a hard court in New York City on September 10. In those finals, she defeated Chris Evert by 6-1, 7-6 in Mel-

bourne; Natalya Zvereva of the Soviet Union by 6-0, 6-0 in Paris; Navratilova by 5-7, 6-2, 6-1 in Wimbledon; and Gabriela Sabatini of Argentina by 6-3, 3-6, 6-1 in New York City.

In men's play, Wilander won the first two grand-slam titles—the Australian Open over Pat Cash of Australia, 6-3, 6-7, 3-6, 6-1, 8-6, and the French Open over Henri Leconte of France, 7-5, 6-2, 6-1. But Wilander seldom played his best on grass, and he lost in the Wimbledon quarterfinals to Miloslav Mecir of Czechoslovakia, 6-3, 6-1, 6-3. Stefan Edberg of Sweden won that final on July 4 from Boris Becker of West Germany, 4-6, 7-6, 6-4, 6-2.

For the second straight year, the U.S. Open final produced a marvelous match between Wilander and Ivan Lendl, a Czechoslovak who lives in Greenwich, Conn. In 1987, Lendl won in four sets that lasted 4 hours 47 minutes. This time, Wilander won in five sets, 6-4, 4-6, 6-3, 5-7, 6-4, in a record 4 hours 54 minutes.

Lendl lost more than the title. He had been number one in the computer rankings for 156 weeks, exactly three years, and was approaching Connors' record of 159 weeks. But when Wilander won the U.S. Open, he took over the number-one ranking.

Andre Agassi, an 18-year-old American, started the year ranked 25th in the world. By year-end, he was ranked 3rd. He reached the Wimbledon and U.S. Open semifinals.

Agassi won all his matches as the United States defeated Peru by 3 matches to 0 and Argentina by 4-1 in Davis Cup regional competition. Those victories qualified the United States for the 16-nation championship competition in 1989. In December, Becker and Eric Jelen led West Germany to victory over Sweden in the 1988 Davis Cup final at Göteborg, Sweden.

The women's tour experienced a youth movement. In the French Open, seven quarterfinalists and all four semifinalists were 18 years or younger.

It was a difficult year for the 34-year-old Evert and the 32-year-old Navratilova. Evert failed to reach the French Open semifinals for the first time in 16 years. Although Navratilova won nine tournaments, she could not win a record ninth Wimbledon singles title and her seventh straight.

Men's tour. The men's competition was conducted by the Men's Tennis Council. The council had nine members—three from the Association of Tennis Professionals (ATP), the players' union; three from the ITF; and three tournament directors.

The ATP wanted a greater voice. When its plan was rejected, it said it would start its own tour in 1990 patterned after the Professional Golfers' Association tour in the United States. ATP members would continue to play in the grand-slam tournaments. The ATP had 520 members, and the top players pledged to support the proposed tour. The ITF declared it would fight any change. Frank Litsky

West Germany's Steffi Graf makes a return, as tennis returned to the Olympics for the first time since 1924. Graf won the gold in singles in October.

In *World Book*, see **Tennis.**

Texas. See **Houston; State government.**

Striking railroad workers sit on tracks to prevent trains from departing from a station in Bangkok, Thailand, on June 21.

Thailand.

Thailand. Prime Minister Prem Tinsulanonda gave up his post in 1988 after overseeing more than eight years of increasing prosperity and political stability in Thailand. He was succeeded on August 11 by Chatichai Choonhavan, the first civilian leader elected since 1976.

Parliamentary coalitions had named Prem, a retired general, prime minister for three terms even though he had not been elected to parliament. His appointment, though constitutional, was increasingly opposed by students, academics, and other Thais, who wanted an elected leader.

Prem was credited with having eliminated a Communist internal security threat and beginning a crackdown on corruption. But in April 1988, he found himself faced with a parliamentary debate on corruption, poor performance from the troops fighting Laos, and pressure from the United States to enact a law protecting U.S. copyrights. The issues prompted dissension among members of parliament, and on April 9, Prem dissolved parliament and his cabinet. He set elections for July 24.

Election results. The coalition supporting Prem won 215 out of 357 seats in the lower house of parliament. The parliamentarians offered Prem a fourth term as prime minister on July 27, a few hours after 3,000 students angrily demonstrated in front of his house. Prem, however, rejected the coalition's offer of a fourth term.

Because Chatichai was the leader of the largest party in the coalition, the 87-seat Thai Nation party, King Bhumibol Adulyadej named him prime minister on August 4. Chatichai, a 66-year-old retired major general, diplomat, businessman, and motorcycle enthusiast, was sworn in on August 10.

Border fighting with Laos, which had flared from time to time in recent years over disputed villages among the region's jungle-covered hills, began again in December 1987 and worsened in early 1988. On February 19, the two nations agreed on a cease-fire and a troop withdrawal to 3 kilometers (1.9 miles) from the battle lines. Talks intended to settle the dispute were not immediately successful, however.

Two U.S. publications reported in October that the United States had a secret program to aid anti-Communist guerrillas from Kampuchea (formerly Cambodia) based in Thailand. The reports said that U.S. funds had been funneled through the Thai government and that Thai army officers and businessmen had stolen about $3.5 million of the money. A Thai army spokesman said that there was no basis for the charge.

Other news. Economic growth surged at a rate of about 8 per cent in 1988 as foreign investment poured into Thailand. Four days of heavy rain on deforested hillsides in southern Thailand in November caused floods that killed hundreds. Henry S. Bradsher

See also **Asia** (Facts in brief table). In *World Book*, see **Thailand.**

Theater.

Theater. On Broadway and around the United States, 1988 was a lively year for theater. There were new shows and stars galore and theater festivals of unusual scope and ambition.

The fantastic *Phantom*. For sheer spectacle, the event of the year was the Broadway premiere of British composer Andrew Lloyd Webber's 1986 musical *The Phantom of the Opera*. In this operatic retelling of an old horror tale, Michael Crawford portrayed a horribly disfigured man who haunts the Paris Opéra. Sarah Brightman, Lloyd Webber's wife, played the beautiful singer with whom the Phantom falls in love.

The lavish show was a Disneyland of special scenic effects, including an eerie underground river. Crawford's sensitive portrayal of the masked Phantom and his tender way with the show's melodic love songs made him the most popular star on Broadway in 1988.

West Coast connections. Although *Phantom* came to Broadway from London, a number of other shows opening on Broadway in 1988 originated in regional U.S. theaters. This trend was encouraging to theater professionals concerned about the many shows imported from Great Britain during the past five years.

Playwright Neil Simon was among the major figures who took this regional route to Broadway. His new comedy, *Rumors*, was developed at the Old Globe Theater in San Diego. Written as a rollicking farce about the wild goings-on at an anniversary party,

461

A French diplomat (played by John Lithgow) comforts his Chinese lover (B. D. Wong), in reality a male spy in disguise, in the Tony-winning *M. Butterfly*.

Rumors proved to be full of funny lines but was rather insubstantial.

The Old Globe also brought *The Cocktail Hour* to Broadway. The play by A. R. Gurney, Jr., starred Nancy Marchand and Keene Curtis as the well-to-do parents of a playwright who wants to expose their privileged life to the world.

More from California. Another California theater, the La Jolla Playhouse, forwarded Lee Blessing's *A Walk in the Woods*, which depicted the friendship between two diplomats, one Russian, the other American. Another Blessing play, *Two Rooms*, about American hostages held in Lebanon, opened in June at the La Jolla. A third theater in the San Diego area—the South Coast Repertory of Costa Mesa, Calif.—won the 1988 Tony Award for outstanding regional theater.

Another West Coast regional theater that sent a successful show to New York City was the Seattle Repertory Theater. Some critics praised *Eastern Standard*, Richard Greenberg's satire about yuppies and their social values, as very witty.

East Coast offerings. The Yale Repertory Theater in New Haven, Conn., guided August Wilson's new play, *Joe Turner's Come and Gone*, to Broadway, where it won the 1988 New York Drama Critics Circle Award for best new play. The critics also praised another Yale production that transferred to New York City—Athol Fugard's *The Road to Mecca*. The play featured Amy Irving as a South African schoolteacher who tries to prevent an eccentric old artist from being sent to a nursing home.

Home-grown productions. New York City's own nonprofit theaters were another valuable source of exciting new material. The Lincoln Center for the Performing Arts presented *Sarafina!*, a charming South African musical with a cast of children, and David Mamet's *Speed-the-Plow*, a funny and foul-mouthed satire about Hollywood film producers. Appearing in Mamet's comedy with Joe Mantegna and Ron Silver was rock star Madonna in her Broadway debut.

Lincoln Center also produced a star-studded show that few theatergoers got to see. Mike Nichols' limited-run production of Samuel Beckett's *Waiting for Godot*—with comedians Robin Williams and Steve Martin as the existential tramps—was such a draw that 25,000 people were turned away.

The Second Stage Theater, a small nonprofit off-Broadway theater, commissioned Michael Weller to write *Spoils of War*, a play about a 16-year-old boy who tries to reconcile his divorced parents. Propelled by Kate Nelligan's star performance as the exotic and eccentric mother, the show was restaged for a Broadway opening in November.

Romance Romance, an unpretentious production consisting of two one-act musicals, originated at the modestly sized Actor's Outlet Theater. It went on to charm Broadway audiences with its old-fashioned stories and songs.

Composer Andrew Lloyd Webber, center, and the stars of the Broadway smash
The Phantom of the Opera acknowledge opening-night cheers in January.

Plays opening in small theaters did not have to move to Broadway to have an impact, however. The Manhattan Theater Club, for example, scored a hit with *Italian American Reconciliation*, in which playwright John Patrick Shanley continued the family themes he raised in his 1987 film, *Moonstruck*.

Costly flops. As in other recent years, fewer new musicals opened on Broadway as production costs continued to rise. Among those that did, there were some costly failures. One ambitious musical that failed to live up to critical expectations was the $5-million *Legs Diamond*. This spectacle starred nightclub performer Peter Allen—who also wrote the music—as the 1920's gangster famous for his flashy style and his ambition to be a professional dancer.

Two British imports were also expensive flops. Lyricist Tim Rice, who had teamed up with composer Lloyd Webber to create *Jesus Christ Superstar* (1971) and other shows, introduced *Chess*, a behind-the-scenes look at an international chess match. Audiences stayed away from the $6-million show, however, after reviewers judged it eye-catching but empty.

Carrie was shallow as well as weird. This Royal Shakespeare Company production, based on Stephen King's 1974 horror novel, could not decide whether it wanted to scare its audience or exploit their interest in a chorus line of sexy high-school girls. Betty Buckley was beautiful but wasted as Carrie's fanatically religious mother in this $7-million fiasco.

Chinese puzzle. Other lavish productions were more successful. David Henry Hwang's drama, *M. Butterfly*, was conceived on a grand, operatic scale. This unusual play starred John Lithgow as a French foreign service officer involved in a bizarre affair with a Chinese opera star—played by B. D. Wong—who is not only a spy but a man in disguise. The play won the 1988 Tony Award for best play and was one of the few shows produced on Broadway in 1988 without previous preparation in a regional theater.

Midwest events. The Guthrie Theater in Minneapolis, Minn., celebrated its 25th anniversary by introducing a major new production of William Shakespeare's *Richard III*. The Milwaukee Repertory Theater christened its new, three-stage $12.5-million theater complex with *The Tale of Lear*, a new version of the Shakespearean tragedy created by Japanese director Tadashi Suzuki.

Special festivals presented during the summer were highly ambitious. One of the highlights of the International Theater Festival held in Chicago in May was *The War of the Roses*. This 22-hour dramatic marathon consisted of seven historical plays by Shakespeare performed over 2½ days by the English Shakespeare Company. In New York City, the First New York International Festival of the Arts presented more than 350 productions in June and early July.

The city of Atlanta, Ga., hosted the First National Black Arts Festival in August. Among its highlights was

Comedians Robin Williams, left, and Steve Martin portray tragicomical tramps in Samuel Beckett's *Waiting for Godot* at New York City's Lincoln Center.

the Negro Ensemble Company's production of *Sally*, a play about racial and class prejudice by Charles Fuller, who won a Pulitzer Prize in 1982 for his drama *A Soldier's Play*.

American themes were sounded in many new plays produced in 1988 by U.S. regional theaters. Steppenwolf Theatre in Chicago presented an adaptation of John Steinbeck's Pulitzer Prize-winning novel, *The Grapes of Wrath* (1939). The Arena Stage in Washington, D.C., introduced Heather McDonald's *The Rivers and Ravines*, a play about the economic crisis in U.S. farm communities. The Cleveland Play House produced *On the Waterfront*, a stage version of Budd Schulberg's 1954 Academy Award-winning film about union corruption. Barbara Damashek's *Whereabouts Unknown*, about the homeless, was the high point of the Humana Festival of New American Plays held in Louisville, Ky., by the Actors Theater of Louisville.

Both the Long Wharf Theatre in New Haven and Lincoln Center, among other theaters, mounted 50th-anniversary productions of *Our Town*, Thornton Wilder's classic. On Broadway, one of the most popular shows of 1988 was also a revival— the Fats Waller musical *Ain't Misbehavin'*, with Nell Carter and the entire original cast from the 1978 production. The joint, as they sing in one of Waller's songs, was genuinely jumping.　　Marilyn Stasio

See also **Awards and prizes** (Arts awards); **Lloyd Webber, Andrew.** In *World Book*, see **Theater.**

Thornburgh, Richard Lewis (1932-　　), a former governor of Pennsylvania, was sworn in as United States attorney general on Aug. 12, 1988, succeeding Edwin Meese III. Thornburgh had been director of the Institute of Politics at Harvard University's John F. Kennedy School of Government in Cambridge, Mass. In the fall, it was announced that he would be staying on in the Administration of President George Bush.

Thornburgh was born on July 16, 1932, in Pittsburgh, Pa. He graduated from Yale University in New Haven, Conn., in 1954 with a degree in engineering and earned a law degree in 1957 from the University of Pittsburgh.

In 1959, after two years as an attorney for the Aluminum Company of America, Thornburgh joined a law firm in Pittsburgh. He left private practice in 1969 to become U.S. attorney for western Pennsylvania. Six years later, President Gerald Ford named him head of the Justice Department's criminal division.

Thornburgh was elected governor of Pennsylvania in 1978 and reelected in 1982. While in office, he initiated nationally acclaimed programs for education and welfare reform. His calm leadership in 1979 during the Three Mile Island nuclear power plant mishap was widely credited with averting public panic.

Thornburgh and his wife, Virginia, have four sons and two grandchildren.　　David L. Dreier

Togo. See **Africa.**

Toronto, Canada's most heavily populated urban area and chief manufacturing and financial center, continued to prosper in 1988—and continued to struggle with a housing crisis brought about by its prosperity. Another unwanted by-product of prosperity appeared in 1988—a garbage crisis. And a public financing crunch loomed as neighboring municipalities stiffened their competition for federal and provincial dollars.

World leaders visit. From June 19 to 21, Toronto spotlighted its emergence as an international financial center by playing host to the annual economic summit conference of the leaders of seven major industrial nations—Canada, France, Great Britain, Italy, Japan, the United States, and West Germany. Canada spent more than $15 million on arrangements for the meeting. (All monetary amounts in this article are Canadian dollars with $1 = U.S. 84 cents on Dec. 31, 1988.)

Investment boosted. Federal laws passed in 1986 and 1987 strengthened Toronto's position as a financial center. These laws allowed Canadian banks to sell stocks and bonds, and permitted foreign firms to buy Canadian companies that deal in securities. By the end of 1988, Canada's six largest banks had entered the securities business, and 10 of the largest United States and Japanese brokerage firms had registered as securities dealers in Canada.

Housing crisis. Toronto's prosperity and a sharp increase in population pushed the price of an average

Runners wearing business suits compete in April in the Rat Race, a 3-mile (4.8-kilometer) run through the Toronto, Canada, financial district.

wing New Democrats scored an upset victory and won a majority of the seats on the City Council.

The garbage crisis surfaced in January, when Metropolitan Toronto began to divert to its western landfill one-third of the garbage it normally deposited in its eastern landfill. Officials expected that they would have to close the eastern landfill as early as 1990, and that the western landfill would be closed by the mid-1990's. Metropolitan Toronto officials began a desperate search to find new sites for landfills, but wherever they looked, they ran into bitter opposition from local residents.

Subway nixed. On May 31, the Ontario provincial government announced that it would not fund the $1.5-million Sheppard Avenue Subway project, which the Metro had approved. The Sheppard Avenue Subway line would have run east and west across most of Metropolitan Toronto, north of the city of Toronto.

Rather than fund the Sheppard project, the province decided to back a project to build Highway 407 to the north of Metropolitan Toronto. This decision made Metropolitan Toronto officials realize that they now face strong competition for provincial and federal money from the three surrounding regional municipalities of Peel, York (not the same as the city of York), and Durham.   David Lewis Stein

See also **Ontario.** In *World Book,* see **Ontario; Toronto.**

new house toward $300,000, the highest in Canada. Furthermore, only 1 out of every 1,000 apartments was vacant. The housing crisis prompted the government of the province of Ontario to work with the city of Toronto in a plan to take over 66 acres (27 hectares) of land on Toronto's industrial east side as a site for 7,000 units of new housing.

In September, John McDermid, Canada's minister of housing, announced that the federal government would turn 123 acres (50 hectares) of Downsview Military Airport over to housing. This airport is located in North York, a city just north of Toronto.

Direct vote for the Metro. In 1988, a governmental unit that includes the city of Toronto changed the system for electing members of its legislative council. Toronto, York, North York, the cities of Etobicoke and Scarborough, and the borough of East York make up the Municipality of Metropolitan Toronto, commonly called Metropolitan Toronto. The governing body of this unit is the Metropolitan Council—popularly called the Metro.

Under a two-tier system in effect since Metropolitan Toronto came into existence in 1954, the governments of the city of Toronto and the other municipalities in Metropolitan Toronto sent representatives to the Metro. On Nov. 14, 1988, however, voters for the first time elected separate representatives to the Metro and their own municipal councils. In the city of Toronto, a coalition of moderate reformers and left

Toys and games. Retail toy sales in the United States had another year of slow growth in 1988, increasing only about 3 per cent over 1987 sales. One factor in the small increase was the return to popularity of lower-priced, traditional toys.

New twists on such classic toys as dolls and action figures sold well in 1988. Mattel Incorporated of Hawthorne, Calif., had success with a doll called Lil Miss Makeup. When cold water is applied to the doll's face, color "makeup" appears, only to disappear when warm water is applied. Kenner Products Company of Cincinnati, Ohio, introduced a line of collectible action figures called Starting Lineup, based on well-known baseball, football, and basketball players. Each figure, 3¾ inches (9.5 centimeters) tall, comes with its own statistics card. A popular comic book series titled "Teenage Mutant Ninja Turtles" inspired Playmates Toys Incorporated of La Mirada, Calif., to introduce a line of action figures of the same name in 1988. As the story goes, the turtles mutated after radioactive waste was dumped into the sewer where they live.

The old-fashioned play store got a new look in 1988 when Fisher-Price of East Aurora, N.Y., unveiled the Magic Scan Checkout Counter. The counter features a replica of the electronic scanner found in supermarkets. The scanner beeps and flashes when play groceries, moving on a conveyor belt, pass over it. Hasbro Incorporated of Pawtucket, R.I., presented a portable rhythm-and-sound machine called Body Rap. Body Rap

Toys and games

consists of eight pressure-sensitive pads that attach to a person's body or clothing. When the pads are tapped, they make a drum or cymbal sound.

Some old favorites enjoyed renewed popularity in 1988. Among them were Hula Hoops, manufactured by Wham-O Incorporated of San Gabriel, Calif.; train sets from Lionel Trains Incorporated; and yoyos.

Video games, which peaked in popularity in the early 1980's, made a strong comeback in 1988. Sales for both the game systems that hook up to television sets and the game cartridges rang up at just under $2 billion during the year. One of the most popular video games was Super Mario Bros. 2 from Nintendo. New and better graphics and lower prices contributed to the video-game boom.

The high-tech toy category saw the introduction in 1988 of video-game versions of TV game shows that enable fans at home to play against the show's real contestants. Players at home, however, do not actually participate in the show. One such game was Mattel's TV Play-Along Wheel of Fortune, which receives invisible light signals from the evening version of the popular "Wheel of Fortune" television show.

Doll wars. In March, Hasbro introduced Maxie, a blue-eyed, blond-haired teen-aged doll designed to compete head-on with Mattel's ever-popular Barbie doll. Barbie has been the top-selling fashion doll since she was introduced in 1959.   Diane P. Cardinale

In *World Book*, see **Doll; Game; Toy.**

Track and field. Even before the Summer Olympic Games began in September 1988 in Seoul, South Korea, Florence Griffith Joyner and Butch Reynolds, two sprinters from the United States, broke world records by large margins. During the Olympic track competition, Griffith Joyner broke another world record, and Reynolds helped tie one.

Griffith Joyner and family. The 28-year-old Griffith Joyner, from Los Angeles, had been a good 200-meter runner better known for her flamboyant running outfits and long fingernails. On July 15 and 16 in the U.S. Olympic trials in Indianapolis, she ran the four fastest 100 meters by a woman—10.60 seconds (wind aided) in her heat; 10.49, a world record, in the quarterfinals; 10.70 in the semifinals; and 10.61 in the final.

On September 29, in the Olympics, Griffith Joyner set world 200-meter records of 21.56 seconds in the semifinals and 21.34 in the final. Again she won by a wide margin as she wiped out the world record of 21.71 seconds first set in 1979 by Marita Koch of East Germany.

Griffith Joyner is the wife of Al Joyner, the 1984 Olympic triple-jump champion. Joyner's 26-year-old sister, Jackie Joyner-Kersee of Long Beach, Calif., broke the world record heptathlon record with 7,215 points in the U.S. Olympic trials and 7,291 in the Olympics. That gave her world records in four of her last five heptathlons. Joyner-Kersee also won the Olympic

World outdoor track and field records established in 1988

Men

Event	Holder	Country	Where set	Date	Record
400 meters	Butch Reynolds	U.S.A.	Zurich, Switzerland	Aug. 17	:43.29
Marathon	Belayneh Densimo	Ethiopia	Rotterdam, Netherlands	April 17	2:06:49*
1,600-meter relay	Everett, Steve Lewis, Robinzine, Reynolds	U.S.A.	Seoul, S. Korea	Oct. 1	2:56.16†
High jump	Javier Sotomayor	Cuba	Salamanca, Spain	Sept. 8	7 ft. 11½ in. (2.43 m)
Pole vault	Sergei Bubka	Soviet Union	Nice, France	July 10	19 ft. 10½ in. (6.06 m)
Shot-put	Ulf Timmermann	E. Germany	Canea, Crete	May 22	75 ft. 8 in. (23.05 m)

Women

Event	Holder	Country	Where set	Date	Record
100 meters	Florence Griffith Joyner	U.S.A.	Indianapolis	July 16	:10.49
200 meters	Florence Griffith Joyner	U.S.A.	Seoul, S. Korea	Sept. 29	:21.34
100-meter hurdles	Jordanka Donkova	Bulgaria	Stara Zagora, Bulgaria	Aug. 21	:12.21
1,600-meter relay	Ledovskaia, Nazarova, Piniguina, Bryzgina	Soviet Union	Seoul, S. Korea	Oct. 1	3:15.18
Long jump	Galina Christyakova	Soviet Union	Leningrad	June 11	24 ft. 8¼ in. (7.52 m)
Discus throw	Gabriele Reinsch	E. Germany	Neubrandenburg, E. Germany	July 9	252 ft. (76.80 m)
Javelin throw	Petra Felke	E. Germany	Potsdam, E. Germany	Sept. 9	262 ft. 5 in. (80.00 m)
Heptathlon	Jackie Joyner-Kersee	U.S.A.	Seoul, S. Korea	Sept. 23-24	7,291 pts.

m = meters; *unofficial record; †tied world record.

Track-and-field star Florence Griffith Joyner sets a women's world record of 10.49 seconds in the 100-meter dash at the Olympic trials in Indianapolis.

Three days later, Johnson was disqualified because a drug test disclosed the anabolic steroid stanozolol—a banned performance-enhancing drug—in his system. Johnson lost his new world record, and his gold medal went to Lewis. In addition, Lewis won an Olympic gold medal in the long jump at 28 feet 7¼ inches (8.72 meters) and a silver medal behind his training partner, Joe DeLoach, in the 200 meters (19.75 seconds to 19.79).

Medal totals. In the 42 Olympic track-and-field events, the United States won 13 gold medals; the Soviet Union, 10; and East Germany, 6. In total medals, East Germany won 27; the United States, 26; and the Soviet Union, 26.

Jumpers came close to two milestones—the first 20-foot (6.10-meter) pole vault and the first 8-foot (2.44-meter) high jump. Sergei Bubka of the Soviet Union broke the world record for the pole vault twice, raising it to 19 feet 10½ inches (6.06 meters). Javier Sotomayor of Cuba improved the world record for the high jump to 7 feet 11½ inches (2.43 meters).

Mixed fortunes resulted for Edwin Moses of Newport Beach, Calif., and Said Aouita of Morocco. At age 33, Moses, the best 400-meter hurdler ever, finished a disappointing third in the Olympics. Aouita, the Grand Prix overall champion, won only a bronze medal in the Olympics.   Frank Litsky

See also **Olympic Games.** In *World Book*, see **Track and field.**

women's long jump at 24 feet 3½ inches (7.40 meters), and Griffith Joyner won a gold medal and a silver in Olympic relays.

Other record breakers. The 24-year-old Reynolds, from Akron, Ohio, shattered the oldest running record —Lee Evans' 43.86 seconds for 400 meters. Evans set that record for the United States in the 1968 Olympics at an altitude of 7,575 feet (2,309 meters) above sea level in Mexico City, where the thinner air helped sprinters run faster. Reynolds ran the 400 meters in 43.29 seconds on Aug. 17, 1988, in Zurich, Switzerland, at an altitude of 1,345 feet (410 meters).

In the Olympic 400-meter race, Steve Lewis of Los Angeles upset Reynolds, 43.87 seconds to 43.93. Then Reynolds anchored the United States to victory in the 1,600-meter relay. The relay team equaled the world record of 2 minutes 56.16 seconds set in the 1968 Olympics with Evans anchoring.

Lewis versus Johnson. In the Zurich meet in which Reynolds broke the world record, Carl Lewis of Houston beat Ben Johnson of Canada in a 100-meter dash in 9.93 seconds. Johnson, recovering from an injury, finished third in 10.00.

That was their first meeting since Johnson beat Lewis in the 1987 world championships and set a world record of 9.83 seconds. Their next meeting was in the Olympics on September 24, when Johnson ran 9.79, an apparent world record, and Lewis was second in 9.92, his fastest time ever.

Transit systems in the United States reported growing ridership in 1988. The American Public Transit Association (APTA), a trade group based in Washington, D.C., that represents public transit systems, estimated that from January to June, ridership increased 2.3 per cent over the same period in 1987.

Among the areas reporting a rise in ridership were Los Angeles County, where ridership increased 3.8 per cent; San Francisco and Oakland, where ridership rose 3.2 per cent; and New York City, where the number of passenger trips went up 2.3 per cent.

Some cities, however, saw a decline in ridership in 1988, according to APTA. In Atlanta, Ga., and Chicago, the number of passenger trips fell 1.3 per cent.

New projects. Maryland officials in 1988 approved plans to construct a 27-mile (43-kilometer) light-rail line linking downtown Baltimore with other cities in Baltimore and Anne Arundel counties. (Light-rail systems—or trolleys—use electrically powered cars that run on tracks at street level.) Construction of the new line was expected to begin in 1989.

In May, the Los Angeles County Transportation Commission approved a 20-mile (32-kilometer) trolley line for the center median of the Century Freeway. It is expected to be in operation by 1993. Work also began on a 21.5-mile (34.5-kilometer) rail line connecting the Long Beach Civic Center with downtown Los Angeles and on a 20-mile rail link between Los Angeles and the Los Angeles International Airport.

Trinidad and Tobago

In June, a 2.6-mile (4.1-kilometer) rail extension to the South Line in Atlanta was completed. The extension brings transit service from the city to Hartsfield International Airport. The cost was $86 million.

Train scrapped. Plans to construct a 93-mile (150-kilometer) rail system in the Dallas area suffered a setback on June 25 when voters rejected a referendum calling for the use of long-term bonds to finance the project. Officials of the Dallas Area Rapid Transit said that the financing would be necessary to build the $2.9-billion system by 2010. Many voters, however, were concerned about whether a rail system could effectively link up the sprawling Dallas metropolitan area.

Federal funding. The Congress of the United States in 1988 once again resisted attempts by President Ronald Reagan's Administration to cut federal funds for public transit systems around the country. In its fiscal 1989 budget, the Administration proposed $1.52 billion in funding for the Urban Mass Transportation Administration (UMTA), which makes federal grants to cities for their mass transportation systems. If that sum had been approved, it would have forced transit authorities to raise fares and cut service, according to industry experts. But in September, Congress approved an UMTA allocation of $3.16 billion, considerably more than the Reagan Administration proposal, but still less than the $3.22 billion allocated in fiscal 1988.

Service for the disabled. Many United States transit authorities improved their service to disabled riders in 1988. In most cases, action was taken because of growing pressure from disabled activists and because of new federal requirements mandating improvements.

On January 6, a federal judge in Philadelphia ruled that public transit authorities must provide services for handicapped people no matter what the cost. The measure overturned a 1986 U.S. Department of Transportation regulation that allowed transit authorities to limit expenditures on handicapped service to 3 per cent of their operating budget.

The Chicago Transit Authority (CTA) in March decided to buy nearly 500 new buses equipped with wheelchair lifts. CTA officials had long resisted proposals to install lifts on regular buses, citing the high cost of such a move. Instead, it offered disabled riders a limited door-to-door service called Dial-A-Ride. On January 18, however, the Illinois Human Rights Commission ruled that the CTA was discriminating against disabled people because Dial-A-Ride was inferior to regular CTA bus service.

In June, the Greater Cleveland Regional Transit Authority rolled out 77 new buses with wheelchair lifts. The vehicles operate on the city's main bus routes.   Gary Washburn

In *World Book*, see **Bus; Electric railroad; Subway; Transportation.**

Trinidad and Tobago. See **Latin America.**

Tunisia. President Zine El-Abidine Ben Ali continued in 1988 to revitalize Tunisia's political system, a process begun on Nov. 7, 1987, when he declared ailing President-for-Life Habib Bourguiba mentally incompetent and seized power. In February 1988, the ruling Socialist Destour Party changed its name to the Democratic Constitutional Assembly (RCD) in an attempt to broaden its appeal. The first RCD congress, held in July, was billed as a "Congress of Salvation." Posters announcing the meeting depicted a strong hand rescuing Tunisia from the sea. On the hand's wrist was a watch with the date "November 7."

Presidential limits. In July, the National Assembly, Tunisia's legislature, approved constitutional amendments that abolished the position of president-for-life and set an age limit of 70 for eligibility to the presidency. Future presidents would be limited to three five-year terms in office, with only two terms to run consecutively.

Political changes. On July 26, Ben Ali formed a new Cabinet that included nonparty members and opponents of Bourguiba. The only holdover from the Bourguiba regime was Prime Minister Hedi Baccouche. The new ministers included Ahmad Mestiri, the leader of the opposition Social Democratic Movement, and other opposition leaders jailed by Bourguiba for political activity.

In April, the Assembly passed a law permitting the formation of new political parties, subject to government approval. To win approval, a party must respect Tunisia's Arab-Islamic identity and heritage, operate within the framework of law, and support the 1956 law that replaced Islamic law with modern secular law. Two new leftist parties, the Progressive Socialist Assembly and the Party of Social Progress, were approved in September 1988.

Exiles return. The political changes prompted former opponents of Bourguiba to return from exile. The most prominent was Ahmad Ben Salah, a former finance minister who fled Tunisia in 1973.

Ben Ali also issued an amnesty for all political prisoners in March, and some 3,000 were released. They included Rached Ghanouchi, the leader of the outlawed fundamentalist Islamic Tendency Movement (MTI). In August, Ghanouchi announced that the MTI would obey the new law on political parties, paving the way for government approval of the MTI.

Increasingly, Bourguiba's image faded from public view. Statues of him were removed from public parks, and streets named after him were renamed.

The economy received a boost from closer cooperation with other North African states, notably Algeria and Libya. The latter agreed in February to pay $12-million in compensation for 21,000 Tunisian workers expelled from Libya in 1985 and to give precedence to up to 70,000 Tunisian workers when recruiting foreign labor.   William Spencer

See also **Middle East** (Facts in brief table). In *World Book*, see **Tunisia.**

Turkey. Prime Minister Turgut Ozal was wounded slightly in an assassination attempt on June 18, 1988, while addressing a convention of the ruling Motherland Party (ANAP) in Ankara. The gunman, an escaped convict, was a member of the outlawed Gray Wolves, a far-right terrorist group responsible for much of the political violence in Turkey in the 1970's.

Referendum. Although the ANAP maintained its majority in parliament in 1988, its popular support continued to decline. In September, Turkish voters defeated a referendum on local elections sought by Ozal by a 65 to 35 per cent margin. Ozal had asked that the Turkish Constitution be amended to advance local elections from March 1989 to November 1988. Many Turks viewed the referendum as an opportunity to vote on Ozal's performance in office and express their disapproval of economic problems and of Ozal's attempts to improve relations with Greece.

Kurdish problems. At least 60,000 Kurds fled into Turkey from neighboring areas of Iraq in August and September after Iraqi military forces—freed from action in the Iran-Iraq War by an August cease-fire with Iran—attacked Kurdish villages. The Kurds, who have waged a guerrilla war against Iraq since 1961, also fought alongside Iranian forces during the Iran-Iraq War. Although Turkey welcomed the refugees, partly as a way of demonstrating its commitment to human rights, the government continued to have problems with its own Kurds. In February 1988, 20

members of the Kurdish Workers' Party, which advocates an independent state for Kurds in Turkey and elsewhere, were sentenced to death.

Foreign relations. In February, Turkey's parliament ratified a two-year extension of the 1980 Defense and Economic Cooperation Agreement with the United States. The government had delayed ratifying the extension, which was signed in 1987, in protest against what Turkey considered insufficient U.S. aid. United States aid for Turkey in 1988 was $525.3 million, less than in 1987 and well below what Turkey said it needed to modernize its armed forces.

In January, Ozal met with Greece's Prime Minister Andreas Papandreou in the first direct meeting of leaders of the two feuding countries since 1978. In June, Ozal made the first visit to Greece by a Turkish leader in 36 years.

The economy. Turkey's continuing economic problems were an important factor in the September referendum. Inflation, though down from previous years, averaged 55 per cent, and price increases of 150 per cent on basic goods turned voters against the government. In October, Ozal ordered Turkey's largest public corporations—Sumerbank, a textile manufacturer, and Petkim, a petrochemical concern—sold to private investors as a means of stimulating the economy.   William Spencer

See also **Iraq; Middle East** (Facts in brief table). In *World Book*, see **Turkey.**

Prime Minister Turgut Ozal attends a political convention on June 19, one day after being slightly wounded in an assassination attempt.

Tyson, Mike (1966-   ), remained the undisputed heavyweight boxing champion of the world with a victory on June 27, 1988, over challenger Michael Spinks in Atlantic City, N.J. The powerful Tyson, a 3½-to-1 favorite, won by a knockout after just 91 seconds of the first round.

Michael Gerald Tyson was born on June 30, 1966, in New York City. He began learning to box at a reformatory in Johnstown, N.Y., where he was sent at the age of 13 after being convicted of a series of burglaries and robberies.

In September 1980, Tyson was paroled to the custody of trainer Constantine (Cus) D'Amato. Under his tutelage, Tyson, then 17, won the 1984 Golden Gloves amateur championship. In November 1985, D'Amato died, but by then Tyson was an accomplished professional fighter with 11 victories, all knockouts.

In 1986, Tyson won the World Boxing Council heavyweight title, becoming—at age 20—the youngest heavyweight boxing champion in history. He became undisputed champion by defeating James (Bonecrusher) Smith for the World Boxing Association title in March 1987 and Tony Tucker for the International Boxing Federation crown in August 1987. By the time Tyson faced Spinks, his record was 34-0.

Tyson married actress Robin Givens in February 1988. She filed for divorce in October.   David L. Dreier

Uganda. See Africa.

Unemployment. See Economics; Labor.

Union of Soviet Socialist Republics

(U.S.S.R.). Communist Party General Secretary Mikhail S. Gorbachev established his mastery of the Soviet political scene more clearly in the fall of 1988 than at any time since coming to power in 1985. He pushed through sweeping changes in the party, the government, and even the armed forces. With Gorbachev's mastery came a drastic reduction of conservative influences hindering his program of *perestroika* (political and economic restructuring).

At a meeting of the Communist Party Central Committee on Feb. 17 and 18, 1988, Gorbachev called for a "complete overhaul" of the Soviet political system. "We are not retreating from Socialism [Communism]," he told opponents who had claimed that Gorbachev's policies of perestroika and *glasnost* (openness in the flow of information) threatened Communism. "The idea is not to replace the existing system, but to change it qualitatively with new structures and features to give it renewed content and dynamism." Resistance to glasnost and perestroika among political diehards grew even stronger, however, and an increase in ethnic discontent in some of the Soviet Union's most sensitive regions added a new dimension to Gorbachev's difficulties (see **Close-Up**).

Gorbachev presented details of his political restructuring plan to the 5,000 delegates attending the 19th All-Union Conference of the Soviet Communist Party in June—the first such conference since 1941. Gorbachev said that he wanted the Communist Party to transfer considerable power to elected legislative bodies to give citizens a weapon against the bureaucracies that currently run the Soviet Union.

The Supreme Soviet, the national legislature, overwhelmingly endorsed Gorbachev's restructuring plan on December 1. This body currently has 1,500 members and meets briefly twice each year. The changes include the creation of a 2,250-member Congress of People's Deputies. This Congress will meet once a year, and will elect a smaller Supreme Soviet of 400 to 450 members, who will debate and decide all legislative and administrative questions. The Congress also will elect a president of the U.S.S.R., who will have overall responsibility for foreign policy, defense, and social and economic programs.

Gorbachev campaigned in September for support of his program. He stumped through the eastern regions of the Soviet Union, seeking direct contact with people in the streets. He worked to overcome their skepticism and to win their acceptance and active support of perestroika. Only through perestroika, he warned them, could the system cure some of the most chronic social ills suffered by the Soviet people, such as shortages of food. And in a speech to Soviet newspaper editors on September 23, Gorbachev acknowledged that there was a big gap between plans and deeds.

Gorbachev cleans house. On September 30, however, at a hurriedly convened meeting of the Central Committee, Gorbachev apparently won the kind of victory he needed to narrow this gap. Gorbachev removed from the Politburo—the Communist Party's policymaking body—four members identified with the economically stagnant era of Leonid I. Brezhnev, who ruled the Soviet Union from 1964 until 1982. Among the four was 79-year-old Andrei A. Gromyko, who was foreign minister from 1957 until 1985, when he became head of state as chairman of the Presidium of the Supreme Soviet.

The Central Committee on October 1 elected Gorbachev to succeed Gromyko as Presidium chairman. Until this time, the chairmanship had been a largely ceremonial position. Under the planned reforms, it would be vested with wide-ranging executive power.

Pullout from Afghanistan. On April 14, Afghanistan and Pakistan signed agreements intended to restore peace to Afghanistan, and the Soviet Union and the United States signed a separate pact guaranteeing the agreements. The Soviet Union began to withdraw its troops from Afghanistan in mid-May, as called for in the agreement. See **Afghanistan.**

Moscow summit. Gorbachev and United States President Ronald Reagan met in Moscow from May 29 to June 2 for their fourth summit. The two leaders exchanged documents ratifying a December 1987 treaty eliminating intermediate-range nuclear missiles. See **Armed forces.**

Relations with China. On Sept. 16, 1988, Gorbachev called for "full normalization" of relations with China. These relations were strained by ideological and border disputes in the 1960's. China has said repeatedly that it will not normalize relations unless the Soviets withdraw their troops from Afghanistan and reduce their forces along the Soviet border with China; and unless Vietnam—a Soviet ally—withdraws from Kampuchea (Cambodia). As Gorbachev spoke, the Soviets and Vietnamese were meeting China's conditions, and Moscow reportedly was pressing Vietnam for a quicker withdrawal from Kampuchea.

China responded favorably, sending Foreign Minister Qian Qichen to Moscow in early December for talks with Soviet Foreign Minister Eduard A. Shevardnadze. The two ministers agreed that their countries would prepare for a summit meeting of their leaders in Beijing (Peking) in the first half of 1989.

Military cuts. On Dec. 7, 1988, Gorbachev announced unilateral reductions in the Soviet armed forces. Addressing the United Nations General Assembly in New York City, he said that, within two years, the Soviets would eliminate 500,000 troops, 10,000 tanks, 8,500 artillery systems, and 800 combat aircraft. Gorbachev said also that Soviet forces would be reorganized to "become clearly defensive."

Gorbachev met with Reagan and President-elect George Bush on December 7. On the same day, an earthquake devastated the Armenian Soviet Socialist Republic (S.S.R.), a region of the U.S.S.R. already torn by ethnic conflict. Gorbachev cut short his visit to the

Armenians in Moscow in March demand that control over a region near the Turkish border be transferred from Azerbaijani to Armenian authorities.

United States on December 8 to return to the Soviet Union.

Earthquake. The earthquake's center was near Spitak, a city of about 16,000 people. The quake destroyed that city; demolished more than two-thirds of the buildings in Leninakan, whose population is about 220,000; and smashed about half the buildings in Kirovakan, a city of about 162,000. About 25,000 people died in the quake, and 500,000 were left homeless.

Speaking from Spitak on December 11, Gorbachev said that the earthquake had caused $8 billion worth of property damage and that reconstruction could take two years. He said a special commission would investigate methods used to construct some of the newer buildings that collapsed.

Gorbachev visited Yugoslavia from March 14 to 18. In a joint declaration with his hosts, Gorbachev renewed pledges made by previous Soviet leaders not to interfere in the affairs of Yugoslavia, which since 1948 has developed its own type of Communism, free of Soviet control. In this declaration, the Soviets promised not to "interfere in the internal affairs of other states under any pretext whatsoever." Thus, Gorbachev came close to renouncing the *Brezhnev Doctrine*, under which the Soviet Union in 1968 had asserted a right to intervene to preserve Communist rule in Soviet-bloc countries.

Gorbachev visited Poland from July 11 to 16, 1988. He disappointed his hosts by failing to mention

so-called "blank spots" in the official Soviet history of relations with Poland during and since World War II (1939-1945). The Soviet Union had agreed in 1987 to correct these omissions.

The most sensitive omission is a record of the massacre in 1941 of 4,000 Polish military officers in the Katyn forest in the Soviet Union. The Soviets have always insisted that invading German soldiers committed the murders. The Germans blame the Soviets.

Ethnic conflict. Gorbachev's reform program included a review of Soviet policy regarding ethnic minorities. About 48 per cent of the Soviet people belong to more than 90 non-Russian ethnic groups. These groups have some rights of self-government. In 1988, some of them demanded more such rights. Ethnic Armenians, the majority group in the Nagorno-Karabakh Autonomous (self-governing) Region of the Azerbaijan S.S.R. in February demanded the transfer of the region to the Armenian S.S.R.

The Estonian, Latvian, and Lithuanian S.S.R.'s, which were independent states from 1918 to 1940, demanded far-reaching local authority in 1988. In fact, the Supreme Soviet of the Estonian S.S.R. went beyond merely stating a demand and declared that the Estonian S.S.R. was "sovereign" and had a right to veto laws passed by the government of the Soviet Union. Moscow said that the declaration was illegal.

Glasnost advanced more rapidly than perestroika in 1988. More of the murky history of Stalinism came

Ethnic Conflict Confronts Gorbachev

When Soviet leader Mikhail S. Gorbachev set out in 1988 to implement *perestroika*, the economic and social restructuring of all branches of Soviet life, a tremendous problem emerged in an unexpected and unprecedented flare-up of ethnic conflict. The problem involved the political structures established to govern the more than 90 ethnic groups that live in the Soviet Union.

About 52 per cent of the Soviet people are ethnic Russians. Most of the remaining ethnic groups have substantial populations concentrated in certain regions. These groups have their own languages and cultures, and most also have a sense of belonging together as a people.

The Soviets have organized their country along ethnic lines. The largest political division in the Soviet Union is the *union republic*, of which there are 15. Because of the great number of ethnic Russians, the largest union republic by far is the Russian Soviet Federative Socialist Republic.

Many other union republics, however, have substantial percentages of ethnic Russians. Up to 40 per cent of the people living in the Estonian Soviet Socialist Republic (S.S.R.), for example, reportedly are Russian, and these people fill a similar percentage of that republic's government and management positions. The number of Russians in top posts is a source of acute resentment on the part of ethnic Estonians.

Within some union republics, minorities live in areas called *autonomous* (self-governing) *regions*. The government of a union republic has the power to overrule the government of an autonomous region within that republic—another source of conflict.

The Soviets easily managed ethnic problems before the call for perestroika. But several ethnic groups saw in perestroika and its twin policy of *glasnost* (openness in the flow of information) an opportunity to correct old grievances.

In early 1988, conflict that had long seethed beneath the surface erupted in violent confrontations in the Armenian and Azerbaijan S.S.R.'s, which lie next to each other on the Soviet border with Turkey and Iran. At issue was the status of the Nagorno-Karabakh Autonomous Region in the Azerbaijan S.S.R. About 75 per cent of the residents of this region are ethnic Armenians; most of the rest are ethnic Azerbaijani. The ethnic Armenians want the Soviet government to transfer the region to the Armenian S.S.R.

There has long been an intense dislike between Armenians, whose background is Christian, and Azerbaijani, most of whom are Muslim. Armenians tend to link Azerbaijani with a neighboring Muslim people, the Turks, who massacred several hundred thousand Armenians in 1915.

In February 1988, demonstrators in Nagorno-Karabakh and the Armenian S.S.R. demanded that the transfer of Nagorno-Karabakh to Armenia be made. On February 20, the legislature of Nagorno-Karabakh surprised Moscow by asking the Soviet government to make the transfer.

Initially, Gorbachev assured the Armenians of his "direct attention" and seemed sympathetic with their cause. The region's Communist Party chief, an ethnic Russian, was dismissed for neglecting long-smoldering tensions, and was replaced by an ethnic Armenian. Then violence erupted. On February 28, 32 people died in ethnic clashes in Sumgait, an Azerbaijani city. Labor unrest followed. On March 27, the Soviet press revealed that railroad and factory strikes had virtually paralyzed the region.

Moscow's attitude stiffened. The Soviet government did not want to favor one side or the other for fear of making the local conflict worse. Moscow was careful not to make any major concessions to the Armenians that might set a precedent for other dissatisfied ethnic groups.

Other groups in many parts of the Soviet Union already were speaking out in defense of their cultures and local rights. The most dramatic agitation occurred in three union republics lo-

Ethnic conflict erupted in three Soviet Socialist Republics (S.S.R.'s) on the Baltic coast, and in the Nagorno-Karabakh region of the Azerbaijan S.S.R.

cated northeast of Poland on the Baltic Sea—the Estonian, Latvian, and Lithuanian S.S.R.'s. These three republics had been independent countries between 1918 and 1940, and they had achieved —and maintained—higher standards of living than the Soviet Union.

The Soviets seized the three countries in June 1940, about nine months after the start of World War II, under secret clauses of a 1939 treaty between the Soviet Union and Nazi Germany. Later in 1940, the Soviets made the three countries part of the Soviet Union.

Hundreds of thousands of Estonians, Latvians, and Lithuanians were sent to labor camps in Siberia for resisting Soviet rule or for opposition to Communism. The Soviet government also encouraged the immigration of ethnic Russians to the Baltic republics. Under Soviet rule, the Russian language has become dominant in all three republics.

Beginning in the spring of 1988 and continuing throughout the remainder of the year, ethnic Estonians, Latvians, and Lithuanians protested against Moscow's immigration and language policies, which they said were a threat to their national identity; Moscow's economic management, which they said had damaged their environment and lowered their living standard; and their loss of independence.

Soviet reactions to these outbursts were astonishingly tolerant, even though the protesters demanded far-reaching local authority, especially in the economic sphere. The Soviets seemed prepared to grant the Baltic S.S.R.'s wide self-rule in economic planning and management, and more respect for national cultures and languages. It was clear, however, that Gorbachev would not allow any significant challenge to the three republics' political status. After the Estonian legislature on November 16 declared Estonia *sovereign*—that is, not subject to any other government—the Soviet government ruled the declaration invalid.

A transfer of Nagorno-Karabakh to the Armenian S.S.R. also seemed out of the question, though this region's troubles multiplied. After bloody clashes between the ethnic groups in late November, Moscow sent troops to put down the violence, imposing curfews and bans on demonstrations in Azerbaijan and Armenia.

On December 7, a natural disaster added to Armenia's miseries. A tremendous earthquake killed about 25,000 people there and left 500,000 homeless. Ethnic conflict continued even as rescue workers and badly needed supplies poured into the area. As 1988 drew to a close, the many-headed monster of ethnic conflict showed every sign that it would follow Gorbachev into 1989— and beyond.   Eric Bourne

to light in waves of accusations and disclosures, and in the restoration of the reputations of many of Stalin's millions of victims.

Glasnost was increasingly apparent in literature, motion pictures, and other arts; and in education, particularly in the fields of history and sociology. Glasnost showed itself also in the Soviet news media's sharpened focus on problems faced by ordinary citizens, such as a low standard of living; and in an announcement that labor camps for convicts would undergo "radical" reform to improve conditions and eliminate abuses.

The government even admitted that for decades, maps of the Soviet Union produced for general use— including distribution to foreigners—contained false details. In some cases, various maps of the same area showed that rivers and towns had mysteriously "moved" from place to place.

Church and state. The Soviet government is officially atheistic. But as Christians celebrated the 1,000th anniversary of the introduction of Christianity to what is now the Soviet Union, the state continued to extend its tolerance of religion. At an unprecedented meeting on April 29 with the Russian Orthodox Patriarch Pimen, Gorbachev announced the drafting of a "new law on freedom of conscience."

Budget deficit revealed. On October 27, the Soviet government disclosed for the first time vital details of the state budget, including a likely deficit. Finance Minister Boris I. Gostev told the Supreme Soviet that the deficit in 1989 was expected to be $59-billion. Gostev cited a number of items that were responsible for the deficit, including vast subsidies for inefficient industries and farms, the fall in international oil prices, crash programs to cut shortages in food and housing, and greatly increased allocations for environmental protection.

The economy registered almost zero growth in 1988. Gorbachev told the June conference that the "most painful and acute" problem of Soviet society was its failure to provide consumers with adequate goods and services. Inadequacies included shortages, poor quality, and a lack of choice of products and services.

Farm reform. In July, Gorbachev launched a plan to allow individuals, families, and other groups to rent land and equipment from state-owned collective farms and to work the land independent of state control. This plan represented a dramatic turn to private farming and a revolutionary break with 70 years of rigid collectivization of agriculture.

The Central Committee backed the plan, and, a month later, the government approved it. Early results included some gains in productivity. There was no immediate indication, however, that the program was encouraging young and able-bodied individuals to stay on the land or to return to it.   Eric Bourne

See also **Europe** (Facts in brief table). In *World Book*, see **Russia; Union of Soviet Socialist Republics.**

United Nations

United Nations (UN) served as a powerful instrument for peace in 1988. UN mediators paved the way to peace in Afghanistan, Iran, and Iraq. The UN General Assembly served as a forum for a stunning announcement of Soviet troop reductions and an offer by the Palestine Liberation Organization (PLO) for a settlement of the Palestinian-Israeli conflict. The signing of an Angola peace pact took place at the UN in December. And an operation of the UN itself won the 1988 Nobel Peace Prize.

UN negotiations to end warfare in Afghanistan bore fruit on April 14, when the Soviet Union agreed to withdraw its troops from that country. The Soviets invaded Afghanistan in December 1979 to support that country's Communist government. They quickly raised their troop level to about 115,000 and maintained that level. The Soviet Union, the United States, Afghanistan, and Pakistan on April 14, 1988, signed accords in Geneva, Switzerland, calling for the withdrawal of all Soviet troops by Feb. 15, 1989. The agreements also prohibit foreign nations from interfering in the internal affairs of Afghanistan and provide for the voluntary return of 5 million Afghan refugees presently living in Pakistan and Iran.

Soviet troops began returning home when the accords went into effect on May 15, but the war continued. Afghan rebels, armed and financed by many countries including the United States, battled the Afghan Army, which is supported by the Soviet Union.

United Nations Secretary-General Javier Pérez de Cuéllar announces on August 8 that Iran and Iraq have accepted a cease-fire proposal.

Iran-Iraq talks. The signing of the Geneva agreements encouraged UN Secretary-General Javier Pérez de Cuéllar to press for a peaceful solution to the war between Iran and Iraq, which began in September 1980. Starting on July 26, 1988, the secretary-general mediated negotiations between Iran's Foreign Minister Ali Akbar Velayati and Iraqi Foreign Minister Tariq Aziz at UN Headquarters in New York City. The negotiators agreed on August 8 to begin a cease-fire on August 20, and to start peace talks in Geneva on August 25. The talks began on time and lasted until September 13.

A second session, in New York City, ran from October 1 to 8. The secretary-general, with the backing of the Security Council, insisted that the cease-fire be strengthened by troop withdrawals and the repatriation of prisoners of war. The International Committee of the Red Cross estimated that Iran has detained about 70,000 Iraqis and that Iraq is holding 30,000 Iranians. (The permanent members of the Security Council are China, France, Great Britain, the Soviet Union, and the United States. The nonpermanent members during 1988 were Algeria, Argentina, Brazil, Italy, Japan, Nepal, Senegal, West Germany, Yugoslavia, and Zambia.)

The Geneva talks ended on November 11, after producing only one agreement. Iraq agreed to repatriate 411 sick and wounded Iranian prisoners, while Iran promised to return 1,115 Iraqis.

General Assembly. The 43rd session of the UN General Assembly opened on September 20. Argentina's Foreign Minister Dante Caputo was elected president for the session. During the first three weeks of debate, 12 heads of state, 10 prime ministers, and dozens of foreign ministers addressed the Assembly.

United States President Ronald Reagan, addressing the General Assembly on September 26, urged that the UN make an effort to end the use of chemical weapons, which have been banned since 1925 by an agreement known as the Geneva Protocol. Of the 159 members of the UN, 110 had signed that accord. Reagan said, "The use of chemical weapons in the Iran-Iraq war, beyond its tragic human toll, jeopardizes the moral and legal strictures [restrictions] that have held these weapons in check since World War I."

Reagan congratulated the UN for its work against international terrorism and AIDS (acquired immune deficiency syndrome). "The United Nations is a better place than it was eight years ago," he said.

Gorbachev pledges to cut troops. Soviet leader Mikhail S. Gorbachev told the General Assembly on December 7 that the Soviet Union will slash its armed forces by 10 per cent and shift its military units in Europe from positions of attack to a defensive posture. He also promised to improve human rights in the Soviet Union, pledged financial relief for developing nations that are deeply in debt, and called for the UN to expand its role in space, international law, and the environment.

Actress Audrey Hepburn, in her real-life role as a UNICEF ambassador, visits Ethiopia to help raise funds to aid that drought-stricken land.

The Soviet leader invited U.S. President-elect George Bush to move forward with the Soviet Union to forge new agreements on the reduction of long-range nuclear arms and the elimination of chemical weapons. See **Union of Soviet Socialist Republics.**

Arafat visa denied. PLO leader Yasir Arafat in November applied to the U.S. government for a visa permitting him to enter the United States to address the UN General Assembly. Arafat wanted to explain the PLO's November 15 declaration of an independent Palestinian state and PLO plans for a peace settlement in the Middle East.

On November 26, however, the U.S. Department of State denied Arafat the visa on the grounds that he condoned and encouraged terrorism. The General Assembly responded to the U.S. action on November 30, voting 151 to 2 for a resolution that "deplores the failure of the host country to approve granting of the requested entry visa." The United States and Israel voted against the resolution, and Great Britain and five other nations did not vote.

Arafat renounces terrorism. The General Assembly held a special session in Geneva from December 13 to 15 so that Arafat could address it. Arafat on December 13 offered the Assembly his plan for peace with Israel, including an international peace conference and replacement of Israeli troops in the West Bank and Gaza Strip with UN peacekeeping forces. Although Arafat set what many diplomats called a

more moderate tone than ever before, he stopped short of renouncing terrorism or recognizing Israel's right to exist.

At a press conference the next day, however, Arafat said that he accepted "the right of all parties concerned in the Middle East conflict to exist in peace and security, including the state of Palestine and Israel and other neighboring states," and that "we totally and absolutely renounce all forms of terrorism, including individual, group, and state terrorism." Arafat also endorsed two UN Security Council resolutions, 242 and 338, as a basis for peace negotiations. President Reagan responded by declaring that the United States would open direct talks with the PLO, lifting a ban that the United States imposed in 1975.

United States to pay dues. The White House announced on September 13 that the United States would pay $44 million in dues for fiscal year 1988, which ended on September 30. The United States had withheld payments to protest what it viewed as mismanagement and overstaffing at the UN. The White House also ordered the State Department to work out a plan for paying the remaining $520 million of the U.S. debt to the UN.

On October 14, the United States paid the UN $85.6-million of the $144 million that the U.S. Congress appropriated for UN dues for fiscal year 1989. The Reagan Administration said it would withhold the remainder until the UN committee that oversees UN finances approved a tight budget for the organization and set a limit on emergency expenditures.

Reagan signs genocide bill. President Reagan on November 4 signed a bill making genocide a federal offense, thereby enabling the United States to ratify a UN agreement called the Genocide Convention. The agreement, which bans genocide, received the General Assembly's approval on Dec. 9, 1948. Since then, 97 countries have ratified it. The U.S. law defines genocide as acting with a "specific intent to destroy, in whole or in substantial part, a national, ethnic, racial, or religious group."

UN peacekeeping forces on Sept. 29, 1988, won the Nobel Peace Prize. The Nobel Committee in Oslo, Norway, said in announcing the award, "United Nations peacekeeping forces represent the manifest will of the community of nations to achieve peace through negotiations, and the forces have, by their presence, made a decisive contribution towards the initiations of actual peace negotiations." As the committee announced the award, about 10,000 troops from 35 countries were serving in UN forces in the Middle East and Asia.

New health chief. Hiroshi Nakajima, a Japanese physician, on July 21 became director-general of the World Health Organization (WHO), a specialized agency of the UN. WHO supports public health programs throughout the world and initiates research to counter the spread of new diseases. WHO has become actively involved in the fight against AIDS.

UNICEF appeals. The United Nations Children's Fund (UNICEF) issued an appeal in April for $39.4-million to help children in Mozambique and $16 million for children in Angola. These two African countries are torn by civil war, and they have the highest child mortality rates in the world. About 375 of every 1,000 children in Mozambique and Angola die of disease or malnutrition before they reach the age of 5. The children's fund has an annual budget of about $250 million, all of which comes from voluntary contributions.

UNICEF continued its worldwide vaccination campaign to immunize children against measles, polio, whooping cough, diphtheria, tetanus, and tuberculosis. These so-called childhood diseases and other afflictions such as dehydration caused by diarrhea and pneumonia kill between 14 million and 15 million children under the age of 5 every year. UNICEF plans to vaccinate all children by the year 1990.

AIDS day. UNICEF and WHO proclaimed Dec. 1, 1988, as World AIDS Day and urged people throughout the world to speak out on that day—in schools, families, and local communities—about efforts to fight AIDS. UNICEF is especially concerned about the spread of AIDS from mothers to their infants during pregnancy, and has also set up programs to protect children from contaminated needles and infected blood.   J. Tuyet Nguyen

In *World Book*, see **United Nations.**

United States, Government of the. The first trillion-dollar budget in United States history—for the 1988 fiscal year, which ended on September 30—produced a deficit of $155.1 billion. That shortfall was more than $5 billion higher than the deficit in the 1987 fiscal year and about $11 billion above the $144-billion target ordered by the 1985 Gramm-Rudman budget-balancing law, named for two of its sponsors, Senators Phil Gramm (R., Tex.) and Warren B. Rudman (R., N.H.).

The rise in the deficit, following a marked decline from the record $220.7-billion deficit of fiscal 1986, spelled potential trouble in 1989 for President-elect George Bush. The new President must aim at a Gramm-Rudman deficit target of $100 billion in fiscal 1990, down sharply from a 1989 deficit expected to range between $135 billion and $160 billion.

Mindful of that daunting budgetary task, and of the nation's need to reduce a trade deficit sticking stubbornly at more than $100 billion a year, international financial markets greeted Bush's election warily. Stock prices declined temporarily, interest rates rose, and the global value of the U.S. dollar continued to erode. Many observers interpreted those developments as an effort by the markets to pressure Bush into taking stronger measures against the budget and trade deficits than his campaign rhetoric suggested was likely. During the campaign, Bush emphasized a plan to deal with the budget deficit through a relatively painless "flexible freeze" on spending that would spare defense programs and social security from budgetary cutbacks while avoiding tax increases. He told cheering audiences that his message to Congress would be, "Read my lips: no new taxes."

The postelection developments in the international markets, however, prompted Bush to pledge that he would work closely with the Democratic-controlled Congress to reduce the budget deficit and promote stability for the dollar. Added pressure in that direction came from former Presidents Jimmy Carter and Gerald R. Ford, who, as cochairmen of a prestigious bipartisan panel called American Agenda, met with Bush on November 21 and urged him to "face reality." Carter and Ford presented the President-elect with an American Agenda report recommending tax hikes, smaller annual cost-of-living increases in social security benefits, and spending cuts in many other programs.

Setbacks for Reagan associates. President Ronald Reagan saw some of his oldest and closest political associates plagued by ethical and legal problems in 1988. Lyn Nofziger, former White House political director whose service to Reagan dated back to the 1960's, was convicted on Feb. 11, 1988, by a federal jury of illegal lobbying at the White House in 1982 after he had become a private consultant. On April 8, 1988, Nofziger was sentenced to 90 days in prison and fined $30,000. He appealed his case.

Michael K. Deaver, Reagan's former deputy chief of staff, in December 1987 was convicted on perjury charges connected with his questionable lobbying efforts. On Jan. 22, 1988, Deaver's lawyers sought dismissal of the case as a federal appeals court upheld, 2 to 1, an Administration argument that the special-prosecutor law under which he was convicted was unconstitutional.

On June 29, however, the Supreme Court of the United States disagreed with the appeals-court decision. In a stunning setback for the Reagan Administration and for Deaver, the high court ruled 7 to 1 that the special-prosecutor law was constitutionally valid. The majority ruling was written by Chief Justice William H. Rehnquist, who had been nominated chief justice in 1986 by Reagan. On September 23, Deaver received a three-year suspended prison sentence and was fined $100,000.

On October 21, Congress passed an ethics bill designed to tighten curbs on lobbying by former federal officials, including for the first time former members of Congress and their top aides. Reagan pocket-vetoed the bill, arguing that it was too restrictive.

The beleaguered attorney general. The Nofziger and Deaver cases were fleeting in impact compared with a months-long hubbub over the status of Attorney General Edwin Meese III, another Reagan intimate. Ethical questions figured prominently in Meese's 1985 confirmation hearings and were never put to rest, so an independent counsel, James C. McKay, was named to investigate his activities. On

March 29, 1988, Deputy Attorney General Arnold I. Burns, the Department of Justice's second-ranking official, and William F. Weld, head of the department's criminal division, resigned abruptly out of frustration over the detrimental effect that Meese's continuing legal difficulties were having on Justice Department operations. Four top aides left with them. A day later, Solicitor General Charles Fried, the department's fourth-ranking official, reportedly urged Meese to resign, arguing that the turmoil arising from the investigations was harming the department.

On April 1, independent counsel McKay made a surprise announcement, stating that he did not plan to seek an indictment of Meese "based on the evidence developed to date." Three months later, on July 5, Meese declared that he had been "completely vindicated" by McKay's 14-month investigation and said he would resign in August. But on July 18, when McKay's 830-page report of the probe was made public, the counsel said Meese "probably violated the criminal law" on four occasions while serving as the chief U.S. law-enforcement officer. Those alleged violations included intentionally filing a false income tax return and failing to pay capital gains taxes when due. McKay told reporters: "It all came down really to the question, 'If this were an ordinary person, would he be prosecuted?' And we concluded that he probably would not be."

Meese said he was "outraged at the tarnishing of

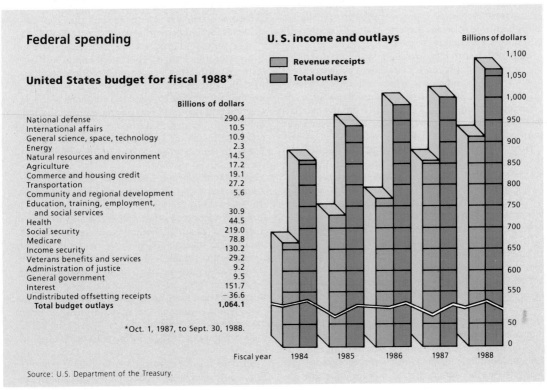

Federal spending

United States budget for fiscal 1988*

	Billions of dollars
National defense	290.4
International affairs	10.5
General science, space, technology	10.9
Energy	2.3
Natural resources and environment	14.5
Agriculture	17.2
Commerce and housing credit	19.1
Transportation	27.2
Community and regional development	5.6
Education, training, employment, and social services	30.9
Health	44.5
Social security	219.0
Medicare	78.8
Income security	130.2
Veterans benefits and services	29.2
Administration of justice	9.2
General government	9.5
Interest	151.7
Undistributed offsetting receipts	−36.6
Total budget outlays	**1,064.1**

*Oct. 1, 1987, to Sept. 30, 1988.

U. S. income and outlays

Billions of dollars

☐ Revenue receipts
☐ Total outlays

Fiscal year   1984   1985   1986   1987   1988

Source: U.S. Department of the Treasury.

our system of justice" by McKay. He accused the counsel of violating "every principle of fairness and decency" in asserting that Meese was probably guilty of crimes without indicting him.

In one of his final official acts, Meese announced on August 12 that he had established an independent-prosecutor system—similar to the one for investigating executive-branch officials—to review suspected criminal conduct by members of Congress. He issued an order requiring the attorney general to appoint an independent counsel whenever there were "reasonable grounds to believe" that a senator or representative may have violated the law. But Meese's successor, former Pennsylvania Governor Richard L. Thornburgh, who was to stay on as Bush's attorney general, did not follow through on the idea.

Other key officials also resigned as time ran out on Reagan's tenure. Secretary of the Treasury James A. Baker III departed in August to manage Bush's presidential campaign and was succeeded by investment banker Nicholas F. Brady. Bush decided to keep Brady in his Cabinet and to nominate Baker for secretary of state. Secretary of Education William J. Bennett resigned in mid-September and was replaced by Lauro F. Cavazos, president of Texas Tech University in Lubbock, who became the first Hispanic American ever to hold Cabinet rank. Bush also kept Cavazos in his Cabinet. Departing in mid-October was James C. Miller III, director of the Office of Management and Budget, who was succeeded in that post by his deputy, Joseph R. Wright, Jr. As his budget director, the President-elect named Richard G. Darman, a Wall Street investment banker who worked as one of Bush's advisers during the presidential campaign.

Embezzler convicted. William John Burns, a financial officer at the State Department's Agency for International Development, which administers most U.S. foreign-aid programs, pleaded guilty on August 11 to embezzling nearly $1.4 million from the government over a six-year period. On October 14, Burns was sentenced to five years in prison.

House impeaches Florida judge. On August 3, U.S. District Court Judge Alcee L. Hastings of the Southern District of Florida was impeached by the House of Representatives. By a vote of 413 to 3, the House adopted 17 articles of impeachment, including a charge that Hastings conspired to obtain a $150,000 bribe in a 1981 criminal case. He was the 15th federal official and 11th judge to be impeached since 1787. The Senate was due to try Hastings in 1989, with a two-thirds vote needed for conviction.

The Federal Bureau of Investigation (FBI) came under fire in January 1988 from a New York City lawyers' group, the Center for Constitutional Rights. The organization released 1,200 pages of FBI documents showing that the law-enforcement agency conducted a wide-ranging investigation from 1981 to 1985 of more than 100 individuals and groups opposed to Reagan Administration policies in Central America. The FBI inquiry centered initially on the Washington, D.C.-based Committee in Solidarity with the People of El Salvador but was expanded to include a number of other organizations—among them, the National Council of Churches, the United Automobile Workers, and the National Education Association—and numerous individuals.

No one was prosecuted as a result of the bureau's surveillance, but Representative Don Edwards (D., Calif.) said the investigation "had an odor of harassment about it." FBI Director William S. Sessions acknowledged that the probe "might not have been properly directed" in all instances.

Defense contracting exposures. The scandal of the year erupted on June 14 when the FBI and the Naval Investigative Service conducted coordinated raids at about 30 locations in 12 states and the District of Columbia. The investigators' targets included five high-level civilian employees of the Department of Defense and the offices of 14 leading defense contractors, including the McDonnell Douglas Corporation, United Technologies Corporation, Unisys Corporation, and the Northrop Corporation.

The raids came at the end of a secret two-year investigation, which turned up evidence that defense contractors had routinely bribed Pentagon officials for confidential information that helped the companies obtain lucrative military contracts. A number of former Pentagon officials working as consultants to the defense industry had apparently served as intermediaries between the contractors and the Pentagon. A federal grand jury in Virginia took charge of the evidence, and indictments were expected in 1989.

In an unrelated incident of cheating by a defense contractor, the Justice Department announced on October 12 that the Sundstrand Corporation of Rockford, Ill., agreed to plead guilty to a four-count criminal indictment that charged the company with contracting and tax fraud and paying more than $100,000 in bribes to Defense Department employees and their spouses. Sundstrand and a subsidiary agreed to pay $127.3 million in what was described as the largest fraud recovery in history.

Stealth airplanes. The U.S. Air Force, after years of secrecy, acknowledged in November that it had developed an F-117A fighter plane and a B-2 bomber using "stealth" technology that makes the aircraft virtually invisible to radar. The bombers will reportedly cost about $500 million each, making them literally worth their weight in gold.

Meanwhile, the Air Force faced problems with its B-1 bomber fleet, built at the order of the Reagan Administration after being rejected by Carter. The Air Force was spending billions of dollars in an effort to make the planes more airworthy. Two of the $280-million bombers crashed during a 10-day period in November; another B-1 went down in October 1987.

Shuttle flights resume. On Sept. 29, 1988, U.S. astronauts returned to space for the first time since

Selected agencies and bureaus of the U.S. government*

Executive Office of the President
President, Ronald Reagan
  Vice President, George Bush
  White House Chief of Staff, Kenneth M. Duberstein
  Presidential Press Secretary, James S. Brady
  Assistant to the President for National Security Affairs, Colin
  L. Powell
  Council of Economic Advisers—Beryl W. Sprinkel, Chairman
  Office of Management and Budget—Joseph R. Wright, Jr., Director
  Office of Science and Technology Policy—William R. Graham,
  Director
  U.S. Trade Representative, Clayton K. Yeutter

Department of Agriculture
Secretary of Agriculture, Richard E. Lyng

Department of Commerce
Secretary of Commerce, C. William Verity, Jr.
  Bureau of Economic Analysis—Allan H. Young, Director
  Bureau of the Census—John G. Keane, Director

Department of Defense
Secretary of Defense, Frank C. Carlucci III
  Secretary of the Air Force, Edward C. Aldridge, Jr.
  Secretary of the Army, John O. Marsh, Jr.
  Secretary of the Navy, William L. Ball III
  Joint Chiefs of Staff—
    Admiral William J. Crowe, Jr., Chairman
    General Larry D. Welch, Chief of Staff, Air Force
    General Carl E. Vuono, Chief of Staff, Army
    Admiral Carlisle A. H. Trost, Chief of Naval Operations
    General Alfred M. Gray, Jr., Commandant, Marine Corps

Department of Education
Secretary of Education, Lauro F. Cavazos

Department of Energy
Secretary of Energy, John S. Herrington

Department of Health and Human Services
Secretary of Health and Human Services, Otis R. Bowen
  Public Health Service—Robert E. Windom, Assistant Secretary
  Centers for Disease Control—James O. Mason, Director
  Food and Drug Administration—Frank E. Young, Commissioner
  National Institutes of Health—James B. Wyngaarden, Director
  Surgeon General of the United States, C. Everett Koop
  Social Security Administration—Dorcas R. Hardy, Commissioner

Department of Housing and Urban Development
Secretary of Housing and Urban Development, Samuel R. Pierce, Jr.

Department of the Interior
Secretary of the Interior, Donald P. Hodel

Department of Justice
Attorney General, Richard L. Thornburgh
  Bureau of Prisons—J. Michael Quinlan, Director
  Drug Enforcement Administration—John C. Lawn, Administrator
  Federal Bureau of Investigation—William S. Sessions, Director
  Immigration and Naturalization Service—Alan C. Nelson,
    Commissioner
  Solicitor General, Charles Fried

Department of Labor
Secretary of Labor, Ann Dore McLaughlin

Department of State
Secretary of State, George P. Shultz
  U.S. Representative to the United Nations, Vernon A. Walters

Department of Transportation
Secretary of Transportation, James H. Burnley IV
  Federal Aviation Administration—T. Allan McArtor, Administrator
  U.S. Coast Guard—Admiral Paul A. Yost, Jr., Commandant

*As of Jan. 3, 1989.

Department of the Treasury
Secretary of the Treasury, Nicholas F. Brady
  Internal Revenue Service—Lawrence B. Gibbs, Commissioner
  Treasurer of the United States, Katherine D. Ortega
  U.S. Secret Service—John R. Simpson, Director

Supreme Court of the United States
Chief Justice of the United States, William H. Rehnquist
  Associate Justices

William J. Brennan, Jr.	John Paul Stevens
Byron R. White	Sandra Day O'Connor
Thurgood Marshall	Antonin Scalia
Harry A. Blackmun	Anthony M. Kennedy

Congressional officials
President of the Senate pro tempore, John C. Stennis
  Senate Majority Leader, George J. Mitchell
  Senate Minority Leader, Robert J. Dole
  Speaker of the House, James C. Wright, Jr.
  House Minority Leader, Robert H. Michel
  Congressional Budget Office—James L. Blum, Acting Director
  General Accounting Office—Charles A. Bowsher, Comptroller
    General of the United States
  Library of Congress—James H. Billington, Librarian of Congress
  Office of Technology Assessment—John H. Gibbons, Director

Independent agencies
ACTION—Donna M. Alvarado, Director
Agency for International Development—Alan Woods, Admin-
  istrator
Central Intelligence Agency—William H. Webster, Director
Commission on Civil Rights—William Barclay Allen, Chairman
Commission of Fine Arts—J. Carter Brown, Chairman
Commodity Futures Trading Commission—Wendy Lee
  Gramm, Chairman
Consumer Product Safety Commission—Terrence M. Scanlon,
  Chairman
Environmental Protection Agency—Lee M. Thomas, Administrator
Equal Employment Opportunity Commission—Clarence Thom-
  as, Chairman
Federal Communications Commission—Dennis R. Patrick,
  Chairman
Federal Deposit Insurance Corporation—L. William Seidman,
  Chairman
Federal Election Commission—Thomas J. Josefiak, Chairman
Federal Emergency Management Agency—Julius W. Becton,
  Jr., Director
Federal Home Loan Bank Board—M. Danny Wall, Chairman
Federal Reserve System Board of Governors—Alan
  Greenspan, Chairman
Federal Trade Commission—Daniel Oliver, Chairman
General Services Administration—Richard G. Austin, Acting
  Administrator
Interstate Commerce Commission—Heather J. Gradison, Chairman
National Aeronautics and Space Administration—James C.
  Fletcher, Administrator
National Endowment for the Arts—Francis S. M. Hodsoll, Chairman
National Endowment for the Humanities—Lynne V. Cheney,
  Chairman
National Labor Relations Board—James M. Stephens, Chairman
National Railroad Passenger Corporation (Amtrak)—W. Gra-
  ham Claytor, Jr., Chairman
National Science Foundation—Erich Bloch, Director
National Transportation Safety Board—James L. Kolstad,
  Acting Chairman
Nuclear Regulatory Commission—Lando W. Zech, Jr., Chairman
Peace Corps—Loret Miller Ruppe, Director
Postal Rate Commission—Janet D. Steiger, Chairman
Securities and Exchange Commission—David S. Ruder, Chairman
Selective Service System—Samuel K. Lessey, Jr., Director
Small Business Administration—James Abdnor, Administrator
Smithsonian Institution—Robert McC. Adams, Secretary
Tennessee Valley Authority—Marvin T. Runyon, Chairman
U.S. Arms Control and Disarmament Agency—William F.
  Burns, Director
U.S. Information Agency—Charles Z. Wick, Director
U.S. Postal Service—Anthony M. Frank, Postmaster General
Veterans Administration—Thomas K. Turnage, Administrator

Uruguay

the *Challenger* space shuttle exploded Jan. 28, 1986. The shuttle *Discovery* and its five-man crew launched a $100-million communications satellite during a four-day mission.

Also on the science front, Secretary of Energy John S. Herrington announced on Nov. 10, 1988, that the world's largest and most expensive scientific tool, the $4.4-billion Superconducting Super Collider, would be built in Texas south of Dallas. The enormous particle accelerator, or atom smasher, will be 20 times more powerful than any accelerator now in existence.

Warming to the PLO. The Reagan Administration on December 14 authorized U.S. talks with the Palestine Liberation Organization (PLO), which the United States has long considered a terrorist group. The U.S. decision came after PLO Chairman Yasir Arafat renounced terrorism and recognized Israel's right to exist. See **Middle East.**

The Supreme Court of the United States, shy one member since the retirement in 1987 of Justice Lewis F. Powell, Jr., once again had nine members in 1988. The Senate voted 97 to 0 on February 3 to confirm Anthony M. Kennedy, a moderately conservative appeals court judge from Sacramento, Calif., to succeed Powell.   Frank Cormier and Margot Cormier

See also **Cabinet, United States; Congress of the United States; Reagan, Ronald Wilson; Supreme Court of the United States.** In *World Book*, see **United States, Government of the.**

Uruguay. Former Tupamaro guerrillas, who had terrorized Uruguay from the late 1960's to the early 1970's with acts of bank robbery, kidnapping, and murder, in 1988 were permitted to open their political headquarters in the capital city of Montevideo. The once-dreaded terrorists have opted to work within the democratic system and support their own candidate in presidential elections scheduled for 1989. The Tupamaros' former leader, Raúl Sendic, now in his mid-60's, heads a rural assistance organization for poverty-stricken peasants.

Uruguayan President Julio María Sanguinetti, who took office in March 1985, in 1988 became the country's first chief executive to visit the Soviet Union. Sanguinetti met with Soviet officials, including Communist Party General Secretary Mikhail S. Gorbachev, from March 21 to 23.

Uruguay's Supreme Court of Justice on May 5 upheld a controversial 1986 law that granted amnesty to those accused of committing human rights abuses when Uruguay was under military rule from 1973 to 1985. The high court ruled in a 3 to 2 decision that the amnesty law, which President Sanguinetti had fashioned, "coincides perfectly with constitutional principles."   Nathan A. Haverstock

See also **Latin America** (Facts in brief table). In *World Book*, see **Uruguay.**

Utah. See **State government.**

Vanuatu. See **Pacific Islands.**

Venezuela. Former Venezuelan President Carlos Andrés Pérez handily won election to the presidency for the second time on Dec. 4, 1988, defeating his principal rival, Eduardo Fernandez of the Social Christian Party. Pérez, 66 years old and the candidate of the Democratic Action (AD) party, was to take office in February 1989.

Pérez' most urgent task will be the renegotiation of Venezuela's nearly $35-billion foreign debt. Payment on the debt has been absorbing half of Venezuela's export earnings, which are derived mostly from oil. This will be a new role for Pérez. During his previous term in office, from 1974 to 1979, Pérez' administration was the beneficiary of windfall profits resulting from the near quadrupling of oil prices. Pérez presided over a boom in the economy and the nationalization of the petroleum and steel industries.

Venezuelan law prevents a president from seeking reelection for 10 years. While out of office, Pérez remained popular with workers, and during his reelection campaign, he defended his previous administration from charges of corruption. In achieving victory, Pérez had to distance himself from the administration of President Jaime Lusinchi. Lusinchi, also of the AD, did not support Pérez in his bid to become the AD's candidate.   Nathan A. Haverstock

See also **Latin America** (Facts in brief table). In *World Book*, see **Venezuela.**

Vermont. See **State government.**

Veterans. A proposal to transform the United States Veterans Administration (VA) into the Cabinet-level Department of Veterans Affairs was enacted in 1988, to take effect in March 1989. The legislation, passed by Congress in October, will not change the VA's functions, but proponents maintained that Cabinet status would give 27 million veterans and their dependents a stronger voice in the government.

Benefits appeals. Also in October, Congress passed a bill that would allow veterans to contest VA benefit decisions in a new special federal court. Veterans' last resort has been a VA appeals board that historically has ruled in favor of veterans less than 13 per cent of the time.

Agent Orange claims. On July 5, a U.S. District Court in New York approved a plan to settle claims of Vietnam veterans who argued they had medical problems from exposure to the defoliant Agent Orange. The suit was tentatively settled in 1984 when seven chemical companies, without admitting fault, agreed to pay $180 million into a fund. Veterans and their families were to begin receiving benefits from that fund—which, with interest, had grown to $240 million—by 1989.   Frank Cormier and Margot Cormier

In *World Book*, see **Veterans Administration; Veterans' organizations.**

Vice President of the United States. See **Bush, George H. W.** In the World Book Supplement section, see **Quayle, Dan.**

Coffins bearing remains purported to be those of U.S. servicemen killed
in the Vietnam War await shipment to the United States from Hanoi in April.

Vietnam suffered grave economic problems
throughout 1988 that lowered the nation's already
depressed living standards. Vietnam's leaders seemed
unable to cope with the country's problems, which
included runaway inflation, declining industrial production, and a shortage of investment capital. Another problem was a population growth rate that
gave Vietnam an additional 1 million mouths to feed
every year while its agriculture industry remained
primitive and stagnant.

Economic mismanagement was widespread and
unemployment high. An official report said that about
1 million people sought jobs "while those employed in
factories and government offices need only one-half
or two-thirds of their hours to finish their work."

During 1988, Vietnam defaulted on almost all of its
foreign debt of more than $3 billion. The country
depended on about $2 billion a year in economic aid
from the Soviet Union, but Moscow sought to reduce
this amount.

Food shortages were the most acute problem.
Three years of poor crop yields cut the amount of
food available per person. In early May, Vietnam
issued an international appeal for emergency food
aid, saying that more than 3 million people were "at
the edge of starvation." The United Nations World
Food Program provided $9.1 million in food.

Reformers thwarted. Reform efforts by Vietnam's
top leader, Communist Party General Secretary
Nguyen Van Linh, seemed to lose momentum in 1988.
Pham Hung, who became chairman of the Council of
Ministers in June 1987 and was hoped to be a bridge
between reformers and Communist hard-liners, died
on March 10, 1988. A June 22 National Assembly
election to fill his post became a showdown between
reformers and conservatives. The conservatives won by
296 to 200, electing Do Muoi.

Other developments. Truong Chinh, who, along
with Ho Chi Minh, had founded Vietnam's Communist
Party in 1930, died on September 30. A rigid ideologist
who was Ho's deputy for many years, Truong Chinh
had been Vietnam's Council of State chairman—a
ceremonial position—from 1981 to 1987.

In May 1988, Vietnam said it would withdraw
50,000 of its troops propping up the government of
Kampuchea (formerly called Cambodia). Several thousand soldiers left Kampuchea in 1988. All Vietnamese
troops were to be evacuated by 1990.

Vietnam agreed on June 8, 1988, to intensify its
lagging efforts to account for the remains of 1,758
United States servicemen still listed as missing in action in Vietnam. Vietnam turned over the remains of
130 human beings in 1988, but only 25 of them had
been identified as Americans.   Henry S. Bradsher

See also **Asia** (Facts in brief table); **Kampuchea.** In
World Book, see **Vietnam.**

Virginia. See **State government.**

Washington. See **State government.**

481

Washington, D.C.

Washington, D.C., voters on Nov. 8, 1988, returned five incumbents and elected one newcomer to the 13-member District of Columbia Council. William P. Lightfoot, Jr., an independent, won an at-large council seat vacated by Republican member Carol Schwartz, who did not seek reelection. Schwartz had been the Republican candidate for mayor in 1986.

Lightfoot, previously a Democrat, defeated former council member Jerry Moore, a Republican, and Tom Chorlton, a gay rights activist running on the D.C. Statehood Party ticket, as well as three other candidates who ran far behind. A lawyer and former City Council staff aide, Lightfoot carried all eight wards in the district.

Incumbent John Ray, a Democrat, was reelected easily to the other at-large seat on the ballot. The other incumbents winning reelection, all Democrats, were John A. Wilson in the Second Ward, Charlene Drew Jarvis in the Fourth Ward, H. R. Crawford in the Seventh Ward, and Wilhelmina J. Rolark in the Eighth.

Walter E. Fauntroy, a Democrat, won a ninth full term as the District of Columbia's delegate to the Congress of the United States with 71 per cent of the vote. Fauntroy defeated three other candidates.

New superintendent. The District of Columbia School Board on May 24 approved Andrew Jenkins as school superintendent, after months of delays and internal conflict. Jenkins, who had worked for the district's school system for 27 years, succeeded Floretta D. McKenzie, who had left the superintendent's post in February to start an education consulting firm.

In the November 8 elections, voters reelected David H. Eaton, a clergyman and long-time school board member, to his at-large seat on the board. Karen Shook, PTA president at a junior high school, won the second at-large seat in her first campaign for public office. Shook defeated incumbent Phyllis Etheridge Young. Eaton and Shook were among five candidates running for the two seats.

Murder record. In 1988, 372 people were murdered in the District of Columbia, setting a district record for the number of murders in a single year. The previous record of 287, set in 1969, was exceeded on Oct. 31, 1988. Mayor Marion S. Barry, Jr., and other officials blamed the rising rate of homicide on growing problems involving illegal drugs, especially territorial wars between rival gangs of drug dealers.

The victims and their assailants were primarily young black men. Police reported that in 1985, 16.9 per cent of the 148 homicides that occurred in the district were drug-related, and 72 per cent of the victims were black men. In 1988, about 60 per cent of the homicides were drug-related, and more than 80 per cent of the victims were black men.

Barry to be investigated. On December 29, the U.S. Department of Justice announced that it would investigate whether Mayor Barry had committed a crime during visits to the hotel room of a suspected drug dealer. Barry denied using drugs but admitted

Buses carrying the Washington Redskins football team —victors in the 1988 Super Bowl— inch through swarms of fans on Pennsylvania Avenue in February.

"poor judgment" in visiting the suspect, a former District of Columbia employee named Charles Lewis.

Budget bill amended. Congress on September 30 approved the district's $3.2-billion budget for fiscal year 1989 but amended the budget bill to prohibit the district from using its own funds to pay for abortions —except to save the life of the woman—and to require the City Council to repeal a residency requirement for district employees by Sept. 30, 1989. President Ronald Reagan had threatened to veto the bill unless it prohibited abortion funding. Another amendment forced the district to change its human-rights law to deny funding and use of facilities to homosexual student groups.

Congress also required the district to repeal an insurance law prohibiting insurance companies from routinely testing applicants for the virus that causes AIDS (acquired immune deficiency syndrome). Many insurers had stopped writing insurance to district residents.

Train station reopens. Washington's 81-year-old Union Station reopened on Sept. 29, 1988, more than seven years after the U.S. Department of the Interior closed it as a public hazard. A $181-million renovation—a cooperative effort of the federal government and the private sector—restored historical elements of the train station and created a 110-store shopping mall.   Sandra Evans

See also **City.** In *World Book,* see **Washington, D.C.**

Water. One of the most serious droughts of the century withered vast areas of the United States and southern Canada in the summer of 1988. In the United States, the widespread drought affected California, the Northwest, the northern Great Plains, the Midwestern grain belt, and parts of Texas, the Southeast, and the Northeast. The Midwest was particularly hard-hit, with the drought spelling disaster for crops and livestock.

River flows in June were below normal in 41 of the 43 key large river gauging stations monitored by the U.S. Geological Survey. Water levels along the Mississippi River fell to record lows, forcing at least one hydroelectric plant to shut down and leaving hundreds of barges stranded.

Urban water shortages. As reservoirs shrank and stream flows dwindled, city water supplies dropped to critical levels. Many city governments were compelled to impose water-conservation measures.

Because 1988 was the second consecutive critically dry year in northern California, San Francisco officials in April imposed water rationing to reduce by 25 per cent the use of water from the Hetch Hetchy reservoir and aqueduct system. A voluntary effort begun in 1987 had failed to reduce water consumption at all. The 1988 rationing program, which affected more than 2 million residents of San Francisco and 30 other Bay Area communities, imposed stiff penalties on people using more than their allotted ration of water.

The Los Angeles City Council also instituted water-conservation measures in April. The council banned the serving of water in restaurants except on demand, forbade hosing down patios and driveways, required property owners to repair leaky faucets and toilets, and banned the use of decorative fountains that did not recycle water. Southern California's Metropolitan Water District instituted a voluntary conservation program that included distributing water-saving kits for faucets, toilets, and showers; providing leak-detection services; and using advertising to promote conservation.

Citing long-term concerns about the effect of drought on New York City's water supplies, Mayor Edward I. Koch inaugurated "the first permanent water-conservation campaign in city history" in May. The program—which included an advertising campaign featuring a picture of a shriveled apple and the slogan "Don't Drip New York Dry"—focused on the installation of water meters on residential and commercial property.

Property owners were then billed for the water used, giving them a financial incentive to avoid wasting water. The program was designed to conserve water not only during the 1988 drought but also in the future, when developing new water supplies will be more difficult and more costly.

Shrinking Aral Sea. The Soviet Union's Aral Sea, once the fourth-largest lake in the world, shrank

A Chicago worker places a locking cap on a fire hydrant in June to prevent unauthorized use and keep water pressure high for fighting fires.

drastically between 1960 and 1987, according to a September 1988 report by Philip P. Micklin, professor of geography at Western Michigan University in Kalamazoo. The size of the lake decreased from 68,000 to 41,000 square kilometers (26,000 to 16,000 square miles), and it became nearly three times more salty. The lake, about 175 miles (282 kilometers) east of the Caspian Sea, is shrinking because almost all the water in its tributary streams is diverted for irrigation.

The shrinkage has had a severe environmental impact. Most of the lake's fish have died, destroying the Aral Sea fishing industry. The surrounding wetlands have dried up, while the deserts have expanded—encroaching upon pastureland vital to the livestock industry. The shrinkage also has exposed large areas of salt-covered lake bottom to the wind, which has carried toxic salts to nearby cultivated lands, poisoning the crops.

Micklin warned that if inflow to the Aral Sea remains limited, the lake will shrink during the next century into several small, lifeless, briny lakes. In recent years, however, the Soviets undertook a project to bring agricultural runoff to the lake. The Soviets also considered a controversial plan to divert two large rivers in Siberia to irrigate croplands near the Aral Sea, allowing the lake's tributaries to replenish it once again.   Iris Priestaf

See also **Conservation; Weather.** In *World Book*, see **Water.**

Weather. The outstanding weather news in the United States in 1988 was the extreme heat and drought that prevailed over most of the northern part of the nation. Crop yields showed their largest yearly decline since record-keeping began. See **Close-Up.**

The first nine months of 1988 featured exceptionally warm weather in the northern and western parts of North America. In central Alaska, for example, average monthly temperatures were more than 6 Fahrenheit degrees (3.3 Celsius degrees) above normal from January through September. And in every month of 1988, the desert regions of the Southwestern United States reported temperatures more than 3 Fahrenheit degrees (1.6 Celsius degrees) above normal. Arid conditions persisted in the West and in the southern Appalachians and spread into the northern states of the Midwest and the Ohio Valley during the late spring and summer. Water levels in the Great Lakes, which had risen in 1987 to their highest levels in 300 years, fell back to normal by the autumn of 1988.

Many forest fires raged through the West during the summer and autumn, with flames approaching to within a few hundred yards of the Old Faithful geyser in Yellowstone Park. See **Forest fires.**

The hurricane season was more active in 1988 than in the two previous years. Gilbert, the most intense hurricane ever recorded in the Western Hemisphere, formed near Barbados on September 10. The hurricane devastated Jamaica, which until then had

escaped a direct encounter with a hurricane for 31 years. Property damage totaled more than $1 billion, and 20 per cent of Jamaica's inhabitants were left homeless. Gilbert then intensified. Its central barometric pressure dropped to the lowest point ever recorded in a hurricane—26.13 inches (663.7 millimeters) of mercury, or 888 millibars—and it produced sustained winds of 190 miles (306 kilometers) per hour. The storm flattened parts of the island of Cancun, off the Yucatán Peninsula, and on September 16 Gilbert struck the Mexican coast about 130 miles (210 kilometers) south of Brownsville, Tex. Heavy rains produced by Gilbert in Monterrey, Mexico, swept four buses into a river, drowning as many as 190 people.

In late October, Hurricane Joan made a direct hit on Nicaragua, causing extensive flooding. Upon reaching the Pacific Ocean as a tropical storm, the former hurricane was renamed Miriam. The only hurricane to reach the United States in 1988 was Florence, which struck the Mississippi Delta in September. Tropical storms Beryl and Chris also reached the United States in August, and a weakened Gilbert brought as much as 8 inches (20 centimeters) of rain to much of the Mississippi Valley, which had been badly parched earlier in the year.

The hurricane season in the eastern Pacific started late. The first storm, Aletta, developed on June 16, the latest start since 1968. Hawaii was threatened by two hurricanes—a much weakened Fabio in early August and the powerful Uleki, which passed a few hundred miles to the south in early September, sending huge swells to Hawaii's south shores.

Tornado activity in the United States in 1988 was less than average. April and May, normally the height of the season, saw only one event—but it was a big one. On May 9, 81 tornadoes were spotted in Arkansas, Illinois, Indiana, Iowa, and Wisconsin. Astonishingly, there were no fatalities. The year's most destructive tornado in the United States hit Raleigh, N.C., in November, killing seven people. The remnants of Hurricane Gilbert spawned more than 35 small tornadoes in the area around San Antonio on September 17 and 18.

Weather highlights. On January 17, southern California was hit by a Pacific storm with a barometric reading in Los Angeles of 29.25 inches (742.95 millimeters) of mercury, or 990 millibars, the lowest ever recorded there. Waves up to 14 feet (4.3 meters) high in addition to a 7-foot (2.1-meter) high tide caused extensive flooding and at least 10 injuries in coastal regions. The same storm later dumped 3 feet (1 meter) of snow on the north rim of the Grand Canyon and brought severe blizzard conditions to the north central states. Marquette, Mich., was hit with a record snowfall of 19.5 inches (49.5 centimeters).

The second week of February brought the Deep South its coldest weather of the year. Temperatures fell to 19°F. (−7°C) in Mobile, Ala., and to 25°F. (−4°C) in New Orleans. The cold wave was accompanied by

A satellite photograph shows Gilbert—the most intense hurricane ever recorded in the Western Hemisphere—as it sweeps into Mexico in September.

snow and ice—2 inches (5 centimeters) in Lake Charles, La., and 0.5 inch (1.3 centimeters) in Mobile—the heaviest snow in these areas in 15 years.

Two fierce storms in mid-March buried the central Rockies under as much as 6 feet (2 meters) of snow. Snow depths reached 53 inches (135 centimeters) at Lead, S. Dak., in the Black Hills. Another intense storm produced a severe blizzard in Edmonton, Canada, crippling the city with 50 centimeters (20 inches) of powdery snow on March 26 and 27. In April, unusually heavy snows fell in southern California, Nevada, and New England. Mount Washington in New Hampshire had its snowiest April on record with 89.9 inches (228 centimeters).

During the drought, record high temperatures and record low levels of rainfall were set in the United States. Reno, Nev., was without rain from March 1 to April 14—a cold-season record. Billings, Mont., recorded only 2.43 inches (6.17 centimeters) of precipitation for the entire winter—the second driest on record. As the drought in the Midwest worsened in May and June, Chicago had 23 consecutive days without rain. On June 21, the first full day of summer, more than 60 cities set maximum temperature records. Five new monthly records were also set. Tucson, Ariz., broke its high-temperature record twice in June, finally reaching 114°F. (46°C).

July was hot and dry throughout the United States except in a few areas, including the southern Rockies

and Florida. During a midmonth surge of hot air, record maximum temperatures were logged in many cities, including Alpena, Mich.; Charleston, W. Va.; Cleveland; Duluth, Minn.; Marquette, Mich.; Milwaukee; and San Francisco. The Middle Atlantic States, which were not severely affected by the drought, had widespread showers from July 19 to 30. A flash flood in the New York City area caused sewage to escape into the Hudson River and harbor area. A final surge of heat and humidity spread into the Ohio Valley and East Coast states during the first two weeks of August. Baltimore and Philadelphia broke records for consecutive days of temperatures at or above 90°F. (32°C).

October was the second-coldest month on record for the Northeast but the warmest ever along the West Coast. November, on the other hand, was unusually stormy, with 144 tornadoes, a record, striking the United States and killing 15 people. Precipitation was also unusually great in some areas. By the end of November, 164 inches (417 centimeters) of snow had fallen at Alta, Utah, the greatest November snowfall since record-keeping began in 1944. Heavy rain soaked much of the Mississippi Valley.

December was unusually dry. Harrisburg and Allentown, Pa., received no precipitation until December 21. Record cold temperatures hit the Northeast on December 12 and 13. Cold air also invaded Florida, bringing Apalachicola its first snow shower in 10 years. The month concluded with numerous avalanche

Summer of 1988:
Too Darn Dry

From April through August 1988, record heat seared farmland across the Midwestern and North Central United States. On the Mississippi, barges lay stranded in shallow riverbeds. In 10 Western states, forest fires raged through a natural tinderbox of dry brush. Altogether, the drought of 1988 shriveled fields, forests, and water reserves across North America and dried up food supplies worldwide.

Yet even as tales of the devastation dominated the news, meteorologists were quick to note that this drought was hardly the worst of the century; that record went to the Dust Bowl drought of the 1930's. And while some people speculated that the heat and dryness were the first signs of a new global warming trend, scientists generally attributed the weather to an unfortunate combination of natural cyclical patterns.

No single cause is responsible for all droughts. Scientists suggest that the 1988 drought was mainly due to a change in the position of the jet stream—a swift, high-altitude air current that flows from west to east across North America—which moved into central Canada, far north of its usual route. As a result, storms also went north, leaving an unusual high-pressure zone over much

A cow wanders over the parched bed of a dried-up pond on a farm near Prairie Home, Nebr., one of the areas hardest hit by the drought of 1988.

of the United States. That meant more heat and less rain, which combined to cause a drought—an abnormal shortage of moisture.

According to scientific indexes for measuring drought, the proportion of the continental United States suffering severe or extreme drought in 1988 peaked in July at nearly 40 per cent, to tie with 1977 as the seventh worst drought year of the 1900's. The affected area stretched in a nearly unbroken band from the Appalachians in the East, across the Ohio Valley and the northern plains, to the Pacific coastal states. The coasts of Oregon and Washington, hard-hit by drought in the past two years, escaped in 1988 thanks to rain in the early summer.

The greatest damage occurred in the North Central farm states, where a record lack of spring rain deprived crops of moisture in their crucial early phase of growth. Some counties in Iowa, Illinois, and Wisconsin had no measurable rain from late March until late June.

While conditions in the Midwest attracted the most attention, the Southeast was in the fourth year of a dry spell. The Tennessee Valley was especially hard-hit; since the winter of 1984, precipitation in Nashville had been below normal by a total of nearly 65 inches (165 centimeters)—about 18 months' normal rainfall.

The entire Mississippi River system suffered, too. River transportation, disrupted in June, was restored only by extensive dredging at Memphis, where river height had fallen to its lowest level since measurements were first taken in 1845. The drop in the Mississippi's level in the Louisiana Delta allowed tides in the Gulf of Mexico to push salt water upstream, threatening the supply of drinking water in New Orleans.

By June 23, half of the U.S. agricultural counties—1,390 counties in 30 states—had been declared drought-disaster areas. In August, President Ronald Reagan signed legislation to provide billions of dollars of relief to farmers who suffered heavy losses. According to government estimates released in September, the drought reduced the total U.S. grain harvest by 31 per cent. In turn, food prices were predicted to rise by 3 to 5 per cent in 1989, reflecting not only the grain shortfall but also meat shortages, as many farmers were forced to slaughter livestock early because of the lack of feed grain.

Meteorologists noted that even a moderate shortage of rain in 1989 might contribute to another serious drought. But if the weather improved, U.S. officials predicted a production-led recovery and new stability for the farm economy because the drought's shortfalls would produce a 1989 rebound in prices for crops and farmland as well as in worldwide demand for grain.   Alfred K. Blackadar and Paul G. Knight

alerts in the Sierra Nevada as a series of Pacific storms dumped several feet of snow there.

World highlights. Severe flooding struck Bangladesh several times during the autumn of 1988. Cyclones in September and November flooded the country, and an active summer monsoon in India combined with erosion along the foothills of the Himalaya to cause excessive runoff into Bangladesh's Ganges River Delta. Thousands of lives were lost.

Southern and eastern Europe experienced an early winter as unseasonably cold weather set in during October. Temperatures averaged as much as 14.3 Celsius degrees (25.7 Fahrenheit degrees) below normal in Turkey and Bulgaria.

Greenhouse effect? For years, scientists have warned that increasing amounts of carbon dioxide and other gases in the atmosphere may lead to an increase in the global average temperatures because these gases tend to trap the sun's radiation. This process is generally called the *greenhouse effect*. Several studies completed in 1988 showed that global average temperatures during the 1980's have been the highest in recent history. Scientists hastened to point out that these high temperatures are a trend that began in the 1890's. The greenhouse effect is also too slight to be solely responsible for the increases.

Alfred K. Blackadar and Paul G. Knight

In *World Book*, see **Weather.**

Weight lifting. See **Olympic Games; Sports.**

Welfare. A major, years-long effort to overhaul the United States welfare system reached fruition on Oct. 13, 1988, when President Ronald Reagan signed the Family Support Act, a law designed to help welfare parents get jobs through education, job training, and work programs. The Senate had voted 96 to 1 to pass the measure on September 29, and the House of Representatives passed it 347 to 53 a day later. Daniel P. Moynihan (D., N.Y.), the bill's chief sponsor in the Senate, had been pressing for welfare reform since he was a White House assistant under President Richard M. Nixon in 1969 and 1970. The National Governors Conference endorsed the idea in 1987.

The revised program, estimated to cost $3.3 billion over five years, represents the first basic restructuring of the welfare system since it began in 1935. It replaces the Aid to Families with Dependent Children program and the Work Incentive Program.

A key provision requires welfare parents with children over the age of 3 to participate, if government funds are available, in basic-education, job-training, work-experience, and job-search programs operated by the states. Child-care assistance would be provided by the states. By 1995, 20 per cent of those eligible will be required to enter such programs. Federal contributions for the programs will increase from $600-million in the 1989 fiscal year to $1.3 billion in 1995.

The compromise measure also requires states to automatically withhold child-support payments from the paychecks of absent parents even if they are not in arrears. At White House insistence, the House agreed to a Senate provision requiring at least one parent in a two-parent welfare family to perform 16 hours a week of unpaid community service starting in 1994. The Senate accepted a House proposal to require states to continue providing child-care assistance and Medicaid benefits for one year after a family works its way off welfare rolls.

Poverty. The poverty rate in the United States edged downward in 1987 for the fourth straight year, the Bureau of the Census reported on Aug. 31, 1988. The 1987 rate of 13.5 per cent continued a decline from a recent peak of 15.2 per cent in 1983, but the drop from 13.6 per cent in 1986 was so small it was not statistically significant.

Median family income increased for the fifth year in a row, to a record $30,853 from $29,458. The incomes of blacks and Hispanics declined. The income losses were so small, however, that they fell within the margin of statistical error, meaning that black and Hispanic incomes may have stayed the same or even risen slightly.

The Census Bureau said 32.5 million Americans had 1987 incomes below the government's official poverty line, defined as an annual cash income of $11,611 or less for a family of four. For white Americans, the poverty rate was 10.5 per cent, down from 11 per cent in 1986. But the poverty rate for blacks increased—for the first time since 1982—from 31.1 to 33.1 per cent, and for Hispanics it rose from 27.3 to 28.2 per cent. On May 5, 1988, the National Urban League, an organization that works to end racial discrimination, charged that the Reagan Administration had conducted a "disastrous eight-year experiment" that featured "retrogressive policies that make black people poorer."

Doing more with less? In August 1988, the American Federation of State, County, and Municipal Employees, a labor union of government workers, contended that spending for federal domestic programs was $158.6 billion less than what was needed to maintain the levels of service that existed at the start of the Reagan Administration in 1981. The federation reported that an analysis by Fiscal Planning Services, an independent group, found the following shortfalls: Medicaid, $14.8 billion less than the $178 billion needed; job training, $40 billion below a required $63 billion; welfare and child support, $6.5 billion below a required $72 billion; food stamps, $5 billion below a required $80 billion; and subsidized housing, $3.3 billion below a required $7.8 billion.

Samuel R. Pierce, Jr., secretary of housing and urban development, said earlier, in April, that his department was doing "more with less" by scrapping programs of questionable effectiveness and streamlining others. His department's spending authority dropped from $33.4 billion in 1981 to a proposed $13.6 billion for 1989. Frank Cormier and Margot Cormier

In *World Book*, see **Welfare.**

West Indies. Hurricane Gilbert—the fiercest hurricane of this century—devastated the island nation of Jamaica on Sept. 12, 1988, killing 45 people. The storm left an estimated 500,000 people homeless—nearly a fifth of Jamaica's entire population.

The storm hit as Jamaica headed toward national elections that must take place by April 1989, in keeping with the parliamentary system. Prime Minister Edward Seaga of the free-enterprise Jamaica Labor Party took full credit for a massive inpouring of international assistance. His opponent—former Prime Minister Michael N. Manley of the socialist People's National Party—was reportedly the favorite before the disaster struck. But Manley was at a disadvantage as the incumbent Seaga extracted political benefits from coordinating relief efforts.

Dominican Republic. The 81-year-old President Joaquín Balaguer further enhanced his reputation as a builder while serving his fourth term as the elected Dominican leader. During his first two years in office, Balaguer, though blind and barely able to walk, proved vigorous in managing new investments worth $250 million in public works. These projects are aimed at boosting tourism and offsetting losses in sugar crop earnings.   Nathan A. Haverstock

See also **Haiti; Latin America** (Facts in brief table). In *World Book*, see **West Indies.**

West Virginia. See **State government.**

Wisconsin. See **State government.**

Witt, Katarina (1965-   ), topped her impressive figure-skating career on Feb. 27, 1988, when she captured the gold medal at the Winter Olympics in Calgary, Canada. Witt, gold medalist at the 1984 games, became the first woman figure skater to win a gold in two consecutive Olympics since Sonja Henie, who won in 1928, 1932, and 1936.

The final free-skating competition in Calgary was dubbed the "battle of the Carmens" because both Witt and her closest rival, Debi Thomas of the United States, chose to skate to music from the opera *Carmen*. Witt repeated her winning program in Budapest, Hungary, on March 26 to win the 1988 world championship. See **Ice skating; Olympic Games.**

Born on Dec. 3, 1965, in Staaken, East Germany, Witt started skating at age 5. When she was 11, she began training with Jutta Müller, East Germany's top skating coach. Since winning her first European championship in 1983, Witt has dominated the international skating scene. She holds six European titles and four world titles. Witt's technical ability, flirtatious manner, movie-star looks, and provocative costumes have made her a popular star. In March 1988, Witt, who lives in Karl-Marx-Stadt, East Germany, retired from amateur competition to study acting. In July, she became an envoy for the United Nations Children's Fund.   Mary A. Krier

Wyoming. See **State government.**

Yemen (Aden or **Sana).** See **Middle East.**

Yugoslavia in 1988 became more deeply mired in economic recession, with the strains of a huge foreign debt, an inflation rate that exceeded 100 per cent, and seemingly endless strikes amid widespread unemployment aggravating ethnic conflict. In fact, ethnic conflict became so severe that it threatened the very existence of Yugoslavia as a multinational federation.

Modern Yugoslavia is a creation of Josip Broz Tito, who emerged as the country's leader after World War II (1939-1945). To minimize wrangling among ethnic groups, Tito divided the country into six republics. To prevent ethnic Serbs from dominating Yugoslav affairs, as they had before the war, Tito granted limited powers of self-government to Kosovo and Vojvodina, provinces in the Republic of Serbia. And to prevent quarrels among individuals who might wish to succeed him after his death, Tito created an eight-member council called the Presidency—made up of one representative of each republic and self-governing province—to run the country.

Trouble in Kosovo. Even before Tito's death in 1980, however, ethnic rivalries had begun to grow. By 1988, one rivalry—between Kosovo's majority of ethnic Albanians and minority of ethnic Serbs—had grown into an intense conflict. One cause of this conflict was the wish of many ethnic Albanians to elevate Kosovo to the status of a republic.

Another cause was economic. Kosovo is rich in coal and other natural resources but has the poorest econ-

Steelworkers in Yugoslavia's Montenegro region strike in October in support of an ethnic Serb minority in the province of Kosovo.

omy in all Yugoslavia. The most industrially advanced republics—Croatia and Slovenia—increasingly resented having to aid Kosovo. Furthermore, Serbia wanted Kosovo put back under its direct rule to make Serbia more competitive with Croatia and Slovenia.

Rallies and rebukes. In mid-1988, Serb nationalists began to hold mass rallies, demanding the resignation of officials who opposed their policy in Kosovo. These rallies drew sharp protests from other republics as well as stern rebukes from the federal government and the Yugoslav Communist Party. The Presidency on September 22 called on regional leaders to stop squabbling. The Yugoslav Communist Party Central Committee, meeting from October 17 to 19, criticized Serbian leaders for exploiting the economic crisis. The committee also excluded the Serbian representative from consideration in a vote of confidence in the 10-member Politburo—the party's policymaking body.

The economy. Federal Executive Council President (prime minister) Branko Mikulić in May produced his fourth package of economic reforms, including wage controls and curbs on public spending. As a result of these reforms, the International Monetary Fund—an agency of the United Nations—in July granted Yugoslavia $235 million in credit. On December 30, however, Mikulić and his entire cabinet resigned because of opposition to their economic policies.   Eric Bourne

See also **Europe** (Facts in brief table). In *World Book*, see **Yugoslavia**.

Yukon Territory. The Council of Yukon Indians, representing 5,500 Indians living in the Yukon Territory, accepted an agreement-in-principle for settling long-standing land claims in July 1988. The agreement will transfer about 16,000 square miles (41,500 square kilometers) of Yukon land to some form of control by the Indians. For some of the land the Indians would have only surface rights; for other areas they would gain full title and mineral rights. In addition, the Indians would also receive more than $200 million in compensation (Canadian dollars; $1 = U.S. 84 cents as of Dec. 31, 1988). The agreement required further negotiations to determine the precise allocation of land and amount of money.

The heaviest rainfall experienced in the Yukon since weather records were first kept in 1942 fell in the first two weeks of July, washing out sections of the Alaska Highway west of Whitehorse, the territorial capital. Traffic on the key route into the Yukon and Alaska was halted for five days.

The mining town of Faro (population 1,300) finally found a physician in June. After having gone without a doctor since 1985, the community conducted a national advertising campaign to recruit a general practitioner.   David M. L. Farr

In *World Book*, see **Yukon Territory**.

Zaire. See Africa.
Zambia. See Africa.
Zimbabwe. See Africa.

Zoology. A debate raged in 1988 over the possible reclassification of chimpanzees from the status of *threatened species* to *endangered species*. A threatened species may be abundant in some areas, but its overall numbers worldwide are on the decline. An endangered species requires protection because it faces the most serious threat of extinction.

A change in the chimpanzees' status from *threatened* to *endangered* would lead to restrictions that could drastically curtail biomedical research in the United States, according to George Galasso of the National Institutes of Health in Bethesda, Md. Because chimpanzees resemble human beings more closely than does any other animal, researchers consider them essential to the study of human diseases.

Conservationists, however, have pressed for the more protective *endangered* classification. The number of chimpanzees living in the wild worldwide may be as low as 150,000, according to a report by the Committee for the Conservation and Care of Chimpanzees. Their slide toward extinction seems primarily due to the drastic loss of habitat in Africa as forests are cleared for lumber and agriculture. But conservationists have charged that the capture of chimpanzees for biomedical research is another contributing factor. British zoologist Jane Goodall believes wild chimps should be protected and that the current breeding population of captive chimpanzees in the United States would be adequate for biomedical research.

© 1988 Malcolm Hancock; reprinted with permission.

489

Zoos

By mid-December, it appeared likely that the United States Fish and Wildlife Service would issue a compromise judgment whereby wild chimpanzee populations would be classified as *endangered* while breeding populations of captive chimpanzees would be classified only as *threatened,* thus allowing continued use of the animals in biomedical research without undue regulations.

Resetting a biological clock. Biologists Martin R. Ralph and Michael Menaker of the University of Oregon in Eugene reported in September the first evidence of a genetic mutation in a *vertebrate* (an animal with a backbone) that affects the animal's *circadian rhythm* (pattern of daily activity). Most animals maintain daily activity patterns about 24 hours in length—even when they are isolated in complete darkness and so are not cued by the 24-hour cycle of day and night.

Many scientists believe these circadian rhythms are partially controlled by *genes* (units of heredity). During a study of golden hamsters, the Oregon biologists discovered a male hamster with a circadian rhythm of 22 hours, rather than 24. Using breeding experiments, the biologists determined that the male had a *gene mutation*—a change in one hereditary unit—that produced the 22-hour pattern. Hamsters with two such mutations had a circadian rhythm shortened even further to 20 hours.   Clyde Freeman Herreid II

In ***World Book***, see **Zoology.**

Zoos. New zoos opened in two major cities in the United States during 1988, and other zoos opened exciting new exhibits. On June 11, the New Indianapolis Zoo welcomed the public to its 64-acre (26-hectare) site in the city's downtown area. More than 2,000 animals live in exhibits representing four types of habitats.

The Plains exhibit, for example, features giraffes, elephants, lions, and antelope from the African savanna, and kangaroos and *emus* (ostrichlike birds) from Australia's grasslands. The Temperate Forest exhibit displays Siberian tigers and Kodiak bears from Alaska. In the Desert Conservatory, visitors walk among flying birds and a variety of harmless reptiles. The Water Complex brings to the Midwest bottlenosed dolphins, *beluga* (white whales), and large dolphins called *killer whales*. Their natural intelligence and abilities are displayed in regular demonstrations that delight visitors.

The oldest zoo in the United States became the newest on August 8 when New York City's Central Park Zoo unveiled its new ultramodern look. The new zoo, which replaced a menagerie begun in 1864, is a collaboration between the New York Zoological Society, which operates the Bronx Zoo, and the city.

Instead of displaying animals in old-fashioned cages, the Central Park Zoo now features three *biomes*, or climate zones, within its 5.5 acres (2.23 hectares). The Polar Circle, for instance, presents polar bears in rocky

Arctic tundra and penguins on an Antarctic ice shelf. Visitors can view the bears and birds through windows below the water's surface as well as from above. In the Temperate Territory, a lively colony of *Japanese macaques* (also known as snow monkeys) scramble around a rocky island. Among the territory's other residents are Asian red pandas and *muntjacs* (small Asian deer that make a barking noise when frightened) and North American otters and sea lions.

The Tropic Zone reveals life in the multiple layers of a rain forest, as colorful tropical birds and Indian fruit bats fly amid the dense tropical vegetation. The tropical setting also offers visitors glimpses of black-and-white colobus monkeys, pythons, alligatorlike *caimans*, and—with the help of television monitors—close-up views of the nonstop bustle of a colony of leaf-cutter ants.

Rain forests. On March 26, the San Diego Zoo opened its new Tiger River exhibit. The display uses 300 concealed high-pressure water nozzles to transform 5,000 exotic plants into a misty forest. About 100 animals prowl the foggy terrain, including Sumatran tigers (the world's smallest and rarest tigers), Malayan *tapirs* (bulky, long-nosed relatives of horses), and Asian *fishing cats* (cats that live in marshes and catch fish with their paws).

Marine World Africa USA in Vallejo, Calif., opened Butterfly World on May 27. Some 600 butterflies, such as green malachites, African monarchs, and Western

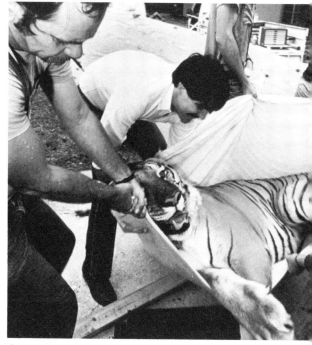

Shane, a Bengal tiger, is carefully moved to his new home at the renovated Lowry Park Zoological Garden, which opened in February in Tampa, Fla.

Visitors enjoy the new look of New York City's renovated Central Park
Zoo, which opened on August 8. The zoo features three climate zones.

tiger swallowtails, flit among tropical trees and plants
inside the 6,000-square-foot (560-square-meter) enclosed exhibit.

On June 11, Zoo Atlanta in Georgia premiered its
African Rain Forest, the most ambitious artificial habitat ever created for gorillas. The exhibit covers 1.5
acres (0.6 hectare) of hilly, wooded countryside complete with streams and waterfalls. Three gorilla families and a solitary male, who had spent 29 years alone
in a small cage, occupy four separate territories in the
exhibit. The gorillas can see and react to one another
as well as to human visitors who move through the
exhibit via enclosed walkways and platforms.

Zoo Atlanta followed the opening of the rain forest
with another premier two months later. On August 6,
the zoo opened another naturalistic primate display
featuring 12 orangutans.

Condor conservation. After more than 61 hours
of struggle, the first California condor ever bred in
captivity emerged from its shell on April 29 at the San
Diego Wild Animal Park. The last adult condor was
removed from the wild in 1987 in a last-ditch effort to
establish a breeding program and save the species
from extinction. The entire world population of
condors—28 birds at the end of 1988, including the
new chick—live at the San Diego park and the Los
Angeles Zoo. Conservationists hope to continue increasing the condor population and, ultimately, to
restore the species to its habitat on the West Coast.

Another rare hatching occurred at the Cincinnati
(Ohio) Zoo on Feb. 1, 1988, when a white-breasted
kingfisher chick hatched. It was the first time the bird
had been successfully bred in captivity. On March 5, a
maleo (a large-footed bird from Indonesia that normally nests in sandy beaches) hatched at the New
York Zoological Society's Wildlife Survival Center on
Saint Catherines Island, Georgia. The new maleo chick
resulted from the first captive breeding of the bird
outside its native Indonesia.

Two Vietnamese box turtles hatched on July 18 at
the Bronx Zoo in New York City. Little is known about
this turtle species. The July hatching was the first
recorded breeding in a zoo.

Mammal populations. On January 9, the Brook-
field Zoo near Chicago tallied the 200th birth of a
callimico, or Goeldi's monkey, since 1977. The Phoenix
Zoo produced its 200th *Arabian oryx* (antelope) on
Feb. 8, 1988. The zoo's program began as a rescue
operation in 1963, when the species was found to be
nearly extinct. Ten North American zoos now breed
the oryx, and many offspring have been sent to Oman
and Israel in an effort to reintroduce the species. The
San Diego Wild Animal Park shipped three pairs of
oryxes to Oman on January 21—its fifth such delivery
since 1980. The San Diego park also sent six *addaxes*,
another highly endangered African antelope, to Tunisia on March 24.   Eugene J. Walter, Jr.

In **World Book**, see **Zoo**.

1982
1985
1986
1987
1988

Dictionary Supplement

This section lists important words from the 1989 edition of *The World Book Dictionary.* This dictionary, first published in 1963, keeps abreast of our living language with a program of continuous editorial revision. The following supplement has been prepared under the direction of the editors of *The World Book Encyclopedia* and Clarence L. Barnhart, editor in chief of *The World Book Dictionary.* It is presented as a service to owners of the dictionary and as an informative feature to subscribers to *The World Book Year Book.*

A a

an|gi|o|gen|in (an′jē ō jen′in), *n.* a protein that promotes the growth of new blood vessels, discovered in human cancer tissue: *Artificially administered angiogenin could be of great benefit to the victims of heart disease by causing new blood vessels to grow in the heart* (Thomas H. Maugh II).

antinoise, *—n.* a sound used to eliminate noise by having its wavelength neutralize the wavelength of the noise: *Digisonix . . . can send antinoise into a fan duct, canceling sounds that would otherwise spread throughout a factory or building* (New York Times).

an|ti|sense (an′tē sens′), *adj. Genetics.* that does not code for a genetic product but serves only to preserve the coding sequence: *Antisense transcription has been described in bacteria [and] in higher forms of life* (Scientific American).

appliance garage, *U.S.* a kitchen cabinet designed to hold appliances such as food processors and toasters: *A popular way to conceal appliances but still keep them handy is the appliance garage . . . Appliance garages keep counter tops neat and uncluttered* (Rodale Home Design).

automatic teller, an electronic machine that releases cash, records, deposits, makes change, etc., upon insertion of an identification card and the pressing of appropriate buttons: *Bankers big and small are rushing to install automatic tellers in their branches* (Time).

az|i|do|thy|mi|dine (az′ī dō thī′mə din, -dēn), *n.* an antiviral drug used in the treatment of AIDS.

AZT (no periods), *Trademark.* azidothymidine: *AZT appeared to extend the life of some AIDS patients* (Michael Woods).

B b

bash, *v.t, v.i.* **2** to set upon vigorously with hostile words, arguments, or abuse; assail: *The premier knew he could* "*win votes by bashing Brits,*" *now that Canada was a multi-ethnic society* (Tom McArthur).

bimbo (bim′bō), *n., pl.* **-boes,** *adj. Slang.* *—n.* **1** a stupid or ineffectual person. *—adj.* of, for, or by bimbos; stupid; unintelligent: *The era of the big three networks and . . .* "*bimbo programming*" *is passing* (Desmond Smith).

bird cage or **bird|cage** (bėrd′kāj′), *n.* **3** *U. S. Slang.* the congested airspace of an airport or air terminal: *. . . one of the busy* "*bird-cages*" *near New York, Chicago, and Los Angeles* (Time).

b quark, = up quark: *The upsilons are . . . made up of a b quark and an anti-b quark* (Science News).

buck|min|ster|ful|ler|ene (buk′min stər fûl′ə rēn′), *n. Chemistry.* a highly stable molecule consisting of sixty carbon atoms arranged as interlocking pentagons and hexagons: *Scientists suspect that buckminsterfullerene has unusual properties that could lead to the development of new lubricants and catalysts* (Peter J. Andrews). [< *Buckminster Fuller,* 1895-1983, an American designer who developed the geodesic dome, which this molecule resembles in structure + *-ene*]

bunker[1] *n., adj., v. —adj.* characterized by or adopting a strongly defensive attitude or position in the face of a threat; last-ditch: *a bunker atmosphere, a bunker philosophy. The reactionary regime has already receded into a bunker mentality* (Time).

C c

care|giv|er (kãr′giv′ər), *n.* a person who provides care for the very young, sick, or elderly: *. . . the link between early* "*attachments*" *to a primary caregiver and later adaptation at school* (Science News). *—***care′giv|ing,** *n., adj.*

cash|point (kash′point′), *n.* an electronic machine from which money can be withdrawn after inserting an identification card and keying in an account number; automatic teller machine: *Its cashpoints feed out notes so new and clean they rasp the hand like fine sandpaper* (Sunday Times).

chaos, *n.* **3** *Mathematics, Physics.* random behavior generated within any deterministic system: *The determinism inherent in chaos implies that many random phenomena are more predictable than has been thought . . . Chaos allows order to be found in such diverse systems as the atmosphere, dripping faucets and the heart* (Scientific American).

charmed quark, a quark having an electric charge of + 2/3 and charm of + 1: *The psi particle is a hadron consisting of a charmed quark and a charmed antiquark* (Scientific American).

charmonium, *n.* any particle with the characteristic of charm; a charmed particle.

Cinderella services, medical and social care provided to the mentally and physically handicapped, the aged, and the chronically ill: *The Cinderella services of primary care include . . . services directed to people in their homes, and special programs for identified groups of medically and socially dependent people* (Journal of the American Medical Association).

co|coon|ing (kə kü′ning), *n.* a tendency to withdraw into the privacy of one's home, expecially during leisure time: *Gandy says his clients are spending a lot more time at home, curled up with good books, good music, and VCR movies. Some refer to this as cocooning* (Christian Science Monitor).

com|mod|i|fi|ca|tion (kə mod′ə fə kā′-shən), *n.* the turning of works of artistic or cultural value into commodities or articles of trade: *Guilbaut's cultural analysis . . . consists of routine attacks on the commodification and trivialization of art* (New Republic). [< *commodi*(ty) + *-fication*]

composite, *n.* **4** a strong, lightweight, plasticlike material used for building a very light aircraft: *Composites—nonmetallic materials that are built up in thin layers—call for entirely different design, production, testing, and inspection facilities* (Jerry Grey).

couch potato, *U.S. Informal.* a person who spends much time watching television or videotapes: *Couch potatoes, as their name implies, are happiest when vegetating* "*all eyes*" *in front of Television* (Jack Mingo).

c quark, = charmed quark: *Other studies of meson states, in which the b quark and the c quark are components, had been carried out at electron-positron colliders* (Lawrence W. Jones).

cy|ber|pho|bia (sī′bər fō′bē ə), *n.* an excessive fear of computers: *Our surveys indicate a strong relationship between creativity and cyberphobia: people scoring on the very top and very bottom of a creativity scale seem most anxious about computers* (Discover). *—***cy′ber-pho′bic,** *adj.*

D d

defective virus, any one of a class of viruses that contain only a small amount of genetic material and can therefore replicate only in the presence of a normal virus: *The delta agent [is] a defective virus that exists only in conjunction with the hepatitis B virus* (Science News).

delta agent or **virus,** a defective virus that can exist only in combination with the virus which causes serum hepatitis: *The delta agent . . . believed to be on the rise world-wide, can make chronic hepatitis B infection lethal* (J. Silberner).

docu|tain|ment (dok′yə tān′mənt), *n. U.S.* television or other entertainment based on or including documentary material: "*I call it 'variety docutainment ',*" *says the production's executive producer . . .* "*We'll be using documentary inserts combined on stage with drama, song, and dance*" (Washington Post). [< *docu-* + (enter)*tainment*]

d quark, = down quark: *Weak interactions can convert an s quark into a u or a d quark* (Scientific American).

E e

ear|bash|ing (ir′bash′ing), *n., adj. British Informal. —n.* a long or noisy speech; harangue; tirade: *Sometimes these occasions are used to give the audience a political earbashing* (London Times). *—adj.* earsplitting; deafening: *an earbashing . . . score, which sounds as if it is being played by a Marine Band . . .* (Manchester Guardian).

e|co|fact (ē′kō fakt′, ek′ō-), *n.* a natural object, such as a bone or grain, found together with artifacts at an archaeological site: *The evaluation of ecofacts reveals such information as what food people ate and whether they grew crops or gathered wild plants* (Barbara Voorhies). [< *eco-* + (arti)*fact*]

ED (no periods) **1** Education Department (the U.S. Department of Education): *Some 60 percent of ED's assistant secretaries and other top officials are women and minorities* (New York Times). *Eventually, 11,000 persons in . . . overseas dependents schools would also become part of ED* (J.L. Burdin).

e|lec|tro|glow (i lek′trə glō′), *n. Astronomy.* a strong emission of ultraviolet light occurring on the sunlit side of various planets, especially Uranus.

E|LI|SA or **E|li|sa** (i lē′sə), *n.* a test for blood supplies to check for the presence of the virus that causes AIDS: *In an ELISA, broken-up pieces of the AIDS-related virus are stuck on a solid surface and washed with blood. If AIDS antibodies are in the blood, they'll stick to the virus* (J. Silberner). [< *e*(nzyme)-*l*(inked) *i*(mmuno)*s*(orbent) *a*(ssay)]

F f

finding, *n.* 4 *U.S.* an authorization for covert governmental action: *McMahon was a scrupulous professional who demanded a Presidential "finding" to justify C.I.A. logistical help to the operation* (William Safire).

fuzzball, *n.* 2 *U.S. Slang.* a derogatory term for a police officer: *"Ten years ago, police were pigs,"* said Moell, who works at criminal hearings. *"Now they are fuzzballs ... "* (Fort Wayne Journal-Gazette).

G g

gab line, *U.S.* a telephone service that provides a person with another party or parties to have a conversation for a fixed charge per minute; talk line: *He might have ... the opportunity to listen in on 976-MEET, ... or almost any of the other so-called gab lines* (Philadelphia Inquirer).

Gaia hypothesis or **theory**, the theory that the planet earth is the core of a unified living system which regulates itself much like an organism does: *It is the Gaia theory's insistence that the earth is a self-controlling, whole system, not a conglomeration of disconnected parts and discontinuous functions, that has drawn the interests of scientists* (Lawrence E. Joseph).

gar|bol|o|gy (gär bol′ə jē), *n.* the study of a culture or society by examining and recording the contents of its garbage or refuse: *Among aficionados and practitioners of the new pop science of garbology ... there's a saying: garbage doesn't lie* (Suburbia Today).

ge|o|tex|tile (jē′ō teks′təl, -tīl), *n.* a very strong, impermeable synthetic fabric, used in the construction of highways, bridges, railroad tracks, and the like: *Polypropylene fibers are finding a hot new market in what is called geotextiles* (Business Week). *Geotextiles ... can take a lot of weight —up to 40 tonnes per metre width* (Economist).

go|mer (gō′mər), *n. U.S. Slang.* an obnoxious undesirable person (used in an unfriendly way): *In hospital parlance, a "gomer" is a disgusting, filthy old man* (St. Louis Post-Dispatch). [perhaps < *gomerel*]

greenhouse gas, a gas that warms the atmosphere by trapping heat of the longwave solar radiation reflected from the earth's surface: *Carbon dioxide and other radiatively active gases such as methane, ozone, fluorocarbons and oxides of nitrogen ... are the greenhouse gases* (Scientific American).

Grinch or **grinch** (grinch), *n. U.S. Informal.* a person or thing that spoils the enjoyment or plans of others; spoilsport; killjoy: *No print-medium Grinch is arguing that humor aimed at the young doesn't have a place in the video spectrum* (Newsweek). [< the name of the character in *How the Grinch Stole Christmas* (1957), a children's story by Dr. Seuss (Theodor Seuss Geisel), an American writer and illustrator].

grunt|work (grunt′wėrk′), *n. U.S. and Canadian Informal.* low, menial work: *Humble Baluchi and Pakistani workers ... do the gruntwork of the [Gulf] states' lavish modernization programs* (Mac-

lean's). ... *the dirty, tedious gruntwork needed to make a campaign successful* (New York Times).

H h

hair shirt 2 *Figurative.* an imposing of penance, austerity, or self-sacrifice: *If low real interest rates and falling inflation are so important ... then the hair shirt is the only answer* (Financial Times). 3 *Figurative.* a person who advocates austere and self-sacrificing remedies: *Although Orwell was certainly a bit of a hair shirt himself, he seemed to have a hair shirt's impatience with other hair shirts* (Christian Science Monitor).

home confinement, *U.S.* a term of imprisonment served in one's home and carried out by monitoring signals from an electronic transmitter attached to the prisoner to determine his or her whereabouts: *A growing number of states have introduced ... home confinement as a punishment, generally for nonviolent crime* (L.S. Gray).

hub-and-spoke (hub′ənd spōk′), *adj.* of or having to do with a system of transportation, especially of small airlines, by which passengers or freight are carried on branch routes to a central city to make connections for transportation to a large metropolitan area.

I i

ice-mi|nus (īs′mī′nəs), *adj.* of or designating a strain of bacteria developed by genetic engineering to resist the effect of ice formation on plants: *The researchers believe that spraying this ice-minus bacteria on plants ... will prevent the growth of the normal bacteria which do catalyze frost formation, and thereby minimize frost damage to crops* (Thomas H. Maugh II).

I.N.F. or **INF** (no periods), Intermediate-range Nuclear Forces (the European-based nuclear weapons of the United States and the Soviet Union).

inflationary, *adj.* 2 *Astronomy.* of or having to do with a model of the big bang theory which postulates that in the first fraction of a second following the cosmic explosion in which it originated, the universe underwent an extremely rapid expansion: *the inflationary universe, the inflationary model. Even more "dark matter" is implied in the inflationary concept of the universe* (Walter Sullivan).

in|fo|tain|ment (in′fə tān′mənt), *n. U.S.* television or other entertainment based on or including factual information: *The airwaves are now flooded with syndicated "infotainment" shows that give TV viewers ... peeks at the public and private lives of their favorite celebrities* (Newsweek). [< *info* + (enter)*tainment*]

interactive fiction, a computer or video game in which an adventure, mystery, or other story is developed through the player's interaction with the story's characters.

K k

kindling, *n.* 3 a physiological process in which a series of small events, actions, or reactions lead up to, and perhaps

stimulate a larger event, such as a seizure or permanent pattern of behavior: *Some scientists believe true kindling represents a kind of learning process and speculate that it may hold clues to the way permanent memories are formed in the brain* (Harold M. Schmeck, Jr.).

kinetic kill vehicle, a weapon designed to destroy a nuclear warhead by force of impact: *This system would not employ directed-energy weapons at the outset; instead it would rely on kinetic kill vehicles* (Scientific American). *Such data is critical for a "kinetic kill vehicle," a vital weapon of the Star Wars system* (Philadelphia Inquirer).

M m

ma|gain|in (mə gā′nin), *n.* any one of a group of broad-spectrum antibiotics obtained from secretions in the skin of certain species of frogs: *The magainins ... kill bacteria, funguses, the yeast that often infects AIDS patients, and protozoans like those that cause malaria* (New York Times). [< Hebrew *māgēn* shield + English *-in²*]

max|sav|er (mak′sā′vər), *n. U.S.* the lowest airfare, usually requiring advance purchase of nonrefundable round-trip tickets for weekday flights: *The range of ticket prices widened ... when major airlines in competitive markets reduced their lowest fares, known throughout the industry as maxsavers* (New York Times).

N n

nar|co-ter|ror|ism (när′kō ter′ə riz-əm), *n.* terrorist practices used by narcotics smugglers and dealers against government interdiction: *Narco-terrorism ... originated in the "Golden Triangle," the opium-producing areas of Burma, Thailand, and Laos, but reached a new high in the 1980's in certain Latin-American countries* (Walter Laqueur). —**nar′-co-ter′ror|ist**, *n.*, *adj.*

ne|o|ex|pres|sion|ism (nē′ō ek spresh′ə niz əm), *n.* a style of painting characterized by bold forms, strong color and a crude and heavy technique. It is a reaction to minimalism and began to appear in the late 1970's.

network, *n.* 6 a system that links together a number of computers: *Networks enable computer users to share files and expensive peripheral equipment* (Howard Wolff).

neural network, 1 a network of units in a computer that are thought of as resembling the interconnections among nerve cells: *Improvements in neural networks ... have sharpened computers' ability to discern or absorb information* (New York Times). 2 a computer having such a network: *The new computers are called neural networks because they contain units that function roughly like the intricate network of neurons in the brain* (Andrew Pollack).

Pronunciation Key: hat, āge, cãre, fär; let, ēqual, tėrm; it, īce; hot, ōpen, ôrder; oil, out; cup, pút, rüle; child; long; thin; ᵺen; zh, measure; ə represents **a** in about, **e** in taken, **i** in pencil, **o** in lemon, **u** in circus.

New Age or **new age music**, a form of popular music influenced by jazz and characterized by soft, restrained playing, slow rhythms, and improvisation on such instruments as the piano, flute, harp, and synthesizer: *George Winton's pastoral piano is the essence of New Age music — serene, introspective and quietly inventive* (Washington Post).

New A|ger (ā'jər), a person who plays or enjoys listening to New Age music.

nuke, *v.t.* **2** *Figurative.* to destroy: *That play, too, was quickly nuked by poor ticket sales* (Dan Hulbert).

O o

os|so|bu|co or **os|so|buc|co** (os'ō bü'-kō, ō'sō-), *n.* an Italian dish of braised veal shanks, prepared with olive oil, white wine, vegetables, anchovies, and seasoned stock. [< Italian *osso buco* (literally) bone marrow]

ovoid, *n.* **2** *Geology.* a region or body having a rectangular shape with rounded corners: *Each of these ovoids [on one of the moons of Uranus] is 200 to 300 kilometers (120 to 180 miles) across, and they are unlike anything ever seen in the solar system* (Laurence A. Soderblom).

P p

parallel processing, performance of many operations simultaneously on a computer by linking together a number of microprocessors: *Another way to handle the series of small steps is to assign each to a different microprocessor so that they can be computed simultaneously; this is called parallel processing* (Science News).

parking, *n.* **5** *U.S. Finance.* the fraudulent practice of holding stocks of another person or company to conceal ownership: *"Parking can be even more damaging than insider trading,"* Lynch said. *If used to conceal stock ownership before a takeover bid . . . it can throw a company into upheaval* (Barbara Bradley).

per|e|stroi|ka (per'ə stroi'kə), *n.* a restructuring of Soviet society, especially in economic policy: *Bukharin's greatest importance today, by far, is as the intellectual forerunner of perestroika* (Manchester Guardian Weekly). [< Russian *perestroika* (literally) rebuilding]

program trading or **trades**, the trading of stocks in a stock market by computer programs set at various levels to buy and sell: *Traders said the broad selloff had been caused by . . . program trading and general nervousness about the market* (Lawrence J. DeMaria).

pro|so|pag|no|si|a (prə sō'pag nō'sē ə), *n.* a brain disorder characterized by an inability to recognize familiar faces: *Some people, primarily certain victims of Alzheimer's disease, amnesia, strokes, or herpes encephalitis, also suffer from prosopagnosia* (Science News). [< Greek *prósōpon* person, face + New Latin *agnosia*] —**pro|so'pagno'si|ac**, *n.*

Q q

quark matter, *Nuclear Physics.* a hypothetical form of matter consisting entirely of free quarks: *The time when the form-*

less particles turned into quark matter . . . *was an amazingly short time — less than one-billionth of one-trillionth of one-trillionth of one second — after the big bang* (Robert H. March).

R r

RFLP (no periods; *often pronounced* rif' lip), *n.* any one of a class of inherited characteristics that can be traced from one generation to another and are defective genes. [< *r*(estriction) *f*(ragment) *l*(ength) *p*(olymorphism)]

rust belt or **rust bowl**, a region with a large concentration of heavy industries, especially in the northeastern and north central United States: *A new Census Bureau report shows population growth has resumed in the rust belt states* (U.S. News & World Report).

S s

seismic tomography, the use of seismic waves to form images of the earth's interior which are then synthesized into a single cross-sectional view: *The three-dimensional maps of the interior produced by seismic tomography have created a revolution in earth sciences by giving geologists a much clearer picture of the inner Earth* (Don L. Anderson).

shadow matter, *Astronomy.* a hypothetical form of matter that interacts with ordinary matter only through gravity and not through electromagnetism or the strong or weak interactions: *Shadow matter . . . interacts with us extremely feebly and is virtually undetectable* (Dietrick E. Thomsen). Compare **dark matter.**

shepherd moon, *Astronomy.* a moon that orbits near the inner and outer edges of the rings of a planet with rings probably holding the ring material together with the moon's gravity: *Among the first discoveries of Voyager 2 were two shepherd moons . . . that orbit the outermost Epsilon ring [of Uranus]* (Laurence A. Soderblom).

sleaze|ball (slēz'bôl'), *n.* *U.S. Slang.* a slovenly, disreputable, or coarse person: *"We're trying to reach upscale people,"* said Farrell. *"No dodos, no porn, no sleazeballs"* (Philadelphia Inquirer).

smokestack, *n.*, *adj.* —*adj.* of, having to do with, or made up of factories of heavy industry, associated with the burning of coal as in making steel or machinery: *smokestack industries.*

snow|board (snō'bôrd, -bōrd), *n.* a long, narrow board somewhat like a ski, used for riding or racing over snow: *"Once people get onto the snowboard they just fall in love with it,"* said Thomas J. Hsieh, Jr., editor of the International Snowboard Association magazine (Yonkers Herald-Statesman). —*v.i.* to ride a snowboard.

space frame, a building constructed of glass walls supported by a frame of large interlocking metal tubes and struts fastened together by nodes: *The largest space frame ever built [is] the five-block long Jacob K. Javits Convention Center in New York City* (R. Robison).

s quark, = strange quark: *An s quark and an s antiquark . . . respectively carry strangeness quantum numbers of -1 and + 1* (Scientific American).

standard candle 2 *Astronomy.* any

celestial object of known brightness that can be used to measure astronomical distances: *Supernovas are interesting both for their own development as giant stellar explosions and also as standard candles . . . used to calibrate distance scales* (Science News).

steel-col|lar (stēl'kol'ər), *adj.* of or having to do with robots as part of the labor force: *Tomorrow's "steel-collar" workers should be able to react to their environment, combining sensing devices to "see" and "feel" and AI software to "think"* (Christian Science Monitor). *Eventually . . . they will make possible the full automation of many factories, displacing millions of blue-collar workers with a new "steel-collar" class* (Newsweek).

T t

talk line, = gab line: *The use of nicknames is common on the talk lines, all of which have monitors who listen to, and sometimes direct, the conversation* (John Woestendick).

t quark, = top quark: *Whereas some theories could be forced to accommodate only five quarks, the t quark would round out the symmetry of the particles* (Lawrence W. Jones).

trade|craft (trād'kraft', -kräft'), *n.* the specialized skill of espionage: *Howard learned the "tradecraft" of intelligence, practicing the recruitment of agents and the use of "dead drops" to pass messages* (David Wise).

trans|gen|ic (trans jen'ik), *adj.* of, produced by, or containing genes transferred from one species to another by means of genetic engineering: *Another very promising tool in molecular genetics is a . . . technique that leads to the creation of transgenic mice: mice that contain single genes or groups of genes from humans* (Scientific American).

Trojan horse 3 a set of unauthorized instructions inserted in a computer program to perform some illegal operation: *One form of Trojan horse, called "a logic bomb," is designed to release voluminous amounts of sensitive data to open terminals at a given time in the future* (Progressive).

U u

u quark, = up quark: *The proton . . . can be constructed with two u quarks and one d quark* (H. T. Simmons).

W w

water farm, *U.S.* a tract of land purchased by a city or state to draw from the water table beneath it.

water farming, the act or practice of using or developing a water farm.

WIMP (no periods; *pronounced* wimp), *n.* *Nuclear Physics.* any one of a class of weakly interacting massive particles thought to be present in the sun's core and strongly affecting the amount of energy found there: *WIMP is a generic term; a specific kind of particle that could fill the bill is a hypothetical one known as a photino* (Dietrick E. Thomsen). [< *W*(eakly) *I*(nteracting) *M*(assive) *P*(article)]

1988

World Book Supplement

To help *World Book* owners keep their
encyclopedias up to date, the following
articles are reprinted from the 1989
edition of the encyclopedia.

See page 533 ▶

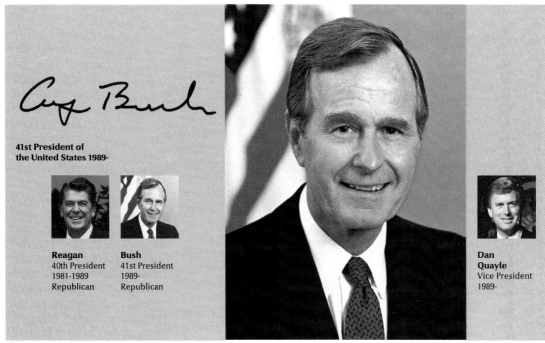

**41st President of
the United States 1989-**

Reagan
40th President
1981-1989
Republican

Bush
41st President
1989-
Republican

**Dan
Quayle**
Vice President
1989-

David Valdez, The White House

Bush, George Herbert Walker (1924-   ), was elected President of the United States in 1988. Bush served as Vice President under Ronald Reagan from 1981 to 1989. After easily winning the Republican nomination for President, Bush defeated his Democratic opponent, Governor Michael S. Dukakis of Massachusetts, in the 1988 election.

Bush became President at a time when many Americans were uncertain about their country's future. The federal government was badly in debt, the result of several years of budget *deficits* (shortages). In addition, the value of goods imported into the United States far exceeded the value of exports, leading many people to fear that the nation was becoming a second-rate economic power. Many Americans also were concerned over foreign policy, particularly the country's involvement in strife-torn areas of the Middle East and Central America.

Bush convinced a majority of voters that he was the best candidate to solve the nation's economic problems and provide direction in foreign affairs. He also took advantage of his association with Reagan, who was an extremely popular President. Bush profited as well from the fact that relations between the United States and the Union of Soviet Socialist Republics (U.S.S.R.) had improved greatly during the final years of the Reagan presidency.

Bush was the 14th former Vice President who became President. Before his election as Vice President, Bush

had a long career of government service. A Texas Republican, he served two terms in the United States House of Representatives. Bush also held several key appointed positions in the national government. These posts included United States ambassador to the United Nations (UN) and director of the Central Intelligence Agency (CIA).

Bush was a successful businessman in the oil industry before entering politics. A native of New England, Bush was drawn to Texas by the booming oil industry. He worked his way up from equipment clerk to become president of an independent offshore oil drilling company.

Bush enjoyed sports, especially tennis and baseball. He liked to jog several miles before work each morning. Bush also enjoyed boating, fishing, and spending time

Important dates in Bush's life

1924   (June 12) Born in Milton, Mass.
1942-1945   Served in the U.S. Navy during World War II.
1945   (Jan. 6) Married Barbara Pierce.
1948   Graduated from Yale University.
1954   Became president of Zapata Off-Shore Company.
1967-1971   Served in U.S. House of Representatives.
1971-1973   Served as U.S. ambassador to the United Nations.
1973-1974   Served as chairman of the Republican National Committee.
1974-1975   Served as U.S. envoy to Communist China.
1976-1977   Served as head of Central Intelligence Agency.
1980   Elected Vice President of the United States.
1984   Reelected Vice President.
1988   Elected President of the United States.

Lee Thornton, the contributor of this article, is Adjunct Professor of Journalism at Howard University and a former Washington correspondent for CBS News.

WORLD BOOK photo by Jennifer Podis

Bush's birthplace was this house in Milton, Mass. When Bush was less than a year old, his family moved to Greenwich, Conn., where he spent his boyhood years.

with his family at their vacation home in Kennebunkport, Me.

Early life

Boyhood. Bush was born on June 12, 1924, in Milton, Mass. He had three brothers—Prescott, Jr. (1922-   ); Jonathan (1931-   ); and William (1938-   )—and a sister, Nancy (1926-   ).

George's parents, Prescott Sheldon Bush (1895-1972) and Dorothy Walker Bush (1901-   ), married in 1921. Prescott Bush was a successful businessman, who eventually became a managing partner in the New York City investment banking firm of Brown Brothers, Harriman and Company. He later developed an interest in politics

and represented Connecticut in the United States Senate from 1952 to 1963.

When George was less than a year old, his family moved to a 9-bedroom house in Greenwich, Conn. His upbringing was comfortable but strict. Prescott and Dorothy Bush expected their children to be modest, fair, and respectful of others. At the same time, the children were taught to play competitively in sports and games. The Bush family spent summers at the Kennebunkport, Me., home of Dorothy Bush's father, George Herbert Walker, for whom young George was named.

George attended the private Greenwich Country Day School. He then entered Phillips Academy at Andover, Mass., an exclusive preparatory school. Bush earned good grades and was well liked by other students. He was elected president of the senior class and captain of the baseball and soccer teams. Bush also played varsity basketball. He graduated from Phillips Academy in 1942.

War hero. Following his graduation from prep school, Bush had planned to attend Yale University. But with the U.S. entrance into World War II (1939-1945) in December 1941, Bush chose to delay his college education and enlisted in the United States Naval Reserve. He received flight training and was commissioned an ensign in June 1943. At that time, Bush was the Navy's youngest pilot.

In 1943, Bush became a fighter pilot with Torpedo Bomber Squadron VT-51, aboard the aircraft carrier U.S.S. *San Jacinto* in the Pacific Ocean. He participated in dangerous fighting. On Sept. 2, 1944, his plane was shot down during an attack on a Japanese-held island. Before escaping from his plane, Bush scored damaging hits on his target, a radio station. A U.S. submarine, the U.S.S. *Finback,* rescued Bush from the ocean, but his two crew

AP/Wide World

Young George, at about age 5, appears in this family photograph with his sister Nancy. The future President also had three brothers—Prescott, Jr.; Jonathan; and William.

The White House

Ensign Bush was the youngest fighter pilot in the United States Navy at the time of his commission in June 1943. He flew combat missions over the Pacific Ocean and was decorated for heroism.

The White House

Bush married Barbara Pierce of Rye, N.Y., on Jan. 6, 1945, after he returned from active duty in the Pacific. The two first met at a Christmas dance in 1941.

members did not survive. Bush received the Distinguished Flying Cross for his heroism in the incident. He returned to flying eight weeks after being shot down. Bush later served at the Oceana Naval Air Station in Virginia until the war ended in August 1945.

Bush's family. Bush met Barbara Pierce (June 8, 1925-   ) of Rye, N.Y., at a Christmas dance in 1941. Her father, Marvin Pierce, was the publisher of *McCall's* and *Redbook* magazines. George and Barbara became engaged in August 1943 and were married on Jan. 6, 1945, after Bush's return from the Pacific. The couple had six children—George (1946-   ); Robin (1949-1953), who died of leukemia; John (1953-   ); Neil (1955-   ); Marvin (1956-   ); and Dorothy (1959-   ).

College education. In the fall of 1945, Bush entered Yale University. He worked hard and did well in his studies. One classmate observed, "George was not an intellectual. He was more of an achiever." Bush played first base on the Yale baseball team for three seasons, and he was elected captain of the team during his senior year.

Bush graduated from Yale in 1948 with a bachelor's

degree in economics. He also was elected to the honor society Phi Beta Kappa.

Business career

Entry into the oil business. Following his graduation from Yale, Bush received an offer to join his father's investment banking firm. But he turned down this secure position and decided to try his luck in the oil fields of Texas. Neil Mallon—a family friend and the head of Dresser Industries, an oil equipment company—offered Bush a position as a trainee. Bush started with Dresser Industries as an equipment clerk in Odessa, a town in western Texas.

After a little less than a year, Bush was transferred to California, where he worked as an assemblyman in an oil-equipment factory and as a salesman of drilling bits. In 1950, Bush was transferred back to Texas. He and his family settled in Midland.

Independent oilman. In late 1950, Bush left Dresser Industries. He and a friend, John Overbey, formed the Bush-Overbey Oil Development Company. The company bought a percentage of mineral rights on land where oil was being drilled, and sought investors to finance its ventures.

In 1953, Bush and Overbey joined forces with brothers Hugh and William Liedtke and formed the Zapata Petroleum Corporation. The new company absorbed Bush-Overbey. The following year, the corporation created Zapata Off-Shore Company, to drill for oil in the Gulf of Mexico. Bush became president of this company, which was made independent of the Zapata Petroleum Corporation in 1959. That year, Bush moved its headquarters to Houston.

Bush's career as an independent oilman made him wealthy. Years later, he credited his experience at Zapata with teaching him leadership in dealing with people and in making decisions.

Early political career

Bush grew increasingly interested in politics during the late 1950's. In 1962, he was elected chairman of the Republican Party of Harris County—the county in which

UPI/Bettmann Newsphotos

Candidate Bush greeted supporters during the Texas campaign for the U.S. Senate in 1964. He lost that race but was elected to the U.S. House of Representatives in 1966 and 1968.

most of Houston lies. In 1964, Bush became the Republican candidate for the U.S. Senate. Liberal Democratic incumbent Ralph Yarborough defeated Bush in the general election.

In 1966, Bush ran for election to the U.S. House of Representatives from Texas' Seventh Congressional District. He defeated his Democratic opponent, conservative Frank Briscoe. Bush generally voted conservatively in the House. But he supported some liberal bills, including those which called for elimination of the military draft and for adoption of a code of ethics for members of Congress. In perhaps his most controversial vote, Bush supported a bill to guarantee open housing to minorities. Bush was reelected to the House without opposition in 1968.

In 1970, partly due to encouragement by President Richard M. Nixon, Bush gave up his seat in the House to make another run for the Senate. He expected to challenge Yarborough again. But conservative Democrat Lloyd Bentsen upset Yarborough in his party's primary election. Bentsen went on to defeat Bush in the general election.

Appointive positions

United Nations ambassador. President Nixon appointed Bush U.S. ambassador to the UN in December 1970. At the UN, Bush was responsible for advocating the policies of the United States.

In 1971, Bush worked to allow Nationalist China, a government descended from one of the original founding members of the UN, to keep its position in the organization. He supported a "dual representation" plan that would accept the entry of Communist China to the UN while preserving Nationalist China's position there. However, the members of the UN voted to expel Nationalist China. Bush's efforts were complicated by gestures of friendship made toward Communist China by the Nixon Administration.

Republican Party chairman. After his reelection in 1972, President Nixon appointed Bush chairman of the Republican National Committee. Bush took over the post in January 1973—just before the events of the Watergate scandal became known to the public. This scandal involved illegal activities by key Republicans working to reelect President Nixon. Their actions included burglary, wiretapping, and sabotage, and the subsequent cover-up of these criminal activities (see **Watergate**).

Bush believed Nixon's claim that he had played no part in either the break-in or the cover-up, and he defended the President against harsh criticism. Bush also worked to separate the illegal actions of a few Republicans from the integrity of the Republican Party. But when secret White House tape recordings provided convincing evidence that Nixon had played a part in the scandal, Bush requested Nixon's resignation in the name of the Republican Party. A letter he gave the President on Aug. 7, 1974, stated: ". . . I now feel that resignation is best for the country. . . ." Nixon announced his resignation from the presidency the following day and officially left office on August 9.

Envoy to China. In 1974, Nixon's successor, Gerald R. Ford, let Bush select his next government assignment. Ford did so in appreciation for Bush's loyalty to the Republican Party. Bush chose to head the United States Li-

As U.S. ambassador to the United Nations, Bush, *second from right,* conferred with advisers during a Security Council debate. Bush served as U.N. ambassador from 1971 to 1973.

aison Office in Beijing, the capital of Communist China. Bush worked to continue developing relations between the two countries, which had opened diplomatic offices in each other's capital in 1973.

CIA director. In November 1975, President Ford requested that Bush return to Washington to head the Central Intelligence Agency. Bush accepted. The Senate confirmed his appointment in January 1976 after imposing the condition that Bush not be considered as a candidate for Vice President in 1976.

When Bush took over the CIA, congressional committees were carefully examining its past activities. Bush's

Bush served as U.S. envoy to China during 1974 and 1975. He is shown here leaving for the United States to become director of the Central Intelligence Agency.

most vital contribution was in raising staff morale during this difficult period. He worked to improve the management of the agency. Bush left the CIA in January 1977, having resigned after the election of Democratic President Jimmy Carter in November 1976.

The 1980 election

Campaign for the presidential nomination. In the fall of 1977, Bush and his advisers began to raise funds for the 1980 campaign for the presidency. Bush officially announced his candidacy in May 1979. He campaigned early and continuously. In January 1980, Bush defeated his chief rival for the nomination, former California Governor Ronald Reagan, in the Iowa caucuses, the first contest in the nominating process. But Bush could not maintain this advantage, as Reagan accumulated victories in primary elections. Bush withdrew his candidacy on May 26, 1980.

Vice presidential candidate. The Republican National Convention, held in Detroit in July 1980, officially nominated Reagan as the party's presidential candidate. Reagan invited Bush to be his vice presidential running mate. Bush accepted and was formally nominated by the convention.

Bush did not completely share Reagan's views on such issues as cutting federal taxes, abortion, and the Equal Rights Amendment. However, Bush minimized his differences with Reagan during the campaign and avoided controversy over them. Reagan and Bush defeated the Democratic ticket of President Jimmy Carter and Vice President Walter Mondale in the general election in November 1980.

Vice President

Reagan's first Administration. Reagan and Bush quickly established a warm, friendly working relationship. Bush was given an office in the White House and allowed free access to the President. In addition, Reagan and Bush had a private lunch each Thursday.

Reagan gave Bush a more active role than most previous Vice Presidents had enjoyed. Bush attended daily security briefings held for the President and received key intelligence information. Reagan appointed Bush chairman of several important groups, including the National Security Council's crisis management team and a special task force that investigated drug smuggling and illegal immigration in Florida.

Bush attended Reagan's Cabinet meetings. But he rarely spoke there, so as not to differ publicly with the President. Rather than contradict Reagan, Bush advised him privately and confidentially. In particular, Bush encouraged Reagan to be open to the possibility of negotiation with the Soviet Union.

On March 30, 1981, Reagan was shot in an attempted assassination. The event thrust Bush into the national spotlight. Just after the shooting, Bush assured the United States and the world that national affairs were under control. Bush also took over some of Reagan's public duties during the President's recovery. But Bush did not use his temporary position to assume excessive amounts of power. Bush's performance won him much respect during this period.

Reagan's second Administration. Reagan and Bush easily won renomination at the 1984 convention of the

David Valdez, The White House

Vice President Bush and President Ronald Reagan had a friendly working relationship. Bush frequently offered the President confidential advice on foreign policy matters.

Republican Party in Dallas. The Democrats nominated former Vice President Mondale for President and Representative Geraldine Ferraro of New York for Vice President. Reagan and Bush won the general election by a landslide. During the second Reagan Administration, Bush continued to influence Reagan from behind the scenes. On July 13, 1985, Bush served as acting President for about eight hours when Reagan underwent cancer surgery.

Election as President

The Republican nomination. Bush entered the 1988 campaign with distinct advantages over his Republican rivals. He had served as Vice President under an enormously popular President. In addition, his name was well known among voters. Bush also had a well-organized, well-financed campaign. His chief rivals included Senator Robert Dole of Kansas and Pat Robertson, a former television evangelist.

Dole dealt Bush a surprising defeat in the Iowa caucuses in February 1988. He questioned Bush's claim of ignorance in the *Iran-contra affair*—a complex, illegal scheme in which U.S. officials indirectly sold weapons to Iran and then used the profits to assist the *contras,* a group of rebels fighting to overthrow the government of Nicaragua. Nevertheless, Bush's campaign quickly recaptured momentum with a string of primary victories. The remaining Republican candidates soon withdrew from the campaign as it became apparent that Bush had won enough delegates to ensure his nomination.

At the Republican National Convention in New Orleans in August 1988, Bush was named the Republican presidential nominee. At his request, Senator Dan Quayle of Indiana was nominated for Vice President. The Democrats nominated Governor Michael S. Dukakis of Massachusetts for President and Senator Lloyd Bentsen of Texas, who had defeated Bush in the 1970 Senate race, for Vice President.

The 1988 election. Many Republicans hoped that Bush could win the support of the conservative Democrats who had crossed party lines to vote for Reagan in 1980 and 1984. Many of Bush's conservative views, particularly those concerning the smuggling of illegal

Trippett/Witt, Sipa

Bush and Senator Dan Quayle of Indiana, *left,* became the Republican nominees for President and Vice President at the party's national convention in New Orleans in August 1988.

drugs into the United States, were similar to those of Reagan. But he took a more moderate position on other issues, including taxation. Bush announced an intention to decrease some taxes, though not to the extent that Reagan had. Bush further promised not to increase any taxes.

Dukakis questioned Bush's lack of knowledge of the Iran-contra affair. The Democrats also criticized Bush for his role in the Reagan presidency, claiming that illegal drug trafficking had flourished and that social services had been cut during Reagan's Administration. Bush, in turn, criticized Dukakis' record as governor of Massachusetts, charging—among other things—that the governor had been lax in protecting the environment and had been too "soft" on criminals. Bush also questioned Dukakis' lack of experience in foreign policy and argued that the Democrats would increase taxes and weaken the nation's military. In the general election, Bush and Quayle defeated Dukakis and Bentsen.　　Lee Thornton

Related articles in *World Book* include:
President of the United States
Quayle, Dan
Reagan, Ronald Wilson

Bush's election

Place of nominating convention ....New Orleans
Ballot on which nominated 1st
Democratic opponent ....Michael S. Dukakis
Age at inauguration 64

The *table* in the **Electoral College** article gives the electoral vote by states for both Bush, the winner, and Dukakis.

Republican Party
Vice President of the United States

Outline

I. Early life
　A. Boyhood　　　　　　C. Bush's family
　B. War hero　　　　　　D. College education
II. Business career
　A. Entry into the oil business
　B. Independent oilman
III. Early political career
IV. Appointive positions
　A. United Nations ambassador
　B. Republican Party chairman
　C. Envoy to China
　D. CIA director
V. The 1980 election
　A. Campaign for the presidential nomination
　B. Vice presidential candidate
VI. Vice President
　A. Reagan's first Administration
　B. Reagan's second Administration
VII. Election as President
　A. The Republican nomination
　B. The 1988 election

Questions

Who encouraged Bush to run for the U.S. Senate in 1970?
What was Bush's most vital contribution to the CIA?
What were some of the key events in Bush's career as an oilman?
What was Bush's chief role as ambassador to the United Nations?
Why did Bush receive the Distinguished Flying Cross?
How did Bush deal with the attempted assassination of President Reagan in 1981?
Why did Bush ask President Nixon to resign?
How did the Iran-contra affair affect Bush's candidacy for President in 1988?
Who defeated Bush in the 1970 Texas election to the U.S. Senate?
Why did President Ford let Bush select his next government assignment in 1974?

The White House

The Bush family gathered in Kennebunkport, Me., for this portrait. The President and the first lady, *third and fourth adults from right,* are surrounded by their children and their families.

Congress, the lawmaking branch of the United States government, consists of the Senate and the House of Representatives. During joint sessions, *above,* all members meet in the House chamber.

Congress of the United States

Congress of the United States makes the nation's laws. Congress consists of two bodies, the *Senate* and the *House of Representatives*. Both bodies have about equal power. The people elect the members of Congress.

Although Congress's most important task is making laws, it also has other major duties. For example, the Senate approves or rejects the U.S. President's choices for the heads of government departments, Supreme Court justices, and certain other high-ranking jobs. The Senate also approves or rejects treaties that the President makes.

Each member of Congress represents many citizens. Therefore, members must know the views of the voters and be guided by those views when considering proposed laws. Being a member of Congress also means answering citizens' letters, appearing at local events, and having local offices to handle people's problems with the government.

This article provides a broad description of Congress. For more information, see the separate *World Book* articles **House of Representatives** and **Senate.**

How Congress is organized

Congress is a *bicameral* (two-chamber) legislature. The 100-member Senate consists of 2 senators from each of the 50 states. The House of Representatives, usually called simply the *House,* has 435 members. House members, or *representatives,* are elected from *congres-*

sional districts of about equal population into which the states are divided. Every state must have at least one House seat. Representatives are often called *congressmen* or *congresswomen,* though technically the titles also apply to senators.

The Democratic and Republican parties have long been the only major political parties in Congress. In each house of Congress, the party with more members is the *majority party.* The other one is the *minority party.* Before every new session of Congress, Republicans and Democrats in each house meet in what is called a *caucus* or *conference* to choose party leaders and to consider legislative issues and plans.

Committees form an important feature of each chamber's organization. They prepare the bills to be voted on. The committee system divides the work of processing legislation and enables members to specialize in particular types of issues. The majority party in each chamber elects the head of each committee and holds a majority of the seats on most committees.

The Senate. According to Article I, Section 3 of the Constitution, the Vice President of the United States serves as head of the Senate with the title *president of the Senate.* However, the Vice President is not considered a member of that body and, except on ceremonial occasions or to break a tie vote, rarely appears there. The Senate elects a *president pro tempore* (temporary president) to serve in the Vice President's absence. The Senate usually elects the majority party senator with the longest continuous service. The president pro tempore signs official papers for the Senate but presides infrequently. Most of the time, the president pro tempore appoints a junior senator as temporary president.

Democrats and Republicans each elect a chief officer

Roger H. Davidson, the contributor of this article, is Professor of Government and Politics at the University of Maryland and co-author of Congress and Its Members.

called a *floor leader.* A floor leader is also known as the *majority leader* or the *minority leader,* depending on the senator's party. Each party elects an officer called a *whip* to assist the floor leaders. Floor leaders or whips are typically at their desks at the front of the chamber. They arrange the Senate's schedule, work for passage of their party's legislative program, and look after the interests of absent senators.

Senators treasure their right to be consulted on bills, to offer amendments, and to speak at length in debate. Just one senator can slow down or halt the entire work of the Senate. Thus, Senate leaders spend much time considering their fellow senators' needs and arranging compromises that will enable the work of the chamber to go on.

Sixteen permanent *standing committees* and several temporary *special* or *select committees* help the Senate make laws. Most committees have *subcommittees* to handle particular topics. Typically, a senator sits on four committees and six subcommittees.

The House of Representatives. The *Speaker of the House,* mentioned in Article I, Section 2 of the Constitution, serves as presiding officer and party leader. The majority party nominates the Speaker, who is then elected by a party-line vote of the entire House. The Speaker is the most important member of Congress because of the office's broad powers. The Speaker refers bills to committees, names members of special committees, and nominates the majority party's members of the powerful Rules Committee. In addition, the Speaker votes in case of ties and grants fellow representatives the right to speak during debates. With the help of assistants, the Speaker also influences committee assignments, arranges committee handling of bills, and schedules bills for House debate. As in the Senate, the House majority and minority parties each choose a floor leader and a whip.

The House has 22 standing committees and several special or select committees. Typically, a representative serves on 2 committees and 5 subcommittees.

When Congress meets. A new Congress is organized every two years, after congressional elections in November of even-numbered years. Voters elect all the representatives, resulting in a new House of Representatives. About a third of the senators come up for election every two years. The Senate is a *continuing body* because it is never completely new. Beginning with the First Congress (1789-1791), each Congress has been numbered in order. The lawmakers elected in 1988 made up the 101st Congress.

Congress holds one regular session a year. The session begins on January 3 unless Congress sets a different date. During the year, Congress recesses often so members can visit their home states or districts. Congress adjourns in early fall in election years and in late fall in other years. After Congress adjourns, the President may call a *special session.* The President may adjourn Congress only if the two houses disagree on an adjournment date.

The Senate and the House meet in separate chambers in the Capitol in Washington, D.C. The building stands on Capitol Hill, often called simply *the Hill.* Senators and representatives occasionally meet in a *joint session* in the larger House of Representatives chamber, mainly to hear an address by the President or a foreign official. The Constitution requires Congress to meet jointly to count the electoral votes after a presidential election. Legislation is never acted on in a joint session.

Congress's power to make laws

Origin of power. The Constitution gives Congress "all legislative powers" of the federal government. At the heart of Congress's lawmaking powers is its "power of the purse"—its control over government taxing and spending. Article I, Section 8 of the Constitution lists a wide range of powers granted to Congress. These *delegated,* or *expressed, powers* include the authority to coin money, regulate trade, declare war, and raise and equip military forces.

Article I, Section 8 also contains an *elastic clause* that gives Congress authority to "make all laws which shall be necessary and proper" to carry out the delegated powers. The elastic clause grants Congress *implied powers* to deal with many matters not specifically mentioned in the Constitution. For example, Congress has the expressed power to coin money. It has the implied power to create a treasury department to print money and manufacture coins.

Limitations of power. Congress is limited in the use of its powers. The Constitution prohibits some types of laws outright. For example, Congress may not pass trade laws that favor one state of the United States over another state. The Bill of Rights, the first 10 amendments to the Constitution, forbids certain other laws. For instance, the First Amendment bars Congress from establishing a national religion; preventing religious freedom; or limiting freedom of speech, press, assembly, or petition.

The executive and judicial branches of government also limit Congress's powers. The President may veto any bill Congress passes. Congress can *override* (reverse) a veto only by a two-thirds vote in each chamber, which is usually difficult to obtain. The President's power to propose legislation acts as another check on

---

Facts in brief about members of Congress

Number: The Senate has 100 members, and the House of Representatives has 435.

Qualifications: Senate: (1) at least 30 years old, (2) a U.S. citizen for at least 9 years, and (3) a resident of the state from which the candidate seeks election. House: (1) at least 25 years old, (2) a U.S. citizen for at least 7 years, and (3) a resident of the state from which the candidate seeks election.

Nomination: Nearly all candidates for Congress are nominated in primary elections, but a few are chosen by party conventions.

Election: A senator is elected by the voters from all parts of the state. A representative may (1) be elected by the voters of one congressional district of the state or (2) be elected *at large* (by voters throughout the state).

Term: Senators are elected to six-year terms, and representatives to two-year terms. There is no legal limit to the number of terms a member of Congress can serve.

Income: The Speaker of the House receives $115,000 a year. Majority and minority leaders of the House and of the Senate and the president pro tempore of the Senate earn $99,500 a year. Other members of Congress receive $89,500. All members receive free office space and allowances for office expenses, staff salaries, travel, and similar expenses.

Removal from office: Members of Congress may be expelled by a two-thirds vote of their particular chamber.

Congress. By its implied power of *judicial review,* the Supreme Court may declare a law passed by Congress to be unconstitutional. The courts also shape laws through their interpretations of them.

Finally, the power of public opinion limits what Congress can do. Lawmakers know that their actions must, in general, reflect the will of the people.

How Congress makes laws

Congress passes and the President signs about 650 laws during every two-year Congress. During that period, senators and representatives introduce about 10,000 bills. The legislative process sifts the proposals at every stage in the development of a bill to a law. To be enacted, a bill must survive committee and floor debates in both houses. It often must win the support of *special-interest groups,* or *lobbies.* A lobby represents a particular group, such as farmers or labor unions, and tries to influence legislators to pass laws favorable to that group. A bill must also gain a majority of votes in Congress and the President's signature. If the President vetoes the bill, it needs overwhelming support in Congress to override the veto.

Proposing new laws. Laws can be proposed by anyone, including lawmakers or their staffs, executive officials, or special-interest groups. The President can propose laws in speeches or public appearances. At a national convention, a political party may suggest laws to reflect the party's position on major issues. But to become a law, a bill must be sponsored and formally introduced in Congress by a member. Any number of senators or representatives may co-sponsor a bill.

A bill may be *public* or *private.* A public bill deals with matters of concern to people in general. Such matters include taxation, national defense, and foreign affairs. A private bill applies only to specific individuals, as in an immigration case or a claim against the government. To become a law, either kind of bill must be passed in exactly the same form by both houses of Congress and then signed by the President. Each proposed bill is printed and assigned a number, such as S. 1 in the Senate and H.R. 1 in the House of Representatives. Bills are also often known by popular names or by the names of their sponsors or authors.

Working in committees. After being introduced, a bill goes to a committee that deals with the matters the bill covers. Some bills involve various subjects and may be handled by several committees. For example, a trade bill may include sections on taxes, commerce, and banking. The bill may thus interest congressional tax, commerce, and banking committees.

The chief congressional committees are the 16 Senate and the 22 House standing committees. They handle most major fields of legislation, such as agriculture, banking, foreign policy, and transportation. Most standing committees have subcommittees, which hold hearings and work on bills on specialized matters.

The select and special committees of Congress propose laws on particular subjects or conduct investigations. In 1987, for example, each house appointed a select committee to examine the Iran-contra affair. The affair involved the sale of U.S. weapons to Iran in exchange for hostages, and the use of profits from the weapons sale to help the contra rebel forces in Nicara-

gua. *Joint committees* have members from both the House and the Senate. Such committees handle mainly research and administrative matters.

A proposed law reaches a critical stage after being referred to a committee. Committees *report* (return) only about 15 per cent of all bills they receive to the full Senate or House for consideration. Most bills are *tabled,* or *pigeonholed*—that is, never acted on. A committee's failure to act on a bill almost always spells death for the measure.

If committee leaders decide to proceed with a bill, they usually hold public hearings to receive testimony for and against the proposal. Testimony may be heard from a range of people, such as members of the President's Cabinet, scholars, representatives of special-interest groups, or lawmakers themselves.

Some bills go from committee to the full House or Senate without change. But most bills must be revised in committee *markup* sessions. In a markup session, members debate the sections of a measure and write amendments, thereby "marking up" the bill. When a majority of the committee's members vote for the revised bill, they report it to the full chamber with the recommendation that it be passed.

Legislative bargaining. To gain passage of a congressional bill, its sponsors must bargain for their fellow lawmakers' support. They need to give other legislators good reason to vote for the measure. To win a majority vote, the bill must be attractive to members with widely differing interests. Skillful legislators know how to draft a bill with broad appeal.

In a bargaining technique called *compromise,* legislators agree to take a position between two viewpoints. For example, lawmakers who want a major new government program and those who oppose any program at all might agree on a small trial project to test the idea.

In another form of legislative bargaining, *logrolling,* lawmakers write a bill so that everyone benefits. For in-

Standing committees of Congress

Senate	House of Representatives
Agriculture, Nutrition, and Forestry	Agriculture
Appropriations	Appropriations
Armed Services	Armed Services
Banking, Housing, and Urban Affairs	Banking, Finance, and Urban Affairs
Budget	Budget
Commerce, Science, and Transportation	District of Columbia
Energy and Natural Resources	Education and Labor
Environment and Public Works	Energy and Commerce
Finance	Foreign Affairs
Foreign Relations	Government Operations
Governmental Affairs	House Administration
Judiciary	Interior and Insular Affairs
Labor and Human Resources	Judiciary
Rules and Administration	Merchant Marine and Fisheries
Small Business	Post Office and Civil Service
Veterans' Affairs	Public Works and Transportation
	Rules
	Science, Space, and Technology
	Small Business
	Standards of Official Conduct
	Veterans' Affairs
	Ways and Means

The buildings where Congress works include the United States Capitol (1), the House office buildings (2), and the Senate office buildings (3). The floor plan shows the layout of the Capitol. The House of Representatives wing, *left,* includes the House Chamber, where the House holds its sessions. Senators meet in the Senate Chamber, located in the Senate wing, *right.*

Shostal

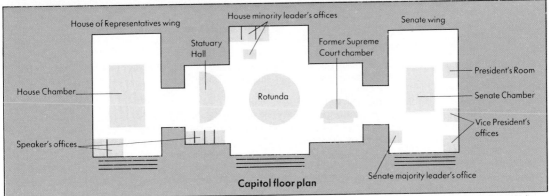

House of Representatives wing
House minority leader's offices
Senate wing
Statuary Hall
Former Supreme Court chamber
President's Room
House Chamber
Rotunda
Senate Chamber
Vice President's offices
Speaker's offices
Senate majority leader's office

Capitol floor plan

WORLD BOOK diagram

stance, a 1987 highway bill in the House included projects in so many members' districts that few representatives dared vote against it. *Pork barrel* is another term for this something-for-everyone legislation.

Some congressional bargaining involves an exchange of support over time. Lawmakers may vote for a fellow member's bill expecting that they will need that person's support later on another measure. Or a member who is ill-informed on a bill may follow the lead of a lawmaker who is an expert on the subject. Some other time, the influence may flow the other way. The technique is called *cue giving* and *cue taking.* Lawmakers cannot be experts on every bill, and so they rely on trusted associates who have worked on the measure.

Passing a bill. After a committee reports a bill, it is placed on a *calendar* (list of business) of whichever house of Congress is considering it. The Senate assigns all public and private bills to one calendar. It has a separate calendar for matters originating in the executive branch, such as treaties and presidential appointments. The House has five calendars. They involve (1) bills that raise or spend money, (2) all other major public bills, (3) private bills, (4) noncontroversial bills, and (5) motions to remove a bill from committee.

Committees screen out bills that lack broad support. Therefore, most measures that reach the House or Senate floor for debate and voting eventually pass. Senators usually call a bill up for consideration by a simple motion or by *unanimous consent*—that is, without anyone's objection. The objection of one senator can block unanimous consent, and so Senate leaders work to make sure

the bill is acceptable to their associates. Senators, however, cherish their tradition of free and sometimes lengthy debate. Senators opposed to a bill may make *filibusters*—long speeches designed to kill the bill or force its sponsors to compromise. To halt a filibuster, the Senate can vote *cloture*—that is, to limit the debate.

The House considers most bills by unanimous consent, like the Senate, or by the *suspension-of-rules procedure*. Both methods speed up legislation on largely noncontroversial bills. Representatives consider controversial bills under rules made by the Rules Committee. The rules control debate on a bill by setting time limits, restricting amendments, and, occasionally, barring objections to sections of the bill. Debate time is divided between the bill's supporters and opponents.

Legislators use various methods to vote on a bill. In a *voice vote,* all in favor say aye together, and those opposed say no. In *division,* the members stand as a group to indicate if they are for or against a bill. In a *roll-call vote,* the lawmakers each vote yes or no after their name is called. The House usually records and counts votes electronically. Members vote by pushing a button.

Senators and representatives tend to vote according to their party's position on a bill. If legislators know the views of their *constituents*—that is, of the people who elected them—they may vote accordingly. The President and powerful lobbies also influence how members vote.

From bill to law. After a bill passes one house of Congress, it goes to the other. The second house approves many bills without change. Some bills go back to the first house for further action. At times, the second house asks for a meeting with the first house to settle differences. Such a *conference committee* brings together committee leaders from both chambers to decide on the final bill. The two chambers then approve the bill, and it is sent to the President.

The President has 10 days—not including Sundays—to sign or veto a bill after receiving it. The veto is most powerful when used as a threat—lawmakers working on a bill want to know if the President is likely to approve it. If the President fails to sign or return the bill within 10 days and Congress is in session, the bill becomes law. But if Congress adjourns during that time, the bill does not become law. Such action is called a *pocket veto*.

Presidents veto about 3 per cent of the bills they receive. Only about 4 per cent of all vetoes are overridden by Congress. Presidents may veto a bill because it differs from their legislative program, or because they feel it is unconstitutional, costs too much, or is too hard to enforce.

Other duties of Congress

Passing laws lies at the heart of Congress's duties. But Congress also has nonlegislative tasks that influence national government and shape public policies.

Approving federal appointments. The Constitution requires the President to submit nominations of Cabinet members, federal judges, ambassadors, and certain other officials to the Senate for approval. A majority vote of the senators present confirms a presidential appointment. Senators approve almost all nominations to the executive branch because they believe that the President deserves loyal people in top jobs. The Senate examines judicial appointments more critically. About a fourth of all Supreme Court nominees have failed to win Senate confirmation. Some were rejected by a vote, but more commonly the Senate delayed acting on the nomination, often leading the President to withdraw it.

Approving treaties. According to Article II, Section 2 of the Constitution, the President has the power to make treaties "by and with the advice and consent of the Senate." A treaty requires the approval of two-thirds of the senators voting on it. The Senate has rejected outright very few treaties since the First Congress met in 1789. More often, the Senate amends the treaty or simply fails to act.

The most famous treaty rejection was the Senate's refusal to approve the Treaty of Versailles, which established peace with Germany at the end of World War I (1914-1918). The treaty included President Woodrow Wilson's proposal for the League of Nations, an international association to maintain peace. Senators proposed reservations to the treaty—particularly the League—but Wilson rejected them, leading to the treaty's downfall.

Presidents today try to keep the Senate informed as they arrange treaties. For example, President Ronald Reagan invited senators to follow negotiations for the Intermediate-Range Nuclear Forces (INF) Treaty, which called for the destruction of certain nuclear weapons in the United States and the Soviet Union. Objections from the senators sent U.S. diplomats back to the bargaining table to revise the treaty. Signed in December 1987, the treaty won Senate approval by the following May.

Conducting investigations. Congress has the implied power to investigate executive actions and public

and private wrongdoing because such inquiries may lead to new laws. Congressional committees conduct the investigations. Congress has launched investigations to uncover scandals, spotlight certain issues, embarrass the President, or advance the reputations of the lawmakers themselves. Televised congressional investigations have aroused great public interest and highlighted Congress's role in keeping the people informed. An early televised investigation took place in 1954, when millions of TV viewers watched Senator Joseph R. McCarthy charge the U.S. Army with "coddling Communists."

Proposing constitutional amendments. Congress can propose amendments to the U.S. Constitution by a two-thirds vote in both houses. Congress can also call a constitutional convention to propose amendments if at least two-thirds of the states formally request it. In addition, Congress determines whether the states vote on an amendment by means of state legislatures or special state conventions. Congress also decides how long the states have to consider an amendment. It allows seven years in most cases.

Handling presidential election results. Congress counts and checks the votes cast by the Electoral College, the group of electors that chooses the U.S. President and Vice President. Congress then announces the results of the election. In most cases, the public knows the winners from the outcome of the popular election. If no candidate has a majority of Electoral College votes, Congress selects the winners. The House chooses the President, and the Senate elects the Vice President.

Impeaching and trying federal officials. An impeachment is a charge of serious misconduct in office. The House of Representatives has the power to draw up charges of impeachment against officials of the national government. If a majority of representatives vote for impeachment, the Senate then sits as a court to hear the charges against the accused official. Impeachments rarely occur. The House voted to impeach President Andrew Johnson in 1868, but the Senate narrowly acquitted him. President Richard M. Nixon resigned in 1974 before representatives voted on impeachment charges recommended by the House Judiciary Committee.

Reviewing its own members. Congress can review the election and judge the qualifications of its own members. It can also *censure* (officially condemn) or expel members for improper conduct as well as apply a milder form of discipline, such as a fine or reprimand. Congress has censured members for such reasons as the conviction of crimes, *unethical* (morally wrong) conduct, or disgracing Congress.

Members of Congress at work

A typical day. The daily schedule of members of Congress reflects their jobs both as lawmakers and as representatives for their districts and states. Most members work at least 11 hours a day. Mornings involve office work and committee meetings, often with two or three meetings scheduled at the same time. Members choose which meeting to attend. They make brief appearances at other meetings or send aides to take notes. During the afternoon, and many mornings and evenings, the Senate and House are in session. Most legislators, busy with other work, do not stay in their particular chamber for debates. Instead, they follow them on

Representation in Congress

The Constitution of the United States provides for a *bicameral* (two chamber) legislature. In the Senate, each state has equal representation—two senators per state. In the House of Representatives, population determines the number of representatives sent from each state.

State	Senate	House	State	Senate	House	State	Senate	House
Alabama	2	7	Louisiana	2	8	Ohio	2	21
Alaska	2	1	Maine	2	2	Oklahoma	2	6
Arizona	2	5	Maryland	2	8	Oregon	2	5
Arkansas	2	4	Massachusetts	2	11	Pennsylvania	2	23
California	2	45	Michigan	2	18	Rhode Island	2	2
Colorado	2	6	Minnesota	2	8	South Carolina	2	6
Connecticut	2	6	Mississippi	2	5	South Dakota	2	1
Delaware	2	1	Missouri	2	9	Tennessee	2	9
Florida	2	19	Montana	2	2	Texas	2	27
Georgia	2	10	Nebraska	2	3	Utah	2	3
Hawaii	2	2	Nevada	2	2	Vermont	2	1
Idaho	2	2	New Hampshire	2	2	Virginia	2	10
Illinois	2	22	New Jersey	2	14	Washington	2	8
Indiana	2	10	New Mexico	2	3	West Virginia	2	4
Iowa	2	6	New York	2	34	Wisconsin	2	9
Kansas	2	5	North Carolina	2	11	Wyoming	2	1
Kentucky	2	7	North Dakota	2	1			

closed-circuit TV. Members must be ready to go to their chamber for a vote or a *quorum call*—that is, a count taken to determine if the minimum number of lawmakers needed to hold a vote is present.

Telephone calls, letters, and visits from constituents take up much of a legislator's time. Many people contact members to give their views on bills. Other people seek help with jobs, immigration problems, social security payments, or appointments to military academies.

Senators and representatives have assistants in their Washington, D.C., offices and in their state or district offices. The size of a senator's staff depends on the population of the senator's state—the larger the population, the larger the staff. The average staff consists of about 40 to 50 people. By law, representatives may employ up to 18 aides. Party and committee leaders in Congress have additional aides. Most members also accept students who work without pay to gain political experience. The students work either in Washington or in local offices on legislation and relations with constituents.

Congressional travel. Members of Congress travel often to their home states or districts to appear at public events, study area problems, and talk with voters or local officials. In fact, about a third of all representatives return to their districts nearly every weekend. Sessions of the Senate and House are scheduled to accommodate the members' need to appear frequently before their constituents, and legislators receive allowances to cover their expenses. If members fail to visit their home states or districts fairly often, they are apt to be criticized for forgetting their constituents.

Fact-finding missions at home or abroad—sometimes called *junkets*—also crowd the schedules of senators and representatives. Critics charge that legislators enjoy foreign travel at public expense. Legislators argue that experience gained by travel abroad helps them understand world developments and legislate wisely.

Social responsibilities. Membership in Congress carries many social obligations. Both at home and in Washington, individuals and groups interview legisla-

tors and expect them to attend social events. One questionable social practice involves members' speeches before interest groups to earn *honorariums* (honorary fees). Critics argue that such payments may be used to influence lawmakers.

History of Congress

The founding of Congress grew out of a tradition of representative assemblies that was brought from Great Britain and took root in the American Colonies in the early 1600's. Colonial assemblies had a wide range of powers, including authority to collect taxes, issue money, and provide for defense. In time, the assemblies increasingly voiced the colonists' interests against those of the British-appointed colonial governors.

As tensions worsened between Great Britain and the American Colonies in the 1760's, the colonial assemblies took up the colonists' cause. The First Continental Congress met in Philadelphia in 1774. It brought together lawmakers from every colony but Georgia and could be considered the country's first national legislature. In 1776, the Second Continental Congress declared the colonies' independence from Britain. The Second Continental Congress served as the national government until 1781, when the states adopted the Articles of Confederation and established the Congress of the Confederation. The Congress of the Confederation functioned without an independent executive or judicial branch and soon showed its weakness.

In 1787, the Constitutional Convention met to strengthen the Articles of Confederation. But the delegates drew up a new plan of government instead—the Constitution of the United States. The power of the legislature remained important, but it was balanced by executive and judicial branches. The Constitution called for two chambers for the new Congress—earlier Congresses had one house—with equal representation in one chamber and representation by population in the other. The establishment of a two-house legislature became known as the *Great Compromise*. It solved a bitter dispute between delegates from small states, who favored equal representation for every state, and those from large states, who wanted representation based on state population.

Growth and conflict. When the new Congress met for the first time in New York City in 1789, the two chambers were small and informal. At the end of the First Congress, the Senate had only 26 members, and the House of Representatives 65. As new states joined the Union, the House grew faster than the Senate and developed strong leaders. Such House Speakers as Henry Clay in the early 1800's and Thomas B. Reed in the late 1800's brought power and high honor to their office. They also increased the House's power. The Senate enjoyed a golden age from about the 1830's to the 1860's, when it had such great speechmakers as Clay, Daniel Webster, and John C. Calhoun. Those men and their fellow senators debated the existence of slavery in the United States and other burning issues of the day.

Relations between Congress and the President shifted wildly throughout the 1800's. Most Presidents yielded to Congress and initiated few policies. During the early and middle 1800's, however, several strong Presidents sought to deal with Congress as an equal. Thomas Jefferson worked with congressional supporters to enact legislation drafted by the executive branch. Andrew Jackson promoted his policies through *patronage*—that is, his authority to make federal job appointments—and through his use of the veto. Abraham Lincoln used emergency authority to force Congress to accept his policies during the Civil War (1861-1865). Congress recaptured power after each of the strong Presidents. Following the Civil War, the House ruled supreme, with the Speaker almost as important as the President. Indeed, the Speaker became so strong that House members revolted in 1910 to limit the power of the office.

Continued struggle for power. During the early to middle 1900's, voters elected several strong-willed men who established the President as a leader in the legislative process. The Presidents included Theodore Roosevelt, Woodrow Wilson, and especially Franklin D. Roosevelt. Each proposed a package of new laws and worked to persuade or pressure Congress to enact that package. Congress began to rely increasingly on its committees to process legislation. Partly to keep its position as an equal branch of government, Congress passed the Legislative Reorganization Act of 1946 and a similar act in 1970. The two laws authorized additional staff and made other reforms to help Congress match the growing power and skill of the executive branch.

Relations between Congress and the presidency changed markedly in the late 1960's and early 1970's. Such events as the Vietnam War (1957-1975) and the Watergate scandal led Congress to limit the President's authority. The Vietnam War had never been officially declared by Congress. But Presidents Lyndon B. Johnson and Nixon, as commanders in chief of the nation's armed forces, had sent hundreds of thousands of U.S. troops into the conflict. Public opposition to the war spurred Congress to pass the War Powers Resolution in 1973 over Nixon's veto. The resolution restricts the President's authority to keep U.S. troops in a hostile area

© Frank Fisher, Gamma/Liaison

Hearings on the Watergate scandal led the House Judiciary Committee, *above,* to recommend impeachment of the President in 1974. Congressional power increased as a result.

without Congress's consent. The law reasserted Congress's role in foreign affairs, but has had mixed success in curbing the President's warmaking authority.

In 1973, a Senate select committee began hearings on the Watergate scandal. The scandal involved illegal campaign activities during the 1972 presidential race. The investigation led the House to begin impeachment proceedings against President Nixon. Nixon was charged with obstructing justice, abusing presidential powers, and illegally withholding evidence. He resigned before an impeachment vote was held. Congress further declared its authority in 1974, when it passed the Congressional Budget and Impoundment Control Act. The act restricts the President's freedom to *impound* (refuse to spend) funds for projects approved by Congress.

Congress today. During the 1980's, conflict arose between Congress and the President. President Ronald Reagan pursued a strong anti-Communist foreign policy and called for increased defense spending, lower taxes, and cuts in welfare programs at home. Congress approved some of Reagan's program in 1981, but opposition mounted as international tensions and the shortage of funds in the federal budget increased. Disputes between the legislative and executive branches erupted over a variety of issues, including aid to Nicaraguan rebels, and Reagan's judicial appointments.

Continuing problems involve congressional ethics. The soaring cost of congressional campaigns has led to questions about the power of special-interest groups and their *political action committees* (PAC's). A PAC obtains voluntary contributions from its members or employees of the interest group and then gives the funds to candidates it favors. Critics fear that the system results in a Congress representing special interests. But lawmakers benefit from PAC's, and so they hesitate to support reforms. Another controversial congressional activity involves members who increase their incomes by accepting honorariums from interest groups for giving speeches. The practice raises questions of ethics and damages voters' opinion of Congress.   Roger H. Davidson

Related articles. See the articles **House of Representatives** and **Senate** and their *Related articles.* See also:

Outline

Questions

Why are there two houses of Congress?
In what ways is the power of Congress limited?
What powers does the Speaker of the House have?
What are *delegated powers* of Congress? *Implied powers?*
How does Congress influence the President's treaty-making
  power?
What techniques are used in legislative bargaining?
How did relations between Congress and the presidency
  change markedly in the late 1960's and early 1970's?
Why does Congress conduct investigations?
What is a *standing committee?* A *conference committee?*
Why do members travel often to their home states or districts?

Reading and Study Guide

See *Congress of the United States* in the Research Guide/Index,
Volume 22, for a *Reading and Study Guide.*

Additional resources

Level I
Coy, Harold. *Congress* Rev. ed. Watts, 1981.
Goode, Stephen. *The New Congress.* Messner, 1980.

Level II
Congress and the Nation: A Review of Government and Politics.
  6 vols. Congressional Quarterly, 1965-1985.
Davidson, Roger H., and Oleszek, W. J. *Congress and Its Mem-*
  bers. 2nd ed. Congressional Quarterly, 1985.
How Congress Works. Congressional Quarterly, 1983.
Mikva, Abner J., and Saris, P. B. *The American Congress: The*
  First Branch. Watts, 1983.

Quayle, Dan (1947-   ), was elected Vice President of the United States in 1988. Quayle and his presidential running mate, Vice President George Bush, defeated their Democratic opponents, Governor Michael S. Dukakis of Massachusetts and Senator Lloyd Bentsen of Texas. Before becoming Vice President, Quayle represented Indiana in the United States Senate from 1981 to 1989. He previously had served two terms in the U.S. House of Representatives.

Early life. Quayle, whose full name is James Danforth Quayle, was born on Feb. 4, 1947, in Indianapolis, Ind. Quayle's maternal grandfather, Eugene Pulliam, was an influential and wealthy publisher of several newspapers in Indiana and Arizona.

Quayle graduated from DePauw University in Green-castle, Ind., in 1969 with a degree in political science. In 1974, Quayle received a law degree from Indiana University in Indianapolis. While attending law school at night, Quayle worked in the offices of the governor and attorney general of Indiana and directed the state's Inheritance Tax Division. From 1974 to 1976, he was associate publisher of *The Huntington Herald-Press,* a paper published by his family.

© R. Maiman, Sygma

Dan Quayle

In 1972, Quayle married Marilyn Tucker (1949-   ) of Indianapolis, Ind. The Quayles had three children—Tucker Danforth (1974-   ), Benjamin Eugene (1976-   ), and Mary Corinne (1978-   ).

Political career. Quayle was elected to the U.S. House of Representatives in 1976 and in 1978 from a district in northeastern Indiana. In the House, he had a consistently conservative voting record.

In 1980, Quayle won election to the U.S. Senate, defeating Democratic Senator Birch E. Bayh, Jr. Quayle was reelected in 1986. He served on the Senate's Budget, Armed Services, and Labor and Human Resources committees. In 1982, Quayle and Senator Edward M. Kennedy of Massachusetts developed the Job Training Partnership Act (JTPA), under which private employers and government joined to provide job training for the unskilled, disadvantaged, and unemployed.

In August 1988, the Republican National Convention nominated Quayle for Vice President at Bush's request. The selection sparked immediate controversy. Much of the controversy centered on Quayle's service in the Indiana National Guard from 1969 to 1975. Charges were raised that Quayle used his family's influence to get into the Guard and thereby avoid being drafted into the Regular Army and possibly seeing combat in the Vietnam War (1957-1975). Quayle, however, defended his service in the National Guard and retained Bush's support and his place on the ticket.   Lee Thornton

Jerusalem is Israel's capital and largest city. This photograph shows West Jerusalem, the more modern section that is home to most of the city's Jewish population.

Steven Lucas, Southern Stock Photos

Israel

Israel is a small country in southwestern Asia. It occupies a narrow strip of land on the eastern shore of the Mediterranean Sea. Israel was founded in 1948 as a homeland for Jews from all parts of the world, and more than 4 out of 5 of its people are Jews. Even Jews who live elsewhere consider Israel their spiritual home. Almost all the non-Jews in Israel are Arabs. Jerusalem is Israel's capital and largest city.

Israel makes up most of the Biblical Holy Land, the place where the religious and national identity of the Jews developed. According to the Bible, Abraham, the father of the Jewish people, established a Semitic population in the Holy Land. Many scholars believe this happened between 1900 and 1700 B.C.

Eventually this land fell to a series of conquerors, including—in 63 B.C.—the Romans, who called the region Palestine. Following unsuccessful Jewish revolts against Roman rule in A.D. 66-70 and A.D. 132-135, the Romans forced most of the Jews from Palestine. Palestine was ruled by the Roman and then the Byzantine empires until the A.D. 600's, when Arabs conquered the region. From that time until the mid-1900's, the majority of people in Palestine were Arabs. For more information on the ancient history of Israel, see the **Palestine** article.

In the late 1800's, European Jews formed a movement called Zionism, which sought to establish a Jewish state in Palestine. Jewish immigrants began arriving in Palestine in large numbers, and by the early 1900's friction

had developed between the Jewish and Arab populations. In 1947, the United Nations (UN) proposed dividing the region into an Arab state and a Jewish state.

On May 14, 1948, the nation of Israel officially came into being. The surrounding Arab nations immediately attacked the new state, in the first of several Arab-Israeli wars. Except for Egypt, with whom Israel signed a peace treaty in 1979, Israel has remained technically at war with its Arab neighbors throughout its history. In addition, since 1967 Israel has held the Gaza Strip and the

Facts in brief

Capital: Jerusalem.
Official languages: Hebrew and Arabic.
Area: 8,019 sq. mi. (20,770 km²), not including 3,900 sq. mi. (10,100 km²) of Arab territory occupied since 1967. *Greatest distances*—north-south, 260 mi. (420 km); east-west, 70 mi. (110 km). *Coastline*—170 mi. (273 km).
Elevation: *Highest*—Mount Meron, 3,963 ft. (1,208 m) above sea level. *Lowest*—shore of the Dead Sea, about 1,310 ft. (399 m) below sea level.
Population: *Estimated 1989 population*—4,447,000; distribution, 90 per cent urban, 10 per cent rural; density, 555 persons per sq. mi. (214 per km²). *1983 census*—4,037,620. *Estimated 1994 population*—4,803,000. Population figures do not include people living in occupied Arab territories, except for Israeli citizens.
Chief products: *Agriculture*—citrus and other fruits, cotton, eggs, grains, poultry, vegetables. *Manufacturing*—chemical products, electronic equipment, fertilizer, finished diamonds, paper, plastics, processed foods, scientific and optical instruments, textiles and clothing. *Mining*—potash, bromine, salt, phosphates.
National anthem: "Hatikva" ("The Hope").
Money: *Basic unit*—shekel. See **Money** (table: Exchange rates). See also **Shekel**.

Bernard Reich, the contributor of this article, is Professor of Political Science and International Affairs at George Washington University.

West Bank—territories that are home to more than 1 million Palestinian Arabs. Israel's occupation of these territories has further inflamed Arab-Israeli tensions.

Israel has few natural resources and imports more goods than it exports. Still, it has achieved a relatively high standard of living. More than 90 per cent of its people can read and write and the level of unemployment is low. Jewish settlers have established major industries, drained swamps, and irrigated deserts.

Although it is a small country, Israel has a diverse terrain that includes mountains, deserts, seashores, and valleys. Israel has a pleasant climate, with hot, dry summers, and cool, mild winters.

Government

National government. Israel is a democratic republic with a parliament-cabinet form of government (see **Cabinet** [The cabinet system of government]). It has no written constitution. Instead, the government follows several "basic laws" that have been passed by the Knesset, the Israeli parliament. The Knesset is a *unicameral* (one-house) body made up of 120 members, each elected to a term not to exceed four years. The Knesset passes legislation, participates in the formation of national policy, and approves budgets and taxes.

All Israeli citizens 18 years or older may vote. Voters do not cast ballots for individual candidates in Knesset elections. Instead, they vote for a *party list,* which includes all the candidates of a particular political party. The list may range from a single candidate to a full slate of 120 candidates. Elections are determined by the percentage of the vote received by each list. For example, if a particular party list received 33 per cent of the vote, it would get 40 Knesset seats.

The prime minister is the head of Israel's government and normally the leader of the party that controls the most seats in the Knesset. The prime minister must maintain the support of a majority of the Knesset to stay in office. He or she forms and heads the Cabinet, Israel's top policymaking body. The Cabinet is composed of the heads of each government department. Appointments to the Cabinet must be approved by the Knesset. The prime minister determines the topics of Cabinet meetings and has the final word in policy decisions.

The president, who functions as the head of state, is elected by the Knesset to a five-year term and may not serve more than two consecutive terms. Most of the president's duties are ceremonial.

Local government. Elected councils are the units of local government in Israel. Municipal councils serve the larger cities, and local councils govern the smaller urban areas. Regional councils serve rural areas. Councils are responsible for providing education, health and sanitation services, water, road maintenance, fire protection, and park and recreation facilities. They also set and collect local taxes and fees.

The national government divides the country into 6 administrative districts and 14 subdistricts. The Minister of Interior, one of the Cabinet members, appoints officials to head the districts and subdistricts. These officials oversee and approve the actions of the councils.

Politics. Israel has many political parties, representing a wide range of views. But two parties—the Labor Party and the Likud bloc—dominate national elections.

The Labor Party supports government control of the economy, but also believes in a limited amount of free enterprise. The party favors a negotiated settlement with the Arab states and compromising with the Arabs over the fate of the occupied territories.

The Likud bloc is an alliance of a number of smaller parties. It supports limited government involvement in the economy. Likud favors a hard-line policy toward the Arab states and believes that Israel should retain the occupied territories.

Israel also has a number of smaller religious and special-interest parties. Each of these parties focuses on a particular subject or theme. If one of the major parties

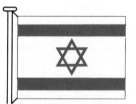 

Israel's flag shows the Star of David, an ancient Jewish symbol. The colors are those of a *tallit* (prayer shawl).

Coat of arms shows the *Menorah* (ancient holy candleholder) and olive branches. Hebrew letters spell Israel.

WORLD BOOK map

Israel lies along the eastern coast of the Mediterranean Sea. It is bordered by Jordan, Lebanon, Syria, and Egypt.

Israel Government Tourist Bureau

The Knesset Building, home of the Israeli parliament, glows in floodlights at night. It stands on a low hill in Jerusalem.

controls too few seats in the Knesset to form a majority, it usually seeks support from the religious parties. These parties thus have considerable power.

Courts. Israel's court system consists of religious and *secular* (nonreligious) courts. The Supreme Court is the highest secular court. The secular court system also includes magistrate and district courts, in addition to municipal and other specialized courts. The Supreme Court hears appeals from these courts and acts to protect the rights of Israeli citizens.

Religious courts hear cases involving certain personal matters, such as marriage problems, divorces, alimony settlements, and inheritances. Jews, Christians, Muslims, and Druses each have their own religious courts.

Most religious court justices and all secular court justices are appointed by the president. The appointments are based on recommendations made by nomination committees consisting of officials from all branches of the Israeli government. Justices must retire at age 70.

Armed forces. Because it is surrounded by hostile Arab states, a strong military is vital to Israel's survival. However, the large amount of money Israel spends on defense puts a strain on the nation's economy.

Israel's army, navy, and air force have about 141,000 members. The country requires almost all Jewish men and most unmarried Jewish women to enter the military at age 18. Men must serve for three years, and women for two years. Annual reserve service is required of men up to age 55 and women up to age 34.

People

When Israel was established in 1948, it had about 806,000 people. In 1989, Israel's population numbered about 4.4 million. Israel's population is very unevenly distributed—with about 90 per cent of the people living in urban areas. The area along the Mediterranean coast is Israel's most densely populated region. The Negev Desert, in the southwestern part of the country, is the least densely populated region.

Jews. About 83 per cent of Israel's people are Jews. The modern state of Israel was created as a homeland for the Jewish people. Between 1948 and the mid-1980's, about 1.8 million Jews migrated to Israel, many to escape persecution in their home countries. In 1950, the Knesset passed the Law of the Return, which allows any Jew, with a few minor exceptions, to settle in Israel. A 1970 amendment to this law defined a Jew as "a person who was born of a Jewish mother or has become converted to Judaism and who is not a member of another religion." The Israeli government provides temporary housing and job training to immigrants.

Israel's Jewish population shares a common spiritual and historical heritage. But because they have come from many countries, Israel's Jews belong to a number of different *ethnic groups,* each with its own cultural, political, and recent historical background.

The two main groups in Israel's Jewish population are the *Ashkenazim* and the *Sephardim,* or *Orientals.* The Ashkenazim, who came to Israel from all parts of Europe and from North America, are descended from members of the Jewish communities of central and eastern Europe. The Sephardim came from the countries of the Middle East and the Mediterranean. Today, most of Israel's Jews are Sephardim. But at the time of independ-

ence, most were Ashkenazim. As a result, the nation's political, educational, and economic systems are primarily Western in orientation. Israel's Sephardic population has had to adapt to this society.

Arabs make up nearly all of the remaining 17 per cent of the population of Israel. Most are Palestinians whose families remained in Israel after the 1948-1949 Arab-Israeli war. They usually live in their own farm villages or in the Arab neighborhoods of Israeli cities.

The nation's Jewish and Arab communities are generally suspicious of one another. Arab and Jewish Israelis have limited contact, in part, because the Arabs have had difficulty adjusting to Israel's Jewish, Western-oriented society. Most Arabs and Jews live in separate areas, attend separate schools, speak different languages, and follow different cultural traditions.

Language. Israel has two official languages—Hebrew, the language spoken by most of the Jewish population, and Arabic, spoken mainly by the Arabs. Many Israelis also speak English and many Ashkenazi Jews speak *Yiddish,* a Germanic language that developed in the Jewish communities of Europe.

Way of life

Israel has a relatively high standard of living, with income levels similar to those in such countries as Spain

Alex Borodulin, De Wys, Inc.

Modern apartment buildings, such as these in Tel Aviv, are common in Israeli cities. Most urban Israelis live in apartments.

© Richard Lobell

A moshav in the Galilee region of Israel houses several rural families. Moshavim are cooperative farming communities.

School attendance is required of all Israelis between the ages of 5 and 16, with free education provided through age 18. The students above are attending class at a rural high school.

Cameramann International, Ltd.

or Greece. Israel's life expectancy levels rank among the highest in the world. The country has an excellent system of health and medical care.

City life. About 90 per cent of Israel's people live in urban areas. In fact, the country's three largest cities—Jerusalem, Tel Aviv, and Haifa—account for about 25 per cent of the nation's population. Many of Israel's cities are built on ancient sites and include historic buildings, but they also have large, modern sections built by Jewish settlers during the mid-1900's. Many feature high-rise apartment and office buildings. Most urban Israelis live in apartments.

Like urban areas in most countries, Israel's major cities face problems brought on by rapid growth. Roads, housing, and municipal services sometimes fail to keep pace with the expanding population. Traffic congestion and, to a lesser degree, pollution have become problems in Israel's larger cities.

Jerusalem, the capital and largest city, is the spiritual center of the Jewish religion. It is also a holy city of Christians and Muslims. The city is divided into two sections, West Jerusalem and East Jerusalem. West Jerusalem, inhabited mainly by Jews, is the newer part of the city. It contains concrete apartment houses and modern public buildings. It also has several ancient holy places. East Jerusalem, which was captured by Israel in 1967, is inhabited mainly by Arabs. This older section of the city includes many ancient holy places. See **Jerusalem.**

Tel Aviv, Israel's second largest city in size and importance, serves as the nation's commercial, financial, and industrial center. Haifa is Israel's major port city and the administrative and industrial center of northern Israel. Beersheba is the most important city in the Negev Desert region.

In the 1950's, the Israeli government began creating "development towns." These towns, which include Arad and Carmiel, were established to attract industry to lightly populated parts of Israel and to provide homes for new immigrants.

Rural life. Only about 10 per cent of the people of Israel live in rural areas. More than half of the rural population live in *collective* or *cooperative* communities. In a collective community, called a *kibbutz,* members receive food, housing, education, child care, and medical care in exchange for labor. All property is shared. In many kibbutzim, the children live in a separate section. The kibbutz is traditionally agricultural, but many now have industrial activity as well. In a cooperative community, called a *moshav,* each family works its land separately and has its own living quarters. The village administration provides the family's equipment and supplies, and markets its produce.

Clothing. Most Israelis wear Western-style clothing, although styles in Israel are generally less formal than in Western countries. But some Israelis still dress in the traditional clothing of their ethnic or religious group.

Food and drink. Israel's food and drink reflect the ethnic diversity of its population. Traditional European Jewish dishes, such as chopped liver, chicken soup, and gefilte fish, are common. But so also are traditional Middle Eastern foods such as *felafel*—small, deep-fried patties of ground chickpeas. Raw vegetables and fruits are among the most popular foods.

All government buildings and most hotels and restaurants serve only *kosher* foods, which are prepared according to Jewish dietary laws (see **Kosher**). But there are nonkosher restaurants as well. Israel also has fast-food restaurants, which serve local dishes in addition to Western foods. Popular beverages in Israel include Turkish coffee, cola, beer, and wine.

Religion. Israeli law guarantees religious freedom and allows members of all faiths to have days of rest on their Sabbath and holy days. Many public facilities are closed on the Jewish Sabbath—from sunset Friday to sunset Saturday.

About one-fifth of Israel's Jewish population strictly observe the principles of Judaism. These people are called *Orthodox* Jews. About half of the country's Jews observe some of the principles. The rest are *secular,* or nonreligious. Israel's Jews disagree on the proper relationship between religion and the state. Orthodox Jews tend to believe that Jewish religious values should play an important role in shaping government policy. But many other members of the Jewish population, including almost all secular Jews, seek to limit the role of religion in the state.

About 77 per cent of Israel's non-Jewish populace are Arab Muslims, most of whom follow the Sunni sect of Islam (see **Islam** [Sects]). About 13 per cent of the non-Jews are Arab Christians, mostly Greek Catholic and Greek Orthodox. Most of the remaining 10 per cent are Druses, an Arabic-speaking people who follow a religion that developed out of Islam. A few are members of the Bahá'ís or other smaller religious communities.

Education. Education is given a high priority in Israel. One of the first laws passed in Israel established free education and required school attendance for all children between the ages of 5 and 14. Attendance is now required to age 16.

Israeli children normally attend one year of nursery school, one year of kindergarten, six years of elementary school, three years of junior high school, and three years of high school. Education is free until age 18.

Israel has a Jewish school system in which instruction is in Hebrew, and an Arab/Druse school system in which instruction is in Arabic. The government recognizes and funds both systems.

The Jewish system consists of state schools, state-religious schools, and independent religious schools. State and state-religious schools offer similar academic programs, but state-religious schools emphasize Jewish studies. Independent religious schools are affiliated with Orthodox Judaism and offer more intensive religious instruction.

The Arab/Druse school system includes separate schools for Arab and Druse students. These schools emphasize Arab or Druse history and culture. The Arab schools also provide religious instruction in Islam or Christianity. In Druse schools, community elders choose whether or not to provide religious training.

Israel has a number of well-known institutions of higher education. They include Haifa University, Hebrew University of Jerusalem, Tel Aviv University, and the Weizmann Institute of Science.

The arts. In music, dance, theater, literature, painting, and sculpture, many Israeli artists work within the traditions of their ethnic group. Other artists have blended different cultural art forms to create a uniquely Israeli artistic tradition. The arts in Israel not only reflect the country's immigrant diversity, they also draw upon Jewish history and religion and address the social and political problems of modern Israel.

The number of books published per person in Israel is among the highest in the world. Most Israeli authors write in Hebrew, and some have achieved international fame. Shmuel Yosef Agnon, a novelist and short-story writer, shared the 1966 Nobel Prize for literature. Other prominent Israeli writers include Chaim Nachman Bialik, Shaul Tchernichovsky, Amos Oz, and A. B. Yehoshua.

Israel has several theatrical companies. *Habimah,* the national theater, was founded in Moscow in 1917. It moved permanently to Tel Aviv in 1932. The Israel Philharmonic Orchestra performs throughout Israel and often tours abroad. Jerusalem has a symphony orchestra. Israel also has several professional ballet and modern dance companies. Haifa and Tel Aviv boast a number of outstanding museums.

The land

Israel has four major land regions. They are (1) the Coastal Plain, (2) the Judeo-Galilean Highlands, (3) the Rift Valley, and (4) the Negev Desert.

The Coastal Plain is a narrow strip of fertile land along the Mediterranean Sea. Most Israelis live in the Coastal Plain, and most of the nation's industry and agriculture are located there. Haifa, Israel's major port, is on the northern coast. The northern part of the Coastal Plain includes part of the fertile Plain of Esdraelon. The Qishon, a broad stream, flows through this plain. Most of Israel's important citrus crop is produced in the Plain of Sharon, which forms part of the central Coastal Plain. Farther south is the city of Tel Aviv.

The Judeo-Galilean Highlands include a series of mountain ranges that run from Galilee—the northernmost part of Israel—to the edge of the Negev Desert in the south. The southern part of the highlands includes the Israeli-occupied West Bank.

The mountains of Galilee stretch southward to the Plain of Esdraelon. Galilee is the home of most of Israel's Arabs and includes the city of Nazareth, the largest Arab center. Galilee also contains the highest mountain in Israel, 3,963-foot (1,208-meter) Mount Meron.

Jerusalem is located in the northern part of the Judean Hills. Rural residents of these hills farm on the hillsides and in the broad valleys. The land to the south is more rugged and agriculture is limited to grazing.

The Rift Valley is a long, narrow strip of land in far eastern Israel. It makes up a small part of the Great Rift Valley, a series of valleys that extends from Syria to Mozambique (see **Great Rift Valley**).

The edges of the Rift Valley are steep, but the floor is largely flat. Much of the region lies below sea level. The region includes the Dead Sea, a saltwater lake. The shore of the Dead Sea lies about 1,310 feet (399 meters) below sea level—the lowest land area on earth.

Few areas of the Rift Valley are fertile. The most fertile section is about 10 miles (16 kilometers) north of the Sea

Frank Folwell, Click/Chicago

A group of Orthodox Jews in Jerusalem read the *Torah,* the first five books of the Bible. Orthodox Jews strictly observe the principles of Judaism. They make up about one-fifth of Israel's Jewish population.

Israel

map index

Cities and towns

Afula ....21,200. .C 5
Akko ....39,000. .B 4
Arad ....12,900. .F 4
Arara* ....5,800. .C 4
Arraba* ....9,500. .B 5
Ashdod ....68,000. .E 3
Ashqelon ....54,100. .E 3
Azor* ....6,600. .D 3
Baqa el
  Gharbiyya* ...11,200. .C 4
Bat Yam ....134,500. .D 3
Beersheba .....112,600. .F 4
Bene Beraq .....94,800. .D 3
Bet Shean ......13,500. .C 5
Bet Shemesh ...13,000. .E 4
Daliyat
  el Karmel* ....8,600. .C 4
Dimona ....27,600. .G 4
Elat ....19,600. .K 4
Er Reina* ....5,800. .B 5
Et Taiyiba .....17,200. .C 4
Et Tira ....11,300. .D 4
Ganne Tiqwa* ...6,000. .D 3
Gedera ....6,200. .E 3
Givat
  Shemuel* ......8,400. .D 3
Givatayim* ....48,300. .D 3
Hadera ....39,400. .C 4
Haifa ....266,100. .B 4
Hazor ....6,500. .A 5
Herzliyya ......63,200. .D 3
Hod
  HaSharon* ...20,100. .D 4
Holon ....134,600. .D 3
Ibillin* ....5,600. .B 4
Iksal* ....5,600. .B 5
Isfiya* ....6,100. .B 4
Jerusalem .....424,400. .E 4
Kafr Kanna* .....7,900. .B 5
Kafr Manda* .....6,500. .B 4
Kafr Qari* ......7,400. .C 4
Kafr Qasim* .....7,600. .D 4
Kafr Yasif* .....5,500. .B 4
Karmiel* ....15,700. .B 5
Kefar Ata ......32,700. .B 4
Kefar Sava .....43,200. .D 4
Lod ....40,900. .D 4
Maalot-
  Tarshiha* .....7,700. .A 4
Maghar* ....9,900. .B 5
Majd
  el Kurum* .....6,300. .B 4
Mevasseret
  Ziyyon* ....7,100. .E 4
Migdal
  Ha Emeq .....14,100. .B 4
Nahariyya ......28,600. .A 4
Nazareth ....45,600. .B 5
Nazerat
  Illit* ....23,400. .B 4
Nes Ziyyona ...14,600. .D 3
Nesher* ....9,400. .B 4
Netivot* ....8,500. .F 3
Netanya ....101,700. .C 3
Ofaqim ....12,700. .F 4
Or Aqiva ....8,100. .C 4
Or Yehuda* ....19,800. .D 3
Pardes Hanna ..15,900. .C 4
Petah Tiqwa ..124,000. .D 4
Qalansuwa* .....7,800. .C 3
Qiryat Ata, see
  Kefar Ata
Qiryat
  Bialik ....30,500. .B 4
Qiryat-Gat .....24,900. .E 3
Qiryat-
  Malakhi ....12,400. .E 3
Qiryat
  Motzkin ....26,300. .B 4
Qiryat Ono .....22,800. .D 3
Qiryat-
  Shemona ......15,900. .A 5
Qiryat Tivon ...11,000. .B 4
Qiryat Yam .....30,300. .B 4
Raananna ....37,200. .D 3
Ramat Gan ....118,950. .D 3
Ramat
  Ha-Sharon ...32,600. .D 3
Ramla ....43,200. .D 4
Rehovot ....68,400. .E 3
Rishon
  LeZiyyon ....100,000. .D 3
Rosh
  HaAyin* ......12,600. .D 4
Sakhnin ....12,700. .B 5
Sederot* ....9,000. .F 3
Shefaram ....16,800. .B 4
Tamra* ....13,100. .B 4
Tel Aviv ......325,700. .D 3
Tiberias ....29,300. .B 5
Tirat
  Karmel ....15,500. .B 4
Turan* ....5,700. .B 5
Umm el Fahm ..20,600. .C 4
Yavne ....13,700. .E 3
Yehud* ....13,000. .D 4
Yeroham ....6,600. .G 4
Yirka* ....6,400. .B 4
Zefat ....16,900. .B 5

*Does not appear on map;
key shows general location.
Source: 1983 official estimates.

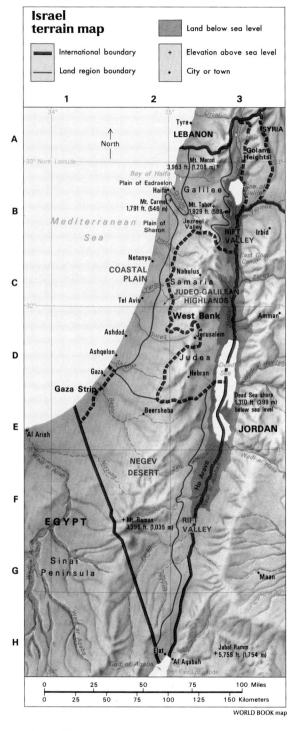

Israel terrain map

▬▬▬ International boundary	▨ Land below sea level
——— Land region boundary	+ Elevation above sea level
	• City or town

```
1        2        3
```

WORLD BOOK map

```
0    25    50    75    100 Miles
0  25  50  75  100  125  150 Kilometers
```

Physical features

Bay of Haifa	A 2	Mount Carmel	B 2
Besor (stream)	E 1	Mount Meron	A 3
Dead Sea	E 3	Mount Ramon	F 2
Gulf of Aqaba	H 2	Mount Tabor	B 3
Ha Arava (depression)	F 3	Plain of Esdraelon	B 2
Jezreel Valley	B 2	Plain of Sharon	B 2
Jordan, River	A 3	Qishon (stream)	B 2
Lake Hula	A 3	Sea of Galilee	B 3
Mediterranean Sea	B 1	Yarqon (stream)	C 2

of Galilee. There, during the 1950's, Israel drained Lake Hula and nearby swamps to create about 15,000 acres (6,100 hectares) of farmland.

The River Jordan, the longest of Israel's few rivers, flows through the northern Rift Valley. It travels through the Sea of Galilee and empties into the Dead Sea.

The Negev Desert, Israel's driest region, is an arid area of flatlands and mountains. The Negev has traditionally been used for grazing because its limited rainfall cannot support crops. But sections of the Negev are being brought under cultivation by means of irrigation. Water from the Sea of Galilee is pumped southward through the National Water Carrier, an extensive system of canals, pipelines, and tunnels. Regional systems connect with the carrier and extend to the northern Negev.

Climate

Israel has hot, dry summers and cool, mild winters. The climate varies somewhat from region to region, partly because of altitude. Temperatures are generally cooler at higher altitudes and warmer at lower altitudes. In August, the hottest month, the temperature may reach 98° F. (37° C) in the hilly regions and as high as 120° F. (49° C) near the Dead Sea. July temperatures average 73° F. (23° C) in Jerusalem and 81° F. (27° C) in Tel Aviv. In January, the coldest month, temperatures average 48° F. (9° C) in Jerusalem and 57° F. (14° C) in Tel Aviv.

Israel has almost continuous sunshine from May through mid-October. A hot, dry, dusty wind called the

Gary Braasch, Wheeler Pictures

Olive groves grow north of the Sea of Galilee in the Rift Valley, a long, narrow lowland in far eastern Israel.

Richard Lobell

The Negev Desert in southern Israel is the nation's driest region, receiving an average yearly rainfall of only 1 inch (25 millimeters). Irrigation is used to cultivate some parts of the Negev.

khamsin sometimes blows in from deserts to the east, particularly in the spring and fall.

Almost all of Israel's rain falls between November and March, much of it in December. There are great regional variations in rainfall. In general, rainfall declines from north to south and from west to east. In the driest area, the southern Negev Desert, the average yearly rainfall is only 1 inch (25 millimeters). In the wettest area, the hilly parts of Upper Galilee, average annual rainfall is $42\frac{1}{2}$ inches (1,080 millimeters). Brief snowfalls also sometimes occur in the hilly regions.

Economy

At independence, Israel was a poor country with little agricultural or industrial production. But Israel's economy has grown tremendously since 1948. The nation now enjoys a relatively high standard of living, despite having few natural resources and a limited water supply.

Large numbers of immigrants came to Israel in the years immediately after independence. Many of these immigrants were skilled laborers and professionals who greatly aided the nation's economic development. Financial assistance from Western nations, especially the United States, is also vital to Israel's economic well-being.

About half of the businesses in Israel are privately owned, and a fourth are owned by the government. The *Histadrut* (General Federation of Labor), a powerful organization of trade unions, also owns about a fourth of the businesses, farms, and industries.

Service industries—economic activities that produce services, not goods—account for about 67 per cent of Israel's net domestic product (NDP). NDP is basically the value of all goods and services produced yearly within the country. Service industries employ about 65 per cent of all workers. Many of Israel's service industry workers are employed by the government or by businesses owned by the government. Government workers provide many of the services needed by Israel's large

immigrant population, such as housing, education, and vocational training.

Tourism is a major service industry in Israel. Trade and transportation are also important service industries, in part because the country imports many of its goods.

Manufacturing accounts for about 23 per cent of Israel's NDP and employs about 22 per cent of its work force. Israeli factories produce such goods as chemical products, electronic equipment, fertilizer, paper, plastics, processed foods, scientific and optical instruments, and textiles and clothing. The cutting of imported diamonds is a major manufacturing industry. Government-owned plants manufacture equipment used by Israel's large armed forces. Tel Aviv and Haifa are Israel's major manufacturing centers.

Agriculture accounts for about 4 per cent of Israel's NDP and employs about 5 per cent of its workers. Agriculture formerly employed a much larger percentage of Israel's work force. But much of the work once performed by people is now performed by machines. Important agricultural products include citrus and other fruits, cotton, eggs, grain, poultry, and vegetables.

Israel's gross national product

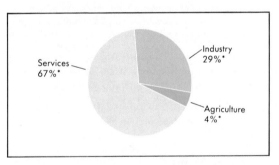

Services 67%*

Industry 29%*

Agriculture 4%*

The gross national product (GNP) is the total value of goods and services produced by a country in a year. The GNP measures a nation's total economic performance and can also be used to compare the economic output and growth of countries. Israel's GNP was $21,290,000,000 in 1984.

Production and workers by economic activities

Economic activities	Per cent of NDP* produced	Employed workers Number of persons	Per cent of total
Community, government, & personal services	45	484,500	36
Manufacturing	23	306,100	22
Trade	13	169,900	12
Transportation & communication	7	89,600	7
Construction	6	79,400	6
Agriculture, forestry, & fishing	4	72,100	5
Utilities	2	12,800	1
Finance, insurance, & real estate	†	129,500	9
Mining	‡	5,600	1
Other	—	9,800	1
Total	100	1,359,000	100

*Based on net domestic product (NDP). NDP is gross national product less net income from abroad, indirect taxes, and depreciation.
†Included in Community, government, & personal services.
‡Included in Manufacturing.
Sources: International Labor Organization; United Nations; World Bank.

Cameramann International, Ltd.

A mineral recovery plant removes such compounds as bromine, potash, and salt from the waters of the Dead Sea. The Dead Sea is Israel's leading source of minerals.

The government develops, helps finance, and controls agricultural activity, including fishing and forestry. Israel produces most of the food needed to feed its people. Agricultural exports provide enough income to pay for any necessary food imports. Most Israeli farmers use modern agricultural methods. Water drawn from the River Jordan irrigates large amounts of land in Israel.

Most Israeli farms are organized as moshavim or kibbutzim (see the *Rural life* section of this article). Israel also has some private farms, mostly owned by Arabs.

Mining. The Dead Sea, the world's saltiest body of water, is Israel's leading mineral source. Compounds drawn from the sea yield bromine, magnesium, potash, and table salt. Potash, used chiefly in fertilizers, is the most important mineral. Phosphates, copper, clay, and gypsum are mined in the Negev Desert.

Energy sources. Israel is poor in energy sources. It has no coal deposits or hydroelectric power resources and only small amounts of crude oil and natural gas. As a result, Israel depends primarily on imported crude oil and coal to meet its energy needs.

Trade. Because it has few natural resources, Israel imports more goods than it exports. The country's chief imports include aircraft, chemical products, rough diamonds, grains, iron and steel, machinery, military equipment, oil, ships, and vehicles. Israel's main exports are citrus fruits and other fruits and vegetables, chemical products, cut diamonds, electronic equipment, fertilizer, military equipment, processed foods, and textiles and clothing. The nation's main trading partners include the United States, Great Britain, West Germany, Italy, France, Belgium, and Luxembourg.

Transportation and communication. Israel has a well-developed transportation system. This system developed in part because of the need to move military troops and equipment quickly to any part of the country.

Most middle-class Israeli families either own an automobile or have one provided by their employer. Overall, Israel has about one car for every six people. Paved roads reach almost all parts of the country. Public transportation both in and between cities is provided primarily by bus. Most rail lines in Israel haul freight.

Ben-Gurion Airport, Israel's international terminal, is located at Lod, near Tel Aviv. Smaller airports are located at Atarot, near Jerusalem, and at Elat. El Al, Israel's international airline, flies regularly to the United States, Canada, Europe, and parts of Africa and Asia. Israel has three major deepwater ports—Haifa, Ashdod, and Elat.

Israel's communication system is one of the best in the Middle East. Israel has more than 20 daily newspapers, about half of which are in Hebrew. The rest are in Arabic, Yiddish, or one of several foreign languages. The Israel Broadcasting Authority, a public corporation set up by the government, runs the TV and nonmilitary radio stations. Israelis own about one TV set for every three people, and one radio for every two people.

History

For detailed information on the early history of what is now Israel, see the *World Book* article on **Palestine**. See also **Zionism.**

Cameramann International, Ltd.

Haifa's deepwater harbor has made this city Israel's chief port and a center of international trade.

Beginnings of a new state. European Jews began to settle in Palestine in the mid-1800's, out of a desire to live in the Holy Land. By 1880, about 24,000 Jews lived in Palestine, which was controlled by the Turkish Ottoman Empire. In the late 1800's, oppression of Jews in eastern Europe triggered the Zionist movement and eventually led to a mass emigration of Jews to Palestine. By 1914, there were about 85,000 Jews in Palestine, out of a total population of about 700,000.

In 1917, during World War I (1914-1918), Great Britain issued the Balfour Declaration, which expressed Britain's support for a national homeland for the Jews in Palestine. Britain was fighting to win control of Palestine from the Ottoman Empire as part of the war. The British hoped the declaration would rally Jewish leaders in Britain and the United States to support the British war efforts. At the same time, however, Britain promised independence to various Arab groups in the Middle East, hoping to gain their support against the Ottomans. The promises were vague, but Arab leaders assumed they included Palestine.

Following the Ottoman defeat in World War I, the League of Nations made Palestine a mandated territory of Britain (see **Mandated territory**). According to the mandate, Britain was to help Palestinian Jews build a national home. Many Zionists viewed the mandate as support for increased Jewish immigration to Palestine. But the British, fearful of the hostility of the large Arab population, proposed limits on Jewish immigration. These limitations, however, were not enforced.

Large numbers of European Jews came to Palestine in the 1930's to escape persecution by the Nazis. Alarmed by the Jewish immigration, the Palestinian Arabs revolted against British rule during 1936-1939. In 1939, Britain began attempting to limit Jewish immigration to Palestine. Jews strongly opposed this policy.

During World War II (1939-1945), the Nazis killed about 6 million European Jews. This led to increased de-

AP/Wide World

Jewish immigrants, *above,* began flocking to Israel after the nation was created in 1948. Israel opened its doors to Jews from anywhere in the world.

mands for a Jewish state, but Britain continued to limit Jewish immigration to Palestine. In 1947, Britain submitted the problem to the United Nations (UN).

Independence and conflict. On Nov. 29, 1947, the UN General Assembly agreed to divide Palestine into an Arab state and a Jewish state and to place Jerusalem under international control. The Jews in Palestine accepted this plan, but the Arabs rejected it. Fighting broke out immediately.

Israel officially came into existence on May 14, 1948, under the leadership of David Ben-Gurion. On May 15, Arab armies, chiefly from Egypt, Syria, Lebanon, Iraq,

In the 1948 war, Israel gained much territory in addition to the area that had been given to it by the United Nations (UN) Partition Plan of 1947.

The 1967 war resulted in Israel's occupation of Egypt's Sinai Peninsula and Syria's Golan Heights, and of the West Bank and Gaza Strip.

WORLD BOOK maps

Israel withdrew from the Sinai in three stages. It pulled back from parts of the peninsula in 1975 and 1979 and completed its withdrawal in 1982.

and Jordan (called Transjordan until 1949), attacked Israel, aiming to destroy the new nation. By early 1949, Israel had defeated the Arabs and gained control of about half the land planned for the new Arab state. Egypt and Jordan held the rest of Palestine. Israel controlled the western half of Jerusalem, and Jordan held the eastern half. Israel incorporated the gained territory into the fledgling country, adding about 150,000 resentful Arabs to its population. Hundreds of thousands of other Palestinian Arabs fled their homes and settled as refugees in parts of Palestine not under Israeli control and in neighboring Arab countries.

By mid-1949, Israel had signed armistice agreements with Egypt, Syria, Jordan, and Lebanon. But formal peace treaties were not signed because the Arab nations refused to recognize the existence of Israel.

Israel held its first election in January 1949. In February, the Knesset elected Chaim Weizmann president, and he officially appointed Ben-Gurion prime minister.

The Sinai invasion. Border clashes between Arab and Israeli troops occurred frequently in the early 1950's. In the mid-1950's, the Egyptian government began giving financial aid and military supplies to Palestinian Arab *fedayeen* (commandos). The fedayeen raided Israel from the Gaza Strip, the Egyptian-occupied part of Palestine. The Israelis raided the Gaza Strip in return. Egypt also blocked Israeli ships from using the Suez Canal and stopped Israeli ships at the entrance to the Gulf of Aqaba. In July 1956, Egypt nationalized the Suez

Important dates in Israel

1917 Great Britain issued the Balfour Declaration, expressing its support for a Jewish homeland in Palestine.
1920 Palestine became a mandated territory of Great Britain.
1947 The United Nations (UN) divided Palestine into a Jewish state and an Arab state.
1948 Israel came into existence on May 14.
1948 Egypt, Syria, Lebanon, Iraq, and Jordan attacked Israel on May 15, starting the first Arab-Israeli war. Israel defeated the Arabs and gained much territory before the UN ended the conflict.
1949 Israel held its first parliamentary elections.
1956 After Egypt nationalized the Suez Canal, Israel attacked Egypt, initiating the second Arab-Israeli war. Britain and France also attacked Egypt. The UN ended the fighting.
1967 Israel defeated Egypt, Jordan, and Syria in the Six-Day War. Israel captured the Sinai Peninsula, Gaza Strip, West Bank, and Golan Heights.
1967 Israel made the eastern half of Jerusalem, captured in the Six-Day War, part of the nation.
1972 Palestinian terrorists killed 11 Israeli athletes at the Summer Olympic Games in Munich, West Germany.
1973 Egypt and Syria attacked Israeli forces along the Suez Canal and in the Golan Heights, starting the Yom Kippur War.
1974 Prime Minister Golda Meir resigned because of public criticism of the government's handling of the Yom Kippur War. Yitzhak Rabin succeeded her.
1977 The Likud bloc gained control of Israel's government, ending 29 years of Labor Party rule. Menachem Begin succeeded Rabin as prime minister.
1978 Israel and Egypt signed the Camp David Accords, a major agreement designed to end the dispute between the two countries.
1979 Egyptian-Israeli peace treaty signed in Washington, D.C.
1982 Israel launched a major attack on Palestine Liberation Organization (PLO) forces in Lebanon.
1984 Labor and Likud formed a unity government after neither was able to achieve a majority in parliamentary elections.

Canal, which at the time was owned mainly by the British and French governments.

In response to the Egyptian actions, on Oct. 29, 1956, Israeli forces invaded Egypt. Britain and France attacked Egypt two days later. By November 5, the Israelis occupied the Gaza Strip and the Sinai Peninsula, and the British and French controlled the northern entrance to the Suez Canal. The United Nations—backed by the United States and the Soviet Union—ended the fighting and arranged the withdrawal of Israeli, British, and French troops from Egyptian territory. The UN also established a multinational peacekeeping force in the Gaza Strip and Sinai Peninsula. This force helped prevent another Arab-Israeli war for 10 years.

The Six-Day War. In late 1966 and early 1967, border clashes took place between Israeli and Syrian forces. In May 1967, the UN removed its peacekeeping force from the Gaza Strip and Sinai Peninsula in response to demands by Egyptian President Gamal Abdel Nasser. Nasser then sent large numbers of troops into the Sinai. He also announced the closing of the Strait of Tiran to Israeli ships, thus blocking the Israeli port of Elat.

Fearing that Arabs would soon attack, Israel launched air strikes against Egypt, Jordan, and Syria on June 5, 1967. Israeli planes almost completely destroyed the air forces of the three nations. Israel's ground forces then defeated those of the Arab states. The UN arranged a cease-fire, ending the brief war after six days.

At the war's conclusion, Israel held the Sinai Peninsula and Gaza Strip, as well as Syria's Golan Heights. It also occupied the West Bank, which had been controlled by Jordan and which included the eastern half of Jerusalem. Israel vowed not to withdraw from these territories until the Arab states recognized Israel's right to exist. In June 1967, Israel officially made the eastern half of Jerusalem part of Israel.

The Six-Day War again proved the superiority of Israel's military forces, but it also planted the seeds of continued Arab-Israeli problems. The occupation of the Gaza Strip and West Bank placed Israel in control of about 1 million hostile Palestinian inhabitants.

The rise of the PLO. Following the Six-Day War, the Palestine Liberation Organization (PLO) became prominent in the Middle East. Founded in 1964, the PLO is a confederation of Palestinian Arab groups that work to establish an Arab state in Palestine. The PLO is dominated by groups of fighters who use *guerrilla* tactics, including terrorist attacks and commando raids.

After the defeat of the regular Arab armies in the 1967 war, Arab leaders began increasing their support of the PLO's forces. These forces then stepped up guerrilla activity against Israel. Israel has retaliated with raids against PLO bases in neighboring Arab countries.

The Yom Kippur War. Israeli and Egyptian forces engaged in intense border fighting along the Suez Canal between April 1969 and August 1970. The Soviet Union provided military assistance to Egypt in the conflict, which was ended by a U.S.-sponsored cease-fire. On October 6, 1973, full-scale war broke out again when Egyptian and Syrian forces attacked Israeli positions along the Suez Canal and in the Golan Heights. The attack occurred on Yom Kippur, the most sacred Jewish holy day. Despite initial Egyptian and Syrian advances, Israel ultimately pushed back the Arab forces. It recaptured the

Israeli soldiers gather at the Wailing Wall following Israel's capture of East Jerusalem in the Six-Day War of 1967. The Wailing Wall is all that remains of the Jews' holy Temple of Biblical times.

Cornell Capa, Magnum

Golan Heights and some additional Syrian territory. A cease-fire was signed on October 24.

The Yom Kippur War had far-reaching effects. The Israeli economy suffered severely. Although Israel won the war, it suffered heavy losses of men and equipment. Many Israelis criticized the government's handling of the conflict. These criticisms caused Prime Minister Golda Meir to resign in April 1974. Yitzhak Rabin succeeded her in June. The Yom Kippur War also greatly increased Israel's dependence on the United States, which supplied Israel with arms and helped negotiate the cease-fire.

Recent developments. The Labor Party controlled Israel's government from independence until 1977. That year, parliamentary elections transferred control of the government to the Likud bloc. Menachem Begin, leader of the Likud, succeeded Rabin as prime minister.

Israeli-Egyptian tensions eased following the Yom Kippur War. In November 1977, Egyptian President Anwar el-Sadat announced that he was ready to negotiate a peace settlement with Israel. Later the same month, Sadat went to Jerusalem to address the Knesset and to meet with Begin. In September 1978, Begin, Sadat, and U.S. President Jimmy Carter held discussions at Camp David in the United States at meetings arranged by Carter. The discussions resulted in the Camp David Accords. The Camp David Accords focused on two objectives: (1) achieving peace between Egypt and Israel, and (2) achieving a comprehensive peace in the Middle East.

The first objective was met when, after negotiations, Egypt and Israel signed a peace treaty in Washington, D.C., in March 1979. In February 1980, the two nations exchanged diplomatic representatives for the first time. In addition, Israel completely withdrew from Egypt's Sinai Peninsula in 1982. Efforts toward meeting the second objective—a broader peace agreement that would deal with the problems of the West Bank and the Gaza Strip—have not been successful.

Tensions between Israel and the PLO escalated in the late 1970's and early 1980's. In 1978, Israel invaded southern Lebanon in an attempt to drive out Palestinian terrorists who had been launching attacks against Israel for several years. In June 1982, a large Israeli force attacked

southern and central Lebanon in retaliation for PLO attacks on northern Israel. The PLO withdrew most of its forces from Lebanon in August 1982. In 1985, Israel withdrew its forces from all of Lebanon except a security zone along the Lebanon-Israeli border. Although the Lebanon invasion removed many PLO bases from Israel's northern border, it resulted in numerous Israeli casualties and severely strained the nation's economy.

Begin resigned as prime minister in September 1983. Yitzhak Shamir of the Likud bloc succeeded him. Parliamentary elections were held in July 1984. The Labor Party won slightly more seats than the Likud bloc, but neither party won a majority and neither was able to form a coalition government. In September, Labor and Likud formed a unity government that was scheduled to last for 50 months. Under the unity government agreement, Shimon Peres, leader of the Labor Party, was named prime minister for a term of 25 months. Shamir became vice prime minister and foreign minister. Under the agreement, the roles of Peres and Shamir were reversed after 25 months—in October 1986.

The unity government included Cabinet members of both parties. One of its major achievements was in reducing Israel's high inflation rate, which had soared to more than 400 per cent in 1984. But the government was divided on how to attain peace with the Arabs. The Labor camp favored giving up portions of the occupied territories in return for peace agreements. The Likud bloc, however, supported Jewish settlements in the territories and their retention by Israel.

In late 1987, Arab residents of the Gaza Strip and West Bank began staging widespread—often violent—demonstrations and strikes against Israel's occupation. Israeli troops killed a number of protesters. A few Israelis were also killed, and hundreds of Palestinians and Israelis suffered injuries. The violence continued in 1988.

In July 1988, Jordan's King Hussein cut his nation's financial and administrative links to the West Bank. The king called on the PLO to take over the functions abandoned by Jordan. The king's action disappointed many Israelis, and others, who had hoped to settle the West Bank problem by granting the region some form of self-rule in confederation with Jordan.   Bernard Reich

Robert Frerck, Woodfin Camp, Inc.

Cairo, the capital and largest city in Egypt, is also the largest city on the African continent. The Nile River, the longest river in the world, flows northward through the Cairo metropolitan area. It provides precious water for agriculture and industry.

Egypt

Egypt is a Middle Eastern country located in the northeast corner of Africa. Little rain falls in Egypt, and dry, windswept desert covers most of the land. But the Nile River flows northward through the desert and serves as a vital source of life for most Egyptians. Almost all of Egypt's people live near the Nile or along the Suez Canal, the country's other important waterway.

Egypt ranks as Africa's second largest country in population. Only Nigeria has more people. Cairo, Egypt's capital and largest city, is the largest city in Africa.

Egypt's population has increased tremendously since the mid-1900's. In addition, many people have moved from rural villages to cities in search of work. As a result, the cities of Egypt overflow with people.

Most Egyptians consider themselves Arabs. About 90 per cent are Muslims. Islam, the Muslim religion, influences family life, social relationships, business activities, and government affairs. Al-Azhar University in Cairo is the world's leading center of Islamic teaching.

For thousands of years, floodwaters from the Nile deposited rich soil on the riverbanks. As a result, the Nile Valley and Delta region of Egypt contains extraordinarily fertile farmland. Agriculture provides jobs for more Egyptians than any other economic activity. Cotton is Egypt's most important agricultural export. Other crops grown in Egypt include oranges, rice, and sugar cane.

Egypt has expanded a variety of manufacturing industries since the mid-1900's. Cotton textiles and processed

---

Robert L. Tignor, the contributor of this article, is Professor of History at Princeton University and the author of a number of works on Egypt.

foods are the chief manufactured products. Petroleum provides much energy, as does hydroelectric power from the Aswan High Dam on the Nile River.

Egypt can rightly boast of being a birthplace of civilization. The ancient Egyptians developed an outstanding culture about 5,000 years ago. They created the world's first national government, as well as early forms of mathematics and writing. For the story of this great civilization, see **Egypt, Ancient.**

Egypt's hot, dry climate has helped preserve many products of ancient Egyptian culture. Tourists from all

Facts in brief

Capital: Cairo.
Official language: Arabic.
Form of government: Republic.
Head of state: President.
Head of government: Prime minister.
Area: 386,662 sq. mi. (1,001,449 km²). *Greatest distances*—east-west, 770 mi. (1,240 km); north-south, 675 mi. (1,086 km). *Coastline*—Mediterranean Sea, 565 mi. (909 km); Red Sea, 850 mi. (1,370 km).
Elevation: *Highest*—Jabal Katrinah, 8,651 ft. (2,637 m) above sea level. *Lowest*—Qattara Depression, 436 ft. (133 m) below sea level.
Population: *Estimated 1989 population*—51,405,000; density, 133 persons per sq. mi. (51 persons per km²); distribution, 51 per cent rural, 49 per cent urban. *1986 census*—48,205,049. *Estimated 1994 population*—56,956,000.
Chief products: *Agriculture*—corn, cotton, oranges, potatoes, rice, sugar cane, tomatoes, wheat. *Manufacturing*—chemicals, cotton textiles, fertilizers, processed foods, steel. *Mining*—petroleum.
National anthem: "Beladi, Beladi" ("My Country, My Country").
Money: *Basic unit*—pound. One hundred piasters equal one pound. For the price of the Egyptian pound in U.S. dollars, see **Money** (table: Exchange rates).

over the world travel to Egypt to see such wonders as the Great Sphinx, an enormous stone sculpture with the head of a human and the body of a lion. They can also marvel at the huge pyramids that the ancient Egyptians built as tombs for their *pharaohs* (rulers).

After ancient times, Egypt was ruled by a series of foreign invaders. In 1953, Egypt became an independent republic. Since then, it has played a leading role in the Middle East, especially in Arab affairs. Egypt's official name is the Arab Republic of Egypt.

Government

Egypt is a republic with a strong national government. According to the Constitution adopted in 1971, Egypt is a democratic and socialist society, and Egyptians are part of the Arab nation.

Egypt's national government has three branches. They are (1) an executive branch headed by a president, (2) a legislative branch called the People's Assembly, and (3) a judicial branch, or court system.

National government. The president serves as the center of power in Egypt. A candidate for president must be nominated by at least one-third of the members of the People's Assembly and confirmed by at least two-thirds of the members. The people then vote the candidate into office in a public referendum. Only one candidate is presented to the people. Egypt's president may serve an unlimited number of six-year terms.

The president may appoint one or more vice presidents, as well as the members of the Council of Ministers (cabinet). In turn, the central government selects all local administrators. Thus, the president has great influence and authority at all levels of government. The president also commands Egypt's armed forces.

The People's Assembly has 448 members elected by Egyptian voters. The president may appoint 10 more members. All members serve five-year terms. At least half the members must be workers or farmers. In theory, the People's Assembly has great lawmaking powers. In practice, the Assembly generally does little but approve the president's policies.

Local government. Egypt is divided into 26 political units called *governorates*. A governor appointed by the president heads each governorate. The governorates are divided into districts and villages, which also are run by appointed officials. Elected councils at each level of local government assist the appointed leaders.

Politics. The National Democratic Party is Egypt's largest political party. The president and most top government officials belong to this party. The National Democratic Party supports a mixture of public and private ownership, and strong ties with Western countries. Opposition parties may participate in general elections. Such parties include the New Wafd and Socialist Labor parties. All Egyptian citizens aged 18 or older may vote.

Courts. The Supreme Constitutional Court is the highest court in Egypt. Lower courts include appeals courts, *tribunals of first instance* (regional courts), and district courts. The president appoints judges on the recommendation of the minister of justice. The courts are otherwise independent of presidential control or influence. There are no juries in Egypt's court system.

Armed forces. Egypt maintains a large military, consisting of an army, a navy, an air force, and an air de-

© Marc Bernheim, Woodfin Camp, Inc.

Outdoor market places called *bazaars* are found in Egyptian towns and in old sections of the cities. Many kinds of goods are offered for sale or trade at bazaars.

Symbols of Egypt include the flag, *above left,* and the coat of arms, *above right.* The eagle is a symbol of Saladin, a Muslim warrior who lived during the 1100's. The eagle's claws hold a panel bearing the country's name.

WORLD BOOK map

Egypt lies in the northeast corner of Africa. It is bordered by the Mediterranean Sea, Israel, the Red Sea, Sudan, and Libya.

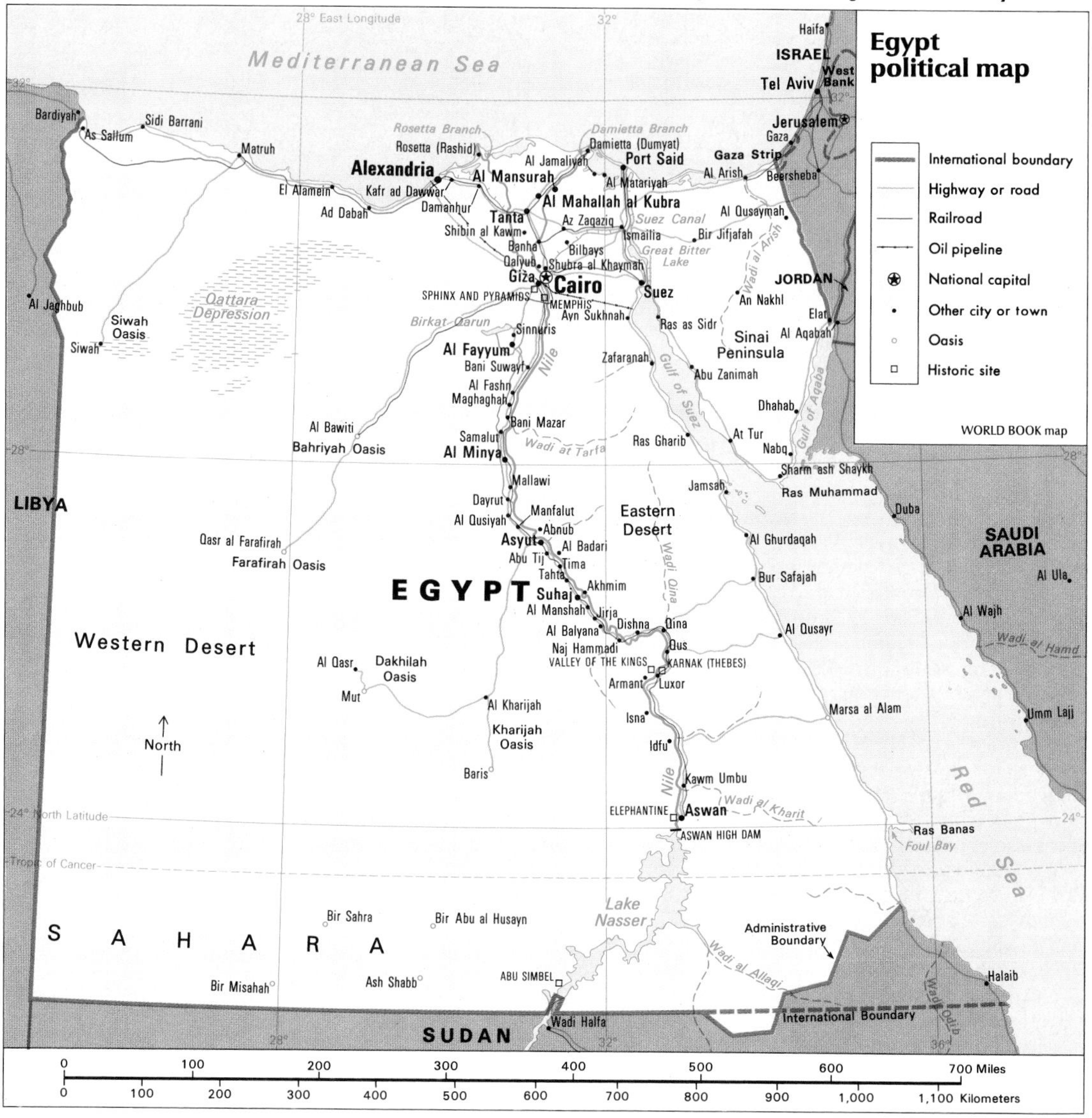

Egypt map index

Cities and towns

Abnub	39,440	C	4
Abu Tij	36,173	D	4
Abu Zanimah		C	5
Abu Kabir*	54,858	B	4
Ad Dabah		B	3
Akhmim	53,371	D	4
Al Arish		A	5
Al Badari	28,134	D	4
Al Balyana	26,101	D	4
Al Bawiti		C	3
Alexandria (Al Is-kandari-yah)	2,705,000	A	3
Al Fashn	33,549	C	4
Al Fayyum	213,000	B	4
Al Ghurdaqah		D	5
Al Hawamidiyah*	48,030	B	4
Al Iskanda-riyah, see Alexandria			
Al Jamaliyah		A	4
Al Jizah, see Giza			
Al Kharijah	26,647	D	4
Al Mahallah al Kubra	355,000	B	4
Al Manshah	27,945	D	4
Al Mansurah	323,000	A	4
Al Manzilah*	43,789	A	4
Al Matariyah	61,197	A	4
Al Minya	183,000	C	4
Al Qahirah, see Cairo			
Al Qasr		D	3
Al Qusaymah		B	6
Al Qusayr	12,548	D	6
Al Qusiyah	31,481	C	4
An Nakhl		B	5
Armant	42,434	D	5
Ashmun*	39,507	B	4
Ash Shabb		F	3
As Sallum		A	1
As Sinbillawayn*	49,346	B	4
Aswan	181,000	E	5
Asyut	257,000	D	4
At Tur		C	5
Ayn Sukhnah		B	4
Az Zaqazig	256,000	B	4
Banha	88,845	B	4
Bani Mazar	39,350	C	4
Bani Suwayf	146,000	C	4
Baris		E	4
Bilbays	69,112	B	4
Bilqas Qism Awwal*	50,230	A	4
Bir Abu al Husayn		F	3
Bir Jifjafah		B	5
Bir Misaha		F	2
Bir Sahra Biyala*	38,593	A	4
Bur Safajah		D	5
Bur Said, see Port Said			
Cairo (Al Qahirah)	5,875,000	B	4
Damanhur	203,000	B	3
Damietta (Dumyat)	93,488	A	4
Dayrut	31,627	C	4
Dhahab		C	6
Dikirnis*	38,433	A	4
Dishna	29,268	D	5
Disuq*	58,665	A	4
El Alamein		A	2
Faqus*	39,090	B	4
Giza (Al Jizah)	1,640,000	B	4
Hawsh Isa*	38,467	B	3
Hihya*	41,296	B	4
Idfu	36,828	E	5
Idku*	56,559	A	3
Ismailia	214,000	B	5
Isna	34,154	E	5
Jamsah		C	5
Jirja	50,961	D	4
Kafr ad Dawwar	174,000	A	3
Kafr ash Shaykh*	77,486	A	4
Kafr az Zayyat*	45,059	B	4
Kawm Umbu	47,155	E	5
Luxor	93,798	D	5
Maghaghah	39,743	C	4
Mallawi	74,197	C	4
Manfalut	41,196	C	4
Marsa al Alam		E	6
Matruh	27,608	A	2
Minuf*	55,208	B	4
Mit Ghamr*	72,168	B	4
Mut		D	3
Nabq		C	6
Naj Hammadi	19,384	D	4
Nasr*	40,234	B	3
Port Said (Bur Said)	364,000	A	5
Qalyub	62,564	B	4
Qasr al Farafirah		D	2
Qina	93,680	D	5
Qus	33,147	D	5
Ras as Sidr		B	5
Ras Gharib	14,237	C	5
Rosetta (Rashid)	39,129	A	3
Samalut	48,851	C	4
Sharm ash Shaykh		C	6
Shibin al Kawm	126,000	B	4
Shubra al Khaymah	497,000	B	4
Sidi Barrani		A	1
Sinnuris	42,010	B	4
Siwah		B	1
Suez	274,000	B	5
Suhaj	128,000	D	4
Tahta	44,841	D	4
Tanta	344,000	B	4
Tel al-Kabir (At Tall al Kabir)*		B	4
Tima	34,979	D	4
Zafaranah		B	5
Zifta*	50,559	B	4

*Does not appear on map; key shows general location.
Sources: 1983 official estimates for places with more than 100,000 people; 1976 census for other places with populations. Places listed without populations have less than 10,000 people; exact populations for these places not available.

fense command. It does so because of its desire to be the most powerful Arab country and because of its relationship with Israel, which remains tense despite the existence of the Egyptian-Israeli peace treaty. The spending necessary to maintain the armed forces has been a drag on the Egyptian economy.

About 445,000 people serve in Egypt's armed forces. Men between the ages of 18 and 30 may be drafted for three years of military service.

People

Population. Egypt has about 51 million people. The population is increasing rapidly—at a rate of about $2\frac{1}{2}$ per cent each year. About 99 per cent of all Egyptians live along the Nile River and the Suez Canal, in an area that covers only about 4 per cent of Egypt's total land. The rest of the people live in the deserts and mountains east and west of the Nile.

Most Egyptians consider themselves Arabs (see **Arabs**). The Beduoins make up a distinct ethnic minority among the Arab population. Bedouins are *nomads* (wanderers) who traditionally lived in small groups in the Egyptian deserts. Most of them have settled and become farmers, but some wandering tribes remain. The major non-Arab minority are the Nubians. These people originally lived in villages along the Nile in northern Sudan and the extreme south of Egypt, in a region called the Nubian Valley. Construction of the Aswan High Dam in the 1960's forced them to move north along the Nile.

Ancestry. Over the years, many groups of people have invaded Egypt and intermarried with the native Egyptians. As a result, present-day Egyptians can trace their ancestry not only to the ancient Egyptians, but also to such groups as Arabs, Ethiopians, Persians, and Turks; and Greeks, Romans, and other Europeans.

Language. Arabic is the official language of Egypt. Regional Arabic dialects have different sounds and words. The dialect of Cairo is the most widely spoken dialect throughout Egypt. The Bedouin dialects differ from those spoken by the settled residents of the Nile Valley. People in some desert villages speak Berber rather than Arabic. Many educated Egyptians speak English or French as a second language. See **Arabic language**.

Way of life

Life styles in Egypt's cities differ greatly from those in its villages. Egyptian city dwellers cope with such typical urban problems as housing shortages and traffic congestion. Although many live in poverty, others enjoy modern conveniences and government services that the cities offer. Villagers generally live much as their ancestors did hundreds of years ago. Most of them make a bare living by growing crops and tending animals. For people throughout Egypt, the beliefs and traditions of Islam form a unifying bond.

City life. About half of all Egyptians live in cities. Cairo, Egypt's largest city, is also the largest city in Africa. It has a population of about 6 million. About 10 million people live in the Cairo metropolitan area. The port city of Alexandria is Egypt's second largest city. Cities in Egypt are extremely overcrowded. Traffic moves slowly, and public transportation is inadequate. Riders crowd onto streetcars and trains.

Population density

The population distribution of Egypt is extremely uneven. The vast majority of the people live along the Nile River and its delta. Egypt's deserts are thinly populated.

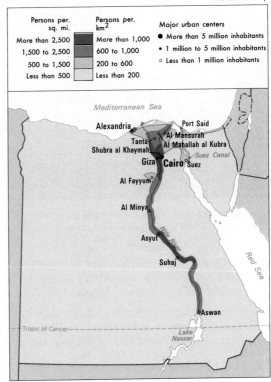

WORLD BOOK map

Persons per. sq. mi.	Persons per. km^2	Major urban centers
More than 2,500	More than 1,000	● More than 5 million inhabitants
1,500 to 2,500	600 to 1,000	• 1 million to 5 million inhabitants
500 to 1,500	200 to 600	○ Less than 1 million inhabitants
Less than 500	Less than 200	

Great extremes of wealth and poverty characterize Egyptian cities. Attractive residential areas exist beside vast slums. Lack of sufficient housing is a serious problem. Many people crowd into small apartments. Many more build makeshift huts on land that belongs to other people, or on the roofs of apartment buildings. Some of the poorest people in Cairo take refuge in historic tombs on the outskirts of the city, in an area known as the City of the Dead.

The cities provide a variety of jobs. Educated Egyptians work in such professions as business and government. Workers with little or no education find jobs at factories or as unskilled laborers.

Rural life. Until the 1900's, the vast majority of Egyptians lived in the countryside. Today, about half of Egypt's population lives in rural areas. Almost all of them are peasants called *fellahin*. They live in villages along the Nile River or the Suez Canal. Most of the fellahin farm small plots of land or tend animals. Many fellahin do not own land. They rent land or work as laborers in the fields of more prosperous landowners. A small minority of Egypt's rural people are Bedouin nomads who wander the deserts with their herds of camels, goats, and sheep.

The fellahin generally live in small huts built of mud bricks with thatched straw roofs. In southern Egypt, some huts are made of stones. Most huts consist of one to three rooms and a courtyard that the family may share

Norman Owen Tomalin, Bruce Coleman Ltd.

Many Egyptian fellahin farm small plots of land in the fertile valley along the Nile River and in the river's low-lying delta. The farm workers shown above are tending crops in the Valley of the Kings, near Luxor.

Thomas Nebbia, Woodfin Camp, Inc.

The slums of Cairo house many poor people. Egypt's crowded cities lack sufficient housing for the increasing population.

with its animals. Most homes have few furnishings and may contain only a few mats and benches, a low table, some earthenware pots, wooden dishes, and a copper kettle.

Each member of a village family performs certain duties. The husband organizes the planting, weeding, and harvesting of crops. The wife cooks, carries water, and helps in the fields. Children look after the animals and help bring water to the fields.

Egyptian villages are characterized by a strong sense of community. People come together to celebrate feasts, festivals, marriages, and births. Islam, the religion of most Egyptians, provides a strong unifying bond. *Mosques* (Islamic houses of worship) serve as centers of both religious and social life.

Clothing. Styles of clothing in Egypt reflect the different ways of life. Many well-to-do city dwellers wear clothing similar to that worn in the United States and Europe. Rural villagers and many poor city dwellers wear

Erich Lessing, Magnum

Peasant women bake bread in outdoor ovens in Luxor, *above.* The diet of most Egyptian villagers and poor city dwellers is based on bread and *ful* or *fool* (broad beans).

traditional clothing. Fellahin men wear pants and a long, full shirtlike garment called a *galabiyah.* Women wear long, flowing gowns in dark or bright colors.

Some Egyptians follow Islamic customs in their appearance. Men grow beards and wear long, light-colored gowns and skullcaps. Women wear robes and cover their hair, ears, and arms with a veil.

Food and drink. Most villagers and poor city dwellers in Egypt eat a simple diet based on bread and *ful* or *fool* (broad beans). At a typical evening meal, each person dips bread into a large bowl of hot vegetable stew.

Government-run stores in the cities distribute such food as meat, cheese, and eggs at controlled prices. However, supplies at these stores often run out. The well-to-do city people have more varied diets. They can afford to buy large quantities of meat and imported fruits and vegetables.

Sweetened coffee and tea are favorite beverages throughout Egypt. People also drink the milk of goats, sheep, and buffaloes.

Recreation. Soccer is very popular in Egypt. Many people attend matches or watch their favorite teams on television. But the main form of recreation in both cities and villages is socializing. People enjoy going to the *bazaar* (outdoor market place) to make purchases and to visit with friends. They also like to sit and talk while drinking cups of coffee or tea.

Religion. Islam is the official religion of Egypt. About 90 per cent of the Egyptian people are Muslims—followers of Islam. Almost all of them follow the *Sunni,* or orthodox, branch of Islam. Coptic Christians make up the largest religious minority group in Egypt.

Islam influences many aspects of life in Egypt. Religious duties include praying five times a day, *almsgiving* (giving money or goods to the poor), fasting, and, if possible, making a pilgrimage to Mecca, Saudi Arabia, the sacred city of Islam. Muslim traditions also affect government and law. For example, the government collects contributions from the wealthy and gives the money to the poor to fulfill the almsgiving requirement of Islam.

The government officially controls Islam in Egypt, and it appoints major Muslim religious leaders. In villages and city neighborhoods, some Muslims form brotherhoods and hold festivals and ceremonies outside of official control. Some of these groups use force in opposing the government and its religious leaders, whom they view as corrupted by non-Islamic values.

By law, Coptic Christians and other religious minorities may worship freely. But some Muslim groups have committed acts of violence against the Coptic community in Cairo and in parts of southern Egypt. See **Islam; Copts; Muslims; Mosque.**

Education. About 55 per cent of Egypt's adult population cannot read and write. During the 1940's, about 80 per cent of the people could not do so. Illiteracy is highest in rural areas. The government is working to improve the quality and availability of education in Egypt.

According to law, all children between the ages of 6 and 15 must go to school. But attendance is enforced only for children between the ages of 6 and 12. About 85 per cent of this age group actually attends school. About half of the children who complete elementary school go on to high school, and about 20 per cent continue their education beyond high school. Elementary and high school education in Egypt are free.

Egypt has 12 universities. Cairo University is the largest. Al-Azhar University, one of the world's oldest universities, was founded around A.D. 970. It is a center of Islamic scholarship.

Egypt's educational system has problems from the elementary through the university level because of overcrowding and lack of funds. There is a shortage of

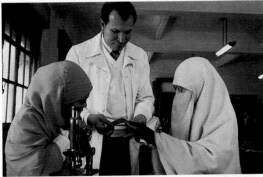
Female university students, wearing traditional Islamic clothing, study in a science laboratory at Cairo University, *above*. The school is Egypt's largest university.

teachers and school buildings, especially in rural areas. Despite these problems, Egypt's university graduates are among the best trained in the Arab world.

The arts. Egypt has a rich artistic tradition. The ancient Egyptians created many fine paintings and statues. They also produced and enjoyed music and stories. For more information about the arts of ancient Egypt, see **Egypt, Ancient** (Painting and sculpture; Music and literature).

Today, Egypt is a center of the Arab publishing and film industries. The celebrated works of Egyptian writers and filmmakers have spread Egypt's culture throughout the Arab world. During the mid-1900's, the works of such writers as Tawfiq al-Hakim and Taha Hussein realistically described Egyptian and Arab society. In 1988, Egyptian author Naguib Mahfouz became the first Arabic-language writer to win the Nobel Prize in literature.

Egyptians enjoy traditional and classical music, as well as modern Egyptian and Western music. Egypt's most popular singer of the 1900's, Um Kulthum, blended Eastern and Western themes in her songs.

The land

Egypt has an area of 386,662 square miles (1,001,449 square kilometers). It consists mostly of sparsely settled deserts. But the inhabited areas—along the Nile River and the Suez Canal—are densely populated.

Egypt has four major land regions: (1) the Nile Valley and Delta, (2) the Western Desert, (3) the Eastern Desert, and (4) the Sinai Peninsula.

The Nile Valley and Delta region extends along the course of the Nile River, which measures about 1,000 miles (1,600 kilometers) in Egypt. The Nile flows northward into Egypt from Sudan to Cairo. Just north of Cairo, the river splits into two main branches and forms a delta. The Nile River delta measures about 150 miles (240 kilometers) at its base along the Mediterranean Sea, and about 100 miles (160 kilometers) from north to south. See **Nile River; Delta.**

The valley and delta region contains most of Egypt's farmland. Without the precious waters of the Nile, Egypt would be little more than a desert wasteland. For thousands of years, annual floods of the Nile deposited valuable soils upon the narrow plain on either side of the

Muslims pray in a *mosque* (Islamic house of worship) in Cairo, *above*. Islam, the Muslim religion, is the official religion of Egypt. About 90 per cent of all Egyptians are Muslims.

Timothy O'Keefe, Bruce Coleman Ltd.

The Nile Valley and Delta region contains most of Egypt's usable farmland. A narrow plain on either side of the river has extremely fertile soil. Barren desert lies beyond the farmland.

Albano Guatti, The Stock Market

The Western Desert covers about two-thirds of Egypt's total area. It consists mainly of a large, sandy plateau. Scattered oases support small villages in the desert.

river and upon the low-lying delta. Almost all of Egypt's people live in the valley and delta region. Many of them farm its fertile soil.

In the southern part of the valley, the Aswan High Dam provides water for irrigation of the lands along the Nile. It also prevents severe damage from the Nile's annual flooding. Lake Nasser, a huge lake created behind the dam, catches and stores the floodwaters. The Aswan High Dam allows Egyptians to cultivate usable farmland more thoroughly. But the dam also collects a great deal

of valuable soil. As a result, this soil is no longer deposited on the farmland that borders the Nile. See **Aswan High Dam; Lake Nasser.**

The Western Desert, also called the *Libyan Desert,* is part of the huge Sahara that stretches across northern Africa. It covers about two-thirds of Egypt's total area. The Western Desert consists almost entirely of a large, sandy plateau with some ridges and basins, and pit-shaped areas called *depressions.* The Qattara Depression, Egypt's lowest point, drops 436 feet (133 meters)

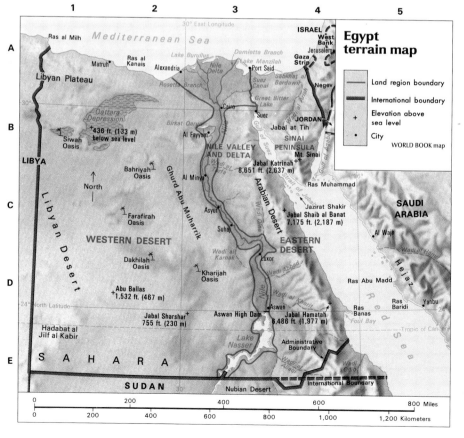

Physical features

Abu Ballas (mountain)	D	2
Arabian Desert	C	3
Aswan High Dam	D	3
Bahriyah Oasis	C	2
Birkat Qarun (lake)	B	2
Dakhilah Oasis	D	2
Damietta Branch	A	3
Farafirah Oasis	C	2
Foul Bay	D	5
Ghurd Abu Muharrik (dune)	C	2
Great Bitter Lake	B	3
Gulf of Aqaba	B	4
Gulf of Suez	B	3
Hadabat al Jilf al Kabir (plateau)	E	1
Jabal at Tih (plateau)	B	4
Jabal Hamatah (mountain)	D	4
Jabal Katrinah (mountain)	B	4
Jabal Shaib al Banat (mountain)	C	4
Jazirat Shakir (island)	C	4
Kharijah Oasis	D	3
Lake Burullus	A	3
Lake Manzilah	B	3
Lake Nasser	E	3
Libyan Desert	C	1
Libyan Plateau	A	1
Mediterranean Sea	A	2
Mount Sinai	B	4
Nile River	B	3
Nile Delta	A	3
Qattara Depression	B	1
Ras al Kanais (cape)	A	2
Ras Banas (cape)	B	4
Ras Muhammad (cape)	C	4
Red Sea	D	5
Rosetta Branch	A	2
Sabkhat al Bardawil (marsh)	A	4
Sahara (desert)	E	1
Siwah Oasis	B	1
Strait of Jubal	C	4
Suez Canal	A	3
Wadi al Allaqi (dry stream)	E	4
Wadi al Kharit (dry stream)	D	4
Wadi at Tarfa (dry stream)	C	3

Egypt terrain map

Land region boundary
International boundary
+ Elevation above sea level
• City

WORLD BOOK map

ISRAEL
West Bank
Jerusalem
Gaza Strip
Negev

Ras al Milh
Mediterranean Sea
Ras al Kanais
Matruh
Alexandria
Lake Burullus
Damietta Branch
Lake Manzilah
Port Said
Nile Delta
Rosetta Branch
Sabkhat al Bardawil

Libyan Plateau

Qattara Depression
+436 ft. (133 m) below sea level
Cairo
Suez Canal
Great Bitter Lake
Suez
Birkat Qarun
JORDAN
Jabal at Tih

Siwah Oasis
Al Fayyum
SINAI PENINSULA
Mt. Sinai
Jabal Katrinah 8,651 ft. (2,637 m)

LIBYA
Bahriyah Oasis
Al Minya
NILE VALLEY AND DELTA
Ras Muhammad

North
Ghurd Abu Muharrik

Farafirah Oasis
Asyut
Jazirat Shakir
Jabal Shaib al Banat 7,175 ft. (2,187 m)
SAUDI ARABIA
Al Wajh

WESTERN DESERT
Suhaj
EASTERN DESERT

Dakhilah Oasis
Wadi al Karnak
Luxor
Wadi Qena

Kharijah Oasis

Hejaz
Ras Abu Madd
Abu Ballas
1,532 ft. (467 m)
Ras Banas
Ras Baridi
Yanbu

Libyan Desert
Jabal Sharshar 755 ft. (230 m)
Aswan High Dam
Aswan
Jabal Hamatah 6,486 ft. (1,977 m)
Foul Bay
Tropic of Cancer

Hadabat al Jilf al Kabir

Red Sea

S A H A R A
Lake Nasser
Administrative Boundary

SUDAN
Nubian Desert
International Boundary

0   200   400   600   800 Miles
0 200 400 600 800 1,000 1,200 Kilometers

30° East Longitude
30°
24° North Latitude

Kevin Fleming, Woodfin Camp, Inc.

The Sinai Peninsula is a desolate desert region in northeast Egypt. Its terrain includes a sandy coastal plain, a high limestone plateau, and mountains.

below sea level. It contains salty marshes, lakes, and *badlands* (regions of small, steep hills and deep gullies). Small villages occupy scattered oases in the desert.

The **Eastern Desert,** or *Arabian Desert,* is also part of the Sahara. The desert rises eastward from the Nile as a sloping, sandy plateau for about 50 to 80 miles (80 to 130 kilometers). It then turns into a series of rocky hills and deep valleys called *wadis.* The land in this region is virtually impossible to cultivate. As a result, the Eastern Desert is mostly uninhabited, except for a few villages on the coast of the Red Sea.

The **Sinai Peninsula** is a desert area that lies east of the Suez Canal and the Gulf of Suez. It consists of a flat, sandy coastal plain in the north, a high limestone plateau in the central area, and mountains in the south. Egypt's highest point, Jabal Katrinah, rises 8,651 feet (2,637 meters) above sea level in the southern Sinai.

Though desolate, the Sinai Peninsula has valuable oil deposits. About 200,000 people live on the peninsula.

Climate

Egypt has a hot, dry climate with only two seasons—scorching summers and mild winters. Summer lasts from around May to October, and winter lasts from around November to April. January temperatures range from an average high of 65° F. (18° C) in Cairo to an average high of 74° F. (23° C) in Aswan. July temperatures reach an average high of 96° F. (36° C) in Cairo, and 106° F. (41° C) in Aswan. Daily temperatures in the deserts vary greatly. The average daytime high temperature is 104° F. (40° C), while the temperature may drop to 45° F. (7° C) after sunset. North winds from the Mediterranean Sea cool the coast of Egypt during the summer, so many wealthy Egyptians spend the hot summer months of July and August in Alexandria.

Average monthly weather

	Cairo						Aswan				
	Temperatures				Days of rain or snow		Temperatures				Days of rain or snow
	F°		C°				F°		C°		
	High	Low	High	Low			High	Low	High	Low	
Jan.	65	47	18	8	1	Jan.	74	50	23	10	0
Feb.	69	48	21	9	1	Feb.	78	52	26	11	0
Mar.	75	52	24	11	1	Mar.	87	58	31	14	0
Apr.	83	57	28	14	0	Apr.	96	66	36	19	0
May	91	63	33	17	0	May	103	74	39	23	1
June	95	68	35	20	0	June	107	78	42	26	0
July	96	70	36	21	0	July	106	79	41	26	0
Aug.	95	71	35	22	0	Aug.	106	79	41	26	0
Sept.	90	68	32	20	0	Sept.	103	75	39	24	0
Oct.	86	65	30	18	0	Oct.	98	71	37	22	0
Nov.	78	58	26	14	1	Nov.	87	62	31	17	0
Dec.	68	50	20	10	1	Dec.	77	53	25	12	0

Average January temperatures

Temperatures in Egypt are mild during winter. The southeast has the warmest winter temperatures.

Degrees Fahrenheit	Degrees Celsius
Over 61	Over 16
57 to 61	14 to 16
54 to 57	12 to 14
Below 54	Below 12

Alexandria
Port Said
Cairo
Suez
Al Minya
Aswan
Tropic of Cancer

Average July temperatures

Most of Egypt has hot summers, but winds from the Mediterranean Sea cool the northern coast.

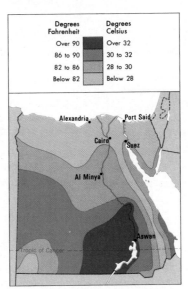

Degrees Fahrenheit	Degrees Celsius
Over 90	Over 32
86 to 90	30 to 32
82 to 86	28 to 30
Below 82	Below 28

Alexandria
Port Said
Cairo
Suez
Al Minya
Aswan
Tropic of Cancer

Average yearly precipitation

Very little rain falls throughout most of Egypt. But winter rainstorms sometimes strike the Mediterranean coast.

WORLD BOOK maps

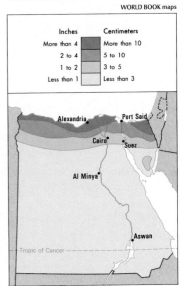

Inches	Centimeters
More than 4	More than 10
2 to 4	5 to 10
1 to 2	3 to 5
Less than 1	Less than 3

Alexandria
Port Said
Cairo
Suez
Al Minya
Aswan
Tropic of Cancer

Most of Egypt receives very little rain. Winter rainstorms occasionally strike the Mediterranean coast, where about 8 inches (20 centimeters) of rain fall each year. Inland, rainfall decreases. Annual rainfall in Cairo averages about 1 inch (2.5 centimeters). Southern Egypt receives only a trace of rain each year.

Around the month of April, a hot windstorm called the *khamsin* sweeps through Egypt. Its driving winds blow large amounts of sand and dust at high speeds. The khamsin may raise temperatures as much as 68 Fahrenheit degrees (38 Celsius degrees) in two hours, and it can damage crops.

Economy

Egypt is a developing country with difficult economic problems. But government policies have helped stimulate the economy in some areas, such as encouraging private investment in business. Service industries—such areas as banking, education, government, trade, and transportation—account for almost half of Egypt's *gross domestic product* (GDP). The GDP is the total value of all goods and services produced within a country in a year. Mining and agriculture each contribute about a fifth of the GDP. But agriculture has been Egypt's most important economic activity since ancient times.

During the 1950's and 1960's, the government of Egypt took over almost all large-scale business and industry. Today, government ownership still dominates in most

Economy of Egypt

Agriculture is an important economic activity in Egypt's Nile Valley and Delta region. This map shows the country's major farm products and indicates its chief mineral deposits.

WORLD BOOK map

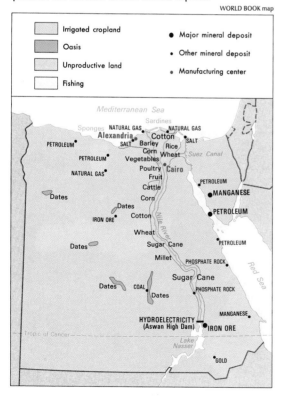

Egypt's gross national product

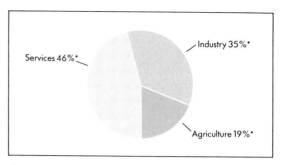

The gross national product (GNP) is the total value of goods and services produced by a country in a year. The GNP measures a nation's total economic performance and can also be used to compare the economic output and growth of countries. Egypt's GNP was $32,861,000,000 in 1983.

Production and workers by economic activities

Economic activities	Per cent of GDP* produced	Employed workers† Number of persons	Per cent of total
Agriculture, forestry, & fishing	19	4,006,000	38
Mining	17	20,700	1
Government	13	(‡)	(‡)
Manufacturing	13	1,577,000	15
Wholesale & retail trade	12	848,100	8
Transportation & communication	8	552,300	5
Construction	5	515,200	5
Finance, insurance, & real estate	5	131,100	1
Community, social, & personal services	4	2,046,000	19
Housing	2	(‡)	(‡)
Hotels & restaurants	1	(§)	(§)
Utilities	1	69,500	1
Other	—	751,000	7
Total	100	10,516,900	100

*Based on gross domestic product (GDP). GDP is gross national product adjusted for net income sent or received from abroad.
†Figures are for 1981.
‡Included in community, social, & personal services.
§Included in wholesale & retail trade.
Sources: International Monetary Fund; State Informational Services, Cairo.

major industries, including food processing, textiles, and steel. But most farms and small businesses are privately owned.

Egypt must import much of its food supply to feed its increasing population. At the same time, its petroleum exports have been hurt by falling prices on the international market and by increased demand within the country. Thus, Egypt faces a huge foreign debt, as the cost of its imports far exceeds its income from exports.

Service industries are economic activities that produce services, not goods. Such industries have become increasingly important to the Egyptian economy. Today, they account for about 46 per cent of Egypt's GDP and employ about 44 per cent of its workers. Many Egyptians work in such service industries as banking, government, and trade. Other important service industries include transportation, communication, and education.

Agriculture accounts for only about 19 per cent of Egypt's GDP. But it employs about 38 per cent of the country's workers. Egypt has about 6 million acres (2.4 million hectares) of farmland, almost all of it along the Nile. About 90 per cent is privately owned. Most of the farms in Egypt cover about 2 acres (0.8 hectare).

For centuries, Egyptian farmers relied on the annual floods of the Nile River to irrigate their fields and renew the topsoil. Each year, before the Nile flooded in July and August, farmers created a series of basins on surrounding farmland. When the Nile overflowed, these basins trapped the floodwaters and the *silt* (tiny particles of soil) that they carried. After the floodwaters withdrew, farmers planted their fields.

Beginning in the 1800's, Egyptians replaced the basin irrigation system with a system of year-round irrigation. They built dams, canals, and reservoirs to capture Nile water and make it available throughout the year. The changeover was completed with the building of the Aswan High Dam, which began operation in 1968. The dam has increased the amount of land irrigated all year by about $2\frac{1}{4}$ million acres (910,000 hectares). Today, nearly all of Egypt's farmland has continuous irrigation. As a result, farmers can plant crops the year around.

Cotton is Egypt's most valuable cash crop, and the country is one of the world's leading cotton producers. Egypt leads all countries in the production of high quality *long-staple* (long-fibered) cotton. Such cotton is known for its strength and durability. Egypt greatly increased its export of cotton during the American Civil War (1861-1865), when the Union blockade of ports interrupted cotton exports from the Southern States of America.

The Egyptian government requires farmers to use some land for growing food crops to feed the expanding population. Important crops include corn, oranges, potatoes, rice, sugar cane, tomatoes, and wheat. Egypt leads the world in the production of dates, which are grown mainly in the desert oases. Goats and sheep are raised for meat, milk, and wool. Cattle and water buffaloes, kept chiefly as work animals, also provide some milk. Many farmers raise chickens for meat and eggs.

Albert Moldvay, PSI FotoFile

Giant pyramids and other ancient wonders of Egypt attract visitors from all over the world. Many tourists ride camels on sightseeing trips through the deserts.

Mining contributes about 17 per cent of Egypt's GDP. Egypt has few natural resources, aside from the fertile farmland along the Nile River. Its most important minerals are petroleum and natural gas. Oil is found in the Eastern and Western deserts, the Sinai Peninsula, and offshore in the Gulf of Suez and the Red Sea. Natural gas is plentiful near Alexandria, in the Delta, and in the Western Desert. Egypt also has some valuable deposits of iron ore, manganese, and phosphate rock.

Manufacturing accounts for about 13 per cent of Egypt's GDP and employs about 15 per cent of the Egyptian labor force. Manufacturing has expanded rapidly in Egypt since the 1950's, when the government took a leading role in promoting industrialization. Egypt's government owns and operates most of the country's large and medium-sized businesses.

Food processing and textile production are the most important industries. Egypt also manufactures chemicals, fertilizers, pharmaceuticals, and steel. Cairo and Alexandria rank as the leading manufacturing centers.

Tourism. Egypt's warm, dry climate and its beautiful relics from ancient times attract visitors from all over the world. Large numbers of people travel to Egypt to admire such wonders as the giant pyramids and the Great Sphinx at Giza. Near Luxor, ancient tombs in the Valley of the Kings and magnificent temples draw many tourists. Visitors to the city of Cairo admire its beautiful

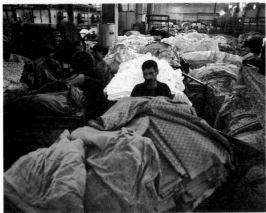

Topham from The Image Works

The manufacturing of cotton textiles ranks as one of Egypt's most important industries. Egypt leads all countries in the production of strong, durable *long-staple* (long-fibered) cotton.

Carl Purcell

The Aswan High Dam captures water from the Nile River and makes it available for year-round farming. The dam's hydroelectric plant generates much electricity at low cost.

mosques, city walls and gates, and traditional Islamic homes. See **Pyramids; Sphinx; Valley of the Kings.**

Energy sources. Petroleum provides most of Egypt's energy. Natural gas is also an important power source. The hydroelectric plant of the Aswan High Dam generates a large amount of low-cost electricity (see **Aswan High Dam**).

Foreign trade. Egypt imports more goods than it exports. Major imports include food, machinery, and transportation equipment. Egypt's major suppliers of imports are the United States, West Germany, France, Japan, and Italy. Important Egyptian exports include petroleum, cotton fibers and products, and fruits. Major markets for exports include Italy, Romania, France, the United States, and the Soviet Union.

Transportation and communication. For thousands of years, the Nile River was the primary means of transportation within Egypt. Today, transportation in Egypt takes many forms. Roads and railroads connect all of Egypt's important cities and towns. Two main highways link Alexandria and Cairo. One stretches across the desert, and the other passes through the densely populated Nile Delta. People use various forms of local transportation. Buses, cars, and motorcycles share Egypt's roads with bicycles, donkeys, and carts. Fewer than 2 per cent of Egypt's people own automobiles.

Cairo has an international airport where many airlines provide service to major cities of the world. Egypt's government-run airline, EgyptAir, provides service throughout the country and to and from foreign cities. Alexandria, on the Mediterranean Sea, ranks as Egypt's leading port. The country's two other major ports, Port Said and Suez, lie on the Suez Canal.

Cairo serves as the center of Egypt's communications industries. Egypt has more than 15 daily newspapers. The three most important papers—*Al-Ahram, Al-Akhbar,* and *Al-Jumhuriyah*—circulate throughout the major cities and into the countryside. Although the government does not allow complete freedom of expression, a number of newspapers express political dissent. The Egyptian government owns and controls the nation's radio and television stations. Only about 1 out of every 5 Egyptians owns a radio, and only about 1 out of every 10 owns a television set.

History

Egypt's long, colorful history goes back more than 5,000 years to about 3100 B.C. For the story of Egypt until it was conquered by Muslim Arab armies between A.D. 639 and 642, see **Egypt, Ancient** (History).

Muslim rule. In A.D. 639, Arab Muslims, inspired by the birth of Islam, burst out of Syria and invaded Egypt. At the time, Egypt was a province of the Byzantine, or East Roman, Empire. The Arabs captured Alexandria, which was then the capital of Egypt, in 642. Their commander, Amr ibn al-As, established a military camp and settlement in what is now part of Cairo. The Arab conquest transformed Egypt. The Egyptian people gradually adopted the Arabic language and converted from the Coptic Christian religion to Islam. See **Muslims.**

Egypt became an important province of the Islamic empire, which was ruled by Arab Muslim leaders called *caliphs.* Caliphs of the Umayyad *dynasty* (family of rulers) governed Egypt from Damascus (now the capital of Syria). They were followed by the Abbasid dynasty, which ruled from Baghdad (now the capital of Iraq).

In the mid-800's, the Abbasids began to lose control over their territories. For most of the period between 868 and 969, two Turkish dynasties—the Tulunid dynasty and the Ikhshidid dynasty—ruled Egypt almost independently of the Abbasid caliphs in Baghdad.

In 969, Fatimid rulers seized Egypt. The Fatimids, who had conquered other lands in northern Africa, made Egypt the center of their expanding empire and broke its ties with the Abbasid state. The Fatimids claimed to be descendants of Fatima, daughter of the prophet Muhammad, the founder of Islam. They were members of an Islamic minority group known as Shiites. The Fatimids founded the city of Al-Qahirah (modern-day Cairo), and they made it their capital in 973. They also built Al-Azhar mosque, which quickly became the center of Fatimid culture and religion. See **Fatimid dynasty.**

By the mid-1100's, the Fatimid empire was weakened by fighting among various factions and with the Christian Crusaders from Europe (see **Crusades**). In 1168, the Fatimid caliph asked Muslims in Syria to send an army to help defend Egypt from the Crusaders. Saladin, an officer in that army, helped drive the Crusaders out of Egypt. Then in 1171, he overthrew the Fatimid ruler, restored the *Sunni* (orthodox) form of Islam, and created an independent state. He became the *sultan* (prince) of Egypt. Saladin was a generous and just ruler. He and his descendants formed the Ayyubid dynasty, which ruled Egypt until 1250.

A group known as the Mamelukes served as the sultan's bodyguard. They were Turkish, Mongol, and Circassian slaves who were given special military training and rose to high positions in the army and government. In 1250, the Mamelukes revolted against the Ayyubid sultan and seized control of Egypt. The Mameluke general Baybars, who later became sultan, saved Egypt from ruin when his forces defeated invading Mongol troops at the battle of Ayn Jalud in Palestine in 1260.

For more than 200 years, rival Mameluke groups competed for authority, with the largest, best-organized, and most ruthless group taking power. But Egypt achieved more in art, architecture, and literature under the Mameluke rulers than at any time since the beginning of the Islamic period. See **Mamelukes.**

Turkish and French control. The Mameluke empire was declining by 1517. That year, Ottoman Turks under Sultan Selim invaded Egypt from Syria and overthrew the Mamelukes. But the Ottomans could not eliminate Mameluke influence. Mamelukes became *beys* (governors) of the regions of Egypt and held the real governing power. By the mid-1700's, Egypt's government was in disarray as Ottoman and Mameluke leaders competed for power. At the same time, the economy suffered from European control of Indian Ocean trade routes that bypassed Egypt.

In 1798, Napoleon Bonaparte led French forces into Egypt. They defeated the Mamelukes in the Battle of the Pyramids (see **Napoleon I** [Egypt invaded]). Napoleon hoped to disrupt the trade routes of Great Britain, France's chief enemy. He also wanted to establish a French colony in Egypt. Napoleon brought many French scholars with him to Egypt. Their scientific investigations helped revive the study of Egyptian relics, and their writings provided thorough descriptions of the country at the end of the 1700's.

Napoleon returned to France in 1799, leaving his troops behind. But military defeat, Egyptian resistance, and disease weakened them. The Ottomans, with British assistance, forced the French to withdraw in 1801.

Muhammad Ali and modernization. Muhammad Ali was an officer in the Turkish army sent to drive the French out of Egypt in 1801. In the disorder following the departure of the French, he gained power rapidly. By 1805, Muhammad Ali had established himself as Egypt's ruler. His killing of Mameluke rivals in 1811 made his rule secure from rebellion. From then on, he carried out a breathtaking program of modernization.

Muhammad Ali was an outstanding military and political leader. Many of his reforms came from a desire to strengthen Egypt's army. Muhammad Ali knew that his position in Egypt remained secure only as long as his army was more powerful than that of the Ottoman sultan. To achieve this goal, he brought in French military experts and patterned his army on that of France. In addition, Muhammad Ali introduced Western education into Egypt. He sent educational missions to Europe and brought European teachers to Egypt. Muhammad Ali also worked to improve agriculture. He began the transformation from basin irrigation to year-round irrigation. He also promoted the industrialization of Egypt.

Many of Muhammad Ali's reforms failed, partly because he tried to do too much too fast. He aroused the hostility of Great Britain, which feared the rise of a strong state in an important part of the Mediterranean Sea area. In 1841, the British forced Muhammad Ali to accept a decree that limited his army to 18,000 men. At the time of his death in 1849, Muhammad Ali's industries had collapsed, his educational missions had been disbanded, and many schools had been closed. See **Muhammad Ali.**

Muhammad Ali's immediate successors did not provide strong leadership. His son Said, also called Said Pasha, ruled from 1854 to 1863. Said granted a French company a contract to build a canal through the Isthmus of Suez. The canal was designed to shorten the sailing

route between Europe and eastern Asia by linking the Red Sea and the Mediterranean Sea. Construction of the Suez Canal began in 1859, and the canal opened in 1869.

Ismail, Said's nephew, ruled Egypt from 1863 to 1879 and became the *khedive* (ruler). Ismail successfully expanded the educational system, built many roads, canals, and railroads, and increased the export of cotton. But he spent large amounts of money on palaces, boulevards, and public displays. By the 1870's, Ismail's lavish spending had created a large national debt. To help pay off the debt, Ismail sold Egypt's shares of ownership in the increasingly profitable Suez Canal Company to the British government in 1875. As a result, Great Britain became the largest shareholder in the canal. See **Suez Canal** (History).

British control. During the 1800's, Great Britain's interests in Egypt steadily increased. When Ismail tried to combat European influence in Egypt, the British helped bring about his removal in favor of his son Tawfiq. In 1881 and again in 1882, Egyptian army officers led by Colonel Ahmad Urabi staged uprisings in an attempt to establish a more independent and reformist regime in Egypt. The breakdown in local order and acts of violence against foreigners eventually led the British to invade Egypt. In September 1882, British forces defeated the Egyptian army at the battle of At Tall al-Kabir and marched into Cairo. The British exiled Urabi and re-

Important dates in Egypt

(For events before A.D. 642, see **Egypt, Ancient.**)

A.D. 639-642 Muslim Arab armies conquered Egypt.

969-1171 The Fatimid dynasty ruled Egypt and made Cairo a leading Muslim city.

1171-1250 Egypt was governed by the Ayyubid dynasty.

1250-1517 The Mamelukes ruled Egypt.

1517 The Ottoman Turks invaded and occupied Egypt.

1798 Napoleon conquered Egypt.

1801 British and Ottoman troops drove the French out of Egypt.

1869 The Suez Canal was completed.

1875 Egypt sold its share of the Suez Canal to Great Britain.

1882 British troops occupied Egypt.

1914 Great Britain made Egypt a protectorate after World War I began.

1922 Great Britain gave Egypt nominal independence.

1940-1942 British forces fought Italian and German troops in Egypt during World War II.

1948-1949 Egypt and other Arab League countries invaded Israel after the United Nations (UN) divided Palestine into Jewish and Arab nations. The Israelis drove back the invaders, and the UN ended the war.

1952 Army officers forced King Faruk to give up the throne.

1953 Egypt became a republic.

1954 Gamal Abdel Nasser came to power in Egypt.

1956 The Egyptian government nationalized the Suez Canal. Israel, France, and Great Britain invaded Egypt, but the United Nations ended the fighting.

1958 Egypt and Syria formed the United Arab Republic. Syria withdrew from the union in 1961.

1960 Construction began on the Aswan High Dam. The dam began operation in 1968.

1967 Egypt and other Arab nations lost a war against Israel.

1970 Nasser died, and Anwar el-Sadat succeeded him as president.

1973 Egypt and other Arab nations fought Israel in the fourth Arab-Israeli war.

1978 Egypt and Israel reached a major agreement designed to end the disputes between the two countries.

1981 Sadat was assassinated, and Hosni Mubarak succeeded him as president.

turned Tawfiq to power.

During the late 1800's and early 1900's, the khedive ruled Egypt in name only. A series of powerful British administrators actually directed the country's affairs. They improved many aspects of life in Egypt. They put Egypt's finances in order, constructed a series of dams to modernize its irrigation system, and provided efficient government. But educated Egyptians criticized the British for neglecting such social concerns as education and public health. Egyptian nationalism began to emerge, and some people called for independence.

World War I (1914-1918) had a powerful impact on Egypt's relationship with Great Britain. Egypt was still actually a part of the Ottoman Empire when the war began. After the Ottomans allied with Germany, the British declared Egypt a *protectorate* (protected country). Britain wanted to protect its interests in Egypt and the Suez Canal. British and Indian troops defended the canal, and British warships prevented enemy ships from using it. Egypt became an important base of Allied operations against Ottoman territory and an important source of labor and supplies. This involvement of Egypt in the war led to outpourings of anti-British sentiment.

Independence. From 1919 to 1922, Egypt was in political turmoil. Nationalists led by Saad Zaghlul renewed demands for independence. When the British arrested and exiled Zaghlul, discontent against the British turned into revolt. For a few months in 1919, government broke down. Negotiations produced few results.

Finally in 1922, Great Britain granted Egypt its independence. But the British kept many powers, including the right to station troops in Egypt. A new constitution took effect in 1923 that established Egypt as a constitutional monarchy. However, Egypt made little progress toward ridding the country of British forces or improving living standards and economic growth. The monarch struggled with the British and with various political parties for supremacy.

In 1936, Egypt and Great Britain agreed to a treaty that reaffirmed Egypt's independence. This treaty reduced the number of British troops stationed in Egypt and restricted them to the Suez Canal region.

The 1940's. During World War II (1939-1945), Italian and German armies invaded Egypt in efforts to capture the Suez Canal. In 1942, the Allies halted the German advance into Egypt in the Battle of El Alamein. Many Egyptians blamed the British for the violence and hunger in Egypt during the war. For more information on Egypt's involvement in World War II, see **World War II** (Fighting in Africa; In northern Africa).

Egypt became a founding member of the United Nations (UN) in 1945. That same year, Egypt and other Arab nations established the Arab League (see **Arab League**).

After World War II, Egypt's parliamentary parties tried unsuccessfully to dislodge British forces from Egypt. They also had little success in dealing with such problems as poverty, illiteracy, and disease.

In 1947, the UN voted to divide Palestine into Jewish and Arab states. Israel was established in Palestine in 1948. Egypt and other Arab countries immediately went to war against Israel and were defeated. Egyptians, including army officers, blamed the government for the defeat, and support for such groups as the Muslim Brotherhood increased. The Muslim Brotherhood

wanted to establish a strictly Islamic government in Egypt and to reclaim all of Palestine for the Arabs.

Republic. In July 1952, a discontented army group known as the Free Officers seized power and sent the reigning monarch, King Faruk, into exile (see **Faruk I**). Gamal Abdel Nasser led the revolt. Nasser believed that Egypt's government was corrupt and that only a change in government could bring economic progess and complete political independence to Egypt.

The Free Officers organized in a body called the Revolutionary Command Council (RCC). The RCC officially took charge of Egypt in September 1952. The army's popular commander in chief, Muhammad Naguib, became prime minister. The council banned all political parties that had participated in elections before 1952, including the Muslim Brotherhood. In June 1953, Egypt was declared a republic, with Naguib serving as both president and prime minister.

During the first two years of military rule, Naguib shared power with Nasser, the deputy prime minister. However, Naguib and Nasser could not agree on policies. In April 1954, Nasser became prime minister. In October, Great Britain agreed to remove all its troops from Egypt by June 18, 1956. In November 1954, Naguib lost the presidency, and Nasser established unchallenged authority over Egypt. See **Nasser, Gamal Abdel**.

Nasser promoted economic progress in many ways. He increased government spending on education and took over all foreign-run schools. To encourage poor Egyptians to get an education, he provided government jobs for all university graduates. He also wanted to construct a huge new dam on the Nile River to increase the supply of water for irrigation and to provide hydroelectric power (see **Aswan High Dam**).

Nasser sought financing from other countries for the Aswan High Dam project. The United States and Great Britain expressed support for the project, but later, in July 1956, withdrew their offers of financial assistance. In retaliation, the Egyptian government seized control of the Suez Canal Company from its British and French owners later that month. Nasser announced that tolls from the canal would provide money for the Aswan High Dam project.

In the meantime, Egypt's relations with Israel worsened. During the 1950's, Egypt supported Palestinian Arabs who raided Israel from the Gaza Strip, the Egyptian-occupied part of Palestine. To retaliate, Israel raided the Gaza Strip. Egypt blocked Israeli ships from the Suez Canal and the Gulf of Aqaba.

In October 1956, Israel invaded Egypt and quickly occupied most of the Sinai Peninsula. Great Britain and France were anxious to regain control over the Suez Canal, and so they sent forces that captured Port Said. But the United States and the Soviet Union condemned the invasion and brought pressure to bear on Britain, France, and Israel. The invading troops withdrew, and the Suez Canal Company eventually was compensated for the loss of its property. A UN peacekeeping force was sent to patrol the Egyptian-Israeli border.

The United Arab Republic. Nasser emerged from the Suez incident as a powerful leader of both Egypt and the Arab world. He strongly believed in the importance of unity among the Arab countries. In 1958, a group of Syrian leaders asked Nasser to form a political union between Egypt and Syria. Nasser agreed. The two countries became the United Arab Republic (U.A.R.), and Nasser was elected president of the new nation. Later in 1958, Yemen (Sana) joined the U.A.R. in a loose union called the United Arab States. Syria eventually grew unhappy with Nasser's economic policies and his increasing power, and so they withdrew from the U.A.R. in 1961. Nasser kept United Arab Republic as Egypt's official name, however. Later in 1961, Nasser dissolved Egypt's ties with Yemen (Sana).

In 1962, Egypt intervened in a bitter civil war in Yemen (Sana). Egyptian soldiers could not end the conflict, but they remained in Yemen (Sana) until 1967.

Progress and conflict. The 1960's marked a period of economic and social change in Egypt. By 1962, Nasser's government had taken over almost all of Egypt's large-scale industries, banks, and businesses. Industry, especially textiles and food processing, expanded. Nasser turned to the Soviet Union for help in building the Aswan High Dam. Construction began in 1960, and the dam began operating in 1968. The dam improved and expanded Egypt's irrigation system and enabled Egypt to greatly increase its agricultural production.

Nasser took steps to narrow the gap between rich and poor Egyptians through land reform programs and expansion of the educational system. A law passed in 1952 made it illegal to own more than 200 *feddans* of land. (A feddan equals 1.038 acres, or 0.4201 hectare.) The government distributed any additional land to the *fellahin* (peasants). Land reform acts in the 1960's eventually limited land ownership to 50 feddans by any single landowner or to 100 feddans by a family. At the same time, the government built more schools in an attempt to improve educational opportunities. Many poor Egyptians were able to receive an education and eventually rise to professional and bureaucratic positions.

On June 5, 1967, Arab-Israeli tensions erupted again in what became known as the Six-Day War. Israel attacked and almost completely destroyed the air forces of Egypt and other Arab countries. The Israeli army then invaded the Sinai Peninsula and positioned itself on the eastern bank of the Suez Canal. When the fighting ended on June 10, Israel also occupied the Gaza Strip, the West Bank of the River Jordan, and the Golan Heights of Syria. The UN arranged a cease-fire.

The war was a territorial and military disaster for the Arab countries. Nasser had overestimated Egypt's military preparedness. The swift Israeli assaults took the Egyptian forces by surprise.

After the Six-Day War, Nasser resigned. But the Egyptian people refused to accept his resignation. Nasser remained president until his sudden death in 1970.

Renewed warfare and peace. Vice President Anwar el-Sadat won the struggle for power that followed Nasser's death. He restored Egypt's official name to the Arab Republic of Egypt in 1971.

Sadat proved to be a shrewd politician. He worked toward two goals: (1) the restoration of lands lost to Israel, and (2) economic growth. To achieve these goals, he believed that the support of the United States was vital. Thus, Sadat broke the ties with the Soviet Union that Nasser had maintained.

In October 1973, along with Syria, Sadat launched a bold and unexpected military assault across the Suez

Canal against the Israelis in the Sinai Peninsula. His early success helped win support from other Arab countries. But the Israeli army, resupplied by the United States, eventually drove Egyptian forces back across the Suez Canal. Nevertheless, Sadat drew U.S. attention to the importance of stability in the Middle East and emerged as a powerful world leader. Egypt and Israel agreed to a separation of their forces in the Sinai in 1974. In 1975, they reached an agreement in which Israel removed its troops from a part of the Sinai that it had occupied since 1967. The Suez Canal, which had been closed as a result of the Six-Day War in 1967, reopened in June 1975.

Sadat sought to regain the entire Sinai Peninsula and to end the state of war readiness that existed between Egypt and Israel. In 1977, he made a historic trip to Israel and addressed the Israeli *Knesset* (parliament). The following year, Sadat and Israeli Prime Minister Menachem Begin met in the United States for discussions with U.S. President Jimmy Carter. The discussions resulted in a major agreement called the Camp David Accords. It was the first such agreement between Israel and an Arab state. The agreement guaranteed the return of the Sinai Peninsula to Egypt, and called for the creation of a peace treaty between Egypt and Israel. The treaty was signed in 1979.

At home, Sadat worked to revitalize the private sector of the economy. His economic policy, called *infitah* ("opening" in Arabic), was designed to allow foreign investment in Egypt and greater private participation in the economy. With this policy, Sadat hoped to improve relations with the United States and initiate a new wave of economic growth.

Despite Sadat's vision, his policies did not meet with great success. Other Arab states rejected his treaty with Israel and criticized Sadat for negotiating independently of them. They removed Egypt from membership in the Arab League in 1979. Many Egyptians felt that Sadat had given up too much to Israel in his desire to regain the Sinai Peninsula. In addition, prosperity did not follow the signing of the Accords, as many had hoped. Discontent grew, led by Islamic extremists. A group of extremists assassinated Sadat in October 1981 as he watched a military parade.

Egypt today. Vice President Hosni Mubarak succeeded Sadat as president. He reaffirmed Sadat's peace treaty with Israel, sustained ties with the United States, and encouraged the private sector of the economy. But Mubarak was much less outspoken on many controversial issues and worked to repair Egypt's ties with other Arab nations. He also made the government more responsive to the opinions of the Egyptian people.

While Nasser and Sadat were leaders of world importance, neither brought great economic progress to Egypt. Today, Egypt's social problems remain much the same as they have throughout the 1900's. The population is too large for the resources of the country, and it continues to grow rapidly. Egypt's strategic importance enables its rulers to gain economic and military assistance from the Soviet Union and the United States. But so far, these alliances have not produced great benefits for the people.   Robert L. Tignor

1883
1884
1885
1886
1887

1888

A Year in Perspective

From the perspective of 1988, *The World Book Year Book* looks at some of the political developments and popular culture of 100 years ago and, in a special section, casts a backward glance at events of 50 years ago as reported in *The World Book Encyclopedia Annual for 1938.*

See page 549 ▶

Scandals of 1888 include U.S. pension fraud (depicted as a greedy pig, *right*) and the failure of London police to catch Jack the Ripper (shown as one artist imagined him, *below right*) despite posters asking the public to help, *below*.

An 1888 portrait by Paul Gauguin shows his friend Vincent van Gogh painting one of several versions of *Sunflowers* done that year, the most fertile in van Gogh's life. Gauguin painted this portrait while visiting van Gogh in Arles, France.

By Sara Dreyfuss

1888: A Year in Perspective

Jack the Ripper terrorized London, and Benjamin Harrison edged out Grover Cleveland in a close U.S. presidential election.

Tariffs are the chief issue in the 1888 U.S. presidential race. Republicans Benjamin Harrison and Levi P. Morton support high tariffs, which they call "protection" for domestic industry. Under the banner of "tariff reform," Democrats Grover Cleveland and Allen Thurman propose lower tariffs.

The author:
Sara Dreyfuss is Associate Editor of *The World Book Year Book.*

Knife in hand, the killer prowled the dark streets of London in search of victims. Between Aug. 31 and Nov. 9, 1888, he found five of them, all women who worked as prostitutes in Whitechapel, a notorious slum with an incongruously lovely name. The killer cut their throats, then slashed and mutilated the bodies so brutally that he came to be called Jack the Ripper.

The police received hundreds of letters from people who claimed to be Jack the Ripper, but only one seemed authentic. The writer gave his address as "From Hell" and enclosed part of a kidney of one of the victims. The press, the public, and even Queen Victoria protested what *The Illustrated London News* called "the failure of the police either to detect the criminal or to guard against the commission of the atrocities." The charges of police incompetence caused the head of Scotland Yard, Sir Charles Warren, to resign on November 8.

Many people have pored over the evidence and written thousands of books and articles trying to solve the case. Suspects include the Duke of Clarence, an eccentric nephew of Queen Victoria; and Montague J. Druitt, an alcoholic schoolmaster who drowned in the River Thames on Dec. 1, 1888. But the identity of Jack the Ripper may never be known.

Sharing headlines with the Ripper murders in 1888 was a presidential election in the United States. The Democrats nominated Grover Cleveland, the tough-minded and hard-working President, for what they hoped would be his second term. Allen

G. Thurman, a former Ohio senator, became Cleveland's running mate. The Republicans nominated Benjamin Harrison for President and Levi P. Morton, a Wall Street banker, for Vice President. Harrison's great-grandfather, also named Benjamin, had been a signer of the Declaration of Independence. The candidate's grandfather, William Henry Harrison, had been a popular President of the United States. Benjamin Harrison himself had served heroically in the Union Army during the Civil War (1861-1865), rising to the rank of brigadier general. More important, he had a clean and nearly blank political record and had done nothing to offend anyone. *Frank Leslie's Illustrated Newspaper* commented, "This meritorious grandson of a popular President is an available candidate, because, being a negative statesman and a rather colorless public man, he could probably unite [voters] from all the elements and in all the sections."

Cleveland and the art of making enemies

President Cleveland, in contrast, had made more than his share of enemies. He had alienated party politicians by awarding government jobs on the basis of merit, not party service. *Life*, then a magazine of humor and opinion, said, "Grover Cleveland, as President of the United States, has humiliated the politicians, disappointed the spoilsmen, and has done what he considered to be for the best interests of the people at large."

Cleveland had also antagonized many veterans by taking a firm stand against pension fraud. Congress set aside each Friday night to approve veterans' pension claims. Cleveland once received 240 pension bills from Congress in a single day, 198 of them covering claims already rejected by the Bureau of Pensions.

Cleveland reviewed each claim individually and vetoed hundreds of them, staying up until 2 or 3 a.m. to write his vetoes. The Grand Army of the Republic, a politically powerful society of veterans who had fought for the North in the Civil War, opposed the President because of his stand on pensions.

French Prime Minister Charles Floquet wins a duel with Georges Boulanger, a member of Parliament, wounding him in the neck in July 1888. Georges Clemenceau, far right, who later became prime minister, serves as Floquet's second.

Worst of all, Cleveland had made many enemies among wealthy manufacturers, who wanted the protection of high *tariffs* (taxes on imports) for their industries. Cleveland called for tariffs to be lowered because the government was collecting more money than it spent. The bloated Treasury kept too much cash out of circulation and provided a constant temptation for extravagance.

Tariffs became the main issue in the campaign. Harrison and the Republicans supported high tariffs, which they called *protection* because high tariffs shield domestic industries from foreign competition. The Republican Party platform declared, "We are uncompromisingly in favor of the American system of protection."

All the votes money can buy

Even with Cleveland's many enemies, the President received about 90,000 more votes than Harrison. But, by carrying such key states as Indiana and New York, Harrison won the election in the Electoral College, 233 to 168. Many observers then—and many historians today—believe fraud also helped the Republicans win. After the election, *Harper's Weekly* magazine declared, "Knowing, as we all know, the great number of purchasable and purchased votes, it would be impossible to interpret peremptorily the defeat of Mr. Cleveland . . . as a deliberate rejection of the policy of reducing [tariffs] which his candidacy represented."

President-elect Harrison remarked to Chairman Matthew S. Quay of the Republican National Committee, "Providence has given us the victory." Quay later repeated the conversation to a colleague and exclaimed, "Think of the man! He ought to know that Providence hadn't a damn thing to do with it." Quay added that Harrison would never know how many Republicans "were compelled to approach the gates of the penitentiary to make him President!"

Buying votes was easy in 1888, when most people in the United States did not vote by secret ballot. "Under our present system," said *Scribner's Magazine*, "whole squads of voters are marched to the polls with their ballots in their hands so that the boss can see them from the time they are received till they are deposited in the ballot-boxes." In an effort to reduce fraud, Kentucky and Massachusetts that year adopted

Here are your

1989 *Year Book* Cross-Reference Tabs

For insertion in your *World Book*

Each year, *The World Book Year Book* adds a valuable dimension to your *World Book* set. The Cross-Reference Tab System is designed especially to help youngsters and parents alike link *The Year Book*'s new and revised *World Book* articles, its Special Reports, and its Close-Ups to the related *World Book* articles they update.

How to use these Tabs

First, remove this page from *The Year Book*. The top Tab on this page is ADOLESCENT. Turn to the A volume of your *World Book* and find the page with the ADOLESCENT article on it. Affix the ADOLESCENT Tab to that page.

Note that the QUAYLE, DAN, Tab should go on a *World Book* page where there is no such article. Put it in the Q-R volume on the same page as the QUASIMODO, SALVATORE, article.

Put all of your Tabs in your *World Book* volumes, and your new *Year Book* will be linked to your encyclopedia set.

Special Report
ADOLESCENT
1989 Year Book, p. 56

Special Report
ART AND THE ARTS
1989 Year Book, p. 70

Year Book Close-Up
AUSTRALIA
1989 Year on File (Australia)

Year Book Close-Up
BERLIN, IRVING
1989 Year on File (Popular Music)

New Article
BUSH, GEORGE HERBERT WALKER
1989 Year Book, p. 498

New Article
CONGRESS OF THE U.S.
1989 Year Book, p. 504

Year Book Close-Up
DROUGHT
1989 Year on File (Weather)

Special Report
DRUG ABUSE
1989 Year Book, p. 56

Special Report
EAR
1989 Year Book, p. 140

New Article
EGYPT
1989 Year Book, p. 524

Special Report
GERMANY
1989 Year Book, p. 108

Special Report
HEARING
1989 Year Book, p. 140

New Article
ISRAEL
1989 Year Book, p. 512

Special Report
KOREA
1989 Year Book, p. 124

New Article
QUAYLE, DAN
1989 Year Book, p. 511

Year Book Close-Up
RUSSIA
1989 Year on File (Union of Sov. S. R.)

Year Book Close-Up
SMOKING
1989 Year on File (Public Health)

Special Report
SPACE TRAVEL
1989 Year Book, p. 38

Special Report
TROPICAL RAIN FOREST
1989 Year Book, p. 88

Year Book Close-Up
WEATHER
1989 Year on File (Weather)

the secret, or Australian, ballot system, in which the voter marks the ballot in a private booth to guarantee secrecy. The new system, *Scribner's* said, would "practically put an end to bribery, for no briber will pay money to a voter whom he cannot follow to the polls to see if he votes as he is bribed."

Dueling politicians

The U.S. presidential election, however corrupt, seemed immensely dignified compared with a clash between two French politicians. In July 1888, General Georges Boulanger, a military hero and member of Parliament, challenged Prime Minister Charles Floquet to a duel with swords. Boulanger thought Floquet had insulted him in Parliament. Floquet, at the age of 65, was 15 years older than Boulanger and less experienced with a sword. Nevertheless, the prime minister wounded Boulanger in the neck and won the duel. Floquet's second, the future Prime Minister Georges Clemenceau, roared with laughter. *Harper's Weekly* told its readers, "That civilized statesmen and soldiers should hack and hew at each other after exchanging insults is, in this age, a remarkable fact."

Colonizing the world . . . and exploring it

The major European nations continued to grab for overseas colonies in 1888, with much of the action taking place among the islands of the Pacific Ocean. Germany took over the South Pacific island of Nauru, and Great Britain annexed Christmas Island (now part of Kiribati) and the Cook Islands. Britain also made protectorates of North Borneo and Sarawak (now the Malaysian state of Sarawak and Sabah) and of what is now the independent nation of Brunei. In the Caribbean Sea, Trinidad and Tobago became a single colony under British rule.

In January 1888, a group of explorers, scientists, educators, and other prominent men met in Washington, D.C., and founded the National Geographic Society, "a society for the increase and diffusion of geographical knowledge." The society became the world's largest scientific and educational organization, with more than 10 million members. It has sponsored exploration and research throughout the world.

Storms and plagues

The winter of 1888 brought unusually severe weather. In mid-January, a terrible blizzard swept across the Dakotas, Iowa, Minnesota, Montana, and Nebraska. It was called the Schoolchildren's Storm because it struck while many children were in school or just starting home. More than 200 youngsters froze to death. On February 19, a cyclone reduced the city of Mount Vernon, Ill., to rubble, killing 25 people.

The most famous storm in New York City history, the Blizzard of '88, struck on March 11, catching New Yorkers unprepared because the previous day had been warm and springlike. The

New York City residents dig out after the Blizzard of '88 buries the city in huge snowdrifts in March.

storm dumped 20 inches (50 centimeters) of snow on the city, and howling winds drove the snow into drifts as high as 20 to 30 feet (6 to 9 meters). The blizzard killed more than 200 people and left the city without transportation, communication, or food supplies. "There was no footfall, no sound of busy wheels or bells, no voice nor cry in the long white drifts, where the streets had been," said *Leslie's* newspaper. "It might have seemed, but for the roar of the wind, like a dream of sudden death."

Beginning in August 1888, a yellow fever epidemic swept through Jacksonville, Fla., causing nearly 5,000 cases of illness and at least 427 deaths. The epidemic was even more frightening because no one knew what caused the disease or how to prevent it. It would be 12 years before a U.S. Army physician named Walter Reed showed that mosquitoes carried yellow fever, and 39 years before researchers proved that a virus caused the disease. In 1888, *Harper's Weekly* could only speculate, "Yellow-fever is undoubtedly the offspring of heat, humidity, and filth."

To combat the epidemic, health officials lit huge bonfires of pine and tar and fired round after round of heavy ammunition in efforts to "purify the air." The authorities also quarantined Jacksonville. People who tried to leave were held in a detention camp for 10 days and released only if they showed no disease.

Meanwhile, medical science was making dramatic progress in learning the causes and prevention of illness. The Pasteur Institute, one of the world's leading centers for the study of disease, was founded in Paris on Nov. 14, 1888. It was named for the great French scientist Louis Pasteur, who had developed the first rabies vaccine and who became the institute's first director.

New uses for electricity

Inventors in 1888 rapidly developed new uses for electricity, a recently harnessed form of energy. The first electric motors ran on direct current (DC), which flows in only one direction. In 1888, Nikola Tesla, an electrical engineer born in Austria-Hungary, patented a motor that ran on alternating current (AC), which regularly changes direction. Today, nearly all household appliances in the United States and Canada use AC motors similar to the one designed by Tesla.

Frank J. Sprague, a former assistant to the great inventor Thomas A. Edison, developed the first practical electric streetcar system in 1888. Electric motors at that time were too erratic to be used for transportation, alternately creeping and roaring at high speeds. Nevertheless, Sprague signed a contract with the city of Richmond, Va., to develop and install an electric trolley system. He devised innovations to enable a streetcar motor to use current efficiently and to accelerate smoothly, including a device called a *rheostat* that furnished progressively more current to the motor as the streetcar got underway.

One night, Sprague took an experimental model of his streetcar for a trial run on one of Richmond's steepest hills. Despite the late hour, a crowd gathered and watched, to Sprague's embarrassment, as the test vehicle jerked to a halt. "Unwilling to admit serious trouble," Sprague later wrote, "I [said] in a tone that could be overheard, that there was some slight trouble in the circuits, and would [an assistant] go for the instruments. . . . Then, turning out the light, I lay down on a seat to wait, while the crowd gradually dispersed. After waiting a long time, [my assistant returned] with those 'instruments' . . . four of them—big powerful mules." The mules towed the streetcar back to Sprague's shop for more work.

A Red Cross nurse tends her patient during a yellow fever epidemic that killed at least 427 people in Jacksonville, Fla., in 1888.

Sprague ironed out the problems and on Feb. 2, 1888, opened the streetcar line for regular service. For 5 cents, a person could ride anywhere on the system's 12 miles (19 kilometers) of track at speeds up to 20 miles (30 kilometers) an hour. Cars left every 10 minutes and climbed smoothly up the steepest hills. The system was so successful that the city of Boston soon ordered 20 streetcars from Sprague. By 1890, trolleys based on Sprague's design were either running or being built in nearly 200 cities.

And for a smoother ride . . .

Another invention of 1888 revolutionized other transportation. On October 31, Scottish veterinarian John B. Dunlop received a patent for "an improvement in Tyres for the wheels of bicycles, tricycles and other road cars." The improvement was the *pneu-*

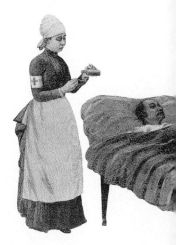

One of the first successful electric streetcar systems, developed by Frank J. Sprague in 1888, links Boston and its suburb of Brookline.

Scottish veterinarian John B. Dunlop takes a spin on a bicycle equipped with the smooth-riding *pneumatic* (air-filled) tires that he patented in October 1888.

matic (air-filled) tire, which provided a smoother ride and made pedaling easier than the solid rubber tires then used. Dunlop made his first tires from a length of garden hose after watching his 10-year-old son ride a tricycle around the yard.

Photography for all

In 1888, the only photographers were a few enthusiasts who knew how to use complicated equipment and could afford to buy it. The inventor George Eastman changed all that by marketing the first camera for amateur photographers. The camera, called the Kodak, was lightweight and easy to use. It produced 100 round snapshots on a single roll of film installed at the factory. After finishing the roll, the photographer sent the entire camera to an Eastman plant. The plant developed the film, made prints, reloaded the camera with new film, and returned it to the customer. "You Press the Button, We Do the Rest," the Kodak slogan declared.

Suddenly, picture-taking became a hobby or pastime for millions. *Scientific American* said, "We believe this system . . . promises to make the practice of photography well nigh universal. . . . The pleasures of journeys through foreign countries will be increased by knowing that any novel sight the traveler may see can be caught and preserved to show to his friends . . . while for affording endless amusement to young people, nothing could be devised that would be more profitable and interesting."

The camera mightier than the pen

Jacob A. Riis, a crusading Danish-born newspaper reporter in New York City, put the camera to serious use and demonstrated

The Kodak Camera

the power of photography as a weapon for social reform. Riis's work as a police reporter often took him into the slums, where, according to *Leslie's,* "From six to nine adults were frequently found huddled together in one small room . . . and the filth and smell are described as most disgusting."

Riis wrote story after story for the *New York Tribune* describing the dirt and overcrowding of the slums, which he believed caused disease and crime, and charging that officials did too little about the conditions. "The wish kept cropping up in me that there were some way of putting before the people what I saw there," he said. "I wrote, but it seemed to make no impression."

Then Riis found a way to draw attention to the slums. Armed with the new magnesium flash powder to provide artificial light, he began in 1888 to photograph the dark alleys, flophouses, and

Advertising for the Kodak camera, introduced in 1888, stresses its ease of use, *left.* Inventor George Eastman, *above,* holds a Kodak identical to the one used to take his picture. The camera made round snapshots, 100 on each roll of film.

An 1888 photograph by Jacob A. Riis called *Bandits' Roost* is one of Riis's many photographs of New York City's Mulberry Bend slum that shocked the public about conditions there.

549

The World Book Encyclopedia Annual 50 Years Ago

Excerpts from *The World Book Encyclopedia Annual for 1938* are printed here in boldface type. The words in lightface type did not appear in the annual but are included here to help identify or explain the events described.

AIRCRAFT. In 1938 Howard Hughes decided to make a scientific world flight to test new aids to navigation and see for himself what further improvements should be made to advance long distance flying. He succeeded gloriously. The Hughes world flight was the outstanding event of the year. . . . This world flight was made in 91 hours at an average flying speed of 206 miles an hour. . . . In every sense of the word it demonstrated the progress made in aviation, and it pointed the way to still further progress. Hughes, a motion-picture producer and aviator, flew around the world in a record time of 3 days 19 hours 14 minutes.

AIRCRAFT. Ever since Charles A. Lindbergh flew to Paris in 1927, young Douglas Corrigan of California had hoped to emulate him [by making a solo flight across the Atlantic Ocean]. **. . . Early on the morning of July 17, Corrigan boarded his plane at Floyd Bennett Field, New York, ostensibly to return to the Pacific Coast. . . . But to the amazement of field attendants he headed out toward the open sea and kept on going. Twenty-five hours later, he landed in Dublin, Ireland, explaining with a smile, "My compass must have been wrong. I must have flown in the wrong direction."** Few people believed the young pilot, who has been known ever since as "Wrong Way" Corrigan.

AMERICAN LEGION. Other activities included . . . helping win the long fight for a Federal law making Armistice Day a national holiday. The federal holiday created in 1938 is now known as Veterans Day.

AUSTRIA. The year saw the end of Austria as an independent country. The nation . . . lost its independence on March 12, 1938, when Adolf Hitler, dictator of Nazi Germany, sent his army into Austria to annex it to the German Reich. Germany was defeated in World War II (1939-1945), and Austria was then occupied for 10 years by France, Great Britain, the Soviet Union, and the United States. Austria finally regained its independence in 1955.

GERMANY. A wave of destruction, looting, and incendiarism [arson]— **unparalleled in Germany since the Thirty Years' War** [1618-1648]—**began to sweep over Greater Germany** [Germany, Austria, and the Sudetenland region of Czechoslovakia] **about 2 A.M. on November 10. Bands of men, wearing Nazi boots and moving in organized groups, set fire to or otherwise sought to destroy all Jewish synagogues throughout the Reich. They also toured the streets, smashing the windows of Jewish shops and hurling furniture, typewriters, and all sorts of property onto the sidewalk. Thousands of Jews were arrested and hustled to prison or concentration camps.** The incident became known as *Kristallnacht* (Night of Glass) because so many windows were broken.

GREAT BRITAIN. There [at a meeting in Munich] **Hitler got all he wanted, and peace was preserved. . . .** [British Prime Minister Neville] **Chamberlain returned to London . . . announcing that he had brought "peace with honor."** At the meeting, France, Great Britain, and Italy signed a pact with Nazi Germany called the Munich Agreement, which forced Czechoslovakia to give much of its land to Germany. The pact kept peace for only a year, until World War II began in 1939.

INVENTIONS AND DISCOVERIES. The most important single invention of the year is nylon, an artificial silk made of common substances, which surpasses rayon in numerous ways—such as in elasticity—and is better than natural silk in some respects. It will have a great economic influence, as it should make for United States independence of Japan for silk.

LABOR. First rank in importance in the field of legislation for the year clearly belongs to the Fair Labor Standards Act, approved on June 25, and effective on October 24. . . . It applies to industries en-

gaged in interstate commerce or in the production of goods for such commerce, fixing a minimum wage and a maximum work week. The wage is to be not less than 25 cents per hour. . . . The hours of employment may not exceed 44 per week for the first year. . . . The Act bars the employment of children under sixteen in the industries affected, and those under eighteen in hazardous or injurious employments.

The conflict between the two major organizations of workers showed no signs of abatement. The Committee for Industrial Organization met in convention in Pittsburgh, on November 14, changing its name to the Congress of Industrial Organizations, thus retaining its familiar initials. The CIO was a group of industrial unions that had been expelled from the American Federation of Labor (AFL), made up mostly of craft unions. Conflict between the AFL and CIO continued until 1955, when the two groups merged to form the American Federation of Labor and Congress of Industrial Organizations (AFL-CIO).

LITERATURE. Most popular among novels of general character, and for many months the most popular novel in the United States, was Marjorie Kinnan Rawlings' *The Yearling.* **It is lively . . . and given special effectiveness by its charming depiction of a tender father-son relationship and by its vigorous portrayal of hunting and outdoor life.**

METEOROLOGY. The year 1938 probably will be known in New England as the time of the great hurricane, generally believed to be the most destructive ever to strike the United States. The storm reached the New England coast on the morning of September 21, and before it had abated over 500 lives had been lost, 100 persons were missing, and the damage, including the destruction of 16,740 structures and 2,605 boats, amounted to about $300,000,000. The final death toll from the hurricane and an accompanying tidal wave was more than 700.

MOTION PICTURES. Alfred Hitchcock received from the New York Film Critics the award for the best staging for his tensely melodramatic *The Lady Vanishes.* **. . . Spencer Tracy and Mickey Rooney in** *Boys Town* **and Bette Davis in** *Jezebel* **gave outstanding performances, which are apt to be remembered long after the offerings. . . . The New York Film Critics selected** *The Citadel* **as the best motion picture of the year;** *Grand Illusion* **as the best foreign language film; James Cagney's performance in** *Angels With Dirty Faces* **as the best piece of male acting, and that of Margaret Sullavan in** *Three Comrades* **as the best feminine portrayal.**

RADIO. The memorable "unbelievable" performance of the year was "the Martian invasion," dramatized as H. G. Wells's "The War of the Worlds" to sound like live news of the moment, and done with such conviction by Orson Welles that a wave of jitters swept the country. The broadcast, which described a fictional invasion of New Jersey by creatures from Mars, was so realistic that thousands of listeners panicked. Its director, 23-year-old Orson Welles, went on to become one of the greatest directors in the history of motion pictures.

SPORTING AND ATHLETIC EVENTS. John Vander Meer, a Cincinnati Reds rookie, pitched two consecutive no-hit, no-run games for the first time in baseball history.

Donald Budge was the first [tennis player in history] **to take the world's four major tennis titles** [the Australian, French, British, and United States championships, also known as the grand slam].

Joe Louis retained the heavyweight championship with the first two-minute four-second knockout on record. The bout was a rematch between Louis and German challenger Max Schmeling, who knocked out Louis in 1936 in one of boxing's biggest upsets.

THEATER. In the winter and spring the best new plays [included] **Thornton Wilder's novel and human play without scenery,** *Our Town.* The play received the 1938 Pulitzer Prize for drama. [S.D.]

Orson Welles directs the radio program that panicked listeners in October 1938 by describing a Martian invasion.

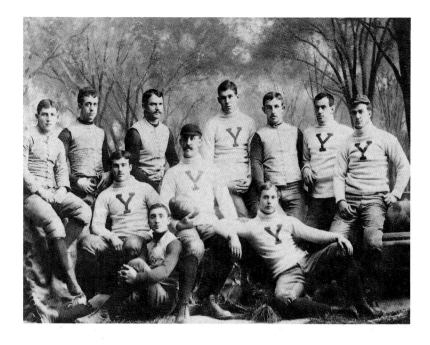

Yale's championship football team of 1888 includes W. Walter (Pudge) Heffelfinger —back row, center— and Amos Alonzo Stagg—extreme left.

tenements of New York City. Riis's pictures shocked the public as his words never could. Through his efforts, the city tore down Mulberry Bend, one of the most miserable tenement districts, which *Leslie's* called "a seat of iniquity, poverty and dirt." In its place, New York built a public park and the Jacob A. Riis Neighborhood House.

Van Gogh at Arles

The year 1888 marked the climax—and the beginning of the end—of the career of one of the greatest painters in modern art, the Dutch-born Vincent van Gogh. In February, van Gogh moved from Paris to Arles in southern France, where he had the most productive period of his career. Between his arrival and a mental collapse in December that put him into a hospital, he completed more than 100 of his most famous paintings, including several versions of *Sunflowers*.

In October, the French painter Paul Gauguin, a friend of van Gogh's, came for a long visit. The two artists got along well at first but then began to quarrel. On Dec. 23, 1888, van Gogh threatened to kill Gauguin with an open razor. Gauguin fled to a hotel to spend the night. Van Gogh then cut off part of his own left ear and carried the severed ear, wrapped in newspaper, to a nearby brothel. According to an Arles newspaper, he "asked for a girl called Rachel, and handed her his ear with these words: 'Keep this object like a treasure.'" The police found the artist at home the next morning and took him to a hospital. Van Gogh continued to suffer from emotional problems, as well as occasional seizures that were diagnosed after his death as epilepsy. He committed suicide in 1890.

Football gains yardage

During the 19 years since the first college football game had been played in 1869, football had developed from a strange mixture of European soccer and Rugby into a uniquely American sport with growing popularity. *The Century Illustrated Monthly Magazine* said, "The game has taken a high place in the affections of the American undergraduate," and *Leslie's* added, "Not only among collegians, but with the public, football has grown to enjoy remarkable favor."

Football fans of 1888 had an opportunity to see perhaps the greatest team in the history of college football. The Yale team of that year finished undefeated, untied, and unscored upon, and piled up 698 points in 13 games. Yale coach Walter Camp, later called the father of American football, developed many of the rules and strategies used today. The team included two of football's all-time greats, W. Walter (Pudge) Heffelfinger at guard and Amos Alonzo Stagg, later coach for 40 years at the University of Chicago, at right end.

Here she comes, Miss Spa of 1888

What may have been the first beauty contest in history was held in September 1888 at the fashionable resort of Spa, Belgium. A jury of eight men made an initial selection from photographs of 350 contestants, choosing 21 finalists. *Leslie's* reported, "Grace, carriage, and toilette were taken into consideration, as well as beauty of face." The winner was 18-year-old Marthe Soucaret of Guadeloupe, a French possession in the West Indies. *Leslie's* described her as "a dusky-skinned, dark-eyed blonde, possessing a faultless form and a figure a little over the average height." The paper added that she received more than 100 marriage proposals after winning the contest, including offers from "ten marquises and a dozen counts and viscounts."

Changing fashions

In 1888, fashionable women began to wear simpler, less artificial clothing as some of the extreme styles of the previous years fell out of favor. One fashion that began to fade was the use of tightly laced corsets to make the waist as small as possible—typically 15 to 18 inches (38 to 46 centimeters). *The Century* criticized the practice of tight lacing, saying, "It suggests disproportion and invalidism rather than grace and beauty."

Another passing fashion was the *bustle*, a small cushion or wire frame worn to puff out the back of a woman's skirt below the waist. "My, how the bustle did rise! It grew like a watermelon under a hot Summer sun," *Leslie's* remarked. "The greatest proportions it ever reached was when it topped the bushel-basket. Now it is a very modest affair, and looks like a small-sized rat trap. By next Fall it will be gone entirely." The newspaper's prediction proved nearly correct. Bustles disappeared by 1890.

The winner of what may have been the first beauty contest in history, held in September 1888 in Spa, Belgium, is 18-year-old Marthe Soucaret of Guadeloupe.

Still another fashion that met increasing ridicule was the trimming of hats with stuffed birds, a custom that resulted in the slaughter of millions of songbirds. The practice died away partly due to the passage of bird protection laws and partly because of satire like that in *Life* in March 1888. The magazine advised, in a mock "Household Hints" column, "Do not throw away your dead canary unless your Spring bonnet is already trimmed."

Casey got no hits, but others did

One of the most popular poems in the English language—"Casey at the Bat" by Ernest Lawrence Thayer—was first printed on June 3, 1888, in *The Daily Examiner* of San Francisco, for which Thayer wrote a humor column. His poem describes how the Mudville baseball team trailed 4 to 2 in the ninth inning when "mighty Casey" came to bat with two men on base and two outs. The last stanza is one of the most famous in American poetry:

> *Oh! somewhere in this favored land the sun is shining bright,*
> *The band is playing somewhere, and somewhere hearts are light;*
> *And somewhere men are laughing, and somewhere children shout,*
> *But there is no joy in Mudville—mighty Casey has struck out.*

Popular songs of 1888 included the comic "Where Did You Get That Hat?" and the sentimental "With All Her Faults I Love Her Still." John Philip Sousa wrote one of his best marches that year, "Semper Fidelis," now the official march of the U.S. Marine Corps.

The most popular and influential novel of 1888 was *Looking Backward* by the American author Edward Bellamy, which sold more than 1 million copies. The novel tells the story of a young man who falls into a hypnotic sleep in 1887 and awakens in the year 2000. He finds that the United States has become a happy socialist state in which all wealth is equally distributed. In *Looking Backward*, Bellamy attacked the economic and social inequality that he saw in the world of his time. Swedish dramatist August Strindberg explored similar themes in his 1888 play *Miss Julie*, the tragedy of a woman who loves a man beneath her social class.

British historian James Bryce took a more favorable view in his 1888 book *The American Commonwealth*, long regarded as a classic study of American political and social institutions. Bryce described both the strengths and the weaknesses of the American system but concluded, "America marks the highest level not only of material well-being, but of intelligence and happiness, which the race has yet attained."

The majority of Americans would probably have agreed with Bryce's assessment of their nation. Most people in 1888 would probably also have joined in Bryce's cautious optimism about the years to come: "We may look forward to the future, not indeed without anxiety, when we mark the clouds that hang on the horizon, yet with a hope that is stronger than anxiety."

Index

How to use the index
This index covers the contents of the 1987, 1988, and 1989 editions of *The World Book Year Book.*

There are two basic kinds of index entries. One kind of entry is followed immediately by an edition year and a page number, as:

Computer, 89-242

This means that an article on computers begins on page 242 of the 1989 *Year Book.*

The other kind of entry has a key word or words between it and the edition year, as:

Einstein ring: astronomy, 89-182

This means that information about Einstein rings can be found on page 182 of the **Astronomy** article in the 1989 *Year Book.*

The "See" and "See also" cross-references are to other entries within the index, as:

Third World. See Developing countries.

Clue words or phrases are used when two or more references to the same subject appear in the same edition of *The Year Book,* as:

Aspirin: drugs, 89-277; hearing, Special Report, 89-151

The indication "il." means that the reference is to an illustration only, as:

Lauper, Cyndi: il., 89-385

An index entry followed by "WBE" refers to a new or revised *World Book Encyclopedia* article in the supplement section, as:

Quayle, Dan: WBE, 89-511

Index

A

Index

Index

Index

Index

Acknowledgments

The publishers acknowledge the following sources for illustrations. Credits read from top to bottom, left to right, on their respective pages. An asterisk (*) denotes illustrations and photographs that are the exclusive property of *The Year Book*. All maps, charts, and diagrams were prepared by *The Year Book* staff unless otherwise noted.

4 Reuters/Bettmann Newsphotos; Art on File; © Gary Braasch
5 © James Nachtwey, Magnum; Tom Hertzberg*; Albert Moldvay, PSI FotoFile
9 NASA
12 UPI/Bettmann Newsphotos
13 © David Moore, Black Star; © Trippett, Sipa Press
14 Sportschrome, Inc.
16 © Jack McKigney, Picture Group; © Shepard Sherbell, Picture Group
17 © B. Bisson, Sygma
18 © Gamma/Liaison; Focus on Sports
19 © Argyropoulos, Sipa Press; Reuters/Bettmann Newsphotos
20 Laski, Sipa Press
21 © Dieter Ludwig, Sipa Press; UPI/Bettmann Newsphotos; Canapress
22 Focus on Sports; © Boccon-Gibod, Sipa Press
23 Touchstone from Shooting Star; © Gamma/Liaison
24 © Shepard Sherbell, Picture Group
25 © M. Shandiz, Sygma; © Gamma/Liaison; © Sygma
26 © Berman, Sipa Press
27 © Trippett, Sipa Press; © Chitrakar, Sipa Press; © Sipa Press
28 NASA
29 © Andy Hernandez, Picture Group; UPI/Bettmann Newsphotos; © Tom Haley, Sipa Press
30 © C. Carrion, Sygma
31 © Will Hart, *Time* magazine; AP/Wide World
32 © Mike Clemmer, Picture Group
33 AP/Wide World; AP/Wide World; © Canada Wide from Sipa Press
34 © Alfred, Sipa Press
35 Reuters/Bettmann Newsphotos; © Sygma
37 Artstreet
38 AP/Wide World; Bobby Coker, *The Orlando Sentinel;* Chris Usher, *The Orlando Sentinel*
42 AP/Wide World; AP/Wide World; NASA
43 AP/Wide World; Keith Meyers, NYT Pictures
44 NASA
46 L. Kizim and V. Solovyov, TASS from Sovfoto; ESA
47 NASA
48 Martin Marietta; Martin Marietta; Rockwell International
52 Joe Van Severen*
55-61 Mark Chickinelli*
63 Steven Spicer*
67 Mark Chickinelli*
70 Art on File
73 Acquired from NEA Community Development Block Grant Program of the Department of Housing and Urban Development and the City of Houston (Art on File); Texas Commerce Towers, Houston, Texas, funded by Texas Commerce Bank Bancshares Inc., United Energy Resources Inc. and Gerald D. Hines (Art on File)
74 © The Detroit Institute of Arts, Founders Society Purchase, with funds from *Sports Illustrated;* Art on File
77 Art on File; © Roy Morsch, The Stock Market
78 Richard Baron, Sculpture Placement, Washington, D.C.; © Nicholas Devore III, Bruce Coleman Inc.
79 © Michael George, Bruce Coleman Inc.; The Ydessa Hendeles Gallery, Toronto
80 Gianfranco Gorgoni; Art on File
81 © D. Gorton, Onyx
82 Art on File
83 Artstreet; Art on File
84 © Martha Cooper
85 Art on File
86 © Howard Woody, University of South Carolina; Hal Bromm Gallery, New York City
87 © Randy Taylor, Sygma
88 © Carl Frank, Photo Researchers; © Michael K. Nichols, Magnum
90 © Gary Braasch, The Nature Conservancy
91 © Gary Braasch; © Gregory G. Dimijian, Photo Researchers
96 © Loren McIntyre
97 © Stephanie Maze, Woodfin Camp, Inc.
98 © Loren McIntyre
99 NASA
101 © Joy Spurr, Bruce Coleman Inc.; © Andrew Young and World Wildlife Fund
102 © Gary Braasch; © Gary Braasch, The Nature Conservancy
103 © Kjell B. Sandved, Photo Researchers
104 © Loren McIntyre
105 © Gary Braasch, The Nature Conservancy
106 UPI/Bettmann Newsphotos

108 © James Nachtwey, Magnum
111 UPI/Bettmann Newsphotos; © Interfoto
115 Owen Franken, German Information Center
116 © Cotton Coulson, Woodfin Camp, Inc.
119 Julian Calder, TSW Click/Chicago
120 Eastfoto
122 © Bruno Widen, TSW Click/Chicago
124 © Michael Langford, Horizon; © Kim Newton, Woodfin Camp, Inc.
127 UPI/Bettmann Newsphotos; AP/Wide World
128 © T. Matsumoto, Sygma
132 © H. Kubota, Magnum
133 © Anthony Suau, Black Star
134 © T. Matsumoto, Sygma; © H. Kubota, Magnum
136 © J. P. Laffont, Sygma
137 © H. Kubota, Magnum
138 Korean Overseas Information Service
140-147 Tom Hertzberg*
148 Starkey Laboratories, Inc.; Starkey Laboratories, Inc.; Beltone Electronics
149 Cameramann International, Ltd.; © Brent Jones
150 Tom Hertzberg*; © Ron Kinmonth; Tom Hertzberg*; 3M Corporation
155 AP/Wide World
156 © 1988 Crain Communications, Inc. Reprinted with permission from *Advertising Age.*
159 Reuters/Bettmann Newsphotos
160 © Steven Greenhouse, NYT Pictures
161 Reuters/Bettmann Newsphotos
164 AP/Wide World
166 Louise Gubb, JB Pictures
168 Bill Ballenberg © 1988 National Geographic Society
169 © Bruce Zuckerman; West Semitic Research Project
170 © E. Otto, Miller Comstock
171 © R. Wollmann, Gamma/Liaison
172 Battelle's Pacific Northwest Laboratories
173 Agence France-Presse
174 © B. Riha, Gamma/Liaison
175 Tom Cinoman
177 © Chip Hires, Gamma/Liaison
178 Agence France-Presse
180-182 AP/Wide World
183 © David Moore, Black Star
184 © Oliver Strewe, Wildlight
185 © Andy Hernandez, Picture Group
187 AP/Wide World
188 Trudy Rogers*
189-190 AP/Wide World
191 Deutsche Presse Agentur
193 Jose R. Lopez, NYT Pictures
194 © Sygma
196-197 AP/Wide World
198 Trudy Rogers*
201 AP/Wide World
202 Focus on Sports
205 © J. Bourg, Gamma/Liaison
207 © Robert Brown, Allsport
209 AP/Wide World
211 Reuters/Bettmann Newsphotos
212 Bouvet, Gamma/Liaison
213 Seth Mydans, NYT Pictures
214 © Savas Ay, Sipa Press
216 Sportschrome, Inc.
218 Trudy Rogers*
221 Canapress
222 Macmillan of Canada, Toronto
224 Photo Assignments Unlimited
225 AP/Wide World
226 UPI/Bettmann Newsphotos
228 Diego Goldberg, Sygma
229 Pan-Asia Newspaper Alliance
230 AP/Wide World
232 © *The Milwaukee Journal*
236 © Chicago Tribune Company, all rights reserved, used with permission.
238 Bayreuther Festspiele
240 Numismatic Guaranty Corporation of America
241 © Parga, Sipa Press
242 Earl W. Engleman, © Cartoon Features Syndicate, used by permission of *The Wall Street Journal*
243 NEC Home Electronics (U.S.A.) Inc.
244 © Paul Hosefros, NYT Pictures

Family milestones of 1988

In the preceding pages, *The World Book Year Book* reported the major events and trends of 1988. Use these two pages to record the developments that made the year memorable for *your* family.

Family members (names)   **Ages**   **Family pets**

_____   _____   _____
_____   _____   _____
_____   _____   _____
_____   _____   _____
_____   _____   _____
_____   _____   _____
_____   _____   _____

Births (name)   **Date**   **Where born**   **Weight**   **Height**

_____   _____   _____   _____   _____
_____   _____   _____   _____   _____
_____   _____   _____   _____   _____

Weddings (names)   **Date**   **Where held**

_____   _____   _____
_____   _____   _____
_____   _____   _____

Religious events   _____   _____
                         _____   _____

Graduations   _____   _____
                         _____   _____

Anniversaries   _____   _____
                         _____   _____

In memoriam   _____   _____

Awards, honors, and prizes   _____   _____
                                    _____   _____
                                    _____   _____

Sports and club achievements   _____   _____
                                      _____   _____

Vacations and trips   _____   _____
                            _____   _____

Most enjoyable books

_____

_____

_____

_____

_____

Most-played recordings and tapes

_____

_____

_____

_____

_____

Most unforgettable motion pictures

_____

_____

_____

_____

_____

Most-watched television programs

_____

_____

_____

_____

_____

Paste a favorite family photograph
or snapshot here.

Date

_____

Location

_____

Occasion

_____

_____

World Book Encyclopedia, Inc., provides high-quality educational and reference products for the family and school. They include Science Year, which presents information about developments in science and technology; The World Book Medical Encyclopedia, a 1,040-page, fully illustrated family health reference; the Student Information Finder and How to Study Video, a fast-paced video presentation of key study skills, with information students need to succeed in school; and Play It Safe! With the Alphabet Pals™, a book, audio tape, and activity-based program designed to help young children develop good safety habits. For further information, write to World Book Encyclopedia, Inc., P.O. Box 3576, Chicago, IL 60654.